THE
SMALL CRAFT
ALMANAC
1997

Incorporating the Channel West & Solent Almanac

Editor Brian Goulder

Consultant Editor Edward Lee-Elliott

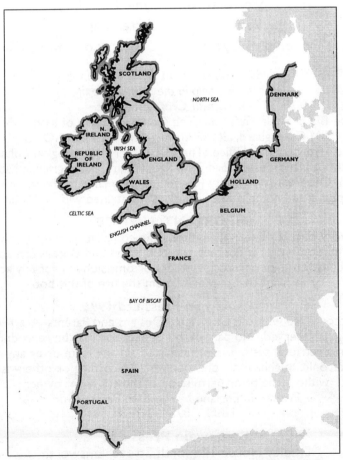

COVERING THE UK & IRELAND
DENMARK TO GIBRALTAR

THE
SMALL CRAFT
ALMANAC
1997

incorporating
The Channel West & Solent Almanac
Corrected to Notice to Mariners 39-96

Editor	Brian Goulder
Consultant editor	Edward Lee-Elliott
Design & production	Jamie Russell
Jacket design	Slatter-Anderson
Cover photograph	Courtesy of Bowman Yachts Ltd

*The publishers would like to thank the followiing for
their kind help in the compilation of*
The Small Craft Almanac:
The BBC, British Telecom, The Commissioners of Irish Lights,
HM Coastguard, HM Customs, HM Stationery Office,
The Hydrographic Office, The IBA, The Meteorological Office,
The Northern Lighthouse Board, The Proudman Oceanographic Laboratory,
The Royal Observatory, Trinity House and the many individuals who kindly
helped in the compilation of the data contained within this book

IMPORTANT NOTICE
Whilst every care has been taken during the compilation stage to check that
the information within is correct, the publishers and editors can accept no
responsibility for any inaccuracies, errors or omissions or for any accidents
or mishaps that may arise from the use of this book.

Printed in England by the Bath Press, Avon
ISBN 1-873432-77-1

Boatswain Press Ltd
Dudley House 12 North Street Emsworth
Hampshire PO10 7DQ
Tel: 01243 377977 Fax: 01243 379136

CONTENTS

PLANNING SECTION

Tidal time differences on Dover 4
Contents 5
Standard ports defined positions 6
Tide tables 7   to 150
Tidal calculations 151
Tidal curves .... 152 to 177
Secondary port tidal differences .... 178 to 198
Tidal stream charts .... 199 to 236
Small Craft chart key 237
Small Craft charts with waypoints, principal
   lights, radiobeacons, ports etc .... 238 to 277
Sunrise/set, moonrise/set .... 278 to 297
Marinas .... 298 to 300

POSITION SECTION

Contents 301
Principal lights visible 15M and over .... 302 to 317
Radiobeacons .... 318 to 321
Emergency D/F service .... 322 & 323
Emergency D/F service charts .... 324 & 325
Distance from dipping light table 326
Speed, time and distance table 327

COMMUNICATION SECTION

Contents 328
HM Coastguard chart 329
Radio operation .... 330 & 331
Port and coastal radio stations .... 332 to 345
Vessel Traffic Service charts .... 346 to 355

WEATHER SECTION

Contents 356
Shipping forecast areas .... 357 to 361
Broadcast weather forecasts - marine .... 362 to 380
Broadcast weather forecasts
- main UK radio stations .... 381 to 383
Navtex and Marinecall 384
Weather forecast terms in 5 languages .... 385 & 386

REFERENCE SECTION

Contents 387
Foreign glossary of general terms .... 388 to 395
Common conversion tables 396
Marine VHF transmitting frequencies 397
Index .... 398 & 399
Sounds and shapes signals 400

TIME DIFFERENCES

Approximate HW time differences between **Dover** and various main ports are given below.
They may be used to calculate *approximate* HW time differences relative to each other.

UK South	
Isles of Scilly	-0635
Penzance	-0635
Falmouth	-0610
Fowey	-0555
Plymouth	-0540
Salcombe	-0535
Dartmouth	-0505
Torquay	-0500
Exmouth Approaches	-0445
Lyme Regis	-0450
Portland	-0430
Portsmouth	+0020
Newhaven	0000

UK East	
Ramsgate	+0020
Sheerness	+0130
Burnham-on-Crouch	+0115
Brightlingsea	+0050
Harwich	+0040
Lowestoft	-0145
Spurn Point	-0550
Bridlington	+0545
Whitby	+0500
North Shields	+0430

UK West	
Barrow-in-Furness	+0025
Liverpool	+0015
Douglas	+0015
Holyhead	-0050
Aberystwyth	-0330
Fishguard	-0400
Milford Haven	-0500
Swansea	-0500
Avonmouth	-0410
Ilfracombe	-0525
St Ives	-0610

Ireland	
Rosslare	-0525
Wicklow	-0020
Dublin Bar	+0015
Carlingford Lough	+0010
Strangford Lough	+0200
Belfast	+0010
Londonderry	-0300
Lough Swilly	-0455
Killybegs	-0530
Broadhaven	-0533
Galway	-0510
Tarbert Island	-0535
Bantry	+0555
Cobh	-0600

Scotland	
Leith	+0340
Dundee	+0350
Aberdeen	+0220
Inverness	+0100
Wick	+0015
Kirkwall	-0040
Lerwick	-0010
Stornoway	-0420
Castle Bay	-0510
Ullapool	-0415
Portree	-0440
Fort William	-0505
Tobermory	-0510
Oban	-0510
Campbeltown	+0045
Rothesay	+0100
Stranraer	+0055

Germany	
Cuxhaven	+0200
Wilhelmshaven	+0155
Borkum	0000

Belgium & Holland	
Oostende	+0110
Delfzijl	-0020
Harlingen	-0240
Den Helder	-0340
Hoek van Holland	+0310
Vlissingen (Flushing)	+0200

France & Channel Islands	
Calais	+0025
Boulogne	0000
Dieppe	-0035
Le Havre	-0120
Cherbourg	-0320
Alderney - Braye	-0410
Guernsey - St Peter Port	-0450
Jersey - St Helier	-0455
St Malo	-0515
Les Héaux de Bréhat	-0525
Morlaix	-0610
Ouessant (Ushant)	+0505
Brest	+0510

PLANNING SECTION
CONTENTS

Standard ports defined positions 6
Tide Tables:
UK South 7
St Helier, St Mary's, Plymouth, Portland, Poole, Southampton, Portsmouth, Shoreham, Dover
UK East 31
Margate, Sheerness, London Bridge, Walton-on-the-Naze, Harwich, Lowestoft, Immingham, R.Tees, R. Tyne
UK Scotland 55
Leith, Rosyth, Aberdeen, Wick, Lerwick, Ullapool, Oban, Greenock, Liverpool
UK West & Ireland 79
Holyhead, Milford Haven, Swansea, Avonmouth, Dublin, Belfast, Londonderry, Galway, Cobh
North Europe 103
Esbjerg, Helgoland, Cuxhaven, Bremerhaven, Hoek van Holland, Rotterdam,Vlissingen,Antwerpen,Dunkerque
South Europe 127
Calais, Dieppe, Le Havre, Cherbourg, St Malo, Brest, Pointe de Grave, Lisboa, Gibraltar
Tidal calculations 151
Tidal curves 152
Secondary port tidal differences 178
Tidal stream charts 199
Small Craft chart key 237
Small Craft charts with waypoints, principal
lights, radiobeacons, ports etc 238
Sunrise/set, moonrise/set 278
Marinas 298

TIDAL NOTES

The tidal data herein is supplied by The Proudman Oceanographic Laboratory whose work is accepted as authoritative. Please note that heights and times of tides can be considerably affected by barometric pressure and prevailing winds.

When there are two low waters, eg Portland and Hoek van Holland, the time shown is for the first. Where there are two high waters, eg Southampton, the time shown is for the first. However, for Rotterdam the low water time shown is the mean of the two low waters.

SMALL CRAFT ALMANAC STANDARD PORTS

Defined positions of height predictions:

Isles of Scilly	49°55'N	6°19'W	Galway	53°16'N	9°03'W
Plymouth	50°22'N	4°11'W	Cobh	51°50'N	8°18'W
Portland	50°34'N	2°26'W	Leith	55°59'N	3°11'W
Poole	50°40'N	1°56'E	Rosyth	56°01'N	3°27'W
Southampton	50°54'N	1°24'W	Aberdeen	57°09'N	2°05'W
Portsmouth	50°48'N	1°07'W	Wick	58°26'N	3°05'W
Shoreham	50°50'N	0°15'W	Lerwick	60°09'N	1°08'W
Dover	51°07'N	1°19'W	Ullapool	57°54'N	5°09'W
Margate	51°24'N	1°23'E	Greenock	55°58'N	4°49'W
Sheerness	51°27'N	0°45'E	Oban	56°25'N	5°29'W
London Bridge	51°30'N	0°05'W	Cuxhaven	53°52'N	8°43'E
Walton on Naze	51°51'N	1°16'E	Bremerhaven	53°32'N	8°35'E
Harwich	51°57'N	1°17'E	Helgoland	53°52'N	8°43'E
Lowestoft	52°28'N	1°45'E	Esbjerg	55°29'N	8°28'E
Immingham	53°38'N	0°11'W	Antwerpen	51°21'N	4°14'E
River Tees	54°38'N	1°09'W	Hoek van Holland	51°59'N	4°07'E
River Tyne	55°00'N	1°26'W	Vlissingen (Flushing)	51°27'N	3°36'E
Liverpool	53°25'N	3°00'W	Rotterdam	51°55'N	4°30'E
Holyhead	53°19'N	4°37'W	Dunkerque	51°03'N	2°22'E
Milford Haven	51°42'N	5°03'W	Calais	50°58'N	1°51'E
Swansea	51°27'N	3°55'W	Dieppe	49°56'N	1°05'E
Avonmouth	51°31'N	2°43'W	Le Havre	49°29'N	0°06'E
Dublin	53°21'N	6°13'W	Cherbourg	49°39'N	1°37'W
Belfast	54°36'N	5°55'W	St Malo	48°38'N	2°02'W
Londonderry	55°00'N	7°19'W	Brest	48°23'N	4°30'W
			St Helier - Jersey	49°11'N	2°07'W

DISTANCE TO HORIZON TABLE

feet	metres	distance NM	feet	metres	distance NM
1	0.31	1.1	41	12.51	7.3
3	0.92	2.0	43	13.12	7.5
5	1.53	2.6	45	13.73	7.7
7	2.14	3.0	47	14.34	7.8
9	2.75	3.4	49	14.95	8.0
11	3.36	3.8	51	15.56	8.2
13	3.97	4.1	53	16.17	8.3
15	4.58	4.4	55	16.78	8.5
17	5.19	4.7	57	17.39	8.6
19	5.80	5.0	59	18.00	8.8
21	6.41	5.2	61	18.61	8.9
23	7.02	5.5	63	19.22	9.1
25	7.63	5.7	65	19.83	9.2
27	8.24	5.9	67	20.44	9.4
29	8.85	6.2	69	21.05	9.5
31	9.46	6.4	71	21.66	9.6
33	10.07	6.6	73	22.27	9.8
35	10.68	6.8	75	22.88	9.9
37	11.29	7.0	77	23.49	10.0
39	11.90	7.1	79	24.10	10.2

SOUTH COAST OF ENGLAND Time Zone UT

St Helier * St Mary's * Plymouth * Portland * Poole * Southampton * Portsmouth * Shoreham * Dover

JANUARY 1997 TIDE TABLES JANUARY 1997

ST HELIER		ST MARYS SCILLY		PLYMOUTH		PORTLAND		POOLE ENTRANCE		SOUTHAMPTON		PORTSMOUTH		SHOREHAM		DOVER			
Time	m	Time	m	Time	m	Time	m	Time	m	Time	m	Time	m	Time	m	Time	m		
0445	3.5	0300	1.8	0344	1.9	0309	0.6	0319	1.8	0315	3.9	0334	4.2	0313	5.3	0308	5.9	1	W
1030	8.9	0900	4.7	0944	4.8	1017	1.6	0809	1.1	0837	1.6	0848	1.7	0937	1.7	1027	1.8		
1706	3.5	1531	1.9	1611	1.9	1539	0.5	1535	1.7	1527	3.8	1542	3.9	1537	5.0	1527	5.5		
2300	8.5	2129	4.5	2218	4.5	2300	1.4	2032	1.0	2058	1.5	2109	1.6	2157	1.7	2239	2.0		
0530	3.8	0350	2.0	0430	2.1	0348	0.7	0457	1.7	0408	3.8	0427	4.0	0401	5.1	0355	5.7	2	TH
1117	8.6	0953	4.5	1035	4.7	1100	1.5	0909	1.2	0932	1.7	0942	1.9	1029	1.8	1115	2.0		
1756	3.4	1628	2.0	1702	2.1	1629	0.6	1722	1.6	1627	3.7	1642	3.8	1632	4.8	1624	5.4		
2355	8.3	2230	4.3	2318	4.4	2359	1.3	2138	1.1	2158	1.7	2209	1.8	2252	1.8	2333	2.2		
0629	4.1	0454	2.1	0527	2.2	0452	0.7	0643	1.7	0511	3.8	0540	4.0	0502	5.0	0456	5.5	3	F
1219	8.3	1059	4.4	1140	4.5	1203	1.4	1027	1.2	1039	1.8	1057	2.0	1133	1.9	1213	2.1		
1900	4.0	1739	2.1	1803	2.2	1743	0.6	1910	1.6	1737	3.7	1805	3.8	1737	4.7	1732	5.3		
		2345	4.4					2256	1.2	2310	1.8	2326	1.9						
0108	8.2	0609	2.1	0029	4.4	0119	1.4	0742	1.7	0619	3.8	0646	4.0	0001	1.9	0039	2.2	4	SA
0742	4.1	1215	4.5	0637	2.3	0623	0.8	1135	1.2	1152	1.8	1208	1.9	0611	5.0	0604	5.5		
1339	8.3	1851	1.9	1254	4.5	1327	1.4	1957	1.6	1851	3.7	1916	3.8	1243	1.8	1323	2.0		
2018	3.9			1916	2.1	1906	0.6	2357	1.1					1849	4.9	1842	5.4		
0227	8.5	0057	4.5	0138	4.5	0242	1.5	0807	1.7	0024	1.7	0031	1.7	0112	1.7	0156	2.1	5	SU
0902	3.9	0719	1.9	0754	2.1	0747	0.7	1228	1.0	0724	4.0	0749	4.1	0720	5.2	0711	5.7		
1458	8.7	1323	4.7	1404	4.6	1454	1.5	2011	1.7	1302	1.6	1306	1.6	1348	1.5	1436	1.8		
2136	3.6	1953	1.7	2030	1.9	2018	0.5			1957	3.9	2022	4.0	1956	5.1	1945	5.7		
0337	9.1	0157	4.8	0243	4.8	0351	1.7	0048	1.0	0131	1.5	0129	1.5	0217	1.5	0312	1.9	6	M
1016	3.3	0819	1.6	0905	1.8	0854	0.6	0812	1.8	0821	4.1	0848	4.3	0821	5.5	0811	5.9		
1605	9.3	1421	5.0	1510	4.8	1607	1.6	1315	0.8	1404	1.3	1400	1.3	1448	1.2	1546	1.5		
2245	3.0	2048	1.4	2134	1.5	2118	0.4	2013	1.8	2053	4.1	2119	4.3	2054	5.5	2042	6.0		
0436	9.8	0249	5.2	0345	5.0	0450	1.9	0135	0.8	0230	1.2	0223	1.3	0313	1.2	0418	1.5	7	TU
1119	2.6	0913	1.3	1006	1.4	0951	0.5	0814	1.9	0910	4.3	0936	4.5	0917	5.8	0903	6.2		
1702	10.0	1512	5.3	1612	5.0	1710	1.8	1401	0.6	1459	0.9	1453	1.0	1542	1.0	1646	1.2		
2344	2.3	2139	1.1	2233	1.2	2213	0.3	2017	1.9	2142	4.3	2205	4.5	2147	5.9	2133	6.3		
0527	10.6	0337	5.5	0441	5.3	0545	2.0	0222	0.6	0324	0.9	0316	1.0	0405	0.9	0515	1.2	8	W
1213	1.8	1003	0.9	1102	1.0	1044	0.3	0820	2.0	0956	4.5	1020	4.7	1007	6.2	0953	6.5		
1753	10.7	1600	5.6	1709	5.2	1808	1.9	1447	0.5	1549	0.6	1544	0.7	1633	0.8	1739	1.0		
		2227	0.8	2327	0.8	2305	0.2	2029	2.0	2228	4.5	2248	4.7	2238	6.2	2222	6.6		
0036	1.7	0424	5.8	0532	5.5	0637	2.2	0309	0.5	0414	0.7	0407	0.8	0454	0.8	0606	0.9	9	TH
0615	11.2	1052	0.6	1154	0.6	1133	0.2	0837	2.1	1041	4.6	1103	4.9	1056	6.4	1042	6.8		
1303	1.2	1646	5.8	1800	5.4	1901	2.1	1533	0.3	1638	0.4	1633	0.5	1722	0.7	1828	0.8		●
1840	11.3	2315	0.6			2354	0.1	2056	2.1	2314	4.6	2333	4.8	2329	6.4	2310	6.8		
0124	1.3	0509	6.0	0017	0.6	0727	2.3	0356	0.4	0503	0.5	0456	0.6	0543	0.8	0653	0.8	10	F
0702	11.7	1141	0.5	0621	5.7	1221	0.1	0909	2.1	1124	4.7	1148	4.9	1145	6.5	1130	6.9		
1349	0.9	1732	5.9	1244	0.4	1951	2.1	1621	0.2	1726	0.2	1721	0.4	1810	0.6	1915	0.7		
1927	11.5			1848	5.5			2141	2.1	2358	4.7					2359	7.0		
0209	1.1	0002	0.5	0105	0.4	0041	0.1	0445	0.3	0552	0.4	0019	4.9	0018	6.5	0739	0.6	11	SA
0747	11.8	0555	6.1	0707	5.8	0813	2.3	0959	2.1	1209	4.7	0544	0.6	0631	0.7	1221	6.9		
1434	0.8	1228	0.4	1331	0.3	1309	0.1	1709	0.2	1813	0.2	1234	5.0	1234	6.6	2000	0.7		
2012	11.6	1818	5.9	1935	5.5	2038	2.1	2244	2.1			1807	0.4	1859	0.6				
0254	1.1	0049	0.5	0151	0.5	0126	0.1	0534	0.4	0044	4.8	0106	4.9	0108	6.5	0048	7.0	12	SU
0832	11.7	0641	6.1	0753	5.8	0857	2.3	1108	2.1	0639	0.4	0630	0.6	0720	0.7	0824	0.6		
1518	0.9	1315	0.4	1416	0.3	1354	0.1	1800	0.3	1256	4.7	1321	4.9	1325	6.5	1311	6.8		
2057	11.3	1903	5.8	2021	5.4	2121	2.1			1857	0.2	1853	0.5	1947	0.6	2043	0.7		
0339	1.4	0136	0.6	0235	0.5	0210	0.1	0009	2.1	0131	4.7	0156	4.9	0155	6.5	0136	6.9	13	M
0917	11.4	0727	5.9	0838	5.6	0940	2.2	0625	0.5	0723	0.4	0716	0.7	0810	0.7	0909	0.6		
1603	1.3	1402	0.6	1501	0.6	1440	0.1	1231	2.0	1344	4.6	1408	4.8	1414	6.4	1401	6.6		
2143	10.8	1950	5.5	2106	5.3	2202	2.0	1851	0.4	1940	0.4	1939	0.6	2035	0.7	2127	0.8		
0424	1.9	0223	0.8	0318	0.8	0254	0.3	0149	2.0	0221	4.6	0248	4.8	0240	6.4	0223	6.8	14	TU
1003	10.8	0815	5.7	0924	5.4	1021	2.1	0718	0.6	0807	0.6	0803	0.9	0858	0.8	0956	0.8		
1649	1.9	1451	0.9	1545	0.9	1527	0.2	1409	1.9	1436	4.4	1458	4.6	1503	6.1	1451	6.4		
2230	10.2	2039	5.2	2153	5.0	2243	1.8	1946	0.5	2025	0.6	2027	0.9	2121	0.8	2213	1.1		
0511	2.5	0313	1.1	0403	1.1	0340	0.4	0352	2.0	0315	4.5	0351	4.6	0326	6.1	0312	6.5	15	W
1053	10.1	0906	5.3	1012	5.1	1103	1.9	0816	0.7	0853	0.9	0854	1.2	0950	1.0	1044	1.1		
1738	2.5	1543	1.2	1631	1.2	1617	0.4	1603	1.8	1534	4.2	1557	4.4	1553	5.7	1543	6.1		
2323	9.6	2133	4.9	2242	4.8	2328	1.7	2046	0.7	2113	0.9	2121	1.1	2213	1.0	2303	1.4		

● ● Time UT. For British Summer Time (shaded) March 30th to October 26th ADD ONE HOUR ● ●

JANUARY 1997 TIDE TABLES JANUARY 1997

Time: UT. For British Summer Time (shaded) March 30th to October 26th ADD ONE HOUR

Day	ST HELIER Time	m	ST MARYS SCILLY Time	m	PLYMOUTH Time	m	PORTLAND Time	m	POOLE ENTRANCE Time	m	SOUTHAMPTON Time	m	PORTSMOUTH Time	m	SHOREHAM Time	m	DOVER Time	m
16 TH	0603	3.1	0410	1.5	0451	1.5	0430	0.6	0551	1.9	0416	4.3	0501	4.5	0416	5.7	0405	6.2
	1149	9.4	1005	5.0	1104	4.9	1151	1.7	0922	0.9	0947	1.2	0954	1.4	1046	1.2	1138	1.4
	1833	3.1	1643	1.5	1722	1.6	1713	0.5	1810	1.8	1640	4.0	1714	4.1	1650	5.4	1642	5.8
			2239	4.6	2340	4.6			2152	0.9	2213	1.3	2223	1.4	2313	1.3		
17 F	0023	9.0	0518	1.7	0548	1.8	0021	1.6	0706	1.8	0524	4.1	0601	4.3	0518	5.4	0000	1.7
	0703	3.6	1115	4.7	1207	4.6	0532	0.7	1034	1.0	1053	1.4	1104	1.6	1154	1.5	0507	5.9
	1256	8.6	1754	1.7	1824	1.8	1248	1.5	1931	1.7	1757	3.9	1830	4.0	1759	5.1	1241	1.6
	1936	3.5	2357	4.5			1819	0.6	2305	1.0	2327	1.5	2336	1.7			1751	5.6
18 SA	0133	8.7	0634	1.8	0050	4.5	0127	1.5	0753	1.8	0639	4.0	0706	4.2	0025	1.5	0106	1.9
	0815	3.8	1234	4.6	0658	2.0	0650	0.8	1147	1.1	1209	1.5	1221	1.7	0629	5.2	0620	5.7
	1413	8.6	1909	1.8	1323	4.5	1401	1.5	2005	1.7	1916	3.9	1942	4.0	1310	1.6	1352	1.8
	2048	3.7			1936	1.9	1934	0.7							1916	5.0	1906	5.5
19 SU	0248	8.7	0115	4.6	0206	4.6	0247	1.5	0016	1.1	0044	1.6	0053	1.7	0139	1.6	0221	1.9
	0933	3.7	0747	1.7	0815	1.9	0814	0.8	0810	1.8	0750	4.0	0810	4.2	0742	5.2	0735	5.7
	1527	8.8	1345	4.6	1441	4.5	1521	1.5	1252	1.2	1322	1.5	1333	1.6	1419	1.5	1506	1.7
	2200	3.5	2015	1.7	2050	1.8	2043	0.6	2012	1.7	2025	4.0	2045	4.1	2024	5.1	2016	5.7
20 M	0354	9.0	0218	4.8	0317	4.7	0359	1.6	0113	1.0	0155	1.5	0158	1.6	0245	1.5	0333	1.7
	1041	3.3	0848	1.6	0927	1.7	0921	0.7	0813	1.8	0848	4.1	0904	4.3	0844	5.3	0840	5.8
	1627	9.1	1444	4.8	1548	4.7	1630	1.5	1340	0.9	1425	1.3	1429	1.4	1518	1.4	1612	1.6
	2301	3.1	2109	1.5	2154	1.6	2139	0.6	2014	1.8	2120	4.1	2135	4.2	2122	5.4	2112	5.9
21 TU	0447	9.5	0310	5.0	0416	4.9	0456	1.7	0200	0.9	0252	1.4	0251	1.5	0340	1.3	0433	1.5
	1136	2.8	0939	1.4	1024	1.5	1012	0.6	0815	1.9	0935	4.2	0948	4.4	0939	5.5	0933	6.0
	1716	9.6	1531	5.0	1642	4.9	1724	1.6	1422	0.8	1518	1.1	1516	1.2	1607	1.2	1706	1.4
	2351	2.6	2155	1.3	2247	1.4	2226	0.5	2019	1.8	2206	4.2	2215	4.3	2211	5.6	2158	6.1
22 W	0533	10.0	0353	5.2	0503	5.1	0544	1.8	0240	0.8	0339	1.2	0336	1.3	0426	1.2	0523	1.3
	1221	2.3	1022	1.2	1112	1.3	1055	0.5	0822	1.9	1015	4.3	1027	4.4	1024	5.7	1018	6.2
	1800	10.0	1612	5.1	1725	5.0	1812	1.7	1500	0.6	1600	0.9	1558	1.0	1649	1.0	1752	1.3
			2235	1.1	2331	1.2	2309	0.4	2031	1.9	2243	4.3	2252	4.4	2254	5.9	2238	6.3
23 TH O	0033	2.2	0431	5.3	0541	5.2	0627	1.9	0318	0.7	0419	1.0	0417	1.1	0505	1.1	0604	1.2
	0614	10.4	1100	1.1	1154	1.1	1136	0.4	0837	1.9	1049	4.3	1103	4.5	1103	5.9	1057	6.3
	1300	1.9	1649	5.2	1801	5.1	1854	1.8	1537	0.6	1635	0.8	1637	0.9	1724	0.9	1829	1.2
	1839	10.3	2311	1.0			2350	0.3	2052	1.9	2318	4.4	2328	4.5	2329	6.0	2315	6.5
24 F	0110	1.9	0506	5.4	0010	1.1	0705	2.0	0355	0.6	0452	0.9	0455	1.0	0539	1.0	0639	1.1
	0651	10.6	1134	1.0	0612	5.3	1215	0.3	0901	1.9	1122	4.3	1139	4.6	1137	6.0	1133	6.3
	1335	1.7	1723	5.3	1230	1.0	1930	1.8	1614	0.5	1707	0.7	1714	0.8	1758	0.9	1900	1.2
	1915	10.5	2344	1.0	1830	5.1			2125	1.9	2349	4.4					2351	6.5
25 SA	0144	1.8	0539	5.5	0044	1.0	0029	0.2	0432	0.6	0522	0.8	0005	4.6	0003	6.0	0712	1.0
	0727	10.7	1206	1.0	0639	5.3	0739	2.0	0936	1.9	1153	4.4	0531	1.0	0611	1.0	1207	6.4
	1406	1.7	1755	5.3	1303	1.0	1253	0.2	1649	0.5	1738	0.6	1215	4.6	1209	6.0	1927	1.1
	1951	10.4			1857	5.1	2003	1.9	2209	1.9			1748	0.8	1829	0.9		
26 SU	0215	1.8	0015	1.0	0115	1.0	0106	0.2	0506	0.6	0019	4.4	0042	4.6	0034	6.0	0026	6.6
	0801	10.6	0611	5.5	0706	5.4	0810	2.0	1021	1.9	0553	0.8	0604	1.0	0643	1.0	0743	1.0
	1436	1.8	1238	1.0	1333	1.0	1327	0.2	1725	0.5	1223	4.3	1250	4.5	1240	5.9	1239	6.3
	2023	10.2	1827	5.3	1926	5.1	2032	1.8	2301	1.9	1807	0.7	1821	0.9	1901	0.9	1955	1.1
27 M	0245	2.0	0047	1.1	0145	1.1	0139	0.2	0540	0.7	0050	4.3	0117	4.5	0103	6.0	0059	6.5
	0832	10.4	0642	5.4	0736	5.4	0839	1.9	1111	1.9	0622	0.8	0635	1.1	0716	1.0	0816	1.0
	1503	2.0	1308	1.1	1403	1.1	1358	0.2	1756	0.6	1253	4.3	1323	4.5	1313	5.8	1309	6.2
	2052	10.0	1857	5.2	1957	5.1	2100	1.8	2356	1.9	1836	0.7	1850	0.9	1934	0.9	2027	1.1
28 TU	0313	2.2	0118	1.2	0213	1.2	0206	0.3	0612	0.7	0120	4.3	0149	4.5	0132	5.9	0128	6.4
	0900	10.0	0713	5.3	0809	5.3	0906	1.8	1205	1.9	0652	0.9	0704	1.1	0749	1.0	0849	1.1
	1529	2.3	1339	1.2	1433	1.2	1422	0.2	1829	0.6	1326	4.2	1354	4.4	1346	5.7	1337	6.1
	2119	9.6	1930	5.1	2030	5.0	2127	1.7			1906	0.8	1919	1.0	2007	1.0	2058	1.3
29 W	0341	2.6	0151	1.3	0244	1.3	0227	0.3	0054	1.9	0154	4.3	0220	4.4	0202	5.8	0156	6.3
	0927	9.7	0746	5.2	0842	5.2	0933	1.7	0647	0.8	0724	1.0	0735	1.2	0821	1.1	0922	1.3
	1556	2.7	1413	1.4	1504	1.4	1442	0.3	1308	1.8	1404	4.1	1427	4.3	1420	5.5	1406	6.0
	2147	9.3	2005	4.9	2103	4.9	2155	1.6	1905	0.7	1938	1.0	1951	1.1	2039	1.1	2130	1.4
30 TH	0412	2.9	0226	1.5	0317	1.5	0249	0.4	0201	1.8	0233	4.1	0254	4.3	0234	5.6	0226	6.1
	0957	9.4	0823	5.0	0915	5.0	1000	1.6	0727	0.8	0759	1.2	0811	1.3	0857	1.3	0956	1.5
	1627	3.0	1451	1.6	1539	1.6	1507	0.3	1424	1.7	1446	4.0	1506	4.1	1454	5.3	1442	5.9
	2218	9.1	2045	4.7	2139	4.7	2225	1.5	1948	0.8	2016	1.3	2029	1.3	2116	1.3	2203	1.7
31 F	0448	3.3	0308	1.7	0354	1.8	0319	0.4	0323	1.8	0320	4.0	0336	4.2	0311	5.3	0304	6.0
	1034	9.1	0906	4.7	0951	4.8	1030	1.5	0816	0.9	0843	1.5	0854	1.5	0940	1.5	1033	1.7
	1708	3.4	1537	1.8	1620	1.8	1545	0.4	1558	1.7	1554	4.0	1554	4.0	1537	5.0	1529	5.7
	2300	8.7	2135	4.5	2221	4.5	2304	1.4	2040	1.0	2106	1.6	2116	1.5	2201	1.6	2245	1.9

SOUTH COAST OF ENGLAND Time Zone UT
St Helier * St Mary's * Plymouth * Portland * Poole * Southampton * Portsmouth * Shoreham * Dover

FEBRUARY 1997 TIDE TABLES FEBRUARY 1997

ST HELIER	ST MARYS, SCILLY	PLYMOUTH	PORTLAND	POOLE ENTRANCE	SOUTHAMPTON	PORTSMOUTH	SHOREHAM	DOVER	
Time m	Time m	Time m	Time m	Time m	Time m	Time m	Time m	Time m	
0538 3.7	0400 1.9	0441 2.0	0405 0.5	0500 1.7	0415 3.9	0429 4.1	0403 5.1	0357 5.8	1 SA
1124 8.6	1001 4.5	1038 4.6	1115 1.4	0918 1.1	0942 1.7	0951 1.7	1034 1.7	1121 1.9	
1804 3.7	1638 2.0	1711 2.0	1640 0.5	1745 1.6	1643 3.7	1657 3.8	1637 4.8	1631 5.5	
	2242 4.4	2320 4.4		2153 1.1	2214 1.8	2224 1.7	2306 1.8	2343 2.1	
0000 8.4	0512 2.0	0542 2.2	0006 1.3	0643 1.7	0524 3.9	0540 4.0	0514 4.9	0506 5.6	2 SU
0646 4.0	1116 4.4	1148 4.4	0516 0.6	1043 1.1	1056 1.8	1113 1.8	1147 1.8	1227 2.0	
1235 8.3	1757 2.0	1820 2.1	1225 1.3	1922 1.6	1802 3.7	1818 3.8	1755 4.8	1747 5.4	
1921 3.9			1804 0.6	2317 1.1	2336 1.8	2348 1.8			
0127 8.2	0006 4.4	0038 4.4	0136 1.4	0748 1.7	0638 3.9	0657 4.0	0024 1.8	0100 2.2	3 M
0812 4.0	0635 2.0	0704 2.2	0654 0.7	1155 1.0	1219 1.7	1229 1.7	0635 5.0	0624 5.6	
1412 8.3	1242 4.5	1313 4.4	1404 1.4	2005 1.6	1923 3.8	1942 3.9	1308 1.7	1348 2.0	
2052 3.8	1917 1.8	1947 2.0	1939 0.6				1919 5.0	1906 5.5	
0302 8.6	0124 4.6	0200 4.6	0309 1.5	0021 1.0	0057 1.6	0058 1.6	0143 1.6	0230 2.0	4 TU
0942 3.5	0750 1.7	0831 1.9	0825 0.6	0810 1.7	0748 4.0	0813 4.1	0752 5.3	0739 5.7	
1539 8.8	1354 4.7	1436 4.6	1539 1.5	1252 0.9	1335 1.4	1334 1.4	1421 1.4	1511 1.7	
2218 3.2	2024 1.5	2106 1.7	2057 0.5	2012 1.8	2029 4.0	2057 4.1	2031 5.4	2018 5.9	
0415 9.4	0227 5.0	0315 4.8	0424 1.7	0117 0.9	0207 1.3	0202 1.4	0251 1.2	0351 1.6	5 W
1058 2.7	0853 1.3	0942 1.4	0934 0.5	0813 1.9	0846 4.2	0915 4.4	0857 5.7	0844 6.1	
1646 9.7	1454 5.1	1551 4.9	1653 1.7	1345 0.7	1438 1.0	1434 1.1	1523 1.0	1621 1.3	
2327 2.4	2121 1.1	2212 1.2	2200 0.3	2015 1.9	2124 4.3	2151 4.4	2132 5.9	2118 6.2	
0514 10.4	0320 5.4	0421 5.2	0526 1.9	0207 0.7	0305 0.9	0300 1.0	0350 0.9	0454 1.2	6 TH
1159 1.8	0948 0.9	1045 0.9	1031 0.3	0817 2.0	0937 4.4	1004 4.6	0953 6.1	0939 6.4	
1741 10.6	1545 5.5	1653 5.2	1755 1.9	1433 0.4	1533 0.6	1529 0.7	1619 0.7	1721 1.0	
	2212 0.7	2311 0.8	2253 0.2	2025 2.0	2212 4.5	2235 4.7	2226 6.3	2209 6.6	
0023 1.5	0409 5.8	0516 5.5	0622 2.2	0256 0.5	0358 0.6	0354 0.7	0441 0.7	0549 0.8	7 F
0604 11.2	1039 0.5	1139 0.5	1122 0.1	0829 2.1	1023 4.6	1048 4.8	1044 6.4	1029 6.7	
1251 1.0	1633 5.8	1745 5.4	1851 2.1	1520 0.3	1622 0.3	1619 0.4	1709 0.6	1815 0.8	●
1830 11.3	2301 0.4		2342 0.0	2045 2.1	2256 4.7	2318 4.9	2317 6.5	2257 6.9	
0112 0.9	0455 6.1	0003 0.4	0714 2.3	0342 0.3	0448 0.4	0442 0.5	0530 0.6	0642 0.6	8 SA
0651 11.8	1127 0.2	0606 5.7	1210 0.0	0856 2.1	1109 4.7	1133 5.0	1132 6.6	1118 6.9	
1338 0.4	1718 5.9	1230 0.2	1940 2.2	1606 0.1	1711 0.1	1706 0.2	1757 0.5	1906 0.6	
1915 11.8	2348 0.2	1834 5.5		2123 2.1	2342 4.8			2345 7.1	
0158 0.5	0540 6.2	0052 0.2	0029 -0.0	0428 0.2	0537 0.2	0003 5.0	0005 6.6	0730 0.4	9 SU
0736 12.1	1213 0.1	0653 5.9	0801 2.4	0939 2.1	1153 4.8	0528 0.4	0618 0.5	1206 7.0	
1422 0.2	1802 6.0	1318 0.0	1257 -0.1	1652 0.1	1758 0.0	1218 5.0	1220 6.7	1952 0.5	
2000 11.9		1921 5.6	2025 2.2	2218 2.1		1751 0.2	1846 0.4		
0242 0.5	0033 0.2	0137 0.1	0113 -0.1	0515 0.2	0025 4.9	0048 5.0	0052 6.7	0031 7.1	10 M
0819 12.1	0624 6.2	0739 5.9	0845 2.4	1040 2.1	0623 0.1	0612 0.4	0707 0.5	0816 0.3	
1505 0.4	1257 0.2	1402 0.1	1341 -0.1	1739 0.2	1238 4.8	1303 4.9	1309 6.6	1255 6.9	
2042 11.7	1845 5.9	2005 5.6	2106 2.2	2331 2.1	1842 0.0	1834 0.3	1932 0.4	2035 0.5	
0324 0.8	0118 0.3	0220 0.2	0156 -0.0	0602 0.3	0110 4.8	0135 4.9	0137 6.6	0117 7.1	11 TU
0902 11.7	0708 6.1	0824 5.8	0924 2.3	1154 2.1	0706 0.2	0655 0.5	0752 0.5	0859 0.4	
1546 0.9	1342 0.4	1444 0.3	1423 -0.0	1827 0.3	1324 4.7	1348 4.8	1356 6.5	1341 6.6	
2124 11.2	1928 5.7	2048 5.4	2144 2.1			1923 0.2	1917 0.4	2015 0.6	2114 0.6	
0406 1.4	0201 0.6	0301 0.5	0236 0.1	0056 2.1	0156 4.7	0221 4.8	0218 6.5	0200 6.9	12 W
0944 11.1	0752 5.7	0907 5.5	1003 2.1	0651 0.4	0746 0.4	0739 0.7	0836 0.6	0940 0.6	
1627 1.6	1426 0.7	1524 0.7	1505 0.1	1323 2.0	1414 4.5	1435 4.6	1440 6.2	1426 6.5	
2206 10.5	2013 5.3	2131 5.2	2219 1.9	1917 0.4	2002 0.5	2002 0.7	2057 0.6	2153 0.9	
0447 2.1	0247 0.9	0340 0.9	0318 0.2	0234 2.0	0246 4.5	0311 4.6	0257 6.2	0244 6.6	13 TH
1028 10.3	0839 5.3	0950 5.2	1039 1.9	0744 0.6	0825 0.7	0826 1.0	0920 0.8	1021 0.9	
1710 2.4	1512 1.1	1603 1.1	1547 0.3	1506 1.9	1507 4.3	1527 4.4	1522 5.8	1512 6.2	
2251 9.7	2102 4.9	2212 4.9	2256 1.7	2011 0.7	2045 0.9	2050 1.1	2142 0.9	2233 1.2	
0532 2.9	0338 1.4	0421 1.4	0400 0.4	0425 1.9	0342 4.2	0409 4.4	0340 5.8	0333 6.3	14 F
1115 9.4	0931 4.9	1033 4.8	1118 1.6	0842 0.8	0912 1.1	0918 1.3	1009 1.2	1106 1.3	
1757 3.1	1605 1.6	1645 1.6	1633 0.5	1707 1.7	1609 4.0	1633 4.1	1611 5.4	1605 5.9	
2342 9.0	2200 4.6	2259 4.6	2336 1.5	2115 0.9	2137 1.3	2148 1.5	2235 1.3	2321 1.6	
0624 3.6	0439 1.7	0509 1.8	0450 0.6	0616 1.8	0446 4.0	0518 4.2	0434 5.3	0430 5.9	15 SA
1214 8.6	1036 4.5	1125 4.5	1203 1.4	0953 1.0	1012 1.5	1024 1.6	1111 1.5	1200 1.7	
1854 3.8	1713 1.9	1738 1.9	1730 0.6	1901 1.6	1722 3.8	1756 3.9	1715 5.0	1710 5.5	
	2317 4.3			2232 1.1	2246 1.7	2302 1.8	2344 1.7		

● ● Time UT. For British Summer Time (shaded) March 30th to October 26th ADD ONE HOUR ● ●

FEBRUARY 1997 TIDETABLES FEBRUARY 1997

	ST HELIER		ST MARYS, SCILLY		PLYMOUTH		PORTLAND		POOLE ENTRANCE		SOUTHAMPTON		PORTSMOUTH		SHOREHAM		DOVER	
	Time	m	Time	m	Time	m	Time	m	Time	m	Time	m	Time	m	Time	m	Time	m
16 SU	0046	8.4	0559	2.0	0000	4.4	0031	1.4	0730	1.7	0601	3.8	0629	4.0	0546	4.9	0023	2.0
	0730	4.1	1200	4.3	0612	2.1	0603	0.7	1118	1.1	1129	1.7	1149	1.8	1229	1.8	0543	5.5
	1333	8.2	1836	2.0	1239	4.3	1310	1.3	1956	1.6	1848	3.7	1914	3.8	1838	4.8	1312	2.0
	2003	4.1			1852	2.2	1849	0.7	2355	1.2							1830	5.3
17 M	0209	8.2	0046	4.3	0121	4.3	0152	1.4	0805	1.6	0011	1.9	0029	1.9	0107	1.9	0144	2.1
	0852	4.1	0722	1.9	0739	2.2	0744	0.8	1230	1.1	0721	3.8	0742	3.9	0709	4.8	0708	5.4
	1500	8.2	1324	4.3	1407	4.3	1450	1.3	2011	1.6	1253	1.7	1309	1.8	1349	1.8	1436	2.0
	2125	4.0	1951	1.9	2020	2.1	2013	0.7			2008	3.8	2027	3.9	1959	4.9	1950	5.4
18 TU	0329	8.4	0200	4.5	0246	4.5	0324	1.5	0058	1.1	0131	1.8	0140	1.8	0222	1.8	0309	1.9
	1015	3.8	0830	1.7	0902	2.0	0903	0.7	0812	1.7	0828	3.9	0845	4.0	0825	4.9	0822	5.5
	1608	8.6	1427	4.5	1524	4.5	1611	1.4	1323	1.0	1405	1.6	1409	1.6	1455	1.6	1550	1.8
	2237	3.6	2051	1.6	2131	1.8	2115	0.6	2013	1.7	2107	4.0	2122	4.0	2104	5.2	2051	5.7
19 W	0428	9.0	0254	4.7	0351	4.8	0429	1.6	0144	1.0	0235	1.6	0233	1.6	0321	1.6	0415	1.6
	1115	3.2	0921	1.5	1003	1.6	0954	0.6	0814	1.7	0919	4.0	0933	4.1	0925	5.2	0918	5.8
	1659	9.2	1515	4.7	1621	4.7	1706	1.5	1404	0.8	1459	1.3	1456	1.3	1547	1.4	1648	1.5
	2331	2.9	2137	1.4	2225	1.5	2204	0.5	2017	1.8	2152	4.1	2202	4.2	2156	5.5	2139	6.0
20 TH	0515	9.6	0336	5.0	0439	5.0	0518	1.7	0223	0.9	0321	1.3	0317	1.4	0408	1.3	0506	1.3
	1202	2.5	1003	1.2	1051	1.3	1035	0.4	0818	1.8	0959	4.1	1010	4.3	1011	5.6	1003	6.0
	1741	9.8	1554	5.0	1703	5.0	1752	1.6	1441	0.7	1541	1.0	1537	1.1	1629	1.1	1733	1.3
			2215	1.2	2309	1.2	2247	0.4	2025	1.8	2227	4.2	2235	4.4	2238	5.8	2219	6.2
21 F	0014	2.3	0412	5.2	0517	5.2	0603	1.9	0259	0.7	0358	1.1	0357	1.1	0446	1.1	0547	1.1
	0555	10.2	1039	1.0	1132	1.1	1114	0.3	0828	1.9	1032	4.2	1044	4.4	1049	5.8	1039	6.2
	1240	1.9	1629	5.2	1738	5.1	1833	1.8	1516	0.6	1616	0.8	1615	0.9	1705	0.9	1811	1.2
	1819	10.2	2250	1.0	2348	1.0	2328	0.2	2039	1.9	2258	4.3	2308	4.5	2312	6.0	2255	6.4
22 SA ○	0051	1.8	0445	5.4	0548	5.3	0643	2.0	0333	0.6	0430	0.9	0433	1.0	0519	0.9	0622	1.0
	0632	10.6	1112	0.9	1208	0.9	1153	0.2	0845	1.9	1103	4.3	1118	4.5	1120	5.9	1113	6.3
	1315	1.6	1701	5.3	1807	5.2	1911	1.9	1551	0.5	1646	0.6	1651	0.8	1738	0.8	1842	1.1
	1854	10.6	2322	0.9					2104	1.9	2327	4.4	2343	4.5	2343	6.1	2330	6.5
23 SU	0125	1.5	0516	5.5	0022	0.9	0008	0.1	0407	0.6	0500	0.7	0507	0.9	0550	0.9	0654	0.9
	0707	10.8	1143	0.8	0617	5.4	0720	2.0	0914	1.9	1133	4.4	1154	4.5	1149	6.0	1145	6.4
	1346	1.4	1732	5.4	1241	0.9	1230	0.1	1624	0.5	1715	0.6	1724	0.8	1808	0.7	1909	1.0
	1928	10.7	2353	0.8	1836	5.2	1945	1.9	2139	1.9	2355	4.4						
24 M	0157	1.5	0546	5.5	0053	0.9	0045	0.1	0440	0.6	0530	0.7	0018	4.6	0011	6.1	0003	6.6
	0739	10.8	1213	0.8	0646	5.5	0753	2.0	0950	1.9	1201	4.4	0539	0.9	0620	0.8	0724	0.9
	1415	1.4	1801	5.4	1311	0.9	1305	0.1	1656	0.5	1746	0.5	1227	4.5	1220	6.0	1215	6.4
	1959	10.6			1905	5.3	2015	1.9	2222	1.9			1754	0.8	1839	0.7	1937	0.9
25 TU	0225	1.6	0023	0.8	0123	0.9	0119	0.1	0509	0.6	0023	4.5	0051	4.5	0039	6.0	0033	6.6
	0809	10.7	0616	5.5	0718	5.5	0824	2.0	1035	1.9	0601	0.6	0607	0.8	0651	0.9	0757	0.8
	1441	1.6	1242	0.9	1340	0.9	1336	0.1	1726	0.5	1229	4.4	1300	4.5	1250	5.9	1242	6.4
	2027	10.4	1831	5.3	1937	5.3	2044	1.9	2308	1.9	1815	0.6	1822	0.8	1909	0.7	2006	0.9
26 W	0252	1.8	0054	0.9	0152	0.9	0147	0.1	0541	0.6	0052	4.5	0121	4.5	0106	6.0	0100	6.5
	0836	10.4	0646	5.4	0751	5.4	0851	1.9	1121	1.9	0630	0.7	0636	0.9	0721	0.8	0828	0.9
	1506	1.9	1313	1.0	1410	1.0	1400	0.1	1758	0.5	1301	4.4	1329	4.5	1321	5.8	1308	6.3
	2053	10.1	1902	5.2	2009	5.2	2110	1.8			1844	0.6	1851	0.9	1939	0.8	2036	1.0
27 TH	0318	2.1	0125	1.0	0222	1.1	0209	0.2	0000	1.9	0123	4.4	0151	4.5	0133	5.9	0124	6.4
	0903	10.1	0718	5.3	0823	5.3	0918	1.8	0614	0.6	0659	0.8	0706	1.0	0752	0.8	0858	1.0
	1531	2.3	1345	1.2	1440	1.2	1420	0.2	1218	1.9	1334	4.3	1401	4.4	1351	5.7	1336	6.2
	2118	9.8	1936	5.1	2041	5.0	2135	1.7	1833	0.6	1914	0.8	1923	1.0	2010	0.9	2106	1.2
28 F	0347	2.5	0159	1.2	0254	1.3	0229	0.2	0102	1.9	0200	4.3	0224	4.4	0202	5.7	0153	6.3
	0930	9.8	0753	5.1	0853	5.1	0944	1.6	0654	0.7	0731	1.0	0741	1.0	0824	1.0	0928	1.2
	1600	2.6	1420	1.4	1512	1.4	1442	0.3	1331	1.8	1415	4.1	1439	4.3	1422	5.5	1410	6.1
	2148	9.5	2013	4.9	2111	4.9	2200	1.6	1914	0.7	1947	1.1	1959	1.1	2044	1.1	2136	1.5

● ● Time: UT. For British Summer Time (shaded) March 30th to October 26th ADD ONE HOUR ● ●

SOUTH COAST OF ENGLAND Time Zone UT

St Helier * St Mary's * Plymouth * Portland * Poole * Southampton * Portsmouth * Shoreham * Dover

MARCH 1997 TIDE TABLES MARCH 1997

ST HELIER	ST MARYS, SCILLY	PLYMOUTH	PORTLAND	POOLE ENTRANCE	SOUTHAMPTON	PORTSMOUTH	SHOREHAM	DOVER	
Time m	Time m	Time m	Time m	Time m	Time m	Time m	Time m	Time m	
0421 2.9	0238 1.5	0327 1.5	0256 0.3	0218 1.8	0243 4.2	0303 4.3	0237 5.5	0229 6.2	**1 SA**
1004 9.4	0833 4.8	0922 4.8	1011 1.5	0739 0.8	0810 1.3	0821 1.2	0903 1.2	1000 1.5	
1637 3.1	1502 1.6	1548 1.6	1515 0.3	1502 1.7	1504 4.0	1525 4.1	1502 5.2	1453 6.0	
2226 9.1	2059 4.7	2143 4.7	2231 1.5	2005 0.8	2033 1.4	2044 1.3	2127 1.4	2214 1.7	
0506 3.3	0326 1.7	0409 1.8	0336 0.4	0358 1.7	0335 4.0	0354 4.1	0324 5.1	0318 5.9	**2 SU**
1050 8.9	0924 4.6	0959 4.6	1048 1.4	0836 0.9	0903 1.6	0912 1.5	0954 1.5	1043 1.7	
1730 3.5	1557 1.8	1633 1.9	1601 0.4	1652 1.7	1607 3.8	1624 3.9	1557 4.9	1551 5.7	
2319 8.6	2200 4.4	2231 4.5	2321 1.4	2110 1.0	2136 1.7	2143 1.6	2226 1.7	2306 1.9	
0611 3.7	0432 1.9	0504 2.0	0438 0.6	0547 1.7	0441 3.9	0458 4.0	0432 4.9	0426 5.6	**3 M**
1155 8.3	1035 4.3	1102 4.4	1149 1.3	0956 1.1	1015 1.8	1027 1.7	1106 1.7	1145 2.0	
1845 3.9	1715 2.0	1739 2.1	1719 0.6	1844 1.6	1727 3.7	1741 3.8	1717 4.8	1709 5.5	
	2324 4.3	2350 4.4		2243 1.1	2301 1.9	2313 1.8	2349 1.8		
0043 8.2	0600 1.9	0627 2.1	0044 1.4	0722 1.6	0601 3.9	0619 3.9	0602 4.9	0020 2.1	**4 TU**
0737 3.9	1209 4.3	1235 4.4	0622 0.6	1128 1.1	1146 1.7	1200 1.7	1235 1.7	0551 5.5	
1339 8.1	1847 1.8	1913 2.1	1327 1.3	1957 1.6	1856 3.8	1916 3.9	1852 5.0	1309 2.0	
2021 3.9			1915 0.6					1839 5.5	
0236 8.4	0055 4.5	0122 4.5	0230 1.5	0002 1.1	0031 1.7	0037 1.7	0118 1.6	0157 2.0	**5 W**
0915 3.5	0726 1.7	0804 1.9	0809 0.6	0807 1.7	0720 3.9	0749 4.0	0730 5.2	0718 5.6	
1522 8.6	1333 4.6	1412 4.5	1516 1.4	1235 0.9	1311 1.4	1314 1.5	1358 1.4	1442 1.8	
2157 3.3	2003 1.5	2044 1.7	2042 0.5	2012 1.7	2009 4.0	2040 4.1	2014 5.4	2000 5.8	
0359 9.2	0206 4.9	0250 4.8	0358 1.7	0104 0.9	0147 1.3	0147 1.4	0233 1.3	0325 1.6	**6 TH**
1039 2.7	0834 1.2	0922 1.4	0921 0.4	0812 1.8	0825 4.1	0900 4.3	0841 5.6	0830 6.0	
1633 9.5	1436 5.0	1534 4.8	1638 1.6	1331 0.7	1418 1.0	1418 1.1	1505 1.0	1558 1.4	
2312 2.3	2103 1.0	2154 1.2	2146 0.3	2014 1.9	2105 4.3	2136 4.4	2117 5.9	2102 6.2	
0459 10.2	0302 5.4	0401 5.2	0506 1.9	0156 0.7	0248 0.9	0247 1.1	0334 0.9	0432 1.1	**7 F**
1142 1.6	0931 0.8	1027 0.9	1018 0.2	0815 1.9	0917 4.3	0949 4.6	0939 6.1	0926 6.4	
1727 10.5	1528 5.4	1636 5.2	1742 1.9	1420 0.5	1513 0.6	1514 0.7	1602 0.7	1700 1.0	
	2156 0.6	2254 0.7	2239 0.2	2020 2.0	2151 4.5	2219 4.7	2210 6.3	2154 6.6	
0009 1.4	0351 5.8	0457 5.5	0604 2.1	0243 0.4	0340 0.5	0339 0.7	0426 0.6	0530 0.7	**8 SA**
0549 11.2	1021 0.4	1123 0.4	1109 0.1	0824 2.0	1004 4.5	1033 4.8	1027 6.4	1015 6.7	
1235 0.8	1615 5.7	1728 5.4	1836 2.1	1505 0.3	1603 0.3	1603 0.4	1653 0.5	1758 0.7	
1815 11.4	2244 0.3	2347 0.4	2328 0.0	2036 2.1	2236 4.7	2302 4.9	2258 6.6	2241 6.9	
0058 0.6	0437 6.1	0548 5.7	0656 2.3	0327 0.3	0429 0.2	0426 0.4	0515 0.4	0625 0.5	**9 SU**
0636 11.9	1109 0.1	1213 0.1	1155 -0.1	0844 2.1	1049 4.7	1116 4.9	1115 6.6	1103 6.9	
1321 0.2	1659 5.9	1815 5.6	1923 2.2	1548 0.1	1651 0.0	1648 0.2	1740 0.3	1851 0.5	
1859 11.9	2330 0.1			2106 2.1	2319 4.8	2345 5.0	2345 6.7	2327 7.1	●
0142 0.2	0521 6.2	0034 0.1	0013 -0.1	0409 0.2	0516 0.1	0509 0.3	0601 0.4	0715 0.3	**10 M**
0719 12.2	1153 0.0	0635 5.9	0742 2.4	0920 2.1	1134 4.8	1200 5.0	1201 6.7	1149 7.0	
1405 0.0	1742 6.0	1259 -0.0	1240 -0.2	1632 0.1	1738 -0.0	1731 0.2	1826 0.3	1936 0.4	
1942 12.0		1900 5.7	2006 2.3	2150 2.1					
0225 0.2	0014 0.1	0118 0.0	0057 -0.1	0454 0.2	0002 4.9	0027 5.0	0029 6.7	0011 7.1	**11 TU**
0802 12.1	0603 6.2	0720 5.9	0825 2.4	1011 2.1	0602 0.0	0552 0.3	0647 0.4	0800 0.2	
1445 0.0	1236 0.1	1342 0.1	1322 -0.2	1715 0.2	1218 4.8	1243 4.9	1248 6.6	1235 6.9	
2022 11.8	1823 5.9	1944 5.6	2045 2.3	2252 2.1	1823 -0.0	1812 0.3	1910 0.3	2016 0.4	
0305 0.6	0056 0.2	0200 0.2	0138 -0.1	0538 0.3	0046 4.8	0111 4.9	0111 6.6	0054 7.1	**12 W**
0842 11.7	0645 6.0	0804 5.7	0904 2.3	1118 2.1	0644 0.1	0633 0.4	0729 0.4	0840 0.3	
1524 0.8	1318 0.4	1422 0.3	1403 -0.1	1801 0.3	1303 4.7	1327 4.8	1333 6.5	1318 6.8	
2102 11.3	1905 5.7	2026 5.5	2121 2.1		1902 0.2	1854 0.4	1950 0.4	2054 0.5	
0344 1.2	0139 0.5	0239 0.5	0217 0.0	0005 2.0	0131 4.7	0154 4.8	0150 6.5	0135 6.9	**13 TH**
0923 11.0	0728 5.6	0846 5.5	0939 2.1	0623 0.4	0722 0.3	0714 0.6	0810 0.5	0918 0.5	
1603 1.5	1359 0.7	1500 0.7	1441 0.1	1237 2.0	1351 4.5	1411 4.7	1412 6.2	1359 6.6	
2141 10.6	1947 5.3	2106 5.3	2154 1.9	1848 0.5	1940 0.5	1936 0.7	2029 0.6	2129 0.8	
0422 2.0	0221 0.9	0315 0.9	0254 0.2	0129 2.0	0217 4.5	0238 4.6	0225 6.1	0217 6.6	**14 F**
1003 10.2	0812 5.2	0925 5.1	1013 1.8	0712 0.6	0759 0.6	0757 0.9	0850 0.8	0954 0.9	
1641 2.4	1442 1.1	1535 1.2	1518 0.3	1411 1.9	1441 4.3	1459 4.4	1450 5.9	1442 6.3	
2220 9.8	2032 4.9	2142 5.0	2224 1.7	1939 0.7	2017 0.9	2021 1.1	2110 1.0	2205 1.2	
0502 2.8	0307 1.3	0352 1.4	0333 0.4	0306 1.8	0309 4.2	0327 4.4	0304 5.7	0303 6.2	**15 SA**
1045 9.3	0900 4.7	1003 4.8	1045 1.6	0807 0.8	0839 1.1	0846 1.3	0933 1.2	1033 1.4	
1723 3.2	1529 1.6	1612 1.6	1556 0.5	1605 1.8	1540 4.0	1558 4.1	1534 5.4	1533 5.9	
2303 8.9	2124 4.5	2220 4.7	2257 1.5	2039 1.0	2103 1.4	2115 1.5	2158 1.4	2247 1.6	

● ● Time UT. For British Summer Time (shaded) March 30th to October 26th ADD ONE HOUR ● ●

MARCH 1997 TIDE TABLES MARCH 1997

	ST HELIER	ST MARYS, SCILLY	PLYMOUTH	PORTLAND	POOLE ENTRANCE	SOUTHAMPTON	PORTSMOUTH	SHOREHAM	DOVER
	Time m	Time m	Time m	Time m	Time m	Time m	Time m	Time m	Time m
16 SU	0548 3.6	0403 1.7	0433 1.8	0416 0.6	0502 1.7	0408 3.9	0430 4.1	0353 5.2	0358 5.8
	1136 8.5	1000 4.3	1047 4.4	1122 1.4	0913 1.0	0933 1.5	0946 1.6	1028 1.6	1119 1.8
	1813 3.9	1630 1.9	1657 2.1	1642 0.6	1823 1.6	1648 3.8	1724 3.9	1634 4.9	1633 5.5
		2235 4.2	2310 4.4	2339 1.4	2156 1.2	2207 1.8	2227 1.9	2303 1.9	2342 2.0
17 M	0000 8.3	0519 2.0	0530 2.2	0522 0.7	0653 1.6	0520 3.7	0549 3.8	0502 4.7	0509 5.4
	0646 4.1	1122 4.1	1154 4.2	1218 1.2	1044 1.2	1047 1.8	1114 1.9	1142 2.0	1225 2.2
	1252 7.9	1754 2.1	1806 2.4	1757 0.8	1938 1.6	1813 3.6	1839 3.7	1757 4.7	1752 5.2
	1918 4.3				2332 1.3	2332 2.0			
18 TU	0126 7.9	0009 4.1	0029 4.2	0048 1.3	0753 1.6	0642 3.6	0004 2.0	0028 2.1	0100 2.2
	0806 4.4	0648 2.1	0659 2.3	0712 0.8	1206 1.2	1215 1.9	0706 3.7	0632 4.6	0639 5.2
	1428 7.8	1252 4.1	1325 4.1	1407 1.2	2008 1.6	1937 3.7	1242 1.9	1308 2.0	1356 2.3
	2042 4.4	1918 2.0	1945 2.3	1937 0.8			1957 3.8	1926 4.7	1917 5.3
19 W	0257 8.1	0128 4.2	0200 4.3	0232 1.4	0038 1.2	0058 2.0	0118 1.9	0149 2.0	0235 2.1
	0938 4.1	0800 1.9	0830 2.1	0838 0.7	0811 1.6	0757 3.7	0819 3.8	0757 4.7	0758 5.3
	1542 8.3	1400 4.3	1450 4.3	1546 1.3	1300 1.1	1334 1.7	1343 1.7	1423 1.9	1519 2.0
	2205 3.9	2022 1.8	2101 2.0	2047 0.7	2012 1.7	2040 3.8	2100 3.9	2037 5.0	2024 5.5
20 TH	0402 8.6	0226 4.5	0314 4.6	0351 1.5	0124 1.1	0205 1.7	0210 1.7	0252 1.8	0347 1.7
	1046 3.4	0854 1.6	0933 1.7	0927 0.6	0813 1.7	0853 3.8	0912 4.0	0902 5.0	0857 5.6
	1633 8.9	1449 4.6	1548 4.7	1640 1.5	1341 0.9	1431 1.4	1430 1.5	1518 1.6	1619 1.7
	2303 3.2	2109 1.5	2156 1.6	2137 0.5	2014 1.8	2124 4.0	2141 4.1	2130 5.4	2114 5.9
21 F	0449 9.3	0309 4.8	0405 4.9	0445 1.7	0201 0.9	0253 1.4	0253 1.4	0340 1.5	0439 1.4
	1134 2.7	0935 1.3	1021 1.4	1008 0.4	0815 1.8	0934 4.0	0949 4.1	0949 5.4	0941 5.9
	1715 9.6	1528 4.8	1631 5.0	1724 1.6	1417 0.8	1513 1.1	1511 1.2	1601 1.2	1705 1.4
	2348 2.5	2148 1.2	2240 1.3	2220 0.4	2019 1.8	2159 4.1	2213 4.3	2211 5.7	2155 6.1
22 SA	0530 10.0	0345 5.1	0444 5.2	0531 1.8	0235 0.8	0330 1.1	0331 1.2	0418 1.1	0520 1.2
	1214 2.1	1011 1.1	1102 1.1	1046 0.3	0821 1.8	1007 4.1	1022 4.3	1025 5.7	1017 6.1
	1752 10.2	1603 5.1	1706 5.1	1805 1.7	1451 0.6	1548 0.9	1548 1.0	1637 1.0	1742 1.2
		2223 1.0	2319 1.1	2301 0.2	2028 1.9	2229 4.3	2245 4.4	2246 5.9	2230 6.3
23 SU	0027 1.9	0418 5.3	0518 5.3	0614 1.9	0308 0.6	0401 0.8	0406 1.0	0452 0.9	0556 1.0
	0610 10.5	1044 0.9	1139 0.9	1124 0.2	0834 1.9	1037 4.2	1057 4.4	1056 5.9	1048 6.2
	1248 1.6	1634 5.3	1739 5.3	1844 1.9	1524 0.5	1617 0.7	1623 0.9	1710 0.8	1815 1.1
	1827 10.6	2255 0.8	2354 0.9	2342 0.1	2046 1.9	2259 4.4	2319 4.5	2315 6.0	2303 6.4
24 M O	0101 1.5	0449 5.4	0551 5.4	0653 2.0	0339 0.5	0432 0.7	0439 0.9	0522 0.8	0630 0.9
	0641 10.8	1115 0.8	1212 0.8	1202 0.1	0855 1.9	1107 4.4	1131 4.5	1124 5.9	1118 6.3
	1321 1.4	1704 5.4	1810 5.3	1920 2.0	1554 0.5	1649 0.5	1654 0.8	1741 0.7	1845 1.0
	1901 10.8	2327 0.7			2113 1.9	2327 4.5	2353 4.6	2344 6.1	2334 6.5
25 TU	0133 1.3	0519 5.5	0027 0.8	0019 0.1	0409 0.5	0505 0.6	0509 0.8	0553 0.7	0702 0.8
	0714 10.9	1145 0.7	0624 5.5	0730 2.0	0925 1.9	1137 4.4	1205 4.5	1155 6.0	1145 6.4
	1350 1.3	1734 5.4	1245 0.8	1237 0.1	1624 0.5	1721 0.5	1724 0.8	1812 0.7	1915 0.9
	1932 10.8	2358 0.7	1843 5.4	1953 2.0	2146 1.9	2356 4.5			
26 W	0203 1.4	0549 5.5	0059 0.8	0054 0.1	0440 0.5	0537 0.5	0024 4.6	0011 6.1	0003 6.5
	0747 10.9	1217 0.8	0659 5.5	0803 2.0	1002 1.9	1207 4.5	0539 0.8	0624 0.7	0734 0.8
	1418 1.5	1805 5.4	1316 0.8	1308 0.1	1656 0.5	1753 0.5	1236 4.5	1226 6.0	1214 6.4
	2000 10.7		1917 5.4	2023 2.0	2226 1.9		1754 0.8	1842 0.7	1946 0.9
27 TH	0231 1.6	0030 0.8	0131 0.8	0124 0.1	0512 0.5	0025 4.5	0054 4.6	0040 6.1	0030 6.5
	0812 10.6	0621 5.4	0733 5.4	0833 1.9	1047 1.9	0609 0.6	0609 0.8	0655 0.7	0806 0.8
	1445 1.7	1248 0.9	1348 0.9	1335 0.1	1729 0.5	1238 4.4	1308 4.5	1258 5.9	1242 6.4
	2027 10.4	1837 5.4	1950 5.3	2051 1.9	2316 1.9	1823 0.6	1825 0.8	1913 0.7	2016 0.9
28 F	0300 1.8	0103 0.9	0203 1.0	0148 0.1	0546 0.5	0057 4.5	0126 4.5	0108 6.0	0057 6.5
	0840 10.4	0654 5.3	0805 5.3	0901 1.8	1144 1.9	0639 0.6	0641 0.8	0726 0.7	0836 0.9
	1512 2.1	1321 1.0	1418 1.1	1358 0.2	1806 0.6	1313 4.3	1342 4.5	1329 5.9	1312 6.4
	2054 10.2	1912 5.2	2021 5.2	2117 1.8		1854 0.8	1859 0.9	1946 0.9	2045 1.1
29 SA	0330 2.2	0138 1.1	0234 1.2	0212 0.2	0016 1.9	0133 4.4	0200 4.5	0138 5.8	0128 6.4
	0910 10.0	0730 5.1	0835 5.1	0929 1.7	0627 0.6	0711 0.8	0717 0.9	0800 0.9	0905 1.1
	1543 2.5	1357 1.2	1450 1.3	1423 0.2	1256 1.9	1354 4.2	1421 4.4	1402 5.7	1348 6.3
	2126 9.8	1951 5.0	2050 5.0	2143 1.7	1848 0.7	1929 1.0	1936 1.1	2021 1.1	2118 1.3
30 SU	0406 2.6	0218 1.3	0308 1.4	0241 0.3	0137 1.8	0216 4.2	0242 4.4	0215 5.6	0209 6.2
	0946 9.6	0812 4.9	0904 4.9	0958 1.6	0713 0.7	0749 1.1	0758 1.1	0841 1.1	0939 1.3
	1622 2.9	1440 1.5	1526 1.6	1455 0.3	1428 1.8	1443 4.1	1508 4.2	1443 5.4	1432 6.1
	2206 9.4	2037 4.8	2121 4.8	2213 1.6	1940 0.8	2014 1.4	2022 1.3	2106 1.4	2156 1.5
31 M	0452 3.0	0306 1.5	0348 1.6	0321 0.4	0314 1.8	0309 4.1	0331 4.2	0304 5.3	0256 6.0
	1032 9.0	0903 4.6	0942 4.7	1036 1.4	0809 0.8	0840 1.4	0848 1.3	0931 1.4	1023 1.6
	1715 3.4	1535 1.7	1611 1.8	1541 0.5	1620 1.7	1547 3.9	1606 4.1	1539 5.1	1530 5.8
	2300 8.8	2137 4.6	2209 4.7	2259 1.5	2046 1.0	2117 1.6	2121 1.6	2207 1.6	2248 1.8

● ● Time: UT. For British Summer Time (shaded) March 30th to October 26th ADD ONE HOUR ● ●

SOUTH COAST OF ENGLAND Time Zone UT

St Helier * St Mary's * Plymouth * Portland * Poole * Southampton * Portsmouth * Shoreham * Dover

APRIL 1997 TIDE TABLES APRIL 1997

ST HELIER Time m	ST MARYS, SCILLY Time m	PLYMOUTH Time m	PORTLAND Time m	POOLE ENTRANCE Time m	SOUTHAMPTON Time m	PORTSMOUTH Time m	SHOREHAM Time m	DOVER Time m		
0556 3.4	0412 1.7	0444 1.9	0424 0.5	0507 1.7	0415 3.9	0433 4.0	0411 5.0	0406 5.7	**1**	**TU**
1139 8.4	1013 4.3	1045 4.5	1137 1.3	0928 1.0	0952 1.6	1000 1.6	1041 1.7	1124 1.9		
1829 3.8	1652 1.9	1716 2.0	1700 0.6	1823 1.7	1707 3.8	1724 3.9	1659 5.0	1648 5.6		
	2300 4.4	2324 4.5		2222 1.1	2241 1.8	2252 1.8	2329 1.7			
0024 8.3	0539 1.8	0605 2.0	0016 1.4	0702 1.6	0536 3.8	0557 3.9	0541 4.9	0000 1.9	**2**	**W**
0718 3.6	1146 4.3	1216 4.4	0613 0.6	1106 1.0	1122 1.6	1137 1.6	1211 1.7	0536 5.5		
1323 8.1	1824 1.8	1851 2.0	1311 1.3	1951 1.7	1835 3.9	1903 4.0	1834 5.1	1246 2.0		
2000 3.8			1900 0.7	2347 1.1				1820 5.6		
0215 8.4	0030 4.5	0057 4.6	0159 1.5	0803 1.7	0011 1.6	0021 1.7	0059 1.6	0133 1.8	**3**	**TH**
0851 3.3	0705 1.5	0742 1.8	0754 0.5	1219 0.9	0658 3.9	0732 4.0	0712 5.2	0705 5.6		
1504 8.6	1312 4.5	1354 4.6	1457 1.5	2011 1.8	1247 1.4	1256 1.5	1337 1.4	1418 1.8		
2136 3.2	1942 1.4	2022 1.7	2026 0.6		1947 4.1	2023 4.2	1955 5.5	1942 5.8		
0339 9.2	0143 4.9	0228 4.8	0331 1.7	0051 0.9	0126 1.3	0132 1.4	0215 1.2	0300 1.5	**4**	**F**
1017 2.6	0814 1.1	0901 1.3	0904 0.4	0812 1.8	0803 4.1	0842 4.3	0824 5.6	0815 6.0		
1614 9.5	1416 4.9	1515 4.9	1619 1.7	1316 0.7	1355 1.0	1401 1.2	1444 1.0	1533 1.4		
2252 2.3	2043 1.0	2133 1.2	2129 0.4	2013 1.9	2043 4.3	2118 4.5	2059 5.9	2044 6.2		
0439 10.2	0241 5.3	0339 5.2	0442 1.9	0142 0.7	0225 0.8	0231 1.1	0316 0.8	0409 1.0	**5**	**SA**
1122 1.6	0911 0.7	1006 0.8	1000 0.2	0813 1.9	0857 4.3	0932 4.5	0921 6.0	0911 6.4		
1707 10.5	1508 5.3	1616 5.2	1721 1.9	1403 0.5	1449 0.6	1455 0.8	1541 0.7	1637 1.0		
2350 1.4	2136 0.6	2233 0.8	2221 0.2	2016 2.0	2129 4.5	2201 4.7	2150 6.3	2135 6.6		
0530 11.0	0330 5.7	0436 5.5	0541 2.1	0226 0.5	0317 0.5	0321 0.7	0407 0.5	0508 0.7	**6**	**SU**
1215 0.8	1000 0.4	1101 0.5	1050 0.0	0819 2.0	0944 4.5	1015 4.8	1008 6.3	1000 6.6		
1754 11.2	1554 5.7	1707 5.5	1814 2.1	1446 0.3	1540 0.3	1543 0.5	1632 0.4	1735 0.7		
	2224 0.3	2326 0.4	2309 0.1	2027 2.1	2213 4.7	2242 4.9	2237 6.5	2221 6.8		
0039 0.7	0416 6.0	0527 5.7	0633 2.3	0308 0.3	0405 0.2	0406 0.5	0456 0.4	0603 0.5	**7**	**M**
0616 11.7	1047 0.2	1151 0.2	1136 -0.1	0834 2.1	1029 4.6	1057 4.9	1054 6.5	1045 6.8		
1300 0.3	1638 5.9	1754 5.6	1901 2.2	1528 0.2	1627 0.1	1627 0.4	1718 0.3	1827 0.6	●	
1839 11.7	2309 0.1		2355 -0.0	2050 2.1	2256 4.8	2324 5.0	2320 6.6	2306 7.0		
0123 0.3	0500 6.1	0013 0.2	0720 2.4	0349 0.2	0452 0.1	0449 0.4	0541 0.3	0653 0.4	**8**	**TU**
0700 11.9	1131 0.1	0613 5.7	1220 -0.1	0902 2.1	1113 4.7	1140 4.9	1139 6.5	1130 6.9		
1343 0.4	1720 5.9	1236 0.2	1944 2.3	1610 0.2	1714 0.1	1710 0.3	1802 0.3	1912 0.5		
1920 11.8	2352 0.2	1838 5.6		2126 2.1	2339 4.8			2349 7.0		
0205 0.3	0542 6.0	0057 0.2	0038 -0.1	0431 0.2	0538 0.1	0006 5.0	0003 6.6	0737 0.3	**9**	**W**
0742 11.9	1213 0.3	0659 5.7	0803 2.3	0945 2.1	1158 4.7	0530 0.4	0624 0.4	1213 6.8		
1424 0.4	1800 5.8	1318 0.2	1301 -0.1	1652 0.3	1758 0.1	1223 4.9	1225 6.5	1952 0.4		
2000 11.6		1921 5.6	2022 2.3	2216 2.1		1751 0.4	1844 0.4			
0244 0.7	0035 0.3	0137 0.3	0118 -0.0	0513 0.3	0022 4.7	0047 4.9	0043 6.5	0031 6.9	**10**	**TH**
0821 11.4	0624 5.8	0742 5.6	0842 2.2	1044 2.0	0618 0.1	0610 0.5	0704 0.5	0817 0.4		
1501 1.0	1254 0.5	1357 0.5	1340 -0.0	1734 0.4	1243 4.6	1306 4.8	1307 6.4	1255 6.7		
2039 11.1	1842 5.6	2001 5.5	2057 2.2	2318 2.0	1838 0.3	1830 0.6	1923 0.6	2029 0.6		
0321 1.3	0116 0.6	0215 0.6	0157 0.1	0558 0.4	0105 4.6	0127 4.8	0121 6.3	0112 6.8	**11**	**F**
0900 10.8	0705 5.5	0823 5.4	0916 2.0	1154 2.0	0656 0.3	0651 0.7	0742 0.6	0854 0.6		
1538 1.7	1333 0.8	1433 0.8	1417 0.1	1821 0.5	1329 4.4	1348 4.6	1345 6.2	1336 6.5		
2115 10.5	1923 5.3	2039 5.3	2127 2.0		1915 0.6	1912 0.9	2000 0.8	2104 0.8		
0357 2.0	0157 0.9	0251 1.0	0234 0.2	0033 1.9	0149 4.3	0209 4.6	0155 6.0	0152 6.5	**12**	**SA**
0939 10.0	0747 5.1	0900 5.1	0948 1.8	0643 0.6	0731 0.7	0732 0.9	0819 0.9	0928 1.0		
1614 2.5	1414 1.2	1508 1.3	1451 0.3	1323 1.9	1418 4.2	1435 4.4	1424 5.8	1417 6.3		
2152 9.7	2006 4.9	2113 5.0	2155 1.8	1909 0.8	1951 1.0	1955 1.2	2040 1.1	2139 1.2		
0435 2.8	0240 1.3	0326 1.4	0310 0.4	0159 1.8	0238 4.1	0253 4.3	0232 5.6	0236 6.1	**13**	**SU**
1018 9.2	0833 4.7	0936 4.7	1017 1.6	0735 0.8	0810 1.0	0818 1.2	0900 1.3	1003 1.4		
1652 3.2	1457 1.6	1542 1.7	1524 0.5	1510 1.8	1513 4.0	1529 4.2	1505 5.4	1503 6.0		
2232 9.0	2054 4.6	2145 4.7	2222 1.6	2006 1.0	2034 1.4	2045 1.6	2126 1.5	2218 1.5		
0516 3.5	0330 1.7	0404 1.8	0351 0.5	0342 1.7	0332 3.8	0346 4.0	0319 5.1	0329 5.7	**14**	**M**
1106 8.4	0927 4.3	1014 4.4	1049 1.4	0836 1.0	0857 1.5	0912 1.6	0950 1.7	1042 1.9		
1737 3.9	1551 1.9	1621 2.1	1601 0.7	1733 1.7	1616 3.7	1649 4.0	1559 5.0	1600 5.6		
2322 8.3	2156 4.2	2227 4.5	2257 1.5	2121 1.2	2131 1.8	2153 1.9	2225 1.9	2305 1.9		
0608 4.0	0436 2.0	0454 2.2	0448 0.7	0554 1.6	0436 3.6	0503 3.8	0422 4.7	0436 5.3	**15**	**TU**
1212 7.9	1039 4.0	1112 4.2	1137 1.2	1001 1.2	1002 1.8	1031 1.9	1056 2.0	1136 2.2		
1836 4.3	1704 2.1	1721 2.4	1704 0.8	1903 1.6	1731 3.6	1758 3.8	1714 4.8	1711 5.3		
	2318 4.1	2335 4.3	2351 1.4	2259 1.3	2247 2.0	2330 2.1	2343 2.2			

● ● Time UT. For British Summer Time (shaded) March 30th to October 26th ADD ONE HOUR ● ●

APRIL 1997 TIDE TABLES APRIL 1997

	ST HELIER		ST MARYS, SCILLY		PLYMOUTH		PORTLAND		POOLE ENTRANCE		SOUTHAMPTON		PORTSMOUTH		SHOREHAM		DOVER	
	Time	m	Time	m	Time	m	Time	m	Time	m	Time	m	Time	m	Time	m	Time	m
16 W	0036	7.9	0558	2.1	0611	2.4	0624	0.7	0723	1.5	0552	3.5	0620	3.6	0547	4.5	0009	2.2
	0717	4.3	1206	4.0	1235	4.1	1303	1.2	1131	1.2	1125	1.9	1203	1.9	1218	2.1	0601	5.1
	1342	7.7	1829	2.1	1854	2.5	1848	0.8	1954	1.6	1850	3.6	1909	3.8	1840	4.7	1254	2.4
	1951	4.4															1835	5.2
17 TH	0209	7.9	0042	4.1	0100	4.3	0116	1.3	0010	1.2	0009	2.0	0046	2.0	0105	2.2	0139	2.2
	0842	4.2	0715	1.9	0745	2.2	0754	0.7	0804	1.5	0710	3.5	0735	3.6	0715	4.5	0722	5.2
	1500	8.1	1318	4.2	1357	4.3	1458	1.3	1230	1.1	1244	1.8	1309	1.8	1336	2.0	1427	2.2
	2115	4.1	1939	1.9	2019	2.2	2008	0.7	2011	1.6	1956	3.7	2017	3.9	1956	4.9	1945	5.4
18 F	0321	8.4	0145	4.4	0218	4.6	0253	1.4	0058	1.1	0119	1.8	0140	1.8	0212	1.9	0301	1.9
	0959	3.7	0812	1.7	0852	1.9	0848	0.6	0812	1.6	0811	3.7	0836	3.8	0824	4.8	0823	5.5
	1556	8.7	1412	4.4	1501	4.6	1600	1.4	1313	1.0	1345	1.5	1358	1.6	1436	1.7	1533	1.9
	2222	3.5	2030	1.6	2116	1.8	2103	0.6	2013	1.7	2044	3.9	2106	4.1	2052	5.3	2039	5.7
19 SA	0412	9.0	0232	4.6	0317	4.9	0358	1.6	0136	1.0	0210	1.5	0224	1.5	0302	1.6	0357	1.6
	1054	3.0	0857	1.4	0942	1.5	0931	0.4	0813	1.7	0856	3.8	0920	4.0	0914	5.2	0909	5.7
	1640	9.3	1454	4.7	1548	4.9	1646	1.6	1349	0.9	1431	1.2	1439	1.4	1522	1.4	1622	1.6
	2312	2.8	2112	1.3	2202	1.5	2148	0.5	2014	1.8	2121	4.1	2143	4.3	2135	5.6	2123	6.0
20 SU	0455	9.6	0312	4.9	0402	5.1	0450	1.7	0208	0.8	0252	1.1	0301	1.3	0343	1.2	0442	1.3
	1137	2.4	0935	1.2	1024	1.2	1011	0.3	0816	1.8	0933	4.0	0957	4.2	0952	5.5	0945	6.0
	1719	9.9	1530	5.0	1628	5.1	1730	1.8	1422	0.7	1509	1.0	1516	1.2	1601	1.1	1703	1.3
	2354	2.2	2150	1.1	2243	1.2	2230	0.3	2020	1.9	2155	4.2	2218	4.4	2210	5.8	2159	6.2
21 M	0534	10.2	0346	5.1	0442	5.3	0537	1.9	0239	0.7	0327	0.9	0335	1.1	0418	1.0	0521	1.1
	1215	1.9	1010	1.0	1103	1.0	1050	0.2	0824	1.9	1007	4.2	1032	4.4	1024	5.7	1017	6.2
	1756	10.4	1603	5.2	1706	5.3	1811	1.9	1453	0.6	1543	0.8	1550	1.0	1637	0.9	1741	1.1
			2224	0.9	2321	1.0	2310	0.2	2032	1.9	2226	4.4	2253	4.5	2242	5.9	2231	6.3
22 TU ○	0032	1.8	0419	5.3	0521	5.4	0621	2.0	0309	0.6	0401	0.7	0407	1.0	0452	0.8	0559	0.9
	0610	10.6	1044	0.8	1140	0.9	1127	0.1	0839	1.9	1039	4.3	1107	4.5	1055	5.8	1045	6.3
	1250	1.6	1636	5.4	1742	5.4	1850	2.0	1523	0.6	1619	0.6	1622	0.9	1711	0.8	1817	1.0
	1830	10.7	2259	0.8	2358	0.9	2349	0.2	2051	1.9	2257	4.5	2326	4.6	2312	6.0	2302	6.5
23 W	0106	1.5	0451	5.4	0559	5.4	0702	2.0	0339	0.5	0437	0.5	0439	0.9	0524	0.7	0636	0.8
	0645	10.8	1118	0.8	1216	0.8	1204	0.1	0903	1.9	1113	4.4	1141	4.5	1127	5.9	1115	6.4
	1323	1.5	1707	5.5	1820	5.5	1927	2.1	1555	0.5	1654	0.5	1655	0.9	1744	0.8	1852	0.9
	1903	10.9	2333	0.7					2117	1.9	2329	4.5	2357	4.6	2343	6.1	2332	6.5
24 TH	0139	1.4	0524	5.5	0034	0.8	0025	0.1	0412	0.5	0512	0.5	0512	0.8	0557	0.7	0711	0.8
	0718	10.9	1151	0.8	0637	5.4	0739	2.0	0936	1.9	1146	4.4	1215	4.6	1202	6.0	1147	6.5
	1354	1.5	1741	5.5	1252	0.8	1239	0.1	1628	0.5	1731	0.5	1728	0.8	1816	0.8	1926	0.9
	1935	10.9			1856	5.5	2000	2.0	2154	2.0								
25 F	0212	1.5	0008	0.7	0110	0.8	0058	0.1	0447	0.5	0001	4.5	0030	4.6	0015	6.1	0003	6.5
	0750	10.8	0558	5.4	0714	5.4	0814	2.0	1021	1.9	0548	0.5	0546	0.8	0632	0.7	0744	0.8
	1427	1.7	1227	0.8	1327	0.9	1310	0.1	1706	0.5	1220	4.4	1250	4.6	1237	6.0	1221	6.5
	2006	10.7	1816	5.4	1930	5.4	2032	2.0	2243	2.0	1805	0.6	1804	0.9	1851	0.8	1957	0.8
26 SA	0245	1.7	0045	0.8	0145	0.9	0129	0.2	0526	0.5	0035	4.5	0105	4.6	0048	6.1	0036	6.5
	0823	10.5	0634	5.3	0748	5.3	0846	1.9	1121	1.9	0623	0.5	0622	0.8	0707	0.8	0815	0.9
	1459	2.0	1303	1.0	1401	1.0	1341	0.2	1748	0.6	1259	4.4	1329	4.5	1314	5.9	1257	6.5
	2039	10.5	1854	5.3	2003	5.3	2102	1.9	2347	1.9	1842	0.7	1842	0.9	1928	1.0	2030	1.0
27 SU	0321	2.0	0124	1.0	0220	1.0	0200	0.2	0607	0.6	0114	4.4	0144	4.5	0125	5.9	0113	6.4
	0858	10.2	0715	5.2	0821	5.1	0918	1.8	1239	1.9	0658	0.7	0700	0.9	0747	0.9	0848	1.0
	1536	2.3	1344	1.1	1436	1.2	1413	0.3	1833	0.7	1342	4.3	1412	4.5	1353	5.8	1337	6.3
	2115	10.1	1936	5.2	2036	5.1	2132	1.8			1920	1.0	1923	1.1	2009	1.1	2106	1.1
28 M	0400	2.3	0207	1.2	0257	1.3	0236	0.3	0108	1.9	0159	4.3	0227	4.4	0206	5.7	0157	6.2
	0939	9.7	0800	4.9	0856	4.9	0952	1.7	0658	0.7	0739	0.9	0745	1.1	0830	1.1	0926	1.2
	1618	2.8	1430	1.4	1513	1.4	1451	0.4	1412	1.8	1433	4.1	1500	4.3	1439	5.6	1425	6.2
	2159	9.6	2026	4.9	2112	5.0	2206	1.7	1927	0.8	2008	1.2	2011	1.3	2058	1.3	2148	1.3
29 TU	0449	2.7	0259	1.4	0339	1.5	0322	0.4	0248	1.8	0253	4.1	0318	4.3	0258	5.4	0251	6.0
	1029	9.2	0854	4.7	0939	4.7	1036	1.5	0758	0.8	0831	1.2	0838	1.3	0922	1.3	1013	1.5
	1713	3.2	1527	1.6	1600	1.7	1542	0.5	1609	1.8	1537	4.0	1600	4.2	1537	5.4	1526	5.9
	2256	9.1	2127	4.7	2201	4.8	2254	1.6	2037	1.0	2109	1.5	2113	1.6	2159	1.5	2241	1.6
30 W	0550	3.1	0403	1.5	0436	1.7	0430	0.5	0445	1.7	0359	4.0	0420	4.1	0404	5.1	0403	5.7
	1137	8.6	1003	4.5	1041	4.6	1136	1.5	0915	0.9	0939	1.4	0948	1.5	1029	1.5	1113	1.7
	1821	3.5	1639	1.7	1706	1.9	1702	0.7	1825	1.7	1653	4.0	1725	4.1	1651	5.2	1640	5.7
			2242	4.6	2312	4.7			2209	1.1	2227	1.6	2239	1.7	2316	1.6	2350	1.7

● ● Time: UT. For British Summer Time (shaded) March 30th to October 26th ADD ONE HOUR ● ●

SOUTH COAST OF ENGLAND Time Zone UT

St Helier * St Mary's * Plymouth * Portland * Poole * Southampton * Portsmouth * Shoreham * Dover

MAY 1997 TIDE TABLES MAY 1997

ST HELIER	ST MARYS, SCILLY	PLYMOUTH	PORTLAND	POOLE ENTRANCE	SOUTHAMPTON	PORTSMOUTH	SHOREHAM	DOVER	Day
Time m	Time m	Time m	Time m	Time m	Time m	Time m	Time m	Time m	
0016 8.6	0522 1.6	0553 1.8	0006 1.5	0648 1.7	0517 3.9	0544 4.0	0526 5.0	0527 5.6	**1 TH**
0703 3.3	1127 4.4	1206 4.5	0605 0.6	1046 1.0	1100 1.4	1116 1.5	1151 1.5	1231 1.8	
1310 8.4	1803 1.7	1833 1.9	1300 1.4	1944 1.8	1813 4.0	1849 4.2	1817 5.3	1803 5.7	
1942 3.5			1842 0.7	2331 1.0	2348 1.5				
0153 8.7	0006 4.7	0039 4.7	0136 1.6	0756 1.7	0635 3.9	0003 1.6	0040 1.5	0115 1.6	**2 F**
0828 3.1	0642 1.4	0720 1.6	0731 0.5	1158 0.9	1219 1.3	0712 4.1	0651 5.2	0649 5.7	
1439 8.8	1247 4.6	1336 4.7	1434 1.5	2009 1.8	1923 4.2	1233 1.4	1313 1.3	1355 1.7	
2110 3.1	1918 1.4	1957 1.6	2003 0.6			2000 1.4	1934 5.5	1919 5.9	
0312 9.2	0118 4.9	0205 4.9	0303 1.7	0033 0.9	0100 1.2	0112 1.4	0154 1.2	0236 1.4	**3 SA**
0949 2.5	0750 1.1	0836 1.3	0839 0.4	0811 1.8	0742 4.1	0820 4.3	0803 5.5	0757 6.0	
1548 9.5	1351 4.9	1452 5.0	1553 1.7	1256 0.8	1327 1.0	1338 1.2	1422 1.0	1507 1.4	
2226 2.4	2019 1.0	2108 1.3	2106 0.5	2012 1.9	2019 4.4	2054 4.5	2035 5.9	2021 6.2	
0415 10.0	0217 5.2	0315 5.2	0415 1.9	0124 0.7	0200 0.8	0210 1.1	0256 0.9	0342 1.1	**4 SU**
1056 1.8	0847 0.8	0939 0.9	0936 0.3	0813 1.9	0837 4.3	0911 4.5	0859 5.9	0851 6.3	
1643 10.3	1445 5.3	1552 5.2	1655 1.9	1344 0.6	1424 0.7	1433 0.9	1518 0.7	1610 1.1	
2326 1.6	2113 0.7	2209 0.9	2200 0.3	2014 2.0	2106 4.5	2139 4.7	2127 6.2	2112 6.5	
0507 10.7	0308 5.5	0413 5.4	0515 2.0	0207 0.5	0252 0.5	0300 0.9	0348 0.6	0442 0.8	**5 M**
1150 1.2	0938 0.6	1036 0.7	1027 0.1	0816 2.0	0925 4.4	0956 4.7	0948 6.1	0940 6.5	
1731 10.9	1533 5.5	1644 5.4	1749 2.1	1427 0.5	1514 0.4	1522 0.7	1610 0.6	1707 0.9	
	2202 0.5	2302 0.7	2249 0.2	2020 2.1	2150 4.6	2221 4.8	2212 6.3	2200 6.7	
0016 1.0	0354 5.7	0505 5.5	0609 2.1	0249 0.4	0341 0.3	0346 0.7	0436 0.5	0539 0.7	**6 TU**
0554 11.2	1024 0.4	1127 0.5	1114 0.1	0826 2.0	1010 4.5	1039 4.8	1033 6.3	1026 6.7	
1237 0.8	1617 5.7	1731 5.5	1837 2.2	1509 0.4	1602 0.3	1607 0.6	1656 0.5	1800 0.7	●
1815 11.3	2248 0.4	2351 0.5	2335 0.1	2037 2.1	2234 4.7	2303 4.9	2256 6.4	2245 6.8	
0102 0.7	0439 5.8	0552 5.5	0657 2.2	0331 0.3	0427 0.2	0430 0.6	0520 0.5	0629 0.6	**7 W**
0639 11.4	1109 0.4	1212 0.5	1158 0.0	0848 2.0	1056 4.6	1122 4.8	1118 6.3	1110 6.7	
1321 0.7	1659 5.7	1815 5.5	1920 2.2	1549 0.4	1650 0.3	1649 0.6	1740 0.5	1846 0.6	
1857 11.4	2333 0.4			2105 2.1	2317 4.7	2344 4.9	2339 6.4	2328 6.8	
0143 0.7	0521 5.7	0034 0.5	0018 0.1	0410 0.3	0513 0.2	0510 0.6	0602 0.5	0713 0.6	**8 TH**
0721 11.3	1151 0.5	0638 5.5	0741 2.2	0925 2.0	1141 4.6	1205 4.8	1203 6.3	1154 6.7	
1400 0.9	1740 5.6	1254 0.6	1239 0.0	1631 0.4	1734 0.4	1730 0.7	1821 0.6	1927 0.6	
1937 11.2		1857 5.5	1959 2.2	2146 2.0	2359 4.6				
0223 1.0	0015 0.5	0115 0.6	0100 0.2	0451 0.4	0554 0.3	0024 4.8	0017 6.3	0011 6.7	**9 F**
0801 11.0	0603 5.5	0721 5.4	0820 2.1	1016 2.0	1225 4.5	0550 0.6	0641 0.7	0753 0.6	
1438 1.3	1231 0.7	1333 0.7	1319 0.1	1713 0.5	1814 0.5	1247 4.7	1244 6.2	1235 6.6	
2015 10.8	1821 5.5	1937 5.4	2033 2.1	2240 2.0		1810 0.8	1858 0.8	2005 0.7	
0300 1.5	0056 0.7	0153 0.8	0139 0.2	0534 0.5	0042 4.4	0103 4.7	0055 6.2	0052 6.6	**10 SA**
0840 10.4	0644 5.3	0800 5.2	0854 2.0	1123 2.0	0632 0.5	0630 0.8	0717 0.8	0829 0.8	
1514 1.9	1310 1.0	1409 1.0	1355 0.2	1758 0.6	1310 4.4	1330 4.6	1324 6.0	1315 6.5	
2052 10.3	1901 5.2	2012 5.3	2103 2.0	2345 1.9	1851 0.8	1851 1.0	1935 1.0	2041 0.9	
0335 2.1	0136 1.0	0229 1.1	0217 0.3	0620 0.6	0125 4.2	0143 4.5	0130 5.9	0132 6.4	**11 SU**
0918 9.8	0725 5.0	0835 5.0	0925 1.8	1243 1.9	0707 0.7	0711 1.0	0754 1.0	0903 1.1	
1548 2.5	1349 1.2	1443 1.3	1429 0.4	1844 0.8	1356 4.2	1414 4.4	1402 5.8	1355 6.3	
2129 9.7	1943 5.0	2044 5.1	2130 1.8		1927 1.1	1933 1.3	2014 1.3	2115 1.1	
0410 2.7	0216 1.3	0303 1.4	0253 0.4	0106 1.8	0209 4.0	0226 4.3	0208 5.6	0215 6.1	**12 M**
0957 9.2	0809 4.7	0907 4.7	0953 1.6	0708 0.8	0743 1.0	0754 1.2	0833 1.3	0935 1.4	
1624 3.1	1430 1.5	1516 1.7	1500 0.5	1420 1.8	1446 4.0	1504 4.3	1442 5.5	1439 6.0	
2206 9.1	2028 4.7	2113 4.9	2155 1.7	1939 1.0	2006 1.4	2021 1.6	2059 1.6	2151 1.4	
0448 3.2	0300 1.6	0338 1.8	0330 0.5	0238 1.7	0258 3.8	0313 4.1	0252 5.2	0302 5.7	**13 TU**
1039 8.6	0857 4.4	0942 4.5	1024 1.4	0803 0.9	0826 1.4	0843 1.5	0919 1.6	1010 1.8	
1706 3.6	1515 1.8	1552 2.0	1533 0.7	1625 1.7	1541 3.8	1609 4.1	1530 5.2	1528 5.8	
2250 8.5	2120 4.5	2150 4.6	2226 1.6	2041 1.2	2055 1.7	2117 1.8	2152 1.9	2233 1.7	
0533 3.7	0353 1.9	0420 2.1	0415 0.6	0434 1.6	0353 3.6	0414 3.8	0348 4.8	0400 5.4	**14 W**
1132 8.1	0954 4.2	1031 4.3	1106 1.3	0912 1.1	0919 1.6	0945 1.8	1015 1.9	1054 2.1	
1754 4.0	1614 2.0	1639 2.3	1620 0.8	1811 1.6	1643 3.7	1715 3.9	1632 4.9	1628 5.5	
2348 8.1	2224 4.2	2246 4.5	2309 1.4	2206 1.3	2157 1.9	2236 2.0	2257 2.1	2326 2.0	
0628 4.0	0500 2.0	0519 2.2	0523 0.7	0631 1.5	0458 3.5	0530 3.7	0458 4.6	0512 5.2	**15 TH**
1243 7.9	1107 4.1	1141 4.2	1209 1.2	1037 1.2	1027 1.8	1107 1.9	1124 2.1	1152 2.3	
1856 4.2	1727 2.1	1749 2.4	1743 0.9	1919 1.6	1752 3.6	1815 3.8	1746 4.8	1741 5.3	
	2340 4.2	2340 4.2		2328 1.3	2309 1.9				

● ● Time UT. For British Summer Time (shaded) March 30th to October 26th ADD ONE HOUR ● ●

MAY 1997 TIDE TABLES MAY 1997

	ST HELIER		ST MARYS, SCILLY		PLYMOUTH		PORTLAND		POOLE ENTRANCE		SOUTHAMPTON		PORTSMOUTH		SHOREHAM		DOVER	
	Time	m	Time	m	Time	m	Time	m	Time	m	Time	m	Time	m	Time	m	Time	m
16 F	0105	7.9	0613	2.0	0002	4.4	0014	1.4	0737	1.5	0610	3.5	0000	2.0	0009	2.2	0031	2.1
	0736	4.1	1222	4.1	0639	2.2	0648	0.7	1147	1.2	1142	1.8	0638	3.6	0618	4.5	0630	5.2
	1400	8.0	1840	2.0	1256	4.3	1339	1.3	1958	1.6	1857	3.7	1221	1.9	1238	2.1	1305	2.3
	2009	4.2			1915	2.3	1914	0.8					1918	3.9	1859	4.9	1854	5.4
17 SA	0221	8.1	0050	4.3	0116	4.6	0139	1.4	0022	1.2	0019	1.8	0100	1.9	0118	2.0	0148	2.0
	0851	3.9	0718	1.8	0755	2.0	0754	0.6	0806	1.6	0715	3.6	0743	3.7	0730	4.7	0734	5.3
	1503	8.4	1324	4.3	1403	4.6	1501	1.4	1237	1.1	1246	1.6	1316	1.7	1343	1.9	1421	2.1
	2122	3.8	1941	1.8	2023	2.0	2019	0.7	2011	1.7	1951	3.8	2016	4.0	2000	5.1	1954	5.6
18 SU	0322	8.6	0146	4.5	0220	4.8	0300	1.5	0103	1.1	0118	1.5	0146	1.7	0215	1.7	0257	1.8
	0957	3.4	0810	1.6	0851	1.7	0845	0.5	0812	1.6	0810	3.8	0839	3.9	0826	4.9	0824	5.6
	1555	8.9	1412	4.6	1457	4.8	1600	1.6	1314	1.0	1341	1.4	1359	1.6	1436	1.6	1524	1.8
	2224	3.3	2030	1.5	2115	1.7	2109	0.6	2013	1.8	2036	4.0	2105	4.2	2049	5.4	2041	5.8
19 M	0412	9.2	0231	4.7	0314	5.0	0404	1.6	0136	0.9	0206	1.2	0224	1.5	0301	1.4	0352	1.5
	1051	2.9	0854	1.3	0939	1.5	0929	0.4	0813	1.7	0854	3.9	0925	4.1	0909	5.3	0905	5.8
	1639	9.5	1453	4.9	1545	5.1	1649	1.7	1347	0.9	1426	1.1	1437	1.4	1520	1.3	1617	1.5
	2314	2.7	2112	1.3	2201	1.4	2154	0.4	2015	1.8	2115	4.2	2147	4.3	2128	5.6	2120	6.0
20 TU	0456	9.8	0311	5.0	0402	5.2	0458	1.8	0207	0.8	0248	1.0	0259	1.3	0341	1.1	0441	1.2
	1136	2.4	0934	1.1	1023	1.2	1010	0.3	0817	1.8	0933	4.1	1006	4.3	0947	5.5	0939	6.1
	1720	10.1	1530	5.1	1629	5.2	1735	1.9	1419	0.8	1507	0.9	1513	1.2	1600	1.1	1704	1.3
	2358	2.2	2151	1.1	2245	1.2	2236	0.3	2021	1.9	2151	4.3	2224	4.5	2205	5.8	2154	6.2
21 W	0537	10.3	0348	5.2	0448	5.3	0548	1.9	0237	0.7	0328	0.8	0333	1.1	0419	0.9	0526	1.1
	1218	1.9	1012	1.0	1106	1.1	1051	0.2	0827	1.9	1011	4.3	1042	4.4	1023	5.7	1012	6.2
	1758	10.5	1606	5.3	1712	5.4	1819	2.0	1452	0.7	1547	0.8	1549	1.0	1638	0.9	1748	1.1
			2230	0.9	2328	1.0	2316	0.3	2034	1.9	2227	4.4	2257	4.5	2241	5.9	2228	6.4
22 TH ○	0039	1.8	0424	5.3	0533	5.3	0633	2.0	0310	0.6	0408	0.6	0409	0.9	0456	0.8	0609	0.9
	0616	10.6	1050	0.9	1148	0.9	1132	0.2	0845	1.9	1049	4.4	1117	4.5	1100	5.9	1047	6.4
	1256	1.7	1642	5.5	1754	5.5	1900	2.1	1528	0.6	1628	0.7	1627	0.9	1716	0.9	1829	1.0
	1836	10.8	2309	0.8			2356	0.2	2055	2.0	2303	4.5	2331	4.6	2317	6.1	2303	6.5
23 F	0118	1.5	0501	5.4	0010	0.9	0717	2.0	0348	0.5	0449	0.5	0448	0.8	0534	0.8	0648	0.9
	0654	10.8	1129	0.8	0615	5.4	1212	0.2	0914	1.9	1127	4.4	1154	4.6	1141	6.0	1124	6.5
	1334	1.6	1720	5.5	1229	0.8	1940	2.1	1606	0.5	1709	0.6	1706	0.8	1754	0.9	1907	0.9
	1912	11.0	2349	0.7	1835	5.5			2127	2.0	2340	4.5			2355	6.1	2342	6.6
24 SA	0156	1.4	0539	5.4	0051	0.8	0035	0.2	0427	0.4	0530	0.5	0007	4.6	0613	0.8	0724	1.0
	0732	10.9	1209	0.8	0656	5.3	0757	2.0	0958	2.0	1205	4.4	0527	0.7	1224	6.0	1206	6.6
	1412	1.6	1800	5.5	1309	0.8	1251	0.2	1649	0.5	1751	0.6	1233	4.6	1835	1.0	1942	0.9
	1950	10.9			1913	5.5	2017	2.1	2218	2.0			1748	0.9				
25 SU	0235	1.5	0030	0.8	0131	0.8	0114	0.2	0512	0.5	0018	4.5	0048	4.6	0035	6.1	0023	6.6
	0811	10.7	0621	5.4	0735	5.3	0836	2.0	1101	2.0	0610	0.6	0609	0.7	0655	0.9	0800	0.9
	1451	1.8	1251	0.9	1348	0.9	1330	0.2	1734	0.6	1248	4.4	1317	4.6	1306	6.0	1249	6.6
	2029	10.8	1842	5.5	1951	5.4	2053	2.0	2323	2.0	1833	0.7	1830	0.9	1917	1.0	2018	0.9
26 M	0315	1.7	0115	0.8	0211	0.9	0154	0.2	0559	0.5	0100	4.4	0130	4.6	0118	6.0	0108	6.5
	0852	10.4	0704	5.3	0812	5.2	0913	1.9	1224	1.9	0651	0.6	0652	0.8	0740	0.9	0836	0.9
	1533	2.1	1336	1.0	1427	1.1	1410	0.3	1825	0.7	1334	4.3	1404	4.6	1352	6.0	1336	6.5
	2111	10.5	1928	5.3	2028	5.3	2129	1.9			1916	0.9	1916	1.1	2004	1.1	2058	1.0
27 TU	0359	2.0	0201	1.0	0251	1.1	0237	0.3	0048	1.9	0147	4.3	0217	4.5	0204	5.9	0158	6.3
	0937	10.0	0753	5.1	0853	5.0	0953	1.8	0651	0.6	0734	0.8	0739	1.0	0826	1.0	0918	1.1
	1618	2.4	1424	1.2	1509	1.3	1455	0.4	1405	1.9	1426	4.3	1456	4.5	1441	5.8	1427	6.3
	2159	10.0	2018	5.2	2109	5.2	2209	1.8	1923	0.8	2005	1.0	2007	1.3	2055	1.2	2144	1.1
28 W	0448	2.3	0254	1.1	0337	1.3	0328	0.4	0228	1.8	0242	4.2	0308	4.4	0258	5.6	0256	6.1
	1030	9.5	0847	4.9	0939	4.8	1039	1.7	0752	0.7	0825	1.0	0833	1.1	0919	1.2	1007	1.3
	1711	2.8	1520	1.4	1557	1.5	1548	0.5	1609	1.9	1528	4.2	1600	4.4	1537	5.7	1524	6.2
	2255	9.5	2117	5.0	2159	5.0	2257	1.7	2030	0.9	2101	1.2	2107	1.4	2153	1.3	2237	1.3
29 TH	0543	2.6	0354	1.3	0431	1.4	0430	0.4	0425	1.8	0345	4.1	0409	4.2	0358	5.4	0402	5.9
	1133	9.1	0950	4.7	1039	4.7	1135	1.6	0903	0.8	0925	1.1	0937	1.3	1020	1.3	1106	1.5
	1812	3.1	1626	1.5	1657	1.7	1656	0.6	1818	1.8	1636	4.1	1720	4.3	1641	5.5	1629	6.0
			2224	4.8	2303	4.9	2359	1.6	2149	1.0	2209	1.4	2220	1.5	2302	1.4	2342	1.4
30 F	0005	9.1	0503	1.4	0539	1.5	0545	0.5	0630	1.7	0457	4.0	0529	4.1	0509	5.2	0512	5.8
	0648	2.9	1103	4.6	1152	4.7	1245	1.6	1021	0.9	1036	1.2	1051	1.4	1132	1.4	1215	1.6
	1249	8.9	1739	1.5	1812	1.7	1815	0.7	1929	1.8	1749	4.1	1827	4.3	1754	5.5	1739	5.9
	1923	3.3	2339	4.8					2304	1.0	2321	1.4	2335	1.5				
31 SA	0124	9.0	0616	1.4	0020	4.8	0114	1.6	0743	1.7	0611	4.0	0648	4.1	0018	1.4	0056	1.5
	0802	2.9	1218	4.7	0654	1.5	0701	0.5	1131	0.9	1150	1.2	1203	1.4	0625	5.2	0625	5.8
	1409	9.0	1851	1.4	1312	4.8	1404	1.6	2003	1.9	1857	4.2	1932	4.4	1247	1.3	1330	1.6
	2041	3.1			1928	1.6	1932	0.6							1905	5.5	1851	6.0

● ● Time: UT. For British Summer Time (shaded) March 30th to October 26th ADD ONE HOUR ● ●

SOUTH COAST OF ENGLAND Time Zone UT

St Helier * St Mary's * Plymouth * Portland * Poole * Southampton * Portsmouth * Shoreham * Dover

JUNE 1997 TIDE TABLES JUNE 1997

Day	ST HELIER Time	m	ST MARYS SCILLY Time	m	PLYMOUTH Time	m	PORTLAND Time	m	POOLE ENTRANCE Time	m	SOUTHAMPTON Time	m	PORTSMOUTH Time	m	SHOREHAM Time	m	DOVER Time	m
1 SU	0242	9.2	0050	4.9	0139	4.9	0233	1.7	0008	0.9	0031	1.2	0044	1.4	0130	1.2	0209	1.4
	0918	2.7	0724	1.2	0805	1.3	0809	0.4	0808	1.8	0719	4.1	0754	4.2	0736	5.4	0731	5.9
	1518	9.4	1325	4.9	1424	4.9	1521	1.7	1231	0.8	1258	1.0	1310	1.3	1357	1.1	1439	1.4
	2157	2.7	1955	1.2	2039	1.4	2039	0.6	2012	1.9	1955	4.4	2029	4.5	2008	5.7	1954	6.1
2 M	0347	9.7	0152	5.1	0250	5.1	0345	1.8	0103	0.8	0132	0.9	0146	1.2	0233	1.0	0317	1.2
	1027	2.2	0823	1.0	0910	1.1	0909	0.4	0812	1.9	0818	4.2	0849	4.4	0835	5.6	0830	6.1
	1616	9.9	1422	5.1	1527	5.1	1626	1.8	1323	0.7	1357	0.9	1409	1.1	1456	0.9	1543	1.3
	2300	2.1	2051	1.0	2142	1.2	2137	0.5	2013	2.0	2046	4.5	2117	4.6	2102	5.9	2050	6.3
3 TU	0442	10.1	0247	5.3	0351	5.2	0450	1.9	0149	0.7	0228	0.7	0239	1.0	0328	0.8	0418	1.0
	1124	1.8	0916	0.9	1009	1.0	1003	0.3	0814	1.9	0910	4.4	0937	4.5	0927	5.8	0921	6.3
	1706	10.4	1512	5.3	1621	5.3	1723	2.0	1408	0.6	1452	0.7	1501	1.0	1549	0.8	1642	1.1
	2354	1.6	2143	0.8	2238	1.0	2229	0.4	2016	2.0	2133	4.5	2201	4.7	2150	6.0	2139	6.5
4 W	0533	10.5	0336	5.4	0445	5.2	0547	2.0	0232	0.5	0319	0.6	0327	0.9	0418	0.7	0515	0.9
	1214	1.5	1004	0.8	1103	0.9	1051	0.2	0821	1.9	0956	4.4	1022	4.6	1015	6.0	1009	6.4
	1753	10.7	1558	5.5	1711	5.3	1813	2.1	1451	0.6	1543	0.6	1548	0.9	1637	0.8	1736	1.0
			2230	0.7	2328	0.9	2316	0.3	2027	2.0	2215	4.5	2243	4.7	2236	6.1	2226	6.6
5 TH	0041	1.3	0421	5.5	0535	5.2	0637	2.0	0313	0.5	0406	0.4	0412	0.8	0502	0.7	0606	0.9
	0618	10.7	1049	0.7	1150	0.8	1137	0.2	0838	2.0	1042	4.5	1106	4.6	1101	6.0	1053	6.5
	1258	1.3	1642	5.5	1757	5.4	1858	2.1	1532	0.5	1629	0.6	1632	0.9	1721	0.8	1823	0.9
	1836	10.9	2315	0.7					2050	2.0	2259	4.5	2324	4.7	2318	6.1	2311	6.6
6 F	0124	1.2	0504	5.4	0014	0.8	0001	0.2	0354	0.5	0451	0.4	0454	0.7	0544	0.8	0651	0.9
	0701	10.7	1132	0.8	0620	5.2	0722	2.0	0909	2.0	1126	4.5	1148	4.6	1146	6.1	1136	6.6
	1339	1.4	1723	5.5	1233	0.9	1220	0.2	1613	0.6	1712	0.6	1713	0.9	1801	0.9	1905	0.8
	1917	10.8	2357	0.8	1838	5.4	1939	2.1	2123	2.0	2341	4.4			2357	6.1	2354	6.6
7 SA	0203	1.3	0545	5.3	0055	0.9	0043	0.2	0434	0.5	0531	0.5	0003	4.7	0621	0.9	0731	0.9
	0742	10.6	1212	0.9	0700	5.2	0803	2.0	0954	2.0	1210	4.4	0533	0.8	1227	6.0	1217	6.6
	1416	1.6	1803	5.4	1312	0.9	1300	0.2	1655	0.6	1752	0.7	1230	4.6	1838	1.0	1943	0.9
	1955	10.6			1914	5.3	2014	2.1	2209	2.0			1753	1.0				
8 SU	0239	1.6	0037	0.9	0133	1.0	0123	0.2	0516	0.5	0020	4.3	0042	4.6	0034	6.0	0034	6.4
	0821	10.2	0625	5.2	0736	5.1	0837	1.9	1052	1.9	0609	0.6	0613	0.8	0657	1.0	0806	1.0
	1451	2.0	1250	1.1	1348	1.4	1337	0.3	1738	0.7	1252	4.3	1311	4.5	1305	6.0	1256	6.5
	2033	10.2	1842	5.2	1946	5.3	2044	2.0	2308	1.9	1828	0.9	1833	1.1	1915	1.0	2019	0.9
9 M	0314	2.0	0115	1.1	0207	1.1	0200	0.3	0600	0.6	0101	4.2	0121	4.5	0110	5.8	0114	6.3
	0859	9.8	0704	5.0	0808	5.0	0907	1.8	1205	1.9	0643	0.8	0653	1.0	0733	1.1	0839	1.2
	1525	2.4	1327	1.2	1421	1.3	1412	0.4	1822	0.8	1334	4.2	1354	4.5	1342	5.8	1335	6.4
	2109	9.8	1921	5.1	2015	5.2	2110	1.9			1904	1.1	1913	1.3	1954	1.3	2054	1.1
10 TU	0348	2.5	0152	1.3	0240	1.4	0236	0.3	0018	1.8	0141	4.0	0201	4.3	0148	5.6	0153	6.1
	0936	9.3	0744	4.8	0838	4.8	0934	1.6	0644	0.7	0717	1.0	0733	1.1	0811	1.3	0909	1.4
	1559	2.8	1403	1.4	1452	1.6	1443	0.5	1331	1.8	1417	4.0	1439	4.3	1420	5.6	1415	6.2
	2144	9.3	2001	4.9	2044	5.0	2136	1.7	1908	0.9	1939	1.3	1954	1.4	2035	1.5	2128	1.3
11 W	0421	2.9	0230	1.5	0312	1.6	0309	0.4	0141	1.8	0223	3.9	0244	4.2	0229	5.3	0234	5.8
	1013	8.9	0825	4.6	0910	4.7	1004	1.5	0731	0.9	0755	1.2	0814	1.4	0852	1.5	0942	1.6
	1635	3.2	1443	1.6	1524	1.8	1512	0.6	1510	1.8	1503	3.9	1529	4.2	1502	5.4	1457	6.0
	2221	8.9	2044	4.7	2119	4.9	2205	1.6	1959	1.0	2020	1.5	2039	1.5	2120	1.5	2206	1.5
12 TH	0457	3.3	0313	1.7	0348	1.9	0343	0.5	0312	1.7	0310	3.7	0330	4.0	0315	5.0	0321	5.6
	1054	8.5	0912	4.4	0953	4.5	1039	1.4	0822	1.0	0838	1.4	0900	1.6	0938	1.7	1020	1.8
	1715	3.6	1530	1.8	1603	2.1	1545	0.7	1659	1.7	1554	3.8	1628	4.0	1550	5.2	1545	5.7
	2305	8.5	2134	4.5	2206	4.7	2241	1.5	2059	1.2	2109	1.7	2133	1.9	2212	1.9	2249	1.8
13 F	0541	3.6	0405	1.9	0434	2.0	0424	0.6	0504	1.6	0405	3.6	0431	3.8	0409	4.7	0416	5.4
	1144	8.2	1008	4.3	1051	4.4	1127	1.3	0925	1.1	0931	1.6	0957	1.8	1032	1.9	1106	2.0
	1805	3.9	1627	2.0	1654	2.2	1633	0.7	1827	1.7	1652	3.7	1727	3.9	1648	5.0	1642	5.5
			2234	4.3	2309	4.6	2329	1.4	2215	1.2	2209	1.8	2245	2.0	2311	2.0	2341	1.9
14 SA	0000	8.2	0507	2.0	0532	2.1	0524	0.6	0647	1.5	0508	3.6	0543	3.7	0513	4.6	0521	5.2
	0635	3.8	1115	4.2	1158	4.4	1232	1.3	1039	1.2	1036	1.7	1109	1.9	1134	2.0	1203	2.2
	1246	8.1	1735	2.0	1800	2.3	1753	0.8	1925	1.7	1754	3.7	1822	3.9	1753	4.9	1748	5.4
	1904	4.0	2345	4.3					2325	1.2	2316	1.8	2357	1.9				
15 SU	0107	8.1	0615	1.9	0019	4.6	0036	1.4	0742	1.5	0615	3.6	0646	3.7	0017	2.0	0042	2.0
	0739	3.9	1224	4.3	0641	2.1	0639	0.6	1141	1.2	1143	1.7	1214	1.8	0622	4.6	0627	5.2
	1355	8.2	1843	1.9	1304	4.5	1351	1.4	1959	1.7	1854	3.8	1920	4.0	1241	2.0	1309	2.2
	2014	4.0			1914	2.2	1915	0.7							1858	5.0	1852	5.5

● ● Time UT. For British Summer Time (shaded) March 30th to October 26th ADD ONE HOUR ● ●

JUNE 1997 TIDE TABLES JUNE 1997

	ST HELIER	ST MARYS, SCILLY	PLYMOUTH	PORTLAND	POOLE ENTRANCE	SOUTHAMPTON	PORTSMOUTH	SHOREHAM	DOVER
	Time m	Time m	Time m	Time m	Time m	Time m	Time m	Time m	Time m
16 M	0218 8.3	0051 4.4	0125 4.7	0157 1.4	0014 1.2	0021 1.6	0051 1.8	0118 1.9	0150 1.9
	0849 3.7	0718 1.8	0750 2.0	0745 0.6	0807 1.6	0719 3.7	0748 3.8	0726 4.7	0727 5.4
	1459 8.5	1324 4.5	1405 4.7	1506 1.5	1228 1.1	1246 1.5	1306 1.7	1342 1.8	1421 2.0
	2125 3.7	1942 1.7	2020 2.0	2019 0.7	2011 1.7	1948 4.0	2018 4.1	1955 5.1	1948 5.6
17 TU	0321 8.7	0146 4.6	0225 4.8	0314 1.5	0054 1.0	0119 1.4	0136 1.6	0214 1.6	0257 1.7
	0956 3.3	0811 1.6	0849 1.7	0840 0.5	0812 1.7	0813 3.9	0845 4.0	0820 5.0	0817 5.7
	1554 9.1	1413 4.7	1500 4.9	1606 1.6	1307 1.0	1342 1.3	1351 1.6	1436 1.6	1529 1.7
	2229 3.2	2033 1.5	2117 1.7	2112 0.6	2013 1.8	2035 4.1	2109 4.2	2045 5.4	2036 5.9
18 W	0415 9.3	0234 4.8	0321 5.0	0418 1.6	0131 0.9	0210 1.2	0218 1.4	0303 1.3	0359 1.5
	1054 2.8	0857 1.3	0942 1.5	0930 0.4	0814 1.8	0901 4.0	0935 4.1	0908 5.3	0901 5.9
	1643 9.7	1457 5.0	1552 5.1	1700 1.8	1345 0.8	1432 1.1	1435 1.3	1524 1.3	1628 1.5
	2324 2.6	2119 1.2	2209 1.4	2200 0.4	2015 1.9	2118 4.3	2151 4.4	2131 5.6	2118 6.1
19 TH	0505 9.9	0318 5.1	0415 5.1	0515 1.8	0207 0.7	0258 0.9	0300 1.1	0348 1.1	0454 1.2
	1146 2.3	0942 1.1	1033 1.2	1018 0.3	0819 1.8	0945 4.2	1015 4.3	0953 5.6	0942 6.2
	1729 10.3	1539 5.3	1642 5.3	1750 2.0	1424 0.7	1519 0.9	1519 1.1	1609 1.1	1720 1.2
		2203 1.0	2300 1.1	2246 0.3	2023 1.9	2159 4.4	2229 4.5	2214 5.9	2159 6.3
20 F	0012 2.0	0400 5.3	0506 5.2	0609 1.9	0246 0.6	0344 0.7	0343 0.9	0432 0.9	0543 1.0
	0551 10.4	1026 0.9	1123 1.0	1105 0.2	0832 1.9	1028 4.3	1054 4.5	1038 5.8	1024 6.4
	1233 1.9	1621 5.5	1730 5.4	1837 2.1	1506 0.6	1606 0.8	1604 0.9	1653 1.0	1807 1.0
○	1812 10.8	2248 0.8	2348 0.9	2332 0.3	2038 2.0	2240 4.5	2306 4.6	2256 6.1	2241 6.5
21 SA	0058 1.6	0442 5.4	0554 5.3	0658 2.0	0329 0.4	0429 0.5	0428 0.7	0516 0.9	0628 0.9
	0635 10.8	1109 0.8	1210 0.8	1151 0.2	0856 2.0	1110 4.4	1133 4.6	1125 6.0	1107 6.6
	1318 1.6	1703 5.6	1815 5.5	1923 2.1	1549 0.5	1653 0.6	1649 0.8	1737 1.0	1851 0.9
	1856 11.1	2333 0.7			2108 2.0	2321 4.5	2347 4.7	2340 6.2	2325 6.6
22 SU	0142 1.3	0524 5.5	0035 0.7	0017 0.2	0413 0.4	0515 0.4	0513 0.6	0600 0.9	0710 0.8
	0718 11.0	1154 0.7	0640 5.4	0745 2.0	0937 2.0	1153 4.5	1216 4.7	1213 6.1	1153 6.7
	1401 1.4	1746 5.7	1255 0.7	1236 0.2	1637 0.5	1740 0.6	1736 0.8	1822 1.0	1932 0.8
	1939 11.3		1858 5.6	2006 2.2	2154 2.0				
23 M	0226 1.1	0018 0.6	0120 0.6	0102 0.2	0501 0.4	0003 4.5	0030 4.7	0025 6.3	0012 6.7
	0803 11.0	0609 5.5	0723 5.4	0829 2.0	1040 2.0	0601 0.4	0559 0.6	0646 0.9	0750 0.8
	1444 1.4	1240 0.7	1339 0.7	1321 0.2	1725 0.5	1237 4.5	1303 4.7	1301 6.2	1241 6.7
	2022 11.2	1831 5.7	1939 5.6	2048 2.2	2300 2.0	1826 0.6	1821 0.8	1910 1.0	2012 0.7
24 TU	0309 1.2	0105 0.6	0203 0.7	0148 0.2	0551 0.4	0048 4.5	0116 4.7	0113 6.2	0103 6.6
	0847 10.9	0655 5.5	0806 5.3	0911 2.0	1200 2.0	0644 0.4	0645 0.6	0734 0.9	0830 0.8
	1528 1.6	1327 0.8	1421 0.8	1406 0.2	1818 0.6	1324 4.5	1351 4.7	1350 6.2	1331 6.7
	2106 11.0	1918 5.6	2021 5.5	2130 2.1		1912 0.7	1909 0.9	1959 1.0	2054 0.8
25 W	0354 1.4	0153 0.7	0247 0.8	0234 0.2	0022 2.0	0135 4.4	0203 4.6	0202 6.1	0156 6.5
	0933 10.5	0742 5.3	0849 5.2	0953 1.9	0643 0.5	0729 0.5	0732 0.8	0824 0.9	0914 0.9
	1614 1.9	1415 0.9	1505 1.0	1451 0.3	1343 2.0	1415 4.4	1445 4.6	1437 6.1	1421 6.6
	2154 10.6	2008 5.5	2106 5.4	2212 2.0	1912 0.8	1958 0.8	1957 1.0	2050 1.0	2141 0.9
26 TH	0440 1.8	0243 0.9	0333 1.0	0323 0.3	0201 1.9	0228 4.3	0254 4.5	0253 5.9	0251 6.3
	1023 10.1	0834 5.1	0936 5.0	1036 1.8	0739 0.6	0816 0.7	0821 0.9	0913 1.0	1001 1.1
	1703 2.3	1508 1.1	1551 1.2	1541 0.4	1546 1.9	1511 4.4	1548 4.6	1528 6.0	1513 6.4
	2246 10.1	2101 5.2	2154 5.2	2257 1.9	2012 0.8	2049 1.0	2051 1.2	2144 1.1	2231 1.0
27 F	0531 2.2	0338 1.1	0422 1.2	0418 0.3	0354 1.8	0326 4.2	0352 4.3	0347 5.7	0348 6.1
	1119 9.6	0930 4.9	1030 4.9	1125 1.7	0842 0.7	0908 0.9	0918 1.1	1008 1.1	1054 1.3
	1757 2.7	1606 1.3	1644 1.5	1636 0.5	1750 1.9	1613 4.3	1700 4.5	1623 5.8	1609 6.3
	2345 9.5	2201 5.0	2251 5.0	2348 1.7	2121 0.9	2145 1.1	2153 1.4	2243 1.2	2329 1.2
28 SA	0629 2.6	0439 1.3	0518 1.4	0519 0.4	0557 1.9	0433 4.1	0505 4.2	0447 5.4	0448 6.0
	1222 9.2	1035 4.7	1133 4.8	1222 1.6	0950 0.8	1010 1.1	1021 1.3	1109 1.2	1155 1.5
	1900 3.1	1712 1.4	1745 1.6	1742 0.6	1905 1.9	1721 4.2	1800 4.4	1725 5.5	1711 6.1
		2310 4.8	2359 4.9		2233 0.9	2251 1.3	2303 1.5	2351 1.3	
29 SU	0054 9.1	0547 1.4	0623 1.5	0049 1.6	0722 1.7	0546 4.0	0619 4.1	0555 5.2	0033 1.4
	0733 2.9	1148 4.7	1244 4.8	0627 0.5	1101 0.9	1119 1.2	1132 1.4	1219 1.3	0554 5.8
	1333 9.0	1824 1.5	1855 1.7	1330 1.6	1950 1.9	1830 4.2	1901 4.4	1833 5.4	1302 1.6
	2010 3.2			1856 0.7	2341 0.9				1818 6.0
30 M	0209 9.0	0022 4.8	0112 4.8	0200 1.6	0801 1.7	0000 1.3	0014 1.5	0103 1.4	0142 1.4
	0845 3.0	0657 1.4	0732 1.5	0737 0.5	1206 0.9	0659 4.0	0728 4.1	0706 5.2	0703 5.8
	1445 9.0	1259 4.8	1355 4.8	1445 1.6	2009 1.9	1230 1.3	1242 1.4	1329 1.4	1411 1.6
	2125 3.1	1932 1.4	2006 1.6	2009 0.7		1934 4.3	2002 4.4	1940 5.4	1927 6.0

● ● Time: UT. For British Summer Time (shaded) March 30th to October 26th ADD ONE HOUR ● ●

SOUTH COAST OF ENGLAND Time Zone UT

St Helier * St Mary's * Plymouth * Portland * Poole * Southampton * Portsmouth * Shoreham * Dover

JULY 1997 TIDE TABLES JULY 1997

ST HELIER		ST MARYS, SCILLY		PLYMOUTH		PORTLAND		POOLE ENTRANCE		SOUTHAMPTON		PORTSMOUTH		SHOREHAM		DOVER		Day
Time	m	Time	m	Time	m	Time	m	Time	m	Time	m	Time	m	Time	m	Time	m	
0319	9.2	0130	4.9	0224	4.9	0317	1.6	0041	0.9	0108	1.2	0121	1.4	0211	1.3	0251	1.4	1 TU
0957	2.8	0800	1.3	0840	1.5	0843	0.5	0812	1.8	0804	4.1	0830	4.2	0812	5.3	0807	5.9	
1549	9.4	1402	4.9	1502	5.0	1557	1.7	1304	0.9	1336	1.2	1347	1.4	1435	1.3	1519	1.5	
2235	2.7	2033	1.2	2115	1.5	2116	0.6	2012	1.9	2030	4.3	2056	4.5	2040	5.5	2029	6.1	
0421	9.5	0230	5.0	0331	4.9	0427	1.7	0133	0.8	0209	1.0	0221	1.2	0310	1.2	0358	1.3	2 W
1059	2.5	0857	1.2	0945	1.3	0941	0.4	0813	1.8	0859	4.2	0922	4.3	0910	5.5	0904	6.1	
1645	9.8	1456	5.1	1603	5.1	1700	1.8	1353	0.8	1436	1.0	1443	1.3	1532	1.2	1622	1.3	
2333	2.3	2127	1.1	2216	1.3	2212	0.5	2014	1.9	2119	4.4	2143	4.5	2133	5.7	2124	6.2	
0514	9.9	0321	5.1	0430	5.0	0527	1.8	0217	0.7	0303	0.8	0311	1.1	0403	1.0	0458	1.2	3 TH
1152	2.1	0948	1.1	1042	1.2	1032	0.4	0818	1.9	0949	4.3	1009	4.4	1002	5.7	0954	6.2	
1733	10.1	1544	5.2	1656	5.2	1752	1.9	1436	0.7	1527	0.9	1532	1.1	1622	1.1	1718	1.2	
		2216	1.0	2309	1.2	2300	0.4	2022	1.9	2203	4.4	2226	4.6	2222	5.8	2212	6.3	
0022	1.9	0407	5.2	0522	5.1	0620	1.8	0259	0.6	0351	0.7	0357	0.9	0448	1.0	0550	1.1	4 F
0601	10.2	1033	1.0	1131	1.1	1118	0.3	0831	1.9	1033	4.4	1051	4.5	1050	5.8	1038	6.4	
1238	1.9	1627	5.3	1742	5.3	1839	2.0	1517	0.7	1614	0.9	1616	1.1	1705	1.0	1806	1.1	●
1817	10.4	2300	0.9	2356	1.1	2345	0.3	2038	1.9	2245	4.4	2306	4.6	2304	5.9	2256	6.4	
0106	1.6	0449	5.3	0606	5.1	0706	1.9	0338	0.5	0435	0.6	0438	0.8	0528	0.9	0635	1.1	5 SA
0644	10.3	1115	1.0	1215	1.1	1200	0.3	0855	1.9	1115	4.4	1131	4.5	1133	5.9	1119	6.5	
1319	1.7	1708	5.4	1821	5.3	1921	2.1	1557	0.6	1655	0.8	1657	1.0	1745	1.1	1848	1.0	
1858	10.6	2341	0.9					2105	1.9	2324	4.3	2344	4.6	2342	6.0	2337	6.4	
0145	1.5	0529	5.2	0037	1.0	0026	0.3	0418	0.5	0513	0.6	0518	0.8	0605	1.0	0713	1.1	6 SU
0724	10.4	1153	1.0	0642	5.1	0746	1.9	0932	1.9	1154	4.4	1211	4.5	1212	6.0	1158	6.5	
1357	1.7	1746	5.4	1254	1.1	1241	0.3	1637	0.6	1732	0.9	1736	1.0	1821	1.1	1924	1.0	
1936	10.5			1853	5.3	1957	2.1	2143	1.9									
0221	1.6	0018	0.9	0114	1.0	0106	0.2	0458	0.5	0001	4.3	0021	4.5	0017	5.9	0016	6.4	7 M
0802	10.2	0606	5.2	0713	5.1	0821	1.9	1021	1.9	0548	0.6	0556	0.8	0640	1.0	0745	1.1	
1430	1.9	1229	1.1	1327	1.1	1319	0.3	1718	0.7	1232	4.3	1250	4.5	1248	5.9	1236	6.5	
2013	10.3	1822	5.3	1921	5.3	2027	2.0	2234	1.9	1806	0.9	1815	1.1	1857	1.2	1959	1.0	
0253	1.9	0052	1.0	0147	1.1	0142	0.2	0538	0.6	0037	4.2	0059	4.5	0052	5.8	0054	6.3	8 TU
0838	10.0	0642	5.1	0741	5.0	0850	1.8	1123	1.9	0621	0.7	0633	0.9	0715	1.1	0815	1.2	
1503	2.1	1303	1.2	1359	1.3	1354	0.3	1758	0.7	1309	4.2	1330	4.5	1323	5.9	1313	6.5	
2048	10.0	1857	5.2	1948	5.3	2054	1.9	2335	1.9	1838	1.0	1851	1.2	1933	1.3	2032	1.1	
0324	2.2	0126	1.2	0217	1.3	0217	0.3	0616	0.6	0112	4.1	0137	4.4	0127	5.7	0130	6.2	9 W
0912	9.6	0717	5.0	0809	5.0	0917	1.7	1233	1.9	0653	0.9	0708	1.0	0751	1.1	0844	1.3	
1533	2.5	1337	1.3	1427	1.4	1425	0.4	1837	0.8	1344	4.1	1409	4.4	1357	5.8	1349	6.3	
2121	9.7	1933	5.1	2018	5.2	2121	1.8			1911	1.1	1926	1.3	2010	1.3	2106	1.2	
0353	2.5	0200	1.3	0247	1.4	0247	0.3	0043	1.8	0149	4.0	0214	4.3	0204	5.5	0204	6.0	10 TH
0945	9.3	0752	4.8	0842	4.9	0944	1.6	0655	0.7	0724	1.0	0742	1.2	0827	1.3	0915	1.4	
1605	2.8	1412	1.4	1457	1.6	1451	0.4	1349	1.8	1422	4.0	1448	4.3	1432	5.6	1424	6.2	
2152	9.3	2009	4.9	2052	5.1	2148	1.7	1915	0.9	1945	1.3	2000	1.4	2049	1.4	2140	1.3	
0423	2.9	0236	1.5	0318	1.6	0312	0.4	0155	1.7	0229	3.9	0251	4.1	0242	5.3	0240	5.8	11 F
1017	8.9	0831	4.7	0920	4.8	1015	1.5	0734	0.9	0801	1.2	0817	1.4	0905	1.4	0950	1.6	
1639	3.2	1451	1.6	1531	1.8	1514	0.5	1506	1.8	1506	3.9	1527	4.2	1509	5.4	1502	6.0	
2225	8.9	2049	4.7	2133	4.9	2217	1.6	1958	1.0	2025	1.4	2038	1.5	2130	1.6	2218	1.5	
0458	3.2	0318	1.7	0357	1.8	0336	0.5	0316	1.7	0316	3.8	0332	3.9	0324	5.0	0321	5.6	12 SA
1052	8.6	0915	4.5	1006	4.7	1050	1.4	0818	1.0	0844	1.4	0856	1.5	0946	1.6	1029	1.8	
1718	3.5	1536	1.8	1613	2.0	1543	0.6	1636	1.7	1556	3.8	1615	4.0	1554	5.1	1545	5.8	
2305	8.6	2137	4.5	2224	4.8	2253	1.5	2049	1.1	2114	1.6	2124	1.8	2216	1.8	2300	1.8	
0541	3.5	0408	1.9	0442	2.0	0413	0.5	0452	1.6	0411	3.7	0424	3.8	0412	4.7	0411	5.4	13 SU
1137	8.3	1009	4.3	1103	4.5	1136	1.3	0914	1.1	0937	1.6	0947	1.7	1036	1.9	1115	2.0	
1809	3.8	1633	2.0	1706	2.2	1631	0.7	1817	1.7	1653	3.8	1719	4.0	1646	4.9	1639	5.6	
2357	8.3	2236	4.3	2324	4.6	2342	1.4	2159	1.2	2214	1.7	2230	1.9	2313	2.0	2351	1.9	
0636	3.8	0511	2.0	0539	2.1	0512	0.6	0646	1.6	0517	3.6	0542	3.7	0512	4.6	0513	5.3	14 M
1238	8.2	1118	4.3	1207	4.5	1242	1.3	1030	1.2	1042	1.8	1100	1.9	1137	2.0	1214	2.1	
1912	4.0	1742	2.0	1809	2.3	1747	0.7	1926	1.7	1757	3.8	1823	3.9	1751	4.8	1743	5.5	
		2348	4.3					2314	1.2	2324	1.8	2345	1.9					
0106	8.2	0621	1.9	0031	4.6	0052	1.3	0746	1.6	0627	3.7	0652	3.7	0018	2.0	0054	2.0	15 TU
0745	3.9	1230	4.4	0646	2.1	0631	0.6	1136	1.2	1154	1.7	1209	1.8	0622	4.6	0621	5.3	
1354	8.3	1853	1.9	1312	4.6	1404	1.4	2000	1.7	1900	3.9	1924	4.0	1246	2.0	1324	2.2	
2027	3.9			1923	2.2	1915	0.7							1900	4.9	1850	5.5	

● ● Time UT. For British Summer Time (shaded) March 30th to October 26th ADD ONE HOUR ● ●

JULY 1997 TIDE TABLES JULY 1997

	ST HELIER	ST MARYS, SCILLY	PLYMOUTH	PORTLAND	POOLE ENTRANCE	SOUTHAMPTON	PORTSMOUTH	SHOREHAM	DOVER
	Time m	Time m	Time m	Time m	Time m	Time m	Time m	Time m	Time m
16 W	0226 8.3 0902 3.7 1509 8.7 2145 3.5	0059 4.4 0727 1.8 1333 4.6 1955 1.7	0137 4.6 0759 2.0 1415 4.7 2035 1.9	0219 1.4 0749 0.5 1522 1.5 2029 0.6	0010 1.1 0809 1.6 1230 1.1 2011 1.7	0033 1.6 0735 3.8 1303 1.6 1959 4.1	0046 1.7 0759 3.9 1308 1.7 2026 4.1	0125 1.8 0731 4.8 1353 1.8 2005 5.2	0205 1.9 0727 5.5 1442 2.0 1952 5.7
17 TH	0338 8.8 1016 3.2 1612 9.3 2253 2.9	0159 4.7 0824 1.5 1427 4.9 2050 1.4	0242 4.8 0906 1.8 1516 4.9 2139 1.6	0340 1.5 0855 0.5 1627 1.7 2130 0.5	0058 0.9 0813 1.7 1318 0.9 2013 1.8	0136 1.4 0833 4.0 1404 1.3 2050 4.2	0140 1.5 0902 4.1 1403 1.4 2119 4.3	0227 1.6 0833 5.2 1452 1.5 2101 5.5	0318 1.7 0826 5.8 1554 1.7 2047 6.0
18 F	0439 9.5 1119 2.6 1706 10.0 2351 2.1	0251 4.9 0916 1.2 1515 5.2 2141 1.0	0345 4.9 1006 1.4 1615 5.2 2236 1.2	0448 1.7 0953 0.4 1724 1.9 2224 0.4	0143 0.8 0815 1.8 1403 0.7 2017 1.9	0233 1.1 0924 4.2 1457 1.1 2136 4.4	0232 1.2 0951 4.3 1455 1.2 2203 4.5	0321 1.3 0928 5.6 1545 1.2 2152 5.9	0423 1.4 0918 6.1 1654 1.3 2136 6.3
19 SA	0532 10.2 1214 1.9 1756 10.7	0339 5.2 1005 1.0 1602 5.5 2230 0.8	0443 5.1 1101 1.1 1708 5.4 2330 0.9	0548 1.8 1046 0.3 1818 2.1 2315 0.3	0227 0.6 0824 1.9 1448 0.6 2028 2.0	0324 0.8 1009 4.3 1548 0.8 2220 4.5	0322 0.9 1033 4.5 1545 0.9 2245 4.7	0412 1.0 1020 5.9 1634 1.0 2239 6.2	0519 1.1 1005 6.4 1747 1.1 2223 6.5
20 SU ○	0042 1.5 0621 10.8 1303 1.4 1842 11.3	0425 5.5 1053 0.7 1647 5.8 2318 0.5	0536 5.3 1153 0.8 1756 5.6	0642 2.0 1136 0.2 1909 2.2	0313 0.4 0844 2.0 1534 0.4 2052 2.0	0413 0.5 1054 4.5 1638 0.6 2303 4.6	0412 0.6 1115 4.7 1634 0.7 2328 4.8	0500 0.9 1110 6.2 1723 0.9 2326 6.3	0610 0.9 1051 6.7 1836 0.8 2310 6.7
21 M	0129 1.0 0707 11.3 1350 1.1 1927 11.6	0510 5.7 1140 0.6 1732 5.9	0020 0.6 0624 5.5 1242 0.6 1842 5.7	0003 0.2 0733 2.1 1224 0.1 1956 2.3	0359 0.3 0918 2.0 1621 0.4 2133 2.1	0501 0.3 1138 4.6 1727 0.5 2347 4.6	0459 0.5 1158 4.8 1721 0.6	0548 0.8 1200 6.3 1811 0.9	0658 0.8 1139 6.9 1922 0.7 2359 6.8
22 TU	0215 0.7 0752 11.5 1434 0.9 2012 11.7	0005 0.4 0555 5.7 1227 0.5 1818 6.0	0108 0.4 0709 5.5 1327 0.5 1927 5.8	0051 0.1 0820 2.1 1309 0.1 2041 2.3	0446 0.2 1014 2.1 1711 0.4 2234 2.1	0549 0.2 1222 4.7 1815 0.4	0012 4.8 0545 0.4 1245 4.8 1808 0.6	0014 6.4 0637 0.8 1250 6.4 1900 0.8	0742 0.7 1227 6.9 2006 0.6
23 W	0258 0.7 0836 11.4 1518 1.1 2056 11.5	0051 0.4 0640 5.7 1313 0.5 1903 5.9	0153 0.4 0754 5.5 1412 0.5 2012 5.7	0136 0.0 0903 2.1 1354 0.1 2123 2.3	0534 0.3 1128 2.1 1800 0.4 2349 2.0	0032 4.6 0634 0.2 1308 4.7 1900 0.4	0059 4.8 0630 0.4 1333 4.8 1853 0.7	0103 6.4 0725 0.7 1337 6.4 1950 0.8	0050 6.8 0825 0.7 1316 6.9 2050 0.5
24 TH	0342 0.9 0921 11.1 1603 1.5 2141 11.1	0138 0.5 0727 5.6 1400 0.7 1950 5.7	0237 0.5 0839 5.4 1455 0.7 2057 5.6	0222 0.1 0945 2.1 1438 0.1 2204 2.1	0624 0.3 1302 2.0 1851 0.5	0119 4.6 0719 0.3 1355 4.6 1944 0.5	0145 4.8 0715 0.5 1424 4.8 1939 0.8	0152 6.4 0813 0.7 1425 6.4 2038 0.8	0142 6.7 0908 0.7 1404 6.8 2134 0.6
25 F	0427 1.4 1007 10.6 1648 2.0 2229 10.4	0225 0.7 0814 5.4 1448 0.9 2040 5.4	0321 0.7 0925 5.2 1539 1.0 2144 5.3	0309 0.2 1024 1.9 1523 0.3 2245 2.0	0123 2.0 0717 0.5 1450 2.0 1946 0.6	0209 4.5 0801 0.5 1447 4.5 2030 0.7	0235 4.6 0802 0.7 1519 4.7 2027 1.0	0239 6.2 0900 0.9 1509 6.2 2127 0.9	0233 6.5 0951 0.9 1451 6.7 2220 0.8
26 SA	0513 2.0 1057 9.9 1737 2.5 2321 9.7	0315 1.0 0906 5.1 1542 1.2 2135 5.1	0405 1.1 1014 5.0 1624 1.3 2235 5.1	0357 0.3 1106 1.8 1611 0.4 2330 1.8	0310 1.9 0814 0.6 1659 1.9 2048 0.8	0305 4.3 0848 0.8 1545 4.4 2119 1.0	0329 4.5 0852 1.0 1628 4.5 2123 1.3	0326 5.9 0948 0.9 1556 5.9 2218 1.1	0323 6.3 1038 1.1 1542 6.4 2310 1.1
27 SU	0605 2.6 1152 9.3 1833 3.1	0411 1.3 1005 4.8 1644 1.4 2239 4.8	0453 1.4 1108 4.8 1717 1.6 2335 4.8	0450 0.4 1154 1.7 1707 0.6	0512 1.8 0918 0.8 1830 1.9 2157 0.9	0408 4.1 0943 1.1 1650 4.2 2220 1.3	0436 4.3 0951 1.3 1729 4.4 2228 1.5	0418 5.5 1041 1.2 1651 5.5 2320 1.4	0417 6.0 1130 1.4 1639 6.1
28 M	0022 9.1 0704 3.2 1258 8.9 1939 3.5	0516 1.5 1116 4.6 1757 1.6 2356 4.6	0549 1.7 1212 4.7 1821 1.9	0022 1.6 0552 0.5 1254 1.6 1818 0.7	0657 1.7 1030 1.0 1931 1.8 2313 1.0	0521 4.0 1050 1.4 1803 4.1 2331 1.4	0552 4.1 1100 1.5 1830 4.3 2344 1.6	0520 5.2 1148 1.5 1758 5.2	0007 1.4 0519 5.8 1232 1.7 1746 5.9
29 TU	0136 8.7 0813 3.5 1414 8.7 2056 3.6	0630 1.7 1236 4.5 1912 1.6	0045 4.7 0657 1.9 1325 4.7 1936 1.9	0129 1.5 0706 0.6 1410 1.5 1944 0.7	0752 1.7 1144 1.0 2004 1.9	0639 4.0 1206 1.5 1915 4.1	0705 4.0 1217 1.7 1937 4.2	0033 1.6 0635 5.0 1304 1.6 1911 5.1	0114 1.7 0633 5.7 1343 1.8 1903 5.7
30 W	0256 8.7 0928 3.4 1527 8.9 2212 3.3	0112 4.6 0741 1.6 1346 4.7 2018 1.5	0202 4.6 0813 1.9 1439 4.8 2053 1.8	0251 1.5 0821 0.6 1532 1.6 2102 0.7	0022 1.0 0811 1.7 1249 1.0 2012 1.8	0047 1.4 0753 4.0 1321 1.5 2019 4.2	0100 1.6 0815 4.1 1330 1.6 2039 4.2	0148 1.6 0750 5.0 1415 1.6 2022 5.2	0229 1.7 0747 5.7 1459 1.7 2014 5.8
31 TH	0404 8.9 1037 3.1 1627 9.3 2315 2.8	0217 4.7 0842 1.5 1444 4.9 2115 1.3	0315 4.7 0924 1.7 1546 5.0 2159 1.6	0410 1.5 0924 0.6 1639 1.7 2159 0.6	0118 0.9 0813 1.8 1340 0.9 2013 1.8	0155 1.3 0854 4.1 1424 1.4 2111 4.2	0203 1.5 0912 4.2 1429 1.5 2128 4.3	0253 1.5 0856 5.2 1517 1.5 2122 5.4	0342 1.6 0850 5.9 1608 1.5 2112 6.0

●●Time: UT. For British Summer Time (shaded) March 30th to October 26th ADD ONE HOUR●●

SOUTH COAST OF ENGLAND Time Zone UT

St Helier * St Mary's * Plymouth * Portland * Poole * Southampton * Portsmouth * Shoreham * Dover

AUGUST 1997 TIDE TABLES AUGUST 1997

ST HELIER Time m	ST MARYS, SCILLY Time m	PLYMOUTH Time m	PORTLAND Time m	POOLE ENTRANCE Time m	SOUTHAMPTON Time m	PORTSMOUTH Time m	SHOREHAM Time m	DOVER Time m		
0459 9.4	0309 4.9	0418 4.9	0512 1.6	0203 0.8	0254 1.1	0255 1.2	0348 1.3	0445 1.4	1	F
1133 2.7	0933 1.3	1024 1.5	1014 0.5	0816 1.8	0943 4.3	0957 4.3	0951 5.5	0939 6.1		
1716 9.8	1532 5.1	1642 5.1	1733 1.8	1423 0.8	1518 1.2	1517 1.3	1609 1.3	1705 1.3		
	2203 1.1	2253 1.3	2245 0.5	2018 1.9	2155 4.3	2209 4.4	2210 5.6	2200 6.1		
0006 2.3	0354 5.0	0509 5.0	0604 1.7	0244 0.7	0341 0.9	0340 1.0	0434 1.2	0537 1.3	2	SA
0545 9.8	1018 1.1	1114 1.3	1058 0.4	0825 1.9	1025 4.3	1036 4.4	1038 5.7	1022 6.3		
1220 2.2	1613 5.2	1726 5.3	1820 1.9	1502 0.7	1601 1.0	1600 1.1	1652 1.2	1753 1.2		
1800 10.2	2244 1.0	2339 1.2	2326 0.4	2029 1.9	2233 4.3	2247 4.5	2253 5.8	2242 6.3		
0048 1.9	0433 5.2	0549 5.1	0648 1.8	0322 0.6	0421 0.7	0421 0.9	0512 1.1	0621 1.2	3	SU
0626 10.2	1057 1.0	1157 1.1	1139 0.3	0842 1.9	1102 4.4	1112 4.5	1118 5.9	1101 6.5		
1300 1.9	1651 5.3	1801 5.3	1901 2.0	1539 0.6	1638 0.9	1639 1.0	1729 1.1	1833 1.1		●
1839 10.5	2321 0.9			2049 1.9	2308 4.3	2323 4.5	2328 5.9	2320 6.4		
0126 1.6	0509 5.2	0018 1.1	0006 0.3	0359 0.5	0455 0.7	0459 0.8	0548 1.0	0657 1.2	4	M
0704 10.4	1133 1.0	0621 5.2	0727 1.9	0910 1.9	1137 4.4	1149 4.5	1154 6.0	1138 6.6		
1336 1.7	1725 5.4	1233 1.1	1219 0.2	1617 0.6	1712 0.9	1717 1.0	1804 1.1	1906 1.0		
1916 10.7	2355 0.9	1830 5.4	1937 2.1	2120 1.9	2341 4.3			2356 6.4		
0159 1.5	0543 5.3	0053 1.0	0044 0.2	0436 0.5	0528 0.7	0000 4.5	0001 5.9	0725 1.2	5	TU
0740 10.4	1206 1.0	0648 5.2	0801 1.9	0949 1.9	1208 4.3	0535 0.8	0620 1.0	1214 6.6		
1409 1.7	1758 5.4	1306 1.1	1257 0.2	1654 0.6	1742 0.9	1226 4.5	1226 6.0	1938 1.0		
1951 10.6		1855 5.4	2009 2.0	2202 1.9		1752 1.0	1836 1.1			
0230 1.6	0027 0.9	0124 1.1	0120 0.2	0512 0.5	0012 4.3	0036 4.5	0033 5.9	0030 6.4	6	W
0814 10.3	0615 5.2	0714 5.2	0830 1.9	1040 1.9	0557 0.7	0609 0.8	0653 1.0	0751 1.1		
1439 1.6	1237 1.0	1335 1.1	1333 0.2	1728 0.7	1240 4.3	1303 4.5	1258 6.0	1248 6.6		
2024 10.4	1830 5.3	1923 5.4	2036 2.0	2252 1.9	1814 0.9	1824 1.0	1909 1.0	2009 1.0		
0257 1.9	0057 1.0	0152 1.2	0153 0.2	0545 0.6	0043 4.2	0111 4.5	0105 5.8	0102 6.3	7	TH
0845 10.0	0648 5.2	0743 5.2	0857 1.8	1137 1.9	0628 0.7	0640 0.9	0726 1.0	0820 1.2		
1507 2.1	1309 1.1	1403 1.2	1403 0.2	1801 0.7	1310 4.3	1338 4.5	1329 5.9	1321 6.5		
2054 10.1	1902 5.2	1954 5.4	2103 1.9	2349 1.9	1843 0.9	1854 1.1	1942 1.1	2041 1.0		
0324 2.2	0129 1.2	0221 1.3	0221 0.2	0618 0.7	0115 4.2	0145 4.4	0136 5.7	0132 6.2	8	F
0914 9.7	0720 5.1	0816 5.1	0923 1.7	1235 1.9	0656 0.9	0709 1.0	0759 1.1	0851 1.2		
1535 2.4	1341 1.3	1431 1.4	1427 0.3	1834 0.8	1343 4.2	1410 4.4	1359 5.8	1349 6.3		
2121 9.7	1935 5.1	2029 5.3	2129 1.8		1913 1.0	1924 1.2	2015 1.2	2114 1.2		
0350 2.5	0201 1.3	0251 1.5	0240 0.3	0046 1.8	0151 4.1	0216 4.3	0209 5.5	0200 6.0	9	SA
0940 9.3	0754 4.9	0851 5.0	0949 1.6	0651 0.7	0727 1.0	0739 1.2	0831 1.2	0922 1.4		
1604 2.8	1415 1.4	1503 1.6	1445 0.4	1337 1.8	1421 4.1	1442 4.3	1429 5.6	1418 6.2		
2148 9.3	2010 4.9	2105 5.1	2155 1.6	1912 0.8	1948 1.2	1957 1.3	2049 1.3	2148 1.4		
0419 2.9	0237 1.5	0324 1.7	0259 0.4	0155 1.7	0233 4.0	0251 4.1	0242 5.2	0232 5.9	10	SU
1008 9.0	0832 4.7	0930 4.8	1018 1.5	0730 0.8	0803 1.3	0813 1.3	0905 1.5	0956 1.6		
1639 3.2	1455 1.7	1539 1.8	1506 0.5	1448 1.8	1505 4.0	1518 4.2	1504 5.3	1451 6.0		
2221 9.0	2051 4.7	2144 4.9	2224 1.5	1955 0.9	2028 1.5	2035 1.5	2127 1.6	2223 1.7		
0456 3.3	0320 1.8	0403 1.9	0327 0.4	0321 1.7	0323 3.8	0335 4.0	0319 5.0	0313 5.7	11	M
1044 8.7	0918 4.5	1012 4.7	1052 1.4	0817 1.0	0848 1.6	0855 1.5	0947 1.7	1035 1.9		
1723 3.6	1544 1.9	1623 2.1	1543 0.5	1622 1.7	1559 3.9	1607 4.1	1550 5.0	1537 5.8		
2303 8.6	2141 4.4	2230 4.7	2301 1.4	2049 1.1	2122 1.7	2124 1.7	2217 1.8	2306 1.9		
0545 3.7	0414 1.9	0450 2.1	0411 0.5	0507 1.6	0425 3.7	0433 3.8	0412 4.7	0409 5.5	12	TU
1135 8.4	1018 4.3	1106 4.5	1142 1.3	0918 1.1	0951 1.8	0951 1.8	1042 2.0	1126 2.1		
1823 3.9	1648 2.0	1719 2.3	1642 0.6	1809 1.7	1703 3.8	1713 3.9	1652 4.8	1642 5.5		
	2249 4.3	2332 4.5	2359 1.3	2209 1.2	2232 1.8	2239 1.9	2322 2.0			
0005 8.2	0527 2.0	0552 2.3	0524 0.6	0659 1.6	0541 3.7	0554 3.8	0524 4.6	0004 2.1	13	W
0654 3.9	1136 4.3	1215 4.5	1300 1.4	1048 1.2	1109 1.9	1118 1.9	1155 2.1	0523 5.4		
1251 8.2	1807 2.0	1833 2.3	1815 0.7	1933 1.7	1817 3.9	1832 3.9	1811 4.8	1235 2.2		
1940 4.0				2332 1.1	2354 1.8			1800 5.5		
0135 8.1	0014 4.3	0048 4.5	0128 1.3	0757 1.6	0702 3.8	0004 1.8	0039 2.0	0118 2.1	14	TH
0818 3.9	0647 1.9	0713 2.2	0705 0.6	1159 1.1	1231 1.8	0716 3.8	0647 4.8	0644 5.5		
1429 8.3	1256 4.5	1330 4.6	1436 1.5	2006 1.7	1926 4.0	1234 1.8	1315 1.9	1400 2.1		
2108 3.7	1922 1.8	1959 2.1	1957 0.7			1945 4.0	1930 5.0	1918 5.6		
0309 8.5	0130 4.5	0207 4.6	0307 1.4	0032 1.0	0110 1.5	0111 1.6	0154 1.7	0241 1.9	15	F
0945 3.5	0756 1.7	0835 2.0	0831 0.5	0812 1.7	0809 4.0	0833 4.0	0803 5.1	0758 5.7		
1548 9.0	1400 4.8	1444 4.8	1556 1.6	1256 1.0	1342 1.5	1338 1.5	1425 1.6	1524 1.8		
2227 3.0	2026 1.4	2113 1.7	2111 0.5	2012 1.8	2024 4.1	2052 4.2	2037 5.5	2024 5.9		

● ● Time UT. For British Summer Time (shaded) March 30th to October 26th ADD ONE HOUR ● ● ●

AUGUST 1997 TIDE TABLES AUGUST 1997

	ST HELIER	ST MARYS, SCILLY	PLYMOUTH	PORTLAND	POOLE ENTRANCE	SOUTHAMPTON	PORTSMOUTH	SHOREHAM	DOVER
	Time m	Time m	Time m	Time m	Time m	Time m	Time m	Time m	Time m
16 SA	0421 9.3 / 1058 2.7 / 1649 9.9 / 2332 2.1	0230 4.9 / 0854 1.3 / 1454 1.6 / 2121 1.0	0321 4.9 / 0944 1.6 / 1551 5.2 / 2216 1.3	0426 1.6 / 0936 0.4 / 1700 1.9 / 2209 0.4	0124 0.8 / 0813 1.8 / 1346 0.8 / 2014 1.9	0213 1.2 / 0904 4.2 / 1441 1.1 / 2115 4.3	0210 1.3 / 0930 4.3 / 1436 1.2 / 2143 4.5	0258 1.4 / 0907 5.6 / 1525 1.3 / 2132 5.9	0355 1.5 / 0858 6.1 / 1630 1.4 / 2118 6.3
17 SU	0517 10.2 / 1157 1.9 / 1741 10.8	0321 5.3 / 0946 0.9 / 1543 5.6 / 2212 0.6	0424 5.1 / 1043 1.1 / 1647 5.5 / 2312 0.8	0530 1.8 / 1031 0.3 / 1758 2.1 / 2300 0.2	0212 0.6 / 0819 1.9 / 1433 0.6 / 2022 2.0	0308 0.8 / 0951 4.4 / 1532 0.8 / 2200 4.5	0305 0.9 / 1015 4.6 / 1529 0.9 / 2227 4.7	0353 1.0 / 1002 6.0 / 1618 1.0 / 2222 6.3	0457 1.2 / 0948 6.5 / 1727 1.0 / 2208 6.6
18 M ○	0026 1.3 / 0606 11.0 / 1248 1.2 / 1828 11.6	0409 5.6 / 1035 0.6 / 1630 5.9 / 2300 0.3	0517 5.4 / 1137 0.7 / 1737 5.7	0627 2.0 / 1121 0.1 / 1851 2.3 / 2348 0.1	0257 0.4 / 0833 2.0 / 1519 0.4 / 2040 2.1	0357 0.5 / 1034 4.6 / 1622 0.5 / 2245 4.6	0355 0.6 / 1056 4.8 / 1618 0.6 / 2309 4.9	0444 0.8 / 1052 6.5 / 1707 0.8 / 2309 6.5	0551 0.9 / 1035 6.8 / 1819 0.7 / 2254 6.9
19 TU	0114 0.6 / 0652 11.6 / 1335 0.7 / 1912 12.0	0454 5.8 / 1122 0.4 / 1715 6.1 / 2347 0.2	0004 0.5 / 0606 5.6 / 1226 0.4 / 1824 5.9	0718 2.2 / 1208 0.0 / 1940 2.4	0342 0.2 / 0901 2.1 / 1605 0.3 / 2114 2.1	0445 0.2 / 1118 4.7 / 1711 0.3 / 2330 4.7	0442 0.3 / 1139 4.9 / 1705 0.4 / 2354 5.0	0533 0.7 / 1142 6.5 / 1756 0.7 / 2357 6.6	0643 0.7 / 1121 7.0 / 1909 0.5 / 2342 7.0
20 W	0159 0.3 / 0736 11.9 / 1419 0.5 / 1957 12.1	0537 6.0 / 1209 0.3 / 1759 6.2	0052 0.2 / 0651 5.7 / 1312 0.3 / 1910 6.0	0035 -0.0 / 0805 2.2 / 1253 -0.0 / 2025 2.4	0427 0.1 / 0946 2.1 / 1650 0.3 / 2205 2.1	0533 0.1 / 1202 4.8 / 1758 0.2	0527 0.2 / 1224 5.0 / 1749 0.4	0622 0.6 / 1230 6.6 / 1844 0.6	0731 0.6 / 1208 7.1 / 1955 0.4
21 TH	0242 0.3 / 0820 11.8 / 1503 0.7 / 2039 11.9	0032 0.3 / 0621 5.9 / 1254 0.3 / 1843 6.1	0137 0.2 / 0736 5.7 / 1356 0.3 / 1956 5.9	0120 -0.1 / 0848 2.3 / 1336 -0.0 / 2107 2.4	0515 0.2 / 1050 2.1 / 1738 0.3 / 2315 2.1	0013 4.7 / 0618 0.1 / 1245 4.8 / 1844 0.2	0039 4.9 / 0612 0.3 / 1310 5.0 / 1833 0.5	0046 6.6 / 0709 0.6 / 1317 6.6 / 1932 0.6	0031 7.0 / 0814 0.6 / 1254 7.1 / 2039 0.4
22 F	0324 0.7 / 0902 11.5 / 1545 1.2 / 2122 11.4	0117 0.3 / 0705 5.8 / 1339 0.5 / 1928 5.8	0220 0.5 / 0821 5.6 / 1438 0.5 / 2042 5.7	0203 -0.0 / 0927 2.2 / 1418 0.1 / 2147 2.2	0601 0.3 / 1211 2.1 / 1825 0.4	0059 4.7 / 0702 0.2 / 1331 4.7 / 1926 0.4	0125 4.9 / 0654 0.4 / 1357 4.9 / 1916 0.7	0133 6.5 / 0754 0.6 / 1401 6.5 / 2018 0.7	0119 6.8 / 0854 0.6 / 1339 7.0 / 2121 0.5
23 SA	0407 1.3 / 0945 10.8 / 1628 1.8 / 2206 10.6	0202 0.6 / 0750 5.5 / 1425 0.8 / 2015 5.4	0302 0.6 / 0907 5.4 / 1519 0.9 / 2127 5.4	0247 0.1 / 1004 2.0 / 1500 0.2 / 2226 2.0	0039 2.0 / 0650 0.4 / 1345 2.0 / 1916 0.6	0147 4.6 / 0743 0.4 / 1420 4.6 / 2006 0.6	0212 4.7 / 0738 0.7 / 1446 4.7 / 2001 0.9	0218 6.3 / 0838 0.7 / 1442 6.3 / 2102 0.8	0206 6.6 / 0934 0.8 / 1424 6.8 / 2202 0.8
24 SU	0451 2.0 / 1030 10.1 / 1714 2.6 / 2254 9.7	0248 1.0 / 0838 5.1 / 1515 1.2 / 2107 5.0	0342 1.1 / 0952 5.2 / 1601 1.3 / 2215 5.1	0330 0.3 / 1042 1.8 / 1543 0.4 / 2306 1.8	0218 1.9 / 0742 0.6 / 1533 1.9 / 2012 0.8	0241 4.4 / 0824 0.7 / 1515 4.4 / 2052 1.0	0303 4.5 / 0824 1.0 / 1541 4.5 / 2051 1.2	0301 6.0 / 0921 0.9 / 1525 5.9 / 2150 1.1	0252 6.4 / 1016 1.1 / 1512 6.4 / 2246 1.2
25 M	0539 2.8 / 1119 9.3 / 1806 3.3 / 2351 8.9	0340 1.4 / 0933 4.8 / 1615 1.5 / 2209 4.6	0425 1.5 / 1041 4.9 / 1648 1.7 / 2309 4.7	0416 0.4 / 1124 1.7 / 1633 0.6 / 2354 1.6	0416 1.8 / 0844 0.9 / 1738 1.8 / 2121 1.0	0341 4.1 / 0915 1.2 / 1620 4.1 / 2148 1.3	0404 4.3 / 0919 1.4 / 1652 4.3 / 2153 1.5	0346 5.6 / 1011 1.3 / 1614 5.5 / 2246 1.5	0343 6.1 / 1103 1.5 / 1606 6.1 / 2339 1.6
26 TU	0634 3.5 / 1221 8.6 / 1909 3.8	0444 1.7 / 1045 4.6 / 1730 1.8 / 2330 4.3	0515 1.9 / 1140 4.6 / 1747 2.1	0513 0.6 / 1218 1.5 / 1743 0.8	0631 1.7 / 0957 1.1 / 1907 1.7 / 2243 1.1	0456 3.9 / 1021 1.6 / 1734 3.9 / 2304 1.6	0530 4.1 / 1028 1.7 / 1802 4.1 / 2313 1.8	0445 5.1 / 1115 1.7 / 1720 5.1 / 2359 1.8	0445 5.7 / 1201 1.8 / 1715 5.7
27 W	0106 8.3 / 0742 4.0 / 1343 8.3 / 2027 4.0	0603 1.9 / 1212 4.4 / 1852 1.8	0018 4.5 / 0622 2.2 / 1254 4.5 / 1908 2.2	0059 1.4 / 0632 0.7 / 1334 1.5 / 1927 0.8	0741 1.7 / 1123 1.2 / 1956 1.7	0620 3.8 / 1144 1.8 / 1855 3.9	0645 3.9 / 1155 1.9 / 1914 4.0	0602 4.8 / 1235 2.0 / 1843 4.9	0045 1.9 / 0601 5.5 / 1315 2.0 / 1840 5.5
28 TH	0236 8.2 / 0901 4.0 / 1507 8.5 / 2151 3.8	0055 4.3 / 0722 1.9 / 1330 4.5 / 2003 1.7	0140 4.4 / 0749 2.2 / 1417 4.6 / 2035 2.1	0233 1.4 / 0801 0.8 / 1507 1.5 / 2055 0.8	0004 1.1 / 0809 1.7 / 1235 1.2 / 2011 1.7	0027 1.7 / 0743 3.9 / 1306 1.8 / 2006 4.0	0039 1.8 / 0800 4.0 / 1314 1.9 / 2022 4.0	0120 1.9 / 0727 4.8 / 1354 2.0 / 2003 4.9	0206 2.0 / 0725 5.5 / 1440 1.9 / 2001 5.6
29 F	0350 8.6 / 1016 3.6 / 1610 9.0 / 2257 3.2	0203 4.5 / 0826 1.7 / 1429 4.7 / 2100 1.4	0300 4.6 / 0906 2.0 / 1528 4.9 / 2142 1.8	0359 1.4 / 0906 0.7 / 1617 1.6 / 2145 0.6	0102 1.0 / 0813 1.7 / 1325 1.1 / 2013 1.8	0143 1.6 / 0847 4.0 / 1414 1.6 / 2102 4.1	0145 1.6 / 0902 4.1 / 1412 1.7 / 2113 4.2	0232 1.8 / 0838 5.1 / 1500 1.8 / 2107 5.2	0324 1.9 / 0832 5.8 / 1552 1.7 / 2102 5.8
30 SA	0442 9.2 / 1114 3.0 / 1658 9.6 / 2346 2.6	0255 4.7 / 0917 1.4 / 1515 5.0 / 2144 1.2	0402 4.8 / 1006 1.6 / 1621 5.1 / 2233 1.4	0457 1.6 / 0954 0.6 / 1709 1.8 / 2224 0.5	0146 0.9 / 0814 1.8 / 1407 0.9 / 2015 1.8	0242 1.3 / 0935 4.2 / 1506 1.4 / 2143 4.2	0236 1.4 / 0945 4.3 / 1459 1.4 / 2152 4.3	0329 1.6 / 0934 5.4 / 1551 1.5 / 2157 5.5	0428 1.6 / 0922 6.0 / 1649 1.4 / 2148 6.1
31 SU	0525 9.7 / 1200 2.4 / 1739 10.1	0337 5.0 / 0958 1.2 / 1554 5.2 / 2222 1.0	0448 5.1 / 1053 1.4 / 1703 5.3 / 2316 1.2	0542 1.7 / 1035 0.5 / 1753 1.9 / 2302 0.4	0224 0.7 / 0820 1.9 / 1443 0.8 / 2022 1.9	0327 1.0 / 1011 4.3 / 1546 1.1 / 2218 4.2	0319 1.2 / 1018 4.4 / 1539 1.2 / 2227 4.2	0414 1.3 / 1020 5.7 / 1632 1.3 / 2236 5.8	0519 1.4 / 1003 6.3 / 1735 1.2 / 2225 6.2

● ● Time: UT. For British Summer Time (shaded) March 30th to October 26th ADD ONE HOUR

SOUTH COAST OF ENGLAND Time Zone UT

St Helier * St Mary's * Plymouth * Portland * Poole * Southampton * Portsmouth * Shoreham * Dover

SEPTEMBER 1997 TIDE TABLES SEPTEMBER 1997

ST HELIER Time m	ST MARYS, SCILLY Time m	PLYMOUTH Time m	PORTLAND Time m	POOLE ENTRANCE Time m	SOUTHAMPTON Time m	PORTSMOUTH Time m	SHOREHAM Time m	DOVER Time m	Day
0026 2.0	0413 5.2	0525 5.2	0624 1.8	0300 0.6	0403 0.8	0358 0.9	0451 1.1	0600 1.3	1 M
0604 10.2	1035 1.1	1133 1.2	1115 0.3	0831 1.9	1044 4.9	1051 4.5	1058 5.9	1040 6.5	●
1238 1.9	1629 5.3	1736 5.4	1833 2.0	1519 0.6	1618 0.9	1618 1.0	1708 1.1	1812 1.1	
1817 10.6	2257 0.9	2354 1.0	2339 0.3	2036 1.9	2250 4.3	2301 4.5	2309 5.9	2300 6.4	
0102 1.6	0446 5.3	0555 5.3	0702 1.9	0336 0.5	0434 0.7	0436 0.8	0526 1.0	0633 1.2	2 TU
0639 10.6	1108 0.9	1209 1.1	1154 0.2	0850 1.9	1114 4.4	1125 4.6	1130 6.0	1115 6.6	
1312 1.6	1701 5.4	1803 5.5	1910 2.1	1553 0.6	1648 0.8	1653 0.9	1740 1.0	1845 1.0	
1853 10.8	2328 0.9			2058 1.9	2319 4.3	2336 4.6	2339 6.0	2332 6.4	
0133 1.5	0518 5.4	0027 1.0	0016 0.2	0410 0.5	0503 0.6	0510 0.8	0557 0.9	0700 1.1	3 W
0714 10.7	1139 0.9	0621 5.4	0735 2.0	0920 2.0	1142 4.4	1200 4.6	1201 6.1	1148 6.7	
1344 1.5	1732 5.5	1240 1.0	1231 0.2	1626 0.6	1717 0.8	1726 0.9	1810 1.0	1914 1.0	
1927 10.9	2358 0.9	1830 5.6	1943 2.1	2132 1.9	2347 4.4				
0203 1.5	0548 5.4	0057 1.0	0052 0.2	0443 0.5	0532 0.6	0011 4.6	0008 5.9	0003 6.5	4 TH
0746 10.7	1210 0.9	0649 5.4	0806 2.0	1000 1.9	1210 4.4	0542 0.8	0628 0.9	0726 1.1	
1413 1.6	1802 5.4	1309 1.0	1306 0.2	1657 0.6	1748 0.7	1235 4.6	1230 6.0	1221 6.6	
1957 10.7		1900 5.6	2012 2.0	2214 1.9		1755 1.0	1841 0.9	1944 0.9	
0230 1.7	0028 0.9	0126 1.1	0124 0.2	0513 0.6	0017 4.4	0045 4.5	0038 5.9	0032 6.4	5 F
0815 10.4	0618 5.3	0720 5.4	0833 1.9	1046 1.9	0602 0.7	0610 0.9	0659 0.9	0755 1.1	
1440 1.9	1240 1.0	1337 1.1	1337 0.2	1727 0.6	1238 4.4	1307 4.5	1259 6.0	1249 6.6	
2026 10.4	1832 5.3	1933 5.5	2040 2.0	2300 1.9	1817 0.8	1823 1.0	1912 0.9	2015 1.0	
0254 2.0	0058 1.0	0154 1.2	0150 0.2	0542 0.6	0046 4.3	0116 4.5	0107 5.8	0058 6.3	6 SA
0842 10.1	0648 5.3	0754 5.3	0859 1.8	1133 1.9	0630 0.7	0637 1.0	0728 1.0	0825 1.2	
1507 2.2	1312 1.1	1406 1.3	1400 0.3	1758 0.7	1309 4.4	1336 4.5	1325 5.9	1314 6.4	
2051 10.1	1903 5.2	2007 5.4	2106 1.8	2351 1.9	1846 0.9	1851 1.1	1941 1.0	2048 1.1	
0320 2.4	0130 1.2	0224 1.4	0209 0.3	0614 0.7	0119 4.2	0146 4.4	0136 5.7	0124 6.2	7 SU
0906 9.8	0721 5.1	0827 5.2	0924 1.7	1227 1.9	0659 0.9	0706 1.1	0758 1.1	0856 1.3	
1534 2.6	1345 1.3	1438 1.5	1417 0.3	1833 0.7	1343 4.3	1406 4.4	1353 5.7	1339 6.3	
2117 9.7	1936 5.0	2039 5.2	2133 1.7		1916 1.1	1923 1.2	2013 1.2	2118 1.3	
0347 2.8	0203 1.4	0255 1.6	0226 0.3	0056 1.8	0159 4.1	0221 4.3	0205 5.5	0154 6.1	8 M
0932 9.4	0757 4.9	0858 5.0	0949 1.6	0652 0.8	0731 1.2	0740 1.2	0830 1.4	0927 1.6	
1606 3.0	1422 1.5	1511 1.7	1438 0.4	1337 1.8	1424 4.1	1442 4.3	1424 5.5	1410 6.2	
2147 9.3	2015 4.8	2110 4.9	2200 1.6	1915 0.8	1953 1.3	2000 1.3	2048 1.4	2150 1.6	
0421 3.2	0242 1.7	0330 1.8	0251 0.4	0218 1.7	0246 4.0	0303 4.1	0241 5.2	0232 6.0	9 TU
1006 9.1	0839 4.7	0930 4.8	1017 1.5	0738 0.9	0814 1.5	0820 1.4	0909 1.6	1002 1.8	
1648 3.5	1507 1.8	1550 2.0	1511 0.5	1508 1.8	1514 4.0	1528 4.2	1508 5.1	1453 5.9	
2227 8.8	2102 4.5	2144 4.7	2232 1.4	2006 1.0	2042 1.6	2045 1.5	2134 1.7	2230 1.9	
0509 3.7	0333 1.9	0412 2.1	0330 0.5	0403 1.7	0345 3.8	0357 4.0	0330 4.9	0324 5.7	10 W
1053 8.6	0935 4.5	1014 4.6	1058 1.4	0836 1.1	0913 1.8	0912 1.7	1003 1.9	1049 2.1	
1748 3.9	1608 2.0	1640 2.2	1602 0.6	1700 1.7	1618 3.9	1629 4.0	1610 4.9	1554 5.6	
2324 8.3	2206 4.3	2239 4.5	2326 1.3	2115 1.1	2152 1.9	2148 1.8	2238 2.0	2324 2.1	
0618 4.0	0444 2.1	0510 2.3	0433 0.7	0607 1.6	0503 3.7	0512 3.8	0442 4.7	0438 5.5	11 TH
1206 8.2	1052 4.3	1123 4.4	1211 1.4	1002 1.2	1034 2.0	1032 1.9	1118 2.1	1157 2.2	
1908 4.0	1730 2.0	1754 2.4	1736 0.7	1853 1.6	1737 3.8	1749 3.9	1732 4.8	1721 5.4	
	2337 4.2			2257 1.2	2319 1.9	2327 1.9			
0058 8.0	0614 2.0	0005 4.4	0056 1.3	0743 1.6	0633 3.8	0648 3.9	0001 2.0	0041 2.2	12 F
0748 4.1	1224 4.5	0636 2.4	0634 0.7	1136 1.2	1206 1.9	1209 1.9	0615 4.8	0610 5.4	
1359 8.2	1856 1.8	1250 4.6	1354 1.5	1958 1.7	1857 3.9	1917 4.0	1245 2.0	1325 2.2	
2040 3.8		1929 2.2	1940 0.7				1901 5.0	1853 5.5	
0250 8.4	0104 4.5	0139 4.6	0244 1.4	0011 1.0	0046 1.6	0047 1.7	0127 1.8	0210 2.0	13 SA
0921 3.6	0732 1.7	0810 2.1	0816 0.6	0810 1.7	0748 4.0	0812 4.1	0740 5.2	0735 5.7	
1530 8.9	1336 4.8	1417 4.8	1527 1.6	1240 1.0	1324 1.6	1320 1.6	1404 1.6	1456 1.8	
2206 3.1	2005 1.4	2051 1.8	2057 0.5	2012 1.8	2003 4.1	2032 4.2	2015 5.5	2006 5.9	
0405 9.3	0209 4.9	0303 4.9	0409 1.6	0107 0.8	0155 1.2	0151 1.3	0236 1.4	0330 1.6	14 SU
1039 2.8	0833 1.3	0924 1.6	0921 0.5	0813 1.9	0844 4.2	0912 4.4	0847 5.7	0839 6.2	
1633 10.0	1434 5.3	1530 5.2	1636 1.9	1332 0.8	1424 1.1	1420 1.3	1505 1.2	1605 1.3	
2312 2.1	2102 0.9	2157 1.2	2154 0.4	2013 1.9	2055 4.3	2124 4.5	2113 6.0	2103 6.3	
0500 10.3	0302 5.3	0406 5.2	0513 1.9	0156 0.6	0250 0.8	0247 0.9	0334 1.0	0433 1.2	15 M
1140 1.8	0927 0.9	1024 1.1	1015 0.3	0816 2.0	0930 4.5	0957 4.7	0941 6.2	0930 6.6	
1724 11.0	1524 5.7	1627 5.6	1736 2.1	1418 0.6	1515 0.7	1512 0.9	1559 0.8	1703 0.9	
	2152 0.5	2254 0.7	2243 0.2	2018 2.0	2141 4.5	2209 4.8	2202 6.3	2151 6.7	

● ● Time UT. For British Summer Time (shaded) March 30th to October 26th ADD ONE HOUR ● ●

SEPTEMBER 1997 TIDE TABLES SEPTEMBER 1997

	ST HELIER	ST MARYS, SCILLY	PLYMOUTH	PORTLAND	POOLE ENTRANCE	SOUTHAMPTON	PORTSMOUTH	SHOREHAM	DOVER
	Time m	Time m	Time m	Time m	Time m	Time m	Time m	Time m	Time m
16 TU ○	0007 1.2 0549 11.2 1230 1.0 1810 11.8	0349 5.7 1015 0.5 1610 6.0 2240 0.2	0458 5.5 1118 0.7 1717 5.8 2345 0.4	0609 2.1 1103 0.1 1829 2.3 2330 0.0	0240 0.4 0826 2.1 1502 0.4 2031 2.1	0338 0.4 1014 4.7 1604 0.4 2225 4.7	0336 0.6 1038 4.9 1600 0.6 2251 5.0	0425 0.7 1031 6.5 1649 0.6 2248 6.6	0529 0.9 1016 6.9 1757 0.7 2237 6.9
17 W	0054 0.5 0633 11.8 1317 0.5 1854 12.2	0433 6.0 1102 0.3 1654 6.2 2325 0.1	0545 5.7 1207 0.4 1804 6.0	0658 2.3 1149 0.0 1918 2.4	0324 0.2 0847 2.1 1545 0.2 2058 2.2	0425 0.2 1056 4.8 1651 0.2 2308 4.8	0423 0.3 1120 5.0 1645 0.4 2335 5.0	0513 0.5 1118 6.6 1737 0.5 2335 6.7	0622 0.7 1101 7.1 1848 0.5 2323 7.1
18 TH	0139 0.2 0717 12.1 1400 0.4 1937 12.3	0516 6.1 1148 0.2 1738 6.3	0033 0.2 0630 5.8 1253 0.2 1850 6.0	0015 -0.1 0744 2.3 1233 -0.0 2003 2.5	0407 0.1 0923 2.2 1628 0.2 2139 2.1	0512 0.1 1138 4.9 1738 0.1 2353 4.8	0507 0.2 1203 5.1 1728 0.4	0600 0.5 1204 6.7 1824 0.5	0710 0.6 1145 7.2 1936 0.4
19 F	0221 0.3 0758 12.0 1442 0.6 2019 12.0	0010 0.1 0559 6.0 1232 0.2 1821 6.1	0117 0.2 0715 5.8 1336 0.3 1936 5.9	0059 -0.1 0825 2.3 1315 -0.0 2045 2.4	0450 0.2 1015 2.2 1713 0.3 2240 2.1	0559 0.1 1221 4.9 1822 0.2	0018 5.0 0549 0.3 1246 5.0 1810 0.4	0023 6.7 0646 0.5 1250 6.7 1909 0.5	0009 7.0 0754 0.5 1230 7.2 2018 0.4
20 SA	0303 0.7 0839 11.6 1523 1.1 2100 11.4	0054 0.3 0642 5.9 1316 0.5 1905 5.8	0159 0.3 0800 5.7 1418 0.5 2022 5.7	0140 -0.0 0903 2.3 1357 0.1 2124 2.2	0535 0.3 1123 2.1 1758 0.4 2354 2.0	0038 4.8 0641 0.2 1305 4.8 1904 0.3	0103 4.9 0631 0.5 1330 4.9 1851 0.6	0109 6.6 0729 0.6 1332 6.6 1953 0.6	0054 6.9 0833 0.6 1312 7.0 2059 0.6
21 SU	0343 1.4 0919 10.9 1604 1.9 2142 10.5	0136 0.6 0725 5.6 1401 0.8 1950 5.4	0239 0.7 0845 5.5 1457 0.9 2108 5.4	0221 0.1 0939 2.1 1436 0.2 2202 2.0	0622 0.5 1244 2.0 1847 0.6	0125 4.8 0721 0.4 1353 4.6 1943 0.6	0148 4.8 0713 0.7 1415 4.8 1935 0.9	0151 6.4 0810 0.7 1411 6.3 2034 0.9	0137 6.7 0912 0.8 1355 6.8 2139 0.9
22 M	0425 2.3 1000 10.1 1648 2.7 2227 9.6	0221 1.0 0811 5.2 1450 1.2 2039 4.9	0318 1.2 0928 5.2 1537 1.4 2152 5.0	0300 0.3 1015 1.9 1516 0.4 2239 1.7	0125 1.9 0713 0.7 1418 1.9 1941 0.8	0217 4.4 0801 0.8 1446 4.3 2024 1.0	0236 4.6 0758 1.1 1503 4.5 2023 1.2	0231 6.0 0853 1.0 1452 5.9 2118 1.2	0222 6.4 0951 1.2 1442 6.4 2220 1.3
23 TU	0509 3.1 1046 9.2 1736 3.5 2320 8.7	0310 1.5 0904 4.8 1547 1.6 2139 4.5	0357 1.7 1012 4.9 1621 1.9 2242 4.6	0339 0.5 1051 1.7 1602 0.6 2323 1.5	0317 1.8 0810 0.9 1614 1.8 2044 1.0	0316 4.1 0848 1.3 1546 4.0 2118 1.4	0333 4.3 0849 1.5 1603 4.2 2119 1.6	0314 5.6 0940 1.5 1538 5.4 2211 1.6	0311 6.1 1035 1.6 1536 6.0 2308 1.4
24 W	0602 3.9 1144 8.5 1836 4.1	0411 1.9 1012 4.4 1700 1.9 2300 4.2	0443 2.1 1104 4.6 1715 2.3 2348 4.3	0427 0.7 1136 1.5 1709 0.8	0604 1.7 0924 1.2 1831 1.7 2209 1.2	0428 3.9 0953 1.7 1700 3.8 2231 1.8	0510 4.1 0956 1.9 1730 4.0 2239 1.9	0410 5.2 1041 1.9 1644 5.0 2320 2.0	0410 5.7 1130 2.0 1644 5.5
25 TH	0036 8.1 0708 4.3 1309 8.1 1954 4.3	0531 2.1 1142 4.3 1827 2.0	0548 2.4 1218 4.4 1839 2.5	0027 1.3 0545 0.9 1246 1.4 1909 0.9	0724 1.7 1059 1.3 1942 1.6 2340 1.2	0554 3.7 1116 2.0 1826 3.7	0621 3.9 1130 2.1 1846 3.8	0528 4.8 1202 2.2 1809 4.7	0012 2.2 0526 5.4 1243 2.2 1815 5.3
26 F	0213 8.0 0829 4.4 1442 8.2 2122 4.1	0030 4.2 0655 2.1 1304 4.4 1939 1.8	0112 4.3 0722 2.5 1344 4.5 2012 2.3	0216 1.3 0732 0.9 1429 1.5 2039 0.8	0804 1.7 1217 1.3 2009 1.6	0000 1.9 0721 3.8 1243 2.0 1945 3.8	0013 2.0 0738 3.9 1254 2.0 2000 3.9	0046 2.1 0656 4.8 1326 2.2 1935 4.8	0135 2.3 0655 5.4 1413 2.1 1941 5.4
27 SA	0327 8.4 0948 4.0 1546 8.8 2229 3.5	0141 4.4 0802 1.8 1404 4.6 2035 1.6	0234 4.5 0842 2.2 1459 4.8 2117 1.9	0342 1.4 0842 0.8 1543 1.6 2121 0.7	0041 1.1 0812 1.7 1307 1.1 2012 1.7	0120 1.8 0828 3.9 1353 1.8 2042 3.9	0121 1.8 0843 4.1 1351 1.8 2055 4.1	0202 2.0 0810 5.0 1433 2.0 2044 5.0	0258 2.1 0806 5.7 1528 1.8 2042 5.7
28 SU	0418 9.0 1048 3.3 1633 9.4 2318 2.8	0232 4.6 0851 1.6 1450 4.9 2118 1.3	0335 4.8 0939 1.8 1551 5.1 2206 1.5	0433 1.6 0927 0.7 1633 1.7 2156 0.5	0125 1.0 0813 1.8 1346 1.0 2014 1.8	0221 1.5 0914 4.1 1443 1.5 2124 4.0	0212 1.6 0927 4.3 1436 1.5 2133 4.2	0300 1.7 0908 5.4 1524 1.7 2135 5.4	0401 1.8 0858 6.0 1623 1.5 2128 6.0
29 M	0459 9.7 1132 2.7 1713 10.1 2357 2.2	0312 4.9 0932 1.3 1528 5.1 2154 1.1	0419 5.1 1024 1.5 1631 5.3 2247 1.2	0513 1.7 1007 0.5 1716 1.9 2231 0.4	0202 0.8 0816 1.9 1421 0.8 2017 1.9	0304 1.2 0949 4.2 1521 1.2 2156 4.2	0254 1.3 0957 4.4 1515 1.3 2205 4.4	0345 1.4 0953 5.7 1605 1.3 2213 5.7	0450 1.5 0939 6.3 1706 1.2 2203 6.2
30 TU	0536 10.3 1210 2.1 1750 10.6	0347 5.2 1007 1.1 1602 5.3 2227 0.9	0454 5.3 1104 1.2 1704 5.5 2324 1.1	0551 1.8 1045 0.4 1757 2.0 2307 0.3	0237 0.7 0822 1.9 1454 0.7 2026 1.9	0338 0.9 1018 4.3 1552 0.9 2226 4.3	0333 1.1 1027 4.5 1551 1.1 2238 4.5	0424 1.1 1029 5.9 1640 1.1 2244 5.9	0530 1.3 1015 6.5 1743 1.1 2236 6.4

● ● Time: UT. For British Summer Time (shaded) March 30th to October 26th ADD ONE HOUR ● ●

SOUTH COAST OF ENGLAND Time Zone UT

St Helier * St Mary's * Plymouth * Portland * Poole * Southampton * Portsmouth * Shoreham * Dover

OCTOBER 1997 TIDE TABLES OCTOBER 1997

ST HELIER	ST MARYS, SCILLY	PLYMOUTH	PORTLAND	POOLE ENTRANCE	SOUTHAMPTON	PORTSMOUTH	SHOREHAM	DOVER	
Time m	Time m	Time m	Time m	Time m	Time m	Time m	Time m	Time m	
0032 1.8	0419 5.3	0524 5.4	0628 2.0	0310 0.6	0408 0.8	0408 0.9	0456 1.0	0602 1.2	**1 W**
0611 10.7	1040 1.0	1139 1.1	1124 0.3	0835 2.0	1047 4.4	1100 4.6	1101 6.0	1049 6.6	
1245 1.7	1633 5.4	1734 5.6	1836 2.0	1527 0.6	1621 0.8	1626 1.0	1712 0.9	1815 1.0	●
1825 10.9	2259 0.9	2357 1.0	2344 0.2	2042 2.0	2254 4.4	2312 4.6	2312 6.0	2305 6.5	
0104 1.6	0450 5.5	0554 5.5	0703 2.0	0342 0.6	0437 0.7	0442 0.9	0529 0.9	0630 1.1	**2 TH**
0645 10.9	1112 0.9	1212 1.0	1202 0.2	0857 2.0	1114 4.5	1134 4.7	1129 6.1	1121 6.7	
1316 1.5	1703 5.5	1806 5.7	1911 2.1	1557 0.6	1651 0.7	1657 1.0	1742 0.8	1846 1.0	
1858 11.0	2329 0.8			2108 2.0	2323 4.5	2347 4.6	2340 6.0	2334 6.5	
0133 1.5	0520 5.5	0029 1.0	0019 0.2	0412 0.6	0507 0.6	0512 0.9	0558 0.9	0700 1.1	**3 F**
0716 10.9	1142 0.9	0625 5.6	0736 2.1	0928 2.0	1141 4.5	1208 4.7	1158 6.1	1150 6.7	
1346 1.6	1733 5.5	1242 1.0	1237 0.2	1626 0.6	1722 0.6	1726 1.0	1812 0.8	1918 0.9	
1929 10.9		1839 5.6	1945 2.1	2142 2.0	2352 4.5				
0201 1.7	0000 0.9	0100 1.0	0051 0.2	0441 0.6	0537 0.6	0020 4.6	0009 5.9	0001 6.5	**4 SA**
0745 10.7	0550 5.5	0659 5.5	0806 2.0	1004 2.0	1210 4.5	0540 0.9	0628 0.9	0730 1.1	
1415 1.8	1214 1.0	1314 1.1	1308 0.2	1656 0.6	1753 0.6	1238 4.6	1226 6.0	1217 6.6	
1957 10.7	1804 5.4	1914 5.6	2015 2.0	2222 1.9		1754 1.0	1842 0.9	1950 1.0	
0228 2.0	0030 1.0	0130 1.1	0118 0.2	0512 0.6	0023 4.4	0051 4.6	0039 5.9	0028 6.5	**5 SU**
0812 10.5	0621 5.4	0733 5.4	0834 2.0	1046 1.9	0608 0.7	0609 1.0	0658 1.0	0802 1.1	
1443 2.1	1246 1.1	1345 1.2	1333 0.3	1728 0.6	1240 4.5	1307 4.6	1254 6.0	1242 6.5	
2024 10.3	1836 5.3	1948 5.4	2044 1.9	2311 1.9	1823 0.7	1824 1.0	1912 0.9	2021 1.1	
0254 2.3	0102 1.2	0201 1.3	0139 0.3	0545 0.7	0055 4.3	0123 4.5	0109 5.8	0056 6.4	**6 M**
0837 10.1	0654 5.3	0805 5.3	0900 1.9	1138 1.9	0637 0.9	0640 1.1	0728 1.1	0833 1.3	
1512 2.5	1320 1.2	1417 1.4	1354 0.3	1804 0.7	1314 4.4	1339 4.5	1324 5.8	1309 6.4	
2051 10.0	1910 5.1	2018 5.2	2112 1.8		1853 0.9	1857 1.1	1944 1.1	2051 1.3	
0324 2.8	0137 1.4	0232 1.5	0200 0.4	0014 1.9	0134 4.2	0159 4.4	0140 5.7	0128 6.3	**7 TU**
0906 9.8	0730 5.1	0833 5.1	0925 1.7	0624 0.8	0711 1.1	0715 1.2	0803 1.3	0903 1.5	
1545 2.9	1358 1.5	1449 1.7	1418 0.4	1248 1.9	1354 4.2	1417 4.4	1358 5.6	1343 6.2	
2124 9.6	1949 4.9	2045 5.0	2140 1.6	1847 0.8	1930 1.2	1935 1.2	2021 1.3	2124 1.6	
0400 3.2	0217 1.6	0305 1.8	0227 0.5	0137 1.8	0221 4.1	0242 4.3	0218 5.4	0206 6.1	**8 W**
0941 9.4	0814 4.9	0903 4.9	0951 1.6	0710 0.9	0753 1.5	0756 1.4	0843 1.6	0939 1.7	
1628 3.3	1444 1.7	1527 1.9	1452 0.5	1418 1.8	1444 4.1	1503 4.3	1443 5.3	1426 6.0	
2205 9.1	2037 4.6	2117 4.8	2215 1.5	1938 0.9	2017 1.5	2020 1.4	2108 1.6	2203 1.8	
0448 3.7	0307 1.9	0345 2.0	0304 0.6	0323 1.7	0319 3.9	0336 4.1	0307 5.2	0257 5.9	**9 TH**
1029 8.9	0909 4.6	0942 4.8	1030 1.5	0809 1.1	0850 1.8	0848 1.7	0938 1.8	1026 2.0	
1727 3.7	1544 1.9	1615 2.1	1543 0.6	1611 1.7	1545 3.9	1601 4.1	1544 5.0	1527 5.7	
2303 8.5	2142 4.4	2210 4.6	2311 1.4	2046 1.1	2123 1.8	2121 1.7	2210 1.8	2258 2.1	
0558 4.0	0417 2.0	0443 2.3	0404 0.7	0535 1.7	0436 3.8	0450 4.0	0420 5.0	0411 5.6	**10 F**
1142 8.4	1024 4.5	1048 4.6	1139 1.5	0932 1.2	1011 1.9	1004 2.0	1053 2.0	1132 2.2	
1846 3.9	1705 1.9	1728 2.3	1722 0.7	1817 1.7	1705 3.8	1719 4.0	1706 4.9	1657 5.5	
	2310 4.3	2336 4.5		2227 1.2	2251 1.8	2257 1.8	2334 1.9		
0039 8.1	0548 2.0	0609 2.3	0040 1.4	0733 1.7	0606 3.8	0632 4.0	0551 5.0	0015 2.2	**11 SA**
0725 4.1	1155 4.6	1218 4.6	0615 0.8	1117 1.2	1142 1.9	1148 1.9	1221 1.9	0545 5.5	
1335 8.3	1832 1.7	1904 2.1	1321 1.5	1947 1.7	1829 3.9	1855 4.0	1837 5.1	1300 2.1	
2015 3.7			1925 0.7	2350 1.1				1833 5.6	
0230 8.5	0040 4.5	0117 4.6	0227 1.5	0807 1.8	0020 1.6	0024 1.7	0101 1.7	0145 2.0	**12 SU**
0859 3.7	0709 1.7	0746 2.1	0758 0.7	1223 1.1	0724 4.0	0752 4.2	0717 5.4	0712 5.8	
1508 9.0	1312 4.9	1352 4.9	1457 1.7	2010 1.9	1301 1.5	1301 1.5	1340 1.5	1429 1.8	
2142 3.0	1943 1.4	2028 1.7	2038 0.5		1940 4.1	2012 4.3	1954 5.5	1949 5.9	
0345 9.4	0147 4.9	0243 4.9	0349 1.7	0049 0.9	0131 1.2	0130 1.4	0212 1.3	0303 1.6	**13 M**
1018 2.8	0812 1.3	0901 1.6	0903 0.6	0812 1.9	0820 4.3	0852 4.5	0824 5.8	0818 6.2	
1611 10.0	1411 5.3	1507 5.2	1609 1.9	1316 0.8	1402 1.1	1401 1.3	1445 1.1	1539 1.3	
2249 2.1	2040 0.9	2135 1.2	2133 0.3	2013 1.9	2034 4.3	2106 4.6	2053 6.0	2045 6.3	
0439 10.3	0241 5.4	0345 5.3	0451 1.9	0138 0.6	0226 0.8	0226 1.0	0311 0.9	0406 1.2	**14 TU**
1118 1.9	0906 0.9	1003 1.1	0956 0.4	0814 2.0	0907 4.5	0937 4.8	0918 6.2	0909 6.6	
1703 10.9	1502 5.7	1606 5.6	1709 2.1	1402 0.6	1454 0.7	1454 1.0	1539 0.7	1637 0.9	
2345 1.3	2131 0.5	2232 0.7	2222 0.2	2015 2.0	2120 4.5	2150 4.8	2140 6.4	2133 6.7	
0527 11.2	0328 5.7	0437 5.6	0545 2.1	0222 0.4	0316 0.5	0316 0.7	0403 0.6	0502 0.9	**15 W**
1210 1.1	0954 0.5	1057 0.7	1044 0.2	0820 2.1	0950 4.7	1018 5.0	1006 6.5	0955 6.9	
1749 11.7	1548 6.0	1656 5.8	1803 2.3	1444 0.4	1542 0.4	1541 0.7	1628 0.5	1732 0.7	
	2218 0.3	2323 0.4	2309 0.1	2024 2.1	2205 4.7	2233 5.0	2226 6.5	2218 6.9	

● ● Time UT. For British Summer Time (shaded) March 30th to October 26th ADD ONE HOUR ● ●

OCTOBER 1997 TIDE TABLES OCTOBER 1997

Day	ST HELIER Time m	ST MARYS, SCILLY Time m	PLYMOUTH Time m	PORTLAND Time m	POOLE ENTRANCE Time m	SOUTHAMPTON Time m	PORTSMOUTH Time m	SHOREHAM Time m	DOVER Time m
16 TH ○	0033 0.7	0412 6.0	0524 5.8	0634 2.3	0304 0.3	0404 0.2	0402 0.5	0450 0.5	0554 0.8
	0612 11.8	1041 0.3	1145 0.5	1129 0.1	0835 2.2	1031 4.9	1059 5.1	1052 6.6	1039 7.1
	1256 0.6	1633 6.2	1743 5.9	1854 2.4	1526 0.3	1629 0.2	1625 0.5	1716 0.4	1824 0.5
	1833 12.1	2303 0.2		2353 -0.0	2044 2.2	2249 4.8	2315 5.0	2311 6.6	2302 7.0
17 F	0117 0.4	0455 6.1	0010 0.3	0719 2.4	0345 0.2	0451 0.1	0445 0.4	0537 0.5	0643 0.7
	0654 12.0	1126 0.2	0609 5.8	1212 0.1	0903 2.2	1114 4.9	1141 5.1	1137 6.7	1122 7.2
	1339 0.5	1716 6.2	1231 0.3	1939 2.4	1607 0.3	1715 0.1	1707 0.4	1801 0.5	1911 0.5
	1916 12.1	2347 0.3	1830 5.9		2119 2.1	2334 4.8	2359 5.0	2358 6.6	2347 7.0
18 SA	0159 0.6	0537 6.0	0054 0.3	0035 -0.0	0427 0.3	0537 0.2	0527 0.4	0621 0.5	0727 0.6
	0736 11.9	1211 0.3	0654 5.8	0800 2.4	0945 2.2	1157 4.9	1223 5.1	1220 6.6	1206 7.1
	1421 0.8	1800 6.0	1315 0.4	1254 0.1	1649 0.3	1759 0.2	1748 0.5	1845 0.6	1954 0.5
	1958 11.8		1917 5.8	2021 2.3	2209 2.1				
19 SU	0239 1.0	0030 0.3	0136 0.5	0115 0.1	0512 0.4	0019 4.8	0042 4.9	0042 6.5	0030 6.9
	0815 11.5	0619 5.9	0739 5.7	0839 2.3	1043 2.1	0620 0.3	0609 0.6	0702 0.7	0809 0.7
	1500 1.3	1254 0.6	1356 0.6	1335 0.2	1734 0.4	1241 4.7	1305 4.9	1302 6.5	1248 6.9
	2039 11.1	1842 5.7	2003 5.6	2100 2.2	2316 2.0	1840 0.3	1830 0.7	1924 0.7	2035 0.7
20 M	0318 1.7	0112 0.8	0216 0.8	0154 0.2	0558 0.5	0106 4.6	0126 4.8	0124 6.3	0112 6.7
	0854 10.8	0703 5.6	0821 5.5	0913 2.1	1151 2.0	0659 0.6	0651 0.9	0743 0.9	0848 0.9
	1540 2.0	1339 0.9	1436 1.0	1414 0.2	1821 0.6	1327 4.5	1346 4.7	1341 6.2	1330 6.7
	2119 10.4	1927 5.3	2046 5.3	2136 1.9		1919 0.6	1912 0.9	2006 1.0	2114 1.1
21 TU	0358 2.5	0156 1.2	0254 1.3	0230 0.4	0039 1.9	0156 4.4	0212 4.6	0205 6.0	0156 6.4
	0933 10.0	0748 5.2	0902 5.3	0945 1.9	0646 0.8	0738 0.9	0734 1.2	0824 1.2	0927 1.2
	1621 2.8	1425 1.3	1515 1.4	1452 0.5	1315 1.9	1417 4.2	1431 4.5	1421 5.9	1415 6.3
	2202 9.5	2015 4.9	2127 4.9	2212 1.7	1912 0.8	1957 1.0	1957 1.3	2047 1.3	2153 1.5
22 W	0440 3.3	0242 1.6	0332 1.7	0305 0.6	0222 1.8	0252 4.1	0305 4.3	0247 5.7	0242 6.1
	1016 9.2	0837 4.8	0941 4.9	1015 1.7	0742 1.0	0822 1.4	0824 1.6	0910 1.6	1008 1.6
	1706 3.6	1518 1.7	1555 1.9	1534 0.7	1458 1.8	1513 4.0	1523 4.2	1507 5.4	1506 5.9
	2251 8.7	2110 4.5	2211 4.6	2250 1.5	2011 1.0	2047 1.4	2050 1.6	2136 1.6	2236 1.9
23 TH	0529 4.0	0336 1.9	0413 2.2	0344 0.8	0515 1.7	0357 3.9	0438 4.1	0340 5.3	0337 5.8
	1108 8.5	0939 4.5	1024 4.6	1051 1.6	0849 1.2	0920 1.8	0924 1.9	1008 2.0	1057 2.0
	1801 4.1	1624 2.0	1645 2.3	1632 0.8	1722 1.7	1619 3.7	1642 3.9	1607 5.0	1611 5.5
	2359 8.1	2221 4.2	2308 4.3	2345 1.3	2128 1.2	2152 1.8	2200 1.9	2239 2.0	2331 2.3
24 F	0629 4.5	0448 2.2	0509 2.5	0442 0.9	0651 1.7	0515 3.7	0547 4.0	0450 5.0	0445 5.5
	1224 8.1	1058 4.3	1127 4.4	1144 1.5	1022 1.4	1035 2.1	1052 2.2	1122 2.2	1202 2.2
	1912 4.4	1744 2.1	1758 2.5	1813 0.9	1911 1.6	1739 3.6	1806 3.8	1727 4.7	1736 5.2
		2348 4.1			2301 1.3	2315 2.0	2332 2.0	2359 2.2	
25 SA	0131 7.9	0612 2.2	0026 4.2	0126 1.3	0748 1.7	0640 3.7	0657 3.9	0614 4.9	0048 2.5
	0744 4.6	1221 4.3	0638 2.6	0632 1.0	1147 1.3	1201 2.1	1221 2.1	1245 2.3	0610 5.4
	1357 8.1	1859 2.0	1251 4.4	1312 1.4	1959 1.6	1902 3.6	1921 3.8	1855 4.7	1328 2.3
	2034 4.3		1932 2.4	1951 0.8					1904 5.3
26 SU	0248 8.3	0102 4.3	0148 4.4	0305 1.4	0011 1.2	0037 1.9	0047 1.9	0118 2.1	0213 2.3
	0903 4.3	0722 2.0	0804 2.4	0800 0.9	0809 1.7	0749 3.8	0804 4.0	0730 5.0	0727 5.5
	1507 8.5	1327 4.5	1409 4.6	1444 1.5	1241 1.2	1312 1.9	1321 1.9	1353 2.1	1447 2.0
	2145 3.9	1957 1.8	2039 2.1	2041 0.7	2011 1.7	2005 3.7	2023 3.9	2007 4.9	2009 5.5
27 M	0342 8.8	0157 4.5	0254 4.7	0354 1.5	0058 1.1	0141 1.7	0141 1.7	0220 1.9	0319 2.0
	1007 3.7	0815 1.8	0903 2.0	0852 0.8	0812 1.8	0837 3.9	0854 4.2	0829 5.3	0824 5.8
	1558 9.1	1415 4.8	1508 4.9	1543 1.6	1322 1.1	1405 1.6	1408 1.7	1447 1.8	1544 1.7
	2238 3.2	2042 1.5	2129 1.7	2118 0.6	2013 1.7	2051 3.9	2106 4.1	2100 5.2	2057 5.8
28 TU	0425 9.5	0240 4.8	0340 5.0	0434 1.7	0136 0.9	0226 1.4	0224 1.5	0309 1.6	0409 1.7
	1056 3.1	0858 1.5	0948 1.7	0934 0.6	0813 1.9	0915 4.1	0929 4.4	0915 5.6	0909 6.1
	1640 9.8	1456 5.0	1551 5.2	1630 1.8	1356 0.9	1445 1.3	1447 1.4	1530 1.4	1628 1.4
	2320 2.6	2121 1.3	2211 1.4	2154 0.4	2014 1.8	2126 4.1	2140 4.3	2139 5.5	2135 6.1
29 W	0503 10.1	0317 5.1	0417 5.3	0512 1.9	0210 0.8	0304 1.1	0303 1.3	0349 1.3	0449 1.5
	1136 2.5	0935 1.3	1029 1.4	1014 0.5	0817 1.9	0946 4.3	1002 4.5	0953 5.8	0947 6.3
	1718 10.3	1532 5.2	1629 5.4	1715 1.9	1428 0.8	1520 1.0	1523 1.3	1606 1.1	1706 1.2
	2357 2.2	2155 1.1	2248 1.2	2231 0.3	2019 1.9	2158 4.2	2215 4.5	2212 5.7	2207 6.3
30 TH	0539 10.6	0351 5.3	0451 5.5	0551 2.0	0242 0.7	0336 0.9	0338 1.1	0424 1.1	0525 1.3
	1213 2.0	1009 1.1	1106 1.2	1053 0.4	0825 2.0	1016 4.4	1035 4.6	1026 6.0	1020 6.5
	1754 10.7	1604 5.4	1704 5.6	1757 2.0	1458 0.7	1552 0.8	1556 1.1	1640 0.9	1742 1.1
		2228 1.0	2324 1.1	2308 0.2	2030 1.9	2229 4.4	2250 4.6	2242 5.9	2236 6.4
31 F ●	0031 1.9	0422 5.5	0526 5.6	0629 2.1	0311 0.7	0408 0.8	0410 1.0	0457 0.9	0559 1.2
	0613 10.9	1043 1.0	1141 1.1	1131 0.3	0840 2.0	1045 4.5	1109 4.7	1056 6.0	1050 6.6
	1248 1.7	1636 5.5	1741 5.6	1838 2.0	1528 0.6	1624 0.7	1627 1.0	1712 0.8	1817 1.0
	1828 10.9	2300 0.9	2359 1.0	2344 0.2	2050 2.0	2259 4.5	2324 4.6	2313 5.9	2304 6.5

● ● Time: UT. For British Summer Time (shaded) March 30th to October 26th ADD ONE HOUR ● ●

SOUTH COAST OF ENGLAND Time Zone UT

St Helier * St Mary's * Plymouth * Portland * Poole * Southampton * Portsmouth * Shoreham * Dover

NOVEMBER 1997 TIDE TABLES NOVEMBER 1997

Day	ST HELIER Time m	ST MARYS SCILLY Time m	PLYMOUTH Time m	PORTLAND Time m	POOLE ENTRANCE Time m	SOUTHAMPTON Time m	PORTSMOUTH Time m	SHOREHAM Time m	DOVER Time m
1 SA	0104 1.7	0453 5.6	0602 5.6	0706 2.1	0341 0.6	0441 0.7	0441 1.0	0529 0.9	0633 1.1
	0646 11.0	1116 0.9	1217 1.0	1206 0.3	0903 2.0	1115 4.6	1141 4.7	1127 6.1	1119 6.6
	1321 1.7	1708 5.5	1818 5.6	1915 2.0	1557 0.6	1658 0.6	1657 1.0	1744 0.8	1852 1.0
	1901 11.0	2333 0.9			2117 2.0	2331 4.5	2357 4.6	2344 6.0	2333 6.6
2 SU	0136 1.8	0525 5.6	0034 1.0	0018 0.2	0412 0.6	0516 0.7	0512 1.0	0600 1.0	0707 1.1
	0717 10.9	1151 1.0	0639 5.6	0739 2.1	0933 2.0	1145 4.6	1212 4.7	1158 6.1	1148 6.6
	1353 1.8	1740 5.5	1252 1.0	1239 0.3	1629 0.6	1732 0.6	1729 0.9	1816 0.9	1925 1.0
	1933 10.8		1856 5.5	1951 2.0	2155 2.0				
3 M	0206 2.0	0007 1.0	0109 1.1	0048 0.3	0446 0.6	0004 4.5	0031 4.6	0017 6.0	0004 6.6
	0747 10.7	0558 5.5	0714 5.5	0811 2.1	1014 2.0	0549 0.7	0545 1.0	0632 1.0	0740 1.1
	1424 2.0	1225 1.0	1327 1.1	1309 0.3	1705 0.6	1217 4.6	1245 4.7	1230 6.1	1218 6.6
	2003 10.6	1815 5.4	1930 5.3	2024 1.9	2244 1.9	1805 0.7	1803 0.9	1849 0.9	1957 1.1
4 TU	0237 2.3	0042 1.1	0142 1.2	0116 0.3	0525 0.7	0039 4.4	0106 4.6	0051 5.9	0037 6.5
	0818 10.5	0634 5.4	0746 5.4	0841 2.0	1106 2.0	0623 0.8	0621 1.1	0706 1.2	0812 1.2
	1457 2.3	1303 1.2	1401 1.3	1338 0.4	1744 0.6	1253 4.5	1320 4.6	1304 6.0	1251 6.5
	2036 10.2	1852 5.2	2002 5.2	2056 1.8	2351 1.9	1839 0.8	1839 1.0	1926 1.1	2029 1.2
5 W	0311 2.7	0120 1.3	0216 1.4	0145 0.4	0607 0.8	0119 4.3	0146 4.5	0127 5.8	0113 6.4
	0851 10.1	0714 5.3	0816 5.2	0909 1.9	1216 1.9	0700 1.1	0700 1.2	0746 1.3	0846 1.4
	1535 2.7	1344 1.3	1436 1.5	1409 0.4	1830 0.7	1334 4.3	1400 4.5	1344 5.8	1329 6.3
	2112 9.8	1934 5.0	2033 5.0	2128 1.7		1917 1.0	1920 1.2	2006 1.2	2104 1.5
6 TH	0350 3.1	0203 1.5	0251 1.6	0218 0.5	0117 1.9	0206 4.2	0232 4.4	0209 5.7	0155 6.2
	0930 9.7	0759 5.1	0848 5.1	0939 1.8	0656 0.9	0743 1.3	0743 1.4	0830 1.5	0925 1.6
	1620 3.1	1432 1.5	1515 1.7	1449 0.5	1349 1.8	1423 4.2	1448 4.3	1432 5.5	1416 6.1
	2157 9.3	2024 4.8	2108 4.8	2208 1.6	1923 0.9	2003 1.3	2007 1.4	2055 1.4	2147 1.7
7 F	0440 3.5	0254 1.7	0333 1.9	0259 0.6	0306 1.8	0303 4.0	0327 4.3	0300 5.5	0248 6.0
	1021 9.2	0854 4.9	0929 4.9	1019 1.7	0757 1.0	0838 1.6	0837 1.7	0926 1.6	1013 1.8
	1717 3.4	1530 1.7	1604 1.9	1545 0.6	1541 1.8	1523 4.0	1545 4.2	1532 5.3	1518 5.8
	2257 8.8	2127 4.6	2200 4.6	2305 1.5	2031 1.0	2105 1.5	2108 1.6	2155 1.6	2242 1.9
8 SA	0545 3.8	0401 1.9	0429 2.1	0402 0.8	0517 1.8	0414 3.9	0439 4.2	0408 5.3	0358 5.8
	1132 8.7	1004 4.7	1030 4.8	1124 1.6	0917 1.2	0950 1.8	0950 1.9	1036 1.7	1116 1.9
	1828 3.6	1645 1.8	1712 2.0	1716 0.7	1745 1.7	1637 3.9	1657 4.1	1647 5.1	1643 5.6
		2247 4.5	2318 4.5		2201 1.1	2223 1.6	2231 1.7	2311 1.7	2354 2.1
9 SU	0024 8.4	0523 1.9	0549 2.2	0027 1.5	0719 1.8	0538 3.9	0615 4.2	0530 5.3	0521 5.7
	0705 3.9	1127 4.7	1154 4.7	0552 0.9	1053 1.2	1114 1.7	1123 1.8	1159 1.7	1237 1.9
	1309 8.6	1806 1.7	1839 1.9	1254 1.6	1933 1.7	1759 3.9	1833 4.1	1811 5.2	1811 5.7
	1950 3.5			1857 0.7	2323 1.0	2348 1.5	2355 1.6		
10 M	0201 8.7	0012 4.6	0054 4.6	0201 1.6	0801 1.8	0653 4.1	0727 4.3	0034 1.5	0118 2.0
	0832 3.6	0642 1.7	0718 2.0	0730 0.8	1201 1.0	1231 1.5	1236 1.7	0649 5.5	0643 5.8
	1438 9.1	1243 5.0	1327 4.9	1424 1.7	2007 1.8	1913 4.0	1948 4.3	1317 1.4	1401 1.7
	2112 3.0	1918 1.4	2000 1.6	2010 0.5				1927 5.5	1924 5.9
11 TU	0316 9.4	0121 4.9	0218 4.9	0321 1.7	0025 0.9	0100 1.2	0103 1.4	0146 1.2	0233 1.7
	0951 2.9	0748 1.3	0834 1.6	0838 0.7	0811 1.9	0754 4.3	0827 4.6	0757 5.8	0751 6.2
	1545 9.8	1346 5.3	1442 5.2	1539 1.9	1257 0.9	1334 1.1	1339 1.4	1422 1.1	1510 1.3
	2222 2.3	2017 1.0	2108 1.2	2108 0.4	2012 1.9	2011 4.3	2044 4.5	2028 5.8	2023 6.2
12 W	0414 10.2	0218 5.3	0321 5.3	0424 1.9	0118 0.7	0159 0.9	0203 1.1	0247 0.9	0337 1.3
	1054 2.1	0844 1.0	0937 1.2	0933 0.5	0813 2.0	0843 4.5	0915 4.8	0851 6.1	0845 6.5
	1639 10.6	1439 5.6	1543 5.5	1642 2.0	1344 0.7	1428 0.8	1433 1.1	1518 0.8	1610 1.0
	2319 1.6	2109 0.7	2206 0.9	2158 0.3	2013 2.0	2100 4.5	2130 4.7	2118 6.1	2113 6.5
13 TH	0504 10.9	0306 5.6	0415 5.5	0518 2.1	0202 0.5	0251 0.6	0254 0.9	0340 0.7	0434 1.1
	1147 1.5	0934 0.7	1033 0.8	1022 0.4	0816 2.1	0928 4.7	0957 5.0	0941 6.4	0933 6.8
	1727 11.2	1528 5.9	1636 5.6	1738 2.2	1426 0.5	1518 0.5	1521 0.8	1609 0.6	1706 0.8
		2157 0.5	2300 0.6	2245 0.2	2019 2.1	2147 4.6	2215 4.9	2205 6.3	2159 6.8
14 F ○	0009 1.1	0352 5.9	0503 5.6	0609 2.3	0245 0.4	0341 0.4	0342 0.7	0429 0.6	0527 0.9
	0549 11.4	1022 0.5	1124 0.6	1109 0.3	0826 2.2	1011 4.8	1039 5.1	1027 6.5	1018 6.9
	1235 1.0	1614 6.0	1725 5.7	1829 2.2	1508 0.4	1607 0.3	1606 0.6	1657 0.5	1758 0.7
	1813 11.6	2243 0.4	2348 0.6	2330 0.1	2034 2.1	2234 4.7	2258 4.9	2251 6.4	2244 6.9
15 SA	0054 0.9	0436 6.0	0551 5.7	0654 2.3	0327 0.4	0429 0.3	0426 0.6	0515 0.6	0617 0.8
	0633 11.6	1108 0.5	1211 0.6	1153 0.2	0847 2.2	1054 4.8	1121 5.1	1113 6.5	1102 7.0
	1318 0.9	1658 6.0	1813 5.8	1916 2.3	1548 0.4	1653 0.2	1648 0.6	1741 0.5	1846 0.7
	1857 11.6	2327 0.5			2103 2.1	2317 4.7	2342 4.9	2337 6.4	2328 6.9

● ● Time UT. For British Summer Time (shaded) March 30th to October 26th ADD ONE HOUR ● ●

NOVEMBER 1997 TIDE TABLES NOVEMBER 1997

	ST HELIER	ST MARYS, SCILLY	PLYMOUTH	PORTLAND	POOLE ENTRANCE	SOUTHAMPTON	PORTSMOUTH	SHOREHAM	DOVER
	Time m	Time m	Time m	Time m	Time m	Time m	Time m	Time m	Time m
16 SU	0136 1.0 0714 11.6 1400 1.1 1939 11.3	0519 5.9 1153 0.6 1742 5.8	0033 0.6 0636 5.7 1255 0.6 1900 5.6	0012 0.1 0737 2.3 1236 0.2 2000 2.2	0409 0.4 0922 2.1 1631 0.4 2146 2.1	0515 0.4 1137 4.8 1736 0.3	0509 0.7 1202 5.0 1730 0.6	0557 0.7 1155 6.5 1822 0.7	0703 0.8 1146 7.0 1930 0.7
17 M	0217 1.4 0754 11.2 1440 1.5 2019 10.9	0010 0.7 0601 5.8 1236 0.7 1824 5.6	0115 0.7 0719 5.6 1336 0.8 1944 5.4	0053 0.2 0815 2.3 1316 0.3 2039 2.1	0451 0.5 1009 2.1 1714 0.5 2246 2.0	0003 4.7 0559 0.5 1221 4.6 1818 0.4	0024 4.9 0550 0.8 1242 4.9 1811 0.8	0021 6.4 0639 0.8 1236 6.4 1902 0.8	0012 6.8 0745 0.8 1228 6.8 2012 0.9
18 TU	0256 1.9 0833 10.7 1518 2.1 2100 10.2	0052 0.9 0644 5.6 1319 1.0 1907 5.3	0155 0.9 0800 5.5 1416 1.0 2024 5.2	0131 0.3 0849 2.1 1355 0.3 2114 1.9	0537 0.6 1110 2.0 1800 0.6	0049 4.5 0638 0.7 1304 4.4 1856 0.7	0107 4.7 0632 1.0 1322 4.7 1853 1.0	0103 6.2 0719 1.1 1315 6.1 1940 1.0	0053 6.7 0825 1.0 1310 6.6 2049 1.2
19 W	0333 2.6 0911 10.1 1557 2.7 2140 9.5	0133 1.2 0727 5.3 1403 1.3 1951 4.9	0233 1.3 0836 5.2 1454 1.4 2100 4.9	0206 0.4 0918 2.0 1433 0.5 2145 1.7	0000 2.0 0624 0.8 1226 1.9 1848 0.8	0136 4.4 0716 1.0 1351 4.2 1934 1.0	0151 4.6 0715 1.2 1405 4.5 1936 1.2	0142 6.0 0800 1.3 1355 5.9 2021 1.3	0134 6.5 0903 1.2 1353 6.3 2125 1.5
20 TH	0412 3.2 0951 9.4 1637 3.4 2224 8.9	0215 1.6 0812 5.0 1448 1.6 2040 4.6	0308 1.7 0908 5.0 1530 1.8 2135 4.6	0240 0.6 0945 1.8 1512 0.6 2218 1.5	0133 1.9 0716 1.0 1355 1.8 1942 0.9	0227 4.1 0756 1.3 1440 4.0 2015 1.3	0240 4.4 0801 1.5 1451 4.2 2024 1.5	0224 5.8 0843 1.6 1439 5.5 2105 1.5	0218 6.2 0942 1.5 1439 5.9 2202 1.9
21 F	0454 3.8 1036 8.8 1723 3.9 2318 8.3	0302 1.9 0903 4.7 1541 1.9 2137 4.3	0345 2.0 0941 4.7 1612 2.1 2218 4.4	0315 0.8 1013 1.7 1557 0.7 2259 1.4	0335 1.8 0816 1.2 1546 1.7 2046 1.1	0322 3.9 0843 1.7 1535 3.7 2107 1.6	0342 4.2 0854 1.8 1548 4.0 2121 1.8	0311 5.4 0935 1.8 1533 5.1 2200 1.8	0306 5.9 1024 1.9 1535 5.6 2245 2.2
22 SA	0544 4.3 1133 8.3 1818 4.2	0358 2.1 1005 4.4 1645 2.1 2248 4.2	0429 2.4 1030 4.5 1706 2.4 2324 4.3	0356 0.9 1052 1.5 1700 0.8	0551 1.7 0930 1.3 1806 1.6 2205 1.2	0424 3.7 0942 1.9 1639 3.6 2212 1.9	0501 4.0 1002 2.1 1711 3.8 2235 2.0	0408 5.2 1037 2.1 1639 4.8 2305 2.0	0403 5.6 1115 2.1 1644 5.3 2342 2.4
23 SU	0029 8.0 0646 4.5 1249 8.1 1927 4.3	0509 2.2 1120 4.3 1759 2.1	0533 2.6 1144 4.4 1825 2.4	0003 1.3 0509 1.0 1153 1.5 1828 0.8	0708 1.7 1058 1.3 1926 1.6 2325 1.3	0536 3.6 1054 2.0 1754 3.5 2329 1.9	0603 4.0 1128 2.1 1823 3.7 2357 2.0	0519 5.0 1149 2.2 1758 4.6	0514 5.4 1221 2.3 1806 5.2
24 M	0146 8.1 0758 4.5 1406 8.3 2039 4.1	0005 4.2 0624 2.2 1233 4.4 1905 2.0	0041 4.3 0700 2.5 1302 4.5 1944 2.2	0133 1.3 0650 1.0 1316 1.5 1940 0.7	0752 1.7 1206 1.3 2002 1.6	0645 3.7 1208 2.0 1906 3.6	0705 4.0 1242 2.0 1929 3.8	0020 2.1 0632 5.0 1301 2.1 1912 4.7	0054 2.5 0633 5.4 1337 2.2 1919 5.3
25 TU	0250 8.5 0909 4.1 1509 8.7 2143 3.7	0110 4.4 0727 2.0 1331 4.6 1958 1.8	0151 4.5 0812 2.3 1409 4.8 2042 1.9	0251 1.5 0803 0.9 1437 1.5 2031 0.6	0022 1.2 0809 1.7 1252 1.2 2011 1.7	0038 1.8 0744 3.8 1310 1.8 2003 3.7	0100 1.9 0803 4.1 1333 1.8 2025 4.0	0128 2.0 0737 5.1 1400 1.9 2011 5.0	0209 2.3 0738 5.6 1445 2.0 2014 5.6
26 W	0341 9.0 1009 3.6 1558 9.2 2235 3.2	0201 4.7 0818 1.8 1419 4.8 2042 1.5	0248 4.8 0903 1.9 1504 5.0 2128 1.6	0344 1.6 0855 0.7 1539 1.6 2113 0.5	0105 1.1 0812 1.8 1328 1.0 2013 1.8	0134 1.6 0830 4.0 1359 1.5 2049 3.9	0148 1.7 0851 4.3 1415 1.6 2110 4.2	0223 1.7 0829 5.4 1449 1.6 2058 5.2	0312 2.0 0830 5.9 1539 1.7 2058 5.8
27 TH	0425 9.6 1057 3.0 1642 9.8 2318 2.7	0243 5.0 0900 1.5 1459 5.1 2122 1.3	0335 5.1 0948 1.6 1551 5.2 2209 1.4	0430 1.8 0939 0.6 1632 1.8 2153 0.4	0138 1.0 0813 1.9 1359 0.9 2015 1.8	0220 1.3 0908 4.2 1442 1.2 2127 4.1	0227 1.5 0932 4.4 1450 1.4 2151 4.3	0309 1.5 0912 5.6 1530 1.3 2135 5.5	0402 1.7 0912 6.1 1626 1.4 2133 6.1
28 F	0505 10.1 1140 2.5 1721 10.3 2359 2.4	0320 5.2 0939 1.3 1536 5.3 2159 1.1	0418 5.3 1030 1.4 1634 5.3 2250 1.2	0513 1.9 1019 0.5 1721 1.9 2233 0.3	0210 0.9 0818 1.9 1429 0.8 2022 1.9	0300 1.1 0943 4.3 1520 1.0 2203 4.3	0303 1.4 1009 4.6 1524 1.3 2228 4.5	0349 1.2 0950 5.8 1609 1.0 2211 5.7	0447 1.5 0947 6.3 1709 1.2 2206 6.3
29 SA	0542 10.6 1220 2.1 1800 10.6	0355 5.4 1016 1.1 1611 5.4 2235 1.0	0458 5.4 1111 1.2 1717 5.4 2331 1.1	0556 2.1 1059 0.4 1807 2.0 2311 0.3	0241 0.9 0828 2.0 1459 0.7 2037 1.9	0339 0.9 1018 4.5 1558 0.8 2239 4.4	0337 1.2 1044 4.6 1557 1.1 2303 4.6	0425 1.1 1026 5.9 1644 0.9 2246 5.9	0529 1.3 1018 6.4 1749 1.1 2236 6.4
30 SU ●	0037 2.0 0618 10.9 1258 1.8 1836 10.8	0430 5.6 1054 1.0 1645 5.5 2311 1.0	0539 5.5 1152 1.0 1759 5.4	0637 2.1 1137 0.3 1851 2.0 2349 0.3	0313 0.7 0844 2.0 1532 0.6 2100 2.0	0417 0.8 1051 4.6 1636 0.6 2314 4.5	0412 1.1 1116 4.7 1632 0.9 2338 4.6	0500 1.0 1100 6.0 1719 0.9 2322 6.0	0609 1.2 1051 6.5 1829 1.0 2310 6.5

● ● Time: UT. For British Summer Time (shaded) March 30th to October 26th ADD ONE HOUR ● ●

SOUTH COAST OF ENGLAND Time Zone UT

St Helier * St Mary's * Plymouth * Portland * Poole * Southampton * Portsmouth * Shoreham * Dover

DECEMBER 1997 TIDE TABLES DECEMBER 1997

	ST HELIER	ST MARYS, SCILLY	PLYMOUTH	PORTLAND	POOLE ENTRANCE	SOUTHAMPTON	PORTSMOUTH	SHOREHAM	DOVER	
	Time m	Time m	Time m	Time m	Time m	Time m	Time m	Time m	Time m	
	0114 1.9 0654 11.0 1336 1.8 1913 10.9	0505 5.6 1131 1.0 1722 5.5 2349 1.0	0012 1.0 0619 5.5 1233 1.0 1839 5.4	0717 2.2 1215 0.3 1932 2.0	0350 0.6 0910 2.0 1610 0.5 2135 2.0	0456 0.7 1125 4.6 1714 0.6 2350 4.5	0450 1.0 1150 4.7 1710 0.9	0537 1.0 1136 6.1 1755 0.9	0648 1.1 1124 6.6 1905 1.0 2347 6.6	**1 M**
	0150 1.9 0730 11.0 1412 1.9 1950 10.8	0542 5.7 1210 1.0 1800 5.5	0051 1.0 0657 5.5 1313 1.0 1917 5.3	0027 0.3 0754 2.1 1251 0.3 2010 2.0	0429 0.6 0949 2.0 1650 0.5 2226 2.0	0534 0.7 1201 4.6 1752 0.6	0014 4.7 0529 1.0 1226 4.7 1749 0.8	0000 6.0 0613 1.1 1214 6.1 1834 0.9	0723 1.1 1201 6.6 1939 1.0	**2 TU**
	0227 2.1 0806 10.8 1450 2.0 2028 10.5	0028 1.0 0621 5.6 1251 1.0 1841 5.4	0130 1.0 0732 5.5 1351 1.1 1951 5.2	0103 0.3 0829 2.1 1329 0.3 2048 1.9	0512 0.6 1044 2.0 1734 0.6 2335 2.0	0028 4.5 0614 0.8 1238 4.5 1831 0.7	0054 4.7 0609 1.0 1306 4.7 1830 0.9	0039 6.1 0653 1.1 1254 6.1 1916 1.0	0026 6.6 0757 1.1 1242 6.5 2013 1.1	**3 W**
	0305 2.4 0845 10.6 1530 2.2 2109 10.2	0109 1.2 0703 5.5 1336 1.1 1925 5.2	0207 1.2 0806 5.4 1430 1.2 2027 5.1	0141 0.4 0903 2.0 1408 0.4 2125 1.8	0558 0.7 1156 2.0 1823 0.6	0110 4.4 0653 0.9 1321 4.4 1911 0.8	0137 4.6 0651 1.1 1349 4.6 1914 1.0	0122 6.0 0737 1.2 1339 6.0 2001 1.1	0108 6.5 0834 1.2 1325 6.4 2052 1.3	**4 TH**
	0347 2.7 0928 10.2 1615 2.6 2156 9.7	0155 1.3 0750 5.4 1424 1.3 2015 5.0	0245 1.3 0842 5.2 1511 1.4 2106 4.9	0221 0.5 0939 1.9 1453 0.4 2207 1.7	0102 1.9 0650 0.8 1327 1.9 1917 0.7	0156 4.3 0738 1.1 1409 4.3 1956 0.9	0224 4.5 0738 1.3 1437 4.5 2002 1.2	0207 5.9 0825 1.2 1428 5.8 2050 1.1	0154 6.4 0916 1.3 1415 6.2 2136 1.4	**5 F**
	0435 3.1 1018 9.7 1707 2.9 2253 9.2	0246 1.5 0843 5.2 1519 1.5 2112 4.8	0328 1.6 0924 5.1 1558 1.5 2157 4.8	0306 0.6 1021 1.8 1548 0.5 2300 1.6	0248 1.9 0750 0.9 1512 1.8 2020 0.8	0249 4.2 0828 1.3 1505 4.1 2049 1.2	0318 4.4 0831 1.5 1530 4.3 2058 1.3	0257 5.8 0918 1.3 1524 5.6 2145 1.3	0245 6.2 1005 1.5 1515 6.0 2229 1.7	**6 SA**
	0533 3.4 1121 9.2 1809 3.2	0346 1.7 0945 5.0 1624 1.6 2221 4.7	0421 1.8 1019 4.9 1659 1.7 2303 4.7	0404 0.7 1118 1.7 1658 0.6	0457 1.8 0901 1.0 1714 1.8 2135 0.9	0353 4.1 0929 1.4 1612 4.0 2156 1.4	0427 4.4 0935 1.6 1637 4.2 2207 1.5	0357 5.6 1021 1.4 1629 5.4 2251 1.3	0346 6.1 1103 1.6 1625 5.8 2333 1.8	**7 SU**
	0003 8.9 0642 3.6 1239 9.0 1921 3.3	0457 1.7 1057 4.9 1737 1.6 2339 4.7	0528 1.9 1133 4.8 1812 1.7	0007 1.6 0523 0.8 1230 1.6 1820 0.6	0655 1.8 1021 1.1 1908 1.8 2253 1.0	0505 4.3 1041 1.5 1728 4.0 2311 1.4	0550 4.3 1051 1.7 1803 4.1 2323 1.5	0505 5.5 1134 1.4 1743 5.3	0455 5.9 1215 1.7 1740 5.8	**8 M**
	0125 8.9 0800 3.5 1401 9.1 2038 3.1	0612 1.7 1212 5.0 1849 1.4	0027 4.7 0647 1.8 1258 4.9 1928 1.6	0125 1.6 0649 0.8 1351 1.7 1934 0.6	0748 1.9 1134 1.0 1958 1.8 2358 0.9	0619 4.1 1155 1.4 1844 4.0	0657 4.4 1206 1.6 1918 4.2	0005 1.3 0619 5.5 1250 1.3 1858 5.4	0048 1.8 0609 5.9 1331 1.6 1852 5.8	**9 TU**
	0242 9.2 0918 3.2 1514 9.5 2151 2.7	0052 4.9 0722 1.5 1321 5.2 1953 1.2	0148 4.9 0802 1.6 1415 5.0 2038 1.3	0245 1.7 0804 0.7 1507 1.8 2038 0.5	0809 1.9 1233 0.9 2011 1.9	0026 1.3 0725 4.3 1303 1.2 1949 4.2	0033 1.4 0759 4.5 1312 1.4 2021 4.4	0119 1.2 0727 5.7 1359 1.1 2003 5.6	0202 1.7 0718 6.1 1442 1.4 1957 6.0	**10 W**
	0346 9.8 1027 2.6 1615 10.0 2254 2.2	0154 5.1 0823 1.2 1419 5.4 2049 1.0	0256 5.1 0909 1.3 1521 5.2 2141 1.1	0353 1.8 0907 0.6 1615 1.9 2134 0.4	0055 0.8 0812 2.0 1325 0.8 2013 1.9	0131 1.1 0822 4.4 1403 0.9 2045 4.4	0137 1.3 0851 4.7 1411 1.2 2112 4.6	0224 1.0 0826 5.9 1459 0.9 2058 5.8	0308 1.5 0819 6.3 1545 1.2 2053 6.3	**11 TH**
	0440 10.3 1125 2.0 1707 10.5 2347 1.8	0248 5.4 0917 1.0 1511 5.6 2140 0.8	0354 5.3 1010 1.1 1619 5.3 2237 0.9	0452 2.0 1001 0.5 1715 2.0 2224 0.3	0144 0.7 0814 2.0 1410 0.6 2016 2.0	0229 0.9 0910 4.6 1458 0.7 2135 4.5	0233 1.1 0938 4.8 1503 1.0 2200 4.7	0320 0.8 0920 6.1 1552 0.8 2149 6.1	0409 1.3 0912 6.5 1644 1.1 2143 6.5	**12 F**
	0529 10.8 1216 1.6 1755 10.9	0336 5.6 1007 0.8 1559 5.7 2227 0.8	0448 5.4 1105 0.9 1713 5.3 2329 0.8	0545 2.1 1051 0.4 1809 2.0 2311 0.3	0229 0.6 0820 2.1 1453 0.5 2028 2.0	0322 0.7 0955 4.7 1549 0.5 2221 4.6	0324 1.0 1021 4.9 1550 0.8 2244 4.8	0412 0.7 1009 6.2 1640 0.7 2237 6.2	0505 1.1 1001 6.6 1739 1.0 2230 6.6	**13 SA**
	0034 1.5 0614 11.1 1301 1.3 1839 11.0	0421 5.8 1054 0.7 1644 5.7 2312 0.8	0537 5.5 1154 0.8 1803 5.3	0633 2.2 1136 0.3 1858 2.1 2354 0.2	0311 0.6 0837 2.1 1533 0.5 2052 2.0	0412 0.6 1039 4.7 1635 0.4 2307 4.6	0410 0.9 1103 4.9 1633 0.7 2327 4.8	0458 0.7 1055 6.3 1724 0.7 2323 6.2	0557 1.0 1048 6.7 1828 0.9 2314 6.7	**14 SU** O
	0118 1.4 0656 11.2 1344 1.4 1922 10.9	0505 5.8 1139 0.8 1727 5.6 2354 0.8	0015 0.8 0623 5.5 1239 0.8 1848 5.3	0718 2.2 1219 0.3 1942 2.1	0354 0.5 0905 2.1 1615 0.4 2129 2.0	0458 0.6 1122 4.6 1719 0.4 2351 4.6	0454 0.9 1144 4.9 1715 0.7	0541 0.8 1137 6.3 1805 0.8	0643 0.9 1131 6.7 1912 0.9 2356 6.7	**15 M**

● ● Time UT. For British Summer Time (shaded) March 30th to October 26th ADD ONE HOUR ● ●

DECEMBER 1997 TIDE TABLES DECEMBER 1997

Time: UT. For British Summer Time (shaded) March 30th to October 26th ADD ONE HOUR

	ST HELIER	ST MARYS SCILLY	PLYMOUTH	PORTLAND	POOLE ENTRANCE	SOUTHAMPTON	PORTSMOUTH	SHOREHAM	DOVER
	Time m	Time m	Time m	Time m	Time m	Time m	Time m	Time m	Time m
16 TU	0158 1.6 0736 11.0 1423 1.6 2003 10.6	0547 5.7 1221 0.9 1809 5.5	0058 0.9 0703 5.5 1321 0.9 1927 5.2	0036 0.3 0757 2.2 1300 0.3 2021 2.0	0436 0.6 0945 2.0 1658 0.5 2222 2.0	0540 0.6 1204 4.5 1759 0.5	0009 4.8 0535 0.9 1223 4.8 1756 0.8	0006 6.2 0621 1.0 1216 6.2 1843 0.9	0726 0.9 1213 6.6 1952 1.0
17 W	0236 1.9 0815 10.7 1500 1.9 2042 10.2	0034 1.0 0627 5.6 1301 1.0 1848 5.3	0137 1.0 0739 5.4 1358 1.0 2002 5.1	0114 0.3 0830 2.1 1339 0.3 2055 1.9	0519 0.6 1038 2.0 1741 0.6 2328 2.0	0035 4.5 0619 0.8 1245 4.4 1835 0.7	0051 4.7 0616 1.0 1302 4.7 1836 0.9	0046 6.2 0700 1.1 1256 6.1 1920 1.0	0036 6.6 0805 1.0 1254 6.5 2027 1.2
18 TH	0312 2.4 0853 10.2 1535 2.4 2121 9.7	0112 1.2 0707 5.4 1339 1.3 1928 5.1	0212 1.2 0809 5.2 1433 1.3 2031 4.9	0150 0.4 0859 2.0 1416 0.4 2124 1.7	0604 0.7 1144 1.9 1827 0.7	0117 4.4 0655 1.0 1326 4.2 1910 0.9	0133 4.6 0657 1.2 1342 4.5 1917 1.1	0124 6.1 0738 1.2 1334 5.9 1959 1.1	0115 6.3 0842 1.1 1333 6.3 2059 1.4
19 F	0346 2.9 0930 9.7 1609 2.9 2159 9.2	0150 1.4 0746 5.2 1418 1.5 2009 4.8	0245 1.5 0836 5.1 1505 1.5 2100 4.7	0224 0.5 0924 1.9 1451 0.5 2151 1.6	0046 1.9 0651 0.9 1302 1.8 1914 0.8	0200 4.2 0729 1.2 1407 4.0 1945 1.1	0216 4.5 0739 1.4 1424 4.3 1959 1.3	0202 5.9 0819 1.4 1415 5.6 2039 1.3	0155 6.4 0917 1.4 1414 6.0 2130 1.7
20 SA	0421 3.3 1008 9.2 1645 3.4 2240 8.7	0228 1.7 0828 4.9 1459 1.7 2053 4.6	0315 1.8 0905 4.9 1538 1.8 2134 4.6	0255 0.6 0949 1.7 1527 0.5 2224 1.5	0218 1.8 0740 1.0 1430 1.7 2003 1.0	0243 4.0 0807 1.4 1451 3.9 2024 1.4	0303 4.3 0822 1.6 1509 4.1 2043 1.5	0241 5.6 0903 1.6 1500 5.3 2123 1.5	0237 6.1 0953 1.6 1459 5.7 2205 1.9
21 SU	0500 3.8 1050 8.7 1726 3.8 2327 8.1	0312 1.9 0915 4.7 1547 1.9 2145 4.4	0350 2.0 0945 4.8 1618 2.1 2226 4.4	0326 0.7 1021 1.6 1604 0.6 2306 1.4	0411 1.8 0835 1.2 1618 1.6 2100 1.1	0332 3.8 0850 1.7 1542 3.7 2111 1.6	0401 4.1 0911 1.8 1605 3.9 2134 1.8	0326 5.4 0952 1.8 1550 5.0 2214 1.7	0323 5.9 1034 1.8 1550 5.5 2248 2.1
22 M	0548 4.1 1141 8.4 1817 4.1	0404 2.1 1011 4.5 1647 2.1 2251 4.3	0434 2.3 1044 4.6 1711 2.2 2333 4.4	0406 0.8 1103 1.5 1657 0.7	0559 1.7 0942 1.3 1820 1.6 2212 1.2	0427 3.7 0944 1.8 1641 3.6 2211 1.8	0506 4.0 1013 2.0 1721 3.7 2242 1.9	0420 5.1 1049 2.0 1651 4.7 2314 1.9	0417 5.6 1123 2.0 1653 5.2 2341 2.3
23 TU	0027 8.1 0646 4.3 1246 8.2 1920 4.2	0511 2.2 1121 4.4 1757 2.1	0536 2.4 1157 4.5 1821 2.3	0006 1.3 0512 0.9 1203 1.4 1811 0.7	0709 1.7 1102 1.3 1929 1.6 2323 1.3	0529 3.7 1050 1.9 1750 3.5 2321 1.9	0604 4.0 1133 2.1 1827 3.7 2355 2.0	0524 5.0 1154 2.0 1801 4.6	0522 5.4 1221 2.2 1806 5.2
24 W	0136 8.2 0754 4.3 1359 8.2 2030 4.1	0006 4.3 0624 2.2 1233 4.4 1904 2.0	0045 4.4 0654 2.4 1308 4.6 1935 2.2	0124 1.4 0645 0.9 1323 1.4 1924 0.6	0751 1.7 1206 1.3 2002 1.6	0634 3.7 1200 1.9 1901 3.6	0702 4.0 1241 2.0 1930 3.8	0022 2.0 0631 4.9 1300 2.0 1910 4.7	0045 2.3 0633 5.4 1329 2.1 1913 5.3
25 TH	0243 8.5 0907 4.1 1505 8.6 2139 3.8	0112 4.4 0729 2.0 1335 4.6 2000 1.8	0151 4.6 0806 2.2 1412 4.7 2036 1.9	0242 1.5 0800 0.8 1444 1.5 2023 0.6	0018 1.2 0809 1.7 1249 1.2 2012 1.7	0031 1.8 0735 3.8 1305 1.7 2002 3.8	0055 1.9 0801 4.1 1330 1.8 2032 3.9	0128 1.9 0734 5.0 1401 1.8 2008 4.9	0158 2.2 0736 5.5 1439 2.0 2009 5.5
26 F	0340 8.9 1012 3.6 1601 9.1 2237 3.3	0205 4.7 0822 1.8 1424 4.8 2048 1.6	0249 4.8 0903 1.9 1510 4.9 2128 1.7	0345 1.6 0857 0.7 1551 1.6 2112 0.5	0059 1.1 0812 1.8 1324 1.0 2013 1.7	0131 1.6 0826 4.0 1401 1.4 2054 4.0	0142 1.8 0856 4.2 1410 1.6 2124 4.1	0224 1.7 0829 5.3 1452 1.5 2058 5.2	0309 2.0 0827 5.7 1542 1.7 2055 5.8
27 SA	0429 9.5 1106 3.0 1650 9.7 2328 2.7	0249 5.0 0909 1.5 1508 5.0 2130 1.3	0342 5.0 0954 1.6 1604 5.0 2218 1.4	0438 1.8 0944 0.6 1649 1.7 2159 0.4	0136 1.0 0814 1.9 1358 0.9 2017 1.8	0223 1.4 0910 4.2 1450 1.1 2137 4.2	0224 1.6 0941 4.4 1449 1.4 2207 4.3	0313 1.4 0915 5.5 1537 1.2 2141 5.5	0410 1.7 0910 6.0 1636 1.4 2135 6.0
28 SU	0514 10.1 1155 2.4 1735 10.2	0330 5.3 0951 1.3 1548 5.3 2212 1.1	0431 5.2 1044 1.3 1654 5.1 2306 1.2	0527 1.9 1029 0.4 1742 1.8 2245 0.3	0213 0.8 0820 1.9 1434 0.7 2027 1.9	0311 1.1 0951 4.4 1534 0.9 2219 4.3	0306 1.3 1019 4.5 1530 1.1 2243 4.5	0356 1.2 0958 5.8 1619 1.0 2223 5.8	0502 1.4 0948 6.2 1724 1.2 2212 6.3
29 M ●	0014 2.3 0556 10.6 1239 1.9 1817 10.7	0409 5.5 1033 1.0 1627 5.4 2253 1.0	0518 5.4 1131 1.1 1741 5.2 2352 1.0	0614 2.1 1112 0.4 1832 1.9 2329 0.2	0251 0.7 0832 2.0 1513 0.6 2046 2.0	0355 0.9 1030 4.5 1617 0.7 2258 4.4	0348 1.1 1053 4.6 1612 0.9 2319 4.6	0437 1.1 1039 6.0 1659 0.9 2305 6.0	0548 1.2 1027 6.4 1809 1.1 2251 6.5
30 TU	0057 1.9 0637 11.0 1321 1.6 1859 10.9	0448 5.7 1115 0.9 1707 5.6 2335 0.9	0601 5.5 1217 0.9 1824 5.3	0659 2.1 1155 0.3 1919 2.0	0331 0.6 0854 2.0 1554 0.4 2117 2.0	0438 0.7 1108 4.6 1659 0.5 2338 4.5	0431 0.9 1130 4.7 1654 0.7 2357 4.7	0517 1.0 1119 6.2 1741 0.8 2348 6.2	0631 1.1 1106 6.6 1850 1.0 2332 6.7
31 W	0139 1.7 0718 11.3 1403 1.4 1940 11.1	0528 5.8 1158 0.8 1748 5.6	0036 0.8 0642 5.6 1301 0.7 1904 5.3	0012 0.2 0742 2.2 1239 0.3 2003 2.0	0415 0.5 0929 2.0 1640 0.4 2205 2.0	0522 0.6 1147 4.6 1742 0.4	0515 0.8 1209 4.8 1739 0.6	0600 1.0 1201 6.3 1824 0.8	0711 1.0 1148 6.7 1927 0.9

● ● Time: UT. For British Summer Time (shaded) March 30th to October 26th ADD ONE HOUR ● ●

EAST COAST OF ENGLAND Time Zone UT

Margate * Sheerness * London Bridge *Walton-on-the-Naze * Harwich * Lowestoft * Immingham * RiverTees * RiverTyne

JANUARY 1997 TIDE TABLES JANUARY 1997

	MARGATE	SHEERNESS	LONDON BRIDGE	WALTON-ON-THE-NAZE	HARWICH	LOWESTOFT	IMMINGHAM	RIVER TEES	RIVER TYNE
	Time m	Time m	Time m	Time m	Time m	Time m	Time m	Time m	Time m
1 W	0406 4.3	0433 5.1	0558 6.2	0344 3.8	0345 3.6	0132 2.4	0406 2.1	0208 1.7	0148 1.5
	1029 1.1	1042 1.1	1220 0.9	1003 0.8	0951 0.7	0756 0.8	1017 6.0	0823 4.4	0802 4.2
	1640 4.2	1707 5.0	1831 6.2	1617 3.7	1618 3.5	1428 2.1	1610 2.5	1415 2.1	1353 1.9
	2236 1.4	2249 1.4		2213 1.1	2200 1.1	1951 1.2	2222 6.1	2036 4.5	2012 4.3
2 TH	0454 4.2	0516 4.9	0032 1.3	0430 3.7	0430 3.5	0221 2.3	0448 2.3	0257 1.8	0239 1.7
	1118 1.2	1127 1.1	0638 6.0	1054 0.9	1043 0.8	0845 0.9	1109 5.8	0918 4.3	0854 4.1
	1733 4.1	1757 4.8	1301 1.1	1708 3.6	1707 3.4	1526 2.1	1700 2.7	1510 2.2	1450 2.1
	2333 1.5	2340 1.5	1918 6.0	2310 1.2	2259 1.2	2049 1.3	2318 5.9	2133 4.4	2109 4.2
3 F	0552 4.0	0611 4.8	0117 1.4	0526 3.6	0524 3.4	0321 2.3	0545 2.5	0357 2.0	0339 1.8
	1221 1.3	1225 1.3	0728 5.8	1157 0.9	1147 0.9	0945 1.0	1215 5.7	1018 4.3	0955 4.0
	1836 4.0	1858 4.7	1351 1.2	1809 3.5	1809 3.3	1630 2.1	1806 2.9	1617 2.3	1600 2.2
			2016 5.9			2200 1.3		2238 4.4	2214 4.1
4 SA	0044 1.6	0047 1.6	0212 1.6	0018 1.2	0012 1.2	0429 2.2	0032 5.9	0503 2.0	0448 1.8
	0658 4.0	0718 4.7	0837 5.7	0633 3.5	0633 3.3	1054 0.9	0659 2.5	1122 4.4	1101 4.1
	1330 1.2	1338 1.3	1457 1.3	1307 0.9	1256 0.8	1733 2.2	1328 5.8	1732 2.3	1717 2.1
	1944 4.1	2008 4.8	2127 5.9	1921 3.6	1921 3.4	2318 1.2	1927 2.8	2344 4.4	2322 4.2
5 SU	0159 1.5	0207 1.6	0327 1.6	0131 1.2	0123 1.1	0536 2.3	0148 6.0	0612 1.8	0557 1.7
	0807 4.0	0833 4.9	0954 5.8	0748 3.6	0748 3.4	1159 0.9	0815 2.3	1224 4.5	1206 4.3
	1435 1.1	1455 1.2	1618 1.2	1417 0.9	1400 0.8	1829 2.3	1435 6.1	1844 2.0	1827 1.8
	2050 4.2	2117 5.0	2234 6.2	2030 3.7	2030 3.5		2042 2.4		
6 M	0305 1.3	0324 1.3	0449 1.4	0240 1.0	0227 0.9	0024 1.1	0254 6.3	0047 4.6	0027 4.4
	0912 4.2	0942 5.1	1102 6.1	0857 3.7	0857 3.5	0636 2.3	0919 2.0	0715 1.6	0657 1.5
	1534 1.0	1602 1.0	1730 0.9	1516 0.8	1459 0.7	1254 0.8	1533 6.5	1320 4.8	1302 4.5
	2149 4.4	2220 5.3	2337 6.5	2130 3.9	2133 3.7	1919 2.3	2145 2.0	1945 1.7	1924 1.5
7 TU	0403 1.1	0428 1.1	0600 1.0	0339 0.9	0324 0.8	0121 1.0	0354 6.6	0145 4.9	0124 4.6
	1010 4.4	1044 5.4	1204 6.5	0955 3.9	1000 3.7	0732 2.4	1016 1.6	0809 1.4	0750 1.3
	1627 0.8	1700 0.8	1836 0.7	1607 0.7	1553 0.6	1345 0.7	1624 6.9	1411 5.1	1351 4.8
	2242 4.6	2315 5.6		2224 4.0	2230 3.8	2004 2.4	2243 1.6	2037 1.3	2016 1.2
8 W	0456 0.8	0527 0.8	0035 6.9	0431 0.7	0418 0.6	0216 0.8	0448 7.0	0236 5.2	0216 4.9
	1104 4.6	1139 5.7	0709 0.7	1048 4.1	1056 3.9	0824 2.4	1109 1.3	0859 1.1	0839 1.0
	1717 0.7	1752 0.7	1300 6.9	1654 0.6	1642 0.5	1434 0.7	1712 7.2	1457 5.4	1436 5.1
	2330 4.8		1939 0.5	2312 4.2	2321 4.0	2047 2.5	2338 1.2	2126 0.9	2105 0.9
9 TH ●	0547 0.6	0006 5.8	0127 7.1	0519 0.5	0507 0.4	0309 0.6	0538 7.2	0326 5.4	0304 5.1
	1155 4.8	0621 0.6	0811 0.5	1137 4.3	1147 4.1	0914 2.5	1200 1.1	0945 0.9	0925 0.8
	1806 0.6	1229 5.9	1351 7.3	1738 0.5	1728 0.4	1522 0.6	1756 7.4	1542 5.6	1520 5.3
		1842 0.6	2036 0.3	2359 4.2		2130 2.6		2212 0.6	2152 0.6
10 F	0017 4.9	0053 5.9	0214 7.4	0606 0.4	0009 4.0	0400 0.4	0030 0.8	0413 5.6	0352 5.3
	0637 0.4	0714 0.4	0906 0.2	1225 4.4	0555 0.3	1004 2.5	0627 7.4	1030 0.8	1011 0.7
	1246 4.9	1318 6.0	1439 7.5	1822 0.5	1235 4.2	1609 0.6	1248 0.9	1627 5.8	1603 5.4
	1854 0.5	1929 0.5	2126 0.3		1812 0.4	2212 2.7	1839 7.6	2258 0.4	2239 0.4
11 SA	0104 5.0	0138 5.9	0259 7.5	0044 4.3	0055 4.1	0450 0.3	0119 0.6	0500 5.7	0439 5.3
	0727 0.3	0805 0.3	0955 0.1	0654 0.3	0641 0.1	1053 2.5	0715 7.4	1115 0.7	1057 0.7
	1336 5.0	1405 6.1	1526 7.7	1312 4.4	1321 4.2	1656 0.6	1334 0.9	1712 5.8	1648 5.5
	1942 0.5	2015 0.5	2212 0.0	1906 0.5	1856 0.5	2257 2.7	1924 7.7	2345 0.4	2327 0.3
12 SU	0151 5.0	0223 6.0	0344 7.6	0128 4.3	0139 4.1	0538 0.2	0206 0.5	0548 5.6	0527 5.3
	0818 0.3	0854 0.2	1041 0.0	0741 0.2	0727 0.1	1143 2.5	0803 7.4	1200 0.8	1142 0.8
	1427 4.9	1451 6.1	1612 7.7	1359 4.4	1407 4.2	1741 0.7	1418 1.0	1757 5.8	1735 5.4
	2030 0.6	2059 0.5	2255 0.4	1951 0.6	1940 0.4	2342 2.7	2008 7.6		
13 M	0237 4.9	0307 5.9	0429 7.5	0214 4.3	0223 4.1	0625 0.2	0251 0.6	0031 0.4	0014 0.4
	0907 0.3	0939 0.2	1124 0.1	0829 0.2	0812 0.1	1234 2.4	0851 7.2	0636 5.5	0617 5.1
	1514 4.8	1539 5.9	1700 7.5	1446 4.3	1453 4.1	1825 0.7	1501 1.1	1246 1.0	1227 0.9
	2116 0.8	2142 0.5	2334 0.7	2038 0.6	2026 0.5		2054 7.4	1845 5.6	1824 5.3
14 TU	0321 4.9	0353 5.8	0515 7.3	0300 4.2	0307 4.1	0029 2.7	0336 0.8	0120 0.6	0103 0.6
	0955 0.4	1024 0.3	1203 0.4	0917 0.3	0900 0.1	0712 0.3	0939 6.9	0728 5.2	0708 4.9
	1601 4.6	1627 5.8	1748 7.2	1534 4.2	1539 4.0	1327 2.3	1544 1.4	1334 1.2	1315 1.2
	2201 0.9	2225 0.8		2125 0.8	2113 0.6	1911 0.8	2142 7.2	1937 5.3	1916 5.1
15 W	0406 4.7	0441 5.6	0011 0.8	0348 4.1	0354 4.0	0118 2.6	0421 1.2	0212 0.9	0153 0.9
	1045 0.6	1109 0.5	0602 7.0	1008 0.4	0951 0.3	0802 0.4	1031 6.6	0823 5.0	0803 4.6
	1649 4.4	1718 5.5	1240 0.6	1626 4.0	1630 3.8	1427 2.2	1630 1.8	1427 1.5	1406 1.4
	2250 1.1	2311 1.0	1839 6.9	2217 0.9	2205 0.7	2002 1.0	2234 6.8	2034 5.0	2015 4.8

● ● Time UT. For British Summer Time (shaded) March 30th to October 26th ADD ONE HOUR ● ●

JANUARY 1997 TIDE TABLES JANUARY 1997

	MARGATE	SHEERNESS	LONDON BRIDGE	WALTON-ON-THE-NAZE	HARWICH	LOWESTOFT	IMMINGHAM	RIVER TEES	RIVER TYNE
	Time m	Time m	Time m	Time m	Time m	Time m	Time m	Time m	Time m
16 TH	0456 4.6 1139 0.7 1744 4.3 2348 1.2	0533 5.4 1158 0.7 1815 5.3	0050 1.1 0654 6.7 1321 0.8 1935 6.6	0441 4.0 1104 0.6 1723 3.8 2316 1.0	0445 3.8 1048 0.4 1726 3.6 2305 0.9	0215 2.5 0856 0.6 1533 2.2 2101 1.0	0510 1.6 1130 6.2 1724 2.1 2338 6.5	0308 1.2 0923 4.7 1527 1.8 2139 4.8	0250 1.2 0903 4.4 1509 1.7 2121 4.6
17 F	0555 4.4 1244 0.9 1849 4.1	0005 1.1 0634 5.2 1257 1.0 1918 5.1	0137 1.2 0751 6.5 1414 1.0 2037 6.4	0541 3.8 1212 0.8 1830 3.6	0544 3.6 1155 0.6 1830 3.5	0322 2.4 1000 0.8 1643 2.2 2214 1.1	0609 2.0 1239 6.0 1830 2.4	0412 1.5 1029 4.5 1638 1.9 2249 4.6	0356 1.5 1011 4.3 1623 1.8 2235 4.4
18 SA	0102 1.2 0706 4.2 1357 1.0 2003 4.1	0111 1.3 0744 5.0 1407 1.1 2030 5.0	0241 1.3 0900 6.3 1524 1.1 2148 6.3	0030 1.1 0653 3.7 1332 0.9 1945 3.6	0018 1.0 0653 3.5 1312 0.7 1942 3.4	0442 2.3 1117 0.9 1751 2.2 2343 1.1	0055 6.2 0720 2.2 1352 6.0 1953 2.5	0523 1.7 1138 4.5 1757 1.9	0512 1.7 1122 4.2 1744 1.8 2351 4.3
19 SU	0223 1.2 0825 4.1 1509 1.0 2117 4.2	0230 1.3 0900 5.0 1522 1.2 2140 5.1	0357 1.3 1020 6.2 1638 1.1 2303 6.4	0157 1.1 0812 3.6 1443 0.9 2057 3.7	0140 1.0 0812 3.4 1428 0.8 2057 3.5	0605 2.3 1230 1.0 1853 2.3	0215 6.1 0837 2.3 1501 6.1 2112 2.3	0002 4.5 0634 1.7 1244 4.5 1908 1.8	0625 1.7 1230 4.3 1855 1.7
20 M	0339 1.1 0942 4.2 1612 1.0 2218 4.3	0349 1.2 1011 5.1 1627 1.1 2242 5.2	0516 1.1 1134 6.4 1753 1.0	0310 1.0 0922 3.7 1541 0.9 2155 3.8	0256 0.8 0927 3.5 1530 0.8 2157 3.6	0100 1.0 0718 2.3 1328 0.9 1943 2.4	0327 6.2 0943 2.2 1558 6.4 2215 2.0	0109 4.6 0735 1.7 1342 4.7 2006 1.6	0059 4.4 0725 1.6 1327 4.5 1952 1.5
21 TU	0440 0.9 1043 4.3 1702 0.9 2306 4.4	0454 1.0 1109 5.3 1718 1.0 2333 5.4	0006 6.6 0631 0.9 1233 6.6 1854 0.9	0407 0.8 1019 3.8 1627 0.8 2244 3.9	0355 0.7 1024 3.6 1618 0.7 2247 3.7	0157 0.9 0812 2.3 1414 0.9 2024 2.4	0424 6.4 1035 2.0 1644 6.7 2305 1.7	0205 4.7 0824 1.6 1430 4.9 2052 1.3	0154 4.5 0812 1.5 1415 4.7 2039 1.3
22 W	0526 0.8 1130 4.4 1739 0.9 2343 4.5	0545 0.9 1156 5.4 1759 1.0	0057 6.8 0726 0.7 1320 6.8 1940 0.7	0454 0.7 1106 3.9 1706 0.8 2325 4.0	0442 0.6 1110 3.7 1658 0.7 2330 3.8	0242 0.8 0857 2.3 1453 0.9 2101 2.5	0510 6.6 1118 1.8 1723 6.9 2348 1.5	0253 4.8 0906 1.5 1512 5.0 2133 1.1	0239 4.7 0853 1.4 1454 4.8 2118 1.1
23 TH ○	0603 0.7 1208 4.4 1809 0.9	0015 5.5 0628 0.8 1236 5.5 1835 0.9	0139 6.9 0809 0.6 1400 6.9 2020 0.8	0533 0.6 1146 4.0 1741 0.8	0522 0.5 1151 3.8 1733 0.7	0323 0.7 0937 2.4 1528 0.9 2136 2.5	0549 6.7 1157 1.6 1757 7.0	0333 4.9 0941 1.4 1548 5.1 2209 1.0	0318 4.8 0928 1.3 1530 4.9 2154 1.0
24 F	0017 4.6 0636 0.6 1243 4.5 1841 0.8	0053 5.6 0706 0.7 1313 5.6 1909 0.8	0215 7.0 0848 0.5 1436 7.0 2056 0.7	0001 4.0 0608 0.5 1221 4.0 1812 0.7	0007 3.8 0558 0.4 1227 3.8 1806 0.6	0400 0.6 1014 2.4 1600 0.8 2209 2.6	0026 1.4 0624 6.8 1231 1.5 1831 7.1	0409 5.0 1013 1.3 1621 5.2 2242 0.9	0354 4.8 1000 1.2 1603 5.0 2227 0.9
25 SA	0049 4.7 0710 0.6 1316 4.5 1914 0.8	0127 5.6 0740 0.6 1346 5.6 1941 0.8	0249 7.1 0924 0.5 1509 7.1 2130 0.7	0034 4.1 0642 0.5 1254 4.1 1845 0.7	0042 3.8 0632 0.4 1301 3.8 1838 0.6	0436 0.6 1048 2.3 1629 0.8 2241 2.6	0101 1.3 0657 6.9 1304 1.5 1903 7.2	0441 5.0 1044 1.2 1651 5.3 2313 0.9	0427 4.8 1032 1.2 1633 5.0 2259 0.9
26 SU	0123 4.7 0745 0.6 1349 4.5 1947 0.9	0159 5.6 0812 0.6 1418 5.6 2012 0.8	0321 7.1 0956 0.5 1542 7.1 2202 0.8	0106 4.1 0714 0.5 1326 4.1 1917 0.7	0114 3.9 0703 0.5 1333 3.8 1909 0.6	0509 0.6 1119 2.3 1656 0.8 2313 2.6	0135 1.2 0729 6.9 1336 1.4 1935 7.1	0512 5.0 1115 1.2 1722 5.2 2345 1.0	0459 4.8 1102 1.2 1705 5.0 2330 0.9
27 M	0155 4.7 0818 0.7 1419 4.5 2018 0.9	0230 5.6 0843 0.6 1451 5.6 2043 0.8	0352 7.0 1026 0.6 1614 7.0 2232 0.9	0136 4.1 0747 0.5 1357 4.0 1949 0.7	0144 3.8 0736 0.3 1403 3.8 1939 0.6	0541 0.6 1149 2.3 1725 0.9 2347 2.5	0206 1.3 0800 6.8 1406 1.5 2006 7.0	0545 4.9 1148 1.3 1754 5.2	0531 4.8 1131 1.2 1737 4.9
28 TU	0226 4.6 0849 0.7 1449 4.4 2048 1.0	0300 5.5 0913 0.7 1522 5.4 2113 0.9	0424 6.9 1055 0.6 1647 6.9 2300 0.9	0207 4.1 0820 0.5 1430 4.0 2022 0.8	0213 3.8 0808 0.4 1434 3.7 2012 0.7	0612 0.6 1221 2.2 1757 0.9	0236 1.4 0830 6.7 1436 1.7 2036 6.9	0018 1.0 0619 4.9 1221 1.4 1829 5.0	0002 1.0 0605 4.6 1202 1.3 1811 4.8
29 W	0257 4.5 0918 0.8 1522 4.4 2119 1.1	0330 5.4 0942 0.8 1555 5.3 2142 1.0	0457 6.7 1124 0.7 1721 6.8 2330 1.0	0239 4.0 0853 0.6 1503 3.9 2056 0.8	0244 3.8 0841 0.5 1508 3.7 2045 0.8	0022 2.5 0644 0.7 1256 2.2 1834 0.9	0306 1.6 0902 6.5 1506 1.9 2108 6.7	0053 1.2 0657 4.7 1257 1.5 1906 4.9	0035 1.1 0640 4.5 1235 1.5 1847 4.7
30 TH	0330 4.4 0951 0.9 1600 4.3 2156 1.2	0403 5.3 1012 0.9 1631 5.2 2213 1.1	0529 6.5 1154 0.8 1755 6.5	0314 3.9 0929 0.7 1541 3.8 2134 0.9	0318 3.7 0916 0.6 1545 3.6 2121 0.9	0100 2.4 0719 0.8 1336 2.2 1917 1.0	0335 1.8 0936 6.3 1538 2.1 2142 6.4	0130 1.4 0738 4.6 1336 1.7 1948 4.7	0111 1.3 0718 4.4 1312 1.6 1928 4.5
31 F	0410 4.3 1029 1.0 1646 4.2 2241 1.4	0439 5.1 1045 1.0 1713 5.0 2252 1.3	0000 1.1 0603 6.3 1227 0.9 1834 6.3	0354 3.8 1010 0.8 1626 3.7 2221 1.0	0358 3.6 0957 0.7 1629 3.5 2206 1.0	0142 2.3 0801 0.8 1427 2.1 2007 1.1	0408 2.0 1016 6.0 1618 2.3 2227 6.2	0213 1.6 0826 4.4 1421 1.9 2040 4.5	0153 1.5 0804 4.2 1359 1.8 2018 4.3

● ● Time UT. For British Summer Time (shaded) March 30th to October 26th ADD ONE HOUR ● ●

EAST COAST OF ENGLAND Time Zone UT

Margate * Sheerness * London Bridge *Walton-on-the-Naze * Harwich * Lowestoft * Immingham * RiverTees * RiverTyne

FEBRUARY 1997 TIDE TABLES FEBRUARY 1997

MARGATE	SHEERNESS	LONDON BRIDGE	WALTON-ON-THE-NAZE	HARWICH	LOWESTOFT	IMMINGHAM	RIVER TEES	RIVER TYNE	
Time m	Time m	Time m	Time m	Time m	Time m	Time m	Time m	Time m	
0500 4.1 1121 1.2 1742 4.1 2343 1.5	0525 5.0 1130 1.1 1807 4.8 2348 1.4	0038 1.2 0645 6.0 1309 1.1 1923 6.1	0443 3.7 1104 0.9 1721 3.6 2323 1.1	0446 3.5 1049 0.8 1724 3.4 2309 1.0	0233 2.3 0854 0.9 1530 2.1 2112 1.2	0452 2.3 1112 5.8 1713 2.6 2330 5.9	0304 1.8 0924 4.3 1520 2.1 2145 4.3	0245 1.7 0859 4.1 1500 2.0 2121 4.2	**1 SA**
0602 4.0 1233 1.3 1851 4.0	0627 4.8 1236 1.3 1917 4.8	0125 1.4 0742 5.8 1404 1.3 2030 5.9	0545 3.6 1213 1.0 1828 3.5	0548 3.3 1203 0.9 1832 3.3	0344 2.2 1004 1.0 1643 2.1 2233 1.2	0557 2.5 1227 5.8 1830 2.7	0409 1.9 1030 4.3 1635 2.2 2300 4.3	0351 1.8 1006 4.1 1619 2.0 2235 4.1	**2 SU**
0108 1.5 0719 3.9 1351 1.2 2008 4.1	0109 1.5 0746 4.8 1405 1.3 2034 4.9	0230 1.6 0903 5.7 1528 1.4 2150 6.0	0039 1.1 0700 3.5 1330 0.9 1945 3.5	0034 1.1 0704 3.3 1321 0.8 1948 3.3	0500 2.2 1121 1.0 1749 2.2 2353 1.1	0058 5.9 0724 2.4 1351 5.9 2000 2.5	0527 1.9 1141 4.4 1803 2.0	0510 1.8 1121 4.1 1746 1.9 2354 4.3	**3 M**
0229 1.3 0838 4.1 1502 1.1 2118 4.3	0243 1.4 0908 5.0 1529 1.1 2148 5.1	0405 1.5 1026 6.0 1656 1.1 2306 6.3	0159 1.1 0821 3.6 1443 0.9 2059 3.7	0151 0.9 0823 3.4 1429 0.7 2100 3.5	0610 2.2 1226 0.9 1848 2.3	0223 6.1 0845 2.2 1503 6.3 2118 2.1	0015 4.5 0645 1.8 1249 4.6 1920 1.7	0627 1.6 1230 4.4 1900 1.6	**4 TU**
0339 1.1 0949 4.3 1604 0.9 2218 4.5	0402 1.1 1020 5.3 1636 0.9 2252 5.4	0528 1.1 1141 6.4 1809 0.8	0312 0.9 0931 3.8 1544 0.7 2200 3.9	0259 0.7 0936 3.6 1530 0.6 2207 3.7	0100 0.9 0715 2.3 1323 0.8 1939 2.4	0335 6.5 0953 1.8 1603 6.7 2226 1.6	0124 4.7 0749 1.5 1348 5.0 2021 1.2	0103 4.5 0729 1.4 1328 4.7 1959 1.2	**5 W**
0440 0.8 1050 4.6 1700 0.7 2312 4.7	0509 0.8 1121 5.6 1735 0.7 2348 5.7	0013 6.7 0648 0.8 1244 6.9 1921 0.6	0413 0.7 1030 4.0 1636 0.6 2254 4.1	0400 0.5 1039 3.8 1625 0.5 2303 3.8	0201 0.7 0813 2.4 1416 0.7 2027 2.5	0436 6.9 1053 1.4 1654 7.1 2325 1.1	0222 5.1 0843 1.1 1441 5.3 2112 0.8	0201 4.8 0822 1.1 1418 5.0 2051 0.8	**6 TH**
0535 0.5 1145 4.8 1751 0.6	0610 0.5 1215 5.9 1828 0.5	0109 7.1 0759 0.4 1338 7.3 2021 0.4	0506 0.4 1123 4.2 1723 0.5 2342 4.2	0454 0.3 1133 4.0 1713 0.4 2354 4.0	0257 0.5 0905 2.5 1507 0.6 2111 2.6	0528 7.2 1146 1.0 1741 7.5	0314 5.4 0932 0.8 1528 5.6 2200 0.4	0251 5.1 0911 0.8 1503 5.3 2140 0.4 ●	**7 F**
0000 4.9 0626 0.3 1236 4.9 1839 0.5	0037 5.9 0705 0.4 1304 6.1 1917 0.4	0159 7.4 0854 0.1 1426 7.6 2113 0.2	0554 0.3 1212 4.4 1808 0.4	0542 0.1 1221 4.2 1757 0.3	0348 0.3 0953 2.5 1555 0.6 2156 2.7	0018 0.6 0617 7.4 1235 0.8 1825 7.7	0401 5.6 1017 0.6 1613 5.9 2246 0.2	0339 5.3 0957 0.6 1548 5.5 2227 0.2	**8 SA**
0048 5.0 0715 0.2 1326 5.0 1927 0.4	0123 6.0 0754 0.1 1351 6.2 2003 0.3	0245 7.6 0944 -0.1 1512 7.8 2200 0.2	0029 4.3 0641 0.1 1258 4.5 1852 0.4	0040 4.1 0627 -0.0 1307 4.3 1841 0.2	0436 0.1 1039 2.5 1641 0.5 2240 2.8	0107 0.4 0703 7.5 1321 0.7 1909 7.8	0447 5.7 1101 0.5 1657 6.0 2330 0.1	0425 5.4 1041 0.5 1632 5.6 2312 0.1	**9 SU**
0135 5.0 0803 0.1 1412 5.0 2012 0.5	0206 6.1 0841 -0.0 1436 6.2 2045 0.3	0328 7.7 1029 -0.2 1557 7.8 2242 0.3	0113 4.4 0727 0.1 1343 4.5 1936 0.4	0124 4.2 0712 -0.1 1351 4.2 1924 0.2	0521 0.1 1125 2.5 1724 0.5 2325 2.8	0152 0.3 0748 7.5 1403 0.7 1952 7.8	0532 5.7 1144 0.6 1741 5.9	0510 5.4 1124 0.6 1718 5.6 2357 0.2	**10 M**
0220 5.0 0848 0.2 1457 4.8 2055 0.6	0250 6.1 0924 0.0 1520 6.0 2126 0.4	0412 7.7 1109 -0.1 1642 7.6 2318 0.5	0157 4.4 0812 0.1 1427 4.4 2020 0.5	0206 4.2 0755 -0.1 1435 4.2 2007 0.3	0606 0.1 1212 2.4 1806 0.6	0235 0.4 0831 7.3 1444 0.9 2035 7.6	0015 0.2 0617 5.6 1227 0.7 1827 5.7	0556 5.2 1207 0.7 1804 5.4	**11 TU**
0302 4.9 0932 0.3 1539 4.7 2137 0.7	0333 6.0 1003 0.2 1604 5.8 2204 0.6	0456 7.5 1144 0.2 1727 7.3 2351 0.7	0241 4.4 0857 0.2 1512 4.2 2104 0.6	0248 4.2 0839 0.0 1518 4.0 2051 0.4	0011 2.7 0649 0.3 1300 2.3 1849 0.7	0315 0.7 0914 7.0 1523 1.2 2120 7.3	0100 0.5 0703 5.3 1312 1.0 1915 5.4	0041 0.5 0643 5.0 1251 0.9 1854 5.2	**12 W**
0343 4.8 1015 0.5 1621 4.5 2221 0.9	0418 5.8 1041 0.5 1650 5.5 2243 0.8	0539 7.2 1215 0.6 1812 6.9	0326 4.2 0942 0.4 1558 4.0 2151 0.8	0332 4.1 0926 0.2 1603 3.8 2139 0.6	0059 2.6 0733 0.5 1351 2.2 1936 0.8	0354 1.1 0957 6.6 1603 1.6 2207 6.8	0146 0.8 0753 5.0 1359 1.3 2007 5.1	0126 0.8 0732 4.7 1338 1.2 1948 4.8	**13 TH**
0429 4.6 1100 0.8 1708 4.2 2312 1.1	0505 5.5 1121 0.8 1739 5.2 2328 1.0	0023 0.9 0626 6.9 1246 0.9 1900 6.6	0415 4.0 1032 0.7 1649 3.7 2245 0.9	0418 3.9 1016 0.5 1653 3.6 2233 0.8	0154 2.5 0823 0.7 1450 2.2 2030 0.9	0436 1.6 1047 6.2 1648 2.0 2305 6.3	0236 1.3 0847 4.7 1452 1.7 2106 4.7	0215 1.2 0827 4.4 1433 1.5 2049 4.5	**14 F**
0524 4.3 1157 1.0 1807 4.1	0600 5.2 1209 1.1 1837 4.9	0100 1.1 0718 6.5 1327 1.1 1956 6.3 2354 1.1	0510 3.8 1132 0.9 1750 3.5 2354 1.1	0512 3.6 1116 0.7 1751 3.3 2342 0.9	0301 2.3 0921 0.9 1558 2.1 2140 1.0	0525 2.1 1149 5.9 1748 2.4	0332 1.7 0948 4.4 1557 1.9 2216 4.4	0315 1.6 0930 4.2 1545 1.8 2203 4.2	**15 SA**

FEBRUARY 1997 TIDE TABLES FEBRUARY 1997

	MARGATE		SHEERNESS		LONDON BRIDGE		WALTON-ON-THE-NAZE		HARWICH		LOWESTOFT		IMMINGHAM		RIVER TEES		RIVER TYNE	
	Time	m	Time	m	Time	m	Time	m	Time	m	Time	m	Time	m	Time	m	Time	m
16 SU	0021	1.2	0029	1.3	0151	1.3	0620	3.6	0620	3.4	0424	2.2	0021	5.9	0442	2.0	0433	1.9
	0633	4.1	0708	4.9	0821	6.2	1253	1.1	1233	0.9	1041	1.0	0633	2.6	1059	4.3	1045	4.1
	1314	1.2	1318	1.3	1428	1.4	1907	3.4	1903	3.2	1712	2.1	1308	5.7	1721	2.1	1715	1.9
	1921	3.9	1948	4.7	2102	6.1					2320	1.0	1916	2.6	2333	4.3	2326	4.1
17 M	0151	1.3	0152	1.4	0312	1.5	0128	1.1	0112	1.0	0556	2.2	0151	5.8	0603	2.1	0558	2.0
	0759	3.9	0829	4.8	0940	6.0	0745	3.5	0745	3.3	1209	1.1	0802	2.7	1212	4.3	1203	4.1
	1436	1.3	1444	1.4	1554	1.5	1415	1.1	1400	1.0	1824	2.2	1429	5.8	1845	2.0	1836	1.8
	2043	4.0	2107	4.8	2226	6.1	2027	3.4	2027	3.2			2049	2.5				
18 TU	0317	1.1	0324	1.3	0441	1.3	0250	1.0	0237	0.9	0045	0.9	0312	5.9	0048	4.3	0042	4.2
	0924	4.0	0948	4.9	1109	6.1	0902	3.5	0906	3.3	0712	2.2	0918	2.5	0715	2.0	0706	1.8
	1549	1.2	1600	1.3	1712	1.3	1518	1.0	1509	0.9	1311	1.1	1535	6.1	1318	4.5	1308	4.3
	2153	4.1	2217	5.0	2340	6.3	2132	3.6	2135	3.4	1921	2.3	2157	2.2	1948	1.7	1937	1.6
19 W	0424	0.9	0436	1.1	0602	1.0	0351	0.8	0339	0.7	0141	0.8	0412	6.2	0148	4.5	0140	4.3
	1028	4.2	1050	5.2	1212	6.5	1001	3.7	1005	3.5	0806	2.3	1015	2.2	0807	1.8	0757	1.7
	1644	1.1	1656	1.2	1821	1.1	1608	0.9	1559	0.8	1357	1.0	1624	6.5	1410	4.7	1357	4.5
	2245	4.3	2311	5.2			2222	3.8	2226	3.6	2006	2.3	2247	1.8	2035	1.5	2023	1.3
20 TH	0511	0.8	0529	0.9	0034	6.6	0437	0.7	0425	0.5	0225	0.7	0457	6.5	0236	4.6	0224	4.5
	1115	4.3	1138	5.4	0701	0.7	1048	3.8	1051	3.6	0848	2.3	1058	1.9	0848	1.6	0836	1.5
	1722	1.0	1739	1.0	1300	6.7	1647	0.8	1639	0.7	1436	1.0	1703	6.7	1453	4.9	1438	4.7
	2324	4.4	2354	5.4	1914	0.9	2303	3.9	2309	3.7	2042	2.4	2328	1.5	2114	1.2	2100	1.1
21 F	0547	0.7	0610	0.8	0117	6.8	0515	0.6	0503	0.4	0303	0.6	0533	6.6	0315	4.8	0302	4.6
	1153	4.4	1218	5.5	0746	0.5	1126	3.9	1130	3.7	0924	2.3	1136	1.7	0922	1.5	0910	1.3
	1752	0.9	1816	0.9	1340	6.9	1720	0.8	1714	0.7	1509	0.9	1738	6.9	1528	5.1	1512	4.8
	2357	4.5			1957	0.8	2339	4.0	2345	3.8	2114	2.5			2148	1.0	2134	1.0
22 SA	0618	0.6	0032	5.5	0154	6.9	0547	0.5	0537	0.4	0339	0.6	0005	1.3	0349	4.9	0334	4.8
	1225	4.5	0646	0.7	0826	0.5	1200	4.0	1206	3.8	0955	2.3	0605	6.8	0954	1.3	0941	1.2
○	1821	0.9	1252	5.6	1415	7.0	1751	0.7	1745	0.6	1538	0.8	1210	1.5	1600	5.2	1542	4.9
			1849	0.8	2035	0.7					2145	2.5	1810	7.1	2219	0.9	2205	0.9
23 SU	0029	4.6	0106	5.6	0227	7.0	0012	4.1	0019	3.8	0412	0.5	0039	1.2	0419	5.0	0405	4.8
	0648	0.6	0718	0.6	0902	0.4	0618	0.4	0608	0.3	1024	2.3	0635	6.9	1024	1.1	1011	1.1
	1255	4.5	1324	5.6	1447	7.1	1231	4.1	1239	3.8	1606	0.8	1243	1.3	1629	5.2	1612	5.0
	1851	0.8	1921	0.7	2111	0.7	1822	0.6	1814	0.5	2217	2.6	1841	7.2	2250	0.8	2236	0.8
24 M	0100	4.7	0136	5.7	0258	7.1	0042	4.1	0051	3.9	0444	0.5	0112	1.1	0448	5.0	0435	4.9
	0720	0.6	0750	0.5	0936	0.5	0650	0.4	0638	0.3	1051	2.3	0704	6.9	1054	1.1	1040	1.0
	1324	4.6	1355	5.7	1517	7.1	1302	4.1	1309	3.9	1634	0.7	1315	1.3	1657	5.3	1642	5.0
	1923	0.8	1952	0.7	2144	0.7	1854	0.5	1844	0.5	2250	2.5	1912	7.2	2321	0.8	2305	0.8
25 TU	0131	4.7	0206	5.7	0328	7.1	0113	4.2	0121	3.9	0514	0.5	0143	1.1	0518	5.0	0505	4.8
	0751	0.6	0821	0.5	1006	0.5	0722	0.4	0709	0.2	1118	2.3	0733	6.9	1124	1.1	1109	1.0
	1352	4.6	1425	5.7	1548	7.2	1333	4.1	1339	3.9	1704	0.7	1345	1.3	1727	5.2	1712	5.0
	1954	0.8	2024	0.7	2214	0.8	1927	0.6	1915	0.5	2323	2.5	1942	7.2	2351	0.9	2336	0.8
26 W	0201	4.7	0236	5.6	0400	7.1	0144	4.1	0151	3.9	0543	0.6	0213	1.2	0549	5.0	0536	4.8
	0821	0.7	0851	0.5	1036	0.6	0754	0.4	0741	0.3	1148	2.3	0803	6.9	1156	1.1	1138	1.1
	1421	4.6	1457	5.6	1619	7.1	1403	4.1	1409	3.8	1736	0.7	1415	1.4	1800	5.1	1744	4.9
	2024	0.9	2053	0.7	2242	0.8	1958	0.6	1947	0.5	2357	2.5	2012	7.0				
27 TH	0230	4.6	0306	5.5	0430	6.9	0215	4.1	0221	3.8	0614	0.6	0241	1.3	0024	1.0	0006	1.0
	0850	0.7	0920	0.6	1103	0.6	0826	0.5	0812	0.4	1221	2.3	0833	6.7	0624	4.9	0607	4.6
	1451	4.5	1527	5.5	1651	7.0	1435	4.0	1441	3.8	1812	0.8	1444	1.5	1230	1.2	1209	1.2
	2054	1.0	2120	0.9	2307	0.9	2030	0.7	2018	0.6			2042	6.8	1835	5.0	1818	4.8
28 F	0300	4.5	0337	5.4	0502	6.8	0248	4.0	0254	3.8	0033	2.4	0309	1.6	0100	1.2	0039	1.1
	0921	0.8	0945	0.8	1128	0.7	0858	0.6	0845	0.5	0647	0.7	0904	6.5	0702	4.7	0642	4.5
	1526	4.4	1601	5.3	1724	6.8	1510	3.9	1517	3.7	1259	2.2	1514	1.8	1306	1.4	1244	1.4
	2128	1.1	2146	1.0	2333	0.9	2103	0.8	2052	0.7	1851	0.9	2115	6.6	1916	4.8	1857	4.6

● ● Time UT. For British Summer Time (shaded) March 30th to October 26th ADD ONE HOUR ● ●

EAST COAST OF ENGLAND Time Zone UT

Margate * Sheerness * London Bridge *Walton-on-the-Naze * Harwich * Lowestoft * Immingham * RiverTees * RiverTyne

MARCH 1997 TIDE TABLES MARCH 1997

	MARGATE		SHEERNESS		LONDON BRIDGE		WALTON-ON-THE-NAZE		HARWICH		LOWESTOFT		IMMINGHAM		RIVER TEES		RIVER TYNE	
	Time	m	Time	m	Time	m	Time	m	Time	m	Time	m	Time	m	Time	m	Time	m
1 SA	0335	4.4	0412	5.3	0536	6.5	0325	3.9	0331	3.7	0113	2.3	0339	1.8	0139	1.4	0117	1.3
	0956	1.0	1012	0.9	1157	0.8	0934	0.7	0921	0.6	0726	0.8	0941	6.3	0748	4.6	0725	4.4
	1608	4.3	1641	5.2	1802	6.5	1551	3.8	1558	3.6	1343	2.2	1551	2.0	1350	1.6	1327	1.5
	2208	1.2	2220	1.1			2145	0.9	2133	0.8	1938	0.9	2156	6.3	2006	4.6	1945	4.4
2 SU	0421	4.3	0457	5.1	0006	1.0	0412	3.8	0417	3.5	0202	2.3	0419	2.1	0228	1.7	0205	1.6
	1041	1.1	1051	1.0	0617	6.3	1022	0.9	1008	0.7	0815	0.9	1030	6.0	0842	4.4	0818	4.2
	1701	4.2	1730	5.0	1233	1.0	1642	3.6	1648	3.4	1439	2.1	1640	2.3	1445	1.8	1424	1.7
	2303	1.4	2311	1.2	1846	6.2	2242	1.0	2228	0.9	2039	1.0	2255	6.0	2110	4.4	2047	4.2
3 M	0524	4.1	0555	4.9	0050	1.2	0512	3.6	0515	3.4	0311	2.2	0518	2.4	0330	1.9	0309	1.8
	1148	1.3	1153	1.2	0711	6.0	1130	1.0	1116	0.9	0923	1.0	1141	5.8	0948	4.3	0924	4.1
	1809	4.0	1836	4.8	1324	1.3	1748	3.5	1753	3.3	1554	2.1	1754	2.5	1557	2.0	1542	1.9
					1948	6.0	2359	1.1	2351	1.0	2200	1.0			2227	4.3	2204	4.1
4 TU	0028	1.4	0030	1.3	0149	1.4	0627	3.5	0630	3.3	0435	2.2	0024	5.8	0449	2.0	0434	1.8
	0644	4.0	0714	4.8	0829	5.8	1251	1.0	1244	0.9	1048	1.0	0646	2.5	1103	4.3	1045	4.1
	1316	1.3	1326	1.3	1444	1.5	1906	3.4	1911	3.2	1709	2.1	1313	5.8	1727	1.9	1716	1.8
	1932	4.0	1958	4.8	2112	5.9					2327	0.9	1930	2.4	2349	4.4	2331	4.2
5 W	0201	1.3	0211	1.3	0327	1.5	0126	1.0	0121	0.9	0553	2.2	0203	6.0	0617	1.9	0602	1.7
	0814	4.1	0842	4.9	0959	6.0	0753	3.6	0754	3.3	1202	1.0	0818	2.3	1218	4.5	1203	4.3
	1436	1.2	1500	1.2	1625	1.3	1415	0.9	1402	0.8	1815	2.2	1436	6.2	1855	1.6	1839	1.4
	2050	4.2	2120	5.0	2237	6.2	2030	3.5	2030	3.3			2057	2.0				
6 TH	0318	1.0	0339	1.0	0502	1.1	0251	0.8	0236	0.7	0041	0.8	0321	6.4	0103	4.7	0047	4.5
	0932	4.3	1000	5.3	1121	6.5	0912	3.8	0915	3.6	0704	2.3	0934	1.9	0729	1.6	0710	1.4
	1544	1.0	1615	0.9	1743	1.0	1523	0.8	1509	0.7	1304	0.9	1542	6.7	1324	4.9	1307	4.6
	2154	4.5	2230	5.3	2352	6.6	2139	3.8	2144	3.5	1914	2.3	2211	1.4	2001	1.1	1942	1.0
7 F	0424	0.7	0454	0.7	0632	0.7	0357	0.6	0342	0.4	0145	0.6	0424	6.8	0205	5.1	0146	4.8
	1036	4.6	1105	5.7	1228	7.0	1014	4.0	1022	3.8	0803	2.4	1036	1.4	0825	1.2	0805	1.1
	1642	0.7	1718	0.7	1903	0.7	1618	0.6	1606	0.5	1400	0.8	1635	7.1	1420	5.3	1359	5.0
	2249	4.7	2328	5.6			2235	4.0	2245	3.8	2004	2.5	2311	0.9	2054	0.7	2035	0.6
8 SA	0520	0.4	0557	0.4	0051	7.1	0451	0.3	0437	0.2	0242	0.4	0516	7.2	0257	5.4	0236	5.1
	1130	4.8	1200	5.9	0745	0.3	1107	4.1	1116	4.0	0853	2.4	1130	1.0	0914	0.9	0854	0.8
	1733	0.6	1812	0.5	1322	7.4	1706	0.5	1655	0.3	1451	0.6	1722	7.5	1509	5.6	1445	5.3
	2339	4.8			2006	0.4	2324	4.2	2336	4.0	2051	2.6			2142	0.3	2124	0.3
9 SU	0609	0.2	0018	5.9	0141	7.4	0539	0.2	0525	0.0	0332	0.2	0003	0.5	0343	5.6	0322	5.3
	1221	4.9	0650	0.2	0840	0.0	1155	4.4	1205	4.2	0937	2.5	0603	7.4	0959	0.6	0939	0.5
	1821	0.5	1248	6.1	1410	7.6	1751	0.4	1739	0.2	1539	0.5	1218	0.7	1554	5.8	1530	5.5
			1900	0.4	2057	0.2					2136	2.7	1806	7.7	2227	0.1	2209	0.1
10 M	0027	5.0	0104	6.0	0226	7.6	0010	4.4	0022	4.1	0418	0.1	0050	0.2	0427	5.8	0406	5.4
	0656	0.1	0737	0.0	0927	-0.1	0624	0.1	0609	-0.1	1020	2.5	0646	7.5	1042	0.5	1022	0.4
	1308	5.0	1333	6.2	1454	7.8	1240	4.5	1249	4.3	1623	0.5	1303	0.5	1638	5.9	1613	5.6
	1906	0.4	1945	0.3	2142	0.2	1834	0.3	1822	0.2	2221	2.8	1850	7.9	2310	0.1	2253	0.0
11 TU	0114	5.1	0147	6.1	0309	7.7	0054	4.5	0105	4.2	0500	0.1	0133	0.2	0509	5.8	0449	5.3
	0741	0.1	0821	-0.0	1010	-0.2	0708	0.0	0652	-0.2	1103	2.5	0727	7.5	1124	0.5	1104	0.4
	1352	4.9	1415	6.2	1538	7.8	1324	4.4	1332	4.2	1705	0.4	1344	0.6	1721	5.9	1658	5.6
	1950	0.4	2027	0.3	2222	0.2	1918	0.3	1904	0.1	2307	2.8	1933	7.8	2352	0.3	2335	0.2
12 W	0158	5.1	0229	6.1	0351	7.7	0137	4.5	0146	4.3	0542	0.1	0213	0.4	0552	5.6	0532	5.2
	0824	0.2	0900	0.0	1048	0.0	0751	0.1	0734	-0.1	1146	2.4	0806	7.3	1206	0.7	1146	0.5
	1433	4.8	1457	6.1	1620	7.6	1406	4.3	1412	4.1	1746	0.5	1423	0.7	1805	5.7	1744	5.4
	2032	0.5	2106	0.3	2257	0.3	2000	0.4	1947	0.2	2353	2.7	2015	7.6				
13 TH	0240	5.0	0311	6.0	0434	7.6	0220	4.4	0227	4.2	0623	0.3	0251	0.7	0034	0.6	0016	0.5
	0904	0.4	0937	0.2	1118	0.3	0833	0.3	0816	0.1	1230	2.3	0845	7.0	0635	5.4	0615	5.0
	1512	4.7	1538	5.8	1702	7.3	1447	4.2	1453	4.0	1828	0.6	1500	1.0	1248	0.9	1227	0.8
	2112	0.6	2142	0.5	2327	0.4	2043	0.5	2030	0.3			2058	7.2	1851	5.4	1831	5.1
14 F	0321	4.8	0353	5.8	0516	7.3	0303	4.3	0308	4.1	0041	2.5	0326	1.2	0117	1.0	0057	0.9
	0943	0.6	1011	0.5	1145	0.7	0915	0.5	0900	0.3	0704	0.5	0924	6.7	0720	5.1	0701	4.7
	1549	4.5	1619	5.6	1743	6.9	1530	3.9	1534	3.8	1316	2.3	1536	1.4	1331	1.2	1312	1.1
	2153	0.8	2218	0.7	2355	0.8	2127	0.7	2115	0.5	1912	0.7	2143	6.7	1940	5.1	1923	4.7
15 SA	0403	4.6	0438	5.5	0600	6.9	0349	4.0	0352	3.8	0136	2.4	0401	1.7	0201	1.4	0141	1.3
	1023	0.9	1045	0.9	1212	0.9	0959	0.8	0945	0.6	0749	0.8	1007	6.3	0809	4.7	0751	4.4
	1632	4.3	1703	5.2	1826	6.6	1616	3.7	1618	3.5	1408	2.2	1617	1.9	1420	1.6	1403	1.4
	2240	1.0	2257	1.0			2216	0.9	2204	0.7	2004	0.8	2236	6.2	2036	4.7	2021	4.4

● ● Time UT. For British Summer Time (shaded) March 30th to October 26th ADD ONE HOUR ● ●

MARCH 1997 TIDE TABLES MARCH 1997

	MARGATE		SHEERNESS		LONDON BRIDGE		WALTON-ON THE-NAZE		HARWICH		LOWESTOFT		IMMINGHAM		RIVER TEES		RIVER TYNE	
	Time	m	Time	m	Time	m	Time	m	Time	m	Time	m	Time	m	Time	m	Time	m
16 SU	0455	4.3	0529	5.2	0028	1.0	0442	3.8	0442	3.5	0243	2.2	0444	2.3	0251	1.8	0234	1.7
	1112	1.2	1126	1.2	0648	6.5	1052	1.0	1038	0.9	0842	1.0	1100	5.9	0906	4.4	0850	4.1
	1725	4.0	1756	4.9	1248	1.2	1710	3.5	1710	3.3	1509	2.1	1711	2.3	1518	1.9	1509	1.7
	2343	1.2	2350	1.2	1915	6.2	2320	1.0	2306	0.9	2111	0.9	2349	5.7	2142	4.4	2130	4.0
17 M	0602	4.0	0632	4.8	0111	1.2	0546	3.5	0545	3.3	0406	2.1	0545	2.7	0354	2.2	0346	2.0
	1222	1.4	1228	1.5	0746	6.1	1206	1.2	1148	1.1	0959	1.2	1217	5.6	1013	4.2	1003	3.9
	1836	3.9	1903	4.6	1338	1.5	1822	3.3	1818	3.1	1621	2.1	1836	2.6	1636	2.1	1639	1.9
					2015	5.9					2250	0.9			2258	4.2	2253	3.9
18 TU	0112	1.3	0112	1.4	0215	1.5	0051	1.1	0035	1.0	0536	2.1	0122	5.6	0516	2.3	0521	2.1
	0727	3.9	0753	4.6	0858	5.9	0712	3.3	0711	3.1	1140	1.2	0719	2.9	1128	4.2	1125	3.9
	1354	1.5	1400	1.6	1502	1.7	1336	1.2	1321	1.1	1740	2.1	1348	5.6	1806	2.1	1807	1.8
	2000	3.9	2026	4.6	2133	5.8	1950	3.3	1947	3.1			2018	2.6				
19 W	0243	1.2	0252	1.4	0403	1.5	0220	1.0	0207	0.9	0017	0.9	0246	5.7	0015	4.2	0014	4.0
	0857	3.9	0917	4.6	1033	6.0	0834	3.4	0837	3.2	0654	2.2	0847	2.7	0639	2.3	0638	2.0
	1516	1.4	1525	1.5	1635	1.5	1448	1.1	1438	1.0	1246	1.1	1503	5.9	1239	4.3	1237	4.1
	2117	4.0	2144	4.8	2306	6.0	2100	3.5	2103	3.2	1849	2.2	2129	2.2	1915	1.8	1910	1.6
20 TH	0354	1.0	0406	1.1	0524	1.1	0322	0.8	0311	0.7	0114	0.8	0348	6.1	0118	4.4	0115	4.2
	1003	4.1	1022	5.1	1144	6.4	0935	3.6	0939	3.4	0748	2.2	0947	2.4	0737	2.1	0730	1.8
	1615	1.2	1627	1.3	1745	1.2	1540	1.0	1532	0.9	1333	1.1	1556	6.3	1335	4.5	1330	4.3
	2214	4.2	2242	5.1			2153	3.7	2157	3.4	1937	2.2	2219	1.9	2003	1.6	1956	1.3
21 F	0443	0.8	0500	0.9	0006	6.4	0409	0.7	0358	0.5	0159	0.7	0433	6.3	0206	4.6	0200	4.4
	1051	4.3	1111	5.3	0627	0.8	1021	3.8	1025	3.6	0828	2.3	1031	2.0	0818	1.8	0811	1.5
	1656	1.1	1713	1.1	1233	6.7	1621	0.9	1613	0.8	1411	1.0	1636	6.6	1420	4.8	1411	4.5
	2256	4.3	2327	5.3	1842	1.0	2235	3.8	2241	3.6	2015	2.3	2300	1.6	2042	1.3	2033	1.1
22 SA	0519	0.8	0542	0.8	0050	6.7	0447	0.6	0436	0.4	0236	0.6	0509	6.6	0245	4.7	0236	4.6
	1127	4.4	1151	5.5	0715	0.6	1059	3.9	1104	3.7	0902	2.3	1109	1.7	0854	1.6	0845	1.3
	1727	1.0	1751	0.9	1313	6.9	1654	0.7	1648	0.7	1443	0.9	1712	6.8	1457	5.0	1445	4.7
	2330	4.5			1928	0.8	2311	4.0	2318	3.7	2047	2.4	2337	1.3	2116	1.1	2106	1.0
23 SU	0550	0.7	0005	5.5	0127	6.9	0519	0.5	0509	0.4	0311	0.6	0539	6.8	0319	4.9	0308	4.7
	1158	4.5	0618	0.7	0757	0.5	1133	4.0	1139	3.8	0930	2.3	1144	1.5	0927	1.3	0916	1.1
	1755	0.9	1225	5.6	1348	7.0	1726	0.6	1718	0.6	1512	0.8	1744	7.0	1530	5.1	1517	4.8
			1825	0.8	2009	0.7	2344	4.1	2352	3.8	2119	2.5			2149	1.0	2137	0.8
24 M ○	0002	4.6	0038	5.7	0200	7.0	0551	0.4	0539	0.3	0343	0.5	0012	1.2	0350	5.0	0338	4.8
	0619	0.7	0651	0.6	0834	0.5	1204	4.1	1212	3.9	0954	2.3	0609	6.9	0958	1.2	0947	1.0
	1227	4.5	1257	5.7	1419	7.1	1757	0.5	1748	0.5	1541	0.7	1218	1.3	1600	5.2	1547	4.9
	1825	0.8	1857	0.7	2046	0.7					2151	2.5	1815	7.1	2221	0.8	2208	0.7
25 TU	0033	4.6	0110	5.7	0231	7.0	0017	4.2	0024	3.9	0414	0.5	0045	1.1	0418	5.1	0408	4.9
	0650	0.6	0722	0.5	0909	0.5	0623	0.3	0609	0.2	1020	2.4	0637	7.0	1030	1.1	1016	1.0
	1255	4.6	1328	5.7	1449	7.2	1235	4.2	1242	3.9	1612	0.6	1251	1.2	1630	5.3	1617	5.0
	1857	0.8	1930	0.6	2121	0.6	1830	0.5	1818	0.4	2225	2.5	1847	7.2	2252	0.8	2238	0.7
26 W	0104	4.7	0141	5.7	0301	7.1	0048	4.2	0056	3.9	0444	0.5	0117	1.0	0448	5.1	0437	4.9
	0721	0.6	0754	0.6	0942	0.5	0655	0.3	0641	0.2	1048	2.4	0706	7.0	1100	1.0	1046	0.9
	1324	4.7	1359	5.8	1520	7.2	1306	4.2	1314	3.9	1644	0.6	1324	1.1	1701	5.3	1648	4.9
	1929	0.8	2003	0.6	2153	0.7	1903	0.5	1851	0.4	2259	2.5	1918	7.2	2324	0.8	2309	0.7
27 TH	0134	4.7	0212	5.7	0333	7.1	0121	4.2	0127	3.9	0515	0.5	0148	1.0	0520	5.1	0507	4.8
	0752	0.6	0827	0.6	1013	0.5	0728	0.4	0713	0.3	1119	2.4	0736	7.0	1133	1.0	1117	0.9
	1353	4.7	1431	5.7	1552	7.2	1338	4.2	1345	3.9	1718	0.6	1355	1.2	1735	5.2	1720	4.9
	2001	0.8	2034	0.7	2222	0.7	1936	0.5	1923	0.4	2334	2.4	1949	7.1	2358	1.0	2340	0.8
28 F	0204	4.7	0243	5.6	0406	7.1	0152	4.1	0159	3.9	0546	0.6	0218	1.2	0555	5.0	0539	4.7
	0824	0.7	0857	0.6	1041	0.6	0800	0.5	0746	0.4	1153	2.3	0807	6.9	1208	1.1	1149	1.0
	1424	4.7	1503	5.6	1624	7.1	1409	4.1	1418	3.8	1754	0.7	1426	1.3	1812	5.1	1755	4.8
	2035	0.9	2103	0.7	2247	0.8	2008	0.5	1956	0.5			2021	6.9				
29 SA	0236	4.6	0316	5.5	0439	7.0	0226	4.1	0233	3.8	0011	2.4	0247	1.4	0035	1.1	0014	1.0
	0857	0.8	0924	0.7	1106	0.7	0832	0.6	0819	0.5	0620	0.7	0840	6.7	0635	4.9	0615	4.6
	1459	4.6	1537	5.4	1659	6.9	1445	4.0	1452	3.7	1230	2.3	1458	1.5	1246	1.2	1225	1.1
	2110	1.0	2130	0.8	2312	0.8	2042	0.7	2032	0.6	1833	0.7	2057	6.7	1856	4.9	1836	4.6
30 SU	0314	4.5	0354	5.4	0516	6.8	0304	4.0	0311	3.7	0052	2.3	0319	1.6	0116	1.4	0052	1.2
	0934	1.0	0952	0.9	1132	0.8	0908	0.7	0857	0.6	0658	0.8	0918	6.5	0721	4.7	0658	4.5
	1540	4.4	1617	5.3	1736	6.7	1524	3.8	1533	3.6	1313	2.2	1535	1.7	1331	1.4	1309	1.3
	2150	1.1	2205	0.9	2344	0.9	2124	0.8	2114	0.6	1921	0.8	2141	6.4	1949	4.7	1927	4.4
31 M	0402	4.4	0439	5.2	0600	6.5	0351	3.8	0357	3.6	0144	2.2	0400	2.0	0206	1.6	0140	1.5
	1020	1.2	1033	1.0	1209	1.0	0955	0.9	0944	0.8	0747	0.9	1006	6.2	0815	4.5	0751	4.3
	1633	4.2	1706	5.0	1821	6.3	1615	3.7	1621	3.4	1405	2.2	1624	2.0	1427	1.6	1406	1.5
	2245	1.2	2257	1.1			2220	0.9	2209	0.8	2021	0.8	2242	6.0	2054	4.5	2030	4.2

● ● Time UT. For British Summer Time (shaded) March 30th to October 26th ADD ONE HOUR ● ●

EAST COAST OF ENGLAND Time Zone UT

Margate * Sheerness * London Bridge *Walton-on-the-Naze * Harwich * Lowestoft * Immingham * RiverTees * RiverTyne

APRIL 1997 TIDE TABLES APRIL 1997

MARGATE		SHEERNESS		LONDON BRIDGE		WALTON-ON-THE-NAZE		HARWICH		LOWESTOFT		IMMINGHAM		RIVER TEES		RIVER TYNE			
Time	m	Time	m	Time	m	Time	m	Time	m	Time	m	Time	m	Time	m	Time	m		
0505	4.2	0539	5.0	0027	1.0	0451	3.7	0454	3.4	0255	2.1	0459	2.3	0307	1.9	0245	1.7	**1**	**TU**
1126	1.4	1135	1.2	0655	6.2	1102	1.0	1050	0.9	0854	1.0	1115	6.0	0921	4.4	0858	4.1		
1742	4.1	1811	4.8	1259	1.3	1719	3.5	1724	3.3	1514	2.1	1737	2.2	1536	1.7	1524	1.6		
				1922	6.0	2336	0.9	2327	0.8	2139	0.8			2209	4.4	2148	4.1		
0009	1.3	0015	1.2	0127	1.3	0606	3.5	0609	3.3	0420	2.1	0013	5.8	0424	2.0	0412	1.8	**2**	**W**
0625	4.0	0656	4.9	0812	6.0	1224	1.1	1215	1.0	1020	1.1	0624	2.5	1034	4.4	1018	4.1		
1252	1.4	1303	1.4	1417	1.5	1838	3.4	1841	3.2	1630	2.1	1245	5.9	1703	1.9	1657	1.5		
1903	4.1	1931	4.8	2045	5.9					2306	0.8	1911	2.2	2328	4.5	2315	4.2		
0142	1.2	0152	1.1	0303	1.3	0103	0.9	0056	0.7	0542	2.2	0150	6.0	0551	1.9	0540	1.7	**3**	**TH**
0756	4.1	0823	5.0	0940	6.2	0733	3.6	0733	3.4	1139	1.0	0756	2.3	1148	4.6	1138	4.3		
1414	1.2	1436	1.2	1559	1.4	1349	1.0	1336	0.9	1742	2.2	1410	6.2	1830	1.5	1819	1.2		
2023	4.2	2055	5.0	2212	6.2	2004	3.5	2002	3.3			2039	1.8						
0300	0.9	0321	0.9	0439	1.0	0231	0.7	0214	0.6	0021	0.6	0307	6.4	0041	4.7	0030	4.4	**4**	**F**
0914	4.4	0942	5.3	1103	6.6	0853	3.8	0855	3.6	0653	2.3	0914	1.9	0704	1.6	0649	1.4		
1524	1.0	1552	1.0	1718	1.0	1501	0.8	1446	0.7	1244	0.9	1518	6.6	1256	4.9	1245	4.6		
2128	4.5	2207	5.3	2330	6.6	2116	3.7	2120	3.5	1845	2.3	2153	1.3	1936	1.1	1922	0.9		
0405	0.6	0436	0.6	0614	0.7	0339	0.5	0322	0.3	0127	0.5	0409	6.8	0142	5.1	0129	4.7	**5**	**SA**
1018	4.6	1046	5.7	1209	7.1	0956	4.1	1003	3.8	0749	2.3	1017	1.5	0802	1.3	0745	1.1		
1623	0.8	1657	0.7	1842	0.7	1558	0.7	1545	0.5	1342	0.8	1613	7.1	1354	5.2	1338	4.9		
2224	4.7	2306	5.6			2214	4.0	2223	3.7	1940	2.4	2252	0.9	2030	0.7	2015	0.5		
0500	0.4	0538	0.4	0030	7.0	0433	0.3	0418	0.2	0222	0.3	0459	7.1	0233	5.4	0218	5.0	**6**	**SU**
1112	4.8	1140	5.9	0727	0.3	1048	4.3	1057	4.0	0836	2.4	1110	1.0	0851	0.9	0833	0.8		
1713	0.6	1751	0.6	1303	7.4	1647	0.5	1635	0.4	1433	0.7	1701	7.4	1445	5.5	1425	5.2		
2315	4.8	2357	5.8	1946	0.5	2304	4.2	2315	4.0	2029	2.6	2342	0.5	2118	0.4	2103	0.3		
0548	0.3	0630	0.2	0121	7.3	0520	0.2	0505	0.0	0311	0.2	0543	7.3	0320	5.6	0303	5.2	**7**	**M**
1201	4.9	1227	6.1	0821	0.1	1136	4.4	1145	4.2	0917	2.5	1158	0.8	0937	0.7	0918	0.5		●
1800	0.5	1840	0.4	1351	7.6	1732	0.4	1720	0.2	1520	0.5	1746	7.6	1531	5.7	1510	5.4		
				2036	0.3	2350	4.3			2116	2.7			2203	0.3	2148	0.1		
0003	4.9	0042	6.0	0206	7.4	0604	0.1	0001	4.1	0355	0.1	0028	0.3	0403	5.7	0345	5.3	**8**	**TU**
0633	0.2	0715	0.1	0906	0.0	1220	4.4	0548	-0.1	0958	2.5	0624	7.4	1020	0.6	1002	0.4		
1245	4.9	1311	6.1	1435	7.6	1815	0.3	1229	4.2	1604	0.4	1242	0.6	1615	5.8	1554	5.5		
1844	0.4	1924	0.3	2121	0.2			1803	0.2	2203	2.7	1830	7.7	2245	0.3	2230	0.2		
0051	5.0	0125	6.1	0249	7.5	0034	4.4	0044	4.2	0437	0.1	0110	0.4	0444	5.7	0426	5.3	**9**	**W**
0715	0.2	0756	0.1	0947	0.1	0647	0.1	0630	-0.1	1039	2.5	0703	7.4	1102	0.6	1044	0.4		
1327	4.9	1352	6.1	1517	7.6	1302	4.4	1310	4.2	1646	0.4	1324	0.6	1659	5.8	1639	5.4		
1927	0.4	2006	0.3	2159	0.2	1859	0.3	1845	0.1	2249	2.7	1913	7.6	2327	0.5	2311	0.3		
0136	5.0	0207	6.1	0331	7.6	0117	4.4	0124	4.2	0518	0.3	0148	0.6	0524	5.6	0507	5.1	**10**	**TH**
0757	0.3	0834	0.2	1021	0.2	0728	0.2	0712	0.0	1121	2.5	0741	7.3	1142	0.7	1125	0.5		
1407	4.8	1433	6.0	1557	7.5	1343	4.3	1349	4.1	1728	0.4	1403	0.8	1742	5.6	1724	5.2		
2009	0.5	2045	0.3	2233	0.3	1942	0.4	1927	0.2	2336	2.6	1956	7.4			2350	0.6		
0218	4.9	0248	6.0	0412	7.5	0159	4.4	0205	4.2	0557	0.4	0224	0.9	0006	0.8	0548	4.9	**11**	**F**
0836	0.5	0909	0.4	1050	0.5	0809	0.4	0753	0.2	1203	2.4	0818	7.1	0606	5.4	1207	0.7		
1444	4.7	1512	5.8	1636	7.3	1422	4.1	1427	3.9	1810	0.5	1439	1.0	1224	0.9	1811	4.9		
2049	0.6	2121	0.5	2302	0.5	2024	0.5	2010	0.3			2039	7.0	1827	5.3				
0300	4.8	0330	5.8	0454	7.3	0242	4.2	0245	4.0	0026	2.4	0257	1.4	0047	1.2	0028	1.0	**12**	**SA**
0913	0.8	0942	0.7	1115	0.7	0848	0.7	0833	0.5	0636	0.6	0856	6.7	0648	5.1	0632	4.7		
1520	4.5	1551	5.5	1715	6.9	1502	3.9	1506	3.7	1245	2.3	1514	1.4	1306	1.2	1250	1.0		
2130	0.8	2156	0.7	2330	0.7	2106	0.6	2053	0.5	1854	0.6	2123	6.6	1915	5.0	1900	4.6		
0342	4.5	0413	5.5	0535	6.9	0325	4.0	0327	3.8	0121	2.3	0330	1.8	0128	1.6	0109	1.4	**13**	**SU**
0951	1.0	1013	1.0	1142	1.0	0928	0.9	0915	0.7	0717	0.9	0935	6.4	0735	4.8	0718	4.4		
1558	4.3	1632	5.2	1754	6.5	1545	3.7	1546	3.5	1331	2.2	1552	1.8	1352	1.5	1338	1.3		
2215	1.0	2231	1.0			2151	0.8	2139	0.7	1942	0.7	2212	6.1	2009	4.7	1954	4.3		
0429	4.3	0501	5.1	0001	0.8	0414	3.7	0413	3.5	0225	2.2	0409	2.3	0215	2.0	0157	1.7	**14**	**M**
1036	1.3	1050	1.3	0621	6.5	1015	1.1	1003	1.0	0804	1.1	1022	6.0	0828	4.6	0812	4.2		
1647	4.1	1718	4.9	1217	1.2	1633	3.5	1631	3.3	1424	2.1	1641	2.2	1446	1.8	1436	1.6		
2311	1.2	2317	1.2	1839	6.2	2247	0.9	2234	0.8	2043	0.8	2317	5.7	2110	4.4	2056	4.0		
0530	4.0	0558	4.8	0039	1.1	0512	3.5	0509	3.3	0339	2.1	0502	2.7	0310	2.3	0259	2.0	**15**	**TU**
1136	1.5	1144	1.5	0714	6.2	1116	1.3	1103	1.2	0910	1.2	1127	5.7	0930	4.4	0916	3.9		
1751	3.9	1818	4.6	1302	1.5	1735	3.3	1728	3.1	1527	2.1	1755	2.5	1551	2.0	1552	1.7		
				1934	5.9			2348	0.9	2208	0.9			2218	4.3	2211	3.8		

● ● Time UT. For British Summer Time (shaded) March 30th to October 26th ADD ONE HOUR ● ●

APRIL 1997 TIDE TABLES APRIL 1997

Day	MARGATE	SHEERNESS	LONDON BRIDGE	WALTON-ON-THE-NAZE	HARWICH	LOWESTOFT	IMMINGHAM	RIVER TEES	RIVER TYNE
	Time m	Time m	Time m	Time m	Time m	Time m	Time m	Time m	Time m
16 W	0027 1.3	0027 1.4	0131 1.4	0003 1.0	0625 3.1	0502 2.1	0041 5.5	0421 2.4	0425 2.2
	0647 3.8	0710 4.6	0819 5.9	0627 3.3	1224 1.2	1056 1.3	0624 3.0	1039 4.3	1034 3.9
	1257 1.6	1306 1.7	1404 1.8	1241 1.3	1851 3.0	1639 2.1	1253 5.6	1709 2.0	1718 1.7
	1909 3.8	1934 4.5	2045 5.7	1857 3.2		2335 0.8	1931 2.5	2328 4.3	2330 3.9
17 TH	0155 1.3	0205 1.4	0304 1.5	0133 1.0	0118 0.9	0619 2.1	0204 5.6	0542 2.4	0551 2.1
	0812 3.9	0832 4.7	0939 5.9	0752 3.4	0753 3.2	1210 1.2	0759 2.9	1147 4.3	1151 4.0
	1424 1.6	1439 1.6	1550 1.8	1402 1.2	1351 1.2	1757 2.1	1415 5.7	1821 1.9	1827 1.6
	2026 3.9	2057 4.6	2212 5.8	2016 3.4	2016 3.1		2045 2.3		
18 F	0306 1.1	0322 1.2	0441 1.2	0240 0.8	0228 0.7	0036 0.8	0309 5.9	0031 4.4	0036 4.0
	0921 4.1	0942 4.9	1103 6.1	0857 3.5	0900 3.3	0717 2.2	0905 2.6	0648 2.2	0651 1.9
	1530 1.4	1546 1.4	1704 1.4	1500 1.1	1452 1.0	1300 1.1	1515 6.1	1246 4.5	1250 4.1
	2128 4.1	2201 4.9	2326 6.1	2114 3.5	2118 3.3	1856 2.1	2139 2.0	1915 1.7	1916 1.4
19 SA	0359 1.0	0419 1.0	0543 0.9	0330 0.7	0319 0.6	0123 0.7	0356 6.2	0123 4.6	0124 4.2
	1012 4.2	1033 5.2	1157 6.5	0945 3.7	0950 3.5	0759 2.2	0954 2.2	0737 2.0	0735 1.6
	1615 1.2	1636 1.2	1802 1.1	1545 0.9	1538 0.8	1339 1.0	1600 6.4	1336 4.7	1334 4.3
	2215 4.3	2250 5.2		2159 3.7	2205 3.5	1939 2.2	2224 1.7	1959 1.5	1956 1.2
20 SU	0439 0.9	0504 0.8	0015 6.4	0411 0.6	0400 0.5	0202 0.7	0434 6.5	0205 4.7	0202 4.4
	1051 4.4	1115 5.4	0635 0.7	1025 3.9	1030 3.7	0832 2.3	1035 1.9	0818 1.7	0812 1.4
	1651 1.1	1718 1.0	1239 6.7	1622 0.8	1615 0.7	1410 0.9	1639 6.6	1418 4.9	1412 4.5
	2254 4.4	2330 5.4	1851 0.9	2238 3.9	2245 3.6	2015 2.3	2303 1.4	2038 1.3	2032 1.1
21 M	0513 0.8	0543 0.7	0054 6.6	0446 0.5	0434 0.4	0236 0.6	0507 6.7	0242 4.9	0236 4.6
	1123 4.5	1152 5.6	0720 0.6	1100 4.0	1107 3.8	0858 2.3	1113 1.6	0855 1.5	0846 1.2
	1723 1.0	1754 0.8	1315 6.9	1657 0.7	1647 0.6	1441 0.8	1713 6.9	1455 5.0	1445 4.7
	2329 4.5		1936 0.8	2314 4.0	2321 3.8	2049 2.4	2339 1.2	2115 1.1	2105 0.8
22 TU ○	0545 0.7	0006 5.5	0128 6.8	0520 0.4	0506 0.3	0309 0.5	0538 6.9	0316 5.1	0307 4.8
	1154 4.6	0618 0.6	0800 0.5	1134 4.1	1142 3.9	0922 2.3	1149 1.3	0930 1.2	0919 1.0
	1756 0.9	1226 5.7	1347 7.0	1731 0.6	1719 0.5	1513 0.7	1747 7.0	1530 5.2	1518 4.8
		1830 0.7	2016 0.7	2348 4.1	2356 3.9	2124 2.4		2150 1.0	2138 0.7
23 W	0003 4.6	0041 5.6	0200 6.9	0554 0.4	0539 0.3	0341 0.5	0015 1.1	0348 5.2	0339 4.9
	0618 0.7	0652 0.6	0839 0.5	1208 4.2	1215 4.0	0949 2.4	0609 7.0	1004 1.1	0951 0.9
	1224 4.7	1300 5.8	1419 7.1	1806 0.5	1753 0.4	1548 0.6	1226 1.2	1603 5.2	1551 4.9
	1830 0.8	1905 0.6	2054 0.6			2200 2.4	1821 7.1	2224 0.9	2211 0.7
24 TH	0036 4.7	0115 5.7	0233 7.1	0024 4.2	0030 3.9	0414 0.5	0049 1.0	0421 5.2	0410 4.9
	0651 0.6	0727 0.5	0916 0.5	0628 0.4	0613 0.3	1020 2.4	0641 7.1	1039 1.0	1024 0.8
	1256 4.7	1334 5.8	1453 7.2	1242 4.2	1249 4.0	1625 0.6	1302 1.1	1638 5.3	1624 4.9
	1906 0.7	1941 0.6	2131 0.6	1840 0.5	1827 0.4	2236 2.4	1855 7.1	2300 0.9	2244 0.7
25 F	0110 4.8	0149 5.7	0309 7.2	0058 4.2	0106 3.9	0448 0.5	0123 1.0	0455 5.2	0442 4.9
	0727 0.7	0802 0.5	0951 0.5	0702 0.5	0648 0.3	1054 2.4	0713 7.1	1114 1.0	1058 0.8
	1330 4.8	1408 5.8	1527 7.3	1315 4.2	1323 4.0	1703 0.6	1337 1.1	1715 5.2	1700 4.9
	1942 0.7	2017 0.6	2205 0.6	1915 0.5	1903 0.4	2314 2.4	1930 7.1	2336 1.0	2318 0.8
26 SA	0145 4.8	0224 5.7	0345 7.2	0133 4.1	0141 3.9	0522 0.6	0157 1.1	0533 5.2	0517 4.8
	0803 0.7	0836 0.6	1024 0.6	0736 0.5	0723 0.4	1130 2.4	0748 7.0	1152 1.0	1135 0.8
	1405 4.7	1443 5.7	1603 7.2	1348 4.1	1358 3.9	1742 0.6	1412 1.2	1757 5.1	1740 4.8
	2021 0.8	2051 0.6	2234 0.6	1951 0.5	1939 0.4	2354 2.3	2007 6.9		2355 0.9
27 SU	0223 4.7	0301 5.6	0422 7.1	0210 4.1	0218 3.8	0559 0.6	0231 1.3	0017 1.2	0556 4.7
	0842 0.8	0909 0.7	1051 0.7	0812 0.6	0800 0.5	1209 2.3	0824 6.9	0615 5.1	1215 0.9
	1443 4.6	1520 5.5	1640 7.0	1425 4.0	1435 3.8	1825 0.6	1449 1.3	1234 1.1	1826 4.6
	2101 0.9	2125 0.7	2301 0.7	2030 0.6	2018 0.5		2049 6.7	1845 5.0	
28 M	0306 4.6	0343 5.5	0504 6.9	0251 4.0	0258 3.8	0039 2.3	0308 1.5	0101 1.4	0037 1.1
	0923 1.0	0943 0.9	1118 0.9	0852 0.8	0841 0.6	0640 0.8	0906 6.7	0704 4.9	0642 4.6
	1527 4.5	1602 5.3	1721 6.7	1507 3.9	1516 3.6	1252 2.3	1531 1.5	1323 1.2	1303 1.1
	2146 1.0	2206 0.8	2334 0.8	2115 0.7	2105 0.5	1915 0.6	2139 6.4	1941 4.8	1919 4.4
29 TU	0357 4.4	0432 5.3	0551 6.6	0340 3.9	0346 3.7	0136 2.2	0353 1.9	0153 1.6	0128 1.4
	1012 1.2	1028 1.0	1156 1.1	0942 0.9	0931 0.8	0730 0.9	0957 6.4	0800 4.7	0736 4.4
	1619 4.3	1652 5.1	1809 6.4	1558 3.7	1606 3.5	1343 2.2	1624 1.7	1419 1.4	1402 1.2
	2244 1.1	2300 0.9		2213 0.7	2202 0.6	2015 0.6	2244 6.1	2045 4.6	2023 4.3
30 W	0459 4.3	0532 5.2	0018 1.0	0441 3.7	0444 3.5	0248 2.1	0451 2.2	0254 1.8	0233 1.6
	1115 1.3	1130 1.2	0649 6.3	1046 1.0	1035 0.9	0836 1.0	1102 6.2	0903 4.6	0841 4.2
	1724 4.2	1756 5.0	1248 1.3	1702 3.6	1706 3.4	1446 2.2	1733 1.9	1527 1.5	1515 1.3
			1909 6.1	2324 0.8	2315 0.7	2127 0.6		2156 4.6	2137 4.2

● ● Time UT. For British Summer Time (shaded) March 30th to October 26th ADD ONE HOUR ● ●

EAST COAST OF ENGLAND Time Zone UT

Margate * Sheerness * London Bridge *Walton-on-the-Naze * Harwich * Lowestoft * Immingham * RiverTees * RiverTyne

MAY 1997 TIDE TABLES MAY 1997

MARGATE	SHEERNESS	LONDON BRIDGE	WALTON-ON-THE-NAZE	HARWICH	LOWESTOFT	IMMINGHAM	RIVER TEES	RIVER TYNE		
Time m	Time m	Time m	Time m	Time m	Time m	Time m	Time m	Time m		
0002 1.1	0013 1.0	0119 1.1	0553 3.6	0555 3.5	0409 2.1	0008 6.0	0406 1.9	0353 1.7	1	TH
0615 4.2	0645 5.1	0802 6.2	1202 1.1	1153 1.0	0955 1.1	0608 2.4	1012 4.6	0957 4.2		
1233 1.4	1248 1.3	1404 1.5	1818 3.5	1819 3.3	1559 2.1	1222 6.1	1645 1.5	1639 1.3		
1840 4.2	1912 4.9	2027 6.1			2245 0.6	1857 1.9	2309 4.6	2257 4.2		
0125 1.0	0140 0.9	0251 1.1	0048 0.8	0036 0.6	0527 2.2	0134 6.1	0525 1.9	0515 1.6	2	F
0738 4.3	0806 5.1	0923 6.4	0715 3.7	0715 3.5	1112 1.0	0732 2.3	1123 4.7	1114 4.3		
1351 1.2	1412 1.2	1536 1.3	1324 1.0	1311 0.9	1711 2.2	1343 6.3	1803 1.3	1756 1.1		
1955 4.3	2031 5.1	2148 6.3	1939 3.6	1936 3.4	2358 0.5	2018 1.6				
0240 0.8	0301 0.8	0419 0.8	0212 0.6	0153 0.5	0636 2.2	0247 6.4	0017 4.8	0009 4.4	3	SA
0853 4.4	0921 5.4	1041 6.7	0832 3.9	0833 3.6	1219 0.9	0848 1.9	0637 1.6	0624 1.4		
1501 1.0	1526 1.0	1652 1.0	1437 0.9	1421 0.8	1818 2.3	1451 6.6	1229 4.9	1221 4.6		
2101 4.5	2142 5.3	2305 6.6	2052 3.8	2053 3.5		2129 1.3	1909 1.1	1900 0.8		
0344 0.6	0414 0.6	0547 0.6	0318 0.4	0300 0.3	0104 0.4	0347 6.7	0116 5.1	0107 4.7	4	SU
0956 4.6	1024 5.7	1147 7.1	0935 4.0	0941 3.8	0730 2.3	0953 1.6	0736 1.4	0721 1.1		
1600 0.9	1632 0.8	1814 0.8	1536 0.7	1522 0.6	1319 0.8	1549 6.9	1328 5.1	1316 4.8		
2200 4.6	2243 5.6		2151 4.0	2159 3.7	1917 2.4	2228 1.0	2004 0.8	1954 0.6		
0439 0.4	0515 0.4	0008 6.9	0412 0.3	0357 0.2	0200 0.3	0437 7.0	0208 5.3	0157 4.9	5	M
1051 4.7	1118 5.8	0703 0.4	1028 4.2	1036 4.0	0815 2.4	1048 1.2	0827 1.1	0812 0.8		
1652 0.7	1728 0.6	1243 7.3	1627 0.6	1614 0.5	1413 0.7	1639 7.2	1421 5.4	1406 5.0		
2252 4.7	2335 5.7	1922 0.6	2243 4.1	2253 3.9	2009 2.5	2318 0.8	2053 0.7	2041 0.4		
0527 0.4	0606 0.3	0101 7.1	0500 0.3	0445 0.1	0248 0.3	0521 7.1	0255 5.4	0241 5.0	6	TU
1139 4.8	1206 5.9	0757 0.3	1116 4.3	1124 4.1	0856 2.4	1136 0.9	0914 0.9	0858 0.6		
1739 0.6	1817 0.5	1332 7.3	1714 0.5	1700 0.3	1501 0.6	1726 7.4	1509 5.5	1452 5.2		
2342 4.8		2013 0.5	2330 4.3	2340 4.0	2058 2.6		2137 0.6	2125 0.4	●	
0610 0.4	0021 5.9	0148 7.2	0543 0.3	0528 0.1	0333 0.3	0004 0.7	0338 5.5	0323 5.1	7	W
1221 4.8	0649 0.3	0842 0.3	1200 4.3	1207 4.1	0936 2.5	0601 7.2	0958 0.8	0942 0.5		
1823 0.5	1250 6.0	1415 7.3	1758 0.4	1744 0.2	1546 0.4	1221 0.8	1554 5.6	1537 5.2		
	1902 0.4	2057 0.4			2146 2.6	1811 7.4	2220 0.7	2207 0.4		
0029 4.8	0105 6.0	0230 7.3	0015 4.3	0024 4.1	0414 0.3	0045 0.7	0419 5.5	0403 5.1	8	TH
0651 0.4	0730 0.3	0921 0.4	0625 0.3	0609 0.1	1017 2.5	0639 7.3	1040 0.8	1025 0.5		
1302 4.8	1330 6.0	1456 7.3	1242 4.3	1248 4.1	1630 0.4	1303 0.8	1638 5.5	1621 5.1		
1906 0.5	1945 0.3	2136 0.3	1842 0.4	1827 0.2	2234 2.5	1855 7.3	2300 0.9	2247 0.6		
0115 4.9	0148 6.0	0312 7.4	0058 4.3	0104 4.1	0453 0.3	0124 0.9	0459 5.4	0444 5.0	9	F
0730 0.5	0807 0.4	0954 0.5	0706 0.4	0651 0.3	1058 2.5	0718 7.2	1121 0.8	1107 0.6		
1340 4.8	1410 5.9	1535 7.3	1321 4.2	1327 4.0	1712 0.4	1343 0.9	1721 5.4	1706 5.0		
1948 0.5	2025 0.4	2209 0.3	1924 0.4	1910 0.2	2323 2.4	1939 7.1	2339 1.1	2325 0.8		
0158 4.8	0229 5.9	0352 7.4	0140 4.3	0145 4.1	0531 0.6	0200 1.2	0539 5.3	0524 4.9	10	SA
0809 0.7	0843 0.6	1023 0.6	0745 0.6	0730 0.4	1139 2.4	0755 7.0	1202 1.0	1148 0.7		
1418 4.7	1448 5.7	1613 7.2	1400 4.1	1403 3.9	1754 0.5	1421 1.1	1806 5.2	1751 4.8		
2030 0.6	2103 0.5	2240 0.5	2006 0.5	1952 0.3		2021 6.8				
0240 4.7	0310 5.7	0433 7.2	0221 4.1	0224 3.9	0012 2.3	0232 1.5	0018 1.1	0003 1.1	11	SU
0846 0.9	0915 0.9	1049 0.8	0822 0.8	0810 0.6	0609 0.7	0832 6.8	0621 5.1	0606 4.7		
1454 4.5	1527 5.5	1650 6.9	1437 3.9	1441 3.7	1218 2.4	1456 1.4	1244 1.2	1230 0.9		
2111 0.7	2138 0.7	2309 0.7	2047 0.6	2034 0.5	1836 0.5	2104 6.5	1853 5.0	1838 4.5		
0321 4.5	0351 5.4	0513 6.9	0303 3.9	0304 3.7	0105 2.2	0304 1.9	0059 1.7	0040 1.4	12	M
0924 1.1	0946 1.0	1118 1.0	0900 1.0	0849 0.8	0646 0.9	0909 6.5	0706 4.9	0648 4.5		
1530 4.4	1604 5.2	1727 6.6	1516 3.8	1518 3.6	1300 2.3	1533 1.7	1329 1.5	1313 1.2		
2153 0.9	2211 0.9	2339 0.8	2129 0.7	2116 0.6	1922 0.6	2150 6.1	1944 4.7	1927 4.3		
0405 4.3	0436 5.2	0555 6.6	0347 3.7	0346 3.5	0202 2.1	0340 2.2	0143 2.0	0123 1.7	13	TU
1005 1.3	1020 1.3	1152 1.2	0941 1.1	0930 1.0	0727 1.1	0952 6.2	0757 4.7	0736 4.3		
1614 4.2	1646 5.0	1807 6.2	1559 3.6	1557 3.4	1345 2.2	1615 2.0	1418 1.7	1403 1.4		
2242 1.1	2250 1.1		2216 0.8	2204 0.7	2014 0.7	2243 5.8	2039 4.5	2020 4.0		
0456 4.1	0524 4.9	0015 1.0	0436 3.6	0433 3.3	0305 2.1	0426 2.6	0234 2.2	0215 1.9	14	W
1056 1.5	1106 1.5	0643 6.3	1033 1.2	1021 1.1	0818 1.2	1045 5.9	0853 4.5	0832 4.1		
1709 4.0	1737 4.8	1233 1.4	1650 3.4	1645 3.2	1439 2.1	1714 2.3	1514 1.9	1503 1.6		
2342 1.2	2345 1.2	1857 6.0	2315 0.9	2303 0.8	2118 0.8	2349 5.6	2139 4.4	2122 3.9		
0559 3.9	0624 4.7	0100 1.2	0536 3.4	0532 3.2	0414 2.1	0528 2.9	0334 2.4	0323 2.1	15	TH
1200 1.6	1209 1.7	0741 6.0	1137 1.3	1127 1.2	0932 1.3	1153 5.7	0954 4.4	0937 3.9		
1816 3.9	1840 4.6	1324 1.6	1754 3.3	1746 3.1	1539 2.1		1618 1.9	1615 1.7		
		1959 5.7			2238 0.8		2240 4.4	2231 3.8		

MAY 1997 TIDE TABLES MAY 1997

	MARGATE	SHEERNESS	LONDON BRIDGE	WALTON-ON-THE-NAZE	HARWICH	LOWESTOFT	IMMINGHAM	RIVER TEES	RIVER TYNE
	Time m	Time m	Time m	Time m	Time m	Time m	Time m	Time m	Time m
16 F	0054 1.3	0102 1.3	0158 1.4	0027 0.9	0014 0.8	0527 2.1	0104 5.6	0443 2.4	0444 2.1
	0712 3.9	0733 4.6	0847 5.9	0650 3.4	0648 3.1	1110 1.3	0652 2.9	1057 4.4	1049 3.9
	1316 1.6	1332 1.7	1432 1.8	1256 1.3	1243 1.2	1645 2.1	1311 5.7	1723 1.9	1726 1.6
	1927 3.9	1954 4.6	2112 5.7	1912 3.3	1906 3.1	2346 0.8	1948 2.4	2340 4.4	2339 3.9
17 SA	0205 1.2	0222 1.2	0336 1.4	0142 0.9	0125 0.8	0631 2.1	0212 5.7	0551 2.3	0555 1.9
	0820 4.0	0843 4.8	0958 6.0	0803 3.5	0803 3.3	1211 1.2	0808 2.8	1157 4.5	1154 4.0
	1427 1.5	1449 1.6	1609 1.6	1407 1.2	1354 1.1	1753 2.1	1419 5.9	1822 1.8	1824 1.5
	2031 4.0	2104 4.7	2224 5.8	2021 3.4	2021 3.2		2048 2.1		
18 SU	0302 1.1	0326 1.1	0451 1.1	0241 0.8	0225 0.7	0037 0.8	0306 6.0	0034 4.6	0035 4.1
	0916 4.1	0943 5.0	1103 6.2	0859 3.6	0902 3.4	0718 2.2	0906 2.4	0649 2.1	0650 1.7
	1521 1.4	1548 1.3	1713 1.4	1501 1.0	1449 0.9	1254 1.1	1514 6.2	1250 4.6	1248 4.2
	2125 4.1	2202 5.0	2325 6.1	2115 3.6	2118 3.4	1849 2.2	2139 1.9	1913 1.6	1912 1.3
19 M	0349 1.0	0418 0.9	0545 0.9	0329 0.6	0314 0.6	0119 0.7	0351 6.3	0122 4.7	0120 4.3
	1002 4.3	1032 5.3	1153 6.4	0945 3.8	0949 3.6	0754 2.2	0954 2.1	0738 1.8	0733 1.5
	1607 1.2	1636 1.1	1806 1.1	1545 0.9	1533 0.8	1330 1.0	1559 6.4	1337 4.8	1332 4.4
	2212 4.3	2249 5.2		2200 3.8	2206 3.6	1935 2.2	2222 1.6	1959 1.4	1954 1.1
20 TU	0430 0.9	0502 0.8	0011 6.3	0410 0.6	0355 0.5	0156 0.7	0430 6.6	0204 4.9	0159 4.5
	1042 4.4	1115 5.5	0635 0.7	1025 4.0	1031 3.8	0821 2.3	1037 1.8	0821 1.6	0813 1.3
	1648 1.0	1720 0.9	1234 6.7	1626 0.7	1612 0.6	1406 0.9	1639 6.7	1420 5.0	1412 4.6
	2254 4.4	2331 5.4	1855 0.9	2241 4.0	2248 3.7	2016 2.3	2303 1.4	2040 1.3	2031 0.9
21 W	0509 0.8	0543 0.7	0051 6.6	0448 0.5	0433 0.4	0231 0.6	0506 6.8	0243 5.1	0235 4.7
	1120 4.6	1154 5.6	0722 0.6	1103 4.1	1110 3.9	0849 2.3	1119 1.5	0902 1.4	0850 1.1
	1727 0.9	1800 0.8	1312 6.9	1704 0.6	1651 0.5	1445 0.7	1718 6.8	1500 5.1	1449 4.7
	2333 4.6		1942 0.8	2321 4.1	2327 3.8	2056 2.4	2343 1.2	2121 1.1	2109 0.8
22 TH ○	0547 0.7	0011 5.6	0130 6.8	0526 0.5	0511 0.4	0308 0.5	0542 7.0	0321 5.2	0309 4.8
	1157 4.7	0622 0.6	0807 0.5	1141 4.2	1148 4.0	0921 2.4	1200 1.2	0941 1.2	0927 0.9
	1806 0.8	1233 5.7	1351 7.0	1742 0.6	1729 0.4	1527 0.6	1757 7.0	1539 5.2	1526 4.8
		1841 0.7	2028 0.6			2135 2.4		2200 1.0	2145 0.7
23 F	0012 4.7	0050 5.7	0209 7.0	0000 4.1	0007 3.9	0345 0.5	0022 1.1	0357 5.3	0345 4.9
	0625 0.7	0702 0.6	0851 0.5	0603 0.5	0549 0.4	0955 2.5	0618 7.1	1020 1.0	1005 0.7
	1234 4.8	1312 5.8	1430 7.2	1218 4.2	1227 4.0	1609 0.5	1241 1.0	1619 5.3	1605 4.9
	1846 0.7	1922 0.6	2112 0.5	1820 0.5	1808 0.4	2215 2.4	1836 7.1	2239 1.0	2223 0.7
24 SA	0051 4.8	0130 5.8	0248 7.2	0039 4.2	0047 4.0	0424 0.5	0101 1.0	0436 5.3	0421 5.0
	0705 0.7	0741 0.6	0933 0.4	0639 0.5	0627 0.4	1032 2.5	0654 7.2	1100 0.9	1044 0.7
	1312 4.8	1349 5.8	1508 7.3	1255 4.2	1306 4.0	1651 0.5	1322 1.0	1702 5.3	1646 4.9
	1928 0.7	2003 0.5	2152 0.5	1900 0.5	1848 0.4	2257 2.4	1917 7.0	2321 1.0	2303 0.7
25 SU	0133 4.8	0209 5.8	0329 7.3	0118 4.2	0127 4.0	0503 0.6	0140 1.1	0517 5.3	0500 4.9
	0747 0.7	0820 0.6	1011 0.5	0718 0.6	0706 0.5	1111 2.5	0733 7.1	1142 0.9	1126 0.6
	1353 4.8	1428 5.7	1548 7.2	1333 4.1	1344 3.9	1736 0.5	1403 1.0	1748 5.2	1730 4.8
	2012 0.7	2045 0.5	2230 0.5	1941 0.5	1928 0.3	2342 2.3	2000 7.0		2344 0.9
26 M	0218 4.8	0251 5.7	0411 7.3	0200 4.1	0208 3.9	0545 0.6	0221 1.2	0004 1.1	0542 4.9
	0830 0.8	0859 0.7	1046 0.7	0758 0.7	0746 0.5	1152 2.4	0814 7.0	0603 5.2	1211 0.7
	1436 4.7	1509 5.6	1628 7.1	1414 4.1	1424 3.8	1822 0.4	1446 1.1	1228 0.9	1819 4.7
	2059 0.7	2127 0.6	2306 0.6	2025 0.5	2012 0.4		2048 6.8	1839 5.1	
27 TU	0304 4.7	0337 5.6	0457 7.1	0245 4.1	0251 3.9	0033 2.3	0302 1.4	0051 1.3	0030 1.1
	0916 1.0	0940 0.8	1119 0.9	0842 0.8	0831 0.6	0629 0.8	0859 6.9	0652 5.1	0630 4.8
	1521 4.6	1554 5.5	1712 6.8	1458 3.9	1507 3.7	1236 2.4	1533 1.2	1318 1.0	1300 0.8
	2148 0.8	2213 0.6	2341 0.6	2114 0.5	2100 0.4	1913 0.5	2140 6.6	1935 4.9	1913 4.6
28 W	0356 4.5	0427 5.5	0546 6.8	0336 4.0	0340 3.8	0131 2.2	0349 1.7	0143 1.5	0121 1.3
	1006 1.1	1027 0.9	1157 1.1	0933 0.9	0921 0.7	0719 0.9	0950 6.7	0747 5.0	0724 4.6
	1611 4.5	1645 5.3	1802 6.6	1550 3.8	1556 3.6	1327 2.3	1625 1.4	1415 1.1	1357 0.9
	2245 0.9	2307 0.7		2211 0.6	2157 0.4	2009 0.5	2243 6.3	2036 4.8	2014 4.4
29 TH	0453 4.4	0526 5.3	0024 0.9	0433 3.9	0436 3.7	0239 2.2	0444 2.0	0242 1.7	0221 1.4
	1104 1.2	1124 1.1	0643 6.6	1033 1.0	1021 0.9	0818 1.0	1050 6.5	0848 4.8	0826 4.5
	1709 4.4	1745 5.2	1246 1.3	1650 3.7	1654 3.5	1425 2.3	1727 1.6	1518 1.2	1503 1.0
	2352 0.9		1900 6.4	2316 0.6	2302 0.5	2113 0.5	2357 6.2	2141 4.7	2121 4.3
30 F	0600 4.3	0012 0.8	0122 0.9	0539 3.8	0542 3.6	0354 2.2	0550 2.1	0348 1.8	0331 1.6
	1212 1.3	0633 5.2	0749 6.5	1141 1.0	1130 0.9	0928 1.0	1200 6.4	0953 4.8	0935 4.4
	1816 4.3	1232 1.2	1352 1.3	1758 3.7	1800 3.5	1532 2.2	1837 1.6	1627 1.3	1616 1.1
		1853 5.1	2008 6.3			2222 0.5		2248 4.7	2234 4.3
31 SA	0105 0.8	0124 0.8	0238 0.9	0030 0.6	0015 0.5	0506 2.2	0112 6.2	0459 1.8	0446 1.5
	0715 4.3	0745 5.3	0902 6.6	0654 3.8	0653 3.6	1042 1.0	0704 2.2	1100 4.8	1048 4.4
	1325 1.3	1345 1.2	1510 1.2	1257 1.0	1244 0.9	1644 2.3	1315 6.4	1738 1.2	1730 1.0
	1927 4.4	2006 5.1	2123 6.4	1913 3.7	1911 3.5	2333 0.5	1950 1.6	2352 4.8	2343 4.4

● ● Time UT. For British Summer Time (shaded) March 30th to October 26th ADD ONE HOUR ● ●

EAST COAST OF ENGLAND Time Zone UT

Margate * Sheerness * London Bridge *Walton-on-the-Naze * Harwich * Lowestoft * Immingham * RiverTees * RiverTyne

JUNE 1997 TIDE TABLES JUNE 1997

MARGATE	SHEERNESS	LONDON BRIDGE	WALTON-ON-THE-NAZE	HARWICH	LOWESTOFT	IMMINGHAM	RIVER TEES	RIVER TYNE	Day
Time m	Time m	Time m	Time m	Time m	Time m	Time m	Time m	Time m	
0216 0.7	0238 0.7	0355 0.7	0148 0.6	0130 0.4	0612 2.2	0221 6.3	0609 1.7	0557 1.4	1 SU
0826 4.4	0856 5.4	1015 6.8	0807 3.9	0806 3.7	1151 1.0	0818 2.0	1205 4.9	1157 4.5	
1435 1.1	1457 1.0	1624 1.0	1412 0.9	1355 0.8	1754 2.3	1425 6.5	1842 1.1	1835 0.9	
2034 4.4	2117 5.3	2238 6.6	2026 3.8	2025 3.6		2100 1.4			
0321 0.6	0348 0.6	0513 0.6	0257 0.5	0238 0.4	0039 0.5	0321 6.5	0052 5.0	0043 4.6	2 M
0931 4.5	1000 5.5	1123 7.0	0912 4.0	0915 3.8	0708 2.3	0926 1.7	0710 1.5	0658 1.2	
1538 0.9	1605 0.9	1740 0.9	1515 0.8	1500 0.7	1257 0.9	1527 6.7	1306 5.0	1257 4.7	
2136 4.5	2220 5.4	2345 6.7	2130 3.9	2135 3.7	1857 2.3	2202 1.3	1939 1.0	1931 0.8	
0418 0.6	0449 0.6	0633 0.6	0353 0.4	0337 0.3	0138 0.5	0414 6.7	0145 5.1	0136 4.7	3 TU
1028 4.6	1057 5.7	1221 7.1	1009 4.1	1014 3.9	0754 2.3	1024 1.5	0805 1.2	0752 1.0	
1633 0.8	1704 0.8	1855 0.7	1610 0.7	1556 0.6	1355 0.8	1621 6.9	1400 5.2	1350 4.8	
2234 4.5	2315 5.6		2224 4.0	2232 3.8	1954 2.4	2254 1.2	2030 1.0	2021 0.8	
0507 0.6	0540 0.6	0042 6.8	0441 0.4	0427 0.3	0227 0.5	0500 6.9	0233 5.2	0221 4.9	4 W
1118 4.6	1146 5.7	0730 0.6	1057 4.2	1103 4.0	0836 2.4	1116 1.2	0854 1.1	0841 0.8	
1722 0.7	1757 0.6	1312 7.1	1659 0.6	1645 0.4	1446 0.6	1710 7.0	1451 5.3	1438 4.9	
2327 4.6		1950 0.6	2314 4.1	2321 3.9	2045 2.4	2341 1.1	2115 0.9	2106 0.7	
0550 0.6	0004 5.7	0130 6.9	0524 0.5	0510 0.3	0311 0.5	0540 7.0	0318 5.3	0304 5.0	5 TH
1200 4.6	0624 0.5	0817 0.6	1142 4.2	1148 4.0	0917 2.5	1203 1.1	0939 1.0	0927 0.7	
1806 0.6	1231 5.8	1357 7.0	1744 0.5	1730 0.3	1533 0.5	1757 7.1	1536 5.3	1524 5.0	●
	1843 0.5	2036 0.5			2136 2.5		2157 1.0	2147 0.8	
0014 4.7	0049 5.8	0214 7.0	0000 4.2	0006 4.0	0352 0.5	0023 1.1	0359 5.3	0345 5.0	6 F
0630 0.7	0705 0.6	0856 0.7	0606 0.5	0551 0.4	0957 2.5	0619 7.1	1022 0.9	1010 0.6	
1239 4.7	1312 5.8	1437 7.1	1224 4.2	1229 4.0	1616 0.4	1246 1.0	1621 5.3	1608 4.9	
1849 0.5	1927 0.5	2115 0.5	1827 0.4	1813 0.3	2224 2.4	1841 7.0	2237 1.1	2226 0.8	
0058 4.7	0132 5.8	0255 7.1	0042 4.2	0048 4.0	0431 0.6	0102 1.2	0439 5.3	0424 5.0	7 SA
0708 0.7	0742 0.6	0930 0.7	0645 0.6	0631 0.4	1038 2.5	0657 7.1	1103 0.9	1051 0.7	
1317 4.7	1351 5.7	1515 7.1	1303 4.1	1307 4.0	1659 0.4	1327 1.0	1703 5.2	1651 4.8	
1931 0.5	2009 0.5	2151 0.4	1909 0.4	1856 0.3	2312 2.4	1924 6.9	2315 1.3	2303 1.0	
0141 4.7	0212 5.7	0335 7.2	0123 4.1	0127 3.9	0508 0.7	0138 1.4	0518 5.3	0503 4.9	8 SU
0746 0.8	0819 0.7	1000 0.7	0722 0.7	0710 0.6	1117 2.5	0735 7.0	1143 1.0	1130 0.8	
1354 4.7	1429 5.7	1552 7.1	1339 4.1	1344 3.9	1739 0.5	1405 1.2	1745 5.1	1733 4.7	
2012 0.6	2048 0.6	2222 0.5	1950 0.5	1936 0.3	2358 2.3	2006 6.7	2353 1.4	2339 1.2	
0221 4.6	0252 5.6	0413 7.1	0202 4.1	0205 3.9	0542 0.8	0211 1.6	0558 5.2	0542 4.8	9 M
0823 0.9	0852 0.8	1029 0.8	0758 0.8	0748 0.7	1154 2.4	0811 6.8	1224 1.2	1209 0.9	
1431 4.6	1506 5.5	1627 6.9	1415 4.0	1419 3.8	1819 0.5	1440 1.4	1830 4.9	1815 4.5	
2052 0.7	2122 0.7	2251 0.6	2028 0.6	2015 0.4		2045 6.5			
0300 4.5	0331 5.4	0451 6.9	0241 3.9	0242 3.7	0044 2.2	0242 1.8	0032 1.6	0015 1.3	10 TU
0900 1.1	0923 1.0	1058 1.0	0833 1.0	0824 0.8	0615 0.9	0847 6.6	0641 5.0	0621 4.6	
1507 4.4	1541 5.3	1703 6.6	1451 3.9	1454 3.7	1230 2.4	1515 1.6	1306 1.3	1248 1.0	
2132 0.8	2153 0.8	2321 0.8	2106 0.6	2054 0.5	1900 0.6	2124 6.2	1915 4.8	1857 4.3	
0339 4.3	0410 5.2	0530 6.7	0320 3.8	0321 3.6	0131 2.1	0316 2.0	0113 1.8	0052 1.5	11 W
0936 1.2	0954 1.2	1130 1.1	0911 1.0	0901 0.9	0650 1.0	0925 6.4	0727 4.9	0703 4.4	
1545 4.3	1618 5.1	1740 6.4	1528 3.8	1529 3.5	1310 2.3	1552 1.8	1350 1.5	1330 1.2	
2213 1.0	2227 1.0	2354 0.9	2146 0.7	2134 0.6	1942 0.7	2207 6.0	2005 4.6	1943 4.0	
0421 4.2	0451 5.1	0612 6.4	0401 3.7	0400 3.5	0221 2.1	0354 2.3	0159 2.0	0136 1.7	12 TH
1019 1.4	1033 1.3	1207 1.2	0954 1.1	0944 1.0	0730 1.1	1009 6.1	0818 4.7	0751 4.3	
1630 4.2	1700 4.9	1822 6.1	1611 3.6	1609 3.4	1356 2.2	1636 2.1	1439 1.7	1418 1.4	
2300 1.1	2309 1.1		2233 0.8	2221 0.7	2028 0.7	2257 5.8	2057 4.5	2034 4.0	
0511 4.0	0539 4.9	0033 1.0	0448 3.6	0445 3.4	0315 2.1	0441 2.6	0251 2.2	0228 1.9	13 F
1111 1.5	1121 1.5	0700 6.2	1046 1.2	1036 1.1	0820 1.2	1101 5.9	0912 4.6	0845 4.1	
1725 4.0	1751 4.8	1250 1.4	1700 3.5	1655 3.3	1449 2.2	1730 2.3	1532 1.8	1514 1.5	
2357 1.2		1912 5.9	2328 0.8	2318 0.7	2124 0.8	2357 5.6	2154 4.4	2131 3.9	
0609 4.0	0004 1.2	0120 1.1	0543 3.5	0540 3.3	0415 2.0	0541 2.6	0350 2.3	0333 2.0	14 SA
1212 1.6	0634 4.7	0756 6.0	1148 1.2	1141 1.2	0924 1.3	1205 5.8	1009 4.5	0947 4.0	
1827 3.9	1222 1.6	1340 1.5	1800 3.4	1755 3.2	1549 2.1	1838 2.4	1630 1.9	1618 1.6	
	1851 4.7	2014 5.7			2231 0.9		2251 4.4	2234 3.9	
0059 1.2	0111 1.2	0216 1.2	0033 0.9	0023 0.8	0518 2.1	0103 5.7	0454 2.3	0445 2.0	15 SU
0712 4.0	0737 4.7	0857 5.9	0649 3.5	0648 3.2	1044 1.3	0656 2.8	1109 4.5	1051 4.0	
1321 1.6	1336 1.6	1441 1.6	1257 1.2	1249 1.1	1654 2.1	1315 5.8	1731 1.8	1724 1.5	
1933 3.9	1958 4.7	2121 5.7	1911 3.4	1909 3.2	2336 0.9	1947 2.3	2348 4.5	2336 4.0	

● ●Time UT. For British Summer Time (shaded) March 30th to October 26th ADD ONE HOUR ● ●

JUNE 1997 TIDE TABLES JUNE 1997

	MARGATE	SHEERNESS	LONDON BRIDGE	WALTON-ON-THE-NAZE	HARWICH	LOWESTOFT	IMMINGHAM	RIVER TEES	RIVER TYN
	Time m	Time m	Time m	Time m	Time m	Time m	Time m	Time m	Time m
16 M	0200 1.2 0814 4.0 1424 1.4 2033 4.0	0222 1.2 0842 4.8 1448 1.5 2105 4.8	0330 1.3 0959 6.0 1600 1.6 2223 5.8	0142 0.8 0758 3.6 1406 1.1 2020 3.5	0127 0.7 0758 3.3 1353 1.0 2020 3.3	0615 2.1 1153 1.2 1757 2.2	0206 5.8 0807 2.6 1420 6.0 2046 2.1	0558 2.2 1206 4.6 1829 1.7	0554 1.? 1154 4.? 1824 1.?
17 TU	0257 1.1 0910 4.2 1521 1.3 2128 4.2	0326 1.1 0942 5.1 1550 1.3 2204 5.1	0445 1.1 1057 6.2 1709 1.3 2320 6.1	0242 0.8 0857 3.7 1504 1.0 2118 3.7	0224 0.7 0859 3.5 1448 0.9 2121 3.5	0027 0.8 0701 2.2 1245 1.1 1854 2.2	0301 6.1 0906 2.3 1515 6.2 2139 1.9	0041 4.6 0657 2.0 1259 4.7 1922 1.6	0032 4.? 0650 1.? 1249 4.? 1914 1.?
18 W	0347 1.0 1001 4.4 1612 1.1 2219 4.3	0421 0.9 1036 5.4 1643 1.0 2256 5.3	0545 0.9 1150 6.4 1809 1.1	0333 0.7 0948 3.9 1553 0.8 2208 3.9	0316 0.6 0951 3.7 1539 0.7 2213 3.7	0112 0.8 0741 2.3 1333 0.9 1944 2.3	0351 6.4 0959 2.0 1606 6.5 2227 1.6	0130 4.8 0749 1.7 1348 4.9 2011 1.4	0120 4.? 0738 1.? 1337 4.? 1959 1.?
19 TH	0434 0.9 1048 4.5 1659 1.0 2306 4.5	0509 0.8 1124 5.6 1733 0.9 2344 5.5	0012 6.3 0642 0.7 1239 6.7 1908 0.9	0418 0.6 1033 4.0 1638 0.7 2254 4.0	0403 0.5 1039 3.8 1624 0.6 2300 3.8	0155 0.7 0818 2.4 1420 0.8 2030 2.3	0435 6.7 1049 1.6 1652 6.7 2314 1.3	0215 5.0 0836 1.5 1436 5.0 2057 1.2	0203 4.6 0822 1.2 1422 4.? 2042 0.?
20 F O	0519 0.8 1133 4.7 1745 0.8 2352 4.6	0556 0.7 1209 5.7 1820 0.7	0101 6.6 0737 0.6 1326 6.9 2004 0.7	0500 0.6 1116 4.1 1721 0.6 2338 4.1	0446 0.5 1124 3.9 1709 0.5 2346 3.9	0238 0.6 0855 2.4 1507 0.6 2115 2.4	0517 6.9 1137 1.3 1737 6.9 2359 1.1	0257 5.2 0921 1.2 1520 5.2 2141 1.1	0242 4.8 0905 0.9 1505 4.8 2124 0.?
21 SA	0603 0.7 1215 4.8 1830 0.7	0029 5.7 0640 0.6 1252 5.8 1907 0.5	0148 6.9 0829 0.4 1410 7.1 2055 0.5	0540 0.6 1158 4.2 1803 0.5	0529 0.5 1208 4.0 1753 0.4	0321 0.6 0933 2.5 1554 0.5 2200 2.4	0557 7.1 1224 1.0 1822 7.1	0339 5.3 1006 1.0 1605 5.3 2224 1.0	0322 5.0 0948 0.? 1548 5.0 2206 0.7
22 SU	0038 4.8 0648 0.6 1259 4.8 1918 0.6	0114 5.8 0724 0.6 1335 5.8 1954 0.4	0233 7.2 0917 0.4 1454 7.3 2143 0.3	0022 4.2 0621 0.6 1239 4.2 1848 0.4	0031 4.0 0610 0.4 1251 4.0 1836 0.3	0405 0.5 1013 2.5 1642 0.4 2246 2.4	0044 1.0 0639 7.2 1311 0.9 1908 7.1	0421 5.4 1050 0.8 1651 5.4 2308 0.9	0403 5.1 1032 0.5 1633 5.0 2250 0.7
23 M	0124 4.8 0734 0.6 1342 4.9 2006 0.5	0158 5.9 0808 0.5 1417 5.8 2041 0.3	0317 7.4 1002 0.4 1536 7.3 2228 0.3	0106 4.3 0703 0.6 1322 4.2 1933 0.4	0115 4.1 0652 0.4 1333 4.0 1920 0.2	0449 0.6 1054 2.6 1729 0.3 2334 2.4	0127 1.0 0721 7.3 1357 0.8 1955 7.1	0505 5.5 1135 0.7 1739 5.3 2353 1.0	0445 5.1 1118 0.4 1720 5.0 2334 0.8
24 TU	0212 4.8 0821 0.7 1427 4.8 2054 0.5	0243 5.9 0851 0.6 1500 5.8 2128 0.3	0403 7.4 1044 0.5 1619 7.2 2311 0.4	0151 4.3 0746 0.6 1406 4.2 2020 0.3	0159 4.1 0735 0.5 1415 4.0 2006 0.2	0533 0.6 1137 2.6 1816 0.3	0212 1.0 0804 7.3 1443 0.8 2044 7.0	0551 5.5 1222 0.7 1829 5.2	0530 5.1 1204 0.4 1809 4.9
25 W	0300 4.8 0908 0.8 1512 4.7 2145 0.6	0330 5.8 0936 0.7 1545 5.7 2216 0.4	0449 7.3 1123 0.6 1704 7.1 2351 0.5	0238 4.2 0833 0.7 1451 4.1 2109 0.4	0244 4.0 0821 0.5 1459 3.9 2053 0.2	0025 2.4 0618 0.7 1222 2.5 1905 0.3	0256 1.2 0850 7.2 1530 0.9 2135 6.8	0040 1.1 0639 5.4 1312 0.8 1923 5.1	0021 0.9 0618 5.0 1254 0.5 1902 4.8
26 TH	0350 4.6 0956 1.0 1600 4.6 2236 0.6	0420 5.7 1021 0.8 1635 5.5 2305 0.5	0538 7.1 1200 1.0 1752 6.8	0327 4.1 0922 0.8 1541 4.0 2203 0.4	0332 3.9 0909 0.6 1546 3.8 2145 0.3	0120 2.3 0706 0.8 1311 2.5 1957 0.3	0341 1.4 0939 7.0 1618 1.1 2231 6.6	0130 1.3 0733 5.2 1405 0.9 2020 4.9	0109 1.1 0709 4.9 1346 0.7 1957 4.6
27 F	0442 4.5 1047 1.1 1651 4.5 2333 0.7	0514 5.5 1112 0.9 1729 5.4 2359 0.5	0031 0.7 0630 6.8 1242 1.1 1845 6.8	0421 4.0 1016 0.9 1636 3.9 2301 0.5	0424 3.8 1003 0.8 1639 3.8 2244 0.4	0221 2.2 0759 0.9 1405 2.4 2053 0.4	0430 1.7 1033 6.8 1711 1.3 2334 6.3	0224 1.5 0830 5.1 1503 1.1 2120 4.8	0204 1.3 0807 4.7 1444 0.9 2059 4.4
28 SA	0540 4.4 1145 1.2 1751 4.5	0613 5.4 1209 1.0 1830 5.3	0117 0.8 0730 6.7 1335 1.2 1945 6.5	0521 3.9 1117 1.0 1736 3.8	0523 3.7 1104 0.9 1739 3.7 2351 0.4	0330 2.2 0900 1.0 1508 2.4 2156 0.5	0527 1.9 1136 6.6 1811 1.5	0324 1.6 0932 4.9 1606 1.2 2224 4.7	0306 1.4 0912 4.6 1550 1.1 2206 4.3
29 SU	0039 0.7 0645 4.3 1254 1.2 1857 4.4	0100 0.7 0718 5.3 1315 1.1 1939 5.2	0215 0.8 0836 6.6 1440 1.2 2054 6.5	0008 0.6 0627 3.8 1227 1.0 1845 3.8	0628 3.6 1215 0.9 1845 3.6	0439 2.2 1009 1.0 1621 2.3 2305 0.6	0042 6.2 0633 2.1 1248 6.4 1919 1.7	0431 1.7 1038 4.8 1713 1.3 2328 4.7	0415 1.5 1023 4.5 1701 1.2 2315 4.3
30 M	0148 0.7 0754 4.3 1408 1.1 2008 4.3	0209 0.8 0827 5.3 1427 1.1 2051 5.2	0324 0.8 0945 6.6 1552 1.2 2209 6.5	0124 0.6 0739 3.8 1346 1.0 2000 3.8	0105 0.5 0738 3.6 1329 0.9 1959 3.6	0545 2.2 1124 1.0 1735 2.3	0150 6.2 0746 2.1 1400 6.4 2030 1.8	0542 1.7 1145 4.8 1819 1.3	0529 1.5 1134 4.5 1811 1.2

● ● Time UT. For British Summer Time (shaded) March 30th to October 26th ADD ONE HOUR ● ●

EAST COAST OF ENGLAND Time Zone UT

Margate * Sheerness * London Bridge *Walton-on-the-Naze * Harwich * Lowestoft * Immingham * RiverTees * RiverTyne

JULY 1997 TIDE TABLES JULY 1997

Day	MARGATE Time	m	SHEERNESS Time	m	LONDON BRIDGE Time	m	WALTON-ON-THE-NAZE Time	m	HARWICH Time	m	LOWESTOFT Time	m	IMMINGHAM Time	m	RIVER TEES Time	m	RIVER TYNE Time	m
1 TU	0256	0.8	0319	0.8	0436	0.8	0234	0.6	0216	0.5	0015	0.7	0254	6.3	0030	4.8	0019	4.4
	0904	4.3	0934	5.3	1056	6.7	0849	3.9	0850	3.7	0645	2.3	0900	2.0	0648	1.6	0638	1.4
	1517	1.0	1540	1.0	1707	1.0	1457	0.9	1441	0.8	1240	0.9	1509	6.5	1248	4.9	1240	4.5
	2118	4.3	2159	5.3	2322	6.5	2110	3.8	2114	3.6	1846	2.3	2136	1.7	1920	1.3	1912	1.2
2 W	0358	0.8	0424	0.8	0556	0.8	0334	0.6	0320	0.5	0118	0.7	0352	6.5	0127	4.9	0116	4.6
	1007	4.4	1036	5.4	1200	6.8	0949	4.0	0952	3.8	0736	2.3	1004	1.7	0748	1.4	0737	1.2
	1620	0.9	1645	0.9	1827	0.9	1557	0.8	1543	0.7	1344	0.8	1609	6.6	1347	4.9	1338	4.6
	2224	4.4	2300	5.4			2210	3.9	2215	3.7	1948	2.3	2233	1.6	2012	1.2	2004	1.1
3 TH	0452	0.8	0518	0.8	0024	6.6	0425	0.6	0412	0.5	0209	0.7	0441	6.7	0218	5.0	0206	4.7
	1100	4.4	1129	5.6	0702	0.8	1041	4.0	1045	3.8	0821	2.4	1100	1.5	0840	1.2	0829	1.0
	1712	0.8	1741	0.8	1254	6.8	1648	0.6	1635	0.5	1436	0.7	1701	6.7	1439	5.0	1429	4.7
	2319	4.4	2351	5.5	1929	0.7	2302	4.0	2307	3.8	2042	2.4	2321	1.5	2059	1.2	2049	1.1
4 F	0536	0.8	0603	0.8	0115	6.7	0509	0.7	0457	0.6	0254	0.7	0523	6.9	0304	5.1	0249	4.8
	1144	4.5	1215	5.6	0751	0.8	1127	4.1	1131	3.9	0901	2.5	1148	1.3	0926	1.1	0915	0.9
	1757	0.7	1829	0.7	1339	6.8	1733	0.6	1720	0.4	1522	0.6	1747	6.8	1525	5.1	1514	4.8
					2016	0.6	2347	4.1	2352	3.9	2130	2.4			2140	1.2	2130	1.0
●																		
5 SA	0005	4.5	0036	5.6	0200	6.8	0548	0.7	0536	0.6	0333	0.7	0003	1.4	0345	5.2	0329	4.9
	0613	0.8	0644	0.8	0832	0.8	1207	4.1	1212	3.9	0940	2.5	0602	7.0	1008	1.0	0957	0.8
	1221	4.6	1257	5.7	1421	6.9	1814	0.5	1802	0.4	1604	0.5	1232	1.2	1607	5.1	1555	4.8
	1837	0.6	1912	0.6	2057	0.5					2215	2.4	1830	6.8	2218	1.2	2207	1.0
6 SU	0045	4.6	0118	5.7	0240	6.9	0028	4.1	0033	3.9	0411	0.7	0042	1.4	0423	5.3	0406	5.0
	0649	0.8	0721	0.7	0908	0.8	0624	0.7	0615	0.6	1018	2.6	0639	7.1	1048	0.9	1035	0.8
	1257	4.6	1335	5.7	1457	7.0	1244	4.1	1250	3.9	1645	0.5	1312	1.1	1647	5.1	1634	4.8
	1916	0.6	1953	0.5	2134	0.5	1853	0.5	1841	0.3	2258	2.3	1909	6.8	2254	1.3	2242	1.1
7 M	0124	4.6	0157	5.7	0318	7.1	0106	4.1	0110	3.9	0446	0.8	0118	1.4	0500	5.3	0442	4.9
	0724	0.8	0757	0.8	0941	0.8	0700	0.8	0651	0.6	1054	2.5	0715	7.0	1124	1.0	1111	0.8
	1334	4.6	1411	5.6	1533	7.0	1319	4.1	1325	3.9	1723	0.5	1348	1.2	1725	5.0	1712	4.7
	1954	0.6	2030	0.6	2207	0.5	1930	0.5	1918	0.3	2339	2.3	1946	6.7	2329	1.3	2316	1.2
8 TU	0202	4.6	0233	5.6	0354	7.1	0142	4.1	0146	3.8	0518	0.8	0151	1.5	0536	5.2	0518	4.9
	0800	0.9	0830	0.8	1012	0.8	0733	0.8	0726	0.7	1130	2.5	0750	7.0	1202	1.0	1146	0.9
	1409	4.6	1445	5.5	1606	6.9	1352	4.1	1359	3.8	1759	0.5	1422	1.3	1803	4.9	1749	4.6
	2032	0.7	2103	0.6	2236	0.6	2006	0.5	1954	0.4			2021	6.6			2348	1.3
9 W	0238	4.5	0309	5.5	0429	7.0	0216	4.0	0221	3.8	0017	2.2	0222	1.7	0005	1.4	0554	4.8
	0835	1.0	0901	0.9	1041	0.9	0808	0.9	0759	0.7	0546	0.9	0824	6.8	0615	5.1	1221	0.9
	1443	4.5	1518	5.4	1639	6.8	1425	4.0	1430	3.8	1203	2.5	1454	1.4	1239	1.2	1827	4.5
	2107	0.8	2133	0.7	2304	0.7	2040	0.6	2028	0.4	1833	0.6	2056	6.5	1844	4.8		
10 TH	0312	4.4	0343	5.4	0504	6.8	0251	3.9	0254	3.7	0054	2.2	0254	1.8	0043	1.6	0022	1.4
	0909	1.1	0931	1.1	1110	1.0	0842	0.9	0833	0.8	0616	1.0	0858	6.6	0655	5.0	0632	4.6
	1518	4.4	1551	5.3	1714	6.6	1459	3.9	1503	3.7	1239	2.4	1527	1.6	1318	1.3	1257	1.1
	2142	0.9	2203	0.8	2334	0.8	2115	0.6	2104	0.5	1907	0.6	2131	6.3	1927	4.7	1906	4.4
11 F	0346	4.3	0419	5.2	0541	6.6	0327	3.8	0328	3.6	0133	2.1	0327	2.0	0123	1.7	0059	1.5
	0943	1.2	1004	1.2	1143	1.1	0919	1.0	0909	0.9	0652	1.0	0935	6.4	0739	4.8	0713	4.5
	1556	4.3	1627	5.1	1750	6.3	1536	3.8	1537	3.6	1320	2.4	1601	1.9	1400	1.5	1336	1.3
	2219	1.0	2237	0.9			2154	0.7	2143	0.6	1945	0.7	2211	6.1	2013	4.5	1950	4.2
12 SA	0427	4.2	0458	5.1	0009	0.8	0406	3.8	0406	3.5	0216	2.1	0403	2.3	0207	1.9	0142	1.7
	1024	1.3	1042	1.3	0621	6.4	1002	1.1	0951	1.0	0736	1.1	1016	6.2	0827	4.6	0759	4.3
	1641	4.2	1706	5.0	1219	1.2	1617	3.7	1617	3.5	1406	2.3	1640	2.1	1448	1.7	1423	1.4
	2303	1.1	2318	1.1	1830	6.1	2239	0.8	2230	0.7	2028	0.8	2257	5.9	2104	4.4	2039	4.1
13 SU	0515	4.1	0543	4.9	0047	0.9	0451	3.6	0451	3.4	0308	2.1	0448	2.5	0258	2.1	0233	1.9
	1115	1.5	1129	1.5	0704	6.1	1053	1.2	1043	1.1	0829	1.2	1106	5.9	0921	4.5	0852	4.2
	1733	4.0	1755	4.8	1300	1.3	1707	3.6	1706	3.4	1501	2.2	1730	2.3	1540	1.8	1518	1.6
	2359	1.2			1915	5.9	2335	0.9	2327	0.8	2121	0.9	2356	5.7	2200	4.3	2134	4.0
14 M	0611	4.0	0009	1.2	0132	1.1	0546	3.5	0546	3.3	0408	2.1	0546	2.7	0357	2.2	0337	2.0
	1219	1.5	0638	4.8	0755	5.9	1154	1.2	1150	1.2	0934	1.3	1212	5.8	1020	4.4	0953	4.1
	1833	3.9	1228	1.6	1349	1.5	1808	3.5	1808	3.3	1606	2.2	1836	2.4	1641	1.9	1622	1.7
			1857	4.7	2013	5.7					2227	0.9			2300	4.4	2237	4.0
15 TU	0102	1.3	0115	1.3	0227	1.2	0042	0.9	0034	0.8	0510	2.1	0104	5.7	0505	2.2	0451	2.0
	0715	4.0	0743	4.8	0858	5.8	0653	3.5	0654	3.3	1053	1.2	0702	2.7	1122	4.4	1100	4.1
	1330	1.5	1344	1.6	1451	1.6	1306	1.2	1301	1.1	1713	2.2	1326	5.8	1745	1.9	1731	1.7
	1941	3.9	2009	4.8	2124	5.7	1921	3.5	1922	3.3	2336	0.9	1950	2.4			2342	4.1

● ● Time UT. For British Summer Time (shaded) March 30th to October 26th ADD ONE HOUR ● ●

JULY 1997 TIDE TABLES JULY 1997

	MARGATE	SHEERNESS	LONDON BRIDGE	WALTON-ON-THE-NAZE	HARWICH	LOWESTOFT	IMMINGHAM	RIVER TEES	RIVER TYN
	Time m	Time m	Time m	Time m	Time m	Time m	Time m	Time m	Time m
16 W	0206 1.2	0232 1.2	0342 1.3	0152 0.9	0139 0.8	0609 2.2	0212 5.9	0000 4.5	0604 1.8
	0821 4.1	0852 4.9	1004 6.0	0805 3.6	0806 3.4	1204 1.1	0818 2.5	0615 2.1	1207 4.2
	1436 1.4	1503 1.4	1612 1.5	1418 1.1	1407 1.0	1817 2.2	1435 6.0	1224 4.6	1835 1.5
	2047 4.1	2120 4.9	2232 5.9	2033 3.6	2036 3.4		2056 2.1	1849 1.7	
17 TH	0307 1.1	0341 1.1	0500 1.1	0255 0.8	0240 0.7	0033 0.9	0313 6.3	0057 4.7	0041 4.3
	0923 4.3	0957 5.2	1108 6.2	0909 3.8	0912 3.6	0703 2.3	0924 2.1	0720 1.8	0705 1.8
	1538 1.2	1609 1.1	1727 1.2	1521 0.9	1507 0.8	1304 1.0	1536 6.3	1323 4.7	1306 4.4
	2148 4.2	2224 5.2	2337 6.2	2136 3.8	2140 3.6	1916 2.2	2154 1.8	1946 1.5	1930 1.3
18 F	0403 1.0	0439 0.9	0606 0.9	0349 0.8	0335 0.6	0124 0.8	0407 6.6	0150 4.9	0133 4.6
	1019 4.5	1055 5.5	1209 6.5	1004 3.9	1010 3.7	0748 2.4	1022 1.7	0815 1.5	0757 1.2
	1634 1.0	1707 0.9	1836 0.9	1614 0.8	1601 0.7	1358 0.8	1632 6.7	1415 5.0	1359 4.6
	2244 4.5	2320 5.5		2230 4.0	2237 3.8	2009 2.3	2249 1.5	2037 1.3	2019 1.1
19 SA	0456 0.8	0533 0.7	0037 6.6	0436 0.7	0425 0.6	0212 0.7	0454 6.9	0238 5.2	0218 4.8
	1109 4.6	1147 5.7	0710 0.6	1054 4.1	1102 3.9	0831 2.5	1118 1.3	0905 1.1	0846 0.5
	1727 0.9	1802 0.7	1304 6.9	1703 0.6	1651 0.5	1451 0.6	1722 6.9	1505 5.2	1447 4.8
	2336 4.7		1943 0.7	2319 4.1	2328 3.9	2100 2.4	2340 1.2	2124 1.0	2106 0.9
20 SU	0545 0.7	0011 5.7	0130 7.0	0521 0.6	0512 0.5	0300 0.6	0539 7.2	0323 5.4	0302 5.1
	1157 4.8	0622 0.6	0810 0.4	1140 4.2	1151 4.0	0913 2.6	1210 1.0	0952 0.8	0933 0.6
	1817 0.6	1235 5.8	1354 7.1	1749 0.5	1739 0.3	1541 0.5	1810 7.1	1552 5.4	1533 5.1
○		1854 0.5	2042 0.4			2147 2.5		2210 0.9	2151 0.7
21 M	0025 4.8	0059 5.9	0218 7.3	0006 4.3	0016 4.1	0348 0.6	0029 1.0	0406 5.6	0345 5.3
	0633 0.6	0710 0.5	0903 0.3	0604 0.6	0555 0.4	0954 2.6	0623 7.4	1038 0.6	1019 0.4
	1242 4.9	1320 5.9	1439 7.4	1225 4.3	1236 4.1	1630 0.3	1300 0.7	1639 5.5	1619 5.2
	1906 0.4	1945 0.3	2133 0.2	1836 0.3	1824 0.2	2234 2.5	1858 7.3	2254 0.8	2236 0.6
22 TU	0114 4.9	0145 6.0	0305 7.5	0053 4.4	0102 4.2	0434 0.6	0115 0.9	0451 5.7	0428 5.4
	0720 0.6	0757 0.5	0951 0.3	0648 0.6	0639 0.4	1037 2.7	0706 7.5	1124 0.4	1106 0.2
	1328 4.9	1404 6.0	1523 7.5	1309 4.3	1321 4.1	1717 0.2	1347 0.5	1725 5.5	1706 5.2
	1954 0.3	2034 0.3	2221 0.0	1922 0.2	1909 0.1	2321 2.5	1945 7.3	2339 0.8	2321 0.6
23 W	0203 4.9	0232 6.1	0350 7.6	0139 4.4	0148 4.2	0519 0.6	0200 0.9	0536 5.7	0513 5.4
	0807 0.6	0842 0.5	1036 0.4	0733 0.6	0721 0.4	1121 2.7	0750 7.5	1209 0.4	1151 0.2
	1414 4.9	1448 6.0	1606 7.5	1354 4.3	1403 4.1	1803 0.2	1433 0.5	1813 5.5	1754 5.1
	2042 0.3	2121 0.1	2305 0.1	2009 0.2	1953 0.0		2032 7.2		
24 TH	0250 4.9	0318 6.0	0436 7.5	0225 4.4	0232 4.2	0009 2.4	0243 1.0	0024 0.9	0005 0.7
	0853 0.7	0925 0.5	1116 0.6	0818 0.6	0805 0.4	0603 0.7	0835 7.5	0623 5.6	0600 5.3
	1458 4.9	1532 5.9	1651 7.3	1439 4.3	1446 4.1	1206 2.7	1517 0.6	1257 0.5	1239 0.3
	2130 0.4	2206 0.2	2345 0.2	2057 0.2	2039 0.1	1849 0.2	2119 7.0	1903 5.3	1843 5.0
25 F	0336 4.7	0405 5.9	0523 7.3	0312 4.3	0318 4.1	0100 2.4	0327 1.2	0111 1.0	0051 0.9
	0938 0.8	1008 0.7	1153 0.8	0906 0.7	0851 0.5	0648 0.7	0921 7.3	0712 5.4	0651 5.2
	1542 4.8	1618 5.8	1736 7.1	1525 4.2	1531 4.0	1253 2.6	1600 0.9	1347 0.7	1327 0.6
	2217 0.5	2250 0.3		2145 0.3	2127 0.2	1936 0.3	2209 6.7	1956 5.1	1935 4.8
26 SA	0423 4.6	0454 5.7	0021 0.5	0402 4.1	0406 3.9	0154 2.3	0411 1.5	0201 1.3	0141 1.1
	1024 1.0	1052 0.8	0612 6.9	0955 0.8	0940 0.7	0736 0.8	1012 7.0	0807 5.2	0745 4.9
	1630 4.7	1708 5.6	1228 1.0	1615 4.1	1619 3.9	1345 2.5	1647 1.2	1440 1.0	1419 0.9
	2307 0.7	2336 0.6	1825 6.9	2239 0.5	2220 0.3	2027 0.5	2303 6.4	2053 4.8	2031 4.5
27 SU	0513 4.4	0547 5.4	0058 0.7	0455 3.9	0458 3.8	0257 2.2	0500 1.8	0257 1.5	0237 1.4
	1116 1.1	1142 1.0	0705 6.7	1051 1.0	1036 0.8	0831 0.9	1110 6.6	0908 4.9	0847 4.7
	1724 4.5	1804 5.4	1309 1.1	1712 3.9	1715 3.8	1448 2.4	1739 1.7	1540 1.3	1520 1.2
			1920 6.6	2340 0.7	2322 0.5	2125 0.6		2156 4.6	2135 4.3
28 M	0006 0.8	0028 0.8	0143 0.8	0557 3.8	0558 3.6	0406 2.2	0006 6.2	0403 1.7	0345 1.6
	0612 4.3	0648 5.2	0804 6.5	1158 1.1	1145 0.9	0937 1.0	0600 2.1	1015 4.7	0957 4.4
	1221 1.2	1242 1.2	1404 1.2	1818 3.8	1819 3.6	1603 2.3	1221 6.3	1647 1.5	1631 1.5
	1830 4.3	1910 5.2	2024 6.5			2236 0.8	1845 2.0	2303 4.5	2245 4.2
29 TU	0117 0.9	0133 1.0	0245 1.0	0055 0.8	0036 0.7	0514 2.2	0117 6.1	0517 1.8	0505 1.6
	0721 4.2	0755 5.1	0911 6.4	0709 3.7	0707 3.5	1100 1.0	0716 2.3	1127 4.6	1114 4.3
	1341 1.2	1357 1.2	1517 1.2	1322 1.1	1304 1.0	1725 2.3	1340 6.2	1758 1.6	1748 1.6
	1944 4.2	2025 5.1	2138 6.3	1936 3.7	1935 3.5	2354 0.9	2001 2.2		2356 4.3
30 W	0230 1.0	0249 1.1	0359 1.0	0212 0.9	0154 0.8	0620 2.3	0228 6.1	0010 4.6	0622 1.6
	0836 4.2	0907 5.1	1025 6.4	0824 3.7	0823 3.5	1228 1.0	0839 2.2	0632 1.7	1227 4.4
	1500 1.1	1519 1.1	1636 1.1	1442 1.0	1425 0.9	1846 2.4	1457 6.2	1236 4.6	1856 1.5
	2105 4.2	2141 5.1	2259 6.3	2054 3.7	2056 3.5		2114 2.1	1905 1.6	
31 TH	0340 1.0	0400 1.1	0516 1.0	0317 0.9	0304 0.8	0101 0.9	0333 6.3	0112 4.7	0059 4.5
	0946 4.3	1015 5.3	1136 6.5	0930 3.8	0933 3.6	0718 2.4	0950 2.0	0736 1.5	0727 1.4
	1610 0.9	1632 1.0	1801 0.9	1545 0.8	1533 0.7	1335 0.8	1603 6.4	1338 4.7	1330 4.5
	2217 4.3	2245 5.3		2157 3.9	2201 3.7	1951 2.3	2214 2.0	2000 1.5	1951 1.4

● ● Time UT. For British Summer Time (shaded) March 30th to October 26th ADD ONE HOUR ● ●

EAST COAST OF ENGLAND Time Zone UT

Margate * Sheerness * London Bridge *Walton-on-the-Naze * Harwich * Lowestoft * Immingham * RiverTees * RiverTyne

AUGUST 1997 TIDE TABLES AUGUST 1997

MARGATE	SHEERNESS	LONDON BRIDGE	WALTON-ON-THE-NAZE	HARWICH	LOWESTOFT	IMMINGHAM	RIVER TEES	RIVER TYNE		
Time m	Time m	Time m	Time m	Time m	Time m	Time m	Time m	Time m		
0439 1.0	0500 1.0	0006 6.5	0409 0.8	0359 0.7	0154 0.9	0425 6.6	0206 4.9	0151 4.6	1	F
1044 4.4	1112 5.4	0632 0.9	1024 4.0	1028 3.7	0805 2.4	1047 1.7	0830 1.3	0819 1.2		
1706 0.8	1730 0.9	1234 6.7	1637 0.7	1626 0.6	1426 0.7	1655 6.6	1430 4.9	1420 4.6		
2312 4.4	2339 5.5	1908 0.7	2249 4.0	2253 3.8	2042 2.3	2303 1.8	2046 1.4	2036 1.3		
0525 1.0	0546 1.0	0100 6.7	0453 0.8	0443 0.7	0238 0.9	0508 6.8	0252 5.0	0236 4.8	2	SA
1129 4.4	1200 5.5	0727 0.8	1109 4.0	1114 3.8	0845 2.5	1134 1.4	0914 1.1	0903 1.0		
1749 0.7	1818 0.7	1322 6.8	1721 0.6	1709 0.5	1509 0.6	1738 6.7	1515 5.0	1503 4.7		
2355 4.4		1957 0.6	2333 4.0	2337 3.8	2124 2.3	2345 1.6	2125 1.3	2114 1.2		
0600 0.9	0024 5.6	0145 6.8	0530 0.8	0521 0.7	0316 0.9	0545 7.0	0332 5.2	0314 4.9	3	SU
1205 4.5	0626 0.9	0809 0.8	1149 4.1	1154 3.9	0921 2.6	1215 1.3	0954 1.0	0941 0.9		
1825 0.6	1240 5.6	1403 6.9	1758 0.5	1747 0.4	1548 0.5	1815 6.8	1554 5.0	1540 4.8		
	1857 0.7	2039 0.5			2203 2.4		2200 1.2	2148 1.2	●	
0032 4.5	0103 5.6	0224 6.9	0011 4.1	0016 3.9	0351 0.8	0022 1.5	0407 5.2	0348 5.0	4	M
0630 0.9	0701 0.9	0848 0.8	0603 0.8	0556 0.7	0957 2.6	0621 7.1	1029 0.9	1015 0.8		
1239 4.6	1317 5.7	1439 7.0	1224 4.1	1231 3.9	1626 0.5	1253 1.2	1628 5.0	1615 4.8		
1858 0.6	1934 0.6	2115 0.5	1833 0.5	1822 0.3	2239 2.4	1851 6.8	2233 1.2	2221 1.1		
0106 4.6	0138 5.7	0259 7.0	0045 4.1	0051 3.9	0423 0.8	0057 1.5	0439 5.3	0421 5.0	5	TU
0703 0.9	0736 0.8	0922 0.7	0636 0.8	0629 0.6	1030 2.6	0654 7.1	1103 0.9	1048 0.8		
1312 4.7	1351 5.7	1512 7.0	1257 4.2	1305 3.9	1700 0.5	1327 1.1	1701 5.0	1648 4.8		
1933 0.6	2008 0.6	2148 0.5	1906 0.5	1856 0.3	2313 2.3	1923 6.9	2306 1.2	2252 1.1		
0139 4.6	0211 5.7	0332 7.1	0118 4.1	0124 3.9	0451 0.8	0129 1.4	0512 5.3	0454 5.0	6	W
0736 0.9	0808 0.8	0954 0.8	0709 0.7	0701 0.6	1103 2.6	0727 7.1	1136 0.9	1120 0.8		
1345 4.6	1422 5.6	1543 7.0	1328 4.2	1336 3.9	1733 0.5	1400 1.2	1734 5.0	1721 4.8		
2006 0.7	2039 0.6	2218 0.6	1939 0.5	1928 0.3	2344 2.3	1954 6.8	2338 1.2	2322 1.2		
0210 4.5	0243 5.6	0403 7.0	0150 4.1	0156 3.9	0519 0.9	0200 1.5	0545 5.2	0526 4.9	7	TH
0808 0.9	0839 0.9	1022 0.8	0742 0.8	0733 0.6	1136 2.6	0759 7.0	1209 1.0	1151 0.9		
1417 4.6	1453 5.6	1614 6.9	1359 4.1	1406 3.9	1803 0.6	1430 1.3	1809 4.9	1754 4.7		
2039 0.8	2109 0.6	2245 0.7	2012 0.5	2000 0.4		2025 6.7		2353 1.2		
0239 4.5	0315 5.5	0436 6.9	0221 4.1	0226 3.8	0015 2.3	0230 1.6	0012 1.3	0600 4.8	8	F
0839 1.0	0908 0.9	1050 0.9	0814 0.8	0804 0.7	0548 0.9	0830 6.9	0621 5.1	1224 1.0		
1448 4.6	1524 5.5	1646 6.7	1430 4.1	1436 3.8	1211 2.5	1500 1.5	1244 1.2	1830 4.6		
2109 0.9	2137 0.7	2312 0.7	2044 0.6	2033 0.5	1833 0.6	2057 6.5	1846 4.8			
0311 4.4	0347 5.4	0509 6.7	0253 4.0	0257 3.8	0048 2.2	0300 1.8	0048 1.5	0026 1.4	9	SA
0909 1.1	0937 1.1	1118 1.0	0847 0.9	0836 0.8	0622 0.9	0903 6.7	0658 4.9	0637 4.7		
1521 4.4	1554 5.3	1719 6.5	1503 4.0	1508 3.8	1248 2.4	1529 1.7	1321 1.4	1259 1.2		
2140 1.0	2206 0.9	2342 0.8	2118 0.7	2107 0.6	1906 0.7	2130 6.3	1927 4.6	1908 4.4		
0347 4.3	0421 5.2	0543 6.5	0328 3.9	0332 3.7	0126 2.2	0331 2.1	0126 1.7	0103 1.5	10	SU
0944 1.2	1008 1.2	1150 1.0	0922 1.0	0912 0.9	0703 1.0	0936 6.4	0741 4.7	0718 4.5		
1600 4.3	1629 5.2	1753 6.3	1540 3.9	1544 3.7	1330 2.4	1600 2.0	1403 1.6	1339 1.4		
2216 1.1	2239 1.0		2156 0.8	2145 0.7	1945 0.8	2208 6.1	2015 4.4	1951 4.3		
0429 4.2	0500 5.1	0015 0.8	0409 3.8	0412 3.6	0212 2.2	0408 2.3	0211 1.9	0147 1.7	11	M
1027 1.4	1044 1.3	0620 6.3	1006 1.1	0952 1.0	0750 1.1	1017 6.1	0831 4.5	0806 4.3		
1645 4.2	1711 5.0	1225 1.1	1624 3.7	1627 3.5	1418 2.3	1639 2.3	1451 1.8	1427 1.6		
2303 1.2	2319 1.2	1832 6.1	2245 0.9	2233 0.8	2033 0.9	2257 5.9	2109 4.3	2042 4.1		
0520 4.1	0548 4.9	0054 1.0	0458 3.7	0501 3.4	0309 2.2	0456 2.6	0305 2.1	0244 1.9	12	TU
1122 1.5	1133 1.5	0703 6.1	1101 1.2	1048 1.1	0849 1.2	1114 5.9	0931 4.4	0903 4.1		
1741 4.0	1806 4.8	1307 1.3	1721 3.6	1723 3.4	1522 2.2	1735 2.5	1551 2.0	1527 1.8		
		1921 5.8	2348 1.0	2339 0.9	2134 1.0		2212 4.3	2144 4.1		
0007 1.4	0016 1.3	0142 1.2	0600 3.5	0603 3.3	0418 2.2	0005 5.8	0414 2.2	0357 2.0	13	W
0623 4.0	0651 4.8	0800 5.8	1212 1.2	1209 1.2	1006 1.2	0606 2.7	1041 4.3	1013 4.1		
1238 1.6	1245 1.6	1401 1.5	1832 3.5	1835 3.3	1636 2.2	1236 5.8	1703 2.0	1642 1.8		
1851 3.9	1919 4.8	2030 5.7			2251 1.0	1855 2.6	2321 4.3	2255 4.1		
0121 1.4	0139 1.4	0250 1.4	0103 1.1	0056 1.0	0525 2.2	0127 5.9	0536 2.1	0521 1.9	14	TH
0736 4.0	0806 4.8	0915 5.8	0715 3.5	0718 3.3	1129 1.1	0734 2.6	1154 4.4	1130 4.1		
1357 1.5	1418 1.5	1521 1.6	1333 1.2	1329 1.1	1748 2.2	1401 5.9	1819 1.9	1800 1.7		
2010 4.0	2041 4.9	2152 5.8	1953 3.5	1956 3.4		2018 2.4				
0233 1.3	0304 1.3	0421 1.4	0218 1.0	0206 0.9	0000 1.0	0240 6.2	0027 4.5	0006 4.3	15	F
0849 4.2	0921 5.1	1031 6.0	0832 3.6	0833 3.5	0626 2.3	0853 2.2	0654 1.8	0636 1.6		
1509 1.2	1539 1.2	1653 1.3	1450 1.0	1438 0.9	1238 1.0	1514 6.3	1300 4.7	1242 4.4		
2123 4.2	2156 5.2	2309 6.1	2108 3.7	2111 3.5	1854 2.3	2127 2.0	1925 1.6	1905 1.5		

● ● Time UT. For British Summer Time (shaded) March 30th to October 26th ADD ONE HOUR ● ●

AUGUST 1997 TIDE TABLES AUGUST 1997

Day	MARGATE Time	m	SHEERNESS Time	m	LONDON BRIDGE Time	m	WALTON-ON THE-NAZE Time	m	HARWICH Time	m	LOWESTOFT Time	m	IMMINGHAM Time	m	RIVER TEES Time	m	RIVER TYN Time	m
16 SA	0337	1.1	0412	1.0	0536	1.0	0322	0.9	0309	0.8	0058	0.9	0342	6.6	0125	4.8	0106	4.6
	0952	4.4	1028	5.4	1144	6.4	0937	3.8	0942	3.7	0719	2.4	1001	1.7	0756	1.4	0736	1.2
	1612	1.0	1645	0.9	1809	0.9	1552	0.8	1539	0.7	1338	0.8	1615	6.7	1359	5.0	1340	4.7
	2224	4.5	2259	5.6			2209	4.0	2215	3.8	1954	2.4	2228	1.6	2020	1.3	1959	1.0
17 SU	0435	0.9	0512	0.8	0018	6.7	0415	0.8	0404	0.6	0151	0.8	0433	7.0	0217	5.2	0156	4.9
	1045	4.7	1125	5.7	0646	0.7	1032	4.0	1040	3.9	0806	2.5	1102	1.2	0848	1.0	0828	0.8
	1709	0.7	1746	0.6	1245	6.9	1645	0.6	1633	0.4	1434	0.6	1708	7.0	1450	5.3	1430	5.0
	2318	4.8	2354	5.8	1927	0.6	2302	4.2	2310	4.0	2045	2.4	2323	1.2	2108	1.0	2048	0.9
18 M ○	0527	0.7	0605	0.6	0113	7.1	0503	0.7	0453	0.5	0242	0.7	0520	7.3	0304	5.5	0242	5.2
	1134	4.8	1215	5.9	0753	0.4	1121	4.2	1132	4.0	0851	2.6	1156	0.8	0936	0.6	0916	0.5
	1800	0.5	1842	0.4	1336	7.2	1733	0.4	1722	0.2	1525	0.4	1757	7.3	1536	5.5	1517	5.2
					2028	0.2	2350	4.4			2133	2.5			2153	0.8	2133	0.7
19 TU	0009	4.9	0043	6.1	0203	7.5	0548	0.6	0000	4.2	0331	0.6	0012	0.9	0348	5.8	0324	5.4
	0615	0.6	0655	0.5	0848	0.3	1207	4.3	0538	0.4	0934	2.7	0604	7.6	1021	0.3	1003	0.2
	1221	5.0	1302	6.0	1421	7.5	1820	0.2	1219	4.2	1614	0.2	1245	0.5	1621	5.7	1602	5.4
	1849	0.3	1933	0.2	2120	-0.0			1807	0.1	2218	2.6	1843	7.5	2236	0.6	2218	0.6
20 W	0058	5.0	0130	6.2	0248	7.7	0036	4.5	0046	4.3	0418	0.6	0100	0.8	0432	5.9	0408	5.6
	0701	0.5	0742	0.5	0936	0.2	0631	0.5	0621	0.3	1018	2.8	0648	7.8	1106	0.2	1048	0.1
	1308	5.1	1346	6.1	1505	7.6	1252	4.5	1303	4.3	1659	0.1	1331	0.3	1706	5.7	1647	5.4
	1936	0.2	2020	0.1	2206	-0.1	1906	0.2	1851	-0.0	2302	2.6	1927	7.5	2320	0.6	2301	0.5
21 TH	0146	5.0	0215	6.2	0333	7.7	0122	4.5	0131	4.3	0502	0.6	0143	0.7	0515	5.9	0453	5.6
	0747	0.5	0827	0.4	1021	0.2	0716	0.5	0703	0.3	1102	2.8	0731	7.8	1150	0.2	1133	0.1
	1354	5.1	1429	6.1	1548	7.7	1336	4.5	1346	4.3	1743	0.1	1415	0.3	1751	5.6	1732	5.3
	2023	0.3	2104	0.1	2249	-0.1	1951	0.1	1934	-0.0	2347	2.5	2011	7.4			2345	0.6
22 F	0233	4.9	0259	6.1	0418	7.6	0206	4.5	0214	4.3	0545	0.6	0225	0.8	0003	0.7	0539	5.5
	0832	0.6	0909	0.5	1100	0.4	0800	0.5	0746	0.4	1147	2.8	0815	7.7	0601	5.8	1217	0.3
	1439	5.1	1512	6.1	1632	7.5	1420	4.5	1428	4.3	1827	0.2	1457	0.5	1235	0.4	1818	5.1
	2108	0.4	2146	0.2	2327	0.2	2036	0.2	2018	0.0			2054	7.2	1837	5.4		
23 SA	0316	4.8	0343	6.0	0502	7.3	0251	4.3	0257	4.2	0033	2.4	0306	1.0	0048	0.9	0029	0.8
	0915	0.8	0948	0.6	1135	0.6	0845	0.6	0830	0.5	0627	0.7	0900	7.4	0649	5.6	0628	5.3
	1522	4.9	1556	5.9	1716	7.3	1505	4.4	1511	4.2	1234	2.7	1536	0.9	1322	0.7	1302	0.6
	2151	0.6	2225	0.4			2122	0.4	2103	0.2	1911	0.4	2139	6.9	1927	5.2	1907	4.9
24 SU	0358	4.6	0428	5.7	0000	0.5	0337	4.1	0342	4.0	0124	2.3	0347	1.4	0136	1.2	0115	1.1
	0959	0.9	1029	0.8	0548	7.0	0932	0.8	0917	0.6	0713	0.8	0948	7.1	0742	5.2	0721	5.0
	1606	4.7	1643	5.7	1206	0.9	1553	4.2	1557	4.0	1327	2.6	1618	1.4	1412	1.1	1351	1.0
	2237	0.8	2305	0.7	1802	7.0	2211	0.6	2152	0.5	1957	0.6	2227	6.5	2021	4.9	2000	4.6
25 M	0444	4.4	0517	5.4	0030	0.8	0427	3.9	0430	3.8	0220	2.3	0431	1.8	0229	1.5	0209	1.4
	1048	1.1	1113	1.0	0636	6.6	1024	0.9	1009	0.8	0806	0.9	1044	6.6	0842	4.9	0821	4.6
	1658	4.5	1736	5.4	1242	1.0	1647	4.0	1648	3.8	1430	2.4	1705	1.9	1508	1.5	1447	1.4
	2330	1.0	2351	1.0	1853	6.7	2308	0.9	2250	0.7	2052	0.8	2326	6.2	2123	4.6	2102	4.3
26 TU	0538	4.2	0613	5.1	0106	1.0	0524	3.7	0525	3.6	0326	2.2	0528	2.2	0333	1.8	0317	1.6
	1150	1.2	1209	1.2	0730	6.3	1129	1.1	1115	1.0	0910	1.0	1156	6.2	0951	4.6	0933	4.3
	1803	4.3	1841	5.1	1327	1.2	1751	3.8	1751	3.6	1550	2.3	1807	2.4	1615	1.8	1559	1.8
					1954	6.4					2203	1.0			2233	4.4	2214	4.2
27 W	0040	1.2	0054	1.3	0159	1.2	0021	1.1	0002	0.9	0437	2.2	0039	6.0	0451	1.9	0442	1.8
	0645	4.1	0720	4.9	0833	6.1	0636	3.6	0633	3.4	1039	1.0	0648	2.5	1108	4.4	1054	4.2
	1314	1.3	1327	1.4	1435	1.3	1257	1.1	1239	1.0	1718	2.3	1322	5.9	1736	2.0	1724	1.9
	1922	4.1	1959	4.9	2106	6.1	1912	3.6	1911	3.4	2332	1.1	1931	2.6	2346	4.4	2331	4.2
28 TH	0203	1.3	0216	1.4	0318	1.4	0146	1.1	0128	1.0	0550	2.3	0200	6.0	0617	1.9	0607	1.7
	0806	4.1	0838	4.9	0948	6.1	0757	3.6	0754	3.4	1215	0.9	0821	2.4	1223	4.5	1213	4.2
	1441	1.2	1500	1.3	1606	1.3	1424	1.0	1409	0.9	1844	2.3	1446	6.0	1850	1.9	1839	1.8
	2051	4.1	2121	5.0	2233	6.2	2035	3.7	2038	3.5			2053	2.5				
29 F	0320	1.2	0336	1.4	0442	1.3	0256	1.1	0244	1.0	0045	1.1	0312	6.2	0053	4.6	0040	4.4
	0924	4.0	0952	5.1	1111	6.3	0907	3.7	0910	3.5	0654	2.3	0936	2.1	0724	1.6	0714	1.5
	1556	1.0	1617	1.1	1733	1.0	1530	0.8	1518	0.7	1319	0.8	1553	6.3	1327	4.6	1318	4.4
	2204	4.3	2228	5.3	2346	6.5	2139	3.8	2144	3.6	1946	2.3	2155	2.2	1947	1.8	1935	1.7
30 SA	0423	1.1	0439	1.2	0559	1.0	0350	1.0	0340	0.9	0138	1.1	0406	6.5	0148	4.8	0135	4.6
	1024	4.4	1052	5.3	1212	6.6	1003	3.9	1007	3.7	0745	2.4	1030	1.8	0815	1.4	0804	1.3
	1652	0.6	1715	0.9	1844	0.7	1621	0.7	1609	0.6	1408	0.7	1643	6.5	1417	4.8	1406	4.5
	2258	4.4	2321	5.5			2230	3.8	2235	3.8	2032	2.3	2244	2.0	2030	1.6	2018	1.5
31 SU	0509	1.0	0527	1.1	0041	6.8	0433	0.9	0424	0.8	0219	1.0	0448	6.8	0233	5.0	0218	4.8
	1109	4.5	1139	5.5	0659	0.8	1048	4.0	1053	3.8	0824	2.5	1115	1.5	0856	1.2	0845	1.1
	1733	0.7	1759	0.8	1300	6.8	1701	0.6	1657	0.6	1449	0.7	1722	6.7	1458	4.9	1445	4.7
	2339	4.5			1933	0.5	2312	4.1	2317	3.8	2109	2.4	2324	1.7	2106	1.4	2054	1.4

● ● Time UT. For British Summer Time (shaded) March 30th to October 26th ADD ONE HOUR ● ●

EAST COAST OF ENGLAND Time Zone UT

Margate * Sheerness * London Bridge *Walton-on-the-Naze * Harwich * Lowestoft * Immingham * RiverTees * RiverTyne

SEPTEMBER 1997 TIDE TABLES SEPTEMBER 1997

MARGATE Time m	SHEERNESS Time m	LONDON BRIDGE Time m	WALTON-ON-THE-NAZE Time m	HARWICH Time m	LOWESTOFT Time m	IMMINGHAM Time m	RIVER TEES Time m	RIVER TYNE Time m	
0542 1.0	0004 5.6	0124 7.0	0507 0.9	0500 0.8	0255 1.0	0525 7.0	0311 5.2	0254 4.9	**1 M**
1145 4.6	0605 1.0	0744 0.7	1126 4.1	1132 3.9	0859 2.6	1154 1.3	0932 1.0	0919 0.9	
1806 0.7	1219 5.6	1341 7.0	1735 0.6	1725 0.4	1526 0.6	1756 6.9	1534 5.0	1520 4.8	
	1836 0.7	2014 0.4	2348 4.1	2354 3.9	2143 2.4		2139 1.3	2127 1.2	●
0013 4.5	0041 5.7	0202 7.0	0539 0.8	0533 0.7	0327 0.9	0000 1.6	0345 5.3	0327 5.0	**2 TU**
0609 1.0	0639 0.9	0823 0.7	1200 4.2	1207 3.9	0931 2.6	0558 7.1	1004 0.9	0951 0.8	
1215 4.6	1254 5.7	1416 7.0	1806 0.5	1757 0.4	1600 0.6	1228 1.2	1605 5.1	1551 4.9	
1835 0.7	1909 0.7	2051 0.4			2214 2.4	1827 6.9	2209 1.2	2157 1.1	
0042 4.6	0114 5.7	0236 7.1	0020 4.2	0027 3.9	0357 0.8	0033 1.4	0415 5.3	0357 5.1	**3 W**
0637 0.9	0711 0.8	0859 0.7	0610 0.7	0604 0.6	1004 2.6	0630 7.2	1036 0.8	1021 0.8	
1246 4.7	1326 5.7	1447 7.1	1231 4.2	1240 4.0	1633 0.5	1301 1.1	1634 5.1	1622 4.9	
1905 0.7	1940 0.6	2124 0.5	1838 0.5	1828 0.3	2242 2.4	1856 7.0	2240 1.1	2227 1.1	
0110 4.6	0145 5.7	0306 7.1	0051 4.2	0059 4.0	0424 0.8	0105 1.4	0443 5.3	0427 5.1	**4 TH**
0708 0.9	0742 0.8	0931 0.7	0642 0.7	0634 0.6	1036 2.6	0702 7.2	1106 0.8	1051 0.8	
1317 4.7	1356 5.7	1517 7.1	1302 4.3	1310 4.0	1703 0.6	1333 1.1	1703 5.1	1652 4.9	
1936 0.7	2011 0.6	2154 0.6	1910 0.5	1858 0.3	2309 2.4	1925 7.0	2310 1.1	2257 1.1	
0138 4.6	0215 5.7	0335 7.1	0121 4.2	0129 4.0	0453 0.8	0136 1.4	0513 5.3	0458 5.0	**5 F**
0739 0.9	0813 0.8	1000 0.8	0715 0.7	0704 0.6	1109 2.6	0733 7.2	1137 0.9	1121 0.8	
1347 4.7	1426 5.7	1546 7.0	1333 4.2	1339 4.0	1731 0.6	1403 1.2	1734 5.0	1723 4.8	
2006 0.8	2040 0.6	2221 0.6	1942 0.5	1930 0.4	2338 2.4	1954 6.9	2342 1.2	2326 1.1	
0206 4.6	0245 5.7	0406 7.0	0151 4.2	0158 3.9	0524 0.8	0206 1.5	0545 5.2	0530 4.9	**6 SA**
0809 1.0	0843 0.9	1027 0.8	0746 0.7	0736 0.7	1144 2.5	0803 7.0	1209 1.1	1152 1.0	
1417 4.7	1455 5.6	1617 6.9	1403 4.2	1409 3.9	1800 0.7	1431 1.4	1809 4.9	1755 4.7	
2035 0.9	2109 0.7	2248 0.7	2013 0.6	2001 0.5		2024 6.8		2357 1.3	
0236 4.6	0316 5.5	0437 6.9	0221 4.1	0228 3.9	0009 2.3	0234 1.7	0015 1.3	0604 4.8	**7 SU**
0840 1.1	0912 1.0	1054 0.9	0818 0.8	0806 0.7	0557 0.9	0833 6.8	0621 5.0	1224 1.1	
1448 4.6	1526 5.5	1649 6.7	1434 4.1	1440 3.9	1219 2.5	1458 1.6	1244 1.3	1830 4.6	
2106 1.0	2137 0.9	2316 0.7	2044 0.7	2033 0.6	1832 0.7	2054 6.6	1846 4.8		
0309 4.5	0348 5.4	0509 6.7	0254 4.0	0301 3.8	0045 2.3	0303 1.9	0051 1.5	0031 1.4	**8 M**
0913 1.2	0939 1.1	1121 0.9	0849 0.9	0839 0.8	0636 0.9	0903 6.6	0700 4.8	0642 4.6	
1523 4.5	1559 5.3	1723 6.5	1509 4.0	1515 3.8	1258 2.4	1527 1.9	1323 1.5	1301 1.4	
2140 1.1	2204 1.0	2345 0.8	2118 0.9	2106 0.7	1908 0.8	2128 6.4	1930 4.6	1910 4.4	
0349 4.4	0424 5.2	0545 6.5	0332 3.9	0339 3.7	0127 2.3	0337 2.2	0133 1.7	0112 1.6	**9 TU**
0951 1.3	1009 1.2	1153 1.0	0927 1.0	0916 0.9	0721 1.0	0940 6.3	0748 4.5	0728 4.4	
1606 4.3	1639 5.2	1801 6.3	1551 3.8	1557 3.6	1345 2.3	1602 2.2	1409 1.8	1345 1.6	
2223 1.3	2238 1.2		2200 1.0	2148 0.9	1953 0.9	2212 6.1	2023 4.4	1959 4.3	
0438 4.2	0509 5.0	0020 1.0	0418 3.7	0424 3.5	0219 2.2	0421 2.4	0226 2.0	0206 1.8	**10 W**
1041 1.4	1054 1.4	0626 6.2	1018 1.1	1005 1.0	0816 1.1	1033 6.0	0851 4.3	0826 4.2	
1701 4.1	1732 5.0	1233 1.1	1645 3.7	1649 3.5	1447 2.2	1654 2.5	1508 2.0	1445 1.8	
2323 1.4	2331 1.4	1848 6.0	2301 1.1	2247 1.0	2052 1.0	2315 5.9	2128 4.3	2101 4.1	
0541 4.1	0609 4.9	0104 1.2	0518 3.6	0523 3.4	0327 2.2	0527 2.6	0335 2.1	0318 1.9	**11 TH**
1155 1.6	1203 1.5	0718 5.9	1130 1.2	1120 1.1	0930 1.1	1156 5.8	1006 4.2	0939 4.1	
1814 4.0	1843 4.8	1324 1.4	1755 3.5	1758 3.3	1607 2.2	1812 2.7	1624 2.1	1603 1.9	
		1954 5.8			2212 1.1		2242 4.3	2216 4.1	
0045 1.5	0054 1.5	0207 1.5	0021 1.2	0012 1.1	0442 2.2	0043 5.8	0502 2.1	0448 1.9	**12 F**
0659 4.0	0726 4.8	0833 5.7	0633 3.5	0637 3.3	1058 1.0	0659 2.6	1127 4.3	1103 4.1	
1327 1.5	1341 1.5	1440 1.5	1255 1.2	1253 1.1	1726 2.2	1336 5.9	1749 2.0	1730 1.8	
1942 4.1	2009 4.9	2121 5.8	1920 3.6	1922 3.4	2331 1.1	1946 2.5	2354 4.5	2334 4.3	
0205 1.4	0230 1.4	0346 1.5	0145 1.1	0134 1.0	0548 2.3	0209 6.1	0629 1.8	0612 1.6	**13 SA**
0820 4.2	0849 5.0	1000 5.9	0757 3.6	0757 3.4	1213 0.9	0828 2.2	1239 4.6	1221 4.4	
1446 1.2	1512 1.2	1624 1.3	1422 1.0	1410 0.9	1838 2.3	1456 6.3	1903 1.8	1842 1.6	
2102 4.3	2131 5.2	2247 6.2	2043 3.8	2044 3.6		2104 2.1			
0315 1.1	0347 1.1	0508 1.1	0257 1.0	0242 0.9	0034 1.0	0315 6.6	0058 4.8	0040 4.6	**14 SU**
0926 4.5	1002 5.3	1120 6.4	0911 3.8	0912 3.6	0648 2.4	0942 1.7	0735 1.3	0715 1.2	
1554 0.9	1624 0.9	1746 0.9	1531 0.8	1516 0.6	1317 0.7	1559 6.7	1339 5.0	1321 4.7	
2206 4.6	2239 5.6	2358 6.8	2148 4.0	2154 3.8	1939 2.4	2209 1.7	2000 1.4	1939 1.2	
0414 0.9	0450 0.9	0623 0.9	0354 0.8	0341 0.7	0130 0.9	0410 7.1	0153 5.2	0133 4.9	**15 M**
1021 4.7	1102 5.6	1223 6.9	1009 4.0	1017 3.8	0739 2.5	1044 1.1	0828 0.9	0809 0.7	
1651 0.6	1729 0.6	1910 0.5	1627 0.5	1612 0.4	1415 0.5	1651 7.1	1430 5.4	1412 5.1	
2300 4.9	2334 6.0		2242 4.3	2251 4.1	2028 2.5	2303 1.2	2048 1.0	2027 0.9	

● ●Time UT. For British Summer Time (shaded) March 30th to October 26th ADD ONE HOUR ● ●

SEPTEMBER 1997 TIDE TABLES SEPTEMBER 1997

	MARGATE	SHEERNESS	LONDON BRIDGE	WALTON-ON THE-NAZE	HARWICH	LOWESTOFT	IMMINGHAM	RIVER TEES	RIVER TYNE
	Time m	Time m	Time m	Time m	Time m	Time m	Time m	Time m	Time m
16 TU ○	0506 0.7 1109 4.9 1740 0.4 2350 5.0	0545 0.7 1154 5.9 1824 0.3	0055 7.3 0733 0.4 1315 7.3 2011 0.1	0443 0.7 1100 4.3 1715 0.3 2331 4.5	0431 0.5 1110 4.1 1702 0.2 2341 4.3	0222 0.8 0826 2.7 1506 0.3 2113 2.6	0458 7.5 1137 0.7 1739 7.4 2354 0.9	0241 5.6 0915 0.5 1516 5.6 2133 0.8	0220 5.3 0857 0.4 1457 5.3 2112 0.7
17 W	0553 0.6 1156 5.1 1827 0.3	0024 6.2 0636 0.5 1240 6.1 1914 0.2	0144 7.6 0830 0.2 1401 7.6 2102 -0.1	0528 0.6 1147 4.4 1801 0.2	0517 0.4 1158 4.2 1746 0.0	0311 0.7 0911 2.8 1553 0.2 2156 2.6	0542 7.8 1225 0.4 1822 7.6	0326 5.9 1000 0.2 1600 5.8 2216 0.6	0303 5.6 0942 0.1 1541 5.5 2157 0.7
18 TH	0038 5.1 0639 0.5 1243 5.1 1913 0.2	0109 6.3 0722 0.5 1324 6.2 1959 0.1	0230 7.7 0918 0.2 1445 7.7 2147 -0.1	0017 4.6 0612 0.5 1232 4.5 1845 0.2	0027 4.4 0600 0.3 1242 4.3 1830 -0.0	0357 0.6 0956 2.9 1637 0.1 2239 2.6	0039 0.7 0626 7.9 1310 0.2 1904 7.6	0409 6.0 1043 0.1 1642 5.9 2258 0.5	0347 5.7 1027 0.0 1624 5.5 2239 0.5
19 F	0124 5.1 0724 0.5 1330 5.2 1958 0.3	0153 6.3 0806 0.4 1406 6.2 2041 0.1	0313 7.7 1000 0.2 1527 7.8 2227 -0.0	0101 4.6 0656 0.5 1315 4.6 1930 0.2	0111 4.4 0642 0.3 1325 4.4 1912 0.0	0442 0.5 1042 2.9 1720 0.1 2321 2.6	0123 0.6 0709 7.9 1352 0.3 1945 7.5	0453 6.0 1126 0.2 1725 5.8 2341 0.7	0431 5.7 1109 0.1 1707 5.5 2322 0.5
20 SA	0209 5.0 0808 0.6 1416 5.1 2042 0.5	0236 6.2 0848 0.5 1449 6.2 2120 0.3	0356 7.6 1039 0.3 1610 7.7 2303 0.2	0145 4.5 0740 0.5 1359 4.6 2013 0.3	0152 4.3 0725 0.3 1406 4.4 1954 0.1	0524 0.6 1128 2.8 1801 0.3	0204 0.7 0753 7.8 1432 0.6 2026 7.3	0537 5.9 1209 0.5 1809 5.6	0518 5.6 1152 0.4 1751 5.2
21 SU	0251 4.8 0851 0.7 1500 5.0 2124 0.7	0318 6.0 0927 0.6 1533 6.0 2156 0.6	0439 7.3 1112 0.5 1654 7.4 2332 0.6	0227 4.3 0824 0.6 1443 4.4 2056 0.6	0233 4.2 0809 0.5 1448 4.2 2038 0.4	0006 2.5 0608 0.6 1216 2.7 1843 0.5	0244 1.0 0838 7.5 1509 1.1 2107 7.0	0024 0.9 0624 5.6 1253 0.9 1855 5.3	0006 0.7 0606 5.3 1235 0.8 1838 4.9
22 M	0330 4.6 0934 0.9 1545 4.7 2206 1.0	0400 5.7 1005 0.8 1618 5.7 2232 0.9	0522 7.0 1142 0.8 1739 7.0	0311 4.1 0909 0.8 1530 4.2 2140 0.8	0315 4.0 0854 0.6 1533 4.0 2124 0.6	0052 2.4 0653 0.7 1310 2.5 1928 0.8	0323 1.4 0925 7.0 1547 1.6 2151 6.6	0109 1.2 0715 5.2 1339 1.3 1947 4.9	0052 1.0 0658 4.9 1321 1.2 1929 4.6
23 TU	0412 4.4 1021 1.1 1635 4.5 2254 1.2	0445 5.4 1045 1.1 1709 5.4 2312 1.2	0000 0.9 0607 6.6 1215 1.0 1827 6.6	0357 3.9 0958 0.9 1621 4.0 2232 1.1	0400 3.7 0944 0.8 1621 3.8 2216 0.9	0144 2.3 0744 0.8 1416 2.4 2019 1.0	0405 1.8 1020 6.5 1630 2.2 2245 6.2	0201 1.5 0814 4.8 1432 1.8 2046 4.6	0145 1.3 0757 4.6 1413 1.6 2027 4.4
24 W	0503 4.2 1121 1.2 1737 4.2	0538 5.1 1136 1.3 1812 5.0	0033 1.1 0655 6.2 1254 1.2 1924 6.3	0450 3.7 1100 1.1 1723 3.7 2340 1.3	0450 3.5 1045 1.0 1721 3.5 2322 1.2	0245 2.3 0847 0.9 1536 2.3 2127 1.2	0458 2.3 1131 6.0 1727 2.7 2357 5.9	0303 1.9 0923 4.5 1538 2.1 2155 4.4	0250 1.6 0907 4.2 1523 2.0 2139 4.2
25 TH	0000 1.5 0609 4.0 1245 1.3 1857 4.1	0010 1.5 0642 4.8 1253 1.5 1928 4.8	0119 1.4 0754 5.9 1351 1.4 2032 6.0	0557 3.5 1225 1.2 1843 3.5	0554 3.3 1208 1.0 1842 3.3	0354 2.2 1015 1.0 1704 2.2 2303 1.3	0618 2.6 1300 5.8 1855 2.9	0422 2.0 1042 4.3 1702 2.3 2312 4.4	0415 1.8 1029 4.1 1653 2.1 2300 4.1
26 F	0127 1.6 0730 4.0 1415 1.2 2028 4.1	0136 1.7 0801 4.7 1433 1.4 2052 4.9	0231 1.6 0906 5.8 1531 1.5 2158 6.0	0109 1.4 0721 3.5 1356 1.1 2008 3.6	0051 1.3 0717 3.3 1342 1.0 2010 3.4	0509 2.3 1148 0.9 1826 2.3	0124 5.9 0757 2.5 1426 5.9 2025 2.8	0552 2.0 1200 4.4 1825 2.3	0544 1.8 1151 4.1 1815 2.0
27 SA	0251 1.5 0853 4.1 1530 1.0 2141 4.3	0304 1.6 0921 4.9 1550 1.2 2202 5.2	0407 1.5 1038 6.0 1700 1.1 2320 6.4	0225 1.3 0836 3.6 1503 0.9 2114 3.8	0213 1.2 0839 3.4 1451 0.8 2118 3.6	0020 1.2 0621 2.3 1252 0.8 1927 2.3	0242 6.1 0912 2.2 1532 6.2 2130 2.5	0022 4.5 0701 1.8 1304 4.5 1923 2.1	0013 4.3 0651 1.6 1255 4.3 1912 1.8
28 SU	0357 1.3 0955 4.3 1626 0.8 2233 4.5	0409 1.4 1024 5.2 1647 1.0 2254 5.4	0523 1.2 1145 6.4 1810 0.7	0321 1.1 0933 3.8 1554 0.7 2204 3.9	0312 1.0 0938 3.6 1542 0.6 2209 3.7	0113 1.2 0716 2.4 1341 0.8 2011 2.4	0340 6.4 1005 1.9 1620 6.5 2218 2.1	0119 4.7 0750 1.5 1353 4.7 2006 1.8	0109 4.5 0739 1.4 1343 4.5 1954 1.6
29 M	0442 1.1 1042 4.5 1706 0.8 2313 4.6	0458 1.2 1112 5.4 1730 0.9 2337 5.6	0015 6.8 0624 0.8 1234 6.8 1901 0.4	0405 1.0 1019 4.0 1633 0.7 2245 4.1	0357 0.9 1024 3.7 1623 0.5 2250 3.9	0154 1.1 0757 2.4 1421 0.7 2046 2.4	0423 6.7 1048 1.6 1657 6.7 2257 1.9	0204 4.9 0828 1.3 1433 4.9 2041 1.6	0153 4.7 0818 1.2 1421 4.7 2029 1.4
30 TU	0515 1.1 1117 4.6 1737 0.8 2345 4.6	0537 1.1 1151 5.6 1806 0.8	0059 7.0 0712 0.7 1315 7.0 1943 0.4	0440 0.9 1057 4.1 1706 0.6 2320 4.2	0434 0.8 1104 3.9 1657 0.5 2326 3.9	0228 1.0 0831 2.5 1457 0.6 2117 2.4	0459 7.0 1124 1.4 1730 6.9 2332 1.6	0242 5.1 0903 1.1 1506 5.0 2112 1.4	0229 4.8 0851 1.0 1454 4.8 2101 1.3

● ● Time UT. For British Summer Time (shaded) March 30th to October 26th ADD ONE HOUR ● ●

EAST COAST OF ENGLAND Time Zone UT

Margate * Sheerness * London Bridge *Walton-on-the-Naze * Harwich * Lowestoft * Immingham * RiverTees * RiverTyne

OCTOBER 1997 TIDE TABLES OCTOBER 1997

MARGATE		SHEERNESS		LONDON BRIDGE		WALTON-ON-THE-NAZE		HARWICH		LOWESTOFT		IMMINGHAM		RIVER TEES		RIVER TYNE		Day
Time	m	Time	m	Time	m	Time	m	Time	m	Time	m	Time	m	Time	m	Time	m	
0542	1.0	0012	5.7	0136	7.1	0512	0.8	0506	0.7	0259	0.9	0532	7.1	0315	5.2	0300	5.0	1 W
1148	4.7	0612	0.9	0754	0.6	1130	4.2	1139	3.9	0903	2.6	1159	1.2	0934	0.9	0922	0.9	●
1805	0.7	1225	5.7	1349	7.0	1737	0.5	1727	0.4	1530	0.6	1759	7.0	1536	5.1	1524	4.9	
		1838	0.7	2020	0.4	2351	4.2			2143	2.4			2144	1.2	2132	1.1	
0012	4.6	0045	5.8	0207	7.1	0543	0.7	0000	4.0	0328	0.9	0006	1.5	0345	5.3	0331	5.1	2 TH
0609	0.9	0643	0.9	0830	0.6	1203	4.3	0536	0.6	0936	2.6	0603	7.2	1005	0.9	0952	0.8	
1217	4.7	1257	5.8	1419	7.1	1808	0.5	1212	4.0	1600	0.6	1232	1.2	1605	5.2	1554	5.0	
1833	0.7	1909	0.7	2054	0.5			1757	0.4	2208	2.5	1827	7.1	2214	1.1	2202	1.1	
0039	4.7	0115	5.8	0236	7.1	0022	4.3	0030	4.0	0357	0.8	0038	1.4	0414	5.3	0401	5.1	3 F
0639	0.9	0715	0.8	0904	0.6	0615	0.7	0606	0.6	1009	2.6	0635	7.3	1036	0.9	1023	0.8	
1247	4.8	1327	5.8	1448	7.1	1235	4.3	1242	4.0	1630	0.6	1303	1.1	1633	5.2	1623	5.0	
1903	0.8	1939	0.6	2126	0.5	1840	0.5	1827	0.4	2235	2.5	1855	7.1	2244	1.1	2231	1.0	
0106	4.7	0145	5.8	0306	7.1	0053	4.3	0100	4.0	0428	0.8	0110	1.3	0443	5.3	0432	5.0	4 SA
0711	0.9	0747	0.8	0935	0.7	0648	0.7	0636	0.6	1043	2.6	0706	7.2	1106	0.9	1053	0.8	
1317	4.8	1358	5.8	1518	7.1	1306	4.3	1313	4.0	1659	0.6	1334	1.2	1703	5.2	1653	4.9	
1934	0.8	2011	0.7	2156	0.6	1912	0.6	1859	0.4	2305	2.5	1924	7.1	2315	1.2	2301	1.1	
0133	4.7	0217	5.8	0336	7.1	0123	4.3	0130	4.0	0502	0.8	0142	1.4	0515	5.2	0504	5.0	5 SU
0743	0.9	0819	0.8	1005	0.7	0721	0.7	0709	0.6	1118	2.5	0736	7.1	1138	1.1	1124	1.0	
1348	4.8	1430	5.7	1550	7.0	1337	4.2	1344	4.0	1729	0.7	1403	1.4	1736	5.1	1724	4.9	
2006	0.9	2042	0.8	2224	0.6	1943	0.7	1930	0.5	2338	2.4	1954	7.0	2348	1.3	2333	1.2	
0205	4.7	0248	5.7	0408	7.0	0154	4.2	0201	4.0	0537	0.8	0212	1.6	0550	5.1	0539	4.8	6 M
0816	1.0	0849	0.9	1032	0.8	0751	0.8	0741	0.7	1154	2.5	0806	6.9	1212	1.3	1155	1.1	
1419	4.7	1501	5.6	1624	6.9	1409	4.1	1417	3.9	1801	0.8	1432	1.6	1813	4.9	1758	4.7	
2039	1.0	2110	0.9	2252	0.7	2014	0.8	2003	0.7			2025	6.8					
0239	4.6	0321	5.5	0442	6.9	0226	4.1	0235	3.9	0014	2.4	0242	1.8	0024	1.4	0008	1.3	7 TU
0851	1.1	0917	1.0	1058	0.8	0824	0.9	0814	0.8	0615	0.9	0839	6.7	0631	4.9	0617	4.7	
1455	4.6	1536	5.4	1659	6.7	1445	4.0	1452	3.8	1233	2.4	1501	1.8	1251	1.5	1231	1.4	
2115	1.1	2138	1.0	2319	0.8	2047	0.9	2037	0.8	1837	0.9	2059	6.6	1856	4.7	1838	4.6	
0318	4.5	0357	5.3	0518	6.6	0303	3.9	0312	3.7	0054	2.4	0316	2.0	0107	1.6	0049	1.5	8 W
0929	1.2	0948	1.2	1129	1.0	0902	1.0	0852	0.9	0700	0.9	0918	6.4	0721	4.6	0704	4.5	
1539	4.4	1618	5.3	1739	6.5	1527	3.9	1534	3.7	1321	2.3	1538	2.1	1338	1.8	1315	1.6	
2157	1.3	2213	1.2	2352	1.0	2128	1.1	2118	0.9	1922	1.0	2142	6.3	1949	4.5	1927	4.4	
0407	4.3	0442	5.1	0559	6.3	0348	3.8	0357	3.6	0142	2.3	0400	2.2	0200	1.8	0142	1.7	9 TH
1018	1.4	1033	1.3	1207	1.1	0952	1.1	0941	0.9	0755	1.0	1012	6.1	0824	4.4	0803	4.3	
1637	4.3	1711	5.1	1828	6.2	1621	3.7	1626	3.5	1424	2.2	1628	2.5	1436	2.0	1415	1.8	
2256	1.5	2306	1.4			2228	1.2	2215	1.1	2021	1.1	2242	6.1	2054	4.4	2029	4.2	
0511	4.2	0540	4.9	0036	1.2	0447	3.6	0453	3.4	0245	2.2	0504	2.5	0309	2.0	0254	1.8	10 F
1132	1.5	1142	1.4	0651	6.0	1102	1.1	1051	1.0	0907	1.0	1134	5.8	0941	4.3	0917	4.1	
1751	4.1	1821	4.9	1259	1.3	1731	3.6	1733	3.4	1547	2.2	1743	2.7	1552	2.2	1535	2.0	
				1934	5.9	2348	1.3	2336	1.2	2140	1.2			2207	4.4	2145	4.2	
0017	1.6	0026	1.5	0139	1.5	0601	3.5	0604	3.4	0359	2.2	0007	6.0	0434	1.9	0422	1.7	11 SA
0630	4.1	0655	4.8	0804	5.8	1227	1.1	1221	1.0	1032	0.9	0633	2.5	1102	4.4	1042	4.2	
1306	1.4	1316	1.4	1415	1.5	1855	3.6	1855	3.4	1708	2.3	1315	5.9	1720	2.1	1704	1.9	
1921	4.2	1945	5.0	2100	5.9					2303	1.2	1918	2.6	2322	4.6	2305	4.3	
0141	1.4	0200	1.5	0318	1.5	0113	1.2	0103	1.1	0511	2.3	0136	6.2	0602	1.7	0547	1.5	12 SU
0752	4.2	0819	5.0	0933	6.0	0726	3.6	0724	3.4	1148	0.8	0804	2.1	1216	4.7	1159	4.4	
1427	1.1	1447	1.1	1601	1.2	1357	0.9	1342	0.8	1820	2.3	1436	6.3	1836	1.8	1818	1.6	
2042	4.4	2108	5.3	2226	6.4	2019	3.8	2018	3.6			2039	2.2					
0253	1.2	0318	1.2	0442	1.1	0230	1.1	0214	0.9	0009	1.1	0248	6.6	0029	4.9	0014	4.6	13 M
0900	4.5	0934	5.3	1055	6.4	0844	3.8	0842	3.6	0614	2.4	0919	1.6	0710	1.3	0652	1.1	
1534	0.8	1602	0.8	1724	0.8	1509	0.7	1451	0.6	1253	0.6	1539	6.8	1317	5.0	1300	4.8	
2145	4.7	2215	5.7	2337	6.9	2127	4.1	2130	3.9	1919	2.4	2145	1.8	1935	1.5	1915	1.3	
0353	0.9	0424	0.9	0557	0.7	0330	0.9	0315	0.7	0106	0.9	0345	7.1	0127	5.2	0109	5.0	14 TU
0955	4.8	1036	5.7	1200	7.0	0945	4.0	0950	3.8	0709	2.5	1021	1.1	0804	0.8	0746	0.7	
1630	0.5	1707	0.6	1850	0.4	1606	0.5	1549	0.3	1351	0.5	1631	7.2	1408	5.4	1351	5.1	
2239	4.9	2312	6.0			2221	4.3	2229	4.1	2007	2.5	2241	1.3	2025	1.1	2005	1.0	
0444	0.7	0521	0.7	0035	7.4	0421	0.7	0407	0.6	0200	0.8	0433	7.5	0217	5.6	0157	5.3	15 W
1044	5.0	1130	5.9	0712	0.5	1037	4.2	1046	4.0	0800	2.7	1115	0.7	0851	0.5	0835	0.4	
1719	0.4	1802	0.4	1253	7.3	1654	0.3	1639	0.2	1442	0.3	1717	7.4	1454	5.7	1436	5.3	
2328	5.0			1951	0.1	2311	4.5	2320	4.3	2051	2.6	2331	1.0	2111	0.8	2051	0.7	

● ● Time UT. For British Summer Time (shaded) March 30th to October 26th ADD ONE HOUR ● ●

OCTOBER 1997 TIDE TABLES OCTOBER 1997

	MARGATE	SHEERNESS	LONDON BRIDGE	WALTON-ON THE-NAZE	HARWICH	LOWESTOFT	IMMINGHAM	RIVER TEES	RIVER TYNE
	Time m	Time m	Time m	Time m	Time m	Time m	Time m	Time m	Time m
16 TH ○	0530 0.6 1131 5.1 1804 0.3	0002 6.1 0612 0.6 1217 6.1 1850 0.3	0124 7.6 0808 0.3 1340 7.5 2041 0.0	0507 0.6 1124 4.4 1739 0.2 2356 4.5	0454 0.4 1136 4.2 1724 0.1	0250 0.7 0848 2.8 1530 0.2 2132 2.6	0519 7.8 1202 0.5 1759 7.6	0303 5.8 0936 0.3 1536 5.8 2154 0.6	0242 5.5 0920 0.2 1518 5.4 2135 0.6
17 F	0015 5.0 0615 0.5 1218 5.2 1848 0.3	0047 6.2 0659 0.5 1301 6.2 1933 0.2	0209 7.6 0856 0.2 1424 7.6 2124 0.1	0552 0.5 1210 4.6 1824 0.2	0006 4.3 0538 0.3 1221 4.3 1807 0.1	0336 0.6 0935 2.8 1613 0.2 2214 2.6	0018 0.8 0603 7.9 1246 0.4 1839 7.6	0348 6.0 1019 0.3 1618 5.9 2236 0.6	0327 5.7 1003 0.2 1600 5.5 2218 0.5
18 SA	0059 5.0 0700 0.5 1306 5.2 1932 0.4	0130 6.2 0743 0.5 1344 6.2 2014 0.3	0252 7.6 0938 0.2 1506 7.7 2203 0.2	0040 4.5 0636 0.5 1254 4.6 1906 0.3	0048 4.3 0621 0.3 1303 4.4 1849 0.1	0422 0.5 1022 2.8 1655 0.3 2257 2.6	0101 0.7 0648 7.9 1327 0.5 1919 7.5	0431 6.0 1101 0.4 1700 5.8 2318 0.7	0412 5.6 1046 0.3 1642 5.4 2302 0.6
19 SU	0142 5.0 0745 0.5 1354 5.1 2015 0.6	0212 6.1 0825 0.5 1427 6.1 2052 0.5	0334 7.5 1015 0.3 1550 7.6 2236 0.4	0122 4.4 0720 0.5 1338 4.5 1948 0.5	0130 4.3 0705 0.3 1345 4.3 1931 0.3	0506 0.5 1111 2.8 1736 0.5 2339 2.5	0142 0.8 0733 7.7 1406 0.9 1959 7.3	0515 5.8 1142 0.7 1742 5.6	0458 5.5 1127 0.6 1725 5.2 2345 0.7
20 M	0224 4.8 0830 0.6 1439 4.9 2056 0.8	0253 5.9 0905 0.6 1511 5.9 2127 0.8	0416 7.3 1048 0.4 1633 7.4 2304 0.6	0203 4.3 0804 0.6 1421 4.4 2029 0.7	0209 4.1 0749 0.4 1427 4.2 2014 0.5	0550 0.6 1201 2.6 1816 0.7	0222 1.0 0818 7.3 1442 1.2 2039 7.0	0001 0.9 0601 5.5 1224 1.1 1826 5.3	0546 5.2 1209 1.0 1810 5.0
21 TU	0303 4.6 0913 0.8 1524 4.7 2136 1.1	0334 5.7 0942 0.8 1556 5.6 2200 1.1	0458 7.0 1119 0.7 1718 7.1 2333 0.9	0245 4.1 0848 0.7 1507 4.2 2110 1.0	0249 3.9 0833 0.6 1509 4.0 2057 0.8	0024 2.5 0636 0.6 1257 2.5 1859 0.9	0301 1.4 0906 6.9 1518 1.8 2121 6.7	0046 1.2 0651 5.2 1308 1.5 1914 5.0	0031 1.0 0637 4.9 1251 1.4 1858 4.7
22 W	0344 4.4 0959 1.0 1612 4.5 2221 1.4	0416 5.4 1021 1.1 1645 5.3 2237 1.4	0539 6.6 1151 0.9 1804 6.7	0327 3.9 0935 0.9 1556 3.9 2156 1.2	0330 3.7 0921 0.8 1556 3.7 2144 1.1	0112 2.4 0725 0.8 1401 2.3 1946 1.1	0342 1.8 0958 6.4 1557 2.3 2209 6.3	0135 1.5 0748 4.8 1357 2.0 2009 4.7	0121 1.3 0733 4.5 1340 1.8 1953 4.4
23 TH	0430 4.2 1054 1.2 1709 4.2 2318 1.6	0504 5.1 1106 1.3 1741 5.0 2327 1.6	0006 1.2 0624 6.2 1227 1.2 1856 6.3	0416 3.7 1030 1.0 1653 3.7 2254 1.4	0416 3.5 1016 0.9 1651 3.5 2241 1.3	0206 2.3 0824 0.9 1515 2.2 2047 1.3	0430 2.2 1103 5.9 1648 2.8 2312 5.9	0233 1.8 0853 4.5 1456 2.3 2115 4.5	0221 1.6 0837 4.2 1442 2.1 2058 4.2
24 F	0531 4.0 1209 1.4 1823 4.0	0602 4.8 1213 1.5 1850 4.8	0047 1.5 0717 5.9 1316 1.4 1958 6.0	0515 3.5 1142 1.1 1803 3.5	0512 3.3 1127 1.0 1801 3.3 2357 1.4	0308 2.3 0941 0.9 1634 2.2 2218 1.4	0542 2.6 1224 5.7 1806 3.1	0344 2.0 1006 4.3 1612 2.5 2227 4.3	0336 1.8 0952 4.0 1605 2.3 2215 4.1
25 SA	0039 1.7 0648 4.0 1336 1.3 1949 4.0	0042 1.8 0715 4.6 1348 1.5 2009 4.8	0145 1.7 0824 5.7 1438 1.6 2113 5.9	0013 1.5 0631 3.4 1310 1.1 1926 3.5	0627 3.2 1255 1.0 1927 3.3	0418 2.2 1109 0.9 1753 2.2 2342 1.3	0036 5.8 0715 2.6 1348 5.8 1940 3.0	0507 2.1 1121 4.3 1738 2.5 2338 4.5	0501 1.8 1112 4.0 1732 2.2 2332 4.2
26 SU	0206 1.6 0808 4.0 1450 1.2 2103 4.2	0215 1.8 0835 4.7 1506 1.3 2121 5.0	0322 1.8 0947 5.8 1621 1.3 2239 6.1	0138 1.4 0752 3.5 1421 1.0 2036 3.7	0125 1.3 0751 3.3 1409 0.9 2039 3.5	0533 2.3 1215 0.9 1855 2.3	0159 5.9 0831 2.4 1455 6.0 2051 2.7	0618 1.9 1226 4.4 1843 2.3	0611 1.7 1218 4.2 1835 2.0
27 M	0315 1.4 0914 4.2 1547 1.0 2157 4.4	0327 1.6 0943 5.0 1605 1.1 2218 5.3	0444 1.4 1108 6.2 1727 0.9 2341 6.5	0242 1.2 0854 3.7 1515 0.8 2129 3.9	0233 1.2 0858 3.4 1504 0.7 2133 3.6	0039 1.3 0636 2.3 1306 0.8 1942 2.3	0302 6.2 0927 2.1 1545 6.4 2142 2.4	0038 4.6 0711 1.7 1317 4.6 1930 2.0	0033 4.3 0702 1.5 1309 4.4 1921 1.8
28 TU	0404 1.3 1003 4.4 1628 0.9 2238 4.5	0420 1.3 1034 5.3 1651 1.0 2302 5.5	0545 1.0 1201 6.6 1820 0.6	0329 1.1 0943 3.9 1557 0.7 2211 4.0	0322 1.0 0948 3.6 1547 0.6 2216 3.8	0121 1.2 0721 2.4 1347 0.8 2017 2.4	0349 6.5 1012 1.8 1624 6.6 2223 2.1	0127 4.8 0751 1.5 1358 4.8 2009 1.8	0120 4.5 0742 1.3 1349 4.6 1958 1.6
29 W	0439 1.1 1042 4.6 1701 0.8 2311 4.6	0503 1.2 1116 5.5 1729 0.9 2339 5.6	0026 6.8 0635 0.7 1242 6.8 1904 0.5	0408 0.9 1023 4.0 1633 0.6 2247 4.1	0401 0.9 1030 3.8 1623 0.5 2254 3.9	0156 1.1 0758 2.4 1422 0.7 2046 2.4	0427 6.8 1050 1.6 1657 6.8 2300 1.8	0207 5.0 0828 1.3 1433 5.0 2043 1.5	0158 4.7 0818 1.1 1423 4.8 2033 1.4
30 TH ●	0509 1.0 1115 4.7 1731 0.8 2339 4.7	0539 1.0 1152 5.6 1803 0.8	0103 6.9 0718 0.7 1317 6.9 1944 0.4	0442 0.8 1059 4.1 1706 0.6 2321 4.2	0435 0.8 1107 3.9 1654 0.5 2328 4.0	0227 1.0 0832 2.5 1454 0.7 2110 2.5	0502 7.0 1125 1.4 1727 7.0 2336 1.6	0243 5.2 0902 1.1 1506 5.1 2116 1.4	0232 4.9 0851 1.0 1454 4.9 2105 1.2
31 F	0540 0.9 1148 4.7 1801 0.8	0012 5.7 0613 0.9 1226 5.7 1835 0:7	0136 7.0 0758 0.6 1348 7.0 2021 0.4	0516 0.7 1133 4.2 1738 0.6 2353 4.3	0506 0.7 1142 4.0 1725 0.5	0257 0.9 0906 2.6 1525 0.7 2135 2.5	0535 7.1 1200 1.3 1757 7.1	0316 5.3 0934 1.0 1536 5.2 2148 1.2	0304 5.0 0923 0.9 1524 5.0 2136 1.1

● ● Time UT. For British Summer Time (shaded) March 30th to October 26th ADD ONE HOUR ● ●

EAST COAST OF ENGLAND Time Zone UT

Margate * Sheerness * London Bridge *Walton-on-the-Naze * Harwich * Lowestoft * Immingham * RiverTees * RiverTyne

NOVEMBER 1997 TIDE TABLES NOVEMBER 1997

MARGATE	SHEERNESS	LONDON BRIDGE	WALTON-ON-THE-NAZE	HARWICH	LOWESTOFT	IMMINGHAM	RIVER TEES	RIVER TYNE		
Time m	Time m	Time m	Time m	Time m	Time m	Time m	Time m	Time m		
0008 4.7	0045 5.8	0206 7.1	0550 0.7	0000 4.0	0331 0.8	0010 1.4	0347 5.3	0336 5.0	**1**	**SA**
0613 0.9	0647 0.8	0835 0.6	1208 4.3	0538 0.6	0942 2.6	0608 7.2	1007 1.0	0954 0.9		
1221 4.8	1300 5.8	1419 7.1	1811 0.6	1215 4.0	1557 0.6	1233 1.2	1606 5.3	1555 5.0		
1834 0.8	1909 0.7	2057 0.5		1757 0.5	2204 2.5	1827 7.2	2221 1.1	2209 1.0		
0038 4.8	0118 5.8	0237 7.2	0026 4.3	0033 4.1	0406 0.8	0045 1.4	0419 5.3	0409 5.0	**2**	**SU**
0647 0.9	0722 0.8	0911 0.6	0624 0.7	0611 0.6	1018 2.6	0640 7.2	1039 1.0	1027 0.9		
1252 4.8	1333 5.8	1452 7.1	1242 4.3	1248 4.0	1629 0.7	1306 1.2	1636 5.3	1626 5.0		
1907 0.8	1943 0.7	2131 0.5	1844 0.6	1830 0.5	2236 2.5	1858 7.2	2254 1.1	2241 1.0		
0109 4.8	0151 5.8	0310 7.2	0057 4.3	0106 4.0	0444 0.7	0120 1.4	0453 5.2	0443 5.0	**3**	**M**
0723 0.9	0757 0.8	0945 0.6	0657 0.7	0645 0.6	1055 2.5	0713 7.1	1113 1.1	1059 1.0		
1326 4.8	1407 5.8	1527 7.1	1315 4.2	1323 4.0	1702 0.7	1339 1.3	1711 5.2	1658 5.0		
1942 0.9	2017 0.7	2204 0.5	1916 0.7	1904 0.6	2312 2.5	1930 7.1	2329 1.2	2315 1.1		
0143 4.8	0225 5.7	0345 7.1	0130 4.2	0139 4.0	0522 0.8	0154 1.4	0530 5.1	0520 4.9	**4**	**TU**
0800 0.9	0832 0.8	1017 0.7	0732 0.7	0720 0.6	1133 2.5	0748 7.0	1150 1.2	1133 1.2		
1402 4.8	1443 5.7	1604 7.1	1350 4.1	1358 3.9	1737 0.8	1411 1.5	1750 5.1	1734 4.9		
2020 1.0	2049 0.9	2235 0.7	1949 0.8	1939 0.7	2349 2.5	2003 7.0		2353 1.2		
0220 4.7	0300 5.6	0421 7.0	0204 4.1	0214 3.9	0603 0.8	0228 1.6	0008 1.3	0601 4.7	**5**	**W**
0838 1.0	0905 0.9	1045 0.8	0808 0.8	0757 0.7	1216 2.4	0825 6.8	0614 4.9	1212 1.3		
1442 4.7	1521 5.5	1643 6.9	1428 4.0	1436 3.9	1815 0.9	1445 1.7	1230 1.5	1815 4.7		
2059 1.1	2122 1.0	2302 0.8	2026 0.9	2017 0.8		2041 6.8	1833 4.9			
0301 4.6	0339 5.4	0458 6.8	0242 4.0	0252 3.8	0030 2.4	0306 1.8	0053 1.4	0037 1.3	**6**	**TH**
0920 1.1	0942 1.0	1115 0.9	0849 0.9	0839 0.7	0650 0.8	0909 6.5	0706 4.7	0651 4.6		
1529 4.5	1606 5.4	1727 6.7	1513 3.9	1520 3.8	1306 2.3	1524 2.0	1318 1.7	1258 1.6		
2144 1.3	2201 1.2	2335 1.0	2110 1.1	2101 0.9	1900 1.0	2126 6.6	1926 4.8	1906 4.6		
0350 4.4	0424 5.2	0542 6.4	0328 3.8	0337 3.6	0117 2.4	0353 2.0	0146 1.6	0130 1.4	**7**	**F**
1012 1.3	1029 1.1	1153 1.0	0941 0.9	0930 0.8	0745 0.8	1006 6.2	0809 4.5	0750 4.4		
1626 4.4	1700 5.2	1818 6.4	1608 3.8	1612 3.6	1411 2.2	1615 2.3	1416 2.0	1357 1.8		
2241 1.5	2254 1.3		2209 1.2	2158 1.0	1959 1.1	2224 6.3	2028 4.6	2006 4.4		
0451 4.3	0521 5.0	0019 1.3	0426 3.7	0433 3.5	0214 2.3	0454 2.2	0252 1.7	0239 1.6	**8**	**SA**
1123 1.3	1134 1.2	0634 6.1	1048 1.0	1035 0.9	0852 0.8	1122 6.0	0921 4.4	0900 4.3		
1736 4.2	1807 5.1	1245 1.2	1715 3.7	1717 3.5	1529 2.2	1724 2.6	1527 2.1	1512 1.9		
2355 1.5		1923 6.1	2321 1.3	2310 1.1	2112 1.2	2339 6.2	2139 4.6	2118 4.3		
0605 4.2	0006 1.5	0122 1.5	0537 3.6	0540 3.4	0322 2.3	0614 2.2	0411 1.7	0358 1.5	**9**	**SU**
1248 1.2	0633 4.9	0745 6.0	1207 1.0	1156 0.8	1008 0.8	1252 6.1	1037 4.5	1018 4.3		
1900 4.3	1258 1.2	1403 1.3	1833 3.7	1833 3.5	1648 2.3	1848 2.6	1649 2.1	1635 1.9		
	1925 5.1	2042 6.2			2231 1.2		2252 4.7	2236 4.4		
0115 1.4	0130 1.4	0253 1.5	0042 1.2	0031 1.1	0434 2.3	0103 6.3	0533 1.5	0519 1.4	**10**	**M**
0723 4.3	0751 5.0	0909 6.1	0657 3.6	0655 3.5	1121 0.7	0737 2.0	1149 4.7	1134 4.5		
1406 1.0	1422 1.0	1540 1.1	1332 0.8	1315 0.7	1757 2.3	1410 6.3	1806 1.9	1749 1.7		
2018 4.5	2042 5.3	2203 6.5	1954 3.8	1951 3.7	2339 1.1	2009 2.3		2346 4.6		
0228 1.2	0247 1.2	0415 1.1	0200 1.1	0144 1.0	0542 2.4	0216 6.6	0000 4.9	0627 1.1	**11**	**TU**
0831 4.5	0905 5.3	1028 6.5	0815 3.8	0810 3.6	1227 0.6	0851 1.6	0642 1.2	1236 4.7		
1512 0.7	1536 0.8	1700 0.7	1445 0.7	1424 0.5	1856 2.4	1514 6.7	1251 5.0	1850 1.4		
2122 4.7	2151 5.6	2314 7.0	2103 4.1	2103 3.8		2118 1.9	1909 1.5			
0330 1.0	0355 1.0	0529 0.8	0305 0.9	0248 0.8	0040 1.0	0317 7.0	0101 5.2	0045 4.9	**12**	**W**
0929 4.7	1009 5.6	1136 6.9	0919 4.0	0921 3.8	0642 2.5	0955 1.2	0739 0.9	0723 0.8		
1609 0.5	1642 0.6	1824 0.4	1544 0.5	1525 0.4	1327 0.5	1607 7.0	1344 5.3	1328 5.0		
2218 4.8	2248 5.8		2200 4.2	2205 4.0	1945 2.5	2216 1.5	2002 1.2	1942 1.1		
0422 0.8	0455 0.8	0013 7.3	0400 0.8	0343 0.6	0136 0.9	0410 7.3	0154 5.5	0137 5.2	**13**	**TH**
1021 4.9	1105 5.8	0646 0.6	1014 4.2	1022 4.0	0736 2.6	1050 0.9	0828 0.7	0812 0.6		
1658 0.5	1736 0.5	1232 7.2	1633 0.4	1617 0.3	1419 0.4	1654 7.3	1432 5.5	1415 5.2		
2308 4.9	2339 6.0	1927 0.3	2250 4.4	2257 4.2	2028 2.5	2309 1.2	2050 1.0	2030 0.9		
0510 0.7	0548 0.7	0105 7.4	0448 0.7	0433 0.5	0230 0.7	0458 7.6	0243 5.7	0224 5.4	**14**	**F**
1110 4.9	1154 5.9	0745 0.5	1104 4.4	1113 4.1	0827 2.7	1138 0.8	0914 0.6	0859 0.5		
1743 0.4	1824 0.4	1321 7.3	1719 0.4	1703 0.2	1506 0.4	1736 7.4	1515 5.7	1457 5.3		
2353 4.9		2018 0.3	2336 4.4	2344 4.2	2109 2.6	2357 0.7	2135 0.6	2116 0.7		○
0556 0.6	0026 6.0	0151 7.4	0534 0.6	0519 0.4	0319 0.6	0545 7.7	0330 5.8	0310 5.5	**15**	**SA**
1159 5.0	0636 0.6	0833 0.4	1151 4.5	1200 4.2	0918 2.7	1222 0.7	0957 0.6	0942 0.5		
1826 0.5	1241 6.0	1406 7.4	1802 0.4	1746 0.2	1550 0.4	1816 7.5	1557 5.7	1539 5.4		
	1907 0.4	2100 0.3			2152 2.6		2218 0.7	2201 0.6		

● ● Time UT. For British Summer Time (shaded) March 30th to October 26th ADD ONE HOUR ● ●

NOVEMBER 1997 TIDE TABLES NOVEMBER 1997

	MARGATE		SHEERNESS		LONDON BRIDGE		WALTON-ON THE-NAZE		HARWICH		LOWESTOFT		IMMINGHAM		RIVER TEES		RIVER TYNE	
	Time	m	Time	m	Time	m	Time	m	Time	m	Time	m	Time	m	Time	m	Time	m
16 SU	0036	4.9	0109	6.0	0233	7.4	0020	4.4	0027	4.2	0406	0.5	0042	0.8	0414	5.8	0356	5.4
	0642	0.5	0722	0.5	0916	0.3	0619	0.5	0604	0.3	1007	2.7	0631	7.6	1039	0.7	1024	0.6
	1248	5.0	1325	6.1	1449	7.5	1236	4.5	1243	4.3	1632	0.5	1303	0.9	1638	5.7	1621	5.3
	1909	0.5	1948	0.5	2138	0.4	1844	0.5	1828	0.3	2234	2.6	1857	7.5	2300	0.8	2245	0.6
17 M	0118	4.9	0150	6.0	0315	7.4	0101	4.4	0108	4.2	0451	0.5	0124	0.9	0458	5.6	0442	5.3
	0727	0.5	0806	0.5	0954	0.3	0703	0.5	0648	0.3	1057	2.6	0717	7.5	1119	0.9	1105	0.9
	1336	5.0	1409	6.0	1532	7.5	1320	4.4	1325	4.2	1712	0.6	1342	1.1	1718	5.6	1703	5.2
	1951	0.7	2025	0.6	2210	0.5	1924	0.7	1910	0.5	2317	2.6	1936	7.3	2342	0.9	2329	0.8
18 TU	0200	4.8	0230	5.8	0355	7.3	0142	4.2	0147	4.0	0536	0.5	0205	1.1	0543	5.4	0530	5.1
	0812	0.6	0847	0.6	1028	0.4	0747	0.6	0733	0.4	1148	2.5	0803	7.2	1159	1.3	1145	1.1
	1422	4.9	1452	5.8	1615	7.4	1403	4.3	1407	4.1	1751	0.8	1418	1.5	1801	5.3	1745	5.0
	2031	0.9	2100	0.9	2240	0.7	2003	0.8	1951	0.7			2015	7.1				
19 W	0239	4.7	0311	5.6	0436	7.0	0221	4.1	0226	3.9	0000	2.5	0243	1.4	0026	1.2	0013	1.0
	0855	0.7	0925	0.8	1100	0.6	0829	0.7	0816	0.5	0620	0.6	0848	6.8	0630	5.1	0618	4.8
	1506	4.7	1536	5.6	1658	7.1	1445	4.1	1448	3.9	1242	2.4	1452	1.9	1240	1.6	1225	1.5
	2110	1.1	2133	1.1	2309	0.9	2042	1.0	2032	0.9	1830	1.0	2055	6.8	1846	5.1	1830	4.8
20 TH	0318	4.5	0351	5.4	0515	6.7	0301	3.9	0304	3.7	0042	2.4	0322	1.7	0112	1.5	0058	1.2
	0939	0.9	1000	1.0	1131	0.9	0912	0.8	0900	0.7	0706	0.7	0935	6.4	0722	4.8	0708	4.5
	1550	4.4	1620	5.3	1741	6.7	1530	3.9	1532	3.7	1340	2.3	1528	2.3	1324	2.0	1308	1.8
	2151	1.3	2206	1.3	2342	1.2	2122	1.2	2114	1.1	1912	1.1	2138	6.4	1936	4.8	1919	4.5
21 F	0400	4.3	0433	5.1	0555	6.3	0344	3.8	0345	3.6	0129	2.4	0405	2.1	0203	1.7	0148	1.5
	1027	1.1	1038	1.2	1205	1.1	1000	0.9	0948	0.8	0758	0.8	1027	6.0	0819	4.5	0803	4.3
	1639	4.2	1709	5.0	1827	6.3	1620	3.7	1618	3.5	1443	2.2	1612	2.6	1415	2.3	1359	2.0
	2239	1.6	2247	1.6			2211	1.3	2202	1.2	2001	1.3	2228	6.1	2034	4.6	2015	4.3
22 SA	0452	4.1	0522	4.9	0019	1.4	0433	3.6	0431	3.4	0221	2.3	0500	2.4	0302	1.9	0248	1.7
	1127	1.3	1129	1.4	0642	6.0	1055	1.0	1043	0.9	0858	0.9	1133	5.7	0922	4.4	0905	4.1
	1740	4.0	1805	4.8	1246	1.3	1716	3.6	1714	3.3	1551	2.2	1709	3.0	1518	2.5	1504	2.2
	2342	1.7	2345	1.8	1922	6.0	2312	1.4	2301	1.3	2106	1.4	2334	5.9	2139	4.5	2121	4.1
23 SU	0557	4.0	0621	4.7	0106	1.7	0533	3.5	0529	3.3	0321	2.3	0615	2.6	0409	2.1	0358	1.8
	1240	1.3	1241	1.5	0741	5.7	1205	1.0	1151	1.0	1013	0.9	1248	5.7	1029	4.3	1015	4.0
	1853	3.9	1911	4.7	1342	1.5	1826	3.5	1824	3.2	1703	2.2	1830	3.1	1631	2.5	1625	2.3
					2026	5.9					2238	1.4			2245	4.4	2233	4.1
24 M	0100	1.7	0103	1.8	0211	1.8	0027	1.4	0015	1.4	0425	2.4	0054	5.8	0518	2.0	0511	1.8
	0711	4.0	0732	4.6	0851	5.7	0647	3.4	0643	3.2	1125	0.9	0732	2.5	1133	4.4	1124	4.1
	1353	1.3	1403	1.4	1519	1.5	1322	1.0	1306	0.9	1811	2.2	1400	5.8	1745	2.4	1740	2.2
	2006	4.0	2022	4.8	2138	5.9	1941	3.5	1940	3.3	2349	1.4	1951	3.0	2348	4.5	2341	4.2
25 TU	0215	1.6	0225	1.7	0351	1.7	0145	1.3	0130	1.3	0533	2.2	0207	5.9	0618	1.9	0612	1.7
	0819	4.1	0845	4.7	1008	5.8	0800	3.5	0800	3.3	1221	0.9	0836	2.4	1230	4.5	1223	4.2
	1452	1.1	1509	1.3	1637	1.2	1424	0.9	1410	0.8	1903	2.3	1457	6.1	1844	2.2	1837	2.0
	2106	4.2	2126	5.0	2248	6.2	2042	3.7	2044	3.5			2053	2.7				
26 W	0312	1.4	0330	1.5	0458	1.4	0244	1.2	0233	1.1	0038	1.3	0304	6.2	0043	4.7	0036	4.3
	0915	4.2	0945	5.0	1114	6.1	0858	3.7	0901	3.4	0632	2.3	0927	2.1	0708	1.7	0700	1.5
	1539	1.0	1603	1.1	1732	0.9	1514	0.8	1501	0.7	1306	0.9	1542	6.3	1317	4.7	1309	4.4
	2153	4.4	2217	5.2	2342	6.4	2130	3.8	2134	3.6	1941	2.3	2142	2.4	1931	2.0	1922	1.7
27 TH	0356	1.3	0420	1.3	0551	1.1	0330	1.0	0320	1.0	0116	1.2	0349	6.5	0130	4.8	0122	4.5
	1002	4.4	1034	5.2	1202	6.4	0945	3.8	0950	3.6	0719	2.4	1010	1.9	0751	1.5	0742	1.4
	1619	0.9	1647	1.0	1819	0.7	1556	0.7	1543	0.6	1342	0.8	1621	6.6	1359	4.9	1348	4.6
	2231	4.5	2300	5.4			2212	4.0	2216	3.8	2010	2.4	2224	2.0	2012	1.7	2001	1.5
28 F	0435	1.1	0503	1.1	0024	6.7	0411	0.9	0400	0.8	0152	1.0	0429	6.7	0212	5.0	0201	4.7
	1042	4.5	1116	5.4	0638	0.9	1026	4.0	1033	3.8	0800	2.4	1049	1.6	0830	1.3	0819	1.2
	1656	0.9	1727	0.9	1240	6.6	1634	0.7	1620	0.6	1416	0.8	1654	6.8	1436	5.1	1424	4.8
	2307	4.6	2339	5.6	1903	0.5	2249	4.1	2255	3.9	2036	2.4	2303	1.8	2050	1.5	2038	1.3
29 SA	0512	1.0	0542	1.0	0100	6.9	0449	0.8	0436	0.7	0228	0.9	0506	6.9	0250	5.1	0238	4.8
	1121	4.6	1156	5.6	0723	0.7	1105	4.1	1112	3.9	0839	2.5	1127	1.5	0907	1.2	0854	1.1
	1732	0.8	1804	0.8	1316	6.8	1710	0.6	1655	0.6	1450	0.7	1728	7.0	1510	5.2	1457	4.9
	2342	4.7			1947	0.5	2325	4.2	2332	4.0	2105	2.5	2343	1.5	2127	1.3	2113	1.2
30 SU	0550	0.9	0017	5.7	0136	7.0	0525	0.7	0512	0.6	0307	0.8	0542	7.0	0326	5.2	0313	4.9
●	1158	4.7	0621	0.8	0806	0.6	1143	4.2	1150	4.0	0918	2.5	1204	1.3	0943	1.1	0930	1.0
	1809	0.8	1233	5.7	1354	7.0	1745	0.6	1731	0.5	1526	0.7	1802	7.2	1543	5.3	1530	5.0
			1842	0.7	2030	0.4					2138	2.5			2203	1.2	2148	1.0

● ● Time UT. For British Summer Time (shaded) March 30th to October 26th ADD ONE HOUR ● ●

EAST COAST OF ENGLAND Time Zone UT

Margate * Sheerness * London Bridge *Walton-on-the-Naze * Harwich * Lowestoft * Immingham * RiverTees * RiverTyne

DECEMBER 1997 TIDE TABLES DECEMBER 1997

	MARGATE		SHEERNESS		LONDON BRIDGE		WALTON-ON-THE-NAZE		HARWICH		LOWESTOFT		IMMINGHAM		RIVER TEES		RIVER TYNE	
	Time	m	Time	m	Time	m	Time	m	Time	m	Time	m	Time	m	Time	m	Time	m
1 M	0018	4.8	0054	5.8	0213	7.1	0001	4.2	0009	4.0	0348	0.7	0022	1.4	0401	5.3	0349	5.0
	0629	0.8	0701	0.8	0850	0.5	0602	0.7	0550	0.6	0957	2.5	0619	7.1	1019	1.1	1005	1.0
	1235	4.8	1312	5.8	1432	7.1	1221	4.2	1228	4.0	1603	0.7	1242	1.3	1618	5.4	1603	5.1
	1847	0.7	1919	0.7	2111	0.4	1820	0.7	1808	0.5	2213	2.6	1836	7.2	2239	1.1	2225	1.0
2 TU	0054	4.9	0131	5.8	0251	7.2	0037	4.2	0046	4.0	0430	0.7	0102	1.3	0439	5.3	0427	5.0
	0709	0.8	0741	0.7	0931	0.5	0639	0.7	0627	0.5	1036	2.5	0657	7.1	1057	1.1	1042	1.0
	1313	4.8	1350	5.8	1511	7.2	1258	4.2	1306	4.0	1641	0.7	1318	1.3	1654	5.4	1639	5.1
	1926	0.8	1957	0.7	2151	0.5	1855	0.7	1845	0.6	2251	2.6	1912	7.2	2318	1.0	2303	0.9
3 W	0131	4.9	0209	5.7	0329	7.2	0112	4.2	0123	4.0	0513	0.7	0141	1.3	0520	5.2	0507	4.9
	0750	0.8	0821	0.7	1010	0.5	0718	0.6	0706	0.5	1118	2.4	0736	7.0	1136	1.2	1120	1.1
	1354	4.8	1430	5.7	1551	7.2	1337	4.2	1345	4.0	1720	0.8	1357	1.4	1734	5.3	1718	5.0
	2007	0.9	2034	0.8	2227	0.6	1933	0.8	1922	0.6	2330	2.5	1949	7.2			2345	1.0
4 TH	0211	4.8	0247	5.6	0407	7.1	0150	4.1	0201	3.9	0558	0.6	0221	1.3	0000	1.1	0551	4.9
	0833	0.8	0901	0.7	1045	0.7	0759	0.7	0747	0.5	1205	2.4	0818	6.9	0606	5.1	1201	1.2
	1437	4.7	1512	5.7	1633	7.1	1418	4.1	1427	3.9	1800	0.8	1436	1.6	1219	1.3	1801	4.9
	2050	1.0	2112	0.9	2259	0.8	2013	0.9	2003	0.7			2030	7.0	1819	5.2		
5 F	0253	4.7	0327	5.5	0448	6.9	0231	4.0	0241	3.8	0012	2.5	0304	1.4	0046	1.1	0031	1.0
	0920	0.9	0944	0.8	1118	0.8	0844	0.7	0831	0.5	0645	0.6	0906	6.7	0657	4.9	0641	4.7
	1524	4.6	1559	5.6	1719	6.9	1505	4.0	1512	3.8	1257	2.3	1518	1.8	1306	1.5	1248	1.4
	2136	1.2	2154	1.0	2330	1.1	2100	1.0	2050	0.8	1846	1.0	2116	6.8	1910	5.0	1851	4.8
6 SA	0339	4.6	0414	5.4	0532	6.6	0318	3.9	0326	3.7	0058	2.4	0351	1.6	0139	1.3	0123	1.2
	1011	1.0	1032	0.9	1154	1.0	0936	0.7	0922	0.6	0738	0.7	1000	6.5	0756	4.7	0737	4.6
	1618	4.4	1651	5.4	1810	6.6	1559	3.9	1603	3.7	1357	2.3	1607	2.1	1401	1.7	1342	1.6
	2228	1.3	2245	1.2			2154	1.1	2143	0.9	1940	1.1	2209	6.6	2008	4.9	1948	4.6
7 SU	0434	4.4	0508	5.2	0012	1.3	0413	3.8	0418	3.6	0151	2.4	0447	1.8	0239	1.4	0223	1.3
	1112	1.0	1130	1.0	0624	6.4	1036	0.8	1021	0.6	0837	0.7	1106	6.2	0901	4.6	0841	4.4
	1722	4.3	1753	5.2	1244	1.1	1700	3.8	1703	3.6	1509	2.2	1706	2.3	1505	1.9	1448	1.8
	2332	1.4	2347	1.3	1910	6.4	2259	1.2	2247	1.0	2045	1.1	2314	6.5	2113	4.7	2054	4.5
8 M	0539	4.4	0611	5.1	0110	1.4	0517	3.7	0520	3.6	0252	2.4	0553	1.9	0348	1.5	0333	1.3
	1225	1.0	1239	1.0	0727	6.2	1147	0.9	1131	0.7	0943	0.7	1224	6.2	1011	4.6	0952	4.4
	1835	4.3	1902	5.2	1352	1.1	1810	3.8	1811	3.6	1623	2.2	1818	2.4	1618	2.0	1602	1.8
					2022	6.4			2359	1.0	2156	1.2			2224	4.7	2206	4.5
9 TU	0045	1.3	0058	1.3	0227	1.4	0011	1.2	0629	3.5	0402	2.4	0030	6.4	0503	1.4	0448	1.3
	0651	4.4	0722	5.1	0842	6.3	0629	3.7	1247	0.6	1052	0.7	0706	1.9	1121	4.7	1104	4.4
	1340	0.9	1353	1.0	1515	0.9	1305	0.8	1923	3.6	1731	2.3	1339	6.3	1734	1.9	1717	1.7
	1949	4.4	2015	5.2	2137	6.6	1926	3.8			2307	1.1	1934	2.3	2334	4.8	2318	4.6
10 W	0200	1.2	0212	1.3	0346	1.2	0128	1.1	0113	1.0	0513	2.4	0145	6.6	0614	1.3	0559	1.2
	0800	4.5	0836	5.2	1000	6.5	0745	3.8	0741	3.6	1200	0.6	0821	1.7	1225	4.9	1210	4.6
	1448	0.7	1506	0.9	1632	0.7	1420	0.7	1358	0.5	1831	2.3	1446	6.5	1843	1.6	1824	1.5
	2057	4.5	2124	5.4	2248	6.8	2037	3.9	2036	3.7			2047	2.1				
11 TH	0306	1.0	0324	1.1	0500	0.9	0240	1.0	0221	0.9	0014	1.0	0251	6.8	0039	5.0	0024	4.8
	0903	4.6	0944	5.4	1111	6.7	0854	3.9	0854	3.7	0619	2.5	0928	1.5	0715	1.1	0700	1.1
	1547	0.6	1614	0.8	1752	0.6	1522	0.6	1503	0.5	1303	0.6	1543	6.6	1323	5.1	1306	4.8
	2157	4.6	2225	5.6	2351	7.1	2138	4.1	2142	3.9	1923	2.4	2152	1.7	1942	1.4	1923	1.3
12 F	0403	0.9	0430	0.9	0618	0.8	0340	0.8	0323	0.7	0118	0.9	0351	7.0	0137	5.2	0121	5.0
	1003	4.6	1044	5.6	1212	6.9	0954	4.1	1000	3.8	0719	2.5	1026	1.3	0809	1.0	0754	0.9
	1639	0.6	1712	0.7	1901	0.6	1615	0.5	1559	0.4	1358	0.6	1633	7.0	1414	5.3	1356	5.0
	2250	4.7	2319	5.7			2231	4.2	2236	4.0	2009	2.5	2248	1.4	2033	1.1	2015	1.0
13 SA	0456	0.8	0528	0.8	0046	7.1	0433	0.7	0417	0.6	0215	0.8	0444	7.2	0230	5.4	0212	5.1
	1059	4.7	1137	5.7	0724	0.6	1048	4.2	1056	4.0	0815	2.6	1116	1.2	0856	0.9	0842	0.9
	1726	0.6	1801	0.6	1305	7.0	1701	0.5	1647	0.4	1446	0.6	1717	7.2	1500	5.4	1441	5.1
	2337	4.7			1954	0.5	2319	4.2	2325	4.0	2051	2.6	2339	1.2	2121	0.9	2103	0.9
14 SU	0544	0.6	0007	5.8	0134	7.1	0521	0.6	0506	0.4	0307	0.7	0533	7.3	0318	5.5	0300	5.2
	1150	4.8	0619	0.7	0815	0.5	1136	4.3	1144	4.1	0907	2.6	1201	1.1	0940	0.9	0926	0.9
	1809	0.6	1226	5.8	1352	7.1	1744	0.6	1730	0.4	1530	0.6	1758	7.3	1542	5.5	1524	5.2
			1844	0.6	2038	0.6					2133	2.6			2205	0.8	2149	0.8
15 M	0019	4.8	0051	5.8	0218	7.1	0003	4.3	0009	4.1	0354	0.6	0026	1.0	0403	5.5	0346	5.2
	0629	0.5	0706	0.6	0858	0.4	0606	0.5	0551	0.4	0958	2.6	0620	7.3	1021	1.0	1007	0.9
	1238	4.8	1311	5.9	1436	7.2	1221	4.3	1228	4.1	1612	0.7	1243	1.2	1623	5.5	1604	5.2
	1850	0.7	1924	0.6	2115	0.6	1824	0.6	1812	0.5	2215	2.6	1839	7.3	2247	0.8	2233	0.7

(14 SU — RIVER TYNE column: O)

● ● Time UT. For British Summer Time (shaded) March 30th to October 26th ADD ONE HOUR ● ●

DECEMBER 1997 TIDE TABLES DECEMBER 1997

	MARGATE	SHEERNESS	LONDON BRIDGE	WALTON-ON THE-NAZE	HARWICH	LOWESTOFT	IMMINGHAM	RIVER TEES	RIVER TYNE
	Time m	Time m	Time m	Time m	Time m	Time m	Time m	Time m	Time m
16 TU	0100 4.8 0714 0.5 1323 4.8 1930 0.7	0133 5.8 0750 0.5 1354 5.8 2002 0.7	0258 7.2 0937 0.4 1518 7.3 2149 0.6	0044 4.2 0649 0.5 1304 4.3 1903 0.7	0050 4.0 0635 0.3 1309 4.1 1851 0.6	0439 0.5 1048 2.5 1651 0.7 2257 2.6	0109 1.0 0705 7.2 1322 1.3 1917 7.3	0446 5.4 1100 1.1 1702 5.5 2328 0.9	0430 5.1 1047 1.0 1645 5.2 2315 0.8
17 W	0139 4.8 0757 0.5 1406 4.8 2009 0.8	0212 5.7 0832 0.6 1436 5.7 2038 0.9	0337 7.2 1012 0.4 1558 7.3 2221 0.7	0122 4.2 0730 0.5 1345 4.2 1939 0.8	0128 4.0 0718 0.4 1350 4.0 1931 0.7	0523 0.5 1136 2.4 1728 0.8 2337 2.6	0150 1.1 0748 7.0 1357 1.5 1955 7.1	0528 5.3 1138 1.3 1741 5.3	0514 5.0 1124 1.2 1724 5.0 2354 0.9
18 TH	0218 4.7 0839 0.6 1447 4.6 2046 1.0	0251 5.6 0909 0.7 1516 5.6 2109 1.0	0415 7.1 1045 0.5 1639 7.1 2250 0.9	0200 4.1 0810 0.6 1424 4.1 2016 0.9	0206 3.9 0759 0.4 1429 3.9 2009 0.8	0604 0.6 1224 2.3 1803 1.0	0227 1.3 0828 6.8 1430 1.8 2032 6.9	0009 1.1 0611 5.1 1215 1.5 1822 5.2	0557 4.8 1200 1.4 1805 4.9
19 F	0254 4.6 0919 0.8 1526 4.4 2123 1.2	0328 5.4 0942 0.9 1555 5.4 2139 1.2	0451 6.8 1114 0.8 1718 6.8 2321 1.1	0236 4.0 0849 0.7 1504 3.9 2052 1.0	0242 3.8 0838 0.5 1507 3.7 2045 0.9	0015 2.5 0645 0.6 1312 2.3 1837 1.1	0303 1.6 0909 6.5 1503 2.1 2109 6.6	0049 1.3 0655 4.9 1255 1.8 1906 5.0	0034 1.1 0640 4.6 1238 1.6 1847 4.7
20 SA	0333 4.4 1000 1.0 1607 4.4 2203 1.4	0405 5.2 1013 1.0 1636 5.1 2213 1.3	0528 6.5 1145 0.9 1758 6.5 2354 1.3	0314 3.9 0929 0.7 1545 3.8 2133 1.1	0318 3.6 0918 0.6 1547 3.6 2125 1.0	0055 2.4 0727 0.7 1401 2.2 1915 1.2	0339 1.9 0949 6.2 1539 2.3 2150 6.4	0133 1.5 0743 4.6 1338 2.0 1954 4.8	0115 1.3 0726 4.4 1318 1.8 1933 4.5
21 SU	0415 4.2 1045 1.1 1654 4.1 2251 1.5	0445 5.0 1050 1.1 1721 4.9 2256 1.5	0609 6.2 1220 1.1 1844 6.2	0355 3.8 1012 0.8 1630 3.6 2221 1.2	0356 3.5 1002 0.7 1630 3.4 2212 1.1	0139 2.4 0813 0.8 1454 2.1 2000 1.3	0420 2.1 1036 5.9 1621 2.7 2238 6.1	0219 1.7 0835 4.4 1427 2.2 2048 4.6	0200 1.5 0815 4.2 1407 2.0 2025 4.3
22 M	0506 4.1 1139 1.2 1750 3.9 2352 1.6	0531 4.8 1139 1.3 1812 4.7 2351 1.7	0033 1.5 0657 5.9 1303 1.2 1937 6.0	0442 3.6 1104 0.9 1721 3.5 2318 1.3	0439 3.4 1054 0.8 1720 3.3 2311 1.2	0229 2.3 0906 0.9 1552 2.1 2058 1.4	0509 2.4 1132 5.7 1715 2.9 2339 5.8	0312 1.9 0932 4.3 1525 2.4 2149 4.4	0254 1.7 0911 4.0 1508 2.2 2126 4.1
23 TU	0608 4.0 1243 1.3 1855 3.9	0627 4.7 1242 1.4 1912 4.6	0121 1.6 0757 5.7 1357 1.4 2039 5.8	0537 3.5 1207 1.0 1824 3.4	0533 3.3 1157 0.9 1823 3.3	0327 2.2 1011 1.0 1657 2.1 2215 1.4	0615 2.6 1240 5.6 1828 3.1	0412 2.0 1033 4.3 1633 2.4 2252 4.4	0358 1.9 1015 4.0 1623 2.3 2233 4.1
24 W	0102 1.6 0715 3.9 1346 1.3 2000 4.0	0102 1.8 0733 4.6 1357 1.4 2018 4.7	0219 1.8 0904 5.6 1511 1.4 2142 5.9	0027 1.3 0645 3.4 1320 1.0 1936 3.5	0020 1.3 0643 3.2 1303 0.9 1934 3.3	0431 2.2 1120 1.0 1759 2.2 2333 1.3	0053 5.8 0728 2.6 1349 5.7 1947 3.0	0516 2.0 1134 4.3 1744 2.4 2354 4.4	0507 1.9 1121 4.0 1738 2.2 2341 4.1
25 TH	0209 1.6 0819 4.0 1443 1.2 2058 4.1	0221 1.7 0842 4.7 1506 1.3 2122 4.9	0342 1.7 1009 5.7 1633 1.2 2242 6.1	0142 1.3 0759 3.5 1424 0.9 2039 3.6	0129 1.2 0758 3.3 1406 0.8 2040 3.4	0536 2.2 1215 1.0 1849 2.2	0204 5.9 0832 2.5 1449 6.0 2051 2.7	0618 1.9 1232 4.5 1847 2.2	0610 1.8 1220 4.2 1839 2.0
26 F	0307 1.4 0917 4.1 1533 1.1 2149 4.3	0330 1.5 0945 4.9 1603 1.1 2218 5.2	0457 1.5 1107 6.0 1730 1.0 2335 6.3	0246 1.1 0900 3.6 1518 0.8 2132 3.8	0230 1.0 0903 3.4 1500 0.7 2135 3.6	0030 1.2 0636 2.3 1259 0.9 1929 2.3	0304 6.1 0925 2.2 1539 6.3 2144 2.3	0051 4.6 0712 1.8 1322 4.7 1940 1.9	0039 4.3 0703 1.6 1309 4.4 1928 1.7
27 SA	0359 1.2 1008 4.3 1620 0.9 2236 4.5	0425 1.2 1039 5.2 1652 1.0 2306 5.4	0553 1.2 1159 6.3 1822 0.7	0337 1.0 0952 3.8 1603 0.8 2217 3.9	0322 0.9 0957 3.6 1547 0.7 2222 3.7	0117 1.1 0728 2.3 1339 0.9 2004 2.4	0354 6.4 1012 1.9 1622 6.6 2232 2.0	0142 4.7 0800 1.6 1407 4.9 2026 1.6	0128 4.5 0748 1.4 1352 4.6 2011 1.5
28 SU	0446 1.0 1055 4.4 1704 0.8 2319 4.7	0514 1.0 1127 5.4 1737 0.8 2351 5.6	0024 6.6 0647 0.9 1246 6.6 1915 0.6	0422 0.9 1038 3.9 1644 0.7 2300 4.1	0408 0.8 1044 3.7 1630 0.6 2306 3.9	0203 1.0 0814 2.4 1419 0.8 2039 2.5	0439 6.7 1056 1.6 1702 6.9 2318 1.6	0227 4.9 0844 1.4 1448 5.1 2109 1.3	0212 4.7 0829 1.3 1431 4.8 2051 1.2
29 M ●	0531 0.9 1139 4.6 1748 0.7	0559 0.9 1212 5.6 1819 0.7	0109 6.9 0741 0.7 1331 6.9 2006 0.4	0504 0.8 1121 4.0 1722 0.7	0451 0.6 1128 3.9 1710 0.6 2348 3.9	0248 0.9 0857 2.4 1500 0.7 2116 2.5	0521 6.9 1139 1.4 1740 7.1	0309 5.1 0925 1.2 1526 5.3 2149 1.1	0252 4.8 0908 1.1 1508 5.0 2132 1.0
30 TU	0000 4.8 0615 0.7 1222 4.7 1830 0.7	0034 5.7 0644 0.7 1254 5.7 1900 0.7	0153 7.1 0833 0.5 1415 7.1 2054 0.4	0545 0.7 1203 4.1 1800 0.7	0533 0.5 1211 4.0 1750 0.5	0333 0.7 0940 2.4 1542 0.7 2154 2.6	0003 1.3 0603 7.0 1221 1.2 1818 7.3	0349 5.2 1005 1.0 1603 5.4 2230 0.9	0333 5.0 0948 1.0 1545 5.1 2212 0.8
31 W	0041 4.9 0659 0.6 1304 4.8 1913 0.7	0115 5.8 0729 0.6 1337 5.8 1942 0.6	0236 7.3 0921 0.4 1459 7.3 2140 0.4	0020 4.2 0625 0.6 1244 4.2 1839 0.6	0030 4.0 0615 0.4 1253 4.0 1830 0.5	0419 0.6 1024 2.5 1624 0.7 2233 2.6	0048 1.1 0645 7.1 1304 1.1 1857 7.4	0430 5.3 1045 1.0 1623 5.2 2312 0.8	0413 5.1 1028 0.9 1623 5.2 2254 0.7

● ● Time UT. For British Summer Time (shaded) March 30th to October 26th ADD ONE HOUR ● ●

SCOTLAND & NORTH WEST ENGLAND Time Zone UT

Leith * Rosyth * Aberdeen * Wick * Lerwick * Ullapool * Oban * Greenock * Liverpool

JANUARY 1997 TIDE TABLES JANUARY 1997

LEITH	ROSYTH	ABERDEEN	WICK	LERWICK	ULLAPOOL	OBAN	GREENOCK	LIVERPOOL	
Time m	Time m	Time m	Time m	Time m	Time m	Time m	Time m	Time m	
0019 1.6	0723 4.9	0557 3.6	0342 2.9	0321 1.8	0520 2.1	0404 1.6	0455 3.0	0321 7.9	**1 W**
0713 4.7	1159 2.0	1133 1.8	0912 1.6	0906 1.1	1121 4.3	0954 3.3	1027 1.0	0948 2.8	
1219 2.0	1942 4.8	1804 3.7	1554 3.1	1531 1.9	1803 2.1	1648 1.9	1650 3.4	1538 7.9	
1930 4.7			2208 1.4	2200 0.9		2242 3.0	2248 0.9	2226 2.7	
0112 1.8	0103 1.8	0017 1.5	0434 2.9	0414 1.7	0024 4.1	0456 1.7	0542 2.9	0412 7.6	**2 TH**
0803 4.6	0814 4.8	0651 3.5	1012 1.7	1008 1.1	0612 2.3	1052 3.1	1123 1.1	1040 3.0	
1321 2.2	1325 2.3	1231 1.9	1649 3.0	1628 1.8	1229 4.2	1747 1.9	1736 3.2	1632 7.7	
2022 4.6	2037 4.7	1903 3.6	2314 1.4	2306 0.9	1903 2.2	2356 2.9	2348 0.9	2325 2.9	
0218 2.0	0209 1.9	0118 1.6	0534 2.9	0515 1.7	0136 4.1	0557 1.8	0638 2.9	0513 7.4	**3 F**
0900 4.5	0911 4.7	0753 3.5	1130 1.7	1133 1.1	0719 2.4	1206 3.1	1230 1.1	1146 3.2	
1440 2.3	1440 2.3	1342 2.0	1754 3.0	1735 1.8	1346 4.1	1858 1.9	1833 3.0	1739 7.5	
2121 4.5	2138 4.7	2010 3.6			2013 2.2				
0330 2.0	0317 2.0	0227 1.7	0024 1.4	0015 0.9	0243 4.1	0125 3.0	0057 0.9	0038 2.9	**4 SA**
1002 4.6	1010 4.7	0900 3.5	0640 2.9	0621 1.8	0837 2.4	0706 1.8	0751 2.8	0624 7.5	
1605 2.2	1551 2.2	1458 1.9	1248 1.7	1249 1.1	1457 4.2	1329 3.1	1342 1.1	1305 3.1	
2228 4.6	2241 4.8	2120 3.6	1902 3.0	1845 1.8	2124 2.1	2012 1.8	1946 3.0	1852 7.7	
0442 1.9	0437 1.8	0334 1.6	0129 1.3	0115 0.9	0342 4.3	0235 3.1	0207 0.8	0151 2.7	**5 SU**
1108 4.7	1109 4.9	1003 3.7	0745 3.0	0724 1.8	0948 2.2	0812 1.7	0912 2.9	0733 7.8	
1716 2.0	1705 2.0	1605 1.7	1356 1.5	1347 1.0	1557 4.4	1438 3.3	1447 0.9	1416 2.7	
2337 4.8	2342 5.0	2224 3.8	2007 3.1	1951 1.9	2224 1.8	2112 1.6	2108 3.0	1959 8.0	
0545 1.6	0555 1.6	0433 1.4	0225 1.2	0206 0.8	0433 4.6	0328 3.3	0307 0.7	0254 2.2	**6 M**
1209 5.0	1206 5.2	1057 3.9	0842 3.2	0819 2.0	1047 1.9	0912 1.5	1013 3.1	0833 8.3	
1814 1.7	1811 1.7	1700 1.4	1452 1.3	1437 0.8	1651 4.6	1534 3.5	1542 0.7	1518 2.2	
		2321 4.0	2107 3.3	2048 2.0	2316 1.5	2202 1.3	2214 3.1	2057 8.5	
0039 5.0	0040 5.2	0524 1.2	0314 1.1	0255 0.7	0518 4.9	0414 3.6	0359 0.6	0350 1.8	**7 TU**
0638 1.4	0654 1.4	1146 4.1	0933 3.4	0909 2.1	1138 1.5	1006 1.2	1104 3.3	0926 8.9	
1304 5.2	1300 5.4	1751 1.1	1542 1.1	1524 0.7	1739 4.9	1624 3.7	1630 0.5	1614 1.7	
1906 1.3	1911 1.3		2201 3.4	2140 2.1		2247 1.0	2309 3.2	2150 9.0	
0130 5.3	0134 5.5	0012 4.2	0400 0.9	0342 0.7	0003 1.2	0457 3.9	0445 0.4	0442 1.3	**8 W**
0728 1.1	0747 1.1	0612 1.0	1021 3.6	0956 2.2	0601 5.2	1057 0.9	1151 3.4	1015 9.4	
1351 5.4	1350 5.7	1231 4.3	1628 0.8	1610 0.5	1226 1.1	1712 3.9	1715 0.3	1706 1.2	
1956 0.9	2012 0.9	1838 0.8	2251 3.6	2231 2.2	1824 5.2	2330 0.8		2239 9.4	
0218 5.6	0224 5.8	0100 4.4	0445 0.8	0428 0.6	0048 1.0	0539 4.1	0000 3.3	0530 0.9	**9 TH**
0816 0.9	0837 0.9	0657 0.8	1108 3.7	1043 2.3	0644 5.5	1145 0.7	0530 0.3	1103 9.7	
1436 5.7	1439 5.9	1315 4.5	1714 0.6	1657 0.4	1312 0.8	1757 4.0	1236 3.5	1757 0.7	
2045 0.6	2106 0.6	1925 0.6	2341 3.7	2321 2.3	1909 5.3		1759 0.1	2327 9.7	●
0303 5.8	0313 6.0	0146 4.5	0530 0.7	0514 0.5	0133 0.8	0014 0.5	0051 3.4	0618 0.7	**10 F**
0904 0.7	0924 0.7	0743 0.7	1154 3.9	1129 2.4	0727 5.7	0621 4.3	0615 0.3	1150 10.0	
1519 5.9	1528 6.0	1358 4.6	1800 0.5	1743 0.3	1357 0.6	1233 0.6	1320 3.7	1845 0.4	
2135 0.4	2155 0.4	2012 0.4			1954 5.4	1841 4.1	1842 0.0		
0348 5.9	0402 6.1	0233 4.5	0029 3.7	0010 2.3	0216 0.7	0057 0.4	0142 3.4	0015 9.8	**11 SA**
0951 0.6	1010 0.7	0829 0.7	0615 0.7	0600 0.5	0811 5.7	0705 4.3	0659 0.2	0703 0.6	
1604 5.9	1618 6.1	1442 4.7	1239 3.9	1215 2.4	1442 0.5	1321 0.5	1403 3.8	1236 10.1	
2222 0.3	2242 0.3	2100 0.4	1848 0.4	1830 0.3	2040 5.4	1923 4.0	1928 -0.0	1933 0.3	
0435 5.9	0451 6.1	0321 4.5	0117 3.7	0059 2.2	0300 0.7	0141 0.4	0231 3.5	0103 9.8	**12 SU**
1036 0.7	1054 0.8	0915 0.8	0700 0.8	0645 0.5	0858 5.7	0748 4.3	0745 0.3	0748 0.6	
1651 5.9	1708 6.0	1528 4.6	1326 3.9	1303 2.4	1528 0.6	1409 0.6	1447 3.8	1324 10.1	
2309 0.4	2327 0.4	2148 0.4	1935 0.5	1918 0.3	2128 5.2	2004 3.9	2015 0.0	2018 0.4	
0524 5.7	0541 5.9	0411 4.4	0206 3.6	0148 2.2	0346 0.9	0226 0.5	0318 3.5	0149 9.6	**13 M**
1119 0.9	1135 1.0	1001 0.9	0745 0.9	0733 0.6	0948 5.5	0834 4.1	0832 0.4	0833 0.8	
1741 5.8	1759 5.9	1617 4.5	1413 3.8	1353 2.3	1615 0.8	1458 0.8	1530 3.8	1411 9.8	
2354 0.6		2237 0.6	2024 0.6	2007 0.4	2221 4.9	2046 3.7	2106 0.1	2104 0.7	
0615 5.5	0009 0.7	0502 4.2	0255 3.4	0238 2.0	0433 1.2	0314 0.7	0403 3.5	0237 9.2	**14 TU**
1202 1.2	0633 5.7	1050 1.1	0833 1.1	0821 0.7	1042 5.2	0923 3.8	0922 0.5	0919 1.2	
1835 5.5	1128 1.2	1709 4.3	1503 3.6	1445 2.2	1704 1.1	1548 1.0	1617 3.8	1459 9.4	
	1853 5.6	2330 0.9	2118 0.8	2100 0.5	2320 4.6	2130 3.4	2200 0.3	2151 1.1	
0039 1.0	0051 1.0	0558 4.0	0348 3.2	0330 1.9	0526 1.5	0405 1.0	0450 3.4	0327 8.8	**15 W**
0711 5.2	0729 5.4	1145 1.3	0925 1.2	0916 0.8	1146 4.9	1019 3.5	1017 0.7	1009 1.7	
1246 1.5	1211 1.5	1809 4.1	1558 3.4	1542 2.1	1758 1.5	1641 1.3	1706 3.6	1551 9.0	
1933 5.3	1952 5.4		2218 1.1	2200 0.7		2218 3.2	2303 0.5	2242 1.6	

● ● Time UT. For British Summer Time (shaded) March 30th to October 26th ADD ONE HOUR ● ●

JANUARY 1997 TIDE TABLES JANUARY 1997

Day	LEITH	ROSYTH	ABERDEEN	WICK	LERWICK	ULLAPOOL	OBAN	GREENOCK	LIVERPOOL
	Time m	Time m	Time m	Time m	Time m	Time m	Time m	Time m	Time m
16 TH	0129 1.4	0048 1.3	0028 1.1	0445 3.1	0426 1.8	0030 4.4	0503 1.3	0539 3.3	0424 8.3
	0812 5.0	0830 5.1		1030 1.4		0626 1.9	1133 3.2	1121 0.8	1106 2.2
	1342 1.8	1317 1.8	1248 1.5	1700 3.3	1642 1.9	1257 4.6	1739 1.5	1803 3.4	1650 8.4
	2036 5.0	2057 5.1	1916 3.9	2330 1.3	2312 0.8	1900 1.9	2325 2.9		2342 2.1
17 F	0234 1.7	0319 1.6	0135 1.4	0551 3.0	0527 1.8	0148 4.3	0612 1.5	0011 0.6	0529 7.9
	0916 4.8	0934 5.0	0808 3.7	1151 1.5	1142 1.0	0739 2.1	1315 3.1	0636 3.2	1215 2.5
	1459 2.0	1538 1.9	1402 1.7	1810 3.1	1750 1.8	1412 4.4	1846 1.6	1233 0.9	1759 8.0
	2144 4.9	2203 5.0	2030 3.8			2015 2.1		1910 3.2	
18 SA	0401 1.9	0435 1.8	0250 1.6	0048 1.4	0032 0.9	0303 4.3	0148 2.9	0125 0.7	0053 2.4
	1024 4.8	1039 4.9	0919 3.7	0701 3.0	0637 1.8	0903 2.2	0737 1.6	0743 3.1	0643 7.7
	1629 2.0	1650 1.9	1522 1.7	1318 1.5	1306 0.9	1526 4.4	1434 3.1	1354 1.0	1333 2.6
	2255 4.8	2309 4.9	2145 3.7	1926 3.1	1908 1.8	2136 2.1	2003 1.6	2034 3.1	1915 7.9
19 SU	0518 1.9	0542 1.8	0403 1.6	0158 1.4	0140 0.9	0409 4.4	0312 3.0	0237 0.7	0207 2.5
	1133 4.8	1143 4.9	1025 3.7	0809 3.1	0750 1.8	1020 2.1	0900 1.6	0903 3.1	0757 7.8
	1742 1.8	1756 1.8	1633 1.6	1430 1.4	1412 0.9	1629 4.4	1531 3.2	1508 0.9	1446 2.4
			2253 3.8	2036 3.1	2023 1.8	2242 2.0	2111 1.5	2154 3.1	2026 8.0
20 M	0004 4.8	0013 5.0	0501 1.5	0253 1.4	0236 0.9	0501 4.6	0403 3.2	0338 0.7	0313 2.3
	0615 1.8	0643 1.8	1121 3.9	0907 3.2	0850 1.9	1118 1.9	1000 1.5	1014 3.1	0900 8.2
	1236 5.0	1242 5.1	1729 1.4	1522 1.3	1506 0.8	1719 4.6	1617 3.3	1605 0.7	1548 2.1
	1840 1.6	1903 1.6	2348 3.9	2133 3.2	2120 1.9	2333 1.8	2204 1.3	2257 3.1	2124 8.3
21 TU	0103 5.0	0111 5.1	0548 1.4	0336 1.3	0323 0.9	0543 4.8	0439 3.4	0428 0.6	0407 2.0
	0701 1.7	0659 1.7	1208 4.0	0955 3.4	0937 2.0	1206 1.7	1046 1.4	1107 3.3	0951 8.5
	1327 5.1	1333 5.3	1815 1.2	1604 1.1	1550 0.7	1800 4.7	1654 3.5	1651 0.6	1639 1.8
	1927 1.4	1909 1.5		2221 3.3	2205 1.9		2247 1.2	2348 3.1	2212 8.6
22 W	0150 5.1	0157 5.3	0033 4.0	0412 1.2	0403 0.8	0015 1.6	0508 3.6	0511 0.6	0451 1.8
	0739 1.5	0644 1.5	0627 1.3	1037 3.5	1018 2.1	0618 5.0	1125 1.3	1148 3.4	1033 8.8
	1411 5.3	1415 5.5	1247 4.1	1641 1.0	1629 0.6	1246 1.5	1729 3.6	1731 0.5	1722 1.6
	2007 1.2	2008 1.3	1854 1.1	2301 3.3	2244 2.0	1836 4.9	2325 1.0		2253 8.8
23 TH ○	0230 5.2	0236 5.4	0112 4.0	0445 1.2	0439 0.8	0053 1.4	0535 3.7	0030 3.1	0529 1.6
	0814 1.4	0723 1.3	0703 1.2	1115 3.5	1055 2.2	0650 5.1	1200 1.2	0548 0.6	1111 9.0
	1449 5.3	1454 5.5	1323 4.2	1715 0.9	1704 0.6	1322 1.3	1801 3.7	1224 3.4	1759 1.4
	2042 1.1	1957 1.1	1930 1.0	2338 3.4	2320 2.0	1910 5.0		1806 0.5	2329 8.9
24 F	0305 5.3	0312 5.4	0147 4.1	0518 1.1	0512 0.7	0127 1.3	0001 0.9	0109 3.2	0603 1.5
	0845 1.3	0803 1.2	0736 1.2	1150 3.6	1130 2.2	0720 5.2	0604 3.8	0622 0.5	1145 9.2
	1523 5.4	1531 5.7	1356 4.3	1749 0.9	1737 0.5	1355 1.2	1234 1.1	1257 3.5	1833 1.3
	2112 1.0	2037 1.0	2003 0.9		2354 2.0	1942 5.0	1833 3.8	1837 0.4	
25 SA	0336 5.3	0345 5.5	0221 4.1	0012 3.4	0542 0.7	0200 1.3	0035 0.9	0143 3.2	0003 9.0
	0914 1.2	0842 1.2	0809 1.1	0550 1.1	1202 2.2	0749 5.2	0633 3.9	0654 0.5	0633 1.4
	1555 5.4	1606 5.7	1427 4.3	1223 3.6	1809 0.5	1427 1.2	1307 1.1	1330 3.6	1218 9.2
	2141 0.9	2114 1.0	2035 0.9	1821 0.8		2012 5.0	1905 3.8	1906 0.4	1903 1.3
26 SU	0409 5.3	0417 5.5	0252 4.1	0045 3.4	0025 2.0	0230 1.3	0109 0.9	0215 3.2	0035 9.0
	0943 1.2	0917 1.2	0839 1.1	0621 0.7	0611 0.7	0818 5.1	0704 3.9	0725 0.5	0703 1.4
	1627 5.3	1639 5.6	1458 4.2	1255 3.6	1231 2.2	1458 1.2	1339 1.2	1403 3.6	1249 9.2
	2210 0.9	2145 1.0	2106 0.9	1853 0.9	1839 0.5	2043 4.9	1936 3.8	1936 0.4	1933 1.4
27 M	0442 5.2	0449 5.4	0324 4.0	0117 3.3	0055 2.0	0302 1.3	0142 0.9	0245 3.2	0106 8.9
	1012 1.2	0949 1.3	0909 1.2	0652 1.1	0640 0.7	0847 5.1	0734 3.9	0757 0.5	0733 1.5
	1700 5.3	1711 5.6	1530 4.2	1327 3.5	1300 2.1	1530 1.3	1411 1.3	1435 3.6	1320 9.0
	2241 1.0	2215 1.1	2137 1.0	1924 0.9	1912 0.6	2115 4.8	2006 3.7	2009 0.4	2003 1.5
28 TU	0518 5.1	0524 5.4	0357 4.0	0149 3.2	0126 1.9	0333 1.4	0215 1.1	0315 3.2	0137 8.8
	1039 1.3	1018 1.4	0940 1.3	0723 1.2	0712 0.8	0918 4.9	0806 3.7	0831 0.6	0806 1.6
	1733 5.2	1744 5.4	1603 4.1	1359 3.4	1332 2.1	1603 1.4	1443 1.4	1507 3.6	1351 8.9
	2312 1.2	2245 1.2	2210 1.1	1957 1.0	1946 0.6	2150 4.6	2037 3.6	2044 0.5	2034 1.7
29 W	0555 5.0	0603 5.3	0433 3.9	0223 3.2	0200 1.9	0407 1.6	0250 1.2	0345 3.1	0209 8.6
	1105 1.5	1045 1.6	1014 1.4	0756 1.3	0747 0.9	0954 4.8	0838 3.6	0908 0.6	0839 1.9
	1809 5.0	1821 5.3	1641 4.0	1433 3.3	1408 2.0	1638 1.6	1518 1.5	1542 3.5	1422 8.6
	2342 1.4	2315 1.4	2247 1.2	2033 1.1	2024 0.7	2230 4.5	2109 3.4	2122 0.5	2108 2.0
30 TH	0636 4.8	0645 5.2	0513 3.7	0301 3.1	0239 1.8	0444 1.8	0328 1.4	0420 3.1	0245 8.3
	1133 1.7	1115 1.7	1052 1.5	0833 1.4	0825 0.9	1036 4.5	0915 3.4	0949 0.7	0916 2.2
	1848 4.9	1901 5.1	1723 3.8	1514 3.2	1450 1.9	1718 1.8	1557 1.7	1618 3.4	1458 8.3
		2351 1.6	2329 1.4	2114 1.3	2106 0.8	2321 4.3	2148 3.2	2206 0.6	2145 2.3
31 F	0019 1.6	0731 5.0	0559 3.6	0345 3.0	0324 1.8	0527 2.0	0412 1.6	0457 3.0	0325 8.0
	0721 4.7	1154 2.0	1139 1.7	0919 1.5	0913 1.0	1128 4.3	0957 3.3	1036 0.8	0959 2.6
	1213 1.9	1948 4.9	1813 3.7	1602 3.1	1540 1.8	1806 2.0	1645 1.8	1657 3.2	1542 8.0
	1936 4.7			2209 1.4	2200 0.9		2239 3.0	2257 0.7	2232 2.7

● ● Time UT. For British Summer Time (shaded) March 30th to October 26th ADD ONE HOUR ● ●

SCOTLAND & NORTH WEST ENGLAND Time Zone UT
Leith * Rosyth * Aberdeen *Wick * Lerwick * Ullapool * Oban * Greenock * Liverpool
FEBRUARY 1997 TIDE TABLES FEBRUARY 1997

Day	LEITH Time m	ROSYTH Time m	ABERDEEN Time m	WICK Time m	LERWICK Time m	ULLAPOOL Time m	OBAN Time m	GREENOCK Time m	LIVERPOOL Time m
1 SA	0109 1.8	0042 1.8	0021 1.5	0439 2.9	0421 1.7	0028 4.1	0506 1.7	0543 2.9	0418 7.7
	0813 4.6	0824 4.9	0655 3.5	1024 1.6	1018 1.0	0623 2.2	1055 3.1	1136 0.9	1054 2.9
	1316 2.2	1252 2.2	1242 1.8	1703 3.0	1645 1.7	1241 4.2	1746 1.9	1746 3.0	1642 7.7
	2033 4.5	2047 4.8	1916 3.6	2322 1.5	2311 0.9	1910 2.2			2336 2.9
2 SU	0222 2.0	0221 2.0	0130 1.6	0545 2.9	0529 1.7	0148 4.1	0002 2.9	0003 0.8	0527 7.5
	0914 4.5	0924 4.8	0803 3.5	1152 1.6	1154 1.0	0737 2.4	0612 1.8	0645 2.8	1209 3.0
	1454 2.3	1449 2.3	1402 1.8	1816 2.9	1801 1.7	1407 4.1	1218 3.0	1251 1.0	1800 7.5
	2142 4.5	2155 4.8	2033 3.5			2030 2.2	1906 1.8	1851 2.9	
3 M	0353 2.0	0346 2.0	0248 1.6	0043 1.4	0033 0.9	0301 4.2	0152 3.0	0120 0.8	0102 2.9
	1024 4.6	1028 4.9	0918 3.6	0658 3.0	0640 1.8	0904 2.3	0730 1.7	0811 2.8	0648 7.6
	1639 2.1	1615 2.1	1527 1.7	1319 1.5	1315 0.9	1527 4.2	1403 3.1	1410 0.9	1336 2.8
	2300 4.6	2303 4.9	2152 3.6	1933 3.0	1918 1.8	2151 2.0	2034 1.7	2018 2.8	1923 7.7
4 TU	0518 1.8	0531 1.8	0403 1.5	0156 1.3	0139 0.9	0405 4.5	0303 3.2	0234 0.7	0221 2.5
	1136 4.8	1131 5.0	1027 3.7	0808 3.1	0748 1.9	1021 2.0	0847 1.5	0936 2.9	0802 8.1
	1754 1.7	1753 1.8	1636 1.4	1430 1.3	1415 0.8	1633 4.5	1521 3.3	1515 0.6	1451 2.3
			2300 3.9	2045 3.2	2027 1.9	2255 1.7	2140 1.4	2141 2.9	2033 8.2
5 W	0013 4.9	0009 5.2	0504 1.3	0256 1.2	0236 0.8	0459 4.8	0357 3.5	0336 0.6	0326 1.9
	0621 1.6	0637 1.5	1123 4.0	0909 3.3	0846 2.0	1121 1.5	0951 1.2	1038 3.1	0904 8.7
	1239 5.1	1231 5.3	1733 1.1	1527 1.0	1507 0.6	1726 4.8	1618 3.5	1609 0.4	1555 1.7
	1852 1.3	1904 1.3	2356 4.1	2145 3.4	2125 2.0	2348 1.3	2231 1.0	2246 3.1	2133 8.8
6 TH	0112 5.3	0109 5.5	0556 1.0	0346 1.0	0327 0.6	0545 5.2	0443 3.8	0427 0.4	0424 1.4
	0715 1.2	0732 1.2	1212 4.3	1002 3.5	0939 2.1	1212 1.1	1045 0.9	1130 3.3	0958 9.3
	1331 5.4	1328 5.6	1824 0.7	1616 0.7	1556 0.4	1813 5.1	1707 3.8	1657 0.2	1652 1.0
	1945 0.9	2004 0.9		2238 3.6	2218 2.1		2316 0.7	2344 3.2	2226 9.3
7 F	0200 5.6	0203 5.8	0045 4.3	0432 0.8	0415 0.5	0035 1.0	0527 4.1	0514 0.3	0516 0.8
	0803 0.8	0822 0.9	0644 0.8	1051 3.8	1028 2.3	0630 5.5	1135 0.6	1218 3.5	1048 9.8
	1417 5.7	1421 6.0	1257 4.5	1702 0.5	1643 0.3	1259 0.7	1751 4.0	1742 -0.0	1745 0.5
	2035 0.4	2055 0.5	1912 0.4	2327 3.7	2308 2.2	1857 5.4			2315 9.7 ●
8 SA	0245 5.9	0254 6.1	0133 4.5	0516 0.7	0500 0.4	0119 0.7	0000 4.4	0039 3.3	0605 0.4
	0850 0.6	0909 0.6	0730 0.7	1138 3.9	1115 2.4	0712 5.8	0611 4.4	0558 0.2	1136 10.1
	1501 6.0	1512 6.2	1342 4.7	1748 0.3	1728 0.1	1343 0.4	1222 0.4	1305 3.6	1833 0.1
	2122 0.2	2142 0.2	1959 0.2		2356 2.3	1939 5.5	1833 4.1	1826 -0.1	
9 SU	0330 6.0	0342 6.3	0218 4.6	0015 3.8	0544 0.4	0203 0.5	0043 0.2	0131 3.4	0002 10.0
	0936 0.4	0953 0.5	0814 0.6	0600 0.6	1202 2.4	0755 5.9	0653 4.5	0642 0.1	0651 0.2
	1546 6.1	1602 6.3	1426 4.8	1224 4.0	1813 0.1	1427 0.3	1309 0.3	1350 3.8	1222 10.3
	2209 0.1	2227 0.1	2045 0.2	1832 0.3		2022 5.5	1911 4.1	1909 -0.2	1919 -0.1
10 M	0416 6.0	0431 6.3	0303 4.6	0100 3.7	0042 2.2	0245 0.5	0126 0.2	0218 3.4	0048 10.0
	1019 0.4	1035 0.5	0857 0.6	0642 0.6	0627 0.4	0839 5.8	0735 4.4	0725 0.1	0734 0.2
	1633 6.1	1651 6.3	1511 4.8	1309 4.0	1248 2.4	1510 0.4	1354 0.4	1433 3.8	1307 10.3
	2252 0.2	2309 0.3	2130 0.3	1916 0.4	1858 0.2	2106 5.3	1948 4.0	1955 -0.1	2003 0.0
11 TU	0503 5.8	0519 6.1	0349 4.4	0145 3.6	0127 2.2	0327 0.6	0209 0.3	0301 3.5	0131 9.8
	1100 0.6	1113 0.7	0941 0.7	0725 0.7	0712 0.4	0925 5.6	0817 4.2	0810 0.2	0817 0.4
	1722 5.9	1740 6.1	1557 4.6	1355 3.9	1335 2.3	1553 0.6	1438 0.6	1515 3.8	1351 10.1
	2333 0.5	2348 0.6	2215 0.5	2000 0.5	1944 0.3	2152 5.1	2024 3.8	2042 -0.0	2044 0.4
12 W	0552 5.5	0609 5.8	0436 4.2	0230 3.5	0212 2.0	0412 0.9	0254 0.6	0342 3.5	0215 9.4
	1139 0.9	1057 1.0	1026 0.9	0809 0.9	0758 0.5	1015 5.3	0859 3.9	0858 0.3	0859 0.8
	1812 5.6	1831 5.8	1647 4.4	1442 3.7	1423 2.2	1637 1.0	1523 0.9	1557 3.8	1436 9.6
		2321 1.0	2301 0.8	2046 0.8	2033 0.5	2244 4.7	2101 3.6	2134 0.2	2126 0.9
13 TH	0011 0.9	0700 5.5	0526 4.0	0316 3.3	0259 1.9	0458 1.3	0342 0.9	0423 3.4	0300 8.9
	0643 5.2	1133 1.3	1115 1.2	0856 1.1	0848 0.7	1114 4.8	0945 3.5	0950 0.4	0943 1.4
	1215 1.3	1925 5.5	1742 4.1	1532 3.4	1515 2.0	1724 1.4	1609 1.2	1642 3.6	1523 9.0
	1907 5.3		2353 1.2	2137 1.1	2125 0.7	2348 4.4	2142 3.3	2233 0.4	2210 1.6
14 F	0047 1.4	0002 1.4	0622 3.7	0408 3.1	0350 1.8	0552 1.8	0434 1.3	0506 3.3	0348 8.3
	0739 4.9	0757 5.1	1212 1.4	0954 1.3	0947 0.8	1224 4.5	1041 3.2	1050 0.6	1033 2.0
	1302 1.7	1225 1.7	1846 3.8	1630 3.2	1612 1.8	1819 1.8	1700 1.5	1731 3.3	1616 8.3
	2006 5.0	2026 5.1		2242 1.4	2229 0.8		2233 3.2	2339 0.6	2303 2.3
15 SA	0136 1.9	0102 1.9	0054 1.5	0509 2.9	0448 1.7	0108 4.2	0538 1.6	0554 3.1	0447 7.8
	0839 4.7	0900 4.8	0728 3.6	1113 1.5	1106 0.9	0659 2.1	1224 2.9	1201 0.8	1137 2.6
	1414 2.0	1446 2.0	1325 1.6	1739 3.0	1718 1.7	1344 4.2	1802 1.7	1830 3.0	1722 7.7
	2113 4.7	2132 4.9	2000 3.6		2356 1.0	1930 2.2			

● ● Time UT. For British Summer Time (shaded) March 30th to October 26th ADD ONE HOUR ● ●

FEBRUARY 1997 TIDE TABLES FEBRUARY 1997

	LEITH	ROSYTH	ABERDEEN	WICK	LERWICK	ULLAPOOL	OBAN	GREENOCK	LIVERPOOL
	Time m	Time m	Time m	Time m	Time m	Time m	Time m	Time m	Time m
16 SU	0308 2.2	0354 2.1	0211 1.7	0006 1.5	0557 1.7	0231 4.1	0015 2.8	0056 0.8	0011 2.8
	0948 4.5	1006 4.7	0842 3.5	0621 2.9	1242 0.9	0830 2.3	0706 1.8	0652 3.0	0603 7.4
	1603 2.1	1620 2.1	1454 1.7	1253 1.5	1841 1.6	1504 4.1	1414 2.9	1327 0.9	1259 2.9
	2227 4.5	2240 4.8	2121 3.5	1900 2.9		2103 2.3	1922 1.8	1957 2.8	1844 7.4
17 M	0453 2.2	0503 2.1	0336 1.8	0133 1.6	0118 1.0	0346 4.2	0301 2.9	0216 0.9	0134 3.0
	1103 4.6	1114 4.7	0957 3.6	0739 2.9	0720 1.7	1002 2.2	0848 1.8	0818 2.8	0727 7.4
	1729 2.0	1731 2.0	1615 1.6	1414 1.4	1356 0.9	1612 4.2	1516 3.0	1450 0.9	1421 2.7
	2343 4.6	2350 4.8	2236 3.6	2018 2.9	2009 1.7	2224 2.2	2047 1.7	2136 2.8	2004 7.5
18 TU	0558 2.1	0603 2.1	0444 1.7	0236 1.5	0221 0.9	0444 4.4	0353 3.1	0321 0.8	0250 2.7
	1215 4.7	1219 4.9	1100 3.7	0845 3.1	0828 1.8	1104 2.0	0953 1.6	0947 2.9	0839 7.1
	1828 1.7	1850 1.8	1714 1.4	1508 1.3	1451 0.8	1705 4.4	1603 3.2	1550 0.7	1529 2.4
				2334 3.7	2118 3.0	2104 1.8	2318 2.0	2146 1.5	2243 2.9	2107 7.9
19 W	0047 4.8	0052 5.0	0532 1.6	0321 1.4	0308 0.9	0527 4.6	0427 3.3	0412 0.7	0348 2.4
	0645 1.9	0557 1.9	1150 3.9	0936 3.2	0918 1.9	1151 1.7	1036 1.5	1045 3.1	0932 8.2
	1311 4.9	1314 5.2	1758 1.3	1549 1.1	1535 0.7	1745 4.6	1639 3.4	1635 0.6	1621 2.0
	1914 1.5	1940 1.6		2204 3.2	2146 1.8	2359 1.7	2230 1.3	2332 3.0	2155 8.3
20 TH	0135 4.9	0141 5.2	0018 3.8	0357 1.3	0347 0.8	0601 4.8	0454 3.5	0454 0.6	0433 2.0
	0722 1.6	0628 1.7	0611 1.4	1018 3.3	0958 2.0	1229 1.5	1112 1.3	1127 3.2	1015 8.6
	1354 5.1	1358 5.4	1229 4.0	1624 1.0	1611 0.6	1818 4.8	1713 3.6	1712 0.5	1703 1.6
	1951 1.3	1927 1.4	1835 1.1	2243 3.2	2224 1.9		2307 1.1		2235 8.7
21 F	0212 5.1	0219 5.3	0054 3.9	0428 1.2	0421 0.7	0035 1.5	0519 3.7	0012 3.0	0510 1.7
	0754 1.4	0706 1.4	0645 1.2	1055 3.4	1036 2.1	0631 4.9	1145 1.2	0529 0.5	1051 8.9
	1431 5.3	1436 5.6	1303 4.1	1655 0.9	1643 0.5	1303 1.3	1745 3.7	1203 3.3	1739 1.4
	2021 1.1	2020 1.2	1909 0.9	2318 3.3	2258 2.0	1849 4.9	2342 0.9	1745 0.4	2309 8.9
22 SA ○	0245 5.2	0252 5.4	0127 4.0	0459 1.1	0451 0.7	0108 1.3	0546 3.8	0047 3.1	0542 1.5
	0824 1.2	0745 1.2	0718 1.1	1129 3.5	1109 2.1	0700 5.1	1216 1.1	0600 0.4	1124 9.1
	1503 5.3	1512 5.7	1335 4.2	1727 0.8	1714 0.5	1333 1.1	1815 3.9	1237 3.4	1810 1.2
	2050 0.9	2019 1.1	1940 0.8	2350 3.4	2330 2.0	1918 5.0		1813 0.4	2341 9.1
23 SU	0314 5.3	0322 5.5	0157 4.1	0529 1.0	0519 0.6	0139 1.2	0014 0.8	0120 3.1	0612 1.3
	0854 1.0	0824 1.1	0748 1.0	1201 3.5	1139 2.1	0727 5.1	0615 3.9	0630 0.4	1156 9.2
	1534 5.4	1546 5.7	1405 4.2	1757 0.7	1742 0.4	1403 1.0	1246 1.1	1309 3.5	1840 1.1
	2119 0.8	2054 1.0	2010 0.8			1947 5.0	1845 3.9	1841 0.3	
24 M	0345 5.3	0351 5.6	0227 4.1	0021 3.4	0000 2.0	0209 1.1	0046 0.8	0151 3.2	0011 9.1
	0925 1.0	0859 1.1	0817 1.0	0559 0.9	0546 0.6	0754 5.2	0643 4.0	0659 0.3	0642 1.2
	1605 5.4	1617 5.7	1435 4.2	1232 3.5	1208 2.1	1433 1.0	1315 1.1	1341 3.5	1226 9.3
	2150 0.8	2124 1.0	2040 0.8	1827 0.7	1811 0.4	2015 5.0	1914 3.9	1909 0.3	1909 1.1
25 TU	0417 5.3	0422 5.6	0257 4.1	0051 3.4	0027 2.0	0238 1.1	0118 0.8	0219 3.2	0041 9.1
	0955 1.0	0929 1.1	0845 1.0	0629 0.9	0615 0.6	0821 5.1	0712 3.9	0729 0.3	0712 1.2
	1636 5.3	1647 5.6	1506 4.2	1303 3.5	1236 2.1	1502 1.0	1345 1.1	1412 3.5	1256 9.2
	2220 0.8	2150 1.0	2109 0.8	1856 0.8	1842 0.5	2045 4.9	1942 3.8	1940 0.3	1939 1.2
26 W	0451 5.2	0456 5.6	0328 4.0	0121 3.3	0056 2.0	0308 1.1	0149 0.9	0248 3.2	0111 9.0
	1021 1.1	0954 1.2	0915 1.0	0659 1.0	0647 0.6	0851 5.0	0740 3.8	0802 0.3	0744 1.3
	1708 5.2	1718 5.6	1538 4.1	1333 3.4	1306 2.0	1533 1.1	1414 1.2	1442 3.5	1325 9.1
	2248 1.0	2215 1.1	2140 0.9	1927 0.9	1915 0.5	2117 4.8	2009 3.7	2014 0.3	2009 1.4
27 TH	0526 5.1	0533 5.5	0401 3.9	0153 3.2	0127 1.9	0340 1.3	0222 1.1	0316 3.2	0142 8.9
	1039 1.2	1017 1.3	0946 1.1	0730 1.0	0721 0.7	0924 4.8	0810 3.7	0837 0.3	0817 1.5
	1741 5.1	1754 5.4	1613 4.0	1406 3.3	1339 2.0	1606 1.3	1445 1.3	1515 3.4	1355 8.9
	2310 1.2	2241 1.3	2214 1.0	1959 1.0	1950 0.6	2153 4.6	2038 3.6	2050 0.3	2040 1.7
28 F	0603 5.0	0613 5.4	0438 3.8	0228 3.1	0203 1.9	0415 1.5	0259 1.2	0348 3.1	0215 8.6
	1101 1.4	1045 1.5	1021 1.2	0806 1.1	0758 0.7	1003 4.6	0843 3.5	0915 0.4	0851 1.8
	1818 4.9	1833 5.3	1653 3.9	1445 3.2	1418 1.9	1642 1.5	1522 1.5	1549 3.3	1429 8.6
	2335 1.4	2312 1.4	2252 1.2	2036 1.1	2030 0.7	2237 4.4	2112 3.4	2130 0.4	2114 2.0

● ● Time UT. For British Summer Time (shaded) March 30th to October 26th ADD ONE HOUR ● ●

SCOTLAND & NORTH WEST ENGLAND Time Zone UT
Leith * Rosyth * Aberdeen *Wick * Lerwick * Ullapool * Oban * Greenock * Liverpool
MARCH 1997 TIDE TABLES MARCH 1997

	LEITH	ROSYTH	ABERDEEN	WICK	LERWICK	ULLAPOOL	OBAN	GREENOCK	LIVERPOOL
	Time m	Time m	Time m	Time m	Time m	Time m	Time m	Time m	Time m
1 SA	0645 4.8 1136 1.6 1903 4.8	0657 5.2 1121 1.6 1918 5.1 2353 1.7	0521 3.7 1105 1.4 1741 3.7 2341 1.4	0309 3.0 0847 1.3 1531 3.1 2124 1.3	0244 1.8 0842 0.8 1506 1.8 2118 0.8	0456 1.7 1051 4.4 1727 1.8 2338 4.2	0341 1.4 0921 3.3 1606 1.6 2156 3.2	0422 3.0 1000 0.5 1627 3.2 2218 0.5	0253 8.4 0930 2.2 1511 8.3 2155 2.4
2 SU	0015 1.7 0735 4.6 1227 1.9 2000 4.6	0747 5.0 1209 1.9 2014 4.9	0612 3.6 1202 1.6 1842 3.6	0400 2.9 0944 1.4 1630 2.9 2235 1.4	0336 1.7 0941 0.9 1609 1.7 2224 0.9	0546 2.0 1200 4.1 1824 2.1	0432 1.6 1012 3.1 1702 1.8 2306 3.0	0503 2.9 1055 0.7 1715 3.0 2319 0.7	0341 8.0 1019 2.6 1606 7.8 2253 2.8
3 M	0124 2.0 0835 4.5 1359 2.1 2109 4.5	0100 2.0 0845 4.8 1345 2.2 2122 4.8	0047 1.6 0719 3.5 1323 1.7 2001 3.5	0503 2.9 1112 1.5 1745 2.9	0445 1.7 1106 0.9 1731 1.6 2356 0.9	0101 4.0 0657 2.2 1334 4.0 1948 2.2	0537 1.7 1129 2.9 1820 1.8	0557 2.8 1209 0.8 1817 2.8	0447 7.7 1129 2.8 1724 7.5
4 TU	0315 2.1 0947 4.5 1612 2.0 2233 4.6	0315 2.2 0953 4.8 1539 2.1 2235 4.9	0214 1.7 0841 3.5 1457 1.6 2129 3.6	0007 1.5 0620 2.9 1252 1.4 1911 2.9	0604 1.7 1247 0.8 1855 1.7	0227 4.1 0831 2.2 1505 4.1 2124 2.1	0114 3.0 0700 1.7 1343 2.9 2000 1.7	0039 0.8 0719 2.7 1336 0.8 1942 2.8	0019 3.0 0612 7.6 1301 2.8 1855 7.6
5 W	0457 1.9 1106 4.7 1737 1.6 2352 4.9	0513 1.9 1102 4.9 1745 1.7 2345 5.1	0339 1.5 0958 3.6 1615 1.3 2242 3.8	0133 1.4 0738 3.0 1412 1.2 2028 3.1	0118 0.9 0720 1.8 1354 0.7 2010 1.8	0339 4.3 1000 1.9 1618 4.4 2237 1.7	0243 3.2 0827 1.5 1512 3.2 2118 1.4	0202 0.8 0859 2.8 1449 0.6 2113 2.8	0151 2.6 0735 7.9 1427 2.3 2014 8.1
6 TH	0605 1.6 1215 5.0 1838 1.2	0620 1.6 1209 5.2 1854 1.3	0446 1.3 1100 3.9 1716 1.0 2340 4.1	0239 1.2 0845 3.2 1512 0.9 2130 3.3	0219 0.7 0825 1.9 1450 0.5 2112 1.9	0439 4.7 1103 1.4 1712 4.7 2332 1.3	0339 3.5 0937 1.2 1609 3.4 2213 1.0	0311 0.6 1012 3.0 1548 0.3 2226 3.0	0305 2.0 0844 8.6 1536 1.6 2118 8.7
7 F	0052 5.3 0658 1.2 1310 5.4 1930 0.7	0048 5.5 0713 1.2 1309 5.6 1950 0.8	0539 1.0 1152 4.2 1808 0.6	0330 1.0 0942 3.5 1600 0.6 2223 3.5	0311 0.6 0921 2.1 1539 0.3 2203 2.1	0528 5.1 1155 0.9 1758 5.1	0427 3.9 1033 0.8 1656 3.7 2259 0.6	0406 0.5 1109 3.2 1637 0.1 2328 3.1	0406 1.4 0941 9.2 1636 0.9 2211 9.3
8 SA	0142 5.6 0746 0.8 1357 5.7 2019 0.3	0143 5.8 0802 0.8 1403 5.9 2039 0.4	0030 4.3 0627 0.8 1239 4.5 1855 0.3	0416 0.7 1033 3.7 1645 0.3 2311 3.6	0358 0.5 1012 2.2 1625 0.2 2251 2.2	0018 0.9 0612 5.5 1242 0.5 1840 5.4	0512 4.2 1121 0.5 1737 4.0 2342 0.3	0454 0.3 1200 3.4 1722 -0.1	0500 0.8 1032 9.8 1729 0.3 2259 9.8
9 SU	0227 5.9 0832 0.5 1442 6.0 2105 0.0	0233 6.1 0846 0.5 1453 6.2 2123 0.2	0115 4.5 0712 0.6 1323 4.7 1940 0.1	0459 0.6 1121 3.9 1729 0.2 2356 3.7	0442 0.3 1058 2.3 1709 0.1 2336 2.2	0103 0.5 0654 5.7 1325 0.2 1921 5.5	0554 4.4 1206 0.3 1815 4.2	0024 3.2 0539 0.1 1248 3.6 1806 -0.2	0548 0.3 1119 10.2 1816 -0.1 2345 10.0 ●
10 M	0310 6.0 0916 0.3 1527 6.1 2149 -0.0	0320 6.3 0930 0.4 1542 6.4 2205 0.1	0159 4.6 0754 0.4 1406 4.8 2024 0.1	0541 0.5 1206 3.9 1812 0.2	0524 0.3 1144 2.4 1752 0.1	0145 0.3 0736 5.8 1407 0.1 2000 5.5	0025 0.2 0636 4.5 1250 0.3 1851 4.2	0113 3.3 0621 0.0 1333 3.7 1848 -0.2	0633 0.0 1204 10.4 1900 -0.2
11 TU	0355 5.9 1000 0.3 1613 6.1 2230 0.1	0407 6.3 1011 0.4 1630 6.4 2245 0.3	0242 4.5 0837 0.4 1451 4.7 2106 0.2	0039 3.7 0622 0.5 1251 3.9 1853 0.3	0018 2.2 0607 0.3 1228 2.3 1835 0.1	0226 0.3 0818 5.8 1448 0.2 2042 5.4	0108 0.1 0715 4.4 1333 0.3 1926 4.1	0157 3.4 0703 -0.0 1415 3.7 1933 -0.2	0027 10.0 0715 0.0 1248 10.3 1941 -0.0
12 W	0440 5.8 1040 0.5 1701 5.9 2309 0.5	0455 6.1 1018 0.6 1718 6.2 2239 0.7	0324 4.4 0918 0.5 1537 4.6 2148 0.5	0121 3.6 0704 0.5 1335 3.8 1933 0.5	0100 2.1 0650 0.3 1313 2.2 1919 0.3	0307 0.4 0902 5.5 1528 0.5 2124 5.1	0150 0.3 0754 4.2 1414 0.6 2000 3.9	0237 3.4 0748 -0.0 1455 3.7 2018 -0.0	0109 9.8 0757 0.2 1330 10.0 2020 0.4
13 TH	0527 5.5 1117 0.8 1751 5.6 2341 1.0	0542 5.8 1028 0.9 1807 5.9 2247 1.1	0408 4.2 1002 0.7 1624 4.3 2231 0.8	0202 3.4 0745 0.7 1419 3.5 2015 0.8	0142 2.0 0735 0.4 1400 2.1 2004 0.5	0349 0.7 0950 5.1 1609 0.9 2210 4.7	0233 0.6 0833 3.8 1455 0.8 2033 3.7	0315 3.5 0833 0.1 1536 3.6 2107 0.2	0151 9.5 0836 0.7 1412 9.5 2058 1.0
14 F	0615 5.2 1149 1.2 1842 5.2	0631 5.5 1102 1.2 1858 5.5 2325 1.2	0454 4.0 1048 1.0 1717 4.0 2318 1.2	0245 3.2 0830 0.9 1507 3.3 2059 1.1	0226 1.9 0824 0.6 1448 1.9 2053 0.7	0433 1.2 1045 4.7 1653 1.4 2306 4.4	0318 0.9 0912 3.5 1538 1.2 2110 3.4	0353 3.4 0923 0.3 1617 3.4 2201 0.4	0231 9.0 0918 1.3 1455 8.9 2138 1.7
15 SA	0006 1.5 0706 4.9 1228 1.6 1938 4.9	0724 5.1 1148 1.6 1954 5.1	0545 3.7 1142 1.3 1818 3.7	0331 3.0 0924 1.1 1601 3.0 2154 1.4	0313 1.8 0920 0.7 1542 1.7 2150 0.9	0523 1.6 1154 4.3 1742 1.8	0407 1.3 1000 3.1 1625 1.5 2155 3.1	0433 3.3 1018 0.5 1702 3.2 2304 0.5	0315 8.4 1003 2.0 1544 8.2 2224 2.4

● ● Time UT. For British Summer Time (shaded) March 30th to October 26th ADD ONE HOUR ● ●

MARCH 1997 TIDE TABLES MARCH 1997

	LEITH		ROSYTH		ABERDEEN		WICK		LERWICK		ULLAPOOL		OBAN		GREENOCK		LIVERPOOL	
	Time	m	Time	m	Time	m	Time	m	Time	m	Time	m	Time	m	Time	m	Time	m
16 SU	0048	1.9	0018	2.0	0013	1.6	0427	2.9	0407	1.7	0024	4.1	0507	1.7	0515	3.1	0408	7.8
	0803	4.6	0823	4.7	0648	3.5	1039	1.3	1033	0.8	0624	2.0	1115	2.8	1126	0.7	1101	2.6
	1333	1.9	1303	2.0	1251	1.5	1708	2.8	1645	1.6	1314	4.0	1722	1.7	1754	2.9	1645	7.5
	2039	4.5	2057	4.8	1930	3.5	2315	1.6	2308	1.0	1845	2.2	2310	2.8			2327	3.0
17 M	0205	2.3	0305	2.3	0127	1.8	0538	2.8	0514	1.6	0152	3.9	0633	1.9	0019	0.9	0518	7.3
	0907	4.4	0929	4.6	0800	3.4	1218	1.4	1209	0.9	0752	2.3	1337	2.8	0604	2.9	1221	3.0
	1530	2.1	1549	2.1	1419	1.7	1830	2.7	1807	1.5	1436	3.9	1839	1.8	1249	0.9	1807	7.1
	2151	4.4	2206	4.6	2051	3.3					2020	2.4			1913	2.6		
18 TU	0417	2.4	0418	2.4	0300	1.9	0057	1.6	0044	1.6	0312	4.0	0233	2.9	0144	1.0	0054	3.3
	1022	4.3	1038	4.6	0919	3.4	0700	2.8	0638	1.6	0934	2.2	0826	1.9	0718	2.7	0648	7.2
	1704	2.0	1659	2.0	1548	1.6	1345	1.3	1327	0.8	1547	4.0	1446	2.9	1420	0.9	1348	2.9
	2311	4.4	2317	4.6	2209	3.4	1952	2.7	1942	1.6	2155	2.3	2011	1.8	2107	2.6	1935	7.2
19 W	0531	2.2	0506	2.2	0418	1.8	0211	1.5	0154	1.0	0415	4.1	0325	3.1	0254	0.9	0218	3.1
	1142	4.5	1146	4.8	1029	3.5	0812	2.9	0756	1.7	1039	2.0	0933	1.7	0905	2.8	0807	7.5
	1803	1.7	1815	1.8	1648	1.4	1442	1.2	1425	0.7	1641	4.2	1534	3.1	1523	0.8	1459	2.6
					2309	3.5	2054	2.9	2039	1.6	2253	2.0	2118	1.6	2215	2.7	2041	7.7
20 TH	0020	4.6	0023	4.8	0508	1.6	0258	1.4	0245	0.9	0500	4.3	0359	3.3	0346	0.8	0319	2.6
	0619	1.9	0537	2.0	1121	3.7	0907	3.0	0848	1.8	1125	1.7	1015	1.5	1011	2.9	0904	8.0
	1243	4.7	1244	5.0	1732	1.2	1523	1.1	1508	0.6	1721	4.4	1613	3.3	1608	0.6	1552	2.1
	1847	1.5	1912	1.6	2354	3.7	2140	3.0	2120	1.7	2335	1.7	2204	1.3	2303	2.8	2130	8.1
21 F	0109	4.8	0112	5.1	0547	1.4	0334	1.3	0324	0.8	0536	4.5	0426	3.4	0427	0.6	0406	2.2
	0656	1.7	0610	1.8	1203	3.8	0951	3.2	0931	1.9	1203	1.4	1049	1.4	1057	3.1	0948	8.4
	1328	4.9	1331	5.3	1809	1.1	1557	0.9	1543	0.6	1754	4.6	1648	3.5	1644	0.5	1634	1.7
	1921	1.4	1945	1.4			2218	3.1	2157	1.8			2242	1.2	2341	3.0	2208	8.5
22 SA	0146	5.0	0151	5.3	0029	3.8	0406	1.1	0357	0.7	0011	1.5	0453	3.6	0501	0.5	0443	1.8
	0728	1.4	0648	1.5	0621	1.2	1028	3.3	1009	2.0	0606	4.7	1121	1.2	1135	3.2	1024	8.8
	1405	5.1	1412	5.5	1237	4.0	1629	0.8	1615	0.5	1236	1.2	1720	3.7	1715	0.4	1710	1.4
	1951	1.2	1950	1.2	1841	0.9	2251	3.2	2230	1.9	1824	4.8	2316	1.0			2242	8.8
23 SU	0217	5.1	0224	5.4	0100	4.0	0436	1.0	0425	0.6	0043	1.2	0521	3.8	0016	3.0	0516	1.5
	0759	1.1	0727	1.2	0653	1.1	1103	3.3	1042	2.0	0633	4.9	1151	1.1	0532	0.4	1057	9.0
	1437	5.3	1448	5.6	1309	4.1	1659	0.7	1643	0.4	1306	1.0	1751	3.9	1211	3.3	1742	1.2
	2021	0.8	1957	1.1	1912	0.8	2323	3.3	2302	1.9	1853	4.9			1744	0.3	2314	9.1
24 M ○	0247	5.2	0255	5.6	0130	4.0	0506	0.9	0453	0.5	0114	1.1	0550	3.9	0050	3.1	0547	1.3
	0831	0.9	0804	1.1	0723	0.9	1135	3.4	1113	2.0	0700	5.0	1220	1.0	0601	0.3	1129	9.2
	1508	5.4	1521	5.7	1339	4.1	1728	0.6	1712	0.4	1336	0.9	1821	3.9	1245	3.3	1812	1.1
	2053	0.7	2029	1.0	1942	0.7	2354	3.4	2330	2.0	1921	5.0			1812	0.2	2344	9.2
25 TU	0318	5.3	0324	5.6	0200	4.1	0535	0.8	0521	0.5	0144	0.9	0020	0.8	0121	3.1	0618	1.1
	0904	0.8	0839	1.0	0751	0.9	1206	3.4	1142	2.1	0727	5.0	0618	4.0	0630	0.2	1200	9.3
	1539	5.4	1552	5.7	1410	4.2	1758	0.6	1741	0.4	1405	0.8	1248	1.0	1316	3.3	1842	1.0
	2125	0.7	2058	1.0	2012	0.7			2358	2.0	1948	5.0	1848	4.0	1841	0.2		
26 W	0351	5.3	0355	5.6	0229	4.1	0024	3.3	0551	0.5	0213	0.9	0051	0.8	0151	3.1	0015	9.3
	0936	0.8	0907	1.0	0821	0.8	0606	0.7	1211	2.0	0756	5.0	0647	4.0	0701	0.1	0651	1.0
	1612	5.4	1623	5.7	1441	4.2	1238	3.4	1813	0.4	1434	0.8	1317	1.0	1347	3.3	1230	9.3
	2157	0.7	2124	1.0	2042	0.7	1828	0.6			2018	5.0	1915	4.0	1912	0.1	1914	1.0
27 TH	0425	5.3	0429	5.7	0300	4.1	0054	3.3	0027	2.0	0244	0.9	0123	0.9	0220	3.2	0045	9.2
	1003	0.9	0930	1.1	0851	0.8	0637	0.7	0624	0.5	0827	4.9	0716	3.9	0734	0.1	0724	1.1
	1644	5.3	1655	5.6	1515	4.1	1311	3.3	1242	2.0	1506	0.9	1347	1.1	1418	3.3	1300	9.2
	2224	0.9	2148	1.1	2113	0.8	1859	0.7	1847	0.5	2049	4.8	1943	3.9	1945	0.1	1945	1.2
28 F	0500	5.2	0506	5.6	0333	4.0	0127	3.2	0059	2.0	0317	1.0	0157	1.0	0249	3.2	0117	9.1
	1021	1.0	0954	1.1	0924	0.9	0710	0.8	0700	0.5	0901	4.8	0746	3.8	0809	0.1	0757	1.3
	1718	5.2	1732	5.5	1551	4.0	1345	3.2	1318	2.0	1539	1.1	1419	1.2	1451	3.3	1333	9.0
	2245	1.1	2214	1.2	2147	0.9	1933	0.8	1923	0.5	2126	4.7	2012	3.7	2022	0.2	2018	1.5
29 SA	0536	5.1	0547	5.6	0410	3.9	0203	3.2	0133	1.9	0353	1.2	0236	1.1	0321	3.1	0151	8.9
	1042	1.2	1022	1.2	1000	0.9	0747	0.9	0739	0.6	0942	4.5	0819	3.6	0848	0.2	0832	1.6
	1757	5.0	1812	5.3	1633	3.9	1425	3.1	1357	1.9	1616	1.3	1457	1.3	1527	3.2	1409	8.7
	2309	1.3	2246	1.4	2226	1.1	2012	1.0	2003	0.6	2211	4.4	2048	3.5	2103	0.3	2051	1.9
30 SU	0618	4.9	0630	5.3	0453	3.7	0244	3.1	0214	1.8	0434	1.4	0319	1.3	0356	3.1	0230	8.6
	1116	1.4	1100	1.4	1044	1.2	0830	1.0	0824	0.7	1034	4.3	0858	3.4	0933	0.3	0910	1.9
	1844	4.8	1859	5.1	1721	3.7	1513	3.0	1446	1.8	1700	1.6	1541	1.6	1607	3.1	1451	8.4
	2349	1.6	2327	1.7	2315	1.3	2100	1.1	2053	0.8	2311	4.2	2132	3.3	2151	0.5	2133	2.3
31 M	0707	4.7	0718	5.0	0545	3.6	0334	2.9	0304	1.7	0526	1.7	0412	1.5	0437	3.0	0319	8.2
	1209	1.7	1149	1.7	1142	1.3	0927	1.1	0923	0.7	1147	4.0	0948	3.1	1029	0.5	1000	2.3
	1940	4.6	1954	4.9	1824	3.5	1612	2.8	1552	1.7	1757	1.9	1637	1.6	1657	3.0	1548	7.9
							2209	1.3	2158	0.9			2241	3.1	2253	0.7	2230	2.7

● ● Time UT. For British Summer Time (shaded) March 30th to October 26th ADD ONE HOUR ● ●

SCOTLAND & NORTH WEST ENGLAND Time Zone UT

Leith * Rosyth * Aberdeen *Wick * Lerwick * Ullapool * Oban * Greenock * Liverpool

APRIL 1997 TIDE TABLES APRIL 1997

LEITH Time m	ROSYTH Time m	ABERDEEN Time m	WICK Time m	LERWICK Time m	ULLAPOOL Time m	OBAN Time m	GREENOCK Time m	LIVERPOOL Time m	Day
0101 1.9	0029 2.0	0023 1.5	0436 2.8	0413 1.7	0033 4.0	0517 1.6	0529 2.9	0424 7.8	1 TU
0808 4.5	0816 4.8	0651 3.5	1055 1.2	1045 0.8	0636 1.9	1107 2.9	1144 0.6	1108 2.6	
1347 1.9	1319 1.9	1303 1.4	1729 2.8	1714 1.6	1320 3.9	1751 1.7	1800 2.8	1705 7.6	
2051 4.5	2102 4.8	1945 3.5	2344 1.4	2328 0.9	1922 2.1			2351 2.9	
0257 2.1	0300 2.1	0151 1.6	0553 2.8	0536 1.6	0200 4.1	0048 3.0	0011 0.8	0548 7.7	2 W
0920 4.5	0926 4.7	0812 3.4	1234 1.1	1223 0.7	0810 1.9	0641 1.7	0644 2.8	1237 2.5	
1555 1.8	1529 1.9	1436 1.4	1855 2.8	1838 1.6	1448 4.0	1330 2.9	1307 0.6	1836 7.6	
2213 4.6	2216 4.9	2112 3.5			2103 2.0	1930 1.6	1923 2.8		
0436 1.9	0456 1.9	0318 1.5	0112 1.3	0057 0.8	0315 4.3	0220 3.2	0133 0.8	0126 2.6	3 TH
1039 4.6	1041 4.9	0932 3.6	0712 2.9	0654 1.7	0939 1.7	0810 1.5	0824 2.8	0712 8.0	
1717 1.4	1734 1.5	1556 1.1	1354 0.9	1334 0.6	1600 4.3	1456 3.1	1421 0.5	1404 2.1	
2331 4.9	2327 5.1	2224 3.7	2012 3.0	1954 1.7	2217 1.6	2053 1.4	2053 2.8	1955 8.1	
0543 1.5	0559 1.5	0426 1.3	0219 1.1	0200 0.7	0416 4.6	0318 3.5	0245 0.7	0242 2.1	4 F
1150 5.0	1151 5.2	1037 3.8	0823 3.1	0803 1.8	1044 1.2	0920 1.1	0945 3.0	0822 8.6	
1818 1.0	1838 1.1	1657 0.8	1453 0.7	1430 0.4	1655 4.6	1551 3.4	1524 0.2	1516 1.5	
		2322 4.0	2113 3.2	2054 1.9	2312 1.2	2150 1.0	2207 3.0	2059 8.7	
0032 5.3	0030 5.4	0520 1.0	0312 0.9	0252 0.6	0507 5.0	0407 3.9	0344 0.5	0345 1.4	5 SA
0636 1.1	0651 1.2	1130 4.1	0921 3.3	0901 2.0	1136 0.8	1014 0.8	1047 3.2	0921 9.2	
1247 5.3	1251 5.5	1748 0.5	1542 0.5	1520 0.2	1740 5.0	1636 3.7	1615 0.0	1616 0.9	
1910 0.6	1931 0.7		2205 3.4	2144 2.0	2359 0.8	2238 0.6	2309 3.1	2152 9.3	
0121 5.6	0122 5.7	0011 4.2	0357 0.7	0339 0.4	0551 5.3	0452 4.1	0433 0.3	0439 0.8	6 SU
0724 0.8	0738 0.8	0608 0.7	1013 3.5	0952 2.1	1221 0.4	1101 0.5	1139 3.4	1012 9.7	
1336 5.7	1343 5.8	1218 4.4	1625 0.3	1604 0.1	1821 5.2	1717 3.9	1701 -0.1	1708 0.4	
1958 0.3	2018 0.4	1836 0.3	2251 3.5	2230 2.1		2322 0.4		2239 9.7	
0206 5.8	0210 6.0	0055 4.4	0439 0.5	0422 0.3	0043 0.5	0534 4.3	0003 3.2	0528 0.4	7 M
0811 0.5	0820 0.6	0652 0.5	1101 3.7	1039 2.2	0634 5.5	1145 0.4	0518 0.1	1059 10.0	
1421 5.9	1432 6.1	1303 4.5	1707 0.2	1648 0.1	1304 0.2	1754 4.1	1228 3.5	1754 0.1	●
2043 0.1	2101 0.3	1919 0.2	2334 3.6	2312 2.1	1900 5.4		1744 -0.2	2324 9.9	
0249 5.9	0257 6.1	0137 4.4	0521 0.4	0504 0.2	0125 0.3	0005 0.3	0051 3.3	0612 0.2	8 TU
0856 0.3	0901 0.4	0735 0.4	1146 3.7	1124 2.3	0715 5.6	0615 4.3	0600 -0.0	1143 10.2	
1507 6.0	1520 6.2	1347 4.6	1748 0.2	1730 0.1	1345 0.2	1227 0.3	1312 3.6	1836 0.0	
2127 0.1	2141 0.3	2001 0.2		2354 2.1	1939 5.4	1829 4.2	1827 -0.2		
0333 5.8	0344 6.1	0218 4.4	0016 3.6	0546 0.2	0206 0.3	0047 0.3	0132 3.3	0006 9.9	9 W
0939 0.3	0944 0.4	0816 0.4	0603 0.4	1209 2.2	0757 5.5	0654 4.3	0642 -0.1	0654 0.1	
1554 5.9	1609 6.2	1432 4.5	1231 3.7	1811 0.2	1424 0.3	1309 0.4	1354 3.6	1226 10.1	
2207 0.3	2219 0.5	2042 0.3	1828 0.3		2018 5.2	1902 4.1	1910 -0.1	1916 0.2	
0418 5.7	0431 6.0	0259 4.3	0056 3.5	0033 2.1	0247 0.4	0130 0.4	0209 3.4	0046 9.7	10 TH
1021 0.4	1012 0.6	0858 0.5	0644 0.4	0630 0.3	0841 5.2	0731 4.0	0726 -0.1	0735 0.3	
1641 5.7	1656 6.0	1517 4.4	1314 3.6	1253 2.1	1504 0.5	1348 0.6	1434 3.5	1307 9.8	
2244 0.7	2148 0.8	2122 0.6	1907 0.6	1854 0.4	2058 5.0	1935 4.0	1954 0.0	1954 0.6	
0503 5.5	0518 5.7	0341 4.1	0136 3.3	0114 2.0	0328 0.7	0212 0.7	0246 3.4	0126 9.4	11 F
1057 0.7	1003 0.9	0941 0.6	0726 0.6	0715 0.4	0927 4.8	0807 3.8	0811 0.0	0815 0.8	
1729 5.5	1744 5.7	1604 4.1	1358 3.3	1338 2.0	1544 0.9	1428 0.9	1513 3.4	1348 9.3	
2312 1.1	2218 1.2	2203 0.9	1945 0.8	1937 0.5	2142 4.7	2009 3.7	2041 0.2	2030 1.2	
0548 5.2	0605 5.4	0424 3.9	0216 3.2	0155 1.9	0411 1.1	0256 1.2	0324 3.4	0205 9.0	12 SA
1128 1.1	1036 1.2	1025 0.9	0810 0.8	0803 0.5	1020 4.4	0845 3.4	0857 0.2	0854 1.3	
1818 5.1	1833 5.4	1654 3.9	1443 3.1	1425 1.9	1625 1.3	1509 1.1	1554 3.2	1430 8.8	
2333 1.5	2254 1.6	2245 1.2	2026 1.1	2023 0.7	2231 4.3	2045 3.5	2131 0.5	2108 1.8	
0636 4.9	0654 5.0	0512 3.7	0300 3.0	0239 1.8	0458 1.5	0343 1.4	0402 3.3	0246 8.5	13 SU
1202 1.5	1118 1.5	1115 1.2	0900 1.0	0857 0.6	1124 4.1	0929 3.1	0949 0.4	0937 2.0	
1909 4.8	1924 5.0	1751 3.6	1535 2.9	1515 1.7	1711 1.7	1554 1.4	1637 3.0	1515 8.1	
	2340 2.0	2336 1.5	2114 1.3	2115 0.9	2337 4.0	2128 3.2	2228 0.7	2149 2.5	
0009 1.9	0748 4.7	0608 3.5	0351 2.8	0330 1.7	0554 1.8	0439 1.7	0442 3.2	0335 7.9	14 M
0728 4.6	1224 1.9	1217 1.4	1007 1.2	1001 0.7	1239 3.8	1030 2.9	1049 0.7	1029 2.6	
1257 1.8	2021 4.7	1857 3.4	1636 2.7	1612 1.5	1807 2.1	1647 1.7	1726 2.8	1611 7.5	
2005 4.5			2221 1.5	2221 1.0		2233 3.0	2335 0.9	2242 3.1	
0115 2.3	0117 2.4	0042 1.8	0454 2.7	0430 1.6	0102 3.8	0554 1.9	0527 3.0	0437 7.4	15 TU
0827 4.4	0849 4.5	0715 3.3	1132 1.3	1120 0.8	0709 2.1	1223 2.8	1200 0.8	1139 3.0	
1433 2.0	1512 2.0	1336 1.5	1751 2.6	1724 1.5	1356 3.7	1756 1.8	1834 2.6	1724 7.1	
2109 4.3	2124 4.5	2011 3.3	2357 1.6	2346 1.0	1927 2.3				

● ● Time UT. For British Summer Time (shaded) March 30th to October 26th ADD ONE HOUR ● ●

APRIL 1997 TIDE TABLES APRIL 1997

Day	LEITH	ROSYTH	ABERDEEN	WICK	LERWICK	ULLAPOOL	OBAN	GREENOCK	LIVERPOOL
	Time m	Time m	Time m	Time m	Time m	Time m	Time m	Time m	Time m
16 W	0306 2.4	0328 2.4	0209 1.9	0611 2.6	0545 1.6	0224 3.8	0115 2.9	0052 1.1	0001 3.4
	0934 4.3	0955 4.5	0830 3.3	1258 1.2	1239 0.8	0845 2.1	0736 1.9	0625 2.8	0557 7.2
	1617 2.0	1619 2.0	1503 1.5	1911 2.6	1854 1.5	1508 3.8	1355 2.9	1325 0.9	1301 3.0
	2221 4.3	2230 4.5	2127 3.3			2107 2.3	1921 1.8	2016 2.5	1850 7.1
17 TH	0444 2.3	0424 2.3	0334 1.8	0126 1.5	0110 1.0	0332 3.9	0233 3.0	0209 1.0	0128 3.3
	1050 4.3	1101 4.6	0942 3.3	0727 2.7	0709 1.6	0959 1.9	0852 1.8	0802 2.7	0720 7.3
	1719 1.8	1713 1.9	1609 1.4	1401 1.1	1342 0.7	1605 4.0	1451 3.0	1439 0.9	1412 2.7
	2333 4.4	2336 4.6	2230 3.4	2016 2.7	1959 1.6	2215 2.1	2035 1.7	2130 2.7	2000 7.5
18 F	0539 2.0	0507 2.1	0432 1.6	0222 1.4	0208 0.9	0423 4.1	0313 3.2	0306 0.9	0235 2.9
	1159 4.5	1202 4.8	1041 3.5	0827 2.8	0809 1.7	1048 1.7	0939 1.6	0924 2.8	0823 7.6
	1805 1.5	1757 1.7	1655 1.2	1446 1.0	1429 0.6	1648 4.2	1536 3.2	1528 0.7	1509 2.3
			2318 3.6	2105 2.8	2044 1.7	2301 1.8	2127 1.5	2220 2.8	2052 7.9
19 SA	0028 4.6	0030 4.9	0514 1.4	0303 1.2	0250 0.8	0502 4.3	0347 3.4	0350 0.7	0325 2.5
	0620 1.7	0546 1.8	1126 3.6	0915 2.9	0856 1.8	1128 1.4	1017 1.5	1017 3.0	0910 8.2
	1250 4.7	1253 5.1	1733 1.1	1524 0.9	1506 0.6	1724 4.4	1615 3.4	1607 0.5	1554 1.9
	1842 1.3	1828 1.5	2355 3.7	2145 3.0	2122 1.8	2339 1.5	2208 1.3	2302 2.9	2133 8.4
20 SU	0109 4.9	0112 5.1	0550 1.2	0336 1.1	0324 0.7	0534 4.5	0418 3.6	0427 0.5	0406 2.0
	0655 1.4	0625 1.6	1203 3.8	0954 3.1	0935 1.8	1203 1.2	1050 1.3	1101 3.1	0949 8.5
	1329 5.0	1337 5.3	1808 0.9	1557 0.8	1539 0.5	1755 4.6	1649 3.6	1640 0.4	1633 1.6
	1915 1.1	1857 1.3		2219 3.1	2157 1.8		2244 1.1	2341 3.0	2209 8.8
21 M	0143 5.0	0149 5.3	0028 3.9	0409 0.9	0354 0.6	0013 1.3	0450 3.7	0500 0.4	0442 1.7
	0730 1.2	0705 1.3	0623 1.1	1031 3.2	1010 1.9	0604 4.6	1121 1.2	1140 3.1	1024 8.8
	1404 5.1	1416 5.4	1238 3.9	1628 0.7	1609 0.4	1235 1.0	1722 3.8	1711 0.3	1708 1.3
	1948 0.9	1930 1.1	1840 0.8	2252 3.2	2229 1.9	1824 4.8	2318 1.0		2242 9.0
22 TU ○	0217 5.2	0223 5.5	0100 4.0	0439 0.8	0424 0.5	0045 1.1	0521 3.8	0017 3.1	0518 1.4
	0805 0.9	0743 1.1	0654 0.9	1106 3.2	1042 2.0	0633 4.8	1151 1.1	0531 0.2	1058 9.1
	1439 5.3	1452 5.5	1311 4.0	1659 0.6	1640 0.4	1306 0.8	1752 3.9	1216 3.2	1742 1.1
	2024 0.7	2003 1.0	1912 0.7	2324 3.2	2259 2.0	1853 4.9	2351 0.9	1742 0.2	2314 9.2
23 W	0251 5.3	0256 5.6	0130 4.1	0511 0.7	0455 0.5	0118 0.9	0552 3.9	0051 3.1	0553 1.1
	0840 0.8	0818 1.0	0726 0.8	1140 3.3	1115 2.0	0702 4.9	1220 1.0	0602 0.1	1131 9.2
	1513 5.3	1525 5.6	1345 4.1	1730 0.6	1712 0.4	1337 0.7	1821 4.0	1250 3.2	1816 1.0
	2059 0.7	2033 1.0	1944 0.6	2357 3.3	2330 2.0	1923 5.0		1812 0.1	2347 9.3
24 TH	0326 5.3	0330 5.6	0203 4.1	0544 0.6	0529 0.4	0149 0.8	0024 0.9	0123 3.1	0628 1.0
	0915 0.8	0847 1.0	0758 0.7	1215 3.3	1148 2.0	0733 4.9	0622 4.0	0635 0.0	1204 9.3
	1548 5.3	1559 5.6	1418 4.1	1802 0.6	1748 0.4	1409 0.7	1251 0.9	1323 3.2	1851 1.0
	2133 0.7	2101 1.0	2017 0.7			1954 4.9	1851 4.0	1846 0.1	
25 F	0401 5.3	0406 5.7	0236 4.1	0030 3.3	0002 2.0	0223 0.7	0059 0.9	0154 3.2	0021 9.4
	0947 0.8	0911 1.0	0832 0.7	0618 0.6	0605 0.4	0808 4.8	0654 3.9	0709 0.0	0705 1.0
	1622 5.3	1634 5.6	1455 4.1	1251 3.2	1224 2.0	1442 0.8	1324 1.0	1357 3.2	1239 9.2
	2206 0.8	2127 1.0	2051 0.7	1837 0.6	1824 0.4	2029 4.9	1921 4.0	1923 0.1	1925 1.1
26 SA	0437 5.3	0445 5.6	0311 4.0	0106 3.3	0036 2.0	0258 0.8	0136 0.9	0226 3.2	0057 9.3
	1015 0.9	0938 1.0	0908 0.7	0655 0.6	0644 0.4	0848 4.7	0727 3.8	0748 0.0	0742 1.1
	1700 5.2	1714 5.5	1535 4.0	1330 3.2	1303 1.9	1518 0.9	1400 1.0	1432 3.2	1315 9.1
	2235 1.0	2157 1.2	2128 0.9	1915 0.7	1903 0.5	2109 4.7	1955 3.8	2003 0.2	2000 1.4
27 SU	0516 5.1	0526 5.5	0350 3.9	0145 3.2	0113 1.9	0337 1.0	0218 1.1	0300 3.2	0135 9.1
	1042 1.0	1011 1.1	0948 0.8	0736 0.7	0726 0.5	0934 4.5	0804 3.6	0830 0.1	0819 1.4
	1742 5.1	1757 5.4	1620 3.9	1413 3.1	1347 1.8	1558 1.2	1440 1.2	1512 3.1	1356 8.8
	2306 1.3	2232 1.4	2211 1.0	1957 0.9	1947 0.6	2158 4.5	2034 3.6	2047 0.3	2038 1.7
28 M	0600 5.0	0610 5.3	0434 3.8	0227 3.1	0155 1.9	0422 1.2	0306 1.2	0338 3.2	0218 8.8
	1121 1.2	1052 1.2	1036 0.9	0824 0.8	0815 0.5	1031 4.2	0847 3.4	0918 0.2	0901 1.7
	1831 4.9	1845 5.2	1712 3.7	1504 2.9	1440 1.7	1645 1.4	1527 1.3	1557 3.1	1442 8.5
	2355 1.6	2317 1.6	2303 1.2	2048 1.0	2038 0.7	2300 4.3	2123 3.4	2138 0.5	2122 2.1
29 TU	0650 4.8	0659 5.1	0527 3.7	0318 3.0	0247 1.8	0516 1.4	0400 1.4	0421 3.1	0309 8.5
	1224 1.4	1148 1.4	1137 1.1	0926 0.9	0915 0.6	1145 4.0	0941 3.1	1017 0.3	0953 2.0
	1929 4.8	1942 5.0	1816 3.6	1605 2.8	1547 1.7	1745 1.7	1622 1.5	1650 3.0	1540 8.1
				2157 1.2	2144 0.8		2234 3.2	2240 0.7	2219 2.5
30 W	0111 1.8	0029 1.9	0011 1.4	0420 2.9	0356 1.7	0018 4.1	0506 1.5	0515 3.0	0413 8.1
	0750 4.7	0757 4.9	0633 3.5	1048 1.0	1031 0.6	0626 1.6	1100 2.9	1129 0.4	1059 2.2
	1357 1.6	1324 1.6	1254 1.2	1718 2.7	1702 1.6	1309 3.9	1733 1.6	1755 2.9	1654 7.8
	2037 4.7	2049 4.9	1933 3.5	2324 1.3	2306 0.8	1906 1.9		2353 0.8	2335 2.7

● ● Time UT. For British Summer Time (shaded) March 30th to October 26th ADD ONE HOUR ● ●

SCOTLAND & NORTH WEST ENGLAND   Time Zone UT
Leith * Rosyth * Aberdeen * Wick * Lerwick * Ullapool * Oban * Greenock * Liverpool
MAY 1997 TIDE TABLES MAY 1997

	LEITH	ROSYTH	ABERDEEN	WICK	LERWICK	ULLAPOOL	OBAN	GREENOCK	LIVERPOOL
	Time m	Time m	Time m	Time m	Time m	Time m	Time m	Time m	Time m
1 TH	0241 1.9	0251 2.0	0133 1.5	0533 2.8	0515 1.7	0136 4.1	0025 3.2	0625 2.9	0530 8.0
	0900 4.6	0909 4.8	0751 3.5	1215 0.9	1159 0.6	0752 1.6	0624 1.5	1244 0.4	1220 2.2
	1534 1.5	1552 1.6	1418 1.1	1839 2.8	1819 1.6	1429 4.0	1302 2.9	1912 2.8	1817 7.8
	2154 4.7	2203 4.9	2053 3.6			2037 1.8	1901 1.5		
2 F	0408 1.8	0433 1.8	0254 1.4	0047 1.2	0032 0.8	0249 4.3	0153 3.3	0108 0.8	0102 2.5
	1016 4.7	1026 4.9	0906 3.6	0649 2.9	0630 1.7	0914 1.4	0747 1.4	0755 2.9	0648 8.2
	1651 1.3	1717 1.3	1533 1.0	1331 0.8	1310 0.5	1539 4.2	1428 3.1	1356 0.4	1341 1.9
	2308 4.9	2311 5.1	2203 3.7	1952 2.9	1931 1.7	2151 1.6	2022 1.3	2034 2.9	1933 8.2
3 SA	0515 1.5	0535 1.5	0401 1.2	0155 1.0	0137 0.7	0352 4.5	0254 3.5	0219 0.7	0218 2.0
	1125 5.0	1134 5.1	1012 3.8	0759 3.0	0739 1.8	1019 1.1	0855 1.2	0918 3.1	0757 8.6
	1753 1.0	1818 1.0	1636 0.7	1431 0.6	1408 0.4	1634 4.5	1525 3.3	1500 0.2	1451 1.4
			2301 3.9	2052 3.1	2031 1.8	2248 1.2	2124 1.0	2146 3.0	2036 8.7
4 SU	0009 5.2	0011 5.4	0458 1.0	0249 0.9	0231 0.6	0445 4.8	0344 3.8	0321 0.6	0321 1.5
	0610 1.2	0627 1.2	1109 4.0	0859 3.2	0839 1.9	1112 0.8	0950 0.9	1023 3.2	0857 9.1
	1224 5.3	1233 5.4	1728 0.6	1520 0.5	1458 0.3	1721 4.8	1612 3.6	1554 0.1	1552 1.0
	1846 0.7	1911 0.8	2350 4.1	2143 3.2	2121 1.9	2338 0.9	2214 0.8	2247 3.1	2130 9.1
5 M	0100 5.4	0103 5.6	0547 0.8	0336 0.7	0318 0.4	0532 5.0	0430 4.0	0413 0.4	0417 1.1
	0701 0.8	0712 0.9	1158 4.2	0952 3.4	0932 2.0	1200 0.6	1038 0.7	1118 3.3	0950 9.4
	1315 5.5	1324 5.6	1815 0.4	1604 0.4	1543 0.2	1802 5.0	1653 3.8	1641 -0.0	1645 0.7
	1935 0.5	1957 0.6		2229 3.3	2207 2.0		2300 0.6	2339 3.2	2218 9.4
6 TU ●	0145 5.6	0150 5.8	0034 4.2	0420 0.5	0403 0.3	0024 0.6	0513 4.1	0459 0.2	0506 0.7
	0749 0.6	0735 0.7	0633 0.6	1042 3.5	1021 2.1	0616 5.2	1122 0.6	1207 3.4	1038 9.7
	1403 5.7	1412 5.8	1245 4.3	1645 0.3	1626 0.2	1242 0.4	1730 3.9	1724 -0.1	1730 0.5
	2021 0.4	2037 0.6	1858 0.4	2312 3.4	2250 2.1	1841 5.1	2345 0.5		2303 9.6
7 W	0229 5.7	0236 5.9	0115 4.3	0503 0.4	0445 0.3	0106 0.5	0554 4.1	0025 3.3	0551 0.5
	0836 0.4	0757 0.6	0716 0.5	1128 3.5	1107 2.1	0658 5.2	1204 0.5	0542 0.1	1122 9.8
	1449 5.7	1500 5.9	1330 4.4	1725 0.4	1708 0.3	1324 0.4	1806 4.0	1253 3.4	1812 0.5
	2104 0.4	2052 0.6	1939 0.4	2353 3.4	2330 2.1	1920 5.2		1807 -0.0	2345 9.6
8 TH	0313 5.7	0322 5.9	0156 4.3	0545 0.4	0529 0.2	0148 0.4	0028 0.6	0106 3.3	0634 0.5
	0921 0.4	0837 0.6	0759 0.4	1212 3.4	1151 2.1	0741 5.1	0633 4.0	0624 0.0	1205 9.7
	1536 5.7	1548 5.9	1415 4.3	1804 0.5	1749 0.3	1403 0.5	1245 0.6	1335 3.4	1852 0.6
	2144 0.6	2048 0.7	2019 0.5			1958 5.1	1839 4.0	1850 0.0	
9 F	0357 5.6	0409 5.8	0236 4.2	0033 3.4	0009 2.1	0230 0.5	0110 0.7	0143 3.4	0024 9.5
	1003 0.5	0951 0.7	0841 0.5	0627 0.4	0612 0.3	0824 4.9	0709 3.9	0707 0.0	0715 0.6
	1622 5.5	1635 5.8	1500 4.2	1255 3.3	1236 2.0	1442 0.7	1324 0.7	1415 3.3	1246 9.4
	2219 0.9	2123 1.0	2058 0.7	1842 0.6	1831 0.5	2037 4.9	1913 3.9	1933 0.2	1929 1.0
10 SA	0441 5.4	0455 5.6	0317 4.1	0112 3.3	0049 2.0	0310 0.7	0152 0.9	0220 3.4	0103 9.3
	1040 0.8	1037 1.0	0923 0.6	0709 0.5	0657 0.4	0909 4.6	0746 3.7	0751 0.1	0754 1.0
	1708 5.3	1721 5.5	1545 4.0	1338 3.1	1318 1.9	1521 1.0	1403 0.9	1455 3.2	1326 9.1
	2246 1.2	2154 1.3	2137 1.0	1920 0.8	1912 0.6	2118 4.6	1948 3.8	2018 0.4	2005 1.4
11 SU	0524 5.1	0540 5.3	0359 3.9	0151 3.2	0129 1.9	0352 1.0	0235 1.2	0257 3.4	0142 8.9
	1110 1.0	1018 1.2	1005 0.8	0752 0.7	0743 0.5	0957 4.3	0824 3.5	0836 0.2	0833 1.4
	1753 5.1	1806 5.2	1633 3.8	1421 3.0	1403 1.8	1601 1.3	1443 1.1	1535 3.1	1406 8.6
	2307 1.5	2230 1.6	2218 1.2	1958 1.0	1955 0.7	2203 4.4	2024 3.6	2105 0.6	2041 1.9
12 M	0609 4.9	0625 5.0	0442 3.7	0233 3.0	0211 1.8	0436 1.3	0320 1.5	0336 3.4	0221 8.5
	1139 1.3	1058 1.4	1051 1.0	0839 0.8	0832 0.6	1052 4.1	0906 3.2	0922 0.4	0913 1.9
	1839 4.8	1854 4.9	1724 3.5	1508 2.8	1448 1.7	1645 1.6	1527 1.4	1617 2.9	1449 8.2
	2342 1.8	2312 1.9	2303 1.5	2041 1.2	2042 0.9	2254 4.1	2107 3.3	2154 0.8	2118 2.4
13 TU	0657 4.7	0714 4.8	0532 3.6	0318 2.9	0256 1.7	0526 1.6	0411 1.7	0415 3.3	0306 8.1
	1225 1.6	1157 1.7	1143 1.2	0933 1.0	0927 0.7	1155 3.8	0958 3.0	1013 0.6	0958 2.4
	1930 4.5	1943 4.7	1820 3.4	1601 2.6	1538 1.6	1733 1.9	1615 1.6	1703 2.8	1539 7.7
			2357 1.7	2135 1.4	2137 0.9		2202 3.1	2249 0.9	2203 2.9
14 W	0036 2.1	0019 2.2	0630 3.4	0413 2.7	0348 1.6	0001 3.9	0512 1.9	0457 3.1	0359 7.7
	0749 4.4	0808 4.6	1246 1.4	1040 1.1	1029 0.7	0625 1.9	1112 2.9	1111 0.8	1053 2.8
	1331 1.8	1353 1.9	1923 3.3	1704 2.5	1636 1.5	1304 3.7	1713 1.7	1759 2.7	1639 7.3
	2024 4.4	2039 4.5		2248 1.5	2245 1.0	1836 2.2	2324 3.0	2353 1.1	2303 3.3
15 TH	0152 2.1	0206 2.4	0108 1.8	0518 2.6	0450 1.6	0120 3.8	0631 2.0	0547 2.9	0504 7.4
	0847 4.3	0906 4.5	0736 3.3	1155 1.1	1136 0.8	0741 2.0	1242 2.9	1219 0.9	1202 2.9
	1458 1.9	1518 2.0	1400 1.5	1815 2.5	1748 1.5	1414 3.7	1824 1.8	1913 2.6	1751 7.2
	2124 4.3	2136 4.5	2030 3.2			1958 2.3			

● ● Time UT. For British Summer Time (shaded) March 30th to October 26th ADD ONE HOUR ● ●

MAY 1997 TIDE TABLES MAY 1997

Date	LEITH Time	m	ROSYTH Time	m	ABERDEEN Time	m	WICK Time	m	LERWICK Time	m	ULLAPOOL Time	m	OBAN Time	m	GREENOCK Time	m	LIVERPOOL Time	m
16 F	0327	2.3	0324	2.4	0229	1.8	0013	1.5	0002	1.0	0232	3.8	0107	3.0	0105	1.1	0021	3.3
	0950	4.3	1007	4.5	0844	3.3	0628	2.6	0606	1.0	0858	1.9	0751	1.9	0652	2.8	0618	7.3
	1615	1.8	1617	1.9	1512	1.4	1304	1.1	1242	0.7	1515	3.8	1355	3.0	1333	0.9	1312	2.8
	2229	4.3	2235	4.5	2135	3.3	1922	2.6	1903	1.5	2118	2.1	1938	1.7	2031	2.7	1903	7.3
17 SA	0442	2.1	0423	2.2	0339	1.7	0127	1.4	0112	0.9	0332	3.9	0212	3.1	0212	1.0	0134	3.1
	1056	4.4	1107	4.7	0948	3.4	0733	2.7	0718	1.6	0959	1.8	0850	1.8	0821	2.8	0727	7.5
	1711	1.6	1703	1.8	1607	1.3	1359	1.0	1336	0.7	1606	4.0	1450	3.1	1434	0.8	1413	2.5
	2330	4.5	2331	4.7	2229	3.5	2018	2.7	1958	1.6	2216	1.9	2039	1.6	2131	2.8	2003	7.7
18 SU	0534	1.8	0511	2.0	0431	1.5	0219	1.3	0203	0.8	0419	4.1	0259	3.3	0304	0.8	0233	2.7
	1157	4.6	1203	4.9	1040	3.5	0828	2.8	0812	1.7	1045	1.5	0935	1.6	0930	2.9	0822	7.9
	1755	1.4	1743	1.6	1651	1.2	1443	0.9	1421	0.6	1647	4.2	1535	3.3	1522	0.6	1506	2.2
					2314	3.6	2103	2.8	2042	1.7	2300	1.7	2126	1.5	2220	2.9	2050	8.1
19 M	0021	4.7	0021	5.0	0512	1.3	0300	1.1	0245	0.7	0457	4.2	0339	3.5	0348	0.6	0321	2.3
	0617	1.6	0556	1.7	1125	3.7	0915	2.9	0856	1.7	1124	1.3	1012	1.4	1021	3.0	0908	8.3
	1245	4.8	1253	5.1	1730	1.0	1521	0.8	1458	0.6	1722	4.4	1615	3.5	1602	0.5	1551	1.8
	1836	1.2	1822	1.4	2352	3.8	2142	3.0	2119	1.8	2339	1.4	2206	1.3	2304	3.0	2130	8.5
20 TU	0105	4.9	0106	5.2	0549	1.1	0337	1.0	0321	0.6	0533	4.4	0415	3.6	0426	0.4	0406	1.9
	0657	1.3	0639	1.5	1205	3.8	0956	3.0	0935	1.8	1201	1.1	1047	1.3	1106	3.0	0948	8.6
	1328	5.0	1338	5.3	1806	1.0	1555	0.7	1534	0.5	1754	4.6	1650	3.7	1638	0.3	1632	1.5
	1915	1.0	1901	1.2			2219	3.1	2154	1.9			2244	1.2	2345	3.1	2208	8.9
21 W	0145	5.1	0148	5.4	0027	3.9	0412	0.8	0355	0.5	0015	1.1	0451	3.7	0502	0.3	0447	1.5
	0736	1.1	0721	1.2	0625	1.0	1036	3.1	1012	1.9	0606	4.6	1120	1.1	1146	3.0	1026	8.9
	1408	5.2	1419	5.4	1243	3.9	1630	0.6	1610	0.5	1236	0.9	1724	3.8	1712	0.2	1712	1.3
	1954	0.9	1940	1.1	1842	0.8	2255	3.2	2228	2.0	1827	4.8	2321	1.0			2245	9.1
22 TH ○	0224	5.3	0226	5.5	0103	4.0	0448	0.7	0431	0.5	0051	0.9	0526	3.9	0022	3.1	0527	1.2
	0815	0.9	0800	1.1	0701	0.8	1115	3.2	1050	2.0	0639	4.7	1153	1.0	0536	0.1	1103	9.1
	1447	5.3	1457	5.5	1321	4.0	1704	0.6	1647	0.4	1311	0.8	1757	4.0	1224	3.1	1751	1.1
	2033	0.8	2016	1.0	1918	0.7	2332	3.3	2303	2.0	1900	4.9	2359	0.9	1748	0.2	2322	9.4
23 F	0302	5.4	0305	5.7	0138	4.1	0524	0.6	0509	0.4	0127	0.8	0602	3.9	0057	3.2	0609	1.0
	0854	0.7	0835	0.9	0738	0.7	1154	3.2	1129	2.0	0716	4.8	1228	0.9	0613	0.0	1142	9.2
	1524	5.4	1536	5.6	1400	4.1	1741	0.6	1726	0.4	1347	0.7	1830	4.0	1302	3.1	1830	1.0
	2113	0.7	2048	1.0	1956	0.7			2341	2.1	1936	5.0			1826	0.1		
24 SA	0339	5.4	0345	5.7	0215	4.1	0009	3.3	0549	0.4	0205	0.7	0039	0.9	0133	3.2	0001	9.5
	0934	0.7	0903	0.9	0817	0.6	0604	0.5	1211	2.0	0756	4.8	0638	3.9	0651	-0.0	0649	0.9
	1603	5.4	1616	5.7	1440	4.1	1236	3.2	1806	0.5	1424	0.7	1305	0.9	1340	3.1	1221	9.3
	2153	0.8	2118	1.0	2035	0.7	1821	0.6			2015	4.9	1906	4.0	1906	0.2	1909	1.1
25 SU	0418	5.4	0426	5.7	0253	4.1	0049	3.3	0019	2.0	0245	0.7	0121	0.9	0209	3.3	0042	9.4
	1015	0.7	0934	0.9	0858	0.6	0646	0.5	0631	0.3	0840	4.7	0717	3.8	0733	-0.0	0730	1.0
	1645	5.3	1659	5.6	1524	4.0	1319	3.2	1254	1.9	1504	0.8	1345	0.9	1421	3.2	1303	9.2
	2234	0.9	2152	1.2	2117	0.8	1903	0.7	1849	0.5	2100	4.8	1944	3.9	1950	0.2	1948	1.2
26 M	0500	5.3	0510	5.6	0335	4.1	0131	3.3	0100	2.0	0328	0.8	0207	1.0	0247	3.3	0124	9.3
	1058	0.8	1012	0.9	0943	0.6	0732	0.5	0717	0.4	0930	4.5	0758	3.7	0818	0.0	0812	1.1
	1730	5.3	1745	5.5	1612	3.9	1406	3.1	1343	1.9	1548	1.0	1428	1.0	1506	3.2	1348	9.0
	2318	1.1	2231	1.3	2203	1.0	1948	0.8	1936	0.6	2151	4.7	2028	3.8	2037	0.4	2030	1.5
27 TU	0546	5.2	0556	5.4	0421	4.0	0216	3.2	0145	1.9	0415	0.9	0257	1.1	0327	3.3	0211	9.1
	1146	0.9	1057	1.1	1034	0.7	0823	0.6	0809	0.4	1029	4.3	0844	3.5	0909	0.1	0858	1.3
	1821	5.1	1835	5.3	1706	3.8	1457	3.0	1439	1.8	1637	1.3	1516	1.1	1554	3.1	1438	8.7
			2321	1.5	2257	1.1	2041	0.9	2028	0.7	2252	4.5	2120	3.6	2130	0.5	2117	1.8
28 W	0009	1.4	0647	5.2	0515	3.8	0307	3.1	0240	1.9	0510	1.2	0352	1.3	0413	3.3	0303	8.8
	0638	5.0	1158	1.2	1133	0.9	0924	0.7	0907	0.5	1136	4.2	0939	3.2	1008	0.2	0950	1.6
	1242	1.1	1931	5.1	1808	3.7	1557	2.9	1540	1.7	1736	1.5	1611	1.3	1649	3.1	1535	8.4
	1918	5.0			2359	1.4	2144	1.1	2130	0.7			2228	3.4	2229	0.6	2212	2.1
29 TH	0107	1.6	0056	1.7	0618	3.7	0406	3.0	0345	1.8	0001	4.4	0454	1.4	0506	3.2	0403	8.5
	0736	4.9	0745	5.1	1242	0.9	1036	0.8	1015	0.5	0615	1.3	1048	3.1	1114	0.3	1051	1.8
	1350	1.3	1329	1.3	1918	3.6	1704	2.8	1646	1.7	1251	4.0	1716	1.4	1750	3.0	1642	8.1
	2022	4.8	2036	5.0			2259	1.2	2241	0.8	1848	1.7	2358	3.3	2335	0.7	2320	2.3
30 F	0217	1.7	0231	1.8	0111	1.4	0513	2.9	0456	1.7	0114	4.3	0603	1.4	0612	3.1	0510	8.4
	0843	4.8	0857	5.0	0729	3.7	1152	0.8	1132	0.5	0729	1.4	1221	3.0	1223	0.4	1201	1.9
	1507	1.3	1536	1.4	1356	1.0	1816	2.8	1754	1.7	1405	4.2	1832	1.4	1857	3.0	1754	8.0
	2133	4.8	2146	5.0	2030	3.6					2007	1.7						
31 SA	0333	1.7	0404	1.7	0225	1.4	0016	1.2	0001	0.8	0224	4.3	0123	3.4	0045	0.8	0036	2.3
	0954	4.9	1010	5.0	0842	3.7	0624	2.9	0606	1.7	0844	1.4	0717	1.4	0730	3.1	0622	8.4
	1622	1.2	1653	1.2	1508	0.9	1305	0.7	1245	0.5	1514	4.2	1351	1.1	1332	0.4	1315	1.8
	2242	4.9	2252	5.1	2138	3.7	1926	2.9	1903	1.7	2121	1.4	1950	1.3	2010	3.0	1906	8.2

● ● Time UT. For British Summer Time (shaded) March 30th to October 26th ADD ONE HOUR ● ●

SCOTLAND & NORTH WEST ENGLAND Time Zone UT

Leith * Rosyth * Aberdeen *Wick * Lerwick * Ullapool * Oban * Greenock * Liverpool

JUNE 1997 TIDE TABLES JUNE 1997

	LEITH	ROSYTH	ABERDEEN	WICK	LERWICK	ULLAPOOL	OBAN	GREENOCK	LIVERPOOL
	Time m	Time m	Time m	Time m	Time m	Time m	Time m	Time m	Time m
1 SU	0444 1.5 1102 5.0 1727 1.1 2345 5.1	0509 1.5 1116 5.1 1754 1.1 2351 5.3	0334 1.3 0949 3.8 1612 0.9 2238 3.8	0127 1.1 0734 3.0 1407 0.7 2027 3.0	0112 0.7 0715 1.8 1345 0.5 2005 1.8	0328 4.4 0951 1.2 1612 4.4 2224 1.4	0228 3.5 0825 1.3 1458 3.2 2057 1.2	0156 0.7 0851 3.1 1438 0.3 2121 3.0	0149 2.1 0731 8.5 1424 1.6 2011 8.5
2 M	0545 1.3 1204 5.2 1823 1.0	0603 1.4 1215 5.3 1850 1.0	0436 1.1 1049 3.9 1707 0.8 2330 4.0	0227 0.9 0838 3.1 1459 0.6 2121 3.1	0210 0.6 0818 1.9 1437 0.4 2058 1.9	0426 4.6 1049 1.1 1702 4.6 2318 1.1	0323 3.6 0923 1.1 1549 3.4 2152 1.0	0302 0.6 0959 3.2 1535 0.2 2224 3.1	0256 1.7 0833 8.8 1527 1.3 2108 8.8
3 TU	0039 5.3 0639 1.0 1259 5.3 1913 0.8	0045 5.4 0648 1.2 1307 5.3 1937 1.0	0529 0.9 1142 4.1 1756 0.7	0318 0.8 0934 3.2 1545 0.6 2208 3.2	0300 0.5 0915 1.9 1524 0.4 2146 2.0	0516 4.8 1139 0.9 1745 4.8	0412 3.7 1014 0.9 1633 3.6 2242 0.9	0357 0.5 1057 3.2 1625 0.2 2317 3.2	0354 1.4 0929 9.1 1621 1.1 2158 9.1
4 W	0127 5.4 0730 0.8 1348 5.4 1959 0.8	0133 5.5 0655 1.0 1355 5.5 1905 0.9	0015 4.1 0617 0.8 1231 4.1 1839 0.7	0405 0.6 1025 3.3 1626 0.6 2252 3.3	0348 0.4 1007 2.0 1608 0.4 2230 2.0	0007 0.9 0602 4.9 1224 0.8 1826 4.9	0457 3.8 1100 0.8 1712 3.8 2328 0.8	0445 0.3 1149 3.3 1710 0.2	0446 1.1 1018 9.2 1708 1.0 2243 9.3
5 TH	0213 5.5 0819 0.7 1436 5.5 2042 0.8	0218 5.6 0731 0.9 1442 5.6 1944 0.9	0057 4.2 0702 0.6 1318 4.2 1921 0.7	0448 0.5 1112 3.3 1705 0.6 2333 3.4	0431 0.4 1054 2.0 1650 0.4 2311 2.1	0052 0.8 0645 4.9 1306 0.7 1904 5.0	0538 3.8 1142 0.8 1747 3.9	0003 3.3 0530 0.2 1237 3.3 1753 0.2	0533 0.9 1104 9.3 1750 1.0 2326 9.3
6 F	0257 5.5 0904 0.6 1521 5.5 2121 0.8	0304 5.7 0814 0.8 1529 5.7 2024 1.0	0138 4.2 0745 0.6 1402 4.1 2000 0.8	0531 0.5 1157 3.3 1744 0.7	0515 0.3 1138 2.0 1731 0.5 2351 2.1	0134 0.7 0727 4.8 1346 0.8 1942 5.0	0012 0.9 0616 3.8 1223 0.8 1821 3.9	0044 3.3 0612 0.2 1321 3.2 1835 0.3	0616 0.9 1148 9.3 1830 1.1
7 SA	0340 5.4 0946 0.7 1604 5.4 2156 1.0	0349 5.6 0933 0.9 1614 5.6 2102 1.1	0218 4.2 0826 0.6 1445 4.0 2038 0.9	0013 3.3 0612 0.5 1239 3.2 1821 0.8	0557 0.3 1220 1.9 1811 0.6	0215 0.7 0809 4.7 1424 0.9 2019 4.8	0054 0.9 0653 3.8 1302 0.8 1855 3.9	0121 3.4 0653 0.2 1401 3.2 1917 0.4	0006 9.3 0657 1.0 1228 9.1 1906 1.2
8 SU	0422 5.3 1022 0.8 1646 5.2 2223 1.2	0433 5.5 1009 1.0 1657 5.4 2136 1.3	0257 4.1 0906 0.7 1527 3.9 2115 1.0	0051 3.3 0653 0.6 1318 3.1 1857 0.9	0029 2.0 0640 0.4 1300 1.9 1851 0.6	0254 0.8 0851 4.6 1502 1.0 2057 4.7	0135 1.1 0729 3.7 1340 0.9 1930 3.8	0158 3.5 0734 0.2 1441 3.1 1958 0.5	0044 9.2 0736 1.2 1306 8.9 1942 1.5
9 M	0503 5.2 1051 1.0 1727 5.1 2246 1.4	0516 5.4 1006 1.2 1739 5.3 2212 1.5	0336 4.0 0945 0.8 1610 3.8 2152 1.2	0130 3.2 0733 0.7 1359 3.0 1934 1.0	0107 2.0 0722 0.4 1339 1.8 1929 0.7	0333 1.0 0933 4.4 1539 1.3 2135 4.5	0215 1.3 0806 3.5 1419 1.1 2006 3.7	0235 3.5 0815 0.3 1520 3.1 2040 0.6	0121 9.0 0813 1.4 1345 8.6 2015 1.9
10 TU	0543 5.0 1118 1.2 1809 4.9 2318 1.6	0557 5.2 1043 1.3 1821 5.0 2251 1.7	0415 3.8 1025 1.0 1654 3.6 2232 1.4	0208 3.1 0813 0.8 1440 2.8 2012 1.2	0145 1.9 0805 0.5 1420 1.7 2008 0.8	0414 1.2 1017 4.2 1619 1.5 2217 4.3	0257 1.5 0845 3.4 1500 1.3 2045 3.5	0312 3.4 0855 0.4 1559 3.0 2123 0.7	0159 8.7 0849 1.8 1424 8.3 2050 2.2
11 W	0626 4.8 1156 1.4 1853 4.7	0639 5.0 1130 1.5 1904 4.8 2340 2.0	0457 3.7 1109 1.1 1740 3.5 2317 1.5	0248 3.0 0857 0.9 1525 2.7 2055 1.3	0225 1.8 0850 0.6 1502 1.6 2053 0.9	0456 1.5 1106 4.0 1702 1.8 2306 4.1	0341 1.6 0929 3.2 1543 1.4 2130 3.3	0350 3.4 0938 0.6 1639 2.9 2208 0.8	0239 8.4 0927 2.1 1506 8.0 2128 2.6
12 TH	0002 1.8 0712 4.6 1246 1.6 1941 4.5	0726 4.8 1239 1.7 1952 4.7	0546 3.6 1158 1.3 1832 3.4	0334 2.8 0949 1.0 1615 2.6 2149 1.4	0310 1.7 0941 0.7 1550 1.6 2148 0.9	0543 1.7 1205 3.9 1751 2.0	0431 1.8 1021 3.1 1633 1.6 2227 3.2	0431 3.3 1025 0.7 1723 2.8 2300 1.0	0323 8.0 1009 2.4 1554 7.6 2215 2.9
13 F	0058 2.0 0802 4.5 1348 1.7 2033 4.4	0101 2.2 0818 4.7 1344 1.9 2045 4.6	0011 1.7 0642 3.4 1257 1.4 1930 3.3	0427 2.7 1050 1.1 1713 2.6 2259 1.5	0401 1.7 1039 0.7 1645 1.5 2257 1.0	0008 3.9 0639 1.9 1311 3.8 1851 2.1	0529 1.9 1128 3.0 1730 1.7 2339 3.1	0512 3.1 1121 0.8 1813 2.7	0414 7.7 1101 2.7 1651 7.4 2313 3.1
14 SA	0209 2.2 0856 4.4 1459 1.8 2130 4.4	0212 2.3 0913 4.6 1445 1.9 2139 4.6	0116 1.8 0743 3.4 1402 1.5 2032 3.3	0527 2.7 1157 1.1 1816 2.6	0501 1.6 1142 0.8 1751 1.5	0121 3.8 0745 1.9 1416 3.8 2003 2.2	0636 1.9 1246 3.0 1836 1.8	0000 1.0 0603 3.0 1224 0.9 1916 2.7	0515 7.5 1204 2.8 1756 7.3
15 SU	0328 2.2 0954 4.4 1608 1.7 2229 4.4	0318 2.3 1010 4.6 1549 1.9 2235 4.7	0230 1.8 0848 3.4 1507 1.4 2133 3.4	0015 1.5 0631 2.7 1300 1.1 1918 2.7	0010 0.9 0610 1.6 1242 0.7 1858 1.6	0230 3.8 0854 1.9 1515 3.9 2115 2.1	0058 3.1 0745 1.9 1357 3.0 1941 1.7	0109 1.0 0703 2.9 1333 0.8 2031 2.7	0024 3.2 0621 7.4 1312 2.7 1902 7.5

● ● Time UT. For British Summer Time (shaded) March 30th to October 26th ADD ONE HOUR ● ●

JUNE 1997 TIDE TABLES JUNE 1997

Date	LEITH	ROSYTH	ABERDEEN	WICK	LERWICK	ULLAPOOL	OBAN	GREENOCK	LIVERPOOL
	Time m	Time m	Time m	Time m	Time m	Time m	Time m	Time m	Time m
16 M	0439 2.0	0421 2.2	0336 1.7	0124 1.4	0113 0.9	0328 3.9	0203 3.2	0212 0.9	0134 2.9
	1057 4.5	1108 4.7	0949 3.4	0733 2.7	0718 1.6	0954 1.8	0844 1.7	0821 2.8	0726 7.6
	1707 1.6	1653 1.8	1603 1.3	1356 1.0	1334 0.7	1604 4.1	1452 3.2	1433 0.7	1413 2.5
	2329 4.6	2330 4.9	2227 3.5	2013 2.8	1953 1.7	2214 1.9	2038 1.6	2135 2.8	2000 7.9
17 TU	0535 1.8	0518 1.9	0430 1.5	0219 1.2	0203 0.8	0418 4.1	0255 3.3	0306 0.7	0234 2.6
	1158 4.6	1203 4.9	1044 3.6	0830 2.8	0812 1.7	1043 1.6	0931 1.6	0934 2.9	0822 8.0
	1757 1.4	1748 1.6	1651 1.2	1442 1.0	1420 0.7	1647 4.3	1539 3.4	1524 0.6	1508 2.1
			2314 3.7	2101 2.9	2038 1.8	2303 1.6	2127 1.5	2227 2.9	2050 8.3
18 W	0024 4.8	0021 5.1	0515 1.3	0306 1.1	0247 0.7	0500 4.3	0341 3.5	0353 0.5	0328 2.1
	0623 1.5	0609 1.7	1133 3.7	0920 2.9	0859 1.8	1127 1.3	1012 1.4	1029 2.9	0911 8.7
	1251 4.9	1257 5.1	1734 1.0	1524 0.8	1502 0.6	1726 4.6	1620 3.6	1607 0.4	1557 1.8
	1843 1.2	1838 1.4	2357 3.9	2145 3.1	2119 1.9	2346 1.3	2212 1.3	2313 3.1	2135 8.7
19 TH	0113 5.0	0110 5.3	0557 1.1	0348 0.9	0328 0.6	0541 4.5	0424 3.6	0435 0.3	0418 1.4
	0708 1.2	0658 1.4	1217 3.9	1006 3.1	0944 1.9	1208 1.1	1051 1.2	1116 3.0	0956 8.7
	1339 5.1	1345 5.4	1815 0.9	1603 0.7	1544 0.5	1803 4.8	1658 3.8	1648 0.3	1644 1.4
	1927 1.0	1927 1.2		2227 3.2	2200 2.0		2255 1.1	2355 3.2	2218 9.1
20 F ○	0158 5.2	0157 5.5	0036 4.0	0428 0.7	0409 0.5	0027 1.1	0506 3.8	0515 0.2	0505 1.4
	0752 1.0	0748 1.1	0639 0.8	1051 3.2	1028 2.0	0621 4.7	1130 1.0	1200 3.1	1039 9.0
	1422 5.3	1430 5.6	1300 4.0	1643 0.7	1626 0.5	1248 0.9	1736 3.9	1729 0.3	1728 1.2
	2012 0.9	2019 1.1	1857 0.8	2309 3.3	2241 2.1	1841 5.0	2339 0.9		2301 9.4
21 SA	0239 5.4	0241 5.7	0116 4.2	0509 0.6	0452 0.4	0109 0.8	0548 3.9	0036 3.2	0551 1.1
	0837 0.7	0848 0.9	0721 0.6	1136 3.3	1113 2.0	0703 4.8	1209 0.8	0556 0.1	1124 9.3
	1504 5.4	1515 5.7	1343 4.1	1724 0.6	1709 0.5	1329 0.8	1815 4.1	1245 3.1	1812 1.0
	2057 0.7	2112 1.0	1939 0.7	2351 3.4	2324 2.1	1921 5.1		1810 0.2	2345 9.6
22 SU	0321 5.5	0325 5.8	0157 4.3	0553 0.4	0536 0.3	0151 0.6	0024 0.8	0116 3.3	0636 0.8
	0923 0.6	0941 0.7	0805 0.5	1222 3.3	1200 2.0	0746 4.9	0629 3.9	0637 0.0	1208 9.4
	1546 5.5	1559 5.8	1427 4.2	1808 0.6	1752 0.5	1410 0.7	1250 0.7	1330 3.2	1856 0.9
	2142 0.7	2159 1.0	2022 0.7			2003 5.1	1854 4.1	1854 0.2	
23 M	0402 5.6	0411 5.8	0239 4.3	0034 3.5	0006 2.1	0234 0.6	0109 0.8	0157 3.4	0029 9.7
	1010 0.5	1027 0.7	0850 0.4	0638 0.4	0621 0.3	0832 4.9	0711 3.9	0721 -0.0	0722 0.7
	1630 5.6	1645 5.8	1514 4.2	1309 3.3	1248 2.0	1453 0.7	1333 0.7	1417 3.2	1253 9.4
	2227 0.8	2244 1.0	2107 0.7	1852 0.6	1837 0.5	2050 5.1	1936 4.1	1939 0.3	1939 1.0
24 TU	0446 5.5	0457 5.8	0322 4.3	0118 3.5	0051 2.1	0319 0.6	0157 0.8	0238 3.5	0115 9.6
	1057 0.5	1112 0.7	0937 0.4	0725 0.4	0708 0.3	0921 4.8	0754 3.8	0808 0.0	0807 0.7
	1717 5.5	1732 5.8	1603 4.1	1357 3.2	1337 2.0	1538 0.9	1418 0.8	1505 3.3	1340 9.3
	2313 0.9	2326 1.2	2154 0.8	1939 0.7	1924 0.5	2140 5.0	2022 4.0	2027 0.4	2024 1.1
25 W	0533 5.5	0545 5.7	0410 4.2	0205 3.4	0139 2.1	0407 0.7	0248 0.9	0321 3.5	0202 9.5
	1145 0.6	1155 0.8	1028 0.5	0815 0.4	0758 0.3	1016 4.6	0839 3.6	0858 0.1	0854 0.9
	1807 5.4	1822 5.6	1655 4.0	1448 3.1	1430 1.9	1627 1.1	1505 0.9	1554 3.3	1430 9.0
			2245 1.0	2029 0.6	2015 0.6	2237 4.8	2113 3.8	2117 0.5	2110 1.4
26 TH	0000 1.1	0003 1.4	0502 4.1	0255 3.3	0233 2.0	0459 0.9	0341 1.0	0407 3.5	0252 9.2
	0624 5.3	0636 5.5	1122 0.7	0911 0.6	0852 0.4	1118 4.4	0928 3.4	0954 0.2	0942 1.1
	1235 0.8	1233 1.0	1752 3.8	1542 3.0	1525 1.8	1721 1.3	1557 1.0	1644 3.2	1522 8.7
	1902 5.2	1917 5.4	2342 1.2	2124 1.0	2110 0.7	2340 4.6	2213 3.6	2212 0.6	2201 1.7
27 F	0050 1.3	0033 1.5	0600 4.0	0351 3.2	0332 1.9	0556 1.2	0437 1.2	0458 3.4	0347 8.9
	0721 5.2	0734 5.3	1223 0.8	1014 0.7	0953 0.5	1227 4.2	1024 3.2	1054 0.3	1036 1.4
	1330 1.0	1312 1.2	1855 3.7	1642 2.9	1624 1.7	1824 1.6	1657 1.2	1737 3.2	1621 8.4
	2003 5.0	2018 5.2		2230 1.1	2213 0.7		2327 3.4	2314 0.7	2300 2.0
28 SA	0148 1.5	0151 1.7	0045 1.3	0452 3.1	0435 1.8	0049 4.5	0538 1.3	0557 3.3	0447 8.6
	0824 5.0	0841 5.1	0706 3.8	1124 0.8	1103 0.5	0700 1.4	1135 3.0	1201 0.4	1137 1.7
	1435 1.3	1504 1.4	1330 1.0	1748 2.8	1725 1.7	1338 4.1	1804 1.3	1836 3.1	1727 8.1
	2109 4.9	2124 5.1	2003 3.6	2344 1.2	2329 0.8	1935 1.7			
29 SU	0257 1.7	0330 1.8	0155 1.4	0600 3.0	0541 1.8	0159 4.4	0052 3.3	0021 0.8	0008 2.2
	0932 4.9	0951 5.1	0817 3.8	1237 0.9	1218 0.6	0811 1.5	0644 1.4	0705 3.2	0554 8.4
	1551 1.4	1625 1.4	1440 1.1	1856 2.9	1831 1.7	1448 4.2	1310 3.0	1310 0.4	1246 1.9
	2216 4.9	2229 5.1	2111 3.7			2051 1.7	1920 1.4	1941 3.0	1837 8.1
30 M	0414 1.6	0442 1.7	0308 1.4	0100 1.2	0047 0.8	0308 4.3	0208 3.3	0135 0.8	0121 2.2
	1041 4.9	1056 5.1	0928 3.8	0711 3.0	0651 1.8	0923 1.5	0753 1.4	0822 3.1	0705 8.3
	1703 1.4	1730 1.4	1549 1.0	1345 0.9	1324 0.6	1552 4.3	1437 3.1	1419 0.5	1357 1.9
	2321 5.0	2330 5.1	2215 3.7	2001 2.9	1938 1.8	2203 1.6	2034 1.3	2052 3.0	1946 8.2

● ● Time UT. For British Summer Time (shaded) March 30th to October 26th ADD ONE HOUR ● ●

SCOTLAND & NORTH WEST ENGLAND Time Zone UT

Leith * Rosyth * Aberdeen *Wick * Lerwick * Ullapool * Oban * Greenock * Liverpool

JULY 1997 TIDE TABLES JULY 1997

Date	LEITH Time m	ROSYTH Time m	ABERDEEN Time m	WICK Time m	LERWICK Time m	ULLAPOOL Time m	OBAN Time m	GREENOCK Time m	LIVERPOOL Time m
1 TU	0524 1.5	0541 1.6	0416 1.3	0209 1.1	0152 0.7	0411 4.4	0309 3.4	0246 0.7	0232 2.0
	1147 5.0	1157 5.1	1034 3.8	0819 3.0	0801 1.8	1028 1.4	0857 1.3	0936 3.1	0812 8.4
	1803 1.3	1830 1.4	1649 1.1	1442 0.9	1421 0.6	1647 4.5	1537 3.3	1521 0.5	1503 1.8
			2311 3.9	2059 3.1	2038 1.8	2303 1.4	2138 1.3	2200 3.1	2048 8.5
2 W	0021 5.1	0027 5.2	0515 1.1	0307 0.9	0248 0.6	0506 4.5	0402 3.5	0348 0.6	0335 1.8
	0624 1.3	0636 1.5	1132 3.9	0920 3.1	0904 1.8	1123 1.3	0954 1.2	1042 3.1	0912 8.6
	1247 5.1	1254 5.2	1741 1.1	1529 3.1	1511 0.6	1733 4.7	1624 3.4	1615 0.4	1600 1.6
	1856 1.2	1920 1.4		2150 3.2	2130 1.9	2355 1.2	2231 1.2	2259 3.2	2142 8.7
3 TH	0115 5.2	0119 5.4	0000 4.0	0355 0.8	0337 0.5	0553 4.6	0447 3.6	0438 0.5	0430 1.5
	0718 1.1	0719 1.3	0606 1.0	1013 3.1	0957 1.9	1210 1.2	1042 1.0	1138 3.1	1004 8.8
	1339 5.2	1344 5.4	1223 4.0	1610 0.9	1555 0.6	1814 4.8	1701 3.6	1702 0.4	1649 1.5
	1941 1.1	1843 1.3	1825 1.0	2235 3.3	2215 2.0		2318 1.1	2347 3.2	2229 9.0
4 F	0202 5.3	0205 5.5	0043 4.1	0439 0.7	0421 0.5	0041 1.1	0527 3.6	0522 0.4	0519 1.3
	0806 0.9	0712 1.1	0651 0.8	1100 3.2	1043 1.9	0636 4.7	1124 0.9	1227 3.1	1051 8.9
	1425 5.3	1430 5.5	1308 4.0	1648 0.8	1636 0.6	1252 1.1	1735 3.7	1744 0.4	1732 1.4
	2023 1.1	1922 1.2	1906 1.0	2317 3.4	2256 2.1	1851 4.9			2311 9.1 ●
5 SA	0245 5.4	0249 5.6	0124 4.2	0518 0.6	0503 0.4	0122 1.0	0000 1.1	0028 3.3	0602 1.2
	0849 0.8	0754 1.0	0732 0.7	1142 3.2	1124 2.0	0715 4.8	0604 3.7	0603 0.3	1132 9.0
	1507 5.3	1512 5.5	1350 4.0	1725 0.8	1715 0.6	1330 1.0	1204 0.9	1311 3.1	1811 1.4
	2100 1.1	2003 1.2	1943 1.0	2356 3.4	2335 2.1	1927 4.9	1807 3.8	1824 0.4	2350 9.2
6 SU	0326 5.4	0332 5.6	0201 4.2	0557 0.6	0543 0.4	0201 0.9	0039 1.1	0105 3.4	0642 1.2
	0928 0.8	0839 1.0	0811 0.7	1221 3.2	1203 1.9	0751 4.7	0639 3.7	0641 0.3	1211 9.0
	1546 5.3	1554 5.5	1430 4.0	1801 0.9	1753 0.6	1407 1.0	1242 0.8	1351 3.1	1846 1.4
	2133 1.1	2043 1.2	2019 1.0			2000 4.9	1839 3.9	1902 0.5	
7 M	0404 5.3	0413 5.6	0237 4.2	0033 3.4	0012 2.1	0237 0.9	0117 1.1	0140 3.5	0027 9.2
	1001 0.8	0918 1.0	0848 0.7	0634 0.6	0621 0.4	0827 4.7	0712 3.7	0717 0.3	0718 1.2
	1624 5.2	1633 5.4	1507 4.0	1259 3.1	1239 1.9	1442 1.1	1318 0.9	1428 3.1	1247 8.9
	2200 1.2	2120 1.3	2054 1.1	1836 0.9	1827 0.7	2033 4.8	1912 3.8	1939 0.5	1919 1.5
8 TU	0441 5.2	0452 5.5	0312 4.1	0108 3.3	0046 2.0	0312 1.0	0154 1.2	0216 3.5	0102 9.0
	1028 0.9	0951 1.1	0922 0.8	0709 0.7	0657 0.5	0903 4.6	0747 3.7	0752 0.4	0751 1.4
	1700 5.1	1709 5.3	1544 3.9	1335 3.1	1314 1.9	1517 1.2	1355 1.0	1503 3.1	1321 8.8
	2226 1.3	2154 1.4	2127 1.2	1909 1.0	1900 0.7	2106 4.7	1945 3.8	2015 0.6	1951 1.7
9 W	0518 5.1	0529 5.4	0348 4.0	0143 3.2	0120 2.0	0348 1.2	0230 1.3	0251 3.5	0136 8.9
	1056 1.0	1024 1.2	0957 0.9	0745 0.8	0733 0.5	0940 4.4	0821 3.6	0828 0.4	0824 1.6
	1737 5.0	1746 5.2	1621 3.8	1411 3.0	1348 1.8	1552 1.4	1433 1.1	1537 3.1	1357 8.6
	2256 1.4	2229 1.6	2202 1.3	1942 1.1	1934 0.8	2141 4.5	2021 3.6	2051 0.6	2023 1.9
10 TH	0555 5.0	0606 5.2	0424 3.9	0219 3.1	0154 1.9	0424 1.3	0309 1.5	0326 3.5	0211 8.6
	1129 1.2	1100 1.4	1033 1.0	0821 0.9	0811 0.6	1021 4.3	0858 3.4	0905 0.5	0856 1.8
	1818 4.8	1825 5.1	1700 3.7	1448 2.9	1425 1.7	1629 1.6	1512 1.3	1611 3.1	1433 8.3
	2330 1.6	2307 1.8	2239 1.4	2019 1.2	2011 0.8	2220 4.4	2059 3.5	2130 0.7	2057 2.2
11 F	0636 4.8	0645 5.1	0506 3.8	0257 3.0	0233 1.8	0503 1.5	0349 1.6	0402 3.4	0248 8.3
	1208 1.4	1145 1.6	1115 1.2	0902 1.0	0853 0.7	1107 4.1	0938 3.3	0945 0.6	0931 2.1
	1900 4.7	1909 5.0	1744 3.5	1530 2.8	1506 1.7	1709 1.8	1554 1.5	1645 3.0	1512 8.0
		2352 2.0	2322 1.6	2101 1.3	2054 0.9	2308 4.2	2141 3.3	2214 0.8	2136 2.5
12 SA	0012 1.8	0730 4.9	0552 3.6	0341 2.9	0317 1.8	0547 1.7	0435 1.8	0439 3.3	0328 8.0
	0719 4.7	1245 1.8	1201 1.3	0950 1.1	0942 0.7	1205 4.0	1026 3.1	1031 0.7	1012 2.4
	1256 1.6	1957 4.9	1833 3.4	1618 2.7	1554 1.6	1757 2.0	1642 1.6	1725 2.9	1558 7.7
	1948 4.6			2154 1.4	2150 0.9		2233 3.2	2305 0.9	2224 2.8
13 SU	0104 2.0	0110 2.2	0015 1.7	0432 2.8	0409 1.7	0009 4.0	0527 1.9	0522 3.1	0416 7.7
	0807 4.5	0821 4.8	0646 3.5	1050 1.2	1041 0.8	0639 1.9	1129 3.0	1125 0.8	1103 2.7
	1354 1.8	1348 1.9	1257 1.5	1712 2.7	1649 1.6	1312 3.9	1737 1.7	1812 2.8	1654 7.5
	2039 4.5	2051 4.8	1930 3.4	2306 1.5	2304 1.0	1855 2.2	2338 3.1		2322 3.0
14 M	0215 2.2	0220 2.3	0119 1.8	0532 2.7	0510 1.6	0122 3.9	0630 1.9	0006 1.0	0517 7.5
	0902 4.4	0918 4.7	0749 3.4	1157 1.3	1149 0.8	0744 2.0	1251 3.0	0611 3.0	1209 2.8
	1503 1.9	1451 2.0	1403 1.5	1815 2.7	1752 1.6	1419 3.9	1841 1.8	1231 0.9	1800 7.4
	2137 4.5	2147 4.8	2034 3.4			2008 2.2		1912 2.7	
15 TU	0337 2.2	0324 2.3	0233 1.8	0024 1.5	0024 1.0	0234 3.9	0057 3.1	0118 0.9	0036 3.1
	1003 4.4	1018 4.7	0857 3.4	0639 2.7	0619 1.6	0855 2.0	0742 1.8	0712 2.9	0627 7.5
	1616 1.8	1600 2.0	1511 1.5	1304 1.2	1251 0.8	1520 4.0	1409 3.1	1342 0.8	1322 2.8
	2239 4.5	2244 4.9	2139 3.5	1920 2.8	1858 1.7	2123 2.1	1948 1.7	2036 2.8	1909 7.6

● ● Time UT. For British Summer Time (shaded) March 30th to October 26th ADD ONE HOUR ● ●

JULY 1997 TIDE TABLES JULY 1997

Date	LEITH Time	m	ROSYTH Time	m	ABERDEEN Time	m	WICK Time	m	LERWICK Time	m	ULLAPOOL Time	m	OBAN Time	m	GREENOCK Time	m	LIVERPOOL Time	m
16 W	0453	2.0	0435	2.2	0345	1.6	0136	1.4	0126	0.9	0338	4.0	0212	3.2	0225	0.8	0149	2.8
	1112	4.5	1118	4.9	1004	3.5	0745	2.8	0727	1.7	1001	1.8	0848	1.7	0833	2.8	0737	7.7
	1721	1.7	1718	1.9	1612	1.4	1404	1.1	1345	0.8	1613	4.3	1507	3.2	1446	0.7	1429	2.4
	2344	4.7	2340	5.1	2237	3.7	2020	2.9	1957	1.8	2227	1.9	2051	1.6	2148	2.9	2012	8.0
17 TH	0554	1.7	0542	1.9	0443	1.4	0236	1.2	0218	0.8	0433	4.2	0313	3.3	0321	0.6	0254	2.4
	1218	4.8	1217	5.1	1103	3.7	0847	2.9	0827	1.8	1056	1.6	0942	1.5	0950	2.9	0838	8.1
	1817	1.4	1821	1.6	1706	1.2	1456	1.0	1435	0.7	1700	4.5	1554	3.5	1539	0.6	1527	2.0
					2327	3.9	2113	3.1	2048	1.9	2319	1.5	2145	1.4	2243	3.0	2106	8.5
18 F	0043	5.0	0035	5.3	0533	1.1	0326	1.0	0305	0.7	0521	4.5	0405	3.5	0411	0.5	0352	1.9
	0645	1.3	0642	1.5	1154	3.9	0942	3.1	0920	1.9	1145	1.3	1028	1.2	1048	3.0	0931	8.6
	1312	5.1	1313	5.4	1754	1.0	1542	0.9	1522	0.6	1742	4.8	1638	3.7	1627	0.5	1620	1.6
	1907	1.2	1917	1.4			2201	3.3	2136	2.0			2236	1.1	2331	3.2	2156	9.0
19 SA	0133	5.3	0127	5.5	0013	4.1	0412	0.8	0351	0.5	0007	1.2	0453	3.7	0457	0.3	0445	1.4
	0735	1.0	0742	1.2	0620	0.8	1033	3.3	1010	2.0	0606	4.7	1111	1.0	1139	3.1	1021	9.0
	1400	5.4	1405	5.7	1242	4.1	1626	0.8	1608	0.5	1230	1.0	1720	3.9	1712	0.4	1709	1.2
	1955	0.9	2010	1.1	1839	0.9	2248	3.5	2222	2.1	1824	5.1	2324	0.9			2243	9.4
20 SU	0218	5.5	0218	5.8	0057	4.3	0456	0.5	0436	0.4	0053	0.8	0538	3.9	0017	3.3	0536	1.0
	0824	0.7	0839	0.8	0706	0.6	1121	3.4	1100	2.1	0650	5.0	1153	0.7	0540	0.1	1108	9.4
	1445	5.6	1454	5.9	1328	4.3	1710	0.6	1654	0.5	1313	0.8	1801	4.2	1230	3.2	1757	0.9
○	2042	0.7	2100	1.0	1924	0.7	2333	3.6	2308	2.2	1906	5.3			1756	0.3	2329	9.8
21 M	0301	5.7	0306	6.0	0139	4.4	0540	0.4	0521	0.2	0137	0.5	0011	0.7	0101	3.4	0625	0.6
	0912	0.4	0930	0.6	0752	0.4	1209	3.5	1148	2.1	0733	5.1	0621	4.0	0623	0.0	1154	9.6
	1528	5.8	1540	6.1	1414	4.4	1754	0.6	1738	0.4	1357	0.6	1236	0.5	1321	3.3	1843	0.7
	2129	0.6	2147	0.8	2009	0.6			2354	2.3	1949	5.4	1844	4.3	1840	0.3		
22 TU	0344	5.8	0354	6.1	0222	4.5	0018	3.7	0607	0.2	0221	0.4	0058	0.6	0145	3.6	0015	9.9
	1000	0.2	1017	0.4	0838	0.3	0626	0.3	1236	2.1	0818	5.2	0703	4.0	0707	-0.0	0712	0.4
	1613	5.8	1627	6.1	1500	4.4	1255	3.5	1823	0.4	1440	0.6	1318	0.5	1411	3.3	1241	9.7
	2215	0.5	2231	0.8	2054	0.6	1823	0.6			2034	5.5	1927	4.3	1928	0.6	1928	0.6
23 W	0429	5.8	0443	6.1	0307	4.5	0104	3.7	0039	2.3	0306	0.4	0146	0.6	0229	3.6	0102	10.0
	1046	0.2	1101	0.4	0925	0.3	0712	0.3	0653	0.2	0905	5.1	0745	3.9	0753	-0.0	0757	0.3
	1700	5.8	1715	6.1	1548	4.3	1342	3.4	1323	2.1	1524	0.7	1403	0.5	1458	3.4	1327	9.6
	2259	0.6	2312	1.0	2139	0.7	1923	0.7	1909	0.5	2122	5.3	2011	4.2	2010	0.3	2012	0.7
24 TH	0517	5.8	0532	6.0	0354	4.5	0150	3.7	0127	2.2	0351	0.5	0234	0.7	0312	3.7	0148	9.9
	1132	0.3	1142	0.6	1012	0.4	0800	0.3	0741	0.2	0954	4.9	0825	3.8	0841	0.0	0842	0.5
	1749	5.6	1804	5.9	1636	4.2	1430	3.3	1412	2.0	1610	0.9	1450	0.6	1543	3.4	1414	9.3
	2342	0.9	2345	1.2	2227	0.8	2009	0.8	1956	0.5	2215	5.1	2058	4.0	2058	0.4	2057	1.0
25 F	0607	5.6	0622	5.8	0444	4.3	0239	3.5	0218	2.1	0439	0.8	0323	0.8	0357	3.7	0235	9.6
	1217	0.6	1153	0.9	1103	0.6	0849	0.5	0831	0.3	1051	4.6	0908	3.6	0933	0.2	0927	0.8
	1842	5.3	1856	5.6	1729	4.0	1520	3.2	1502	1.9	1700	1.2	1539	0.8	1627	3.4	1503	9.0
			2346	1.4	2318	1.1	2100	1.0	2048	0.6	2315	4.8	2149	3.7	2150	0.5	2143	1.4
26 SA	0027	1.2	0717	5.5	0539	4.2	0330	3.4	0312	2.0	0530	1.1	0414	1.1	0444	3.6	0325	9.2
	0702	5.4	1214	1.2	1157	0.8	0945	0.7	0927	0.5	1157	4.4	0954	3.3	1031	0.3	1015	1.3
	1303	1.0	1953	5.4	1827	3.8	1615	3.0	1556	1.8	1756	1.5	1634	1.1	1715	3.3	1555	8.5
	1939	5.1					2159	1.1	2146	0.7			2251	3.4	2249	0.6	2236	1.8
27 SU	0118	1.5	0042	1.6	0017	1.3	0428	3.2	0412	1.9	0024	4.5	0509	1.3	0536	3.5	0420	8.7
	0803	5.1	0819	5.3	0642	3.9	1051	1.0	1031	0.6	0627	1.5	1051	3.1	1136	0.5	1109	1.8
	1400	1.4	1315	1.6	1300	1.1	1715	2.9	1654	1.7	1310	4.2	1737	1.3	1806	3.2	1655	8.1
	2042	4.9	2057	5.1	1932	3.7	2313	1.3	2259	0.8	1903	1.8			2357	0.8	2339	2.2
28 M	0224	1.7	0250	1.9	0126	1.4	0535	3.0	0516	1.8	0137	4.3	0020	3.2	0637	3.3	0524	8.2
	0909	4.9	0927	5.1	0754	3.8	1206	1.1	1151	0.8	0736	1.8	0609	1.5	1249	0.6	1215	2.2
	1516	1.7	1554	1.8	1411	1.3	1824	2.9	1800	1.7	1425	4.1	1224	2.9	1906	3.1	1806	7.9
	2148	4.8	2203	5.0	2042	3.6					2024	1.9	1854	1.5				
29 TU	0350	1.8	0418	1.9	0245	1.5	0039	1.3	0026	1.0	0251	4.2	0115	3.1	0115	0.8	0054	2.4
	1021	4.8	1036	5.0	0910	3.7	0650	2.9	0630	1.7	0855	1.9	0721	1.6	0753	3.1	0639	8.0
	1642	1.8	1705	1.8	1527	1.4	1324	1.2	1306	0.8	1536	4.2	1433	3.0	1404	0.7	1330	2.4
	2258	4.8	2309	5.0	2152	3.7	1935	2.9	1912	1.8	2146	1.9	2021	1.6	2021	3.0	1921	7.9
30 W	0512	1.7	0525	1.8	0401	1.4	0200	1.2	0139	0.8	0400	4.3	0303	3.1	0234	0.8	0212	2.4
	1133	4.8	1142	5.0	1023	3.7	0805	2.9	0750	1.7	1012	1.8	0836	1.5	0919	3.0	0754	8.0
	1750	1.7	1809	1.8	1634	1.4	1427	1.2	1408	0.8	1635	4.4	1537	3.2	1511	0.7	1442	2.3
					2254	3.8	2039	3.0	2021	1.8	2253	1.7	2134	1.5	2139	3.0	2030	8.1
31 TH	0005	4.9	0011	5.1	0505	1.3	0300	1.1	0239	0.7	0457	4.4	0357	3.3	0339	0.7	0321	2.1
	0617	1.5	0635	1.7	1125	3.8	0909	3.0	0856	1.8	1110	1.7	0939	1.4	1033	3.0	0859	8.2
	1237	4.9	1243	5.1	1728	1.4	1517	1.2	1500	0.8	1722	4.6	1622	3.3	1606	0.6	1543	2.1
	1842	1.6	1905	1.8	2346	3.9	2133	3.2	2115	1.9	2345	1.5	2227	1.4	2245	3.1	2128	8.3

● ● Time UT. For British Summer Time (shaded) March 30th to October 26th ADD ONE HOUR ● ●

SCOTLAND & NORTH WEST ENGLAND Time Zone UT

Leith * Rosyth * Aberdeen *Wick * Lerwick * Ullapool * Oban * Greenock * Liverpool

AUGUST 1997 TIDE TABLES AUGUST 1997

LEITH	ROSYTH	ABERDEEN	WICK	LERWICK	ULLAPOOL	OBAN	GREENOCK	LIVERPOOL		
Time m	Time m	Time m	Time m	Time m	Time m	Time m	Time m	Time m		
0103 5.1	0106 5.3	0556 1.1	0348 1.0	0329 0.6	0544 4.5	0439 3.4	0431 0.6	0418 1.8	1	F
0709 1.3	0734 1.5	1215 3.9	1003 3.1	0947 1.9	1157 1.5	1027 1.2	1130 3.1	0952 8.5		
1330 5.1	1336 5.3	1812 1.3	1557 1.1	1545 0.7	1802 4.8	1656 3.5	1653 0.6	1634 1.8		
1926 1.4	1827 1.6		2219 3.3	2200 2.0		2310 1.2	2334 3.3	2215 8.8		
0151 5.2	0154 5.5	0030 4.1	0427 0.8	0411 0.5	0030 1.3	0516 3.5	0514 0.5	0506 1.5	2	SA
0754 1.1	0733 1.3	0639 1.0	1047 3.2	1029 1.9	0623 4.7	1108 1.0	1218 3.1	1037 8.8		
1414 5.2	1419 5.4	1257 4.0	1633 1.0	1623 0.7	1238 1.3	1724 3.7	1733 0.6	1716 1.6		
2003 1.3	1905 1.5	1850 1.2	2300 3.4	2240 2.1	1836 4.9	2348 1.2		2257 9.1		
0233 5.3	0236 5.6	0108 4.2	0503 0.7	0448 0.5	0108 1.1	0550 3.7	0014 3.3	0548 1.3	3	SU
0833 0.9	0824 1.1	0717 0.8	1126 3.2	1107 2.0	0657 4.8	1145 0.9	0551 0.5	1116 8.9		
1452 5.3	1457 5.5	1335 4.0	1706 1.0	1659 0.7	1315 1.2	1752 3.8	1259 3.2	1753 1.5		
2037 1.2	1945 1.3	1925 1.1	2337 3.5	2317 2.1	1907 5.0		1809 0.5	2333 9.2		●
0310 5.4	0315 5.7	0143 4.2	0537 0.7	0524 0.5	0143 1.0	0023 1.1	0049 3.4	0624 1.2	4	M
0906 0.8	0818 1.0	0752 0.8	1202 3.3	1142 2.0	0730 4.8	0621 3.8	0624 0.4	1151 9.0		
1526 5.3	1533 5.6	1410 4.1	1739 0.9	1732 0.6	1348 1.1	1221 0.8	1336 3.2	1825 1.4		
2108 1.1	2024 1.2	1959 1.0		2351 2.1	1937 5.0	1821 3.9	1843 0.5			
0345 5.4	0352 5.7	0216 4.2	0012 3.5	0557 0.4	0216 1.0	0057 1.1	0123 3.5	0007 9.2	5	TU
0936 0.8	0854 1.0	0825 0.7	0610 0.7	1215 2.0	0801 4.8	0653 3.8	0656 0.4	0656 1.2		
1558 5.3	1606 5.6	1443 4.0	1236 3.3	1802 0.6	1421 1.1	1256 0.8	1409 3.2	1225 9.0		
2136 1.1	2101 1.3	2030 1.0	1812 0.9		2006 5.0	1852 3.9	1915 0.5	1856 1.4		
0417 5.3	0427 5.7	0248 4.2	0045 3.4	0022 2.1	0248 1.0	0129 1.1	0156 3.5	0039 9.2	6	W
1003 0.8	0927 1.0	0856 0.8	0642 0.7	0629 0.5	0833 4.8	0724 3.8	0727 0.4	0727 1.3		
1631 5.2	1639 5.5	1515 4.0	1308 3.2	1246 1.9	1452 1.2	1330 0.9	1440 3.2	1257 8.9		
2205 1.1	2134 1.3	2101 1.1	1842 1.0	1831 0.7	2036 4.9	1923 3.9	1948 0.5	1926 1.5		
0450 5.3	0500 5.6	0320 4.1	0117 3.4	0052 2.1	0319 1.1	0202 1.2	0228 3.6	0111 9.1	7	TH
1031 0.9	0957 1.1	0927 0.8	0714 0.7	0700 0.5	0904 4.7	0755 3.7	0758 0.5	0755 1.4		
1706 5.1	1712 5.4	1548 3.9	1340 3.1	1316 1.9	1524 1.3	1403 1.0	1509 3.2	1328 8.8		
2233 1.2	2205 1.4	2132 1.2	1914 1.0	1902 0.7	2106 4.8	1954 3.8	2021 0.6	1957 1.6		
0524 5.2	0533 5.4	0354 4.0	0149 3.3	0123 2.0	0351 1.2	0235 1.3	0300 3.5	0142 8.9	8	F
1101 1.0	1029 1.3	1000 1.0	0746 0.7	0733 0.6	0939 4.5	0827 3.6	0832 0.5	0825 1.6		
1744 5.0	1748 5.4	1623 3.8	1413 3.1	1348 1.9	1557 1.4	1439 1.2	1539 3.2	1400 8.6		
2300 1.4	2234 1.6	2205 1.3	1946 1.1	1936 0.8	2141 4.6	2027 3.6	2056 0.6	2029 1.9		
0600 5.0	0609 5.3	0430 3.9	0223 3.2	0157 1.9	0425 1.4	0309 1.5	0333 3.5	0213 8.6	9	SA
1133 1.2	1101 1.4	1035 1.1	0820 1.0	0810 0.7	1017 4.4	0900 3.4	0908 0.6	0857 1.9		
1823 4.9	1829 5.3	1701 3.7	1449 3.0	1425 1.8	1633 1.6	1516 1.4	1609 3.1	1434 8.3		
2328 1.6	2304 1.8	2242 1.4	2022 1.2	2014 0.8	2221 4.4	2101 3.4	2134 0.7	2105 2.2		
0639 4.8	0648 5.1	0511 3.8	0301 3.1	0237 1.9	0503 1.6	0347 1.6	0408 3.4	0248 8.3	10	SU
1208 1.5	1136 1.7	1115 1.3	0859 1.1	0851 0.8	1105 4.2	0936 3.2	0948 0.7	0933 2.3		
1906 4.7	1915 5.1	1745 3.6	1530 2.9	1508 1.7	1714 1.9	1559 1.5	1645 3.1	1512 8.0		
	2339 2.0	2326 1.6	2106 1.4	2059 0.9	2311 4.2	2142 3.3	2218 0.8	2145 2.6		
0004 1.8	0736 4.9	0559 3.6	0347 2.9	0324 1.8	0548 1.9	0431 1.6	0446 3.2	0328 8.0	11	M
0723 4.7	1220 1.9	1203 1.5	0948 1.3	0941 0.9	1209 4.0	1024 3.1	1035 0.8	1016 2.6		
1254 1.8	2006 5.0	1837 3.5	1621 2.8	1600 1.7	1804 2.1	1648 1.7	1725 2.9	1600 7.7		
1954 4.6			2205 1.5	2159 1.0		2233 3.1	2312 0.9	2236 2.9		
0100 2.1	0029 2.3	0023 1.7	0443 2.8	0424 1.7	0020 4.0	0526 1.9	0530 3.1	0421 7.6	12	TU
0816 4.5	0831 4.8	0658 3.5	1056 1.4	1046 0.9	0645 2.1	1137 2.9	1134 0.9	1113 2.9		
1400 2.0	1400 2.2	1305 1.6	1721 2.8	1701 1.7	1325 4.0	1750 1.8	1815 2.8	1703 7.5		
2051 4.5	2102 4.9	1940 3.5	2330 1.5	2328 1.0	1911 2.2	2346 3.0		2343 3.1		
0233 2.2	0235 2.4	0138 1.8	0551 2.8	0534 1.7	0145 3.9	0638 1.9	0023 1.0	0533 7.4	13	W
0919 4.4	0934 4.7	0810 3.4	1216 1.4	1208 0.9	0800 2.2	1327 3.0	0626 2.9	1232 3.0		
1526 2.1	1518 2.2	1421 1.7	1831 2.8	1811 1.7	1438 4.0	1903 1.8	1249 1.0	1821 7.5		
2156 4.5	2203 4.9	2052 3.5			2036 2.2		1930 2.8			
0415 2.1	0353 2.3	0303 1.7	0057 1.5	0052 0.9	0305 4.0	0132 3.0	0144 0.9	0108 3.0	14	TH
1033 4.5	1039 4.8	0929 3.5	0709 2.8	0651 1.7	0923 2.1	0805 1.8	0742 2.8	0657 7.5		
1651 1.9	1655 2.1	1538 1.6	1331 1.3	1316 0.9	1542 4.2	1442 3.1	1409 0.9	1353 2.7		
2306 4.7	2303 5.0	2202 3.6	1942 2.9	1920 1.8	2156 2.1	2021 1.7	2106 2.8	1937 7.9		
0530 1.8	0524 2.0	0415 1.5	0211 1.3	0153 0.8	0411 4.2	0255 3.2	0252 0.8	0224 2.6	15	F
1148 4.8	1144 5.1	1039 3.6	0821 3.0	0802 1.8	1031 1.8	0915 1.5	0914 2.9	0810 7.9		
1757 1.6	1808 1.8	1642 1.4	1433 1.2	1413 0.8	1636 4.5	1536 3.4	1513 0.8	1500 2.2		
		2300 3.9	2044 3.1	2021 1.9	2257 1.6	2127 1.4	2215 3.0	2041 8.4		

AUGUST 1997 TIDE TABLES AUGUST 1997

	LEITH	ROSYTH	ABERDEEN	WICK	LERWICK	ULLAPOOL	OBAN	GREENOCK	LIVERPOOL
	Time m	Time m	Time m	Time m	Time m	Time m	Time m	Time m	Time m
16 SA	0014 5.0	0003 5.3	0512 1.1	0307 1.0	0245 0.7	0505 4.5	0353 3.4	0348 0.5	0330 2.0
	0628 1.4	0633 1.5	1136 3.9	0922 3.2	0901 1.9	1125 1.4	1007 1.2	1024 3.0	0911 8.5
	1249 5.1	1245 5.4	1734 1.1	1524 1.0	1504 0.7	1723 4.9	1621 3.7	1607 0.6	1558 1.7
	1850 1.3	1903 1.5	2351 4.1	2138 3.4	2114 2.1	2349 1.2	2221 1.1	2308 3.2	2136 9.0
17 SU	0109 5.3	0101 5.6	0603 0.8	0355 0.7	0333 0.5	0551 4.9	0442 3.6	0437 0.3	0427 1.3
	0720 0.9	0733 1.1	1225 4.2	1015 3.4	0954 2.1	1212 1.1	1052 0.9	1121 3.2	1003 9.1
	1339 5.5	1341 5.8	1822 0.9	1610 0.8	1551 0.6	1806 5.3	1704 4.0	1654 0.5	1651 1.2
	1939 0.9	1954 1.1		2227 3.6	2203 2.2		2310 0.8	2357 3.4	2225 9.6
18 M ○	0156 5.6	0155 5.9	0036 4.4	0440 0.5	0420 0.3	0036 0.7	0527 3.9	0522 0.1	0521 0.8
	0809 0.5	0826 0.7	0649 0.5	1105 3.5	1043 2.2	0634 5.2	1136 0.6	1216 3.3	1052 9.5
	1424 5.8	1431 6.1	1312 4.4	1654 0.7	1637 0.5	1257 0.7	1747 4.3	1739 0.3	1741 0.7
	2026 0.6	2041 0.9	1907 0.7	2314 3.8	2251 2.3	1848 5.5	2357 0.5		231210.0
19 TU	0239 5.9	0245 6.1	0120 4.6	0524 0.3	0504 0.2	0121 0.4	0609 4.0	0045 3.6	0610 0.3
	0857 0.2	0914 0.4	0736 0.2	1151 3.6	1130 2.2	0716 5.4	1218 0.3	0605 -0.0	1139 9.8
	1509 6.0	1518 6.3	1357 4.5	1736 0.6	1721 0.4	1340 0.5	1829 4.4	1309 3.4	1827 0.4
	2112 0.4	2126 0.7	1951 0.6		2336 2.4	1930 5.7		1821 0.3	235810.2
20 W	0323 6.1	0335 6.3	0203 4.7	0000 3.9	0548 0.1	0203 0.2	0043 0.4	0130 3.7	0656 0.1
	0943 -0.0	0959 0.2	0821 0.1	0608 0.2	1217 2.2	0758 5.4	0648 4.1	0648 -0.1	1224 9.9
	1553 6.0	1606 6.4	1441 4.6	1237 3.7	1804 0.4	1422 0.4	1301 0.2	1357 3.5	1912 0.3
	2157 0.4	2209 0.6	2035 0.5	1820 0.5		2014 5.7	1911 4.4	1904 0.2	
21 TH	0409 6.1	0424 6.3	0248 4.7	0045 3.9	0022 2.4	0247 0.2	0129 0.4	0215 3.8	004410.3
	1028 0.0	1041 0.3	0906 0.2	0652 0.2	0633 0.1	0842 5.3	0727 4.1	0733 -0.0	0740 0.1
	1639 5.9	1653 6.3	1526 4.5	1322 3.6	1302 2.2	1505 0.5	1345 0.3	1442 3.5	1308 9.8
	2240 0.5	2248 0.7	2118 0.6	1903 0.6	1848 0.4	2100 5.6	1953 4.3	1948 0.2	1955 0.4
22 F	0456 6.0	0512 6.2	0333 4.7	0131 3.8	0109 2.3	0330 0.4	0215 0.5	0257 3.8	012810.1
	1112 0.2	1120 0.5	0951 0.3	0736 0.3	0718 0.2	0927 5.1	0804 3.9	0818 0.1	0822 0.3
	1727 5.7	1741 6.1	1612 4.3	1407 3.5	1347 2.1	1549 0.7	1430 0.5	1523 3.5	1352 9.6
	2321 0.7	2236 1.0	2203 0.8	1947 0.7	1934 0.5	2149 5.3	2036 4.0	2035 0.3	2038 0.7
23 SA	0546 5.8	0602 6.0	0422 4.5	0218 3.7	0158 2.2	0414 0.7	0300 0.7	0340 3.8	0213 9.8
	1153 0.6	1055 0.9	1037 0.6	0822 0.6	0806 0.4	1019 4.8	0842 3.7	0909 0.2	0904 0.7
	1818 5.4	1830 5.8	1701 4.1	1453 3.3	1435 2.0	1636 1.1	1518 0.8	1603 3.5	1437 9.1
		2312 1.2	2252 1.0	2034 0.9	2024 0.6	2248 4.9	2121 3.7	2125 0.4	2121 1.2
24 SU	0003 1.1	0654 5.6	0516 4.2	0308 3.4	0250 2.1	0501 1.1	0347 1.0	0424 3.7	0300 9.3
	0640 5.5	1135 1.3	1128 1.0	0912 0.9	0858 0.6	1122 4.5	0923 3.4	1004 0.4	0948 1.4
	1233 1.1	1925 5.4	1756 3.9	1543 3.1	1525 1.9	1729 1.5	1609 1.1	1646 3.4	1525 8.6
	1912 5.1		2348 1.3	2130 1.1	2121 0.7	2358 4.5	2215 3.3	2222 0.6	2211 1.8
25 M	0048 1.5	0000 1.6	0618 3.9	0404 3.2	0348 1.9	0554 1.6	0437 1.3	0512 3.5	0351 8.6
	0739 5.1	0754 5.3	1227 1.3	1013 1.2	0959 0.8	1240 4.2	1012 3.1	1109 0.7	1039 2.0
	1320 1.6	1227 1.8	1900 3.7	1641 3.0	1621 1.8	1833 1.9	1711 1.4	1732 3.3	1622 8.1
	2012 4.9	2027 5.1		2245 1.3	2233 0.8		2339 3.0	2330 0.8	2311 2.4
26 TU	0154 1.8	0218 2.0	0058 1.5	0511 3.0	0451 1.8	0117 4.2	0536 1.6	0608 3.2	0454 8.0
	0845 4.8	0903 5.0	0731 3.7	1133 1.4	1120 0.9	0700 2.0	1135 2.9	1224 0.9	1142 2.6
	1437 2.0	1519 2.1	1339 1.6	1751 2.9	1727 1.7	1402 4.1	1832 1.7	1826 3.1	1733 7.7
	2119 4.7	2136 4.9	2012 3.6			1957 2.1			
27 W	0333 2.0	0357 2.0	0222 1.6	0021 1.4	0009 0.9	0237 4.1	0143 2.9	0052 0.9	0029 2.7
	0958 4.7	1013 4.9	0852 3.6	0630 2.9	0609 1.7	0827 2.2	0650 1.7	0723 3.0	0613 7.6
	1624 2.1	1637 2.2	1504 1.7	1302 1.5	1246 1.0	1518 4.2	1433 2.9	1345 0.9	1303 2.9
	2232 4.7	2245 4.9	2127 3.6	1908 2.9	1845 1.8	2133 2.1	2017 1.7	1939 3.0	1857 7.6
28 TH	0505 1.8	0512 1.9	0348 1.5	0148 1.3	0127 0.8	0349 4.1	0254 3.0	0220 0.9	0153 2.7
	1115 4.7	1123 4.9	1010 3.6	0751 2.9	0740 1.7	0956 2.1	0816 1.6	0906 2.9	0736 7.6
	1736 2.0	1744 2.1	1619 1.7	1413 1.4	1354 1.0	1621 4.3	1533 3.1	1457 0.9	1422 2.7
	2345 4.8	2351 5.0	2235 3.7	2018 3.0	2001 1.8	2242 1.9	2133 1.6	2115 3.0	2012 7.9
29 F	0609 1.6	0626 1.7	0454 1.4	0249 1.2	0227 0.8	0446 4.3	0344 3.2	0327 0.8	0305 2.3
	1224 4.8	1229 5.1	1114 3.7	0857 3:0	0844 1.8	1056 1.9	0923 1.5	1023 3.0	0845 8.0
	1827 1.8	1843 2.0	1713 1.6	1503 1.3	1447 0.9	1707 4.5	1614 3.3	1553 0.8	1527 2.4
			2329 3.9	2114 3.2	2056 1.9	2331 1.6	2221 1.5	2226 3.1	2112 8.4
30 SA	0047 5.0	0049 5.3	0542 1.2	0333 1.0	0315 0.7	0529 4.5	0424 3.3	0417 0.7	0403 1.9
	0657 1.4	0723 1.5	1202 3.8	0948 3.1	0930 1.9	1141 1.7	1010 1.2	1116 3.1	0937 8.4
	1315 5.0	1322 5.3	1755 1.4	1541 1.2	1529 0.8	1744 4.7	1642 3.5	1637 0.8	1617 2.0
	1908 1.6	1815 1.8		2200 3.3	2140 2.0		2258 1.3	2314 3.3	2157 8.8
31 SU	0135 5.2	0136 5.5	0012 4.0	0409 0.9	0353 0.6	0012 1.4	0458 3.5	0457 0.6	0448 1.6
	0737 1.2	0802 1.3	0621 1.0	1029 3.2	1008 1.9	0604 4.7	1048 1.1	1200 3.2	1019 8.7
	1357 5.2	1403 5.4	1240 4.0	1614 1.1	1605 0.8	1219 1.5	1706 3.7	1715 0.7	1657 1.8
	1941 1.4	1848 1.6	1831 1.3	2239 3.4	2218 2.1	1815 4.9	2330 1.2	2353 3.4	2236 9.1

● ● Time UT. For British Summer Time (shaded) March 30th to October 26th ADD ONE HOUR ● ●

SCOTLAND & NORTH WEST ENGLAND Time Zone UT
Leith * Rosyth * Aberdeen *Wick * Lerwick * Ullapool * Oban * Greenock * Liverpool

SEPTEMBER 1997 TIDE TABLES SEPTEMBER 1997

	LEITH	ROSYTH	ABERDEEN	WICK	LERWICK	ULLAPOOL	OBAN	GREENOCK	LIVERPOOL
	Time m	Time m	Time m	Time m	Time m	Time m	Time m	Time m	Time m
1 M ●	0215 5.3	0218 5.7	0048 4.1	0442 0.8	0427 0.5	0047 1.2	0529 3.7	0531 0.5	0526 1.4
	0809 1.0	0754 1.2	0655 0.9	1105 3.3	1044 2.0	0636 4.8	1124 0.9	1237 3.2	1056 9.0
	1431 5.3	1438 5.6	1314 4.1	1645 1.0	1637 0.7	1254 1.3	1732 3.8	1748 0.6	1731 1.6
	2012 1.2	1926 1.3	1904 1.1	2315 3.5	2254 2.2	1845 5.0			2311 9.2
2 TU	0249 5.4	0255 5.8	0120 4.2	0512 0.7	0500 0.5	0120 1.0	0002 1.1	0027 3.5	0600 1.3
	0839 0.9	0756 1.0	0727 0.8	1138 3.3	1117 2.0	0705 4.9	0600 3.8	0602 0.5	1128 9.1
	1502 5.4	1509 5.6	1345 4.1	1715 1.0	1707 0.7	1325 1.2	1157 0.9	1311 3.3	1801 1.4
	2042 1.1	2004 1.2	1935 1.1	2348 3.5	2327 2.2	1912 5.1	1800 3.9	1819 0.5	2343 9.3
3 W	0320 5.4	0330 5.8	0151 4.3	0543 0.7	0529 0.5	0150 1.0	0033 1.0	0100 3.5	0630 1.2
	0906 0.8	0829 1.0	0757 0.7	1209 3.3	1148 2.0	0733 5.0	0629 3.9	0630 0.5	1200 9.2
	1531 5.4	1539 5.6	1415 4.1	1746 0.9	1735 0.6	1356 1.1	1230 0.8	1342 3.3	1830 1.4
	2112 1.0	2039 1.2	2005 1.0		2356 2.2	1939 5.1	1828 4.0	1848 0.5	
4 TH	0350 5.4	0402 5.7	0221 4.3	0018 3.5	0557 0.5	0219 0.9	0103 1.0	0132 3.5	0014 9.3
	0935 0.7	0900 1.0	0827 0.8	0613 0.7	1215 2.0	0802 5.0	0659 3.9	0659 0.5	0658 1.2
	1603 5.3	1608 5.6	1445 4.1	1239 3.3	1803 0.6	1425 1.1	1302 0.9	1412 3.3	1230 9.1
	2142 1.0	2112 1.2	2033 1.0	1816 0.9		2006 5.0	1857 3.9	1918 0.5	1900 1.4
5 F	0421 5.4	0432 5.6	0252 4.2	0049 3.5	0024 2.1	0249 1.0	0133 1.1	0203 3.5	0043 9.2
	1004 0.8	0930 1.0	0857 0.8	0642 0.7	0627 0.5	0831 4.9	0727 3.8	0728 0.5	0727 1.3
	1637 5.3	1639 5.6	1515 4.1	1309 3.3	1243 2.0	1455 1.2	1334 0.9	1439 3.3	1259 9.0
	2209 1.1	2139 1.3	2103 1.1	1846 1.0	1833 0.7	2035 4.9	1926 3.9	1949 0.5	1931 1.5
6 SA	0454 5.3	0503 5.5	0324 4.1	0120 3.4	0053 2.1	0319 1.1	0203 1.2	0233 3.5	0112 9.1
	1033 1.0	0957 1.2	0927 0.9	0712 0.8	0659 0.6	0901 4.7	0756 3.7	0759 0.5	0756 1.5
	1712 5.2	1715 5.5	1548 4.0	1340 3.2	1313 2.0	1527 1.3	1407 1.1	1506 3.3	1329 8.9
	2231 1.3	2204 1.4	2134 1.2	1917 1.0	1907 0.7	2107 4.7	1956 3.7	2023 0.5	2003 1.7
7 SU	0529 5.1	0537 5.4	0359 4.0	0153 3.3	0126 2.0	0351 1.3	0233 1.3	0304 3.5	0142 8.8
	1057 1.2	1024 1.3	1000 1.1	0744 0.9	0734 0.7	0936 4.6	0825 3.6	0833 0.5	0827 1.8
	1749 5.0	1755 5.4	1624 3.9	1414 3.1	1348 1.9	1601 1.5	1442 1.3	1536 3.3	1400 8.6
	2251 1.5	2230 1.6	2208 1.3	1951 1.1	1944 0.8	2144 4.5	2027 3.6	2059 0.6	2037 2.0
8 M	0606 5.0	0617 5.2	0439 3.9	0230 3.1	0203 2.0	0427 1.5	0308 1.5	0338 3.4	0214 8.5
	1122 1.4	1052 1.5	1036 1.2	0819 1.1	0812 0.8	1018 4.4	0857 3.4	0910 0.6	0900 2.2
	1830 4.9	1839 5.3	1705 3.8	1454 3.0	1427 1.9	1640 1.7	1523 1.5	1609 3.2	1436 8.3
	2321 1.7	2301 1.8	2249 1.5	2030 1.3	2026 0.9	2230 4.3	2102 3.3	2140 0.7	2115 2.4
9 TU	0648 4.8	0702 5.0	0524 3.7	0313 3.0	0249 1.9	0507 1.8	0348 1.6	0415 3.3	0252 8.2
	1157 1.7	1127 1.8	1121 1.4	0903 1.3	0857 0.9	1115 4.2	0938 3.2	0954 0.8	0939 2.6
	1917 4.7	1927 5.1	1754 3.6	1541 2.9	1515 1.8	1727 2.0	1611 1.7	1647 3.1	1521 8.0
		2342 2.0	2343 1.6	2124 1.4	2121 1.0	2336 4.0	2147 3.1	2230 0.9	2201 2.8
10 W	0008 1.9	0755 4.8	0621 3.6	0408 2.9	0348 1.8	0600 2.1	0440 1.8	0457 3.1	0342 7.8
	0741 4.6	1216 2.1	1221 1.6	1006 1.4	0957 1.0	1237 4.0	1040 3.0	1049 0.9	1031 3.0
	1257 2.0	2023 4.9	1856 3.5	1639 2.9	1618 1.8	1831 2.2	1712 1.8	1733 3.0	1620 7.6
	2012 4.6			2247 1.5	2240 1.0		2254 2.9	2339 1.0	2305 3.1
11 TH	0136 2.2	0052 2.3	0058 1.7	0518 2.8	0503 1.7	0111 3.9	0550 1.9	0554 3.0	0452 7.4
	0845 4.5	0900 4.7	0736 3.5	1136 1.5	1124 1.0	0715 2.2	1247 2.9	1203 1.1	1148 3.2
	1444 2.2	1445 2.3	1342 1.8	1751 2.9	1733 1.7	1402 4.0	1830 1.8	1842 2.9	1742 7.5
	2119 4.6	2127 4.8	2012 3.5			2000 2.2			
12 F	0345 2.1	0319 2.2	0230 1.7	0027 1.4	0022 1.0	0241 4.0	0059 2.9	0105 1.0	0033 3.0
	1003 4.5	1009 4.8	0902 3.5	0642 2.8	0624 1.7	0852 2.2	0725 1.8	0712 2.9	0624 7.4
	1627 2.1	1639 2.2	1509 1.7	1303 1.4	1251 1.0	1515 4.2	1421 3.1	1330 1.1	1321 3.0
	2233 4.7	2233 4.9	2130 3.6	1909 3.0	1849 1.8	2131 2.0	1959 1.7	2024 2.9	1907 7.8
13 SA	0512 1.7	0516 1.9	0351 1.4	0148 1.2	0130 0.8	0353 4.2	0242 3.1	0222 0.8	0158 2.6
	1123 4.8	1118 5.0	1017 3.7	0800 3.0	0742 1.8	1009 1.9	0849 1.5	0847 2.9	0747 7.9
	1738 1.7	1751 1.8	1620 1.5	1412 1.3	1354 0.9	1614 4.6	1516 3.4	1445 0.9	1436 2.4
	2345 5.0	2338 5.2	2235 3.9	2017 3.2	1956 1.9	2238 1.6	2110 1.4	2145 3.1	2017 8.4
14 SU	0611 1.3	0624 1.4	0452 1.1	0248 0.9	0225 0.6	0448 4.6	0340 3.3	0324 0.6	0308 1.9
	1227 5.2	1223 5.4	1116 4.0	0904 3.2	0844 2.0	1106 1.5	0945 1.2	1002 3.1	0851 8.5
	1831 1.3	1846 1.4	1715 1.2	1506 1.0	1446 0.7	1703 5.0	1603 3.8	1543 0.8	1538 1.8
			2327 4.2	2115 3.4	2053 2.1	2330 1.1	2206 1.0	2244 3.3	2115 9.1
15 M	0044 5.4	0039 5.6	0543 0.7	0337 0.7	0315 0.5	0534 5.0	0427 3.6	0415 0.3	0409 1.2
	0703 0.8	0719 0.9	1206 4.3	0958 3.4	0936 2.1	1154 1.0	1032 0.8	1103 3.3	0945 9.2
	1318 5.6	1318 5.8	1803 0.9	1551 0.8	1533 0.6	1746 5.4	1645 4.1	1633 0.6	1632 1.2
	1919 0.9	1933 1.1		2206 3.6	2143 2.2		2254 0.7	2336 3.5	2206 9.7

● ● Time UT. For British Summer Time (shaded) March 30th to October 26th ADD ONE HOUR ● ●

SEPTEMBER 1997 TIDE TABLES SEPTEMBER 1997

	LEITH		ROSYTH		ABERDEEN		WICK		LERWICK		ULLAPOOL		OBAN		GREENOCK		LIVERPOOL	
	Time	m	Time	m	Time	m	Time	m	Time	m	Time	m	Time	m	Time	m	Time	m
16 TU ○	0132	5.7	0134	5.9	0014	4.5	0421	0.4	0400	0.3	0016	0.6	0509	3.9	0500	0.1	0502	0.6
	0751	0.4	0809	0.5	0630	0.4	1046	3.6	1024	2.2	0615	5.3	1115	0.5	1159	3.4	1033	9.7
	1403	5.9	1408	6.1	1251	4.5	1634	0.6	1618	0.5	1238	0.7	1728	4.4	1717	0.4	1722	0.7
	2006	0.6	2017	0.7	1847	0.7	2254	3.8	2230	2.4	1828	5.7	2340	0.4			2253	10.1
17 W	0216	6.0	0224	6.2	0058	4.7	0504	0.2	0444	0.2	0100	0.3	0549	4.1	0025	3.7	0551	0.2
	0838	0.1	0854	0.3	0715	0.2	1131	3.7	1109	2.3	0656	5.5	1158	0.2	0544	-0.0	1119	10.0
	1446	6.1	1454	6.3	1335	4.6	1716	0.5	1700	0.4	1320	0.4	1810	4.5	1251	3.5	1808	0.3
	2051	0.4	2058	0.5	1930	0.5	2339	4.0	2316	2.4	1909	5.8			1800	0.3	2338	10.4
18 TH	0300	6.2	0313	6.4	0142	4.8	0547	0.2	0527	0.1	0142	0.1	0024	0.3	0112	3.8	0636	-0.0
	0923	-0.0	0936	0.1	0759	0.1	1215	3.7	1153	2.3	0736	5.6	0627	4.2	0626	-0.1	1203	10.1
	1530	6.1	1541	6.4	1418	4.6	1759	0.5	1743	0.4	1402	0.3	1241	0.2	1336	3.6	1852	0.2
	2136	0.3	2138	0.5	2013	0.5					1952	5.8	1851	4.5	1842	0.2		
19 F	0347	6.2	0402	6.4	0226	4.8	0025	4.0	0002	2.5	0224	0.2	0108	0.3	0155	3.8	0022	10.4
	1006	0.0	1016	0.3	0842	0.2	0629	0.2	0610	0.2	0817	5.5	0703	4.2	0709	-0.0	0718	0.0
	1616	6.0	1628	6.3	1501	4.6	1258	3.7	1236	2.3	1444	0.4	1324	0.2	1418	3.6	1245	10.0
	2219	0.4	2138	0.6	2057	0.6	1841	0.5	1827	0.4	2036	5.6	1931	4.3	1926	0.2	1934	0.3
20 SA	0435	6.1	0451	6.3	0312	4.7	0110	3.9	0048	2.4	0306	0.4	0151	0.4	0237	3.8	0106	10.2
	1048	0.3	1038	0.6	0925	0.4	0711	0.4	0654	0.3	0900	5.2	0739	4.0	0754	0.1	0759	0.3
	1703	5.8	1716	6.1	1545	4.4	1341	3.5	1319	2.2	1527	0.7	1409	0.5	1457	3.6	1328	9.7
	2300	0.7	2208	0.8	2140	0.7	1924	0.7	1912	0.5	2124	5.3	2011	4.0	2012	0.3	2016	0.5
21 SU	0525	5.8	0539	6.0	0400	4.5	0157	3.7	0136	2.3	0348	0.8	0234	0.7	0319	3.8	0149	9.8
	1126	0.8	1024	0.9	1009	0.8	0754	0.7	0741	0.5	0948	4.9	0815	3.8	0843	0.3	0839	0.9
	1752	5.5	1805	5.7	1632	4.2	1424	3.4	1405	2.1	1612	1.0	1455	0.8	1536	3.6	1411	9.2
	2340	1.1	2242	1.2	2228	1.0	2011	0.9	2001	0.6	2221	4.8	2053	3.6	2100	0.4	2059	1.2
22 M	0618	5.4	0632	5.6	0454	4.2	0245	3.4	0227	2.1	0433	1.2	0318	1.0	0401	3.6	0234	9.2
	1200	1.3	1102	1.4	1057	1.1	0839	1.0	0830	0.7	1045	4.5	0854	3.5	0936	0.6	0920	1.6
	1845	5.1	1858	5.3	1724	3.9	1512	3.2	1454	2.0	1703	1.5	1546	1.2	1615	3.6	1456	8.7
					2325	1.5	2105	1.1	2058	0.8	2332	4.4	2140	3.2	2156	0.6	2146	1.9
23 TU	0022	1.5	0730	5.2	0555	3.9	0340	3.1	0324	1.9	0522	1.7	0406	1.3	0448	3.4	0324	8.5
	0715	5.1	1148	1.9	1152	1.5	0933	1.3	0928	0.9	1206	4.2	0939	3.2	1037	0.8	1006	2.3
	1238	1.9	1959	4.9	1826	3.7	1606	3.0	1548	1.9	1805	1.9	1646	1.6	1659	3.4	1549	8.1
	1943	4.9					2220	1.3	2210	0.9			2250	2.9	2302	0.8	2244	2.5
24 W	0125	1.9	0112	2.0	0030	1.5	0446	2.9	0426	1.8	0054	4.1	0503	1.6	0541	3.1	0424	7.8
	0820	4.7	0836	4.9	0708	3.6	1051	1.6	1044	1.1	0625	2.2	1052	2.9	1151	1.1	1108	2.9
	1348	2.3	1442	2.3	1303	1.8	1715	2.9	1652	1.8	1333	4.1	1809	1.8	1748	3.2	1658	7.6
	2048	4.6	2108	4.7	1938	3.6	2357	1.4	2344	0.9	1929	2.2						
25 TH	0313	2.1	0336	2.0	0156	1.6	0606	2.8	0543	1.7	0216	4.0	0115	2.8	0022	1.0	0001	2.9
	0930	4.5	0946	4.7	0828	3.5	1230	1.6	1218	1.1	0754	2.4	0615	1.7	0654	2.9	0544	7.4
	1554	2.4	1604	2.4	1433	1.9	1834	2.9	1810	1.8	1453	4.1	1419	2.9	1315	1.2	1231	3.2
	2200	4.6	2217	4.7	2055	3.6					2110	2.2	2005	1.9	1854	3.1	1824	7.4
26 F	0447	1.9	0451	1.9	0327	1.6	0126	1.3	0104	0.9	0330	4.0	0229	2.9	0154	1.0	0127	2.9
	1048	4.6	1057	4.7	0948	3.5	0730	2.8	0719	1.7	0931	2.3	0745	1.7	0845	2.9	0712	7.4
	1712	2.3	1706	2.3	1555	1.6	1351	1.6	1331	1.1	1557	4.2	1515	3.1	1431	1.2	1355	3.1
	2315	4.7	2324	4.9	2207	3.7	1949	3.0	1931	1.8	2220	2.0	2118	1.7	2036	3.0	1945	7.7
27 SA	0548	1.7	0603	1.7	0432	1.4	0226	1.2	0205	0.8	0425	4.2	0318	3.1	0303	0.9	0239	2.5
	1159	4.7	1203	4.9	1052	3.7	0835	2.9	0821	1.8	1033	2.1	0857	1.5	1001	3.0	0822	7.8
	1803	2.0	1747	2.1	1651	1.4	1442	1.5	1425	1.0	1645	4.4	1551	3.3	1528	1.0	1500	2.7
					2303	3.8	2047	3.1	2028	1.9	2308	1.7	2202	1.5	2154	3.2	2046	8.2
28 SU	0021	4.9	0023	5.1	0518	1.3	0309	1.1	0251	0.8	0506	4.4	0357	3.3	0352	0.8	0336	2.1
	0633	1.5	0659	1.5	1139	3.8	0924	3.1	0903	1.9	1118	1.8	0945	1.3	1051	3.1	0913	8.3
	1251	4.9	1257	5.2	1731	1.5	1519	1.3	1506	0.9	1720	4.6	1616	3.5	1612	0.9	1550	2.3
	1841	1.8	1802	1.9	2345	4.0	2133	3.3	2112	2.0	2346	1.5	2236	1.4	2244	3.3	2132	8.6
29 M	0109	5.1	0112	5.4	0554	1.1	0344	0.9	0327	0.7	0540	4.7	0431	3.5	0431	0.7	0420	1.7
	0709	1.3	0736	1.3	1215	3.9	1003	3.2	0940	2.0	1154	1.6	1023	1.1	1131	3.2	0954	8.7
	1331	5.1	1338	5.4	1806	1.3	1551	1.2	1541	0.8	1751	4.8	1640	3.6	1649	0.8	1630	1.9
	1913	1.5	1831	1.6			2212	3.4	2151	2.1			2306	1.2	2324	3.4	2210	9.0
30 TU	0148	5.3	0153	5.6	0021	4.1	0415	0.8	0400	0.6	0020	1.3	0503	3.7	0504	0.6	0457	1.5
	0738	1.1	0800	1.2	0627	1.0	1038	3.3	1015	2.0	0609	4.8	1057	1.0	1206	3.3	1029	9.0
	1404	5.3	1412	5.5	1247	4.1	1621	1.1	1612	0.7	1227	1.2	1706	3.8	1721	0.7	1703	1.7
	1944	1.3	1907	1.3	1838	1.2	2247	3.4	2227	2.2	1818	5.0	2336	1.1	2359	3.5	2244	9.2

● ● Time UT. For British Summer Time (shaded) March 30th to October 26th ADD ONE HOUR ● ●

SCOTLAND & NORTH WEST ENGLAND Time Zone UT

Leith * Rosyth * Aberdeen * Wick * Lerwick * Ullapool * Oban * Greenock * Liverpool

OCTOBER 1997 TIDE TABLES OCTOBER 1997

	LEITH		ROSYTH		ABERDEEN		WICK		LERWICK		ULLAPOOL		OBAN		GREENOCK		LIVERPOOL	
	Time	m	Time	m	Time	m	Time	m	Time	m	Time	m	Time	m	Time	m	Time	m
1 W ●	221	5.4	0230	5.7	0053	4.2	0444	0.8	0430	0.6	0051	1.1	0533	3.8	0533	0.5	0529	1.3
	806	0.9	0734	1.0	0658	0.9	1109	3.4	1048	2.1	0638	5.0	1130	0.9	1240	3.4	1101	9.1
	433	5.4	1442	5.6	1317	4.2	1651	1.0	1639	0.7	1259	1.2	1733	3.9	1751	0.6	1733	1.5
	015	1.1	1943	1.2	1909	1.1	2320	3.5	2259	2.2	1845	5.0					2315	9.3
2 TH	251	5.4	0304	5.7	0124	4.3	0514	0.7	0457	0.5	0121	1.0	0006	1.0	0033	3.5	0559	1.2
	835	0.8	0804	1.0	0728	0.8	1140	3.4	1117	2.1	0706	5.1	0603	3.9	0601	0.5	1131	9.3
	503	5.4	1510	5.6	1345	4.2	1721	0.9	1707	0.7	1329	1.1	1203	0.9	1312	3.4	1803	1.4
	047	1.0	2018	1.1	1938	1.0	2351	3.5	2327	2.2	1912	5.1	1802	4.0	1820	0.5	2345	9.3
3 F	323	5.5	0336	5.7	0154	4.3	0543	0.7	0526	0.5	0150	0.9	0034	1.0	0105	3.5	0628	1.2
	906	0.7	0835	0.9	0757	0.8	1209	3.4	1145	2.1	0733	5.1	0632	3.9	0629	0.5	1200	9.3
	536	5.4	1539	5.7	1415	4.2	1751	0.9	1736	0.6	1359	1.0	1233	0.9	1341	3.4	1834	1.3
	118	1.0	2049	1.1	2007	1.0			2356	2.2	1939	5.1	1830	4.0	1849	0.5		
4 SA	355	5.4	0406	5.6	0226	4.3	0022	3.5	0557	0.6	0219	0.9	0103	1.0	0136	3.5	0015	9.3
	938	0.8	0904	1.0	0827	0.8	0612	0.7	1212	2.1	0801	5.0	0700	3.9	0657	0.5	0658	1.3
	609	5.4	1611	5.7	1445	4.2	1239	3.4	1809	0.7	1429	1.1	1306	0.9	1409	3.4	1230	9.2
	147	1.0	2115	1.2	2037	1.0	1821	0.9			2009	5.0	1859	3.9	1920	0.5	1907	1.4
5 SU	428	5.3	0437	5.5	0258	4.2	0054	3.4	0027	2.1	0249	1.0	0132	1.1	0206	3.5	0045	9.2
	006	1.0	0931	1.1	0857	0.9	0642	0.8	0630	0.6	0831	4.9	0727	3.8	0729	0.5	0729	1.4
	644	5.3	1648	5.6	1518	4.1	1311	3.3	1243	2.1	1500	1.2	1339	1.1	1437	3.4	1301	9.1
	208	1.2	2139	1.3	2109	1.1	1854	0.9	1843	0.7	2041	4.8	1928	3.8	1954	0.5	1940	1.6
6 M	502	5.2	0512	5.4	0334	4.1	0128	3.3	0101	2.1	0321	1.2	0203	1.2	0237	3.4	0115	8.9
	028	1.2	0956	1.2	0930	1.1	0715	0.9	0705	0.7	0906	4.7	0757	3.7	0803	0.5	0800	1.7
	721	5.2	1727	5.5	1551	4.0	1345	3.2	1317	2.1	1536	1.3	1415	1.2	1507	3.4	1333	8.9
	227	1.3	2204	1.4	2143	1.2	1928	1.0	1921	0.8	2119	4.6	2000	3.6	2030	0.5	2015	1.9
7 TU	540	5.1	0553	5.3	0414	3.9	0206	3.2	0139	2.0	0357	1.4	0238	1.4	0312	3.3	0148	8.7
	050	1.4	1024	1.4	1006	1.2	0750	1.1	0743	0.8	0947	4.5	0829	3.5	0842	0.6	0834	2.1
	800	5.0	1810	5.3	1633	3.9	1424	3.2	1355	2.0	1615	1.6	1456	1.4	1540	3.4	1410	8.6
	257	1.5	2237	1.5	2225	1.3	2009	1.2	2004	0.8	2207	4.3	2034	3.4	2112	0.6	2052	2.3
8 W	624	4.9	0638	5.1	0500	3.8	0251	3.0	0225	1.9	0438	1.7	0319	1.5	0350	3.2	0228	8.3
	124	1.7	1059	1.7	1051	1.4	0833	1.2	0828	0.9	1043	4.3	0909	3.3	0925	0.8	0912	2.5
	847	4.8	1857	5.1	1722	3.7	1512	3.0	1442	1.9	1703	1.8	1545	1.6	1618	3.3	1454	8.2
	345	1.8	2320	1.7	2318	1.5	2102	1.3	2058	0.9	2315	4.1	2118	3.2	2203	0.8	2138	2.6
9 TH	718	4.7	0730	4.9	0559	3.6	0346	2.9	0325	1.8	0530	2.0	0410	1.7	0436	3.1	0318	7.9
	224	2.0	1147	2.0	1151	1.7	0935	1.4	0928	1.0	1203	4.1	1010	3.1	1021	1.0	1003	2.9
	943	4.7	1951	4.9	1823	3.6	1609	2.9	1544	1.8	1806	2.1	1648	1.8	1704	3.1	1553	7.9
							2223	1.4	2214	1.0			2224	2.9	2312	0.9	2241	2.9
10 F	114	2.0	0025	2.0	0033	1.6	0457	2.8	0442	1.7	0049	3.9	0518	1.8	0534	3.0	0428	7.5
	823	4.6	0834	4.7	0714	3.5	1106	1.5	1052	1.1	0646	2.2	1210	3.0	1134	1.1	1117	3.2
	418	2.2	1417	2.3	1315	1.8	1721	2.9	1703	1.8	1332	4.1	1807	1.8	1809	0.9	1712	7.7
	2051	4.8	2057	4.8	1941	3.6			2353	0.9	1936	2.1						
11 SA	321	2.0	0253	2.0	0205	1.6	0003	1.3	0604	1.8	0219	4.0	0030	2.8	0035	0.9	0005	2.9
	940	4.6	0946	4.8	0840	3.6	0621	2.8	1227	1.0	0826	2.2	0650	1.7	0654	2.9	0600	7.5
	602	2.1	1619	2.1	1444	1.7	1237	1.5	1822	1.8	1447	4.3	1355	3.2	1258	1.2	1251	3.0
	2206	4.7	2209	4.9	2100	3.7	1839	3.0			2107	1.9	1938	1.6	1945	3.0	1839	7.9
12 SU	448	1.6	0505	1.7	0327	1.3	0124	1.1	0106	0.8	0333	4.3	0221	3.0	0152	0.8	0133	2.5
	1059	4.9	1057	5.0	0955	3.8	0741	3.0	0722	1.9	0947	1.9	0818	1.5	0825	3.0	0724	7.9
	1713	1.8	1731	1.8	1556	1.5	1349	1.3	1333	0.9	1549	4.6	1453	3.5	1414	1.1	1410	2.5
	2318	5.0	2319	5.1	2208	3.9	1951	3.2	1932	2.0	2215	1.5	2051	1.3	2115	3.2	1951	8.5
13 M	549	1.2	0609	1.2	0430	1.0	0226	0.9	0203	0.6	0429	4.6	0320	3.3	0257	0.6	0245	1.8
	1203	5.3	1203	5.4	1055	4.1	0845	3.2	0824	2.0	1044	1.5	0920	1.1	0942	3.2	0830	8.6
	1808	1.4	1824	1.4	1653	1.2	1444	1.1	1426	0.8	1640	5.0	1540	3.8	1517	0.9	1514	1.8
					2303	4.2	2051	3.4	2030	2.1	2308	1.0	2146	1.0	2218	3.4	2051	9.1
14 TU	018	5.4	0021	5.5	0522	0.7	0315	0.6	0253	0.5	0515	5.0	0406	3.6	0351	0.3	0345	1.2
	641	0.8	0703	0.8	1145	4.3	0937	3.4	0915	2.2	1133	1.1	1008	0.8	1043	3.3	0924	9.2
	1255	5.6	1257	5.7	1741	0.9	1530	0.9	1513	0.6	1726	5.4	1624	4.1	1609	0.7	1610	1.2
	1857	1.0	1911	1.0	2351	4.5	2144	3.6	2122	2.3	2354	0.6	2234	0.7	2312	3.6	2143	9.7
15 W	108	5.7	0114	5.8	0609	0.4	0400	0.4	0339	0.3	0556	5.3	0448	3.8	0438	0.2	0439	0.7
	729	0.4	0750	0.5	1230	4.5	1024	3.6	1002	2.3	1217	0.7	1053	0.5	1138	3.5	1012	9.7
	1341	5.9	1345	6.0	1826	0.7	1613	0.7	1557	0.5	1808	5.6	1707	4.3	1655	0.5	1700	0.7
	1943	0.7	1949	0.7			2233	3.8	2210	2.4			2319	0.4			2231	10.1

● ● Time UT. For British Summer Time (shaded) March 30th to October 26th ADD ONE HOUR ● ●

OCTOBER 1997 TIDE TABLES OCTOBER 1997

		LEITH		ROSYTH		ABERDEEN		WICK		LERWICK		ULLAPOOL		OBAN		GREENOCK		LIVERPOOL	
		Time	m	Time	m	Time	m	Time	m	Time	m	Time	m	Time	m	Time	m	Time	m
16 TH ○		0154	6.0	0203	6.1	0036	4.7	0442	0.3	0422	0.3	0038	0.4	0527	4.1	0003	3.7	0527	0.3
		0815	0.2	0832	0.3	0654	0.3	1109	3.7	1046	2.3	0636	5.5	1136	0.3	0521	0.0	105710.0	
		1424	6.0	1431	6.2	1312	4.6	1656	0.5	1639	0.4	1300	0.5	1749	4.4	1227	3.5	1746	0.4
		2030	0.4	2006	0.5	1909	0.6	2319	3.9	2257	2.4	1850	5.8			1739	0.3	231610.3	
17 F		0239	6.2	0251	6.3	0121	4.8	0524	0.3	0505	0.3	0120	0.2	0003	0.3	0050	3.8	0612	0.2
		0900	0.1	0910	0.2	0736	0.3	1151	3.7	1128	2.4	0715	5.6	0605	4.2	0604	0.0	114110.1	
		1508	6.1	1518	6.3	1354	4.6	1739	0.5	1723	0.4	1342	0.4	1220	0.3	1312	3.6	1830	0.3
		2115	0.4	2036	0.4	1953	0.5			2342	2.4	1933	5.7	1830	4.4	1821	0.3		
18 SA		0326	6.1	0339	6.3	0206	4.8	0005	3.9	0548	0.4	0201	0.3	0045	0.3	0134	3.8	000010.0	
		0944	0.3	0854	0.4	0818	0.4	0605	0.4	1210	2.3	0754	5.5	0641	4.2	0648	0.1	0654	0.0
		1554	5.9	1605	6.2	1436	4.5	1233	3.7	1806	0.4	1424	0.5	1304	0.4	1351	3.7	122310.0	
		2200	0.5	2112	0.5	2036	0.6	1821	0.5			2016	5.5	1909	4.2	1905	0.2	1913	0.5
19 SU		0415	6.0	0429	6.2	0253	4.6	0051	3.8	0029	2.4	0242	0.5	0127	0.5	0216	3.8	004410.1	
		1024	0.6	0927	0.6	0900	0.6	0645	0.6	0631	0.5	0836	5.2	0716	4.0	0732	0.2	0733	0.6
		1639	5.7	1653	5.9	1519	4.4	1315	3.6	1252	2.3	1507	0.7	1348	0.6	1430	3.7	1305	9.7
		2242	0.7	2145	0.8	2120	0.7	1905	0.6	1853	0.5	2104	5.1	1948	3.9	1951	0.3	1955	0.8
20 M		0504	5.7	0518	5.9	0342	4.4	0136	3.6	0117	2.2	0324	0.9	0209	0.7	0257	3.7	0127	9.6
		1100	1.0	0959	1.0	0942	0.9	0726	0.8	0716	0.7	0921	4.9	0752	3.8	0819	0.4	0812	1.1
		1727	5.5	1742	5.6	1604	4.2	1357	3.4	1336	2.2	1552	1.1	1434	1.0	1508	3.7	1346	9.3
		2320	1.1	2219	1.1	2206	0.9	1951	0.6	1942	0.6	2157	4.7	2027	3.6	2039	0.4	2038	1.3
21 TU		0556	5.4	0609	5.5	0433	4.1	0224	3.3	0206	2.1	0406	1.3	0251	1.0	0340	3.5	0210	9.0
		1126	1.5	1034	1.4	1027	1.3	0808	1.1	0804	0.9	1012	4.6	0830	3.6	0909	0.7	0852	1.8
		1818	5.1	1833	5.2	1654	4.0	1442	3.2	1424	2.0	1640	1.5	1524	1.3	1547	3.7	1430	8.7
		2358	1.5	2258	1.5	2259	1.2	2044	1.0	2037	0.8	2303	4.3	2111	3.3	2131	0.6	2124	2.0
22 W		0650	5.0	0704	5.1	0532	3.8	0316	3.1	0300	1.9	0454	1.8	0336	1.3	0426	3.3	0257	8.4
		1157	2.0	1116	1.9	1118	1.6	0857	1.4	0857	1.1	1121	4.3	0914	3.3	1006	1.0	0936	2.5
		1912	4.9	1931	4.9	1751	3.7	1533	3.1	1515	1.9	1737	1.9	1621	1.7	1630	3.5	1518	8.2
								2151	1.2	2142	0.9			2208	3.0	2231	0.9	2218	2.5
23 TH		0051	1.9	0047	1.9	0000	1.5	0418	2.9	0357	1.8	0021	4.0	0429	1.6	0518	3.1	0354	7.8
		0749	4.7	0806	4.8	0639	3.6	1002	1.6	1003	1.2	0551	2.2	1016	3.0	1111	1.2	1031	3.1
		1255	2.3	1220	2.3	1222	1.9	1636	2.9	1615	1.8	1249	4.1	1736	1.9	1716	3.6	1621	7.7
		2013	4.6	2036	4.6	1858	3.6	2315	1.4	2303	0.9	1852	2.2	2359	2.8	2342	1.0	2327	3.0
24 F		0227	2.1	0303	2.0	0118	1.6	0532	2.7	0506	1.7	0141	3.9	0535	1.7	0624	2.9	0506	7.3
		0854	4.5	0912	4.6	0753	3.4	1135	1.7	1127	1.2	0708	2.4	1332	2.9	1227	1.3	1148	3.4
		1444	2.6	1519	2.5	1345	2.0	1751	2.9	1726	1.8	1411	4.0	1922	2.0	1813	3.2	1739	7.4
		2119	4.5	2142	4.6	2012	3.5					2026	2.2						
25 SA		0406	2.0	0415	1.9	0245	1.6	0043	1.3	0024	0.9	0254	4.0	0141	2.9	0106	1.1	0047	3.0
		1005	4.5	1020	4.6	0909	3.5	0651	2.8	0632	1.7	0845	2.4	0657	1.8	0800	2.9	0630	7.3
		1627	2.4	1621	2.4	1513	2.0	1308	1.7	1251	1.2	1519	4.1	1434	3.1	1347	1.4	1312	3.4
		2231	4.6	2248	4.7	2124	3.6	1906	2.9	1846	1.8	2142	2.1	2041	1.8	1938	3.1	1902	7.5
26 SU		0508	1.8	0519	1.8	0354	1.5	0148	1.3	0127	0.9	0351	4.1	0238	3.0	0222	1.1	0158	2.8
		1116	4.6	1124	4.7	1015	3.6	0759	2.9	0742	1.8	0957	2.2	0815	1.6	0920	3.0	0744	7.6
		1724	2.2	1705	2.2	1615	1.8	1407	1.6	1351	1.1	1610	4.3	1511	3.2	1451	1.2	1420	3.0
		2339	4.7	2347	4.9	2224	3.7	2009	3.0	1951	1.9	2233	1.8	2128	1.7	2106	3.1	2007	7.9
27 M		0554	1.6	0617	1.6	0442	1.4	0234	1.1	0215	0.8	0436	4.3	0321	3.2	0315	0.9	0256	2.4
		1212	4.8	1218	4.9	1104	3.7	0850	3.0	0828	1.9	1045	2.0	0909	1.5	1012	3.1	0839	8.0
		1805	1.9	1738	1.9	1700	1.6	1448	1.4	1436	1.0	1649	4.5	1539	3.4	1538	1.1	1512	2.6
						2311	3.8	2058	3.1	2039	2.0	2313	1.6	2204	1.5	2203	3.3	2057	8.3
28 TU		0032	4.9	0038	5.2	0521	1.2	0311	1.0	0253	0.8	0511	4.6	0358	3.4	0357	0.8	0342	2.0
		0630	1.4	0656	1.4	1142	3.9	0930	3.1	0907	2.0	1124	1.7	0951	1.3	1054	3.3	0921	8.5
		1255	5.0	1301	5.2	1736	1.5	1523	1.3	1511	0.9	1721	4.7	1606	3.6	1616	0.9	1554	2.2
		1840	1.6	1811	1.6	2349	4.0	2139	3.3	2119	2.0	2348	1.4	2236	1.3	2248	3.4	2136	8.7
29 W		0113	5.1	0121	5.4	0554	1.1	0343	0.9	0326	0.7	0542	4.8	0433	3.6	0431	0.7	0420	1.7
		0701	1.2	0700	1.3	1215	4.0	1006	3.3	0942	2.0	1159	1.5	1027	1.2	1131	3.4	0957	8.8
		1330	5.2	1337	5.3	1809	1.3	1554	1.1	1542	0.8	1751	4.8	1636	3.7	1651	0.7	1630	1.9
		1913	1.4	1846	1.4			2216	3.3	2156	2.1			2307	1.2	2327	3.4	2212	9.0
30 TH		0149	5.3	0200	5.5	0024	4.1	0414	0.8	0357	0.7	0021	1.2	0505	3.8	0502	0.6	0454	1.5
		0732	1.0	0712	1.1	0627	1.0	1039	3.4	1015	2.1	0611	4.9	1101	1.0	1206	3.4	1030	9.1
		1403	5.3	1409	5.5	1246	4.1	1625	1.0	1612	0.7	1231	1.3	1706	3.9	1721	0.6	1703	1.6
		1947	1.2	1923	1.2	1841	1.1	2251	3.4	2229	2.2	1820	4.9	2337	1.1			2245	9.2
31 F ●		0222	5.4	0236	5.6	0057	4.2	0444	0.8	0426	0.6	0051	1.0	0536	3.9	0003	3.4	0527	1.3
		0805	0.9	0742	1.0	0657	0.9	1110	3.4	1045	2.2	0639	5.1	1134	1.0	0531	0.5	1101	9.2
		1436	5.4	1441	5.6	1316	4.2	1656	0.9	1641	0.7	1303	1.1	1736	4.0	1240	3.5	1736	1.5
		2021	1.0	1958	1.1	1912	1.0	2324	3.4	2300	2.2	1848	5.0			1751	0.5	2316	9.3

● ● Time UT. For British Summer Time (shaded) March 30th to October 26th ADD ONE HOUR ● ●

SCOTLAND & NORTH WEST ENGLAND Time Zone UT
Leith * Rosyth * Aberdeen *Wick * Lerwick * Ullapool * Oban * Greenock * Liverpool
NOVEMBER 1997 TIDE TABLES NOVEMBER 1997

LEITH		ROSYTH		ABERDEEN		WICK		LERWICK		ULLAPOOL		OBAN		GREENOCK		LIVERPOOL			
Time	m	Time	m	Time	m	Time	m	Time	m	Time	m	Time	m	Time	m	Time	m		
0256	5.4	0309	5.6	0129	4.2	0514	0.8	0457	0.6	0122	1.0	0006	1.0	0036	3.4	0559	1.3	**1**	**SA**
0839	0.8	0814	1.0	0729	0.9	1142	3.5	1115	2.2	0708	5.1	0606	4.0	0600	0.5	1133	9.3		
1510	5.5	1512	5.6	1348	4.3	1728	0.9	1713	0.7	1334	1.1	1206	0.9	1311	3.5	1810	1.4		
2055	1.0	2030	1.0	1943	1.0	2358	3.4	2333	2.2	1918	5.0	1806	4.0	1822	0.5	2348	9.3		
0330	5.4	0341	5.6	0203	4.2	0545	0.8	0530	0.6	0153	1.0	0036	1.0	0109	3.4	0632	1.3	**2**	**SU**
0912	0.9	0845	1.0	0800	0.9	1214	3.5	1145	2.2	0738	5.1	0636	4.0	0631	0.5	1205	9.4		
1545	5.5	1547	5.7	1419	4.3	1801	0.8	1748	0.7	1406	1.0	1240	1.0	1341	3.5	1845	1.4		
2127	1.0	2057	1.1	2015	0.9					1949	5.0	1836	4.0	1855	0.4				
0405	5.4	0415	5.5	0238	4.2	0033	3.4	0006	2.2	0224	1.0	0107	1.0	0140	3.4	0021	9.2	**3**	**M**
0944	1.0	0912	1.1	0833	0.9	0618	0.8	0605	0.7	0809	5.0	0705	3.9	0705	0.5	0706	1.4		
1620	5.4	1624	5.6	1453	4.2	1248	3.4	1218	2.2	1440	1.1	1315	1.0	1411	3.5	1239	9.3		
2155	1.1	2123	1.1	2050	1.0	1836	0.9	1825	0.7	2025	4.8	1908	3.9	1930	0.4	1921	1.5		
0442	5.3	0453	5.5	0315	4.1	0109	3.3	0044	2.1	0259	1.2	0140	1.1	0215	3.4	0055	9.1	**4**	**TU**
1011	1.2	0939	1.2	0908	1.1	0653	0.9	0642	0.7	0846	4.9	0736	3.8	0742	0.5	0740	1.6		
1657	5.3	1705	5.5	1530	4.1	1324	3.4	1254	2.2	1517	1.2	1354	1.2	1443	3.5	1314	9.1		
2221	1.2	2151	1.2	2128	1.1	1915	0.9	1905	0.7	2107	4.6	1942	3.7	2009	0.5	1959	1.7		
0521	5.2	0535	5.3	0357	4.0	0151	3.2	0125	2.0	0336	1.4	0217	1.2	0252	3.3	0133	8.8	**5**	**W**
1039	1.4	1009	1.4	0947	1.2	0732	1.1	0723	0.8	0930	4.7	0812	3.7	0823	0.6	0815	2.0		
1738	5.1	1748	5.3	1611	4.0	1405	3.3	1333	2.1	1559	1.4	1439	1.3	1518	3.5	1354	8.8		
2255	1.4	2227	1.3	2212	1.2	1959	1.0	1951	0.8	2159	4.4	2020	3.5	2054	0.6	2039	2.0		
0607	5.0	0621	5.1	0445	3.9	0237	3.1	0213	2.0	0420	1.6	0300	1.3	0334	3.3	0215	8.5	**6**	**TH**
1118	1.7	1047	1.6	1034	1.4	0818	1.2	0810	0.9	1027	4.5	0856	3.5	0910	0.8	0856	2.4		
1825	5.0	1834	5.1	1700	3.9	1452	3.2	1421	2.0	1648	1.7	1530	1.5	1558	3.4	1440	8.5		
2348	1.6	2314	1.5	2307	1.3	2054	1.1	2045	0.8	2306	4.2	2106	3.2	2148	0.7	2126	2.3		
0700	4.9	0713	4.9	0545	3.7	0333	3.0	0315	1.9	0513	1.9	0351	1.5	0424	3.2	0306	8.1	**7**	**F**
1226	2.0	1139	1.9	1134	1.6	0918	1.4	0909	1.0	1140	4.3	0957	3.3	1006	1.0	0947	2.7		
1921	4.8	1927	4.9	1800	3.7	1548	3.1	1522	1.9	1752	1.9	1632	1.6	1645	3.3	1538	8.2		
						2209	1.2	2155	0.9			2212	3.0	2255	0.8	2227	2.5		
0118	1.8	0024	1.7	0018	1.4	0442	2.9	0427	1.8	0030	4.1	0456	1.6	0525	3.1	0414	7.8	**8**	**SA**
0805	4.8	0815	4.8	0657	3.6	1040	1.5	1026	1.1	0626	2.1	1136	3.2	1115	1.1	1056	3.0		
1359	2.1	1348	2.1	1252	1.7	1657	3.0	1639	1.9	1303	4.3	1747	1.7	1748	3.2	1651	8.0		
2027	4.8	2033	4.8	1913	3.7	2337	1.2	2321	0.8	1913	1.9	2355	2.9			2343	2.6		
0254	1.8	0228	1.8	0140	1.4	0601	2.9	0543	1.8	0154	4.1	0618	1.6	0010	0.8	0536	7.7	**9**	**SU**
0918	4.8	0927	4.8	0817	3.7	1207	1.5	1155	1.0	0757	2.1	1321	3.3	0641	3.1	1221	2.9		
1529	2.1	1552	2.0	1415	1.7	1812	3.1	1756	1.9	1418	4.4	1911	1.6	1231	1.2	1810	8.1		
2140	4.8	2148	4.9	2031	3.8					2039	1.8					1914	3.2		
0418	1.5	0445	1.5	0259	1.2	0057	1.1	0039	0.8	0307	4.3	0148	3.0	0123	0.7	0105	2.3	**10**	**M**
1033	5.0	1038	5.0	0930	3.8	0717	3.0	0657	1.9	0917	1.9	0744	1.4	0803	3.1	0657	8.0		
1642	1.8	1706	1.7	1528	1.5	1321	1.3	1307	0.9	1522	4.6	1425	3.5	1344	1.1	1341	2.5		
2251	5.1	2300	5.1	2140	4.0	1924	3.2	1906	2.0	2148	1.5	2024	1.3	2042	3.3	1923	8.5		
0522	1.2	0548	1.1	0404	1.0	0200	0.9	0139	0.6	0406	4.6	0253	3.2	0229	0.5	0217	1.8	**11**	**TU**
1139	5.3	1142	5.3	1032	4.0	0821	3.2	0800	2.0	1019	1.6	0851	1.2	0917	3.2	0804	8.5		
1741	1.5	1801	1.3	1628	1.3	1419	1.1	1403	0.8	1618	4.9	1517	3.8	1451	1.0	1448	1.9		
2353	5.4			2239	4.2	2027	3.4	2007	2.1	2244	1.1	2122	1.0	2151	3.4	2026	9.0		
0617	0.9	0003	5.4	0500	0.8	0253	0.7	0231	0.5	0454	4.9	0343	3.5	0327	0.4	0320	1.3	**12**	**W**
1233	5.5	0642	0.8	1123	4.2	0915	3.4	0852	2.1	1110	1.2	0944	0.9	1020	3.4	0900	9.1		
1833	1.1	1236	5.6	1719	1.1	1509	0.9	1452	0.7	1706	5.2	1603	4.0	1547	0.8	1546	1.4		
		1848	1.0	2330	4.4	2122	3.6	2102	2.2	2333	0.8	2212	0.8	2248	3.6	2121	9.5		
0046	5.6	0055	5.7	0548	0.6	0339	0.6	0318	0.5	0538	5.2	0427	3.7	0417	0.2	0415	0.9	**13**	**TH**
0707	0.7	0730	0.6	1209	4.4	1003	3.5	0940	2.2	1157	0.9	1032	0.7	1115	3.5	0951	9.5		
1320	5.8	1324	5.8	1806	0.8	1554	0.8	1538	0.6	1751	5.4	1648	4.2	1636	0.6	1638	1.0		
1922	0.8	1923	0.8			2213	3.7	2153	2.3			2257	0.6	2341	3.6	2210	9.8		
0135	5.9	0144	5.9	0018	4.6	0421	0.5	0402	0.4	0018	0.6	0507	3.9	0503	0.2	0503	0.6	**14**	**F**
0754	0.5	0811	0.5	0633	0.5	1047	3.6	1024	2.3	0618	5.4	1118	0.5	1203	3.6	1037	9.7		
1404	5.9	1410	5.9	1252	4.5	1638	0.6	1622	0.5	1242	0.7	1730	4.2	1721	0.4	1726	0.7		
2010	0.6	1936	0.6	1851	0.7	2301	3.8	2241	2.4	1834	5.5	2342	0.5			2257	10.0		
																			O
0222	6.0	0232	6.0	0105	4.6	0503	0.5	0445	0.4	0100	0.5	0545	4.1	0029	3.7	0548	0.5	**15**	**SA**
0839	0.5	0751	0.5	0716	0.5	1130	3.7	1106	2.3	0657	5.5	1203	0.5	0546	0.2	1121	9.9		
1448	5.9	1457	6.0	1333	4.5	1722	0.6	1706	0.4	1325	0.6	1812	4.2	1246	3.7	1811	0.6		
2057	0.5	2014	0.5	1936	0.6	2348	3.7	2327	2.3	1918	5.5			1804	0.3	2342	10.0		

● ● Time UT. For British Summer Time (shaded) March 30th to October 26th ADD ONE HOUR ● ●

NOVEMBER 1997 TIDE TABLES NOVEMBER 1997

	LEITH		ROSYTH		ABERDEEN		WICK		LERWICK		ULLAPOOL		OBAN		GREENOCK		LIVERPOOL	
	Time	m	Time	m	Time	m	Time	m	Time	m	Time	m	Time	m	Time	m	Time	m
16 SU	0309	5.9	0321	6.1	0151	4.6	0543	0.6	0527	0.5	0142	0.6	0024	0.5	0114	3.7	0630	0.6
	0922	0.6	0829	0.6	0757	0.6	1212	3.7	1148	2.3	0737	5.4	0621	4.1	0629	0.2	1203	9.8
	1533	5.8	1544	5.9	1415	4.5	1806	0.6	1751	0.5	1408	0.7	1247	0.6	1326	3.7	1854	0.7
	2142	0.6	2054	0.6	2020	0.6					2002	5.3	1851	4.1	1848	0.3		
17 M	0357	5.8	0409	6.0	0237	4.5	0033	3.6	0014	2.3	0222	0.8	0104	0.6	0157	3.6	0024	9.7
	1002	0.9	0906	0.8	0839	0.8	0623	0.8	0611	0.6	0818	5.3	0657	4.0	0713	0.4	0710	0.9
	1619	5.7	1632	5.8	1457	4.4	1252	3.6	1230	2.3	1451	0.8	1331	0.8	1404	3.8	1245	9.6
	2225	0.8	2216	0.8	2103	0.7	1850	0.7	1837	0.5	2048	5.0	1929	3.8	1933	0.3	1936	1.0
18 TU	0445	5.6	0458	5.7	0324	4.3	0118	3.5	0100	2.2	0303	1.0	0145	0.8	0239	3.5	0107	9.4
	1036	1.2	0939	1.1	0919	1.1	0703	1.0	0654	0.8	0900	5.0	0733	3.9	0758	0.5	0749	1.0
	1705	5.4	1720	5.5	1539	4.2	1333	3.5	1312	2.2	1534	1.1	1415	1.1	1442	3.8	1325	9.3
	2303	1.1	2300	1.1	2148	0.9	1935	0.8	1924	0.6	2136	4.7	2007	3.6	2018	0.5	2018	1.4
19 W	0533	5.3	0547	5.4	0414	4.0	0203	3.3	0147	2.1	0344	1.4	0226	1.0	0322	3.4	0149	8.9
	1058	1.6	1013	1.4	1000	1.3	0742	1.2	0739	0.9	0945	4.7	0810	3.7	0845	0.8	0827	1.9
	1752	5.2	1809	5.2	1625	4.0	1416	3.3	1357	2.1	1620	1.5	1502	1.4	1521	3.8	1406	8.8
	2334	1.4	2351	1.4	2235	1.1	2022	1.0	2015	0.7	2230	4.4	2048	3.3	2107	0.6	2102	1.9
20 TH	0622	5.0	0637	5.1	0506	3.8	0251	3.1	0234	1.9	0428	1.7	0309	1.2	0407	3.2	0233	8.4
	1125	1.9	1052	1.8	1045	1.6	0824	1.4	0827	1.0	1036	4.4	0852	3.4	0936	1.0	0907	2.4
	1842	4.9	1900	4.9	1715	3.8	1503	3.2	1443	2.0	1709	1.8	1553	1.7	1603	3.6	1451	8.4
					2327	1.4	2116	1.2	2110	0.8	2333	4.1	2136	3.1	2159	0.8	2149	2.4
21 F	0013	1.7	0036	1.7	0603	3.6	0345	2.9	0324	1.8	0517	2.1	0356	1.5	0455	3.1	0322	7.9
	0715	4.7	0730	4.8	1139	1.8	0915	1.6	0921	1.1	1144	4.2	0944	3.2	1030	1.2	0953	2.9
	1212	2.2	1144	2.1	1813	3.7	1557	3.0	1535	1.9	1809	2.1	1654	1.9	1646	3.5	1543	7.9
	1936	4.7	1957	4.7			2222	1.3	2212	0.9			2241	2.9	2257	1.0	2245	2.8
22 SA	0115	1.9	0206	1.9	0029	1.6	0447	2.8	0421	1.7	0045	4.0	0452	1.7	0551	3.0	0421	7.5
	0810	4.6	0828	4.6	0706	3.5	1024	1.7	1025	1.2	0617	2.4	1100	3.0	1132	1.3	1051	3.3
	1323	2.4	1340	2.4	1246	2.0	1700	2.9	1636	1.8	1305	4.1	1812	2.0	1735	3.3	1646	7.6
	2033	4.6	2058	4.6	1919	3.6	2337	1.4	2320	1.0	1921	2.2					2351	3.0
23 SU	0242	2.1	0319	1.9	0142	1.7	0557	2.8	0528	1.7	0158	4.0	0014	2.9	0004	1.1	0531	7.2
	0910	4.5	0928	4.5	0813	3.4	1151	1.8	1142	1.2	0735	2.5	0600	1.8	0702	2.9	1208	3.5
	1459	2.5	1515	2.4	1406	2.1	1810	2.9	1747	1.8	1420	4.1	1259	3.0	1244	1.4	1759	7.4
	2136	4.5	2159	4.6	2027	3.5					2039	2.2	1936	1.9	1836	3.2		
24 M	0403	2.0	0421	1.9	0254	1.6	0050	1.4	0029	1.0	0303	4.1	0137	2.9	0119	1.2	0100	3.0
	1014	4.5	1027	4.5	0919	3.5	0706	2.8	0643	1.7	0858	2.4	0716	1.8	0821	2.9	0646	7.3
	1623	2.4	1615	2.3	1521	2.0	1311	1.7	1257	1.1	1521	4.1	1408	3.1	1356	1.3	1321	3.3
	2240	4.6	2257	4.7	2132	3.6	1917	2.9	1900	1.8	2144	2.1	2039	1.8	2000	3.1	1911	7.6
25 TU	0500	1.8	0510	1.8	0354	1.5	0147	1.3	0125	0.9	0354	4.2	0236	3.1	0224	1.1	0202	2.7
	1116	4.6	1123	4.7	1016	3.6	0804	2.9	0743	1.8	1000	2.2	0821	1.6	0923	3.1	0749	7.7
	1719	2.1	1701	2.1	1617	1.8	1407	1.6	1353	1.1	1609	4.3	1451	3.3	1453	1.2	1421	3.0
	2342	4.7	2351	4.9	2227	3.7	2014	3.0	1957	1.9	2233	1.8	2124	1.6	2115	3.1	2009	7.9
26 W	0544	1.6	0548	1.7	0439	1.4	0231	1.2	0210	0.9	0436	4.4	0322	3.3	0314	0.9	0254	2.4
	1209	4.8	1212	4.9	1102	3.8	0851	3.1	0829	1.9	1047	2.0	0912	1.5	1012	3.2	0839	8.1
	1803	1.8	1742	1.8	1700	1.6	1449	1.4	1435	1.0	1648	4.5	1530	3.5	1538	1.0	1509	2.6
					2312	3.8	2101	3.1	2044	2.0	2312	1.6	2203	1.5	2209	3.2	2057	8.3
27 TH	0032	4.9	0040	5.1	0519	1.3	0309	1.1	0248	0.8	0512	4.7	0402	3.5	0354	0.8	0338	2.1
	0623	1.4	0618	1.5	1140	3.9	0930	3.2	0908	2.0	1127	1.7	0953	1.4	1055	3.3	0920	8.5
	1251	5.0	1254	5.2	1739	1.4	1526	1.3	1511	0.9	1723	4.7	1605	3.6	1617	0.8	1552	2.2
	1842	1.6	1824	1.6	2353	4.0	2142	3.2	2124	2.0	2348	1.4	2237	1.3	2253	3.3	2136	8.6
28 F	0115	5.1	0124	5.3	0554	1.1	0343	1.0	0323	0.8	0545	4.8	0438	3.6	0430	0.7	0418	1.8
	0700	1.3	0649	1.3	1215	4.1	1006	3.3	0942	2.1	1203	1.5	1031	1.2	1134	3.4	0957	8.8
	1331	5.2	1333	5.4	1813	1.3	1600	1.1	1544	0.8	1755	4.8	1639	3.7	1653	0.7	1632	1.9
	1920	1.4	1903	1.3			2221	3.3	2200	2.1			2310	1.2	2333	3.3	2213	8.9
29 SA	0154	5.3	0204	5.4	0030	4.1	0416	0.9	0357	0.7	0023	1.2	0512	3.8	0503	0.6	0456	1.5
	0736	1.1	0725	1.1	0629	1.0	1041	3.4	1015	2.2	0615	5.0	1107	1.1	1210	3.4	1032	9.1
	1409	5.4	1412	5.5	1249	4.2	1635	1.0	1618	0.7	1238	1.3	1713	3.9	1726	0.5	1710	1.6
	1957	1.2	1944	1.2	1848	1.1	2259	3.4	2236	2.1	1827	4.9	2342	1.1			2249	9.1
30 SU ●	0231	5.4	0242	5.5	0106	4.2	0449	0.9	0431	0.7	0057	1.1	0544	3.9	0009	3.3	0533	1.4
	0814	1.0	0802	1.0	0703	1.0	1115	3.5	1048	2.2	0647	5.1	1143	1.0	0535	0.5	1107	9.3
	1446	5.5	1448	5.6	1323	4.3	1709	0.9	1654	0.7	1312	1.1	1747	3.9	1245	3.6	1749	1.4
	2035	1.0	2021	1.0	1923	1.0	2336	3.4	2313	2.2	1900	5.0			1800	0.4	2325	9.2

SCOTLAND & NORTH WEST ENGLAND Time Zone UT

Leith * Rosyth * Aberdeen *Wick * Lerwick * Ullapool * Oban * Greenock * Liverpool

DECEMBER 1997 TIDE TABLES DECEMBER 1997

Day	LEITH Time m	ROSYTH Time m	ABERDEEN Time m	WICK Time m	LERWICK Time m	ULLAPOOL Time m	OBAN Time m	GREENOCK Time m	LIVERPOOL Time m
1 M	309 5.4	0319 5.6	0143 4.2	0523 0.9	0508 0.7	0130 1.0	0014 1.0	0045 3.3	0610 1.3
	851 1.0	0837 1.0	0739 0.9	1151 3.5	1124 2.3	0720 5.2	0615 4.0	0609 0.5	1144 9.4
	1524 5.5	1527 5.7	1357 4.3	1745 0.8	1731 0.6	1348 1.1	1220 1.0	1318 3.5	1829 1.3
	112 1.0	2054 1.0	2000 0.9		2352 2.2	1936 5.0	1821 3.9	1836 0.4	
2 TU	345 5.4	0357 5.6	0221 4.2	0015 3.4	0546 0.7	0206 1.0	0048 0.9	0121 3.3	0002 9.2
	929 1.0	0906 1.0	0815 1.0	0600 0.9	1200 2.3	0755 5.2	0648 4.0	0647 0.5	0648 1.3
	1600 5.5	1606 5.7	1433 4.3	1229 3.6	1812 0.6	1426 1.0	1259 1.0	1351 3.6	1221 9.4
	151 1.0	2121 1.0	2038 0.9	1824 0.8		2016 4.9	1856 3.9	1914 0.3	1909 1.3
3 W	424 5.4	0437 5.6	0302 4.2	0057 3.4	0033 2.2	0243 1.1	0124 0.9	0200 3.3	0041 9.2
	007 1.1	0935 1.1	0854 1.0	0639 0.9	0627 0.7	0836 5.1	0724 4.0	0728 0.5	0725 1.4
	1639 5.4	1648 5.6	1512 4.3	1308 3.5	1239 2.2	1506 1.1	1342 1.1	1427 3.6	1301 9.4
	230 1.0	2152 1.0	2119 0.9	1907 0.8	1854 0.6	2101 4.8	1933 3.8	1957 0.4	1949 1.4
4 TH	506 5.3	0521 5.5	0346 4.1	0140 3.3	0118 2.1	0324 1.3	0203 1.0	0242 3.3	0122 9.0
	047 1.3	1008 1.3	0936 1.2	0721 1.0	0710 0.8	0921 5.0	0803 3.8	0812 0.6	0804 1.7
	1721 5.3	1732 5.5	1555 4.2	1351 3.5	1320 2.2	1549 1.2	1428 1.2	1504 3.6	1344 9.2
	315 1.2	2230 1.1	2206 1.0	1954 0.9	1942 0.6	2153 4.6	2015 3.6	2044 0.4	2032 1.6
5 F	553 5.2	0607 5.2	0435 4.0	0228 3.2	0208 2.0	0409 1.5	0247 1.1	0327 3.3	0207 8.8
	133 1.5	1048 1.5	1024 1.3	0809 1.2	0758 0.9	1015 4.8	0850 3.7	0900 0.7	0847 2.0
	1809 5.2	1818 5.3	1644 4.1	1438 3.4	1409 2.1	1639 1.4	1520 1.3	1546 3.6	1431 8.9
		2318 1.2	2259 1.1	2047 1.0	2035 0.7	2254 4.4	2103 3.4	2137 0.5	2119 1.8
6 SA	006 1.3	0659 5.2	0532 3.9	0322 3.1	0306 1.9	0500 1.7	0337 1.3	0419 3.2	0259 8.4
	645 5.1	1142 1.7	1120 1.5	0904 1.3	0854 0.9	1120 4.6	0947 3.5	0955 0.9	0937 2.3
	228 1.7	1911 5.1	1740 3.9	1532 3.3	1507 2.0	1738 1.6	1618 1.4	1634 3.5	1526 8.6
	903 5.1			2152 1.0	2136 0.7		2201 3.1	2239 0.6	2215 2.0
7 SU	109 1.5	0021 1.4	0002 1.2	0425 3.0	0410 1.9	0006 4.3	0436 1.4	0518 3.2	0400 8.1
	746 4.9	0758 5.0	0637 3.8	1012 1.4	1000 1.0	0605 2.0	1105 3.3	1057 1.0	1038 2.5
	334 1.9	1303 1.9	1227 1.6	1635 3.2	1618 2.0	1233 4.5	1725 1.5	1733 3.4	1630 8.4
	005 5.0	2013 5.0	1847 3.9	2309 1.1	2249 0.8	1848 1.7	2318 3.0	2347 0.6	2321 2.2
8 M	222 1.5	0147 1.5	0114 1.2	0536 3.0	0518 1.8	0124 4.2	0548 1.5	0624 3.2	0512 8.0
	854 4.9	0906 5.0	0750 3.7	1131 1.5	1118 1.0	0723 2.1	1239 3.3	1206 1.1	1151 2.6
	450 2.0	1512 1.9	1342 1.7	1745 3.2	1730 1.9	1346 4.5	1839 1.5	1848 3.3	1741 8.3
	115 5.0	2128 5.0	2000 3.9			2004 1.7			
9 TU	342 1.5	0416 1.4	0228 1.2	0026 1.1	0008 0.7	0238 4.3	0059 3.0	0056 0.6	0034 2.1
	006 5.0	1016 5.0	0901 3.8	0648 3.0	0627 1.9	0842 2.0	0708 1.4	0735 3.2	0627 8.1
	606 1.8	1636 1.7	1457 1.6	1248 1.4	1237 1.0	1454 4.6	1356 3.4	1317 1.1	1309 2.4
	225 5.1	2240 5.1	2112 4.0	1856 3.2	1839 2.0	2116 1.6	1951 1.4	2009 3.3	1854 8.5
10 W	453 1.4	0524 1.2	0337 1.1	0134 1.0	0115 0.7	0342 4.5	0223 3.1	0204 0.6	0148 1.9
	112 5.1	1120 5.2	1006 3.9	0754 3.2	0732 2.0	0951 1.8	0821 1.3	0848 3.2	0736 8.3
	713 1.6	1736 1.5	1603 1.4	1354 1.3	1340 0.9	1556 4.8	1456 3.6	1427 1.0	1420 2.1
	330 5.2	2343 5.2	2217 4.1	2003 3.3	1945 2.0	2219 1.4	2055 1.2	2124 3.4	2000 8.8
11 TH	554 1.2	0621 1.1	0438 1.0	0231 0.9	0210 0.6	0436 4.8	0323 3.3	0306 0.5	0254 1.6
	211 5.3	1216 5.4	1102 4.1	0851 3.3	0830 2.1	1050 1.5	0924 1.1	0954 3.3	0837 8.7
	812 1.3	1827 1.3	1700 1.2	1451 1.1	1435 0.7	1651 5.0	1548 3.7	1530 0.8	1523 1.7
			2315 4.2	2103 3.4	2045 2.1	2313 1.2	2150 1.0	2227 3.4	2100 9.1
12 F	029 5.4	0039 5.4	0530 0.9	0320 0.8	0300 0.6	0523 5.0	0412 3.6	0400 0.4	0351 1.3
	647 1.1	0713 1.0	1151 4.3	0942 3.5	0921 2.2	1142 1.2	1017 0.9	1051 3.4	0931 9.1
	302 5.5	1306 5.5	1751 1.0	1540 0.9	1524 0.6	1739 5.2	1636 3.9	1622 0.6	1619 1.3
	905 1.1	1909 1.1		2158 3.5	2141 2.2		2239 0.8	2323 3.5	2153 9.4
13 SA	121 5.6	0129 5.6	0006 4.3	0404 0.8	0346 0.6	0001 1.0	0454 3.8	0448 0.3	0443 1.1
	736 0.9	0754 0.9	0617 0.9	1028 3.6	1007 2.2	0606 5.2	1106 0.8	1142 3.5	1020 9.4
	349 5.6	1354 5.7	1236 4.4	1627 0.8	1609 0.6	1229 1.0	1720 3.9	1709 0.5	1709 1.0
	956 0.9	1917 0.9	1839 0.8	2248 3.6	2231 2.2	1824 5.3	2324 0.7		2242 9.5
14 SU	210 5.7	0217 5.7	0054 4.4	0445 0.8	0430 0.6	0045 0.9	0532 3.9	0014 3.5	0529 1.0
	821 0.9	0728 0.8	0700 0.9	1112 3.7	1051 2.3	0645 5.3	1151 0.8	0533 0.3	1105 9.5
	434 5.7	1440 5.8	1318 4.4	1711 0.7	1654 0.5	1314 0.9	1800 4.0	1225 3.6	1756 0.9
	044 0.9	1957 0.8	1924 0.7	2335 3.6	2318 2.2	1908 5.3		1753 0.4	2327 9.5
									○
15 M	257 5.7	0304 5.8	0140 4.4	0525 0.9	0512 0.6	0127 0.9	0006 0.7	0100 3.5	0611 1.0
	903 0.9	0809 0.9	0741 0.9	1154 3.7	1132 2.3	0724 5.4	0608 4.0	0615 0.4	1148 9.6
	518 5.7	1527 5.8	1358 4.5	1754 0.7	1739 0.5	1356 0.9	1236 0.8	1305 3.7	1839 0.9
	129 0.7	2109 0.8	2007 0.7			1950 5.2	1839 3.9	1836 0.3	

● ● Time UT. For British Summer Time (shaded) March 30th to October 26th ADD ONE HOUR ● ●

DECEMBER 1997 TIDE TABLES DECEMBER 1997

	LEITH		ROSYTH		ABERDEEN		WICK		LERWICK		ULLAPOOL		OBAN		GREENOCK		LIVERPOO
	Time	m	Time	m	Time	m	Time	m	Time	m	Time	m	Time	m	Time	m	Time m
16 TU	0342	5.6	0352	5.8	0225	4.3	0019	3.5	0002	2.2	0206	1.0	0045	0.7	0145	3.4	0009 9.4
	0942	1.1	0848	1.0	0821	1.0	0604	0.9	0554	0.7	0803	5.3	0643	4.0	0658	0.5	0651 1.
	1603	5.6	1614	5.7	1439	4.4	1234	3.6	1213	2.3	1437	1.0	1318	1.0	1343	3.8	1228 9.5
	2209	0.9	2139	0.8	2049	0.8	1836	0.7	1823	0.5	2031	5.0	1915	3.8	1918	0.4	1921 1.
17 W	0427	5.5	0438	5.6	0309	4.2	0102	3.4	0045	2.1	0245	1.2	0124	0.8	0227	3.4	0051 9.2
	1013	1.3	0924	1.2	0859	1.1	0642	1.1	0635	0.8	0841	5.1	0718	3.9	0741	0.6	0728 1.
	1645	5.4	1700	5.5	1518	4.3	1313	3.6	1253	2.2	1518	1.1	1359	1.1	1421	3.8	1307 9.3
	2244	1.0	2228	1.0	2130	0.8	1917	0.8	1906	0.6	2113	4.8	1951	3.7	2000	0.4	2001 1.
18 TH	0509	5.3	0523	5.4	0353	4.0	0143	3.3	0126	2.0	0324	1.4	0203	0.9	0307	3.3	0130 8.9
	1036	1.5	0957	1.4	0937	1.3	0718	1.2	0715	0.9	0919	4.9	0753	3.8	0823	0.7	0804 1.
	1727	5.2	1744	5.3	1559	4.1	1353	3.4	1333	2.2	1558	1.4	1440	1.4	1500	3.8	1345 9.
	2310	1.3	2227	1.2	2210	1.1	1958	1.0	1950	0.7	2156	4.6	2027	3.5	2042	0.6	2039 1.
19 F	0552	5.1	0606	5.1	0436	3.9	0224	3.2	0206	1.9	0403	1.6	0242	1.1	0348	3.2	0209 8.
	1102	1.7	1033	1.6	1015	1.5	0756	1.4	0754	1.0	0959	4.7	0830	3.6	0906	0.9	0839 2.
	1811	5.0	1827	5.1	1641	4.0	1433	3.3	1412	2.1	1640	1.6	1523	1.6	1538	3.7	1424 8.
	2340	1.5	2307	1.4	2252	1.2	2040	1.1	2034	0.8	2242	4.4	2107	3.3	2125	0.7	2118 2.
20 SA	0637	4.9	0650	4.9	0522	3.7	0309	3.0	0248	1.8	0445	1.9	0324	1.3	0430	3.2	0250 8.
	1139	1.9	1116	1.9	1057	1.7	0836	1.5	0836	1.0	1044	4.5	0912	3.4	0951	1.0	0916 2.
	1856	4.8	1914	4.9	1727	3.8	1518	3.2	1455	2.0	1725	1.9	1611	1.9	1617	3.6	1506 8.
					2339	1.4	2128	1.3	2122	0.8	2338	4.2	2153	3.1	2212	0.9	2158 2.
21 SU	0024	1.7	0002	1.6	0613	3.6	0357	2.9	0334	1.8	0530	2.2	0412	1.5	0512	3.0	0336 7.
	0724	4.7	0738	4.7	1148	1.9	0924	1.6	0926	1.1	1141	4.3	1003	3.2	1041	1.1	0958 2.
	1229	2.2	1216	2.1	1821	3.7	1609	3.0	1544	1.9	1818	2.1	1706	1.9	1659	3.4	1555 7.
	1945	4.7	2005	4.7			2227	1.4	2217	0.9			2253	3.0	2305	1.0	2246 2.
22 M	0121	1.9	0115	1.9	0035	1.6	0454	2.8	0427	1.7	0045	4.0	0506	1.7	0600	3.0	0430 7.
	0816	4.5	0830	4.6	0709	3.5	1029	1.7	1030	1.2	0626	2.4	1109	3.1	1139	1.3	1052 3.
	1335	2.4	1341	2.3	1250	2.0	1708	2.9	1642	1.8	1257	4.1	1814	2.0	1745	3.2	1652 7.
	2039	4.5	2100	4.6	1922	3.5	2335	1.4	2321	1.0	1922	2.2					2346 3.0
23 TU	0231	2.0	0223	2.0	0140	1.7	0557	2.8	0530	1.7	0157	4.0	0012	2.9	0009	1.1	0533 7.
	0912	4.5	0925	4.5	0812	3.4	1149	1.8	1147	1.2	0736	2.5	0612	1.8	0700	2.9	1201 3.
	1457	2.4	1452	2.4	1406	2.1	1813	2.9	1751	1.8	1413	4.1	1233	3.1	1249	1.3	1759 7.
	2137	4.5	2157	4.6	2028	3.5					2034	2.3	1928	1.9	1840	3.1	
24 W	0347	2.0	0334	2.0	0249	1.7	0044	1.4	0026	1.0	0301	4.1	0136	3.0	0120	1.1	0054 3.0
	1011	4.5	1020	4.6	0915	3.5	0702	2.9	0642	1.7	0855	2.5	0721	1.8	0817	2.9	0642 7.
	1619	2.3	1603	2.3	1519	2.0	1307	1.7	1259	1.1	1518	4.2	1351	3.1	1358	1.2	1315 3.3
	2239	4.5	2253	4.7	2133	3.6	1918	2.9	1903	1.8	2140	2.1	2034	1.8	1954	3.0	1909 7.
25 TH	0452	1.9	0445	1.9	0350	1.6	0143	1.4	0122	0.9	0354	4.3	0241	3.1	0223	1.0	0158 2.8
	1112	4.6	1114	4.8	1013	3.6	0800	3.0	0742	1.8	1000	2.3	0824	1.7	0924	3.0	0746 7.
	1721	2.1	1703	2.1	1618	1.8	1409	1.6	1354	1.0	1610	4.3	1449	3.3	1455	1.0	1418 2.5
	2342	4.7	2348	4.8	2231	3.7	2017	3.0	2003	1.8	2233	2.0	2126	1.7	2117	3.0	2009 7.
26 F	0545	1.7	0539	1.7	0440	1.5	0232	1.3	0209	0.9	0439	4.5	0330	3.3	0314	0.9	0254 2.
	1209	4.8	1206	5.0	1103	3.8	0849	3.1	0829	1.9	1051	2.0	0918	1.6	1017	3.1	0839 8.
	1811	1.8	1756	1.8	1705	1.6	1457	1.4	1439	0.9	1654	4.5	1536	3.4	1543	0.9	1513 2.
					2321	3.8	2107	3.1	2050	1.9	2317	1.7	2208	1.5	2215	3.0	2100 8.2
27 SA	0038	4.9	0042	5.1	0523	1.4	0313	1.2	0251	0.8	0518	4.7	0412	3.5	0357	0.7	0342 2.
	0630	1.5	0627	1.5	1145	4.0	0933	3.3	0909	2.0	1135	1.8	1003	1.4	1102	3.2	0924 8.
	1300	5.0	1256	5.2	1746	1.4	1537	1.3	1518	0.8	1730	4.7	1618	3.6	1625	0.7	1602 2.
	1854	1.6	1845	1.5			2153	3.3	2133	2.0	2357	1.5	2245	1.3	2302	3.1	2144 8.
28 SU	0126	5.1	0131	5.3	0005	4.0	0351	1.1	0330	0.8	0554	4.9	0450	3.7	0436	0.6	0427 1.
	0712	1.3	0714	1.3	0603	1.2	1013	3.4	0948	2.1	1215	1.5	1044	1.3	1142	3.3	1005 8.
	1344	5.3	1342	5.4	1224	4.1	1616	1.1	1557	0.7	1810	4.8	1657	3.7	1703	0.5	1648 1.
	1936	1.3	1934	1.0	1826	1.2	2236	3.4	2215	2.1			2321	1.1	2345	3.2	2225 8.
29 M ●	0209	5.3	0216	5.5	0046	4.0	0428	1.0	0410	0.7	0035	1.3	0526	3.9	0515	0.5	0510 1.
	0754	1.2	0800	1.2	0642	1.1	1052	3.5	1027	2.2	0629	5.1	1124	1.1	1221	3.4	1045 9.
	1425	5.4	1426	5.6	1301	4.3	1654	0.9	1636	0.6	1124	1.1	1735	3.8	1742	0.4	1732 1.
	2018	1.1	2026	1.0	1906	1.0	2318	3.5	2257	2.2	1848	5.0	2356	0.9			2306 9.
30 TU	0248	5.4	0258	5.6	0127	4.2	0506	0.9	0451	0.7	0113	1.1	0601	4.0	0026	3.2	0552 1.
	0836	1.0	0847	1.0	0721	1.0	1132	3.6	1106	2.3	0706	5.3	1206	1.0	0554	0.4	1126 9.
	1504	5.4	1508	5.7	1339	4.4	1734	0.8	1718	0.5	1333	1.0	1812	3.9	1258	3.5	1815 1.
	2101	0.9	2115	0.8	1946	0.8			2340	2.2	1927	5.1			1821	0.3	2348 9.
31 W	0328	5.5	0340	5.8	0208	4.3	0001	3.5	0532	0.6	0151	1.0	0032	0.8	0108	3.3	0633 1.
	0918	0.9	0932	1.0	0801	0.9	0546	0.9	1147	2.3	0744	5.4	0637	4.1	0634	0.4	1208 9.
	1543	5.6	1551	5.8	1418	4.4	1213	3.7	1800	0.5	1414	0.9	1248	0.9	1336	3.6	1859 1.
	2145	0.7	2201	0.7	2028	0.7	1815	0.7			2008	5.1	1851	3.9	1901	0.2	

● ● Time UT. For British Summer Time (shaded) March 30th to October 26th ADD ONE HOUR ● ●

WEST COAST ENGLAND, WALES & IRELAND Time Zone UT
Holyhead * Milford Haven * Swansea * Avonmouth * Dublin * Belfast * Londonderry * Galway * Cobh

JANUARY 1997 TIDE TABLES JANUARY 1997

	HOLYHEAD	MILFORD HAVEN	SWANSEA	AVONMOUTH	DUBLIN	BELFAST	LONDONDERRY	GALWAY	COBH
	Time m	Time m	Time m	Time m	Time m	Time m	Time m	Time m	Time m
1 W	239 4.7 837 2.0 454 4.8 119 1.9	0422 2.0 1030 5.8 1652 2.2 2257 5.4	0413 2.6 1036 7.9 1641 2.8 2302 7.6	0516 2.9 111510.8 1736 3.1 233910.2	0415 3.4 0957 1.5 1639 3.5 2241 1.3	0324 3.0 0931 1.1 1545 3.3 2200 0.9	0033 2.3 0623 1.1 1224 2.5 1926 1.3	0321 2.0 0941 4.2 1559 1.8 2221 4.1	0348 1.1 0952 3.5 1621 1.1 2218 3.4
2 TH	333 4.5 933 2.2 551 4.7 219 2.0	0512 2.3 1121 5.5 1747 2.4 2356 5.3	0505 3.0 1126 7.6 1737 3.0	0554 3.3 115910.3 1818 3.5	0513 3.3 1056 1.6 1739 3.4 2338 1.4	0415 3.0 1025 1.2 1638 3.2 2255 0.9	0135 2.2 0718 1.1 1324 2.4 2035 1.3	0415 2.1 1032 4.0 1657 1.9 2320 4.0	0440 1.2 1043 3.4 1717 1.2 2315 3.3
3 F	439 4.5 040 2.2 700 4.6 327 1.9	0615 2.5 1224 5.4 1855 2.4	0000 7.3 0612 3.2 1230 7.5 1849 3.1	0030 9.9 0642 3.7 130010.1 1915 3.7	0616 3.3 1158 1.6 1842 3.3	0513 2.9 1128 1.2 1737 3.1 2356 1.0	0246 2.2 0822 1.2 1440 2.4 2150 1.2	0521 2.2 1137 3.9 1803 2.0	0542 1.3 1144 3.3 1821 1.2
4 SA	550 4.5 152 2.1 813 4.6	0108 5.3 0730 2.4 1337 5.4 2012 2.3	0112 7.3 0726 3.1 1341 7.5 2003 3.0	0145 9.8 0754 3.9 142110.2 2048 3.7	0036 1.3 0718 3.3 1258 1.5 1944 3.4	0617 2.9 1236 1.2 1840 3.1	0357 2.3 0935 1.1 1600 2.4 2255 1.1	0028 4.0 0633 2.1 1250 4.0 1910 1.9	0020 3.3 0651 1.2 1253 3.3 1931 1.1
5 SU	033 1.8 656 4.7 257 1.9 918 4.8	0221 5.5 0845 2.2 1448 5.7 2120 2.0	0225 7.6 0836 2.8 1451 7.9 2110 2.5	030710.4 0936 3.4 153710.9 2215 2.9	0130 1.2 0814 3.5 1354 1.4 2039 3.6	0059 0.9 0721 3.0 1341 1.1 1942 3.2	0458 2.4 1047 1.0 1708 2.5 2350 1.0	0133 4.2 0739 1.9 1356 4.2 2008 1.6	0130 3.4 0803 1.1 1403 3.4 2038 1.0
6 M	130 1.6 751 5.0 355 1.6 012 5.1	0324 5.9 0948 1.8 1550 6.0 2218 1.6	0330 8.2 0936 2.3 1554 8.4 2207 2.0	041511.3 164211.8 2323 2.1	0221 1.1 0903 3.7 1444 1.1 2130 3.7	0200 0.9 0820 3.1 1440 0.9 2042 3.3	0552 2.6 1151 0.9 1804 2.7	0227 4.4 0833 1.6 1451 4.4 2058 1.4	0236 3.5 0909 0.9 1506 3.6 2136 0.8
7 TU	222 1.3 839 5.3 445 1.2 102 5.3	0421 6.3 1044 1.4 1645 6.4 2310 1.2	0426 8.8 1031 1.7 1649 8.9 2300 1.4	051412.3 1154 1.7 174012.6	0309 0.9 0950 3.9 1532 0.9 2218 3.9	0256 0.8 0914 3.3 1534 0.7 2136 3.3	0038 0.8 0641 2.8 1248 0.8 1854 2.8	0315 4.7 0922 1.2 1540 4.7 2144 1.1	0334 3.8 1005 0.7 1600 3.8 2230 0.6
8 W	309 1.0 924 5.6 533 0.9 148 5.6	0512 6.8 1136 0.9 1736 6.8 2359 0.8	0517 9.3 1123 1.2 1741 9.4 2349 1.0	0026 1.4 060913.1 1257 1.1 183513.2	0354 0.7 1034 4.1 1618 0.6 2304 4.1	0348 0.6 1004 3.4 1624 0.5 2228 3.4	0124 0.7 0727 3.0 1341 0.6 1942 2.9	0400 5.1 1009 0.8 1627 5.0 2229 0.8	0426 4.0 1057 0.5 1649 3.9 2319 0.4
9 TH ●	354 0.7 008 5.8 619 0.6 233 5.7	0600 7.1 1224 0.6 1825 7.1	0606 9.8 1212 0.8 1830 9.7	0126 1.0 070113.7 1354 0.8 192713.7	0439 0.6 1118 4.3 1705 0.4 2351 4.2	0437 0.5 1051 3.6 1712 0.4 2318 3.5	0207 0.6 0812 3.1 1430 0.6 2028 2.9	0445 5.3 1054 0.5 1713 5.2 2312 0.6	0514 4.1 1145 0.3 1736 4.1
10 F	439 0.6 052 6.0 706 0.4 320 5.8	0046 0.5 0648 7.4 1312 0.3 1912 7.3	0036 0.7 065410.0 1300 0.5 1918 9.9	0221 0.7 075014.0 1447 0.5 201513.9	0524 0.5 1203 4.4 1751 0.3	0524 0.4 1137 3.7 1800 0.2	0250 0.5 0855 3.2 1518 0.5 2114 2.9	0531 5.5 1138 0.3 1800 5.3 2357 0.5	0006 0.3 0600 4.3 1231 0.2 1821 4.1
11 SA	524 0.5 138 6.1 752 0.3	0133 0.4 0735 7.5 1400 0.3 1959 7.2	0121 0.5 074110.1 1345 0.4 2003 9.9	0309 0.6 083714.2 1534 0.4 210014.0	0038 4.2 0609 0.4 1249 4.5 1839 0.2	0006 3.5 0611 0.4 1224 3.7 1847 0.1	0333 0.5 0939 3.2 1606 0.6 2200 2.8	0617 5.6 1223 0.3 1846 5.3	0053 0.2 0646 4.3 1318 0.2 1906 4.2
12 SU	008 5.8 611 0.5 226 6.1 841 0.4	0218 0.4 0821 7.4 1445 0.4 2045 7.1	0203 0.5 082710.0 1430 0.5 2047 9.7	0353 0.6 092214.2 1616 0.5 214513.8	0127 4.2 0657 0.5 1338 4.5 1930 0.3	0055 3.5 0658 0.4 1311 3.7 1935 0.1	0418 0.5 1024 3.2 1654 0.7 2247 2.7	0042 0.5 0704 5.6 1309 0.4 1933 5.2	0139 0.2 0731 4.3 1403 0.2 1952 4.1
13 M	057 5.6 659 0.7 315 5.9 930 0.6	0304 0.6 0908 7.2 1532 0.6 2132 6.8	0245 0.8 0912 9.7 1512 0.8 2131 9.3	0432 0.8 100713.8 1654 0.8 222913.3	0218 4.1 0746 0.6 1429 4.4 2022 0.5	0145 3.4 0747 0.5 1401 3.7 2026 0.2	0504 0.6 1110 3.1 1743 0.8 2336 2.5	0128 0.7 0752 5.4 1357 0.6 2021 5.0	0225 0.3 0818 4.2 1449 0.3 2039 4.0
14 TU	147 5.4 750 1.0 406 5.7 2024 0.6	0351 0.9 0956 6.9 1619 1.0 2221 6.4	0329 1.2 0957 9.3 1558 1.3 2218 8.7	0506 1.2 105213.2 1729 1.3 231312.6	0312 4.0 0839 0.8 1525 4.2 2119 0.7	0238 3.3 0839 0.6 1454 3.5 2121 0.3	0554 0.8 1201 2.9 1836 0.9	0218 1.0 0842 5.1 1446 0.9 2113 4.8	0312 0.4 0906 4.1 1538 0.5 2128 3.9
15 W	242 5.1 845 1.3 502 5.4 122 1.2	0439 1.3 1047 6.5 1709 1.4 2314 6.0	0418 1.7 1048 8.7 1649 1.9 2310 8.2	0542 1.7 114012.4 1806 1.8	0412 3.8 0938 1.1 1627 4.0 2221 1.0	0335 3.1 0935 0.7 1553 3.4 2221 0.5	0033 2.4 0648 0.9 1258 2.7 1934 1.1	0311 1.3 0936 4.8 1541 1.3 2209 4.5	0403 0.6 0957 3.9 1630 0.7 2222 3.7

● ● Time UT. For British Summer Time (shaded) March 30th to October 26th ADD ONE HOUR ● ●

JANUARY 1997 TIDE TABLES JANUARY 1997

	HOLYHEAD		MILFORD HAVEN		SWANSEA		AVONMOUTH		DUBLIN		BELFAST		LONDONDERRY		GALWAY		COBH	
	Time	m	Time	m	Time	m	Time	m	Time	m	Time	m	Time	m	Time	m	Time	m
16 TH	0342	4.9	0535	1.7	0516	2.3	0001	11.8	0518	3.7	0437	3.0	0142	2.2	0412	1.6	0500	0.8
	0948	1.6	1143	6.1	1145	8.2	0622	2.3	1044	1.3	1039	0.8	0751	1.1	1036	4.5	1054	3.6
	1606	5.1	1808	1.8	1752	2.5	1232	11.6	1736	3.9	1659	3.3	1409	2.5	1645	1.6	1730	0.9
	2228	1.5					1851	2.4	2327	1.2	2328	0.6	2043	1.1	2317	4.2	2323	3.5
17 F	0454	4.7	0015	5.7	0015	7.7	0056	11.0	0626	3.6	0543	3.0	0309	2.2	0527	1.8	0604	0.9
	1101	1.8	0642	2.0	0630	2.8	0712	2.9	1155	1.4	1151	0.9	0909	1.1	1149	4.2	1158	3.4
	1719	4.9	1248	5.7	1254	7.8	1333	11.0	1846	3.8	1809	3.2	1530	2.4	1800	1.8	1837	1.0
	2340	1.7	1918	2.0	1909	2.8	1949	3.0					2158	1.2				
18 SA	0610	4.7	0126	5.5	0132	7.5	0203	10.6	0038	1.3	0037	0.7	0429	2.2	0035	4.1	0033	3.4
	1218	1.8	0800	2.1	0753	2.9	0823	3.4	0733	3.6	0648	3.0	1031	1.2	0651	1.8	0718	1.0
	1836	4.8	1403	5.6	1412	7.7	1446	10.7	1309	1.4	1302	0.9	1642	2.4	1307	4.1	1312	3.3
			2034	2.1	2029	2.9	2107	3.2	1954	3.7	1917	3.1	2304	1.1	1916	1.8	1951	1.0
19 SU	0052	1.8	0243	5.6	0250	7.7	0321	10.6	0146	1.3	0142	0.8	0530	2.3	0148	4.2	0151	3.4
	0721	4.8	0916	2.0	0906	2.8	0951	3.3	0836	3.7	0749	3.1	1141	1.1	0801	1.9	0832	1.0
	1328	1.7	1517	5.7	1524	7.9	1602	10.9	1418	1.3	1406	0.8	1740	2.5	1415	4.2	1426	3.4
	1945	4.8	2142	1.9	2136	2.7	2229	2.9	2057	3.8	2019	3.1	2357	1.0	2019	1.7	2059	0.9
20 M	0155	1.7	0351	5.8	0356	8.0	0434	11.1	0245	1.2	0239	0.7	0618	2.5	0245	4.4	0300	3.5
	0820	5.0	1018	1.8	1008	2.5	1109	2.8	0931	3.9	0842	3.2	1236	1.0	0857	1.5	0934	0.9
	1427	1.6	1618	5.9	1625	8.2	1709	11.4	1515	1.2	1502	0.8	1829	2.5	1509	4.3	1527	3.5
	2041	5.0	2238	1.7	2232	2.3	2337	2.4	2151	3.8	2114	3.2			2109	1.6	2155	0.8
21 TU	0246	1.5	0444	6.1	0449	8.4	0534	11.7	0333	1.2	0328	0.7	0040	0.9	0333	4.5	0354	3.6
	0906	5.2	1109	1.5	1059	2.2	1209	2.3	1018	4.0	0930	3.3	0659	2.6	0942	1.3	1025	0.8
	1515	1.4	1707	6.2	1715	8.5	1803	12.0	1602	1.0	1550	0.7	1322	0.9	1556	4.5	1615	3.6
	2125	5.1	2323	1.4	2318	2.0			2237	3.8	2202	3.2	1912	2.6	2153	1.4	2242	0.7
22 W	0327	1.4	0528	6.4	0534	8.8	0032	1.9	0415	1.1	0412	0.7	0118	0.9	0415	4.7	0440	3.7
	0944	5.4	1151	1.3	1142	2.0	0623	12.3	1059	4.1	1014	3.4	0736	2.7	1024	1.1	1109	0.7
	1554	1.2	1749	6.4	1757	8.8	1259	1.9	1644	0.9	1632	0.6	1403	0.9	1638	4.6	1657	3.6
	2203	5.2			2357	1.8	1848	12.4	2316	3.8	2244	3.2	1950	2.6	2233	1.2	2323	0.7
23 TH ○	0403	1.2	0002	1.2	0613	9.0	0119	1.6	0453	1.0	0450	0.7	0154	0.8	0454	4.8	0520	3.8
	1018	5.5	0607	6.5	1221	1.8	0704	12.6	1134	4.1	1053	3.5	0809	2.7	1102	0.9	1147	0.7
	1630	1.1	1227	1.1	1836	8.9	1342	1.7	1722	0.8	1709	0.6	1438	0.9	1717	4.7	1734	3.7
	2237	5.3	1826	6.5			1927	12.6	2349	3.8	2321	3.2	2025	2.6	2310	1.1	2359	0.6
24 F	0436	1.1	0037	1.1	0033	1.6	0200	1.5	0530	0.9	0524	0.7	0225	0.8	0532	4.9	0556	3.8
	1051	5.5	0642	6.7	0649	9.1	0741	12.8	1207	4.1	1130	3.6	0839	2.8	1139	0.8	1221	0.6
	1703	1.0	1301	1.0	1255	1.6	1421	1.6	1758	0.8	1742	0.6	1510	0.9	1754	4.8	1809	3.7
	2309	5.3	1900	6.6	1909	9.0	2003	12.7			2353	3.2	2057	2.6	2345	1.0		
25 SA	0508	1.1	0110	1.0	0105	1.5	0236	1.5	0021	3.8	0556	0.7	0254	0.7	0608	5.0	0032	0.6
	1122	5.6	0715	6.7	0723	9.2	0814	12.9	0604	0.8	1203	3.6	0906	2.8	1214	0.8	0629	3.9
	1735	1.0	1333	1.0	1327	1.5	1454	1.6	1238	4.1	1813	0.5	1539	0.9	1831	4.8	1254	0.6
	2341	5.3	1933	6.6	1942	9.0	2034	12.7	1833	0.8			2128	2.6			1841	3.8
26 SU	0539	1.1	0142	1.0	0136	1.4	0308	1.5	0051	3.8	0024	3.2	0324	0.7	0020	1.0	0103	0.6
	1154	5.6	0746	6.7	0754	9.1	0844	12.9	0638	0.8	0626	0.7	0933	2.8	0643	4.9	0701	3.9
	1806	1.0	1403	1.0	1357	1.5	1524	1.6	1310	4.0	1236	3.6	1608	0.9	1248	0.8	1324	0.6
			2003	6.5	2012	9.0	2103	12.7	1906	0.8	1845	0.5	2159	2.6	1906	4.7	1914	3.8
27 M	0012	5.3	0212	1.0	0206	1.5	0336	1.5	0125	3.8	0054	3.2	0355	0.7	0054	1.0	0134	0.6
	0611	1.1	0817	6.6	0824	9.0	0913	12.8	0711	0.9	0657	0.7	1001	2.8	0717	4.8	0732	3.8
	1226	5.4	1433	1.1	1425	1.6	1551	1.6	1345	3.9	1309	3.6	1639	0.9	1321	0.9	1355	0.7
	1839	1.1	2033	6.4	2040	8.8	2132	12.5	1940	0.9	1918	0.5	2233	2.5	1940	4.6	1946	3.7
28 TU	0046	5.2	0243	1.2	0234	1.6	0403	1.6	0202	3.7	0126	3.2	0430	0.8	0128	1.2	0205	0.7
	0644	1.3	0847	6.5	0853	8.9	0943	12.5	0745	1.0	0732	0.7	1033	2.7	0750	4.7	0804	3.8
	1259	5.3	1504	1.3	1453	1.7	1617	1.8	1423	3.8	1344	3.5	1714	1.0	1355	1.1	1427	0.7
	1913	1.2	2104	6.2	2109	8.6	2202	12.1	2015	1.0	1954	0.6	2309	2.4	2015	4.5	2021	3.7
29 W	0121	5.0	0315	1.4	0303	1.8	0428	1.9	0242	3.6	0201	3.2	0509	0.8	0203	1.3	0239	0.8
	0719	1.4	0919	6.3	0923	8.6	1014	12.0	0821	1.1	0809	0.8	1108	2.6	0824	4.5	0838	3.7
	1333	5.2	1536	1.5	1523	1.9	1643	2.1	1505	3.7	1422	3.5	1754	1.1	1430	1.3	1503	0.8
	1950	1.4	2137	6.0	2140	8.3	2232	11.5	2054	1.1	2033	0.6	2352	2.3	2051	4.3	2058	3.6
30 TH	0159	4.9	0349	1.6	0336	2.1	0455	2.3	0327	3.5	0241	3.2	0551	0.9	0241	1.5	0315	0.8
	0758	1.6	0954	6.1	0957	8.3	1045	11.4	0901	1.2	0852	0.9	1148	2.5	0901	4.3	0916	3.6
	1412	5.0	1612	1.8	1557	2.2	1711	2.5	1551	3.5	1505	3.4	1841	1.1	1509	1.5	1542	0.9
	2032	1.6	2215	5.8	2218	8.0	2303	10.9	2140	1.2	2118	0.7			2132	4.1	2140	3.5
31 F	0243	4.7	0428	1.9	0416	2.4	0525	2.7	*0418	3.4	0327	3.1	0042	2.2	0324	1.7	0400	1.0
	0845	1.8	1035	5.8	1039	8.0	1120	10.9	0951	1.4	0941	1.0	0641	1.0	0945	4.1	1000	3.4
	1500	4.8	1654	2.1	1641	2.6	1744	2.9	1646	3.4	1554	3.3	1237	2.4	1557	1.7	1631	1.0
	2124	1.8	2303	5.5	2306	7.7	2341	10.4	2238	1.3	2208	0.8	1937	1.2	2221	4.0	2230	3.3

● ● Time UT. For British Summer Time (shaded) March 30th to October 26th ADD ONE HOUR ● ●

WEST COAST ENGLAND, WALES & IRELAND Time Zone UT
Holyhead * Milford Haven * Swansea * Avonmouth * Dublin * Belfast * Londonderry * Galway * Cobh

FEBRUARY 1997 TIDE TABLES FEBRUARY 1997

HOLYHEAD	MILFORD HAVEN	SWANSEA	AVONMOUTH	DUBLIN	BELFAST	LONDONDERRY	GALWAY	COBH	
Time m	Time m	Time m	Time m	Time m	Time m	Time m	Time m	Time m	
0339 4.6	0519 2.2	0511 2.8	0603 3.1	0515 3.3	0421 3.0	0146 2.1	0420 1.9	0454 1.1	**1 SA**
0945 2.0	1129 5.5	1134 7.7	1207 10.5	1056 1.5	1039 1.1	0739 1.1	1042 3.9	1055 3.3	
1602 4.6	1752 2.3	1744 3.0	1827 3.3	1751 3.4	1653 3.2	1342 2.3	1700 1.9	1732 1.1	
2230 1.9				2345 1.4	2308 1.0	2050 1.2	2326 3.9	2332 3.2	
0451 4.5	0008 5.3	0014 7.4	0040 10.1	0623 3.3	0524 3.0	0308 2.1	0533 2.0	0603 1.1	**2 SU**
1100 2.1	0630 2.4	0627 3.0	0657 3.5	1210 1.5	1150 1.2	0850 1.1	1157 3.8	1203 3.1	
1723 4.5	1241 5.3	1248 7.6	1319 10.2	1903 3.4	1800 3.1	1515 2.2	1820 1.9	1845 1.1	
2348 1.9	1912 2.4	1909 3.1	1936 3.6			2215 1.2			
0612 4.6	0130 5.3	0137 7.4	0212 10.1	0052 1.3	0018 1.0	0429 2.3	0042 3.9	0045 3.2	**3 M**
1220 1.9	0758 2.3	0752 2.9	0835 3.6	0732 3.4	0636 3.0	1015 1.1	0656 1.9	0723 1.1	
1845 4.6	1406 5.4	1411 7.6	1453 10.5	1318 1.3	1306 1.1	1650 2.3	1318 3.9	1321 3.2	
	2041 2.2	2034 2.8	2129 3.3	2010 3.5	1912 3.1	2327 1.0	1936 1.7	2003 1.0	
0100 1.7	0250 5.6	0257 7.8	0339 10.9	0153 1.2	0130 1.0	0533 2.5	0154 4.2	0203 3.3	**4 TU**
0721 4.8	0919 2.0	0907 2.4	1015 2.8	0834 3.6	0748 3.1	1136 0.9	0807 1.6	0840 0.9	
1329 1.6	1523 5.8	1527 8.1	1612 11.4	1419 1.1	1415 1.0	1756 2.5	1428 4.2	1437 3.3	
1951 4.9	2153 1.8	2144 2.2	2251 2.4	2109 3.7	2019 3.2		2038 1.4	2111 0.7	
0200 1.4	0357 6.1	0403 8.5	0449 12.0	0248 1.0	0235 0.9	0023 0.8	0252 4.5	0310 3.6	**5 W**
0818 5.2	1024 1.4	1012 1.8	1128 1.9	0928 3.8	0851 3.2	0627 2.7	0905 1.1	0943 0.6	
1427 1.2	1627 6.3	1631 8.7	1720 12.3	1514 0.8	1515 0.7	1241 0.6	1524 4.6	1539 3.6	
2046 5.2	2252 1.2	2243 1.5		2203 3.9	2121 3.3	1849 2.6	2130 1.0	2209 0.5	
0253 1.0	0454 6.6	0500 9.2	0003 1.6	0338 0.7	0332 0.7	0111 0.6	0344 4.9	0407 3.8	**6 TH**
0906 5.5	1120 0.9	1108 1.1	0551 13.0	1018 4.1	0946 3.4	0715 2.9	0955 0.7	1038 0.4	
1518 0.8	1721 6.8	1727 9.3	1239 1.2	1604 0.5	1609 0.5	1335 0.6	1614 4.9	1631 3.8	
2135 5.5	2344 0.7	2336 0.9	1820 13.2	2251 4.1	2215 3.4	1936 2.8	2216 0.7	2302 0.3	
0339 0.7	0545 7.1	0553 9.8	0111 1.0	0425 0.5	0423 0.5	0157 0.5	0431 5.3	0457 4.1	**7 F**
0952 5.9	1211 0.4	1200 0.6	0646 13.7	1104 4.3	1036 3.6	0800 3.1	1041 0.3	1128 0.2	
1605 0.4	1812 7.1	1818 9.8	1342 0.6	1651 0.3	1657 0.3	1424 0.5	1700 5.2	1720 4.0	
2221 5.8			1913 13.8	2338 4.3	2306 3.5	2021 2.8	2300 0.3	2351 0.1	●
0424 0.4	0033 0.4	0024 0.5	0209 0.5	0510 0.4	0511 0.4	0240 0.4	0517 5.5	0545 4.3	**8 SA**
1037 6.1	0634 7.5	0642 10.2	0736 14.3	1150 4.5	1124 3.7	0843 3.2	1124 0.0	1216 0.2	
1650 0.1	1259 0.1	1248 0.2	1436 0.2	1737 0.2	1744 0.1	1511 0.4	1745 5.4	1806 4.2	
2305 5.9	1858 7.4	1905 10.1	2001 14.2		2354 3.5	2106 2.9	2343 0.2		
0509 0.3	0119 0.1	0109 0.2	0259 0.2	0024 4.3	0557 0.3	0324 0.3	0603 5.7	0038 -0.0	**9 SU**
1122 6.2	0720 7.7	0728 10.4	0823 14.5	0554 0.3	1210 3.8	0926 3.2	1207 -0.0	0630 4.4	
1736 0.1	1345 -0.0	1333 0.1	1523 -0.1	1235 4.6	1830 0.0	1555 0.4	1830 5.4	1302 -0.0	
2351 5.9	1944 7.5	1949 10.1	2045 14.3	1823 0.1		2148 2.8		1851 4.2	
0553 0.3	0204 0.1	0151 0.2	0342 0.1	0109 4.3	0040 3.5	0407 0.4	0026 0.3	0124 -0.0	**10 M**
1208 6.2	0805 7.7	0812 10.3	0906 14.6	0639 0.4	0642 0.3	1009 3.2	0648 5.7	0715 4.4	
1821 0.1	1429 0.1	1414 0.2	1603 0.0	1321 4.6	1256 3.8	1639 0.5	1251 0.0	1347 0.0	
	2027 7.3	2031 10.0	2127 14.2	1909 0.2	1916 0.1	2231 2.7	1914 5.3	1936 4.2	
0036 5.7	0248 0.3	0230 0.4	0418 0.3	0155 4.2	0127 3.5	0451 0.5	0109 0.3	0209 0.0	**11 TU**
0639 0.4	0849 7.4	0854 10.0	0949 14.3	0724 0.5	0728 0.3	1053 3.0	0733 5.5	0800 4.3	
1254 6.1	1512 0.3	1454 0.5	1638 0.4	1409 4.5	1343 3.7	1724 0.6	1334 0.3	1431 0.1	
1908 0.4	2111 7.0	2111 9.6	2208 13.7	1957 0.4	2003 0.2	2315 2.5	1959 5.1	2020 4.1	
0122 5.5	0330 0.6	0309 0.9	0450 0.8	0244 4.0	0215 3.3	0537 0.6	0155 0.6	0253 0.2	**12 W**
0726 0.7	0933 7.1	0936 9.5	1030 13.6	0813 0.7	0816 0.4	1139 2.8	0821 5.2	0845 4.1	
1342 5.8	1554 0.8	1533 1.1	1708 1.0	1500 4.3	1433 3.6	1809 0.8	1420 0.7	1515 0.3	
1957 0.7	2154 6.6	2152 9.1	2248 12.9	2048 0.7	2054 0.3		2046 4.8	2106 3.9	
0211 5.2	0413 1.1	0351 1.5	0519 1.4	0338 3.8	0306 3.2	0002 2.4	0244 1.0	0339 0.4	**13 TH**
0817 1.0	1018 6.6	1019 8.9	1112 12.6	0907 0.9	0908 0.6	0627 0.8	0910 4.8	0931 3.9	
1434 5.4	1638 1.3	1616 1.7	1738 1.7	1559 4.0	1529 3.4	1231 2.6	1510 1.2	1603 0.6	
2049 1.2	2241 6.1	2237 8.4	2329 11.9	2145 1.0	2150 0.6	1858 1.0	2137 4.4	2154 3.7	
0305 4.9	0500 1.6	0439 2.1	0551 2.2	0439 3.7	0403 3.1	0058 2.2	0339 1.4	0430 0.7	**14 F**
0915 1.4	1109 6.0	1109 8.2	1157 11.5	1009 1.2	1006 0.8	0726 1.0	1006 4.3	1022 3.6	
1533 5.0	1727 1.8	1708 2.5	1812 2.5	1705 3.8	1632 3.2	1337 2.4	1607 1.6	1655 0.8	
2150 1.6	2335 5.7	2332 7.8		2249 1.3	2254 0.8	1957 1.1	2237 4.1	2250 3.4	
0410 4.6	0559 2.1	0542 2.6	0015 10.9	0546 3.5	0506 3.0	0221 2.1	0448 1.7	0528 0.9	**15 SA**
1026 1.8	1208 5.5	1210 7.6	0629 3.0	1121 1.4	1117 0.9	0843 1.1	1115 4.0	1121 3.3	
1645 4.6	1831 2.2	1819 3.1	1251 10.6	1817 3.6	1742 3.0	1507 2.2	1721 1.9	1758 1.0	
2303 1.9			1857 3.3			2112 1.2	2355 3.9	2356 3.2	

● ● Time UT. For British Summer Time (shaded) March 30th to October 26th ADD ONE HOUR ● ●

FEBRUARY 1997TIDETABLES FEBRUARY 1997

	HOLYHEAD	MILFORD HAVEN	SWANSEA	AVONMOUTH	DUBLIN	BELFAST	LONDONDERRY	GALWAY	COBH
	Time m	Time m	Time m	Time m	Time m	Time m	Time m	Time m	Time m
16 SU	0532 4.5	0043 5.3	0045 7.3	0115 10.2	0001 1.5	0007 0.9	0406 2.1	0619 1.9	0641 1.1
	1148 2.0	0719 2.3	0706 3.2	0725 3.7	0657 3.5	0613 3.0	1020 1.2	1239 3.8	1234 3.1
	1811 4.5	1324 5.2	1329 7.3	1403 10.0	1239 1.5	1234 0.9	1632 2.2	1851 2.0	1915 1.1
		1956 2.4	1947 3.3	2013 3.8	1929 3.5	1854 3.0	2233 1.1		
17 M	0024 2.0	0209 5.2	0211 7.2	0238 9.9	0116 1.5	0118 0.9	0516 2.2	0123 3.9	0118 3.1
	0656 4.6	0848 2.3	0833 3.2	0908 3.9	0805 3.6	0718 3.0	1139 1.1	0745 1.8	0801 1.1
	1308 1.9	1451 5.3	1454 7.3	1530 10.1	1357 1.4	1344 0.9	1733 2.3	1400 3.9	1356 3.1
	1931 4.6	2116 2.2	2107 3.1	2153 3.6	2037 3.6	1959 3.0	2337 1.0	2006 1.9	2030 1.1
18 TU	0136 1.9	0328 5.5	0329 7.6	0405 10.4	0223 1.4	0218 0.9	0606 2.4	0230 4.0	0236 3.2
	0802 4.8	0958 2.0	0944 2.9	1036 3.2	0907 3.7	0815 3.1	1234 1.0	0845 1.6	0909 1.0
	1412 1.7	1558 5.6	1603 7.7	1645 10.8	1457 1.2	1443 0.8	1821 2.4	1458 4.1	1503 3.2
	2030 4.8	2218 1.9	2209 2.7	2306 2.8	2136 3.6	2056 3.0		2100 1.7	2130 0.9
19 W	0230 1.7	0425 5.8	0428 8.0	0511 11.3	0315 1.3	0309 0.8	0026 0.9	0321 4.2	0334 3.4
	0850 5.0	1050 1.7	1039 2.5	1140 2.4	0959 3.9	0907 3.2	0647 2.5	0930 1.3	1002 0.9
	1500 1.4	1648 5.9	1656 8.2	1741 11.7	1546 1.0	1532 0.7	1318 0.9	1544 4.3	1553 3.3
	2112 4.9	2304 1.5	2257 2.3		2222 3.7	2145 3.0	1903 2.5	2142 1.4	2219 0.8
20 TH	0312 1.5	0509 6.2	0515 8.5	0004 2.0	0358 1.1	0353 0.7	0107 0.8	0402 4.4	0419 3.5
	0927 5.2	1131 1.4	1124 2.1	0601 12.1	1042 4.0	0952 3.3	0724 2.6	1009 1.1	1045 0.7
	1538 1.2	1729 6.2	1739 8.6	1232 1.9	1627 0.9	1614 0.6	1354 0.8	1624 4.5	1635 3.5
	2147 5.1	2342 1.3	2337 1.9	1827 12.3	2300 3.7	2226 3.1	1939 2.5	2218 1.2	2300 0.7
21 F	0347 1.3	0547 6.4	0554 8.8	0053 1.6	0436 1.0	0431 0.7	0143 0.7	0439 4.6	0458 3.7
	1000 5.4	1207 1.1	1201 1.8	0643 12.5	1117 4.0	1033 3.4	0757 2.7	1045 0.9	1123 0.6
	1611 1.1	1805 6.4	1815 8.9	1317 1.6	1703 0.8	1649 0.5	1427 0.7	1700 4.6	1712 3.6
	2218 5.2			1906 12.6	2331 3.8	2301 3.1	2013 2.6	2253 0.9	2336 0.6
22 SA	0417 1.1	0017 1.0	0012 1.6	0136 1.4	0511 0.9	0504 0.6	0215 0.7	0514 4.8	0533 3.8
	1030 5.5	0621 6.6	0629 9.0	0719 12.8	1148 4.0	1108 3.4	0827 2.7	1118 0.7	1157 0.6
○	1641 0.9	1239 1.0	1235 1.5	1357 1.4	1736 0.8	1721 0.5	1458 0.7	1734 4.7	1745 3.7
	2247 5.3	1838 6.6	1848 9.1	1940 12.8	2359 3.8	2332 3.2	2044 2.6	2326 0.8	
23 SU	0446 1.0	0048 0.9	0045 1.4	0214 1.2	0543 0.8	0534 0.6	0245 0.6	0548 4.8	0009 0.5
	1100 5.5	0652 6.7	0701 9.2	0751 12.9	1216 4.0	1140 3.5	0853 2.7	1151 0.6	0606 3.8
	1710 0.9	1309 0.9	1306 1.4	1433 1.4	1807 0.7	1749 0.5	1526 0.7	1807 4.8	1230 0.5
	2316 5.4	1909 6.7	1919 9.2	2010 12.9		2359 3.2	2112 2.6	2358 0.7	1818 3.8
24 M	0515 0.9	0118 0.8	0115 1.3	0248 1.2	0026 3.8	0603 0.6	0312 0.6	0620 4.9	0040 0.5
	1130 5.5	0722 6.8	0731 9.3	0820 13.0	0612 0.8	1211 3.5	0918 2.7	1221 0.6	0636 3.9
	1740 0.9	1339 0.8	1333 1.3	1505 1.3	1245 4.0	1818 0.4	1553 0.7	1839 4.8	1300 0.5
	2347 5.4	1938 6.7	1948 9.2	2039 13.0	1836 0.8		2141 2.6		1850 3.8
25 TU	0546 0.9	0149 0.8	0142 1.3	0318 1.1	0056 3.8	0027 3.2	0342 0.6	0029 0.7	0112 0.5
	1200 5.5	0751 6.8	0800 9.2	0849 13.1	0641 0.8	0632 0.5	0943 2.7	0651 4.8	0707 3.9
	1811 0.9	1409 0.9	1400 1.3	1533 1.3	1316 3.9	1242 3.5	1621 0.8	1251 0.7	1332 0.5
		2008 6.6	2015 9.1	2107 12.9	1905 0.8	1848 0.4	2211 2.5	1911 4.7	1922 3.8
26 W	0018 5.3	0219 0.9	0209 1.3	0345 1.2	0129 3.8	0056 3.3	0413 0.6	0100 0.8	0142 0.6
	0618 1.0	0821 6.7	0827 9.1	0919 12.9	0711 0.9	0705 0.6	1012 2.6	0722 4.7	0738 3.8
	1232 5.4	1438 1.0	1426 1.4	1559 1.4	1351 3.8	1315 3.5	1652 0.8	1322 0.8	1403 0.6
	1842 1.0	2037 6.5	2042 9.0	2137 12.6	1936 0.8	1922 0.5	2245 2.5	1942 4.6	1955 3.8
27 TH	0051 5.2	0250 1.1	0237 1.5	0411 1.4	0206 3.7	0129 3.3	0450 0.7	0133 1.0	0215 0.6
	0651 1.1	0851 6.5	0855 8.9	0950 12.5	0745 0.9	0741 0.6	1045 2.6	0754 4.6	0810 3.8
	1305 5.3	1508 1.3	1453 1.6	1623 1.7	1431 3.7	1351 3.5	1728 0.9	1354 1.0	1436 0.6
	1916 1.2	2109 6.3	2111 8.7	2206 12.1	2012 0.9	2000 0.5	2324 2.3	2017 4.5	2030 3.7
28 F	0126 5.1	0322 1.4	0307 1.7	0435 1.8	0249 3.6	0207 3.3	0530 0.7	0208 1.2	0249 0.7
	0728 1.3	0924 6.3	0927 8.7	1021 11.9	0824 1.0	0821 0.7	1123 2.4	0830 4.4	0845 3.6
	1342 5.1	1540 1.5	1524 1.9	1648 2.1	1516 3.6	1433 3.4	1809 1.0	1432 1.3	1512 0.8
	1955 1.4	2144 6.0	2145 8.4	2236 11.4	2056 1.1	2043 0.6		2055 4.3	2109 3.6

● ● Time UT. For British Summer Time (shaded) March 30th to October 26th ADD ONE HOUR ● ●

WEST COAST ENGLAND, WALES & IRELAND Time Zone UT
Holyhead * Milford Haven * Swansea * Avonmouth * Dublin * Belfast * Londonderry * Galway * Cobh

MARCH 1997 TIDE TABLES MARCH 1997

HOLYHEAD		MILFORD HAVEN		SWANSEA		AVONMOUTH		DUBLIN		BELFAST		LONDONDERRY		GALWAY		COBH		
Time	m	Time	m	Time	m	Time	m	Time	m	Time	m	Time	m	Time	m	Time	m	
0206	4.9	0357	1.7	0343	2.0	0502	2.2	0337	3.5	0251	3.2	0009	2.2	0249	1.4	0329	0.8	**1 SA**
0812	1.5	1003	6.0	1006	8.3	1054	11.3	0911	1.2	0908	0.8	0617	0.9	0912	4.2	0927	3.5	
1425	4.9	1618	1.9	1603	2.3	1716	2.5	1610	3.5	1523	3.3	1209	2.3	1516	1.5	1557	0.9	
2044	1.6	2227	5.7	2230	8.0	2312	10.9	2152	1.2	2133	0.8	1900	1.1	2142	4.0	2157	3.4	
0257	4.7	0443	2.0	0432	2.5	0536	2.7	0434	3.4	0342	3.1	0106	2.1	0340	1.6	0421	1.0	**2 SU**
0908	1.7	1052	5.6	1057	7.8	1135	10.8	1013	1.3	1004	1.0	0712	1.0	1006	3.9	1019	3.3	
1524	4.6	1710	2.2	1700	2.8	1755	2.9	1715	3.4	1621	3.2	1311	2.1	1616	1.8	1654	1.0	
2148	1.9	2326	5.4	2333	7.5			2305	1.4	2231	1.0	2004	1.1	2242	3.9	2256	3.2	
0406	4.5	0549	2.3	0544	2.9	0003	10.4	0541	3.3	0445	3.0	0224	2.1	0451	1.8	0527	1.1	**3 M**
1022	1.9	1201	5.3	1209	7.5	0624	3.1	1134	1.4	1115	1.1	0821	1.1	1119	3.8	1126	3.1	
1646	4.5	1828	2.4	1826	3.1	1240	10.3	1833	3.4	1730	3.1	1450	2.0	1739	1.9	1807	1.1	
2311	1.9					1854	3.4			2344	1.1	2133	1.1					
0533	4.5	0051	5.3	0100	7.4	0130	10.1	0021	1.4	0600	3.0	0404	2.2	0002	3.8	0010	3.2	**4 TU**
1149	1.8	0721	2.3	0718	2.9	0747	3.5	0658	3.4	1238	1.1	0957	1.1	0622	1.8	0651	1.1	
1819	4.5	1333	5.3	1340	7.4	1417	10.3	1252	1.3	1848	3.0	1648	2.1	1250	3.8	1248	3.1	
		2009	2.3	2006	2.9	2045	3.5	1948	3.5			2306	1.0	1911	1.8	1933	1.0	
0033	1.8	0221	5.5	0230	7.7	0308	10.7	0130	1.2	0104	1.1	0518	2.4	0125	4.0	0134	3.3	**5 W**
0654	4.7	0854	2.0	0845	2.5	0943	2.9	0809	3.6	0719	3.1	1133	0.9	0745	1.5	0815	0.9	
1306	1.5	1500	5.6	1506	7.8	1547	11.1	1400	1.0	1354	0.9	1753	2.3	1409	4.1	1412	3.2	
1933	4.8	2131	1.8	2124	2.3	2223	2.6	2052	3.7	2001	3.1			2021	1.4	2048	0.8	
0140	1.4	0336	6.0	0343	8.3	0427	11.8	0230	1.0	0215	0.9	0008	0.8	0233	4.4	0248	3.5	**6 TH**
0756	5.1	1005	1.4	0954	1.8	1105	2.0	0909	3.8	0828	3.2	0612	2.6	0848	1.0	0923	0.6	
1409	1.1	1609	6.2	1615	8.6	1701	12.1	1458	0.7	1456	0.7	1238	0.7	1509	4.5	1518	3.5	
2031	5.2	2234	1.2	2227	1.6	2343	1.7	2148	4.0	2104	3.3	1842	2.5	2114	1.0	2150	0.5	
0235	1.0	0436	6.6	0444	9.1	0533	12.9	0323	0.8	0315	0.7	0057	0.6	0327	4.8	0348	3.8	**7 F**
0848	5.5	1103	0.8	1053	1.1	1221	1.2	1002	4.1	0927	3.4	0659	2.9	0939	0.6	1019	0.3	
1500	0.6	1705	6.7	1712	9.3	1803	13.1	1549	0.5	1549	0.4	1329	0.5	1559	4.9	1612	3.8	
2119	5.5	2327	0.7	2319	0.9			2238	4.1	2200	3.4	1928	2.7	2200	0.5	2244	0.2	
0322	0.6	0528	7.1	0536	9.8	0055	1.0	0409	0.5	0406	0.5	0143	0.4	0415	5.2	0439	4.1	**8 SA**
0934	5.8	1154	0.5	1145	0.5	0630	13.7	1049	4.3	1018	3.6	0743	3.1	1023	0.2	1110	0.1	
1547	0.3	1754	7.2	1802	9.8	1327	0.5	1636	0.3	1638	0.2	1414	0.4	1644	5.2	1701	4.1	
2203	5.8					1857	13.8	2323	4.3	2249	3.5	2011	2.8	2242	0.2	2333	0.0	
0406	0.3	0015	0.3	0007	0.4	0154	0.3	0454	0.4	0454	0.4	0227	0.3	0500	5.5	0527	4.3	**9 SU**
1018	6.1	0616	7.5	0625	10.2	0719	14.3	1134	4.5	1106	3.7	0826	3.2	1106	-0.1	1158	-0.0	
1631	0.0	1241	0.0	1231	0.2	1420	-0.0	1721	0.2	1724	0.1	1457	0.3	1727	5.4	1748	4.2	●
2246	5.9	1840	7.4	1848	10.2	1943	14.2			2336	3.6	2052	2.8	2324	-0.0			
0449	0.2	0101	0.0	0051	0.1	0242	-0.0	0006	4.3	0539	0.3	0309	0.2	0544	5.6	0021	-0.1	**10 M**
1103	6.2	0701	7.7	0711	10.4	0804	14.6	0536	0.3	1152	3.8	0908	3.2	1147	-0.2	0612	4.4	
1715	-0.0	1325	-0.1	1315	0.1	1505	-0.2	1218	4.6	1809	0.0	1538	0.3	1809	5.4	1243	-0.1	
2330	5.9	1924	7.5	1930	10.3	2025	14.4	1803	0.2			2132	2.8			1833	4.3	
0533	0.1	0145	-0.0	0132	0.1	0324	-0.1	0048	4.3	0020	3.6	0352	0.3	0006	-0.0	0106	-0.1	**11 TU**
1148	6.2	0745	7.7	0753	10.4	0846	14.6	0619	0.3	0623	0.3	0949	3.1	0628	5.6	0656	4.4	
1759	0.1	1408	-0.0	1354	0.2	1543	-0.1	1302	4.5	1237	3.8	1618	0.4	1228	-0.0	1327	-0.0	
		2006	7.4	2010	10.1	2105	14.3	1847	0.3	1853	0.1	2212	2.7	1852	5.3	1915	4.3	
0012	5.8	0226	0.1	0210	0.4	0358	0.1	0130	4.2	0103	3.5	0435	0.4	0048	0.1	0149	0.0	**12 W**
0617	0.3	0827	7.4	0833	10.1	0927	14.3	0703	0.4	0706	0.3	1031	2.9	0712	5.4	0739	4.3	
1233	6.0	1448	0.3	1430	0.6	1615	0.3	1348	4.4	1323	3.7	1657	0.5	1310	0.3	1409	0.1	
1843	0.4	2046	7.1	2048	9.8	2144	13.8	1930	0.5	1938	0.2	2251	2.5	1935	5.1	1959	4.2	
0057	5.6	0306	0.5	0247	0.8	0427	0.7	0215	4.1	0148	3.4	0519	0.5	0132	0.4	0231	0.2	**13 TH**
0703	0.6	0909	7.0	0912	9.6	1006	13.6	0748	0.6	0751	0.4	1115	2.7	0757	5.1	0821	4.1	
1319	5.7	1527	0.7	1506	1.1	1642	1.0	1436	4.2	1411	3.5	1737	0.7	1354	0.7	1451	0.3	
1928	0.8	2127	6.7	2126	9.2	2221	13.0	2018	0.8	2025	0.4	2332	2.4	2020	4.8	2042	4.0	
0142	5.3	0346	1.0	0324	1.4	0452	1.3	0303	3.9	0235	3.3	0606	0.7	0218	0.9	0314	0.4	**14 F**
0751	0.9	0951	6.5	0951	9.0	1045	12.5	0839	0.8	0839	0.5	1205	2.4	0845	4.7	0905	3.9	
1407	5.3	1606	1.3	1545	1.7	1708	1.7	1530	3.9	1503	3.3	1821	0.8	1440	1.2	1534	0.6	
2016	1.2	2209	6.2	2206	8.6	2258	11.9	2110	1.1	2117	0.7			2108	4.4	2127	3.7	
0230	4.9	0429	1.5	0407	2.1	0519	2.1	0359	3.7	0327	3.2	0019	2.2	0310	1.3	0400	0.7	**15 SA**
0845	1.4	1036	5.9	1036	8.3	1124	11.3	0939	1.1	0934	0.7	0701	0.9	0938	4.2	0951	3.6	
1502	4.8	1649	1.8	1630	2.5	1736	2.5	1634	3.7	1603	3.1	1306	2.2	1533	1.6	1621	0.8	
2112	1.7	2257	5.7	2254	7.9	2337	10.9	2212	1.4	2218	0.9	1911	1.0	2203	4.0	2218	3.4	

● ● **Time UT. For British Summer Time (shaded) March 30th to October 26th ADD ONE HOUR** ● ●

MARCH 1997 TIDE TABLES MARCH 1997

	HOLYHEAD		MILFORD HAVEN		SWANSEA		AVONMOUTH		DUBLIN		BELFAST		LONDONDERRY		GALWAY		COBH	
	Time	m	Time	m	Time	m	Time	m	Time	m	Time	m	Time	m	Time	m	Time	m
16 SU	0329	4.6	0520	2.1	0502	2.8	0551	2.9	0506	3.5	0427	3.0	0125	2.0	0415	1.7	0453	1.0
	0952	1.8	1130	5.4	1130	7.6	1211	10.3	1049	1.3	1041	0.9	0818	1.1	1042	3.9	1045	3.3
	1610	4.5	1745	2.3	1732	3.1	1812	3.3	1747	3.5	1712	2.9	1440	2.0	1642	2.0	1718	1.1
	2223	2.1			2359	7.3			2324	1.6	2331	1.0	2016	1.1	2313	3.7	2320	3.2
17 M	0446	4.4	0000	5.2	0619	3.3	0029	10.0	0618	3.5	0533	2.9	0327	2.0	0543	1.9	0600	1.2
	1114	2.0	0634	2.4	1243	7.1	0635	3.7	1208	1.4	1200	0.9	1007	1.1	1205	3.7	1153	3.0
	1739	4.3	1242	5.0	1859	3.5	1318	9.6	1901	3.4	1824	2.8	1612	2.0	1817	2.1	1831	1.2
	2348	2.2	1909	2.5			1910	4.0					2145	1.1				
18 TU	0617	4.4	0126	5.0	0124	7.1	0151	9.5	0042	1.6	0045	1.1	0448	2.1	0047	3.7	0039	3.1
	1238	2.0	0811	2.5	0751	3.5	0809	4.2	0730	3.5	0640	2.9	1127	1.0	0717	1.9	0721	1.3
	1905	4.4	1415	5.0	1413	7.1	1451	9.6	1328	1.4	1314	0.9	1714	2.1	1334	3.7	1316	3.0
			2041	2.4	2029	3.4	2113	4.0	2012	3.4	1932	2.8	2303	1.1	1942	2.0	1951	1.2
19 W	0107	2.1	0255	5.2	0251	7.3	0328	9.9	0157	1.5	0149	1.0	0540	2.3	0205	3.8	0202	3.1
	0731	4.6	0927	2.3	0909	3.2	1001	3.6	0837	3.6	0742	3.0	1220	0.9	0821	1.7	0835	1.2
	1345	1.8	1530	5.3	1531	7.4	1613	10.3	1433	1.2	1415	0.8	1801	2.2	1437	3.9	1429	3.1
	2006	4.6	2147	2.1	2137	3.0	2233	3.1	2112	3.5	2030	2.9	2359	0.9	2038	1.8	2056	1.1
20 TH	0205	1.9	0356	5.6	0357	7.7	0439	10.9	0253	1.3	0242	0.9	0622	2.4	0258	4.0	0303	3.3
	0822	4.8	1021	1.8	1009	2.7	1106	2.6	0933	3.7	0836	3.1	1300	0.8	0907	1.4	0930	1.0
	1433	1.8	1621	5.7	1627	7.9	1712	11.3	1522	1.0	1505	0.7	1842	2.4	1523	4.1	1522	3.3
	2048	4.8	2236	1.7	2228	2.5	2332	2.2	2200	3.6	2119	2.9			2120	1.5	2147	0.9
21 F	0248	1.6	0442	6.0	0445	8.2	0531	11.8	0337	1.1	0327	0.8	0043	0.8	0339	4.2	0350	3.5
	0901	5.0	1103	1.4	1054	2.2	1159	1.9	1017	3.8	0924	3.2	0659	2.5	0945	1.1	1014	0.8
	1512	1.3	1702	6.1	1710	8.4	1758	12.1	1603	0.9	1546	0.6	1334	0.7	1601	4.4	1605	3.5
	2122	5.0	2315	1.4	2309	2.0			2237	3.7	2200	3.0	1918	2.5	2157	1.2	2228	0.8
22 SA	0322	1.3	0519	6.3	0525	8.6	0021	1.6	0415	1.0	0405	0.7	0121	0.7	0416	4.5	0429	3.7
	0933	5.2	1139	1.2	1132	1.9	0614	12.3	1053	3.9	1006	3.3	0732	2.6	1020	0.9	1052	0.7
	1544	1.1	1738	6.4	1747	8.8	1246	1.5	1638	0.8	1621	0.5	1406	0.6	1636	4.6	1642	3.6
	2152	5.2	2350	1.1	2345	1.7	1837	12.5	2307	3.7	2235	3.1	1952	2.5	2230	0.9	2306	0.6
23 SU	0352	1.1	0553	6.6	0600	9.0	0106	1.3	0448	0.9	0439	0.6	0154	0.6	0450	4.6	0504	3.8
	1003	5.4	1211	1.0	1206	1.6	0651	12.6	1124	3.9	1042	3.3	0803	2.6	1052	0.7	1127	0.6
	1613	0.9	1810	6.6	1820	9.1	1328	1.3	1709	0.8	1652	0.5	1436	0.6	1709	4.7	1718	3.8
	2221	5.3					1911	12.7	2333	3.8	2305	3.1	2023	2.6	2301	0.7	2340	0.6
24 M	0421	1.0	0021	0.9	0017	1.4	0146	1.1	0518	0.8	0509	0.5	0226	0.5	0522	4.7	0537	3.9
○	1033	5.5	0624	6.7	0633	9.2	0723	12.8	1151	3.9	1114	3.3	0830	2.6	1122	0.6	1201	0.5
	1642	0.8	1242	0.8	1237	1.4	1406	1.2	1737	0.7	1721	0.4	1504	0.5	1740	4.8	1751	3.9
	2249	5.4	1841	6.7	1851	9.3	1942	12.9	2359	3.9	2333	3.2	2052	2.6	2332	0.6		
25 TU	0450	0.8	0053	0.8	0048	1.3	0222	1.0	0545	0.7	0538	0.5	0255	0.5	0553	4.8	0015	0.5
	1103	5.5	0655	6.8	0704	9.3	0753	13.0	1218	3.9	1144	3.4	0855	2.6	1151	0.6	0609	3.9
	1712	0.8	1312	0.8	1306	1.3	1441	1.1	1803	0.7	1749	0.4	1531	0.6	1810	4.8	1235	0.5
	2320	5.4	1911	6.8	1921	9.3	2011	13.1			2359	3.2	2121	2.6			1824	3.9
26 W	0521	0.8	0124	0.7	0117	1.2	0255	0.9	0027	3.8	0608	0.5	0326	0.5	0002	0.6	0048	0.5
	1135	5.5	0725	6.8	0733	9.3	0824	13.1	0612	0.7	1215	3.4	0922	2.6	0623	4.8	0641	3.9
	1742	0.8	1342	0.8	1334	1.2	1512	1.0	1249	3.9	1821	0.4	1600	0.6	1221	0.6	1308	0.5
	2351	5.4	1942	6.8	1949	9.3	2042	13.1	1832	0.7			2151	2.5	1841	4.8	1857	3.9
27 TH	0553	0.8	0156	0.8	0145	1.2	0325	0.9	0100	3.8	0028	3.3	0358	0.5	0033	0.6	0121	0.6
	1207	5.4	0756	6.8	0803	9.3	0855	3.1	0642	0.7	0640	0.5	0952	2.6	0654	4.7	0713	3.9
	1815	0.9	1413	0.9	1400	1.3	1539	1.1	1324	3.8	1248	3.4	1630	0.6	1252	0.7	1341	0.6
			2012	6.7	2018	9.2	2113	12.9	1904	0.7	1854	0.4	2224	2.5	1913	4.7	1931	3.9
28 F	0024	5.3	0227	0.9	0214	1.3	0353	1.1	0137	3.8	0102	3.3	0435	0.6	0106	0.8	0154	0.6
	0627	0.9	0827	6.6	0832	9.1	0927	12.8	0717	0.7	0717	0.5	1027	2.5	0728	4.6	0746	3.8
	1241	5.3	1444	1.1	1429	1.5	1604	1.4	1404	3.8	1327	3.4	1706	0.7	1325	0.9	1415	0.6
	1849	1.1	2045	6.5	2048	9.0	2145	12.5	1942	0.8	1933	0.5	2303	2.4	1948	4.6	2007	3.8
29 SA	0100	5.2	0300	1.2	0245	1.5	0418	1.5	0220	3.7	0141	3.3	0516	0.7	0142	1.0	0229	0.7
	0706	1.1	0902	6.4	0905	8.8	1000	12.2	0758	0.8	0758	0.6	1107	2.3	0806	4.5	0822	3.7
	1319	5.1	1517	1.4	1500	1.8	1628	1.8	1451	3.7	1410	3.3	1746	0.8	1403	1.2	1451	0.7
	1930	1.3	2122	6.2	2124	8.6	2217	11.8	2027	1.0	2016	0.6	2347	2.3	2027	4.4	2047	3.7
30 SU	0141	5.1	0338	1.5	0322	1.9	0444	1.9	0309	3.6	0225	3.2	0603	0.8	0225	1.2	0309	0.8
	0751	1.3	0942	6.1	0945	8.4	1036	11.6	0848	1.0	0845	0.7	1156	2.2	0851	4.3	0904	3.5
	1405	4.9	1556	1.7	1541	2.0	1657	2.2	1547	3.5	1500	3.2	1835	0.9	1449	1.5	1533	0.9
	2018	1.5	2206	5.9	2209	8.2	2255	11.2	2124	1.2	2106	0.8			2115	4.2	2134	3.5
31 M	0232	4.8	0424	1.8	0411	2.3	0518	2.3	0406	3.5	0317	3.2	0042	2.2	0317	1.4	0400	1.0
	0847	1.5	1032	5.7	1036	7.9	1120	11.0	0951	1.1	0942	0.8	0657	0.9	0945	4.0	0956	3.4
	1505	4.6	1648	2.1	1636	2.7	1736	2.6	1653	3.5	1600	3.1	1300	2.0	1550	1.7	1630	1.0
	2122	1.8	2305	5.6	2312	7.7	2347	10.6	2237	1.3	2206	1.0	1934	1.0	2215	4.0	2233	3.4

● ● ● Time UT. For British Summer Time (shaded) March 30th to October 26th ADD ONE HOUR ● ● ●

WEST COAST ENGLAND, WALES & IRELAND Time Zone UT
Holyhead * Milford Haven * Swansea * Avonmouth * Dublin * Belfast * Londonderry * Galway * Cobh

APRIL 1997 TIDE TABLES APRIL 1997

HOLYHEAD	MILFORD HAVEN	SWANSEA	AVONMOUTH	DUBLIN	BELFAST	LONDONDERRY	GALWAY	COBH	
Time m	Time m	Time m	Time m	Time m	Time m	Time m	Time m	Time m	
0339 4.6	0530 2.1	0521 2.7	0607 2.8	0514 3.4	0420 3.1	0154 2.1	0427 1.6	0506 1.1	**1 TU**
1000 1.7	1141 5.4	1148 7.5	122410.4	1113 1.2	1054 0.9	0806 1.0	1057 3.8	1102 3.2	
1627 4.5	1806 2.3	1802 3.0	1836 3.1	1812 3.4	1711 3.0	1445 1.9	1713 1.9	1743 1.1	
2245 1.9				2357 1.4	2321 1.1	2055 1.1	2334 3.9	2347 3.3	
0505 4.6	0027 5.4	0037 7.5	010910.3	0632 3.5	0535 3.0	0336 2.2	0557 1.7	0628 1.1	**2 W**
1127 1.7	0700 2.2	0657 2.8	0727 3.2	1233 1.1	1217 0.9	0952 1.0	1228 3.9	1224 3.2	
1800 4.5	1312 5.3	1319 7.4	135410.4	1929 3.5	1830 3.0	1642 2.0	1848 1.8	1908 1.0	
	1945 2.2	1944 2.9	2015 3.3			2236 1.0			
0009 1.8	0157 5.6	0207 7.7	024310.7	0109 1.2	0044 1.1	0454 2.4	0100 4.1	0111 3.3	**3 TH**
0627 4.8	0832 1.9	0824 2.5	0915 2.8	0746 3.6	0654 3.1	1130 0.8	0723 1.4	0752 0.9	
1245 1.4	1440 5.6	1446 7.8	152411.0	1342 0.9	1332 0.8	1742 2.2	1350 4.1	1348 3.3	
1915 4.8	2109 1.8	2105 2.3	2155 2.6	2035 3.7	1943 3.1	2345 0.8	2000 1.4	2025 0.8	
0118 1.4	0315 6.0	0323 8.3	040411.7	0212 1.0	0155 0.9	0549 2.6	0210 4.4	0226 3.6	**4 F**
0732 5.1	0943 1.4	0935 1.8	1040 1.9	0849 3.9	0805 3.2	1228 0.6	0826 1.0	0901 0.7	
1348 1.0	1549 6.1	1557 8.5	164012.0	1442 0.7	1433 0.6	1829 2.4	1450 4.5	1455 3.6	
2012 5.2	2213 1.2	2207 1.6	2321 1.8	2132 3.9	2047 3.2		2054 1.0	2129 0.5	
0214 1.0	0415 6.6	0424 9.1	051212.7	0305 0.8	0254 0.7	0038 0.6	0306 4.8	0327 3.9	**5 SA**
0825 5.5	1042 0.8	1033 1.2	1200 1.2	0944 4.1	0904 3.4	0637 2.8	0916 0.6	0959 0.4	
1440 1.0	1645 6.7	1653 9.2	174313.0	1533 0.5	1527 0.4	1315 0.4	1539 4.9	1551 3.9	
2100 5.5	2306 0.7	2300 1.0		2221 4.1	2141 3.4	1912 2.6	2139 0.6	2224 0.3	
0302 0.7	0507 7.1	0517 9.7	0035 1.0	0353 0.6	0346 0.6	0124 0.4	0354 5.1	0418 4.1	**6 SU**
0912 5.8	1133 0.4	1124 0.6	060913.5	1032 4.3	0957 3.6	0721 3.0	1001 0.2	1050 0.2	
1526 0.3	1733 7.1	1742 9.8	1306 0.6	1619 0.3	1615 0.2	1357 0.3	1623 5.2	1641 4.1	
2143 5.7	2355 0.3	2348 0.5	183613.6	2306 4.2	2230 3.5	1954 2.7	2222 0.4	2314 0.1	
0346 0.4	0555 7.4	060510.1	0133 0.4	0436 0.4	0433 0.4	0209 0.3	0439 5.4	0506 4.3	**7 M**
0957 6.0	1219 0.1	1211 0.4	065914.0	1117 4.4	1045 3.7	0804 3.0	1043 0.0	1138 0.1	
1610 0.1	1818 7.4	182710.1	1358 0.2	1702 0.3	1701 0.1	1436 0.3	1705 5.3	1727 4.3	
2225 5.8			192114.0	2348 4.3	2315 3.6	2033 2.7	2303 0.1	●	
0429 0.2	0040 0.2	0031 0.4	0221 0.1	0518 0.4	0518 0.3	0252 0.2	0523 5.5	0001 0.0	**8 TU**
1042 6.1	0639 7.5	065010.3	074214.3	1200 4.5	1132 3.7	0845 3.0	1124 -0.0	0551 4.4	
1653 0.1	1303 0.0	1253 0.3	1442 0.0	1743 0.3	1745 0.1	1515 0.3	1747 5.4	1223 0.1	
2307 5.8	1901 7.4	190910.2	200314.1		2357 3.6	2112 2.7	2345 0.1	1812 4.3	
0512 0.2	0123 0.1	0112 0.4	0300 0.1	0027 4.3	0601 0.3	0335 0.3	0606 5.5	0045 0.1	**9 W**
1127 6.0	0722 7.5	073210.2	082414.3	0600 0.3	1217 3.7	0927 2.9	1205 0.1	0635 4.4	
1736 0.3	1343 0.1	1331 0.5	1519 0.2	1243 4.4	1829 0.2	1551 0.3	1829 5.3	1306 0.1	
2350 5.8	1942 7.3	194810.0	204114.1	1824 0.4		2149 2.6		1855 4.3	
0557 0.3	0203 0.2	0149 0.6	0334 0.3	0107 4.2	0039 3.6	0417 0.4	0027 0.2	0128 0.2	**10 TH**
1212 5.8	0803 7.2	0812 9.9	090314.0	0642 0.4	0644 0.3	1009 2.7	0651 5.3	0717 4.3	
1818 0.5	1422 0.4	1407 0.8	1549 0.6	1327 4.3	1301 3.6	1627 0.5	1246 0.4	1347 0.3	
	2022 7.0	2025 9.7	211913.7	1906 0.6	1912 0.4	2225 2.5	1911 5.1	1937 4.2	
0033 5.6	0243 0.6	0225 1.0	0402 0.8	0148 4.1	0121 3.5	0459 0.5	0110 0.5	0209 0.4	**11 F**
0642 0.6	0844 6.9	0849 9.5	094213.3	0727 0.6	0727 0.4	1051 2.5	0736 5.0	0757 4.1	
1257 5.5	1500 0.8	1442 1.3	1615 1.1	1413 4.1	1348 3.4	1703 0.6	1328 0.8	1427 0.5	
1901 0.9	2101 6.7	2102 9.2	215612.9	1950 0.8	1957 0.6	2303 2.4	1955 4.8	2018 4.0	
0115 5.3	0321 1.0	0301 1.5	0427 1.4	0233 3.9	0206 3.4	0544 0.7	0156 0.9	0249 0.6	**12 SA**
0728 0.9	0924 6.4	0927 8.9	102012.3	0816 0.8	0814 0.5	1139 2.3	0822 4.6	0839 3.9	
1343 5.1	1537 1.3	1518 1.8	1640 1.8	1504 3.9	1438 3.2	1743 0.7	1414 1.3	1506 0.7	
1947 1.3	2141 6.2	2140 8.7	223111.9	2039 1.2	2045 0.8	2345 2.3	2041 4.4	2102 3.8	
0201 5.0	0401 1.5	0342 2.1	0452 2.1	0324 3.7	0256 3.3	0635 0.9	0246 1.3	0332 0.9	**13 SU**
0819 1.3	1006 5.9	1008 8.3	105711.2	0914 1.0	0905 0.7	1236 2.1	0912 4.2	0922 3.6	
1433 4.8	1617 1.8	1600 2.4	1706 2.5	1604 3.6	1534 3.0	1828 0.9	1504 1.7	1550 0.9	
2037 1.7	2225 5.7	2225 8.1	230710.9	2139 1.4	2142 1.0		2132 4.1	2149 3.5	
0253 4.7	0447 2.0	0431 2.7	0521 2.8	0427 3.6	0351 3.1	0037 2.1	0346 1.7	0420 1.1	**14 M**
0919 1.7	1055 5.4	1057 7.7	113910.2	1021 1.2	1006 0.8	0742 1.0	1011 3.9	1011 3.3	
1535 4.4	1706 2.2	1655 3.0	1738 3.2	1713 3.4	1639 2.9	1356 1.9	1606 2.0	1640 1.1	
2139 2.1	2321 5.3	2321 7.5	235310.0	2248 1.6	2248 1.1	1923 2.0	2233 3.8	2245 3.3	
0359 4.5	0550 2.4	0538 3.2	0559 3.5	0539 3.5	0453 3.0	0203 2.0	0503 1.9	0518 1.3	**15 TU**
1033 1.9	1200 5.0	1201 7.2	1237 9.5	1134 1.3	1118 0.9	0926 1.1	1124 3.7	1112 3.1	
1654 4.2	1818 2.5	1812 3.5	1824 3.9	1826 3.3	1747 2.8	1530 1.9	1730 2.2	1744 1.3	
2259 2.3						2036 1.1	2355 3.7	2355 3.1	

● ● Time UT. For British Summer Time (shaded) March 30th to October 26th ADD ONE HOUR ● ●

APRIL 1997 TIDE TABLES APRIL 1997

	HOLYHEAD		MILFORD HAVEN		SWANSEA		AVONMOUTH		DUBLIN		BELFAST		LONDONDERRY		GALWAY		COBH	
	Time	m	Time	m	Time	m	Time	m	Time	m	Time	m	Time	m	Time	m	Time	m
16 W	0522	4.4	0036	5.1	0036	7.1	0105	9.5	0004	1.6	0001	1.1	0351	2.1	0630	1.9	0632	1.4
	1153	2.0	0719	2.5	0702	3.4	0703	4.1	0651	3.4	0557	3.0	1051	1.0	1251	3.7	1227	3.0
	1820	4.3	1324	4.9	1323	7.0	1403	9.3	1251	1.3	1230	0.9	1636	2.0	1857	2.1	1859	1.3
			1949	2.5	1939	3.5	2005	4.3	1936	3.3	1854	2.7	2203	1.1				
17 TH	0021	2.3	0204	5.1	0200	7.2	0239	9.6	0119	1.6	0107	1.1	0454	2.2	0120	3.7	0114	3.1
	0641	4.4	0840	2.3	0821	3.3	0912	3.8	0757	3.5	0700	3.0	1145	0.9	0739	1.7	0745	1.3
	1302	1.8	1446	5.1	1445	7.2	1528	9.9	1357	1.2	1333	0.8	1726	2.1	1400	3.8	1341	3.1
	1926	4.4	2102	2.3	2052	3.2	2151	3.5	2036	3.4	1952	2.8	2312	1.0	2000	1.9	2008	1.2
18 F	0124	2.0	0313	5.5	0311	7.5	0356	10.4	0221	1.4	0203	1.0	0541	2.3	0221	3.9	0220	3.3
	0739	4.6	0939	2.0	0924	2.9	1024	2.9	0855	3.6	0757	3.0	1226	0.8	0830	1.5	0845	1.2
	1354	1.6	1543	5.5	1546	7.7	1631	10.8	1448	1.1	1424	0.7	1808	2.3	1449	4.1	1440	3.3
	2012	4.7	2156	1.9	2147	2.7	2251	2.6	2126	3.5	2042	2.9			2047	1.6	2103	1.1
19 SA	0212	1.8	0403	5.8	0404	8.0	0451	11.3	0307	1.2	0249	0.9	0003	0.8	0306	4.1	0310	3.5
	0823	4.9	1024	1.6	1013	2.4	1118	2.2	0942	3.6	0847	3.1	0621	2.4	0912	1.3	0933	1.0
	1436	1.4	1627	5.9	1632	8.2	1720	11.6	1530	1.0	1507	0.6	1300	0.7	1530	4.3	1527	3.5
	2049	4.9	2239	1.5	2230	2.2	2343	1.9	2205	3.6	2125	2.9	1845	2.4	2126	1.3	2149	0.9
20 SU	0248	1.5	0443	6.2	0447	8.4	0536	11.9	0346	1.1	0330	0.7	0045	0.7	0345	4.3	0352	3.7
	0859	5.1	1103	1.3	1054	2.0	1208	1.7	1021	3.7	0930	3.1	0656	2.5	0948	1.0	1015	0.8
	1509	1.1	1703	6.2	1711	8.6	1800	12.2	1605	0.9	1545	0.6	1333	0.6	1605	4.5	1608	3.7
	2121	5.1	2316	1.2	2309	1.8			2237	3.7	2202	3.0	1921	2.5	2200	1.1	2230	0.8
21 M	0321	1.2	0519	6.4	0524	8.8	0030	1.4	0418	0.9	0406	0.6	0123	0.6	0419	4.5	0430	3.8
	0932	5.2	1138	1.1	1130	1.7	0615	12.4	1053	3.7	1009	3.2	0729	2.5	1020	0.9	1054	0.7
	1541	1.0	1738	6.5	1746	9.0	1254	1.4	1636	0.8	1618	0.5	1404	0.5	1638	4.7	1645	3.8
	2151	5.3	2351	1.0	2345	1.5	1836	12.6	2305	3.7	2234	3.1	1954	2.5	2233	0.8	2309	0.7
22 TU ○	0351	1.0	0553	6.6	0600	9.1	0113	1.2	0448	0.8	0440	0.6	0158	0.5	0451	4.6	0506	3.9
	1003	5.3	1211	0.9	1205	1.5	0650	12.7	1122	3.8	1043	3.2	0800	2.5	1051	0.7	1131	0.6
	1612	0.8	1811	6.7	1819	9.2	1335	1.2	1703	0.7	1650	0.4	1435	0.5	1709	4.8	1723	3.9
	2221	5.4					1910	12.9	2332	3.7	2303	3.2	2027	2.6	2303	0.7	2346	0.6
23 W	0423	0.9	0025	0.8	0018	1.3	0154	1.0	0515	0.8	0512	0.5	0233	0.5	0523	4.7	0541	4.0
	1036	5.4	0626	6.7	0634	9.2	0724	12.9	1151	3.8	1116	3.3	0830	2.5	1121	0.7	1208	0.5
	1643	0.8	1244	0.8	1237	1.3	1413	1.0	1732	0.7	1721	0.4	1506	0.5	1739	4.9	1759	4.0
	2253	5.5	1844	6.8	1852	9.4	1944	13.1			2333	3.3	2059	2.6	2335	0.6		
24 TH	0456	0.8	0100	0.8	0051	1.2	0230	0.8	0002	3.9	0545	0.5	0307	0.5	0555	4.8	0024	4.0
	1109	5.4	0659	6.8	0707	9.3	0758	13.1	0545	0.7	1150	3.3	0900	2.5	1152	0.7	0615	4.0
	1716	0.8	1318	0.8	1309	1.3	1449	0.9	1224	3.8	1755	0.4	1536	0.5	1812	4.9	1245	0.6
	2327	5.5	1917	6.8	1924	9.4	2018	13.2	1803	0.7			2132	2.6			1835	4.0
25 F	0531	0.8	0134	0.8	0123	1.2	0306	0.8	0036	3.9	0005	3.3	0343	0.5	0008	0.6	0100	0.6
	1145	5.4	0733	6.8	0740	9.3	0834	13.1	0618	0.6	0621	0.4	0935	2.5	0630	4.8	0651	4.0
	1751	0.8	1351	0.9	1339	1.3	1521	1.0	1303	3.8	1227	3.3	1609	0.5	1226	0.8	1321	0.6
			1952	6.8	1958	9.3	2053	13.1	1839	0.7	1832	0.4	2207	2.5	1847	4.9	1912	4.0
26 SA	0003	5.4	0209	0.9	0156	1.3	0337	1.0	0115	3.9	0042	3.3	0422	0.5	0044	0.7	0137	0.7
	0609	0.8	0809	6.7	0815	9.2	0909	12.9	0657	0.6	0700	0.4	1013	2.4	0707	4.7	0727	3.9
	1223	5.3	1426	1.0	1412	1.4	1549	1.3	1345	3.8	1308	3.3	1646	0.6	1303	0.9	1357	0.7
	1830	1.0	2029	6.6	2033	9.1	2128	12.7	1921	0.8	1912	0.5	2247	2.5	1925	4.8	1950	3.9
27 SU	0042	5.4	0247	1.1	0231	1.4	0406	1.3	0200	3.8	0122	3.3	0506	0.6	0124	0.8	0215	0.8
	0651	0.9	0848	6.4	0852	8.9	0947	12.4	0742	0.7	0743	0.5	1057	2.3	0749	4.6	0806	3.8
	1306	5.1	1503	1.3	1447	1.7	1616	1.6	1435	3.7	1354	3.3	1728	0.7	1345	1.2	1436	0.8
	1913	1.2	2109	6.4	2112	8.8	2206	12.2	2009	0.9	1957	0.6	2332	2.4	2009	4.6	2032	3.8
28 M	0127	5.2	0328	1.3	0312	1.7	0435	1.7	0250	3.8	0209	3.3	0554	0.7	0210	1.1	0258	0.9
	0739	1.1	0931	6.1	0935	8.5	1027	11.8	0836	0.8	0833	0.6	1150	2.2	0837	4.4	0850	3.7
	1355	4.9	1547	1.6	1530	2.1	1648	2.0	1532	3.6	1447	3.2	1816	0.8	1434	1.4	1521	0.9
	2005	1.4	2157	6.1	2201	8.4	2249	11.6	2106	1.1	2050	0.7			2059	4.4	2121	3.7
29 TU	0219	5.0	0418	1.6	0404	2.1	0512	2.1	0348	3.7	0302	3.2	0025	2.3	0305	1.3	0349	1.0
	0837	1.3	1024	5.8	1029	8.0	1115	11.0	0941	0.9	0931	0.7	0648	0.8	0933	4.2	0942	3.5
	1457	4.7	1642	1.9	1627	2.5	1730	2.4	1639	3.5	1548	3.1	1256	2.0	1536	1.7	1618	1.0
	2108	1.7	2257	5.8	2303	7.9	2345	11.0	2218	1.2	2151	0.9	1913	0.9	2159	4.2	2219	3.5
30 W	0325	4.8	0523	1.9	0513	2.5	0604	2.5	0454	3.6	0405	3.1	0133	2.3	0413	1.5	0454	1.1
	0948	1.4	1133	5.5	1138	7.6	1219	10.7	1057	1.0	1042	0.7	0758	0.9	1043	4.0	1047	3.4
	1615	4.6	1755	2.1	1749	2.8	1830	2.8	1755	3.5	1658	3.0	1436	2.0	1654	1.8	1727	1.1
	2225	1.8							2334	1.3	2305	1.0	2026	1.0	2312	4.1	2330	3.4

● ● Time UT. For British Summer Time (shaded) March 30th to October 26th ADD ONE HOUR ● ●

WEST COAST ENGLAND, WALES & IRELAND Time Zone UT
Holyhead * Milford Haven * Swansea * Avonmouth * Dublin * Belfast * Londonderry * Galway * Cobh

MAY 1997 TIDE TABLES MAY 1997

Day	HOLYHEAD	MILFORD HAVEN	SWANSEA	AVONMOUTH	DUBLIN	BELFAST	LONDONDERRY	GALWAY	COBH
	Time m	Time m	Time m	Time m	Time m	Time m	Time m	Time m	Time m
1 TH	0443 4.8	0013 5.6	0022 7.7	0059 10.7	0609 3.6	0517 3.1	0300 2.3	0535 1.5	0610 1.1
	1107 1.4	0644 1.9	0640 2.6	0719 2.7	1212 1.0	1159 0.7	0939 0.9	1206 4.0	1204 3.3
	1739 4.6	1255 5.5	1302 7.5	1339 10.6	1909 3.6	1814 3.0	1616 2.0	1822 1.7	1846 1.0
	2345 1.7	1924 2.1	1924 2.8	1957 3.0			2157 0.9		
2 F	0600 4.9	0135 5.7	0145 7.8	0223 11.0	0045 1.2	0024 1.0	0421 2.4	0034 4.2	0048 3.5
	1221 1.2	0807 1.7	0803 2.5	0851 2.5	0723 3.7	0632 3.1	1109 0.8	0655 1.3	0728 1.0
	1851 4.8	1417 5.7	1424 7.8	1501 11.1	1321 0.8	1309 0.6	1718 2.2	1325 4.2	1322 3.4
		2044 1.8	2042 2.3	2127 2.5	2015 3.7	1925 3.1	2314 0.8	1934 1.4	2001 0.8
3 SA	0054 1.4	0249 6.1	0300 8.3	0340 11.7	0149 1.1	0133 0.9	0520 2.6	0145 4.4	0201 3.7
	0706 5.1	0918 1.4	0912 1.8	1012 1.9	0827 3.9	0742 3.2	1206 0.6	0759 1.0	0837 0.8
	1324 0.9	1525 6.1	1534 8.5	1615 11.9	1421 0.7	1410 0.5	1808 2.3	1426 4.5	1430 3.7
	1950 5.1	2148 1.3	2145 1.7	2251 1.9	2112 3.9	2027 3.2		2030 1.1	2106 0.9
4 SU	0151 1.1	0351 6.5	0401 8.9	0448 12.5	0245 0.9	0233 0.7	0012 0.6	0242 4.7	0303 3.9
	0802 5.4	1017 0.9	1011 1.3	1131 1.4	0924 4.1	0842 3.4	0610 2.7	0851 0.7	0936 0.5
	1418 0.7	1621 6.6	1630 9.1	1718 12.6	1514 0.5	1504 0.4	1252 0.5	1515 4.8	1528 3.9
	2039 5.3	2244 0.9	2238 1.2		2203 4.0	2120 3.4	1852 2.5	2117 0.7	2203 0.4
5 M	0241 0.8	0445 6.9	0455 9.4	0008 1.3	0334 0.7	0325 0.6	0103 0.5	0332 5.0	0357 4.1
	0851 5.6	1109 0.6	1102 0.9	0546 13.1	1014 4.2	0936 3.5	0657 2.8	0936 0.5	1029 0.4
	1505 0.5	1711 6.9	1720 9.5	1239 0.9	1600 0.5	1554 0.3	1333 0.4	1600 5.1	1620 4.1
	2123 5.5	2333 0.6	2326 0.9	1812 13.1	2248 4.1	2208 3.5	1933 2.6	2201 0.5	2254 0.4
6 TU	0327 0.6	0533 7.1	0544 9.8	0106 0.9	0419 0.6	0413 0.5	0149 0.4	0418 5.2	0445 4.3
	0938 5.8	1155 0.4	1148 0.8	0636 13.5	1100 4.3	1026 3.6	0740 2.8	1019 0.3	1117 0.3
	1549 0.4	1756 7.1	1805 9.8	1332 0.7	1643 0.5	1640 0.3	1411 0.4	1643 5.2	1707 4.2
	2205 5.7			1858 13.4	2329 4.2	2252 3.6	2013 2.6	2243 0.3	2341 0.3 ●
7 W	0411 0.4	0018 0.4	0010 0.8	0155 0.7	0502 0.5	0458 0.4	0233 0.4	0503 5.3	0531 4.3
	1023 5.8	0618 7.2	0629 9.9	0721 13.6	1143 4.3	1112 3.6	0823 2.8	1101 0.3	1202 0.3
	1632 0.4	1239 0.3	1230 0.8	1416 0.6	1724 0.5	1724 0.4	1447 0.4	1725 5.3	1752 4.3
	2247 5.7	1839 7.2	1847 9.9	1939 13.6		2335 3.6	2050 2.6	2326 0.3	
8 TH	0454 0.4	0101 0.4	0051 0.8	0236 0.7	0008 4.2	0541 0.4	0315 0.4	0546 5.2	0025 0.4
	1108 5.7	0701 7.1	0711 9.8	0802 13.6	0544 0.5	1157 3.6	0904 2.7	1142 0.5	0614 4.3
	1714 0.5	1319 0.4	1309 0.9	1454 0.7	1225 4.3	1806 0.4	1521 0.4	1806 5.2	1245 0.4
	2329 5.7	1920 7.1	1927 9.7	2018 13.6	1804 0.6		2126 2.6		1835 4.2
9 F	0539 0.5	0142 0.5	0130 1.0	0310 0.8	0046 4.2	0016 3.6	0357 0.5	0008 0.4	0107 0.4
	1152 5.6	0742 7.0	0751 9.5	0842 13.4	0626 0.5	0624 0.4	0945 2.6	0630 5.1	0654 4.2
	1756 0.7	1358 0.6	1345 1.2	1525 1.0	1308 4.1	1242 3.5	1556 0.5	1224 0.7	1324 0.5
		2000 6.9	2004 9.5	2057 13.3	1845 0.8	1848 0.5	2200 2.5	1849 5.0	1916 4.1
10 SA	0011 5.5	0221 0.7	0206 1.3	0339 1.1	0126 4.1	0057 3.6	0438 0.6	0051 0.6	0147 0.6
	0622 0.7	0821 6.7	0828 9.2	0921 12.9	0711 0.6	0706 0.5	1027 2.4	0715 4.8	0734 4.0
	1236 5.3	1436 0.9	1420 1.5	1552 1.4	1352 4.0	1327 3.3	1631 0.6	1306 1.0	1403 0.6
	1837 1.0	2038 6.6	2041 9.1	2133 12.7	1927 0.9	1931 0.7	2236 2.5	1932 4.8	1957 4.0
11 SU	0053 5.3	0259 1.1	0242 1.7	0406 1.6	0209 4.0	0140 3.5	0520 0.7	0137 0.9	0226 0.8
	0707 1.0	0900 6.3	0906 8.8	0958 12.1	0759 0.8	0751 0.5	1112 2.2	0801 4.6	0814 3.8
	1320 5.0	1512 1.3	1457 1.9	1618 1.9	1440 3.8	1413 3.2	1709 0.7	1350 1.3	1441 0.8
	1920 1.4	2116 6.2	2118 8.7	2209 11.9	2015 1.1	2016 0.8	2315 2.4	2017 4.5	2038 3.8
12 M	0135 5.1	0338 1.5	0322 2.1	0431 2.1	0257 3.8	0227 3.4	0605 0.9	0225 1.3	0305 1.0
	0754 1.3	0941 5.9	0945 8.3	1034 11.2	0852 1.0	0838 0.7	1203 2.1	0849 4.3	0854 3.6
	1406 4.8	1550 1.7	1537 2.3	1644 2.4	1534 3.6	1504 3.0	1751 0.8	1438 1.7	1521 1.0
	2005 1.7	2157 5.9	2200 8.2	2244 11.1	2109 1.3	2106 1.0		2104 4.2	2121 3.6
13 TU	0221 4.8	0419 1.9	0407 2.5	0459 2.6	0351 3.7	0316 3.3	0000 2.3	0319 1.6	0348 1.2
	0846 1.6	1025 5.5	1029 7.8	1112 10.4	0952 1.1	0930 0.8	0658 1.0	0941 4.0	0939 3.4
	1459 4.5	1633 2.1	1626 2.8	1713 3.0	1636 3.4	1600 2.9	1304 1.9	1533 1.9	1605 1.1
	2058 1.9	2245 5.7	2251 7.8	2324 10.3	2212 1.5	2202 1.1	1839 0.9	2157 4.0	2211 3.4
14 W	0315 4.6	0510 2.2	0503 2.9	0533 3.1	0456 3.5	0412 3.1	0057 2.2	0421 1.8	0439 1.3
	0947 1.8	1119 5.2	1124 7.4	1200 9.8	1057 1.2	1030 0.9	0809 1.1	1041 3.8	1032 3.3
	1602 4.3	1730 2.4	1728 3.2	1753 3.5	1742 3.3	1700 2.8	1420 1.9	1639 2.1	1659 1.3
	2203 2.2	2346 5.3	2351 7.4		2321 1.6	2306 1.2	1937 1.0	2301 3.8	2309 3.3
15 TH	0421 4.4	0618 2.4	0611 3.2	0020 9.8	0604 3.4	0510 3.0	0215 2.1	0533 1.9	0539 1.4
	1056 1.9	1227 5.0	1230 7.1	0622 3.6	1204 1.3	1135 0.9	0935 1.1	1153 3.7	1134 3.2
	1717 4.2	1844 2.5	1844 3.4	1306 9.4	1848 3.3	1803 2.7	1533 1.9	1757 2.1	1802 1.3
	2318 2.3			1852 3.9			2047 1.1		

● ● Time UT. For British Summer Time (shaded) March 30th to October 26th ADD ONE HOUR ● ●

MAY 1997 TIDE TABLES MAY 1997

	HOLYHEAD	MILFORD HAVEN	SWANSEA	AVONMOUTH	DUBLIN	BELFAST	LONDONDERRY	GALWAY	COBH
	Time m	Time m	Time m	Time m	Time m	Time m	Time m	Time m	Time m
16 F	0535 4.4 1204 1.9 1827 4.4	0100 5.2 0736 2.4 1344 5.1 2002 2.4	0102 7.2 0724 3.2 1345 7.2 1957 3.2	0136 9.6 0743 3.9 1426 9.6 2039 3.9	0030 1.6 0709 3.4 1308 1.2 1948 3.3	0010 1.1 0611 3.0 1237 0.9 1902 2.8	0338 2.1 1043 1.0 1632 2.0 2202 1.0	0017 3.7 0643 1.8 1306 3.8 1909 2.0	0016 3.2 0646 1.4 1243 3.2 1909 1.3
17 SA	0027 2.2 0642 4.5 1303 1.7 1923 4.6	0213 5.3 0842 2.2 1450 5.3 2104 2.1	0212 7.4 0830 3.0 1451 7.5 2057 2.9	0255 10.0 0927 3.4 1536 10.2 2200 3.2	0134 1.5 0808 3.4 1403 1.1 2041 3.4	0110 1.1 0708 3.0 1332 0.8 1955 2.8	0440 2.2 1133 0.9 1721 2.2 2306 0.9	0127 3.8 0742 1.7 1403 4.0 2004 1.8	0123 3.3 0750 1.1 1347 3.3 2010 1.2
18 SU	0122 1.9 0735 4.7 1350 1.5 2007 4.8	0312 5.6 0936 1.9 1541 5.7 2154 1.8	0312 7.7 0925 2.6 1545 7.9 2146 2.5	0358 10.7 1030 2.7 1630 11.0 2257 2.4	0226 1.3 0859 3.5 1447 1.1 2124 3.5	0203 1.0 0801 3.0 1420 0.7 2042 2.9	0530 2.3 1214 0.8 1803 2.3 2358 0.8	0221 4.0 0829 1.5 1449 4.2 2048 1.5	0221 3.5 0845 1.1 1442 3.5 2104 1.0
19 M	0206 1.7 0819 4.9 1430 1.3 2045 5.0	0400 5.9 1021 1.6 1624 6.0 2239 1.5	0401 8.1 1011 2.2 1629 8.4 2229 2.1	0449 11.4 1123 2.0 1717 11.7 2348 1.8	0308 1.2 0942 3.5 1524 1.0 2201 3.6	0249 0.9 0848 3.0 1503 0.6 2123 3.0	0612 2.3 1252 0.7 1844 2.4	0305 4.2 0909 1.3 1527 4.4 2126 1.3	0309 3.6 0933 0.9 1529 3.7 2151 0.9
20 TU	0245 1.4 0857 5.1 1506 1.1 2119 5.2	0441 6.2 1101 1.3 1703 6.4 2318 1.2	0444 8.5 1052 1.9 1709 8.8 2309 1.7	0534 12.0 1213 1.6 1759 12.3	0342 1.1 1018 3.6 1558 0.9 2233 3.7	0331 0.7 0931 3.1 1542 0.6 2200 3.1	0044 0.7 0651 2.4 1328 0.6 1922 2.5	0343 4.3 0945 1.1 1603 4.6 2201 1.0	0353 3.8 1018 0.8 1612 3.8 2236 0.8
21 W	0321 1.1 0933 5.2 1542 0.9 2153 5.4	0519 6.4 1139 1.1 1740 6.6 2357 1.0	0524 8.9 1131 1.6 1747 9.1 2348 1.5	0036 1.4 0615 12.5 1300 1.3 1839 12.8	0415 0.9 1053 3.7 1630 0.8 2306 3.8	0410 0.6 1012 3.2 1618 0.5 2235 3.2	0126 0.6 0727 2.5 1403 0.5 2000 2.6	0418 4.5 1018 0.9 1636 4.8 2236 0.8	0434 3.9 1100 0.7 1654 4.0 2318 0.7
22 TH ○	0357 1.0 1010 5.3 1617 0.8 2228 5.5	0557 6.6 1217 0.9 1818 6.8	0604 9.1 1209 1.4 1825 9.3	0123 1.1 0656 12.8 1345 1.1 1918 13.1	0447 0.8 1127 3.8 1703 0.7 2340 3.9	0448 0.5 1050 3.2 1656 0.4 2310 3.3	0207 0.5 0804 2.5 1439 0.5 2036 2.6	0454 4.7 1052 0.8 1710 4.9 2311 0.7	0513 4.0 1142 0.7 1734 4.0
23 F	0434 0.8 1048 5.4 1654 0.8 2306 5.6	0036 0.8 0636 6.8 1255 0.8 1857 6.9	0026 1.3 0643 9.3 1246 1.3 1903 9.4	0206 0.9 0736 3.0 1427 1.0 1958 13.3	0522 0.7 1205 3.8 1740 0.6	0526 0.5 1130 3.3 1734 0.4 2346 3.3	0248 0.5 0842 2.5 1514 0.5 2114 2.7	0530 4.8 1127 0.8 1747 5.0 2348 0.6	0000 0.6 0552 4.0 1223 0.6 1814 4.1
24 SA	0514 0.7 1127 5.4 1733 0.8 2346 5.6	0116 0.8 0715 6.8 1334 0.8 1936 6.9	0105 1.2 0723 9.3 1323 1.2 1943 9.4	0248 0.8 0817 13.1 1506 1.0 2038 13.3	0018 4.0 0601 0.5 1246 3.9 1821 0.6	0606 0.4 1211 3.3 1815 0.4	0329 0.4 0921 2.5 1551 0.5 2152 2.7	0609 4.8 1206 0.8 1826 5.0	0042 0.6 0631 4.0 1303 0.6 1854 4.1
25 SU	0556 0.7 1210 5.3 1815 0.9	0157 0.9 0757 6.7 1415 0.9 2018 6.8	0144 1.2 0803 9.2 1401 1.3 2024 9.3	0326 0.9 0857 13.0 1542 1.2 2118 13.0	0059 4.0 0645 0.5 1332 3.9 1906 0.9	0026 3.4 0648 0.4 1256 3.3 1858 0.5	0412 0.5 1004 2.5 1630 0.5 2234 2.6	0028 0.6 0651 4.8 1247 0.9 1909 5.0	0123 0.7 0712 4.0 1345 0.6 1936 4.0
26 M	0030 5.5 0642 0.8 1257 5.2 1903 1.0	0239 0.9 0839 6.5 1457 1.1 2103 6.6	0225 1.3 0845 9.0 1441 1.5 2108 9.0	0402 1.1 0939 12.7 1615 1.5 2201 12.6	0145 4.0 0733 0.5 1423 3.8 1955 0.8	0110 3.4 0734 0.4 1344 3.2 1946 0.6	0457 0.5 1051 2.4 1713 0.6 2320 2.6	0112 0.7 0737 4.7 1333 1.1 1956 4.8	0205 0.7 0754 3.9 1427 0.7 2021 3.9
27 TU	0117 5.4 0732 0.9 1349 5.1 1955 1.2	0324 1.1 0927 6.3 1544 1.4 2153 6.4	0309 1.5 0931 8.6 1527 1.8 2158 8.6	0436 1.4 1024 12.2 1650 1.8 2248 12.1	0236 4.0 0827 0.6 1520 3.7 2052 1.0	0158 3.4 0825 0.4 1438 3.1 2039 0.7	0546 0.6 1144 2.2 1801 0.7	0200 0.9 0827 4.6 1424 1.3 2048 4.7	0251 0.8 0839 3.8 1515 0.8 2111 3.8
28 W	0211 5.2 0830 1.0 1450 4.9 2056 1.4	0415 1.4 1021 6.0 1638 1.6 2251 6.1	0401 1.8 1024 8.2 1623 2.2 2257 8.2	0517 1.8 1115 11.7 1733 2.1 2343 11.6	0332 3.9 0930 0.7 1624 3.6 2157 1.1	0252 3.3 0924 0.5 1538 3.1 2140 0.8	0012 2.5 0642 0.8 1248 2.1 1856 0.8	0255 1.1 0923 4.4 1524 1.5 2145 4.5	0342 0.9 0932 3.7 1609 0.9 2207 3.7
29 TH	0312 5.1 0935 1.2 1559 4.7 2205 1.6	0516 1.6 1124 5.8 1744 1.8 2357 6.0	0505 2.1 1127 7.9 1736 2.5	0607 2.1 1212 11.3 1829 2.4	0436 3.8 1039 0.8 1734 3.6 2308 1.2	0353 3.2 1029 0.5 1645 3.0 2250 0.9	0113 2.5 0747 0.8 1409 2.0 2001 0.9	0358 1.3 1027 4.3 1633 1.7 2252 4.3	0442 1.0 1033 3.5 1713 0.9 2312 3.6
30 F	0421 5.0 1045 1.2 1714 4.7 2318 1.6	0626 1.7 1235 5.7 1900 1.9	0006 8.0 0620 2.3 1241 7.7 1900 2.6	0048 11.3 0711 2.3 1321 11.1 1939 2.6	0546 3.8 1149 0.9 1845 3.6	0500 3.2 1139 0.5 1756 3.0	0227 2.4 0910 0.9 1538 2.1 2121 0.9	0509 1.3 1141 4.2 1752 1.6	0550 1.0 1142 3.5 1824 0.9
31 SA	0533 5.0 1156 1.2 1825 4.8	0109 5.9 0740 1.7 1349 5.8 2015 1.7	0121 8.0 0737 2.3 1358 7.9 2015 2.3	0200 11.3 0824 2.2 1435 11.2 2057 2.4	0017 1.2 0657 3.8 1256 0.8 1950 3.7	0003 0.9 0612 3.2 1246 0.5 1904 3.1	0344 2.4 1033 0.8 1647 2.2 2239 0.8	0006 4.3 0624 1.3 1256 4.3 1905 1.5	0023 3.6 0702 1.0 1254 3.5 1936 3.6

● ● Time UT. For British Summer Time (shaded) March 30th to October 26th ADD ONE HOUR ● ●

WEST COAST ENGLAND, WALES & IRELAND Time Zone UT

Holyhead * Milford Haven * Swansea * Avonmouth * Dublin * Belfast * Londonderry * Galway * Cobh

JUNE 1997 TIDE TABLES JUNE 1997

HOLYHEAD Time m	MILFORD HAVEN Time m	SWANSEA Time m	AVONMOUTH Time m	DUBLIN Time m	BELFAST Time m	LONDONDERRY Time m	GALWAY Time m	COBH Time m	Day
0027 1.5	0221 6.1	0233 8.2	0312 11.6	0122 1.1	0111 0.8	0449 2.5	0118 4.4	0134 3.7	**1 SU**
0641 5.1	0850 1.5	0847 2.0	0939 2.0	0803 3.9	0720 3.2	1136 0.7	0730 1.2	0812 0.8	
1300 1.1	1458 6.0	1509 8.3	1547 11.6	1358 0.8	1348 0.5	1742 2.3	1400 4.5	1403 3.7	
1926 5.0	2123 1.5	2120 1.9	2217 2.2	2050 3.8	2005 3.2	2345 0.7	2005 1.2	2042 0.7	
0128 1.3	0325 6.3	0337 8.6	0421 12.1	0223 1.0	0212 0.7	0545 2.6	0218 4.6	0239 3.9	**2 M**
0740 5.3	0951 1.2	0948 1.7	1057 1.8	0902 4.0	0821 3.3	1224 0.6	0825 1.0	0913 0.7	
1357 0.9	1557 6.3	1607 8.8	1651 12.1	1454 0.7	1443 0.4	1830 2.4	1451 4.7	1506 3.9	
2018 5.2	2221 1.2	2215 1.6	2335 1.8	2143 3.9	2058 3.3		2056 1.0	2142 0.6	
0222 1.0	0422 6.5	0433 9.0	0521 12.5	0316 0.9	0306 0.6	0040 0.6	0311 4.8	0336 4.0	**3 TU**
0833 5.4	1045 1.0	1040 1.4	1207 1.5	0956 4.1	0917 3.4	0634 2.6	0913 0.9	1008 0.6	
1446 0.8	1649 6.6	1658 9.1	1748 12.5	1542 0.7	1534 0.4	1307 0.6	1539 4.9	1600 4.0	
2105 5.4	2312 0.9	2306 1.4		2230 4.0	2147 3.4	1913 2.4	2142 0.8	2234 0.5	
0311 0.8	0513 6.7	0523 9.3	0038 1.5	0404 0.8	0355 0.5	0130 0.6	0359 4.9	0426 4.1	**4 W**
0922 5.5	1133 0.8	1127 1.3	0615 12.7	1044 4.1	1009 3.4	0720 2.6	0958 0.8	1057 0.5	
1532 0.7	1736 6.8	1745 9.4	1303 1.3	1626 0.7	1621 0.4	1345 0.5	1622 5.0	1649 4.1	
2148 5.5	2359 0.8	2351 1.3	1836 12.8	2313 4.1	2232 3.5	1953 2.5	2227 0.6	2322 0.5	
0357 0.7	0559 6.8	0609 9.4	0129 1.3	0448 0.7	0441 0.5	0215 0.5	0445 5.0	0512 4.2	**5 TH**
1008 5.5	1217 0.7	1210 1.3	0701 12.9	1128 4.1	1056 3.4	0803 2.6	1041 0.7	1143 0.5	
1615 0.7	1820 6.9	1827 9.4	1350 1.2	1707 0.7	1705 0.5	1421 0.5	1705 5.1	1734 4.1	
2230 5.6			1920 13.0	2352 4.1	2314 3.6	2030 2.5	2310 0.6	●	
0441 0.7	0042 0.7	0033 1.3	0212 1.2	0532 0.7	0524 0.5	0258 0.5	0529 5.0	0006 0.5	**6 F**
1052 5.5	0642 6.8	0653 9.3	0744 13.0	1210 4.1	1141 3.4	0845 2.5	1123 0.8	0554 4.1	
1655 0.8	1258 0.7	1250 1.3	1430 1.2	1747 0.8	1747 0.6	1455 0.5	1748 5.1	1225 0.6	
2312 5.6	1901 6.8	1908 9.4	2000 13.1		2355 3.6	2105 2.6	2353 0.6	1817 4.1	
0523 0.7	0123 0.8	0113 1.4	0249 1.3	0030 4.1	0606 0.5	0339 0.6	0613 4.9	0048 0.6	**7 SA**
1135 5.4	0723 6.7	0733 9.2	0824 12.9	0614 0.6	1223 3.3	0925 2.5	1205 0.9	0634 4.0	
1736 0.9	1336 0.9	1327 1.5	1504 1.3	1251 4.0	1827 0.7	1528 0.5	1830 5.0	1304 0.6	
2351 5.5	1940 6.7	1946 9.2	2039 13.0	1827 0.8		2138 2.6		1857 4.0	
0605 0.8	0201 0.9	0150 1.6	0321 1.5	0108 4.1	0036 3.6	0417 0.7	0036 0.7	0126 0.8	**8 SU**
1216 5.2	0802 6.5	0810 8.9	0903 12.6	0657 0.7	0647 0.5	1005 2.4	0657 4.7	0712 3.9	
1815 1.1	1414 1.0	1402 1.7	1534 1.6	1332 3.9	1305 3.2	1602 0.6	1246 1.1	1341 0.7	
	2017 6.6	2023 9.0	2115 12.6	1909 0.9	1907 0.8	2212 2.5	1912 4.8	1936 3.9	
0031 5.4	0239 1.1	0226 1.8	0349 1.7	0148 4.0	0116 3.6	0454 0.8	0119 0.9	0203 0.9	**9 M**
0646 1.0	0839 6.3	0846 8.7	0939 12.2	0742 0.8	0727 0.6	1045 2.3	0741 4.6	0750 3.8	
1257 5.0	1449 1.3	1437 1.9	1602 1.9	1415 3.7	1347 3.1	1638 0.7	1329 1.3	1416 0.9	
1854 1.3	2054 6.3	2100 8.7	2150 12.1	1952 1.1	1947 0.8	2248 2.5	1954 4.6	2015 3.8	
0109 5.2	0315 1.4	0303 2.0	0416 2.1	0231 3.9	0158 3.5	0533 0.8	0203 1.1	0239 1.0	**10 TU**
0728 1.2	0916 6.0	0923 8.4	1013 11.5	0830 0.9	0809 0.6	1128 2.2	0825 4.4	0828 3.7	
1338 4.8	1524 1.6	1515 2.1	1627 2.3	1501 3.6	1430 3.0	1718 0.7	1412 1.5	1452 1.0	
1934 1.6	2132 6.1	2138 8.4	2223 11.5	2040 1.2	2030 0.9	2327 2.4	2037 4.4	2054 3.7	
0150 5.0	0351 1.7	0342 2.3	0442 2.4	0318 3.8	0242 3.4	0616 0.9	0250 1.4	0317 1.1	**11 W**
0812 1.4	0955 5.7	1002 8.0	1047 10.9	0921 1.0	0854 0.7	1216 2.1	0911 4.2	0909 3.6	
1421 4.6	1603 1.9	1557 2.5	1655 2.6	1552 3.5	1517 2.9	1801 0.8	1500 1.7	1532 1.1	
2019 1.8	2212 5.8	2220 8.0	2258 10.9	2133 1.3	2116 1.0		2123 4.2	2136 3.5	
0234 4.8	0433 2.0	0427 2.6	0514 2.7	0411 3.6	0330 3.3	0011 2.3	0340 1.6	0400 1.2	**12 TH**
0900 1.7	1039 5.4	1047 7.7	1124 10.3	1016 1.1	0944 0.8	0706 1.0	1000 4.0	0954 3.4	
1512 4.5	1648 2.1	1647 2.8	1729 3.0	1649 3.3	1608 2.9	1312 2.0	1553 1.9	1618 1.2	
2110 2.0	2300 5.5	2309 7.7	2340 10.4	2233 1.5	2209 1.1	1850 0.9	2212 4.0	2225 3.4	
0326 4.6	0524 2.2	0521 2.9	0552 3.1	0510 3.4	0421 3.2	0104 2.2	0436 1.7	0451 1.3	**13 F**
0956 1.8	1132 5.2	1140 7.4	1212 9.9	1114 1.2	1037 0.8	0808 1.1	1056 3.9	1046 3.3	
1611 4.4	1743 2.3	1748 3.1	1812 3.4	1751 3.3	1703 2.8	1418 2.0	1655 2.0	1711 1.3	
2211 2.2	2357 5.4			2334 1.5	2307 1.1	1946 1.0	2312 3.8	2320 3.3	
0427 4.5	0625 2.3	0005 7.4	0035 10.0	0613 3.3	0516 3.1	0209 2.2	0539 1.8	0549 1.3	**14 SA**
1058 1.9	1236 5.1	0624 3.0	0642 3.4	1212 1.2	1134 0.9	0919 1.1	1201 3.8	1145 3.3	
1718 4.3	1851 2.4	1242 7.2	1315 9.7	1851 3.3	1800 2.8	1524 2.0	1805 2.0	1811 1.3	
2318 2.2		1855 3.2	1910 3.7			2051 1.0			
0536 4.5	0103 5.3	0109 7.4	0144 9.9	0035 1.5	0009 1.1	0324 2.1	0020 3.8	0021 3.3	**15 SU**
1201 1.8	0734 2.3	0730 3.0	0753 3.6	0714 3.3	0613 3.0	1026 1.0	0642 1.8	0652 1.3	
1824 4.5	1345 5.2	1349 7.3	1428 9.9	1307 1.2	1232 0.9	1625 2.1	1306 3.9	1249 3.3	
	2003 2.3	2000 3.0	2039 3.7	1948 3.3	1857 2.8	2201 1.0	1910 1.9	1915 1.2	

● ● Time UT. For British Summer Time (shaded) March 30th to October 26th ADD ONE HOUR ● ●

JUNE 1997 TIDE TABLES JUNE 1997

	HOLYHEAD	MILFORD HAVEN	SWANSEA	AVONMOUTH	DUBLIN	BELFAST	LONDONDERRY	GALWAY	COBH
	Time m	Time m	Time m	Time m	Time m	Time m	Time m	Time m	Time m
16 M	0024 2.1	0210 5.4	0212 7.5	0255 10.3	0131 1.5	0109 1.1	0430 2.2	0126 3.8	0124 3.4
	0640 4.6	0839 2.1	0831 2.8	0926 3.3	0809 3.3	0709 3.0	1122 0.9	0739 1.6	0754 1.2
	1258 1.7	1448 5.5	1451 7.7	1534 10.5	1357 1.2	1327 0.8	1718 2.2	1401 4.1	1351 3.4
	1919 4.7	2105 2.1	2057 2.7	2203 3.0	2038 3.4	1951 2.9	2306 0.9	2004 1.7	2017 1.1
17 TU	0119 1.8	0309 5.7	0311 7.8	0357 10.9	0221 1.3	0203 1.0	0526 2.2	0220 4.0	0223 3.5
	0736 4.7	0935 1.9	0925 2.5	1034 2.6	0859 3.4	0803 3.0	1210 0.8	0827 1.5	0851 1.0
	1348 1.5	1540 5.8	1545 8.1	1630 11.3	1441 1.1	1418 0.8	1806 2.3	1446 4.3	1448 3.6
	2006 4.9	2158 1.8	2148 2.3	2303 2.3	2122 3.5	2040 3.0		2050 1.5	2113 1.0
18 W	0208 1.6	0400 6.0	0403 8.3	0452 11.6	0303 1.2	0254 0.9	0003 0.8	0306 4.2	0315 3.7
	0823 4.9	1024 1.6	1014 2.1	1132 1.9	0944 3.5	0854 3.1	0615 2.3	0909 1.3	0944 0.8
	1432 1.3	1627 6.2	1632 8.6	1721 12.1	1521 1.0	1506 0.7	1254 0.7	1527 4.5	1539 3.8
	2048 5.1	2246 1.4	2235 1.9		2203 3.6	2125 3.1	1851 2.5	2130 1.2	2205 0.8
19 TH	0252 1.3	0447 6.3	0451 8.7	0000 1.6	0343 1.0	0341 0.7	0055 0.7	0348 4.4	0403 3.8
	0906 5.1	1109 1.3	1100 1.7	0543 12.3	1025 3.6	0942 3.2	0700 2.4	0949 1.1	1032 0.7
	1514 1.1	1712 6.5	1717 9.0	1227 1.4	1600 0.9	1551 0.6	1334 0.6	1606 4.7	1627 3.9
	2127 5.3	2332 1.1	2321 1.5	1810 12.7	2241 3.8	2208 3.2	1934 2.6	2211 0.9	2253 0.7
20 F ○	0334 1.0	0532 6.5	0537 9.0	0054 1.2	0423 0.8	0426 0.6	0143 0.6	0429 4.6	0448 4.0
	0948 5.3	1154 1.0	1144 1.4	0632 12.7	1106 3.8	1027 3.2	0743 2.5	1028 0.9	1118 0.6
	1554 1.0	1755 6.8	1802 9.3	1319 1.1	1640 0.7	1634 0.5	1415 0.5	1645 4.9	1712 4.0
	2207 5.5			1857 13.1	2320 4.0	2249 3.3	2016 2.7	2251 0.7	2339 0.6
21 SA	0416 0.8	0017 0.9	0006 1.2	0145 1.0	0504 0.6	0509 0.5	0230 0.5	0510 4.8	0532 4.0
	1030 5.4	0617 6.7	0623 9.2	0718 13.1	1149 3.9	1112 3.3	0827 2.6	1109 0.8	1203 0.5
	1636 0.7	1237 0.8	1227 1.2	1409 1.0	1722 0.6	1718 0.5	1454 0.4	1727 5.1	1756 4.1
	2248 5.7	1839 7.0	1846 9.5	1942 13.4		2331 3.4	2057 2.8	2333 0.5	
22 SU	0459 0.6	0101 0.7	0051 1.0	0234 0.8	0001 4.1	0553 0.3	0315 0.4	0554 4.9	0024 0.6
	1113 5.5	0701 6.9	0709 9.4	0804 13.5	0547 0.5	1158 3.3	0910 2.6	1151 0.7	0615 4.1
	1718 0.7	1321 0.8	1310 1.0	1456 0.9	1233 4.0	1802 0.4	1534 0.4	1810 5.2	1248 0.5
	2332 5.7	1924 7.1	1931 9.6	2027 13.5	1806 0.5		2139 2.8		1839 4.1
23 M	0544 0.5	0146 0.6	0135 0.9	0320 0.8	0045 4.2	0014 3.5	0401 0.4	0015 0.4	0109 0.5
	1159 5.5	0746 6.9	0754 9.4	0849 13.5	0633 0.4	0638 0.3	0954 2.6	0639 5.0	0658 4.1
	1803 0.7	1405 0.8	1353 1.0	1539 1.0	1320 4.0	1245 3.3	1616 0.4	1234 0.7	1332 0.5
		2009 7.0	2016 9.5	2111 13.5	1851 0.6	1848 0.4	2221 2.8	1856 5.2	1924 4.1
24 TU	0018 5.7	0232 0.7	0219 0.9	0403 0.8	0131 4.2	0100 3.5	0448 0.5	0101 0.5	0154 0.6
	0631 0.5	0833 6.8	0839 9.2	0934 13.2	0722 0.3	0725 0.2	1042 2.5	0726 4.9	0742 4.0
	1248 5.4	1451 0.9	1436 1.1	1618 1.1	1410 3.9	1334 3.3	1700 0.5	1321 0.8	1417 0.5
	1851 0.8	2055 6.9	2102 9.3	2157 13.2	1941 0.6	1936 0.5	2307 2.8	1944 5.1	2010 4.1
25 W	0106 5.7	0318 0.8	0305 1.1	0442 1.0	0221 4.2	0148 3.5	0537 0.6	0149 0.6	0240 0.6
	0721 0.6	0921 6.6	0924 9.0	1019 12.8	0815 0.4	0815 0.2	1133 2.4	0815 4.8	0829 4.0
	1339 5.2	1538 1.1	1521 1.4	1655 1.4	1504 3.9	1427 3.2	1747 0.6	1411 1.0	1505 0.6
	1942 1.0	2145 6.7	2151 9.0	2243 12.8	2034 0.6	2028 0.6	2357 2.7	2034 4.9	2059 4.0
26 TH	0158 5.5	0408 1.0	0353 1.4	0521 1.3	0315 4.1	0241 3.4	0630 0.7	0241 0.8	0330 0.7
	0816 0.8	1011 6.3	1014 8.6	1107 12.3	0912 0.5	0910 0.3	1229 2.2	0908 4.6	0919 3.8
	1435 5.1	1629 1.3	1613 1.8	1735 1.7	1603 3.8	1524 3.1	1839 0.7	1506 1.2	1557 0.7
	2038 1.2	2238 6.5	2244 8.6	2333 12.3	2133 1.0	2126 0.7		2129 4.7	2152 3.9
27 F	0254 5.3	0502 1.3	0448 1.7	0603 1.6	0415 4.0	0339 3.4	0052 2.6	0337 1.0	0425 0.8
	0915 1.0	1107 6.1	1110 8.2	1159 11.8	1015 0.7	1011 0.4	0728 0.8	1006 4.4	1015 3.7
	1536 4.9	1727 1.6	1715 2.2	1821 2.0	1709 3.7	1627 3.1	1336 2.1	1608 1.4	1654 0.8
	2142 1.4	2337 6.2	2344 8.3		2238 1.1	2230 0.8	1939 0.8	2230 4.5	2251 3.8
28 SA	0357 5.2	0603 1.5	0554 2.1	0030 11.8	0521 3.9	0443 3.3	0157 2.5	0440 1.2	0527 0.9
	1021 1.2	1210 5.8	1215 7.9	0654 2.0	1121 0.8	1116 0.5	0836 0.9	1112 4.3	1117 3.6
	1645 4.8	1833 1.8	1830 2.4	1257 11.3	1816 3.6	1734 3.0	1457 2.1	1721 1.6	1758 0.9
	2251 1.5			1916 2.4	2346 1.2	2339 0.8	2050 0.9	2339 4.3	2356 3.7
29 SU	0506 5.0	0042 6.0	0052 8.0	0133 11.4	0630 3.8	0551 3.2	0312 2.4	0551 1.4	0634 1.0
	1129 1.3	0711 1.7	0707 2.3	0754 2.3	1227 0.9	1223 0.5	0953 0.9	1224 4.3	1225 3.6
	1757 4.8	1319 5.8	1328 7.8	1404 11.1	1922 3.6	1840 3.1	1615 2.1	1836 1.5	1908 0.9
		1946 1.8	1946 2.5	2024 2.6			2209 0.9		
30 M	0002 1.5	0152 5.9	0204 8.0	0242 11.3	0054 1.2	0048 0.8	0424 2.4	0052 4.3	0106 3.6
	0617 5.0	0821 1.7	0819 2.3	0905 2.4	0738 3.8	0700 3.2	1102 0.9	0702 1.4	0745 0.9
	1236 1.3	1430 5.8	1441 8.0	1515 11.1	1332 1.0	1327 0.5	1719 2.2	1333 4.3	1337 3.6
	1904 4.9	2058 1.7	2055 2.3	2142 2.6	2025 3.7	1942 3.1	2323 0.9	1944 1.4	2018 0.8

● ● Time UT. For British Summer Time (shaded) March 30th to October 26th ADD ONE HOUR ● ● ●

WEST COAST ENGLAND, WALES & IRELAND Time Zone UT

Holyhead * Milford Haven * Swansea * Avonmouth * Dublin * Belfast * Londonderry * Galway * Cobh

JULY 1997 TIDE TABLES JULY 1997

HOLYHEAD	MILFORD HAVEN	SWANSEA	AVONMOUTH	DUBLIN	BELFAST	LONDONDERRY	GALWAY	COBH	
Time m	Time m	Time m	Time m	Time m	Time m	Time m	Time m	Time m	
0109 1.5	0301 6.0	0312 8.2	0355 11.5	0201 1.2	0152 0.8	0526 2.4	0158 4.3	0215 3.7	**1 TU**
0723 5.0	0928 1.6	0924 2.1	1021 2.3	0842 3.8	0803 3.2	1157 0.8	0803 1.3	0851 0.9	
1338 1.3	1536 6.0	1545 8.4	1624 11.5	1432 1.0	1425 0.6	1812 2.3	1431 4.5	1445 3.7	
2003 5.0	2202 1.5	2155 2.0	2303 2.4	2123 3.8	2037 3.3		2040 1.2	2121 0.8	
0209 1.3	0403 6.2	0412 8.5	0458 11.8	0300 1.1	0249 0.7	0024 0.8	0254 4.5	0317 3.8	**2 W**
0821 5.1	1026 1.4	1021 1.9	1136 2.1	0940 3.9	0902 3.3	0619 2.4	0856 1.2	0949 0.8	
1432 1.2	1632 6.3	1639 8.7	1726 11.9	1524 0.9	1518 0.6	1243 0.7	1521 4.7	1543 3.8	
2052 5.2	2257 1.3	2248 1.8		2214 4.0	2127 3.4	1857 2.4	2130 1.0	2216 0.7	
0301 1.1	0457 6.3	0506 8.8	0010 2.0	0353 1.0	0341 0.6	0117 0.7	0345 4.6	0409 3.9	**3 TH**
0912 5.2	1115 1.2	1109 1.7	0556 12.1	1031 3.9	0954 3.3	0706 2.5	0942 1.1	1039 0.7	
1519 1.1	1721 6.5	1727 9.0	1236 1.8	1610 0.9	1606 0.6	1324 0.7	1606 4.8	1633 3.9	
2136 5.4	2344 1.1	2336 1.7	1818 12.3	2259 4.0	2212 3.5	1938 2.5	2215 0.8	2305 0.7	
0347 1.0	0544 6.5	0553 8.9	0105 1.8	0439 0.9	0427 0.6	0203 0.7	0431 4.7	0455 3.9	**4 F**
0957 5.2	1200 1.1	1154 1.6	0645 12.4	1117 3.9	1042 3.3	0750 2.5	1026 1.0	1125 0.6	
1600 1.0	1805 6.6	1811 9.1	1327 1.6	1652 0.9	1649 0.6	1400 0.6	1649 4.9	1718 4.0	
2217 5.5			1904 12.7	2339 4.1	2255 3.5	2015 2.5	2257 0.7	2348 0.7	●
0429 0.9	0027 1.0	0019 1.6	0151 1.6	0521 0.8	0510 0.5	0244 0.7	0515 4.7	0536 4.0	**5 SA**
1039 5.3	0627 6.5	0636 9.0	0729 12.6	1157 3.9	1125 3.3	0830 2.5	1108 1.0	1206 0.7	
1639 1.0	1239 1.0	1233 1.6	1409 1.5	1732 0.9	1730 0.7	1434 0.6	1730 4.9	1800 4.0	
2255 5.5	1845 6.7	1851 9.1	1945 12.8		2335 3.6	2048 2.6	2339 0.7		
0509 0.9	0106 1.0	0058 1.6	0230 1.6	0015 4.1	0549 0.5	0321 0.7	0557 4.7	0028 0.7	**6 SU**
1118 5.2	0705 6.5	0715 8.9	0809 12.6	0603 0.7	1204 3.2	0908 2.4	1148 1.0	0615 3.9	
1716 1.0	1317 1.0	1309 1.6	1446 1.5	1234 3.9	1807 0.7	1506 0.6	1812 4.9	1245 0.7	
2332 5.5	1921 6.7	1929 9.1	2022 12.8	1811 0.9		2119 2.6		1839 3.9	
0546 0.9	0142 1.0	0134 1.6	0305 1.6	0051 4.1	0013 3.6	0356 0.7	0019 0.7	0105 0.8	**7 M**
1154 5.2	0742 6.5	0751 8.9	0845 12.6	0642 0.7	0627 0.5	0943 2.4	0638 4.7	0651 3.9	
1752 1.1	1352 1.1	1344 1.6	1519 1.6	1310 3.8	1241 3.2	1538 0.6	1227 1.0	1319 0.7	
	1957 6.6	2004 9.0	2057 12.7	1849 0.9	1842 0.7	2150 2.6	1851 4.8	1915 3.9	
0008 5.4	0216 1.1	0208 1.7	0336 1.7	0127 4.1	0051 3.6	0429 0.8	0059 0.8	0139 0.9	**8 TU**
0622 1.0	0816 6.4	0825 8.7	0919 12.3	0722 0.7	0703 0.6	1018 2.4	0718 4.6	0726 3.8	
1230 5.1	1426 1.2	1418 1.7	1548 1.8	1348 3.7	1317 3.1	1611 0.6	1306 1.1	1352 0.8	
1827 1.2	2030 6.5	2039 8.8	2129 12.4	1928 0.9	1918 0.8	2221 2.6	1930 4.7	1950 3.8	
0043 5.3	0249 1.3	0242 1.8	0403 1.9	0204 4.0	0128 3.5	0502 0.8	0138 1.0	0212 0.9	**9 W**
0659 1.1	0850 6.2	0859 8.5	0951 12.0	0803 0.8	0739 0.6	1054 2.3	0759 4.4	0801 3.8	
1307 5.0	1458 1.4	1451 1.9	1613 2.0	1427 3.7	1354 3.1	1647 0.7	1345 1.3	1424 0.9	
1903 1.4	2104 6.3	2112 8.6	2200 12.0	2009 1.0	1954 0.8	2255 2.5	2009 4.5	2025 3.8	
0118 5.2	0322 1.5	0315 2.0	0427 2.1	0245 3.8	0207 3.5	0538 0.9	0218 1.1	0246 1.0	**10 TH**
0736 1.3	0924 6.0	0933 8.3	1021 11.5	0845 0.9	0818 0.6	1134 2.2	0839 4.3	0838 3.7	
1345 4.8	1533 1.6	1527 2.1	1639 2.2	1509 3.5	1433 3.0	1726 0.7	1426 1.5	1500 0.9	
1942 1.6	2139 6.1	2148 8.3	2232 11.5	2052 1.2	2035 0.9	2332 2.4	2048 4.3	2102 3.7	
0157 5.0	0357 1.7	0351 2.2	0454 2.3	0329 3.7	0248 3.4	0619 1.0	0259 1.3	0324 1.1	**11 F**
0817 1.5	1001 5.8	1010 8.0	1053 11.0	0930 1.0	0900 0.7	1218 2.1	0920 4.1	0918 3.6	
1427 4.7	1610 1.9	1606 2.4	1708 2.6	1556 3.4	1515 3.0	1809 0.8	1509 1.7	1539 1.0	
2025 1.8	2218 5.8	2227 8.0	2306 11.0	2139 1.3	2120 1.0		2130 4.1	2143 3.6	
0239 4.8	0438 2.0	0433 2.5	0526 2.7	0418 3.5	0333 3.3	0013 2.3	0344 1.5	0408 1.2	**12 SA**
0903 1.7	1042 5.5	1052 7.7	1129 10.5	1019 1.2	0945 0.8	0708 1.0	1006 4.0	1003 3.5	
1515 4.5	1654 2.1	1654 2.8	1742 2.9	1648 3.3	1603 2.9	1312 2.1	1600 1.8	1626 1.1	
2115 2.0	2303 5.6	2313 7.7	2345 10.5	2233 1.4	2210 1.1	1858 0.9	2216 3.9	2230 3.4	
0330 4.6	0525 2.2	0523 2.8	0603 3.1	0512 3.4	0424 3.2	0102 2.2	0436 1.7	0459 1.3	**13 SU**
0957 1.8	1133 5.3	1144 7.4	1213 10.0	1113 1.3	1036 0.9	0806 1.1	1059 3.9	1054 3.4	
1614 4.4	1749 2.3	1752 3.0	1824 3.4	1746 3.3	1657 2.9	1415 2.0	1659 2.0	1720 1.2	
2215 2.1	2359 5.4			2333 1.5	2309 1.1	1954 1.0	2314 3.8	2325 3.4	
0433 4.5	0625 2.4	0008 7.5	0037 10.1	0613 3.3	0519 3.1	0205 2.2	0538 1.8	0558 1.3	**14 M**
1100 1.9	1238 5.2	0625 3.0	0651 3.4	1210 1.3	1133 0.9	0917 1.1	1202 3.8	1154 3.3	
1722 4.4	1857 2.4	1248 7.3	1315 9.8	1848 3.3	1757 2.9	1527 2.0	1809 2.0	1823 1.2	
2325 2.1		1900 3.1	1921 3.7			2101 1.0			
0545 4.5	0106 5.3	0113 7.4	0148 10.0	0034 1.5	0013 1.1	0327 2.1	0024 3.7	0029 3.3	**15 TU**
1206 1.9	0737 2.4	0735 3.0	0803 3.6	0718 3.3	0619 3.0	1030 1.0	0645 1.8	0704 1.2	
1830 4.6	1350 5.3	1357 7.5	1436 10.1	1306 1.3	1235 0.9	1635 2.1	1308 3.9	1300 3.3	
	2013 2.3	2009 2.9	2058 3.6	1949 3.3	1858 2.9	2217 1.0	1917 1.8	1931 1.2	

● ● Time UT. For British Summer Time (shaded) March 30th to October 26th ADD ONE HOUR ● ●

JULY 1997 TIDE TABLES JULY 1997

	HOLYHEAD	MILFORD HAVEN	SWANSEA	AVONMOUTH	DUBLIN	BELFAST	LONDONDERRY	GALWAY	COBH
	Time m	Time m	Time m	Time m	Time m	Time m	Time m	Time m	Time m
16 W	0034 2.0	0218 5.4	0221 7.6	0307 10.5	0133 1.4	0118 1.1	0445 2.2	0133 3.8	0136 3.4
	0654 4.6	0849 2.2	0842 2.7	0943 3.2	0818 3.3	0721 3.0	1131 0.9	0745 1.6	0812 1.1
	1308 1.7	1457 5.6	1502 7.8	1548 10.8	1400 1.2	1336 0.9	1733 2.3	1405 4.1	1409 3.5
	1929 4.8	2121 2.0	2110 2.5	2223 2.8	2043 3.5	1957 3.0	2328 0.9	2015 1.6	2038 1.0
17 TH	0134 1.7	0323 5.7	0325 8.0	0415 11.2	0227 1.3	0219 1.0	0547 2.3	0231 4.0	0241 3.5
	0753 4.8	0951 1.8	0941 2.3	1054 2.3	0912 3.5	0820 3.1	1223 0.8	0839 1.4	0912 0.9
	1402 1.4	1556 6.0	1600 8.4	1649 11.8	1450 1.1	1433 0.8	1825 2.4	1454 4.4	1509 3.6
	2020 5.0	2218 1.6	2206 2.0	2327 1.9	2133 3.6	2052 3.1		2105 1.2	2137 0.8
18 F	0227 1.4	0420 6.1	0423 8.5	0515 12.0	0315 1.0	0314 0.8	0030 0.7	0321 4.3	0336 3.7
	0843 5.0	1045 1.4	1034 1.8	1157 1.7	1002 3.6	0915 3.2	0639 2.4	0925 1.2	1006 0.7
	1450 1.2	1648 6.4	1652 8.9	1746 12.6	1536 0.9	1526 0.7	1309 0.6	1540 4.7	1603 3.8
	2105 5.3	2310 1.2	2258 1.5		2218 3.8	2142 3.3	1912 2.6	2151 0.9	2230 0.7
19 SA	0314 1.0	0512 6.5	0516 8.9	0028 1.4	0402 0.8	0404 0.6	0124 0.6	0409 4.6	0427 3.9
	0930 5.3	1134 1.1	1124 1.3	0612 12.7	1049 3.8	1007 3.3	0727 2.5	1010 0.9	1057 0.6
	1535 0.9	1736 6.8	1742 9.4	1257 1.2	1621 0.7	1615 0.6	1353 0.5	1625 4.9	1652 4.0
	2148 5.6		2348 1.1	1839 13.2	2302 4.0	2229 3.4	1957 2.8	2235 0.6	2319 0.5
20 SU ○	0400 0.7	0000 0.8	0606 9.3	0128 1.0	0448 0.5	0452 0.4	0214 0.5	0454 4.8	0513 4.0
	1014 5.5	0600 6.8	1212 0.9	0704 13.2	1134 4.0	1056 3.3	0813 2.6	1053 0.6	1145 0.4
	1618 0.7	1221 0.8	1830 9.7	1355 0.9	1706 0.6	1702 0.5	1436 0.4	1709 5.2	1739 4.2
	2231 5.8	1824 7.1		1928 13.7	2345 4.2	2315 3.5	2040 2.9	2318 0.3	
21 M	0444 0.4	0048 0.6	0036 0.7	0224 0.7	0533 0.3	0538 0.3	0302 0.4	0539 5.0	0007 0.4
	1059 5.6	0648 7.0	0654 9.6	0753 13.5	1219 4.1	1144 3.4	0857 2.7	1136 0.5	0558 4.1
	1703 0.5	1308 0.6	1257 0.7	1448 0.7	1750 0.5	1748 0.4	1518 0.3	1754 5.3	1231 0.3
	2316 5.9	1910 7.3	1918 9.9	2015 13.9			2123 3.0		1824 4.2
22 TU	0530 0.3	0134 0.4	0123 0.5	0313 0.5	0029 4.4	0000 3.6	0348 0.4	0002 0.2	0053 0.4
	1145 5.7	0734 7.1	0741 9.7	0839 13.7	0619 0.2	0624 0.1	0942 2.7	0624 5.1	0643 4.2
	1748 0.5	1354 0.5	1342 0.6	1534 0.6	1306 4.1	1231 3.4	1601 0.3	1220 0.4	1317 0.3
		1957 7.4	2004 9.9	2100 14.0	1835 0.4	1834 0.4	2206 3.0	1841 5.4	1909 4.3
23 W	0002 6.0	0221 0.4	0208 0.5	0358 0.4	0115 4.4	0045 3.6	0434 0.4	0046 0.2	0139 0.4
	0616 0.3	0820 7.1	0826 9.6	0924 13.7	0706 0.2	0710 0.1	1027 2.6	0710 5.1	0727 4.2
	1232 5.7	1439 0.6	1424 0.7	1615 0.7	1353 4.1	1319 3.3	1645 0.4	1305 0.5	1403 0.3
	1834 0.6	2042 7.3	2049 9.8	2145 13.9	1922 0.5	1921 0.4	2250 3.0	1928 5.3	1955 4.3
24 TH	0050 5.9	0306 0.5	0251 0.7	0437 0.5	0203 4.4	0133 3.6	0521 0.5	0132 0.3	0225 0.4
	0705 0.4	0906 6.9	0910 9.4	1007 13.4	0756 0.3	0759 0.1	1113 2.5	0757 5.0	0813 4.1
	1321 5.5	1524 0.8	1508 1.0	1651 0.9	1444 4.0	1409 3.3	1731 0.5	1353 0.7	1449 0.4
	1923 0.8	2130 7.1	2136 9.4	2230 13.4	2012 0.6	2011 0.5	2337 2.8	2017 5.1	2042 4.2
25 F	0139 5.8	0352 0.8	0336 1.0	0512 0.9	0254 4.3	0224 3.5	0609 0.6	0220 0.6	0313 0.5
	0755 0.6	0954 6.6	0956 9.0	1051 12.9	0848 0.5	0851 0.2	1203 2.3	0847 4.8	0901 4.0
	1412 5.2	1612 1.1	1554 1.4	1725 1.3	1538 3.9	1503 3.2	1821 0.6	1443 1.0	1538 0.5
	2016 1.0	2218 6.7	2224 9.0	2315 12.8	2106 0.8	2105 0.6		2108 4.8	2132 4.0
26 SA	0233 5.5	0441 1.1	0424 1.5	0548 1.4	0351 4.1	0321 3.4	0029 2.7	0312 0.9	0403 0.7
	0851 0.9	1045 6.3	1045 8.5	1136 12.1	0945 0.7	0947 0.4	0702 0.8	0940 4.5	0953 3.9
	1509 5.0	1703 1.4	1648 2.0	1802 1.9	1639 3.8	1602 3.1	1301 2.2	1541 1.3	1631 0.7
	2115 1.3	2312 6.3	2318 8.5		2207 1.1	2205 0.7	1918 0.8	2205 4.5	2226 3.8
27 SU	0332 5.2	0535 1.5	0522 2.1	0005 12.0	0454 4.0	0422 3.3	0130 2.5	0410 1.3	0500 0.9
	0952 1.2	1141 5.9	1145 8.0	0627 2.0	1048 0.9	1050 0.5	0802 0.9	1042 4.3	1050 3.7
	1615 4.8	1804 1.8	1756 2.5	1227 11.4	1744 3.7	1706 3.0	1416 2.1	1649 1.5	1730 0.9
	2224 1.6			1846 2.5	2315 1.2	2312 0.8	2026 0.9	2312 4.2	2327 3.6
28 M	0441 4.9	0013 5.9	0021 8.0	0102 11.2	0604 3.8	0531 3.2	0246 2.3	0520 1.5	0604 1.0
	1102 1.5	0639 1.9	0633 2.5	0718 2.6	1155 1.1	1159 0.6	0913 1.0	1154 4.1	1156 3.5
	1729 4.7	1248 5.6	1255 7.7	1329 10.8	1852 3.6	1813 3.0	1549 2.0	1811 1.6	1840 1.0
	2339 1.7	1918 2.0	1915 2.7	1945 3.0			2151 1.0		
29 TU	0557 4.8	0123 5.7	0133 7.8	0209 10.8	0027 1.1	0025 0.8	0409 2.3	0029 4.1	0037 3.5
	1215 1.6	0754 2.0	0751 2.7	0827 3.0	0715 3.7	0642 3.1	1030 1.0	0638 1.6	0717 1.1
	1844 4.7	1403 5.6	1412 7.7	1442 10.6	1305 1.2	1307 0.7	1703 2.1	1311 4.1	1311 3.5
		2037 2.1	2031 2.7	2109 3.3	2000 3.7	1916 3.1	2313 1.0	1929 1.6	1955 1.0
30 W	0054 1.7	0239 5.6	0248 7.8	0325 10.8	0142 1.3	0134 0.8	0517 2.3	0143 4.1	0153 3.5
	0712 4.8	0907 2.0	0903 2.6	0951 3.0	0824 3.7	0748 3.1	1134 0.9	0748 1.6	0829 1.0
	1323 1.6	1518 5.7	1523 8.0	1600 10.9	1412 1.2	1409 0.7	1759 2.2	1416 4.3	1426 3.5
	1950 4.9	2148 1.9	2138 2.5	2235 2.9	2103 3.8	2015 3.2		2031 1.4	2103 0.9
31 TH	0200 1.5	0348 5.8	0355 8.1	0439 11.2	0248 1.2	0235 0.7	0018 0.9	0244 4.2	0259 3.6
	0815 4.9	1010 1.7	1003 2.4	1108 2.5	0927 3.7	0848 3.1	0611 2.3	0845 1.5	0931 0.9
	1421 1.5	1618 6.0	1622 8.3	1708 11.5	1509 1.2	1503 0.7	1224 0.8	1509 4.4	1528 3.6
	2042 5.1	2245 1.6	2234 2.2	2345 2.4	2157 3.9	2106 3.3	1844 2.4	2121 1.2	2200 0.8

● ● Time UT. For British Summer Time (shaded) March 30th to October 26th ADD ONE HOUR ● ●

WEST COAST ENGLAND, WALES & IRELAND Time Zone UT
Holyhead * Milford Haven * Swansea * Avonmouth * Dublin * Belfast * Londonderry * Galway * Cobh

AUGUST 1997 TIDE TABLES AUGUST 1997

HOLYHEAD Time m	MILFORD HAVEN Time m	SWANSEA Time m	AVONMOUTH Time m	DUBLIN Time m	BELFAST Time m	LONDONDERRY Time m	GALWAY Time m	COBH Time m	
0253 1.3	0444 6.1	0451 8.4	0540 11.7	0342 1.1	0327 0.7	0109 0.8	0335 4.4	0353 3.7	1 F
0906 5.0	1101 1.5	1054 2.1	1212 2.0	1021 3.7	0941 3.2	0657 2.4	0932 1.3	1023 0.8	
1508 1.4	1707 6.3	1712 8.7	1803 12.1	1556 1.1	1551 0.7	1306 0.7	1554 4.6	1619 3.8	
2126 5.3	2331 1.3	2322 2.0		2245 4.0	2153 3.4	1924 2.5	2205 1.0	2248 0.8	
0337 1.1	0530 6.3	0538 8.7	0042 1.9	0428 0.9	0413 0.6	0153 0.7	0419 4.5	0439 3.8	2 SA
0948 5.1	1144 1.3	1138 1.8	0630 12.2	1106 3.8	1027 3.2	0739 2.4	1014 1.1	1108 0.7	
1548 1.2	1749 6.5	1755 8.9	1304 1.7	1638 1.0	1633 0.7	1344 0.7	1635 4.7	1703 3.8	
2203 5.4			1848 12.5	2324 4.1	2236 3.5	1959 2.6	2245 0.8	2330 0.7	
0415 1.0	0011 1.2	0004 1.8	0130 1.7	0509 0.8	0454 0.5	0230 0.7	0500 4.6	0518 3.9	3 SU
1024 5.2	0609 6.5	0619 8.8	0713 12.5	1143 3.8	1107 3.2	0815 2.5	1052 1.0	1147 0.7	
1623 1.1	1221 1.1	1216 1.7	1348 1.5	1716 0.9	1711 0.7	1417 0.6	1714 4.8	1742 3.9	
2237 5.5	1827 6.6	1834 9.1	1928 12.7	2359 4.1	2314 3.5	2031 2.6	2322 0.7		●
0451 0.9	0047 1.0	0041 1.6	0211 1.6	0547 0.8	0530 0.5	0304 0.7	0539 4.7	0007 0.8	4 M
1057 5.2	0646 6.5	0656 8.9	0751 12.6	1216 3.8	1142 3.2	0849 2.5	1130 0.9	0554 3.9	
1656 1.1	1256 1.0	1251 1.6	1427 1.5	1753 0.9	1745 0.7	1448 0.6	1752 4.9	1223 0.7	
2310 5.5	1901 6.7	1909 9.1	2003 12.8		2350 3.6	2100 2.7	2359 0.6	1817 3.9	
0524 0.9	0120 1.0	0115 1.6	0247 1.6	0030 4.1	0603 0.5	0334 0.7	0617 4.7	0041 0.8	5 TU
1130 5.2	0719 6.6	0730 9.0	0825 12.7	0623 0.7	1215 3.2	0920 2.5	1206 0.9	0628 3.9	
1727 1.1	1329 1.0	1323 1.5	1500 1.5	1246 3.8	1816 0.7	1517 0.6	1829 4.8	1255 0.7	
2342 5.5	1934 6.7	1942 9.1	2036 12.8	1827 0.8		2127 2.7		1851 3.9	
0556 1.0	0151 1.0	0146 1.5	0318 1.6	0102 4.1	0024 3.6	0403 0.7	0034 0.7	0113 0.8	6 W
1203 5.2	0751 6.5	0801 8.9	0856 12.6	0657 0.7	0634 0.5	0951 2.5	0653 4.6	0701 3.9	
1800 1.1	1400 1.1	1354 1.5	1530 1.5	1318 3.8	1245 3.2	1546 0.6	1241 0.9	1326 0.7	
	2005 6.6	2014 9.0	2106 12.7	1901 0.9	1848 0.7	2154 2.6	1904 4.7	1922 3.9	
0015 5.4	0222 1.1	0215 1.6	0345 1.6	0135 4.0	0057 3.5	0431 0.8	0109 0.8	0144 0.8	7 TH
0628 1.1	0822 6.4	0832 8.8	0924 12.5	0731 0.8	0706 0.5	1021 2.4	0729 4.6	0733 3.9	
1235 5.1	1431 1.2	1424 1.6	1556 1.6	1351 3.7	1317 3.2	1619 0.6	1316 1.1	1357 0.8	
1833 1.2	2036 6.5	2044 8.9	2135 12.5	1935 0.9	1921 0.7	2223 2.6	1939 4.6	1954 3.8	
0047 5.3	0252 1.3	0245 1.7	0409 1.8	0211 3.9	0132 3.5	0503 0.8	0143 1.0	0215 0.9	8 F
0701 1.2	0853 6.3	0902 8.6	0953 12.1	0806 0.9	0741 0.6	1056 2.4	0805 4.4	0807 3.8	
1309 5.0	1503 1.4	1455 1.8	1620 1.9	1430 3.7	1351 3.2	1655 0.7	1351 1.2	1428 0.8	
1908 1.4	2106 6.3	2115 8.6	2204 12.1	2010 1.0	1957 0.8	2255 2.5	2014 4.4	2028 3.8	
0121 5.1	0324 1.5	0315 2.0	0434 2.0	0250 3.7	0209 3.5	0539 0.9	0218 1.2	0249 1.0	9 SA
0737 1.4	0925 6.1	0933 8.4	1022 11.6	0842 1.0	0818 0.6	1135 2.3	0841 4.3	0843 3.7	
1346 4.9	1536 1.6	1527 2.1	1646 2.2	1512 3.6	1430 3.2	1735 0.7	1429 1.4	1504 0.9	
1945 1.6	2140 6.1	2148 8.3	2235 11.5	2049 1.2	2038 0.9	2332 2.4	2050 4.2	2104 3.7	
0159 5.0	0357 1.8	0348 2.3	0500 2.4	0334 3.6	0251 3.4	0621 1.0	0257 1.4	0328 1.1	10 SU
0817 1.6	1000 5.8	1008 8.0	1053 10.9	0924 1.1	0901 0.7	1221 2.2	0921 4.1	0924 3.6	
1428 4.7	1613 1.9	1606 2.5	1714 2.7	1559 3.5	1513 3.1	1821 0.8	1512 1.7	1545 1.1	
2030 1.8	2218 5.8	2227 8.0	2307 10.9	2135 1.3	2124 1.0		2131 4.0	2147 3.5	
0243 4.8	0437 2.1	0427 2.6	0530 2.8	0424 3.4	0339 3.3	0015 2.3	0341 1.6	0415 1.2	11 M
0904 1.8	1043 5.5	1052 7.7	1127 10.4	1014 1.3	0948 0.8	0712 1.1	1007 3.9	1010 3.5	
1519 4.6	1659 2.2	1654 2.8	1748 3.1	1651 3.3	1603 3.1	1316 2.1	1603 1.9	1636 1.2	
2124 2.0	2306 5.5	2315 7.7	2347 10.4	2232 1.5	2218 1.1	1913 0.9	2223 3.8	2237 3.4	
0339 4.6	0528 2.4	0523 3.0	0608 3.3	0522 3.3	0433 3.2	0109 2.2	0439 1.8	0511 1.3	12 TU
1005 1.9	1140 5.3	1152 7.4	1215 10.0	1116 1.4	1044 0.9	0815 1.1	1106 3.8	1107 3.3	
1625 4.5	1802 2.5	1803 3.1	1833 3.5	1753 3.3	1703 3.0	1430 2.0	1712 2.0	1737 1.3	
2234 2.1				2342 1.5	2324 1.2	2017 1.0	2331 3.7	2339 3.3	
0455 4.4	0010 5.3	0021 7.4	0047 10.0	0632 3.3	0536 3.1	0231 2.1	0553 1.9	0618 1.3	13 W
1119 2.0	0639 2.5	0639 3.2	0703 3.6	1223 1.4	1148 1.0	0935 1.1	1218 3.8	1215 3.3	
1744 4.5	1257 5.2	1308 7.4	1336 9.9	1902 3.3	1809 3.0	1555 2.1	1833 1.9	1851 1.2	
2354 2.0	1925 2.5	1924 3.1	1949 3.8			2136 1.0			
0618 4.5	0132 5.3	0139 7.4	0218 10.1	0053 1.4	0038 1.1	0416 2.1	0052 3.7	0054 3.3	14 TH
1233 1.9	0807 2.4	0803 3.0	0847 3.7	0744 3.3	0644 3.1	1055 1.0	0710 1.8	0735 1.2	
1856 4.7	1420 5.4	1426 7.7	1509 10.4	1327 1.3	1258 1.0	1706 2.3	1329 4.0	1332 3.4	
	2049 2.2	2039 2.7	2145 3.2	2008 3.4	1918 3.1	2303 0.9	1945 1.6	2008 1.1	
0105 1.8	0252 5.6	0255 7.8	0342 10.8	0157 1.3	0148 1.0	0530 2.3	0204 4.0	0209 3.4	15 F
0728 4.7	0924 2.0	0914 2.5	1021 2.8	0847 3.5	0751 3.1	1157 0.8	0815 1.5	0845 1.0	
1336 1.6	1530 5.9	1533 8.2	1622 11.5	1424 1.1	1405 0.9	1803 2.5	1428 4.3	1443 3.6	
1954 5.0	2156 1.7	2142 2.1	2259 2.2	2106 3.7	2021 3.2		2044 1.2	2113 0.9	

AUGUST 1997 TIDE TABLES AUGUST 1997

	HOLYHEAD		MILFORD HAVEN		SWANSEA		AVONMOUTH		DUBLIN		BELFAST		LONDONDERRY		GALWAY		COBH	
	Time	m	Time	m	Time	m	Time	m	Time	m	Time	m	Time	m	Time	m	Time	m
16 SA	0205	1.4	0359	6.0	0401	8.4	0453	11.8	0253	1.0	0249	0.8	0013	0.8	0302	4.3	0313	3.7
	0824	5.0	1024	1.5	1013	1.8	1131	1.9	0942	3.7	0852	3.2	0626	2.4	0907	1.2	0944	0.8
	1430	1.2	1627	6.4	1631	8.9	1725	12.6	1516	0.9	1503	0.8	1247	0.7	1520	4.7	1542	3.8
	2044	5.4	2252	1.2	2239	1.4			2156	3.9	2117	3.3	1851	2.7	2133	0.8	2209	0.6
17 SU	0255	0.9	0454	6.5	0458	9.0	0007	1.5	0344	0.7	0342	0.6	0109	0.6	0351	4.6	0406	3.9
	0912	5.3	1116	1.0	1106	1.2	0554	12.8	1032	3.9	0948	3.3	0713	2.6	0953	0.8	1037	0.5
	1516	0.9	1719	6.9	1724	9.5	1239	1.3	1603	0.7	1556	0.6	1333	0.5	1607	5.0	1633	4.1
	2129	5.7	2343	0.7	2331	0.9	1821	13.4	2242	4.1	2208	3.5	1936	2.9	2218	0.4	2300	0.4
18 M ○	0342	0.6	0545	7.0	0549	9.5	0113	0.9	0430	0.4	0432	0.4	0200	0.4	0437	4.9	0454	4.1
	0957	5.6	1206	0.6	1155	0.7	0648	13.4	1118	4.1	1039	3.4	0758	2.7	1036	0.5	1126	0.3
	1600	0.6	1807	7.3	1813	10.0	1342	0.8	1648	0.5	1645	0.5	1417	0.3	1652	5.3	1720	4.3
	2212	6.0					1912	14.0	2327	4.4	2255	3.6	2020	3.1	2301	0.1	2348	0.3
19 TU	0426	0.3	0032	0.4	0021	0.4	0211	0.4	0516	0.2	0518	0.2	0246	0.4	0521	5.2	0540	4.3
	1041	5.8	0632	7.3	0638	9.9	0738	13.9	1203	4.2	1126	3.5	0842	2.8	1119	0.2	1213	0.2
	1644	0.4	1252	0.4	1241	0.4	1436	0.4	1732	0.4	1730	0.4	1500	0.3	1737	5.5	1806	4.4
	2257	6.1	1854	7.6	1901	10.2	2000	14.3			2341	3.7	2102	3.2	2344	-0.1		
20 W	0511	0.1	0118	0.1	0106	0.2	0301	0.1	0012	4.5	0603	0.1	0330	0.3	0606	5.3	0035	0.2
	1125	5.8	0718	7.4	0724	10.1	0824	14.1	0600	0.1	1212	3.5	0924	2.8	1202	0.2	0625	4.4
	1728	0.3	1338	0.2	1324	0.3	1522	0.2	1247	4.2	1816	0.3	1543	0.3	1822	5.6	1300	0.1
	2342	6.2	1939	7.7	1947	10.3	2045	14.5	1816	0.3			2145	3.1			1851	4.4
21 TH	0556	0.1	0203	0.1	0150	0.2	0345	0.0	0057	4.6	0027	3.8	0414	0.4	0027	-0.1	0121	0.2
	1211	5.8	0803	7.4	0807	10.0	0906	14.1	0645	0.1	0649	0.1	1006	2.7	0650	5.3	0709	4.4
	1814	0.4	1422	0.3	1406	0.4	1602	0.3	1332	4.2	1258	3.5	1627	0.3	1245	0.2	1345	0.2
			2024	7.5	2030	10.1	2127	14.3	1901	0.4	1902	0.3	2227	3.0	1908	5.5	1936	4.4
22 F	0029	6.1	0248	0.3	0231	0.4	0422	0.3	0143	4.5	0114	3.7	0457	0.5	0110	0.1	0206	0.3
	0642	0.3	0846	7.2	0849	9.7	0948	13.8	0732	0.3	0736	0.1	1049	2.6	0735	5.1	0754	4.3
	1257	5.6	1506	0.6	1447	0.8	1636	0.7	1419	4.1	1345	3.4	1712	0.4	1330	0.5	1430	0.3
	1901	0.6	2109	7.2	2114	9.7	2209	13.8	1948	0.5	1949	0.4	2312	2.9	1955	5.2	2021	4.3
23 SA	0117	5.9	0330	0.7	0312	0.9	0454	0.8	0233	4.4	0203	3.6	0542	0.6	0155	0.5	0251	0.5
	0730	0.6	0931	6.8	0932	9.3	1028	13.2	0821	0.5	0825	0.3	1134	2.4	0822	4.9	0840	4.2
	1346	5.4	1550	1.0	1530	1.3	1706	1.3	1509	4.0	1436	3.3	1801	0.6	1418	0.8	1516	0.5
	1951	0.9	2155	6.8	2158	9.2	2252	12.9	2039	0.8	2039	0.5			2045	4.9	2108	4.1
24 SU	0209	5.5	0415	1.1	0355	1.5	0524	1.5	0327	4.2	0258	3.4	0003	2.6	0244	0.9	0339	0.7
	0823	1.0	1018	6.4	1017	8.7	1110	12.2	0914	0.8	0919	0.5	0630	0.8	0913	4.6	0928	4.0
	1439	5.1	1637	1.4	1618	1.9	1736	2.0	1606	3.8	1532	3.2	1225	2.2	1513	1.2	1606	0.7
	2048	1.3	2245	6.3	2248	8.5	2337	11.9	2139	1.0	2136	0.7	1856	0.8	2140	4.5	2159	3.8
25 M	0306	5.1	0504	1.7	0446	2.2	0557	2.2	0429	3.9	0400	3.3	0102	2.4	0340	1.4	0431	0.9
	0921	1.4	1110	5.9	1111	8.1	1155	11.3	1015	1.1	1021	0.7	0724	1.0	1012	4.2	1022	3.7
	1542	4.8	1733	1.9	1718	2.6	1813	2.7	1711	3.7	1634	3.1	1334	2.1	1620	1.6	1702	0.9
	2157	1.6	2342	5.7	2347	7.9			2247	1.3	2244	0.8	2006	1.0	2245	4.1	2257	3.6
26 TU	0415	4.8	0604	2.1	0553	2.8	0029	10.9	0540	3.7	0509	3.1	0225	2.2	0450	1.7	0533	1.1
	1032	1.8	1215	5.5	1219	7.6	0639	3.0	1123	1.4	1133	0.8	0831	1.1	1124	4.0	1126	3.5
	1659	4.6	1849	2.3	1839	3.1	1251	10.5	1821	3.6	1742	3.0	1525	2.0	1749	1.8	1810	1.1
	2317	1.8					1903	3.5					2142	1.1				
27 W	0539	4.6	0054	5.4	0100	7.5	0136	10.2	0003	1.4	0002	0.9	0401	2.1	0008	3.9	0007	3.4
	1152	2.0	0724	2.4	0718	3.2	0742	3.6	0654	3.6	0623	3.0	0956	1.1	0618	1.9	0647	1.2
	1824	4.6	1336	5.3	1341	7.4	1409	10.1	1237	1.5	1246	0.9	1648	2.1	1251	4.0	1244	3.3
			2018	2.3	2006	3.2	2033	3.9	1933	3.6	1848	3.1	2311	1.0	1919	1.7	1930	1.2
28 TH	0038	1.8	0219	5.3	0224	7.4	0259	10.1	0124	1.4	0115	0.9	0509	2.2	0131	3.9	0128	3.3
	0703	4.6	0848	2.3	0840	3.1	0921	3.6	0808	3.5	0732	3.0	1109	1.0	0739	1.8	0806	1.2
	1307	1.9	1500	5.5	1501	7.6	1536	10.4	1351	1.5	1351	0.9	1743	2.3	1403	4.1	1406	3.4
	1935	4.8	2134	2.1	2119	2.9	2210	3.4	2039	3.8	1949	3.1			2023	1.5	2042	1.1
29 F	0147	1.6	0333	5.6	0337	7.8	0419	10.7	0234	1.3	0218	0.8	0012	0.9	0235	4.1	0240	3.4
	0808	4.8	0954	2.0	0945	2.7	1043	2.9	0915	3.6	0833	3.0	0600	2.3	0836	1.7	0911	1.1
	1408	1.7	1603	5.9	1604	8.1	1649	11.2	1451	1.4	1445	0.8	1202	0.9	1457	4.3	1511	3.5
	2029	5.1	2230	1.8	2217	2.5	2321	2.6	2138	3.9	2043	3.2	1826	2.4	2110	1.3	2139	0.9
30 SA	0239	1.4	0428	5.9	0433	8.2	0522	11.6	0328	1.1	0310	0.7	0058	0.8	0323	4.3	0334	3.6
	0855	4.9	1045	1.6	1036	2.3	1146	2.1	1009	3.7	0924	3.1	0643	2.4	0919	1.4	0945	0.8
	1454	1.5	1650	6.2	1654	8.5	1744	12.1	1540	1.2	1533	0.8	1245	0.8	1539	4.5	1601	3.7
	2109	5.2	2314	1.4	2304	2.1			2226	4.0	2130	3.3	1903	2.6	2150	1.0	2227	0.9
31 SU	0321	1.2	0511	6.2	0519	8.6	0018	1.9	0412	0.9	0354	0.6	0136	0.7	0403	4.5	0418	3.7
	0932	5.1	1124	1.4	1118	2.0	0611	12.2	1051	3.7	1008	3.1	0721	2.5	0958	1.2	1046	0.8
	1530	1.3	1730	6.5	1735	8.9	1241	1.4	1621	1.1	1543	0.7	1323	0.7	1618	4.7	1642	3.8
	2144	5.4	2351	1.2	2343	1.8	1829	12.6	2305	4.1	2212	3.4	1936	2.7	2226	0.8	2306	0.8

Time UT. For British Summer Time (shaded) March 30th to October 26th ADD ONE HOUR ● ●

WEST COAST ENGLAND, WALES & IRELAND Time Zone UT
Holyhead * Milford Haven * Swansea * Avonmouth * Dublin * Belfast * Londonderry * Galway * Cobh

SEPTEMBER 1997 TIDE TABLES SEPTEMBER 1997

HOLYHEAD		MILFORD HAVEN		SWANSEA		AVONMOUTH		DUBLIN		BELFAST		LONDONDERRY		GALWAY		COBH		
Time	m	Time	m	Time	m	Time	m	Time	m	Time	m	Time	m	Time	m	Time	m	
0356	1.1	0548	6.5	0557	8.9	0105	1.6	0451	0.8	0432	0.6	0209	0.7	0441	4.6	0456	3.9	**1 M**
1004	5.2	1200	1.2	1154	1.7	0653	12.6	1125	3.8	1045	3.1	0755	2.6	1033	1.0	1124	0.7	
1603	1.2	1805	6.7	1812	9.1	1323	1.4	1657	1.0	1648	0.7	1357	0.6	1654	4.8	1718	3.9	●
2215	5.5					1907	12.8	2338	4.1	2250	3.5	2007	2.7	2300	0.7	2342	0.8	
0427	1.0	0024	1.0	0018	1.6	0146	1.5	0525	0.8	0505	0.5	0240	0.7	0517	4.7	0530	3.9	**2 TU**
1033	5.3	0622	6.6	0632	9.1	0729	12.8	1154	3.8	1117	3.2	0827	2.6	1108	0.9	1157	0.7	
1632	1.1	1233	1.0	1227	1.5	1403	1.4	1731	0.9	1720	0.7	1427	0.6	1729	4.9	1752	4.0	
2245	5.5	1837	6.8	1845	9.2	1941	12.9			2324	3.5	2034	2.7	2333	0.6			
0457	0.9	0054	1.0	0050	1.5	0223	1.5	0006	4.1	0535	0.5	0308	0.7	0551	4.8	0014	0.7	**3 W**
1103	5.3	0654	6.7	0704	9.2	0800	12.8	0557	0.7	1146	3.2	0855	2.6	1141	0.8	0603	4.0	
1702	1.0	1303	1.0	1259	1.4	1437	1.3	1219	3.8	1748	0.6	1454	0.6	1803	4.9	1229	0.7	
2315	5.5	1908	6.8	1917	9.3	2011	13.0	1803	0.8	2355	3.5	2059	2.7			1824	4.0	
0527	0.9	0124	1.0	0119	1.4	0255	1.4	0034	4.0	0603	0.5	0333	0.7	0006	0.6	0045	0.8	**4 TH**
1133	5.3	0724	6.7	0734	9.2	0829	12.9	0627	0.7	1213	3.2	0922	2.6	0625	4.8	0634	4.0	
1732	1.0	1333	1.0	1328	1.4	1507	1.3	1247	3.8	1818	0.6	1522	0.6	1214	0.8	1259	0.7	
2345	5.5	1937	6.8	1946	9.2	2039	13.0	1832	0.8			2124	2.7	1836	4.8	1854	4.0	
0557	1.0	0153	1.0	0147	1.5	0323	1.4	0104	4.0	0026	3.5	0400	0.7	0037	0.7	0115	0.8	**5 F**
1204	5.3	0754	6.6	0803	9.1	0857	12.8	0656	0.8	0633	0.5	0951	2.5	0657	4.7	0706	4.0	
1803	1.1	1403	1.0	1357	1.5	1534	1.4	1318	3.8	1242	3.3	1553	0.6	1245	0.9	1329	0.8	
		2006	6.7	2015	9.1	2107	12.8	1902	0.9	1849	0.7	2151	2.6	1907	4.7	1924	4.0	
0017	5.4	0223	1.2	0214	1.6	0348	1.5	0138	3.9	0058	3.5	0430	0.8	0108	0.9	0146	0.8	**6 SA**
0628	1.1	0823	6.5	0830	8.9	0925	12.5	0726	0.8	0706	0.5	1024	2.5	0730	4.6	0739	4.0	
1236	5.2	1434	1.2	1424	1.6	1600	1.6	1354	3.8	1314	3.3	1628	0.7	1318	1.1	1400	0.8	
1836	1.3	2036	6.5	2042	8.9	2137	12.4	1933	0.9	1924	0.7	2223	2.6	1940	4.5	1957	3.9	
0050	5.2	0252	1.4	0240	1.8	0412	1.8	0216	3.8	0134	3.5	0504	0.9	0140	1.1	0218	0.9	**7 SU**
0701	1.3	0853	6.3	0859	8.7	0954	12.0	0800	0.9	0742	0.6	1100	2.4	0804	4.4	0812	3.9	
1311	5.1	1506	1.5	1454	1.9	1624	2.0	1435	3.7	1351	3.3	1707	0.7	1353	1.3	1434	0.9	
1912	1.4	2108	6.3	2113	8.6	2206	11.8	2010	1.1	2003	0.8	2259	2.4	2015	4.3	2030	3.8	
0125	5.1	0324	1.7	0310	2.1	0436	2.3	0259	3.6	0215	3.4	0544	1.0	0215	1.3	0254	1.0	**8 M**
0738	1.5	0927	6.0	0931	8.4	1023	11.3	0839	1.1	0823	0.7	1142	2.3	0841	4.3	0850	3.8	
1350	4.9	1540	1.8	1527	2.3	1649	2.5	1520	3.6	1433	3.3	1752	0.9	1433	1.5	1512	1.0	
1954	1.6	2143	6.0	2148	8.3	2237	11.2	2054	1.2	2048	0.9	2342	2.2	2055	4.1	2110	3.6	
0206	4.8	0359	2.0	0345	2.5	0502	2.7	0348	3.5	0302	3.3	0631	1.1	0257	1.6	0336	1.2	**9 TU**
0823	1.7	1006	5.7	1012	8.0	1054	10.7	0927	1.2	0909	0.8	1235	2.2	0925	4.1	0934	3.6	
1437	4.7	1622	2.2	1612	2.7	1719	2.9	1612	3.5	1521	3.2	1845	1.0	1522	1.8	1600	1.2	
2046	1.9	2227	5.7	2235	7.9	2313	10.6	2149	1.3	2140	1.0			2145	3.9	2159	3.5	
0300	4.6	0445	2.3	0435	2.9	0536	3.1	0448	3.4	0357	3.2	0038	2.2	0353	1.9	0430	1.3	**10 W**
0921	2.0	1059	5.4	1109	7.6	1137	10.2	1032	1.4	1004	1.0	0730	1.1	1022	3.9	1029	3.4	
1541	4.6	1721	2.5	1716	3.1	1800	3.4	1712	3.4	1619	3.1	1344	2.1	1629	1.9	1701	1.3	
2156	2.0	2329	5.3	2340	7.5			2304	1.4	2245	1.1	1948	1.1	2253	3.7	2300	3.3	
0417	4.4	0555	2.6	0553	3.2	0007	10.1	0600	3.3	0502	3.1	0201	2.0	0511	2.0	0540	1.4	**11 TH**
1039	2.1	1216	5.3	1229	7.4	0625	3.6	1148	1.5	1110	1.1	0845	1.2	1136	3.9	1139	3.3	
1704	4.5	1848	2.6	1847	3.2	1250	9.9	1824	3.4	1728	3.1	1518	2.1	1757	1.9	1818	1.3	
2321	2.0					1906	3.8					2111	1.1					
0550	4.5	0057	5.2	0106	7.4	0137	9.9	0024	1.4	0004	1.1	0403	2.1	0021	3.8	0019	3.3	**12 F**
1203	2.0	0734	2.5	0732	3.2	0754	3.8	0718	3.4	0615	3.1	1018	1.1	0642	1.9	0703	1.3	
1826	4.7	1349	5.4	1357	7.6	1434	10.2	1300	1.4	1227	1.1	1641	2.3	1257	4.0	1301	3.4	
		2024	2.3	2014	2.8	2108	3.5	1938	3.5	1843	3.1	2249	1.0	1921	1.7	1941	1.2	
0040	1.7	0228	5.5	0232	7.7	0315	10.6	0133	1.2	0121	1.0	0519	2.3	0143	4.0	0142	3.4	**13 SA**
0707	4.7	0900	2.1	0853	2.6	0949	3.1	0827	3.6	0727	3.1	1130	0.9	0754	1.6	0820	1.1	
1312	1.7	1507	5.9	1512	8.1	1557	11.3	1403	1.2	1340	1.0	1739	2.6	1405	4.4	1418	3.6	
1930	5.1	2136	1.8	2124	2.1	2233	2.4	2041	3.7	1952	3.2			2024	1.2	2051	0.9	
0143	1.3	0340	6.0	0342	8.4	0431	11.7	0233	0.9	0224	0.8	0000	0.8	0244	4.4	0251	3.7	**14 SU**
0806	5.1	1004	1.6	0955	1.9	1107	2.1	0924	3.8	0831	3.2	0612	2.5	0848	1.2	0923	0.8	
1409	1.2	1608	6.5	1612	9.0	1704	12.6	1457	1.0	1442	0.9	1224	0.7	1500	4.8	1520	3.9	
2022	5.5	2233	1.1	2221	1.4	2347	1.5	2135	4.0	2052	3.4	1828	2.9	2114	0.7	2149	0.6	
0235	0.8	0436	6.6	0441	9.1	0535	12.8	0325	0.6	0319	0.6	0054	0.6	0333	4.8	0345	4.0	**15 M**
0854	5.4	1058	1.0	1048	1.1	1221	1.3	1015	4.0	0927	3.4	0657	2.7	0934	0.8	1017	0.5	
1456	0.9	1700	7.1	1706	9.7	1803	13.6	1545	0.7	1536	0.7	1310	0.5	1548	5.2	1612	4.2	
2108	5.8	2325	0.6	2314	0.7			2223	4.2	2145	3.6	1912	3.1	2158	0.3	2240	0.4	

● ● Time UT. For British Summer Time (shaded) March 30th to October 26th ADD ONE HOUR ● ●

SEPTEMBER 1997 TIDE TABLES SEPTEMBER 1997

	HOLYHEAD		MILFORD HAVEN		SWANSEA		AVONMOUTH		DUBLIN		BELFAST		LONDONDERRY		GALWAY		COBH	
	Time	m	Time	m	Time	m	Time	m	Time	m	Time	m	Time	m	Time	m	Time	m
16 TU ○	0321	0.5	0527	7.1	0531	9.8	0056	0.8	0412	0.4	0409	0.3	0141	0.4	0418	5.1	0434	4.2
	0938	5.7	1147	0.5	1136	0.6	0630	13.6	1100	4.2	1018	3.5	0740	2.8	1017	0.4	1106	0.3
	1540	0.5	1748	7.5	1755	10.2	1325	0.7	1630	0.5	1624	0.5	1355	0.5	1633	5.5	1700	4.4
	2151	6.1					1854	14.2	2309	4.4	2233	3.7	1955	3.2	2240	0.0	2329	0.2
17 W	0406	0.2	0013	0.2	0001	0.3	0154	0.3	0457	0.2	0455	0.2	0225	0.3	0501	5.4	0521	4.4
	1021	5.9	0613	7.4	0618	10.2	0719	14.1	1144	4.3	1105	3.6	0821	2.9	1059	0.2	1154	0.2
	1623	0.3	1233	0.2	1222	0.3	1418	0.3	1712	0.4	1710	0.4	1439	0.3	1717	5.7	1746	4.5
	2236	6.3	1834	7.7	1842	10.5	1941	14.5	2352	4.6	2320	3.8	2037	3.2	2321	-0.1		
18 TH	0449	0.1	0059	0.0	0046	0.1	0243	-0.0	0540	0.1	0540	0.1	0306	0.3	0544	5.5	0015	0.2
	1103	6.0	0657	7.6	0703	10.4	0803	14.3	1226	4.3	1150	3.6	0902	2.9	1141	0.1	0605	4.5
	1707	0.2	1318	0.1	1304	0.2	1503	0.1	1756	0.3	1754	0.3	1522	0.3	1801	5.7	1240	0.1
	2321	6.3	1919	7.8	1926	10.5	2024	14.6					2119	3.2			1830	4.6
19 F	0533	0.1	0142	0.1	0128	0.2	0325	-0.0	0036	4.6	0006	3.8	0347	0.4	0003	-0.0	0100	0.2
	1148	5.9	0741	7.5	0745	10.3	0844	14.3	0623	0.2	0625	0.1	0942	2.8	0627	5.5	0649	4.5
	1751	0.3	1402	0.2	1345	0.4	1542	0.2	1309	4.3	1234	3.6	1606	0.4	1223	0.2	1324	0.2
			2003	7.6	2009	10.3	2106	14.4	1839	0.4	1839	0.3	2202	3.0	1846	5.6	1915	4.5
20 SA	0007	6.1	0225	0.3	0207	0.5	0400	0.3	0122	4.5	0052	3.8	0427	0.5	0045	0.2	0144	0.3
	0618	0.3	0824	7.3	0826	10.0	0924	14.0	0707	0.3	0710	0.2	1021	2.7	0711	5.3	0733	4.5
	1233	5.7	1444	0.5	1424	0.8	1614	0.7	1353	4.2	1320	3.5	1651	0.5	1307	0.5	1409	0.3
	1838	0.6	2046	7.2	2050	9.9	2147	13.8	1925	0.5	1925	0.4	2246	2.8	1933	5.3	1958	4.4
21 SU	0054	5.9	0306	0.7	0246	1.0	0430	0.9	0211	4.4	0141	3.6	0509	0.7	0130	0.6	0227	0.5
	0705	0.7	0906	6.9	0906	9.5	1003	13.3	0753	0.6	0757	0.4	1102	2.5	0757	5.0	0818	4.3
	1320	5.4	1527	1.0	1504	1.3	1642	1.3	1441	4.1	1408	3.4	1738	0.7	1354	0.9	1453	0.5
	1928	0.9	2130	6.7	2132	9.3	2227	12.9	2015	0.7	2014	0.6	2334	2.5	2021	4.9	2043	4.1
22 M	0145	5.5	0348	1.2	0326	1.6	0457	1.7	0304	4.1	0234	3.4	0552	0.8	0217	1.1	0312	0.7
	0754	1.2	0951	6.4	0948	8.9	1043	12.2	0844	0.9	0849	0.6	1148	2.3	0846	4.6	0903	4.0
	1410	5.1	1612	1.5	1548	2.0	1709	2.1	1535	3.9	1500	3.3	1833	0.9	1448	1.3	1540	0.8
	2024	1.3	2216	6.2	2218	8.6	2309	11.7	2113	1.0	2109	0.7			2115	4.4	2131	3.9
23 TU	0241	5.0	0433	1.8	0412	2.4	0527	2.5	0406	3.8	0335	3.2	0033	2.3	0311	1.6	0401	1.0
	0851	1.6	1039	5.9	1038	8.2	1125	11.1	0942	1.3	0950	0.9	0642	1.0	0942	4.3	0954	3.8
	1510	4.8	1704	2.1	1643	2.7	1742	3.0	1638	3.7	1600	3.2	1247	2.2	1554	1.7	1633	1.1
	2130	1.7	2311	5.6	2312	7.9	2357	10.6	2221	1.3	2214	0.9	1945	1.1	2220	4.1	2226	3.6
24 W	0349	4.7	0529	2.3	0512	3.1	0603	3.3	0517	3.6	0445	3.0	0200	2.1	0419	2.0	0500	1.3
	1000	2.0	1141	5.4	1142	7.6	1217	10.2	1051	1.5	1102	1.0	0743	1.1	1053	4.0	1055	3.5
	1626	4.6	1818	2.5	1800	3.3	1825	3.8	1750	3.6	1707	3.1	1440	2.1	1724	1.9	1739	1.3
	2251	1.9							2339	1.4	2333	0.9	2134	1.2	2343	3.9	2333	3.3
25 TH	0515	4.4	0021	5.2	0024	7.3	0101	9.8	0633	3.5	0600	2.9	0343	2.1	0553	2.2	0612	1.4
	1123	2.2	0650	2.6	0639	3.5	0657	4.0	1208	1.7	1218	1.1	0906	1.2	1224	3.9	1212	3.3
	1754	4.6	1303	5.2	1305	7.3	1333	9.7	1903	3.6	1815	3.1	1620	2.2	1900	1.9	1858	1.4
			1953	2.5	1933	3.5	1947	4.3					2300	1.1				
26 F	0015	2.0	0151	5.1	0151	7.2	0228	9.6	0101	1.4	0050	0.9	0449	2.2	0113	3.9	0057	3.3
	0643	4.5	0821	2.5	0809	3.4	0848	4.2	0748	3.5	0709	2.9	1030	1.1	0721	2.1	0733	1.4
	1243	2.2	1433	5.4	1430	7.4	1508	10.0	1326	1.6	1324	1.1	1714	2.4	1342	4.1	1339	3.3
	1909	4.8	2111	2.3	2052	3.2	2142	3.8	2012	3.7	1918	3.1	2354	1.0	2003	1.7	2013	1.3
27 SA	0124	1.8	0310	5.4	0311	7.5	0354	10.3	0212	1.3	0153	0.8	0538	2.3	0218	4.1	0212	3.4
	0748	4.7	0930	2.2	0919	3.0	1015	3.3	0854	3.5	0809	2.9	1130	1.0	0817	1.9	0842	1.3
	1345	2.0	1538	5.8	1538	7.9	1623	10.9	1430	1.5	1420	1.0	1756	2.5	1436	4.2	1445	3.5
	2003	5.0	2206	1.9	2152	2.7	2251	2.8	2112	3.8	2014	3.2			2048	1.4	2112	1.2
28 SU	0216	1.5	0404	5.8	0409	8.0	0456	11.3	0305	1.1	0245	0.7	0035	0.8	0303	4.3	0307	3.6
	0833	4.9	1019	1.8	1011	2.5	1116	2.3	0947	3.6	0900	3.0	0618	2.5	0859	1.6	0935	1.1
	1430	1.7	1624	6.2	1628	8.4	1718	11.9	1518	1.3	1506	0.9	1215	0.9	1518	4.5	1534	3.7
	2044	5.2	2248	1.5	2237	2.3	2346	2.0	2200	3.9	2103	3.3	1833	2.6	2126	1.2	2158	1.0
29 M	0256	1.3	0446	6.2	0453	8.5	0545	12.1	0348	1.0	0327	0.6	0109	0.8	0342	4.5	0351	3.7
	0908	5.1	1059	1.5	1051	2.1	1208	1.7	1027	3.7	0942	3.1	0654	2.6	0936	1.3	1017	0.9
	1506	1.5	1703	6.5	1709	8.8	1802	12.5	1559	1.1	1546	0.8	1254	0.8	1554	4.6	1615	3.8
	2118	5.3	2324	1.3	2315	1.9			2239	4.0	2145	3.3	1906	2.7	2200	1.0	2236	0.8
30 TU	0329	1.2	0522	6.5	0530	8.9	0033	1.6	0425	0.9	0403	0.6	0140	0.7	0417	4.7	0428	3.9
	0938	5.2	1133	1.2	1127	1.7	0625	12.6	1100	3.8	1018	3.1	0728	2.7	1010	1.1	1054	0.8
	1537	1.3	1738	6.7	1744	9.1	1252	1.4	1635	1.0	1621	0.7	1328	0.7	1629	4.8	1650	4.0
	2148	5.5	2356	1.1	2349	1.6	1839	12.8	2311	4.0	2222	3.4	1936	2.8	2233	0.8	2311	0.8

● ● Time UT. For British Summer Time (shaded) March 30th to October 26th ADD ONE HOUR ● ●

WEST COAST ENGLAND, WALES & IRELAND Time Zone UT
Holyhead * Milford Haven * Swansea * Avonmouth * Dublin * Belfast * Londonderry * Galway * Cobh

OCTOBER 1997 TIDE TABLES OCTOBER 1997

HOLYHEAD Time	m	MILFORD HAVEN Time	m	SWANSEA Time	m	AVONMOUTH Time	m	DUBLIN Time	m	BELFAST Time	m	LONDONDERRY Time	m	GALWAY Time	m	COBH Time	m	Day
0359	1.0	0555	6.7	0603	9.2	0115	1.4	0457	0.8	0436	0.5	0209	0.7	0451	4.8	0503	4.0	1 W
1006	5.4	1206	1.0	1200	1.5	0700	12.8	1127	3.8	1049	3.2	0759	2.7	1043	0.9	1128	0.8	●
1606	1.1	1809	6.8	1817	9.3	1333	1.3	1706	0.9	1652	0.7	1400	0.6	1703	4.9	1723	4.1	
2217	5.5					1912	12.9	2339	4.0	2256	3.4	2003	2.8	2305	0.7	2345	0.8	
0428	1.0	0027	1.0	0021	1.5	0154	1.4	0527	0.8	0505	0.5	0236	0.6	0523	4.9	0536	4.1	2 TH
1035	5.4	0626	6.8	0635	9.3	0731	12.9	1151	3.8	1117	3.2	0827	2.7	1115	0.8	1200	0.7	
1635	1.0	1236	0.9	1231	1.4	1409	1.2	1735	0.9	1721	0.6	1429	0.6	1734	4.9	1755	4.1	
2247	5.6	1840	6.9	1848	9.4	1942	13.0			2326	3.5	2028	2.8	2335	0.7			
0457	0.9	0056	0.9	0051	1.4	0227	1.3	0006	4.0	0533	0.5	0302	0.7	0554	4.9	0017	0.7	3 F
1104	5.5	0656	6.8	0705	9.4	0800	13.0	0554	0.8	1143	3.3	0855	2.7	1145	0.8	0608	4.2	
1705	1.0	1307	0.9	1301	1.4	1442	1.2	1218	3.9	1751	0.6	1458	0.6	1806	4.9	1233	0.7	
2318	5.5	1909	6.9	1918	9.4	2011	13.0	1803	0.8	2357	3.5	2054	2.7			1826	4.1	
0527	1.0	0126	1.0	0118	1.4	0258	1.3	0036	3.9	0602	0.5	0329	0.7	0005	0.8	0048	0.8	4 SA
1135	5.4	0726	6.8	0733	9.3	0829	13.0	0621	0.8	1212	3.4	0924	2.7	0625	4.9	0640	4.1	
1736	1.1	1338	1.0	1330	1.5	1511	1.2	1248	3.9	1822	0.6	1530	0.6	1217	0.9	1304	0.8	
2349	5.4	1939	6.8	1946	9.3	2041	13.0	1831	0.8			2123	2.7	1837	4.8	1857	4.1	
0557	1.1	0156	1.1	0145	1.6	0326	1.4	0109	3.9	0029	3.5	0359	0.7	0035	0.9	0121	0.8	5 SU
1207	5.4	0756	6.7	0802	9.2	0859	12.8	0651	0.8	0635	0.5	0956	2.6	0657	4.8	0713	4.1	
1809	1.2	1409	1.2	1357	1.6	1539	1.5	1324	3.9	1244	3.4	1606	0.7	1249	1.0	1337	0.8	
		2010	6.6	2015	9.1	2112	12.7	1904	0.9	1857	0.7	2157	2.6	1910	4.7	1930	4.0	
0023	5.3	0226	1.3	0212	1.7	0351	1.7	0147	3.8	0106	3.4	0433	0.8	0106	1.1	0154	0.9	6 M
0631	1.2	0827	6.5	0831	9.0	0922	12.4	0726	0.9	0712	0.6	1033	2.5	0731	4.7	0747	4.0	
1242	5.3	1442	1.4	1427	1.8	1604	1.8	1403	3.8	1321	3.4	1646	0.8	1324	1.2	1411	0.9	
1846	1.3	2042	6.4	2046	8.8	2143	12.1	1942	1.0	1936	0.7	2235	2.5	1947	4.5	2004	3.9	
0059	5.1	0257	1.6	0242	2.0	0415	2.1	0231	3.7	0147	3.4	0513	0.9	0143	1.4	0228	1.0	7 TU
0709	1.4	0902	6.2	0904	8.7	1000	11.7	0806	1.0	0752	0.7	1115	2.4	0809	4.5	0824	3.9	
1321	5.1	1517	1.7	1502	2.1	1629	2.3	1450	3.7	1403	3.4	1732	0.9	1405	1.5	1448	1.1	
1929	1.5	2119	6.1	2122	8.5	2216	11.5	2027	1.1	2021	0.8	2321	2.3	2029	4.3	2043	3.7	
0142	4.9	0333	1.9	0318	2.3	0441	2.5	0323	3.6	0235	3.3	0600	1.0	0226	1.7	0309	1.2	8 W
0754	1.7	0942	5.9	0945	8.2	1034	11.1	0857	1.2	0839	0.8	1206	2.3	0854	4.3	0908	3.7	
1409	4.9	1600	2.1	1545	2.5	1659	2.7	1542	3.6	1451	3.3	1826	1.0	1455	1.7	1535	1.2	
2022	1.7	2204	5.7	2209	8.0	2255	10.9	2124	1.2	2114	0.9			2121	4.1	2132	3.6	
0237	4.7	0421	2.3	0406	2.8	0515	2.9	0424	3.4	0330	3.2	0021	2.2	0322	1.9	0401	1.3	9 TH
0853	1.9	1035	5.6	1042	7.8	1118	10.5	1001	1.4	0934	1.0	0657	1.1	0951	4.1	1003	3.6	
1512	4.7	1700	2.4	1648	2.9	1741	3.2	1644	3.5	1549	3.2	1312	2.3	1601	1.9	1635	1.3	
2131	1.9	2306	5.4	2314	7.6	2349	10.3	2241	1.3	2219	1.0	1930	1.1	2229	3.9	2233	3.4	
0354	4.5	0531	2.5	0521	3.2	0604	3.4	0539	3.4	0436	3.1	0148	2.1	0441	2.1	0511	1.4	10 F
1011	2.1	1151	5.4	1202	7.5	1229	10.1	1121	1.5	1042	1.1	0809	1.2	1105	4.0	1112	3.4	
1633	4.7	1826	2.5	1820	3.1	1847	3.6	1756	3.5	1657	3.1	1442	2.3	1729	1.9	1752	1.3	
2255	1.9									2338	1.0	2055	1.1	2357	3.9	2351	3.3	
0527	4.5	0034	5.3	0042	7.4	0113	10.1	0001	1.3	0551	3.1	0350	2.1	0615	2.0	0635	1.4	11 SA
1136	2.0	0709	2.5	0706	3.2	0727	3.7	0657	3.5	1202	1.2	0939	1.1	1228	4.2	1234	3.4	
1757	4.8	1324	5.5	1332	7.6	1406	10.3	1236	1.4	1813	3.2	1610	2.5	1855	1.6	1916	1.2	
		2000	2.2	1951	2.8	2036	3.4	1911	3.6			2237	1.0					
0015	1.6	0206	5.3	0211	7.7	0249	10.6	0112	1.1	0055	0.9	0502	2.3	0121	4.2	0115	3.5	12 SU
0645	4.8	0838	2.1	0831	2.7	0918	3.2	0806	3.6	0706	3.1	1059	1.0	0731	1.7	0754	1.1	
1248	1.7	1443	6.0	1450	8.2	1532	11.3	1341	1.3	1317	1.1	1712	2.7	1340	4.5	1353	3.7	
1903	5.1	2114	1.7	2103	2.1	2206	2.5	2017	3.8	1925	3.3	2345	0.8	1959	1.0	2028	1.0	
0119	1.2	0319	6.1	0324	8.4	0408	11.7	0213	0.8	0200	0.7	0552	2.6	0223	4.6	0226	3.7	13 M
0745	5.2	0943	1.6	0936	1.9	1042	2.2	0905	3.8	0810	3.3	1157	0.8	0826	1.3	0900	0.8	
1345	1.3	1546	6.5	1553	9.0	1642	12.5	1436	1.0	1419	0.9	1801	3.0	1437	4.9	1457	4.0	
1958	5.5	2213	1.1	2203	1.4	2324	1.6	2112	4.1	2027	3.4			2050	0.8	2127	0.7	
0212	0.8	0416	6.6	0421	9.2	0513	12.7	0306	0.6	0255	0.5	0034	0.6	0312	5.0	0323	4.1	14 TU
0833	5.5	1038	1.0	1029	1.2	1159	1.4	0956	4.1	0907	3.4	0637	2.7	0913	0.9	0957	0.6	
1434	0.9	1639	7.1	1646	9.7	1741	13.5	1525	0.8	1514	0.7	1246	0.6	1526	5.3	1551	4.2	
2045	5.9	2304	0.8	2254	0.8			2203	4.3	2121	3.6	1846	3.1	2135	0.4	2220	0.4	
0300	0.5	0506	7.1	0512	9.8	0034	0.9	0353	0.4	0345	0.3	0118	0.5	0356	5.3	0413	4.3	15 W
0917	5.8	1127	0.6	1117	0.7	0609	13.5	1042	4.2	0957	3.6	0719	2.9	0956	0.5	1047	0.3	
1519	0.6	1728	7.5	1735	10.2	1303	0.8	1611	0.6	1603	0.6	1332	0.4	1611	5.6	1639	4.5	
2130	6.1	2352	0.3	2342	0.4	1833	14.1	2249	4.5	2212	3.7	1930	3.2	2217	0.2	2309	0.3	

● ● Time UT. For British Summer Time (shaded) March 30th to October 26th ADD ONE HOUR ● ●

OCTOBER 1997 TIDE TABLES OCTOBER 1997

Date	HOLYHEAD	MILFORD HAVEN	SWANSEA	AVONMOUTH	DUBLIN	BELFAST	LONDONDERRY	GALWAY	COBH
	Time m	Time m	Time m	Time m	Time m	Time m	Time m	Time m	Time m
16 TH ○	0344 0.2	0552 7.4	0558 10.2	0132 0.4	0436 0.3	0432 0.2	0200 0.4	0439 5.5	0500 4.5
	0959 5.9	1214 0.3	1202 0.4	0657 14.0	1124 4.3	1043 3.7	0759 2.9	1038 0.3	1135 0.2
	1603 0.4	1814 7.7	1821 10.5	1356 0.4	1654 0.5	1649 0.4	1416 0.4	1655 5.7	1726 4.6
	2215 6.2			1919 14.4	2333 4.6	2300 3.8	2012 3.2	2258 0.1	2354 0.3
17 F	0427 0.2	0037 0.1	0025 0.3	0220 0.2	0519 0.2	0517 0.2	0239 0.4	0521 5.6	0545 4.6
	1042 6.0	0636 7.6	0642 10.4	0740 14.2	1205 4.4	1127 3.7	0838 2.9	1120 0.2	1221 0.2
	1647 0.4	1258 0.2	1245 0.4	1440 0.3	1736 0.4	1733 0.4	1500 0.4	1740 5.7	1810 4.6
	2300 6.2	1858 7.7	1905 10.5	2003 14.5		2345 3.8	2054 3.1	2339 0.2	
18 SA	0510 0.3	0120 0.2	0106 0.4	0301 0.2	0018 4.6	0601 0.3	0316 0.5	0603 5.6	0039 0.3
	1125 5.9	0719 7.5	0723 10.3	0821 14.2	0600 0.3	1211 3.7	0915 2.9	1203 0.3	0630 4.6
	1732 0.4	1341 0.3	1324 0.6	1518 0.4	1246 4.4	1818 0.4	1543 0.5	1824 5.5	1304 0.3
	2347 6.0	1942 7.5	1947 10.2	2044 14.2	1820 0.4		2136 3.0		1854 4.5
19 SU	0554 0.5	0202 0.3	0145 0.7	0336 0.6	0103 4.5	0032 3.7	0354 0.6	0021 0.5	0122 0.4
	1209 5.8	0801 7.3	0801 10.0	0901 13.9	0643 0.5	0646 0.4	0953 2.8	0648 5.4	0712 4.5
	1818 0.6	1423 0.6	1403 1.0	1551 0.9	1329 4.3	1255 3.6	1627 0.6	1247 0.6	1348 0.4
		2024 7.1	2027 9.8	2124 13.7	1906 0.6	1903 0.5	2219 2.7	1911 5.2	1936 4.4
20 M	0034 5.7	0242 0.8	0222 1.2	0406 1.1	0151 4.3	0120 3.6	0432 0.7	0105 0.9	0204 0.6
	0640 0.9	0842 6.9	0842 9.5	0940 13.2	0727 0.8	0732 0.6	1031 2.6	0733 5.1	0756 4.3
	1255 5.5	1505 1.0	1442 1.5	1618 1.5	1414 4.2	1342 3.5	1713 0.8	1333 1.0	1430 0.6
	1907 1.0	2106 6.6	2108 9.2	2205 12.7	1955 0.8	1951 0.6	2306 2.5	2000 4.9	2019 4.1
21 TU	0123 5.4	0322 1.3	0300 1.8	0433 1.8	0242 4.0	0212 3.4	0513 0.9	0151 1.3	0247 0.8
	0727 1.3	0925 6.4	0923 8.9	1019 12.2	0816 1.1	0821 0.8	1112 2.5	0821 4.8	0840 4.1
	1344 5.2	1548 1.6	1524 2.1	1645 2.3	1505 4.0	1432 3.4	1806 1.0	1426 1.4	1515 0.9
	2000 1.3	2151 6.1	2151 8.6	2246 11.6	2051 1.0	2042 0.7		2052 4.5	2105 3.9
22 W	0216 5.0	0404 1.8	0342 2.4	0500 2.6	0342 3.8	0309 3.2	0002 2.3	0243 1.8	0333 1.1
	0820 1.8	1011 5.9	1009 8.3	1100 11.2	0912 1.4	0917 1.0	0559 1.0	0914 4.4	0928 3.8
	1438 4.9	1636 2.1	1613 2.7	1716 3.0	1605 3.8	1527 3.3	1203 2.4	1527 1.8	1603 1.2
	2102 1.7	2241 5.6	2240 7.9	2330 10.5	2157 1.2	2143 0.9	1913 1.2	2153 4.1	2155 3.6
23 TH	0320 4.6	0455 2.3	0436 3.0	0533 3.4	0451 3.5	0415 3.0	0119 2.1	0347 2.2	0425 1.3
	0923 2.1	1107 5.5	1106 7.7	1147 10.2	1020 1.6	1024 1.2	0654 1.2	1018 4.1	1024 3.5
	1545 4.7	1740 2.3	1720 3.3	1754 3.8	1715 3.7	1630 3.2	1321 2.3	1647 2.0	1703 1.4
	2216 2.0	2344 5.2	2345 7.3		2310 1.4	2256 1.0	2057 1.3	2308 3.9	2257 3.4
24 F	0439 4.4	0606 2.6	0552 3.5	0027 9.7	0604 3.4	0527 2.9	0300 2.1	0510 2.3	0530 1.5
	1041 2.4	1220 5.2	1220 7.3	0618 4.1	1134 1.7	1138 1.2	0806 1.3	1139 4.0	1133 3.4
	1707 4.6	1908 2.6	1846 3.5	1254 9.6	1827 3.6	1736 3.1	1518 2.3	1816 2.0	1815 1.5
	2336 2.0			1856 4.3			2226 1.2		
25 SA	0603 4.4	0106 5.0	0106 7.1	0147 9.4	0027 1.4	0011 1.0	0411 2.2	0035 3.9	0012 3.3
	1202 2.4	0736 2.7	0723 3.6	0748 4.5	0716 3.4	0635 2.8	0931 1.3	0639 2.3	0647 1.5
	1825 4.7	1347 5.3	1345 7.3	1423 9.7	1251 1.7	1246 1.2	1627 2.4	1302 4.0	1254 3.3
		2029 2.4	2009 3.4	2057 4.1	1935 3.6	1839 3.1	2319 1.1	1924 1.9	1930 1.5
26 SU	0045 1.9	0230 5.2	0229 7.3	0138 1.3	0138 1.3	0115 0.9	0501 2.3	0144 4.1	0127 3.3
	0710 4.6	0849 2.4	0839 3.3	0935 3.8	0821 3.5	0735 2.9	1041 2.1	0742 2.1	0758 1.4
	1307 2.2	1458 5.6	1457 7.7	1543 10.5	1359 1.6	1343 1.1	1714 2.5	1402 4.2	1404 3.4
	1924 4.8	2127 2.1	2113 3.0	2211 3.2	2036 3.7	1937 3.1	2358 1.0	2013 1.7	2031 1.3
27 M	0140 1.7	0328 5.6	0332 7.8	0419 10.8	0233 1.1	0207 0.8	0543 2.5	0232 4.3	0228 3.5
	0759 4.8	0942 2.0	0934 2.8	1038 2.9	0913 3.6	0826 3.0	1133 1.0	0829 1.8	0855 1.3
	1357 1.9	1549 6.0	1551 8.1	1641 11.1	1450 1.4	1431 1.0	1753 2.6	1447 4.4	1457 3.6
	2009 5.0	2212 1.7	2202 2.5	2306 2.4	2125 3.8	2027 3.2		2054 1.4	2120 1.2
28 TU	0222 1.5	0413 6.0	0419 8.3	0509 11.6	0316 1.0	0251 0.7	0032 0.8	0312 4.5	0315 3.7
	0836 5.0	1025 1.7	1018 2.3	1130 2.1	0954 3.7	0909 3.0	0621 2.6	0908 1.6	0940 1.1
	1435 1.7	1630 6.3	1634 8.6	1727 12.1	1532 1.2	1513 0.9	1215 0.9	1525 4.6	1540 3.8
	2045 5.2	2250 1.4	2242 2.1	2355 1.9	2206 3.8	2112 3.3	1828 2.7	2130 1.2	2200 1.0
29 W	0257 1.3	0451 6.3	0457 8.8	0551 12.2	0353 0.9	0329 0.6	0103 0.8	0348 4.7	0355 3.9
	0907 5.2	1103 1.4	1055 1.9	1216 1.7	1028 3.7	0945 3.1	0655 2.7	0943 1.3	1020 1.0
	1507 1.4	1706 6.5	1711 9.0	1806 12.5	1607 1.1	1550 0.8	1254 0.8	1600 4.7	1618 3.9
	2118 5.4	2324 1.2	2317 1.8		2239 3.8	2151 3.3	1900 2.8	2203 1.1	2238 0.9
30 TH	0328 1.1	0525 6.6	0532 9.1	0039 1.6	0425 0.9	0403 0.6	0134 0.7	0421 4.9	0433 4.0
	0937 5.4	1137 1.2	1130 1.7	0627 12.6	1056 3.8	1018 3.2	0727 2.8	1016 1.1	1057 0.8
	1538 1.2	1739 6.7	1745 9.2	1258 1.4	1639 1.0	1624 0.7	1328 0.7	1634 4.8	1652 4.1
	2148 5.5	2357 1.1	2351 1.6	1840 12.7	2309 3.9	2226 3.3	1930 2.8	2234 1.0	2314 0.8
31 F ●	0358 1.0	0557 6.8	0605 9.3	0120 1.4	0454 0.8	0434 0.6	0203 0.7	0453 5.0	0508 4.1
	1006 5.5	1210 1.0	1203 1.5	0700 12.8	1123 3.9	1048 3.3	0759 2.8	1048 1.0	1132 0.8
	1609 1.1	1812 6.8	1818 9.4	1337 1.3	1706 0.9	1656 0.6	1400 0.7	1706 4.9	1727 4.1
	2220 5.5			1912 12.9	2339 3.9	2258 3.4	1959 2.8	2305 0.9	2349 0.8

● ● Time UT. For British Summer Time (shaded) March 30th to October 26th ADD ONE HOUR ● ●

WEST COAST ENGLAND, WALES & IRELAND Time Zone UT
Holyhead * Milford Haven * Swansea * Avonmouth * Dublin * Belfast * Londonderry * Galway * Cobh

NOVEMBER 1997 TIDE TABLES NOVEMBER 1997

Day	HOLYHEAD Time m	MILFORD HAVEN Time m	SWANSEA Time m	AVONMOUTH Time m	DUBLIN Time m	BELFAST Time m	LONDONDERRY Time m	GALWAY Time m	COBH Time m
1 SA	0428 1.0	0029 1.0	0022 1.5	0157 1.3	0521 0.8	0504 0.5	0232 0.7	0524 5.1	0542 4.2
	1037 5.6	0629 6.9	0637 9.5	0731 13.0	1151 3.9	1117 3.4	0830 2.8	1119 0.9	1208 0.8
	1640 1.0	1243 1.0	1235 1.4	1414 1.2	1736 0.9	1727 0.6	1435 0.7	1738 4.9	1800 4.1
	2252 5.5	1844 6.9	1851 9.4	1945 13.0		2331 3.4	2029 2.8	2335 1.0	
2 SU	0500 1.0	0101 1.0	0053 1.5	0233 1.3	0010 3.9	0536 0.5	0302 0.7	0555 5.1	0025 0.8
	1109 5.6	0701 6.9	0709 9.5	0803 13.1	0551 0.8	1148 3.4	0900 2.8	1151 1.0	0618 4.2
	1714 1.0	1316 1.0	1306 1.5	1448 1.2	1223 4.0	1801 0.6	1510 0.7	1811 4.9	1243 0.8
	2327 5.5	1916 6.8	1923 9.4	2018 13.0	1806 0.8		2101 2.7		1834 4.1
3 M	0533 1.1	0133 1.1	0122 1.5	0305 1.3	0045 3.9	0006 3.4	0333 0.7	0007 1.1	0100 0.8
	1144 5.5	0734 6.8	0739 9.4	0836 13.0	0624 0.8	0610 0.5	0934 2.8	0629 5.0	0652 4.2
	1750 1.1	1351 1.1	1337 1.5	1520 1.3	1300 4.0	1221 3.5	1548 0.7	1226 1.0	1318 0.8
		1950 6.7	1955 9.2	2052 12.9	1842 0.8	1837 0.6	2137 2.7	1847 4.8	1909 4.0
4 TU	0003 5.4	0207 1.2	0152 1.6	0334 1.6	0125 3.8	0045 3.4	0409 0.8	0042 1.2	0135 0.9
	0609 1.2	0809 6.7	0812 9.2	0910 12.7	0701 0.9	0648 0.6	1012 2.7	0705 4.9	0728 4.1
	1221 5.4	1426 1.3	1410 1.7	1549 1.7	1340 3.9	1300 3.5	1630 0.8	1303 1.2	1354 0.9
	1830 1.2	2026 6.5	2029 9.0	2127 12.4	1923 0.9	1918 0.6	2219 2.6	1927 4.7	1945 3.9
5 W	0042 5.2	0242 1.5	0225 1.8	0400 1.9	0212 3.7	0127 3.4	0451 0.9	0121 1.4	0212 1.0
	0649 1.4	0847 6.4	0848 8.9	0945 12.2	0745 1.0	0731 0.7	1054 2.6	0746 4.8	0807 4.0
	1303 5.3	1505 1.6	1448 1.9	1618 2.1	1427 3.8	1342 3.4	1717 0.9	1347 1.4	1434 1.0
	1915 1.4	2106 6.2	2109 8.6	2205 11.9	2012 0.9	2005 0.7	2309 2.4	2012 4.5	2026 3.8
6 TH	0129 5.0	0321 1.8	0303 2.2	0429 2.3	0304 3.6	0216 3.3	0538 1.0	0207 1.7	0253 1.1
	0737 1.6	0930 6.2	0932 8.5	1025 11.6	0836 1.2	0819 0.8	1146 2.6	0833 4.6	0851 3.8
	1352 5.1	1551 1.8	1533 2.3	1651 2.5	1520 3.7	1432 3.4	1812 1.0	1439 1.6	1520 1.1
	2009 1.5	2154 5.9	2156 8.2	2248 11.2	2110 1.1	2058 0.8		2106 4.3	2115 3.6
7 F	0226 4.8	0412 2.1	0352 2.6	0505 2.7	0406 3.5	0312 3.2	0011 2.3	0304 1.9	0345 1.2
	0836 1.8	1025 5.9	1028 8.1	1114 11.0	0940 1.3	0915 1.0	0634 1.1	0930 4.4	0945 3.7
	1454 4.9	1651 2.1	1634 2.6	1735 2.9	1621 3.7	1529 3.3	1249 2.5	1543 1.7	1618 1.2
	2115 1.7	2257 5.6	2259 7.7	2343 10.7	2223 1.1	2203 0.9	1916 1.1	2212 4.2	2214 3.5
8 SA	0338 4.7	0519 2.3	0503 3.0	0557 3.1	0519 3.5	0418 3.1	0134 2.2	0418 2.1	0451 1.3
	0948 2.0	1137 5.7	1142 7.7	1220 10.6	1057 1.4	1022 1.1	0741 1.2	1039 4.3	1051 3.6
	1608 4.9	1809 2.2	1757 2.8	1840 3.2	1731 3.6	1635 3.2	1409 2.5	1701 1.8	1730 1.3
	2232 1.7				2339 1.1	2316 0.9	2039 1.1	2331 4.2	2327 3.4
9 SU	0502 4.7	0017 5.5	0020 7.5	0058 10.5	0636 3.5	0530 3.1	0321 2.2	0545 2.0	0609 1.3
	1109 1.9	0646 2.3	0640 3.0	0712 3.4	1210 1.4	1139 1.1	0903 1.2	1158 4.4	1208 3.6
	1727 5.0	1300 5.7	1307 7.8	1344 10.7	1845 3.7	1748 3.2	1534 2.6	1823 1.6	1849 1.2
	2348 1.5	1934 2.1	1926 2.7	2009 3.1			2214 1.0		
10 M	0618 4.9	0142 5.6	0146 7.7	0223 10.8	0048 1.0	0030 0.8	0436 2.4	0053 4.4	0046 3.5
	1221 1.7	0811 2.1	0806 2.6	0847 3.1	0743 3.7	0644 3.1	1025 1.0	0702 1.8	0727 1.1
	1836 5.2	1416 6.0	1425 8.2	1501 11.4	1316 1.3	1253 1.1	1640 2.8	1312 4.6	1324 3.7
		2048 1.7	2040 2.2	2135 2.5	1952 3.9	1900 3.3	2321 0.9	1930 1.3	2002 1.0
11 TU	0054 1.2	0254 6.1	0300 8.3	0341 11.6	0151 0.8	0135 0.7	0529 2.6	0157 4.7	0158 3.7
	0720 5.2	0919 1.6	0913 2.0	1010 2.4	0843 3.9	0749 3.3	1129 0.9	0801 1.4	0836 0.9
	1321 1.4	1521 6.5	1530 8.9	1615 12.3	1415 1.1	1357 0.9	1733 3.0	1412 4.9	1431 3.9
	1933 5.5	2149 1.2	2142 1.6	2253 1.8	2051 4.1	2004 3.5		2024 1.0	2105 0.7
12 W	0149 0.9	0354 6.5	0401 9.0	0447 12.4	0245 0.6	0232 0.5	0010 0.7	0248 5.0	0259 4.0
	0812 5.4	1016 1.1	1009 1.4	1130 1.7	0935 4.1	0846 3.4	0615 2.7	0851 1.1	0935 0.5
	1413 1.0	1618 6.9	1626 9.5	1717 13.1	1506 0.9	1453 0.8	1222 0.7	1503 5.2	1529 4.2
	2024 5.8	2242 0.8	2235 1.1		2143 4.3	2101 3.6	1821 3.1	2110 0.7	2200 0.5
13 TH	0238 0.6	0445 6.9	0452 9.6	0006 1.2	0333 0.5	0324 0.4	0054 0.6	0334 5.3	0353 4.3
	0857 5.7	1107 0.8	1058 1.0	0544 13.1	1022 4.2	0937 3.6	0657 2.8	0936 0.7	1028 0.4
	1500 0.8	1708 7.2	1716 9.9	1237 1.1	1553 0.7	1543 0.6	1310 0.6	1551 5.4	1620 4.4
	2111 5.9	2331 0.5	2322 0.7	1810 13.6	2231 4.4	2154 3.7	1906 3.1	2154 0.5	2249 0.4
14 F	0324 0.5	0533 7.2	0539 10.0	0106 0.8	0418 0.4	0412 0.3	0133 0.5	0418 5.5	0442 4.4
	0940 5.8	1155 0.5	1144 0.7	0634 13.6	1105 4.3	1024 3.7	0737 2.9	1019 0.5	1117 0.3
	1545 0.6	1755 7.4	1803 10.1	1331 0.8	1637 0.6	1630 0.5	1356 0.5	1636 5.5	1707 4.5
	2157 6.0			1858 13.9	2317 4.4	2242 3.7	1948 3.1	2237 0.5	2336 0.4 O
15 SA	0408 0.5	0017 0.4	0006 0.7	0155 0.6	0500 0.5	0457 0.3	0211 0.5	0500 5.6	0528 4.5
	1023 5.9	0617 7.4	0623 10.1	0719 13.8	1146 4.4	1108 3.7	0815 2.9	1103 0.5	1203 0.3
	1630 0.5	1239 0.4	1227 0.7	1417 0.7	1721 0.5	1715 0.5	1439 0.6	1721 5.5	1751 4.5
	2243 6.0	1839 7.4	1847 10.1	1942 14.0		2330 3.7	2031 3.0	2319 0.5	

● ● Time UT. For British Summer Time (shaded) March 30th to October 26th ADD ONE HOUR ● ●

NOVEMBER 1997 TIDE TABLES NOVEMBER 1997

	HOLYHEAD	MILFORD HAVEN	SWANSEA	AVONMOUTH	DUBLIN	BELFAST	LONDONDERRY	GALWAY	COBH
	Time m	Time m	Time m	Time m	Time m	Time m	Time m	Time m	Time m
16 SU	0451 0.5	0100 0.4	0047 0.8	0237 0.7	0001 4.4	0542 0.4	0248 0.6	0543 5.6	0021 0.4
	1106 5.9	0700 7.3	0704 10.1	0800 13.9	0542 0.5	1151 3.8	0852 2.9	1145 0.5	0612 4.5
	1715 0.6	1323 0.5	1308 0.9	1456 0.8	1227 4.4	1800 0.5	1522 0.7	1806 5.4	1246 0.4
	2330 5.8	1923 7.2	1929 9.9	2024 13.8	1805 0.5		2113 2.9		1834 4.4
17 M	0534 0.7	0141 0.6	0126 1.0	0313 0.9	0046 4.3	0015 3.6	0323 0.7	0001 0.8	0103 0.5
	1150 5.8	0742 7.1	0745 9.8	0841 13.7	0623 0.7	0626 0.5	0928 2.8	0627 5.4	0655 4.4
	1802 0.7	1405 0.7	1347 1.2	1530 1.1	1308 4.3	1234 3.7	1605 0.8	1230 0.7	1329 0.5
		2005 6.9	2009 9.6	2106 13.4	1850 0.6	1845 0.5	2155 2.7	1853 5.2	1916 4.2
18 TU	0015 5.6	0221 0.9	0203 1.4	0344 1.3	0132 4.2	0102 3.5	0400 0.8	0045 1.1	0144 0.7
	0618 1.0	0822 6.9	0823 9.4	0921 13.1	0706 0.9	0709 0.7	1004 2.8	0711 5.2	0737 4.3
	1234 5.6	1445 1.1	1424 1.6	1559 1.7	1351 4.2	1318 3.6	1648 0.9	1316 1.0	1409 0.7
	1848 1.0	2046 6.5	2048 9.1	2145 12.6	1939 0.8	1930 0.6	2240 2.5	1940 4.9	1957 4.1
19 W	0103 5.3	0300 1.3	0239 1.8	0412 1.9	0221 3.9	0150 3.3	0438 0.9	0130 1.4	0224 0.9
	0702 1.4	0903 6.5	0902 9.0	1000 12.3	0753 1.1	0755 0.9	1043 2.7	0757 4.9	0819 4.1
	1319 5.3	1526 1.5	1504 2.0	1627 2.3	1439 4.0	1406 3.5	1736 1.1	1406 1.4	1451 0.9
	1937 1.3	2127 6.1	2127 8.6	2225 11.7	2031 1.0	2018 0.7	2330 2.3	2030 4.6	2039 3.8
20 TH	0151 5.0	0339 1.8	0318 2.3	0440 2.6	0315 3.7	0242 3.1	0521 1.0	0218 1.8	0306 1.0
	0749 1.7	0945 6.1	0944 8.5	1038 11.4	0845 1.4	0845 1.0	1128 2.6	0847 4.6	0903 3.8
	1406 5.1	1609 1.9	1548 2.5	1656 2.9	1533 3.9	1456 3.4	1832 1.2	1500 1.7	1534 1.1
	2030 1.6	2212 5.7	2212 8.0	2306 10.8	2130 1.1	2111 0.8		2124 4.3	2125 3.6
21 F	0244 4.7	0422 2.2	0406 2.8	0510 3.2	0416 3.5	0339 3.0	0032 2.2	0313 2.1	0351 1.2
	0842 2.1	1033 5.7	1033 8.0	1118 10.6	0946 1.6	0940 1.2	0612 1.2	0941 4.3	0952 3.6
	1501 4.8	1700 2.3	1642 3.0	1729 3.5	1636 3.7	1551 3.3	1225 2.4	1603 1.9	1624 1.3
	2131 1.9	2305 5.3	2304 7.5	2351 10.0	2236 1.3	2211 0.9	1944 1.3	2224 4.1	2217 3.4
22 SA	0347 4.5	0516 2.5	0506 3.2	0546 3.8	0524 3.4	0441 2.9	0150 2.1	0419 2.3	0444 1.4
	0946 2.3	1131 5.4	1133 7.5	1211 9.9	1054 1.7	1044 1.3	0712 1.3	1045 4.1	1048 3.5
	1606 4.6	1806 2.5	1750 3.3	1814 4.0	1744 3.6	1651 3.2	1345 2.4	1715 2.0	1723 1.5
	2240 2.1				2343 1.3	2317 1.0	2112 1.3	2336 4.0	2318 3.3
23 SU	0501 4.4	0010 5.1	0010 7.2	0052 9.5	0631 3.3	0545 2.8	0308 2.2	0537 2.4	0548 1.5
	1100 2.4	0629 2.7	0622 3.5	0640 4.2	1205 1.7	1151 1.3	0823 1.3	1200 4.0	1155 3.3
	1720 4.6	1242 5.3	1244 7.3	1321 9.7	1850 3.6	1751 3.1	1512 2.4	1827 2.0	1829 1.5
	2349 2.0	1924 2.5	1907 3.4	1928 4.3			2220 1.2		
24 M	0613 4.5	0127 5.1	0127 7.2	0209 9.5	0050 1.3	0021 1.0	0409 2.3	0050 4.1	0027 3.3
	1212 2.3	0748 2.6	0740 3.4	0821 4.3	0733 3.4	0646 2.8	0937 1.3	0651 2.3	0657 1.5
	1828 4.7	1358 5.4	1358 7.4	1441 9.9	1314 1.6	1252 1.2	1618 2.5	1311 4.1	1305 3.3
		2032 2.3	2018 3.2	2113 3.9	1951 3.6	1851 3.1	2308 1.1	1926 1.9	1935 1.4
25 TU	0050 1.9	0237 5.4	0239 7.5	0323 10.1	0148 1.2	0118 0.9	0458 2.4	0149 4.2	0133 3.4
	0711 4.7	0853 2.3	0845 3.1	0947 3.6	0828 3.5	0740 2.9	1040 1.2	0748 2.0	0800 1.4
	1309 2.1	1500 5.7	1502 7.8	1548 10.6	1412 1.5	1346 1.1	1706 2.6	1406 4.2	1406 3.5
	1923 4.8	2127 2.0	2115 2.8	2218 3.1	2043 3.5	1945 3.1	2348 1.0	2014 1.7	2031 1.3
26 W	0139 1.7	0330 5.7	0335 7.9	0421 10.8	0236 1.1	0206 0.8	0541 2.6	0236 4.4	0230 3.5
	0756 4.9	0945 2.0	0936 2.7	1044 2.8	0913 3.6	0827 3.0	1132 1.0	0834 1.8	0855 1.2
	1355 1.9	1550 6.0	1552 8.2	1641 11.3	1457 1.3	1434 1.0	1748 2.6	1451 4.4	1457 3.6
	2007 5.0	2212 1.7	2202 2.4	2311 2.5	2128 3.7	2033 3.2		2055 1.5	2120 1.1
27 TH	0219 1.5	0414 6.1	0419 8.4	0508 11.6	0315 1.1	0249 0.8	0025 0.9	0315 4.6	0318 3.7
	0833 5.1	1028 1.7	1018 2.3	1134 2.2	0951 3.7	0909 3.1	0620 2.7	0913 1.6	0942 1.1
	1434 1.6	1631 6.2	1634 8.5	1725 11.9	1535 1.2	1516 0.9	1217 0.9	1530 4.5	1541 3.8
	2046 5.2	2251 1.5	2243 2.1	2359 1.9	2206 3.7	2116 3.2	1826 2.7	2131 1.3	2203 0.9
28 F	0255 1.3	0453 6.4	0458 8.8	0548 12.2	0350 1.0	0328 0.7	0100 0.8	0350 4.8	0400 3.9
	0908 5.3	1107 1.4	1058 1.9	1221 1.7	1024 3.8	0947 3.2	0657 2.8	0949 1.3	1024 0.9
	1509 1.4	1709 6.5	1713 8.9	1805 12.3	1608 1.1	1556 0.8	1257 0.8	1605 4.7	1621 3.9
	2121 5.3	2328 1.3	2321 1.8		2241 3.8	2156 3.3	1901 2.8	2205 1.2	2245 0.8
29 SA	0329 1.2	0529 6.6	0535 9.2	0044 1.6	0421 0.9	0404 0.6	0134 0.7	0423 5.0	0441 4.0
	0941 5.4	1145 1.2	1136 1.7	0627 12.6	1055 3.9	1021 3.3	0733 2.9	1023 1.2	1106 0.8
	1545 1.2	1745 6.7	1751 9.2	1305 1.4	1639 1.0	1633 0.7	1337 0.8	1639 4.8	1700 4.0
	2156 5.4		2357 1.6	1843 12.7	2314 3.8	2234 3.3	1936 2.8	2238 1.1	2324 0.7
30 SU ●	0403 1.1	0004 1.1	0612 9.4	0127 1.3	0453 0.8	0439 0.6	0207 0.7	0456 5.1	0519 4.1
	1014 5.6	0605 6.8	1212 1.5	0704 12.9	1127 4.0	1055 3.4	0808 2.9	1057 1.0	1145 0.7
	1620 1.1	1222 1.0	1827 9.3	1348 1.2	1712 0.9	1709 0.6	1415 0.7	1715 4.9	1738 4.1
	2232 5.5	1821 6.8		1921 12.9	2349 3.9	2311 3.3	2010 2.8	2312 1.1	

WEST COAST ENGLAND, WALES & IRELAND Time Zone UT
Holyhead * Milford Haven * Swansea * Avonmouth * Dublin * Belfast * Londonderry * Galway * Cobh

DECEMBER 1997 TIDE TABLES DECEMBER 1997

HOLYHEAD	MILFORD HAVEN	SWANSEA	AVONMOUTH	DUBLIN	BELFAST	LONDONDERRY	GALWAY	COBH	
Time m	Time m	Time m	Time m	Time m	Time m	Time m	Time m	Time m	
0438 1.0	0040 1.0	0031 1.4	0209 1.2	0526 0.8	0515 0.5	0241 0.7	0530 5.2	0004 0.7	**1 M**
1049 5.6	0641 6.9	0648 9.5	0742 13.2	1202 4.0	1129 3.4	0843 2.9	1132 0.9	0557 4.2	
1657 1.0	1300 1.0	1248 1.4	1428 1.1	1747 0.8	1746 0.6	1455 0.7	1751 5.0	1225 0.7	
2309 5.5	1859 6.8	1905 9.4	1959 13.1		2349 3.4	2047 2.8	2347 1.1	1815 4.1	
0515 1.0	0117 1.0	0106 1.4	0247 1.3	0027 3.9	0553 0.5	0315 0.7	0607 5.2	0043 0.7	**2 TU**
1127 5.7	0718 6.9	0724 9.5	0820 13.2	0603 0.7	1206 3.4	0919 2.9	1209 0.9	0636 4.2	
1736 1.0	1338 1.0	1324 1.3	1507 1.2	1239 4.1	1825 0.5	1536 0.7	1830 4.9	1304 0.7	
2348 5.4	1937 6.8	1942 9.3	2038 13.0	1826 0.7		2127 2.7		1853 4.0	
0554 1.1	0154 1.1	0141 1.4	0323 1.4	0109 3.9	0030 3.4	0353 0.8	0026 1.2	0121 0.7	**3 W**
1207 5.6	0757 6.8	0802 9.4	0858 13.1	0643 0.8	0633 0.5	0958 2.9	0647 5.2	0715 4.1	
1818 1.0	1418 1.1	1402 1.4	1543 1.4	1321 4.1	1245 3.5	1620 0.8	1251 1.0	1343 0.7	
	2018 6.6	2021 9.1	2118 12.8	1910 0.7	1908 0.5	2211 2.6	1914 4.9	1933 4.0	
0032 5.3	0234 1.3	0217 1.5	0356 1.7	0156 3.8	0115 3.3	0435 0.8	0108 1.3	0201 0.8	**4 TH**
0636 1.2	0839 6.7	0842 9.1	0939 12.7	0728 0.9	0718 0.6	1042 2.9	0731 5.1	0756 4.0	
1251 5.5	1500 1.3	1442 1.6	1617 1.7	1409 4.0	1330 3.5	1708 0.9	1336 1.1	1424 0.8	
1905 1.1	2101 6.4	2102 8.8	2200 12.4	2000 0.7	1954 0.5	2301 2.5	2000 4.7	2015 3.9	
0120 5.2	0318 1.5	0257 1.8	0429 2.0	0248 3.7	0204 3.3	0522 0.9	0156 1.5	0244 0.9	**5 F**
0725 1.4	0925 6.5	0927 8.8	1022 12.3	0820 1.0	0806 0.7	1132 2.8	0820 4.9	0840 3.9	
1341 5.4	1547 1.5	1528 1.8	1653 2.1	1501 4.0	1418 3.5	1801 1.0	1427 1.3	1511 0.9	
1957 1.2	2150 6.1	2149 8.5	2245 11.9	2057 0.8	2048 0.6		2053 4.6	2103 3.7	
0215 5.0	0407 1.7	0345 2.1	0506 2.3	0348 3.6	0259 3.2	0000 2.4	0251 1.7	0334 1.0	**6 SA**
0821 1.6	1018 6.2	1020 8.4	1111 11.8	0920 1.2	0901 0.8	0616 1.0	0914 4.7	0932 3.8	
1438 5.2	1642 1.7	1624 2.2	1737 2.4	1600 3.9	1514 3.4	1230 2.7	1525 1.5	1605 1.0	
2058 1.4	2248 5.9	2246 8.0	2338 11.4	2203 0.9	2148 0.6	1903 1.1	2153 4.4	2158 3.6	
0320 4.8	0508 2.0	0448 2.5	0556 2.7	0457 3.6	0400 3.1	0113 2.3	0354 1.9	0433 1.1	**7 SU**
0926 1.7	1121 6.0	1124 8.1	1210 11.3	1029 1.3	1004 1.0	0718 1.1	1016 4.6	1032 3.7	
1543 5.1	1749 1.9	1734 2.5	1834 2.6	1707 3.8	1617 3.3	1340 2.7	1632 1.6	1709 1.1	
2207 1.8	2357 5.7	2357 7.7		2313 1.0	2255 0.7	2017 1.1	2302 4.3	2303 3.5	
0433 4.8	0621 2.1	0610 2.7	0041 11.0	0609 3.6	0509 3.1	0243 2.3	0510 1.9	0543 1.1	**8 M**
1039 1.8	1233 5.9	1239 8.0	0659 2.9	1140 1.4	1116 1.0	0833 1.1	1127 4.5	1141 3.6	
1655 5.1	1904 1.9	1855 2.5	1320 11.2	1819 3.8	1727 3.3	1458 2.7	1746 1.6	1821 1.1	
2319 1.4			1944 2.7			2142 1.1			
0548 4.9	0112 5.7	0117 7.7	0154 11.0	0021 0.7	0006 0.7	0404 2.4	0018 4.4	0015 3.5	**9 TU**
1151 1.7	0740 2.0	0736 2.6	0815 2.9	0717 3.7	0621 3.1	0953 1.1	0628 1.8	0657 1.0	
1806 5.2	1346 6.0	1356 8.1	1436 11.4	1248 1.3	1229 1.0	1611 2.8	1242 4.6	1254 3.6	
	2018 1.7	2012 2.3	2101 2.5	1927 3.9	1838 3.3	2253 1.0	1857 1.4	1933 1.0	
0027 1.3	0225 5.9	0233 8.1	0310 11.3	0126 0.9	0112 0.6	0505 2.5	0128 4.6	0128 3.7	**10 W**
0654 5.0	0852 1.7	0848 2.2	0936 2.6	0818 3.8	0728 3.2	1104 1.0	0735 1.6	0810 0.9	
1257 1.5	1455 6.3	1506 8.5	1547 11.9	1351 1.2	1336 0.9	1710 2.8	1348 4.7	1404 3.8	
1909 5.3	2124 1.4	2119 1.9	2218 2.2	2030 4.0	1945 3.4	2346 0.9	1957 1.3	2040 0.8	
0127 1.1	0330 6.3	0339 8.6	0419 11.9	0224 0.8	0212 0.6	0555 2.6	0225 4.9	0235 3.8	**11 TH**
0751 5.3	0955 1.4	0949 1.8	1057 2.2	0915 4.0	0827 3.3	1203 0.9	0830 1.3	0914 0.7	
1354 1.2	1557 6.5	1606 9.0	1651 12.4	1448 1.0	1434 0.8	1802 2.9	1444 4.9	1507 3.9	
2006 5.5	2222 1.1	2216 1.5	2334 1.8	2126 4.2	2045 3.5		2048 1.1	2139 0.6	
0220 0.9	0426 6.6	0434 9.2	0520 12.5	0315 0.7	0306 0.5	0032 0.8	0314 5.1	0334 4.0	**12 F**
0841 5.5	1050 1.1	1042 1.4	1209 1.7	1004 4.1	0920 3.5	0640 2.7	0919 1.0	1010 0.5	
1446 1.0	1651 6.8	1700 9.4	1749 12.9	1539 0.9	1527 0.7	1254 0.8	1534 5.1	1602 4.1	
2057 5.6	2313 0.9	2306 1.3		2217 4.2	2140 3.6	1849 2.9	2136 0.9	2232 0.5	
0309 0.8	0516 6.9	0523 9.5	0038 1.4	0402 0.7	0356 0.5	0112 0.7	0400 5.3	0426 4.2	**13 SA**
0926 5.6	1140 0.8	1130 1.2	0614 13.0	1049 4.3	1008 3.6	0721 2.8	1005 0.8	1101 0.4	
1534 0.8	1739 6.9	1748 9.6	1306 1.3	1625 0.7	1617 0.6	1342 0.7	1621 5.2	1651 4.2	
2145 5.7		2351 1.1	1840 13.2	2304 4.3	2230 3.6	1933 2.9	2220 0.8	2320 0.5	
0353 0.8	0000 0.8	0608 9.7	0130 1.1	0445 0.7	0442 0.5	0150 0.7	0444 5.4	0514 4.3	**14 SU**
1009 5.8	0602 7.0	1215 1.2	0701 13.3	1131 4.3	1052 3.7	0800 2.9	1049 0.7	1148 0.4	
1620 0.7	1225 0.7	1833 9.6	1355 1.2	1710 0.7	1703 0.5	1426 0.7	1707 5.3	1736 4.2	
2231 5.7	1825 7.0		1927 13.3	2348 4.2	2318 3.6	2016 2.9	2303 0.8	○	
0436 0.8	0042 0.7	0033 1.1	0215 1.1	0526 0.7	0527 0.6	0226 0.7	0527 5.4	0005 0.5	**15 M**
1052 5.8	0645 7.1	0651 9.7	0744 13.4	1211 4.3	1135 3.7	0836 2.9	1133 0.7	0558 4.3	
1704 0.7	1308 0.7	1256 1.2	1436 1.2	1754 0.7	1746 0.5	1508 0.8	1752 5.2	1231 0.5	
2315 5.6	1908 6.9	1915 9.5	2009 13.4			2057 2.8	2345 0.9	1818 4.1	

● ● Time UT. For British Summer Time (shaded) March 30th to October 26th ADD ONE HOUR ● ●

DECEMBER 1997 TIDE TABLES DECEMBER 1997

	HOLYHEAD	MILFORD HAVEN	SWANSEA	AVONMOUTH	DUBLIN	BELFAST	LONDONDERRY	GALWAY	COBH
	Time m	Time m	Time m	Time m	Time m	Time m	Time m	Time m	Time m
16 TU	0518 0.9	0123 0.8	0111 1.3	0254 1.2	0031 4.2	0003 3.5	0300 0.7	0610 5.3	0046 0.5
	1134 5.7	0726 7.0	0730 9.6	0824 13.4	0607 0.8	0609 0.6	0911 2.9	1217 0.8	0640 4.2
	1747 0.8	1348 0.8	1334 1.4	1512 1.4	1251 4.3	1217 3.7	1548 0.9	1837 5.1	1312 0.6
	2359 5.5	1948 6.8	1954 9.3	2050 13.1	1837 0.7	1829 0.5	2137 2.7		1858 4.1
17 W	0558 1.1	0202 0.9	0147 1.4	0327 1.4	0113 4.0	0045 3.4	0335 0.8	0027 1.1	0126 0.6
	1215 5.6	0805 6.8	0808 9.4	0904 13.1	0648 0.9	0650 0.7	0945 2.8	0653 5.2	0720 4.1
	1830 1.0	1427 1.0	1411 1.6	1545 1.7	1330 4.2	1258 3.7	1627 1.0	1300 1.0	1351 0.7
		2027 6.5	2030 9.0	2128 12.7	1922 0.8	1911 0.6	2218 2.6	1921 4.9	1937 3.9
18 TH	0041 5.3	0239 1.2	0222 1.7	0357 1.8	0157 3.9	0128 3.3	0412 0.9	0110 1.3	0203 0.8
	0639 1.3	0842 6.6	0844 9.1	0941 12.6	0731 1.1	0730 0.9	1021 2.8	0736 5.0	0759 4.0
	1255 5.4	1504 1.3	1447 1.8	1613 2.1	1413 4.1	1340 3.6	1708 1.1	1345 1.2	1427 0.8
	1912 1.2	2105 6.2	2106 8.7	2205 12.0	2009 0.9	1953 0.7	2301 2.4	2006 4.7	2015 3.8
19 F	0122 5.0	0315 1.5	0258 2.0	0424 2.3	0242 3.7	0211 3.2	0451 0.9	0154 1.6	0239 0.9
	0719 1.6	0921 6.3	0921 8.7	1016 11.9	0818 1.2	0812 1.0	1100 2.7	0821 4.7	0838 3.8
	1336 5.2	1541 1.6	1524 2.2	1639 2.5	1500 3.9	1424 3.5	1752 1.2	1431 1.5	1505 1.0
	1957 1.5	2143 5.9	2144 8.3	2239 11.3	2100 1.1	2037 0.8	2349 2.3	2053 4.4	2055 3.7
20 SA	0206 4.8	0351 1.8	0338 2.3	0451 2.7	0333 3.5	0257 3.0	0536 1.0	0240 1.8	0317 1.0
	0802 1.8	1000 6.0	1002 8.3	1051 11.2	0909 1.4	0857 1.1	1145 2.6	0906 4.5	0919 3.7
	1418 5.0	1621 2.0	1606 2.5	1707 2.9	1551 3.7	1511 3.4	1845 1.3	1521 1.7	1545 1.2
	2044 1.7	2225 5.6	2226 7.9	2315 10.6	2154 1.2	2125 0.9		2142 4.2	2139 3.5
21 SU	0254 4.6	0433 2.1	0424 2.7	0520 3.2	0430 3.4	0347 2.9	0045 2.2	0332 2.1	0400 1.2
	0851 2.1	1045 5.7	1048 7.9	1129 10.6	1007 1.5	0948 1.1	0626 1.1	0955 4.2	1004 3.5
	1507 4.8	1707 2.2	1657 2.9	1741 3.3	1651 3.6	1602 3.3	1239 2.5	1615 1.9	1632 1.3
	2138 1.9	2315 5.3	2317 7.5	2357 10.0	2253 1.3	2218 0.9	1948 1.3	2236 4.1	2228 3.4
22 M	0350 4.5	0524 2.4	0521 3.1	0557 3.6	0533 3.3	0442 2.8	0152 2.2	0431 2.2	0451 1.3
	0950 2.3	1139 5.4	1143 7.5	1218 10.0	1111 1.6	1045 1.2	0724 1.2	1053 4.0	1056 3.3
	1606 4.6	1806 2.4	1758 3.2	1824 3.8	1756 3.5	1657 3.2	1347 2.4	1718 2.0	1727 1.3
	2239 2.1				2354 1.4	2315 1.0	2100 1.3	2341 4.0	2325 3.3
23 TU	0457 4.4	0015 5.2	0018 7.2	0053 9.6	0636 3.3	0542 2.8	0302 2.2	0542 2.3	0550 1.4
	1058 2.4	0630 2.5	0630 3.3	0648 4.0	1217 1.6	1148 1.2	0830 1.2	1201 3.9	1157 3.3
	1716 4.5	1245 5.3	1248 7.3	1322 9.8	1859 3.4	1756 3.1	1505 2.4	1825 2.0	1829 1.3
	2345 2.1	1917 2.5	1909 3.3	1927 4.1			2206 1.3		
24 W	0607 4.5	0127 5.2	0130 7.2	0206 9.6	0054 1.4	0015 1.0	0405 2.3	0050 4.0	0029 3.3
	1207 2.3	0746 2.5	0742 3.3	0809 4.2	0734 3.4	0642 2.9	0940 1.2	0653 2.2	0656 1.4
	1825 4.6	1355 5.3	1357 7.4	1436 9.9	1319 1.6	1251 1.2	1614 2.4	1311 4.0	1302 3.3
		2027 2.4	2018 3.2	2106 3.9	1957 3.4	1854 3.1	2302 1.2	1926 1.9	1933 1.3
25 TH	0046 1.9	0236 5.4	0239 7.5	0318 10.0	0148 1.3	0113 1.0	0459 2.4	0149 4.2	0135 3.3
	0707 4.7	0854 2.3	0845 3.0	0947 3.7	0827 3.5	0738 2.9	1045 1.1	0752 2.0	0802 1.3
	1308 2.1	1500 5.5	1500 7.7	1543 10.5	1413 1.5	1349 1.1	1709 2.5	1409 4.1	1406 3.4
	1924 4.7	2127 2.1	2117 2.8	2220 3.2	2048 3.5	1950 3.1	2349 1.0	2017 1.8	2034 1.1
26 F	0138 1.7	0332 5.7	0335 7.9	0418 10.8	0234 1.2	0206 0.9	0547 2.6	0237 4.3	0235 3.5
	0757 4.9	0950 2.0	0939 2.7	1049 2.9	0912 3.6	0829 3.0	1141 1.0	0840 1.8	0901 1.1
	1358 1.8	1553 5.8	1554 8.1	1639 11.2	1458 1.3	1441 1.0	1756 2.6	1457 4.3	1502 3.5
	2014 4.9	2216 1.8	2206 2.4	2316 2.4	2133 3.6	2041 3.1		2100 1.6	2127 0.9
27 SA	0223 1.5	0420 6.0	0423 8.4	0509 11.7	0315 1.1	0254 0.8	0031 0.9	0318 4.6	0327 3.7
	0839 5.1	1038 1.7	1025 2.2	1142 2.1	0953 3.7	0915 3.1	0630 2.7	0922 1.5	0954 0.9
	1442 1.6	1639 6.2	1642 8.5	1730 11.9	1537 1.2	1528 0.9	1231 0.9	1538 4.5	1551 3.7
	2057 5.1	2300 1.5	2251 2.0		2215 3.7	2128 3.2	1839 2.7	2139 1.4	2216 0.8
28 SU	0303 1.3	0503 6.4	0507 8.8	0009 1.8	0352 1.0	0337 0.7	0111 0.8	0356 4.8	0415 3.8
	0917 5.3	1121 1.3	1109 1.8	0556 12.4	1030 3.8	0956 3.3	0712 2.8	1000 1.2	1040 0.7
	1523 1.3	1721 6.4	1726 8.9	1234 1.6	1614 1.0	1612 0.7	1317 0.8	1617 4.7	1636 3.8
	2136 5.3	2342 1.2	2333 1.6	1816 12.5	2253 3.8	2212 3.3	1920 2.7	2217 1.2	2301 0.7
29 M	0342 1.1	0543 6.7	0549 9.2	0059 1.4	0429 0.8	0419 0.6	0149 0.7	0433 5.0	0458 4.0
	0954 5.5	1203 1.1	1152 1.5	0640 12.9	1106 4.0	1036 3.4	0751 2.9	1038 1.0	1125 0.6
	1603 1.0	1803 6.7	1809 9.2	1324 1.2	1651 0.8	1653 0.6	1402 0.7	1656 4.8	1718 3.9
●	2215 5.4			1901 12.9	2332 3.9	2255 3.3	2000 2.8	2254 1.0	2345 0.6
30 TU	0420 0.9	0023 1.0	0014 1.3	0148 1.2	0506 0.7	0500 0.5	0227 0.7	0511 5.2	0540 4.1
	1033 5.7	0624 6.9	0630 9.5	0724 13.3	1143 4.1	1114 3.5	0830 3.0	1117 0.8	1208 0.5
	1642 0.8	1245 1.0	1234 1.2	1412 1.1	1730 0.6	1733 0.6	1445 0.7	1736 5.0	1759 4.0
	2254 5.5	1845 6.8	1851 9.4	1945 13.2		2337 3.4	2040 2.8	2333 0.9	
31 W	0500 0.8	0104 0.9	0054 1.1	0234 1.1	0012 4.0	0540 0.5	0305 0.6	0551 5.3	0027 0.5
	1112 5.8	0706 7.0	0712 9.6	0807 13.5	0546 0.7	1153 3.5	0910 3.0	1157 0.7	0621 4.1
	1724 0.7	1327 1.0	1315 1.0	1458 1.0	1222 4.2	1815 0.4	1530 0.7	1818 5.1	1250 0.5
	2336 5.5	1927 6.9	1932 9.5	2028 13.4	1812 0.5		2122 2.8		1839 4.0

● ● Time UT. For British Summer Time (shaded) March 30th to October 26th ADD ONE HOUR ● ●

DENMARK, GERMANY, HOLLAND & BELGIUM Time Zone -0100

Esbjerg * Helgoland * Cuxhaven * Bremerhaven * Hoek van Holland * Rotterdam *Vlissingen * Antwerpen * Dunkerque

JANUARY 1997 TIDE TABLES JANUARY 1997

ESBJERG	HELGOLAND	CUXHAVEN	BREMERHAVEN	HOEK VAN HOLLAND	ROTTERDAM	VLISSINGEN	ANTWERPEN	DUNKERQUE	
Time m	Time m	Time m	Time m	Time m	Time m	Time m	Time m	Time m	
0654 1.7	0354 2.7	0506 3.1	0534 3.5	0101 0.4	0136 0.6	0621 4.1	0142 0.7	0513 5.3	**1 W**
1307 0.2	1038 0.6	1154 0.6	1202 0.4	0703 1.8	0824 1.7	1234 0.6	0747 5.1	1154 1.3	
1916 1.5	1627 2.3	1746 2.7	1806 3.2	1258 0.1	1418 0.3	1847 4.1	1407 0.4	1737 5.2	
	2245 0.7			1936 1.9	2058 1.8		2012 5.1		
0117 0.2	0443 2.6	0002 0.7	0015 0.5	0147 0.4	0425 0.6	0051 0.9	0223 0.8	0010 1.6	**2 TH**
0739 1.7	1127 0.7	0558 3.0	0626 3.4	0753 1.7	0915 1.7	0710 3.9	0833 5.0	0601 5.1	
1351 0.2	1723 2.3	1238 0.7	1247 0.5	1351 0.1	1616 0.3	1322 0.7	1451 0.5	1248 1.5	
2007 1.5	2341 0.8	1842 2.7	1901 3.1	2042 1.8	2203 1.7	1946 3.9	2106 5.0	1830 5.0	
0206 0.2	0545 2.5	0053 0.8	0106 0.5	0236 0.4	0550 0.5	0145 1.0	0310 0.9	0112 1.7	**3 F**
0833 1.6	1229 0.7	0701 2.9	0727 3.3	0910 1.6	1032 1.6	0815 3.8	0934 4.8	0700 4.9	
1445 0.2	1832 2.3	1334 0.7	1343 0.5	1445 0.2	1757 0.3	1424 0.8	1542 0.6	1351 1.6	
2111 1.4		1947 2.7	2006 3.1	2151 1.8	2333 1.7	2055 3.9	2212 4.9	1933 4.9	
0306 0.3	0051 0.8	0157 0.8	0212 0.6	0333 0.4	0700 0.4	0258 1.1	0407 1.0	0222 1.7	**4 SA**
0939 1.6	0657 2.5	0812 2.9	0837 3.2	1021 1.6	1203 1.6	0927 3.8	1045 4.8	0811 4.9	
1551 0.2	1342 0.7	1446 0.7	1457 0.5	1545 0.2	1915 0.3	1548 0.8	1648 0.7	1458 1.6	
2226 1.5	1945 2.4	2056 2.8	2118 3.1	2259 1.8		2206 3.9	2321 5.0	2045 4.9	
0419 0.3	0212 0.7	0319 0.7	0335 0.5	0604 0.4	0043 1.8	0422 1.0	0521 1.0	0331 1.6	**5 SU**
1054 1.6	0812 2.5	0923 3.0	0950 3.3	1129 1.7	0803 0.4	1039 3.9	1152 5.0	0923 5.0	
1704 0.2	1454 0.5	1606 0.4	1617 0.4	1654 0.3	1309 1.7	1700 0.7	1808 0.7	1603 1.4	
2339 1.5	2053 2.5	2203 3.0	2229 3.3		2021 0.3	2312 4.1		2151 5.2	
0534 0.2	0325 0.6	0440 0.5	0451 0.3	0000 1.9	0141 1.9	0530 0.8	0024 5.3	0436 1.4	**6 M**
1205 1.6	0918 2.6	1030 3.2	1058 3.4	0822 0.3	0903 0.3	1139 4.2	0640 0.8	1023 5.2	
1809 0.1	1557 0.4	1715 0.3	1724 0.2	1226 1.8	1403 1.8	1800 0.6	1254 5.3	1703 1.2	
	2152 2.7	2303 3.2	2331 3.5	1754 0.3	2126 0.3		1918 0.6	2246 5.4	
0044 1.6	0427 0.3	0545 0.2	0554 0.1	0053 2.0	0231 2.0	0007 4.4	0122 5.6	0534 1.1	**7 TU**
0639 0.1	1017 2.8	1130 3.3	1159 3.6	0622 0.3	1003 0.3	0627 0.6	0748 0.6	1112 5.5	
1309 1.7	1653 0.2	1812 0.1	1821 -0.0	1315 2.0	1452 2.0	1230 4.4	1348 5.7	1758 1.0	
1906 0.1	2244 2.9	2359 3.4		1837 0.3	2235 0.3	1852 0.4	2019 0.4	2334 5.7	
0140 1.7	0522 0.1	0641 -0.0	0027 3.7	0140 2.0	0316 2.0	0055 4.6	0215 5.8	0627 0.8	**8 W**
0736 0.0	1110 2.9	1227 3.5	0648 -0.1	0656 0.3	1105 0.3	0719 0.4	0848 0.4	1158 5.8	
1408 1.7	1745 0.0	1905 -0.1	1253 3.8	1401 2.1	1536 2.1	1317 4.7	1439 6.0	1848 0.8	
1959 -0.0	2333 3.0		1912 -0.2	1915 0.3	2350 0.3	1941 0.3	2115 0.3		
0232 1.7	0614 -0.0	0051 3.6	0117 3.9	0225 2.1	0359 2.1	0141 4.7	0303 6.0	0019 5.9	**9 TH**
0828 -0.1	1200 2.9	0734 -0.2	0739 -0.3	0732 0.2	1208 0.3	0809 0.2	0943 0.2	0715 0.6	
1503 1.7	1833 -0.0	1320 3.6	1344 3.9	1446 2.2	1621 2.2	1402 4.9	1527 6.2	1242 6.0	
2048 -0.0		1956 -0.2	2000 -0.3	1953 0.3	2234 0.4	2029 0.2	2207 0.2	1936 0.6	●
0321 1.8	0019 3.1	0141 3.7	0204 4.0	0310 2.1	0441 2.1	0225 4.8	0350 6.1	0103 6.1	**10 F**
0918 -0.1	0703 -0.2	0824 -0.3	0827 -0.4	0809 0.1	1115 0.3	0857 0.1	1035 0.1	0802 0.4	
1555 1.7	1248 2.9	1411 3.5	1431 4.0	1531 2.3	1704 2.2	1446 5.0	1612 6.3	1327 6.1	
2134 -0.1	1921 -0.1	2044 -0.3	2048 -0.4	2032 0.3	2330 0.5	2116 0.2	2256 0.2	2021 0.5	
0407 1.8	0104 3.1	0229 3.7	0250 4.2	0356 2.1	0524 2.1	0309 4.9	0436 6.2	0148 6.2	**11 SA**
1006 -0.2	0750 -0.2	0912 -0.4	0914 -0.5	0850 0.0	1214 0.2	0946 -0.0	1124 0.0	0848 0.3	
1645 1.7	1333 2.9	1458 3.5	1516 4.0	1617 2.3	1749 2.3	1532 5.0	1658 6.4	1413 6.2	
2220 -0.1	2005 -0.1	2129 -0.4	2133 -0.4	2114 0.3		2203 0.2	2343 0.2	2106 0.5	
0453 1.8	0148 3.2	0315 3.8	0333 4.2	0442 2.0	0018 0.5	0354 4.8	0521 6.1	0233 6.2	**12 SU**
1052 -0.2	0835 -0.3	0957 -0.5	0959 -0.6	0933 -0.0	0607 2.1	1035 -0.1	1212 0.0	0933 0.3	
1732 1.6	1417 2.9	1543 3.5	1600 4.0	1703 2.3	1312 0.2	1618 4.9	1745 6.3	1500 6.2	
2304 -0.1	2048 -0.1	2212 -0.4	2216 -0.5	2159 0.4	1834 2.3	2250 0.3		2151 0.5	
0538 1.8	0230 3.2	0357 3.8	0416 4.3	0529 2.0	0107 0.4	0441 4.7	0029 0.4	0320 6.2	**13 M**
1138 -0.2	0918 -0.3	1041 -0.5	1043 -0.7	1021 -0.0	0651 2.2	1124 -0.1	0607 6.0	1019 0.3	
1815 1.6	1459 2.9	1624 3.4	1642 4.0	1754 2.2	1430 0.1	1708 4.8	1258 0.0	1550 6.1	
2350 -0.1	2129 -0.1	2254 -0.5	2259 -0.5	2250 0.4	1920 2.3	2336 0.3	1833 6.1	2237 0.7	
0621 1.8	0312 3.2	0439 3.8	0459 4.3	0621 2.0	0210 0.4	0531 4.6	0113 0.5	0409 6.1	**14 TU**
1225 -0.2	1000 -0.2	1123 -0.4	1126 -0.7	1113 -0.0	0736 2.1	1212 0.0	0656 5.8	1108 0.5	
1858 1.5	1540 2.8	1705 3.4	1724 3.9	1850 2.1	1339 0.0	1803 4.7	1344 0.1	1642 5.9	
	2210 -0.1	2334 -0.3	2342 -0.5		2008 2.3		1924 5.8	2326 0.9	
0036 -0.1	0357 3.2	0520 3.7	0542 4.2	0228 0.3	0342 0.4	0024 0.2	0158 0.6	0503 5.9	**15 W**
0708 1.8	1044 -0.1	1204 -0.3	1210 -0.5	0719 1.9	0824 2.1	0627 4.5	0748 5.6	1202 0.7	
1314 -0.1	1624 2.8	1746 3.3	1808 3.8	1227 0.0	1438 0.0	1300 0.2	1431 0.2	1739 5.6	
1943 1.5	2254 0.0			1952 2.0	2100 2.2	1905 4.5	2020 5.5		

● ● Time Zone -0100. For UT subtract 1 hour. For European summer time (shaded) 30/3-26/10 add 1 hour ● ●

JANUARY 1997 TIDE TABLES JANUARY 1997

	ESBJERG		HELGOLAND		CUXHAVEN		BREMERHAVEN		HOEK VAN HOLLAND		ROTTERDAM		VLISSINGEN		ANTWERPEN		DUNKERQUE	
	Time	m	Time	m	Time	m	Time	m	Time	m	Time	m	Time	m	Time	m	Time	m
16 TH	0127	-0.0	0445	3.1	0015	-0.1	0027	-0.4	0230	0.4	0312	0.3	0115	0.6	0247	0.7	0023	1.1
	0800	1.7	1130	0.1	0604	3.6	0628	4.0	0820	1.9	0919	2.0	0728	4.3	0845	5.4	0603	5.6
	1408	0.0	1714	2.7	1248	-0.1	1256	-0.3	1418	0.0	1539	0.0	1355	0.3	1523	0.4	1303	1.0
	2036	1.5	2343	0.2	1831	3.2	1854	3.6	2054	1.9	2202	2.0	2007	4.3	2122	5.3	1845	5.3
17 F	0224	0.0	0538	2.9	0100	0.0	0115	-0.2	0300	0.3	0416	0.3	0215	0.7	0342	0.8	0129	1.3
	0900	1.7	1224	0.2	0654	3.4	0719	3.8	0923	1.8	1026	1.9	0833	4.1	0950	5.1	0715	5.3
	1509	0.1	1810	2.5	1338	0.1	1348	-0.1	1513	0.1	1644	0.1	1459	0.5	1621	0.5	1413	1.3
	2138	1.5			1924	3.1	1946	3.5	2200	1.9	2312	1.9	2113	4.1	2230	5.1	2002	5.1
18 SA	0331	0.1	0043	0.3	0156	0.3	0213	0.0	0354	0.3	0527	0.3	0327	0.8	0446	0.9	0242	1.5
	1008	1.6	0640	2.7	0751	3.2	0816	3.5	1031	1.8	1139	1.8	0942	4.0	1101	5.0	0836	5.1
	1618	0.2	1327	0.4	1440	0.3	1448	0.2	1615	0.2	1757	0.2	1617	0.6	1727	0.7	1526	1.4
	2247	1.5	1915	2.5	2024	2.9	2046	3.3	2308	1.8			2222	4.0	2341	5.0	2117	5.1
19 SU	0446	0.1	0157	0.5	0310	0.4	0323	0.2	0456	0.3	0019	1.9	0451	0.8	0602	0.9	0356	1.4
	1121	1.6	0751	2.6	0856	3.0	0922	3.3	1138	1.9	0648	0.4	1051	4.0	1212	5.0	0946	5.2
	1728	0.2	1439	0.5	1555	0.4	1600	0.3	1718	0.2	1246	1.8	1728	0.7	1845	0.7	1635	1.3
	2357	1.6	2027	2.4	2132	2.9	2156	3.2			1916	0.3	2327	4.1			2219	5.2
20 M	0559	0.1	0316	0.5	0433	0.4	0437	0.3	0010	1.8	0121	1.8	0557	0.7	0045	5.1	0501	1.2
	1234	1.6	0904	2.4	1007	2.9	1035	3.2	0820	0.3	0757	0.4	1154	4.1	0723	0.7	1043	5.3
	1831	0.2	1548	0.5	1706	0.4	1708	0.4	1237	1.8	1346	1.8	1823	0.6	1314	5.2	1733	1.2
			2138	2.5	2242	2.9	2309	3.3	1815	0.3	2030	0.4			1953	0.6	2310	5.3
21 TU	0102	1.7	0426	0.4	0542	0.4	0542	0.4	0106	1.8	0216	1.8	0023	4.2	0142	5.3	0555	1.0
	0702	0.1	1012	2.4	1117	2.8	1148	3.2	0644	0.3	0957	0.4	0648	0.6	0824	0.5	1131	5.5
	1337	1.6	1649	0.4	1807	0.3	1809	0.3	1330	1.9	1440	1.8	1246	4.3	1407	5.4	1821	1.1
	1926	0.1	2239	2.5	2346	3.0			1857	0.3	2129	0.5	1908	0.6	2045	0.5	2354	5.5
22 W	0155	1.7	0524	0.4	0641	0.3	0018	3.3	0156	1.9	0304	1.8	0111	4.3	0232	5.5	0641	0.8
	0755	0.1	1109	2.4	1218	2.8	0640	0.3	0717	0.2	1021	0.4	0733	0.4	0912	0.3	1213	5.6
	1427	1.6	1740	0.4	1900	0.3	1251	3.3	1415	2.0	1527	1.8	1331	4.4	1454	5.6	1902	1.0
	2012	0.1	2329	2.6			1902	0.3	1936	0.3	2227	0.6	1947	0.6	2130	0.4		
23 TH	0238	1.7	0614	0.3	0041	3.0	0115	3.4	0240	1.9	0345	1.7	0152	4.4	0315	5.6	0032	5.6
	0840	0.0	1156	2.4	0732	0.2	0731	0.3	0751	0.2	1112	0.5	0813	0.3	0954	0.2	0723	0.7
(○)	1506	1.6	1825	0.4	1310	2.8	1342	3.4	1455	2.0	1607	1.8	1410	4.5	1535	5.7	1251	5.6
	2053	0.1			1946	0.3	1949	0.4	2014	0.3	2320	0.7	2022	0.5	2208	0.4	1940	1.0
24 F	0313	1.7	0011	2.6	0127	3.0	0201	3.5	0320	2.0	0422	1.7	0230	4.4	0354	5.7	0109	5.7
	0920	0.0	0657	0.3	0817	0.2	0817	0.3	0826	0.1	1206	0.5	0850	0.3	1032	0.1	0801	0.7
	1540	1.6	1236	2.4	1353	2.8	1424	3.3	1531	2.0	1645	1.8	1446	4.6	1612	5.8	1328	5.7
	2129	0.0	1904	0.4	2027	0.3	2032	0.4	2053	0.3			2057	0.5	2243	0.4	2015	1.0
25 SA	0346	1.8	0048	2.6	0206	3.1	0239	3.5	0356	2.0	0009	0.7	0304	4.6	0430	5.7	0145	5.8
	0956	0.0	0736	0.3	0857	0.3	0857	0.4	0901	0.1	0458	1.8	0926	0.2	1107	0.1	0837	0.7
	1612	1.6	1312	2.4	1430	2.8	1459	3.3	1605	2.1	1304	0.5	1520	4.6	1647	5.8	1405	5.7
	2203	0.0	1940	0.4	2105	0.3	2109	0.5	2133	0.3	1721	1.8	2130	0.5	2315	0.4	2048	1.0
26 SU	0418	1.8	0121	2.6	0240	3.1	0310	3.5	0430	2.0	0055	0.7	0337	4.6	0503	5.7	0220	5.8
	1030	-0.0	0809	0.3	0933	0.3	0933	0.4	0935	0.1	0534	1.8	1000	0.2	1140	0.1	0910	0.7
	1641	1.6	1344	2.4	1505	2.9	1529	3.3	1638	2.1	1103	0.4	1552	4.6	1720	5.8	1440	5.7
	2235	-0.0	2012	0.4	2138	0.3	2143	0.5	2213	0.3	1757	1.8	2203	0.5	2345	0.4	2119	1.0
27 M	0450	1.7	0152	2.7	0313	3.1	0338	3.5	0500	1.9	0133	0.6	0409	4.5	0536	5.6	0254	5.8
	1102	-0.0	0841	0.4	1004	0.4	1006	0.4	1009	0.1	0609	1.8	1031	0.2	1209	0.1	0941	0.7
	1709	1.5	1415	2.4	1539	2.9	1557	3.3	1709	2.0	1151	0.4	1624	4.5	1752	5.7	1513	5.7
	2306	-0.0	2043	0.4	2208	0.3	2215	0.4			1833	1.9	2233	0.5			2147	1.0
28 TU	0521	1.7	0224	2.7	0345	3.1	0408	3.5	0057	0.3	0057	0.6	0439	4.5	0014	0.5	0326	5.8
	1132	-0.0	0910	0.4	1034	0.4	1036	0.4	0526	1.9	0645	1.8	1100	0.3	0608	5.6	1010	0.8
	1737	1.5	1446	2.4	1611	2.9	1628	3.3	1045	0.0	1300	0.3	1654	4.5	1238	0.2	1545	5.7
	2336	-0.1	2113	0.4	2238	0.4	2245	0.4	1741	2.0	1909	2.0	2305	0.6	1825	5.6	2217	1.0
29 W	0553	1.7	0255	2.7	0417	3.1	0440	3.6	0140	0.3	0132	0.6	0510	4.4	0045	0.5	0357	5.8
	1202	-0.0	0941	0.4	1103	0.4	1108	0.4	0553	1.9	0722	1.8	1130	0.3	0640	5.5	1042	0.9
	1807	1.5	1518	2.4	1644	2.8	1703	3.3	1124	0.0	1357	0.3	1728	4.4	1309	0.2	1618	5.6
			2146	0.4	2309	0.3	2319	0.3	1814	2.0	1948	1.9	2339	0.6	1858	5.5	2249	1.1
30 TH	0009	-0.1	0330	2.7	0450	3.1	0518	3.5	0031	0.3	0221	0.5	0544	4.3	0117	0.5	0433	5.7
	0625	1.6	1015	0.5	1136	0.4	1142	0.2	0626	1.9	0802	1.8	1204	0.4	0713	5.4	1118	1.0
	1234	-0.0	1555	2.4	1719	2.8	1742	3.3	1210	0.0	1334	0.3	1806	4.3	1341	0.2	1655	5.5
	1839	1.4	2224	0.5	2345	0.5	2357	0.2	1851	2.0	2030	1.9			1934	5.4	2328	1.3
31 F	0046	-0.1	0411	2.6	0529	3.0	0602	3.4	0106	0.3	0305	0.5	0018	0.6	0153	0.6	0514	5.5
	0700	1.6	1055	0.5	1213	0.5	1221	0.2	0706	1.8	0847	1.8	0624	4.2	0750	5.2	1203	1.3
	1312	-0.0	1641	2.4	1803	2.8	1829	3.2	1308	0.0	1436	0.3	1245	0.5	1418	0.3	1740	5.3
	1919	1.4	2309	0.6					1939	1.9	2121	1.8	1852	4.1	2016	5.2		

• • Time Zone -0100. For UT subtract 1 hour. For European summer time (shaded) 30/3-26/10 add 1 hour • •

DENMARK, GERMANY, HOLLAND & BELGIUM Time Zone -0100

Esbjerg * Helgoland * Cuxhaven * Bremerhaven * Hoek van Holland * Rotterdam *Vlissingen * Antwerpen * Dunkerque

FEBRUARY 1997 TIDE TABLES FEBRUARY 1997

ESBJERG Time m	HELGOLAND Time m	CUXHAVEN Time m	BREMERHAVEN Time m	HOEK VAN HOLLAND Time m	ROTTERDAM Time m	VLISSINGEN Time m	ANTWERPEN Time m	DUNKERQUE Time m	Day
0130 -0.0	0504 2.5	0027 0.5	0040 0.3	0151 0.5	0518 0.5	0105 0.7	0235 0.7	0018 1.5	**1 SA**
0745 1.5	1146 0.6	0623 2.9	0654 3.3	0758 1.8	0944 1.7	0716 4.0	0837 5.1	0606 5.2	
1400 0.0	1742 2.3	1259 0.5	1309 0.3	1407 0.0	1724 0.3	1338 0.6	1503 0.5	1300 1.5	
2013 1.4		1901 2.7	1926 3.2	2047 1.8	2232 1.7	1957 3.9	2114 5.0	1838 5.0	
0223 -0.0	0008 0.6	0120 0.6	0133 0.4	0244 0.3	0621 0.4	0205 0.8	0326 0.8	0127 1.6	**2 SU**
0846 1.5	0612 2.5	0729 2.9	0757 3.2	0921 1.7	1107 1.6	0831 3.8	0946 4.9	0713 5.0	
1500 0.0	1251 0.5	1357 0.6	1409 0.4	1507 0.1	1842 0.3	1447 0.7	1601 0.7	1412 1.6	
2126 1.4	1854 2.3	2009 2.8	2032 3.2	2211 1.7		2116 3.8	2230 4.9	1951 4.9	
0331 0.0	0122 0.6	0228 0.6	0244 0.4	0347 0.3	0000 1.7	0324 0.9	0433 0.9	0245 1.6	**3 M**
1006 1.4	0727 2.4	0841 2.9	0907 3.2	1047 1.7	0724 0.3	0954 3.8	1106 4.9	0836 4.9	
1614 0.1	1407 0.5	1514 0.5	1527 0.4	1618 0.2	1230 1.7	1615 0.7	1721 0.8	1524 1.5	
2250 1.4	2007 2.4	2118 2.9	2144 3.2	2326 1.7	1951 0.3	2236 3.9	2346 5.1	2112 4.9	
0453 0.0	0244 0.5	0354 0.5	0409 0.4	0502 0.3	0109 1.8	0453 0.8	0600 0.9	0359 1.5	**4 TU**
1128 1.5	0842 2.5	0952 3.0	1019 3.4	1157 1.8	0824 0.3	1109 4.0	1221 5.2	0951 5.1	
1733 0.0	1521 0.4	1636 0.3	1646 0.3	1742 0.2	1334 1.8	1732 0.6	1844 0.7	1633 1.3	
	2115 2.6	2225 3.1	2253 3.4		2057 0.2	2342 4.1		2221 5.2	
0006 1.5	0356 0.3	0512 0.2	0521 0.1	0029 1.8	0206 1.9	0606 0.6	0056 5.3	0506 1.1	**5 W**
0610 -0.1	0948 2.7	1058 3.2	1126 3.5	0558 0.2	0924 0.2	1209 4.3	0721 0.7	1051 5.4	
1243 1.5	1625 0.2	1743 0.0	1751 0.0	1254 1.9	1428 2.0	1833 0.4	1326 5.5	1736 1.1	
1840 -0.1	2214 2.8	2327 3.3	2355 3.7	1831 0.2	2211 0.3		1956 0.5	2315 5.5	
0112 1.6	0458 0.0	0616 -0.1	0621 -0.1	0122 1.9	0254 2.0	0037 4.4	0156 5.7	0605 0.8	**6 TH**
0715 -0.2	1046 2.8	1200 3.4	1226 3.7	0637 0.2	1027 0.2	0704 0.3	0831 0.4	1142 5.8	
1351 1.5	1721 -0.0	1842 -0.2	1847 -0.2	1344 2.1	1516 2.1	1300 4.6	1422 5.9	1830 0.8	
1939 -0.1	2308 2.9			1904 0.2	2121 0.3	1926 0.3	2058 0.3		
0212 1.6	0553 -0.2	0024 3.5	0051 3.9	0210 1.9	0339 2.0	0125 4.6	0248 5.9	0003 5.8	**7 F**
0812 -0.3	1139 2.9	0713 -0.3	0715 -0.3	0714 0.1	1024 0.2	0755 0.1	0930 0.2	0657 0.5	
1451 1.6	1813 -0.2	1257 3.4	1320 3.9	1430 2.2	1601 2.2	1347 4.8	1512 6.2	1230 6.0	
2030 -0.2	2357 3.0	1936 -0.4	1938 -0.3	1938 0.2	2235 0.4	2015 0.2	2153 0.2	1920 0.6	
								●	
0305 1.7	0644 -0.3	0118 3.6	0141 4.1	0256 2.0	0421 2.1	0210 4.8	0336 6.1	0048 6.1	**8 SA**
0902 -0.3	1228 2.9	0806 -0.5	0806 -0.5	0751 -0.0	1128 0.2	0845 -0.1	1023 0.0	0746 0.2	
1544 1.6	1901 -0.3	1350 3.5	1409 4.0	1516 2.2	1645 2.3	1432 5.0	1558 6.3	1315 6.2	
2118 -0.2		2025 -0.5	2027 -0.5	2014 0.3	2330 0.4	2101 0.1	2243 0.2	2006 0.4	
0355 1.7	0044 3.1	0209 3.7	0229 4.2	0341 2.0	0503 2.2	0254 4.9	0421 6.2	0132 6.2	**9 SU**
0950 -0.3	0731 -0.4	0854 -0.6	0854 -0.6	0830 -0.1	1219 0.2	0932 -0.2	1112 -0.1	0832 0.1	
1632 1.6	1314 2.9	1439 3.5	1455 4.0	1601 2.3	1729 2.3	1516 5.0	1643 6.4	1400 6.3	
2203 -0.3	1946 -0.3	2111 -0.5	2112 -0.6	2054 0.3		2148 0.1	2330 0.1	2051 0.4	
0442 1.8	0128 3.2	0256 3.7	0313 4.3	0425 2.0	0020 0.4	0337 4.9	0504 6.2	0216 6.3	**10 M**
1036 -0.4	0815 -0.4	0939 -0.6	0939 -0.7	0913 -0.1	0547 2.2	1018 -0.3	1158 -0.1	0918 0.0	
1716 1.6	1356 2.9	1523 3.4	1539 4.0	1647 2.2	1309 0.1	1601 5.0	1728 6.3	1445 6.3	
2248 -0.3	2029 -0.3	2154 -0.5	2157 -0.6	2137 0.3	1813 2.3	2233 0.2		2134 0.4	
0526 1.8	0210 3.2	0339 3.7	0357 4.4	0510 2.0	0109 0.4	0421 4.9	0014 0.3	0300 6.3	**11 TU**
1120 -0.3	0857 -0.4	1021 -0.6	1023 -0.7	0959 -0.1	0630 2.2	1104 -0.2	0548 6.1	1003 0.1	
1756 1.5	1436 2.8	1603 3.4	1620 4.0	1733 2.1	1413 0.1	1648 4.9	1242 -0.1	1531 6.2	
2331 -0.3	2109 -0.3	2234 -0.5	2239 -0.6	2225 0.3	1858 2.3	2315 0.2	1814 6.1	2218 0.5	
0607 1.7	0251 3.2	0418 3.7	0439 4.3	0556 2.0	0209 0.3	0508 4.8	0056 0.3	0347 6.3	**12 W**
1203 -0.3	0937 -0.3	1101 -0.5	1104 -0.6	1050 -0.1	0714 2.2	1147 -0.1	0634 5.9	1048 0.3	
1832 1.5	1515 2.8	1641 3.4	1700 3.9	1823 2.1	1317 0.0	1737 4.7	1324 -0.0	1618 6.0	
	2148 -0.2	2312 -0.4	2321 -0.5	2322 0.4	1942 2.2	2358 0.3	1901 5.8	2303 0.7	
0015 -0.3	0333 3.1	0457 3.6	0520 4.2	0647 2.0	0143 0.3	0558 4.6	0137 0.5	0436 6.0	**13 TH**
0648 1.7	1017 -0.1	1139 -0.3	1145 -0.4	1155 -0.0	0759 2.2	1230 0.1	0722 5.7	1137 0.6	
1247 -0.2	1554 2.7	1718 3.3	1741 3.8	1920 2.0	1421 0.0	1832 4.5	1406 0.1	1709 5.7	
1909 1.5	2227 -0.1	2350 -0.2			2030 2.1		1951 5.5	2354 1.0	
0102 -0.2	0416 2.9	0536 3.5	0002 -0.4	0153 0.2	0245 0.3	0043 0.5	0220 0.6	0529 5.7	**14 F**
0733 1.6	1057 0.1	1217 -0.1	0603 4.0	0745 1.9	0848 2.1	0654 4.4	0813 5.4	1232 1.0	
1334 -0.1	1639 2.6	1757 3.1	1227 -0.2	1351 -0.0	1521 0.1	1318 0.3	1450 0.3	1807 5.2	
1953 1.4	2312 0.1		1824 3.6	2021 1.8	2123 1.9	1932 4.2	2047 5.2		
0154 -0.2	0506 2.7	0029 -0.0	0045 -0.1	0224 0.2	0347 0.3	0137 0.7	0308 0.7	0052 1.3	**15 SA**
0825 1.5	1143 0.3	0621 3.2	0649 3.7	0849 1.8	0947 1.9	0758 4.2	0912 5.1	0633 5.3	
1429 0.0	1731 2.5	1257 0.2	1312 0.1	1444 0.0	1622 0.1	1416 0.5	1541 0.6	1335 1.3	
2049 1.4		1845 3.0	1911 3.4	2126 1.7	2232 1.7	2037 3.9	2151 4.9	1921 4.9	

●● Time Zone -0100. For UT subtract 1 hour. For European summer time (shaded) 30/3-26/10 add 1 hour ●●

FEBRUARY 1997 TIDE TABLES FEBRUARY 1997

	ESBJERG		HELGOLAND		CUXHAVEN		BREMERHAVEN		HOEK VAN HOLLAND		ROTTERDAM		VLISSINGEN		ANTWERPEN		DUNKERQUE	
	Time	m	Time	m	Time	m	Time	m	Time	m	Time	m	Time	m	Time	m	Time	m
16 SU	0255	-0.1	0005	0.3	0115	0.3	0137	0.2	0319	0.2	0451	0.3	0245	0.8	0406	0.9	0200	1.5
	0931	1.5	0604	2.5	0715	3.0	0742	3.4	1000	1.7	1103	1.7	0909	3.9	1023	4.8	0757	5.0
	1536	0.1	1241	0.5	1348	0.5	1408	0.5	1549	0.1	1730	0.2	1531	0.7	1642	0.8	1446	1.6
	2201	1.4	1834	2.3	1943	2.8	2008	3.2	2239	1.6	2348	1.6	2151	3.8	2308	4.7	2045	4.7
17 M	0412	0.0	0118	0.5	0224	0.5	0248	0.5	0424	0.2	0600	0.3	0411	0.8	0518	1.0	0317	1.6
	1049	1.4	0715	2.3	0821	2.7	0847	3.1	1115	1.7	1220	1.7	1026	3.8	1145	4.7	0919	4.9
	1653	0.1	1359	0.6	1512	0.6	1525	0.7	1656	0.2	1845	0.3	1656	0.8	1759	0.9	1602	1.6
	2318	1.5	1951	2.3	2054	2.7	2118	3.1	2348	1.6			2303	3.8			2155	4.8
18 TU	0533	0.0	0249	0.6	0406	0.6	0412	0.6	0526	0.2	0057	1.6	0531	0.7	0021	4.8	0431	1.5
	1207	1.4	0839	2.2	0937	2.6	1006	3.0	1219	1.7	0710	0.3	1135	4.0	0652	0.8	1022	5.1
	1805	0.1	1524	0.6	1642	0.6	1644	0.7	1757	0.3	1327	1.7	1800	0.7	1254	5.0	1709	1.5
			2114	2.3	2212	2.7	2242	3.1			2006	0.4			1926	0.8	2251	5.0
19 W	0030	1.5	0409	0.5	0524	0.5	0523	0.5	0049	1.7	0159	1.6	0005	3.9	0121	5.0	0533	1.2
	0642	-0.0	0959	2.2	1058	2.6	1127	3.1	0618	0.2	0811	0.4	0630	0.6	0801	0.5	1114	5.3
	1315	1.5	1631	0.5	1748	0.4	1748	0.6	1314	1.8	1426	1.7	1230	4.1	1349	5.3	1801	1.3
	1903	0.0	2224	2.4	2328	2.8			1844	0.3	2300	0.4	1848	0.7	2023	0.6	2336	5.3
20 TH	0130	1.6	0509	0.4	0624	0.3	0000	3.3	0141	1.7	0251	1.6	0054	4.1	0212	5.3	0621	1.0
	0736	-0.1	1100	2.3	1208	2.7	0622	0.4	0658	0.1	1000	0.4	0715	0.4	0851	0.3	1157	5.5
	1408	1.5	1724	0.4	1842	0.3	1234	3.2	1358	1.9	1515	1.7	1315	4.3	1435	5.5	1845	1.1
	1952	-0.0	2318	2.5			1842	0.4	1922	0.3	2355	0.4	1927	0.6	2107	0.4		
21 F	0216	1.6	0558	0.3	0029	2.9	0100	3.4	0223	1.8	0334	1.7	0134	4.3	0254	5.5	0015	5.5
	0820	-0.1	1146	2.3	0714	0.2	0712	0.3	0733	0.1	1039	0.4	0754	0.3	0932	0.1	0703	0.8
	1448	1.5	1809	0.3	1300	2.8	1326	3.3	1434	1.9	1555	1.8	1351	4.4	1515	5.7	1235	5.6
	2033	-0.1			1928	0.2	1930	0.4	1959	0.3	2230	0.6	2003	0.5	2145	0.3	1923	1.0
22 SA ○	0253	1.6	0000	2.6	0116	3.0	0146	3.5	0259	1.9	0409	1.7	0209	4.4	0332	5.6	0051	5.6
	0858	-0.1	0639	0.2	0757	0.1	0757	0.3	0806	0.1	1127	0.4	0829	0.2	1009	0.1	0742	0.6
	1521	1.5	1225	2.4	1342	2.9	1408	3.4	1508	2.0	1630	1.8	1424	4.5	1550	5.8	1311	5.7
	2108	-0.1	1848	0.2	2009	0.1	2012	0.3	2035	0.3	2317	0.6	2036	0.4	2220	0.3	1957	0.9
23 SU	0325	1.6	0036	2.6	0155	3.1	0224	3.6	0332	1.9	0443	1.7	0241	4.5	0406	5.7	0124	5.7
	0933	-0.2	0716	0.2	0836	0.1	0837	0.3	0837	0.0	1214	0.4	0903	0.2	1044	0.0	0816	0.6
	1549	1.5	1300	2.4	1419	2.9	1443	3.5	1540	2.0	1703	1.8	1456	4.6	1623	5.8	1345	5.8
	2141	-0.2	1924	0.2	2046	0.1	2050	0.3	2110	0.3	2330	0.6	2109	0.4	2252	0.3	2030	0.9
24 M	0357	1.6	0109	2.6	0230	3.1	0256	3.6	0403	1.9	0517	1.8	0312	4.6	0439	5.8	0157	5.8
	1005	-0.2	0749	0.2	0911	0.1	0912	0.3	0908	0.0	1113	0.4	0935	0.1	1116	0.1	0848	0.5
	1617	1.5	1330	2.4	1453	2.9	1513	3.5	1612	2.0	1738	1.9	1526	4.6	1654	5.8	1417	5.8
	2212	-0.2	1957	0.2	2121	0.1	2124	0.3	2141	0.3	2333	0.6	2141	0.4	2323	0.3	2058	0.9
25 TU	0428	1.6	0139	2.6	0303	3.1	0324	3.6	0431	1.9	0551	1.8	0342	4.6	0510	5.8	0227	5.9
	1035	-0.2	0821	0.2	0944	0.2	0945	0.3	0938	0.0	1356	0.3	1006	0.1	1146	0.1	0917	0.5
	1645	1.5	1400	2.5	1525	2.9	1542	3.5	1642	2.0	1812	1.9	1556	4.6	1726	5.8	1446	5.8
	2242	-0.2	2027	0.2	2152	0.1	2157	0.3	2203	0.3			2212	0.4	2353	0.3	2125	0.9
26 W	0500	1.6	0209	2.6	0336	3.1	0354	3.6	0457	1.9	0001	0.6	0412	4.6	0541	5.7	0256	5.9
	1104	-0.2	0850	0.2	1014	0.2	1017	0.3	1009	0.0	0626	1.9	1036	0.2	1216	0.1	0946	0.6
	1713	1.4	1428	2.5	1557	2.9	1612	3.5	1712	2.0	1434	0.3	1627	4.6	1757	5.7	1514	5.8
	2312	-0.2	2058	0.3	2224	0.2	2228	0.2	2227	0.3	1848	1.9	2244	0.4			2153	0.9
27 TH	0530	1.5	0238	2.7	0407	3.1	0426	3.6	0525	1.9	0047	0.5	0442	4.5	0024	0.4	0325	5.9
	1133	-0.2	0920	0.3	1044	0.2	1048	0.2	1043	0.0	0702	1.9	1106	0.2	0612	5.7	1016	0.7
	1741	1.4	1457	2.5	1627	2.9	1645	3.4	1745	2.0	1310	0.3	1659	4.5	1247	0.2	1545	5.8
	2345	-0.3	2130	0.3	2255	0.2	2301	0.2	2259	0.2	1924	1.9	2317	0.4	1829	5.6	2224	0.9
28 F	0559	1.5	0309	2.6	0438	3.0	0500	3.6	0558	2.0	0140	0.5	0515	4.5	0055	0.5	0400	5.9
	1205	-0.2	0952	0.3	1115	0.3	1121	0.2	1121	-0.0	0740	1.9	1139	0.3	0643	5.6	1051	0.8
	1809	1.4	1529	2.5	1657	2.9	1721	3.4	1821	2.0	1410	0.3	1735	4.4	1318	0.3	1621	5.7
			2204	0.3	2328	0.3	2337	0.1	2339	0.2	2005	1.9	2352	0.5	1903	5.6	2300	1.1

● ● Time Zone -0100. For UT subtract 1 hour. For European summer time (shaded) 30/3-26/10 add 1 hour ● ●

PAGE 106

DENMARK, GERMANY, HOLLAND & BELGIUM Time Zone -0100

Esbjerg * Helgoland * Cuxhaven * Bremerhaven * Hoek van Holland * Rotterdam *Vlissingen * Antwerpen * Dunkerque

MARCH 1997 TIDE TABLES MARCH 1997

ESBJERG		HELGOLAND		CUXHAVEN		BREMERHAVEN		HOEK VAN HOLLAND		ROTTERDAM		VLISSINGEN		ANTWERPEN		DUNKERQUE			
Time	m	Time	m	Time	m	Time	m	Time	m	Time	m	Time	m	Time	m	Time	m		
0021	-0.3	0347	2.6	0511	3.0	0540	3.5	0638	1.9	0236	0.5	0553	4.4	0128	0.5	0439	5.7	**1**	**SA**
0630	1.4	1028	0.4	1150	0.3	1159	0.2	1209	-0.0	0823	1.9	1218	0.3	0720	5.5	1130	1.1		
1242	-0.2	1609	2.5	1733	2.8	1803	3.4	1904	1.9	1509	0.3	1818	4.3	1351	0.4	1705	5.4		
1844	1.4	2245	0.4							2051	1.8			1943	5.4	2344	1.3		
0103	-0.3	0435	2.5	0006	0.3	0018	0.2	0036	0.1	0318	0.4	0036	0.5	0206	0.5	0528	5.4	**2**	**SU**
0709	1.4	1114	0.4	0556	3.0	0627	3.4	0725	1.9	0913	1.8	0640	4.2	0804	5.4	1222	1.3		
1327	-0.2	1703	2.5	1230	0.4	1242	0.2	1330	0.0	1657	0.3	1307	0.5	1433	0.5	1759	5.1		
1931	1.3	2338	0.4	1823	2.8	1853	3.3	2000	1.7	2148	1.7	1913	4.0	2034	5.2				
0154	-0.2	0538	2.4	0053	0.4	0106	0.3	0206	0.1	0529	0.4	0133	0.6	0254	0.7	0044	1.5	**3**	**M**
0808	1.3	1212	0.5	0657	2.9	0724	3.3	0831	1.7	1022	1.7	0747	3.9	0904	5.1	0632	5.1		
1424	-0.1	1812	2.4	1322	0.4	1334	0.3	1443	0.1	1806	0.3	1412	0.6	1528	0.7	1333	1.5		
2041	1.3			1928	2.8	1954	3.3	2127	1.6	2315	1.6	2035	3.8	2146	4.9	1912	4.8		
0259	-0.2	0046	0.5	0153	0.4	0208	0.4	0314	0.2	0632	0.3	0248	0.8	0358	0.8	0206	1.6	**4**	**TU**
0932	1.3	0652	2.4	0806	2.9	0830	3.3	1012	1.6	1154	1.7	0919	3.8	1027	5.0	0759	4.9		
1536	-0.1	1326	0.5	1431	0.4	1445	0.4	1600	0.1	1921	0.3	1542	0.7	1646	0.9	1453	1.6		
2210	1.3	1927	2.4	2039	2.9	2103	3.3	2257	1.6			2205	3.7	2313	4.9	2043	4.8		
0422	-0.2	0209	0.4	0315	0.3	0332	0.4	0430	0.2	0038	1.7	0425	0.7	0529	0.9	0328	1.5	**5**	**W**
1102	1.3	0809	2.5	0918	3.0	0943	3.3	1133	1.7	0737	0.3	1045	4.0	1154	5.1	0926	5.1		
1702	-0.1	1447	0.4	1558	0.3	1610	0.3	1839	0.1	1307	1.8	1712	0.6	1817	0.8	1609	1.4		
2333	1.4	2039	2.6	2148	3.1	2215	3.5			2033	0.2	2321	4.0			2159	5.1		
0547	-0.2	0327	0.2	0442	0.1	0451	0.2	0009	1.6	0140	1.8	0548	0.5	0033	5.2	0442	1.2	**6**	**TH**
1224	1.4	0920	2.6	1027	3.1	1054	3.5	0534	0.1	0838	0.2	1151	4.3	0701	0.7	1033	5.4		
1818	-0.2	1558	0.2	1715	0.1	1721	0.1	1235	1.9	1406	2.0	1818	0.4	1306	5.1	1716	1.1		
		2144	2.8	2254	3.3	2323	3.7	2101	0.1	2151	0.2			1937	0.6	2257	5.4		
0047	1.5	0434	-0.1	0552	-0.2	0555	-0.1	0105	1.7	0232	1.9	0019	4.2	0137	5.5	0545	0.8	**7**	**F**
0657	-0.3	1022	2.7	1133	3.3	1158	3.7	0616	0.1	0921	0.1	0650	0.2	0816	0.4	1126	5.8		
1336	1.4	1658	-0.1	1818	-0.2	1821	-0.1	1327	2.0	1455	2.1	1243	4.6	1405	5.9	1813	0.8		
1919	-0.4	2242	2.9	2355	3.5			1852	0.2	2111	0.3	1912	0.2	2043	0.3	2346	5.8		
0151	1.5	0530	-0.4	0651	-0.4	0022	3.9	0153	1.8	0318	2.0	0107	4.5	0230	5.9	0639	0.4	**8**	**SA**
0754	-0.4	1116	2.8	1232	3.4	0651	-0.4	0653	0.0	1030	0.2	0741	-0.0	0916	0.1	1213	6.1		
1438	1.5	1751	-0.2	1914	-0.4	1255	3.9	1413	2.1	1540	2.2	1330	4.8	1455	6.2	1903	0.5		
2012	-0.3	2333	3.0			1914	-0.3	1919	0.2	2221	0.3	2000	0.1	2138	0.2				
0248	1.6	0622	-0.4	0053	3.6	0116	4.2	0238	1.9	0400	2.1	0151	4.7	0317	6.1	0030	6.1	**9**	**SU**
0845	-0.5	1205	2.8	0744	-0.6	0743	-0.5	0730	-0.1	1121	0.2	0828	-0.2	1007	-0.1	0729	0.1		
1529	1.5	1840	-0.3	1327	3.4	1345	4.0	1458	2.2	1624	2.3	1414	5.0	1540	6.3	1258	6.3		●
2100	-0.4			2004	-0.5	2003	-0.4	1954	0.2	2320	0.4	2045	0.0	2227	0.1	1949	0.3		
0339	1.6	0021	3.1	0145	3.6	0205	4.3	0321	2.0	0442	2.2	0234	4.9	0401	6.2	0112	6.3	**10**	**M**
0931	-0.5	0709	-0.4	0832	-0.6	0831	-0.6	0809	-0.1	1209	0.2	0914	-0.3	1054	-0.1	0815	-0.0		
1615	1.5	1250	2.8	1415	3.4	1432	4.1	1542	2.2	1706	2.3	1457	5.0	1624	6.4	1342	6.4		
2145	-0.4	1925	-0.4	2050	-0.6	2051	-0.5	2033	0.2			2129	0.0	2312	0.1	2033	0.3		
0426	1.7	0105	3.1	0233	3.6	0251	4.3	0404	2.0	0013	0.4	0316	4.9	0443	6.2	0155	6.4	**11**	**TU**
1015	-0.4	0752	-0.4	0917	-0.6	0916	-0.6	0852	-0.1	0524	2.2	0958	-0.3	1139	-0.1	0859	-0.1		
1655	1.5	1330	2.8	1458	3.4	1515	4.1	1626	2.2	1259	0.1	1540	5.0	1707	6.3	1424	6.4		
2228	-0.4	2007	-0.3	2133	-0.5	2134	-0.5	2115	0.2	1749	2.3	2212	0.1	2354	0.1	2115	0.3		
0509	1.7	0146	3.1	0315	3.6	0333	4.3	0447	2.1	0107	0.3	0359	4.9	0526	6.1	0238	6.4	**12**	**W**
1057	-0.4	0833	-0.3	0957	-0.5	0959	-0.6	0938	-0.1	0606	2.3	1040	-0.2	1220	-0.1	0942	0.0		
1730	1.5	1409	2.8	1536	3.3	1555	4.0	1709	2.1	1401	0.1	1624	4.8	1751	6.1	1508	6.2		
2311	-0.4	2046	-0.3	2212	-0.5	2216	-0.5	2202	0.3	1832	2.2	2252	0.1			2157	0.4		
0548	1.6	0226	3.0	0354	3.5	0415	4.2	0530	2.1	0215	0.3	0443	4.8	0034	0.3	0322	6.3	**13**	**TH**
1138	-0.3	0911	-0.2	1036	-0.3	1039	-0.4	1028	-0.0	0649	2.2	1120	-0.1	0610	6.0	1026	0.3		
1802	1.5	1445	2.8	1612	3.3	1634	3.9	1754	2.0	1248	0.0	1709	4.6	1259	0.0	1553	6.0		
2353	-0.4	2124	-0.2	2249	-0.3	2256	-0.4	2256	0.2	1915	2.1	2332	0.2	1835	5.8	2240	0.6		
0625	1.6	0306	2.9	0429	3.4	0454	4.1	0616	2.0	0109	0.2	0530	4.7	0112	0.3	0409	6.0	**14**	**F**
1218	-0.2	0946	-0.0	1110	-0.1	1118	-0.2	1130	0.0	0732	2.1	1158	0.1	0654	5.7	1110	0.6		
1835	1.4	1522	2.7	1644	3.2	1712	3.8	1845	1.9	1357	0.1	1759	4.4	1336	0.2	1639	5.6		
		2200	0.0	2324	-0.2	2335	-0.1			1957	2.0			1921	5.5	2326	0.9		
0037	-0.4	0346	2.8	0506	3.3	0534	3.8	0121	0.2	0215	0.2	0013	0.3	0151	0.5	0458	5.7	**15**	**SA**
0705	1.5	1021	0.2	1142	0.1	1155	0.1	0709	2.0	0817	2.0	0622	4.4	0742	5.4	1159	1.0		
1301	-0.2	1603	2.6	1719	3.1	1750	3.6	1321	0.0	1456	0.1	1241	0.4	1415	0.4	1733	5.2		
1914	1.4	2240	0.1	2357	0.1			1945	1.7	2044	1.8	1855	4.1	2010	5.2				

• • Time Zone -0100. For UT subtract 1 hour. For European summer time (shaded) 30/3-26/10 add 1 hour • •

MARCH 1997 TIDE TABLES MARCH 1997

	ESBJERG	HELGOLAND	CUXHAVEN	BREMERHAVEN	HOEK VAN HOLLAND	ROTTERDAM	VLISSINGEN	ANTWERPEN	DUNKERQUE
	Time m	Time m	Time m	Time m	Time m	Time m	Time m	Time m	Time m
16 SU	0125 -0.3	0432 2.6	0547 3.0	0015 0.1	0146 0.1	0315 0.2	0103 0.5	0234 0.6	0018 1.3
	0752 1.4	1100 0.4	1212 0.3	0616 3.5	0814 1.8	0908 1.8	0724 4.1	0833 5.1	0557 5.2
	1350 -0.1	1651 2.5	1803 2.9	1233 0.4	1414 0.1	1554 0.2	1336 0.6	1501 0.6	1256 1.4
	2003 1.4	2327 0.4		1833 3.5	2050 1.6	2142 1.6	2000 3.8	2106 4.8	1838 4.8
17 M	0222 -0.2	0527 2.3	0033 0.3	0059 0.5	0245 0.1	0415 0.3	0210 0.7	0327 0.8	0121 1.6
	0854 1.3	1148 0.6	0637 2.8	0704 3.3	0925 1.7	1022 1.6	0836 3.8	0936 4.8	0714 4.9
	1451 0.0	1752 2.3	1249 0.6	1318 0.7	1522 0.1	1656 0.3	1451 0.8	1559 0.9	1403 1.7
	2113 1.4		1900 2.7	1925 3.2	2205 1.5	2311 1.4	2115 3.6	2221 4.5	2004 4.6
18 TU	0337 -0.1	0034 0.6	0126 0.6	0203 0.8	0355 0.1	0519 0.3	0330 0.8	0436 0.9	0233 1.7
	1015 1.2	0637 2.1	0742 2.5	0806 3.0	1046 1.6	1151 1.5	0957 3.7	1107 4.6	0842 4.7
	1611 0.1	1306 0.8	1351 0.8	1436 1.0	1632 0.2	1807 0.4	1614 0.9	1711 1.0	1518 1.8
	2237 1.4	1909 2.2	2010 2.6	2035 3.1	2322 1.5		2234 3.6	2349 4.5	2123 4.6
19 W	0502 -0.1	0216 0.7	0332 0.7	0342 0.9	0459 0.1	0030 1.4	0454 0.7	0603 0.9	0351 1.7
	1136 1.3	0806 2.0	0900 2.4	0927 2.9	1156 1.7	0628 0.3	1109 3.8	1225 4.8	0953 4.9
	1732 0.1	1450 0.8	1610 0.8	1612 1.0	1733 0.2	1303 1.6	1729 0.8	1842 0.9	1634 1.6
	2353 1.4	2039 2.2	2133 2.5	2203 3.1		1933 0.5	2339 3.8		2223 4.8
20 TH	0614 -0.1	0345 0.6	0500 0.6	0458 0.8	0026 1.5	0136 1.5	0600 0.6	0054 4.8	0501 1.4
	1246 1.3	0936 2.1	1031 2.4	1056 3.0	0553 0.1	0740 0.3	1206 4.0	0727 0.6	1047 5.1
	1836 -0.0	1606 0.6	1724 0.6	1721 0.6	1251 1.8	1405 1.6	1822 0.7	1322 5.2	1734 1.4
		2158 2.3	2258 2.7	2329 3.2	1824 0.2	2230 0.4		1951 0.7	2310 5.1
21 F	0057 1.4	0445 0.4	0600 0.4	0557 0.6	0117 1.6	0231 1.6	0029 4.0	0145 5.2	0554 1.1
	0709 -0.2	1039 2.2	1147 2.6	1207 3.2	0636 0.1	0849 0.3	0649 0.4	0820 0.3	1131 5.4
	1341 1.4	1700 0.4	1818 0.4	1817 0.6	1333 1.8	1454 1.7	1250 4.2	1409 5.5	1820 1.1
	1925 -0.1	2254 2.4			1906 0.2	2324 0.4	1903 0.6	2038 0.4	2350 5.4
22 SA	0146 1.5	0533 0.3	0004 2.8	0031 3.4	0157 1.7	0315 1.6	0109 4.2	0227 5.5	0637 0.8
	0753 -0.2	1126 2.3	0648 0.2	0647 0.5	0712 0.1	1124 0.3	0728 0.3	0903 0.1	1211 5.6
	1422 1.4	1745 0.3	1239 2.8	1300 3.4	1407 1.9	1534 1.8	1326 4.4	1448 5.7	1859 0.9
	2006 -0.2	2337 2.5	1903 0.2	1905 0.4	1943 0.2		1939 0.5	2117 0.3	
23 SU	0226 1.5	0612 0.2	0052 3.0	0120 3.6	0230 1.8	0006 0.4	0142 4.3	0305 5.6	0026 5.6
	0830 -0.3	1204 2.4	0730 0.1	0731 0.3	0743 0.1	0351 1.7	0802 0.2	0941 0.1	0715 0.6
	1455 1.4	1824 0.2	1319 2.9	1343 3.6	1440 1.9	1203 0.3	1357 4.5	1523 5.8	1246 5.7
	2042 -0.2		1944 0.1	1947 0.3	2016 0.2	1609 1.8	2011 0.4	2152 0.3	1934 0.8
24 M ○	0300 1.5	0014 2.6	0132 3.1	0159 3.7	0302 1.9	0040 0.4	0214 4.5	0339 5.7	0100 5.7
	0904 -0.3	0648 0.1	0808 0.0	0811 0.2	0811 0.1	0424 1.8	0835 0.2	1015 0.1	0750 0.5
	1524 1.4	1238 2.5	1356 3.0	1420 3.6	1512 2.0	1235 0.3	1427 4.6	1554 5.8	1319 5.8
	2114 -0.2	1900 0.2	2021 0.0	2025 0.2	2044 0.2	1642 1.9	2043 0.3	2225 0.3	2006 0.8
25 TU	0332 1.5	0048 2.6	0209 3.1	0233 3.8	0332 1.9	0110 0.4	0244 4.6	0411 5.8	0130 5.8
	0936 -0.3	0722 0.1	0844 0.0	0847 0.2	0837 0.1	0457 1.8	0906 0.2	1048 0.1	0822 0.5
	1551 1.4	1309 2.5	1431 3.1	1452 3.7	1543 2.0	1309 0.3	1458 4.6	1626 5.9	1349 5.8
	2146 -0.3	1934 0.1	2057 0.0	2101 0.2	2102 0.2	1715 1.9	2116 0.3	2257 0.3	2035 0.8
26 W	0405 1.5	0119 2.6	0244 3.1	0304 3.8	0401 1.9	0142 0.3	0314 4.6	0442 5.9	0158 5.8
	1006 -0.3	0755 0.2	0918 0.1	0921 0.2	0905 0.1	0530 1.8	0939 0.1	1120 0.1	0852 0.5
	1621 1.4	1339 2.5	1505 3.0	1522 3.6	1615 2.0	1348 0.2	1529 4.6	1657 5.9	1416 5.8
	2218 -0.3	2008 0.2	2131 0.0	2136 0.2	2123 0.2	1750 1.9	2150 0.3	2330 0.3	2103 0.8
27 TH	0438 1.5	0151 2.6	0318 3.1	0336 3.7	0430 2.0	0217 0.3	0345 4.6	0512 5.9	0226 5.9
	1037 -0.3	0827 0.2	0951 0.1	0954 0.2	0936 0.1	0605 1.9	1012 0.2	1153 0.2	0922 0.5
	1651 1.4	1408 2.5	1538 3.0	1554 3.6	1646 2.0	1429 0.2	1600 4.6	1729 5.9	1445 5.9
	2251 -0.3	2041 0.2	2205 0.1	2209 0.2	2151 0.2	1825 1.9	2224 0.3		2133 0.8
28 F	0510 1.4	0221 2.6	0352 3.1	0409 3.7	0501 2.0	0253 0.3	0417 4.6	0003 0.3	0257 6.0
	1108 -0.3	0859 0.2	1023 0.1	1027 0.2	1010 0.1	0642 1.9	1046 0.2	0545 5.8	0954 0.6
	1720 1.4	1437 2.6	1609 3.0	1626 3.6	1720 2.0	1508 0.2	1634 4.6	1225 0.3	1518 5.8
	2324 -0.4	2114 0.2	2238 0.1	2243 0.1	2227 0.1	1902 1.9	2300 0.3	1802 5.8	2206 0.8
29 SA	0539 1.4	0254 2.6	0426 3.1	0443 3.7	0536 2.0	0334 0.3	0451 4.6	0036 0.4	0333 5.9
	1141 -0.3	0931 0.2	1055 0.2	1101 0.1	1050 0.1	0720 1.9	1121 0.2	0618 5.8	1029 0.8
	1748 1.4	1509 2.6	1640 3.0	1701 3.6	1757 1.9	1329 0.4	1711 4.5	1257 0.4	1556 5.7
		2149 0.2	2312 0.1	2319 0.1	2309 0.1	1942 1.9	2336 0.4	1838 5.7	2242 1.0
30 SU	0001 -0.4	0330 2.6	0500 3.0	0521 3.6	0616 2.0	0204 0.4	0530 4.5	0109 0.5	0415 5.8
	0609 1.3	1007 0.3	1130 0.2	1138 0.1	1138 0.0	0802 1.9	1159 0.4	0657 5.7	1109 1.0
	1219 -0.3	1548 2.6	1713 3.0	1741 3.6	1840 1.8	1429 0.3	1754 4.5	1330 0.4	1640 5.5
	1822 1.4	2229 0.3	2350 0.2	2359 0.1		2025 1.8		1920 5.6	2324 1.1
31 M	0044 -0.4	0417 2.5	0542 3.0	0606 3.5	0001 0.0	0336 0.3	0018 0.4	0145 0.5	0503 5.5
	0651 1.3	1050 0.4	1209 0.3	1219 0.2	0703 1.9	0850 1.9	0618 4.3	0742 5.6	1158 1.2
	1304 -0.3	1639 2.5	1758 3.0	1827 3.5	1255 0.0	1644 0.3	1248 0.5	1411 0.6	1734 5.2
	1909 1.3	2319 0.3			1933 1.7	2118 1.7	1848 4.0	2010 5.3	

•• Time Zone -0100. For UT subtract 1 hour. For European summer time (shaded) 30/3-26/10 add 1 hour ••

DENMARK, GERMANY, HOLLAND & BELGIUM Time Zone -0100
Esbjerg * Helgoland * Cuxhaven * Bremerhaven * Hoek van Holland * Rotterdam *Vlissingen * Antwerpen * Dunkerque
APRIL 1997 TIDE TABLES APRIL 1997

ESBJERG	HELGOLAND	CUXHAVEN	BREMERHAVEN	HOEK VAN HOLLAND	ROTTERDAM	VLISSINGEN	ANTWERPEN	DUNKERQUE	
Time m	Time m	Time m	Time m	Time m	Time m	Time m	Time m	Time m	
0135 -0.4 0751 1.2 1400 -0.2 2017 1.3	0515 2.5 1145 0.4 1742 2.5	0034 0.2 0635 2.9 1257 0.3 1857 3.0	0046 0.2 0658 3.4 1309 0.3 1924 3.5	0123 0.1 0807 1.8 1439 0.1 2058 1.5	0346 0.3 0954 1.8 1652 0.3 2236 1.6	0115 0.5 0723 4.0 1352 0.6 2009 3.7	0233 0.6 0842 5.3 1506 0.7 2121 5.0	0021 1.4 0607 5.2 1306 1.4 1848 4.9	**1 TU**
0240 -0.3 0915 1.2 1512 0.4 2143 1.3	0023 0.3 0626 2.4 1255 0.5 1854 2.5	0131 0.2 0739 2.9 1401 0.4 2005 3.0	0146 0.3 0801 3.4 1416 0.4 2030 3.5	0251 0.1 0950 1.7 1707 0.1 2235 1.5	0454 0.2 1124 1.8 1853 0.3	0230 0.6 0857 3.9 1521 0.7 2141 3.7	0339 0.8 1003 5.1 1623 0.9 2248 4.9	0139 1.5 0736 5.0 1427 1.5 2021 4.8	**2 W**
0403 -0.3 1045 1.2 1637 -0.1 2307 1.4	0141 0.3 0740 2.4 1415 0.3 2006 2.6	0248 0.2 0848 3.0 1525 0.3 2115 3.1	0304 0.3 0912 3.4 1538 0.4 2141 3.6	0406 0.1 1112 1.8 1829 0.1 2348 1.5	0007 1.6 0557 0.2 1242 1.9 2010 0.2	0408 0.6 1024 4.0 1654 0.6 2259 3.9	0509 0.9 1131 5.2 1754 0.8	0303 1.4 0904 5.1 1547 1.4 2139 5.0	**3 TH**
0527 -0.3 1209 1.3 1756 -0.2	0300 0.1 0851 2.5 1530 0.2 2114 2.8	0414 0.0 0957 3.1 1646 0.1 2221 3.3	0422 0.1 1023 3.5 1651 0.2 2250 3.8	0511 0.1 1215 1.9 2033 0.1	0113 1.7 0650 0.1 1342 2.0 2129 0.2	0532 0.4 1131 4.3 1802 0.4 2358 4.2	0010 5.2 0644 0.7 1245 5.6 1918 0.6	0420 1.1 1012 5.5 1657 1.1 2237 5.4	**4 F**
0023 1.4 0637 -0.4 1321 1.4 1859 -0.3	0408 -0.1 0955 2.7 1632 -0.0 2214 2.9	0525 -0.2 1103 3.2 1752 -0.2 2325 3.4	0527 -0.1 1129 3.7 1753 -0.1 2352 4.0	0045 1.7 0555 0.0 1307 2.0 2126 0.1	0207 1.9 0731 0.1 1433 2.2 2045 0.3	0633 0.1 1224 4.6 1855 0.2	0115 5.5 0759 0.3 1345 6.0 2025 0.4	0526 0.7 1107 5.9 1756 0.7 2327 5.8	**5 SA**
0131 1.5 0734 -0.5 1420 1.4 1953 -0.3	0505 -0.3 1050 2.8 1727 -0.2 2307 3.0	0626 -0.4 1204 3.3 1849 -0.3	0624 -0.3 1227 3.9 1848 -0.2	0133 1.8 0633 0.0 1354 2.1 1900 0.3	0254 2.0 0809 0.0 1518 2.2 2200 0.3	0047 4.5 0724 -0.1 1310 4.8 1942 0.1	0209 5.9 0857 0.1 1434 6.2 2119 0.2	0621 0.4 1154 6.2 1846 0.5	**6 SU**
0230 1.5 0824 -0.5 1509 1.4 2041 -0.4	0557 -0.4 1139 2.8 1816 -0.3 2355 3.0	0024 3.5 0719 -0.5 1259 3.4 1940 -0.4	0048 4.2 0717 -0.5 1319 4.0 1939 -0.4	0217 1.9 0710 -0.0 1438 2.2 1934 0.2	0337 2.1 1103 0.1 1600 2.3 2304 0.3	0130 4.7 0809 -0.2 1354 4.9 2026 0.1	0256 6.0 0948 -0.0 1520 6.3 2207 0.1	0010 6.0 0710 0.1 1238 6.3 1931 0.3	**7 M** ●
0321 1.6 0909 -0.4 1552 1.5 2125 -0.4	0644 -0.5 1222 2.8 1902 -0.3	0118 3.5 0807 -0.5 1347 3.4 2027 -0.5	0139 4.2 0806 -0.5 1406 4.1 2027 -0.4	0300 2.0 0750 -0.1 1521 2.1 2013 0.2	0418 2.2 0931 -0.0 1153 0.2 1642 2.3	0212 4.8 0853 -0.2 1436 4.9 2108 0.1	0339 6.1 1033 -0.1 1603 6.3 2251 0.1	0051 6.2 0756 0.0 1320 6.3 2014 0.3	**8 TU**
0406 1.6 0952 -0.4 1630 1.5 2209 -0.4	0039 3.0 0727 -0.3 1303 2.8 1944 -0.2	0206 3.5 0851 -0.4 1430 3.3 2110 -0.4	0225 4.2 0851 -0.4 1449 4.0 2111 -0.3	0342 2.1 0833 -0.1 1603 2.1 2056 0.2	0004 0.3 0500 2.2 1245 0.2 1724 2.2	0254 4.9 0935 -0.2 1518 4.9 2150 0.1	0421 6.2 1115 -0.0 1645 6.2 2332 0.1	0133 6.3 0839 0.1 1402 6.2 2056 0.4	**9 W**
0448 1.6 1033 -0.3 1703 1.5 2251 -0.4	0121 2.9 0806 -0.2 1339 2.8 2023 -0.3	0248 3.4 0932 -0.3 1506 3.3 2149 -0.3	0309 4.2 0934 -0.3 1530 4.0 2153 -0.2	0424 2.1 0918 0.0 1645 2.0 2142 0.2	0105 0.3 0542 2.2 1346 0.2 1805 2.1	0336 4.9 1015 -0.1 1600 4.8 2230 0.1	0504 6.1 1155 0.0 1727 6.1	0215 6.2 0921 0.2 1444 6.1 2136 0.5	**10 TH**
0527 1.5 1112 -0.3 1734 1.5 2332 -0.4	0200 2.8 0842 -0.0 1415 2.7 2100 -0.1	0325 3.3 1009 -0.1 1538 3.2 2225 -0.2	0349 4.0 1014 -0.1 1606 3.9 2233 -0.0	0506 2.1 1009 0.1 1728 1.9 2234 0.2	0003 0.2 0624 2.2 1212 0.1 1846 2.0	0420 4.8 1051 0.1 1644 4.6 2308 0.2	0011 0.2 0547 6.0 1232 0.2 1811 5.8	0259 6.1 1002 0.4 1527 5.9 2218 0.7	**11 F**
0603 1.5 1151 -0.2 1806 1.5	0238 2.7 0915 0.1 1451 2.7 2135 0.1	0400 3.2 1040 0.1 1607 3.2 2257 0.0	0427 3.8 1050 0.2 1641 3.8 2309 0.2	0549 2.0 1109 0.1 1815 1.8 2339 0.1	0034 0.2 0706 2.1 1321 0.2 1926 1.9	0505 4.7 1128 0.3 1730 4.4 2348 0.3	0048 0.3 0630 5.8 1308 0.3 1854 5.5	0344 5.9 1043 0.7 1613 5.6 2300 0.9	**12 SA**
0015 -0.4 0640 1.4 1231 -0.2 1842 1.5	0317 2.6 0947 0.3 1530 2.6 2211 0.3	0433 3.1 1106 0.2 1640 3.1 2326 0.2	0503 3.6 1124 0.4 1715 3.7 2345 0.4	0638 2.0 1249 0.1 1910 1.7	0139 0.2 0748 1.9 1423 0.3 2007 1.7	0554 4.4 1207 0.5 1821 4.1	0126 0.4 0715 5.5 1345 0.5 1939 5.2	0432 5.6 1127 1.1 1703 5.2 2348 1.2	**13 SU**
0100 -0.3 0722 1.3 1315 -0.1 1927 1.4	0400 2.4 1020 0.4 1615 2.5 2253 0.4	0513 2.9 1130 0.4 1724 3.0 2357 0.4	0542 3.4 1154 0.7 1754 3.5	0057 0.0 0739 1.9 1344 0.2 2015 1.6	0239 0.2 0833 1.8 1519 0.3 2054 1.5	0034 0.4 0651 4.2 1258 0.7 1921 3.8	0205 0.5 0802 5.2 1426 0.7 2028 4.9	0527 5.2 1218 1.4 1801 4.9	**14 M**
0152 -0.2 0818 1.2 1410 -0.0 2027 1.4	0452 2.2 1102 0.6 1712 2.3 2351 0.6	0601 2.7 1203 0.6 1818 2.8	0021 0.7 0625 3.2 1227 0.9 1841 3.3	0202 0.0 0846 1.7 1456 0.2 2123 1.5	0338 0.2 0933 1.6 1618 0.4 2210 1.3	0139 0.6 0758 3.9 1414 0.9 2032 3.5	0252 0.6 0857 4.9 1518 0.9 2130 4.6	0043 1.5 0633 4.9 1318 1.7 1915 4.6	**15 TU**

● ● Time Zone -0100. For UT subtract 1 hour. For European summer time (shaded) 30/3-26/10 add 1 hour ● ●

APRIL 1997 TIDE TABLES APRIL 1997

	ESBJERG		HELGOLAND		CUXHAVEN		BREMERHAVEN		HOEK VAN HOLLAND		ROTTERDAM		VLISSINGEN		ANTWERPEN		DUNKERQUE	
	Time	m	Time	m	Time	m	Time	m	Time	m	Time	m	Time	m	Time	m	Time	m
16 W	0259	-0.1	0557	2.0	0042	0.6	0111	0.9	0324	0.1	0440	0.3	0255	0.7	0355	0.8	0149	1.7
	0936	1.2	1206	1.8	0703	2.5	0721	3.0	1003	1.6	1115	1.5	0917	3.7	1012	4.7	0754	4.7
	1523	0.1	1824	2.2	1254	0.8	1318	1.1	1608	0.2	1728	0.5	1532	1.0	1629	1.1	1428	1.8
	2148	1.3			1927	2.6	1946	3.2	2244	1.4	2354	1.3	2154	3.5	2259	4.5	2038	4.5
17 TH	0420	-0.1	0127	0.7	0209	0.8	0252	1.1	0431	0.1	0549	0.3	0407	0.7	0515	0.8	0301	1.7
	1056	1.2	0721	2.0	0818	2.3	0837	2.8	1122	1.6	1232	1.5	1034	3.7	1144	4.8	0911	4.8
	1647	0.1	1356	0.9	1459	1.0	1521	1.2	1709	0.2	1857	0.5	1644	0.9	1748	1.0	1544	1.7
	2309	1.3	1951	2.1	2047	2.5	2110	3.1	2351	1.5			2303	3.6			2144	4.7
18 F	0534	-0.1	0304	0.7	0422	0.7	0420	1.0	0527	0.1	0103	1.4	0516	0.6	0015	4.7	0414	1.6
	1204	1.2	0854	2.0	0945	2.4	1008	2.9	1218	1.7	0707	0.3	1133	3.9	0636	0.6	1010	5.0
	1757	-0.0	1527	0.7	1646	0.8	1644	1.0	1803	0.2	1333	1.6	1745	0.8	1246	5.1	1653	1.5
			2115	2.2	2212	2.6	2239	3.2			2030	0.4	2355	3.9	1906	0.8	2235	5.0
19 SA	0014	1.4	0409	0.5	0524	0.5	0522	0.7	0042	1.6	0159	1.5	0611	0.5	0109	5.1	0514	1.3
	0632	-0.1	1003	2.2	1105	2.6	1127	3.1	0613	0.1	0825	0.3	1218	4.1	0739	0.4	1057	5.3
	1301	1.3	1626	0.5	1743	0.5	1743	0.7	1300	1.8	1424	1.7	1831	0.6	1335	5.4	1745	1.2
	1850	-0.1	2217	2.4	2322	2.8	2350	3.4	1851	0.2	2224	0.3			2000	0.6	2318	5.2
20 SU	0107	1.4	0457	0.3	0613	0.3	0613	0.4	0123	1.7	0245	1.6	0036	4.1	0154	5.4	0602	1.0
	0718	-0.3	1052	2.4	1201	2.8	1224	3.4	0651	0.1	0937	0.3	0654	0.4	0827	0.2	1139	5.5
	1347	1.4	1712	0.4	1830	0.3	1833	0.4	1336	1.9	1506	1.8	1254	4.3	1415	5.6	1827	1.0
	1933	-0.2	2303	2.5					1933	0.2	2316	0.3	1909	0.5	2043	0.4	2356	5.5
21 M	0151	1.4	0538	0.2	0015	3.0	0043	3.6	0157	1.8	0324	1.7	0111	4.3	0233	5.6	0642	0.7
	0756	-0.3	1132	2.5	0656	0.1	0659	0.3	0720	0.1	1051	0.2	0730	0.3	0907	0.2	1216	5.7
	1423	1.4	1753	0.2	1245	3.0	1311	3.6	1409	1.9	1542	1.8	1327	4.4	1451	5.8	1903	0.8
	2010	-0.2	2343	2.6	1912	0.1	1917	0.3	2003	0.2	2356	0.3	1943	0.4	2121	0.3		
22 TU ○	0230	1.5	0615	0.1	0059	3.1	0127	3.8	0230	1.9	0359	1.8	0143	4.4	0307	5.7	0030	5.6
	0830	-0.3	1208	2.6	0735	0.2	0740	0.1	0743	0.1	1152	0.2	0803	0.3	0942	0.2	0718	0.6
	1455	1.4	1832	0.1	1324	3.1	1350	3.8	1442	2.0	1616	1.9	1358	4.6	1524	5.8	1249	5.8
	2045	-0.2			1952	0.0	1958	0.2	2014	0.2			2016	0.4	2155	0.3	1937	0.8
23 W	0305	1.5	0020	2.6	0139	3.2	0205	3.8	0301	1.9	0034	0.2	0215	4.6	0340	5.8	0100	5.7
	0904	-0.3	0652	0.1	0813	-0.0	0818	0.1	0806	0.1	0433	1.8	0836	0.2	1017	0.2	0752	0.5
	1526	1.4	1242	2.6	1403	3.2	1426	3.8	1515	2.0	1242	0.2	1430	4.6	1556	5.9	1318	5.8
	2120	-0.3	1909	0.1	2030	-0.0	2036	0.1	2027	0.2	1651	1.9	2051	0.3	2230	0.3	2009	0.7
24 TH	0341	1.5	0056	2.7	0219	3.2	0240	3.8	0333	2.0	0114	0.2	0247	4.7	0412	5.9	0130	5.8
	0938	-0.3	0728	0.1	0850	-0.0	0855	0.1	0835	0.2	0508	1.9	0912	0.2	1052	0.2	0825	0.5
	1559	1.5	1315	2.6	1440	3.2	1500	3.8	1548	2.0	1330	0.2	1503	4.7	1630	6.0	1348	5.8
	2155	-0.3	1946	0.1	2109	-0.1	2113	0.1	2053	0.2	1727	1.9	2128	0.3	2307	0.3	2042	0.7
25 F	0418	1.4	0130	2.6	0257	3.2	0315	3.8	0406	2.0	0154	0.2	0321	4.7	0446	6.0	0200	5.8
	1012	-0.3	0803	0.1	0927	0.0	0931	0.1	0909	0.2	0544	1.9	0949	0.2	1129	0.2	0900	0.6
	1633	1.5	1348	2.6	1516	3.2	1534	3.8	1623	2.0	1415	0.2	1538	4.7	1704	6.0	1420	5.9
	2231	-0.4	2022	0.1	2145	-0.0	2150	0.1	2126	0.2	1803	1.9	2208	0.3	2345	0.3	2115	0.7
26 SA	0454	1.4	0206	2.6	0336	3.2	0351	3.7	0441	2.1	0234	0.2	0356	4.7	0521	6.0	0234	5.9
	1047	-0.3	0839	0.2	1002	0.1	1007	0.1	0945	0.2	0622	1.9	1028	0.2	1205	0.3	0935	0.6
	1705	1.5	1420	2.7	1551	3.1	1609	3.8	1700	2.0	1457	0.2	1615	4.6	1740	5.9	1456	5.8
	2309	-0.4	2059	0.1	2222	-0.0	2227	0.1	2205	0.1	1842	1.9	2248	0.3			2151	0.8
27 SU	0529	1.4	0241	2.6	0412	3.1	0427	3.7	0518	2.1	0310	0.2	0433	4.7	0021	0.4	0313	5.9
	1124	-0.3	0915	0.2	1038	0.1	1043	0.1	1028	0.2	0701	1.9	1107	0.3	0559	6.0	1012	0.7
	1736	1.5	1454	2.7	1625	3.1	1645	3.8	1739	1.9	1537	0.2	1654	4.5	1240	0.4	1537	5.8
	2348	-0.4	2136	0.1	2259	-0.0	2305	0.1	2249	0.1	1921	1.8	2329	0.3	1820	5.8	2230	0.9
28 M	0603	1.3	0321	2.6	0450	3.1	0507	3.6	0600	2.0	0340	0.3	0515	4.5	0057	0.4	0357	5.8
	1203	-0.3	0952	0.2	1115	0.1	1121	0.1	1119	0.2	0745	1.9	1149	0.4	0642	5.9	1054	0.9
	1813	1.4	1534	2.7	1700	3.2	1724	3.8	1824	1.8	1613	0.3	1739	4.3	1317	0.5	1624	5.6
			2218	0.1	2339	0.0	2346	0.1	2342	0.0	2006	1.8			1904	5.6	2315	1.0
29 TU	0033	-0.4	0406	2.6	0531	3.1	0551	3.6	0650	2.0	0205	0.2	0014	0.4	0137	0.5	0449	5.6
	0649	1.3	1036	0.3	1154	0.2	1204	0.2	1445	0.1	0833	1.9	0606	4.2	0730	5.7	1144	1.1
	1250	-0.2	1623	2.7	1744	3.2	1809	3.8	1918	1.6	1645	0.3	1239	0.5	1400	0.6	1720	5.3
	1902	1.4	2307	0.1							2057	1.7	1835	4.0	1958	5.4		
30 W	0125	-0.4	0500	2.5	0023	0.0	0033	0.1	0058	0.0	0309	0.2	0110	0.4	0227	0.6	0011	1.2
	0751	1.2	1127	0.3	0620	3.0	0640	3.5	0758	1.8	0934	1.9	0714	4.1	0832	5.5	0554	5.3
	1345	-0.2	1721	2.7	1241	0.2	1254	0.2	1546	0.2	1604	0.3	1342	0.6	1456	0.8	1248	1.3
	2008	1.4			1837	3.2	1901	3.7	2051	1.5	2207	1.6	1957	3.8	2108	5.1	1833	5.2

• • Time Zone -0100. For UT subtract 1 hour. For European summer time (shaded) 30/3-26/10 add 1 hour • •

DENMARK, GERMANY, HOLLAND & BELGIUM Time Zone -0100
Esbjerg * Helgoland * Cuxhaven * Bremerhaven * Hoek van Holland * Rotterdam *Vlissingen * Antwerpen * Dunkerque

MAY 1997 TIDE TABLES MAY 1997

ESBJERG	HELGOLAND	CUXHAVEN	BREMERHAVEN	HOEK VAN HOLLAND	ROTTERDAM	VLISSINGEN	ANTWERPEN	DUNKERQUE	
Time m	Time m	Time m	Time m	Time m	Time m	Time m	Time m	Time m	
0229 -0.3	0007 0.2	0118 0.1	0131 0.1	0236 0.0	0415 0.1	0224 0.5	0333 0.7	0123 1.3	**1 TH**
0910 1.2	0603 2.5	0717 3.0	0739 3.5	0934 1.8	1057 1.9	0844 4.1	0949 5.3	0718 5.1	
1455 -0.1	1231 0.3	1341 0.2	1355 0.3	1657 0.2	1749 0.3	1507 0.7	1610 0.9	1406 1.4	
2127 1.4	1828 2.7	1939 3.2	2002 3.7	2214 1.5	2335 1.6	2120 3.8	2230 5.1	2000 4.9	
0348 -0.3	0118 0.1	0227 0.1	0240 0.1	0346 0.0	0518 0.1	0353 0.5	0458 0.7	0242 1.3	**2 F**
1032 1.2	0712 2.5	0821 3.0	0844 3.5	1050 1.8	1215 1.9	1002 4.2	1111 5.4	0842 5.2	
1616 -0.1	1345 0.3	1456 0.2	1509 0.3	1815 0.1	1946 0.2	1633 0.6	1735 0.8	1525 1.3	
2246 1.4	1937 2.7	2045 3.3	2109 3.7	2324 1.6		2234 3.9	2347 5.3	2116 5.1	
0508 -0.3	0232 0.0	0345 -0.0	0352 -0.0	0449 0.1	0044 1.7	0511 0.3	0624 0.5	0359 1.1	**3 SA**
1150 1.3	0821 2.5	0927 3.1	0952 3.5	1154 1.9	0619 0.0	1109 4.4	1223 5.6	0951 5.5	
1733 -0.2	1459 0.1	1615 0.1	1620 0.1	1950 0.1	1316 2.1	1741 0.4	1857 0.6	1637 1.1	
		2045 2.8	2151 3.3	2217 3.8	2059 0.2	2334 4.2		2216 5.4	
0000 1.5	0339 -0.1	0456 -0.2	0457 -0.2	0021 1.7	0140 1.9	0612 0.1	0052 5.6	0506 0.7	**4 SU**
0615 -0.4	0925 2.6	1032 3.2	1058 3.7	0536 0.0	0711 0.0	1203 4.6	0737 0.3	1046 5.8	
1300 1.4	1603 -0.0	1723 -0.1	1724 -0.0	1245 2.0	1409 2.2	1834 0.3	1322 5.9	1736 0.8	
1836 -0.2	2146 2.9	2255 3.4	2321 3.9	2045 0.2	2213 0.2		2003 0.4	2306 5.7	
0109 1.5	0437 -0.2	0557 -0.3	0556 -0.3	0110 1.8	0230 2.0	0024 4.4	0146 5.8	0602 0.4	**5 M**
0712 -0.4	1021 2.7	1133 3.3	1158 3.8	0615 0.0	0751 0.0	0703 -0.0	0836 0.1	1134 6.1	
1357 1.4	1700 -0.1	1822 -0.3	1821 -0.2	1333 2.1	1455 2.2	1250 4.7	1413 6.1	1827 0.5	
1931 -0.3	2241 2.9	2356 3.4		1845 0.3	2133 0.3	1921 0.2	2058 0.3	2350 5.9	
0209 1.6	0530 -0.2	0651 -0.3	0020 4.0	0155 1.9	0314 2.1	0109 4.6	0234 5.9	0651 0.3	**6 TU**
0802 -0.4	1111 2.7	1228 3.3	0650 -0.4	0653 0.0	1040 0.2	0748 -0.1	0926 0.1	1218 6.1	
1445 1.5	1751 -0.2	1915 -0.3	1252 3.9	1417 2.1	1538 2.2	1333 4.8	1459 6.2	1912 0.4	
2021 -0.3	2330 2.9		1915 -0.2	1918 0.3	2247 0.3	2005 0.1	2146 0.2	●	
0300 1.6	0618 -0.2	0051 3.4	0113 4.1	0239 2.0	0356 2.1	0152 4.8	0318 6.0	0032 6.1	**7 W**
0847 -0.5	1155 2.7	0741 -0.3	0740 -0.3	0733 0.1	1132 0.2	0830 -0.0	1011 0.1	0736 0.3	
1526 1.5	1839 -0.2	1317 3.3	1341 4.0	1500 2.1	1618 2.1	1415 4.8	1542 6.2	1259 6.1	
2106 -0.3		2003 -0.3	2003 -0.2	1957 0.2	2353 0.4	2048 0.1	2230 0.2	1955 0.4	
0345 1.6	0015 2.8	0139 3.3	0202 4.0	0322 2.1	0437 2.1	0234 4.9	0401 6.1	0113 6.1	**8 TH**
0930 -0.3	0701 -0.1	0826 -0.2	0827 -0.2	0816 0.1	1224 0.3	0911 0.0	1052 0.1	0818 0.3	
1603 1.5	1235 2.7	1359 3.2	1424 3.9	1543 2.0	1659 2.1	1458 4.8	1624 6.1	1340 6.0	
2150 -0.3	1922 -0.1	2048 -0.2	2049 -0.1	2040 0.2		2129 0.1	2311 0.1	2036 0.5	
0427 1.6	0057 2.7	0221 3.2	0246 3.9	0403 2.1	0518 2.1	0317 4.9	0444 6.0	0155 6.0	**9 F**
1009 -0.2	0741 0.0	0907 -0.0	0909 0.0	0903 0.2	1319 0.4	0949 0.2	1130 0.2	0859 0.5	
1636 1.6	1312 2.6	1435 3.1	1504 3.8	1625 2.0	1739 2.0	1540 4.7	1707 6.0	1421 5.9	
2232 -0.3	2002 -0.0	2128 -0.1	2131 0.0	2127 0.2	2304 0.2	2209 0.1	2350 0.1	2118 0.6	
0506 1.5	0136 2.6	0258 3.1	0326 3.7	0445 2.1	0600 2.0	0400 4.8	0527 6.0	0238 5.9	**10 SA**
1048 -0.2	0816 0.2	0943 0.1	0949 0.2	0953 0.2	1134 0.3	1026 0.3	1207 0.3	0938 0.7	
1710 1.6	1347 2.7	1505 3.1	1540 3.8	1707 1.9	1818 1.9	1623 4.6	1749 5.8	1505 5.8	
2313 -0.3	2039 0.1	2204 0.0	2211 0.2	2216 0.1		2248 0.2		2157 0.7	
0543 1.4	0213 2.5	0332 3.0	0402 3.6	0527 2.1	0000 0.2	0445 4.6	0027 0.2	0323 5.7	**11 SU**
1127 -0.2	0848 0.3	1014 0.2	1024 0.4	1052 0.3	0642 1.9	1101 0.4	0609 5.8	1018 0.9	
1744 1.6	1423 2.7	1533 3.1	1612 3.7	1751 1.8	1235 0.3	1707 4.4	1242 0.4	1549 5.6	
2354 -0.3	2114 0.2	2236 0.2	2247 0.4	2312 0.1	1857 1.8	2327 0.3	1831 5.5	2239 0.9	
0618 1.4	0251 2.5	0405 2.9	0436 3.4	0612 2.0	0102 0.2	0530 4.4	0103 0.3	0409 5.5	**12 M**
1206 -0.1	0918 0.3	1037 0.3	1055 0.6	1215 0.3	0722 1.8	1139 0.6	0652 5.6	1057 1.1	
1819 1.5	1502 2.6	1607 3.1	1643 3.6	1842 1.7	1340 0.4	1754 4.1	1318 0.5	1636 5.3	
	2148 0.3	2303 0.3	2320 0.6		1936 1.6		1913 5.3	2321 1.2	
0037 -0.2	0333 2.3	0444 2.8	0510 3.3	0012 0.0	0203 0.2	0011 0.4	0141 0.4	0500 5.3	**13 TU**
0656 1.3	0949 0.4	1100 0.4	1122 0.7	0706 1.9	0804 1.7	0621 4.2	0736 5.3	1142 1.4	
1247 -0.1	1545 2.5	1651 3.0	1718 3.6	1314 0.2	1439 0.4	1224 0.8	1355 0.7	1729 5.0	
1859 1.5	2226 0.4	2332 0.4	2352 0.7	1941 1.6	2017 1.5	1845 3.9	1959 5.0		
0124 -0.2	0420 2.2	0530 2.7	0550 3.2	0109 0.0	0300 0.2	0107 0.6	0221 0.5	0009 1.4	**14 W**
0742 1.2	1029 0.6	1134 0.5	1152 0.9	0806 1.8	0853 1.6	0718 4.0	0826 5.1	0556 5.0	
1333 -0.0	1637 2.4	1743 2.8	1803 3.4	1430 0.3	1539 0.5	1330 0.9	1440 0.9	1236 1.6	
1949 1.4	2315 0.6			2039 1.5	2106 1.4	1945 3.7	2053 4.8	1829 4.8	
0219 -0.1	0518 2.1	0012 0.6	0032 0.9	0235 0.1	0401 0.2	0219 0.7	0314 0.6	0106 1.6	**15 TH**
0845 1.2	1123 0.7	0627 2.5	0642 3.0	0909 1.7	1015 1.5	0824 3.8	0926 4.9	0701 4.8	
1433 0.1	1741 2.2	1222 0.7	1236 1.0	1543 0.3	1649 0.5	1451 1.0	1539 1.0	1339 1.7	
2054 1.4		1847 2.7	1902 3.3	2145 1.4	2257 1.3	2056 3.5	2200 4.6	1939 4.6	

● ● Time Zone -0100. For UT subtract 1 hour. For European summer time (shaded) 30/3-26/10 add 1 hour ● ●

MAY 1997 TIDE TABLES MAY 1997

	ESBJERG	HELGOLAND	CUXHAVEN	BREMERHAVEN	HOEK VAN HOLLAND	ROTTERDAM	VLISSINGEN	ANTWERPEN	DUNKERQUE
	Time m	Time m	Time m	Time m	Time m	Time m	Time m	Time m	Time m
16 F	0328 -0.1	0027 0.7	0112 0.7	0136 1.0	0404 0.1	0511 0.3	0324 0.7	0426 0.7	0210 1.7
	1003 1.2	0631 2.0	0735 2.4	0749 2.9	1024 1.7	1148 1.5	0942 3.7	1041 4.8	0815 4.7
	1547 0.1	1245 0.8	1330 0.9	1352 1.1	1643 0.2	1821 0.5	1557 1.0	1657 1.1	1446 1.8
	2212 1.4	1858 2.2	2000 2.6	2018 3.1	2301 1.4		2213 3.6	2318 4.6	2051 4.6
17 SA	0440 -0.1	0201 0.7	0311 0.8	0318 1.0	0500 0.1	0018 1.3	0426 0.7	0542 0.6	0315 1.6
	1112 1.2	0754 2.0	0852 2.4	0911 2.9	1132 1.7	0633 0.3	1048 3.8	1157 4.9	0921 4.9
	1701 0.1	1426 0.8	1540 0.9	1547 1.1	1739 0.2	1252 1.5	1658 0.8	1811 0.9	1554 1.6
	2323 1.4	2019 2.2	2119 2.6	2142 3.2	2359 0.1	1946 0.4	2312 3.8		2151 4.8
18 SU	0542 -0.1	0316 0.6	0433 0.6	0433 0.8	0549 0.1	0118 1.4	0524 0.6	0023 4.9	0419 1.4
	1212 1.3	0910 2.1	1009 2.6	1033 3.1	1220 1.8	0754 0.3	1137 4.0	0649 0.5	1015 5.1
	1802 0.0	1538 0.6	1656 0.6	1700 0.8		1346 1.7	1751 0.7	1251 5.2	1655 1.4
		2129 2.3	2232 2.8	2259 3.3		2057 0.3	2357 4.0	1913 0.7	2239 5.1
19 M	0021 1.4	0412 0.4	0529 0.4	0532 0.5	0043 1.7	0209 1.6	0613 0.5	0113 5.2	0515 1.1
	0633 -0.2	1007 2.3	1112 2.8	1139 3.4	0630 0.1	0903 0.2	1218 4.2	0742 0.4	1101 5.4
	1302 1.4	1631 0.4	1750 0.4	1756 0.5	1300 1.9	1433 1.8	1834 0.6	1336 5.5	1745 1.1
	1851 -0.1	2222 2.5	2331 2.9		2101 0.2	2203 0.2		2001 0.6	2321 5.3
20 TU	0112 1.5	0457 0.3	0616 0.2	0000 3.5	0121 1.8	0253 1.7	0036 4.2	0155 5.5	0601 0.9
	0716 -0.2	1053 2.5	1203 3.0	0621 0.3	0657 0.2	1008 0.2	0654 0.4	0826 0.3	1140 5.6
	1345 1.4	1718 0.3	1836 0.2	1233 3.6	1337 2.0	1513 1.9	1254 4.4	1415 5.7	1827 0.9
	1933 -0.1	2308 2.6		1844 0.3	2153 0.2	2303 0.2	1912 0.5	2042 0.4	2357 5.5
21 W	0157 1.5	0540 0.1	0021 3.1	0051 3.7	0157 1.9	0331 1.8	0112 4.4	0233 5.7	0642 0.8
	0755 -0.2	1133 2.6	0700 0.1	0707 0.1	0716 0.2	1113 0.2	0730 0.3	0906 0.3	1215 5.7
	1424 1.5	1800 0.1	1248 3.1	1317 3.8	1413 2.0	1551 1.9	1330 4.6	1451 5.8	1906 0.8
	2014 -0.0	2350 2.6	1921 -0.0	1928 0.1	1942 0.3	2356 0.2	1948 0.4	2122 0.4	
22 TH ○	0238 1.5	0621 0.1	0108 3.2	0135 3.8	0232 2.0	0408 1.8	0147 4.6	0309 5.8	0031 5.6
	0833 -0.2	1212 2.6	0742 -0.0	0749 0.0	0740 0.2	1215 0.2	0808 0.3	0945 0.3	0721 0.7
	1501 1.5	1842 0.1	1331 3.2	1358 3.9	1449 2.0	1627 1.9	1405 4.7	1528 5.9	1248 5.8
	2054 -0.2		2003 -0.1	2010 0.0	2000 0.2		2027 0.3	2203 0.3	1943 0.7
23 F	0320 1.5	0030 2.7	0152 3.2	0216 3.8	0308 2.0	0045 0.2	0223 4.7	0347 5.9	0103 5.7
	0912 -0.3	0702 0.1	0824 -0.1	0830 -0.0	0812 0.2	0445 1.9	0847 0.3	1025 0.3	0800 0.6
	1539 1.5	1250 2.7	1413 3.3	1436 3.9	1527 2.0	1309 0.2	1442 4.7	1606 6.0	1322 5.8
	2135 -0.3	1924 0.0	2045 -0.2	2051 -0.0	2031 0.2	1705 1.9	2109 0.2	2245 0.3	2021 0.7
24 SA	0403 1.5	0111 2.7	0236 3.2	0255 3.8	0345 2.1	0131 0.2	0300 4.8	0424 6.0	0138 5.8
	0951 -0.3	0742 0.1	0904 -0.1	0909 -0.0	0848 0.2	0524 1.9	0929 0.2	1106 0.3	0839 0.6
	1618 1.5	1327 2.7	1454 3.3	1514 3.9	1605 2.0	1359 0.2	1520 4.7	1645 6.0	1359 5.9
	2215 -0.3	2005 -0.0	2127 -0.2	2131 -0.0	2107 0.1	1743 1.9	2153 0.2	2328 0.3	2100 0.7
25 SU	0445 1.4	0151 2.6	0318 3.2	0335 3.8	0424 2.1	0214 0.2	0339 4.8	0504 6.1	0217 5.8
	1030 -0.3	0821 0.1	0944 -0.1	0948 -0.0	0927 0.3	0604 1.9	1012 0.3	1148 0.3	0918 0.7
	1656 1.5	1404 2.7	1533 3.3	1551 3.9	1645 2.0	1445 0.2	1600 4.6	1725 6.0	1439 5.9
	2257 -0.4	2045 -0.0	2207 -0.2	2212 -0.1	2148 0.1	1823 1.8	2238 0.2		2139 0.7
26 M	0528 1.4	0230 2.6	0359 3.2	0414 3.7	0506 2.1	0253 0.2	0421 4.7	0010 0.3	0300 5.8
	1111 -0.4	0900 0.1	1024 -0.1	1028 -0.0	1012 0.3	0646 2.0	1056 0.3	0546 6.1	0959 0.7
	1733 1.5	1442 2.8	1612 3.3	1630 3.9	1727 1.9	1527 0.2	1643 4.5	1229 0.4	1524 5.8
	2340 -0.4	2127 -0.1	2248 -0.2	2253 -0.1	2234 0.1	1905 1.8	2324 0.2	1808 5.9	2221 0.8
27 TU	0611 1.3	0312 2.6	0439 3.2	0455 3.7	0551 2.1	0325 0.2	0506 4.6	0053 0.3	0347 5.8
	1154 -0.2	0941 0.1	1103 -0.1	1109 -0.0	1105 0.3	0730 2.0	1142 0.4	0632 6.0	1042 0.8
	1814 1.5	1524 2.8	1650 3.3	1710 4.0	1814 1.8	1606 0.3	1731 4.3	1310 0.5	1612 5.7
		2210 -0.1	2330 -0.2	2336 -0.2	2327 0.0	1949 1.8		1855 5.7	2308 0.9
28 W	0027 -0.4	0356 2.6	0521 3.2	0538 3.7	0644 2.0	0152 0.1	0013 0.2	0137 0.4	0441 5.7
	0659 1.3	1024 0.1	1145 -0.1	1152 -0.0	1442 0.2	0819 2.0	0600 4.4	0723 5.8	1133 1.0
	1241 -0.2	1611 2.8	1733 3.3	1754 4.0	1914 1.7	1641 0.3	1233 0.5	1356 0.6	1709 5.4
	1903 1.5	2257 -0.1				2039 1.8	1830 4.1	1951 5.5	
29 TH	0119 -0.3	0446 2.6	0015 -0.2	0023 -0.2	0037 0.0	0246 0.1	0109 0.3	0228 0.4	0003 1.0
	0756 1.3	1113 0.1	0606 3.1	0625 3.6	0758 1.9	0917 2.0	0712 4.3	0824 5.6	0545 5.5
	1335 -0.2	1704 2.8	1230 -0.0	1240 0.0	1536 0.2	1645 0.3	1333 0.6	1451 0.7	1233 1.2
	2004 1.5	2351 -0.0	1822 3.4	1844 3.9	2041 1.6	2142 1.7	1945 4.0	2057 5.3	1818 5.2
30 F	0220 -0.3	0542 2.5	0106 -0.2	0115 -0.2	0228 0.0	0348 0.0	0217 0.3	0332 0.5	0109 1.1
	0903 1.3	1210 0.1	0657 3.1	0718 3.6	0916 1.9	1031 2.0	0827 4.2	0936 5.5	0700 5.3
	1439 -0.1	1805 2.8	1324 0.0	1336 0.1	1641 0.2	1738 0.3	1447 0.7	1559 0.8	1345 1.3
	2114 1.5		1918 3.3	1939 3.9	2149 1.6	2301 1.7	2057 4.0	2210 5.3	1936 5.1
31 SA	0331 -0.3	0054 -0.0	0206 -0.1	0215 -0.1	0330 0.0	0452 -0.0	0331 0.3	0445 0.5	0223 1.1
	1014 1.3	0645 2.5	0755 3.1	0817 3.5	1025 1.9	1145 2.0	0937 4.3	1050 5.5	0818 5.3
	1554 -0.1	1316 0.1	1429 0.0	1441 0.1	1754 0.2	1914 0.3	1605 0.6	1713 0.8	1501 1.3
	2226 1.5	1909 2.8	2020 3.3	2041 3.8	2256 1.6		2206 4.1	2322 5.3	2051 5.2

• • Time Zone -0100. For UT subtract 1 hour. For European summer time (shaded) 30/3-26/10 add 1 hour • •

DENMARK, GERMANY, HOLLAND & BELGIUM Time Zone -0100

Esbjerg * Helgoland * Cuxhaven * Bremerhaven * Hoek van Holland * Rotterdam *Vlissingen * Antwerpen * Dunkerque

JUNE 1997 TIDE TABLES JUNE 1997

ESBJERG Time m	HELGOLAND Time m	CUXHAVEN Time m	BREMERHAVEN Time m	HOEK VAN HOLLAND Time m	ROTTERDAM Time m	VLISSINGEN Time m	ANTWERPEN Time m	DUNKERQUE Time m	
0445 -0.3	0201 -0.0	0315 -0.1	0321 -0.1	0430 0.0	0012 1.8	0445 0.3	0600 0.4	0338 1.0	**1 SU**
1124 1.4	0750 2.5	0857 3.1	0921 3.6	1128 2.0	0557 -0.0	1043 4.4	1200 5.6	0927 5.5	
1707 -0.1	1427 0.1	1542 -0.0	1550 0.0	1858 0.2	1248 2.0	1715 0.5	1830 0.7	1613 1.1	
2337 1.5	2016 2.7	2124 3.3	2147 3.8	2355 1.7	2022 0.2	2308 4.2		2154 5.4	
0551 -0.3	0308 -0.1	0424 -0.1	0426 -0.2	0520 0.1	0112 1.9	0548 0.2	0027 5.5	0445 0.8	**2 M**
1231 1.4	0854 2.5	1000 3.1	1026 3.6	1223 2.0	0700 0.0	1139 4.5	0711 0.3	1025 5.7	
1813 -0.2	1533 0.0	1652 -0.1	1656 -0.0	1945 0.2	1343 2.1	1812 0.4	1300 5.8	1715 0.9	
	2119 2.7	2227 3.3	2252 3.8		2134 0.2		1939 0.5	2246 5.6	
0046 1.6	0409 -0.1	0527 -0.2	0527 -0.2	0048 1.8	0205 2.0	0002 4.4	0124 5.7	0542 0.6	**3 TU**
0648 -0.2	0952 2.6	1101 3.1	1129 3.7	0602 0.1	0743 0.1	0640 0.1	0812 0.2	1115 5.8	
1329 1.5	1634 -0.1	1754 -0.2	1756 -0.1	1312 2.0	1433 2.1	1230 4.6	1352 5.9	1807 0.7	
1911 -0.1	2217 2.7	2329 3.2	2354 3.8	1838 0.3	2102 0.3	1901 0.3	2037 0.4	2333 5.8	
0147 1.6	0503 -0.1	0624 -0.2	0624 -0.2	0136 1.9	0252 2.0	0050 4.5	0214 5.8	0632 0.6	**4 W**
0740 -0.2	1044 2.6	1157 3.1	1227 3.8	0642 0.2	1012 0.2	0726 0.1	0903 0.2	1159 5.9	
1418 1.5	1729 -0.1	1851 -0.2	1851 -0.1	1359 2.0	1516 2.0	1315 4.6	1440 6.0	1854 0.6	
2002 -0.2	2309 2.7			1909 0.3	2230 0.3	1946 0.2	2127 0.3		
0239 1.6	0553 -0.0	0025 3.2	0051 3.8	0221 2.0	0336 2.0	0135 4.7	0300 5.8	0015 5.8	**5 TH**
0827 -0.2	1130 2.6	0716 -0.1	0716 -0.1	0723 0.3	1105 0.3	0809 0.2	0949 0.3	0717 0.6	
1500 1.6	1818 -0.1	1248 3.1	1318 3.8	1444 2.0	1557 2.0	1400 4.7	1524 6.0	1240 5.9	**●**
2050 -0.2	2355 2.6	1942 -0.2	1942 -0.1	1947 0.2	2337 0.4	2029 0.2	2211 0.2	1937 0.6	
0325 1.6	0638 0.1	0115 3.0	0142 3.7	0305 2.1	0417 2.0	0218 4.7	0345 5.9	0057 5.8	**6 F**
0909 -0.1	1212 2.6	0803 -0.0	0804 0.1	0806 0.2	1158 0.5	0848 0.3	1031 0.3	0758 0.7	
1539 1.6	1904 0.0	1331 3.0	1404 3.7	1527 2.0	1636 1.9	1442 4.7	1608 5.9	1321 5.8	
2134 -0.2		2028 -0.1	2030 0.1	2029 0.2	2259 0.4	2111 0.2	2253 0.2	2019 0.6	
0407 1.5	0038 2.5	0159 2.9	0228 3.6	0348 2.1	0458 1.9	0302 4.7	0427 5.9	0139 5.8	**7 SA**
0950 -0.1	0719 0.2	0845 0.1	0848 0.2	0851 0.3	1251 0.5	0926 0.3	1109 0.3	0838 0.8	
1615 1.6	1251 2.5	1408 3.0	1445 3.7	1610 2.0	1716 1.8	1524 4.6	1650 5.9	1403 5.8	
2217 -0.2	1945 0.1	2110 0.0	2113 0.1	2113 0.1	2238 0.2	2151 0.2	2332 0.1	2100 0.7	
0447 1.5	0117 2.4	0237 2.8	0309 3.5	0428 2.1	0539 1.9	0345 4.7	0510 5.9	0221 5.7	**8 SU**
1028 -0.1	0756 0.2	0923 0.2	0929 0.4	0940 0.3	1347 0.6	1003 0.4	1145 0.4	0917 0.9	
1650 1.6	1327 2.5	1439 3.0	1520 3.6	1653 1.9	1755 1.8	1606 4.5	1731 5.7	1445 5.7	
2257 -0.2	2024 0.2	2148 0.1	2153 0.1	2159 0.1	2329 0.2	2231 0.2		2139 0.8	
0524 1.5	0154 2.3	0312 2.8	0343 3.4	0509 2.1	0620 1.8	0427 4.6	0009 0.2	0305 5.6	**9 M**
1106 -0.1	0829 0.3	0955 0.3	1004 0.6	1034 0.4	1149 0.4	1039 0.5	0551 5.8	0954 1.0	
1725 1.6	1403 2.5	1510 3.0	1550 3.6	1734 1.8	1833 1.7	1647 4.4	1221 0.4	1527 5.6	
2336 -0.2	2058 0.2	2221 0.2	2229 0.5	2247 0.1		2310 0.3	1811 5.6	2218 0.9	
0558 1.4	0231 2.3	0345 2.7	0415 3.3	0550 2.0	0024 0.2	0508 4.4	0045 0.2	0348 5.5	**10 TU**
1143 -0.1	0859 0.3	1021 0.3	1035 0.7	1142 0.3	0700 1.8	1115 0.6	0631 5.6	1031 1.1	
1800 1.6	1441 2.5	1545 3.0	1620 3.6	1818 1.8	1242 0.5	1728 4.3	1254 0.6	1612 5.5	
	2131 0.3	2250 0.3	2300 0.6	2337 0.0	1912 1.6	2348 0.4	1851 5.4	2256 1.1	
0015 -0.1	0310 2.3	0423 2.7	0446 3.2	0635 1.9	0123 0.2	0551 4.3	0118 0.3	0434 5.4	**11 W**
0631 1.3	0930 0.4	1045 0.4	1103 0.7	1254 0.3	0740 1.7	1153 0.7	0712 5.5	1109 1.3	
1221 -0.1	1521 2.5	1627 2.9	1654 3.6	1906 1.7	1342 0.5	1811 4.1	1328 0.7	1657 5.3	
1836 1.6	2206 0.4	2318 0.4	2331 0.6		1950 1.6		1931 5.2	2337 1.2	
0055 -0.1	0353 2.2	0506 2.6	0524 3.2	0029 0.0	0221 0.2	0030 0.5	0154 0.3	0521 5.2	**12 TH**
0708 1.3	1008 0.5	1118 0.4	1133 0.7	0725 1.9	0822 1.7	0637 4.1	0755 5.3	1154 1.4	
1301 -0.0	1608 2.4	1715 2.8	1736 3.5	1424 0.3	1454 0.5	1237 0.8	1406 0.8	1746 5.1	
1918 1.5	2248 0.5	2354 0.5		1957 1.6	2033 1.5	1859 3.9	2018 5.0		
0139 -0.1	0443 2.1	0556 2.6	0006 0.7	0122 0.0	0322 0.2	0126 0.6	0233 0.4	0024 1.4	**13 F**
0754 1.3	1054 0.6	1203 0.5	0610 3.1	0821 1.8	0914 1.6	0730 3.9	0846 5.1	0612 5.0	
1347 0.0	1702 2.3	1812 2.7	1214 0.7	1522 0.3	1613 0.5	1343 1.0	1450 0.9	1248 1.6	
2009 1.5	2341 0.6		1828 3.3	2051 1.5	2129 1.4	1955 3.7	2113 4.8	1842 4.9	
0231 -0.0	0544 2.0	0042 0.6	0053 0.7	0221 0.1	0433 0.3	0236 0.7	0324 0.5	0121 1.5	**14 SA**
0854 1.2	1156 0.7	0656 2.5	0709 3.0	0920 1.7	1042 1.5	0830 3.8	0946 4.9	0712 4.8	
1443 0.1	1809 2.2	1258 0.7	1309 0.8	1618 0.3	1748 0.5	1506 1.0	1545 1.0	1350 1.7	
2111 1.4		1918 2.6	1934 3.2	2152 1.5	2317 1.4	2059 3.6	2217 4.7	1945 4.7	
0333 0.0	0052 0.6	0147 0.7	0159 0.8	0431 0.1	0600 0.3	0336 0.7	0433 0.6	0221 1.6	**15 SU**
1005 1.3	0655 2.0	0803 2.4	0819 3.0	1025 1.7	1203 1.5	0939 3.8	1051 4.9	0818 4.8	
1551 0.1	1316 0.7	1412 0.7	1430 0.9	1712 0.3	1909 0.4	1607 0.9	1702 1.0	1454 1.7	
2221 1.4	1924 2.2	2030 2.6	2050 3.1	2259 1.5		2210 3.7	2323 4.8	2054 4.8	

● ● Time Zone -0100. For UT subtract 1 hour. For European summer time (shaded) 30/3-26/10 add 1 hour ● ●

JUNE 1997 TIDE TABLES JUNE 1997

	ESBJERG	HELGOLAND	CUXHAVEN	BREMERHAVEN	HOEK VAN HOLLAND	ROTTERDAM	VLISSINGEN	ANTWERPEN	DUNKERQUE
	Time m	Time m	Time m	Time m	Time m	Time m	Time m	Time m	Time m
16 M	0439 -0.0 1114 1.3 1701 0.1 2329 1.4	0211 0.6 0810 2.1 1439 0.6 2036 2.3	0316 0.6 0915 2.5 1550 0.6 2142 2.7	0327 0.7 0937 3.1 1603 0.8 2208 3.2	0523 0.1 1129 1.8 1812 0.2 2357 1.6	0031 1.4 0721 0.3 1305 1.6 2015 0.3	0434 0.7 1045 3.9 1703 0.8 2310 3.9	0548 0.6 1155 5.0 1813 0.9	0322 1.5 0922 4.9 1557 1.5 2153 5.0
17 TU	0539 -0.0 1213 1.4 1803 0.0	0319 0.4 0915 2.2 1545 0.4 2139 2.4	0434 0.5 1021 2.7 1702 0.4 2248 2.8	0442 0.5 1050 3.3 1713 0.5 2317 3.4	0611 0.2 1221 1.9 2021 0.2	0129 1.5 0830 0.2 1357 1.7 2118 0.2	0528 0.6 1136 4.1 1754 0.7 2359 4.1	0023 5.0 0647 0.6 1249 5.3 1909 0.7	0422 1.3 1017 5.2 1655 1.3 2242 5.2
18 W	0029 1.5 0632 -0.1 1305 1.5 1856 -0.1	0415 0.3 1009 2.4 1640 0.2 2232 2.5	0533 0.2 1119 2.9 1758 0.2 2345 3.0	0542 0.3 1151 3.5 1809 0.2	0045 1.8 0639 0.2 1305 1.9 2127 0.2	0219 1.6 0933 0.2 1443 1.8 2218 0.2	0616 0.5 1221 4.3 1839 0.6	0113 5.3 0738 0.5 1336 5.5 2000 0.5	0517 1.1 1103 5.4 1747 1.1 2325 5.4
19 TH	0123 1.5 0720 -0.1 1353 1.5 1945 -0.1	0505 0.1 1057 2.5 1730 0.1 2320 2.6	0624 0.0 1211 3.1 1849 -0.1	0015 3.6 0633 0.1 1243 3.7 1859 0.1	0127 1.9 0654 0.3 1346 2.0 1915 0.3	0303 1.7 1039 0.2 1525 1.9 2318 0.2	0042 4.3 0700 0.4 1303 4.5 1922 0.4	0159 5.6 0827 0.4 1421 5.8 2049 0.4	0606 1.0 1143 5.6 1833 0.9
20 F O	0212 1.5 0805 -0.2 1437 1.6 2031 -0.2	0551 0.0 1142 2.6 1817 -0.1	0036 3.1 0712 -0.1 1259 3.2 1937 -0.2	0105 3.7 0721 -0.0 1330 3.8 1945 -0.1	0206 2.0 0721 0.3 1427 2.0 1939 0.2	0344 1.8 1148 0.2 1604 1.9	0122 4.5 0742 0.3 1343 4.7 2006 0.3	0242 5.8 0914 0.3 1504 5.9 2138 0.3	0003 5.5 0652 0.8 1222 5.7 1918 0.7
21 SA	0301 1.5 0849 -0.2 1521 1.6 2116 -0.3	0006 2.6 0637 -0.1 1224 2.7 1903 -0.1	0126 3.2 0758 -0.2 1346 3.3 2024 -0.3	0151 3.8 0806 -0.1 1412 3.9 2030 -0.2	0246 2.1 0755 0.3 1508 2.0 2013 0.1	0016 0.2 0424 1.9 1250 0.2 1644 1.9	0203 4.7 0825 0.3 1424 4.7 2051 0.2	0325 6.0 1001 0.3 1547 6.0 2227 0.2	0042 5.7 0736 0.7 1301 5.8 2001 0.6
22 SU	0349 1.5 0933 -0.2 1605 1.6 2202 -0.3	0051 2.6 0722 -0.1 1306 2.7 1948 -0.2	0214 3.2 0844 -0.3 1431 3.3 2109 -0.4	0236 3.8 0849 -0.1 1454 4.0 2114 -0.2	0327 2.1 0832 0.3 1549 2.0 2051 0.1	0107 0.2 0505 2.0 1342 0.2 1724 1.9	0244 4.8 0910 0.2 1506 4.8 2139 0.1	0408 6.1 1048 0.3 1630 6.1 2315 0.2	0121 5.8 0819 0.7 1342 5.9 2044 0.6
23 M	0437 1.5 1015 -0.2 1648 1.6 2247 -0.3	0135 2.6 0805 -0.1 1348 2.8 2032 -0.3	0300 3.2 0927 -0.3 1515 3.3 2154 -0.5	0318 3.8 0932 -0.2 1535 4.0 2157 -0.3	0410 2.2 0912 0.3 1633 2.0 2132 0.0	0154 0.1 0548 2.0 1430 0.2 1806 1.9	0326 4.8 0957 0.2 1548 4.7 2227 0.0	0451 6.2 1134 0.3 1714 6.0	0203 5.9 0902 0.6 1425 5.9 2127 0.5
24 TU	0526 1.5 1059 -0.2 1732 1.6 2332 -0.3	0218 2.6 0847 -0.1 1430 2.8 2115 -0.3	0344 3.2 1010 -0.3 1557 3.4 2236 -0.5	0400 3.8 1014 -0.2 1615 4.1 2239 -0.4	0454 2.2 0956 0.3 1718 1.9 2217 0.0	0235 0.1 0631 2.1 1512 0.2 1849 1.9	0410 4.8 1044 0.3 1633 4.6 2316 0.0	0002 0.2 0536 6.2 1220 0.4 1758 6.0	0249 5.9 0945 0.7 1512 5.9 2211 0.5
25 W	0613 1.4 1144 -0.2 1816 1.6	0259 2.6 0929 -0.2 1512 2.9 2158 -0.3	0426 3.2 1052 -0.3 1639 3.4 2319 -0.5	0441 3.8 1056 -0.3 1657 4.1 2323 -0.5	0542 2.1 1045 0.4 1807 1.8 2307 0.0	0310 0.1 0716 2.1 1551 0.3 1933 1.9	0458 4.7 1132 0.4 1722 4.5	0048 0.2 0623 6.1 1304 0.5 1846 5.9	0338 5.9 1030 0.7 1601 5.9 2258 0.6
26 TH	0018 -0.3 0700 1.4 1230 -0.2 1903 1.6	0342 2.6 1011 -0.2 1557 2.9 2243 -0.3	0507 3.2 1133 -0.2 1721 3.4	0524 3.8 1139 -0.3 1740 4.1	0636 2.1 1427 0.2 1907 1.8	0136 0.1 0804 2.1 1627 0.3 2021 1.9	0006 0.1 0552 4.6 1222 0.5 1819 4.3	0135 0.2 0714 5.9 1351 0.6 1939 5.7	0431 5.9 1119 0.9 1655 5.7 2351 0.7
27 F	0109 -0.3 0749 1.3 1321 -0.2 1956 1.6	0428 2.6 1057 -0.1 1646 2.9 2332 -0.2	0003 -0.5 0550 3.2 1217 -0.3 1806 3.4	0008 -0.5 0608 3.8 1225 -0.3 1827 4.1	0009 0.0 0745 2.0 1518 0.3 2018 1.7	0227 -0.0 0857 2.1 1617 0.3 2118 1.9	0100 0.1 0658 4.5 1317 0.5 1924 4.2	0225 0.2 0812 5.7 1442 0.7 2039 5.5	0530 5.7 1215 1.0 1757 5.5
28 SA	0205 -0.2 0845 1.3 1420 -0.1 2057 1.6	0518 2.5 1148 -0.1 1741 2.8	0049 -0.4 0637 3.1 1305 -0.2 1857 3.4	0056 -0.4 0656 3.7 1315 -0.2 1918 3.9	0224 -0.0 0851 2.0 1615 0.3 2121 1.7	0327 -0.0 1002 2.0 1613 0.3 2227 1.8	0157 0.2 0805 4.4 1419 0.6 2030 4.2	0321 0.3 0917 5.5 1541 0.7 2147 5.4	0052 0.9 0637 5.5 1321 1.2 1908 5.3
29 SU	0308 -0.2 0946 1.4 1527 -0.1 2203 1.6	0027 -0.1 0615 2.5 1247 -0.0 1842 2.7	0141 -0.3 0729 3.1 1401 -0.2 1954 3.2	0148 -0.3 0749 3.6 1412 -0.1 2015 3.8	0311 -0.0 0957 1.9 1724 0.3 2226 1.7	0432 -0.0 1112 2.0 1755 0.3 2339 1.8	0303 0.3 0909 4.3 1530 0.7 2136 4.1	0423 0.3 1026 5.4 1648 0.7 2257 5.3	0202 1.1 0751 5.3 1434 1.3 2024 5.3
30 M	0416 -0.1 1052 1.4 1639 -0.1 2313 1.6	0129 -0.0 0717 2.4 1354 0.0 1948 2.6	0242 -0.1 0827 3.0 1509 -0.1 2056 3.1	0249 -0.2 0849 3.5 1519 -0.0 2118 3.6	0409 0.0 1101 1.9 1824 0.3 2330 1.8	0542 0.0 1218 2.0 1934 0.3	0415 0.3 1015 4.3 1646 0.6 2242 4.2	0530 0.4 1135 5.4 1800 0.7	0314 1.1 0904 5.3 1546 1.2 2132 5.4

• • Time Zone -0100. For UT subtract 1 hour. For European summer time (shaded) 30/3-26/10 add 1 hour • •

DENMARK, GERMANY, HOLLAND & BELGIUM Time Zone -0100

Esbjerg * Helgoland * Cuxhaven * Bremerhaven * Hoek van Holland * Rotterdam *Vlissingen * Antwerpen * Dunkerque

JULY 1997 TIDE TABLES JULY 1997

ESBJERG	HELGOLAND	CUXHAVEN	BREMERHAVEN	HOEK VAN HOLLAND	ROTTERDAM	VLISSINGEN	ANTWERPEN	DUNKERQUE	
Time m	Time m	Time m	Time m	Time m	Time m	Time m	Time m	Time m	
0524 -0.1 1159 1.5 1749 -0.1	0236 0.0 0822 2.4 1505 0.0 2054 2.5	0351 -0.1 0929 2.9 1622 -0.1 2201 3.0	0355 -0.1 0954 3.5 1628 0.0 2226 3.6	0506 0.1 1200 1.9 1912 0.2	0044 1.8 0700 0.1 1318 1.9 2043 0.3	0523 0.3 1118 4.3 1750 0.5 2342 4.3	0003 5.4 0642 0.4 1238 5.5 1915 0.6	0423 1.0 1006 5.4 1651 1.0 2230 5.5	**1 TU**
0024 1.6 0625 -0.1 1300 1.5 1852 -0.1	0341 0.0 0925 2.4 1611 -0.0 2157 2.5	0458 -0.0 1031 2.9 1730 -0.1 2306 2.9	0501 -0.0 1101 3.5 1733 0.0 2333 3.5	0027 1.9 0557 0.2 1254 1.9 1957 0.2	0142 1.9 0808 0.2 1411 1.9 2211 0.3	0619 0.3 1212 4.4 1842 0.4	0104 5.5 0748 0.4 1333 5.6 2018 0.5	0523 0.9 1059 5.5 1748 0.9 2319 5.6	**2 W**
0128 1.6 0720 -0.1 1354 1.6 1947 -0.1	0440 0.0 1022 2.4 1710 -0.0 2254 2.4	0600 -0.0 1131 2.9 1830 -0.1	0601 0.0 1205 3.5 1832 0.0	0118 1.9 0639 0.3 1344 1.9 1904 0.2	0233 1.9 0936 0.3 1458 1.9 2213 0.4	0035 4.4 0706 0.4 1302 4.5 1930 0.3	0158 5.6 0843 0.4 1424 5.7 2109 0.3	0615 0.9 1145 5.6 1836 0.7	**3 TH**
0223 1.6 0809 -0.0 1440 1.6 2036 -0.1	0533 0.1 1112 2.4 1803 -0.0 2342 2.3	0005 2.9 0654 -0.0 1225 2.9 1924 -0.1	0036 3.5 0656 0.1 1302 3.6 1925 0.1	0206 2.0 0719 0.3 1431 1.9 1940 0.2	0319 1.9 1034 0.5 1540 1.8 2314 0.4	0123 4.5 0749 0.4 1347 4.5 2013 0.3	0247 5.7 0930 0.4 1510 5.7 2155 0.3	0003 5.7 0700 0.9 1226 5.7 1921 0.7	**4 F** ●
0309 1.5 0853 -0.0 1520 1.7 2121 -0.1	0621 0.1 1157 2.4 1851 0.0	0058 2.8 0743 0.0 1312 2.9 2012 -0.0	0130 3.5 0746 0.2 1351 3.6 2014 0.2	0251 2.0 0800 0.3 1516 2.0 2018 0.1	0401 1.9 1128 0.6 1619 1.8 2133 0.3	0207 4.6 0829 0.4 1430 4.6 2054 0.2	0331 5.8 1012 0.4 1554 5.8 2236 0.2	0045 5.7 0741 0.9 1306 5.7 2003 0.7	**5 SA**
0350 1.5 0933 -0.0 1556 1.7 2203 -0.1	0026 2.3 0703 0.2 1237 2.4 1933 0.1	0145 2.7 0828 0.1 1353 2.8 2057 0.0	0218 3.4 0831 0.3 1433 3.5 2058 0.3	0333 2.1 0842 0.3 1558 2.0 2058 0.1	0442 1.8 1221 0.7 1657 1.8 2230 0.3	0248 4.7 0906 0.5 1509 4.6 2134 0.2	0413 5.8 1051 0.4 1634 5.8 2315 0.1	0125 5.7 0820 1.0 1345 5.7 2042 0.7	**6 SU**
0427 1.5 1011 -0.0 1632 1.7 2241 -0.1	0105 2.2 0742 0.2 1313 2.4 2011 0.1	0225 2.6 0908 0.2 1428 2.8 2136 0.1	0257 3.3 0912 0.5 1508 3.5 2137 0.4	0412 2.1 0926 0.4 1638 1.9 2139 0.1	0522 1.8 1312 0.7 1736 1.7 2301 0.2	0328 4.6 0942 0.5 1548 4.6 2213 0.2	0454 5.9 1126 0.4 1713 5.7 2351 0.1	0206 5.6 0857 1.0 1425 5.7 2120 0.8	**7 M**
0503 1.5 1047 -0.0 1706 1.7 2318 -0.1	0141 2.2 0815 0.2 1348 2.4 2045 0.2	0300 2.6 0942 0.2 1501 2.8 2210 0.2	0330 3.3 0948 0.6 1537 3.5 2212 0.5	0450 2.0 1012 0.4 1715 1.9 2220 0.1	0601 1.8 1412 0.7 1814 1.7 2351 0.2	0406 4.6 1017 0.5 1625 4.5 2250 0.2	0531 5.8 1200 0.4 1750 5.6	0246 5.6 0932 1.1 1505 5.7 2156 0.8	**8 TU**
0535 1.4 1121 -0.1 1739 1.6 2352 -0.1	0215 2.2 0846 0.2 1424 2.4 2115 0.2	0335 2.6 1012 0.3 1535 2.9 2239 0.2	0359 3.2 1020 0.6 1606 3.5 2244 0.5	0526 2.0 1106 0.4 1750 1.8 2303 0.0	0639 1.8 1158 0.5 1851 1.7	0442 4.5 1051 0.6 1700 4.4 2323 0.3	0024 0.1 0608 5.7 1231 0.5 1826 5.5	0327 5.6 1006 1.1 1545 5.6 2230 0.9	**9 W**
0604 1.4 1155 -0.1 1812 1.6	0251 2.2 0917 0.3 1500 2.4 2147 0.3	0409 2.6 1039 0.3 1612 2.8 2307 0.3	0429 3.2 1048 0.6 1638 3.5 2313 0.5	0603 2.0 1339 0.3 1823 1.8 2350 0.0	0042 0.2 0717 1.8 1239 0.5 1927 1.7	0518 4.4 1124 0.7 1736 4.3 2354 0.3	0056 0.2 0645 5.6 1302 0.6 1903 5.3	0406 5.5 1039 1.2 1624 5.5 2305 1.0	**10 TH**
0026 -0.1 0636 1.4 1230 -0.0 1848 1.6	0328 2.2 0951 0.3 1541 2.4 2222 0.3	0447 2.6 1109 0.3 1653 2.8 2338 0.3	0503 3.2 1119 0.5 1716 3.5 2345 0.5	0642 1.9 1421 0.3 1859 1.7	0124 0.2 0755 1.8 1319 0.5 2007 1.7	0555 4.3 1158 0.7 1814 4.1	0127 0.2 0723 5.4 1335 0.7 1941 5.2	0445 5.4 1115 1.3 1704 5.4 2344 1.2	**11 F**
0101 -0.0 0712 1.3 1308 -0.0 1930 1.5	0410 2.2 1030 0.4 1627 2.3 2305 0.4	0529 2.6 1147 0.4 1741 2.7	0543 3.2 1156 0.5 1802 3.4	0041 0.0 0726 1.9 1340 0.3 1945 1.7	0206 0.3 0838 1.7 1449 0.5 2052 1.6	0027 0.5 0637 4.1 1239 0.8 1859 4.0	0200 0.3 0805 5.2 1412 0.7 2026 5.0	0527 5.2 1157 1.4 1748 5.2	**12 SA**
0141 -0.0 0758 1.3 1352 0.0 2020 1.5	0500 2.1 1119 0.5 1723 2.2 2359 0.5	0017 0.4 0619 2.5 1233 0.4 1839 2.6	0024 0.5 0633 3.1 1241 0.5 1858 3.3	0134 0.1 0823 1.8 1426 0.3 2050 1.6	0356 0.3 0932 1.6 1715 0.5 2153 1.5	0110 0.6 0730 4.0 1330 0.9 1956 3.8	0239 0.4 0854 5.0 1455 0.8 2121 4.8	0032 1.4 0614 5.0 1252 1.6 1841 5.0	**13 SU**
0229 0.0 0856 1.3 1447 0.1 2121 1.4	0602 2.0 1222 0.5 1831 2.1	0106 0.5 0719 2.5 1329 0.5 1945 2.5	0114 0.5 0734 3.1 1339 0.6 2006 3.2	0227 0.1 0927 1.8 1641 0.3 2157 1.6	0526 0.3 1055 1.6 1830 0.4 2330 1.5	0208 0.7 0832 3.9 1440 1.0 2103 3.7	0325 0.6 0953 4.9 1547 0.9 2223 4.8	0130 1.5 0711 4.9 1357 1.7 1945 4.8	**14 M**
0330 0.0 1006 1.3 1557 0.1 2233 1.4	0108 0.5 0713 2.0 1339 0.5 1946 2.2	0209 0.5 0826 2.5 1442 0.5 2056 2.6	0219 0.6 0845 3.1 1457 0.6 2121 3.2	0327 0.2 1033 1.7 1735 0.3 2306 1.6	0647 0.3 1218 1.6 1936 0.4	0332 0.7 0942 3.9 1606 0.9 2215 3.8	0425 0.7 1056 4.9 1656 1.0 2327 4.9	0232 1.6 0819 4.8 1503 1.6 2058 4.9	**15 TU**

● ● Time Zone -0100. For UT subtract 1 hour. For European summer time (shaded) 30/3-26/10 add 1 hour ● ●

JULY 1997 TIDE TABLES JULY 1997

	ESBJERG		HELGOLAND		CUXHAVEN		BREMERHAVEN		HOEK VAN HOLLAND		ROTTERDAM		VLISSINGEN		ANTWERPEN		DUNKERQUE	
	Time	m	Time	m	Time	m	Time	m	Time	m	Time	m	Time	m	Time	m	Time	m
16 W	0441	0.0	0224	0.4	0330	0.5	0345	0.5	0544	0.2	0045	1.5	0441	0.7	0544	0.7	0336	1.5
	1120	1.4	0824	2.2	0934	2.6	1001	3.2	1139	1.8	0756	0.3	1051	4.0	1200	5.1	0928	5.0
	1712	0.1	1457	0.4	1609	0.4	1625	0.5	1830	0.3	1321	1.7	1711	0.8	1815	0.8	1608	1.5
	2345	1.5	2057	2.3	2206	2.7	2234	3.3			2038	0.3	2321	4.0			2202	5.1
17 TH	0548	-0.0	0332	0.3	0447	0.3	0500	0.4	0008	1.7	0145	1.6	0540	0.6	0030	5.1	0437	1.3
	1225	1.5	0927	2.3	1037	2.8	1110	3.4	0629	0.2	0901	0.2	1150	4.2	0651	0.6	1026	5.2
	1819	-0.0	1603	0.2	1720	0.1	1733	0.3	1234	1.9	1414	1.8	1808	0.6	1300	5.4	1709	1.2
			2157	2.4	2309	2.9	2339	3.5	1842	0.3	2138	0.2			1920	0.6	2254	5.3
18 F	0050	1.5	0431	0.1	0549	0.0	0601	0.1	0059	1.9	0235	1.8	0014	4.3	0127	5.5	0534	1.1
	0647	-0.1	1022	2.5	1134	3.0	1209	3.6	0640	0.3	1009	0.2	0633	0.5	0751	0.5	1115	5.5
	1322	1.5	1700	-0.0	1819	-0.1	1830	0.0	1323	1.9	1500	1.9	1239	4.4	1354	5.6	1804	1.0
	1918	-0.1	2252	2.5					1849	0.2	2241	0.2	1859	0.4	2021	0.5	2341	5.6
19 SA	0149	1.5	0524	-0.1	0006	3.1	0036	3.7	0144	2.0	0321	1.9	0101	4.5	0219	5.8	0626	0.9
	0739	-0.1	1112	2.6	0644	-0.2	0654	-0.0	0708	0.3	1124	0.3	0721	0.4	0848	0.4	1200	5.7
	1414	1.6	1753	-0.2	1228	3.2	1301	3.8	1407	2.0	1543	1.9	1324	4.6	1445	5.9	1854	0.7
	2010	-0.2	2342	2.6	1913	-0.4	1921	-0.2	1919	0.2	2345	0.2	1948	0.3	2118	0.3		
20 SU ○	0244	1.5	0615	-0.2	0100	3.2	0127	3.8	0228	2.1	0403	2.0	0145	4.7	0308	6.1	0024	5.8
	0828	-0.2	1200	2.7	0736	-0.3	0742	-0.2	0740	0.3	1230	0.3	0807	0.3	0942	0.3	0715	0.8
	1503	1.6	1843	-0.3	1319	3.3	1348	3.9	1451	2.0	1624	2.0	1407	4.7	1531	6.1	1243	5.9
	2100	-0.2			2004	-0.5	2009	-0.3	1954	0.1	2227	0.3	2036	0.1	2211	0.2	1941	0.5
21 M	0336	1.5	0030	2.6	0152	3.2	0215	3.9	0312	2.2	0446	2.1	0228	4.9	0354	6.3	0107	5.9
	0915	-0.2	0702	-0.3	0824	-0.5	0829	-0.3	0815	0.3	1054	0.4	0854	0.2	1033	0.2	0800	0.7
	1551	1.7	1245	2.8	1409	3.3	1433	4.1	1535	2.0	1706	2.0	1451	4.8	1616	6.1	1326	6.0
	2147	-0.3	1930	-0.4	2052	-0.6	2055	-0.4	2031	0.0	2331	0.2	2124	-0.0	2302	0.1	2027	0.4
22 TU	0427	1.5	0116	2.6	0241	3.2	0259	3.9	0356	2.2	0530	2.2	0312	5.0	0439	6.4	0151	6.1
	1000	-0.2	0748	-0.5	0911	-0.5	0914	-0.4	0854	0.3	1143	0.4	0942	0.2	1121	0.2	0845	0.6
	1638	1.7	1329	2.8	1456	3.4	1516	4.2	1619	2.0	1748	2.0	1534	4.8	1700	6.2	1410	6.1
	2233	-0.3	2015	-0.5	2138	-0.7	2139	-0.6	2112	-0.0			2213	-0.1	2351	0.0	2112	0.3
23 W	0516	1.5	0200	2.6	0327	3.2	0342	4.0	0441	2.2	0024	0.2	0357	5.0	0523	6.3	0237	6.1
	1045	-0.2	0830	-0.4	0954	-0.6	0957	-0.5	0935	0.4	0615	2.2	1029	0.2	1209	0.3	0930	0.6
	1724	1.7	1412	2.9	1540	3.4	1558	4.1	1704	1.9	1228	0.4	1618	4.8	1745	6.1	1456	6.2
	2318	-0.3	2059	-0.5	2221	-0.7	2223	-0.7	2155	-0.0	1831	2.1	2302	-0.1			2157	0.3
24 TH	0603	1.5	0242	2.6	0409	3.2	0423	4.0	0527	2.2	0119	0.1	0443	4.9	0038	0.0	0324	6.2
	1130	-0.2	0912	-0.4	1036	-0.6	1039	-0.6	1021	0.4	0659	2.2	1116	0.3	0609	6.2	1014	0.6
	1809	1.7	1454	2.9	1622	3.5	1640	4.3	1751	1.9	1315	0.4	1706	4.7	1254	0.4	1544	6.1
			2141	-0.5	2303	-0.7	2306	-0.7	2244	-0.0	1915	2.1	2350	-0.1	1830	6.0	2244	0.4
25 F	0004	-0.3	0322	2.6	0449	3.2	0504	3.9	0618	2.1	0241	0.1	0535	4.7	0124	0.1	0415	6.0
	0646	1.4	0953	-0.4	1117	-0.6	1121	-0.6	1115	0.5	0745	2.2	1203	0.4	0657	6.0	1101	0.7
	1215	-0.2	1538	2.9	1703	3.5	1722	4.2	1844	1.9	1425	0.3	1757	4.5	1338	0.5	1634	6.0
	1853	1.7	2223	-0.4	2345	-0.6	2348	-0.6	2340	0.0	2000	2.1			1920	5.8	2334	0.6
26 SA	0051	-0.2	0405	2.6	0530	3.2	0546	3.9	0718	2.0	0212	-0.0	0038	0.0	0210	0.2	0509	5.8
	0729	1.4	1036	-0.3	1158	-0.5	1205	-0.5	1453	0.3	0833	2.2	0633	4.6	0751	5.7	1153	0.9
	1303	-0.2	1624	2.8	1746	3.4	1806	4.1	1946	1.9	1446	0.3	1251	0.5	1424	0.6	1730	5.8
	1939	1.6	2307	-0.3							2051	2.0	1857	4.4	2015	5.6		
27 SU	0141	-0.2	0451	2.5	0027	-0.5	0033	-0.5	0209	0.0	0311	-0.0	0129	0.2	0259	0.3	0031	0.8
	0815	1.4	1122	-0.2	0612	3.1	0631	3.8	0823	2.0	0930	2.1	0736	4.4	0851	5.5	0609	5.5
	1356	-0.1	1715	2.7	1241	-0.4	1251	-0.4	1451	0.3	1547	0.3	1347	0.6	1517	0.7	1254	1.2
	2034	1.6	2357	-0.1	1833	3.3	1854	3.9	2051	1.8	2151	1.9	2000	4.3	2118	5.3	1836	5.5
28 M	0238	-0.1	0543	2.4	0112	-0.3	0121	-0.3	0245	0.0	0414	0.0	0228	0.3	0354	0.4	0136	1.1
	0911	1.4	1216	-0.1	0700	3.0	0721	3.6	0927	1.9	1036	1.9	0840	4.2	0957	5.3	0721	5.2
	1458	-0.0	1813	2.5	1331	-0.2	1344	-0.2	1528	0.3	1653	0.3	1453	0.7	1616	0.8	1403	1.4
	2137	1.6			1927	3.1	1948	3.7	2157	1.8	2303	1.8	2108	4.1	2227	5.2	1954	5.3
29 TU	0344	0.0	0054	0.0	0206	-0.0	0216	-0.0	0344	0.1	0523	0.1	0340	0.5	0455	0.6	0248	1.3
	1016	1.4	0643	2.3	0755	2.9	0817	3.5	1033	1.8	1148	1.8	0948	4.1	1108	5.2	0840	5.1
	1611	0.0	1322	0.1	1435	-0.0	1448	0.1	1626	0.3	1808	0.3	1615	0.7	1726	0.8	1517	1.4
	2248	1.5	1919	2.4	2027	2.9	2051	3.5	2306	1.8			2218	4.1	2339	5.1	2112	5.2
30 W	0454	0.0	0202	0.2	0315	0.1	0324	0.2	0448	0.2	0015	1.8	0457	0.6	0609	0.7	0359	1.3
	1127	1.5	0751	2.3	0857	2.8	0922	3.3	1139	1.8	0641	0.2	1056	4.1	1215	5.2	0948	5.1
	1727	0.0	1439	0.1	1554	0.1	1602	0.2	1730	0.3	1253	1.8	1728	0.6	1850	0.7	1627	1.3
			2031	2.3	2135	2.7	2200	3.3			1923	0.3	2325	4.2			2215	5.3
31 TH	0003	1.5	0314	0.2	0430	0.1	0436	0.3	0009	1.8	0119	1.8	0559	0.6	0045	5.2	0504	1.2
	0602	0.1	0900	2.3	1004	2.7	1035	3.3	0551	0.3	0808	0.3	1158	4.2	0725	0.6	1045	5.3
	1235	1.6	1553	0.1	1709	0.0	1713	0.2	1238	1.8	1351	1.8	1827	0.5	1316	5.3	1728	1.1
	1836	-0.0	2142	2.2	2245	2.6	2315	3.3	1821	0.2	2006	0.3			1959	0.5	2308	5.5

• • Time Zone -0100. For UT subtract 1 hour. For European summer time (shaded) 30/3-26/10 add 1 hour • •

DENMARK, GERMANY, HOLLAND & BELGIUM Time Zone -0100
Esbjerg * Helgoland * Cuxhaven * Bremerhaven * Hoek van Holland * Rotterdam *Vlissingen * Antwerpen * Dunkerque

AUGUST 1997 TIDE TABLES AUGUST 1997

ESBJERG	HELGOLAND	CUXHAVEN	BREMERHAVEN	HOEK VAN HOLLAND	ROTTERDAM	VLISSINGEN	ANTWERPEN	DUNKERQUE	
Time m	Time m	Time m	Time m	Time m	Time m	Time m	Time m	Time m	
0113 1.5	0420 0.2	0538 0.1	0542 0.3	0105 1.9	0216 1.8	0024 4.3	0143 5.4	0558 1.1	1 F
0701 0.0	1005 2.3	1109 2.7	1148 3.3	0637 0.3	0847 0.4	0650 0.6	0824 0.5	1133 5.4	
1335 1.6	1657 0.0	1814 -0.0	1815 0.2	1331 1.8	1443 1.7	1251 4.3	1409 5.5	1820 0.9	
1934 -0.0	2243 2.2	2351 2.6		1854 0.2	2155 0.4	1915 0.4	2053 0.3	2353 5.6	
0210 1.5	0517 0.1	0636 0.1	0024 3.3	0154 2.0	0306 1.8	0112 4.4	0233 5.6	0644 1.1	2 SA
0752 0.0	1101 2.3	1209 2.8	0639 0.3	0714 0.4	0958 0.5	0733 0.5	0912 0.5	1213 5.6	
1424 1.7	1751 0.0	1909 -0.1	1251 3.4	1419 1.9	1527 1.7	1335 4.4	1456 5.6	1905 0.8	
2023 -0.0	2335 2.2		1909 0.2	1928 0.2	2246 0.5	1958 0.3	2138 0.2		
0256 1.5	0606 0.1	0048 2.6	0121 3.3	0237 2.0	0349 1.8	0154 4.5	0318 5.7	0033 5.6	3 SU
0836 0.0	1148 2.3	0727 0.0	0730 0.3	0751 0.4	1055 0.6	0810 0.5	0954 0.4	0724 1.0	
1503 1.7	1838 0.0	1301 2.8	1342 3.5	1502 1.9	1606 1.7	1415 4.5	1537 5.7	1251 5.7	●
2106 -0.0		1958 -0.1	1958 0.2	2003 0.1	2339 0.5	2037 0.2	2218 0.2	1945 0.7	
0333 1.5	0018 2.2	0136 2.6	0208 3.4	0316 2.0	0428 1.8	0233 4.6	0357 5.9	0111 5.7	4 M
0916 0.0	0649 0.1	0812 0.1	0815 0.3	0828 0.4	1148 0.7	0845 0.5	1030 0.4	0802 1.0	
1538 1.7	1227 2.4	1345 2.8	1424 3.5	1540 2.0	1642 1.7	1451 4.6	1615 5.8	1328 5.7	
2145 -0.0	1919 0.0	2041 -0.0	2042 0.3	2039 0.1	2154 0.3	2114 0.2	2254 0.1	2024 0.7	
0407 1.5	0056 2.2	0217 2.6	0246 3.3	0351 2.1	0506 1.8	0308 4.6	0433 5.9	0148 5.7	5 TU
0951 -0.0	0727 0.1	0852 0.1	0855 0.4	0907 0.4	1237 0.7	0920 0.5	1105 0.4	0837 1.0	
1612 1.7	1303 2.4	1422 2.8	1458 3.5	1616 2.0	1719 1.8	1526 4.6	1651 5.8	1404 5.8	
2221 -0.1	1955 0.1	2119 0.0	2120 0.4	2115 0.1	2237 0.3	2150 0.2	2329 0.1	2100 0.7	
0438 1.5	0130 2.2	0252 2.6	0317 3.3	0426 2.1	0542 1.8	0342 4.6	0509 5.9	0226 5.7	6 W
1025 -0.0	0801 0.1	0927 0.1	0931 0.5	0947 0.4	1327 0.7	0954 0.5	1137 0.4	0910 1.0	
1645 1.7	1336 2.4	1455 2.8	1527 3.5	1648 1.9	1755 1.8	1559 4.6	1725 5.7	1440 5.8	
2254 -0.1	2027 0.1	2153 0.1	2154 0.4	2151 0.1	2324 0.3	2224 0.2		2133 0.8	
0508 1.5	0201 2.2	0325 2.6	0345 3.3	0459 2.0	0619 1.8	0414 4.6	0001 0.1	0301 5.7	7 TH
1057 -0.0	0832 0.2	0959 0.1	1003 0.5	1027 0.4	1129 0.6	1026 0.5	0542 5.8	0940 1.1	
1716 1.7	1408 2.4	1528 2.8	1554 3.5	1717 1.9	1830 1.8	1630 4.5	1207 0.5	1515 5.8	
2325 -0.0	2057 0.1	2222 0.1	2224 0.4	2228 0.1		2254 0.3	1758 5.7	2203 0.8	
0535 1.5	0232 2.2	0357 2.6	0412 3.3	0530 2.0	0007 0.3	0445 4.5	0030 0.1	0336 5.7	8 F
1128 -0.1	0902 0.2	1027 0.2	1033 0.4	1112 0.4	0654 1.8	1056 0.6	0615 5.7	1009 1.1	
1747 1.6	1441 2.4	1600 2.8	1624 3.5	1744 1.9	1330 0.6	1701 4.4	1236 0.5	1548 5.8	
2354 -0.0	2126 0.2	2250 0.2	2254 0.4	2307 0.1	1906 1.8	2321 0.3	1831 5.5	2233 0.9	
0603 1.4	0304 2.2	0430 2.6	0444 3.3	0602 2.0	0139 0.3	0518 4.4	0059 0.2	0409 5.6	9 SA
1200 -0.0	0933 0.2	1057 0.2	1103 0.3	1408 0.3	0730 1.8	1127 0.6	0649 5.6	1040 1.2	
1818 1.6	1515 2.4	1634 2.8	1659 3.5	1814 1.9	1405 0.5	1733 4.3	1307 0.6	1623 5.7	
	2157 0.2	2319 0.2	2324 0.3	2353 0.1	1943 1.8	2351 0.4	1904 5.4	2308 1.0	
0025 -0.0	0339 2.2	0505 2.6	0520 3.3	0636 2.0	0236 0.3	0553 4.3	0130 0.3	0444 5.5	10 SU
0635 1.4	1008 0.3	1130 0.2	1136 0.3	1253 0.3	0809 1.8	1204 0.7	0724 5.4	1116 1.3	
1234 -0.0	1554 2.3	1712 2.7	1739 3.5	1850 1.8	1449 0.5	1810 4.2	1341 0.7	1700 5.5	
1853 1.5	2233 0.3	2352 0.3			2024 1.8		1939 5.2	2348 1.2	
0100 -0.0	0421 2.2	0545 2.6	0000 0.3	0049 0.1	0156 0.3	0030 0.5	0205 0.4	0524 5.3	11 M
0712 1.4	1050 0.3	1209 0.3	0603 3.3	0718 1.9	0853 1.8	0634 4.2	0803 5.2	1201 1.5	
1314 -0.0	1642 2.2	1802 2.6	1216 0.3	1336 0.3	1514 0.5	1247 0.8	1420 0.7	1747 5.3	
1934 1.5	2319 0.4		1828 3.3	1936 1.8	2112 1.7	1856 4.0	2021 5.0		
0142 0.0	0515 2.1	0033 0.3	0042 0.4	0148 0.1	0451 0.4	0117 0.6	0246 0.6	0041 1.5	12 TU
0801 1.4	1142 0.4	0637 2.5	0657 3.2	0816 1.8	0950 1.7	0731 4.0	0852 5.0	0615 5.0	
1403 0.0	1745 2.1	1257 0.4	1304 0.4	1426 0.3	1748 0.5	1342 0.9	1506 0.8	1302 1.6	
2029 1.4		1904 2.5	1927 3.2	2046 1.7	2220 1.6	2003 3.9	2121 4.9	1847 5.0	
0236 0.0	0018 0.5	0126 0.4	0136 0.5	0245 0.2	0610 0.4	0220 0.7	0336 0.7	0146 1.6	13 W
0907 1.4	0623 2.1	0740 2.5	0800 3.1	0940 1.7	1121 1.6	0848 3.8	1000 4.9	0722 4.9	
1506 0.1	1251 0.5	1357 0.4	1407 0.5	1525 0.3	1854 0.4	1456 0.9	1603 0.9	1415 1.7	
2142 1.4	1900 2.1	2014 2.5	2037 3.2	2218 1.6	2357 1.6	2126 3.8	2235 4.9	2005 4.9	
0345 0.1	0132 0.4	0234 0.4	0248 0.6	0354 0.2	0722 0.3	0350 0.8	0447 0.9	0256 1.6	14 TH
1028 1.4	0737 2.1	0850 2.6	0915 3.1	1058 1.7	1243 1.6	1008 3.8	1114 5.0	0843 4.9	
1626 0.1	1412 0.4	1518 0.3	1535 0.5	1734 0.3	1957 0.4	1629 0.9	1726 1.0	1528 1.6	
2305 1.4	2017 2.2	2127 2.6	2153 3.2	2334 1.7		2245 3.9	2351 5.0	2125 5.0	
0506 0.1	0251 0.3	0400 0.3	0418 0.5	0615 0.3	0111 1.7	0508 0.7	0611 0.8	0403 1.5	15 F
1146 1.5	0848 2.3	0957 2.8	1029 3.3	1206 1.8	0830 0.3	1121 4.1	1227 5.2	0955 5.1	
1746 0.0	1529 0.2	1643 0.1	1657 0.3	1753 0.3	1345 1.7	1741 0.7	1847 0.8	1636 1.3	
	2126 2.3	2234 2.8	2304 3.4		2057 0.3	2350 4.2		2229 5.3	

● ● Time Zone -0100. For UT subtract 1 hour. For European summer time (shaded) 30/3-26/10 add 1 hour ● ●

AUGUST 1997 TIDE TABLES AUGUST 1997

	ESBJERG	HELGOLAND	CUXHAVEN	BREMERHAVEN	HOEK VAN HOLLAND	ROTTERDAM	VLISSINGEN	ANTWERPEN	DUNKERQUE
	Time m	Time m	Time m	Time m	Time m	Time m	Time m	Time m	Time m
16 SA	0021 1.5 0616 -0.0 1252 1.6 1854 -0.1	0400 0.1 0949 2.5 1633 -0.1 2225 2.5	0515 0.1 1100 3.0 1751 -0.2 2336 3.0	0528 0.2 1134 3.5 1800 0.1	0034 1.9 0706 0.3 1301 1.9 1824 0.2	0208 1.8 0942 0.3 1436 1.9 2200 0.3	0609 0.5 1218 4.3 1840 0.4	0100 5.4 0721 0.6 1331 5.6 1957 0.5	0507 1.2 1052 5.4 1737 1.0 2321 5.7
17 SU	0128 1.5 0716 -0.1 1351 1.6 1950 -0.2	0458 -0.1 1044 2.6 1730 -0.3 2318 2.6	0617 -0.2 1157 3.2 1849 -0.4	0006 3.6 0626 -0.0 1232 3.8 1855 -0.2	0124 2.0 0653 0.3 1349 1.9 1857 0.1	0257 2.0 1102 0.3 1521 2.0 2128 0.3	0042 4.6 0703 0.4 1306 4.6 1932 0.2	0200 5.8 0827 0.5 1426 5.9 2101 0.3	0604 1.0 1141 5.7 1832 0.7
18 M ○	0228 1.5 0809 -0.1 1445 1.7 2041 -0.2	0551 -0.3 1134 2.8 1821 -0.5	0034 3.2 0712 -0.4 1252 3.3 1942 -0.6	0101 3.8 0718 -0.2 1322 4.0 1945 -0.4	0210 2.2 0721 0.3 1433 2.0 1932 0.0	0342 2.1 0953 0.4 1603 2.1 2247 0.2	0127 4.8 0751 0.3 1350 4.8 2021 0.0	0251 6.2 0925 0.3 1514 6.1 2157 0.1	0006 6.0 0654 0.7 1225 6.0 1921 0.4
19 TU	0323 1.5 0857 -0.2 1535 1.7 2129 -0.3	0008 2.7 0640 -0.4 1221 2.9 1909 -0.6	0128 3.3 0803 -0.6 1345 3.4 2032 -0.8	0151 3.9 0806 -0.4 1409 4.2 2033 -0.6	0254 2.3 0754 0.3 1517 2.0 2009 -0.0	0426 2.2 1054 0.4 1645 2.1 2341 0.2	0211 5.0 0838 0.2 1432 4.9 2108 -0.1	0337 6.4 1018 0.2 1559 6.3 2248 -0.0	0051 6.2 0742 0.6 1308 6.2 2008 0.2
20 W	0413 1.5 0942 -0.2 1624 1.7 2215 -0.3	0054 2.7 0727 -0.4 1307 2.9 1954 -0.6	0218 3.3 0851 -0.7 1434 3.5 2118 -0.8	0236 4.0 0852 -0.5 1454 4.3 2119 -0.7	0338 2.3 0831 0.3 1600 2.0 2049 -0.1	0509 2.3 1145 0.4 1727 2.2	0254 5.1 0924 0.2 1515 4.9 2155 -0.2	0421 6.5 1106 0.2 1642 6.3 2335 -0.1	0135 6.3 0827 0.5 1351 6.3 2054 0.1
21 TH	0500 1.5 1027 -0.2 1709 1.8 2259 -0.3	0137 2.7 0810 -0.5 1350 2.9 2037 -0.6	0304 3.3 0935 -0.7 1519 3.5 2201 -0.8	0319 4.1 0936 -0.6 1537 4.4 2202 -0.7	0422 2.3 0912 0.4 1644 2.0 2133 -0.1	0029 0.2 0553 2.3 1233 0.4 1810 2.2	0338 5.1 1010 0.2 1558 4.9 2241 -0.2	0505 6.5 1152 0.3 1725 6.2	0220 6.4 0912 0.5 1436 6.4 2139 0.1
22 F	0544 1.5 1110 -0.2 1753 1.8 2342 -0.2	0218 2.7 0851 -0.5 1432 2.9 2118 -0.5	0347 3.3 1016 -0.7 1601 3.5 2242 -0.7	0401 4.1 1019 -0.7 1619 4.4 2244 -0.7	0507 2.2 0957 0.4 1728 2.0 2220 -0.0	0118 0.1 0637 2.3 1322 0.4 1853 2.3	0423 5.0 1055 0.3 1642 4.8 2326 -0.1	0021 -0.1 0549 6.3 1236 0.4 1809 6.1	0306 6.3 0955 0.5 1521 6.4 2224 0.3
23 SA	0623 1.5 1154 -0.2 1834 1.7	0257 2.7 0931 -0.4 1514 2.9 2157 -0.4	0426 3.2 1056 -0.6 1641 3.4 2321 -0.6	0442 4.0 1100 -0.6 1701 4.3 2325 -0.6	0554 2.1 1046 0.4 1815 2.0 2314 0.0	0223 0.1 0721 2.3 1431 0.3 1937 2.2	0510 4.8 1139 0.4 1730 4.7	0104 0.1 0636 6.0 1318 0.5 1856 5.8	0353 6.2 1040 0.7 1609 6.2 2312 0.5
24 SU	0026 -0.1 0658 1.5 1239 -0.2 1916 1.7	0337 2.6 1012 -0.4 1558 2.8 2238 -0.2	0503 3.2 1135 -0.5 1721 3.3 2359 -0.4	0522 3.9 1142 -0.5 1743 4.1	0647 2.0 1151 0.4 1911 2.0	0154 0.1 0806 2.2 1417 0.3 2024 2.2	0009 0.1 0603 4.6 1223 0.5 1825 4.5	0146 0.2 0724 5.7 1401 0.6 1946 5.6	0443 5.9 1129 0.9 1701 5.9
25 M	0112 -0.1 0739 1.5 1330 -0.1 2006 1.6	0420 2.5 1055 -0.2 1646 2.6 2322 -0.0	0543 3.1 1215 -0.3 1805 3.1	0006 -0.4 0604 3.8 1225 -0.3 1829 3.9	0137 0.1 0749 1.9 1407 0.3 2018 1.9	0254 0.1 0855 2.0 1516 0.3 2117 2.0	0055 0.3 0703 4.4 1313 0.6 1929 4.3	0230 0.4 0819 5.4 1447 0.8 2044 5.3	0006 0.8 0539 5.5 1225 1.2 1803 5.5
26 TU	0204 0.0 0831 1.5 1429 0.0 2108 1.5	0509 2.4 1145 -0.0 1742 2.4	0039 -0.2 0627 3.0 1259 -0.1 1855 2.9	0050 -0.1 0650 3.6 1313 -0.0 1919 3.6	0215 0.1 0855 1.8 1451 0.3 2127 1.8	0352 0.1 0956 1.8 1617 0.3 2226 1.8	0150 0.5 0808 4.1 1418 0.7 2039 4.1	0318 0.6 0922 5.1 1541 0.9 2153 5.0	0107 1.2 0648 5.1 1331 1.5 1922 5.2
27 W	0307 0.1 0938 1.5 1542 0.1 2223 1.5	0015 0.2 0608 2.3 1250 0.2 1848 2.2	0125 0.1 0720 2.8 1358 0.1 1955 2.7	0142 0.3 0742 3.4 1415 0.3 2019 3.3	0316 0.2 1005 1.7 1554 0.3 2242 1.8	0455 0.2 1112 1.7 1721 0.3 2346 1.7	0302 0.7 0918 3.9 1541 0.8 2154 4.0	0415 0.8 1035 4.9 1648 0.9 2312 4.9	0217 1.5 0814 4.9 1445 1.6 2048 5.1
28 TH	0422 0.2 1054 1.5 1705 0.1 2343 1.5	0124 0.4 0718 2.2 1413 0.3 2006 2.1	0231 0.3 0824 2.7 1527 0.3 2106 2.5	0250 0.5 0848 3.2 1537 0.5 2132 3.1	0426 0.3 1118 1.7 1659 0.2 2352 1.8	0605 0.3 1227 1.6 1827 0.4	0429 0.8 1033 3.9 1706 0.8 2308 4.0	0526 1.0 1150 4.9 1818 0.9	0331 1.6 0929 4.9 1600 1.5 2157 5.2
29 F	0537 0.2 1209 1.6 1818 0.1	0247 0.4 0835 2.2 1536 0.2 2127 2.1	0403 0.4 0935 2.6 1652 0.2 2224 2.4	0411 0.6 1006 3.2 1654 0.5 2254 3.1	0532 0.4 1222 1.7 1754 0.2	0057 1.7 0726 0.4 1332 1.6 1930 0.4	0539 0.8 1141 4.0 1809 0.6	0024 5.1 0657 0.9 1255 5.1 1937 0.6	0442 1.5 1028 5.1 1708 1.3 2252 5.4
30 SA	0057 1.5 0642 0.1 1314 1.7 1917 0.0	0401 0.4 0948 2.2 1642 0.1 2233 2.1	0518 0.3 1049 2.6 1757 0.1 2339 2.5	0521 0.6 1128 3.2 1757 0.4	0051 1.9 0623 0.4 1317 1.8 1836 0.2	0200 1.8 1032 0.5 1428 1.7 2145 0.4	0009 4.2 0632 0.7 1234 4.2 1859 0.4	0125 5.4 0803 0.7 1350 5.4 2031 0.3	0540 1.3 1116 5.3 1801 1.0 2337 5.6
31 SU	0155 1.5 0733 0.1 1405 1.7 2005 -0.0	0500 0.3 1048 2.3 1735 0.1 2324 2.2	0618 0.2 1156 2.7 1851 -0.0	0008 3.2 0620 0.5 1235 3.4 1851 0.3	0139 2.0 0700 0.4 1403 1.9 1911 0.2	0253 1.8 1136 0.4 1514 1.7 2218 0.5	0057 4.4 0714 0.6 1318 4.4 1939 0.3	0215 5.6 0851 0.5 1436 5.6 2115 0.2	0627 1.2 1157 5.5 1845 0.9

• •Time Zone -0100. For UT subtract 1 hour. For European summer time (shaded) 30/3-26/10 add 1 hour• •

DENMARK, GERMANY, HOLLAND & BELGIUM Time Zone -0100

Esbjerg * Helgoland * Cuxhaven * Bremerhaven * Hoek van Holland * Rotterdam *Vlissingen * Antwerpen * Dunkerque

SEPTEMBER 1997 TIDE TABLES SEPTEMBER 1997

Day	ESBJERG	HELGOLAND	CUXHAVEN	BREMERHAVEN	HOEK VAN HOLLAND	ROTTERDAM	VLISSINGEN	ANTWERPEN	DUNKERQUE
	Time m	Time m	Time m	Time m	Time m	Time m	Time m	Time m	Time m
1 M ●	0239 1.5	0548 0.2	0038 2.6	0105 3.3	0218 2.0	0336 1.8	0136 4.5	0258 5.8	0016 5.7
	0817 0.1	1135 2.4	0708 0.1	0710 0.4	0736 0.4	1013 0.6	0749 0.6	0930 0.4	0706 1.0
	1444 1.7	1820 0.0	1249 2.8	1327 3.5	1442 1.9	1553 1.7	1354 4.5	1516 5.8	1233 5.7
	2045 -0.0		1938 -0.1	1939 0.3	1945 0.1	2308 0.5	2015 0.3	2154 0.1	1925 0.7
2 TU	0314 1.5	0006 2.2	0124 2.7	0151 3.4	0253 2.0	0413 1.8	0211 4.6	0336 5.9	0053 5.8
	0854 0.0	0630 0.1	0752 0.0	0755 0.3	0812 0.4	1109 0.7	0823 0.5	1006 0.4	0742 1.0
	1517 1.7	1215 2.4	1332 2.9	1408 3.6	1515 2.0	1627 1.8	1427 4.6	1552 5.8	1307 5.8
	2121 -0.0	1858 0.0	2019 -0.1	2021 0.3	2018 0.1	2358 0.5	2049 0.2	2230 0.1	2002 0.7
3 W	0343 1.5	0042 2.3	0202 2.7	0228 3.5	0326 2.1	0448 1.9	0243 4.6	0410 6.0	0127 5.9
	0929 0.0	0708 0.1	0831 0.0	0835 0.3	0847 0.4	1155 0.7	0856 0.5	1040 0.4	0816 1.0
	1548 1.7	1248 2.4	1409 2.9	1442 3.6	1548 2.0	1701 1.8	1459 4.6	1626 5.9	1341 5.9
	2154 -0.0	1933 0.1	2056 -0.0	2058 0.3	2050 0.1		2122 0.2	2303 0.1	2035 0.7
4 TH	0411 1.5	0114 2.3	0236 2.7	0300 3.5	0358 2.1	0050 0.5	0314 4.7	0442 6.0	0201 5.9
	1000 -0.0	0742 0.1	0906 0.0	0910 0.4	0919 0.4	0522 1.9	0929 0.5	1112 0.4	0847 1.0
	1618 1.7	1320 2.4	1443 2.9	1510 3.6	1618 2.0	1217 0.6	1530 4.7	1657 5.9	1413 5.9
	2226 -0.0	2004 0.1	2129 0.0	2131 0.4	2121 0.1	1736 1.9	2154 0.2	2334 0.1	2106 0.7
5 F	0438 1.5	0143 2.3	0309 2.8	0327 3.4	0430 2.1	0004 0.4	0344 4.7	0513 5.9	0233 5.9
	1031 -0.0	0813 0.1	0939 0.1	0942 0.4	0948 0.4	0556 1.9	1000 0.5	1141 0.4	0915 1.0
	1650 1.7	1351 2.4	1516 2.9	1539 3.6	1645 2.0	1205 0.6	1600 4.6	1729 5.8	1444 5.9
	2254 -0.0	2034 0.1	2159 0.1	2202 0.4	2153 0.1	1810 1.9	2223 0.3		2135 0.7
6 SA	0506 1.5	0212 2.3	0341 2.8	0355 3.4	0459 2.1	0006 0.4	0414 4.6	0003 0.2	0303 5.8
	1101 -0.0	0844 0.2	1009 0.1	1013 0.3	1015 0.4	0630 1.9	1030 0.6	0545 5.8	0942 1.0
	1721 1.7	1421 2.4	1548 2.8	1608 3.6	1712 2.0	1236 0.6	1629 4.6	1211 0.5	1514 5.9
	2323 0.0	2103 0.3	2228 0.2	2232 0.3	2227 0.2	1845 1.9	2251 0.4	1759 5.7	2204 0.8
7 SU	0533 1.5	0241 2.3	0412 2.7	0426 3.4	0530 2.1	0054 0.4	0445 4.6	0032 0.3	0333 5.8
	1132 -0.0	0915 0.2	1040 0.2	1044 0.3	1046 0.4	0706 1.9	1101 0.6	0615 5.7	1012 1.1
	1749 1.6	1452 2.4	1619 2.8	1641 3.6	1742 2.0	1324 0.6	1700 4.5	1241 0.6	1545 5.9
	2352 0.0	2133 0.3	2257 0.2	2303 0.3	2303 0.2	1921 1.9	2323 0.4	1830 5.6	2236 1.0
8 M	0601 1.5	0312 2.3	0442 2.7	0500 3.4	0603 2.1	0150 0.4	0518 4.5	0102 0.4	0406 5.7
	1205 -0.0	0948 0.2	1112 0.2	1117 0.2	1123 0.4	0742 1.9	1136 0.6	0648 5.6	1045 1.2
	1818 1.6	1527 2.4	1651 2.8	1718 3.5	1818 2.0	1419 0.5	1736 4.4	1313 0.7	1622 5.7
		2206 0.3	2329 0.3	2337 0.3	2347 0.2	2000 1.9	2359 0.5	1904 5.5	2315 1.2
9 TU	0026 0.0	0348 2.3	0515 2.7	0539 3.4	0642 2.0	0251 0.4	0557 4.3	0135 0.5	0446 5.5
	0633 1.5	1026 0.3	1148 0.3	1154 0.3	1212 0.3	0824 1.9	1216 0.7	0725 5.4	1126 1.4
	1244 -0.0	1611 2.3	1733 2.7	1802 3.4	1901 2.0	1518 0.5	1818 4.3	1349 0.7	1707 5.5
	1854 1.5	2248 0.4				2045 1.9		1944 5.3	
10 W	0107 0.0	0436 2.3	0006 0.3	0016 0.3	0053 0.2	0357 0.4	0043 0.6	0213 0.7	0001 1.4
	0715 1.5	1113 0.4	0600 2.7	0625 3.3	0730 1.9	0913 1.8	0645 4.1	0810 5.3	0535 5.2
	1331 0.0	1709 2.2	1230 0.3	1239 0.4	1341 0.3	1639 0.5	1307 0.8	1433 0.8	1220 1.6
	1945 1.5	2340 0.5	1830 2.6	1855 3.3	1957 1.8	2142 1.8	1914 4.0	2036 5.2	1804 5.2
11 TH	0158 0.1	0541 2.2	0054 0.4	0104 0.4	0216 0.2	0525 0.4	0142 0.8	0301 0.8	0106 1.6
	0818 1.4	1216 0.4	0700 2.7	0723 3.2	0839 1.7	1024 1.6	0757 3.9	0911 5.0	0640 4.9
	1430 0.1	1824 2.2	1325 0.4	1335 0.5	1448 0.3	1747 0.4	1416 0.9	1528 0.9	1335 1.7
	2101 1.4		1939 2.6	2000 3.2	2133 1.7	2310 1.7	2043 3.8	2149 5.0	1924 5.0
12 F	0304 0.1	0051 0.5	0155 0.4	0207 0.5	0328 0.3	0647 0.4	0306 0.9	0408 1.0	0222 1.7
	0944 1.5	0656 2.3	0809 2.7	0833 3.2	1022 1.6	1204 1.6	0931 3.8	1033 4.9	0808 4.8
	1549 0.1	1336 0.4	1439 0.3	1454 0.5	1602 0.3	1902 0.4	1552 0.9	1648 1.0	1455 1.7
	2232 1.4	1942 2.2	2051 2.7	2114 3.2	2304 1.8		2215 3.9	2316 5.0	2054 5.0
13 SA	0427 0.1	0213 0.4	0318 0.4	0335 0.5	0604 0.3	0039 1.8	0440 0.8	0537 1.0	0336 1.6
	1109 1.5	0810 2.4	0919 2.9	0948 3.3	1141 1.7	0801 0.4	1054 3.9	1158 5.1	0930 5.0
	1718 0.0	1458 0.2	1609 0.1	1622 0.4	1715 0.3	1315 1.7	1718 0.7	1819 0.9	1609 1.4
	2356 1.5	2055 2.4	2201 2.9	2228 3.4		2009 0.3	2327 4.2		2205 5.4
14 SU	0548 0.1	0329 0.2	0443 0.1	0454 0.3	0012 1.9	0142 2.0	0551 0.6	0036 5.4	0444 1.3
	1222 1.6	0917 2.6	1025 3.1	1057 3.6	0833 0.3	0916 0.3	1156 4.3	0657 0.8	1031 5.4
	1830 -0.1	1606 -0.1	1724 -0.2	1730 0.1	1240 1.8	1410 1.9	1823 0.4	1309 5.5	1714 1.0
		2158 2.5	2306 3.1	2335 3.6	1757 0.2	2015 0.3		1939 0.6	2300 5.8
15 M	0109 1.5	0432 -0.0	0551 -0.1	0557 0.1	0104 2.1	0234 2.1	0021 4.6	0139 5.9	0544 1.0
	0653 -0.0	1015 2.8	1126 3.3	1159 3.8	0638 0.4	1036 0.3	0646 0.4	0809 0.5	1121 5.8
	1327 1.7	1705 -0.3	1824 -0.4	1827 -0.2	1329 1.9	1457 2.0	1245 4.5	1405 5.9	1811 0.6
	1930 -0.2	2253 2.7			1833 0.1	2148 0.2	1916 0.2	2045 0.3	2348 6.2

● ● Time Zone -0100. For UT subtract 1 hour. For European summer time (shaded) 30/3-26/10 add 1 hour ● ●

SEPTEMBER 1997 TIDE TABLES SEPTEMBER 1997

	ESBJERG	HELGOLAND	CUXHAVEN	BREMERHAVEN	HOEK VAN HOLLAND	ROTTERDAM	VLISSINGEN	ANTWERPEN	DUNKERQUE
	Time m	Time m	Time m	Time m	Time m	Time m	Time m	Time m	Time m
16 TU ○	0212 1.6 0748 -0.1 1424 1.7 2021 -0.2	0527 -0.2 1107 2.9 1757 -0.5 2342 2.8	0006 3.3 0648 -0.4 1224 3.5 1918 -0.6	0033 3.8 0651 -0.2 1253 4.1 1920 -0.4	0151 2.2 0700 0.4 1414 2.0 1909 0.0	0321 2.3 0942 0.4 1541 2.2 2248 0.2	0108 4.9 0735 0.3 1329 4.8 2003 -0.0	0230 6.3 0909 0.3 1453 6.2 2139 0.1	0636 0.7 1206 6.1 1901 0.3
17 W	0306 1.6 0836 -0.1 1517 1.8 2109 -0.2	0616 -0.4 1156 3.0 1845 -0.6	0101 3.4 0739 -0.5 1318 3.6 2008 -0.7	0124 4.0 0742 -0.4 1342 4.3 2009 -0.6	0234 2.3 0733 0.4 1457 2.1 1947 -0.0	0403 2.4 1045 0.4 1622 2.2 2338 0.2	0151 5.0 0821 0.2 1411 4.9 2049 -0.1	0317 6.6 1000 0.2 1537 6.4 2229 -0.1	0032 6.4 0724 0.5 1248 6.3 1948 0.1
18 TH	0354 1.6 0922 -0.1 1606 1.8 2153 -0.2	0027 2.8 0703 -0.4 1242 3.0 1930 -0.5	0152 3.4 0827 -0.6 1408 3.6 2054 -0.7	0210 4.1 0829 -0.5 1429 4.4 2055 -0.6	0318 2.3 0809 0.4 1539 2.1 2027 -0.1	0446 2.4 1140 0.4 1704 2.3	0233 5.1 0905 0.2 1452 5.0 2134 -0.2	0400 6.6 1048 0.2 1620 6.4 2315 -0.1	0115 6.5 0808 0.4 1330 6.5 2033 0.1
19 F	0439 1.6 1006 -0.2 1651 1.8 2236 -0.1	0110 2.8 0746 -0.4 1325 3.0 2012 -0.5	0238 3.4 0912 -0.6 1454 3.6 2137 -0.7	0254 4.1 0914 -0.6 1513 4.4 2139 -0.6	0401 2.3 0849 0.4 1621 2.1 2111 -0.0	0025 0.2 0529 2.4 1233 0.4 1746 2.3	0316 5.1 0949 0.2 1535 5.0 2218 -0.1	0443 6.6 1133 0.3 1702 6.3 2359 0.0	0159 6.5 0851 0.4 1413 6.5 2118 0.1
20 SA	0518 1.6 1049 -0.2 1733 1.8 2318 -0.1	0150 2.8 0828 -0.4 1407 2.9 2051 -0.3	0319 3.3 0954 -0.6 1536 3.5 2217 -0.5	0336 4.1 0957 -0.6 1555 4.3 2220 -0.5	0445 2.2 0933 0.4 1703 2.1 2158 0.1	0115 0.2 0612 2.4 1330 0.4 1829 2.3	0359 5.0 1032 0.3 1618 5.0 2259 0.1	0527 6.4 1215 0.4 1745 6.2	0242 6.4 0935 0.5 1457 6.4 2203 0.3
21 SU	0552 1.6 1132 -0.1 1812 1.7 2359 -0.0	0228 2.7 0907 -0.3 1448 2.9 2130 -0.2	0357 3.3 1033 -0.5 1614 3.4 2254 -0.3	0416 4.1 1038 -0.5 1636 4.2 2300 -0.3	0528 2.1 1023 0.4 1748 2.1 2251 0.2	0016 0.1 0654 2.3 1237 0.3 1912 2.3	0444 4.8 1113 0.4 1704 4.8 2339 0.3	0039 0.2 0611 6.1 1255 0.5 1830 5.9	0328 6.2 1018 0.7 1544 6.2 2248 0.6
22 M	0624 1.6 1216 -0.1 1851 1.7	0306 2.7 0946 -0.2 1530 2.7 2206 -0.0	0432 3.2 1110 -0.3 1652 3.2 2329 -0.1	0455 4.0 1118 -0.3 1718 4.0 2339 -0.1	0616 2.0 1121 0.4 1839 2.1	0126 0.2 0736 2.1 1342 0.3 1956 2.2	0533 4.6 1154 0.5 1755 4.6	0118 0.4 0657 5.7 1335 0.6 1918 5.6	0416 5.9 1105 0.9 1634 5.9 2338 1.0
23 TU	0042 0.1 0701 1.6 1304 -0.0 1936 1.6	0347 2.6 1027 -0.0 1615 2.5 2245 0.2	0508 3.1 1147 -0.1 1733 3.0	0535 3.8 1159 -0.1 1800 3.7	0003 0.2 0714 1.9 1318 0.3 1944 2.0	0227 0.2 0821 2.0 1442 0.3 2045 2.0	0020 0.5 0629 4.3 1242 0.6 1857 4.3	0158 0.6 0747 5.3 1417 0.8 2010 5.3	0509 5.4 1157 1.2 1732 5.5
24 W	0130 0.2 0749 1.6 1400 0.1 2036 1.5	0433 2.5 1113 0.2 1709 2.3 2332 0.4	0002 0.1 0549 3.0 1226 0.1 1821 2.8	0018 0.2 0617 3.6 1243 -0.3 1847 3.4	0141 0.3 0823 1.8 1412 0.3 2056 1.9	0323 0.3 0913 1.8 1541 0.3 2146 1.8	0111 0.7 0734 4.0 1345 0.8 2008 4.0	0241 0.8 0843 5.0 1506 0.9 2112 5.0	0034 1.4 0614 5.0 1259 1.5 1847 5.1
25 TH	0228 0.3 0856 1.6 1512 0.2 2154 1.4	0530 2.4 1215 0.4 1814 2.1	0039 0.4 0641 2.8 1317 0.4 1920 2.6	0103 0.6 0706 3.4 1341 0.6 1943 3.2	0246 0.3 0933 1.7 1522 0.3 2215 1.8	0421 0.4 1029 1.6 1642 0.3 2315 1.7	0223 1.0 0846 3.8 1506 0.9 2127 3.9	0334 1.0 0953 4.7 1609 1.0 2233 4.8	0141 1.7 0739 4.8 1410 1.7 2018 4.9
26 F	0345 0.3 1018 1.6 1637 0.2 2317 1.5	0038 0.6 0639 2.2 1342 0.5 1935 2.0	0131 0.6 0745 2.7 1454 0.6 2033 2.4	0206 0.9 0808 3.2 1507 0.8 2055 3.0	0400 0.4 1051 1.6 1632 0.3 2330 1.8	0527 0.5 1157 1.5 1747 0.4	0351 1.1 1006 3.7 1633 0.9 2245 3.9	0442 1.2 1117 4.7 1732 1.0 2356 4.9	0256 1.8 0901 4.8 1527 1.7 2131 5.0
27 SA	0507 0.3 1137 1.6 1753 0.2	0213 0.7 0802 2.2 1513 0.5 2104 2.0	0329 0.7 0900 2.6 1629 0.5 2157 2.4	0339 1.0 0927 3.1 1629 0.8 2222 3.0	0508 0.4 1200 1.7 1730 0.3	0033 1.7 0644 0.5 1306 1.5 1855 0.4	0511 1.0 1116 3.9 1742 0.7 2347 4.1	0611 1.1 1227 4.9 1904 0.7	0413 1.7 1003 5.0 1640 1.5 2228 5.3
28 SU	0031 1.5 0615 0.2 1245 1.7 1852 0.1	0337 0.6 0924 2.3 1620 0.3 2214 2.2	0454 0.6 1021 2.7 1734 0.3 2317 2.5	0454 0.9 1055 3.2 1733 0.6 2340 3.1	0030 1.9 0602 0.5 1255 1.8 1815 0.2	0138 1.7 0958 0.6 1405 1.6 2003 0.4	0607 0.9 1211 4.1 1834 0.5	0059 5.3 0730 0.8 1323 5.3 2001 0.4	0515 1.5 1053 5.2 1736 1.2 2314 5.5
29 M	0130 1.6 0709 0.2 1337 1.7 1939 0.0	0437 0.6 1027 2.4 1711 0.2 2304 2.3	0554 0.4 1133 2.8 1827 0.1	0554 0.6 1206 3.4 1826 0.4	0117 2.0 0644 0.4 1339 1.8 1851 0.2	0231 1.8 1106 0.5 1453 1.7 2203 0.4	0035 4.3 0650 0.7 1253 4.3 1914 0.4	0150 5.6 0821 0.6 1409 5.6 2046 0.2	0603 1.2 1133 5.5 1821 0.9 2353 5.7
30 TU	0214 1.6 0751 0.1 1417 1.7 2018 0.0	0525 0.3 1114 2.5 1753 0.1 2345 2.4	0015 2.7 0643 0.2 1227 2.9 1911 0.0	0039 3.3 0645 0.5 1259 3.6 1912 0.3	0154 2.0 0721 0.4 1415 1.9 1924 0.2	0315 1.9 1151 0.5 1533 1.8 2234 0.5	0112 4.5 0724 0.6 1328 4.5 1948 0.4	0233 5.9 0902 0.4 1450 5.8 2125 0.1	0643 1.0 1209 5.7 1859 0.8

● ●Time Zone -0100. For UT subtract 1 hour. For European summer time (shaded) 30/3-26/10 add 1 hour ● ●

PAGE 120

DENMARK, GERMANY, HOLLAND & BELGIUM Time Zone -0100

Esbjerg * Helgoland * Cuxhaven * Bremerhaven * Hoek van Holland * Rotterdam *Vlissingen * Antwerpen * Dunkerque

OCTOBER 1997 TIDE TABLES OCTOBER 1997

ESBJERG	HELGOLAND	CUXHAVEN	BREMERHAVEN	HOEK VAN HOLLAND	ROTTERDAM	VLISSINGEN	ANTWERPEN	DUNKERQUE	Day
Time m	Time m	Time m	Time m	Time m	Time m	Time m	Time m	Time m	
0247 1.6	0606 0.2	0100 2.9	0125 3.5	0226 2.1	0351 1.9	0145 4.6	0309 6.0	0029 5.9	1 W
0829 0.1	1153 2.5	0726 0.1	0730 0.3	0755 0.4	1229 0.5	0757 0.6	0939 0.3	0718 0.9	●
1450 1.7	1830 0.1	1309 3.0	1342 3.7	1447 2.0	1607 1.8	1400 4.6	1525 5.9	1243 5.8	
2053 0.1		1951 0.0	1954 0.3	1955 0.2	2310 0.5	2021 0.3	2201 0.1	1935 0.7	
0315 1.6	0020 2.5	0138 3.0	0204 3.6	0258 2.1	0425 1.9	0215 4.7	0343 6.0	0103 6.0	2 TH
0902 0.1	0643 0.2	0805 0.1	0809 0.3	0826 0.4	1300 0.5	0830 0.5	1012 0.4	0752 0.9	
1521 1.7	1227 2.6	1347 3.0	1417 3.7	1518 2.0	1640 1.9	1430 4.7	1558 5.9	1315 5.9	
2124 0.1	1905 0.1	2027 0.0	2031 0.3	2024 0.2		2052 0.3	2234 0.1	2008 0.6	
0342 1.6	0051 2.5	0212 3.0	0236 3.6	0330 2.1	0054 0.4	0245 4.7	0414 6.0	0135 6.0	3 F
0933 0.1	0718 0.2	0841 0.1	0846 0.3	0851 0.4	0458 2.0	0902 0.5	1044 0.4	0822 0.9	
1551 1.8	1300 2.6	1423 3.1	1449 3.7	1547 2.1	1327 0.5	1500 4.7	1628 5.9	1345 5.9	
2154 0.1	1938 0.1	2101 0.1	2106 0.3	2051 0.2	1714 1.9	2123 0.3	2305 0.2	2038 0.7	
0409 1.6	0121 2.5	0246 3.0	0307 3.6	0400 2.2	0127 0.4	0315 4.7	0444 6.0	0204 5.9	4 SA
1004 0.0	0751 0.2	0915 0.1	0920 0.3	0912 0.4	0533 2.0	0934 0.5	1115 0.5	0851 0.9	
1624 1.7	1331 2.5	1458 3.0	1519 3.7	1615 2.1	1356 0.5	1530 4.7	1659 5.9	1414 5.9	
2224 0.1	2009 0.2	2133 0.2	2139 0.3	2121 0.2	1748 1.9	2154 0.4	2335 0.3	2108 0.7	
0438 1.6	0151 2.5	0319 3.0	0336 3.6	0431 2.1	0206 0.4	0346 4.7	0514 5.9	0232 5.9	5 SU
1036 0.0	0824 0.2	0948 0.2	0953 0.3	0939 0.4	0607 2.0	1007 0.5	1145 0.5	0919 1.0	
1655 1.7	1403 2.5	1532 3.0	1551 3.6	1645 2.1	1430 0.5	1601 4.7	1730 5.9	1443 6.0	
2254 0.1	2039 0.3	2205 0.2	2210 0.3	2154 0.3	1823 2.0	2227 0.4		2139 0.8	
0506 1.6	0219 2.5	0351 3.0	0408 3.6	0503 2.1	0016 0.5	0418 4.7	0006 0.4	0303 5.9	6 M
1108 0.0	0857 0.3	1021 0.2	1026 0.3	1011 0.4	0642 1.9	1040 0.6	0546 5.9	0950 1.1	
1724 1.6	1434 2.5	1606 2.9	1624 3.6	1718 2.1	1245 0.6	1634 4.7	1218 0.6	1516 5.9	
2325 0.1	2111 0.3	2236 0.3	2242 0.3	2230 0.3	1900 2.0	2300 0.5	1802 5.8	2212 1.0	
0534 1.6	0249 2.5	0422 2.9	0442 3.6	0537 2.1	0115 0.5	0452 4.6	0036 0.5	0337 5.8	7 TU
1142 0.0	0930 0.3	1054 0.3	1100 0.3	1049 0.3	0719 1.9	1115 0.6	0620 5.8	1024 1.2	
1752 1.6	1509 2.5	1639 2.9	1700 3.5	1755 2.1	1347 0.5	1710 4.6	1250 0.7	1554 5.8	
	2145 0.4	2309 0.3	2317 0.3	2312 0.3	1939 2.0	2336 0.7	1838 5.7	2249 1.1	
0000 0.1	0324 2.5	0452 2.9	0518 3.6	0617 2.0	0217 0.5	0531 4.4	0109 0.6	0418 5.6	8 W
0606 1.6	1008 0.3	1130 0.3	1137 0.3	1136 0.3	0800 1.9	1155 0.7	0658 5.7	1104 1.3	
1222 0.0	1551 2.4	1718 2.9	1742 3.5	1838 2.1	1511 0.5	1753 4.4	1324 0.7	1639 5.6	
1827 1.5	2224 0.4	2345 0.4	2356 0.3		2024 2.0		1919 5.6	2334 1.3	
0041 0.1	0410 2.5	0532 2.9	0602 3.5	0007 0.3	0340 0.5	0019 0.7	0146 0.7	0507 5.3	9 TH
0646 1.6	1054 0.4	1212 0.3	1221 0.3	0703 1.9	0848 1.8	0618 4.2	0744 5.5	1155 1.5	
1309 0.0	1647 2.4	1809 2.8	1831 3.4	1236 0.3	1445 0.4	1245 0.7	1407 0.8	1736 5.3	
1918 1.5	2315 0.5			1932 1.9	2118 1.9	1847 4.2	2011 5.4		
0132 0.1	0511 2.5	0030 0.4	0042 0.4	0203 0.3	0348 0.5	0118 0.8	0235 0.9	0035 1.6	10 F
0746 1.5	1154 0.4	0629 2.9	0654 3.5	0805 1.7	0950 1.7	0724 3.9	0842 5.2	0612 5.0	
1407 0.1	1755 2.3	1304 0.3	1315 0.4	1417 0.3	1612 0.4	1353 0.9	1504 0.9	1306 1.7	
2036 1.4		1911 2.8	1931 3.3	2059 1.8	2237 1.9	2013 3.9	2121 5.2	1856 5.1	
0236 0.2	0021 0.5	0127 0.5	0140 0.5	0315 0.4	0513 0.4	0236 0.9	0342 1.1	0153 1.7	11 SA
0910 1.5	0622 2.5	0736 3.0	0758 3.4	0954 1.6	1126 1.7	0902 3.8	1004 5.0	0741 4.9	
1524 0.1	1308 0.3	1413 0.3	1427 0.4	1530 0.3	1721 0.3	1526 0.9	1624 1.0	1428 1.6	
2208 1.4	1911 2.4	2020 2.9	2040 3.3	2238 1.8		2148 4.0	2249 5.2	2028 5.1	
0357 0.2	0140 0.5	0245 0.4	0300 0.5	0554 0.4	0009 1.9	0415 0.9	0509 1.1	0312 1.6	12 SU
1036 1.6	0736 2.6	0845 3.1	0909 3.5	1115 1.7	0734 0.4	1026 3.9	1133 5.1	0906 5.0	
1652 0.1	1428 0.2	1539 0.2	1548 0.3	1641 0.3	1244 1.8	1657 0.7	1757 0.9	1545 1.4	
2333 1.5	2024 2.5	2129 3.0	2153 3.4	2348 2.0	1821 0.3	2303 4.3		2142 5.5	
0521 0.2	0258 0.3	0411 0.2	0419 0.3	0801 0.3	0115 2.1	0530 0.7	0012 5.5	0423 1.3	13 M
1153 1.7	0845 2.7	0952 3.3	1019 3.7	1217 1.8	0850 0.3	1131 4.2	0634 0.9	1009 5.4	
1806 -0.0	1538 0.0	1654 -0.1	1658 0.0	1730 0.2	1342 1.9	1804 0.4	1245 5.5	1652 1.0	
	2128 2.7	2235 3.2	2301 3.6		1911 0.2	2359 4.6	1921 0.6	2239 5.9	
0048 1.6	0403 0.1	0521 -0.0	0525 0.1	0042 2.1	0209 2.2	0627 0.5	0116 6.0	0524 0.9	14 TU
0628 0.1	0945 2.9	1055 3.5	1124 3.9	0904 0.3	1006 0.3	1221 4.5	0750 0.6	1100 5.8	
1301 1.8	1637 -0.2	1757 -0.3	1758 -0.3	1306 1.9	1432 2.1	1857 0.2	1342 5.9	1751 0.6	
1906 -0.1	2224 2.8	2336 3.4		1810 0.2	1951 0.2		2027 0.4	2327 6.3	
0152 1.6	0500 0.1	0621 -0.2	0001 3.8	0130 2.3	0257 2.4	0046 4.9	0209 6.3	0618 0.6	15 W
0724 0.1	1040 3.0	1154 3.6	0622 -0.2	0639 0.4	0921 0.4	0716 0.3	0850 0.4	1145 6.1	
1402 1.8	1730 -0.4	1851 -0.5	1221 4.1	1351 2.0	1516 2.2	1306 4.8	1430 6.2	1842 0.3	
1959 -0.1	2314 2.9		1852 -0.4	1848 0.1	2242 0.2	1944 0.0	2120 0.1		

●● Time Zone -0100. For UT subtract 1 hour. For European summer time (shaded) 30/3-26/10 add 1 hour ●●

OCTOBER 1997 TIDE TABLES OCTOBER 1997

	ESBJERG	HELGOLAND	CUXHAVEN	BREMERHAVEN	HOEK VAN HOLLAND	ROTTERDAM	VLISSINGEN	ANTWERPEN	DUNKERQUE
	Time m	Time m	Time m	Time m	Time m	Time m	Time m	Time m	Time m
16 TH ○	0245 1.7	0551 -0.2	0032 3.5	0054 4.0	0214 2.3	0340 2.4	0130 5.0	0255 6.5	0012 6.5
	0815 -0.0	1130 3.1	0714 -0.4	0715 -0.3	0712 0.4	1031 0.4	0801 0.3	0941 0.3	0704 0.5
	1456 1.9	1818 -0.4	1250 3.7	1314 4.2	1435 2.1	1558 2.3	1348 5.0	1515 6.4	1227 6.4
	2045 -0.1		1942 -0.5	1942 -0.5	1927 0.1	2328 0.3	2028 -0.1	2208 0.0	1928 0.1
17 F	0331 1.7	0000 2.9	0122 3.5	0143 4.1	0257 2.3	0422 2.4	0212 5.1	0339 6.6	0054 6.5
	0901 -0.0	0639 -0.3	0803 -0.4	0803 -0.4	0749 0.4	1133 0.4	0845 0.2	1027 0.2	0749 0.4
	1545 1.9	1216 3.1	1340 3.6	1403 4.3	1518 2.2	1640 2.4	1430 5.1	1557 6.4	1309 6.4
	2130 -0.0	1903 -0.3	2028 -0.5	2029 -0.5	2008 0.1	2156 0.1	2111 -0.0	2253 0.0	2013 0.1
18 SA	0412 1.7	0042 2.9	0208 3.5	0228 4.1	0339 2.3	0503 2.4	0254 5.1	0421 6.5	0137 6.5
	0945 -0.1	0723 -0.3	0848 -0.4	0850 -0.4	0830 0.4	1234 0.4	0927 0.3	1111 0.3	0832 0.4
	1630 1.9	1300 3.0	1426 3.6	1448 4.3	1600 2.2	1722 2.4	1512 5.1	1640 6.4	1351 6.4
	2212 0.0	1945 -0.2	2111 -0.3	2113 -0.4	2051 0.1	2246 0.2	2153 0.1	2334 0.1	2057 0.3
19 SU	0449 1.7	0121 2.9	0248 3.4	0310 4.1	0422 2.2	0545 2.3	0337 5.0	0504 6.3	0220 6.3
	1029 -0.0	0805 -0.2	0930 -0.3	0933 -0.4	0915 0.4	1108 0.3	1009 0.3	1152 0.3	0915 0.5
	1711 1.8	1341 2.9	1508 3.4	1531 4.2	1642 2.2	1804 2.3	1556 5.0	1723 6.2	1435 6.3
	2253 0.1	2024 -0.1	2151 -0.2	2155 -0.2	2139 0.2	2342 0.3	2232 0.3		2139 0.5
20 M	0521 1.7	0158 2.8	0324 3.4	0350 4.0	0505 2.1	0627 2.2	0421 4.8	0014 0.3	0304 6.1
	1112 -0.0	0845 -0.1	1010 -0.2	1015 -0.2	1003 0.3	1204 0.3	1049 0.4	0548 6.1	0957 0.7
	1749 1.8	1421 2.8	1545 3.3	1612 4.0	1724 2.2	1847 2.3	1641 4.8	1231 0.4	1521 6.1
	2333 0.1	2100 0.1	2226 0.0	2234 -0.0	2233 0.3		2309 0.5	1808 6.0	2223 0.7
21 TU	0553 1.7	0235 2.8	0357 3.3	0428 3.9	0551 2.0	0046 0.3	0507 4.6	0051 0.5	0351 5.8
	1155 0.0	0922 0.0	1046 -0.0	1055 -0.0	1059 0.3	0708 2.1	1129 0.5	0633 5.7	1042 0.9
	1827 1.7	1502 2.7	1621 3.2	1651 3.8	1812 2.1	1306 0.3	1730 4.6	1310 0.6	1610 5.8
		2134 0.3	2257 0.2	2312 0.2	2339 0.4	1930 2.2	2348 0.7	1854 5.7	2309 1.1
22 W	0014 0.2	0314 2.8	0429 3.2	0505 3.8	0644 1.9	0150 0.4	0559 4.3	0128 0.7	0441 5.6
	0629 1.7	1000 0.2	1121 0.1	1134 0.2	1207 0.3	0750 1.9	1214 0.6	0720 5.4	1130 1.2
	1242 0.1	1545 2.5	1700 3.0	1730 3.6	1912 2.0	1407 0.3	1828 4.3	1350 0.7	1705 5.4
	1909 1.6	2209 0.4	2325 0.4	2347 0.5		2015 2.0		1942 5.4	
23 TH	0059 0.3	0358 2.7	0509 3.1	0542 3.7	0103 0.4	0248 0.4	0034 0.9	0209 0.9	0000 1.4
	0713 1.7	1043 0.4	1154 0.3	1215 0.5	0750 1.8	0835 1.7	0700 4.0	0810 5.0	0540 5.1
	1333 0.2	1635 2.3	1745 2.8	1813 3.3	1324 0.2	1505 0.3	1314 0.8	1435 0.8	1227 1.5
	2003 1.5	2249 0.6	2354 0.6		2021 1.9	2109 1.8	1935 4.1	2038 5.1	1811 5.1
24 F	0151 0.3	0451 2.5	0600 3.0	0023 0.7	0214 0.4	0345 0.5	0143 1.1	0257 1.1	0101 1.7
	0812 1.6	1138 0.6	1236 0.6	0627 3.5	0857 1.7	0935 1.6	0808 3.8	0910 4.8	0654 4.8
	1439 0.3	1736 2.2	1842 2.6	1303 0.8	1445 0.3	1605 0.3	1431 0.9	1532 0.9	1333 1.8
	2117 1.4	2346 0.8		1904 3.1	2135 1.8	2237 1.7	2050 3.9	2146 4.8	1933 4.9
25 SA	0300 0.4	0557 2.3	0038 0.8	0111 1.0	0333 0.5	0448 0.6	0306 1.2	0400 1.2	0212 1.9
	0932 1.6	1300 0.7	0703 2.8	0724 3.3	1012 1.6	1118 1.5	0927 3.6	1028 4.6	0818 4.7
	1558 0.3	1853 2.1	1357 0.8	1422 1.0	1603 0.3	1709 0.4	1547 0.9	1647 1.0	1445 1.8
	2238 1.5		1953 2.5	2010 2.9	2257 1.8		2209 3.8	2313 4.8	2051 4.9
26 SU	0423 0.4	0121 0.9	0203 1.0	0245 1.2	0442 0.5	0001 1.7	0424 1.2	0519 1.2	0327 1.8
	1054 1.7	0718 2.3	0818 2.7	0837 3.1	1127 1.6	0605 0.6	1042 3.7	1148 4.8	0927 4.8
	1715 0.3	1434 0.7	1552 0.8	1549 0.9	1703 0.3	1233 1.5	1700 0.8	1812 0.8	1557 1.7
	2350 1.5	2023 2.1	2115 2.5	2133 2.9		1822 0.4	2315 4.0		2154 5.1
27 M	0537 0.4	0257 0.8	0416 0.9	0415 1.1	0000 1.9	0106 1.7	0530 1.0	0024 5.1	0436 1.6
	1202 1.7	0844 2.3	0939 2.7	1004 3.2	0539 0.5	0747 0.6	1138 4.0	0642 1.0	1020 5.1
	1817 0.2	1545 0.6	1700 0.6	1657 0.6	1224 1.7	1333 1.6	1757 0.7	1248 5.1	1659 1.4
		2139 2.2	2238 2.6	2256 3.1	1752 0.3	1942 0.4		1921 0.5	2242 5.4
28 TU	0050 1.6	0403 0.7	0521 0.7	0519 0.8	0046 2.0	0200 1.8	0003 4.2	0118 5.5	0530 1.3
	0634 0.3	0952 2.4	1054 2.9	1121 3.3	0627 0.4	0957 0.5	0617 0.8	0742 0.7	1103 5.4
	1257 1.7	1637 0.4	1753 0.4	1752 0.5	1307 1.8	1424 1.7	1222 4.2	1337 5.5	1747 1.1
	1906 0.2	2233 2.4	2340 2.9		1833 0.3	2057 0.3	1840 0.6	2010 0.2	2324 5.7
29 W	0136 1.6	0454 0.5	0611 0.4	0001 3.3	0123 2.0	0246 1.9	0042 4.4	0201 5.8	0612 1.1
	0719 0.2	1043 2.6	1152 3.0	0612 0.6	0707 0.4	1102 0.5	0655 0.7	0828 0.5	1142 5.6
	1342 1.8	1720 0.3	1837 0.2	1221 3.5	1343 1.9	1506 1.8	1258 4.4	1419 5.7	1827 0.9
	1945 0.1	2315 2.5		1839 0.3	1906 0.3	2207 0.4	1916 0.5	2052 0.1	
30 TH	0213 1.7	0536 0.4	0026 3.0	0051 3.5	0157 2.1	0325 1.9	0115 4.5	0239 5.9	0001 5.8
	0757 0.2	1124 2.6	0655 0.3	0659 0.4	0742 0.4	1142 0.4	0730 0.6	0907 0.4	0650 0.9
	1419 1.8	1758 0.2	1238 3.2	1308 3.7	1416 2.0	1542 1.9	1330 4.5	1455 5.9	1216 5.7
	2020 0.1	2351 2.6	1918 0.2	1923 0.2	1934 0.3	2324 0.4	1949 0.4	2129 0.2	1903 0.7
31 F ●	0244 1.7	0615 0.3	0106 3.2	0133 3.7	0230 2.1	0400 2.0	0146 4.7	0313 6.0	0036 5.9
	0832 0.2	1202 2.7	0735 0.2	0741 0.3	0809 0.4	1218 0.4	0803 0.6	0942 0.4	0724 0.9
	1452 1.8	1834 0.2	1319 3.2	1348 3.7	1448 2.1	1617 1.9	1402 4.7	1528 5.9	1248 5.8
	2052 0.1		1955 0.1	2002 0.2	1959 0.3		2021 0.4	2203 0.2	1938 0.7

• • Time Zone -0100. For UT subtract 1 hour. For European summer time (shaded) 30/3-26/10 add 1 hour • •

DENMARK, GERMANY, HOLLAND & BELGIUM Time Zone -0100
Esbjerg * Helgoland * Cuxhaven * Bremerhaven * Hoek van Holland * Rotterdam *Vlissingen * Antwerpen * Dunkerque

NOVEMBER 1997 TIDE TABLES NOVEMBER 1997

ESBJERG		HELGOLAND		CUXHAVEN		BREMERHAVEN		HOEK VAN HOLLAND		ROTTERDAM		VLISSINGEN		ANTWERPEN		DUNKERQUE			
Time	m	Time	m	Time	m	Time	m	Time	m	Time	m	Time	m	Time	m	Time	m		
0312	1.7	0025	2.7	0144	3.3	0210	3.8	0302	2.2	0018	0.4	0218	4.7	0344	6.0	0106	6.0	1	SA
0906	0.1	0653	0.3	0814	0.2	0821	0.2	0824	0.4	0434	2.0	0836	0.5	1015	0.4	0756	0.9		
1526	1.8	1238	2.7	1359	3.2	1424	3.8	1518	2.1	1254	0.4	1433	4.7	1600	5.9	1318	5.9		
2124	0.1	1910	0.3	2032	0.2	2039	0.2	2025	0.3	1651	1.9	2054	0.4	2235	0.3	2010	0.7		
0342	1.7	0058	2.7	0221	3.3	0245	3.8	0334	2.2	0106	0.4	0249	4.8	0415	6.0	0136	5.9	2	SU
0939	0.1	0730	0.3	0851	0.2	0857	0.2	0844	0.4	0509	2.0	0910	0.5	1048	0.5	0827	0.9		
1600	1.8	1312	2.7	1437	3.2	1500	3.7	1551	2.2	1332	0.4	1506	4.8	1631	6.0	1347	5.9		
2157	0.1	1945	0.3	2108	0.2	2115	0.2	2055	0.3	1727	2.0	2129	0.4	2308	0.4	2043	0.8		
0415	1.7	0130	2.7	0257	3.2	0318	3.7	0407	2.2	0153	0.4	0322	4.8	0448	6.0	0205	5.9	3	M
1014	0.1	0805	0.3	0928	0.2	0933	0.2	0913	0.4	0545	2.0	0947	0.5	1123	0.5	0859	0.9		
1634	1.7	1347	2.6	1515	3.1	1534	3.7	1624	2.2	1412	0.4	1539	4.8	1705	6.0	1418	5.9		
2230	0.1	2019	0.3	2143	0.3	2150	0.2	2129	0.4	1803	2.0	2206	0.5	2342	0.5	2117	0.8		
0446	1.7	0201	2.7	0332	3.2	0351	3.7	0442	2.1	0236	0.4	0357	4.7	0522	5.9	0238	5.9	4	TU
1050	0.1	0841	0.3	1004	0.2	1009	0.2	0948	0.3	0621	1.9	1025	0.5	1159	0.6	0933	1.0		
1707	1.7	1421	2.6	1552	3.1	1610	3.6	1659	2.2	1449	0.4	1614	4.7	1740	6.0	1454	5.9		
2304	0.1	2054	0.3	2218	0.3	2225	0.2	2208	0.4	1842	2.0	2243	0.5			2152	0.9		
0517	1.7	0234	2.7	0406	3.2	0426	3.7	0518	2.1	0037	0.6	0433	4.6	0017	0.6	0316	5.8	5	W
1127	0.1	0918	0.3	1040	0.2	1046	0.2	1029	0.3	0700	1.9	1104	0.5	0600	5.9	1010	1.1		
1739	1.6	1458	2.6	1629	3.1	1648	3.6	1739	2.2	1312	0.5	1653	4.6	1234	0.6	1535	5.8		
2342	0.1	2130	0.4	2254	0.4	2302	0.2	2252	0.4	1922	2.0	2322	0.6	1819	5.9	2231	1.1		
0550	1.7	0310	2.7	0439	3.2	0503	3.7	0559	2.0	0142	0.6	0515	4.5	0051	0.6	0359	5.7	6	TH
1208	0.1	0957	0.3	1118	0.3	1126	0.2	1115	0.2	0742	1.9	1146	0.6	0640	5.8	1051	1.2		
1817	1.6	1541	2.6	1709	3.1	1729	3.5	1823	2.1	1457	0.4	1737	4.5	1311	0.6	1622	5.7		
		2210	0.5	2332	0.4	2342	0.2	2347	0.4	2007	2.1			1903	5.8	2316	1.2		
0024	0.1	0355	2.8	0518	3.2	0545	3.7	0646	1.9	0303	0.5	0006	0.7	0130	0.7	0450	5.4	7	F
0633	1.7	1043	0.3	1201	0.3	1209	0.2	1212	0.2	0829	1.9	0603	4.2	0728	5.6	1142	1.3		
1256	0.1	1633	2.5	1754	3.0	1815	3.5	1918	2.0	1425	0.3	1236	0.7	1355	0.7	1720	5.5		
1909	1.5	2259	0.5							2101	2.0	1833	4.3	1957	5.6				
0115	0.2	0451	2.7	0015	0.4	0027	0.3	0216	0.4	0316	0.5	0103	0.9	0220	0.9	0014	1.4	8	SA
0730	1.7	1138	0.3	0609	3.3	0634	3.7	0748	1.7	0927	1.8	0707	4.0	0827	5.4	0554	5.2		
1353	0.1	1733	2.5	1251	0.3	1302	0.2	1348	0.2	1536	0.3	1341	0.8	1454	0.8	1247	1.5		
2024	1.5	2359	0.5	1850	3.0	1910	3.4	2044	1.9	2214	2.0	1956	4.1	2105	5.4	1836	5.3		
0216	0.2	0555	2.8	0110	0.4	0123	0.3	0320	0.4	0429	0.4	0216	0.9	0326	1.0	0127	1.6	9	SU
0847	1.7	1245	0.3	0709	3.3	0732	3.7	0930	1.6	1051	1.8	0837	3.9	0945	5.2	0717	5.0		
1505	0.1	1842	2.5	1354	0.2	1405	0.2	1505	0.2	1644	0.2	1505	0.7	1611	0.9	1405	1.5		
2148	1.5			1953	3.1	2012	3.4	2212	1.9	2339	2.0	2123	4.1	2228	5.3	2002	5.3		
0331	0.3	0111	0.5	0219	0.4	0232	0.3	0539	0.4	0708	0.4	0347	0.9	0448	1.0	0247	1.5	10	M
1008	1.7	0705	2.8	0815	3.4	0836	3.7	1047	1.7	1211	1.8	0957	4.0	1108	5.2	0839	5.1		
1627	0.1	1358	0.2	1509	0.1	1517	0.1	1612	0.2	1748	0.2	1632	0.6	1738	0.8	1521	1.3		
2309	1.6	1952	2.6	2059	3.2	2120	3.5	2322	2.0			2235	4.3	2348	5.5	2117	5.5		
0452	0.2	0225	0.3	0338	0.3	0345	0.2	0708	0.4	0047	2.2	0506	0.8	0611	0.9	0400	1.3	11	TU
1124	1.8	0813	2.9	0921	3.5	0944	3.8	1151	1.8	0820	0.3	1103	4.2	1220	5.5	0945	5.4		
1740	0.1	1507	0.0	1622	-0.0	1625	-0.1	1706	0.2	1312	2.0	1741	0.4	1859	0.5	1631	1.0		
		2057	2.8	2203	3.3	2226	3.6			1846	0.1	2334	4.6			2217	5.9		
0023	1.6	0333	0.2	0450	0.1	0453	0.0	0018	2.1	0142	2.3	0606	0.6	0053	5.9	0504	1.0	12	W
0602	0.2	0917	3.0	1025	3.6	1049	3.9	0829	0.4	0930	0.3	1156	4.5	0728	0.7	1039	5.8		
1234	1.8	1608	-0.1	1727	-0.2	1727	-0.3	1242	1.9	1405	2.1	1836	0.2	1318	5.9	1731	0.6		
1842	0.0	2155	2.9	2305	3.5	2328	3.8	1750	0.2	1932	0.1			2005	0.3	2308	6.2		
0126	1.7	0432	0.0	0552	-0.1	0553	-0.2	0107	2.2	0232	2.3	0024	4.8	0146	6.2	0558	0.7	13	TH
0701	0.1	1014	3.1	1126	3.7	1151	4.0	0622	0.5	0854	0.4	0655	0.5	0830	0.5	1125	6.1		
1338	1.9	1702	-0.2	1824	-0.3	1823	-0.4	1330	2.1	1451	2.2	1243	4.7	1408	6.1	1823	0.4		
1935	0.0	2246	2.9					1830	0.2	2012	0.2	1923	0.1	2059	0.2	2353	6.3		
0219	1.8	0526	-0.1	0001	3.5	0024	3.9	0153	2.3	0316	2.4	0109	4.9	0234	6.3	0646	0.5	14	F
0754	0.1	1106	3.1	0648	-0.2	0648	-0.3	0656	0.5	1016	0.4	0741	0.4	0921	0.3	1209	6.2		
1434	1.9	1750	-0.2	1222	3.7	1246	4.1	1414	2.2	1535	2.3	1327	4.9	1454	6.2	1910	0.3		
2023	0.1	2333	3.0	1915	-0.3	1915	-0.4	1910	0.2	2312	0.3	2007	0.1	2147	0.2			O	
0305	1.8	0615	-0.1	0052	3.5	0115	4.0	0237	2.3	0358	2.3	0152	5.0	0318	6.4	0036	6.4	15	SA
0842	0.1	1153	3.0	0739	-0.2	0739	-0.3	0734	0.4	1127	0.5	0825	0.3	1007	0.3	0731	0.4		
1524	1.9	1838	-0.1	1314	3.6	1338	4.1	1458	2.2	1617	2.3	1411	5.0	1537	6.2	1251	6.3		
2107	0.1			2003	-0.2	2004	-0.3	1952	0.2			2049	0.2	2230	0.2	1954	0.4		

• • Time Zone -0100. For UT subtract 1 hour. For European summer time (shaded) 30/3-26/10 add 1 hour • •

NOVEMBER 1997 TIDE TABLES NOVEMBER 1997

	ESBJERG		HELGOLAND		CUXHAVEN		BREMERHAVEN		HOEK VAN HOLLAND		ROTTERDAM		VLISSINGEN		ANTWERPEN		DUNKERQUE	
	Time	m	Time	m	Time	m	Time	m	Time	m	Time	m	Time	m	Time	m	Time	m
16 SU	0345	1.8	0015	3.0	0138	3.5	0203	4.0	0321	2.2	0002	0.4	0236	5.0	0401	6.3	0118	6.3
	0927	0.1	0701	-0.1	0826	-0.2	0827	-0.3	0815	0.4	0439	2.3	0908	0.3	1051	0.3	0814	0.5
	1609	1.9	1237	2.9	1400	3.5	1425	4.0	1541	2.3	1233	0.5	1454	5.0	1621	6.2	1333	6.2
	2149	0.1	1921	0.1	2046	-0.0	2049	-0.2	2037	0.3	1659	2.3	2129	0.3	2312	0.3	2036	0.5
17 M	0421	1.8	0054	2.9	0218	3.4	0246	4.0	0404	2.2	0054	0.5	0318	4.9	0445	6.2	0200	6.2
	1011	0.1	0745	0.0	0909	-0.1	0912	-0.1	0900	0.3	0520	2.2	0949	0.3	1132	0.3	0857	0.6
	1650	1.8	1318	2.8	1441	3.3	1509	3.9	1624	2.3	1041	0.3	1538	4.9	1705	6.1	1417	6.1
	2230	0.2	2000	0.2	2126	0.1	2132	0.0	2125	0.4	1742	2.2	2207	0.4	2350	0.4	2118	0.7
18 TU	0454	1.8	0132	2.9	0252	3.4	0326	3.9	0447	2.1	0154	0.5	0403	4.7	0529	6.0	0243	6.0
	1054	0.1	0824	0.1	0950	0.1	0955	0.0	0948	0.3	0601	2.1	1030	0.4	1211	0.3	0939	0.7
	1728	1.8	1357	2.7	1518	3.2	1550	3.7	1706	2.2	1133	0.3	1623	4.8	1749	6.0	1502	5.9
	2310	0.2	2035	0.3	2201	0.3	2212	0.3	2218	0.4	1824	2.2	2243	0.6			2159	0.9
19 W	0529	1.8	0208	2.9	0322	3.3	0403	3.8	0532	2.0	0004	0.4	0448	4.5	0027	0.5	0329	5.8
	1137	0.1	0903	0.2	1027	0.2	1035	0.2	1040	0.2	0642	2.0	1109	0.5	0612	5.7	1021	0.9
	1805	1.7	1436	2.6	1552	3.1	1627	3.5	1752	2.2	1231	0.3	1710	4.6	1248	0.4	1550	5.7
	2350	0.3	2107	0.4	2231	0.4	2247	0.5	2318	0.5	1907	2.1	2321	0.8	1834	5.7	2241	1.2
20 TH	0605	1.8	0246	2.8	0354	3.3	0436	3.7	0621	1.9	0106	0.5	0535	4.3	0103	0.7	0417	5.5
	1221	0.2	0939	0.3	1059	0.4	1113	0.4	1137	0.2	0722	1.9	1152	0.6	0657	5.4	1106	1.2
	1842	1.6	1518	2.5	1629	3.0	1703	3.4	1845	2.1	1332	0.3	1801	4.4	1327	0.5	1640	5.4
			2139	0.5	2254	0.5	2320	0.6			1950	2.0			1919	5.5	2327	1.4
21 F	0032	0.3	0329	2.8	0433	3.2	0511	3.6	0029	0.5	0206	0.5	0003	0.9	0140	0.8	0509	5.2
	0645	1.8	1018	0.5	1130	0.5	1149	0.6	0719	1.8	0803	1.8	0627	4.1	0742	5.1	1154	1.4
	1308	0.2	1603	2.4	1713	2.9	1741	3.2	1238	0.2	1430	0.3	1244	0.7	1407	0.6	1736	5.2
	1926	1.5	2215	0.7	2322	0.7	2351	0.8	1945	2.0	2038	1.8	1858	4.1	2008	5.2		
22 SA	0118	0.3	0417	2.6	0523	3.1	0551	3.5	0138	0.5	0306	0.6	0100	1.1	0223	1.0	0019	1.7
	0733	1.7	1103	0.6	1206	0.7	1229	0.7	0818	1.7	0851	1.6	0725	3.9	0833	4.9	0609	5.0
	1401	0.3	1657	2.3	1806	2.7	1827	3.1	1343	0.2	1530	0.3	1353	0.8	1455	0.7	1251	1.6
	2024	1.5	2303	0.8					2046	1.9	2144	1.7	2002	3.9	2104	4.9	1840	4.9
23 SU	0213	0.4	0516	2.5	0004	0.8	0029	0.9	0305	0.5	0411	0.6	0221	1.2	0315	1.2	0122	1.8
	0835	1.7	1207	0.8	0622	3.0	0642	3.5	0920	1.6	1012	1.5	0832	3.7	0936	4.7	0718	4.8
	1507	0.4	1805	2.2	1259	0.8	1322	0.9	1532	0.3	1635	0.3	1501	0.9	1600	0.9	1355	1.8
	2141	1.5			1910	2.6	1924	2.9	2158	1.8	2318	1.6	2117	3.8	2214	4.8	1954	4.8
24 M	0323	0.5	0016	1.0	0104	1.0	0130	1.1	0414	0.5	0530	0.6	0332	1.2	0430	1.3	0230	1.9
	0954	1.7	0628	2.4	0733	2.8	0748	3.2	1036	1.6	1148	1.5	0951	3.6	1051	4.6	0833	4.8
	1620	0.4	1333	0.8	1442	0.9	1445	1.0	1635	0.3	1750	0.4	1605	0.9	1719	0.8	1502	1.7
	2254	1.5	1926	2.1	2026	2.6	2038	2.9	2314	1.8			2229	3.9	2333	4.9	2104	4.9
25 TU	0439	0.5	0155	1.0	0303	1.1	0312	1.1	0512	0.5	0026	1.7	0437	1.1	0548	1.2	0340	1.8
	1107	1.7	0750	2.4	0850	2.8	0907	3.1	1140	1.7	0706	0.6	1054	3.8	1203	4.9	0936	4.9
	1727	0.3	1453	0.8	1611	0.8	1606	0.8	1728	0.3	1253	1.6	1706	0.8	1830	0.6	1606	1.6
	2357	1.6	2048	2.3	2145	2.7	2159	3.0			1915	0.4	2323	4.0			2202	5.2
26 W	0545	0.4	0316	0.9	0434	0.9	0433	0.9	0006	1.9	0123	1.8	0534	1.0	0036	5.1	0442	1.5
	1208	1.7	0906	2.4	1006	2.9	1028	3.2	0608	0.4	0823	0.5	1144	4.0	0656	0.9	1027	5.2
	1821	0.3	1553	0.6	1710	0.6	1709	0.6	1229	1.8	1348	1.7	1758	0.7	1258	5.2	1703	1.3
			2151	2.4	2254	2.9	2312	3.2	1815	0.3	2030	0.4			1927	0.4	2249	5.4
27 TH	0049	1.6	0415	0.7	0532	0.7	0534	0.6	0048	2.0	0213	1.9	0006	4.2	0124	5.4	0533	1.3
	0637	0.3	1005	2.6	1111	3.0	1136	3.4	0842	0.4	0930	0.4	0620	0.8	0748	0.7	1110	5.4
	1300	1.8	1641	0.5	1759	0.4	1802	0.4	1309	1.9	1434	1.8	1224	4.2	1343	5.5	1749	1.1
	1905	0.2	2239	2.6	2347	3.1			1852	0.3	2134	0.4	1841	0.6	2013	0.3	2330	5.6
28 F	0133	1.7	0503	0.5	0620	0.4	0011	3.5	0125	2.1	0256	1.9	0043	4.4	0204	5.6	0615	1.0
	0721	0.3	1052	2.7	1203	3.2	0626	0.4	0933	0.3	1033	0.4	0659	0.7	0830	0.5	1148	5.6
	1344	1.8	1724	0.4	1842	0.3	1231	3.6	1345	2.0	1515	1.8	1300	4.4	1422	5.7	1830	0.9
	1943	0.2	2320	2.7			1849	0.2	1919	0.4	2238	0.4	1918	0.5	2052	0.3		
29 SA	0211	1.7	0545	0.4	0032	3.3	0100	3.7	0201	2.1	0335	2.0	0118	4.7	0241	5.8	0006	5.8
	0800	0.2	1135	2.7	0704	0.3	0712	0.2	0801	0.4	1130	0.4	0735	0.6	0908	0.5	0654	0.9
	1424	1.8	1804	0.3	1249	3.3	1318	3.7	1419	2.1	1552	1.9	1334	4.6	1458	5.8	1223	5.7
	2020	0.2	2358	2.8	1924	0.2	1933	0.1	1940	0.1	2345	0.4	1952	0.5	2129	0.4	1908	0.8
30 SU ●	0246	1.8	0627	0.3	0114	3.4	0142	3.8	0236	2.2	0411	2.0	0152	4.7	0315	5.9	0039	5.8
	0839	0.2	1215	2.8	0746	0.2	0754	0.1	0802	0.4	1220	0.4	0811	0.6	0945	0.4	0730	0.8
	1502	1.8	1844	0.3	1333	3.3	1400	3.7	1454	2.1	1629	1.9	1409	4.7	1533	5.9	1254	5.7
	2056	0.2			2005	0.2	2013	0.1	2006	0.4			2028	0.5	2206	0.4	1944	0.8

• • Time Zone -0100. For UT subtract 1 hour. For European summer time (shaded) 30/3-26/10 add 1 hour • •

DENMARK, GERMANY, HOLLAND & BELGIUM Time Zone -0100

Esbjerg * Helgoland * Cuxhaven * Bremerhaven * Hoek van Holland * Rotterdam *Vlissingen * Antwerpen * Dunkerque

DECEMBER 1997 TIDE TABLES DECEMBER 1997

ESBJERG	HELGOLAND	CUXHAVEN	BREMERHAVEN	HOEK VAN HOLLAND	ROTTERDAM	VLISSINGEN	ANTWERPEN	DUNKERQUE	Day
Time m	Time m	Time m	Time m	Time m	Time m	Time m	Time m	Time m	
0321 1.8	0035 2.8	0155 3.4	0221 3.8	0312 2.2	0045 0.4	0227 4.8	0351 5.9	0111 5.9	**1 M**
0918 0.1	0708 0.3	0828 0.1	0835 0.1	0824 0.4	0448 2.0	0849 0.5	1024 0.4	0806 0.8	
1541 1.8	1254 2.8	1416 3.3	1441 3.7	1530 2.2	1308 0.3	1445 4.8	1609 6.0	1326 5.8	
2133 0.1	1923 0.3	2045 0.2	2053 0.1	2037 0.4	1706 2.0	2107 0.4	2245 0.4	2021 0.8	
0357 1.8	0111 2.9	0235 3.4	0259 3.8	0348 2.2	0136 0.4	0303 4.8	0428 5.9	0144 5.9	**2 TU**
0957 0.1	0748 0.2	0909 0.1	0915 0.1	0855 0.3	0525 2.0	0930 0.4	1105 0.4	0842 0.8	
1619 1.7	1333 2.7	1458 3.3	1519 3.7	1606 2.2	1352 0.3	1521 4.8	1646 6.0	1400 5.8	
2211 0.1	2002 0.3	2124 0.2	2132 0.1	2112 0.4	1745 2.0	2148 0.4	2324 0.5	2058 0.8	
0433 1.8	0147 2.9	0314 3.4	0336 3.8	0426 2.1	0224 0.4	0341 4.7	0506 6.0	0221 5.9	**3 W**
1036 0.1	0828 0.2	0949 0.1	0954 0.0	0932 0.3	0604 1.9	1013 0.4	1146 0.5	0920 0.8	
1658 1.7	1411 2.7	1539 3.3	1557 3.7	1645 2.2	1433 0.3	1600 4.8	1726 6.1	1439 5.9	
2249 0.1	2040 0.2	2203 0.2	2210 0.1	2152 0.4	1826 2.1	2230 0.5		2136 0.9	
0508 1.8	0223 2.9	0352 3.4	0413 3.8	0506 2.0	0306 0.4	0421 4.6	0003 0.5	0300 5.9	**4 TH**
1117 0.0	0908 0.2	1030 0.1	1034 -0.0	1013 0.2	0644 1.9	1057 0.4	0546 5.9	0959 0.9	
1736 1.6	1451 2.7	1618 3.2	1637 3.6	1727 2.2	1508 0.3	1642 4.7	1227 0.5	1522 5.9	
2330 0.1	2119 0.3	2242 0.2	2250 0.1	2237 0.4	1909 2.1	2313 0.6	1808 6.1	2218 0.9	
0545 1.8	0301 2.9	0429 3.5	0451 3.9	0548 2.0	0346 0.4	0504 4.5	0042 0.6	0345 5.8	**5 F**
1200 0.0	0949 0.2	1110 0.1	1116 -0.1	1100 0.2	0727 1.9	1143 0.4	0630 5.9	1042 0.9	
1818 1.6	1532 2.7	1659 3.2	1718 3.6	1814 2.1	1427 0.3	1728 4.6	1309 0.5	1611 5.8	
	2200 0.3	2322 0.2	2331 0.0	2330 0.5	1954 2.1		1854 6.0	2303 1.1	
0013 0.1	0345 3.0	0509 3.5	0533 3.9	0637 1.9	0221 0.5	0000 0.7	0124 0.7	0437 5.6	**6 SA**
0628 1.7	1033 0.2	1153 0.1	1200 -0.1	1154 0.2	0813 1.9	0554 4.3	0718 5.7	1130 1.1	
1248 0.0	1619 2.7	1742 3.2	1803 3.6	1910 2.1	1411 0.2	1233 0.5	1355 0.5	1708 5.6	
1909 1.5	2246 0.4				2047 2.1	1825 4.4	1947 5.8	2356 1.2	
0102 0.2	0435 3.0	0006 0.2	0016 0.0	0302 0.4	0409 0.5	0052 0.8	0214 0.8	0537 5.4	**7 SU**
0722 1.7	1124 0.2	0555 3.5	0619 3.9	0741 1.8	0909 1.9	0655 4.1	0815 5.5	1230 1.2	
1342 0.1	1713 2.7	1241 0.1	1248 -0.2	1315 0.2	1513 0.1	1332 0.5	1451 0.6	1815 5.4	
2012 1.5	2339 0.4	1831 3.4	1851 3.6	2030 2.0	2152 2.1	1940 4.2	2052 5.5		
0159 0.2	0533 3.0	0055 0.3	0107 0.0	0401 0.4	0403 0.4	0157 0.9	0315 0.9	0103 1.4	**8 M**
0828 1.7	1222 0.2	0649 3.5	0712 3.8	0906 1.7	1020 1.9	0812 4.0	0926 5.3	0650 5.2	
1446 0.1	1814 2.7	1336 0.1	1344 -0.2	1444 0.2	1618 0.1	1442 0.6	1600 0.6	1342 1.3	
2124 1.5		1927 3.2	1947 3.5	2145 2.0	2309 2.1	2056 4.2	2208 5.4	1934 5.4	
0307 0.2	0042 0.4	0154 0.3	0207 0.0	0513 0.4	0548 0.4	0313 0.9	0428 1.0	0220 1.4	**9 TU**
0942 1.7	0636 3.0	0749 3.5	0810 3.8	1017 1.7	1137 1.9	0925 4.0	1043 5.3	0809 5.2	
1600 0.1	1328 0.2	1440 0.1	1446 -0.2	1548 0.2	1725 0.1	1602 0.5	1717 0.6	1458 1.2	
2238 1.6	1919 2.7	2029 3.3	2048 3.5	2254 2.0		2206 4.3	2324 5.5	2051 5.4	
0422 0.2	0152 0.3	0305 0.2	0314 0.0	0627 0.4	0017 2.2	0434 0.8	0546 0.9	0335 1.3	**10 W**
1055 1.8	0743 3.0	0853 3.5	0914 3.8	1122 1.8	0743 0.3	1033 4.2	1154 5.4	0920 5.4	
1712 0.1	1435 0.1	1550 0.0	1551 -0.2	1646 0.2	1242 2.0	1715 0.5	1833 0.5	1610 1.0	
2350 1.6	2024 2.7	2132 3.3	2152 3.6	2354 2.1	1830 0.1	2308 4.4		2155 5.7	
0535 0.2	0301 0.2	0418 0.2	0421 -0.1	0723 0.4	0116 2.2	0541 0.7	0030 5.7	0442 1.1	**11 TH**
1207 1.8	0848 3.0	0957 3.6	1019 3.8	1218 1.9	0849 0.3	1132 4.4	0705 0.7	1019 5.6	
1816 0.1	1539 0.1	1656 -0.0	1656 -0.2	1736 0.2	1339 2.1	1812 0.3	1255 5.6	1712 0.8	
	2126 2.8	2234 3.4	2256 3.7		1923 0.2		1942 0.4	2250 5.9	
0055 1.7	0406 0.1	0524 0.0	0525 -0.2	0046 2.1	0208 2.2	0003 4.6	0126 5.9	0539 0.8	**12 F**
0639 0.2	0949 3.0	1100 3.5	1123 3.8	0616 0.5	0812 0.4	0635 0.5	0809 0.5	1109 5.9	
1315 1.8	1636 0.0	1756 -0.1	1755 -0.3	1309 2.0	1429 2.1	1224 4.5	1348 5.8	1806 0.6	
1912 0.1	2221 2.9	2333 3.4	2356 3.8	1820 0.3	2000 0.2	1903 0.3	2039 0.3	2337 6.0	
0151 1.8	0503 0.1	0624 -0.0	0624 -0.2	0135 2.1	0254 2.2	0051 4.7	0215 6.0	0630 0.6	**13 SA**
0735 0.1	1045 2.9	1158 3.5	1223 3.8	0648 0.4	1005 0.4	0724 0.4	0903 0.4	1154 6.0	
1414 1.9	1728 0.1	1851 -0.1	1851 -0.2	1357 2.1	1515 2.1	1311 4.7	1437 5.9	1854 0.6	
2003 0.1	2310 2.9			1901 0.3	2247 0.4	1948 0.3	2128 0.4		
0239 1.8	0556 0.1	0026 3.4	0051 3.8	0221 2.2	0337 2.2	0137 4.8	0302 6.0	0021 6.0	**14 SU**
0826 0.1	1134 2.9	0718 -0.0	0718 -0.2	0725 0.4	1116 0.5	0809 0.3	0951 0.4	0715 0.5	
1505 1.8	1816 0.1	1251 3.4	1318 3.8	1442 2.2	1557 2.2	1357 4.8	1522 5.9	1237 6.0	
2048 0.2	2354 2.9	1940 0.0	1942 -0.1	1944 0.3	2337 0.5	2030 0.3	2212 0.4	1937 0.6	
									O
0321 1.9	0645 0.1	0113 3.4	0142 3.8	0307 2.1	0418 2.1	0221 4.8	0346 6.0	0102 6.0	**15 M**
0913 0.1	1219 2.8	0807 0.0	0808 -0.1	0806 0.3	1217 0.5	0852 0.3	1034 0.3	0758 0.6	
1550 1.8	1900 0.2	1339 3.2	1408 3.7	1527 2.2	1639 2.1	1441 4.9	1606 6.0	1320 6.0	
2131 0.2		2025 0.1	2029 0.0	2028 0.4	2152 0.4	2109 0.4	2252 0.4	2019 0.8	

•• Time Zone -0100. For UT subtract 1 hour. For European summer time (shaded) 30/3-26/10 add 1 hour ••

DECEMBER 1997 TIDE TABLES DECEMBER 1997

	ESBJERG		HELGOLAND		CUXHAVEN		BREMERHAVEN		HOEK VAN HOLLAND		ROTTERDAM		VLISSINGEN		ANTWERPEN		DUNKERQUE	
	Time	m	Time	m	Time	m	Time	m	Time	m	Time	m	Time	m	Time	m	Time	m
16 TU	0359	1.9	0035	2.9	0154	3.3	0227	3.8	0351	2.1	0458	2.0	0305	4.7	0430	5.9	0143	6.0
	0957	0.1	0729	0.2	0853	0.1	0855	0.0	0849	0.2	1017	0.3	0933	0.3	1115	0.3	0840	0.6
	1631	1.8	1301	2.7	1421	3.1	1454	3.6	1610	2.2	1722	2.1	1524	4.8	1650	6.0	1403	5.9
	2212	0.2	1940	0.3	2106	0.3	2112	0.2	2115	0.4	2238	0.4	2146	0.5	2330	0.5	2059	0.9
17 W	0435	1.9	0112	2.8	0229	3.3	0308	3.7	0436	2.1	0121	0.7	0348	4.7	0512	5.8	0226	5.9
	1040	0.1	0810	0.2	0935	0.2	0939	0.2	0934	0.2	0539	2.0	1014	0.3	1154	0.2	0921	0.7
	1709	1.7	1339	2.6	1457	3.0	1533	3.5	1652	2.2	1106	0.2	1608	4.7	1733	5.9	1446	5.8
	2251	0.2	2015	0.4	2143	0.4	2152	0.4	2203	0.5	1804	2.0	2222	0.6			2138	1.0
18 TH	0510	1.9	0149	2.8	0300	3.3	0343	3.7	0518	2.0	0007	0.5	0430	4.6	0006	0.5	0309	5.8
	1121	0.1	0848	0.3	1012	0.3	1018	0.3	1021	0.2	0619	1.9	1054	0.4	0554	5.7	1002	0.9
	1743	1.7	1416	2.5	1531	3.0	1608	3.4	1734	2.1	1200	0.2	1651	4.6	1230	0.2	1530	5.7
	2329	0.2	2048	0.5	2213	0.5	2228	0.5	2257	0.5	1846	2.0	2258	0.7	1815	5.8	2216	1.1
19 F	0545	1.8	0226	2.8	0330	3.3	0415	3.6	0602	1.9	0021	0.5	0512	4.4	0040	0.6	0353	5.7
	1201	0.2	0922	0.4	1045	0.4	1054	0.5	1110	0.1	0659	1.8	1133	0.5	0636	5.5	1042	1.0
	1816	1.6	1454	2.5	1606	2.9	1639	3.3	1818	2.1	1257	0.2	1734	4.4	1306	0.3	1616	5.5
			2118	0.5	2237	0.5	2259	0.6	2358	0.5	1927	1.9	2336	0.8	1856	5.6	2254	1.3
20 SA	0007	0.2	0305	2.8	0409	3.3	0446	3.6	0648	1.9	0118	0.6	0554	4.2	0115	0.7	0439	5.5
	0621	1.8	0956	0.5	1114	0.5	1127	0.5	1202	0.1	0739	1.8	1213	0.6	0716	5.3	1123	1.2
	1241	0.2	1535	2.4	1645	2.9	1713	3.2	1907	2.0	1356	0.2	1819	4.2	1341	0.4	1703	5.3
	1850	1.5	2152	0.6	2304	0.6	2329	0.7			2010	1.8			1939	5.4	2337	1.5
21 SU	0046	0.2	0348	2.7	0453	3.2	0523	3.5	0101	0.4	0224	0.6	0018	1.0	0151	0.8	0527	5.2
	0700	1.8	1033	0.6	1145	0.6	1200	0.6	0736	1.8	0820	1.7	0640	4.0	0800	5.1	1209	1.4
	1323	0.2	1621	2.4	1733	2.8	1754	3.1	1256	0.1	1457	0.3	1302	0.7	1419	0.5	1753	5.1
	1930	1.5	2233	0.7	2342	0.7			2000	1.9	2058	1.8	1909	4.0	2026	5.1		
22 M	0130	0.3	0438	2.6	0546	3.0	0003	0.7	0237	0.4	0336	0.6	0111	1.1	0232	1.0	0029	1.7
	0745	1.7	1121	0.7	1225	0.7	0609	3.4	0829	1.7	0911	1.6	0732	3.8	0851	4.8	0621	5.0
	1412	0.3	1718	2.3	1830	2.7	1238	0.7	1354	0.2	1603	0.3	1407	0.8	1505	0.6	1303	1.6
	2022	1.5	2327	0.8			1844	3.1	2057	1.8	2209	1.7	2006	3.8	2122	4.9	1850	4.9
23 TU	0221	0.4	0539	2.5	0032	0.8	0048	0.8	0345	0.4	0459	0.6	0235	1.2	0322	1.1	0130	1.8
	0843	1.7	1224	0.8	0649	2.9	0707	3.2	0926	1.6	1038	1.5	0833	3.7	0951	4.7	0724	4.8
	1509	0.4	1827	2.2	1322	0.9	1332	0.8	1603	0.2	1720	0.4	1512	0.9	1611	0.8	1404	1.7
	2132	1.5			1936	2.6	1948	3.0	2200	1.8	2336	1.6	2113	3.7	2226	4.7	1957	4.8
24 W	0324	0.4	0041	0.9	0138	1.0	0154	0.9	0444	0.4	0630	0.5	0343	1.2	0439	1.2	0236	1.8
	0954	1.6	0652	2.4	0800	2.8	0818	3.1	1034	1.6	1204	1.5	0946	3.6	1059	4.6	0835	4.8
	1617	0.4	1343	0.8	1445	0.9	1450	0.8	1700	0.3	1845	0.4	1612	0.9	1732	0.8	1506	1.7
	2249	1.5	1945	2.2	2050	2.6	2102	3.0	2309	1.8			2226	3.6	2334	4.8	2107	4.9
25 TH	0437	0.4	0211	0.9	0316	1.0	0328	0.8	0542	0.4	0041	1.7	0443	1.1	0558	1.1	0342	1.7
	1109	1.6	0811	2.4	0916	2.8	0936	3.1	1139	1.6	0742	0.5	1054	3.8	1205	4.8	0940	4.9
	1721	0.4	1458	0.7	1614	0.8	1615	0.7	1754	0.3	1307	1.6	1710	0.8	1833	0.7	1609	1.5
	2354	1.6	2100	2.3	2203	2.8	2220	3.1			1958	0.4	2322	4.0			2206	5.1
26 F	0544	0.4	0327	0.8	0443	0.8	0449	0.6	0006	1.9	0137	1.8	0539	0.9	0035	5.0	0442	1.5
	1212	1.7	0921	2.4	1027	2.9	1051	3.3	0745	0.4	0846	0.4	1145	4.0	0657	0.9	1033	5.1
	1817	0.3	1558	0.6	1715	0.6	1721	0.4	1230	1.8	1400	1.7	1801	0.7	1300	5.1	1705	1.3
			2158	2.5	2305	3.0	2328	3.4	1845	0.3	2103	0.3			1925	0.6	2255	5.3
27 SA	0049	1.6	0425	0.6	0542	0.6	0550	0.4	0053	1.9	0227	1.8	0009	4.2	0124	5.3	0535	1.2
	0640	0.3	1018	2.6	1127	3.1	1155	3.4	0904	0.3	0946	0.3	0626	0.8	0746	0.7	1118	5.3
	1307	1.7	1648	0.4	1807	0.4	1815	0.2	1314	1.9	1447	1.8	1230	4.2	1346	5.3	1754	1.1
	1905	0.2	2247	2.7	2357	3.2			1915	0.3	2206	0.3	1845	0.6	2010	0.5	2336	5.5
28 SU	0137	1.7	0515	0.4	0633	0.3	0025	3.6	0134	2.0	0309	1.9	0051	4.4	0208	5.5	0621	1.0
	0729	0.2	1106	2.7	1219	3.3	0642	0.2	0739	0.4	1047	0.3	0708	0.6	0832	0.6	1158	5.5
	1357	1.7	1735	0.3	1854	0.2	1249	3.6	1354	2.0	1528	1.9	1309	4.4	1429	5.6	1839	1.0
	1949	0.1	2330	2.8			1903	0.1	1930	0.4	2316	0.4	1926	0.5	2054	0.5		
29 M	0220	1.7	0603	0.3	0045	3.4	0114	3.7	0214	2.1	0349	1.9	0130	4.6	0250	5.7	0015	5.7
	0814	0.1	1152	2.8	0721	0.1	0729	0.3	0741	0.3	1148	0.3	0748	0.5	0918	0.4	0703	0.8
	1441	1.7	1820	0.2	1308	3.3	1337	3.7	1433	2.1	1608	1.9	1348	4.6	1511	5.8	1234	5.7
	2032	0.1			1940	0.1	1949	-0.0	1953	0.4			2006	0.5	2139	0.4	1921	0.8
30 TU	0300	1.8	0012	2.9	0130	3.5	0158	3.8	0253	2.1	0024	0.4	0209	4.7	0332	5.9	0051	5.8
	0858	0.0	0648	0.2	0806	0.0	0814	-0.1	0806	0.3	0428	2.0	0831	0.4	1004	0.4	0745	0.7
	1524	1.7	1236	2.8	1355	3.4	1421	3.8	1512	2.2	1242	0.3	1427	4.8	1552	6.0	1309	5.8
	2113	0.0	1903	0.2	2024	-0.0	2033	-0.1	2024	0.4	1648	2.0	2048	0.4	2225	0.4	2001	0.8
31 W	0341	1.8	0052	2.9	0215	3.5	0240	3.9	0333	2.1	0120	0.3	0248	4.8	0413	6.0	0127	5.9
	0941	0.0	0731	0.1	0851	-0.1	0857	-0.1	0839	0.2	0507	2.0	0915	0.2	1051	0.3	0825	0.6
	1608	1.7	1318	2.8	1441	3.4	1503	3.8	1552	2.2	1331	0.3	1507	4.8	1633	6.1	1348	5.9
	2154	0.0	1946	0.1	2108	-0.0	2115	-0.1	2058	0.4	1730	2.1	2133	0.3	2311	0.4	2042	0.7

•• Time Zone -0100. For UT subtract 1 hour. For European summer time (shaded) 30/3-26/10 add 1 hour ••

FRANCE, SPAIN, PORTUGAL & GIBRALTAR Time Zone -0100

Calais * Dieppe * Le Havre * Cherbourg * St Malo * Brest * Pointe de Grave * Lisboa * Gibraltar

JANUARY 1997 TIDE TABLES JANUARY 1997

CALAIS Time m	DIEPPE Time m	LE HAVRE Time m	CHERBOURG Time m	ST MALO Time m	BREST Time m	POINTE DE GRAVE Time m	LISBOA Time m	GIBRALTAR Time m		
0437 6.4	0345 7.6	0245 7.0	0103 5.2	0533 3.8	0318 2.6	0312 1.9	0148 1.3	0745 0.8	**1**	**W**
1132 2.0	1023 2.2	0942 2.5	0740 2.4	1109 9.9	0913 5.7	0922 4.4	0830 3.1	1334 0.4		
1701 6.2	1602 7.5	1455 6.8	1313 5.2	1752 3.9	1549 2.7	1544 1.9	1427 1.3	2009 0.7		
2359 2.1	2247 2.2	2203 2.5	2009 2.2	2339 9.4	2145 5.4	2200 4.2	2106 2.9			
0524 6.1	0433 7.3	0335 6.7	0153 5.0	0618 4.2	0410 2.8	0403 2.0	0246 1.5	0159 0.4	**2**	**TH**
1231 2.1	1113 2.5	1033 2.7	0833 2.5	1200 9.4	1006 5.5	1024 4.3	0924 3.0	0843 0.8		
1754 6.0	1656 7.1	1551 6.5	1408 5.0	1846 4.2	1645 2.8	1640 2.0	1530 1.4	1445 0.4		
	2343 2.5	2258 2.7	2105 2.4		2248 5.3	2312 4.2	2208 2.9	2116 0.7		
0102 2.3	0533 7.1	0440 6.5	0254 4.9	0042 9.0	0510 2.9	0504 2.1	0357 1.5	0314 0.4	**3**	**F**
0624 5.9	1217 2.7	1133 2.8	0936 2.6	0722 4.5	1112 5.4	1139 4.2	1032 2.9	0948 0.8		
1336 2.2	1803 6.9	1705 6.3	1515 4.8	1312 9.1	1749 2.8	1745 2.0	1641 1.4	1605 0.3		
1902 5.8			2210 2.4	2000 4.4			2321 2.9	2228 0.8		
0207 2.3	0053 2.6	0003 2.7	0401 4.9	0203 9.0	0000 5.3	0026 4.2	0512 1.5	0430 0.3	**4**	**SA**
0737 5.9	0644 7.1	0603 6.5	1046 2.5	0842 4.4	0618 2.8	0612 2.1	1148 3.0	1054 0.8		
1440 2.1	1333 2.6	1241 2.7	1625 4.9	1434 9.2	1227 5.5	1254 4.3	1747 1.3	1712 0.3		
2018 5.9	1920 7.0	1832 6.4	2318 2.3	2122 4.4	1900 2.7	1852 2.0		2334 0.8		
0312 2.1	0209 2.5	0113 2.6	0509 5.1	0319 9.4	0112 5.6	0131 4.4	0030 3.1	0530 0.3	**5**	**SU**
0850 6.0	0759 7.4	0718 6.7	1155 2.3	1000 4.0	0728 2.6	0718 1.9	0618 1.3	1154 0.8		
1545 1.9	1448 2.3	1351 2.5	1734 5.1	1548 9.7	1339 5.7	1358 4.5	1256 3.1	1806 0.2		
2125 6.1	2034 7.4	1945 6.7		2235 3.6	2004 2.4	1954 1.8	1845 1.1			
0416 1.9	0319 2.1	0222 2.3	0024 2.1	0424 10.2	0215 6.0	0227 4.7	0129 3.3	0031 0.8	**6**	**M**
0951 6.3	0905 7.9	0814 7.1	0611 5.4	1108 3.2	0830 2.2	0818 1.7	0715 1.0	0622 0.2		
1647 1.7	1553 1.8	1458 2.1	1257 1.9	1650 10.5	1439 6.1	1454 4.8	1355 3.3	1248 0.9		
2221 6.5	2136 8.0	2041 7.1	1837 5.4	2338 2.9	2101 2.0	2048 1.6	1936 0.9	1854 0.2		
0517 1.6	0420 1.7	0327 2.0	0123 1.8	0520 11.0	0308 6.4	0318 5.0	0221 3.5	0122 0.9	**7**	**TU**
1045 6.7	1001 8.4	0853 7.4	0705 5.7	1209 2.5	0926 1.8	0912 1.4	0805 0.8	0709 0.2		
1747 1.4	1651 1.3	1602 1.7	1354 1.5	1745 11.2	1532 6.5	1545 5.0	1448 3.5	1339 0.9		
2311 6.8	2230 8.5	2127 7.4	1932 5.7		2153 1.6	2138 1.3	2024 0.7	1939 0.1		
0616 1.4	0517 1.3	0430 1.6	0218 1.5	0036 2.3	0357 6.8	0406 5.3	0310 3.8	0211 0.9	**8**	**W**
1134 7.0	1052 8.9	0921 7.7	0755 6.1	0612 11.8	1018 1.3	1002 1.2	0853 0.6	0754 0.1		
1845 1.2	1747 0.9	1702 1.3	1445 1.1	1306 1.8	1621 6.9	1633 5.2	1536 3.7	1428 1.0		
2359 7.1	2318 9.0	2206 7.6	2023 6.0	1837 11.9	2242 1.2	2226 1.1	2111 0.5	2024 0.0		
0712 1.1	0612 0.9	0528 1.3	0308 1.1	0132 1.7	0445 7.2	0453 5.5	0357 3.9	0258 1.0	**9**	**TH**
1222 7.2	1140 9.3	0954 7.9	0844 6.4	0701 12.4	1107 1.0	1050 0.9	0939 0.4	0839 0.1		
1940 1.0	1840 0.6	1757 0.9	1535 0.8	1400 1.2	1709 7.1	1718 5.4	1624 3.8	1516 1.0		
		2242 7.8	2111 6.3	1926 12.4	2330 0.9	2312 1.0	2156 0.4	2108 0.0	●	
0047 7.3	0006 9.3	0621 1.1	0357 0.9	0225 1.2	0533 7.5	0539 5.6	0443 4.1	0345 1.0	**10**	**F**
0806 0.9	0705 0.6	1033 8.0	0930 6.6	0748 12.8	1156 0.7	1137 0.8	1025 0.3	0924 0.0		
1311 7.4	1227 9.5	1846 0.7	1623 0.5	1451 0.7	1756 7.3	1804 5.4	1710 3.9	1604 1.0		
2031 0.8	1931 0.3		2158 6.4	2012 12.6		2358 0.9	2242 0.4	2153 0.0		
0135 7.4	0052 9.5	0033 7.9	0445 0.8	0314 1.0	0018 0.8	0625 5.7	0528 4.2	0432 1.0	**11**	**SA**
0854 0.8	0754 0.4	0708 0.9	1017 6.7	0833 12.6	0619 7.6	1224 0.7	1112 0.3	1010 0.1		
1400 7.4	1312 9.6	1201 8.0	1709 0.4	1539 0.6	1244 0.6	1851 5.4	1755 3.9	1653 1.0		
2118 0.7	2018 0.1	1931 0.5	2244 6.4	2057 12.6	1842 7.3		2327 0.4	2238 0.0		
0223 7.4	0137 9.5	0124 8.0	0530 0.8	0400 1.0	0105 0.8	0045 0.9	0613 4.1	0521 1.0	**12**	**SU**
0939 0.7	0840 0.4	0752 0.6	1102 6.6	0917 12.0	0706 7.5	0712 5.6	1158 0.4	1058 0.1		
1450 7.4	1357 9.5	1229 8.0	1756 0.5	1624 0.7	1331 0.7	1312 0.8	1841 3.8	1743 1.0		
2202 0.8	2103 0.1	2014 0.6	2329 6.3	2140 12.4	1928 7.1	1938 5.2		2325 0.1		
0312 7.3	0221 9.4	0212 8.0	0617 0.9	0442 1.2	0153 1.0	0133 0.9	0015 0.6	0610 1.0	**13**	**M**
1022 0.7	0924 0.4	0834 0.9	1148 6.5	0959 12.5	0752 7.3	0800 5.4	0700 4.0	1148 0.1		
1540 7.2	1442 9.3	1423 8.0	1842 0.8	1706 1.1	1419 1.0	1400 0.9	1247 0.6	1835 0.9		
2245 0.9	2145 0.3	2054 0.7		2221 11.9	2015 6.8	2028 5.0	1928 3.7			
0402 7.1	0306 9.1	0258 7.8	0015 6.1	0523 1.8	0241 1.3	0224 1.1	0105 0.8	0016 0.1	**14**	**TU**
1107 0.9	1006 0.7	0915 1.2	0704 1.2	1042 11.8	0840 6.9	0853 5.2	0748 3.8	0702 0.9		
1632 7.0	1527 8.9	1508 7.7	1234 6.2	1748 1.8	1508 1.4	1451 1.1	1340 0.8	1244 0.2		
2331 1.2	2228 0.6	2136 1.1	1930 1.1	2307 11.3	2104 6.4	2124 4.8	2020 3.5	1931 0.9		
0455 6.9	0353 8.7	0343 7.6	0103 5.8	0605 2.5	0332 1.7	0318 1.3	0200 1.0	0114 0.2	**15**	**W**
1156 1.2	1050 1.1	0958 1.6	0754 1.6	1129 11.1	0931 6.5	0951 4.9	0842 3.6	0758 0.9		
1728 6.7	1618 8.4	1554 7.4	1324 5.8	1832 2.6	1600 1.8	1547 1.4	1439 1.1	1351 0.2		
	2313 1.1	2220 1.5	2021 1.5	2357 10.5	2158 6.0	2227 4.6	2118 3.3	2033 0.8		

● ● Time Zone -0100. For UT subtract 1 hour. For European summer time (shaded) 30/3-26/10 add 1 hour ● ●

JANUARY 1997 TIDE TABLES JANUARY 1997

	CALAIS	DIEPPE	LE HAVRE	CHERBOURG	ST MALO	BREST	POINTE DE GRAVE	LISBOA	GIBRALTAR
	Time m	Time m	Time m	Time m	Time m	Time m	Time m	Time m	Time m
16 TH	0023 1.5 0554 6.6 1253 1.5 1831 6.3	0446 8.2 1139 1.5 1717 7.8	0431 7.3 1047 2.0 1645 7.0 2312 2.0	0156 5.5 0850 1.9 1421 5.4 2119 1.9	0652 3.2 1225 10.3 1924 3.3	0428 2.1 1030 6.0 1659 2.2 2303 5.7	0417 1.5 1058 4.6 1649 1.6 2341 4.4	0307 1.2 0900 0.8 1549 1.3 2227 3.2	0225 0.3 0900 0.8 1518 0.3 2143 0.8
17 F	0124 1.9 0700 6.3 1400 1.8 1939 6.1	0006 1.6 0551 7.7 1240 2.0 1832 7.4	0524 7.0 1148 2.3 1747 6.8	0257 5.2 0956 2.2 1529 5.1 2228 2.2	0100 9.9 0751 3.7 1336 9.6 2029 3.7	0533 2.4 1139 5.7 1807 2.5	0524 1.7 1212 4.5 1758 1.8	0426 1.4 1059 3.2 1705 1.3 2342 3.2	0351 0.3 1008 0.8 1645 0.3 2256 0.8
18 SA	0236 2.1 0809 6.1 1515 2.0 2048 6.0	0116 2.1 0709 7.5 1404 2.2 1948 7.4	0020 2.4 0627 6.8 1303 2.5 1859 6.6	0410 5.0 1113 2.3 1651 4.9 2345 2.2	0215 9.5 0904 4.0 1457 9.4 2144 3.8	0020 5.6 0647 2.6 1258 5.6 1921 2.5	0056 4.4 0637 1.8 1325 4.4 1910 1.8	0544 1.4 1215 3.2 1813 1.3	0505 0.3 1117 0.8 1747 0.3
19 SU	0353 2.1 0917 6.1 1630 1.9 2153 6.1	0240 2.1 0819 7.6 1521 2.0 2054 7.6	0136 2.5 0739 6.8 1418 2.3 2021 6.7	0534 5.1 1230 2.2 1812 5.0	0333 9.6 1023 3.8 1614 9.7 2255 3.5	0136 5.6 0759 2.5 1409 5.8 2027 2.4	0203 4.5 0747 1.8 1429 4.5 2014 1.8	0052 3.2 0650 1.3 1321 3.2 1909 1.2	0002 0.8 0602 0.3 1218 0.8 1835 0.2
20 M	0500 1.9 1021 6.2 1730 1.7 2252 6.2	0348 1.9 0920 7.8 1621 1.9 2151 7.9	0246 2.3 0854 6.9 1523 2.1 2133 6.9	0056 2.1 0641 5.3 1332 1.9 1912 5.2	0441 10.0 1130 3.4 1716 10.1 2354 3.2	0239 5.9 0900 2.2 1506 6.0 2121 2.1	0259 4.6 0847 1.6 1522 4.6 2106 1.6	0150 3.4 0742 1.2 1415 3.3 1954 1.1	0057 0.8 0647 0.2 1309 0.9 1915 0.2
21 TU	0556 1.7 1116 6.4 1821 1.6 2341 6.4	0443 1.7 1012 8.1 1712 1.4 2239 8.2	0347 2.1 0953 7.1 1619 1.8 2224 7.1	0151 1.9 0731 5.5 1421 1.6 1957 5.5	0536 10.5 1225 2.9 1806 10.5	0328 6.2 0950 2.0 1551 6.2 2206 1.9	0345 4.8 0936 1.5 1605 4.7 2151 1.5	0239 3.5 0825 1.0 1501 3.4 2033 1.0	0144 0.9 0727 0.2 1354 0.9 1951 0.2
22 W	0640 1.5 1200 6.6 1901 1.5	0531 1.5 1057 8.4 1757 1.2 2321 8.4	0439 1.9 1036 7.3 1708 1.6 2304 7.3	0237 1.7 0812 5.7 1503 1.4 2037 5.7	0044 2.8 0622 10.9 1312 2.6 1849 10.8	0411 6.4 1033 1.7 1632 6.4 2247 1.7	0424 4.9 1018 1.4 1642 4.8 2230 1.4	0321 3.6 0902 0.9 1542 3.5 2109 0.9	0224 0.9 0803 0.2 1433 0.9 2025 0.1
23 TH O	0018 6.6 0718 1.5 1236 6.7 1935 1.4	0613 1.4 1136 8.6 1836 1.1 2359 8.6	0525 1.8 1105 7.4 1750 1.3 2334 7.4	0317 1.5 0850 5.9 1540 1.3 2113 5.8	0127 2.6 0701 11.2 1353 2.4 1927 11.0	0449 6.6 1112 1.6 1708 6.5 2324 1.6	0458 5.0 1057 1.3 1714 4.9 2306 1.3	0359 3.7 0936 0.8 1620 3.5 2142 0.8	0302 0.9 0838 0.2 1509 0.9 2059 0.1
24 F	0051 6.7 0750 1.4 1307 6.8 2006 1.4	0651 1.3 1213 8.7 1911 1.1	0604 1.7 1048 7.5 1825 1.5 2347 7.5	0352 1.4 0924 6.0 1614 1.2 2147 5.9	0206 2.4 0739 11.3 1430 2.2 2002 11.1	0524 6.7 1148 1.5 1742 6.6 2358 1.5	0528 5.1 1132 1.2 1743 4.9 2341 1.2	0435 3.7 1009 0.8 1655 3.5 2215 0.8	0336 0.9 0912 0.1 1544 0.9 2133 0.1
25 SA	0121 6.9 0821 1.3 1338 6.9 2035 1.4	0035 8.7 0723 1.3 1248 8.8 1942 1.0	0637 1.7 1115 7.7 1856 1.5 2352 7.6	0425 1.4 0957 6.1 1646 1.2 2219 5.9	0242 2.3 0812 11.4 1502 2.1 2033 11.2	0556 6.8 1221 1.5 1813 6.6	0557 5.1 1206 1.2 1812 4.9	0509 3.7 1041 0.7 1728 3.5 2248 0.8	0410 0.9 0946 0.1 1618 0.9 2205 0.1
26 SU	0152 7.0 0851 1.3 1409 7.0 2104 1.4	0108 8.7 0752 1.2 1320 8.7 2009 1.1	0707 1.7 1148 7.7 1924 1.5	0457 1.4 1027 6.1 1716 1.2 2249 5.9	0314 2.2 0842 11.5 1532 2.1 2102 11.2	0030 1.5 0626 6.8 1252 1.6 1843 6.6	0014 1.2 0626 5.1 1238 1.2 1842 4.9	0542 3.7 1114 0.7 1800 3.5 2321 0.8	0442 0.9 1020 0.1 1651 0.9 2237 0.1
27 M	0223 7.0 0919 1.3 1439 7.0 2132 1.4	0139 8.6 0819 1.2 1351 8.6 2036 1.1	0021 7.6 0736 1.7 1223 7.7 1951 1.5	0527 1.5 1057 6.0 1747 1.3 2319 5.8	0343 2.3 0911 11.4 1600 2.2 2129 11.1	0101 1.6 0656 6.7 1323 1.7 1913 6.4	0047 1.2 0655 5.0 1310 1.3 1913 4.8	0612 3.6 1146 0.8 1830 3.4 2355 0.9	0515 0.9 1054 0.2 1725 0.9 2310 0.2
28 TU	0254 7.0 0948 1.4 1509 6.9 2200 1.5	0210 8.5 0848 1.3 1421 8.5 2104 1.3	0051 7.6 0805 1.7 1256 7.6 2021 1.7	0558 1.6 1126 5.9 1818 1.5 2348 5.7	0412 2.5 0938 11.3 1628 2.4 2156 10.8	0133 1.8 0727 6.5 1355 1.9 1945 6.2	0120 1.3 0727 4.9 1343 1.4 1946 4.7	0642 3.5 1221 0.9 1901 3.3	0549 0.9 1128 0.2 1801 0.8 2343 0.2
29 W	0324 6.9 1018 1.5 1541 6.8 2234 1.7	0240 8.4 0918 1.5 1452 8.2 2136 1.5	0122 7.4 0836 1.9 1329 7.4 2052 1.8	0631 1.8 1156 5.7 1851 1.7	0441 2.7 1006 11.0 1656 2.8 2225 10.5	0206 2.0 0759 6.3 1430 2.1 2020 6.0	0154 1.4 0800 4.7 1419 1.5 2023 4.5	0031 1.0 0712 3.4 1257 1.0 1933 3.2	0626 0.8 1205 0.8 1841 0.8
30 TH	0357 6.8 1055 1.7 1617 6.6 2315 1.9	0313 8.1 0952 1.8 1527 7.9 2212 1.9	0155 7.2 0911 2.1 1406 7.2 2130 2.1	0021 5.5 0707 2.0 1230 5.5 1930 2.0	0510 3.1 1039 10.6 1727 3.3 2300 10.1	0245 2.2 0836 6.0 1509 2.4 2101 5.7	0233 1.6 0839 4.6 1500 1.7 2108 4.3	0111 1.1 0745 3.2 1340 1.2 2012 3.1	0021 0.2 0707 0.8 1248 0.3 1928 0.7
31 F	0436 6.5 1143 1.9 1701 6.3	0351 7.8 1034 2.1 1611 7.5 2258 2.3	0236 7.0 0953 2.4 1453 6.8 2217 2.4	0100 5.3 0750 2.2 1314 5.2 2015 2.2	0545 3.6 1119 10.0 1806 3.8 2348 9.6	0329 2.5 0919 5.7 1558 2.6 2152 5.5	0319 1.8 0928 4.3 1550 1.9 2209 4.2	0159 1.3 0828 3.1 1433 1.3 2104 3.0	0106 0.3 0757 0.8 1344 0.3 2027 0.7

•• Time Zone -0100. For UT subtract 1 hour. For European summer time (shaded) 30/3-26/10 add 1 hour ••

FRANCE, SPAIN, PORTUGAL & GIBRALTAR Time Zone -0100
Calais * Dieppe * Le Havre * Cherbourg * St Malo * Brest * Pointe de Grave * Lisboa * Gibraltar
FEBRUARY 1997 TIDE TABLES FEBRUARY 1997

	CALAIS	DIEPPE	LE HAVRE	CHERBOURG	ST MALO	BREST	POINTE DE GRAVE	LISBOA	GIBRALTAR
	Time m	Time m	Time m	Time m	Time m	Time m	Time m	Time m	Time m
1 SA	0010 2.1	0440 7.4	0331 6.7	0151 5.0	0635 4.1	0424 2.7	0415 1.9	0302 1.4	0209 0.3
	0527 6.2	1129 2.4	1046 2.6	0845 2.4	1215 9.4	1017 5.5	1039 4.2	0929 3.0	0901 0.7
	1244 2.1	1709 7.1	1600 6.5	1415 4.9	1906 4.2	1658 2.8	1653 2.0	1542 1.4	1508 0.3
	1800 6.0		2315 2.7	2116 2.4		2301 5.4	2332 4.1	2217 2.9	2142 0.7
2 SU	0116 2.3	0000 2.6	0452 6.4	0300 4.9	0058 9.1	0530 2.8	0524 2.0	0421 1.5	0346 0.3
	0635 6.0	0548 7.1	1151 2.8	0954 2.5	0748 4.4	1133 5.4	1209 4.2	1052 2.9	1017 0.7
	1351 2.2	1241 2.6	1734 6.4	1533 4.8	1339 9.1	1810 2.8	1806 2.0	1702 1.4	1646 0.3
	1920 5.8	1829 6.9		2230 2.4	2030 4.4			2342 3.0	2303 0.7
3 M	0225 2.3	0121 2.7	0026 2.8	0418 4.9	0232 9.1	0024 5.4	0054 4.3	0542 1.3	0512 0.3
	0801 5.9	0713 7.1	0626 6.5	1113 2.4	0918 4.2	0646 2.7	0639 1.9	1221 3.0	1133 0.8
	1502 2.3	1409 2.5	1306 2.7	1655 4.9	1513 9.3	1300 5.5	1330 4.3	1814 1.2	1754 0.2
	2045 6.0	1957 7.1	1906 6.6	2350 2.3	2200 4.0	1928 2.6	1920 1.9		
4 TU	0337 2.1	0247 2.4	0145 2.6	0536 5.1	0356 9.7	0143 5.8	0202 4.6	0059 3.2	0013 0.8
	0919 6.2	0833 7.5	0736 6.9	1229 2.0	1042 3.6	0802 2.3	0750 1.7	0650 1.1	0613 0.2
	1615 1.9	1527 2.0	1427 2.3	1814 5.2	1630 10.0	1416 5.9	1435 4.6	1333 3.2	1237 0.8
	2154 6.3	2110 7.7	2012 6.9		2318 3.3	2037 2.1	2024 1.6	1915 1.0	1846 0.1
5 W	0449 1.8	0359 1.9	0303 2.2	0101 1.9	0503 10.6	0247 6.2	0300 4.9	0200 3.5	0111 0.8
	1021 6.6	0939 8.1	0825 7.3	0644 5.5	1153 2.7	0906 1.8	0851 1.4	0747 0.8	0703 0.1
	1725 1.6	1633 1.4	1542 1.8	1334 1.5	1732 10.9	1515 6.4	1530 4.9	1430 3.5	1332 0.9
	2251 6.8	2209 8.3	2103 7.3	1917 5.6		2135 1.6	2120 1.3	2008 0.7	1933 0.1
6 TH	0557 1.4	0500 1.3	0414 1.7	0201 1.5	0023 2.4	0342 6.8	0351 5.2	0253 3.8	0201 0.9
	1116 7.0	1033 8.8	0904 7.7	0741 5.9	0559 11.6	1002 1.3	0945 1.1	0838 0.5	0749 0.1
	1830 1.2	1732 0.9	1648 1.3	1430 1.0	1254 1.7	1607 6.8	1619 5.2	1521 3.7	1422 1.0
	2342 7.1	2301 8.9	2157 7.7	2010 6.0	1826 11.8	2227 1.2	2209 1.0	2057 0.5	2017 -0.0
7 F	0659 1.0	0558 0.8	0515 1.2	0254 1.0	0121 1.6	0431 7.2	0439 5.5	0341 4.0	0248 1.0
	1208 7.3	1124 9.3	0940 8.0	0831 6.3	0650 12.4	1053 0.9	1035 0.8	0925 0.3	0833 -0.0
	1928 0.9	1827 0.4	1743 0.8	1521 0.6	1348 0.9	1656 7.2	1705 5.4	1609 3.9	1509 1.0
		2349 9.4	2323 7.9	2059 6.3	1915 12.5	2315 0.8	2257 0.8	2142 0.4	2100 -0.0 ●
8 SA	0032 7.4	0651 0.4	0607 0.8	0343 0.7	0212 0.9	0518 7.6	0524 5.7	0427 4.2	0335 1.0
	0754 0.7	1212 9.6	1115 8.1	0918 6.6	0737 13.0	1142 0.5	1122 0.6	1011 0.2	0917 -0.0
	1257 7.5	1917 -0.0	1832 0.4	1609 0.3	1439 0.3	1742 7.5	1750 5.5	1654 4.0	1556 1.0
	2019 0.6			2145 6.5	2001 12.9		2343 0.6	2227 0.3	2142 -0.1
9 SU	0121 7.6	0036 9.7	0021 8.1	0430 0.5	0301 0.4	0003 0.5	0610 5.7	0512 4.3	0420 1.0
	0842 0.5	0739 0.1	0654 0.6	1003 6.8	0821 13.3	0605 7.8	1208 0.5	1056 0.2	1001 -0.0
	1346 7.6	1257 9.8	1136 8.2	1654 0.2	1526 0.0	1228 0.4	1834 5.5	1738 4.0	1642 1.0
	2104 0.5	2003 -0.2	1916 0.2	2228 6.6	2044 13.0	1827 7.5		2312 0.3	2225 -0.0
10 M	0208 7.6	0120 9.8	0111 8.2	0515 0.5	0345 0.3	0049 0.5	0029 0.6	0557 4.3	0505 1.0
	0924 0.4	0824 -0.0	0736 0.5	1047 6.8	0903 13.2	0649 7.7	0654 5.7	1140 0.3	1045 -0.0
	1434 7.6	1340 9.8	1203 8.2	1739 0.3	1609 0.1	1313 0.5	1254 0.6	1821 4.0	1728 1.0
	2145 0.6	2045 -0.2	1957 0.3	2311 6.5	2125 12.8	1910 7.4	1918 5.4	2357 0.4	2308 -0.0
11 TU	0254 7.5	0203 9.7	0157 8.2	0559 0.6	0427 0.6	0135 0.7	0115 0.7	0641 4.1	0551 1.0
	1005 0.5	0905 0.1	0817 0.6	1129 6.6	0944 12.8	0733 7.5	0740 5.5	1225 0.5	1130 0.0
	1521 7.4	1423 9.6	1411 8.2	1821 0.6	1648 0.6	1358 0.8	1339 0.7	1906 3.8	1815 0.9
	2224 0.7	2124 0.0	2036 0.5	2353 6.3	2204 12.4	1954 7.0	2003 5.1		2353 0.1
12 W	0340 7.4	0245 9.4	0239 8.0	0642 1.0	0505 1.2	0220 1.0	0202 0.9	0042 0.7	0638 0.9
	1045 0.7	0944 0.3	0854 0.9	1212 6.3	1024 12.2	0817 7.1	0827 5.2	0727 3.9	1217 0.1
	1608 7.2	1506 9.1	1452 7.9	1905 1.0	1726 1.4	1444 1.2	1427 1.0	1312 0.8	1905 0.9
	2306 1.0	2203 0.4	2113 1.0		2241 11.6	2037 6.6	2052 4.8	1952 3.6	
13 TH	0429 7.1	0327 8.9	0318 7.7	0036 6.0	0542 2.0	0307 1.5	0252 1.1	0132 0.9	0042 0.1
	1129 1.1	1024 0.8	0933 1.4	0727 1.4	1105 11.3	0903 6.5	0919 4.8	0815 3.6	0728 0.9
	1658 6.8	1550 8.5	1531 7.5	1257 5.8	1805 2.3	1531 1.8	1518 1.3	1403 1.1	1311 0.2
	2351 1.4	2244 1.0	2151 1.5	1950 1.5	2327 10.8	2125 6.1	2149 4.5	2044 3.3	2000 0.8
14 F	0522 6.7	0414 8.3	0357 7.3	0122 5.6	0621 2.9	0358 2.0	0348 1.5	0230 1.2	0143 0.2
	1218 1.5	1106 1.4	1014 1.9	0816 1.9	1152 10.3	0955 6.0	1021 4.5	0913 3.3	0825 0.8
	1756 6.3	1642 7.8	1612 7.0	1348 5.4	1848 3.2	1624 2.3	1615 1.7	1505 1.3	1427 0.3
		2329 1.7	2236 2.2	2040 2.0		2222 5.6	2300 4.3	2147 3.1	2106 0.7
15 SA	0045 1.9	0512 7.6	0439 6.9	0216 5.2	0021 9.9	0457 2.5	0451 1.8	0345 1.4	0317 0.3
	0624 6.2	1158 2.1	1108 2.5	0915 2.3	0711 3.7	1100 5.5	1138 4.2	1024 3.0	0935 0.7
	1318 2.0	1755 7.2	1706 6.6	1449 4.9	1257 9.4	1730 2.7	1722 1.9	1622 1.5	1621 0.3
	1902 6.0		2337 2.7	2144 2.4	1945 4.0	2339 5.3		2306 3.0	2226 0.7

● ● Time Zone -0100. For UT subtract 1 hour. For European summer time (shaded) 30/3-26/10 add 1 hour ● ●

FEBRUARY 1997 TIDE TABLES FEBRUARY 1997

	CALAIS		DIEPPE		LE HAVRE		CHERBOURG		ST MALO		BREST		POINTE DE GRAVE		LISBOA		GIBRALTAR	
	Time	m	Time	m	Time	m	Time	m	Time	m	Time	m	Time	m	Time	m	Time	m
16 SU	0150	2.3	0030	2.3	0536	6.5	0325	4.8	0134	9.1	0613	2.8	0023	4.1	0515	1.5	0453	0.3
	0735	5.9	0632	7.1	1224	2.8	1032	2.5	0821	4.3	1226	5.3	0606	1.9	1147	3.0	1055	0.7
	1431	2.3	1321	2.5	1817	6.3	1612	4.7	1426	8.9	1850	2.8	1300	4.1	1745	1.5	1738	0.3
	2014	5.7	1918	6.9			2308	2.6	2104	4.4			1839	2.0			2346	0.7
17 M	0312	2.4	0205	2.6	0100	2.9	0457	4.8	0305	9.0	0109	5.3	0140	4.2	0026	3.1	0557	0.3
	0847	5.8	0751	7.0	0649	6.4	1203	2.4	0954	4.4	0736	2.7	0724	1.9	0632	1.4	1209	0.7
	1557	2.3	1453	2.5	1351	2.8	1751	4.7	1557	9.0	1350	5.4	1412	4.2	1301	3.0	1830	0.3
	2124	5.8	2032	7.1	1946	6.3			2233	4.2	2006	2.7	1951	2.0	1850	1.4		
18 TU	0433	2.3	0323	2.4	0221	2.8	0034	2.4	0425	9.3	0221	5.6	0241	4.4	0130	3.2	0048	0.8
	0957	5.9	0859	7.3	0818	6.5	0620	4.9	1117	3.9	0842	2.5	0829	1.8	0728	1.3	0644	0.7
	1708	2.1	1558	2.1	1502	2.5	1314	2.2	1705	9.5	1450	5.7	1506	4.4	1358	3.1	1305	0.8
	2230	6.0	2133	7.4	2110	6.6	1855	5.0	2340	3.7	2103	2.4	2048	1.8	1938	1.3	1909	0.2
19 W	0535	2.0	0422	2.1	0326	2.5	0134	2.1	0523	9.9	0312	5.9	0327	4.6	0219	3.4	0136	0.8
	1057	6.2	0954	7.7	0929	6.8	0713	5.2	1213	3.3	0933	2.2	0919	1.6	0810	1.1	0721	0.2
	1800	1.8	1651	1.7	1558	2.1	1403	1.8	1754	10.1	1535	6.0	1548	4.5	1443	3.3	1348	0.8
	2321	6.2	2222	7.8	2204	6.9	1940	5.3			2148	2.1	2133	1.6	2017	1.1	1942	0.2
20 TH	0620	1.7	0510	1.7	0418	2.2	0219	1.8	0029	3.1	0354	6.2	0406	4.7	0301	3.5	0214	0.8
	1142	6.4	1039	8.1	1013	7.1	0754	5.5	0601	10.5	1015	1.9	1000	1.4	0845	1.0	0754	0.2
	1840	1.6	1735	1.4	1645	1.8	1442	1.5	1256	2.8	1613	6.3	1622	4.7	1522	3.4	1423	0.9
			2303	8.2	2242	7.2	2018	5.5	1833	10.6	2227	1.8	2211	1.4	2051	0.9	2013	0.1
21 F	0000	6.5	0551	1.5	0501	1.9	0256	1.6	0109	2.7	0430	6.5	0437	4.9	0339	3.6	0247	0.9
	0657	1.5	1118	8.4	1039	7.3	0830	5.8	0645	10.9	1052	1.6	1036	1.3	0916	0.8	0825	0.1
	1218	6.6	1813	1.1	1724	1.6	1518	1.3	1333	2.4	1648	6.5	1652	4.8	1558	3.5	1455	0.9
	1914	1.4	2339	8.5	2310	7.4	2053	5.8	1909	10.9	2303	1.6	2246	1.2	2124	0.8	2043	0.1
22 SA ○	0033	6.8	0627	1.3	0539	1.7	0330	1.4	0146	2.3	0503	6.7	0507	5.0	0413	3.7	0318	0.9
	0730	1.3	1153	8.6	1027	7.5	0903	6.0	0719	11.3	1125	1.5	1109	1.1	0948	0.7	0855	0.1
	1248	6.8	1848	1.0	1759	1.4	1550	1.1	1408	2.1	1720	6.6	1721	4.9	1632	3.6	1526	0.9
	1946	1.3			2324	7.5	2124	5.9	1941	11.2	2336	1.4	2318	1.1	2155	0.7	2112	0.1
23 SU	0102	6.9	0012	8.7	0612	1.5	0402	1.3	0221	2.1	0533	6.8	0535	5.1	0446	3.7	0347	0.9
	0803	1.2	0700	1.1	1051	7.7	0934	6.1	0751	11.5	1157	1.4	1141	1.1	1018	0.7	0926	0.1
	1318	7.0	1226	8.8	1830	1.3	1621	1.0	1440	1.9	1750	6.7	1750	5.0	1703	3.6	1557	0.9
	2018	1.2	1918	0.9	2325	7.6	2155	6.0	2011	11.4			2350	1.1	2227	0.7	2142	0.1
24 M	0131	7.1	0045	8.8	0643	1.5	0433	1.2	0253	1.9	0006	1.4	0603	5.1	0517	3.7	0416	0.9
	0834	1.1	0730	1.0	1120	7.8	1003	6.2	0820	11.7	0603	6.8	1212	1.1	1048	0.6	0956	0.1
	1346	7.0	1258	8.9	1900	1.3	1651	1.0	1512	1.8	1227	1.4	1818	5.0	1734	3.6	1627	0.9
	2048	1.2	1948	0.9	2346	7.7	2224	6.0	2039	11.5	1819	6.7			2258	0.7	2211	0.1
25 TU	0159	7.1	0116	8.8	0713	1.4	0503	1.2	0325	1.8	0037	1.4	0021	1.1	0546	3.7	0446	0.9
	0903	1.2	0800	1.0	1148	7.8	1031	6.1	0848	11.7	0632	6.8	0632	5.1	1120	0.7	1027	0.1
	1413	7.1	1329	8.8	1930	1.3	1721	1.1	1542	1.8	1257	1.5	1242	1.1	1803	3.5	1659	0.9
	2115	1.3	2016	0.9			2251	6.0	2106	11.5	1848	6.7	1848	4.9	2331	0.7	2240	0.1
26 W	0225	7.1	0146	8.8	0008	7.7	0534	1.3	0356	1.8	0109	1.5	0053	1.1	0615	3.6	0518	0.9
	0930	1.2	0828	1.1	0743	1.5	1058	6.1	0915	11.6	0702	6.7	0701	5.0	1152	0.7	1057	0.1
	1439	7.1	1359	8.7	1215	7.8	1753	1.3	1612	2.0	1328	1.6	1313	1.2	1831	3.5	1733	0.9
	2140	1.4	2045	1.1	2000	1.5	2318	5.9	2133	11.3	1919	6.5	1918	4.8			2309	0.1
27 TH	0253	7.1	0215	8.6	0033	7.6	0606	1.5	0425	2.2	0142	1.7	0126	1.2	0005	0.8	0551	0.8
	0956	1.4	0857	1.2	0812	1.6	1127	5.9	0944	11.4	0733	6.5	0732	4.8	0642	3.5	1130	0.1
	1509	7.0	1428	8.5	1245	7.6	1824	1.5	1639	2.4	1402	1.8	1348	1.3	1227	0.9	1808	0.8
	2209	1.5	2113	1.4	2029	1.7	2347	5.7	2200	11.0	1951	6.3	1951	4.7	1901	3.3	2342	0.2
28 F	0324	7.0	0245	8.4	0103	7.4	0640	1.7	0453	2.7	0218	1.9	0203	1.4	0042	1.0	0627	0.8
	1028	1.5	0927	1.5	0843	1.8	1159	5.7	1014	11.0	0807	6.2	0807	4.6	0714	3.3	1206	0.2
	1543	6.8	1500	8.2	1321	7.4	1859	1.8	1707	3.0	1439	2.1	1427	1.5	1306	1.0	1848	0.8
	2245	1.7	2145	1.7	2102	2.0			2233	10.6	2029	6.0	2031	4.5	1936	3.2		

• • Time Zone -0100. For UT subtract 1 hour. For European summer time (shaded) 30/3-26/10 add 1 hour • •

FRANCE, SPAIN, PORTUGAL & GIBRALTAR Time Zone -0100
Calais * Dieppe * Le Havre * Cherbourg * St Malo * Brest * Pointe de Grave * Lisboa * Gibraltar
MARCH 1997 TIDE TABLES MARCH 1997

CALAIS	DIEPPE	LE HAVRE	CHERBOURG	ST MALO	BREST	POINTE DE GRAVE	LISBOA	GIBRALTAR	
Time m	Time m	Time m	Time m	Time m	Time m	Time m	Time m	Time m	
0402 6.8	0320 8.1	0144 7.2	0021 5.5	0524 3.2	0300 2.2	0248 1.6	0127 1.1	0019 0.2	**1 SA**
1110 1.8	1005 1.9	0920 2.1	0719 2.0	1051 10.4	0847 5.9	0851 4.4	0754 3.2	0712 0.7	
1626 6.5	1539 7.8	1407 7.1	1239 5.4	1740 3.5	1525 2.4	1515 1.7	1354 1.2	1251 0.2	
2333 2.0	2227 2.1	2143 2.3	1941 2.1	2314 10.0	2115 5.7	2126 4.3	2024 3.1	1939 0.7	
0450 6.4	0403 7.6	0239 6.8	0108 5.2	0604 3.8	0351 2.5	0342 1.8	0224 1.3	0110 0.3	**2 SU**
1205 2.0	1054 2.3	1008 2.5	0809 2.2	1139 9.7	0940 5.6	0957 4.2	0851 3.0	0808 0.7	
1721 6.2	1632 7.3	1513 6.6	1336 5.0	1829 4.1	1623 2.7	1615 1.9	1500 1.4	1356 0.3	
	2324 2.5	2324 2.5	2238 2.6	2037 2.4		2221 5.5	2248 4.1	2133 3.0	2045 0.7	
0035 2.2	0506 7.2	0400 6.5	0215 5.0	0014 9.3	0457 2.7	0450 1.9	0343 1.4	0232 0.3	**3 M**
0555 6.1	1203 2.6	1110 2.7	0916 2.4	0708 4.3	1056 5.4	1136 4.1	1016 2.9	0924 0.7	
1312 2.2	1751 6.9	1655 6.4	1457 4.8	1257 9.0	1736 2.8	1731 2.0	1624 1.4	1546 0.3	
1840 5.9		2348 2.9	2154 2.5	1948 4.6	2348 5.4		2306 3.0	2212 0.7	
0148 2.3	0044 2.8	0545 6.5	0342 4.9	0151 9.0	0615 2.7	0024 4.2	0512 1.3	0430 0.3	**4 TU**
0727 5.9	0637 7.0	1229 2.8	1042 2.3	0842 4.4	1233 5.4	0609 1.9	1154 2.9	1056 0.7	
1427 2.2	1337 2.6	1838 6.5	1628 4.8	1446 9.0	1900 2.6	1309 4.2	1748 1.3	1718 0.2	
2015 5.9	1928 7.0		2324 2.4	2133 4.4		1852 1.9		2339 0.7	
0306 2.2	0222 2.6	0113 2.8	0509 5.0	0333 9.4	0118 5.7	0140 4.5	0032 3.2	0546 0.2	**5 W**
0854 6.1	0806 7.3	0705 6.8	1206 2.0	1023 3.8	0739 2.4	0727 1.7	0629 1.1	1213 0.8	
1548 2.0	1506 2.1	1359 2.5	1754 5.1	1613 9.8	1357 5.8	1419 4.5	1312 3.2	1819 0.2	
2130 6.3	2046 7.5	1948 6.9		2303 3.6	2016 2.2	2003 1.6	1856 1.0		
0427 1.9	0340 2.0	0242 2.3	0042 2.0	0446 10.4	0227 6.2	0242 4.8	0138 3.5	0046 0.8	**6 TH**
1001 6.6	0917 8.0	0800 7.2	0624 5.4	1140 2.8	0848 1.8	0833 1.4	0730 0.8	0641 0.1	
1708 1.6	1615 1.4	1524 1.9	1316 1.5	1718 10.8	1459 6.3	1515 4.8	1412 3.5	1313 0.9	
2230 6.7	2148 8.3	2041 7.4	1900 5.5		2117 1.6	2102 1.3	1951 0.7	1908 0.1	
0542 1.4	0445 1.3	0357 1.7	0145 1.4	0009 2.5	0324 6.7	0334 5.2	0233 3.8	0139 0.9	**7 F**
1057 7.0	1015 8.7	0843 7.7	0724 5.9	0543 11.5	0945 1.3	0928 1.0	0821 0.5	0728 0.0	
1815 1.2	1715 0.8	1630 1.2	1414 1.0	1239 1.7	1551 6.8	1603 5.2	1503 3.7	1404 0.9	
2323 7.2	2242 8.9	2130 7.7	1954 6.0	1810 11.8	2210 1.1	2153 0.9	2040 0.5	1953 0.0	
0643 1.0	0542 0.7	0457 1.2	0239 1.0	0105 1.5	0414 7.3	0422 5.5	0322 4.0	0227 1.0	**8 SA**
1149 7.4	1106 9.3	0920 8.0	0814 6.3	0634 12.4	1036 0.8	1018 0.7	0909 0.3	0812 -0.0	
1912 0.8	1809 0.2	1724 0.7	1504 0.5	1333 0.8	1639 7.3	1648 5.4	1550 3.9	1451 1.0	
	2330 9.5	2200 8.0	2041 6.4	1858 12.6	2259 0.7	2240 0.7	2126 0.3	2036 -0.0	
0012 7.5	0633 0.2	0548 0.7	0327 0.6	0155 0.7	0501 7.6	0507 5.6	0409 4.2	0312 1.0	**9 SU**
0736 0.6	1152 9.7	1048 8.2	0900 6.7	0721 13.1	1123 0.4	1104 0.5	0953 0.2	0856 -0.1	
1238 7.8	1857 -0.1	1812 0.3	1551 0.3	1421 0.2	1724 7.5	1731 5.5	1634 4.1	1536 1.0	
2000 0.6		2242 8.1	2125 6.6	1943 13.1	2345 0.4	2325 0.5	2210 0.2	2117 -0.1	●
0100 7.7	0015 9.8	0634 0.4	0412 0.4	0242 0.2	0546 7.8	0551 5.7	0453 4.3	0356 1.1	**10 M**
0822 0.4	0720 -0.1	1115 8.2	0945 6.8	0804 13.4	1209 0.3	1148 0.4	1036 0.2	0937 -0.1	
1326 7.7	1237 9.9	1856 0.2	1635 0.2	1506 -0.1	1806 7.6	1813 5.5	1717 4.1	1621 1.0	
2044 0.5	1942 -0.3		2208 6.7	2025 13.2			2253 0.3	2157 -0.1	
0146 7.7	0059 9.9	0052 8.3	0456 0.4	0326 0.2	0030 0.4	0010 0.5	0536 4.2	0439 1.0	**11 TU**
0904 0.4	0803 -0.2	0716 0.3	1027 6.8	0845 13.3	0630 7.7	0634 5.6	1118 0.3	1018 -0.1	
1412 7.6	1320 9.8	1146 8.1	1718 0.3	1548 0.1	1252 0.4	1232 0.5	1759 4.0	1703 1.0	
2123 0.5	2023 -0.2	1936 0.3	2248 6.6	2104 13.0	1848 7.4	1855 5.4	2336 0.4	2238 -0.0	
0231 7.6	0140 9.8	0136 8.2	0539 0.6	0406 0.4	0114 0.6	0054 0.5	0620 4.1	0521 1.0	**12 W**
0942 0.4	0843 -0.0	0755 0.5	1108 6.6	0924 12.9	0712 7.5	0718 5.4	1159 0.5	1059 -0.0	
1456 7.5	1401 9.6	1352 8.2	1759 0.6	1626 0.6	1336 0.8	1316 0.7	1841 3.9	1746 0.9	
2200 0.7	2102 0.0	2013 0.6	2328 6.4	2142 12.5	1930 7.1	1937 5.2		2318 0.0	
0315 7.4	0221 9.4	0215 8.0	0620 0.9	0442 1.1	0157 1.0	0139 0.8	0018 0.6	0604 0.9	**13 TH**
1020 0.7	0920 0.3	0831 0.9	1148 6.3	1002 12.2	0753 7.0	0801 5.1	0703 3.8	1140 0.1	
1540 7.2	1442 9.2	1430 7.9	1839 1.1	1702 1.4	1418 1.3	1400 1.0	1241 0.8	1830 0.9	
2236 1.0	2138 0.5	2048 1.1		2219 11.8	2010 6.7	2021 4.8	1924 3.6		
0400 7.1	0300 8.9	0248 7.6	0008 6.0	0517 1.9	0242 1.5	0227 1.1	0103 0.9	0000 0.1	**14 F**
1059 1.1	0957 0.8	0905 1.4	0700 1.4	1040 11.3	0836 6.5	0848 4.7	0749 3.5	0649 0.8	
1627 6.8	1524 8.5	1504 7.4	1230 5.8	1736 2.4	1503 1.8	1448 1.3	1326 1.1	1223 0.2	
2318 1.4	2215 1.1	2121 1.4	1919 1.6	2259 10.9	2054 6.1	2111 4.5	2012 3.4	1918 0.8	
0450 6.7	0343 8.2	0314 7.2	0050 5.6	0552 2.9	0329 2.0	0318 1.4	0156 1.2	0048 0.2	**15 SA**
1142 1.6	1035 1.5	0940 2.0	0744 1.9	1123 10.2	0923 5.9	0943 4.3	0842 3.2	0739 0.8	
1719 6.3	1611 7.8	1534 7.0	1317 5.3	1814 3.4	1551 2.4	1541 1.7	1420 1.4	1316 0.3	
	2255 1.8	2158 2.4	2003 2.1	2346 9.9	2145 5.6	2215 4.2	2109 3.1	2014 0.7	

• • Time Zone -0100. For UT subtract 1 hour. For European summer time (shaded) 30/3-26/10 add 1 hour • •

MARCH 1997 TIDE TABLES MARCH 1997

	CALAIS		DIEPPE		LE HAVRE		CHERBOURG		ST MALO		BREST		POINTE DE GRAVE		LISBOA		GIBRALTAR	
	Time	m	Time	m	Time	m	Time	m	Time	m	Time	m	Time	m	Time	m	Time	m
16 SU	0004	1.9	0434	7.5	0342	6.8	0139	5.2	0634	3.8	0424	2.5	0418	1.8	0303	1.4	0158	0.3
	0548	6.2	1120	2.2	1025	2.6	0835	2.3	1220	9.2	1023	5.4	1057	4.0	0948	2.9	0841	0.7
	1235	2.1	1716	7.1	1619	6.5	1415	4.9	1903	4.3	1652	2.8	1645	2.0	1533	1.6	1450	0.3
	1822	5.9	2347	2.5	2251	3.0	2100	2.6			2255	5.3	2342	4.0	2224	3.0	2130	0.6
17 M	0102	2.4	0551	6.8	0437	6.4	0243	4.8	0053	9.0	0536	2.9	0531	2.0	0436	1.6	0403	0.3
	0656	5.8	1227	2.7	1136	3.1	0945	2.6	0735	4.6	1148	5.1	1227	3.9	1112	2.8	1006	0.6
	1341	2.5	1843	6.7	1729	6.2	1533	4.6	1351	8.5	1812	3.0	1803	2.2	1706	1.6	1651	0.3
	1933	5.6					2221	2.8	2018	4.8					2349	2.9	2306	0.6
18 TU	0218	2.6	0114	3.0	0018	3.3	0409	4.6	0230	8.6	0030	5.1	0107	4.0	0603	1.5	0525	0.3
	0809	5.6	0716	6.6	0551	6.2	1122	2.6	0914	4.9	0705	2.9	0651	2.0	1233	2.9	1138	0.3
	1507	2.6	1412	2.8	1317	3.1	1715	4.6	1531	8.6	1321	5.2	1344	4.0	1821	1.5	1754	0.3
	2046	5.6	2002	6.7	1858	6.1			2201	4.8	1937	2.9	1921	2.1				
19 W	0351	2.5	0248	2.9	0153	3.2	0000	2.7	0357	8.9	0153	5.4	0212	4.2	0100	3.1	0021	0.7
	0921	5.7	0830	6.8	0716	6.2	0545	4.7	1054	4.4	0818	2.6	0801	1.9	0703	1.3	0616	0.3
	1632	2.4	1526	2.5	1433	2.8	1244	2.4	1641	9.1	1425	5.5	1439	4.2	1332	3.0	1240	0.7
	2154	5.8	2107	7.1	2036	6.4	1827	4.8	2317	4.2	2038	2.6	2021	1.9	1914	1.4	1836	0.3
20 TH	0501	2.2	0351	2.4	0257	2.8	0107	2.3	0457	9.5	0247	5.7	0259	4.4	0152	3.2	0109	0.8
	1024	6.0	0930	7.3	0848	6.6	0645	5.0	1150	3.7	0909	2.3	0853	1.7	0745	1.2	0653	0.3
	1727	2.0	1621	2.0	1528	2.4	1335	2.0	1729	9.7	1511	5.8	1520	4.4	1417	3.2	1322	0.8
	2250	6.1	2157	7.6	2133	6.8	1914	5.2			2124	2.2	2107	1.6	1953	1.2	1909	0.2
21 F	0548	1.8	0441	2.0	0347	2.4	0151	2.0	0004	3.5	0328	6.0	0337	4.6	0234	3.4	0145	0.8
	1113	6.3	1015	7.8	0939	6.9	0727	5.4	0541	10.1	0949	2.0	0934	1.4	0818	1.0	0724	0.2
	1808	1.7	1704	1.6	1612	2.0	1413	1.6	1229	3.1	1548	6.2	1554	4.6	1456	3.4	1355	0.8
	2332	6.5	2237	8.1	2211	7.2	1951	5.5	1806	10.3	2202	1.9	2145	1.4	2027	1.0	1939	0.2
22 SA	0627	1.5	0521	1.6	0428	2.0	0228	1.7	0042	2.9	0404	6.3	0409	4.8	0312	3.6	0215	0.8
	1151	6.6	1052	8.2	1006	7.2	0803	5.7	0618	10.7	1024	1.7	1009	1.2	0850	0.8	0754	0.2
	1844	1.4	1742	1.3	1650	1.7	1448	1.4	1304	2.6	1621	6.4	1625	4.8	1531	3.5	1426	0.9
			2312	8.4	2239	7.4	2025	5.7	1840	10.8	2236	1.6	2220	1.2	2100	0.8	2009	0.2
23 SU	0006	6.8	0557	1.3	0505	1.7	0301	1.4	0117	2.4	0436	6.6	0440	4.9	0347	3.7	0244	0.9
	0702	1.2	1127	8.5	1007	7.5	0836	5.9	0651	11.1	1057	1.5	1042	1.1	0921	0.7	0824	0.1
	1223	6.9	1817	1.0	1725	1.5	1520	1.2	1338	2.1	1653	6.6	1655	5.0	1605	3.6	1455	0.9
	1919	1.2	2346	8.7	2300	7.6	2057	5.9	1912	11.3	2309	1.4	2253	1.1	2131	0.7	2038	0.1
24 M O	0037	7.0	0631	1.1	0540	1.5	0333	1.2	0152	2.0	0507	6.7	0509	5.0	0419	3.7	0312	0.9
	0737	1.1	1200	8.8	1026	7.7	0906	6.1	0723	11.5	1128	1.3	1113	1.0	0951	0.6	0854	0.1
	1253	7.0	1850	0.9	1800	1.3	1551	1.1	1412	1.8	1723	6.8	1724	5.0	1636	3.7	1526	0.9
	1954	1.1			2254	7.7	2127	6.1	1942	11.6	2340	1.3	2324	1.0	2203	0.6	2106	0.1
25 TU	0106	7.1	0018	8.9	0615	1.3	0406	1.1	0228	1.7	0537	6.8	0539	5.1	0451	3.7	0342	0.9
	0811	1.0	0705	0.9	1048	7.8	0936	6.2	0754	11.7	1200	1.3	1144	1.0	1022	0.6	0924	0.1
	1320	7.1	1233	8.9	1833	1.3	1624	1.0	1448	1.6	1753	6.8	1754	5.0	1707	3.7	1557	0.9
	2026	1.1	1923	0.9	2305	7.7	2154	6.2	2012	11.7	2355	1.0			2235	0.6	2136	0.1
26 W	0132	7.2	0051	8.9	0648	1.3	0438	1.1	0303	1.6	0012	1.3	0609	5.0	0521	3.7	0412	0.9
	0842	1.1	0737	0.9	1110	7.8	1004	6.2	0824	11.9	0607	6.8	1215	1.0	1054	0.6	0954	0.0
	1345	7.1	1306	8.9	1906	1.3	1656	1.1	1521	1.6	1231	1.3	1824	5.0	1736	3.6	1630	0.9
	2055	1.2	1955	0.9	2325	7.7	2222	6.2	2041	11.8	1824	6.8			2308	0.6	2205	0.1
27 TH	0157	7.2	0122	8.9	0721	1.4	0511	1.2	0336	1.7	0045	1.3	0027	1.0	0551	3.6	0443	0.9
	0910	1.2	0809	1.0	1137	7.8	1033	6.1	0853	11.8	0639	6.8	0639	5.0	1126	0.7	1024	0.0
	1412	7.1	1337	8.8	1939	1.4	1728	1.3	1554	1.9	1304	1.5	1247	1.1	1806	3.6	1703	0.9
	2122	1.3	2026	1.1	2353	7.7	2250	6.1	2109	11.7	1856	6.7	1855	4.9	2343	0.7	2236	0.1
28 F	0226	7.1	0153	8.8	0752	1.5	0545	1.3	0408	2.0	0121	1.5	0103	1.1	0621	3.5	0516	0.9
	0938	1.3	0839	1.1	1209	7.7	1103	6.0	0923	11.6	0711	6.6	0710	4.8	1201	0.8	1057	0.1
	1442	7.0	1409	8.6	2009	1.6	1802	1.5	1624	2.3	1339	1.7	1322	1.3	1838	3.5	1737	0.8
	2151	1.5	2056	1.3			2321	5.9	2139	11.4	1930	6.5	1929	4.8			2308	0.1
29 SA	0259	7.0	0224	8.5	0028	7.5	0621	1.5	0439	2.4	0158	1.7	0141	1.2	0021	0.8	0551	0.8
	1010	1.5	0911	1.4	0822	1.7	1137	5.8	0954	11.2	0747	6.3	0746	4.6	0655	3.4	1132	0.1
	1518	6.9	1441	8.3	1248	7.5	1839	1.8	1653	2.8	1418	2.0	1403	1.4	1241	0.9	1816	0.8
	2227	1.6	2129	1.6	2041	1.9	2357	5.7	2212	11.0	2007	6.2	2009	4.6	1915	3.3	2345	0.1
30 SU	0338	6.8	0258	8.2	0111	7.3	0700	1.8	0509	3.0	0242	2.0	0227	1.4	0106	1.0	0633	0.8
	1051	1.7	0948	1.7	0857	2.0	1220	5.5	1031	10.7	0828	6.0	0832	4.4	0738	3.2	1213	0.2
	1602	6.6	1520	7.9	1338	7.1	1921	2.0	1724	3.5	1505	2.3	1451	1.7	1329	1.1	1901	0.7
	2312	1.9	2210	2.0	2120	2.3			2252	10.3	2054	5.9	2104	4.4	2004	3.2		
31 M	0427	6.5	0342	7.8	0206	6.9	0045	5.4	0548	3.6	0333	2.3	0321	1.6	0203	1.2	0030	0.2
	1143	1.9	1036	2.1	0942	2.3	0750	2.0	1118	9.9	0921	5.6	0939	4.2	0837	3.0	0723	0.7
	1658	6.2	1612	7.4	1447	6.7	1318	5.1	1809	4.1	1603	2.6	1552	1.9	1433	1.3	1309	0.2
			2306	2.4	2212	2.6	2017	2.3	2348	9.6	2159	5.6	2226	4.2	2112	3.1	1958	0.7

•• Time Zone -0100. For UT subtract 1 hour. For European summer time (shaded) 30/3-26/10 add 1 hour ••

FRANCE, SPAIN, PORTUGAL & GIBRALTAR Time Zone -0100

Calais * Dieppe * Le Havre * Cherbourg * St Malo * Brest * Pointe de Grave * Lisboa * Gibraltar

APRIL 1997 TIDE TABLES APRIL 1997

	CALAIS		DIEPPE		LE HAVRE		CHERBOURG		ST MALO		BREST		POINTE DE GRAVE		LISBOA		GIBRALTAR	
	Time	m	Time	m	Time	m	Time	m	Time	m	Time	m	Time	m	Time	m	Time	m
1 TU	0012	2.1	0443	7.3	0331	6.6	0153	5.1	0646	4.2	0437	2.5	0429	1.8	0321	1.3	0137	0.3
	0534	6.1	1145	2.4	1042	2.6	0857	2.2	1233	9.1	1038	5.4	1118	4.0	1000	2.9	0831	0.7
	1248	2.1	1730	7.0	1639	6.5	1439	4.9	1923	4.6	1715	2.7	1708	2.0	1559	1.4	1436	0.3
	1819	5.9			2323	2.9	2134	2.4			2325	5.5			2240	3.1	2116	0.7
2 W	0123	2.5	0026	2.7	0518	6.5	0320	4.9	0123	9.1	0555	2.5	0000	4.2	0451	1.3	0324	0.3
	0707	6.0	0614	7.0	1202	2.7	1021	2.2	0819	4.4	1212	5.4	0548	1.8	1134	3.0	1003	0.7
	1404	2.2	1315	2.5	1818	6.6	1610	4.9	1424	9.0	1838	2.6	1251	4.2	1727	1.3	1621	0.2
	1954	6.0	1904	7.1			2303	2.3	2110	4.5			1830	1.9			2248	0.7
3 TH	0243	2.1	0200	2.5	0051	2.8	0447	5.1	0309	9.4	0054	5.7	0119	4.5	0006	3.2	0500	0.2
	0833	6.2	0742	7.3	0640	6.8	1145	1.9	1004	3.9	0718	2.3	0706	1.6	0609	1.1	1133	0.7
	1530	2.0	1443	2.1	1336	2.4	1734	5.1	1553	9.7	1336	5.8	1400	4.5	1251	3.2	1733	0.2
	2108	6.3	2023	7.6	1928	7.0			2244	3.7	1955	2.2	1942	1.6	1836	1.1		
4 F	0410	1.8	0320	1.9	0222	2.3	0023	1.9	0424	10.4	0206	6.2	0221	4.8	0115	3.5	0006	0.8
	0940	6.6	0854	7.9	0739	7.2	0602	5.5	1121	2.8	0827	1.8	0813	1.3	0710	0.8	0604	0.2
	1651	1.6	1554	1.4	1501	1.9	1256	1.5	1656	10.8	1439	6.3	1456	4.8	1351	3.5	1242	0.8
	2208	6.7	2126	8.3	2026	7.4	1839	5.6	2350	2.6	2057	1.6	2042	1.2	1933	0.8	1830	0.1
5 SA	0524	1.4	0425	1.2	0336	1.7	0126	1.4	0522	11.4	0303	6.7	0315	5.1	0211	3.8	0106	0.9
	1036	7.0	0953	8.6	0824	7.6	0702	5.9	1218	1.8	0924	1.3	0909	1.0	0802	0.5	0656	0.1
	1757	1.2	1654	0.8	1606	1.2	1353	1.0	1748	11.8	1530	6.8	1544	5.1	1442	3.8	1337	0.9
	2301	7.2	2219	9.0	2139	7.7	1932	6.0			2150	1.1	2133	0.9	2022	0.5	1918	0.1
6 SU	0624	0.9	0521	0.6	0434	1.1	0219	1.0	0043	1.6	0354	7.2	0403	5.4	0301	4.0	0157	0.9
	1127	7.3	1044	9.2	0900	7.9	0753	6.3	0612	12.3	1015	0.8	0957	0.7	0848	0.4	0742	0.0
	1851	1.1	1746	0.3	1701	0.7	1443	0.6	1309	1.0	1618	7.2	1629	5.3	1528	4.0	1425	1.0
	2350	7.4	2308	9.4	2249	8.0	2019	6.3	1836	12.5	2239	0.7	2221	0.7	2107	0.4	2002	0.0
7 M	0715	0.6	0612	0.2	0525	0.7	0307	0.6	0132	0.9	0440	7.5	0448	5.5	0348	4.1	0242	1.0
	1216	7.5	1131	9.6	1019	8.1	0839	6.6	0658	12.9	1102	0.6	1043	0.6	0931	0.3	0825	-0.0
	1939	0.6	1834	-0.0	1749	0.5	1530	0.4	1357	0.5	1702	7.4	1711	5.4	1612	4.1	1510	1.0
			2353	9.7	2225	8.0	2103	6.6	1920	13.0	2324	0.5	2306	0.5	2150	0.3	2044	-0.0

● (new moon)

	CALAIS		DIEPPE		LE HAVRE		CHERBOURG		ST MALO		BREST		POINTE DE GRAVE		LISBOA		GIBRALTAR	
	Time	m	Time	m	Time	m	Time	m	Time	m	Time	m	Time	m	Time	m	Time	m
8 TU	0037	7.6	0658	0.0	0612	0.5	0353	0.5	0218	0.5	0525	7.6	0531	5.6	0433	4.2	0326	1.0
	0800	0.5	1215	9.7	1051	8.1	0924	6.7	0742	13.1	1146	0.5	1127	0.5	1012	0.3	0906	-0.0
	1303	7.6	1919	-0.1	1833	0.4	1614	0.4	1442	0.3	1745	7.5	1752	5.4	1655	4.1	1553	1.0
	2020	0.6			2304	8.0	2145	6.6	2001	13.1			2350	0.5	2232	0.3	2124	-0.0
9 W	0122	7.6	0036	9.8	0654	0.5	0436	0.5	0302	0.5	0009	0.5	0613	5.5	0516	4.1	0407	1.0
	0840	0.5	0740	0.0	1124	8.0	1006	6.6	0823	13.0	0608	7.6	1210	0.6	1052	0.4	0947	-0.0
	1347	7.5	1257	9.7	1913	0.6	1656	0.6	1523	0.5	1230	0.6	1832	5.3	1736	4.0	1635	1.0
	2058	0.7	2000	0.0	2340	7.9	2224	6.6	2041	12.8	1826	7.3			2313	0.5	2203	0.0
10 TH	0206	7.5	0117	9.6	0733	0.7	0518	0.7	0342	0.8	0053	0.7	0034	0.6	0559	4.0	0448	1.0
	0917	0.6	0820	0.2	1331	8.0	1046	6.5	0902	12.6	0649	7.2	0654	5.3	1132	0.6	1025	0.0
	1430	7.2	1339	9.4	1950	0.9	1736	0.9	1601	1.0	1312	0.9	1252	0.8	1818	3.9	1715	0.9
	2133	0.8	2038	0.3			2303	6.4	2118	12.4	1906	7.0	1912	5.1	2354	0.7	2242	0.1
11 F	0249	7.3	0157	9.3	0148	7.8	0557	1.0	0418	1.4	0136	1.1	0118	0.8	0641	3.7	0528	0.9
	0952	0.9	0857	0.5	0807	1.1	1126	6.1	0939	11.9	0730	6.8	0736	5.0	1211	0.8	1103	0.1
	1512	7.1	1418	9.0	1406	7.7	1814	1.3	1636	1.8	1353	1.4	1335	1.1	1900	3.7	1755	0.9
	2207	1.1	2113	0.8	2022	1.4	2342	6.0	2155	11.7	1945	6.6	1952	4.8			2322	0.1
12 SA	0333	7.0	0236	8.8	0213	7.5	0636	1.4	0452	2.1	0218	1.5	0203	1.1	0037	0.9	0608	0.8
	1028	1.2	0931	1.0	0839	1.6	1206	5.7	1017	11.1	0810	6.3	0818	4.6	0725	3.4	1142	0.2
	1556	6.7	1459	8.4	1433	7.3	1852	1.8	1709	2.6	1435	1.9	1419	1.4	1253	1.1	1836	0.8
	2245	1.5	2148	1.3	2051	2.0			2233	10.8	2025	6.1	2036	4.5	1944	3.4		
13 SU	0419	6.7	0315	8.2	0216	7.2	0022	5.6	0524	3.0	0303	2.0	0251	1.5	0125	1.2	0003	0.2
	1108	1.5	1006	1.6	0909	2.1	0716	1.9	1057	10.2	0854	5.8	0906	4.3	0814	3.2	0650	0.7
	1645	6.3	1543	7.8	1454	6.9	1251	5.3	1742	3.5	1520	2.4	1509	1.7	1341	1.4	1224	0.2
	2327	1.9	2224	1.9	2124	2.6	1931	2.2	2315	9.9	2112	5.7	2129	4.2	2036	3.2	1922	0.7
14 M	0512	6.2	0401	7.5	0253	6.8	0109	5.2	0600	3.9	0353	2.5	0345	1.8	0224	1.4	0053	0.3
	1154	2.1	1046	2.1	0947	2.6	0801	2.3	1147	9.2	0948	5.4	1011	4.0	0914	2.9	0738	0.7
	1741	5.9	1639	7.1	1535	6.5	1345	4.9	1823	4.4	1615	2.8	1606	2.0	1444	1.6	1318	0.3
			2309	2.5	2210	3.1	2021	2.6			2212	5.3	2245	4.0	2142	3.0	2018	0.7
15 TU	0018	2.3	0504	6.8	0346	6.4	0207	4.8	0012	9.1	0456	2.8	0451	2.0	0346	1.6	0209	0.4
	0614	5.8	1140	2.7	1045	3.1	0901	2.6	0649	4.6	1101	5.1	1136	3.8	1029	2.8	0842	0.6
	1252	2.5	1756	6.6	1637	6.2	1455	4.6	1304	8.5	1725	3.0	1717	2.2	1612	1.7	1449	0.4
	1848	5.6			2324	3.5	2130	2.8	1924	5.0	2336	5.1			2301	2.9	2137	0.6

● ● Time Zone -0100. For UT subtract 1 hour. For European summer time (shaded) 30/3-26/10 add 1 hour ● ●

PAGE 133

APRIL 1997 TIDE TABLES APRIL 1997

	CALAIS	DIEPPE	LE HAVRE	CHERBOURG	ST MALO	BREST	POINTE DE GRAVE	LISBOA	GIBRALTAR
	Time m	Time m	Time m	Time m	Time m	Time m	Time m	Time m	Time m
16 W	0125 2.6	0015 3.0	0454 6.1	0322 4.6	0137 8.5	0618 2.9	0012 3.9	0515 1.5	0400 0.4
	0725 5.6	0626 6.5	1220 3.3	1023 2.7	0807 5.0	1232 5.1	0606 2.1	1148 2.8	1011 0.6
	1406 2.7	1305 3.0	1801 6.1	1621 4.6	1441 8.4	1851 3.0	1257 3.9	1736 1.6	1627 0.4
	2000 5.5	1914 6.5		2302 2.8	2055 5.1		1834 2.2		2307 0.7
17 TH	0246 2.6	0147 3.1	0104 3.4	0449 4.7	0306 8.6	0105 5.2	0124 4.0	0015 3.0	0512 0.4
	0836 5.6	0743 6.6	0618 6.1	1150 2.5	0955 4.9	0736 2.8	0718 2.0	0621 1.4	1135 0.6
	1530 2.6	1430 2.8	1345 3.0	1742 4.8	1554 8.8	1345 5.3	1356 4.1	1253 3.0	1728 0.4
	2109 5.7	2024 6.8	1933 6.3		2226 4.7	1959 2.7	1939 2.0	1835 1.4	
18 F	0406 2.3	0300 2.7	0214 3.0	0020 2.5	0411 9.1	0208 5.5	0216 4.3	0113 3.1	0010 0.7
	0941 5.9	0848 7.0	0736 6.4	0600 4.9	1103 4.2	0832 2.5	0814 1.7	0706 1.2	0600 0.3
	1636 2.2	1532 2.4	1442 2.6	1250 2.2	1646 9.4	1435 5.7	1441 4.3	1342 3.2	1229 0.7
	2207 6.0	2119 7.3	2044 6.7	1836 5.1	2321 4.4	2048 2.4	2030 1.7	1918 1.2	1812 0.3
19 SA	0501 1.9	0355 2.3	0304 2.5	0111 2.2	0459 9.7	0253 5.8	0258 4.5	0159 3.3	0052 0.8
	1033 6.2	0939 7.5	0841 6.8	0648 5.2	1147 3.5	0914 2.1	0858 1.5	0743 1.1	0637 0.3
	1724 1.8	1619 1.9	1527 2.2	1333 1.8	172710.0	1515 6.0	1518 4.6	1422 3.3	1309 0.8
	2254 6.4	2202 7.9	2128 7.1	1916 5.4		2128 2.0	2112 1.5	1955 1.1	1848 0.3
20 SU	0545 1.5	0439 1.8	0346 2.1	0151 1.8	0002 3.3	0330 6.1	0334 4.7	0239 3.5	0127 0.8
	1116 6.6	1019 8.0	0922 7.1	0727 5.5	053810.3	0951 1.8	0936 1.3	0817 0.9	0712 0.2
	1806 1.4	1700 1.5	1607 1.8	1409 1.6	1224 2.9	1549 6.3	1552 4.8	1459 3.5	1344 0.8
	2333 6.7	2239 8.3	2203 7.4	1951 5.7	180310.7	2203 1.7	2148 1.3	2030 0.9	1923 0.2
21 M	0626 1.3	0519 1.4	0426 1.7	0226 1.6	0040 2.7	0404 6.4	0408 4.9	0315 3.6	0159 0.9
	1151 6.8	1056 8.4	0948 7.4	0803 5.8	061510.9	1024 1.6	1010 1.2	0849 0.8	0745 0.2
	1845 1.2	1739 1.2	1647 1.5	1445 1.3	1301 2.4	1621 6.5	1625 4.9	1534 3.6	1418 0.9
		2315 8.7	2231 7.6	2024 5.9	183611.2	2238 1.5	2223 1.2	2103 0.8	1956 0.2
22 TU ○	0006 6.9	0558 1.1	0506 1.5	0301 1.3	0119 2.2	0437 6.6	0441 5.0	0351 3.6	0232 0.9
	0706 1.1	1132 8.7	1000 7.6	0835 6.0	064911.4	1057 1.4	1043 1.1	0922 0.7	0818 0.1
	1223 7.0	1818 1.0	1727 1.4	1519 1.2	1340 2.0	1654 6.7	1657 5.0	1608 3.7	1453 0.9
	1924 1.1	2350 8.9	2221 7.6	2055 6.1	191011.6	2312 1.3	2257 1.1	2138 0.7	2029 0.1
23 W	0037 7.0	0636 1.0	0545 1.3	0337 1.2	0158 1.8	0509 6.7	0514 5.0	0424 3.7	0305 0.9
	0743 1.1	1208 8.7	1016 7.7	0907 6.1	072411.7	1131 1.3	1116 1.1	0955 0.6	0851 0.1
	1252 7.0	1856 0.9	1806 1.3	1554 1.1	1419 1.7	1727 6.8	1730 5.1	1641 3.7	1528 0.9
	2000 1.1		2230 7.7	2125 6.2	194411.8	2348 1.2	2330 1.0	2212 0.6	2102 0.1
24 TH	0105 7.1	0025 9.0	0624 1.3	0413 1.1	0238 1.6	0543 6.8	0547 5.0	0457 3.7	0339 0.9
	0819 1.1	0714 0.9	1039 7.7	0939 6.2	075811.9	1206 1.3	1149 1.1	1029 0.6	0925 0.0
	1320 7.0	1243 8.8	1844 1.3	1630 1.2	1457 1.7	1801 6.9	1803 5.1	1714 3.7	1603 0.9
	2035 1.2	1933 1.0	2254 7.7	2156 6.2	201712.0			2248 0.6	2135 0.1
25 F	0133 7.1	0100 9.0	0701 1.3	0449 1.1	0316 1.6	0024 1.2	0006 1.0	0531 3.6	0415 0.9
	0852 1.2	0751 1.0	1109 7.7	1012 6.1	083211.9	0618 6.8	0621 5.0	1104 0.7	0959 0.0
	1349 7.0	1318 8.8	1920 1.4	1707 1.3	1534 1.8	1243 1.4	1224 1.1	1748 3.7	1639 0.9
	2106 1.3	2009 1.1	2327 7.7	2228 6.2	204911.9	1836 6.8	1838 5.0	2326 0.7	2209 0.1
26 SA	0205 7.0	0134 8.8	0736 1.4	0527 1.2	0352 1.8	0103 1.3	0044 1.1	0607 3.5	0451 0.9
	0924 1.3	0827 1.1	1146 7.6	1047 6.0	090611.8	0655 6.6	0657 4.9	1142 0.8	1034 0.0
	1423 6.9	1353 8.7	1954 1.6	1745 1.5	1609 2.2	1322 1.5	1303 1.2	1824 3.6	1717 0.9
	2139 1.4	2045 1.3		2304 6.0	212311.7	1915 6.6	1916 4.9		2245 0.1
27 SU	0242 6.9	0209 8.6	0006 7.6	0607 1.4	0427 2.2	0145 1.5	0126 1.2	0007 0.8	0529 0.9
	1000 1.5	0904 1.3	0810 1.6	1127 5.8	094111.4	0734 6.4	0738 4.7	0647 3.4	1112 0.1
	1503 6.8	1430 8.4	1230 7.4	1826 1.7	1643 2.7	1405 1.8	1347 1.4	1225 0.9	1757 0.8
	2218 1.6	2123 1.6	2029 1.9	2345 5.8	215911.2	1957 6.3	2001 4.7	1906 3.5	2326 0.1
28 M	0324 6.8	0248 8.3	0053 7.3	0651 1.6	0503 2.7	0230 1.8	0214 1.3	0054 0.9	0612 0.8
	1042 1.6	0945 1.5	0846 1.9	1214 5.5	102110.8	0820 6.1	0828 4.5	0734 3.3	1156 0.1
	1550 6.6	1512 8.1	1324 7.1	1912 1.9	1718 3.3	1454 2.1	1437 1.6	1315 1.1	1842 0.8
	2304 1.7	2207 1.9	2109 2.2		224210.6	2047 6.0	2059 4.5	1957 3.3	
29 TU	0418 6.5	0333 7.9	0154 7.0	0037 5.5	0544 3.3	0324 2.0	0309 1.5	0153 1.1	0015 0.2
	1133 1.8	1035 1.9	0931 2.1	0742 1.8	111010.1	0917 5.7	0937 4.3	0834 3.1	0701 0.8
	1650 6.3	1606 7.7	1445 6.8	1315 5.2	1803 3.9	1551 2.4	1538 1.8	1419 1.3	1250 0.2
		2304 2.2	2201 2.5	2010 2.2	2339 9.9	2151 5.8	2215 4.4	2103 3.2	1937 0.7
30 W	0001 1.9	0436 7.5	0322 6.7	0145 5.3	0640 3.9	0426 2.3	0414 1.6	0307 1.2	0118 0.2
	0528 6.2	1139 2.1	1030 2.4	0847 2.0	1221 9.4	1029 5.5	1106 4.2	0950 3.0	0803 0.7
	1236 2.0	1719 7.3	1637 6.6	1430 5.0	1912 4.4	1700 2.5	1649 1.9	1541 1.4	1403 0.2
	1809 6.1		2309 2.7	2123 2.3		2309 5.7	2339 4.4	2221 3.2	2044 0.7

• • Time Zone -0100. For UT subtract 1 hour. For European summer time (shaded) 30/3-26/10 add 1 hour • •

FRANCE, SPAIN, PORTUGAL & GIBRALTAR Time Zone -0100
Calais * Dieppe * Le Havre * Cherbourg * St Malo * Brest * Pointe de Grave * Lisboa * Gibraltar
MAY 1997 TIDE TABLES MAY 1997

	CALAIS		DIEPPE		LE HAVRE		CHERBOURG		ST MALO		BREST		POINTE DE GRAVE		LISBOA		GIBRALTAR	
	Time	m	Time	m	Time	m	Time	m	Time	m	Time	m	Time	m	Time	m	Time	m
1 TH	0109	2.0	0015	2.4	0501	6.7	0303	5.1	0103	9.4	0537	2.3	0528	1.7	0432	1.2	0244	0.3
	0654	6.1	0556	7.3	1147	2.5	1003	2.0	0803	4.1	1153	5.5	1230	4.3	1113	3.1	0924	0.7
	1349	2.1	1257	2.2	1803	6.7	1551	5.0	1359	9.3	1816	2.4	1806	1.8	1706	1.3	1530	0.2
	1934	6.1	1842	7.4			2244	2.2	2046	4.3					2341	3.3	2205	0.8
2 F	0227	2.0	0137	2.2	0032	2.6	0424	5.2	0239	9.6	0030	5.8	0055	4.6	0548	1.0	0415	0.2
	0813	6.1	0718	7.5	0620	6.9	1122	1.8	0936	3.8	0654	2.1	0643	1.5	1227	3.3	1053	0.7
	1512	1.9	1417	1.9	1314	2.3	1709	5.2	1523	9.8	1311	5.8	1338	4.5	1815	1.1	1648	0.2
	2045	6.4	1957	7.8	1913	7.0			2215	3.7	1930	2.1	1918	1.6			2323	0.8
3 SA	0351	1.7	0255	1.8	0157	2.2	0000	1.9	0354	10.4	0141	6.1	0158	4.8	0050	3.5	0525	0.2
	0918	6.6	0829	8.0	0722	7.2	0536	5.5	1051	2.9	0803	1.8	0749	1.3	0648	0.8	1208	0.8
	1631	1.6	1528	1.4	1433	1.8	1231	1.5	1627	10.7	1415	6.2	1433	4.8	1327	3.5	1749	0.2
	2145	6.7	2100	8.3	2015	7.4	1814	5.6	2321	2.7	2033	1.7	2019	1.3	1912	0.9		
4 SU	0503	1.4	0401	1.2	0308	1.7	0103	1.5	0454	11.2	0239	6.6	0253	5.1	0148	3.7	0028	0.9
	1015	6.9	0929	8.5	0814	7.5	0637	5.8	1150	2.1	0900	1.4	0846	1.1	0740	0.7	0622	0.1
	1735	1.3	1628	0.9	1538	1.3	1330	1.1	1721	11.6	1507	6.6	1523	5.1	1419	3.7	1307	0.9
	2239	7.0	2155	8.9	2126	7.7	1908	5.9			2127	1.3	2112	1.0	2002	0.7	1842	0.1
5 M	0602	1.0	0457	0.7	0407	1.2	0158	1.1	0015	1.9	0331	6.9	0342	5.3	0240	3.9	0123	0.9
	1106	7.2	1021	9.0	0945	7.8	0730	6.1	0545	11.9	0952	1.0	0936	0.9	0826	0.5	0711	0.1
	1828	1.0	1721	0.5	1633	0.9	1421	0.9	1241	1.4	1555	7.0	1608	5.2	1506	3.9	1358	0.9
	2329	7.3	2244	9.3	2228	7.9	1956	6.2	1809	12.2	2217	0.9	2200	0.9	2048	0.5	1929	0.1
6 TU	0653	0.8	0548	0.4	0500	0.9	0247	0.9	0105	1.3	0419	7.1	0428	5.4	0327	4.0	0211	0.9
	1155	7.3	1109	9.3	0941	7.8	0818	6.3	0633	12.4	1039	0.9	1022	0.8	0909	0.5	0756	0.0
	1915	0.9	1810	0.3	1724	0.7	1508	0.8	1329	1.1	1640	7.2	1651	5.3	1551	4.0	1445	0.9
			2330	9.5	2321	8.0	2040	6.4	1854	12.5	2304	0.8	2247	0.7	2130	0.5	2013	0.1
●																		
7 W	0016	7.4	0635	0.3	0548	0.7	0333	0.7	0152	1.1	0504	7.2	0512	5.4	0413	4.0	0256	1.0
	0738	0.7	1153	9.4	1018	7.8	0903	6.4	0718	12.5	1124	0.8	1106	0.8	0948	0.5	0838	0.0
	1241	7.3	1855	0.3	1809	0.8	1552	0.8	1415	1.0	1723	7.2	1732	5.3	1634	4.0	1528	0.9
	1957	0.8			2242	7.8	2122	6.5	1937	12.6	2349	0.8	2331	0.7	2212	0.5	2055	0.1
8 TH	0101	7.4	0012	9.5	0631	0.7	0416	0.7	0236	1.1	0547	7.1	0553	5.3	0457	3.9	0339	1.0
	0818	0.8	0718	0.3	1228	7.9	0945	6.4	0800	12.4	1207	0.9	1148	0.8	1027	0.6	0919	0.0
	1325	7.2	1236	9.4	1851	1.0	1634	0.9	1457	1.2	1804	7.1	1811	5.2	1716	4.0	1609	0.9
	2034	0.9	1937	0.5	2321	7.7	2203	6.4	2018	12.4					2252	0.6	2136	0.1
9 F	0144	7.3	0054	9.3	0711	1.0	0458	0.9	0318	1.4	0033	0.9	0014	0.8	0539	3.8	0419	0.9
	0853	0.9	0758	0.5	1308	7.7	1027	6.2	0841	12.1	0628	6.9	0633	5.1	1106	0.7	0959	0.1
	1406	7.1	1318	9.1	1927	1.3	1714	1.2	1536	1.7	1249	1.2	1230	1.0	1757	3.8	1649	0.9
	2107	1.1	2015	0.8			2241	6.3	2056	12.0	1844	6.9	1848	5.1	2332	0.7	2216	0.1
10 SA	0226	7.1	0134	9.0	0117	7.6	0537	1.2	0356	1.8	0115	1.2	0057	1.0	0621	3.6	0459	0.9
	0926	1.1	0835	0.8	0746	1.3	1106	6.0	0919	11.5	0708	6.6	0712	4.9	1144	0.9	1038	0.1
	1447	6.9	1357	8.8	1339	7.5	1751	1.5	1612	2.2	1330	1.5	1311	1.2	1837	3.7	1729	0.8
	2140	1.4	2051	1.1	2000	1.7	2319	6.0	2133	11.5	1922	6.6	1926	4.9			2257	0.2
11 SU	0307	6.9	0213	8.6	0107	7.4	0615	1.5	0429	2.4	0156	1.6	0140	1.2	0013	0.9	0537	0.8
	1000	1.4	0909	1.2	0817	1.7	1146	5.7	0956	10.9	0747	6.2	0751	4.6	0703	3.4	1117	0.2
	1528	6.7	1437	8.3	1356	7.2	1828	1.9	1643	2.9	1409	1.9	1353	1.5	1224	1.1	1808	0.8
	2215	1.5	2123	1.5	2028	2.1	2358	5.7	2209	10.8	2000	6.2	2005	4.6	1919	3.5	2338	0.2
12 M	0351	6.7	0251	8.1	0135	7.2	0652	1.8	0459	3.0	0237	2.0	0224	1.5	0057	1.1	0616	0.8
	1036	1.7	0941	1.6	0845	2.1	1228	5.3	1033	10.2	0828	5.8	0833	4.3	0748	3.2	1158	0.2
	1612	6.4	1518	7.8	1416	7.0	1905	2.2	1713	3.5	1451	2.3	1438	1.7	1308	1.3	1848	0.8
	2254	1.8	2157	1.9	2057	2.6			2248	10.1	2042	5.8	2050	4.4	2006	3.3		
13 TU	0438	6.3	0333	7.6	0218	6.9	0042	5.3	0530	3.7	0322	2.4	0313	1.7	0149	1.3	0023	0.3
	1118	2.1	1017	2.0	0918	2.5	0733	2.2	1116	9.4	0915	5.5	0924	4.1	0839	3.0	0657	0.7
	1702	6.1	1605	7.3	1457	6.7	1318	5.0	1748	4.2	1538	2.7	1528	1.9	1402	1.5	1243	0.3
	2341	2.2	2236	2.4	2139	2.9	1948	2.5	2333	9.4	2133	5.5	2147	4.1	2100	3.1	1932	0.7
14 W	0532	6.0	0422	7.1	0307	6.6	0133	5.0	0608	4.3	0414	2.7	0408	1.9	0254	1.5	0116	0.3
	1210	2.4	1102	2.4	1005	2.9	0822	2.4	1212	8.8	1013	5.2	1033	3.9	0941	2.9	0744	0.7
	1800	5.8	1703	6.9	1551	6.4	1416	4.8	1833	4.7	1635	2.9	1628	2.1	1512	1.6	1339	0.3
			2327	2.6	2237	3.0	2045	2.7			2236	5.2	2300	4.0	2205	3.0	2025	0.7
15 TH	0040	2.4	0526	6.7	0406	6.3	0236	4.8	0036	8.8	0518	2.8	0512	2.0	0412	1.5	0226	0.4
	0635	5.7	1201	2.7	1112	3.1	0926	2.6	0703	4.8	1127	5.1	1150	3.9	1052	2.8	0843	0.7
	1315	2.6	1810	6.6	1703	6.2	1526	4.7	1330	8.5	1745	3.0	1736	2.1	1633	1.6	1451	0.4
	1907	5.7			2354	3.3	2157	2.8	1940	5.0	2354	5.2			2317	3.0	2130	0.7

● ● Time Zone -0100. For UT subtract 1 hour. For European summer time (shaded) 30/3-26/10 add 1 hour ● ●

MAY 1997 TIDE TABLES MAY 1997

	CALAIS	DIEPPE	LE HAVRE	CHERBOURG	ST MALO	BREST	POINTE DE GRAVE	LISBOA	GIBRALTAR
	Time m	Time m	Time m	Time m	Time m	Time m	Time m	Time m	Time m
16 F	0149 2.5	0035 3.0	0521 6.2	0348 4.7	0154 8.6	0632 2.8	0016 4.0	0522 1.5	0344 0.4
	0744 5.7	0637 6.6	1232 3.1	1039 2.5	0823 4.9	1244 5.2	0620 2.0	1200 2.9	0959 0.7
	1425 2.5	1315 2.8	1827 6.3	1640 4.8	1446 8.6	1859 2.8	1257 4.0	1742 1.5	1604 0.4
	2016 5.7	1920 6.7		2312 2.7	2103 4.9		1844 2.1		2240 0.7
17 SA	0300 2.4	0151 2.8	0109 3.1	0459 4.8	0306 8.8	0108 5.3	0119 4.2	0021 3.1	0451 0.4
	0851 5.8	0747 6.8	0642 6.3	1146 2.3	0946 4.6	0738 2.6	0721 1.9	0617 1.3	1113 0.7
	1533 2.3	1425 2.6	1340 2.9	1744 5.0	1547 9.1	1345 5.5	1351 4.3	1255 3.1	1706 0.3
	2118 5.9	2024 7.1	1941 6.6		2216 4.4	1958 2.6	1942 1.9	1834 1.4	2341 0.7
18 SU	0404 2.0	0255 2.5	0209 2.7	0015 2.4	0403 9.3	0204 5.6	0210 4.4	0115 3.2	0544 0.3
	0948 6.1	0848 7.2	0749 6.6	0558 5.1	1048 3.9	0827 2.3	0812 1.7	0700 1.2	1212 0.7
	1632 1.9	1524 2.2	1433 2.3	1240 2.1	1636 9.7	1432 5.8	1436 4.5	1342 3.2	1756 0.3
	2211 6.3	2116 7.6	2037 7.0	1832 5.3	2310 3.7	2045 2.3	2030 1.7	1918 1.2	
19 M	0457 1.7	0349 2.0	0259 2.2	0104 2.1	0451 10.0	0248 5.9	0254 4.6	0200 3.3	0031 0.8
	1035 6.4	0938 7.7	0842 6.9	0645 5.4	1136 3.3	0909 2.1	0856 1.5	0739 1.0	0629 0.3
	1721 1.6	1614 1.8	1521 2.0	1325 1.8	1718 10.4	1511 6.1	1516 4.7	1423 3.4	1301 0.8
	2254 6.6	2201 8.1	2121 7.3	1912 5.6	2357 3.0	2126 2.0	2112 1.5	1957 1.0	1840 0.3
20 TU	0545 1.4	0437 1.6	0346 1.9	0148 1.8	0534 10.6	0327 6.2	0334 4.8	0241 3.4	0115 0.8
	1115 6.7	1021 8.2	0924 7.2	0725 5.6	1221 2.7	0948 1.8	0935 1.3	0816 0.9	0710 0.2
	1807 1.4	1700 1.9	1608 1.7	1406 1.6	1759 11.0	1548 6.4	1554 4.9	1502 3.5	1345 0.8
	2332 6.8	2242 8.5	2157 7.5	1948 5.8		2205 1.7	2151 1.3	2035 0.8	1921 0.2
21 W	0630 1.2	0523 1.3	0432 1.6	0228 1.5	0042 2.4	0405 6.4	0412 4.9	0320 3.5	0157 0.9
	1151 6.8	1102 8.6	0944 7.4	0803 5.8	0615 11.2	1025 1.5	1012 1.2	0853 0.8	0751 0.1
	1851 1.3	1745 1.2	1654 1.5	1447 1.4	1306 2.2	1624 6.6	1631 5.1	1539 3.7	1427 0.8
		2321 8.8	2157 7.6	2024 6.0	1838 11.5	2244 1.4	2229 1.2	2113 0.7	2001 0.2
22 TH ○	0006 6.9	0607 1.1	0518 1.4	0309 1.3	0127 2.0	0443 6.6	0450 5.0	0359 3.6	0238 0.9
	0713 1.2	1142 8.8	0954 7.5	0839 6.0	0655 11.6	1104 1.4	1049 1.2	0930 0.7	0830 0.1
	1224 6.9	1829 1.1	1740 1.4	1527 1.3	1351 1.9	1703 6.8	1708 5.2	1617 3.7	1508 0.9
	1934 1.2		2206 7.7	2059 6.2	1917 11.8	2324 1.2	2307 1.1	2151 0.6	2040 0.2
23 F	0040 7.0	0000 9.0	0603 1.3	0349 1.2	0213 1.7	0521 6.7	0528 5.1	0437 3.6	0319 0.9
	0756 1.0	0652 0.9	1019 7.6	0918 6.1	0736 11.9	1144 1.3	1127 1.1	1007 0.6	0908 0.1
	1257 7.0	1221 8.9	1824 1.4	1608 1.3	1435 1.8	1742 6.9	1746 5.2	1655 3.8	1548 0.9
	2015 1.3	1913 1.1	2235 7.7	2135 6.3	1956 12.1		2348 1.0	2231 0.6	2119 0.1
24 SA	0114 7.0	0039 9.0	0645 1.3	0431 1.1	0257 1.5	0006 1.1	0608 5.0	0517 3.6	0400 0.9
	0836 0.9	0736 0.9	1054 7.6	0957 6.1	0815 11.9	0602 6.8	1207 1.1	1047 0.6	0947 0.0
	1333 6.9	1301 8.9	1906 1.4	1650 1.3	1518 1.8	1225 1.3	1827 5.2	1734 3.8	1629 0.9
	2054 1.3	1957 1.1	2312 7.7	2214 6.3	2034 12.1	1822 6.9		2312 0.6	2159 0.1
25 SU	0151 7.0	0119 8.9	0727 1.3	0513 1.1	0339 1.6	0048 1.2	0030 1.0	0558 3.6	0442 0.9
	0915 1.3	0818 0.9	1135 7.5	1038 6.1	0854 11.9	0643 6.7	0649 5.0	1129 0.7	1027 0.0
	1412 6.9	1342 8.8	1947 1.6	1733 1.4	1559 2.0	1309 1.4	1249 1.2	1816 3.7	1711 0.9
	2133 1.3	2039 1.2	2355 7.6	2256 6.2	2112 11.9	1905 6.8	1909 5.1	2357 0.7	2241 0.1
26 M	0233 6.9	0159 8.8	0806 1.4	0557 1.2	0421 1.9	0134 1.3	0115 1.1	0642 3.5	0524 0.9
	0955 1.4	0902 1.0	1223 7.4	1123 5.9	0934 11.6	0727 6.5	0736 4.8	1214 0.8	1109 0.1
	1456 6.8	1423 8.6	2027 1.7	1818 1.5	1638 2.4	1355 1.6	1336 1.3	1901 3.7	1754 0.9
	2215 1.4	2122 1.3		2342 6.0	2153 11.6	1951 6.6	1958 5.0		2326 0.1
27 TU	0321 6.8	0242 8.5	0046 7.4	0645 1.3	0501 2.3	0222 1.5	0204 1.2	0047 0.8	0611 0.8
	1039 1.4	0946 1.2	0847 1.6	1214 5.7	1017 11.1	0816 6.2	0828 4.6	0731 3.4	1156 0.1
	1547 6.6	1509 8.3	1326 7.1	1907 1.7	1718 2.9	1445 1.8	1427 1.5	1306 1.0	1842 0.8
	2301 1.5	2209 1.5	2109 1.9		2238 11.0	2042 6.3	2054 4.8	1952 3.5	
28 W	0417 6.6	0330 8.2	0151 7.2	0035 5.8	0545 2.8	0315 1.7	0258 1.3	0145 1.0	0018 0.2
	1130 1.6	1035 1.4	0931 1.8	0736 1.5	1107 10.5	0912 6.0	0932 4.5	0828 3.3	0702 0.8
	1648 6.5	1601 8.0	1526 7.0	1312 5.5	1804 3.4	1541 2.1	1525 1.6	1408 1.2	1249 0.2
	2355 1.6	2300 1.8	2158 2.2	2003 1.9	2333 10.4	2142 6.1	2202 4.7	2051 3.4	1935 0.8
29 TH	0525 6.4	0427 7.9	0325 7.0	0136 5.5	0637 3.3	0413 1.9	0359 1.5	0254 1.1	0118 0.2
	1227 1.8	1130 1.6	1026 2.0	0836 1.7	1210 9.9	1016 5.8	1047 4.4	0934 3.2	0801 0.8
	1800 6.3	1704 7.8	1638 6.9	1417 5.3	1903 3.8	1644 2.2	1630 1.7	1522 1.3	1353 0.2
			2259 2.3	2108 2.1		2249 5.9	2315 4.6	2200 3.4	2036 0.8
30 F	0058 1.7	0000 1.9	0451 6.9	0245 5.4	0043 9.9	0518 2.1	0506 1.5	0410 1.1	0230 0.2
	0640 6.3	0536 7.6	1132 2.1	0943 1.8	0745 3.6	1129 5.7	1203 4.4	1048 3.2	0912 0.7
	1335 1.9	1233 1.8	1748 6.9	1527 5.2	1329 9.7	1752 2.2	1742 1.7	1642 1.3	1506 0.2
	1914 6.3	1816 7.7		2220 2.1	2018 3.9			2315 3.4	2143 0.8
31 SA	0211 1.8	0110 1.9	0010 2.4	0357 5.3	0206 9.9	0002 5.9	0028 4.6	0523 1.1	0348 0.2
	0751 6.4	0651 7.7	0603 7.0	1055 1.8	0903 3.5	0627 2.0	0617 1.5	1200 3.3	1030 0.7
	1451 1.9	1346 1.7	1247 2.1	1640 5.3	1448 9.9	1242 5.8	1311 4.6	1752 1.2	1618 0.2
	2022 6.4	1928 7.9	1854 7.1	2333 1.9	2138 3.6	1903 2.1	1852 1.6		2254 0.8

•• Time Zone -0100. For UT subtract 1 hour. For European summer time (shaded) 30/3-26/10 add 1 hour ••

FRANCE, SPAIN, PORTUGAL & GIBRALTAR Time Zone -0100
Calais * Dieppe * Le Havre * Cherbourg * St Malo * Brest * Pointe de Grave * Lisboa * Gibraltar
JUNE 1997 TIDE TABLES JUNE 1997

Time Zone -0100. All times are Time m (Time, metres).

CALAIS	DIEPPE	LE HAVRE	CHERBOURG	ST MALO	BREST	POINTE DE GRAVE	LISBOA	GIBRALTAR	Day
0329 1.7	0226 1.7	0127 2.1	0508 5.5	0321 10.2	0112 6.1	0133 4.8	0024 3.5	0500 0.2	**1 SU**
0857 6.5	0803 7.9	0709 7.1	1204 1.6	1015 3.1	0736 1.9	0724 1.4	0625 1.0	1143 0.8	
1607 1.7	1459 1.4	1401 1.8	1748 5.5	1554 10.5	1348 6.1	1410 4.8	1303 3.5	1722 0.2	
2124 6.6	2033 8.3	1957 7.3		2247 3.0	2009 1.8	1955 1.4	1852 1.0		
0440 1.4	0334 1.4	0237 1.8	0039 1.7	0424 10.8	0215 6.3	0232 4.9	0126 3.6	0000 0.8	**2 M**
0955 6.7	0904 8.3	0815 7.3	0613 5.7	1117 2.5	0836 1.6	0823 1.2	0718 0.8	0600 0.2	
1712 1.4	1602 1.1	1507 1.5	1305 1.4	1652 11.1	1444 6.4	1503 5.0	1357 3.7	1245 0.8	
2219 6.8	2130 8.7	2105 7.5	1845 5.8	2345 2.4	2106 1.5	2051 1.2	1943 0.8	1818 0.2	
0540 1.2	0433 1.0	0339 1.4	0136 1.4	0519 11.3	0309 6.5	0324 5.1	0220 3.7	0057 0.9	**3 TU**
1048 6.9	0958 8.7	0932 7.5	0710 5.9	1211 2.0	0929 1.1	0915 1.1	0804 0.8	0651 0.1	
1806 1.2	1657 0.9	1606 1.2	1359 1.2	1743 11.6	1534 6.7	1550 5.1	1446 3.8	1339 0.8	
2311 7.0	2221 9.0	2206 7.7	1935 6.0		2157 1.3	2142 1.0	2030 0.7	1909 0.2	
0632 1.0	0525 0.8	0435 1.1	0228 1.2	0037 1.9	0359 6.7	0412 5.1	0309 3.8	0149 0.9	**4 W**
1139 7.0	1048 9.0	1033 7.7	0800 6.0	0610 11.7	1018 1.3	1002 1.1	0847 0.7	0738 0.1	
1854 1.1	1747 0.8	1659 1.1	1448 1.2	1301 1.8	1620 6.8	1634 5.2	1533 3.9	1427 0.9	
	2308 9.1	2257 7.8	2021 6.2	1830 11.9	2245 1.1	2230 1.0	2112 0.7	1955 0.2	
0000 7.1	0613 0.7	0526 1.0	0315 1.0	0127 1.7	0445 6.8	0455 5.1	0356 3.8	0236 0.9	**5 TH**
0718 1.0	1133 9.1	1123 7.7	0846 6.1	0657 11.8	1103 1.2	1046 1.0	0927 0.7	0822 0.1	
1224 7.0	1833 0.8	1747 1.2	1533 1.2	1349 1.8	1704 6.9	1715 5.2	1616 3.9	1512 0.9	
1937 1.1	2352 9.1	2342 7.8	2103 6.3	1915 12.0	2330 1.1	2314 1.0	2154 0.7	2040 0.1	●
0045 7.1	0658 0.7	0612 1.0	0359 1.0	0214 1.7	0528 6.8	0536 5.1	0439 3.7	0321 0.9	**6 F**
0757 1.1	1217 9.0	1206 7.7	0929 6.1	0742 11.7	1147 1.3	1128 1.1	1006 0.8	0905 0.1	
1306 7.0	1917 0.9	1830 1.3	1615 1.2	1433 1.9	1745 6.9	1753 5.2	1657 3.9	1554 0.9	
2014 1.2			2143 6.3	1958 11.9		2356 1.0	2233 0.7	2123 0.1	
0126 7.0	0034 9.0	0018 7.7	0440 1.1	0257 1.9	0014 1.2	0614 5.0	0521 3.7	0403 0.9	**7 SA**
0833 1.2	0739 0.9	0653 1.2	1009 6.0	0823 11.5	0609 6.7	1209 1.2	1043 0.8	0945 0.1	
1345 6.9	1259 8.9	1243 7.5	1654 1.4	1514 2.1	1228 1.4	1829 5.1	1737 3.8	1635 0.9	
2046 1.3	1955 1.1	1909 1.6	2221 6.1	2037 11.7	1824 6.7		2312 0.8	2204 0.2	
0205 6.9	0115 8.8	0002 7.5	0518 1.3	0336 2.1	0054 1.4	0037 1.1	0601 3.5	0443 0.9	**8 SU**
0904 1.4	0816 1.0	0729 1.5	1048 5.9	0901 11.2	0648 6.5	0650 4.8	1120 0.9	1026 0.1	
1424 6.8	1339 8.6	1308 7.4	1731 1.6	1549 2.5	1307 1.6	1248 1.3	1816 3.7	1714 0.9	
2118 1.4	2030 1.3	1942 1.8	2259 6.0	2114 11.3	1901 6.5	1903 4.9	2351 0.9	2245 0.2	
0244 6.8	0153 8.6	0024 7.4	0554 1.5	0408 2.5	0133 1.6	0118 1.3	0641 3.4	0521 0.8	**9 M**
0936 1.5	0848 1.3	0800 1.7	1126 5.7	0937 10.8	0724 6.2	0725 4.7	1158 1.1	1106 0.2	
1502 6.7	1417 8.3	1312 7.3	1806 1.9	1620 2.8	1345 1.9	1327 1.5	1855 3.5	1752 0.8	
2151 1.6	2101 1.6	2010 2.1	2336 5.8	2148 10.9	1937 6.3	1939 4.8		2327 0.2	
0324 6.7	0230 8.2	0106 7.3	0629 1.7	0436 2.9	0212 1.9	0158 1.4	0030 1.1	0600 0.8	**10 TU**
1009 1.7	0918 1.5	0826 2.0	1205 5.5	1012 10.3	0801 6.0	0802 4.5	0721 3.2	1145 0.2	
1542 6.6	1454 8.0	1343 7.1	1840 2.1	1648 3.3	1422 2.2	1409 1.6	1239 1.2	1830 0.8	
2226 1.7	2132 1.8	2038 2.4		2222 10.4	2015 6.0	2017 4.6	1936 3.4		
0406 6.5	0306 7.9	0148 7.2	0015 5.5	0504 3.3	0250 2.2	0240 1.6	0115 1.2	0009 0.3	**11 W**
1046 1.9	0950 1.8	0855 2.3	0706 2.0	1047 9.8	0841 5.7	0845 4.3	0804 3.1	0638 0.7	
1626 6.4	1533 7.7	1424 7.0	1247 5.2	1718 3.7	1503 2.4	1452 1.8	1325 1.4	1226 0.2	
2308 1.9	2206 2.1	2114 2.6	1918 2.3	2259 9.9	2056 5.7	2101 4.4	2019 3.2	1909 0.8	
0451 6.3	0346 7.5	0233 6.9	0059 5.3	0536 3.7	0333 2.4	0326 1.8	0206 1.3	0054 0.3	**12 TH**
1132 2.1	1028 2.1	0934 2.5	0747 2.2	1127 9.3	0927 5.4	0936 4.2	0853 3.0	0720 0.7	
1714 6.1	1617 7.3	1511 6.7	1336 5.0	1755 4.1	1549 2.7	1542 1.9	1420 1.5	1311 0.3	
	2249 2.4	2200 2.8	2005 2.5	2342 9.4	2145 5.5	2157 4.2	2111 3.1	1953 0.8	
0000 2.1	0434 7.1	0324 6.6	0150 5.0	0618 4.2	0422 2.6	0418 1.9	0307 1.4	0146 0.3	**13 F**
0543 6.0	1115 2.4	1025 2.8	0837 2.4	1221 8.9	1024 5.3	1040 4.1	0951 2.9	0809 0.7	
1229 2.3	1709 7.0	1609 6.5	1433 4.8	1845 4.5	1644 2.8	1638 2.1	1527 1.6	1403 0.3	
1810 5.9	2342 2.6	2257 3.0	2102 2.7		2244 5.3	2303 4.1	2212 3.0	2043 0.8	
0100 2.3	0532 6.8	0427 6.3	0250 4.9	0042 9.0	0521 2.8	0518 2.0	0415 1.5	0248 0.4	**14 SA**
0644 5.8	1213 2.6	1127 2.9	0937 2.5	0715 4.5	1130 5.2	1150 4.1	1055 2.9	0909 0.7	
1331 2.4	1811 6.9	1722 6.4	1536 4.8	1330 8.7	1747 2.8	1741 2.1	1638 1.6	1507 0.4	
1915 5.8			2208 2.8	1952 4.7	2352 5.2		2318 3.0	2142 0.7	
0203 2.3	0046 2.7	0003 3.0	0355 4.8	0154 8.9	0626 2.7	0013 4.1	0518 1.4	0357 0.3	**15 SU**
0751 5.8	0639 6.8	0544 6.3	1042 2.4	0830 4.5	1239 5.3	0620 2.0	1159 3.0	1019 0.7	
1435 2.3	1320 2.6	1234 2.8	1642 4.9	1440 8.9	1854 2.7	1255 4.2	1742 1.5	1615 0.4	
2021 5.9	1918 7.0	1842 6.5	2314 2.5	2107 4.5		1844 2.0		2247 0.8	

● ● Time Zone -0100. For UT subtract 1 hour. For European summer time (shaded) 30/3-26/10 add 1 hour ● ●

JUNE 1997 TIDE TABLES JUNE 1997

	CALAIS	DIEPPE	LE HAVRE	CHERBOURG	ST MALO	BREST	POINTE DE GRAVE	LISBOA	GIBRALTAR
	Time m	Time m	Time m	Time m	Time m	Time m	Time m	Time m	Time m
16 M	0306 2.1	0155 2.6	0110 2.8	0459 5.0	0303 9.1	0101 5.4	0117 4.3	0021 3.1	0503 0.3
	0855 5.9	0748 7.0	0702 6.5	1143 2.3	0943 4.2	0729 2.6	0720 1.9	0612 1.3	1130 0.7
	1536 2.1	1427 2.4	1339 2.5	1740 5.2	1542 9.4	1339 5.6	1351 4.4	1255 3.1	1719 0.3
	2121 6.1	2023 7.4	1947 6.8		2215 4.0	1953 2.5	1942 1.9	1836 1.3	2349 0.8
17 TU	0406 1.9	0300 2.2	0211 2.4	0015 2.3	0403 9.6	0200 5.6	0212 4.4	0116 3.2	0600 0.3
	0950 6.2	0852 7.5	0805 6.8	0557 5.2	1046 3.6	0823 2.3	0812 1.7	0700 1.1	1231 0.8
	1634 1.8	1527 2.1	1437 2.2	1239 2.1	163510.0	1430 5.9	1439 4.6	1344 3.3	1815 0.3
	2212 6.3	2119 7.9	2039 7.1	1830 5.4	2314 3.3	2045 2.2	2033 1.7	1924 1.1	
18 W	0501 1.6	0357 1.8	0307 2.0	0108 2.0	045510.3	0250 5.9	0300 4.7	0206 3.3	0045 0.8
	1037 6.5	0945 7.9	0855 7.1	0648 5.4	1141 3.0	0910 2.0	0859 1.5	0744 1.0	0651 0.2
	1727 1.6	1622 1.7	1532 1.9	1330 1.8	172410.7	1515 6.2	1524 4.9	1430 3.5	1324 0.8
	2257 6.6	2209 8.3	2119 7.3	1914 5.7		2132 1.8	2119 1.5	2008 0.9	1904 0.2
19 TH	0554 1.4	0450 1.5	0400 1.7	0156 1.7	0008 2.7	0335 6.2	0345 4.8	0251 3.4	0136 0.8
	1120 6.7	1033 8.4	0935 7.3	0733 5.7	054510.9	0955 1.7	0942 1.4	0826 0.8	0737 0.1
	1819 1.4	1714 1.4	1626 1.6	1417 1.6	1233 2.5	1557 6.5	1607 5.1	1513 3.6	1412 0.8
	2339 6.8	2254 8.7	2140 7.5	1955 6.0	181011.3	2218 1.5	2203 1.3	2051 0.8	1950 0.1
20 F ○	0645 1.3	0542 1.2	0454 1.5	0243 1.4	0100 2.1	0419 6.5	0430 5.0	0336 3.5	0224 0.9
	1200 6.9	1118 8.7	0948 7.5	0817 5.9	063211.4	1039 1.4	1025 1.2	0907 0.7	0821 0.1
	1909 1.3	1805 1.2	1718 1.5	1503 1.4	1325 2.1	1641 6.8	1649 5.2	1556 3.8	1457 0.9
		2338 9.0	2154 7.7	2037 6.2	185511.8	2303 1.2	2248 1.1	2133 0.6	2034 0.1
21 SA	0019 7.0	0633 1.0	0545 1.3	0329 1.1	0152 1.7	0503 6.7	0513 5.1	0419 3.6	0311 0.9
	0734 1.2	1202 8.9	1012 7.6	0901 6.1	071811.8	1124 1.2	1108 1.1	0950 0.6	0904 0.1
	1241 7.0	1856 1.1	1809 1.3	1550 1.3	1416 1.7	1724 7.0	1732 5.3	1639 3.9	1542 0.9
	1958 1.2		2225 7.8	2120 6.3	194012.2	2349 1.0	2332 1.0	2217 0.5	2118 0.1
22 SU	0100 7.0	0022 9.1	0634 1.1	0415 1.0	0242 1.4	0548 6.8	0557 5.2	0503 3.7	0356 0.9
	0823 1.2	0722 0.8	1145 7.6	0946 6.2	080312.0	1210 1.1	1151 1.1	1033 0.6	0946 0.0
	1322 7.0	1246 9.0	1857 1.3	1636 1.2	1504 1.6	1809 7.1	1816 5.4	1721 3.9	1626 0.9
	2045 1.2	1945 1.0	2304 7.8	2204 6.4	202312.3			2301 0.5	2202 0.1
23 M	0144 7.1	0106 9.1	0720 1.1	0500 0.9	0330 1.2	0036 0.9	0017 0.9	0548 3.7	0442 0.9
	0909 1.1	0810 0.7	1219 7.6	1031 6.2	084612.1	0633 6.8	0642 5.1	1117 0.6	1030 0.0
	1406 7.0	1330 9.0	1941 1.3	1721 1.2	1550 1.6	1257 1.1	1236 1.1	1806 3.9	1711 0.9
	2129 1.1	2032 0.9	2348 7.8	2249 6.4	210612.3	1855 7.1	1902 5.3	2348 0.5	2247 0.1
24 TU	0230 7.1	0149 9.1	0803 1.1	0547 0.9	0414 1.3	0123 1.0	0103 0.9	0633 3.7	0528 0.9
	0952 1.2	0855 0.7	1252 7.5	1118 6.1	092911.9	0720 6.7	0729 5.0	1204 0.7	1113 0.0
	1454 7.0	1414 8.9	2024 1.4	1808 1.3	1633 1.8	1345 1.2	1324 1.1	1851 3.9	1757 0.9
	2212 1.1	2117 0.9		2336 6.3	214812.0	1942 6.9	1950 5.2		2334 0.1
25 W	0320 7.0	0234 8.9	0041 7.6	0634 1.0	0457 1.6	0211 1.1	0152 1.0	0037 0.7	0616 0.9
	1036 1.2	0939 0.7	0845 1.2	1206 6.0	101211.6	0808 6.5	0819 4.9	0721 3.6	1200 0.1
	1544 6.9	1500 8.8	1442 7.5	1857 1.4	1715 2.2	1434 1.5	1414 1.2	1255 0.9	1845 0.9
	2257 1.1	2201 1.0	2106 1.5		223211.6	2032 6.7	2043 5.1	1941 3.8	
26 TH	0415 6.8	0321 8.7	0242 7.5	0026 6.1	0540 2.1	0302 1.3	0243 1.1	0132 0.8	0025 0.1
	1123 1.3	1024 0.9	0927 1.3	0724 1.2	105911.0	0900 6.3	0917 4.7	0814 3.5	0708 0.8
	1641 6.7	1548 8.5	1533 7.3	1258 5.8	1759 2.7	1527 1.7	1509 1.4	1353 1.0	1251 0.1
	2347 1.3	2248 1.3	2151 1.7	1948 1.7	232111.0	2126 6.4	2142 4.9	2036 3.6	1936 0.9
27 F	0515 6.7	0413 8.3	0339 7.3	0121 5.8	0627 2.6	0355 1.6	0339 1.3	0234 1.0	0122 0.2
	1215 1.5	1113 1.2	1015 1.6	0818 1.5	115310.5	0957 6.0	1022 4.6	0913 3.3	0805 0.8
	1743 6.6	1644 8.2	1627 7.2	1356 5.5	1848 3.2	1624 2.0	1609 1.5	1500 1.2	1350 0.2
		2339 1.5	2242 2.0	2047 1.9		2226 6.1	2249 4.7	2138 3.5	2032 0.9
28 SA	0044 1.5	0513 8.0	0440 7.1	0221 5.6	002110.4	0454 1.9	0442 1.5	0344 1.1	0228 0.2
	0621 6.5	1207 1.5	1110 1.9	0918 1.7	0722 3.1	1100 5.8	1133 4.5	1020 3.3	0909 0.8
	1316 1.7	1748 8.0	1726 7.1	1459 5.4	125810.0	1727 2.1	1715 1.6	1615 1.3	1457 0.2
	1851 6.4		2344 2.2	2153 2.0	1949 3.5	2333 5.9		2248 3.4	2134 0.8
29 SU	0150 1.7	0039 1.8	0545 7.0	0327 5.4	013210.0	0559 2.1	0000 4.7	0456 1.2	0344 0.2
	0729 6.3	0624 7.8	1216 2.0	1025 1.9	0828 3.4	1211 5.8	0549 1.6	1131 3.3	1021 0.8
	1426 1.9	1313 1.7	1828 7.0	1609 5.3	1411 9.9	1836 2.2	1243 4.5	1729 1.2	1610 0.3
	1959 6.4	1900 7.9		2304 2.1	2100 3.6		1825 1.6		2241 0.8
30 M	0303 1.7	0154 1.8	0055 2.2	0440 5.3	024710.0	0044 5.9	0109 4.7	0000 3.4	0457 0.2
	0835 6.3	0736 7.8	0651 7.0	1136 1.9	0939 3.3	0708 2.1	0657 1.6	0602 1.1	1133 0.8
	1540 1.8	1429 1.7	1330 2.0	1721 5.4	152310.1	1321 5.9	1348 4.7	1239 3.4	1718 0.3
	2103 6.4	2008 8.0	1932 7.1		2213 3.3	1944 2.1	1933 1.6	1833 1.1	2347 0.8

• • Time Zone -0100. For UT subtract 1 hour. For European summer time (shaded) 30/3-26/10 add 1 hour • •

FRANCE, SPAIN, PORTUGAL & GIBRALTAR Time Zone -0100
Calais * Dieppe * Le Havre * Cherbourg * St Malo * Brest * Pointe de Grave * Lisboa * Gibraltar

JULY 1997 TIDE TABLES JULY 1997

	CALAIS	DIEPPE	LE HAVRE	CHERBOURG	ST MALO	BREST	POINTE DE GRAVE	LISBOA	GIBRALTAR
	Time m	Time m	Time m	Time m	Time m	Time m	Time m	Time m	Time m
1 TU	0416 1.6	0309 1.6	0209 2.0	0015 1.9	0357 10.2	0152 6.0	0212 4.7	0106 3.4	0559 0.2
	0937 6.4	0842 8.0	0802 7.1	0553 5.4	1046 3.0	0812 2.0	0801 1.5	0658 1.1	1236 0.8
	1649 1.7	1537 1.5	1439 1.9	1242 1.8	1627 10.5	1423 6.1	1445 4.8	1338 3.5	1817 0.2
	2203 6.5	2108 8.3	2041 7.3	1826 5.6	2318 2.9	2046 1.9	2034 1.4	1928 1.0	
2 W	0520 1.5	0411 1.4	0315 1.7	0118 1.7	0459 10.6	0251 6.1	0309 4.8	0203 3.5	0047 0.8
	1035 6.5	0939 8.3	0915 7.2	0655 5.6	1145 2.6	0909 1.8	0857 1.4	0746 1.0	0651 0.2
	1748 1.5	1635 1.3	1542 1.7	1341 1.6	1724 10.9	1517 6.3	1536 4.9	1430 3.6	1332 0.8
	2259 6.7	2202 8.6	2144 7.4	1919 5.8		2140 1.6	2127 1.3	2015 0.9	1908 0.2
3 TH	0615 1.3	0505 1.1	0414 1.5	0212 1.5	0015 2.5	0343 6.3	0358 4.9	0254 3.6	0140 0.9
	1127 6.6	1030 8.5	1015 7.4	0747 5.7	0554 10.9	1000 1.6	0945 1.3	0829 0.9	0736 0.2
	1838 1.4	1727 1.2	1638 1.5	1431 1.5	1239 2.4	1604 6.5	1621 5.0	1516 3.7	1421 0.9
	2348 6.8	2251 8.7	2236 7.5	2006 6.0	1814 11.3	2230 1.5	2215 1.2	2058 0.8	1954 0.2
4 F	0702 1.3	0555 1.0	0507 1.3	0300 1.3	0108 2.3	0430 6.4	0442 4.9	0340 3.6	0228 0.9
	1212 6.7	1117 8.7	1105 7.5	0832 5.9	0642 11.2	1046 1.5	1030 1.3	0909 0.9	0819 0.1
	1921 1.4	1815 1.2	1728 1.5	1516 1.5	1329 2.3	1648 6.6	1701 5.1	1559 3.8	1505 0.9
		2336 8.8	2318 7.6	2048 6.1	1900 11.5	2314 1.4	2258 1.2	2137 0.8	2037 0.2
●									
5 SA	0032 6.8	0640 1.0	0554 1.3	0342 1.2	0156 2.1	0512 6.5	0521 4.9	0422 3.6	0312 0.9
	0742 1.4	1200 8.7	1146 7.5	0913 5.9	0727 11.2	1128 1.5	1110 1.3	0946 0.8	0900 0.1
	1252 6.8	1858 1.2	1813 1.5	1557 1.4	1414 2.2	1728 6.7	1736 5.1	1639 3.8	1546 0.9
	1958 1.4		2349 7.6	2127 6.1	1942 11.5	2356 1.3	2339 1.2	2215 0.8	2118 0.2
6 SU	0110 6.8	0017 8.8	0636 1.3	0422 1.2	0239 2.1	0551 6.5	0556 4.9	0502 3.6	0353 0.9
	0816 1.4	0721 1.1	1218 7.5	0952 5.9	0808 11.2	1208 1.5	1148 1.3	1022 0.9	0939 0.1
	1327 6.8	1241 8.7	1852 1.6	1635 1.5	1454 2.3	1805 6.7	1809 5.1	1718 3.8	1624 0.9
	2030 1.4	1936 1.3	2321 7.6	2203 6.1	2021 11.5			2251 0.8	2157 0.2
7 M	0146 6.8	0056 8.7	0712 1.5	0458 1.3	0317 2.2	0034 1.4	0017 1.2	0539 3.5	0432 0.9
	0846 1.5	0757 1.1	1227 7.4	1028 5.9	0844 11.1	0627 6.4	0628 4.8	1058 0.9	1016 0.1
	1402 6.8	1318 8.6	1924 1.6	1709 1.6	1529 2.4	1245 1.6	1226 1.3	1754 3.7	1701 0.9
	2100 1.4	2009 1.4	2357 7.6	2238 6.1	2055 11.3	1839 6.6	1841 5.0	2327 0.9	2236 0.2
8 TU	0221 6.8	0132 8.6	0742 1.7	0532 1.4	0348 2.4	0110 1.5	0054 1.3	0616 3.4	0509 0.9
	0915 1.5	0828 1.2	1235 7.4	1103 5.8	0917 10.9	0700 6.3	0700 4.8	1134 0.9	1053 0.1
	1437 6.8	1354 8.5	1952 1.9	1742 1.7	1559 2.6	1319 1.7	1302 1.4	1830 3.6	1736 0.9
	2130 1.5	2039 1.5		2312 5.9	2127 11.1	1912 6.4	1912 4.9		2313 0.2
9 W	0257 6.8	0208 8.4	0036 7.5	0604 1.6	0416 2.6	0144 1.7	0130 1.3	0003 0.9	0545 0.8
	0945 1.6	0855 1.4	0807 1.8	1137 5.7	0948 10.6	0733 6.2	0733 4.7	0651 3.3	1129 0.2
	1513 6.8	1428 8.3	1310 7.4	1815 1.9	1627 2.8	1354 1.9	1339 1.5	1211 1.0	1812 0.9
	2203 1.6	2106 1.6	2018 2.1	2345 5.8	2157 10.8	1945 6.2	1945 4.8	1905 3.5	2351 0.2
10 TH	0333 6.7	0239 8.2	0116 7.4	0636 1.8	0442 2.8	0218 1.9	0206 1.5	0041 1.0	0621 0.8
	1018 1.7	0924 1.5	0833 2.0	1213 5.5	1018 10.3	0808 5.9	0809 4.5	0728 3.2	1206 0.2
	1550 6.8	1501 8.1	1348 7.3	1848 2.1	1654 3.1	1429 2.2	1417 1.6	1251 1.2	1848 0.8
	2238 1.7	2137 1.8	2049 2.2		2227 10.5	2021 6.0	2023 4.6	1941 3.3	
11 F	0411 6.5	0314 7.9	0157 7.2	0021 5.5	0511 3.2	0254 2.2	0245 1.6	0123 1.2	0032 0.3
	1057 1.8	0957 1.8	0906 2.2	0712 2.0	1050 10.0	0847 5.7	0851 4.4	0807 3.1	0701 0.8
	1629 6.5	1537 7.8	1430 7.1	1252 5.3	1726 3.5	1509 2.4	1459 1.8	1336 1.3	1245 0.3
	2321 1.9	2214 2.0	2127 2.4	1928 2.3	2302 10.0	2101 5.7	2106 4.5	2021 3.2	1928 0.8
12 SA	0452 6.3	0352 7.6	0242 6.9	0103 5.3	0545 3.6	0336 2.4	0329 1.8	0211 1.3	0117 0.3
	1144 2.0	1036 2.1	0947 2.4	0754 2.2	1127 9.5	0932 5.5	0941 4.2	0853 3.0	0746 0.7
	1713 6.2	1619 7.5	1518 6.8	1339 5.1	1806 3.9	1555 2.6	1546 1.9	1429 1.4	1330 0.3
		2258 2.3	2213 2.6	2015 2.5	2345 9.5	2148 5.5	2159 4.3	2110 3.0	2014 0.8
13 SU	0013 2.0	0439 7.3	0334 6.6	0152 5.1	0629 4.0	0424 2.6	0419 1.9	0309 1.4	0212 0.3
	0540 6.1	1124 2.4	1037 2.6	0845 2.4	1219 9.1	1027 5.3	1044 4.1	0948 2.9	0841 0.7
	1241 2.1	1711 7.2	1617 6.5	1435 4.9	1858 4.3	1650 2.8	1642 2.0	1534 1.5	1429 0.3
	1806 6.0	2354 2.6	2309 2.8	2113 2.6		2247 5.3	2306 4.2	2211 3.0	2109 0.8
14 M	0112 2.2	0537 7.0	0441 6.4	0254 4.9	0044 9.1	0522 2.7	0519 2.0	0416 1.4	0323 0.3
	0640 5.8	1224 2.6	1138 2.8	0945 2.5	0730 4.3	1133 5.3	1157 4.2	1054 2.9	0949 0.7
	1342 2.3	1815 7.0	1735 6.4	1539 4.9	1330 8.9	1752 2.8	1746 2.1	1647 1.5	1545 0.4
	1913 5.8			2219 2.6	2008 4.4	2357 5.3		2322 2.9	2215 0.8
15 TU	0215 2.2	0100 2.7	0014 2.8	0402 4.9	0201 9.0	0629 2.7	0022 4.2	0522 1.4	0442 0.3
	0753 5.8	0650 6.9	0608 6.3	1051 2.5	0845 4.3	1244 5.4	0625 2.0	1203 3.0	1104 0.7
	1445 2.2	1334 2.6	1246 2.7	1646 5.0	1448 9.1	1900 2.6	1305 4.3	1754 1.4	1702 0.3
	2027 5.9	1929 7.2	1856 6.6	2327 2.5	2124 4.2		1853 2.0		2324 0.8

●● Time Zone -0100. For UT subtract 1 hour. For European summer time (shaded) 30/3-26/10 add 1 hour ●●

JULY 1997 TIDE TABLES JULY 1997

Day	CALAIS Time	m	DIEPPE Time	m	LE HAVRE Time	m	CHERBOURG Time	m	ST MALO Time	m	BREST Time	m	POINTE DE GRAVE Time	m	LISBOA Time	m	GIBRALTAR Time	m
16 W	0317	2.1	0213	2.5	0123	2.6	0511	5.0	0318	9.3	0110	5.4	0132	4.3	0032	3.0	0548	0.3
	0903	6.0	0806	7.2	0727	6.6	1157	2.3	1000	3.9	0736	2.5	0729	1.9	0622	1.2	1212	0.7
	1548	2.0	1446	2.4	1355	2.5	1749	5.3	1557	9.7	1349	5.7	1405	4.5	1306	3.2	1805	0.3
	2131	6.1	2039	7.6	1957	6.9			2236	3.6	2005	2.4	1955	1.8	1851	1.2		
17 TH	0419	1.9	0322	2.1	0230	2.3	0031	2.2	0424	9.9	0215	5.7	0231	4.5	0133	3.2	0027	0.8
	1001	6.3	0912	7.7	0827	6.9	0615	5.3	1108	3.4	0836	2.2	0826	1.7	0714	1.0	0642	0.2
	1649	1.8	1551	2.0	1500	2.2	1257	2.1	1656	10.4	1445	6.0	1457	4.8	1400	3.4	1309	0.8
	2225	6.5	2138	8.1	2043	7.2	1844	5.6	2340	2.9	2103	2.0	2051	1.6	1943	0.9	1857	0.2
18 F	0520	1.6	0423	1.7	0333	1.9	0128	1.8	0522	10.6	0309	6.1	0324	4.8	0226	3.3	0123	0.9
	1052	6.6	1006	8.2	0913	7.2	0710	5.6	1209	2.7	0929	1.8	0917	1.5	0803	0.8	0729	0.1
	1749	1.6	1649	1.6	1602	1.8	1353	1.7	1749	11.2	1535	6.5	1545	5.1	1448	3.6	1400	0.9
	2314	6.8	2230	8.6	2116	7.5	1933	5.9			2155	1.5	2142	1.3	2030	0.7	1944	0.2
19 SA	0619	1.4	0521	1.2	0434	1.5	0221	1.4	0039	2.2	0400	6.4	0412	5.0	0315	3.5	0214	0.9
	1139	6.9	1057	8.7	0950	7.5	0800	5.9	0615	11.3	1018	1.4	1004	1.3	0848	0.7	0813	0.1
	1847	1.3	1746	1.3	1702	1.5	1444	1.4	1306	2.1	1622	6.8	1632	5.3	1536	3.8	1447	0.9
			2318	9.0	2142	7.8	2020	6.2	1839	11.8	2245	1.2	2230	1.1	2117	0.5	2029	0.1
20 SU ○	0001	7.0	0615	0.9	0531	1.2	0311	1.1	0136	1.6	0447	6.8	0458	5.2	0402	3.7	0302	0.9
	0716	1.2	1144	9.0	1009	7.7	0847	6.2	0704	11.9	1107	1.1	1051	1.1	0933	0.5	0857	0.0
	1224	7.1	1840	1.0	1757	1.3	1533	1.2	1401	1.5	1709	7.1	1718	5.5	1621	4.0	1533	1.0
	1942	1.1			2214	8.0	2106	6.5	1927	12.4	2333	0.8	2316	0.9	2202	0.4	2113	0.1
21 M	0048	7.2	0005	9.3	0623	0.9	0359	0.8	0229	1.0	0534	7.0	0543	5.3	0448	3.8	0349	1.0
	0809	1.0	0708	0.6	1118	7.8	0933	6.3	0751	12.3	1154	0.9	1136	1.0	1018	0.4	0939	0.0
	1310	7.2	1230	9.3	1845	1.0	1621	1.0	1452	1.1	1756	7.3	1803	5.6	1706	4.1	1618	1.0
	2033	0.9	1932	0.7	2252	8.1	2151	6.6	2012	12.7					2248	0.3	2158	0.0
22 TU	0134	7.3	0051	9.4	0709	0.7	0446	0.6	0318	0.7	0021	0.7	0002	0.8	0533	3.8	0436	1.0
	0858	0.9	0757	0.4	1151	7.8	1018	6.4	0836	12.5	0620	7.1	0628	5.3	1103	0.4	1022	0.0
	1357	7.3	1315	9.4	1930	0.9	1707	0.9	1539	1.0	1242	0.8	1221	0.9	1751	4.1	1703	1.0
	2119	0.9	2019	0.5			2237	6.7	2056	12.8	1842	7.4	1848	5.6	2333	0.4	2243	0.0
23 W	0222	7.3	0135	9.4	0032	8.0	0532	0.6	0403	0.6	0108	0.6	0048	0.8	0618	3.8	0523	1.0
	0942	0.8	0842	0.3	0753	0.6	1104	6.4	0919	12.4	0706	7.1	0714	5.3	1150	0.5	1106	0.0
	1444	7.3	1359	9.4	1347	7.9	1753	1.0	1623	1.1	1330	0.9	1309	0.9	1836	4.0	1748	1.0
	2202	0.7	2103	0.5	2013	0.9	2322	6.6	2138	12.6	1928	7.3	1935	5.5			2330	0.1
24 TH	0310	7.3	0220	9.3	0103	7.9	0618	0.8	0446	0.9	0155	0.8	0135	0.8	0021	0.5	0612	0.9
	1024	0.9	0925	0.3	0833	0.7	1149	6.3	1001	12.1	0752	6.9	0802	5.1	0703	3.7	1152	0.1
	1532	7.2	1443	9.2	1433	7.8	1839	1.2	1704	1.4	1418	1.1	1357	1.0	1239	0.7	1836	1.0
	2245	0.8	2145	0.6	2053	1.1			2220	12.1	2015	7.0	2024	5.3	1924	3.9		
25 F	0401	7.1	0304	9.1	0245	7.8	0009	6.4	0527	1.4	0243	1.1	0224	1.0	0112	0.7	0020	0.1
	1108	1.0	1007	0.5	0913	1.0	0705	1.0	1044	11.6	0840	6.6	0854	4.9	0753	3.6	0703	0.9
	1624	7.0	1529	8.9	1519	7.7	1237	6.0	1745	2.0	1507	1.4	1448	1.2	1333	0.9	1242	0.1
	2331	1.0	2228	0.9	2134	1.4	1928	1.5	2305	11.5	2105	6.6	2119	5.1	2015	3.7	1927	0.9
26 SA	0456	6.8	0352	8.7	0331	7.6	0058	6.0	0610	2.1	0333	1.5	0317	1.2	0208	0.9	0116	0.2
	1156	1.3	1051	0.9	0954	1.4	0755	1.4	1130	10.9	0931	6.2	0953	4.7	0847	3.4	0758	0.8
	1721	6.7	1618	8.5	1606	7.4	1328	5.7	1828	2.7	1600	1.8	1545	1.4	1434	1.1	1340	0.2
			2314	1.3	2219	1.7	2021	1.8	2356	10.7	2200	6.2	2221	4.8	2114	3.5	2022	0.9
27 SU	0023	1.3	0446	8.2	0421	7.2	0153	5.7	0657	2.8	0428	1.9	0415	1.5	0313	1.1	0225	0.2
	0557	6.5	1139	1.4	1042	1.8	0850	1.8	1227	10.2	1030	5.9	1102	4.5	0951	3.3	0901	0.8
	1251	1.6	1718	8.0	1657	7.1	1427	5.4	1921	3.3	1700	2.1	1649	1.6	1547	1.3	1454	0.3
	1826	6.5			2314	2.1	2123	2.1			2303	5.8	2333	4.6	2222	3.3	2124	0.8
28 M	0123	1.6	0009	1.7	0520	7.0	0257	5.3	0059	10.0	0530	2.2	0521	1.7	0427	1.3	0351	0.3
	0704	6.3	0554	7.7	1143	2.2	0954	2.1	0755	3.4	1140	5.7	1217	4.4	1103	3.2	1013	0.8
	1356	1.9	1239	1.9	1755	6.9	1536	5.2	1336	9.7	1809	2.3	1800	1.8	1706	1.3	1618	0.3
	1935	6.2	1830	7.7			2235	2.3	2027	3.7					2339	3.2	2233	0.8
29 TU	0234	1.9	0122	2.1	0024	2.4	0414	5.1	0218	9.6	0018	5.6	0048	4.5	0539	1.3	0509	0.3
	0813	6.1	0712	7.5	0627	6.8	1108	2.3	0906	3.7	0642	2.4	0633	1.8	1217	3.2	1127	0.8
	1511	2.0	1400	2.1	1258	2.4	1657	5.2	1456	9.6	1257	5.6	1329	4.5	1818	1.3	1729	0.3
	2043	6.2	1944	7.7	1902	6.9	2354	2.2	2145	3.8	1923	2.4	1913	1.8			2342	0.8
30 W	0351	1.9	0245	2.0	0142	2.4	0539	5.2	0339	9.6	0135	5.6	0158	4.5	0050	3.2	0608	0.2
	0920	6.1	0821	7.6	0742	6.8	1224	2.2	1021	3.4	0753	2.3	0742	1.8	0642	1.2	1232	0.8
	1627	2.0	1515	2.0	1415	2.4	1812	5.4	1610	9.9	1407	5.8	1431	4.6	1321	3.4	1824	0.3
	2148	6.2	2050	7.8	2015	6.9			2300	3.4	2030	2.2	2019	1.7	1917	1.1		
31 TH	0503	1.8	0351	1.8	0255	2.1	0103	2.0	0448	10.0	0239	5.8	0258	4.6	0150	3.3	0043	0.8
	1022	6.2	0924	7.9	0900	6.9	0645	5.3	1128	3.2	0854	2.1	0841	1.7	0732	1.1	0654	0.2
	1732	1.8	1616	1.9	1522	2.1	1326	2.0	1712	10.4	1503	6.1	1524	4.8	1414	3.5	1326	0.8
	2248	6.4	2147	8.1	2124	7.1	1907	5.6			2127	1.9	2115	1.5	2004	1.0	1910	0.2

●● Time Zone -0100. For UT subtract 1 hour. For European summer time (shaded) 30/3-26/10 add 1 hour ●●

FRANCE, SPAIN, PORTUGAL & GIBRALTAR Time Zone -0100
Calais * Dieppe * Le Havre * Cherbourg * St Malo * Brest * Pointe de Grave * Lisboa * Gibraltar

AUGUST 1997 TIDE TABLES AUGUST 1997

CALAIS	DIEPPE	LE HAVRE	CHERBOURG	ST MALO	BREST	POINTE DE GRAVE	LISBOA	GIBRALTAR	Day
Time m	Time m	Time m	Time m	Time m	Time m	Time m	Time m	Time m	
0600 1.6	0448 1.5	0357 1.8	0158 1.7	0003 3.0	0330 6.1	0347 4.7	0240 3.4	0135 0.9	**1 F**
1116 6.4	1016 8.2	1001 7.2	0736 5.6	054510.4	0945 1.9	0931 1.5	0815 1.0	0735 0.2	
1824 1.6	1709 1.5	1621 1.9	1417 1.8	1224 2.8	1551 6.3	1609 4.9	1500 3.6	1412 0.9	
2339 6.5	2236 8.4	2218 7.3	1953 5.8	180310.8	2215 1.7	2202 1.4	2045 0.9	1951 0.2	
0648 1.5	0538 1.3	0451 1.6	0244 1.5	0055 2.6	0415 6.3	0429 4.8	0324 3.5	0219 0.9	**2 SA**
1200 6.5	1103 8.5	1049 7.4	0818 5.8	063210.8	1030 1.7	1014 1.4	0853 0.9	0812 0.1	
1907 1.5	1757 1.4	1711 1.7	1500 1.6	1313 2.5	1632 6.5	1646 5.0	1542 3.7	1452 0.9	
	2320 8.6	2257 7.5	2032 6.0	184711.2	2257 1.5	2242 1.3	2121 0.8	2028 0.2	
0020 6.7	0622 1.1	0536 1.4	0324 1.4	0140 2.3	0454 6.4	0504 4.9	0403 3.5	0259 0.9	**3 SU**
0727 1.5	1144 8.6	1127 7.5	0856 5.9	071311.0	1109 1.6	1052 1.3	0928 0.8	0847 0.1	
1236 6.7	1839 1.3	1754 1.6	1539 1.5	1355 2.3	1709 6.7	1718 5.1	1620 3.7	1529 0.9	●
1942 1.4	2359 8.7	2251 7.5	2108 6.1	192611.4	2336 1.4	2319 1.2	2154 0.8	2103 0.2	
0054 6.8	0701 1.1	0616 1.4	0401 1.3	0220 2.2	0530 6.5	0535 4.9	0440 3.5	0336 0.9	**4 M**
0759 1.4	1221 8.7	1154 7.5	0931 6.0	075011.2	1146 1.5	1128 1.3	1002 0.8	0921 0.1	
1309 6.8	1915 1.3	1830 1.6	1613 1.5	1433 2.2	1744 6.7	1748 5.1	1656 3.7	1603 0.9	
2013 1.4		2257 7.6	2142 6.2	200211.5		2354 1.2	2228 0.7	2138 0.2	
0126 6.8	0036 8.8	0649 1.4	0434 1.3	0255 2.1	0011 1.4	0604 4.9	0515 3.5	0411 0.9	**5 TU**
0827 1.4	0735 1.1	1136 7.6	1004 6.0	082411.2	0603 6.5	1203 1.2	1036 0.8	0954 0.1	
1340 6.9	1257 8.7	1901 1.7	1645 1.5	1506 2.2	1221 1.5	1817 5.1	1730 3.7	1637 0.9	
2042 1.3	1947 1.3	2330 7.7	2214 6.2	203311.4	1815 6.7		2300 0.7	2212 0.2	
0157 6.9	0109 8.8	0718 1.5	0506 1.3	0326 2.1	0043 1.4	0027 1.2	0548 3.5	0445 0.9	**6 W**
0856 1.4	0804 1.2	1201 7.6	1036 6.0	085411.2	0634 6.5	0633 4.9	1109 0.8	1027 0.1	
1412 7.0	1330 8.7	1928 1.7	1716 1.6	1536 2.3	1253 1.6	1236 1.3	1802 3.6	1709 0.9	
2111 1.3	2014 1.4		2245 6.1	210311.4	1846 6.6	1845 5.0	2333 0.8	2247 0.2	
0229 6.9	0142 8.7	0006 7.7	0536 1.5	0354 2.2	0115 1.6	0100 1.2	0621 3.4	0518 0.9	**7 TH**
0924 1.4	0830 1.2	0742 1.6	1106 5.9	092111.0	0705 6.4	0703 4.8	1143 0.9	1100 0.2	
1443 7.0	1400 8.6	1234 7.6	1746 1.7	1605 2.4	1324 1.7	1309 1.3	1833 3.5	1742 0.9	
2140 1.4	2041 1.4	1954 1.8	2314 6.0	213011.2	1916 6.4	1915 4.9		2321 0.2	
0300 6.8	0212 8.5	0041 7.6	0606 1.6	0421 2.4	0145 1.8	0133 1.3	0008 0.9	0553 0.9	**8 F**
0953 1.5	0857 1.4	0809 1.7	1136 5.8	094810.8	0736 6.2	0736 4.7	0653 3.3	1133 0.2	
1515 6.9	1431 8.4	1308 7.5	1818 1.9	1633 2.7	1357 1.9	1344 1.4	1218 1.0	1817 0.9	
2210 1.5	2109 1.6	2023 1.9	2345 5.8	215810.9	1948 6.2	1948 4.8	1905 3.4	2357 0.2	
0332 6.8	0243 8.3	0116 7.5	0639 1.9	0448 2.8	0218 2.0	0208 1.5	0044 1.0	0631 0.8	**9 SA**
1024 1.6	0927 1.6	0837 1.9	1209 5.6	101610.5	0809 6.0	0811 4.6	0725 3.2	1208 0.3	
1547 6.8	1502 8.2	1342 7.3	1854 2.1	1702 3.0	1433 2.2	1421 1.6	1257 1.1	1855 0.8	
2245 1.7	2142 1.8	2055 2.1		222810.5	2023 6.0	2024 4.6	1939 3.2		
0406 6.6	0316 8.0	0153 7.2	0017 5.6	0518 3.2	0256 2.2	0245 1.7	0125 1.2	0039 0.3	**10 SU**
1102 1.8	1001 1.9	0912 2.2	0715 2.1	104810.1	0848 5.8	0852 4.4	0803 3.1	0715 0.8	
1624 6.5	1537 7.9	1420 7.1	1245 5.4	1735 3.5	1515 2.4	1503 1.8	1343 1.3	1249 0.3	
2328 1.9	2221 2.1	2135 2.4	1935 2.4	230310.0	2104 5.7	2108 4.4	2018 3.1	1940 0.8	
0445 6.3	0355 7.6	0236 6.9	0057 5.3	0553 3.7	0340 2.5	0331 1.8	0214 1.3	0130 0.3	**11 M**
1152 2.1	1043 2.3	0956 2.5	0759 2.4	1128 9.6	0936 5.5	0947 4.2	0850 3.0	0809 0.7	
1708 6.3	1621 7.5	1510 6.7	1333 5.1	1818 4.0	1606 2.6	1554 2.0	1441 1.4	1345 0.4	
	2309 2.4	2224 2.6	2026 2.6	2351 9.5	2156 5.4	2209 4.2	2113 2.9	2036 0.8	
0024 2.1	0445 7.2	0336 6.5	0154 5.0	0643 4.2	0435 2.7	0427 2.0	0318 1.4	0245 0.3	**12 TU**
0537 6.0	1137 2.6	0855 2.6	0855 2.6	1227 9.1	1037 5.3	1101 4.2	0954 2.9	0916 0.7	
1253 2.2	1719 7.2	1622 6.4	1438 5.0	1919 4.4	1706 2.8	1657 2.1	1555 1.5	1511 0.4	
1808 6.0		2324 2.9	2131 2.7		2304 5.3	2333 4.1	2227 2.9	2145 0.8	
0127 2.2	0012 2.7	0507 6.3	0309 4.9	0104 9.0	0541 2.8	0536 2.1	0434 1.4	0421 0.3	**13 W**
0650 5.8	0557 6.9	1157 2.9	1005 2.7	0756 4.5	1154 5.3	1224 4.2	1114 2.9	1036 0.7	
1359 2.3	1248 2.8	1800 6.4	1556 4.9	1357 8.9	1817 2.7	1811 2.1	1715 1.4	1646 0.3	
1931 5.8	1839 7.0		2245 2.6	2041 4.4			2353 2.9	2300 0.8	
0234 2.2	0131 2.7	0036 2.8	0433 4.9	0240 9.0	0028 5.3	0059 4.2	0548 1.3	0531 0.3	**14 TH**
0817 5.8	0726 7.0	0648 6.4	1121 2.5	0923 4.3	0656 2.7	0651 2.0	1230 3.1	1148 0.8	
1507 2.2	1410 2.7	1314 2.8	1713 5.1	1526 9.3	1313 5.6	1336 4.5	1824 1.2	1750 0.3	
2054 6.0	2004 7.3	1918 6.7		2206 4.0	1932 2.5	1923 1.9			
0342 2.0	0253 2.3	0154 2.6	0000 2.4	0402 9.6	0147 5.6	0209 4.5	0105 3.1	0007 0.8	**15 F**
0930 6.1	0842 7.5	0758 6.8	0550 5.2	1044 3.7	0807 2.3	0757 1.8	0649 1.1	0624 0.2	
1617 1.9	1526 2.2	1431 2.5	1232 2.2	163610.2	1419 6.0	1435 4.8	1333 3.3	1247 0.8	
2158 6.4	2112 7.9	2012 7.1	1820 5.5	2321 3.1	2039 2.0	2027 1.6	1921 0.9	1840 0.2	

•• Time Zone -0100. For UT subtract 1 hour. For European summer time (shaded) 30/3-26/10 add 1 hour ••

AUGUST 1997 TIDE TABLES AUGUST 1997

	CALAIS		DIEPPE		LE HAVRE		CHERBOURG		ST MALO		BREST		POINTE DE GRAVE		LISBOA		GIBRALTAR	
	Time	m	Time	m	Time	m	Time	m	Time	m	Time	m	Time	m	Time	m	Time	m
16 SA	0452	1.7	0402	1.8	0309	2.1	0106	1.9	0506	10.5	0249	6.0	0306	4.8	0204	3.3	0104	0.9
	1027	6.6	0943	8.1	0848	7.2	0652	5.6	1153	2.9	0907	1.9	0854	1.5	0742	0.8	0709	0.1
	1724	1.6	1630	1.7	1542	2.0	1333	1.8	1733	11.1	1515	6.5	1527	5.1	1426	3.6	1338	0.9
	2252	6.8	2208	8.6	2050	7.6	1915	5.9			2136	1.5	2121	1.3	2012	0.6	1926	0.1
17 SU	0557	1.4	0502	1.2	0417	1.6	0202	1.4	0024	2.2	0342	6.5	0355	5.1	0255	3.5	0155	1.0
	1118	7.0	1036	8.8	0927	7.6	0743	6.0	0600	11.4	1000	1.4	0945	1.2	0831	0.6	0752	0.1
	1827	1.2	1729	1.5	1646	1.5	1427	1.4	1252	2.0	1605	7.0	1615	5.4	1515	3.8	1425	1.0
	2342	7.2	2259	9.1	2121	7.9	2003	6.3	1824	12.0	2227	1.0	2211	1.0	2100	0.4	2009	0.1
18 M O	0658	1.1	0558	0.7	0516	1.1	0254	1.0	0121	1.4	0430	6.9	0442	5.3	0342	3.7	0243	1.0
	1206	7.3	1124	9.2	0953	7.9	0830	6.3	0650	12.2	1050	1.0	1033	1.0	0917	0.4	0834	0.0
	1924	0.9	1824	0.7	1742	1.1	1516	1.0	1346	1.3	1653	7.4	1700	5.6	1602	4.0	1511	1.0
			2347	9.5	2155	8.2	2050	6.7	1912	12.7	2315	0.7	2258	0.8	2145	0.3	2053	0.0
19 TU	0030	7.4	0651	0.3	0607	0.7	0342	0.6	0214	0.7	0517	7.3	0526	5.4	0428	3.9	0330	1.0
	0752	0.8	1211	9.6	1101	8.0	0916	6.6	0736	12.7	1138	0.7	1118	0.8	1002	0.3	0916	-0.0
	1252	7.5	1915	0.4	1830	0.8	1603	0.8	1436	0.7	1739	7.6	1745	5.7	1647	4.2	1556	1.1
	2016	0.7			2233	8.3	2135	6.9	1957	13.1			2344	0.6	2230	0.2	2136	0.0
20 W	0116	7.6	0033	9.7	0653	0.4	0427	0.5	0302	0.3	0003	0.4	0609	5.5	0513	4.0	0416	1.0
	0840	0.7	0739	0.1	1134	8.1	1000	6.7	0821	13.0	0603	7.4	1204	0.7	1047	0.3	0958	-0.0
	1338	7.6	1256	9.7	1914	0.6	1649	0.7	1523	0.5	1224	0.6	1830	5.7	1732	4.3	1641	1.1
	2101	0.5	2000	0.2			2219	6.9	2041	13.2	1824	7.7			2315	0.2	2221	0.0
21 TH	0203	7.6	0117	9.8	0008	8.2	0513	0.5	0347	0.2	0049	0.4	0029	0.6	0557	4.0	0503	1.0
	0923	0.6	0823	-0.0	0735	0.3	1043	6.7	0903	12.9	0647	7.4	0654	5.4	1132	0.4	1041	0.0
	1424	7.5	1339	9.7	1209	8.0	1734	0.8	1606	0.5	1311	0.6	1250	0.7	1817	4.1	1727	1.1
	2144	0.5	2044	0.2	1955	0.6	2303	6.8	2122	13.0	1909	7.5	1915	5.6			2306	0.1
22 F	0251	7.5	0200	9.7	0039	8.1	0557	0.7	0429	0.5	0135	0.6	0115	0.7	0000	0.4	0551	1.0
	1004	0.7	0904	0.1	0815	0.5	1127	6.6	0942	12.6	0731	7.2	0739	5.3	0642	3.9	1126	0.1
	1512	7.4	1422	9.5	1416	8.1	1818	1.0	1646	1.0	1357	0.9	1337	0.8	1218	0.5	1814	1.0
	2225	0.6	2124	0.4	2033	0.8	2347	6.6	2202	12.5	1954	7.2	2002	5.4	1903	3.9	2354	0.1
23 SA	0339	7.2	0243	9.4	0230	8.0	0642	1.0	0509	1.1	0221	1.0	0202	0.9	0046	0.6	0641	0.9
	1045	0.9	0945	0.4	0852	0.9	1211	6.3	1023	12.0	0816	6.8	0827	5.0	0728	3.7	1215	0.2
	1601	7.2	1505	9.2	1457	7.8	1905	1.4	1725	1.7	1445	1.3	1427	1.1	1308	0.8	1904	1.0
	2308	0.9	2204	0.7	2112	1.2			2243	11.7	2041	6.7	2053	5.1	1953	3.7		
24 SU	0431	6.9	0328	8.9	0313	7.7	0033	6.2	0548	2.0	0309	1.5	0251	1.2	0138	0.9	0049	0.2
	1130	1.2	1025	0.9	0930	1.4	0728	1.5	1105	11.2	0904	6.3	0923	4.8	0820	3.4	0736	0.8
	1656	6.8	1551	8.6	1538	7.5	1258	5.9	1805	2.5	1536	1.8	1521	1.4	1406	1.0	1313	0.2
	2356	1.3	2247	1.3	2152	1.7	1954	1.8	2330	10.7	2132	6.2	2152	4.7	2049	3.4	2000	0.9
25 M	0530	6.5	0418	8.2	0356	7.3	0124	5.7	0630	2.9	0400	2.0	0348	1.5	0238	1.2	0203	0.3
	1221	1.6	1110	1.5	1012	2.0	0820	2.0	1156	10.3	0959	5.9	1030	4.5	0920	3.2	0840	0.8
	1758	6.4	1646	8.0	1621	7.1	1353	5.5	1852	3.4	1633	2.2	1622	1.7	1517	1.3	1440	0.3
			2337	1.9	2242	2.3	2052	2.2			2234	5.7	2305	4.4	2157	3.1	2106	0.8
26 TU	0052	1.7	0525	7.6	0448	6.8	0227	5.2	0029	9.8	0501	2.5	0452	1.8	0354	1.4	0351	0.3
	0636	6.1	1206	2.1	1108	2.6	0921	2.4	0724	3.7	1109	5.5	1150	4.3	1033	3.1	0956	0.8
	1322	2.0	1800	7.4	1715	6.7	1501	5.1	1304	9.5	1743	2.6	1734	1.9	1644	1.4	1621	0.3
	1909	6.1			2351	2.7	2205	2.5	1955	4.0	2353	5.4			2316	3.0	2221	0.8
27 W	0201	2.1	0049	2.4	0556	6.5	0348	5.0	0154	9.1	0616	2.7	0028	4.3	0516	1.4	0509	0.3
	0748	5.9	0647	7.2	1227	2.9	1040	2.6	0836	4.2	1234	5.4	0606	2.0	1154	3.1	1115	0.8
	1439	2.3	1331	2.5	1824	6.6	1630	5.0	1433	9.2	1904	2.6	1310	4.3	1805	1.3	1728	0.3
	2021	5.9	1921	7.2			2332	2.5	2122	4.3			1853	2.0			2334	0.8
28 TH	0325	2.2	0221	2.4	0119	2.8	0526	5.0	0328	9.1	0119	5.4	0144	4.3	0033	3.0	0602	0.3
	0858	5.8	0803	7.3	0718	6.5	1206	2.5	1003	4.2	0734	2.6	0722	2.0	0627	1.4	1220	0.8
	1605	2.2	1454	2.4	1354	2.9	1757	5.2	1558	9.4	1352	5.6	1416	4.5	1302	3.2	1818	0.3
	2130	6.0	2032	7.4	1946	6.6			2249	3.9	2016	2.4	2004	1.8	1906	1.2		
29 F	0444	2.0	0331	2.1	0237	2.5	0048	2.3	0441	9.6	0226	5.6	0245	4.4	0134	3.1	0033	0.8
	1004	6.0	0909	7.6	0845	6.7	0634	5.2	1117	3.7	0838	2.4	0825	1.9	0719	1.2	0642	0.2
	1714	2.0	1557	2.1	1505	2.5	1312	2.3	1701	10.0	1449	5.9	1509	4.7	1356	3.3	1310	0.9
	2233	6.2	2132	7.8	2106	6.9	1853	5.4	2352	3.3	2112	2.1	2100	1.7	1951	1.1	1857	0.3
30 SA	0542	1.8	0429	1.8	0339	2.1	0142	1.9	0533	10.2	0315	5.9	0331	4.6	0222	3.3	0119	0.9
	1100	6.2	1002	8.0	0947	7.0	0721	5.5	1210	3.1	0928	2.1	0914	1.7	0800	1.1	0716	0.2
	1805	1.7	1651	1.8	1601	2.2	1400	2.0	1749	10.6	1533	6.2	1551	4.8	1441	3.5	1351	0.9
	2323	6.4	2221	8.2	2200	7.2	1936	5.7			2157	1.8	2144	1.5	2027	0.9	1930	0.2
31 SU	0627	1.6	0518	1.4	0430	1.8	0224	1.6	0039	2.8	0356	6.2	0409	4.8	0303	3.4	0157	0.9
	1143	6.5	1045	8.4	1030	7.3	0800	5.7	0616	10.7	1010	1.8	0954	1.5	0835	0.9	0748	0.2
	1845	1.5	1736	1.5	1648	1.9	1439	1.7	1254	2.7	1612	6.5	1625	5.0	1520	3.6	1426	0.9
			2301	8.5	2236	7.4	2012	6.0	1829	11.0	2236	1.6	2221	1.3	2100	0.8	2002	0.2

•• Time Zone -0100. For UT subtract 1 hour. For European summer time (shaded) 30/3-26/10 add 1 hour ••

FRANCE, SPAIN, PORTUGAL & GIBRALTAR Time Zone -0100

Calais * Dieppe * Le Havre * Cherbourg * St Malo * Brest * Pointe de Grave * Lisboa * Gibraltar

SEPTEMBER 1997 TIDE TABLES SEPTEMBER 1997

CALAIS Time m	DIEPPE Time m	LE HAVRE Time m	CHERBOURG Time m	ST MALO Time m	BREST Time m	POINTE DE GRAVE Time m	LISBOA Time m	GIBRALTAR Time m	Day
0002 6.6	0559 1.2	0512 1.5	0301 1.4	0118 2.4	0433 6.4	0441 4.9	0340 3.5	0232 0.9	**1 M**
0703 1.4	1124 8.6	1105 7.5	0834 5.9	0653 11.1	1048 1.6	1031 1.3	0908 0.8	0818 0.2	
1217 6.7	1815 1.4	1728 1.7	1515 1.5	1332 2.4	1647 6.7	1655 5.1	1556 3.7	1457 1.0	
1919 1.3	2339 8.7	2220 7.6	2045 6.1	1905 11.3	2311 1.4	2257 1.2	2131 0.7	2033 0.2	●
0033 6.8	0636 1.1	0548 1.4	0335 1.3	0154 2.2	0506 6.6	0510 5.0	0415 3.5	0304 1.0	**2 TU**
0735 1.3	1158 8.8	1128 7.6	0906 6.1	0727 11.3	1121 1.5	1105 1.2	0940 0.7	0848 0.2	
1247 6.9	1849 1.3	1802 1.6	1547 1.4	1407 2.2	1719 6.8	1724 5.1	1630 3.7	1528 1.0	
1950 1.2		2233 7.7	2117 6.3	1937 11.5	2344 1.4	2329 1.1	2202 0.7	2104 0.2	
0103 6.9	0012 8.9	0620 1.4	0406 1.3	0227 2.0	0537 6.7	0538 5.0	0448 3.6	0335 1.0	**3 W**
0804 1.3	0707 1.1	1106 7.7	0937 6.2	0757 11.4	1154 1.4	1137 1.2	1012 0.7	0918 0.2	
1316 7.0	1231 8.9	1831 1.5	1618 1.4	1439 2.0	1749 6.8	1751 5.1	1703 3.7	1557 1.0	
2020 1.2	1919 1.2	2303 7.8	2147 6.3	2007 11.6			2233 0.7	2135 0.2	
0132 7.0	0045 8.9	0648 1.4	0436 1.3	0259 2.0	0015 1.4	0000 1.1	0520 3.6	0406 1.0	**4 TH**
0833 1.3	0736 1.1	1128 7.8	1006 6.2	0826 11.5	0606 6.7	0606 5.0	1044 0.7	0948 0.2	
1345 7.1	1303 8.9	1900 1.5	1648 1.5	1511 2.0	1224 1.5	1209 1.2	1733 3.6	1627 1.0	
2049 1.2	1948 1.2	2333 7.9	2215 6.3	2036 11.6	1818 6.8	1818 5.1	2304 0.7	2206 0.2	
0200 7.0	0116 8.9	0715 1.5	0506 1.4	0329 2.0	0045 1.5	0030 1.2	0550 3.5	0439 0.9	**5 F**
0901 1.3	0804 1.2	1155 7.8	1035 6.2	0854 11.4	0636 6.6	0635 5.0	1116 0.7	1018 0.2	
1413 7.1	1333 8.8	1927 1.6	1718 1.6	1542 2.1	1256 1.6	1240 1.2	1803 3.5	1659 0.9	
2117 1.3	2015 1.3		2243 6.2	2103 11.5	1848 6.6	1847 5.0	2336 0.8	2238 0.2	
0228 7.0	0146 8.8	0002 7.8	0536 1.6	0357 2.2	0115 1.6	0101 1.3	0619 3.4	0513 0.9	**6 SA**
0927 1.4	0831 1.3	0743 1.6	1102 6.1	0920 11.3	0706 6.5	0705 4.9	1150 0.8	1048 0.2	
1441 7.0	1402 8.7	1221 7.7	1750 1.8	1611 2.4	1328 1.8	1312 1.3	1833 3.4	1733 0.9	
2143 1.4	2043 1.4	1957 1.7	2310 6.0	2130 11.3	1918 6.4	1917 4.9		2312 0.2	
0257 6.9	0215 8.6	0031 7.7	0608 1.8	0426 2.6	0147 1.9	0133 1.4	0010 0.9	0550 0.9	**7 SU**
0955 1.5	0900 1.5	0812 1.8	1130 5.9	0946 11.0	0738 6.3	0737 4.7	0649 3.3	1121 0.3	
1511 6.9	1431 8.4	1250 7.5	1824 2.0	1639 2.8	1403 2.0	1348 1.5	1226 1.0	1811 0.9	
2213 1.6	2113 1.7	2026 1.9	2341 5.8	2159 10.9	1951 6.2	1950 4.7	1903 3.2	2349 0.3	
0328 6.8	0245 8.3	0104 7.5	0642 2.1	0454 3.1	0223 2.1	0210 1.6	0048 1.0	0633 0.8	**8 M**
1029 1.7	0930 1.9	0842 2.0	1202 5.7	1016 10.6	0813 6.0	0815 4.6	0723 3.2	1158 0.3	
1545 6.7	1503 8.1	1325 7.3	1902 2.2	1709 3.3	1443 2.3	1429 1.7	1309 1.1	1856 0.8	
2251 1.8	2148 2.0	2100 2.2		2232 10.4	2028 5.9	2030 4.5	1941 3.1		
0406 6.5	0321 7.9	0145 7.1	0018 5.5	0524 3.6	0305 2.4	0254 1.8	0133 1.2	0036 0.3	**9 TU**
1112 2.0	1009 2.2	0921 2.4	0722 2.4	1052 10.0	0857 5.7	0903 4.4	0806 3.0	0724 0.8	
1627 6.4	1542 7.7	1412 6.9	1243 5.4	1746 3.9	1532 2.5	1519 1.9	1402 1.3	1248 0.4	
2342 2.0	2233 2.4	2145 2.5	1949 2.5	2314 9.8	2117 5.6	2126 4.2	2033 2.9	1953 0.8	
0454 6.2	0407 7.4	0242 6.7	0109 5.2	0607 4.2	0358 2.7	0349 2.0	0233 1.4	0146 0.4	**10 W**
1211 2.2	1100 2.6	1012 2.8	0816 2.6	1143 9.4	0956 5.5	1016 4.2	0909 2.9	0831 0.7	
1724 6.1	1636 7.3	1521 6.6	1346 5.1	1841 4.4	1632 2.7	1622 2.0	1515 1.4	1412 0.4	
	2336 2.7	2242 2.8	2053 2.6		2226 5.3	2256 4.1	2149 2.8	2106 0.8	
0047 2.2	0515 7.0	0415 6.3	0228 4.9	0019 9.1	0506 2.9	0500 2.1	0353 1.4	0337 0.4	**11 TH**
0604 5.8	1212 2.9	1118 3.0	0929 2.8	0715 4.7	1116 5.4	1150 4.2	1033 2.9	0952 0.7	
1321 2.3	1759 7.0	1709 6.4	1515 4.9	1310 8.9	1745 2.8	1739 2.1	1642 1.4	1609 0.4	
1849 5.8		2356 3.0	2213 2.6	2006 4.6	2357 5.3		2323 2.9	2227 0.8	
0159 2.2	0058 2.8	0612 6.4	0403 4.9	0208 8.9	0625 2.8	0035 4.2	0518 1.3	0457 0.3	**12 F**
0741 5.8	0653 6.9	1238 3.0	1054 2.7	0852 4.7	1245 5.6	0620 2.1	1159 3.1	1111 0.8	
1434 2.2	1342 2.8	1842 6.6	1644 5.1	1500 9.2	1906 2.5	1310 4.4	1800 1.1	1719 0.3	
2024 6.0	1934 7.2		2336 2.3	2145 4.2		1857 1.9		2338 0.9	
0314 2.1	0229 2.5	0122 2.7	0529 5.2	0343 9.5	0124 5.6	0149 4.4	0042 3.1	0551 0.2	**13 SA**
0903 6.1	0816 7.4	0730 6.8	1212 2.3	1027 4.0	0743 2.4	0733 1.8	0627 1.1	1213 0.9	
1551 2.0	1506 2.3	1406 2.7	1758 5.5	1617 10.1	1357 6.0	1414 4.8	1307 3.3	1810 0.2	
2134 6.4	2048 7.8	1942 7.1		2306 3.3	2018 2.1	2005 1.6	1901 0.9		
0430 1.7	0342 1.8	0248 2.2	0045 1.9	0449 10.5	0230 6.1	0247 4.8	0142 3.3	0036 0.9	**14 SU**
1004 6.6	0921 8.2	0824 7.3	0633 5.6	1137 3.0	0847 1.9	0833 1.5	0724 0.8	0636 0.2	
1704 1.6	1612 1.7	1524 2.1	1315 1.8	1715 11.2	1455 6.6	1507 5.1	1403 3.6	1305 1.0	
2230 6.9	2146 8.6	2025 7.6	1855 6.0		2116 1.5	2101 1.2	1953 0.6	1855 0.1	
0539 1.3	0443 1.2	0358 1.6	0143 1.3	0009 2.2	0324 6.6	0336 5.1	0234 3.5	0127 1.0	**15 M**
1056 7.1	1015 8.9	0905 7.7	0724 6.1	0542 11.6	0941 1.4	0925 1.2	0813 0.5	0719 0.1	
1809 1.1	1711 1.0	1627 1.5	1409 1.3	1235 2.0	1546 7.1	1555 5.5	1453 3.9	1353 1.0	
2321 7.3	2239 9.2	2100 8.0	1945 6.4	1806 12.2	2208 1.0	2151 0.9	2040 0.3	1938 0.1	

● ● Time Zone -0100. For UT subtract 1 hour. For European summer time (shaded) 30/3-26/10 add 1 hour ● ●

SEPTEMBER 1997 TIDE TABLES SEPTEMBER 1997

	CALAIS		DIEPPE		LE HAVRE		CHERBOURG		ST MALO		BREST		POINTE DE GRAVE		LISBOA		GIBRALTAR	
	Time	m	Time	m	Time	m	Time	m	Time	m	Time	m	Time	m	Time	m	Time	m
16 TU ○	0638	1.0	0539	0.6	0456	1.0	0234	0.9	0103	1.2	0412	7.1	0422	5.4	0321	3.8	0215	1.1
	1143	7.4	1103	9.4	0929	8.0	0811	6.5	0631	12.4	1030	0.9	1013	0.9	0900	0.3	0800	0.0
	1904	0.8	1804	0.5	1721	1.0	1457	0.9	1327	1.1	1633	7.5	1641	5.7	1540	4.1	1438	1.1
			2327	9.7	2133	8.3	2030	6.8	1853	12.9	2256	0.6	2238	0.7	2125	0.2	2021	0.0
17 W	0008	7.6	0629	0.2	0546	0.6	0321	0.6	0153	0.5	0457	7.5	0506	5.5	0406	4.0	0300	1.1
	0730	0.7	1150	9.8	1042	8.2	0855	6.8	0716	13.0	1118	0.6	1059	0.7	0944	0.2	0842	0.0
	1230	7.7	1853	0.2	1809	0.6	1544	0.6	1415	0.5	1719	7.8	1725	5.8	1626	4.2	1523	1.1
	1954	0.5			2316	8.3	2115	7.0	1938	13.4	2342	0.4	2323	0.6	2209	0.1	2103	0.0
18 TH	0054	7.7	0012	9.9	0632	0.3	0407	0.4	0240	0.2	0542	7.6	0548	5.6	0451	4.1	0346	1.1
	0817	0.5	0716	-0.0	1117	8.2	0939	6.9	0800	13.3	1204	0.5	1144	0.6	1027	0.2	0923	0.0
	1315	7.7	1234	10.0	1853	0.5	1629	0.6	1501	0.3	1803	7.8	1809	5.8	1712	4.2	1607	1.1
	2039	0.4	1939	0.1	2344	8.3	2158	7.0	2021	13.4					2252	0.1	2145	0.0
19 F	0140	7.7	0056	10.0	0714	0.3	0451	0.5	0324	0.2	0027	0.4	0007	0.6	0535	4.0	0432	1.1
	0859	0.5	0800	-0.0	1152	8.1	1021	6.9	0840	13.2	0625	7.6	0631	5.5	1112	0.3	1004	0.1
	1401	7.7	1317	9.9	1933	0.5	1713	0.7	1544	0.5	1250	0.6	1230	0.6	1756	4.1	1653	1.1
	2120	0.4	2021	0.1			2242	6.9	2101	13.1	1848	7.6	1853	5.6	2335	0.4	2228	0.1
20 SA	0227	7.5	0139	9.8	0016	8.1	0534	0.7	0406	0.6	0112	0.6	0052	0.7	0618	3.9	0518	1.0
	0939	0.6	0841	0.1	0753	0.6	1102	6.7	0920	12.8	0708	7.3	0715	5.4	1156	0.5	1047	0.1
	1448	7.5	1358	9.7	1226	7.9	1757	1.0	1624	0.9	1335	0.9	1316	0.8	1842	3.9	1739	1.0
	2200	0.6	2101	0.4	2012	0.8	2324	6.6	2140	12.5	1931	7.2	1939	5.4			2312	0.2
21 SU	0315	7.3	0221	9.4	0211	8.0	0618	1.2	0445	1.3	0157	1.1	0138	1.0	0018	0.7	0607	0.9
	1018	0.9	0920	0.5	0829	1.0	1144	6.4	0959	12.1	0751	6.9	0800	5.1	0703	3.7	1132	0.2
	1536	7.2	1440	9.2	1432	7.8	1841	1.4	1702	1.7	1421	1.3	1404	1.1	1243	0.7	1829	0.9
	2241	0.9	2140	0.8	2048	1.3			2220	11.7	2015	6.7	2027	5.0	1930	3.6		
22 M	0404	6.9	0303	8.9	0250	7.7	0009	6.1	0523	2.2	0242	1.6	0226	1.3	0106	1.0	0002	0.3
	1100	1.2	0959	1.1	0904	1.6	0701	1.7	1039	11.3	0836	6.4	0852	4.8	0753	3.5	0700	0.8
	1629	6.8	1524	8.6	1506	7.4	1229	5.9	1740	2.6	1511	1.9	1457	1.4	1336	1.0	1226	0.3
	2326	1.4	2220	1.4	2124	1.8	1927	1.9	2304	10.6	2105	6.1	2123	4.6	2024	3.3	1926	0.8
23 TU	0500	6.5	0352	8.2	0327	7.2	0057	5.6	0603	3.2	0333	2.2	0319	1.7	0200	1.3	0108	0.3
	1148	1.7	1042	1.7	0942	2.2	0749	2.2	1126	10.3	0929	5.9	0956	4.4	0850	3.2	0805	0.8
	1729	6.4	1615	7.8	1536	7.0	1320	5.5	1824	3.6	1606	2.4	1556	1.8	1445	1.3	1352	0.4
			2307	2.0	2209	2.5	2021	2.3			2204	5.6	2235	4.3	2129	3.0	2034	0.8
24 W	0018	1.9	0454	7.5	0410	6.7	0158	5.2	0000	9.6	0432	2.7	0421	2.0	0313	1.5	0318	0.4
	0603	6.0	1134	2.4	1032	2.8	0848	2.6	0651	4.1	1036	5.5	1118	4.2	1001	3.0	0924	0.8
	1245	2.1	1727	7.2	1624	6.6	1426	5.1	1230	9.3	1715	2.7	1706	2.0	1615	1.4	1602	0.4
	1837	6.0			2314	3.0	2131	2.7	1923	4.4	2324	5.2			2249	2.9	2157	0.8
25 TH	0123	2.3	0013	2.6	0515	6.4	0318	4.8	0127	8.8	0547	2.9	0003	4.1	0446	1.6	0448	0.4
	0714	5.7	0618	7.0	1153	3.3	1007	2.9	0802	4.7	1205	5.3	0536	2.2	1124	3.0	1050	0.8
	1359	2.5	1255	2.9	1735	6.3	1554	4.9	1406	8.9	1839	2.8	1243	4.2	1744	1.4	1710	0.4
	1950	5.8	1851	6.9			2301	2.7	2054	4.7			1827	2.1			2315	0.8
26 F	0248	2.5	0147	2.6	0051	3.1	0501	4.6	0309	8.6	0056	5.3	0121	4.2	0009	2.9	0537	0.4
	0826	5.7	0737	7.0	0643	6.2	1140	2.8	0939	4.7	0710	2.9	0655	2.2	0604	1.5	1155	0.8
	1531	2.5	1424	2.8	1330	3.2	1730	5.0	1536	9.1	1328	5.5	1351	4.4	1236	3.1	1754	0.4
	2101	5.8	2008	7.0	1903	6.3			2231	4.4	1955	2.6	1940	2.0	1845	1.3		
27 SA	0415	2.3	0303	2.5	0213	2.8	0024	2.5	0421	9.3	0205	5.5	0221	4.3	0110	3.0	0010	0.8
	0934	5.8	0847	7.3	0820	6.5	0612	5.1	1057	4.2	0816	2.6	0800	2.0	0658	1.3	0613	0.3
	1645	2.1	1531	2.5	1440	2.9	1249	2.5	1639	9.7	1427	5.8	1443	4.5	1330	3.2	1240	0.9
	2206	6.0	2111	7.5	2039	6.6	1829	5.3	2331	3.7	2049	2.3	2036	1.8	1929	1.1	1827	0.3
28 SU	0514	2.0	0402	2.1	0312	2.4	0117	2.1	0511	10.0	0253	5.9	0306	4.5	0157	3.2	0051	0.9
	1032	6.1	0940	7.8	0922	6.9	0658	5.4	1147	3.5	0905	2.3	0849	1.8	0738	1.1	0642	0.3
	1735	1.8	1624	2.0	1533	2.4	1336	2.1	1724	10.3	1510	6.1	1523	4.7	1415	3.4	1315	0.9
	2257	6.3	2159	7.9	2134	7.0	1911	5.6			2132	2.0	2118	1.5	2003	0.9	1856	0.3
29 M	0556	1.7	0448	1.6	0359	2.0	0157	1.8	0013	3.1	0332	6.2	0342	4.7	0237	3.4	0124	1.0
	1116	6.5	1021	8.2	1004	7.2	0735	5.7	0550	10.5	0945	1.9	0930	1.5	0812	1.0	0709	0.3
	1814	1.5	1707	1.7	1616	2.1	1412	1.8	1226	3.0	1547	6.4	1557	4.9	1453	3.5	1345	1.0
	2336	6.6	2238	8.4	2209	7.3	1946	5.9	1802	10.8	2209	1.7	2155	1.4	2034	0.8	1924	0.3
30 TU	0631	1.4	0528	1.4	0438	1.7	0232	1.5	0048	2.6	0406	6.5	0412	4.9	0313	3.5	0153	1.0
	1151	6.7	1057	8.6	1036	7.5	0808	6.0	0624	11.0	1021	1.7	1005	1.2	0844	0.8	0737	0.2
	1848	1.2	1744	1.4	1653	1.8	1445	1.6	1300	2.5	1621	6.6	1627	5.0	1529	3.6	1413	1.0
			2312	8.7	2227	7.5	2018	6.1	1835	11.2	2242	1.5	2228	1.2	2104	0.7	1953	0.0

● ● Time Zone -0100. For UT subtract 1 hour. For European summer time (shaded) 30/3-26/10 add 1 hour ● ●

FRANCE, SPAIN, PORTUGAL & GIBRALTAR Time Zone -0100
Calais * Dieppe * Le Havre * Cherbourg * St Malo * Brest * Pointe de Grave * Lisboa * Gibraltar

OCTOBER 1997 TIDE TABLES OCTOBER 1997

CALAIS Time m	DIEPPE Time m	LE HAVRE Time m	CHERBOURG Time m	ST MALO Time m	BREST Time m	POINTE DE GRAVE Time m	LISBOA Time m	GIBRALTAR Time m	Day
0008 6.8	0603 1.2	0512 1.5	0303 1.4	0121 2.3	0438 6.7	0442 5.0	0348 3.6	0222 1.0	1 W
0703 1.2	1131 8.9	1100 7.6	0839 6.2	0656 11.4	1054 1.5	1039 1.2	0915 0.7	0806 0.2	●
1222 7.0	1817 1.2	1727 1.6	1518 1.4	1335 2.2	1651 6.8	1656 5.1	1603 3.6	1441 1.0	
1921 1.1	2346 8.9	2214 7.7	2049 6.3	1907 11.5	2314 1.4	2300 1.2	2135 0.6	2022 0.2	
0038 7.0	0635 1.1	0545 1.4	0335 1.3	0154 2.1	0509 6.8	0511 5.1	0420 3.6	0252 1.0	2 TH
0736 1.1	1203 9.0	1048 7.7	0909 6.3	0727 11.6	1126 1.4	1110 1.2	0947 0.6	0835 0.2	
1251 7.1	1849 1.1	1759 1.5	1548 1.4	1409 2.0	1721 6.8	1724 5.2	1635 3.6	1509 1.0	
1953 1.1		2236 7.8	2119 6.4	1938 11.7	2345 1.4	2331 1.1	2205 0.6	2052 0.2	
0106 7.1	0018 9.0	0616 1.4	0406 1.3	0228 1.9	0539 6.8	0539 5.1	0451 3.6	0324 1.0	3 F
0808 1.1	0706 1.1	1057 7.8	0937 6.4	0756 11.7	1157 1.4	1142 1.2	1019 0.6	0903 0.2	
1318 7.1	1236 9.1	1831 1.4	1620 1.4	1443 1.9	1751 6.8	1753 5.1	1706 3.6	1539 1.0	
2024 1.1	1920 1.1	2301 7.9	2147 6.4	2007 11.8			2236 0.6	2122 0.2	
0133 7.1	0051 9.0	0648 1.4	0437 1.4	0301 2.0	0015 1.4	0001 1.2	0522 3.6	0356 1.0	4 SA
0838 1.2	0737 1.2	1118 7.8	1004 6.3	0824 11.7	0609 6.8	0609 5.1	1051 0.7	0933 0.2	
1345 7.1	1306 9.0	1903 1.5	1652 1.5	1517 2.0	1229 1.5	1213 1.2	1736 3.5	1612 1.0	
2054 1.2	1951 1.2	2327 7.8	2215 6.3	2036 11.7	1821 6.7	1822 5.1	2308 0.7	2154 0.2	
0159 7.0	0121 8.9	0719 1.5	0509 1.5	0333 2.2	0047 1.6	0032 1.3	0551 3.5	0430 0.9	5 SU
0905 1.4	0807 1.3	1142 7.7	1031 6.2	0853 11.6	0639 6.7	0639 5.0	1125 0.7	1003 0.2	
1412 7.1	1336 8.8	1933 1.6	1725 1.6	1549 2.2	1303 1.6	1246 1.3	1806 3.4	1645 0.9	
2121 1.4	2021 1.4	2356 7.7	2244 6.1	2105 11.6	1853 6.6	1852 4.9	2342 0.8	2226 0.2	
0227 6.9	0152 8.7	0750 1.7	0542 1.8	0404 2.5	0121 1.8	0106 1.4	0622 3.4	0507 0.9	6 M
0933 1.5	0837 1.5	1213 7.6	1100 6.1	0921 11.4	0712 6.5	0712 4.9	1202 0.8	1036 0.3	
1442 7.0	1406 8.6	2003 1.8	1800 1.8	1620 2.6	1339 1.9	1323 1.4	1839 3.3	1724 0.9	
2151 1.5	2052 1.6		2315 5.9	2136 11.2	1926 6.3	1926 4.8		2303 0.3	
0300 6.8	0223 8.4	0030 7.6	0617 2.0	0433 3.0	0157 2.0	0143 1.6	0020 0.9	0549 0.8	7 TU
1006 1.7	0909 1.8	0821 2.0	1133 5.8	0951 11.0	0748 6.2	0749 4.7	0657 3.3	1114 0.3	
1518 6.8	1439 8.3	1251 7.4	1839 2.1	1651 3.2	1420 2.1	1405 1.6	1245 1.0	1809 0.8	
2228 1.7	2127 1.9	2036 2.1	2354 5.6	2209 10.7	2005 6.0	2007 4.5	1918 3.1	2347 0.3	
0339 6.6	0258 8.0	0114 7.3	0658 2.2	0503 3.6	0240 2.4	0227 1.8	0104 1.1	0640 0.8	8 W
1048 1.9	0947 2.2	0857 2.3	1215 5.5	1028 10.4	0831 5.9	0838 4.5	0742 3.1	1203 0.4	
1602 6.5	1517 7.9	1339 7.1	1926 2.3	1725 3.7	1509 2.4	1456 1.8	1337 1.2	1908 0.8	
2317 2.0	2212 2.2	2117 2.4		2251 10.0	2054 5.7	2104 4.3	2012 2.9		
0429 6.3	0344 7.6	0211 6.9	0045 5.3	0543 4.2	0334 2.7	0324 2.0	0203 1.3	0050 0.4	9 TH
1144 2.1	1039 2.6	0945 2.7	0751 2.6	1116 9.7	0930 5.6	0950 4.3	0843 3.0	0745 0.8	
1700 6.2	1610 7.4	1447 6.7	1317 5.2	1817 4.3	1610 2.6	1558 2.0	1448 1.3	1317 0.4	
	2314 2.6	2212 2.7	2029 2.5	2354 9.3	2203 5.4	2235 4.1	2128 2.8	2022 0.8	
0020 2.2	0451 7.2	0344 6.5	0205 5.0	0647 4.7	0442 2.8	0433 2.1	0322 1.4	0233 0.4	10 F
0539 5.9	1150 2.8	1049 3.0	0905 2.7	1237 9.1	1050 5.5	1124 4.3	1005 3.0	0905 0.8	
1253 2.2	1732 7.1	1632 6.5	1446 5.0	1939 4.6	1723 2.7	1714 2.0	1615 1.3	1514 0.4	
1824 5.9		2326 2.9	2150 2.5		2335 5.3		2259 2.9	2148 0.8	
0133 2.2	0036 2.7	0541 6.5	0339 4.9	0140 8.9	0601 2.8	0014 4.2	0451 1.3	0409 0.3	11 SA
0714 5.8	0627 7.1	1210 3.0	1031 2.6	0827 4.8	1218 5.7	0554 2.1	1130 3.1	1026 0.8	
1409 2.2	1320 2.8	1809 6.6	1617 5.1	1430 9.2	1843 2.5	1245 4.5	1736 1.1	1638 0.3	
1958 6.0	1907 7.2		2312 2.2	2123 4.3		1832 1.8		2303 0.9	
0251 2.1	0206 2.4	0054 2.7	0505 5.2	0319 9.5	0102 5.6	0128 4.5	0018 1.1	0511 0.3	12 SU
0836 6.1	0750 7.5	0703 6.8	1151 2.3	1006 4.2	0720 2.4	0708 1.8	0606 1.1	1133 0.9	
1529 1.9	1445 2.3	1340 2.7	1733 5.5	1552 10.1	1333 6.1	1351 4.8	1242 3.3	1733 0.2	
2110 6.4	2022 7.8	1916 7.1		2245 3.3	1955 2.0	1942 1.6	1840 0.8		
0410 1.7	0320 1.8	0223 2.2	0024 1.8	0426 10.6	0209 6.1	0226 4.8	0120 3.4	0004 1.0	13 M
0939 6.6	0856 8.2	0802 7.3	0611 5.7	1116 3.1	0825 1.9	0810 1.5	0704 0.8	0559 0.2	
1645 1.5	1551 1.6	1500 2.1	1254 1.8	1652 11.2	1433 6.6	1445 5.2	1339 3.6	1227 1.0	
2208 6.9	2124 8.5	2004 7.6	1833 6.0	2346 2.2	2054 1.5	2039 1.2	1933 0.6	1821 0.2	
0519 1.3	0421 1.1	0333 1.6	0121 1.3	0520 11.6	0303 6.7	0315 5.1	0212 3.6	0056 1.0	14 TU
1032 7.1	0951 8.9	0848 7.7	0703 6.1	1212 2.0	0920 1.4	0903 1.1	0754 0.6	0643 0.1	
1748 1.1	1649 0.9	1603 1.4	1348 1.3	1743 12.2	1524 7.1	1534 5.5	1431 3.9	1316 1.1	
2258 7.3	2216 9.2	2040 8.0	1923 6.4		2146 1.0	2130 0.9	2020 0.4	1904 0.1	
0617 0.9	0515 0.6	0431 1.0	0213 0.9	0039 1.3	0351 7.2	0401 5.4	0300 3.9	0144 1.1	15 W
1121 7.4	1041 9.5	0941 8.0	0750 6.5	0607 12.5	1010 0.9	0952 0.9	0840 0.4	0725 0.1	
1842 0.7	1742 0.5	1657 0.9	1438 0.9	1302 1.2	1612 7.5	1621 5.7	1519 4.1	1402 1.1	
2345 7.6	2305 9.7	2115 8.2	2010 6.7	1830 12.9	2234 0.6	2216 0.7	2104 0.2	1946 0.1	

• • Time Zone -0100. For UT subtract 1 hour. For European summer time (shaded) 30/3-26/10 add 1 hour • •

OCTOBER 1997 TIDE TABLES OCTOBER 1997

	CALAIS		DIEPPE		LE HAVRE		CHERBOURG		ST MALO		BREST		POINTE DE GRAVE		LISBOA		GIBRALTAR	
	Time	m	Time	m	Time	m	Time	m	Time	m	Time	m	Time	m	Time	m	Time	m
16 TH O	0707	0.7	0606	0.2	0522	0.6	0300	0.6	0127	0.7	0436	7.5	0445	5.6	0345	4.0	0229	1.1
	1207	7.7	1127	9.9	1017	8.2	0834	6.8	0652	13.1	1057	0.6	1039	0.7	0924	0.3	0806	0.1
	1930	0.5	1830	0.2	1745	0.6	1524	0.7	1350	0.7	1658	7.7	1705	5.7	1606	4.1	1446	1.1
			2350	9.9	2244	8.3	2055	6.9	1915	13.3	2320	0.5	2302	0.6	2147	0.2	2027	0.0
17 F	0032	7.7	0652	0.1	0609	0.5	0345	0.6	0214	0.5	0520	7.6	0527	5.6	0430	4.1	0314	1.1
	0753	0.6	1211	10.0	1055	8.2	0917	6.9	0736	13.3	1143	0.6	1124	0.6	1008	0.2	0847	0.1
	1253	7.6	1915	0.1	1830	0.5	1609	0.6	1436	0.6	1742	7.7	1748	5.7	1651	4.1	1530	1.1
	2015	0.5			2316	8.2	2139	6.9	1957	13.3			2345	0.7	2229	0.3	2109	0.1
18 SA	0118	7.6	0034	9.9	0651	0.5	0430	0.7	0259	0.6	0005	0.6	0609	5.5	0513	4.0	0358	1.1
	0834	0.6	0736	0.1	1132	8.1	0959	6.9	0817	13.2	0603	7.5	1210	0.7	1051	0.3	0927	0.1
	1339	7.6	1254	9.9	1912	0.6	1653	0.7	1519	0.8	1229	0.7	1832	5.5	1736	4.0	1615	1.1
	2056	0.6	1958	0.2	2348	8.0	2221	6.8	2039	12.9	1826	7.5			2310	0.5	2150	0.1
19 SU	0204	7.4	0117	9.7	0730	0.6	0512	0.9	0341	1.0	0049	0.8	0030	0.8	0557	3.9	0443	1.0
	0913	0.7	0818	0.4	1207	7.9	1039	6.7	0857	12.7	0645	7.3	0651	5.4	1134	0.5	1009	0.2
	1425	7.4	1336	9.6	1950	0.9	1736	1.0	1600	1.3	1314	1.0	1256	0.9	1821	3.8	1700	1.0
	2134	0.8	2038	0.5			2304	6.5	2118	12.3	1909	7.1	1915	5.3	2351	0.7	2231	0.2
20 M	0250	7.2	0159	9.3	0149	7.9	0554	1.3	0420	1.7	0133	1.2	0115	1.1	0641	3.7	0530	0.9
	0951	1.0	0857	0.8	0807	1.2	1121	6.4	0936	12.1	0727	6.9	0736	5.1	1219	0.8	1051	0.3
	1512	7.1	1417	9.1	1403	7.7	1818	1.4	1638	2.0	1359	1.4	1342	1.2	1908	3.5	1748	0.9
	2213	1.1	2116	0.9	2026	1.4	2347	6.1	2158	11.5	1952	6.6	2001	4.9			2315	0.3
21 TU	0337	6.8	0242	8.8	0224	7.6	0636	1.8	0457	2.5	0217	1.8	0200	1.4	0035	1.0	0620	0.8
	1030	1.3	0934	1.3	0841	1.8	1203	5.9	1015	11.3	0810	6.4	0823	4.8	0727	3.5	1140	0.4
	1602	6.8	1459	8.5	1425	7.4	1902	1.9	1715	2.8	1446	1.9	1433	1.5	1309	1.0	1843	0.8
	2255	1.5	2155	1.5	2100	1.9			2240	10.6	2039	6.1	2053	4.5	1959	3.2		
22 W	0428	6.5	0327	8.1	0253	7.2	0033	5.6	0533	3.4	0305	2.3	0251	1.7	0124	1.3	0009	0.4
	1115	1.7	1015	1.9	0915	2.4	0720	2.3	1059	10.3	0859	5.9	0919	4.5	0820	3.2	0720	0.6
	1656	6.4	1547	7.8	1442	7.0	1251	5.5	1754	3.7	1539	2.4	1527	1.8	1410	1.3	1246	0.4
	2342	2.0	2238	2.1	2138	2.5	1951	2.3	2331	9.6	2133	5.6	2157	4.2	2058	3.0	1950	0.6
23 TH	0525	6.0	0424	7.4	0326	6.7	0129	5.2	0617	4.3	0359	2.7	0348	2.0	0228	1.5	0136	0.5
	1206	2.2	1102	2.5	0959	2.9	0813	2.7	1155	9.4	1000	5.5	1033	4.2	0924	3.0	0836	0.8
	1758	6.0	1648	7.2	1530	6.6	1351	5.1	1844	4.5	1642	2.8	1633	2.1	1532	1.5	1454	0.5
			2333	2.6	2233	3.0	2053	2.7			2245	5.2	2320	4.0	2211	2.8	2113	0.7
24 F	0041	2.4	0536	6.9	0422	6.4	0239	4.8	0046	8.8	0508	3.0	0457	2.2	0356	1.6	0350	0.8
	0631	5.7	1207	2.9	1109	3.4	0924	3.0	0717	4.9	1119	5.3	1157	4.2	1040	3.0	1001	0.8
	1312	2.5	1806	6.7	1635	6.3	1506	4.8	1318	8.8	1800	2.9	1747	2.1	1703	1.5	1627	0.5
	1908	5.7					2213	2.8	2001	5.0					2330	2.8	2236	0.8
25 SA	0155	2.6	0053	2.9	0003	3.3	0409	4.8	0223	8.6	0012	5.2	0040	4.1	0523	1.6	0451	0.4
	0742	5.6	0654	6.8	0545	6.2	1051	2.9	0845	5.1	0630	3.0	0613	2.2	1155	3.0	1109	0.8
	1436	2.6	1333	3.1	1247	3.4	1636	4.8	1448	8.8	1245	5.4	1309	4.2	1808	1.3	1714	0.4
	2019	5.7	1925	6.9	1759	6.2	2337	2.6	2142	4.8	1918	2.8	1900	2.1			2332	0.8
26 SU	0321	2.5	0214	2.8	0130	3.1	0531	4.9	0339	9.0	0128	5.4	0142	4.2	0034	3.0	0528	0.4
	0851	5.7	0808	7.0	0724	6.3	1208	2.7	1012	4.7	0740	2.8	0721	2.1	0623	1.4	1155	0.9
	1556	2.3	1446	2.8	1400	3.1	1748	5.1	1556	9.3	1351	5.6	1403	4.4	1254	3.1	1747	0.4
	2124	5.9	2034	7.1	1935	6.4			2250	4.2	2016	2.5	1958	1.9	1854	1.2		
27 M	0427	2.2	0318	2.4	0230	2.7	0038	2.3	0432	9.6	0221	5.7	0228	4.4	0124	3.1	0011	0.9
	0951	6.0	0906	7.5	0838	6.7	0624	5.3	1107	4.1	0832	2.5	0814	1.9	0706	1.2	0559	0.4
	1651	1.9	1543	2.3	1452	2.6	1259	2.3	1645	9.9	1438	5.9	1446	4.6	1342	3.3	1229	0.9
	2219	6.2	2126	7.6	2050	6.7	1836	5.4	2333	3.6	2100	2.2	2044	1.7	1930	1.0	1816	0.4
28 TU	0513	1.8	0407	2.0	0315	2.3	0120	2.0	0512	10.2	0301	6.1	0306	4.7	0206	3.3	0042	1.0
	1040	6.4	0949	8.0	0924	7.1	0703	5.6	1147	3.4	0913	2.2	0857	1.7	0742	1.1	0628	0.3
	1733	1.6	1627	1.9	1534	2.2	1338	2.0	1724	10.5	1516	6.2	1522	4.8	1422	3.4	1258	1.0
	2303	6.5	2207	8.1	2132	7.1	1915	5.7			2137	1.9	2122	1.5	2003	0.9	1845	0.3
29 W	0552	1.5	0448	1.6	0355	1.9	0156	1.7	0008	3.0	0336	6.4	0339	4.9	0243	3.4	0112	1.0
	1120	6.7	1027	8.4	0959	7.4	0737	5.9	0548	10.8	0950	1.9	0934	1.5	0816	0.9	0657	0.3
	1811	1.3	1706	1.5	1612	1.9	1412	1.7	1223	2.8	1550	6.5	1555	5.0	1459	3.5	1327	1.0
	2339	6.8	2243	8.5	2201	7.4	1948	5.9	1800	11.0	2211	1.7	2157	1.3	2035	0.9	1915	0.3
30 TH	0629	1.2	0524	1.3	0432	1.7	0230	1.5	0042	2.6	0409	6.6	0412	5.0	0318	3.6	0143	1.0
	1154	6.9	1101	8.8	1027	7.6	0809	6.1	0621	11.2	1024	1.7	1009	1.3	0849	0.8	0727	0.3
	1848	1.1	1742	1.3	1649	1.6	1446	1.5	1259	2.4	1622	6.7	1627	5.1	1534	3.6	1357	1.0
			2318	8.8	2215	7.6	2021	6.1	1833	11.4	2243	1.5	2230	1.3	2106	0.7	1945	0.2
31 F ●	0011	6.9	0600	1.2	0509	1.5	0303	1.4	0118	2.2	0440	6.8	0443	5.1	0352	3.6	0215	1.0
	0705	1.1	1136	9.0	1047	7.7	0840	6.3	0654	11.6	1057	1.5	1042	1.3	0922	0.7	0757	0.2
	1224	7.0	1818	1.1	1727	1.4	1520	1.4	1336	2.1	1654	6.8	1658	5.1	1609	3.6	1427	1.0
	1924	1.1	2352	9.0	2218	7.7	2052	6.2	1907	11.7	2315	1.4	2302	1.2	2139	0.6	2016	0.2

•• Time Zone -0100. For UT subtract 1 hour. For European summer time (shaded) 30/3-26/10 add 1 hour ••

FRANCE, SPAIN, PORTUGAL & GIBRALTAR Time Zone -0100
Calais * Dieppe * Le Havre * Cherbourg * St Malo * Brest * Pointe de Grave * Lisboa * Gibraltar
NOVEMBER 1997 TIDE TABLES NOVEMBER 1997

CALAIS Time m	DIEPPE Time m	LE HAVRE Time m	CHERBOURG Time m	ST MALO Time m	BREST Time m	POINTE DE GRAVE Time m	LISBOA Time m	GIBRALTAR Time m		
0040 7.0	0636 1.1	0546 1.4	0336 1.4	0156 2.0	0512 6.9	0515 5.2	0425 3.6	0249 1.0	**1**	**SA**
0741 1.1	1209 9.1	1033 7.7	0910 6.4	0726 11.8	1130 1.4	1115 1.2	0956 0.6	0829 0.2		
1254 7.1	1854 1.1	1804 1.4	1554 1.3	1415 1.9	1726 6.8	1730 5.1	1642 3.6	1501 1.0		
2000 1.1		2236 7.7	2123 6.3	1940 11.8	2349 1.4	2334 1.2	2212 0.6	2048 0.2		
0108 7.0	0027 9.0	0624 1.4	0411 1.4	0234 2.0	0545 6.9	0547 5.2	0458 3.6	0324 1.0	**2**	**SU**
0815 1.2	0712 1.2	1049 7.7	0939 6.4	0758 11.9	1206 1.4	1149 1.2	1030 0.6	0900 0.2		
1321 7.1	1243 9.1	1841 1.4	1630 1.4	1453 1.9	1759 6.8	1802 5.1	1715 3.5	1536 1.0		
2033 1.2	1930 1.1	2302 7.7	2154 6.2	2013 11.9			2245 0.7	2121 0.2		
0135 7.0	0100 8.9	0700 1.5	0446 1.5	0311 2.1	0024 1.5	0008 1.3	0531 3.6	0401 1.0	**3**	**M**
0847 1.4	0748 1.3	1116 7.7	1009 6.3	0830 11.9	0618 6.8	0620 5.1	1106 0.7	0933 0.2		
1349 7.0	1316 8.9	1916 1.5	1706 1.5	1530 2.1	1242 1.5	1226 1.3	1749 3.4	1613 0.9		
2103 1.4	2005 1.3	2333 7.7	2226 6.1	2046 11.7	1833 6.7	1836 5.0	2321 0.7	2157 0.2		
0206 6.9	0134 8.8	0735 1.7	0523 1.7	0346 2.4	0100 1.7	0044 1.4	0606 3.5	0440 0.9	**4**	**TU**
0918 1.5	0822 1.5	1151 7.6	1042 6.2	0903 11.7	0654 6.7	0656 5.0	1145 0.8	1009 0.2		
1422 6.9	1349 8.7	1950 1.7	1744 1.6	1605 2.4	1321 1.7	1305 1.4	1826 3.3	1654 0.9		
2137 1.5	2040 1.4		2302 5.9	2120 11.4	1911 6.4	1914 4.8		2236 0.2		
0241 6.8	0209 8.5	0012 7.5	0602 1.9	0420 2.9	0140 1.9	0124 1.5	0001 0.9	0524 0.9	**5**	**W**
0954 1.6	0858 1.7	0809 1.9	1118 6.0	0936 11.4	0733 6.4	0737 4.9	0644 3.4	1051 0.3		
1501 6.8	1424 8.4	1232 7.5	1826 1.8	1639 2.9	1406 1.9	1349 1.5	1230 0.9	1742 0.9		
2216 1.7	2119 1.7	2024 1.9	2345 5.7	2157 11.0	1952 6.2	1959 4.6	1909 3.2	2322 0.3		
0324 6.6	0248 8.2	0059 7.3	0645 2.2	0454 3.4	0225 2.2	0211 1.7	0047 1.0	0616 0.8	**6**	**TH**
1037 1.8	0939 2.0	0846 2.2	1205 5.7	1015 10.8	0818 6.2	0828 4.7	0730 3.3	1142 0.3		
1548 6.6	1506 8.1	1323 7.2	1915 2.0	1718 3.4	1456 2.2	1441 1.7	1322 1.0	1841 0.8		
2304 1.8	2206 2.0	2104 2.2		2241 10.3	2043 5.8	2057 4.4	2003 3.1			
0415 6.3	0335 7.8	0200 7.0	0039 5.4	0534 4.0	0320 2.5	0306 1.9	0144 1.2	0023 0.3	**7**	**F**
1130 1.9	1032 2.3	0933 2.5	0739 2.4	1104 10.2	0917 5.9	0936 4.5	0828 3.2	0719 0.8		
1648 6.3	1559 7.7	1432 6.9	1306 5.4	1807 4.0	1554 2.4	1541 1.8	1430 1.2	1254 0.4		
	2305 2.3	2157 2.4	2015 2.2	2341 9.6	2150 5.6	2220 4.3	2112 3.0	1954 0.8		
0003 2.0	0439 7.4	0331 6.7	0152 5.1	0633 4.5	0424 2.7	0413 2.0	0259 1.3	0151 0.4	**8**	**SA**
0524 6.1	1138 2.5	1033 2.7	0848 2.5	1217 9.6	1030 5.7	1100 4.5	0942 3.1	0833 0.8		
1234 2.0	1713 7.3	1606 6.7	1425 5.2	1921 4.3	1703 2.5	1651 1.9	1551 1.2	1433 0.4		
1808 6.1		2306 2.6	2129 2.2		2312 5.5	2349 4.3	2234 3.0	2117 0.8		
0112 2.1	0017 2.4	0517 6.6	0315 5.1	0112 9.3	0538 2.6	0527 2.0	0425 1.3	0324 0.4	**9**	**SU**
0651 6.0	0601 7.3	1149 2.8	1007 2.5	0802 4.6	1151 5.8	1218 4.6	1102 3.2	0950 0.9		
1348 2.0	1257 2.5	1741 6.7	1547 5.2	1357 9.5	1818 2.4	1806 1.8	1712 1.1	1600 0.3		
1934 6.1	1839 7.4		2246 2.1	2054 4.1			2351 3.2	2234 0.9		
0230 2.0	0137 2.2	0028 2.5	0435 5.3	0246 9.6	0034 5.7	0103 4.5	0541 1.1	0433 0.3	**10**	**M**
0809 6.2	0721 7.6	0638 6.9	1124 2.2	0935 4.1	0654 2.4	0641 1.8	1214 3.4	1058 0.9		
1508 1.9	1418 2.1	1312 2.5	1703 5.5	1520 10.1	1306 6.1	1325 4.8	1817 0.9	1703 0.3		
2045 6.4	1955 7.8	1852 7.1	2357 1.8	2215 3.4	1930 2.0	1915 1.5		2337 0.9		
0349 1.8	0253 1.7	0151 2.1	0543 5.6	0356 10.5	0143 6.1	0203 4.8	0055 3.4	0527 0.2	**11**	**TU**
0914 6.6	0828 8.2	0741 7.3	1231 1.8	1047 3.2	0800 2.0	0746 1.5	0642 0.9	1155 1.0		
1624 1.5	1527 1.6	1430 2.0	1807 5.9	1624 11.0	1409 6.5	1423 5.1	1316 3.6	1753 0.2		
2145 6.8	2058 8.4	1948 7.4		2318 2.4	2030 1.6	2015 1.3	1912 0.7			
0457 1.4	0356 1.1	0303 1.6	0058 1.4	0452 11.4	0239 6.6	0254 5.1	0145 3.6	0030 1.0	**12**	**W**
1009 7.0	0926 8.8	0840 7.6	0639 6.0	1144 2.3	0857 1.5	0842 1.2	0735 0.7	0614 0.2		
1727 1.1	1627 1.0	1535 1.5	1327 1.4	1717 11.9	1503 7.0	1514 5.4	1410 3.8	1245 1.1		
2237 7.1	2154 9.0	2033 7.8	1902 6.2		2124 1.2	2108 1.0	2000 0.5	1838 0.1		
0555 1.1	0451 0.7	0403 1.2	0151 1.1	0010 1.7	0329 7.0	0341 5.3	0239 3.8	0119 1.1	**13**	**TH**
1100 7.3	1018 9.3	0951 7.9	0729 6.4	0542 12.2	0949 1.1	0933 1.0	0822 0.5	0657 0.1		
1821 0.8	1719 0.6	1632 1.0	1418 1.0	1235 1.6	1552 7.3	1601 5.5	1500 3.9	1332 1.1		
2327 7.4	2243 9.4	2129 7.9	1951 6.5	1806 12.5	2213 0.9	2156 0.9	2044 0.4	1921 0.1		
0646 0.9	0542 0.4	0457 0.9	0240 0.9	0100 1.2	0415 7.3	0426 5.5	0326 4.0	0205 1.1	**14**	**F**
1148 7.5	1105 9.7	0941 8.0	0815 6.6	0628 12.7	1038 0.9	1021 0.8	0907 0.4	0739 0.1		
1910 0.7	1808 0.4	1723 0.8	1506 0.8	1324 1.1	1639 7.4	1647 5.6	1548 4.0	1417 1.1		O
	2330 9.6	2203 8.0	2038 6.6	1852 12.8	2300 0.8	2242 0.7	2127 0.4	2002 0.1		
0014 7.4	0630 0.4	0545 0.8	0327 0.9	0148 1.0	0500 7.4	0509 5.5	0411 4.0	0249 1.1	**15**	**SA**
0732 0.8	1150 9.7	1026 8.0	0858 6.7	0712 12.9	1124 0.8	1107 0.8	0951 0.4	0821 0.1		
1236 7.5	1854 0.3	1809 0.7	1552 0.8	1411 1.1	1724 7.4	1730 5.5	1634 4.0	1501 1.1		
1954 0.7			2122 6.6	1936 12.8	2345 0.9	2326 0.9	2207 0.5	2043 0.1		

● ● Time Zone -0100. For UT subtract 1 hour. For European summer time (shaded) 30/3-26/10 add 1 hour ● ●

NOVEMBER 1997 TIDE TABLES NOVEMBER 1997

	CALAIS		DIEPPE		LE HAVRE		CHERBOURG		ST MALO		BREST		POINTE DE GRAVE		LISBOA		GIBRALTAR	
	Time	m	Time	m	Time	m	Time	m	Time	m	Time	m	Time	m	Time	m	Time	m
16 SU	0100	7.4	0014	9.6	0006	8.1	0411	0.9	0233	1.2	0543	7.4	0551	5.5	0454	4.0	0333	1.0
	0813	0.8	0715	0.5	0630	0.8	0940	6.7	0755	12.8	1210	0.9	1152	0.9	1033	0.5	0902	0.2
	1321	7.4	1233	9.6	1105	7.9	1636	0.9	1457	1.2	1807	7.2	1813	5.4	1718	3.8	1545	1.0
	2034	0.8	1938	0.5	1853	0.8	2206	6.5	2019	12.5					2248	0.6	2124	0.1
17 M	0145	7.3	0057	9.5	0049	8.0	0454	1.1	0317	1.5	0028	1.1	0009	1.0	0537	3.9	0418	1.0
	0851	0.9	0757	0.7	0712	1.1	1021	6.5	0836	12.5	0625	7.2	0632	5.3	1115	0.6	0944	0.2
	1406	7.3	1315	9.4	1303	7.9	1718	1.1	1538	1.6	1254	1.2	1237	1.0	1803	3.7	1630	0.9
	2112	1.0	2018	0.7	1933	1.1	2248	6.3	2100	12.0	1849	6.9	1855	5.1	2327	0.8	2206	0.2
18 TU	0229	7.1	0140	9.1	0128	7.8	0535	1.5	0357	2.0	0111	1.4	0053	1.2	0620	3.8	0503	0.9
	0927	1.1	0836	1.0	0750	1.5	1101	6.3	0915	11.9	0706	6.9	0713	5.1	1158	0.8	1027	0.3
	1451	7.0	1357	9.0	1331	7.6	1800	1.4	1616	2.2	1339	1.5	1322	1.2	1847	3.5	1718	0.9
	2148	1.3	2056	1.0	2009	1.5	2329	5.9	2139	11.3	1930	6.5	1937	4.9			2250	0.3
19 W	0312	6.8	0222	8.7	0158	7.5	0615	1.8	0432	2.7	0153	1.8	0136	1.4	0009	1.0	0551	0.9
	1003	1.4	0912	1.4	0824	1.9	1142	5.9	0954	11.3	0747	6.5	0755	4.9	0703	3.5	1115	0.3
	1536	6.8	1438	8.5	1327	7.4	1840	1.8	1651	2.9	1423	1.9	1408	1.5	1243	1.0	1808	0.8
	2225	1.6	2132	1.5	2042	1.9			2220	10.6	2012	6.1	2021	4.6	1933	3.2	2339	0.4
20 TH	0357	6.5	0305	8.2	0216	7.2	0012	5.6	0506	3.4	0236	2.2	0222	1.7	0053	1.2	0644	0.8
	1043	1.7	0948	1.8	0855	2.4	0654	2.2	1034	10.5	0830	6.1	0842	4.6	0751	3.3	1211	0.4
	1623	6.4	1521	7.9	1403	7.1	1225	5.6	1724	3.6	1509	2.3	1457	1.8	1334	1.2	1906	0.8
	2306	2.0	2209	1.9	2114	2.4	1922	2.1	2303	9.8	2059	5.7	2112	4.3	2024	3.0		
21 F	0447	6.2	0351	7.6	0245	6.9	0100	5.2	0541	4.1	0324	2.6	0313	2.0	0145	1.4	0040	0.4
	1129	2.1	1029	2.3	0932	2.8	0738	2.5	1120	9.8	0919	5.7	0938	4.4	0843	3.1	0746	0.8
	1716	6.1	1609	7.4	1448	6.8	1315	5.2	1803	4.2	1601	2.7	1552	2.0	1437	1.4	1327	0.5
	2357	2.3	2254	2.4	2156	2.8	2012	2.5	2358	9.1	2156	5.4	2218	4.1	2124	2.9	2015	0.7
22 SA	0543	5.9	0446	7.1	0333	6.6	0157	4.9	0626	4.7	0420	2.9	0411	2.1	0253	1.6	0206	0.5
	1226	2.4	1118	2.7	1024	3.2	0833	2.8	1220	9.1	1021	5.4	1048	4.2	0947	3.0	0857	0.8
	1817	5.8	1709	6.9	1544	6.4	1416	4.9	1857	4.7	1704	2.9	1655	2.1	1555	1.5	1506	0.5
			2350	2.7	2257	3.1	2113	2.7			2307	5.2	2333	4.0	2233	2.8	2131	0.7
23 SU	0100	2.5	0551	6.8	0436	6.3	0305	4.8	0112	8.7	0528	3.1	0517	2.2	0415	1.6	0335	0.5
	0648	5.7	1222	3.0	1136	3.3	0943	2.9	0729	5.1	1136	5.3	1203	4.2	1057	3.0	1005	0.8
	1334	2.5	1818	6.7	1654	6.2	1527	4.8	1336	8.8	1818	2.9	1803	2.1	1709	1.4	1617	0.5
	1924	5.7					2225	2.7	2012	4.9					2342	2.9	2236	0.8
24 M	0211	2.6	0100	2.9	0015	3.2	0422	4.8	0230	8.7	0027	5.2	0042	4.1	0528	1.5	0433	0.4
	0757	5.7	0703	6.8	0601	6.3	1059	2.8	0850	5.0	0642	3.0	0625	2.2	1204	3.0	1059	0.8
	1447	2.4	1335	3.0	1254	3.2	1642	4.9	1451	8.9	1253	5.4	1306	4.3	1805	1.3	1703	0.4
	2033	5.7	1933	6.8	1818	6.2	2334	2.5	2133	4.7	1927	2.8	1906	2.0			2325	0.8
25 TU	0321	2.4	0210	2.7	0125	2.9	0532	5.0	0334	9.1	0133	5.5	0138	4.3	0041	3.0	0515	0.4
	0902	5.9	0812	7.1	0724	6.5	1203	2.6	1003	4.6	0745	2.8	0726	2.0	0623	1.4	1141	0.9
	1551	2.1	1442	2.7	1355	2.8	1747	5.1	1551	9.3	1353	5.7	1358	4.4	1300	3.1	1740	0.4
	2133	6.0	2039	7.2	1939	6.5			2234	4.1	2018	2.5	2000	1.8	1849	1.2		
26 W	0419	2.0	0311	2.4	0220	2.6	0029	2.2	0424	9.7	0221	5.8	0224	4.5	0128	3.2	0005	0.9
	0957	6.2	0906	7.6	0828	6.9	0622	5.3	1056	3.9	0833	2.5	0816	1.8	0706	1.2	0552	0.4
	1644	1.8	1537	2.2	1445	2.4	1254	2.2	1639	9.9	1438	5.9	1442	4.6	1346	3.3	1218	0.9
	2224	6.3	2129	7.7	2042	6.8	1836	5.4	2320	3.5	2100	2.2	2045	1.7	1928	1.0	1815	0.3
27 TH	0507	1.7	0401	1.9	0306	2.2	0113	2.0	0506	10.3	0301	6.1	0303	4.7	0210	3.4	0042	0.9
	1044	6.5	0951	8.1	0915	7.2	0703	5.6	1140	3.3	0915	2.2	0859	1.7	0745	1.0	0627	0.3
	1730	1.7	1624	1.8	1530	2.0	1336	1.9	1721	10.5	1517	6.2	1521	4.8	1427	3.4	1253	0.9
	2306	6.6	2211	8.2	2128	7.1	1916	5.6			2137	1.9	2124	1.5	2004	0.9	1849	0.3
28 F	0551	1.4	0445	1.6	0351	1.9	0153	1.7	0002	2.9	0338	6.4	0341	4.9	0249	3.5	0118	0.9
	1123	6.7	1030	8.5	0951	7.4	0739	5.9	0545	10.9	0952	1.9	0938	1.5	0823	0.9	0702	0.2
	1813	1.3	1707	1.4	1614	1.7	1415	1.7	1222	2.7	1553	6.4	1558	5.0	1507	3.5	1329	1.0
	2342	6.8	2249	8.6	2206	7.4	1953	5.8	1800	11.0	2212	1.7	2200	1.4	2039	0.8	1924	0.2
29 SA	0633	1.3	0527	1.4	0436	1.6	0232	1.6	0044	2.5	0412	6.6	0417	5.1	0326	3.6	0155	1.0
	1158	6.9	1107	8.8	1024	7.6	0813	6.1	0622	11.4	1029	1.7	1015	1.4	0900	0.9	0736	0.2
	1855	1.2	1749	1.2	1658	1.5	1453	1.5	1306	2.3	1628	6.6	1635	5.1	1545	3.5	1406	1.0
			2327	8.8	2241	7.5	2028	6.0	1839	11.5	2248	1.5	2236	1.3	2115	0.7	2000	0.2
30 SU ●	0016	6.9	0609	1.2	0520	1.5	0310	1.4	0127	2.2	0448	6.8	0453	5.2	0403	3.7	0233	1.0
	0715	1.2	1145	9.0	1036	7.6	0846	6.2	0700	11.7	1107	1.5	1052	1.3	0936	0.7	0812	0.2
	1230	7.0	1831	1.1	1742	1.4	1532	1.3	1349	2.0	1704	6.8	1711	5.1	1622	3.5	1444	1.0
	1936	1.2			2230	7.6	2103	6.1	1917	11.7	2326	1.4	2312	1.3	2151	0.7	2036	0.2

●● Time Zone -0100. For UT subtract 1 hour. For European summer time (shaded) 30/3-26/10 add 1 hour ●●

FRANCE, SPAIN, PORTUGAL & GIBRALTAR Time Zone -0100
Calais * Dieppe * Le Havre * Cherbourg * St Malo * Brest * Pointe de Grave * Lisboa * Gibraltar

DECEMBER 1997 TIDE TABLES DECEMBER 1997

Day	CALAIS Time	m	DIEPPE Time	m	LE HAVRE Time	m	CHERBOURG Time	m	ST MALO Time	m	BREST Time	m	POINTE DE GRAVE Time	m	LISBOA Time	m	GIBRALTAR Time	m
1 M	0048	6.9	0005	8.9	0603	1.5	0349	1.4	0210	2.0	0524	6.9	0530	5.3	0439	3.7	0313	1.0
	0755	1.3	0651	1.2	1033	7.7	0920	6.3	0737	12.0	1146	1.4	1130	1.2	1014	0.6	0848	0.2
	1303	7.0	1222	9.1	1825	1.3	1612	1.2	1433	1.8	1742	6.8	1748	5.1	1700	3.5	1524	1.0
	2015	1.2	1913	1.0	2251	7.6	2139	6.1	1955	11.9			2349	1.3	2228	0.6	2112	0.2
2 TU	0119	6.9	0043	8.9	0646	1.5	0430	1.4	0253	2.0	0005	1.4	0607	5.3	0516	3.7	0354	0.9
	0833	1.3	0733	1.2	1103	7.7	0955	6.3	0814	12.1	0603	7.0	1210	1.2	1053	0.6	0925	0.2
	1336	7.0	1300	9.0	1906	1.4	1652	1.2	1515	1.8	1227	1.4	1827	5.1	1738	3.5	1606	0.9
	2053	1.3	1955	1.0	2324	7.6	2217	6.1	2033	11.9	1821	6.8			2307	0.7	2151	0.2
3 W	0154	6.9	0121	8.9	0727	1.6	0510	1.5	0334	2.2	0045	1.5	0029	1.3	0554	3.7	0436	0.9
	0911	1.4	0814	1.3	1139	7.7	1033	6.3	0851	12.0	0642	6.9	0647	5.2	1134	0.7	1006	0.2
	1412	6.9	1338	8.9	1945	1.5	1733	1.3	1556	2.0	1309	1.4	1252	1.2	1818	3.4	1651	0.9
	2131	1.4	2036	1.1			2258	6.0	2112	11.7	1902	6.6	1909	5.0	2349	0.8	2234	0.2
4 TH	0232	6.8	0200	8.7	0005	7.5	0552	1.6	0413	2.5	0128	1.7	0111	1.4	0636	3.6	0523	0.9
	0949	1.4	0856	1.4	0806	1.7	1115	6.1	0929	11.7	0724	6.7	0731	5.1	1220	0.7	1051	0.2
	1454	6.8	1417	8.7	1224	7.6	1818	1.4	1636	2.3	1355	1.6	1337	1.3	1903	3.4	1742	0.9
	2212	1.5	2118	1.3	2024	1.6	2343	5.8	2151	11.3	1946	6.4	1955	4.8			2323	0.2
5 F	0316	6.7	0242	8.5	0054	7.3	0638	1.8	0452	2.9	0215	1.9	0158	1.5	0036	0.9	0615	0.9
	1032	1.5	0939	1.6	0845	1.9	1202	5.9	1010	11.3	0812	6.5	0821	4.9	0721	3.5	1145	0.3
	1542	6.7	1500	8.4	1315	7.4	1906	1.6	1717	2.8	1445	1.8	1427	1.4	1311	0.9	1839	0.8
	2257	1.6	2204	1.5	2105	1.8			2236	10.8	2036	6.1	2051	4.6	1954	3.3		
6 SA	0409	6.5	0329	8.2	0157	7.1	0036	5.6	0533	3.4	0308	2.1	0251	1.7	0130	1.1	0021	0.3
	1122	1.6	1028	1.8	0930	2.1	0730	2.0	1058	10.7	0906	6.2	0922	4.8	0815	3.4	0714	0.8
	1641	6.5	1552	8.0	1421	7.1	1258	5.7	1804	3.3	1540	2.1	1524	1.6	1412	1.0	1251	0.3
	2351	1.8	2256	1.7	2152	2.0	2002	1.8	2331	10.2	2136	5.9	2200	4.5	2055	3.2	1945	0.8
7 SU	0512	6.4	0426	7.9	0331	6.9	0137	5.4	0626	3.9	0406	2.3	0353	1.8	0238	1.2	0134	0.3
	1221	1.8	1124	2.0	1023	2.3	0830	2.2	1200	10.1	1009	6.0	1033	4.7	0919	3.3	0820	0.8
	1751	6.3	1654	7.7	1547	6.9	1403	5.4	1906	3.7	1642	2.2	1628	1.7	1526	1.1	1413	0.3
			2356	1.9	2251	2.2	2106	1.9			2246	5.7	2319	4.4	2206	3.1	2100	0.8
8 M	0055	1.9	0534	7.7	0459	6.9	0246	5.2	0044	9.8	0513	2.4	0501	1.8	0357	1.3	0255	0.3
	0627	6.2	1230	2.1	1128	2.4	0940	2.2	0736	4.1	1121	6.0	1148	4.7	1033	3.3	0929	0.9
	1329	1.8	1809	7.6	1716	6.9	1515	5.3	1321	9.8	1750	2.2	1738	1.7	1642	1.1	1536	0.3
	1909	6.3					2216	1.9	2021	3.8					2321	3.2	2214	0.8
9 TU	0207	1.9	0106	1.9	0001	2.2	0400	5.3	0206	9.8	0002	5.8	0033	4.5	0514	1.2	0409	0.3
	0742	6.3	0649	7.8	0612	7.0	1054	2.1	0857	4.0	0624	2.3	0613	1.7	1147	3.4	1036	0.9
	1445	1.8	1345	2.0	1242	2.3	1630	5.4	1442	10.0	1236	6.1	1258	4.8	1751	1.0	1644	0.3
	2020	6.4	1925	7.8	1830	7.0	2327	1.8	2139	3.4	1901	2.1	1848	1.6			2320	0.9
10 W	0324	1.8	0222	1.7	0118	2.1	0512	5.5	0321	10.3	0114	6.0	0137	4.7	0030	3.4	0508	0.3
	0850	6.5	0800	8.1	0718	7.2	1205	1.9	1012	3.4	0734	2.1	0721	1.6	0621	1.0	1136	1.0
	1600	1.6	1500	1.7	1359	2.0	1740	5.6	1555	10.6	1343	6.3	1400	5.0	1254	3.5	1739	0.2
	2124	6.6	2033	8.2	1936	7.2			2245	2.8	2006	1.8	1951	1.4	1850	0.9		
11 TH	0436	1.6	0330	1.4	0231	1.8	0033	1.6	0423	10.9	0216	6.4	0233	5.0	0129	3.6	0016	0.9
	0949	6.7	0901	8.5	0823	7.4	0616	5.8	1115	2.7	0836	1.8	0821	1.4	0717	0.9	0559	0.2
	1706	1.3	1603	1.2	1507	1.6	1307	1.5	1652	11.2	1442	6.6	1456	5.1	1352	3.6	1229	1.0
	2221	6.8	2132	8.6	2052	7.4	1842	5.8	2342	2.2	2103	1.5	2048	1.3	1941	0.7	1826	0.2
12 F	0536	1.3	0429	1.0	0336	1.4	0131	1.4	0518	11.6	0309	6.7	0324	5.2	0221	3.7	0107	1.0
	1045	7.0	0956	8.9	0932	7.7	0711	6.0	1210	2.1	0931	1.5	0916	1.2	0807	0.7	0645	0.2
	1804	1.1	1659	0.8	1608	1.2	1402	1.2	1745	11.7	1535	6.9	1547	5.3	1445	3.7	1318	1.0
	2313	7.0	2224	9.0	2204	7.7	1937	6.1			2154	1.3	2139	1.1	2027	0.7	1911	0.1
13 SA	0629	1.1	0521	0.8	0433	1.2	0224	1.2	0035	1.8	0358	7.0	0412	5.3	0310	3.9	0154	1.0
	1136	7.1	1046	9.2	1030	7.8	0800	6.3	0608	12.1	1021	1.2	1006	1.0	0853	0.6	0729	0.2
	1854	1.0	1749	0.6	1703	1.0	1452	1.0	1302	1.7	1623	7.0	1633	5.3	1534	3.8	1405	1.0
			2312	9.2	2300	7.8	2026	6.2	1835	12.0	2242	1.2	2225	1.1	2109	0.6	1954	0.1
14 SU	0003	7.1	0611	0.7	0526	1.1	0312	1.1	0125	1.6	0444	7.1	0455	5.4	0356	3.9	0239	1.0
	0716	1.0	1133	9.3	1120	7.9	0845	6.4	0654	12.3	1109	1.1	1052	1.0	0936	0.6	0812	0.2
	1224	7.2	1837	0.6	1752	0.9	1539	0.9	1351	1.6	1708	7.0	1718	5.3	1620	3.8	1451	1.0
	1939	1.0	2358	9.2	2348	7.8	2111	6.3	1921	12.1	2327	1.2	2309	1.1	2149	0.6	2036	0.1
15 M	0048	7.1	0657	0.8	0613	1.1	0357	1.1	0213	1.7	0527	7.1	0536	5.4	0439	3.9	0324	1.0
	0758	1.1	1217	9.3	1203	7.9	0927	6.4	0739	12.3	1154	1.1	1137	1.0	1018	0.6	0855	0.2
	1309	7.2	1921	0.7	1837	0.9	1622	1.0	1439	1.6	1751	7.0	1758	5.2	1703	3.7	1536	1.0
	2019	1.1					2154	6.2	2005	11.9			2351	1.1	2228	0.7	2118	0.1

Day 14 SU: ○

* * Time Zone -0100. For UT subtract 1 hour. For European summer time (shaded) 30/3-26/10 add 1 hour * *

DECEMBER 1997 TIDE TABLES DECEMBER 1997

	CALAIS	DIEPPE	LE HAVRE	CHERBOURG	ST MALO	BREST	POINTE DE GRAVE	LISBOA	GIBRALTAR
	Time m	Time m	Time m	Time m	Time m	Time m	Time m	Time m	Time m
16 TU	0130 7.0 0835 1.1 1351 7.1 2054 1.2	0042 9.2 0739 0.9 1259 9.1 2002 0.8	0031 7.8 0657 1.3 1239 7.7 1918 1.1	0439 1.2 1007 6.3 1703 1.1 2233 6.1	0257 1.9 082112.1 1521 1.8 204611.6	0010 1.3 0609 7.1 1237 1.3 1831 6.8	0616 5.3 1220 1.1 1836 5.1	0521 3.9 1058 0.7 1745 3.6 2306 0.8	0408 0.9 0938 0.2 1620 0.9 2200 0.2
17 W	0210 7.0 0908 1.3 1430 7.0 2126 1.4	0124 9.0 0818 1.1 1339 8.9 2039 1.0	0107 7.6 0735 1.6 1243 7.6 1955 1.4	0518 1.4 1045 6.2 1742 1.3 2312 5.9	0337 2.2 090011.8 1558 2.2 212411.2	0051 1.5 0648 6.9 1318 1.5 1909 6.5	0033 1.2 0653 5.1 1302 1.2 1914 4.9	0601 3.8 1137 0.8 1825 3.5 2345 0.9	0452 0.9 1021 0.2 1704 0.9 2243 0.3
18 TH	0248 6.8 0941 1.4 1510 6.8 2159 1.6	0203 8.7 0852 1.4 1418 8.6 2111 1.3	0131 7.5 0809 1.9 1252 7.5 2025 1.8	0554 1.7 1122 6.0 1818 1.6 2350 5.7	0411 2.6 093611.4 1630 2.7 220010.7	0130 1.7 0725 6.6 1358 1.8 1947 6.2	0113 1.4 0729 5.0 1343 1.4 1951 4.7	0640 3.6 1218 0.9 1906 3.3	0536 0.9 1106 0.3 1749 0.8 2327 0.3
19 F	0328 6.7 1015 1.6 1551 6.6 2234 1.8	0242 8.3 0924 1.6 1454 8.2 2142 1.6	0139 7.3 0837 2.2 1332 7.3 2052 2.1	0630 2.0 1200 5.7 1854 1.9	0441 3.1 101210.8 1658 3.1 223610.2	0209 2.0 0802 6.3 1437 2.1 2025 5.9	0154 1.6 0806 4.8 1425 1.6 2030 4.5	0024 1.1 0721 3.5 1300 1.1 1948 3.2	0621 0.8 1153 0.3 1836 0.8
20 SA	0410 6.5 1054 1.8 1635 6.4 2316 2.1	0320 7.9 0957 2.0 1533 7.7 2217 2.0	0209 7.1 0907 2.5 1415 7.1 2124 2.4	0030 5.4 0706 2.2 1241 5.4 1932 2.1	0511 3.5 104810.3 1728 3.6 2315 9.6	0248 2.4 0841 6.0 1518 2.5 2108 5.6	0237 1.8 0848 4.6 1510 1.8 2118 4.3	0108 1.3 0803 3.3 1347 1.3 2034 3.0	0015 0.3 0710 0.8 1246 0.4 1928 0.8
21 SU	0457 6.3 1142 2.1 1724 6.1	0401 7.5 1035 2.3 1617 7.3 2259 2.3	0251 6.9 0945 2.7 1502 6.8 2206 2.7	0115 5.1 0747 2.5 1328 5.1 2017 2.4	0544 4.0 1129 9.6 1806 4.1	0332 2.7 0926 5.7 1606 2.7 2200 5.4	0324 1.9 0939 4.4 1600 2.0 2216 4.1	0158 1.4 0851 3.1 1444 1.4 2130 2.9	0110 0.4 0803 0.8 1351 0.4 2027 0.7
22 M	0009 2.3 0549 6.0 1240 2.3 1822 5.8	0449 7.1 1124 2.6 1709 6.9 2353 2.6	0343 6.6 1036 3.0 1558 6.4 2302 2.9	0208 4.9 0839 2.7 1424 4.9 2114 2.5	0003 9.1 0629 4.5 1221 9.1 1857 4.5	0424 2.9 1022 5.4 1703 2.9 2306 5.2	0419 2.1 1042 4.2 1658 2.1 2327 4.1	0301 1.6 0950 3.0 1551 1.5 2234 2.9	0218 0.4 0902 0.8 1506 0.4 2133 0.7
23 TU	0111 2.4 0652 5.8 1344 2.4 1930 5.7	0547 6.9 1224 2.8 1815 6.7	0448 6.4 1139 3.1 1710 6.2	0310 4.8 0944 2.8 1530 4.8 2219 2.6	0107 8.7 0730 4.8 1331 8.8 2007 4.7	0526 3.0 1131 5.3 1811 2.9	0521 2.2 1154 4.2 1803 2.1	0415 1.6 1058 2.9 1700 1.5 2342 2.9	0332 0.4 1003 0.8 1618 0.4 2237 0.8
24 W	0215 2.4 0802 5.7 1448 2.3 2039 5.8	0057 2.8 0657 6.8 1333 2.8 1930 6.8	0009 2.9 0609 6.4 1248 3.0 1835 6.3	0419 4.8 1054 2.7 1639 4.8 2325 2.5	0221 8.7 0845 4.7 1444 8.9 2123 4.5	0021 5.3 0636 3.0 1246 5.4 1919 2.8	0036 4.1 0626 2.1 1301 4.2 1906 2.0	0525 1.5 1206 3.0 1759 1.4	0436 0.4 1059 0.8 1714 0.4 2333 0.8
25 TH	0319 2.2 0908 5.9 1550 2.0 2139 6.0	0206 2.7 0809 7.1 1442 2.5 2041 7.2	0117 2.8 0726 6.6 1352 2.7 1951 6.5	0527 5.0 1159 2.5 1746 5.0	0327 9.1 0957 4.3 1548 9.3 2228 4.0	0129 5.5 0742 2.8 1351 5.6 2015 2.5	0136 4.3 0727 2.0 1359 4.4 2001 1.9	0043 3.0 0624 1.4 1305 3.1 1848 1.2	0528 0.4 1149 0.8 1800 0.3
26 F	0418 2.0 1003 6.2 1646 1.8 2230 6.3	0312 2.3 0909 7.6 1542 2.1 2135 7.7	0218 2.5 0827 6.9 1449 2.3 2051 6.9	0024 2.2 0622 5.3 1254 2.2 1841 5.3	0422 9.7 1057 3.7 1642 9.9 2323 3.4	0222 5.8 0834 2.5 1441 5.9 2101 2.2	0226 4.6 0820 1.9 1448 4.6 2048 1.7	0134 3.2 0712 1.2 1356 3.2 1933 1.1	0022 0.3 0613 0.3 1235 0.9 1842 0.2
27 SA	0512 1.7 1051 6.4 1738 1.6 2314 6.6	0407 1.9 0957 8.1 1635 1.7 2221 8.2	0312 2.1 0914 7.2 1542 1.9 2140 7.2	0117 2.0 0707 5.6 1344 1.8 1927 5.5	051110.4 1149 3.1 173010.6	0306 6.1 0920 2.1 1524 6.2 2143 1.9	0311 4.8 0907 1.7 1533 4.8 2131 1.5	0220 3.4 0757 1.0 1441 3.3 2013 0.9	0106 0.9 0654 0.3 1319 0.9 1921 0.2
28 SU	0603 1.5 1133 6.7 1827 1.4 2353 6.8	0458 1.6 1041 8.6 1724 1.3 2304 8.6	0406 1.8 0954 7.4 1633 1.6 2223 7.4	0203 1.7 0748 5.8 1429 1.5 2009 5.8	0014 2.8 055611.0 1239 2.5 181611.2	0347 6.4 1003 1.8 1606 6.5 2225 1.6	0354 5.0 0950 1.5 1615 5.0 2212 1.4	0302 3.5 0838 0.8 1524 3.4 2054 0.8	0149 0.9 0733 0.2 1402 0.9 2001 0.1
29 M ●	0651 1.3 1211 6.9 1915 1.2	0547 1.3 1123 8.9 1812 1.0 2346 8.9	0457 1.6 1025 7.6 1724 1.4 2306 7.5	0248 1.5 0827 6.0 1512 1.3 2049 6.0	0103 2.3 063911.6 1330 2.0 190011.6	0427 6.7 1046 1.5 1647 6.7 2306 1.4	0434 5.2 1032 1.3 1656 5.1 2252 1.3	0342 3.7 0918 0.7 1605 3.5 2133 0.6	0232 0.9 0812 0.2 1445 0.9 2040 0.1
30 TU	0031 6.9 0739 1.2 1248 7.0 2002 1.2	0635 1.1 1204 9.1 1900 0.8	0548 1.5 1028 7.6 1813 1.2 2351 7.6	0332 1.3 0906 6.2 1556 1.0 2130 6.1	0153 2.0 072212.0 1418 1.6 194312.0	0508 7.0 1129 1.3 1728 6.9 2349 1.3	0515 5.3 1114 1.1 1737 5.2 2333 1.2	0423 3.8 1000 0.6 1645 3.6 2214 0.6	0314 0.9 0852 0.1 1528 0.9 2120 0.1
31 W	0108 7.0 0824 1.1 1327 7.1 2046 1.1	0027 9.0 0721 1.0 1246 9.2 1946 0.7	0636 1.4 1054 7.8 1859 1.1 2356 7.6	0415 1.2 0946 6.4 1639 0.9 2211 6.2	0241 1.7 080312.3 1506 1.3 202512.1	0550 7.1 1213 1.1 1810 7.0	0556 5.4 1156 1.0 1818 5.2	0503 3.9 1041 0.5 1727 3.7 2255 0.6	0357 0.9 0933 0.1 1613 0.9 2201 0.1

●● Time Zone -0100. For UT subtract 1 hour. For European summer time (shaded) 30/3-26/10 add 1 hour ●●

USE OF TIDE TABLES AND CURVES

Calculation of times and heights of tides is by no means precise and there are differences to be found in tables published by different authorities. In addition, a wind from a steady direction or unusually high or low barometric pressures can cause quite large variations in times and heights. It therefore makes very little sense to calculate too scrupulously and very often the old twelfths rule (1/12 in the first hour, 2/12 in the second hour, 3/12 in the third hour, 3/12 in the fourth hour, 2/12 in the fifth hour and 1/12 in the sixth hour) will be perfectly adequate.

However, it may be felt that the best use possible should be made of the published data so that any uncertainties are reduced to natural or unavoidable causes. Hence these notes. Heights calculated by whatever method must be added to the charted depth.

Standard Ports

Say one needs the height of tide at 1030UT (1130DST) at Shoreham on Sunday 1st June 1997. The tables give HW at 0736 of 5·4m and LW at 1357 of 1·1m. Go to the tidal curve for Shoreham and mark the HW height of 5·4 on the top line and the LW height of 1·1 on the bottom line of the graticule to the left of the curve. Draw a diagonal line between these two points. Mark the HW time on the bottom line under the curve and work forwards to 1030 and erect a perpendicular from this time to the curve. Erect a horizontal away to the diagonal and from thence another perpendicular to the top line of the graticule. This shows that the height of tide at 1030 is 3·5m. Incidentally, the twelfths rule would have given 6/12ths for the three hours after HW, ie half of (5·4-1·1)m range or 2·2m on top of the 1·1 LW giving a height of 3·3m.

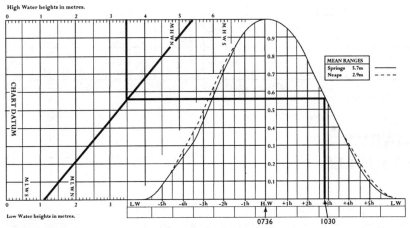

Secondary Ports

The procedure is the same after the times and heights of HW and LW for the port are calculated using the difference tables. *Thus*: find the times and heights of HW and LW at Yarmouth, Isle of Wight, on Sunday 1st June 1997.

Note that the secondary port tables have two columns for HW differences and two for LW differences. Note, especially, that the times in bold opposite the standard port are discrete, ie having found Yarmouth and looked above to the bold times, the HW difference when HW Portsmouth is either 0000 or 1200 is −0105 or when HW Portsmouth is 0600 or 1800 the difference is +0005. At any time between 0600 and 1200, for example, the difference is found by interpolation between +0005 and −0105. This can be done by eye, by calculation or by drawing a straight line graph. On 1st June 1997, HW Portsmouth is at 0754 (4·2m) and LW is at 1310 (1·3m). Hence by interpolation, the HW correction for Yarmouth is −0018 making HW Yarmouth 0736. Similarly LW Yarmouth is at 1242.

Looking now at the height differences and interpolating again between the actual height at Portsmouth of 4·2m and the limits of 4·7m and 3·8m we find a difference of −1·4m, thus the height of tide at HW at Yarmouth is 4·2−1·4, say 2·8m and similarly the height of tide at Yarmouth at LW is 1·3−0·2, say 1·1m. These figures for Yarmouth 0736 (2·8m) and 1242 (1·1m) can be applied to the Portsmouth curve as above to give heights against time or vice versa.

ST HELIER

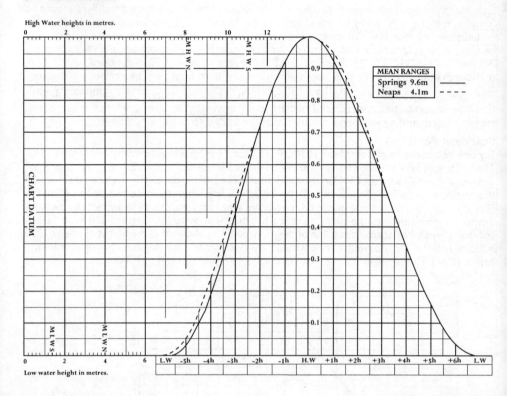

High Water heights in metres.

Low water height in metres.

MEAN RANGES
Springs 9.6m ———
Neaps 4.1m - - - -

ST MARY'S
SCILLY ISLES

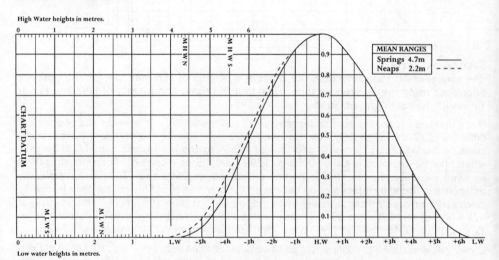

High Water heights in metres.

Low water heights in metres.

MEAN RANGES
Springs 4.7m ———
Neaps 2.2m - - - -

PLYMOUTH

High Water heights in metres.

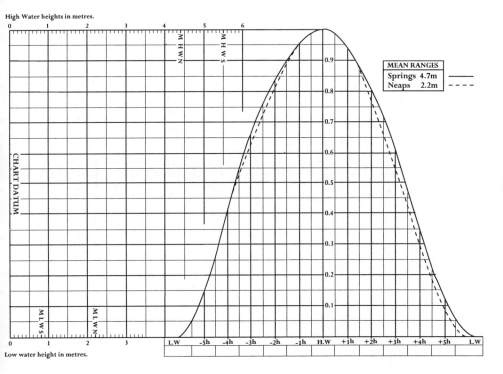

MEAN RANGES
Springs 4.7m ——
Neaps 2.2m - - - -

Low water height in metres.

PORTLAND

High Water heights in metres.

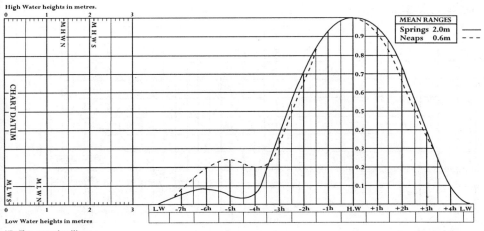

MEAN RANGES
Springs 2.0m ——
Neaps 0.6m - - -

Low Water heights in metres

NB - There are two Low Waters.
The times shown in the Tide Tables are for the first.

POOLE - ENTRANCE

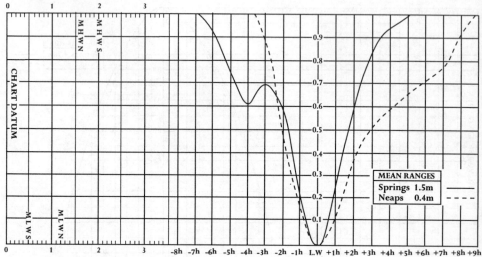

SOUTHAMPTON

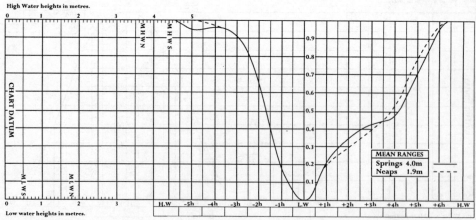

NB - There are two High Waters.
The times shown in the Tide Tables are for the first.

PORTSMOUTH

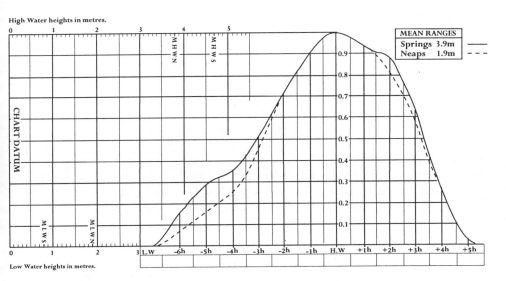

High Water heights in metres.

Low Water heights in metres.

MEAN RANGES
Springs 3.9m
Neaps 1.9m

SHOREHAM

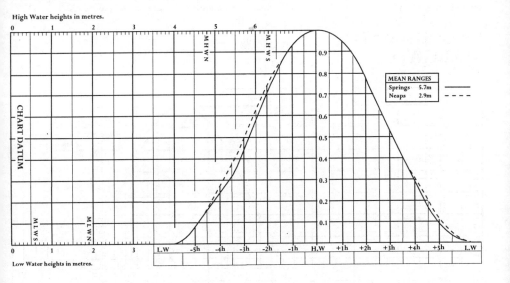

High Water heights in metres.

Low Water heights in metres.

MEAN RANGES
Springs 5.7m
Neaps 2.9m

TIDAL CURVES

DOVER

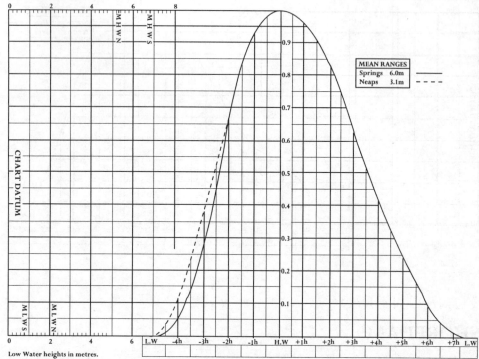

High Water heights in metres.

Low Water heights in metres.

MEAN RANGES
Springs 6.0m
Neaps 3.1m

MARGATE

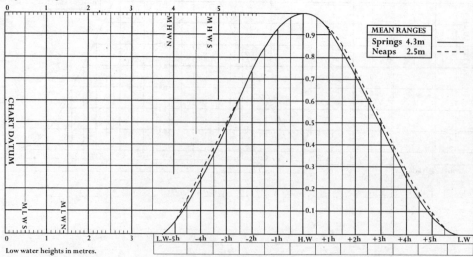

High Water heights in metres.

Low water heights in metres.

MEAN RANGES
Springs 4.3m
Neaps 2.5m

SHEERNESS

High Water heights in metres.

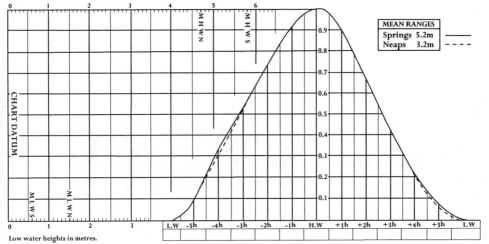

Low water heights in metres.

LONDON BRIDGE

High Water heights in metres.

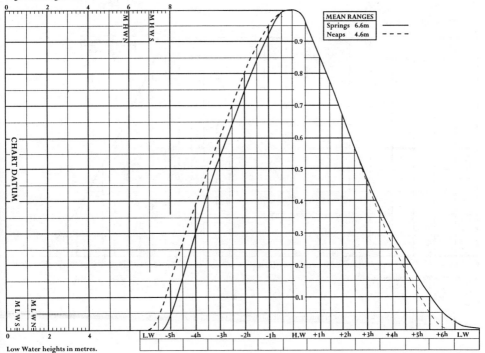

Low Water heights in metres.

WALTON-ON-THE-NAZE

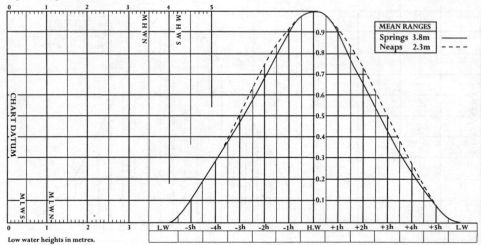

High Water heights in metres.

Low water heights in metres.

MEAN RANGES
Springs 3.8m
Neaps 2.3m

HARWICH

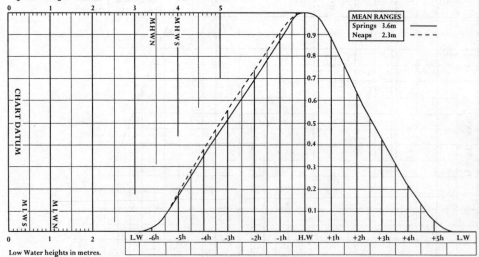

High Water heights in metres.

Low Water heights in metres.

MEAN RANGES
Springs 3.6m
Neaps 2.3m

LOWESTOFT

High Water heights in metres.

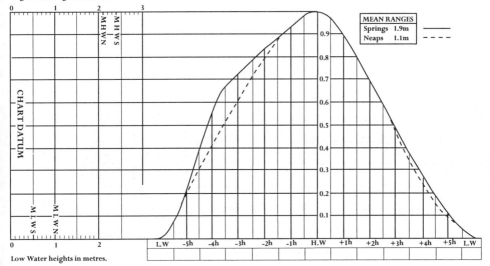

IMMINGHAM

High Water heights in metres.

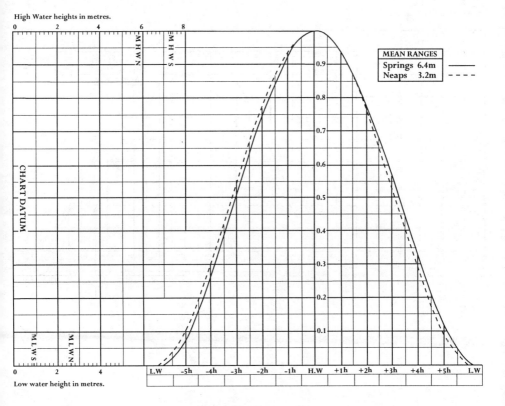

RIVER TEES

High Water heights in metres.

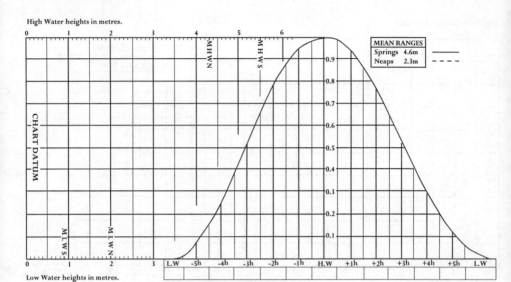

Low Water heights in metres.

RIVER TYNE

High Water heights in metres.

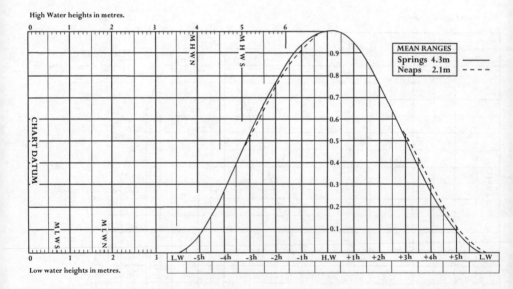

Low water heights in metres.

LEITH

High Water heights in metres.

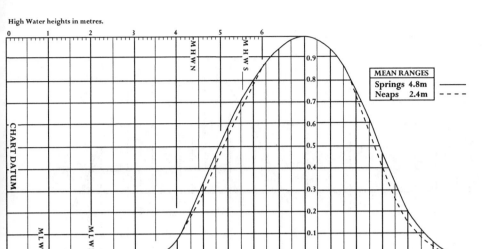

Low water heights in metres.

ROSYTH

High Water heights in metres.

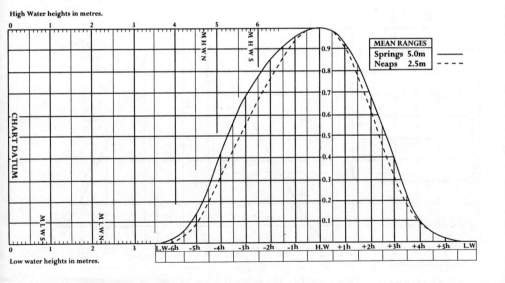

Low water heights in metres.

ABERDEEN

High Water heights in metres.

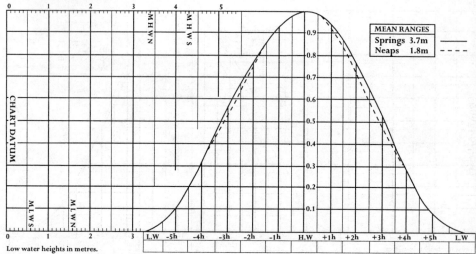

MEAN RANGES
Springs 3.7m ———
Neaps 1.8m - - - -

Low water heights in metres.

WICK

High Water heights in metres.

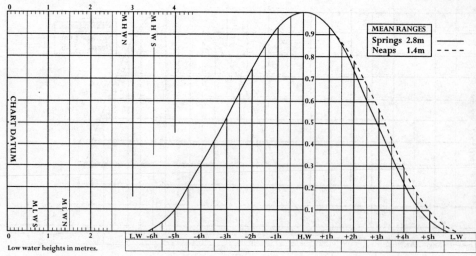

MEAN RANGES
Springs 2.8m ———
Neaps 1.4m - - - -

Low water heights in metres.

LERWICK

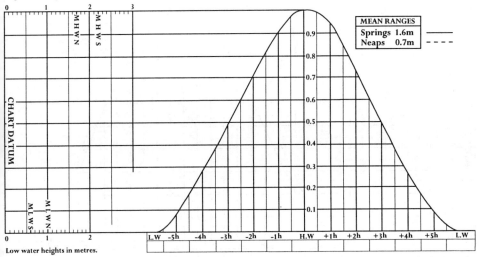

ULLAPOOL

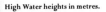

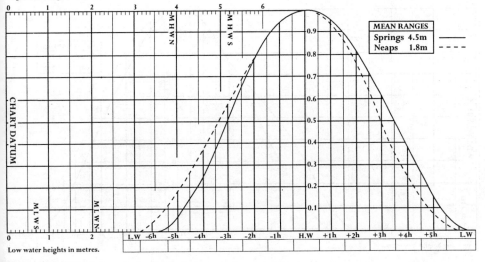

OBAN

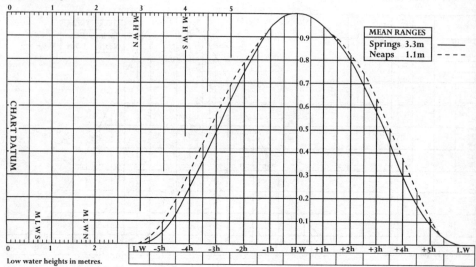

High Water heights in metres.

MEAN RANGES
Springs 3.3m
Neaps 1.1m

Low water heights in metres.

GREENOCK

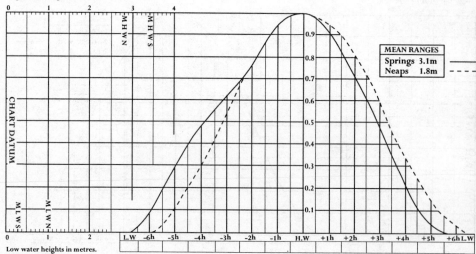

High Water heights in metres.

MEAN RANGES
Springs 3.1m
Neaps 1.8m

Low water heights in metres.

LIVERPOOL

High Water heights in metres.

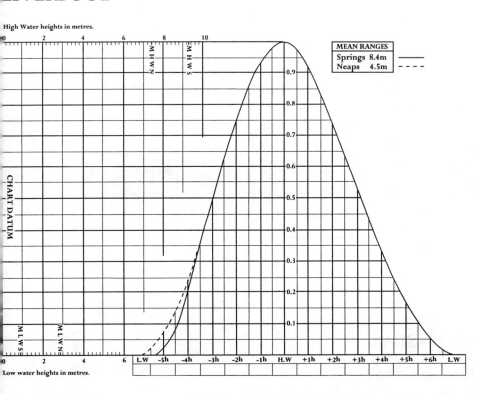

Low water heights in metres.

MEAN RANGES
Springs 8.4m ——
Neaps 4.5m - - - -

HOLYHEAD

High Water heights in metres.

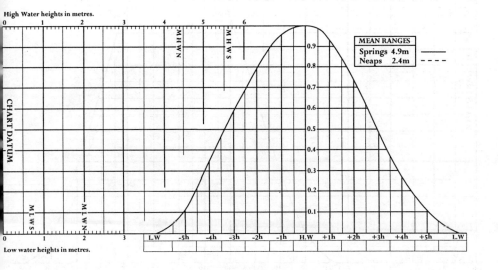

Low water heights in metres.

MEAN RANGES
Springs 4.9m ——
Neaps 2.4m - - - -

MILFORD HAVEN

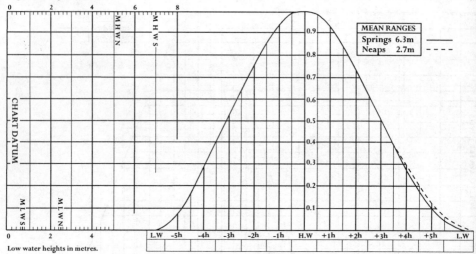

SWANSEA

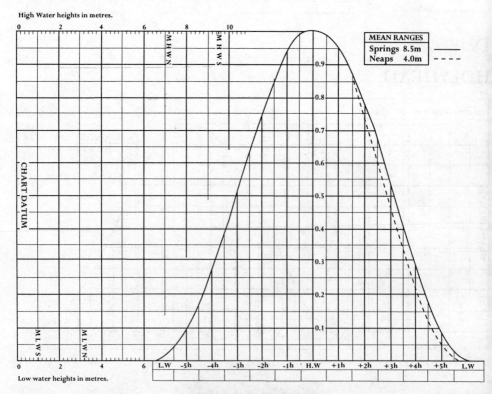

AVONMOUTH

High Water heights in metres.

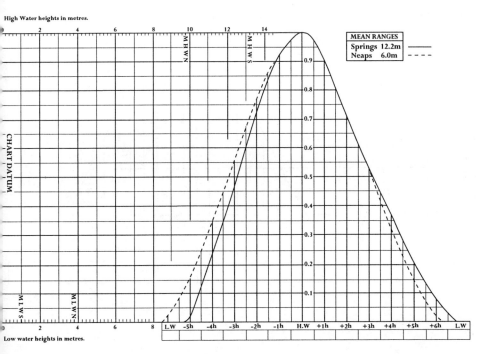

MEAN RANGES
Springs 12.2m ———
Neaps 6.0m ----

CHART DATUM

Low water heights in metres.

DUBLIN

High Water heights in metres.

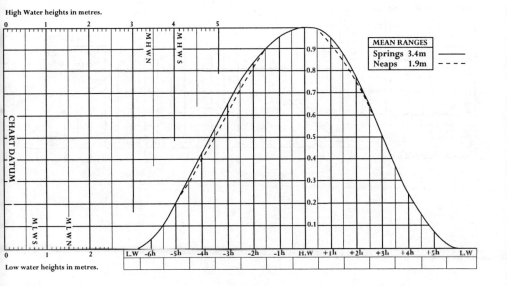

MEAN RANGES
Springs 3.4m ———
Neaps 1.9m ----

CHART DATUM

Low water heights in metres.

BELFAST

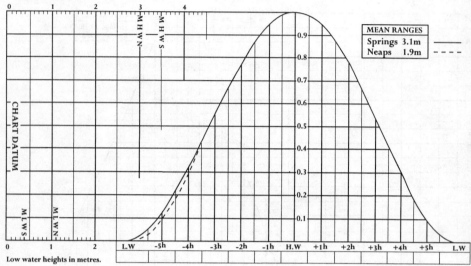

High Water heights in metres.

MEAN RANGES
Springs 3.1m
Neaps 1.9m

Low water heights in metres.

LONDONDERRY

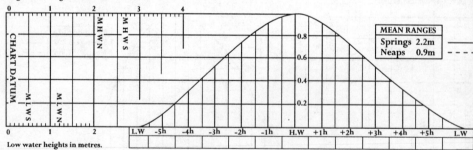

High Water heights in metres.

MEAN RANGES
Springs 2.2m
Neaps 0.9m

Low water heights in metres.

GALWAY

High Water heights in metres.

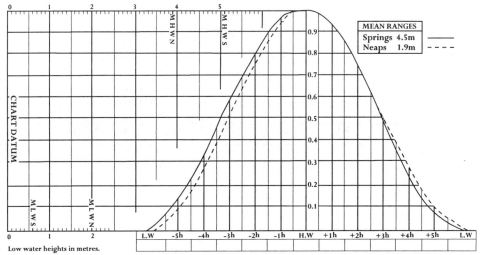

COBH

High Water heights in metres.

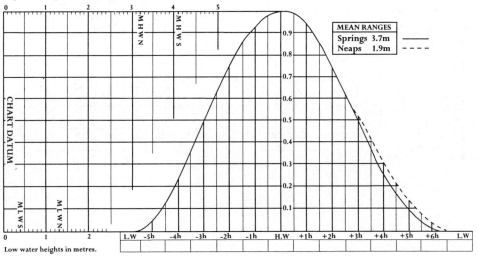

ESBJERG

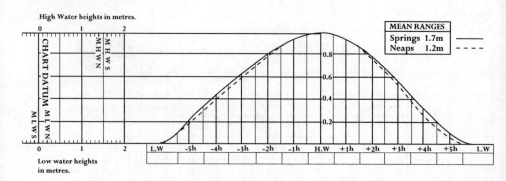

HELGOLAND

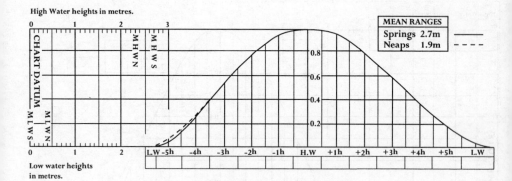

CUXHAVEN

High Water heights in metres.

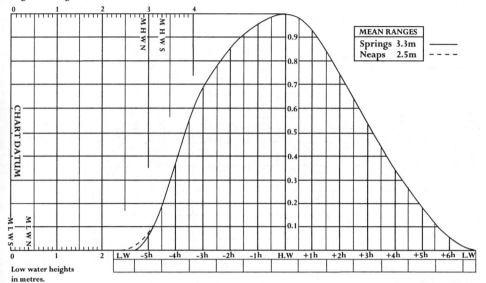

Low water heights in metres.

HOEK VAN HOLLAND

High Water heights in metres.

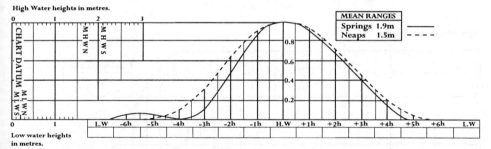

Low water heights in metres.

NB - There are often two Low Waters.
When this occurs the times shown in the Tide Tables are for the first.

ROTTERDAM

High Water heights in metres.

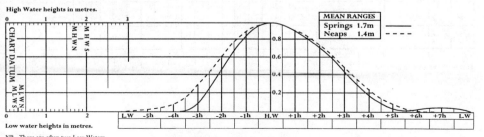

Low water heights in metres.

NB - There are often two Low Waters.
When this occurs the times shown in the Tide Tables are midway between the two.

ANTWERPEN

High Water heights in metres.

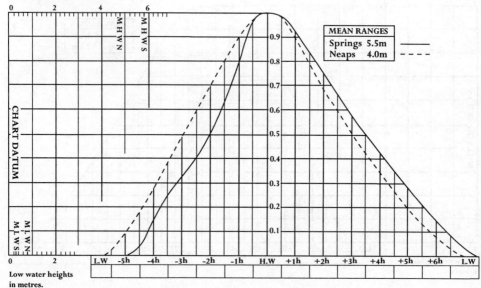

MEAN RANGES
Springs 5.5m ——
Neaps 4.0m ----

Low water heights
in metres.

VLISSINGEN

High Water heights in metres.

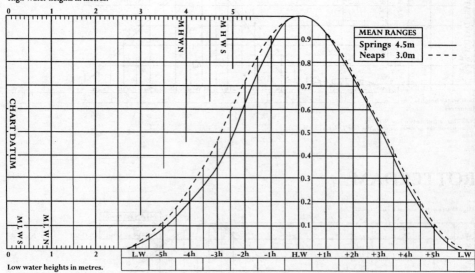

MEAN RANGES
Springs 4.5m ——
Neaps 3.0m ----

Low water heights in metres.

DUNKERQUE

High Water heights in metres.

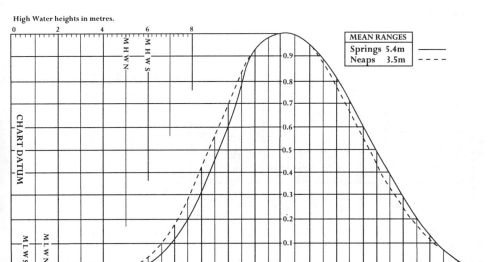

MEAN RANGES
Springs 5.4m
Neaps 3.5m

Low water height in metres.

CALAIS

High Water heights in metres.

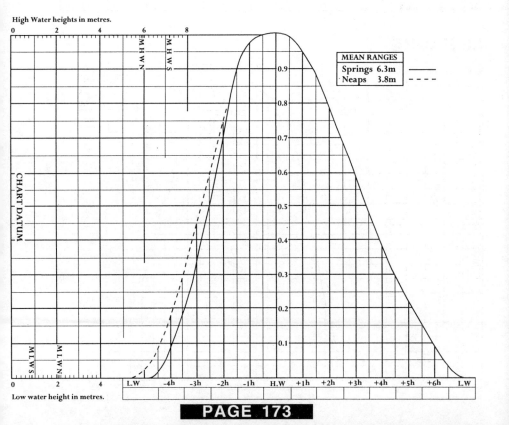

MEAN RANGES
Springs 6.3m
Neaps 3.8m

Low water height in metres.

DIEPPE

High Water heights in metres.

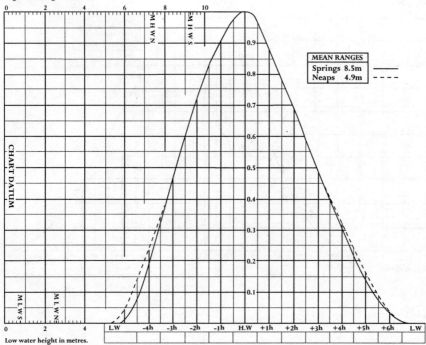

MEAN RANGES
Springs 8.5m
Neaps   4.9m

Low water height in metres.

LE HAVRE

High Water heights in metres.

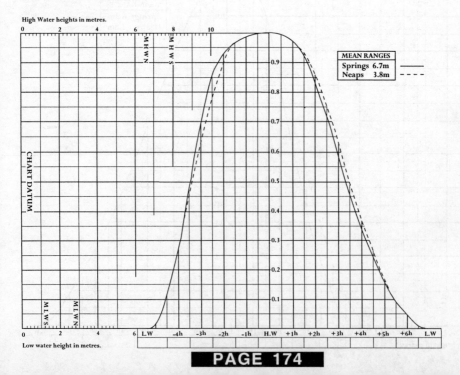

MEAN RANGES
Springs 6.7m
Neaps   3.8m

Low water height in metres.

CHERBOURG

High Water heights in metres.

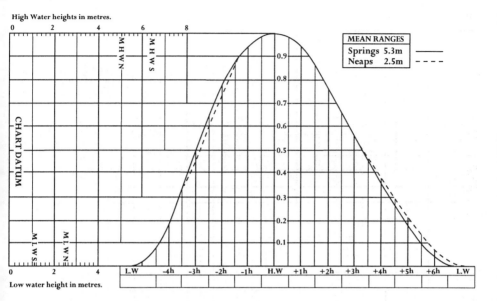

MEAN RANGES
Springs 5.3m ——
Neaps 2.5m - - - -

Low water height in metres.

ST MALO

High Water heights in metres.

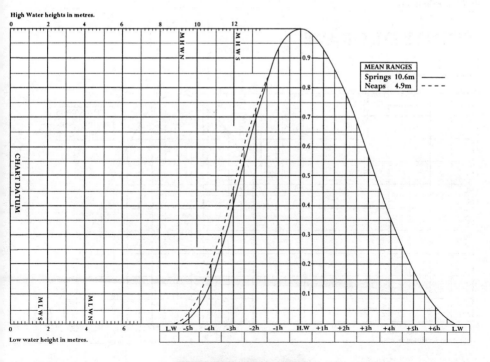

MEAN RANGES
Springs 10.6m ——
Neaps 4.9m - - - -

Low water height in metres.

BREST

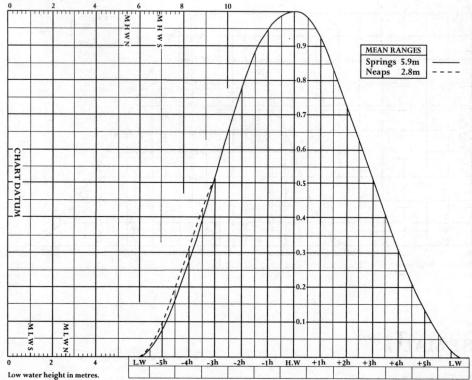

High Water heights in metres.

MEAN RANGES
Springs 5.9m ———
Neaps 2.8m - - - -

Low water height in metres.

POINTE DE GRAVE

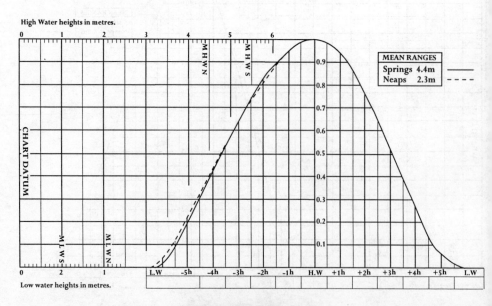

High Water heights in metres.

MEAN RANGES
Springs 4.4m ———
Neaps 2.3m - - - -

Low water heights in metres.

LISBOA

High Water heights in metres.

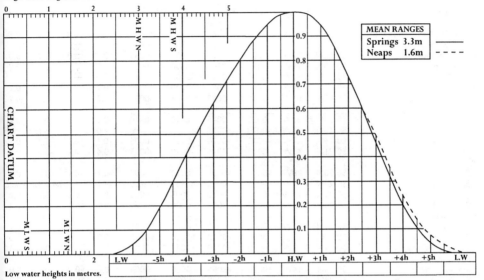

MEAN RANGES	
Springs 3.3m	——
Neaps 1.6m	- - - -

Low water heights in metres.

GIBRALTAR

High Water heights in metres.

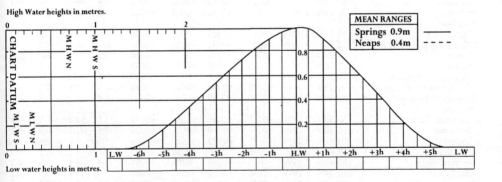

MEAN RANGES	
Springs 0.9m	——
Neaps 0.4m	- - - -

Low water heights in metres.

SECONDARY PORTS & TIDAL DIFFERENCES
SOUTH COAST UK

Location	Lat	Long	High Water 0000	High Water 0600	Low Water 0000	Low Water 0600	MHWS	MHWN	MLWN	MLWS
PLYMOUTH, DEVONPORT	50 22N	4 11W	and	and	and	and	5.5	4.4	2.2	0.8
standard port			1200	1800	1200	1800				
Penzance Newlyn	50 06N	5 33W	-0055	-0115	-0035	-0035	+0.1	0.0	-0.2	0.0
Porthleven	50 05N	5 19W	-0050	-0105	-0030	-0025	0.0	-0.1	-0.2	0.0
Lizard Point	49 57N	5 12W	-0045	-0100	-0030	-0030	-0.2	-0.2	-0.3	-0.2
Coverack	50 01N	5 05W	-0030	-0050	-0020	-0015	-0.2	-0.2	-0.3	-0.2
Helford River (Entrance)	50 05N	5 05W	-0030	-0035	-0015	-0010	-0.2	-0.2	-0.3	-0.2
River Fal										
Falmouth	50 09N	5 03W	-0025	-0045	-0010	-0010	-0.2	-0.2	-0.3	-0.2
Truro	50 16N	5 03W	-0020	-0025	no data	no data	-2.0	-2.0	no data	no data
Mevagissey	50 16N	4 47W	-0015	-0020	-0010	-0005	-0.1	-0.1	-0.2	-0.1
Par	50 21N	4 42W	-0010	-0015	-0010	-0005	-0.4	-0.4	-0.4	-0.2
River Fowey										
Fowey	50 20N	4 38W	-0010	-0015	-0010	-0005	-0.1	-0.1	-0.2	-0.2
Lostwithiel	50 24N	4 40W	+0005	-0010	no data	no data	-4.1	-4.1	no data	no data
Looe	50 21N	4 27W	-0010	-0010	-0005	-0005	-0.1	-0.2	-0.2	-0.2
Whitsand Bay	50 20N	4 15W	0000	0000	0000	0000	0.0	+0.1	-0.1	+0.2
River Tamar										
Saltash	50 24N	4 12W	0000	+0010	0000	-0005	+0.1	+0.1	+0.1	+0.1
Cargreen	50 26N	4 12W	0000	+0010	+0020	+0020	0.0	0.0	-0.1	0.0
Cotehele Quay	50 29N	4 13W	0000	+0020	+0045	+0045	-0.9	-0.9	-0.8	-0.4
River Lynher										
Jupiter Point	50 23N	4 14W	+0010	+0005	0000	-0005	0.0	0.0	+0.1	0.0
St Germans	50 23N	4 18W	0000	0000	+0020	+0020	-0.3	-0.1	0.0	+0.2
Turnchapel	50 22N	4 07W	0000	0000	+0010	-0015	0.0	+0.1	+0.2	+0.1
Bovisand Pier	50 20N	4 08W	0000	-0020	0000	-0010	-0.2	-0.1	0.0	+0.1
River Yealm Entrance	50 18N	4 04W	+0006	+0006	+0002	+0002	-0.1	-0.1	-0.1	-0.1
			0100	0600	0100	0600				
PLYMOUTH, DEVONPORT	50 22N	4 11W	and	and	and	and	5.5	4.4	2.2	0.8
			1300	1800	1300	1800				
Salcombe	50 13N	3 47W	0000	+0010	+0005	-0005	-0.2	-0.3	-0.1	-0.1
Start Point	50 13N	3 39W	+0005	+0030	-0005	+0005	-0.2	-0.4	-0.1	-0.1
River Dart										
Dartmouth	50 21N	3 34W	+0015	+0025	0000	-0005	-0.6	-0.6	-0.2	-0.2
Greenway Quay	50 23N	3 35W	+0030	+0045	+0025	+0005	-0.6	-0.6	-0.2	-0.2
Totnes	50 26N	3 41W	+0030	+0040	+0115	+0030	-2.0	-2.1	dries	dries
Torquay	50 28N	3 31W	+0025	+0045	+0010	0000	-0.6	-0.7	-0.2	-0.1
Teignmouth Approaches	50 33N	3 30W	+0025	+0040	0000	0000	-0.7	-0.8	-0.3	-0.2
Teignmouth Shaldon Bridge	50 33N	3 31W	+0035	+0050	+0020	+0020	-0.9	-0.9	-0.2	0.0
Exmouth Approaches	50 36N	3 23W	+0030	+0050	+0015	+0005	-0.9	-1.0	-0.5	-0.3
River Exe										
Exmouth Dock	50 37N	3 25W	+0035	+0055	+0050	+0020	-1.5	-1.6	-0.9	-0.6
Starcross	50 38N	3 27W	+0040	+0110	+0055	+0025	-1.4	-1.5	-0.8	-0.1
Topsham	50 41N	3 28W	+0045	+0105	no data	no data	-1.5	-1.6	no data	no data
Lyme Regis	50 43N	2 56W	+0040	+0100	+0005	-0005	-1.2	-1.3	-0.5	-0.2
Bridport West Bay	50 42N	2 45W	+0025	+0040	0000	0000	-1.4	-1.4	-0.6	-0.2
Chesil Cove	50 34N	2 28W	+0035	+0050	-0010	+0005	-1.5	-1.6	-0.5	-0.2
Brixham	50 24N	3 31W	+0025	+0045	+0010	0000	-0.6	-0.7	-0.2	-0.1
			0100	0700	0100	0700				
PORTLAND/WEYMOUTH	50 34N	2 26W	and	and	and	and	2.1	1.4	0.8	0.1
standard port			1300	1900	1300	1900				
Lulworth Cove	50 37N	2 15W	+0005	+0015	-0005	0000	+0.1	+0.1	+0.2	+0.1
			0000	0600	0500	1100				
PORTSMOUTH	50 48N	1 07W	and	and	and	and	4.7	3.8	1.9	0.8
standard port			1200	1800	1700	2300				
Swanage	50 37N	1 57W	-0250	+0105	-0105	-0105	-2.7	-2.2	-0.7	-0.3
Poole Harbour										
Town Quay	50 43N	1 59W	-0210	+0140	-0015	-0005	-2.6	-2.2	-0.7	-0.2
Pottery Pier	50 42N	1 59W	-0150	+0200	-0010	0000	-2.7	-2.1	-0.6	0.0
Wareham River Frome	50 41N	2 06W	-0140	+0205	+0110	+0035	-2.5	-2.1	-0.7	+0.1
Cleavel Point	50 40N	2 00W	-0220	+0130	-0025	-0015	-2.6	-2.3	-0.7	-0.3

Location	Lat	Long	High Water		Low Water		MHWS	MHWN	MLWN	MLWS
PORTSMOUTH	50 48N	1 07W	0000	0600	0500	1100				
			and	and	and	and	4.7	3.8	1.9	0.8
standard port			1200	1800	1700	2300				
Bournemouth	50 43N	1 52W	-0240	+0055	-0050	-0030	-2.7	-2.2	-0.8	-0.3
Christchurch *Entrance*	50 43N	1 45W	-0230	+0030	-0035	-0035	-2.9	-2.4	-1.2	-0.2
Christchurch *Tuckton*	50 44N	1 47W	-0205	+0110	+0110	+0105	-3.0	-2.5	-1.0	+0.1
Hurst Point	50 42N	1 33W	-0115	-0005	-0030	-0025	-2.0	-1.5	-0.5	-0.1
Lymington	50 46N	1 32W	-0110	+0005	-0020	-0020	-1.7	-1.2	-0.5	-0.1
Bucklers Hard	50 48N	1 25W	-0040	-0010	+0010	-0010	-1.0	-0.8	-0.2	-0.3
Stansore Point	50 47N	1 21W	-0050	-0010	-0005	-0010	-0.9	-0.6	-0.2	0.0
Isle of Wight										
Yarmouth	50 42N	1 30W	-0105	+0005	-0025	-0030	-1.6	-1.3	-0.4	0.0
Totland Bay	50 41N	1 33W	-0130	-0045	-0040	-0040	-2.0	-1.5	-0.5	-0.1
Freshwater	50 40N	1 31W	-0210	+0025	-0040	-0020	-2.1	-1.5	-0.4	0.0
Ventnor	50 36N	1 12W	-0025	-0030	-0025	-0030	-0.8	-0.6	-0.2	+0.2
Sandown	50 39N	1 09W	0000	+0005	+0010	+0025	-0.6	-0.5	-0.2	0.0
Foreland *Lifeboat Slip*	50 41N	1 04W	-0005	0000	+0005	+0010	-0.1	-0.1	0.0	+0.1
Bembridge Harbour	50 42N	1 06W	-0010	+0005	+0020	0000	-1.6	-1.5	-1.4	-0.6
Ryde	50 44N	1 07W	-0010	+0010	-0005	-0010	-0.2	-0.1	0.0	+0.1
Medina River										
Cowes	50 46N	1 18W	-0015	+0015	0000	-0020	-0.5	-0.3	-0.1	0.0
Folly Inn	50 44N	1 17W	-0015	+0015	0000	-0020	-0.6	-0.4	-0.1	+0.2
			0400	1100	0000	0600				
SOUTHAMPTON	50 54N	1 24W	and	and	and	and	4.5	3.7	1.8	0.5
standard port			1600	2300	1200	1800				
Calshot Castle	50 49N	1 18W	0000	+0025	0000	0000	0.0	0.0	+0.2	+0.3
Redbridge	50 55N	1 28W	-0020	+0005	0000	-0005	-0.1	-0.1	-0.1	-0.1
River Hamble										
Warsash	50 51N	1 18W	+0020	+0010	+0010	0000	0.0	+0.1	+0.1	+0.3
Bursledon	50 53N	1 18W	+0020	+0020	+0010	+0010	+0.1	+0.1	+0.2	+0.2
			0500	1000	0000	0600				
PORTSMOUTH	50 48N	1 07W	and	and	and	and	4.7	3.8	1.9	0.8
standard port			1700	2200	1200	1800				
Lee-on-the-Solent	50 48N	1 12W	-0005	+0005	-0015	-0010	-0.2	-0.1	+0.1	+0.2
Chichester Harbour										
Entrance	50 47N	0 56W	-0010	+0005	+0015	+0020	+0.2	+0.2	0.0	+0.1
Northney	50 50N	0 58W	+0010	+0015	+0015	+0025	+0.2	0.0	-0.2	-0.3
Bosham	50 50N	0 52W	0000	+0010	no data	no data	+0.2	+0.1	no data	no data
Itchenor	50 48N	0 52W	-0005	+0005	+0005	+0025	+0.1	0.0	-0.2	-0.2
Dell Quay	50 49N	0 49W	+0005	+0015	no data	no data	+0.2	+0.1	no data	no data
Selsey Bill	50 43N	0 47W	-0005	-0005	+0035	+0035	+0.6	+0.6	0.0	0.0
Nab Tower	50 40N	0 57W	+0015	0000	+0015	+0015	-0.2	0.0	+0.2	0.0
			0500	1000	0000	0600				
SHOREHAM	50 50N	0 15W	and	and	and	and	6.3	4.8	1.9	0.6
standard port			1700	2200	1200	1800				
Pagham	50 46N	0 43W	+0015	0000	-0015	-0025	-0.7	-0.5	-0.1	-0.1
Bognor Regis	50 47N	0 40W	+0010	-0005	-0005	-0020	-0.6	-0.5	-0.2	-0.1
Littlehampton *Entrance*	50 48N	0 32W	+0010	0000	-0005	-0010	-0.4	-0.4	-0.2	-0.2
Worthing	50 48N	0 22W	+0010	0000	- 0005	-0010	-0.1	-0.2	0.0	0.0
Brighton	50 49N	0 08W	-0010	-0005	-0005	-0005	+0.3	+0.1	0.0	-0.1
Newhaven	50 47N	0 04E	-0015	-0010	0000	0000	+0.4	+0.2	0.0	-0.2
Eastbourne	50 46N	0 17E	-0010	-0005	+0015	+0020	+1.1	+0.6	+0.2	+0.1
			0000	0600	0100	0700				
DOVER	51 07N	1 19E	and	and	and	and	6.8	5.3	2.2	0.8
standard port			1200	1800	1300	1900				
Hastings	50 51N	0 35E	0000	-0010	-0030	-0030	+0.8	+0.5	+0.1	-0.1
Rye *Approaches*	50 55N	0 47E	+0005	-0010	no data	no data	+1.0	+0.7	no data	no data
Rye *Harbour*	50 56N	0 46E	+0005	-0010	dries	dries	-1.4	-1.7	dries	dries
Dungeness	50 54N	0 58E	-0010	-0015	-0020	-0010	+1.0	+0.6	+0.4	+0.1
Folkestone	51 05N	1 12E	-0020	-0005	-0010	-0010	+0.4	+0.4	0.0	-0.1
Deal	51 13N	1 25E	+0010	+0020	+0010	+0005	-0.6	-0.3	0.0	0.0
Ramsgate	51 20N	1 25E	+0030	+0030	+0017	+0007	-1.6	-1.3	-0.8	-0.2

EAST COAST UK

Location	Lat	Long	High Water		Low Water		MHWS	MHWN	MLWN	MLWS
			0100	0700	0100	0700				
MARGATE	51 23N	1 23E	and	and	and	and	4.8	3.9	1.4	0.5
standard port			1300	1900	1300	1900				
Broadstairs	51 21N	1 27E	-0020	-0008	+0007	+0010	-0.2	-0.2	-0.1	-0.1
Herne Bay	51 23N	1 07E	+0034	+0022	+0015	+0032	+0.4	+0.4	0.0	0.0
Whitstable *Approaches*	51 22N	1 02E	+0042	+0029	+0025	+0050	+0.6	+0.6	+0.1	0.0
			0200	0800	0200	0700				
SHEERNESS	51 27N	0 45E	and	and	and	and	5.8	4.7	1.5	0.6
standard port			1400	2000	1400	1900				
River Swale										
Grovehurst Jetty	51 22N	0 46E	-0007	0000	0000	+0016	0.0	0.0	0.0	-0.1
Faversham	51 19N	0 54E	no data	no data	no data	no data	-0.2	-0.2	no data	no data
River Medway										
Bee Ness	51 25N	0 39E	+0002	+0002	0000	+0005	+0.2	+0.1	0.0	0.0
Bartlett Creek	51 23N	0 38E	+0016	+0008	no data	no data	+0.1	0.0	no data	no data
Darnett Ness	51 24N	0 36E	+0004	+0004	0000	+0010	+0.2	+0.1	0.0	-0.1
Chatham *Lock approaches*	51 24N	0 33E	+0010	+0012	+0012	+0018	+0.3	+0.1	-0.1	-0.2
Upnor	51 25N	0 32E	+0015	+0015	+0015	+0025	+0.2	+0.2	-0.1	-0.1
Rochester *Strood Pier*	51 24N	0 30E	+0018	+0018	+0018	+0028	+0.2	+0.2	-0.2	-0.3
Wouldham	51 21N	0 27E	+0030	+0025	+0035	+0120	-0.2	-0.3	-1.0	-0.3
New Hythe	51 19N	0 28E	+0035	+0035	+0220	+0240	-1.6	-1.7	-1.2	-0.3
Allington Lock	51 17N	0 30E	+0050	+0035	no data	no data	-2.1	-2.2	-1.3	-0.4
River Thames										
Southend-on-Sea	51 31N	0 43E	-0005	-0005	-0005	-0005	0.0	0.0	-0.1	-0.1
Coryton	51 30N	0 31E	+0005	+0010	+0010	+0010	+0.4	+0.3	+0.1	-0.1
			0300	0900	0400	1100				
LONDON BRIDGE	51 30N	0 05W	and	and	and	and	7.1	5.9	1.3	0.5
standard port			1500	2100	1600	2300				
Albert Bridge	51 29N	0 10W	+0025	+0020	+0105	+0110	-0.9	-0.8	-0.7	-0.4
Hammersmith Bridge	51 29N	0 14W	+0040	+0035	+0205	+0155	-1.4	-1.3	-1.0	-0.5
Kew Bridge	51 29N	0 17W	+0055	+0050	+0255	+0235	-1.8	-1.8	-1.2	-0.5
Richmond Lock	51 28N	0 19W	+0105	+0055	+0325	+0305	-2.2	-2.2	-1.3	-0.5
			0200	0700	0100	0700				
SHEERNESS	51 27N	0 45E	and	and	and	and	5.8	4.7	1.5	0.6
standard port			1400	1900	1300	1900				
Thames Estuary										
Shivering Sand	51 30N	1 05E	-0025	-0019	-0008	-0026	-0.6	-0.6	-0.1	-0.1
			0100	0700	0100	0700				
MARGATE	51 23N	1 23E	and	and	and	and	4.8	3.9	1.4	0.5
standard port			1300	1900	1300	1900				
SE Long Sand	51 32N	1 21E	-0006	-0003	-0004	-0004	0.0	+0.1	0.0	-0.1
			0000	0600	0500	1100				
WALTON-ON-THE-NAZE	51 51N	1 16E	and	and	and	and	4.2	3.4	1.1	0.4
standard port			1200	1800	1700	2300				
Whitaker Beacon	51 40N	1 06E	+0022	+0024	+0033	+0027	+0.6	+0.5	+0.2	+0.1
Holliwell Point	51 38N	0 56E	+0034	+0037	+0100	+0037	+1.1	+0.9	+0.3	+0.1
River Roach										
Rochford	51 35N	0 43E	+0050	+0040	dries	dries	-0.8	-1.1	dries	dries
River Crouch										
Burnham-on-Crouch	51 37N	0 48E	+0050	+0035	+0115	+0050	+1.0	+0.8	-0.1	-0.2
North Fambridge	51 38N	0 41E	+0115	+0050	+0130	+0100	+1.1	+0.8	0.0	-0.1
Hullbridge	51 38N	0 38E	+0115	+0050	+0135	+0105	+1.1	+0.8	0.0	-0.1
Battlesbridge	51 37N	0 34E	+0120	+0110	dries	dries	-1.8	-2.0	dries	dries
River Blackwater										
Bradwell Waterside	51 45N	0 53E	+0035	+0023	+0047	+0004	+1.1	+0.8	+0.2	+0.1
Osea Island	51 43N	0 46E	+0057	+0045	+0050	+0007	+1.1	+0.9	+0.1	0.0
Maldon	51 44N	0 42E	+0107	+0055	no data	no data	-1.3	-1.1	no data	no data
West Mersea	51 47N	0 54E	+0035	+0015	+0055	+0010	+0.9	+0.4	+0.1	+0.1
River Colne										
Brightlingsea	51 48N	1 00E	+0025	+0021	+0046	+0004	+0.8	+0.4	+0.1	0.0
Colchester	51 53N	0 56E	+0035	+0025	dries	dries	0.0	-0.3	dries	dries
Clacton-on-Sea	51 47N	1 09E	+0012	+0010	+0025	+0008	+0.3	+0.1	0.0	0.0
Bramble Creek	51 53N	1 14E	+0010	-0007	-0005	+0010	+0.3	+0.3	+0.3	+0.3
Sunk Head	51 46N	1 30E	0000	+0002	-0002	+0002	-0.3	-0.3	-0.1	-0.1

Location	Lat	Long	High Water		Low Water		MHWS	MHWN	MLWN	MLWS
			0000	0600	0000	0600				
HARWICH	51 57N	1 17E	and	and	and	and	4.0	3.4	1.1	0.4
standard port			1200	1800	1200	1800				
River Stour										
Mistley	51 57N	1 05E	+0025	+0025	0000	+0020	+0.2	0.0	-0.1	-0.1
River Orwell										
Ipswich	52 03N	1 10E	+0015	+0025	0000	+0010	+0.2	0.0	-0.1	-0.1
			0100	0700	0100	0700				
WALTON-ON-THE-NAZE	51 51N	1 16E	and	and	and	and	4.2	3.4	1.1	0.4
standard port			1300	1900	1300	1900				
Felixstowe Pier	51 57N	1 21E	-0008	-0010	-0020	-0020	-0.4	-0.3	-0.1	0.0
River Deben										
Woodbridge Haven	51 59N	1 24E	0000	-0005	-0020	-0025	-0.5	-0.5	-0.1	+0.1
Woodbridge	52 05N	1 19E	+0045	+0025	+0025	-0020	-0.2	-0.3	-0.2	0.0
Bawdsey	52 00N	1 26E	-0010	-0012	-0028	-0032	-0.8	-0.7	-0.2	-0.2
Orford Haven										
Bar	52 02N	1 28E	-0015	-0017	-0038	-0042	-1.0	-0.8	-0.2	-0.1
Orford Quay	52 05N	1 32E	+0040	+0040	+0055	+0055	-1.6	-1.3	+0.2	0.0
Slaughden Quay	52 08N	1 36E	+0100	+0100	+0115	+0115	-1.3	-1.0	+0.2	0.0
Iken Cliffs	52 09N	1 31E	+0130	+0130	+0155	+0155	-1.3	-1.0	+0.2	0.0
Snape	52 10N	1 30E	+0200	+0200	no data	no data	-1.3	-1.0	-0.3	+0.4
			0300	0900	0200	0800				
LOWESTOFT	52 28N	1 45E	and	and	and	and	2.4	2.1	1.0	0.5
standard port			1500	2100	1400	2000				
Orford Ness	52 05N	1 35E	+0135	+0135	+0135	+0125	+0.4	+0.6	-0.1	0.0
Aldeburgh	52 09N	1 36E	+0130	+0130	+0115	+0120	+0.3	+0.2	-0.1	-0.2
Minsmere	52 14N	1 38E	+0110	+0110	+0110	+0110	0.0	-0.1	-0.2	-0.2
Southwold	52 19N	1 40E	+0105	+0105	+0055	+0055	0.0	0.0	-0.1	0.0
Great Yarmouth										
Gorleston-on-Sea	52 34N	1 44E	-0035	-0035	-0030	-0030	0.0	-0.1	0.0	0.0
Britannia Pier	52 36N	1 45E	-0100	-0100	-0040	-0040	0.0	0.0	0.0	0.0
Caister-on-Sea	52 39N	1 44E	-0130	-0130	-0100	-0100	0.0	-0.1	0.0	0.0
Winterton-on-Sea	52 43N	1 42E	-0225	-0215	-0135	-0135	+0.8	+0.5	+0.2	+0.1
			0100	0700	0100	0700				
IMMINGHAM	53 38N	0 11W	and	and	and	and	7.3	5.8	2.6	0.9
			1300	1900	1300	1900				
Cromer	52 56N	1 18E	+0050	+0030	+0050	+0130	-2.1	-1.7	-0.5	-0.1
Blakeney Bar	52 59N	0 59E	+0035	+0025	+0030	+0040	-1.6	-1.3	no data	no data
Blakeney	52 57N	1 01E	+0115	+0055	no data	no data	-3.9	-3.8	no data	no data
Wells Bar	52 59N	0 49E	+0020	+0020	+0020	+0020	-1.3	-1.0	no data	no data
Wells	52 57N	0 51E	+0035	+0045	+0340	+0310	-3.8	-3.8	no data	no data
Burnham *Overy Staithe*	52 58N	0 48E	+0045	+0055	no data	no data	-5.0	-4.9	no data	no data
The Wash										
Hunstanton	52 56N	0 29E	+0010	+0020	+0105	+0025	+0.1	-0.2	-0.1	0.0
West Stones	52 50N	0 21E	+0025	+0025	+0115	+0040	-0.3	-0.4	-0.3	+0.2
King's Lynn	52 45N	0 24E	+0030	+0030	+0305	+0140	-0.5	-0.8	-0.8	+0.1
Wisbech Cut	52 48N	0 13E	+0020	+0025	+0200	+0030	-0.3	-0.7	-0.4	no data
Lawyer's Creek	52 53N	0 05E	+0010	+0020	no data	no data	-0.3	-0.6	no data	no data
Tabs Head	52 56N	0 05E	0000	+0005	+0125	+0020	+0.2	-0.2	-0.2	-0.2
Boston	52 58N	0 01W	0000	+0010	+0140	+0050	-0.5	-1.0	-0.9	-0.5
Skegness	53 09N	0 21E	+0010	+0015	+0030	+0020	-0.4	-0.5	-0.1	0.0
Inner Dowsing Light Tower	53 20N	0 34E	0000	0000	+0010	+0010	-0.9	-0.7	-0.1	+0.3
River Humber										
Bull Sand Fort	53 34N	0 04E	-0020	-0030	-0035	-0015	-0.4	-0.3	+0.1	+0.2
Grimsby	53 35N	0 04W	-0003	-0011	-0015	-0002	-0.3	-0.2	0.0	+0.1
Hull *King George Dock*	53 44N	0 16W	+0010	+0010	+0021	+0017	+0.3	+0.2	-0.1	-0.2
Hull *Albert Dock*	53 44N	0 21W	+0019	+0019	+0033	+0027	+0.3	+0.1	-0.1	-0.2
Humber Bridge	53 43N	0 27W	+0027	+0022	+0049	+0039	-0.1	-0.4	-0.7	-0.6
River Trent										
Burton Stather	53 39N	0 42W	+0105	+0045	+0335	+0305	-2.1	-2.3	-2.3	dries
Flixborough Wharf	53 37N	0 42W	+0120	+0100	+0400	+0340	-2.3	-2.6	dries	dries
Keadby	53 36N	0 44W	+0135	+0120	+0425	+0410	-2.5	-2.8	dries	dries
Owston Ferry	53 29N	0 46W	+0155	+0145	dries	dries	-3.5	-3.9	dries	dries
River Ouse										
Blacktoft	53 42N	0 43W	+0100	+0055	+0325	+0255	-1.6	-1.8	-2.2	-1.1
Goole	53 42N	0 52W	+0130	+0115	+0355	+0350	-1.6	-2.1	-1.9	-0.6

SECONDARY PORT TIDAL DATA

Location	Lat	Long	High Water 0000 and 1200	0600 and 1800	Low Water 0000 and 1200	0600 and 1800	MHWS	MHWN	MLWN	MLWS
RIVER TEES ENTRANCE	54 38N	1 09W	and	and	and	and	5.5	4.3	2.0	0.9
standard port			1200	1800	1200	1800				
Bridlington	54 05N	0 11W	+0100	+0050	+0055	+0050	+0.6	+0.4	+0.3	+0.2
Filey Bay	54 13N	0 16W	+0042	+0042	+0047	+0034	+0.3	+0.6	+0.4	+0.1
Scarborough	54 17N	0 23W	+0040	+0040	+0030	+0030	+0.2	+0.3	+0.3	0.0
Whitby	54 29N	0 37W	+0015	+0030	+0020	+0005	+0.1	0.0	-0.1	-0.1
River Tees										
Middlesborough Dock *Entrance*	54 35N	1 13W	0000	+0002	0000	-0003	+0.1	+0.2	+0.1	-0.1
Tees Bridge *Newport*	54 34N	1 16W	-0002	+0004	+0005	-0003	+0.1	+0.2	0.0	-0.1
Hartlepool	54 41N	1 11W	-0004	-0004	-0006	-0006	-0.1	-0.1	-0.2	-0.1
Seaham	54 50N	1 19W	-0015	-0015	-0015	-0015	-0.3	-0.2	0.0	-0.2
Sunderland	54 55N	1 21W	-0017	-0017	-0016	-0016	-0.3	-0.1	0.0	-0.1
			0200 and 1400	0800 and 2000	0100 and 1300	0800 and 2000				
RIVER TYNE, NORTH SHIELDS			and	and	and	and	5.0	3.9	1.8	0.7
standard port	55 01N	1 26W	1400	2000	1300	2000				
River Tyne										
Newcastle-upon-Tyne	54 58N	1 36W	+0003	+0003	+0008	+0008	+0.3	+0.2	+0.1	+0.1
Blyth	55 07N	1 29W	+0005	-0007	-0001	+0009	0.0	0.0	-0.1	+0.1
Coquet Island	55 20N	1 32W	-0010	-0010	-0020	-0020	+0.1	+0.1	0.0	+0.1
Amble	55 20N	1 34W	-0023	-0015	-0023	-0014	0.0	+0.2	+0.2	+0.1
N Sunderland *Northumberland*	55 34N	1 38W	-0048	-0044	-0058	-0102	-0.2	-0.2	-0.2	0.0
Holy Island	55 40N	1 47W	-0043	-0039	-0105	-0110	-0.2	-0.2	-0.3	-0.1
Berwick	55 47N	2 00W	-0053	-0053	-0109	-0109	-0.3	-0.1	-0.5	-0.1

WEST COAST UK & IRELAND

Location	Lat	Long	High Water 0000 and 1200	0600 and 1800	Low Water 0200 and 1400	0800 and 2000	MHWS	MHWN	MLWN	MLWS
LIVERPOOL	53 24N	3 01W	and	and	and	and	9.3	7.4	2.9	0.9
standard port			1200	1800	1400	2000				
Portpatrick	54 50N	5 07W	+0018	+0026	0000	-0035	-5.5	-4.4	-2.0	-0.6
Wigtown Bay										
Drummore	54 41N	4 53W	+0030	+0040	+0015	+0020	-3.4	-2.5	-0.9	-0.3
Port William	54 43N	4 40W	+0030	+0030	+0025	0000	-2.9	-2.2	-0.8	*no data*
Isle of Whithorn	54 42N	4 22W	+0020	+0025	+0025	+0005	-2.4	-2.0	-0.8	-0.2
Garlieston	54 47N	4 21W	+0025	+0035	+0030	+0005	-2.3	-1.7	-0.5	*no data*
Solway Firth										
Kirkcudbright Bay	54 48N	4 04W	+0015	+0015	+0010	0000	-1.8	-1.5	-0.5	-0.1
Hestan Islet	54 50N	3 48W	+0025	+0025	+0020	+0025	-1.0	-1.1	-0.5	0.0
Southerness Point	54 52N	3 36W	+0030	+0030	+0030	+0010	-0.7	-0.7	*no data*	*no data*
Annan Waterfoot	54 58N	3 16W	+0050	+0105	+0220	+0310	-2.2	-2.6	-2.7	*no data*
Torduff Point	54 58N	3 09W	+0105	+0140	+0520	+0410	-4.1	-4.9	*no data*	*no data*
Redkirk	54 59N	3 06W	+0110	+0215	+0715	+0445	-5.5	-6.2	*no data*	*no data*
Silloth	54 52N	3 24W	+0030	+0040	+0045	+0055	-0.1	-0.3	-0.6	-0.1
Maryport	54 43N	3 30W	+0017	+0032	+0020	+0005	-0.7	-0.8	-0.4	0.0
Workington	54 39N	3 34W	+0020	+0020	+0020	+0010	-1.2	-1.1	-0.3	0.0
Whitehaven	54 33N	3 36W	+0005	+0015	+0010	+0005	-1.3	-1.1	-0.5	+0.1
Tarn Point	54 17N	3 25W	+0005	+0005	+0010	0000	-1.0	-1.0	-0.4	0.0
Duddon Bar	54 09N	3 20W	+0003	+0003	+0008	+0002	-0.8	-0.8	-0.3	0.0

Location	Lat	Long	High Water 0000 and 1200	0600 and 1800	Low Water 0200 and 1400	0700 and 1900	MHWS	MHWN	MLWN	MLWS
LIVERPOOL	53 24N	3 01W	and	and	and	and	9.3	7.4	2.9	0.9
standard port			1200	1800	1400	1900				
Morecambe Bay										
Ulverston	54 11N	3 04W	+0020	+0040	*no data*	*no data*	0.0	-0.1	*no data*	*no data*
Arnside	54 12N	2 51W	+0100	+0135	*no data*	*no data*	+0.5	+0.2	*no data*	*no data*
Morecambe	54 04N	2 52W	+0005	+0010	+0030	+0015	+0.2	0.0	0.0	+0.2
Heysham	54 02N	2 55W	+0005	+0005	+0015	0000	+0.1	0.0	0.0	+0.2
River Lune										
Glasson Dock	54 00N	2 51W	+0020	+0030	+0220	+0240	-2.7	-3.0	*no data*	*no data*
Lancaster	54 03N	2 49W	+0110	+0030	*dries*	*dries*	-5.0	-4.9	*dries*	*dries*
River Wyre										
Wyre Lighthouse	53 57N	3 02W	-0010	-0010	+0005	0000	-0.1	-0.1	*no data*	*no data*
Fleetwood	53 56N	3 00W	0000	0000	+0005	0000	-0.1	-0.1	+0.1	+0.3
Blackpool	53 49N	3 04W	-0015	-0005	-0005	-0015	-0.4	-0.4	-0.1	+0.1
River Ribble										
Preston	53 46 N	2 45W	+0010	+0010	+0335	+0310	-4.0	-4.1	-2.8	-0.8
Liverpool Bay										
Southport	53 39N	3 01W	-0020	-0010	*no data*	*no data*	-0.3	-0.3	*no data*	*no data*

Location	Lat	Long	High Water		Low Water		MHWS	MHWN	MLWN	MLWS
			0000	0600	0200	0700				
LIVERPOOL	53 24N	3 01W	and	and	and	and	9.3	7.4	2.9	0.9
standard port			1200	1800	1400	1900				
Formby	53 32N	3 07W	-0015	-0010	-0020	-0020	-0.3	-0.1	0.0	+0.1
River Mersey										
Gladstone Dock	53 27N	3 01W	-0003	-0003	-0003	-0003	-0.1	-0.1	0.0	-0.1
Eastham	53 19N	2 57W	+0010	+0010	+0009	+0009	+0.3	+0.1	-0.1	-0.3
Hale Head	53 19N	2 48W	+0030	+0025	no data	no data	-2.4	-2.5	no data	no data
Widnes	53 21N	2 44W	+0040	+0045	+0400	+0345	-4.2	-4.4	-2.5	-0.3
Fiddler's Ferry	53 22N	2 39W	+0100	+0115	+0540	+0450	-5.9	-6.3	-2.4	-0.4
River Dee										
Hilbre Island	53 23N	3 13W	-0015	-0012	-0010	-0015	-0.3	-0.2	+0.2	+0.4
Mostyn Quay	53 19N	3 16W	-0020	-0015	-0020	-0020	-0.8	-0.7	no data	no data
Connah's Quay	53 13N	3 03W	0000	+0015	+0355	+0340	-4.6	-4.4	dries	dries
Chester	53 12N	2 54W	+0105	+0105	+0500	+0500	-5.3	-5.4	dries	dries
Isle of Man										
Peel	54 14N	4 42W	-0015	+0010	0000	-0010	-4.0	-3.2	-1.4	-0.4
Ramsey	54 19N	4 22W	+0005	+0015	-0005	-0015	-1.7	-1.5	-0.6	+0.1
Douglas	54 09N	4 28W	-0004	-0004	-0022	-0032	-2.4	-2.0	-0.5	-0.1
Port St Mary	54 04N	4 44W	+0005	+0015	-0010	-0030	-3.4	-2.7	-1.2	-0.3
Calf Sound	54 04N	4 48W	+0005	+0005	-0015	-0025	-3.2	-2.6	-0.9	-0.3
Port Erin	54 05N	4 46W	-0005	+0015	-0010	-0050	-4.1	-3.2	-1.3	-0.5
Colwyn Bay	53 18N	3 43W	-0035	-0025	no data	no data	-1.5	-1.3	no data	no data
Llandudno	53 20N	3 50W	-0035	-0025	-0025	-0035	-1.9	-1.5	-0.5	-0.2
			0000	0600	0500	1100				
HOLYHEAD	53 19N	4 37W	and	and	and	and	5.6	4.4	2.0	0.7
standard port			1200	1800	1700	2300				
Conwy	53 17N	3 50W	+0020	+0020	no data	+0050	+2.1	+1.6	+0.3	no data
Menai Strait										
Beaumaris	53 16N	4 05W	+0025	+0010	+0055	+0035	+2.0	+1.6	+0.5	+0.1
Menai Bridge	53 13N	4 09W	+0030	+0010	+0100	+0035	+1.7	+1.4	+0.3	0.0
Port Dinorwic	53 11N	4 13W	-0015	-0025	+0030	0000	0.0	0.0	0.0	+0.1
Caernarfon	53 09N	4 16W	-0030	-0030	+0015	-0005	-0.4	-0.4	-0.1	-0.1
Fort Belan	53 07N	4 20W	-0040	-0015	-0025	-0005	-1.0	-0.9	-0.2	-0.1
Trwyn Dinmor	53 19N	4 03W	+0025	+0015	+0050	+0035	+1.9	+1.5	+0.5	+0.2
Moelfre	53 20N	4 14W	+0025	+0020	+0050	+0035	+1.9	+1.4	+0.5	+0.2
Amlwch	53 25N	4 20W	+0020	+0010	+0035	+0025	+1.6	+ 1.3	+0.5	+0.2
Cemaes Bay	53 25N	4 27W	+0020	+0025	+0040	+0035	+1.0	+0.7	+0.3	+0.1
Trearddur Bay	53 16N	4 37W	-0045	-0025	-0015	-0015	-0.4	-0.4	0.0	+0.1
Porth Trecastell	53 12N	4 30W	-0045	-0025	-0005	-0015	-0.6	-0.6	0.0	0.0
Llanddwyn Island	53 08N	4 25W	-0115	-0055	-0030	-0020	-0.7	-0.5	-0.1	0.0
Trefor	53 00N	4 25W	-0115	-0100	-0030	-0020	-0.8	-0.9	-0.2	-0.1
Porth Dinllaen	52 57N	4 34W	-0120	-0105	-0035	-0025	-1.0	-1.0	-0.2	-0.2
Porth Ysgaden	52 54N	4 39W	-0125	-0110	-0040	-0035	-1.1	-1.0	-0.1	-0.1
Bardsey Island	52 46N	4 47W	-0220	-0240	-0145	-0140	-1.2	-1.2	-0.5	-0.1
			0100	0800	0100	0700				
MILFORD HAVEN	51 42N	5 03W	and	and	and	and	7.0	5.2	2.5	0.7
standard port			1300	2000	1300	1900				
Cardigan Bay										
Aberdaron	52 48N	4 43W	+0210	+0200	+0240	+0310	-2.4	-1.9	-0.6	-0.2
St Tudwal's Roads	52 49N	4 29W	+0155	+0145	+0240	+0310	-2.2	-1.9	-0.7	-0.2
Pwllheli	52 53N	4 24W	+0210	+0150	+0245	+0320	-2.0	- 1.8	-0.6	-0.2
Criccieth	52 55N	4 14W	+0210	+0155	+0255	+0320	-2.0	-1.8	-0.7	-0.3
Porthmadog	52 55N	4 08W	+0235	+0210	no data	no data	-1.9	-1.8	no data	no data
Barmouth	52 43N	4 03W	+0215	+0205	+0310	+0320	-2.0	-1.7	-0.7	0.0
Aberdovey	52 32N	4 03W	+0215	+0200	+0230	+0305	-2.0	-1.7	-0.5	0.0
Aberystwyth	52 24N	4 05W	+0145	+0130	+0210	+0245	-2.0	-1.7	-0.7	0.0
New Quay	52 13N	4 21W	+0150	+0125	+0155	+0230	-2.1	-1.8	-0.6	-0.1
Aberporth	52 08N	4 33W	+0135	+0120	+0150	+0220	-2.1	-1.8	-0.6	-0.1
Port Cardigan	52 07N	4 42W	+0140	+0120	+0220	+0130	-2.3	-1.8	-0.5	0.0
Cardigan *Town*	52 05N	4 40W	+0220	+0150	no data	no data	-2.2	-1.6	no data	no data
Fishguard	52 00N	4 58W	+0115	+0100	+0110	+0135	-2.2	-1.8	-0.5	+0.1
Porthgain	51 57N	5 11W	+0055	+0045	+0045	+0100	-2.5	-1.8	-0.6	0.0
Ramsey Sound	51 53N	5 19W	+0030	+0030	+0030	+0030	-1.9	-1.3	-0.3	0.0
Solva	51 52N	5 12W	+0015	+0010	+0035	+0015	-1.5	-1.0	-0.2	0.0
Little Haven	51 46N	5 06W	+0010	+0010	+0025	+0015	-1.1	-0.8	-0.2	0.0
Martin's Haven	51 44N	5 15W	+0010	+0010	+0015	+0015	-0.8	-0.5	+0.1	+0.1
Skomer Island	51 44N	5 17W	-0005	-0005	+0005	+0005	-0.4	-0.1	0.0	0.0
Dale Roads	51 42N	5 09W	-0005	-0005	-0008	-0008	0.0	0.0	0.0	-0.1

SECONDARY PORT TIDAL DATA

Location	Lat	Long	High Water		Low Water		MHWS	MHWN	MLWN	MLWS
			0100	0800	0100	0700				
MILFORD HAVEN	51 42N	5 03W	and	and	and	and	7.0	5.2	2.5	0.7
standard port			1300	2000	1300	1900				
Cleddau River										
Neyland	51 42N	4 57W	+0002	+0010	0000	0000	0.0	0.0	0.0	0.0
Black Tar	51 45N	4 54W	+0010	+0020	+0005	0000	+0.1	+0.1	0.0	-0.1
Haverfordwest	51 48N	4 58W	+0010	+0025	dries	dries	-4.8	-4.9	dries	dries
Stackpole Quay	51 37N	4 54W	-0005	+0025	-0010	-0010	+0.9	+0.7	+0.2	+0.3
Tenby	51 40N	4 42W	-0015	-0010	-0015	-0020	+1.4	+1.1	+0.5	+0.2
Towy River										
Ferryside	51 46N	4 22W	0000	-0010	+0220	0000	-0.3	-0.7	-1.7	-0.6
Carmarthen	51 51N	4 18W	+0010	0000	dries	dries	-4. 4	-4.8	dries	dries
Burry Inlet										
Burry Port	51 41N	4 15W	+0003	+0003	+0007	+0007	+1.6	+1.4	+0.5	+0.4
Llanelli	51 40N	4 10W	-0003	-0003	+0150	+0020	+0.8	+0.6	no data	no data
Mumbles	51 34N	3 58W	+0005	+0010	-0020	-0015	+2.3	+1.7	+0.6	+0.2
Port Talbot	51 35N	3 49W	+0003	+0005	-0013	-0007	+2.6	+2.0	+0.8	+0.2
Porthcawl	51 28N	3 42W	+0005	+0010	-0010	-0005	+2.9	+2.3	+0.8	+0.3
			0600	1100	0300	0800				
PORT OF BRISTOL, AVONMOUTH			and	and	and	and	13.2	9.8	3.8	1.0
standard port	51 30N	2 44W	1800	2300	1500	2000				
Barry	51 23N	3 16W	-0030	-0015	-0125	-0030	-1.8	-1.3	+0.2	0.0
Flat Holm	51 23N	3 07W	-0015	-0015	-0045	-0045	-1.3	-1.1	-0.2	+0.2
Steep Holm	51 20N	3 06W	-0020	-0020	-0050	-0050	-1.6	-1.2	-0.2	-0.2
Cardiff	51 27N	3 09W	-0015	-0015	-0100	-0030	-1.0	-0.6	+0.1	0.0
Newport	51 33N	2 59W	-0020	-0010	0000	-0020	-1.1	-1.0	-0.6	-0.7
River Wye										
Chepstow	51 39N	2 40W	+0020	+0020	no data	no data	no data	no data	no data	no data
			0000	0600	0000	0700				
PORT OF BRISTOL, AVONMOUTH			and	and	and	and	13.2	9.8	3.8	1.0
standard port	51 30N	2 44W	1200	1800	1200	1900				
England										
River Severn										
Sudbrook	51 35N	2 43W	+0010	+0010	+0025	+0015	+0.2	+0.1	-0.1	+0.1
Beachley *Aust*	51 36N	2 38W	+0010	+0015	+0040	+0025	-0.2	-0.2	-0.5	-0.3
Inward Rocks	51 39N	2 37W	+0020	+0020	+0105	+0045	-1.0	-1.1	-1.4	-0.6
Narlwood Rocks	51 39N	2 36W	+0025	+0025	+0120	+0100	-1.9	-2.0	-2.3	-0.8
White House	51 40N	2 33W	+0025	+0025	+0145	+0120	-3.0	-3.1	-3.6	-1.0
Berkeley	51 42N	2 30W	+0030	+0045	+0245	+0220	-3.8	-3.9	-3.4	-0.5
Sharpness Dock	51 43N	2 29W	+0035	+0050	+0305	+0245	-3.9	-4.2	-3.3	-0.4
Wellhouse Rock	51 44N	2 29W	+0040	+0055	+0320	+0305	-4.1	-4.4	-3.1	-0.2
Epney	51 42N	2 24W	+0130	no data	no data	no data	-9.4	no data	no data	no data
Minsterworth	51 50N	2 23W	+0140	no data	no data	no data	-10.1	no data	no data	no data
Llanthony	51 51N	2 21W	+0215	no data	no data	no data	-10.7	no data	no data	no data
			0200	0800	0300	0800				
PORT OF BRISTOL, AVONMOUTH			and	and	and	and	13.2	9.8	3.8	1.0
Royal Portbury Dock	51 30N	2 44W								
standard port			1400	2000	1500	2000				
River Avon										
Shirehampton	51 29N	2 41W	0000	0000	+0035	+0010	-0.7	-0.7	-0.8	0.0
Sea Mills	51 29N	2 39W	+0005	+0005	+0105	+0030	-1.4	-1.5	-0.7	-0.1
Cumberland Basin *Entrance*	51 27N	2 37W	+0010	+0010	dries	dries	-2.9	-3.0	dries	dries
Portishead	51 30N	2 45W	-0002	0000	no data	no data	-0.1	-0.1	no data	no data
Clevedon	51 27N	2 52W	-0010	-0020	-0025	-0015	-0.4	-0.2	+0.2	0.0
St Thomas Head	51 24N	2 56W	0000	0000	-0030	-0030	-0.4	-0.2	+0.1	+0.1
English & Welsh Grounds	51 28N	2 59W	-0008	-0008	-0030	-0030	-0.5	-0.8	-0.3	0.0
Weston-super-Mare	51 21N	2 59W	-0020	-0030	-0130	-0030	-1.2	-1.0	-0.8	-0.2
River Parrett										
Burnham	51 14N	3 00W	-0020	-0025	-0030	0000	-2.3	-1.9	-1.4	-1.1
Bridgwater	51 08N	3 00W	-0015	-0030	+0305	+0455	-8.6	-8.1	dries	dries
Hinkley Point	51 13N	3 08W	-0020	-0025	-0100	-0040	-1.7	-1.4	-0.2	-0.2
Watchet	51 11N	3 20W	-0035	-0050	-0145	-0040	-1.9	-1.5	+0.1	+0.1
Minehead	51 13N	3 28W	-0037	-0052	-0155	-0045	-2.6	-1.9	-0.2	0.0
Porlock Bay	51 13N	3 38W	-0045	-0055	-0205	-0050	-3.0	-2.2	-0.1	-0.1
Lynmouth	51 14N	3 49W	-0055	-0115	no data	no data	-3.6	-2.7	no data	no data

Location	Lat	Long	High Water		Low Water		MHWS	MHWN	MLWN	MLWS
			0100	0700	0100	0700				
MILFORD HAVEN	51 42N	5 03W	and	and	and	and	7.0	5.2	2.5	0.7
standard port			1300	1900	1300	1900				
Ilfracombe	51 13N	4 07W	-0016	-0016	-0041	-0031	+2.3	+1.8	+0.6	+0.3
Rivers Taw & Torridge										
Appledore	51 03N	4 12W	-0020	-0025	+0015	-0045	+0.5	0.0	-0.9	-0.5
Yelland Marsh	51 04N	4 10W	-0010	-0015	+0100	-0015	+0.1	-0.4	-1.2	-0.6
Fremington	51 05N	4 07W	-0010	-0015	+0030	-0030	-1.1	-1.8	-2.2	-0.5
Barnstaple	51 05N	4 04W	0000	-0015	-0155	-0245	-2.9	-3.8	-2.2	-0.4
Bideford	51 01N	4 12W	-0020	-0025	0000	0000	-1.1	-1.6	-2.5	-0.7
Clovelly	51 00N	4 24W	-0030	-0030	-0020	-0040	+1.3	+1.1	+0.2	+0.2
Lundy	51 10N	4 40W	-0030	-0030	-0020	-0040	+1.0	+0.7	+0.2	+0.1
Bude	50 50N	4 33W	-0040	-0040	-0035	-0045	+0.7	+0.6	no data	no data
Boscastle	50 41N	4 42W	-0045	-0010	-0110	-0100	+0.3	+0.4	+0.2	+0.2
Port Isaac	50 35N	4 50W	-0100	-0100	-0100	-0100	+0.5	+0.6	0.0	+0.2
River Camel										
Padstow	50 33N	4 56W	-0055	-0050	-0040	-0050	+0.3	+0.4	+0.1	+0.1
Wadebridge	50 31N	4 50W	-0052	-0052	+0235	+0245	-3.8	-3.8	-2.5	-0.4
Newquay	50 25N	5 05W	-0100	-0110	-0105	-0050	0.0	+0.1	0.0	-0.1
Perranporth	50 21N	5 09W	-0100	-0110	-0110	-0050	-0.1	0.0	0.0	+0.1
St. Ives	50 13N	5 28W	-0050	-0115	-0105	-0040	-0.4	-0.3	-0.1	+0.1
Cape Cornwall	50 08N	5 42 W	-0130	-0145	-0120	-0120	-1.0	-0.9	-0.5	-0.1
Sennen Cove	50 04N	5 42W	-0130	-0145	-0125	-0125	-0.9	-0.4	no data	no data
			0000	0700	0000	0500				
DUBLIN, NORTH WALL	53 21N	6 13W	and	and	and	and	4.1	3.4	1.5	0.7
standard port			1200	1900	1200	1700				
Courtown	52 39N	6 13W	-0328	-0242	-0158	-0138	-2.8	-2.4	-0.5	0.0
Arklow	52 47N	6 08W	-0315	-0201	-0140	-0134	-2.7	-2.2	-0.6	-0.1
Wicklow	52 59N	6 02W	-0019	-0019	-0024	-0026	-1.4	-1.1	-0.4	0.0
Greystones	53 09N	6 04W	-0008	-0008	-0008	-0008	-0.5	-0.4	no data	no data
Dun Laoghaire	53 18N	6 08W	-0006	-0001	-0002	-0003	0.0	0.0	0.0	+0.1
Dublin Bar	53 21N	6 09W	-0006	-0001	-0002	-0003	0.0	0.0	0.0	+0.1
Howth	53 23N	6 04W	-0007	-0005	+0001	+0005	0.0	-0.1	-0.2	-0.2
Malahide	53 27N	6 09W	+0002	+0003	+0009	+0009	+0.1	-0.2	-0.4	-0.2
Balbriggan	53 37N	6 11W	-0021	-0015	+0010	+0002	+0.3	+0.2	no data	no data
River Boyne										
Bar	53 43N	6 14W	-0005	0000	+0020	+0030	+0.9	+0.8	+0.4	+0.3
Dunany Point	53 52N	6 14W	-0028	-0018	-0008	-0006	+0.7	+0.9	no data	no data
Dundalk										
Soldiers Point	54 00N	6 21W	-0010	-0010	0000	+0045	+1.0	+0.8	+0.1	-0.1
Carlingford Lough										
Cranfield Point	54 01N	6 03W	-0027	-0011	+0017	-0007	+0.7	+0.9	+0.3	+0.2
Warrenpoint	54 06N	6 15W	-0020	-0010	+0040	+0040	+1.0	+0.9	+0.1	+0.2
Newry *Victoria Lock*	54 09N	6 19W	-0010	-0010	+0040	dries	+1.1	+1.0	+0.1	dries
			0100	0700	0000	0600				
BELFAST	54 36N	5 55W	and	and	and	and	3.5	3.0	1.1	0.4
standard port			1300	1900	1200	1800				
Kilkeel	54 03N	5 59W	+0040	+0030	+0010	+0010	+1.2	+1.1	+0.4	+0.4
Newcastle	54 12N	5 53W	+0025	+0035	+0020	+0040	+1.6	+1.1	+0.4	+0.1
Killough Harbour	54 15N	5 38W	0000	+0020	no data	no data	+1.8	+1.6	no data	no data
Ardglass	54 16N	5 36W	+0010	+0015	+0005	+0010	+1.7	+1.2	+0.6	+0.3
Strangford Lough										
Killard Point	54 19N	5 31W	+0011	+0021	+0005	+0025	+1.0	+0.8	+0.1	+0.1
Strangford	54 22N	5 33W	+0147	+0157	+0148	+0208	+0.1	+0.1	-0.2	0.0
Quoile Barrier	54 22N	5 41W	+0150	+0200	+0150	+0300	+0.2	+0.2	-0.3	-0.1
Killyleagh	54 24N	5 39W	+0157	+0207	+0211	+0231	+0.3	+0.3	no data	no data
South Rock	54 24N	5 25W	+0023	+0023	+0025	+0025	+1.0	+0.8	+0.1	+0.1
Portavogie	54 28N	5 26W	+0010	+0020	+0010	+0020	+1.2	+0.9	+0.3	+0.2
Donaghadee	54 38N	5 32W	+0020	+0020	+0023	+0023	+0.5	+0.4	0.0	+0.1
Carrickfergus	54 43N	5 48W	+0005	+0005	+0005	+0005	-0.3	-0.3	-0.2	-0.1
Larne	54 51N	5 47W	+0005	0000	+0010	-0005	-0.7	-0.5	-0.3	0.0
Red Bay	55 04N	6 03W	+0022	-0010	+0007	-0017	-1.9	-1.5	-0.8	-0.2
Cushendun	55 08N	6 02W	+0010	-0030	0000	-0025	-1.7	-1.5	-0.6	-0.2
			0200	0900	0300	0700				
LONDONDERRY			and	and	and	and	2.7	2.1	1.2	0.5
standard port	55 00N	7 19W	1400	2100	1500	1900				
Ballycastle Bay	55 12N	6 14W	+0053	-0147	-0125	+0056	-1.5	-1.0	-0.5	-0.2

Location	Lat	Long	High Water		Low Water		MHWS	MHWN	MLWN	MLWS
			0200	0800	0500	1100				
LONDONDERRY			and	and	and	and	2.7	2.1	1.2	0.5
standard port	55 00N	7 19W	1400	2000	1700	2300				
Portrush	55 12N	6 40W	-0105	-0105	-0105	-0105	-0.8	-0.7	-0.4	-0.1
Coleraine	55 08N	6 40W	-0030	-0130	-0110	-0020	-0.5	-0.3	-0.3	-0.1
Lough Foyle										
Warren Point	55 13N	6 57W	-0121	-0139	-0156	-0132	-0.4	-0.2	no data	no data
Moville	55 11N	7 03W	-0046	-0058	-0108	-0052	-0.4	-0.2	-0.2	-0.1
Quigley's Point	55 07N	7 11W	-0025	-0040	-0025	-0040	-0.4	-0.3	-0.3	-0.2
Culmore Point	55 03N	7 15W	-0010	-0030	-0020	-0040	-0.3	-0.3	-0.2	-0.1
River Foyle										
Culdaff Bay	55 18N	7 09W	-0136	-0156	-0206	-0146	+0.1	+0.2	no data	no data
			0200	0900	0200	0800				
GALWAY			and	and	and	and	5.1	3.9	2.0	0.6
standard port	53 16N	9 03W	1400	2100	1400	2000				
Inishtrahull	55 26N	7 14W	+0100	+0100	+0115	+0200	-1.8	-1.4	-0.4	-0.2
Portmore	55 22N	7 20W	+0120	+0120	+0135	+0135	-1.3	-1.1	-0.4	-0.1
Trawbreaga Bay	55 19N	7 23W	+0115	+0059	+0109	+0125	-1.1	-0.8	no data	no data
Lough Swilly										
Rathmullan	55 05N	7 31W	+0125	+0050	+0126	+0118	-0.8	-0.7	-0.1	-0.1
Fanad Head	55 16N	7 38W	+0115	+0040	+0125	+0120	-1.1	-0.9	-0.5	-0.1
Mulroy Bay										
Bar	55 15N	7 46W	+0108	+0052	+0102	+0118	-1.2	-1.0	no data	no data
Fanny's Bay	55 12N	7 49W	+0145	+0129	+0151	+0207	-2.2	-1.7	no data	no data
Seamount Bay	55 11N	7 44W	+0210	+0154	+0226	+0242	-3.1	-2.3	no data	no data
Cranford Bay	55 09N	7 42W	+0329	+0313	+0351	+0407	-3.7	-2.8	no data	no data
Sheephaven										
Downies Bay	55 11N	7 50W	+0057	+0043	+0053	+0107	-1.1	-0.9	no data	no data
Inishbofin Bay	55 10N	8 10W	+0040	+0026	+0032	+0046	-1.2	-0.9	no data	no data
			0600	1100	0000	0700				
GALWAY	53 16N	9 03W	and	and	and	and	5.1	3.9	2.0	0.6
standard port			1800	2300	1200	1900				
Gweedore Harbour	55 04N	8 19W	+0048	+0100	+0055	+0107	-1.3	-1.0	-0.5	-0.1
Burtonport	54 59N	8 26W	+0042	+0055	+0115	+0055	-1.2	-1.0	-0.6	-0.1
Loughros More Bay	54 47N	8 30W	+0042	+0054	+0046	+0058	-1.1	-0.9	no data	no data
Donegal Bay										
Killybegs	54 38N	8 26W	+0040	+0050	+0055	+0035	-1.0	-0.9	-0.5	0.0
Donegal Harbour *Salt Hill Quay*	54 38N	8 13W	+0038	+0050	+0052	+0104	-1.2	-0.9	no data	no data
Mullaghmore	54 28N	8 27W	+0036	+0048	+0047	+0059	-1.4	-1.0	-0.4	-0.2
Sligo Harbour *Oyster Island*	54 18N	8 34W	+0043	+0055	+0042	+0054	-1.0	-0.9	-0.5	-0.1
Ballysadare Bay *Culleenamore*	54 16N	8 36W	+0059	+0111	+0111	+0123	-1.2	-0.9	no data	no data
Killala Bay *Inishcrone*	54 13N	9 06W	+0035	+0055	+0030	+0050	-1.3	-1.2	-0.7	-0.2
Broadhaven	54 16N	9 53W	+0040	+0050	+0040	+0050	-1.4	-1.1	-0.4	-0.1
Blacksod Bay										
Blacksod Quay	54 06N	10 03W	+0025	+0035	+0040	+0040	-1.2	-1.0	-0.6	-0.2
Bull's Mouth	54 02N	9 55W	+0101	+0057	+0109	+0105	-1.5	-1.0	-0.6	-0.1
Clare Island	53 48N	9 57W	+0019	+0013	+0029	+0023	-1.0	-0.7	-0.4	-0.1
Westport Bay										
Inishraher	53 48N	9 38W	+0030	+0012	+0058	+0026	-0.6	-0.5	-0.3	-0.1
Killary Harbour	53 38N	9 53W	+0021	+0015	+0035	+0029	-1.0	-0.8	-0.4	-0.1
Inishbofin										
Bofin Harbour	53 37N	10 13W	+0013	+0009	+0021	+0017	-1.0	-0.8	-0.4	-0.1
Clifden Bay	53 29N	10 04W	+0005	+0005	+0016	+0016	-0.7	-0.5	no data	no data
Slyne Head	53 24N	10 14W	+0002	+0002	+0010	+0010	-0.7	-0.5	no data	no data
Roundstone Bay	53 23N	9 55W	+0003	+0003	+0008	+0008	-0.7	-0.5	-0.3	-0.1
Kilkieran Cove	53 20N	9 44W	+0005	+0005	+0016	+0016	-0.3	-0.2	-0.1	0.0
Aran Islands										
Killeany Bay	53 07N	9 39W	-0008	-0008	+0003	+0003	-0.4	-0.3	-0.2	-0.1
Liscannor	52 56N	9 23W	-0003	-0007	+0006	+0002	-0.4	-0.3	no data	no data
Seafield Point	52 48N	9 30W	-0006	-0014	+0004	-0004	-0.5	-0.4	no data	no data
Kilrush	52 38N	9 30W	+0025	+0016	+0046	+0014	-0.1	-0.2	-0.3	-0.1
Limerick Dock	52 40N	8 38W	+0135	+0141	+0141	+0219	+1.0	+0.7	-0.8	-0.2
			0500	1100	0500	1100				
COBH	51 51N	8 18W	and	and	and	and	4.1	3.2	1.3	0.4
standard port			1700	2300	1700	2300				
Tralee Bay										
Fenit Pier	52 16N	9 52W	-0057	-0017	-0029	-0109	+0.5	+0.2	+0.3	+0.1
Smerwick Harbour	52 12N	10 24W	-0107	-0027	-0041	-0121	-0.3	-0.4	no data	

Location	Lat	Long	High Water 0500	High Water 1100	Low Water 0500	Low Water 1100	MHWS	MHWN	MLWN	MLWS
COBH	51 51N	8 18 W	and	and	and	and	4.1	3.2	1.3	0.4
standard port			1700	2300	1700	2300				
Dingle Harbour	52 07N	10 15W	-0111	-0041	-0049	-0119	-0.1	0.0	+0.3	+0.4
Castlemaine Harbour										
Cromane Point	52 09N	9 54W	-0026	-0006	-0017	-0037	+0.4	+0.2	+0.4	+0.2
Valentia Harbour										
Knights Town	51 56N	10 18W	-0118	-0038	-0056	-0136	-0.6	-0.4	-0.1	0.0
Ballinskelligs Bay										
Castle	51 49N	10 16W	-0119	-0039	-0054	-0134	-0.5	-0.5	-0.1	0.0
Kenmare River										
West Cove	51 46N	10 03W	-0113	-0033	-0049	-0129	-0.6	-0.5	-0.1	0.0
Dunkerron Harbour	51 52N	9 38W	-0117	-0027	-0050	-0140	-0.2	-0.3	+0.1	0.0
Coulagh Bay										
Ballycrovane Harbour	51 43N	9 57W	-0116	-0036	-0053	-0133	-0.6	-0.5	-0.1	0.0
Black Ball Harbour	51 36N	10 02W	-0115	-0035	-0047	-0127	-0.7	-0.6	-0.1	+0.1
Bantry Bay										
Castletown Bearhaven	51 39N	9 54W	-0048	-0012	-0025	-0101	-0.9	-0.6	-0.1	0.0
Bantry	51 41N	9 28W	-0045	-0025	-0040	-0105	-0.9	-0.8	-0.2	0.0
Dunmanus Bay										
Dunbeacon Harbour	51 37N	9 33W	-0057	-0025	-0032	-0104	-0.8	-0.7	-0.3	-0.1
Dunmanus Harbour	51 32N	9 40W	-0107	-0031	-0044	-0120	-0.7	-0.6	-0.2	0.0
Crookhaven	51 28N	9 43W	-0057	-0033	-0048	-0112	-0.8	-0.6	-0.4	-0.1
Schull	51 31N	9 32W	-0040	-0015	-0015	-0110	-0.9	-0.6	-0.2	0.0
Baltimore	51 29N	9 23W	-0025	-0005	-0010	-0050	-0.6	-0.3	+0.1	+0.2
Castletownshend	51 32N	9 10W	-0020	-0030	-0020	-0050	-0.4	-0.2	+0.1	+0.3
Clonakilty Bay	51 35N	8 50W	-0033	-0011	-0019	-0041	-0.3	-0.2	no data	no data
Courtmacsherry	51 38N	8 42W	-0029	-0007	+0005	-0017	-0.4	-0.3	-0.2	-0.1
Kinsale	51 42N	8 31W	-0019	-0005	-0009	-0023	-0.2	0.0	+0.1	+0.2
Roberts Cove	51 45N	8 19W	-0005	-0005	-0005	-0005	-0.1	0.0	0.0	+0.1
Cork Harbour										
Ringaskiddy	51 50N	8 19W	+0005	+0020	+0007	+0013	+0.1	+0.1	+0.1	+0.1
Marino Point	51 53N	8 20W	0000	+0010	0000	+0010	+0.1	+0.1	0.0	0.0
Cork City	51 54N	8 27W	+0005	+0010	+0020	+0010	+0.4	+0.4	+0.3	+0.2
Ballycotton	51 50N	8 01W	-0011	+0001	+0003	-0009	0.0	0.0	-0.1	0.0
Youghal	51 57N	7 51W	0000	+0010	+0010	0000	-0.2	-0.1	-0.1	-0.1
Dungarvan Harbour	52 05N	7 34W	+0004	+0012	+0007	-0001	0.0	+0.1	-0.2	0.0
Waterford Harbour										
Dunmore East	52 09N	6 59W	+0008	+0003	0000	0000	+0.1	0.0	+0.1	+0.2
Cheekpoint	52 16N	7 00W	+0022	+0020	+0020	+0020	+0.3	+0.2	+0.2	+0.1
Kilmokea Point	52 17N	7 00W	+0026	+0022	+0020	+0020	+0.2	+0.1	+0.1	+0.1
Waterford	52 16N	7 07W	+0057	+0057	+0046	+0046	+0.4	+0.3	-0.1	+0.1
New Ross	52 24N	6 57W	+0100	+0030	+0055	+0130	+0.3	+0.4	+0.3	+0.4
Baginbun Head	52 10N	6 50W	+0003	+0003	-0008	-0008	-0.2	-0.1	+0.2	+0.2
Great Saltee	52 07N	6 38W	+0019	+0009	-0004	+0006	-0.3	-0.4	no data	no data
Carnsore Point	52 10N	6 22W	+0029	+0019	-0002	-0008	-1.1	-1.0	no data	no data
Rosslare Harbour	52 15N	6 21W	+0055	+0043	+0022	+0002	-2.2	-1.8	-0.5	-0.1
Wexford Harbour	52 20N	6 27W	+0126	+0126	+0118	+0108	-2.1	-1.7	-0.3	+0.1

SCOTLAND

Location	Lat	Long	High Water 0300	High Water 0900	Low Water 0300	Low Water 0900	MHWS	MHWN	MLWN	MLWS
LEITH	55 59N	3 11W	and	and	and	and	5.6	4.4	2.0	0.8
standard port			1500	2100	1500	2100				
Eyemouth	55 52N	2 05W	-0015	-0025	-0014	-0004	-0.9	-0.8	no data	no data
Dunbar	56 00N	2 31W	-0005	-0010	+0010	+0017	-0.4	-0.3	-0.1	-0.1
Fidra	56 04N	2 47W	-0001	0000	-0002	+0001	-0.2	-0.2	0.0	0.0
Cockenzie	55 58N	2 57W	-0007	-0015	-0013	-0005	-0.2	0.0	no data	no data
Granton	55 59N	3 13W	0000	0000	0000	0000	0.0	0.0	0.0	0.0

Location	Lat	Long	High Water 0300	High Water 1000	Low Water 0300	Low Water 0900	MHWS	MHWN	MLWN	MLWS
ROSYTH	56 01N	3 27W	and	and	and	and	5.8	4.7	2.2	0.8
standard port			1500	2200	1500	2100				
River Forth										
Grangemouth	56 02N	3 41W	+0025	+0010	-0052	-0015	-0.1	-0.2	-0.3	-0.3
Kincardine	56 04N	3 43W	+0015	+0030	-0030	-0030	0.0	-0.2	-0.5	-0.3
Alloa	56 07N	3 48W	+0040	+0040	+0025	+0025	-0.2	-0.5	no data	-0.7
Stirling	56 07N	3 56W	+0100	+0100	no data	no data	-2.9	-3.1	-2.3	-0.7

SECONDARY PORT TIDAL DATA

Location	Lat	Long	High Water		Low Water		MHWS	MHWN	MLWN	MLWS
			0300	0900	0300	0900				
LEITH	55 59N	3 11W	and	and	and	and	5.6	4.4	2.0	0.8
standard port			1500	2100	1500	2100				
Firth of Forth										
Burntisland	56 03N	3 14W	+0013	+0004	-0002	+0007	+0.1	0.0	+0.1	+0.2
Kirkcaldy	56 09N	3 09W	+0005	0000	-0004	-0001	-0.3	-0.3	-0.2	-0.2
Methil	56 11N	3 00W	+0003	-0002	-0004	+0001	0.0	0.0	+0.1	+0.1
Anstruther Easter	56 13N	2 42W	-0018	-0012	-0006	-0008	-0.3	-0.2	0.0	0.0
			0000	0600	0100	0700				
ABERDEEN	57 09N	2 05W	and	and	and	and	4.3	3.4	1.6	0.6
standard port			1200	1800	1300	1900				
River Tay										
Bar	56 27N	2 38W	+0100	+0100	+0050	+0110	+0.9	+0.8	+0.3	+0.1
Dundee	56 27N	2 58W	+0140	+0120	+0055	+0145	+1.1	+0.9	+0.3	+0.1
Newburgh	56 21N	3 14W	+0215	+0200	+0250	+0335	-0.2	-0.4	-1.1	-0.5
Perth	56 24N	3 27W	+0220	+0225	+0510	+0530	-0.9	-1.4	-1.2	-0.3
Arbroath	56 33N	2 35W	+0056	+0037	+0034	+0055	+0.7	+0.7	+0.2	+0.1
Montrose	56 42N	2 27W	+0055	+0055	+0030	+0040	+0.5	+0.4	+0.2	0.0
Stonehaven	56 58N	2 12W	+0013	+0008	+0013	+0009	+0.2	+0.2	+0.1	0.0
Peterhead	57 30N	1 46W	-0035	-0045	-0035	-0040	-0.5	-0.3	-0.1	-0.1
Fraserburgh	57 41N	2 00W	-0105	-0115	-0120	-0110	-0.6	-0.5	-0.2	0.0
			0200	0900	0400	0900				
ABERDEEN	57 09N	2 05W	and	and	and	and	4.3	3.4	1.6	0.6
standard port			1400	2100	1600	2100				
Banff	57 40N	2 31W	-0100	-0150	-0150	-0050	-0.8	-0.6	-0.5	-0.2
Whitehills	57 41N	2 35W	-0122	-0137	-0117	-0127	-0.4	-0.3	+0.1	+0.1
Buckie	57 40N	2 58W	-0130	-0145	-0125	-0140	-0.2	-0.2	0.0	+0.1
Lossiemouth	57 43N	3 18W	-0125	-0200	-0130	-0130	-0.2	-0.2	0.0	0.0
Hopeman	57 43N	3 26W	-0120	-0150	-0135	-0120	-0.2	-0.2	0.0	0.0
Burghead	57 42N	3 29W	-0120	-0150	-0135	-0120	-0.2	-0.2	0.0	0.0
Findhorn	57 40M	3 35W	-0120	-0150	-0135	-0125	-0.1	-0.2	0.0	0.0
Nairn	57 36N	3 52W	-0120	-0150	-0135	-0130	0.0	-0.1	0.0	+0.1
McDermott Base	57 36N	3 59W	-0110	-0140	-0120	-0115	-0.1	-0.1	+0.1	+0.3
			0300	1000	0000	0700				
ABERDEEN	57 09N	2 05W	and	and	and	and	4.3	3.4	1.6	0.6
standard port			1500	2200	1200	1900				
Inverness Firth										
Fortrose	57 35N	4 08W	-0125	-0125	-0125	-0125	0.0	0.0	no data	no data
Inverness	57 30N	4 15W	-0050	-0150	-0200	-0105	+0.5	+0.3	+0.2	+0.1
Cromarty Firth										
Cromarty	57 42N	4 03W	-0120	-0155	-0155	-0120	0.0	0.0	+0.1	+0.2
Invergordon	57 41N	4 10W	-0105	-0200	-0200	-0110	+0.1	+0.1	+0.1	+0.1
Dingwall	57 36N	4 25W	-0045	-0145	no data	no data	+0.1	+0.2	no data	no data
			0300	0800	0200	0800				
ABERDEEN	57 09N	2 05W	and	and	and	and	4.3	3.4	1.6	0.6
standard port			1500	2000	1400	2000				
Dornoch Firth										
Portmahomack	57 50N	3 50W	-0120	-0210	-0140	-0110	-0.2	-0.1	+0.1	+0.1
Meikle Ferry	57 51N	4 08W	-0100	-0140	-0120	-0055	+0.1	0.0	-0.1	0.0
Golspie	57 58N	3 59W	-0130	-0215	-0155	-0130	-0.3	-0.3	-0.1	0.0
			0000	0700	0200	0700				
WICK	58 26N	3 05W	and	and	and	and	3.5	2.8	1.4	0.7
standard port			1200	1900	1400	1900				
Helmsdale	58 07N	3 39W	+0025	+0015	+0035	+0030	+0.4	+0.3	+0.1	0.0
Duncansby Head	58 39N	3 02W	-0115	-0115	-0110	-0110	-0.4	-0.4	no data	no data
Orkney Islands										
Muckle Skerry	58 41N	2 55W	-0025	-0025	-0020	-0020	-0.9	-0.8	-0.4	-0.3
Burray Ness	58 51N	2 52W	+0005	+0005	+0015	+0015	-0.2	-0.3	-0.1	-0.1
Deer Sound	58 58N	2 50W	-0040	-0040	-0035	-0035	-0.3	-0.3	-0.1	-0.1
Kirkwall	58 59N	2 58W	-0042	-0042	-0041	-0041	-0.5	-0.4	-0.1	-0.1
Loth	59 12N	2 42W	-0052	-0052	-0058	-0058	-0.1	0.0	+0.3	+0.4
Kettletoft Pier	59 14N	2 36W	-0025	-0025	-0015	-0015	0.0	0.0	+0.2	+0.2
Stronsay	59 09N	2 35W	-0025	-0025	-0015	-0015	0.0	0.0	+0.2	+0.2
Rapness	59 15N	2 52W	-0205	-0205	-0205	-0205	+0.1	0.0	+0.2	0.0
Pierowall	59 19N	2 58W	-0150	-0150	-0145	-0145	+0.2	0.0	0.0	0.0
Tingwall	59 05N	3 02W	-0200	-0125	-0145	-0125	-0.4	-0.4	-0.1	-0.1

Location	Lat	Long	High Water		Low Water		MHWS	MHWN	MLWN	MLWS
			0000	0700	0200	0700				
WICK	58 26N	3 05W	and	and	and	and	3.5	2.8	1.4	0.7
standard port			1200	1900	1400	1900				
Stromness	58 58N	3 18W	-0225	-0135	-0205	-0205	+0.1	-0.1	0.0	0.0
St Mary's	58 54N	2 55W	-0140	-0140	-0140	-0140	-0.2	-0.2	0.0	-0.1
Widewall Bay	58 49N	3 01W	-0155	-0155	-0150	-0150	+0.1	-0.1	-0.1	-0.3
Bur Wick	58 44N	2 58W	-0100	-0100	-0150	-0150	-0.1	-0.1	+0.2	+0.1
			0000	0600	0100	0800				
LERWICK	60 09N	1 08W	and	and	and	and	2.2	1.7	1.0	0.6
standard port			1200	1800	1300	2000				
Fair Isle	59 32N	1 36W	-0006	-0015	-0031	-0037	0.0	0.0	0.0	0.0
Shetland Islands										
Sumburgh *Grutness Voe*	59 53N	1 17W	+0006	+0008	+0004	-0002	-0.4	-0.3	-0.3	-0.2
Dury Voe	60 21N	1 10W	-0015	-0015	-0010	-0010	-0.1	-0.1	-0.1	-0.3
Out Skerries	60 25N	0 45W	-0025	-0025	-0010	-0010	0.0	0.0	-0.1	-0.2
Toft Pier	60 28N	1 12W	-0105	-0100	-0125	-0115	+0.1	+0.1	-0.2	-0.2
Burra Voe *Yell Sound*	60 30N	1 03W	-0025	-0025	-0025	-0025	+0.1	+0.1	-0.1	-0.2
Mid Yell	60 36N	1 03W	-0030	-0020	-0035	-0025	+0.2	+0.2	+0.1	0.0
Balta Sound	60 45N	0 50W	-0055	-0055	-0045	-0045	+0.1	+0.1	-0.1	-0.2
Burra Firth	60 48N	0 52W	-0110	-0110	-0115	-0115	+0.3	+0.2	-0.1	-0.1
Bluemull Sound	60 42N	1 00W	-0135	-0135	-0155	-0155	+0.4	+0.2	0.0	-0.1
Sullom Voe	60 27N	1 18W	-0135	-0125	-0135	-0120	0.0	0.0	-0.2	-0.2
Hillswick	60 29N	1 29W	-0220	-0220	-0200	-0200	-0.2	-0.1	-0.2	-0.1
Scalloway	60 08N	1 16W	-0150	-0150	-0150	-0150	-0.6	-0.4	-0.4	-0.1
Bay of Quendale	59 54N	1 20W	-0025	-0025	-0030	-0030	-0.5	-0.3	-0.1	0.0
Foula	60 07N	2 03W	-0140	-0130	-0140	-0120	-0.2	-0.1	-0.1	-0.1
			0200	0700	0100	0700				
WICK	58 26N	3 05W	and	and	and	and	3.5	2.8	1.4	0.7
standard port			1400	1900	1300	1900				
Stroma	58 40N	3 08W	-0115	-0115	-0110	-0110	-0.4	-0.5	-0.1	-0.2
Gills Bay	58 38N	3 10W	-0150	-0150	-0202	-0202	+0.7	+0.7	+0.6	+0.3
Scrabster	58 37N	3 33W	-0255	-0225	-0240	-0230	+1.5	+1.2	+0.8	+0.3
Sule Skerry	59 05N	4 24W	-0320	-0255	-0315	-0250	+0.4	+0.3	+0.2	+0.1
Loch Eriboll										
Portnancon	58 30N	4 42W	-0340	-0255	-0315	-0255	+1.6	+1.3	+0.8	+0.4
Kyle of Durness	58 36N	4 47W	-0350	-0350	-0315	-0315	+1.1	+0.7	+0.4	-0.1
Rona	59 08N	5 49W	-0410	-0345	-0330	-0340	-0.1	-0.2	-0.2	-0.1
			0100	0700	0300	0900				
ULLAPOOL	57 54N	5 10W	and	and	and	and	5.2	3.9	2.1	0.7
standard port			1300	1900	1500	2100				
Outer Hebrides										
Stornoway	58 12N	6 23W	-0010	-0010	-0010	-0010	-0.4	-0.2	-0.1	0.0
Loch Shell	58 00N	6 25W	-0023	-0010	-0010	-0027	-0.4	-0.3	-0.2	0.0
E. Loch Tarbert	57 54N	6 48W	-0035	-0020	-0020	-0030	-0.2	-0.2	0.0	+0.1
Loch Maddy	57 36N	7 06W	-0054	-0024	-0026	-0040	-0.4	-0.3	-0.2	0.0
Loch Carnan	57 22N	7 16W	-0100	-0020	-0030	-0050	-0.7	-0.7	-0.2	-0.1
Loch Skiport	57 20N	7 16W	-0110	-0035	-0034	-0034	-0.6	-0.6	-0.4	-0.2
Loch Boisdale	57 09N	7 16W	-0105	-0040	-0030	-0050	-1.1	-0.9	-0.4	-0.2
Barra *North Bay*	57 00N	7 24W	-0113	-0041	-0044	-0058	-1.0	-0.7	-0.3	-0.1
Castle Bay	56 57N	7 29W	-0125	-0050	-0055	-0110	-0.9	-0.8	-0.4	-0.1
Barra Head	56 47N	7 38W	-0125	-0050	-0055	-0105	-1.2	-0.9	-0.3	+0.1
Shillay	57 31N	7 41W	-0113	-0053	-0057	-0117	-1.0	-0.9	-0.8	-0.3
Balivanich	57 29N	7 23W	-0113	-0027	-0041	-0055	-1.1	-0.8	-0.6	-0.2
Scolpaig	57 39N	7 29W	-0043	-0043	-0050	-0050	-1.4	-1.1	-0.6	0.0
Leverburgh	57 46N	7 01W	-0051	-0030	-0025	-0035	-0.6	-0.4	-0.2	-0.1
W. Loch Tarbert	57 55N	6 55W	-0025	-0025	-0056	-0056	-1.5	-1.1	-0.6	0.0
Little Bernera	58 16N	6 52W	-0031	-0021	-0027	-0037	-0.9	-0.8	-0.5	-0.2
Carloway	58 17N	6 47W	-0050	+0010	-0045	-0025	-1.0	-0.7	-0.5	-0.1
			0000	0600	0300	0900				
ULLAPOOL	57 54N	5 10W	and	and	and	and	5.2	3.9	2.1	0.7
standard port			1200	1800	1500	2100				
St Kilda										
Village Bay	57 48N	8 34W	-0050	-0050	-0055	-0055	-1.8	-1.4	-0.9	-0.3
Flannan Isles	58 16N	7 36W	-0036	-0026	-0026	-0036	-1.3	-0.9	-0.7	-0.2
Rockall	57 36N	13 41W	-0105	-0105	-0115	-0115	-2.2	-1.7	-1.0	-0.2
Loch Bervie	58 27N	5 03W	+0030	+0010	+0010	+0020	-0.3	-0.3	-0.2	0.0

Location	Lat	Long	High Water		Low Water		MHWS	MHWN	MLWN	MLWS
			0000	0600	0300	0900				
ULLAPOOL	57 54N	5 10W	and	and	and	and	5.2	3.9	2.1	0.7
standard port			1200	1800	1500	2100				
Loch Laxford	58 24N	5 05W	+0015	+0015	+0005	+0005	-0.3	-0.4	-0.2	0.0
Eddrachillis Bay										
Badcall Bay	58 19N	5 08W	+0005	+0005	+0005	+0005	-0.7	-0.5	-0.5	+0.2
Loch Nedd	58 14N	5 10W	0000	0000	0000	0000	-0.3	-0.2	-0.2	0.0
Loch Inver	58 09N	5 18W	-0005	-0005	-0005	-0005	-0.2	0.0	0.0	+0.1
Summer Isles										
Tanera Mor	58 01N	5 24W	-0005	-0005	-0010	-0010	-0.1	+0.1	0.0	+0.1
Loch Ewe										
Mellon Charles	57 51N	5 38W	-0010	-0010	-0010	-0010	-0.1	-0.1	-0.1	0.0
Loch Gairloch										
Gairloch	57 43N	5 41W	-0020	-0020	-0010	-0010	0.0	+0.1	-0.3	-0.1
Loch Torridon										
Shieldaig	57 31N	5 39W	-0020	-0020	-0015	-0015	+0.4	+0.3	+0.1	0.0
Inner Sound										
Applecross	57 26N	5 49W	-0020	-0015	-0010	-0010	-0.1	0.0	-0.1	0.0
Loch Carron										
Plockton	57 20N	5 39W	+0005	-0025	-0005	-0010	+0.5	+0.5	+0.5	+0.2
Rona										
Loch a' Bhraige	57 35N	5 58W	-0020	0000	-0010	0000	-0.1	-0.1	-0.1	-0.2
Skye										
Broadford Bay	57 15N	5 54W	-0035	-0020	-0025	-0030	+0.3	+0.2	+0.1	-0.1
Portree	57 24N	6 11W	-0025	-0025	-0025	-0025	+0.1	-0.2	-0.2	0.0
Loch Snizort (Uig Bay)	57 35N	6 22W	-0045	-0020	-0005	-0025	+0.1	-0.4	-0.2	0.0
Loch Dunvegan	57 27N	6 38W	-0105	-0030	-0020	-0040	0.0	-0.1	0.0	0.0
Loch Harport	57 20N	6 25W	-0115	-0035	-0020	-0100	-0.1	-0.1	0.0	+0.1
Soay										
Camus nan Gall	57 09N	6 13W	-0055	-0025	-0025	-0045	-0.4	-0.2	*no data*	*no data*
Loch Alsh										
Kyle of Lochalsh	57 17N	5 43W	-0040	-0020	-0005	-0025	+0.1	0.0	+0.1	+0.1
Dornie Bridge	57 17N	5 31W	-0040	-0010	-0005	-0020	+0.1	-0.1	0.0	0.0
Kyle Rhea										
Glenelg Bay	57 13N	5 38W	-0105	-0035	-0035	-0055	-0.4	-0.4	-0.9	-0.1
Loch Hourn	57 06N	5 34W	-0125	-0050	-0040	-0110	-0.2	-0.1	-0.1	+0.1
			0000	0600	0100	0700				
OBAN	56 25N	5 29W	and	and	and	and	4.0	2.9	1.8	0.7
standard port			1200	1800	1300	1900				
Loch Nevis										
Inverie Bay	57 02N	5 41W	+0030	+0020	+0035	+0020	+1.0	+0.9	+0.2	0.0
Mallaig	57 00N	5 50W	+0017	+0017	+0017	+0017	+1.0	+0.7	+0.3	+0.1
Eigg										
Bay of Laig	56 55N	6 10W	+0015	+0030	+0040	+0005	+0.7	+0.6	-0.2	- 0.2
Loch Moidart	56 47N	5 53W	+0015	+0015	+0040	+0020	+0.8	+0.6	- 0.2	-0.2
Coll										
Loch Eatharna	56 37N	6 31W	+0025	+0010	+0015	+0025	+0.4	+0.3	*no data*	*no data*
Tiree										
Gott Bay	56 31N	6 48W	0000	+0010	+0005	+0010	0.0	+0.1	0.0	0.0
			0100	0700	0100	0800				
OBAN	56 25N	5 29W	and	and	and	and	4.0	2.9	1.8	0.7
standard port			1300	1900	1300	2000				
Mull										
Carsaig Bay	56 19N	5 59W	-0015	-0005	-0030	+0020	+0.1	+0.2	0.0	-0.1
Iona	56 19N	6 23W	-0010	-0005	-0020	+0015	0.0	+0.1	-0.3	-0.2
Bunessan	56 19N	6 14W	-0015	-0015	-0010	-0015	+0.3	+0.1	0.0	-0.1
Ulva Sound	56 29N	6 08W	-0010	-0015	0000	-0005	+0.4	+0.3	0.0	-0.1
Loch Sunart										
Salen	56 42N	5 47W	-0015	+0015	+0010	+0005	+0.6	+0.5	-0.1	-0.1
Sound of Mull										
Tobermory	56 37N	6 04W	+0025	+0010	+0015	+0025	+0.4	+0.4	0.0	0.0
Salen	56 32N	5 56W	+0045	+0015	+0020	+0030	+0.2	+0.2	-0.1	0.0
Loch Aline	56 32N	5 46W	+0012	+0012	*no data*	*no data*	+0.5	+0.3	*no data*	*no data*
Craignure	56 28N	5 42W	+0030	+0005	+0010	+0015	0.0	+0.1	-0.1	-0.1
Loch Linnhe										
Corran	56 43N	5 14W	+0007	+0007	+0004	+0004	+0.4	+0.4	-0.1	0.0
Corpach	56 50N	5 07W	0000	+0020	+0040	0000	0.0	0.0	-0.2	-0.2
Loch Eil Head	56 51N	5 20W	+0025	+0045	+0105	+0025	*no data*	*no data*	*no data*	*no data*
Loch Leven Head	56 43N	5 00W	+0045	+0045	+0045	+0045	*no data*	*no data*	*no data*	*no data*

Location	Lat	Long	High Water 0100	0700	Low Water 0100	0800	MHWS	MHWN	MLWN	MLWS
OBAN	56 25N	5 29W	and	and	and	and	4.0	2.9	1.8	0.7
standard port			1300	1900	1300	2000				
Loch Linnhe										
Port Appin	56 33N	5 25W	-0005	-0005	-0030	0000	+0.2	+0.2	+0.1	+0.1
Loch Creran										
Barcaldine Pier	56 32N	5 19W	+0010	+0020	+0040	+0015	+0.1	+0.1	0.0	+0.1
Loch Creran Head	56 33N	5 16W	+0015	+0025	+0120	+0020	-0.3	-0.3	-0.4	-0.3
Loch Etive										
Dunstaffnage Bay	56 27N	5 26W	+0005	0000	0000	+0005	+0.1	+0.1	+0.1	+0.1
Connel	56 27N	5 24W	+0020	+0005	+0010	+0015	-0.3	-0.2	-0.1	+0.1
Bonawe	56 27N	5 13W	+0150	+0205	+0240	+0210	-2.0	-1.7	-1.3	-0.5
Seil Sound	56 18N	5 35W	-0035	-0015	-0040	-0015	-1.3	-0.9	-0.7	-0.3
Colonsay										
Scalasaig	56 04N	6 10W	-0020	-0005	-0015	+0005	-0.1	-0.2	-0.2	-0.2
Jura										
Glengarrisdale Bay	56 06N	5 47W	-0020	0000	-0010	0000	-0.4	-0.2	0.0	-0.2
Islay										
Rubha A'Mhail	55 56N	6 07W	-0020	0000	+0005	-0015	-0.3	-0.1	-0.3	-0.1
Ardnave Point	55 52N	6 20W	-0035	+0010	0000	-0025	-0.4	-0.2	-0.3	-0.1
Orsay	55 41N	6 31W	-0110	-0110	-0040	-0040	-1.4	-0.6	-0.5	-0.2
Bruichladdich	55 48N	6 22W	-0100	-0005	-0110	-0040	-1.7	-1.4	-0.4	+0.1
Port Ellen	55 38N	6 11W	-0530	-0050	-0045	-0530	-3.1	-2.1	-1.3	-0.4
Port Askaig	55 51N	6 06W	-0110	-0030	-0020	-0020	-1.9	-1.4	-0.8	-0.3
Sound of Jura										
Craighouse	55 50N	5 57W	-0230	-0250	-0150	-0230	-3.0	-2.4	-1.3	-0.6
Loch Melfort	56 15N	5 29W	-0055	-0025	-0040	-0035	-1.2	-0.8	-0.5	-0.1
Craobh Haven	56 13N	5 33W	-0100	-0030	-0045	-0040	-1.2	-0.8	-0.5	-0.1
Loch Beag	56 09N	5 36W	-0110	-0045	-0035	-0045	-1.6	-1.2	-0.8	-0.4
Carsaig Bay	56 02N	5 38W	-0105	-0040	-0050	-0050	-2.1	-1.6	-1.0	-0.4
Sound of Gigha	55 41N	5 44W	-0450	-0210	-0130	-0410	-2.5	-1.6	-1.0	-0.1
Machrihanish	55 25N	5 45W	-0520	-0350	-0340	-0540	Mean range 0.5 metres			
			0000	0600	0000	0600				
GREENOCK	55 57N	4 46W	and	and	and	and	3.4	2.8	1.0	0.3
standard port			1200	1800	1200	1800				
Firth of Clyde										
Southend, Kintyre	55 19N	5 38W	-0030	-0010	+0005	+0035	-1.3	-1.2	-0.5	-0.2
Campbeltown	55 25N	5 36W	-0025	-0005	-0015	+0005	-0.5	-0.3	+0.1	+0.2
Carradale	55 36N	5 28W	-0015	-0005	-0005	+0005	-0.3	-0.2	+0.1	+0.1
Loch Ranza	55 43N	5 18W	-0015	-0005	-0010	-0005	-0.4	-0.3	-0.1	0.0
Loch Fyne										
East Loch Tarbert	55 52N	5 24W	+0005	+0005	-0020	+0015	0.0	0.0	+0.1	-0.1
Ardrishaig	56 01N	5 27W	+0007	+0007	-0005	+0020	0.0	0.0	0.0	-0.1
Inveraray	56 14N	5 04W	+0011	+0011	+0034	+0034	-0.1	+0.1	-0.5	-0.2
Kyles of Bute										
Rubha Bodach	55 55N	5 09W	-0020	-0010	-0007	-0007	-0.2	-0.1	+0.2	+0.2
Tighnabruich	55 55N	5 13W	+0007	-0010	-0002	-0015	0.0	+0.2	+0.4	+0.5
Firth of Clyde - continued										
Millport	55 45N	4 56W	-0005	-0025	-0025	-0005	0.0	-0.1	0.0	+0.1
Rothesay Bay	55 51N	5 03W	-0020	-0015	-0010	-0002	+0.2	+0.2	+0.2	+0.2
Wemyss Bay	55 53N	4 53W	-0005	-0005	-0005	-0005	0.0	0.0	+0.1	+0.1
Loch Long										
Coulport	56 03N	4 53W	-0011	-0011	-0008	-0008	0.0	0.0	0.0	0.0
Lochgoilhead	56 10N	4 54W	+0015	0000	-0005	-0005	-0.2	-0.3	-0.3	-0.3
Arrochar	56 12N	4 45W	-0005	-0005	-0005	-0005	0.0	0.0	-0.1	-0.1
Gareloch										
Rosneath *Rhu Pier*	56 01N	4 47W	-0005	-0005	-0005	-0005	0.0	-0.1	0.0	0.0
Faslane	56 04N	4 49W	-0010	-0010	-0010	-0010	0.0	0.0	-0.1	-0.2
Garelochhead	56 05N	4 50W	0000	0000	0000	0000	0.0	0.0	0.0	-0.1
River Clyde										
Helensburgh	56 00N	4 44W	0000	0000	0000	0000	0.0	0.0	0.0	0.0
Port Glasgow	55 56N	4 41W	+0010	+0005	+0010	+0020	+0.2	+0.1	0.0	0.0
Bowling	55 56N	4 29W	+0020	+0010	+0030	+0055	+0.6	+0.5	+0.3	+0.1
Renfrew	55 53N	4 23W	+0025	+0015	+0035	+0100	+0.9	+0.8	+0.5	+0.2
Glasgow	55 51N	4 17W	+0025	+0015	+0035	+0105	+1.3	+1.2	+0.6	+0.4
Firth of Clyde - continued										
Inverkip	55 55N	4 52W	-0005	-0005	-0005	-0005	0.0	0.0	+0.1	+0.1
Largs	55 46N	4 51W	-0020	-0020	-0020	-0020	+0.1	+0.1	+0.1	+0.1
Brodick Bay	55 35N	5 08W	0000	0000	+0005	+0005	-0.2	-0.2	0.0	0.0
Lamlash	55 32N	5 07W	-0016	-0036	-0024	-0004	-0.2	-0.2	no data	no data

Location	Lat	Long	High Water 0000	High Water 0600	Low Water 0000	Low Water 0600	MHWS	MHWN	MLWN	MLWS
GREENOCK	55 57N	4 46W	and	and	and	and	3.4	2.8	1.0	0.3
standard port			1200	1800	1200	1800				
Ardrossan	55 38N	4 49W	-0020	-0010	-0010	-0010	-0.2	-0.2	+0.1	+0.1
Irvine	55 36N	4 41W	-0020	-0020	-0030	-0010	-0.3	-0.3	-0.1	0.0
Troon	55 33N	4 41W	-0025	-0025	-0020	-0020	-0.2	-0.2	0.0	0.0
Ayr	55 28N	4 39W	-0025	-0025	-0030	-0015	-0.4	-0.3	+0.1	+0.1
Girvan	55 15N	4 52W	-0025	-0040	-0035	-0010	-0.3	-0.3	-0.1	0.0
Loch Ryan										
Stranraer	54 55N	5 03W	-0020	-0020	-0017	-0017	-0.4	-0.4	-0.4	-0.2

FRANCE & THE CHANNEL ISLANDS

Location	Lat	Long	High Water 0200	High Water 0800	Low Water 0200	Low Water 0900	MHWS	MHWN	MLWN	MLWS
DUNKERQUE	51 03N	2 22E	and	and	and	and	6.0	5.0	1.5	0.6
standard port			1400	2000	1400	2100				
Gravelines	51 01N	2 06E	-0005	-0015	-0005	+0005	+0.3	+0.1	-0.1	-0.1
Sandettie Bank	51 09N	1 47E	-0015	-0025	-0020	-0005	+0.1	-0.1	-0.1	-0.1
Wissant	50 53N	1 40E	-0035	-0050	-0030	-0010	+2.0	+1.5	+0.8	+0.4

Location	Lat	Long	High Water 0000	High Water 0600	Low Water 0000	Low Water 0600	MHWS	MHWN	MLWN	MLWS
CALAIS	50 58N	1 51E	and	and	and	and	7.2	5.9	2.1	0.9
standard port			1200	1800	1200	1800				
Boulogne	50 44N	1 35E	-0030	-0030	-0030	-0030	+1.7	+1.3	+0.5	+0.2

Location	Lat	Long	High Water 0100	High Water 0600	Low Water 0100	Low Water 0700	MHWS	MHWN	MLWN	MLWS
DIEPPE	49 56N	1 05E	and	and	and	and	9.3	7.4	2.5	0.8
standard port			1300	1800	1300	1900				
Le Touquet, Étaples	50 31N	1 35E	+0007	+0017	+0032	+0032	+0.2	+0.3	+0.4	+0.4
Berck	50 24N	1 34E	+0007	+0017	+0028	+0028	+0.5	+0.5	+0.4	+0.4
La Somme										
Le Hourdel	50 13N	1 34E	+0020	+0020	no data	no data	+0.8	+0.6	no data	no data
St Valéry	50 11N	1 37E	+0035	+0035	no data	no data	+0.9	+0.7	no data	no data
Cayeux	50 11N	1 29E	0000	+0005	+0015	+0010	+0.5	+0.6	+0.4	+0.4
Le Tréport	50 04N	1 22E	+0005	0000	+0007	+0007	+0.1	+0.1	0.0	+0.1
St. Valéry-en-Caux	49 52N	0 42E	-0007	-0007	-0015	-0025	-0.8	-0.6	-0.2	-0.1
Fécamp	49 46N	0 22E	-0015	-0010	-0030	-0040	-1.0	-0.6	+0.3	+0.4
Etretat	49 42N	0 12E	-0020	-0020	-0045	-0050	-1.2	-0.8	+0.3	+0.4

Location	Lat	Long	High Water 0000	High Water 0500	Low Water 0000	Low Water 0700	MHWS	MHWN	MLWN	MLWS
LE HAVRE	49 29N	0 07E	and	and	and	and	7.9	6.6	2.8	1.2
standard port			1200	1700	1200	1900				
Antifer *Le Havre*	49 39N	0 09E	+0025	+0015	+0005	-0007	+0.1	0.0	0.0	0.0
La Seine										
Honfleur	49 25N	0 14E	-0135	-0135	+0015	+0040	+0.1	+0.1	+0.1	+0.3
Tancarville	49 28N	0 28E	-0105	-0100	+0105	+0140	-0.1	-0.1	0.0	+1.0
Quilleboeuf	49 28N	0 32E	-0045	-0050	+0120	+0200	0.0	0.0	+0.2	+1.4
Vatteville	49 29N	0 40E	+0005	-0020	+0225	+0250	0.0	-0.1	+0.8	+2.3
Caudebec	49 32N	0 44E	+0020	-0015	+0230	+0300	-0.3	-0.2	+0.9	+2.4
Heurteauville	49 27N	0 49E	+0110	+0025	+0310	+0330	-0.5	-0.2	+1.1	+2.7
Duclair	49 29N	0 53E	+0225	+0150	+0355	+0410	-0.4	-0.3	+1.4	+3.3
Rouen	49 27N	1 06E	+0440	+0415	+0525	+0525	-0.2	-0.1	+1.6	+3.6
Deauville/Trouville	49 22N	0 05E	-0100	-0010	0000	+0005	+0.4	+0.3	+0.3	+0.1
Dives	49 18N	0 05E	-0100	-0010	0000	0000	+0.3	+0.2	+0.2	+0.1
Ouistreham	49 17N	0 15W	-0045	-0010	-0005	0000	-0.3	-0.3	-0.2	-0.3
Courseulles-sur-Mer	49 20N	0 27W	-0045	-0015	-0020	-0025	-0.5	-0.5	-0.1	-0.1
Arromanches	49 21N	0 37W	-0055	-0025	-0027	-0035	-0.6	-0.6	-0.2	-0.2
Port-en-Bessin	49 21N	0 45W	-0055	-0030	-0005	-0035	-0.7	-0.7	-0.2	-0.1
Grandcamp-Maisy	49 23N	0 07W	+0116	+0052	+0128	+0115	+0.8	+0.8	+0.1	+0.1
Carentan	49 20N	0 10W	+0116	+0052	+0128	+0115	+0.8	+0.8	+0.1	+0.1

Location	Lat	Long	High Water 0300	High Water 1000	Low Water 0400	Low Water 1000	MHWS	MHWN	MLWN	MLWS
CHERBOURG	49 39N	1 38W	and	and	and	and	6.4	5.0	2.5	1.1
standard port			1500	2200	1600	2200				
Rade de la Capelle	49 25N	1 05W	+0115	+0050	+0130	+0117	+0.8	+0.9	+0.1	+0.1
Iles Saint Marcouf	49 30N	1 08W	+0118	+0052	+0125	+0110	+0.6	+0.7	+0.1	+0.1
St. Vaast-la-Hougue	49 34N	1 16W	+0110	+0045	+0050	+0100	+0.2	+0.2	0.0	-0.1
Barfleur	49 40N	1 15W	+0110	+0055	+0052	+0052	+0.1	+0.3	0.0	0.0
Omonville	49 42N	1 50W	-0025	-0030	-0022	-0022	-0.3	-0.2	-0.2	-0.1
Goury	49 43N	1 57W	-0100	-0040	-0105	-0120	+1.7	+1.6	+1.0	+0.3

Location	Lat	Long	High Water 0300	0900	Low Water 0200	0900	MHWS	MHWN	MLWN	MLWS
ST HELIER	49 11N	2 07W	and	and	and	and	11.0	8.1	4.0	1.4
standard port			1500	2100	1400	2100				
Alderney										
Braye	49 43N	2 12W	+0050	+0040	+0025	+0105	-4.8	-3.4	-1.5	-0.5
Sark										
Maseline Pier	49 26N	2 21W	+0005	+0015	+0005	+0010	-2.1	-1.5	-0.6	-0.3
Guernsey										
St Peter Port	49 27N	2 31W	0000	+0012	-0008	+0002	-1.7	-1.1	-0.4	0.0
Jersey										
St Catherine Bay/Gorey	49 13N	2 01W	0000	+0010	+0010	+0010	0.0	-0.1	0.0	+0.1
Bouley Bay	49 14N	2 05W	+0002	+0002	+0004	+0004	-0.3	-0.3	-0.1	-0.1
Les Ecrehou	49 17N	1 56W	+0105	+0109	+0111	+0109	-0.2	+0.1	-0.2	0.0
Les Minquiers	48 57N	2 08W	+0046	+0042	+0059	+0052	+0.5	+0.6	+0.1	+0.1
			0100	0800	0300	0800				
ST MALO	48 38N	2 02W	and	and	and	and	12.2	9.2	4.3	1.6
standard port			1300	2000	1500	2000				
Iles Chausey	48 52N	1 49W	+0010	+0010	+0020	+0015	+0.8	+0.7	+0.5	+0.4
Flamanville	49 32N	1 53W	+0050	+0050	+0025	+0045	-2.7	-1.8	-1.1	-0.5
Carteret	49 22N	1 47W	+0035	+0025	+0020	+0035	-1.6	-1.1	-0.6	-0.3
Portbail	49 18N	1 45W	+0035	+0030	+0030	+0035	-0.8	-0.5	-0.3	-0.1
St. Germain sur Ay	49 14N	1 36W	+0030	+0030	+0040	+3040	-0.7	-0.4	-0.1	0.0
Le Sénéquet	49 05N	1 40W	+0020	+0020	+0028	+0028	-0.3	-0.2	0.0	0.0
Regnéville sur Mer	49 01N	1 33W	+0018	+0018	+0028	+0028	-0.2	-0.1	0.0	0.0
Granville	48 50N	1 36W	+0010	+0010	+0025	+0015	+0.7	+0.6	+0.2	-0.1
Cancale	48 40N	1 51W	-0002	-0002	+0012	+0006	+0.8	+0.7	+0.3	+0.1
Dinard	48 38N	2 03W	0000	-0002	-0018	-0006	-0.1	-0.1	0.0	0.0
St Cast	48 38N	2 15W	-0002	-0002	-0005	-0005	-0.2	-0.1	-0.1	-0.1
Erquy	48 38N	2 28W	-0005	0000	-0018	-0012	-0.6	-0.4	-0.1	-0.1
Dahouët	48 35N	2 34W	-0006	-0006	-0020	-0015	-0.9	-0.6	-0.3	-0.3
Le Légué	48 32N	2 44W	+0005	+0005	-0013	-0003	-0.7	-0.3	-0.2	-0.2
Binic	48 36N	2 49W	-0003	-0003	-0025	-0010	-0.8	-0.6	-0.3	-0.3
Portrieux	48 38N	2 49W	-0005	0000	-0020	-0010	-1.0	-0.6	-0.3	-0.2
Paimpol	48 47N	3 02W	-0005	-0010	-0035	-0025	-1.4	-0.8	-0.5	-0.2
Ile de Bréhat	48 51N	3 00W	-0008	-0013	-0040	-0037	-1.8	-1.2	-0.5	-0.3
Les Héaux de Bréhat	48 55N	3 05W	-0018	-0017	-0050	-0050	-2.4	-1.6	-0.7	-0.3
Lézardrieux	48 47N	3 06W	-0010	-0010	-0047	-0037	-1.7	-1.2	-0.6	-0.3
Port-Béni	48 51N	3 10W	-0017	-0022	-0100	-0045	-2.4	-1.5	-0.6	-0.2
Tréguier	48 47N	3 13W	-0005	-0010	-0055	-0040	-2.3	-1.5	-0.7	-0.3
Perros-Guirec	48 49N	3 28W	-0030	-0040	-0115	-0055	-2.9	-1.8	-0.9	-0.3
Ploumanac'h	48 50N	3 29W	-0023	-0033	-0112	-0053	-2.9	-1.8	-0.7	-0.2
			0000	0600	0000	0600				
BREST	48 23N	4 30W	and	and	and	and	6.9	5.4	2.6	1.0
standard port			1200	1800	1200	1800				
Trébeurden	48 46N	3 35W	+0100	+0110	+0120	+0100	+2.3	+1.9	+0.9	+0.4
Locquirec	48 42N	3 38W	+0058	+0108	+0100	+0100	+2.2	+1.8	+0.8	+0.3
Anse de Primel	48 43N	3 50W	+0100	+0110	+0120	+0100	+2.1	+1.7	+0.8	+0.3
Rade de Morlaix										
Morlaix *Chateau du Taureau*	48 41N	3 53W	+0055	+0105	+0115	+0055	+2.0	+1.7	+0.8	+0.3
Roscoff	48 43N	3 58W	+0055	+0105	+0115	+0055	+1.9	+1.6	+0.8	+0.3
Ile de Batz	48 44N	4 00W	+0045	+0100	+0105	+0055	+2.0	+1.6	+0.9	+0.4
Brignogan	48 40N	4 19W	+0040	+0045	+0055	+0040	+1.1	+0.9	+0.3	+0.1
L'Aber Wrac'h										
Ile Cézon	48 36N	4 34W	+0030	+0030	+0038	+0037	+0.8	+0.7	+0.2	0.0
Aber Benoît	48 35N	4 37W	+0022	+0025	+0035	+0020	+1.0	+0.9	+0.4	+0.2
Portsall	48 33N	4 42W	+0015	+0020	+0025	+0015	+0.6	+0.5	+0.1	0.0
L'Aber Ildut	48 28N	4 45W	+0010	+0010	+0023	+0010	+0.4	+0.3	0.0	0.0
Port du Moulin Blanc			as Standard Port Brest							
Ouessant										
Baie de Lampaul	48 27N	5 06W	+0005	+0005	-0005	+0003	0.0	-0.1	-0.1	0.0
Molene	48 24N	4 58W	+0012	+0012	+0017	+0017	+0.4	+0.3	+0.2	+0.1
Le Conquet	48 22N	4 47W	-0005	0000	+0007	+0007	-0.1	-0.1	-0.1	0.0
Camaret	48 16N	4 36W	-0010	-0010	-0013	-0013	-0.3	-0.3	-0.1	0.0
Morgat	48 13N	4 30W	-0008	-0008	-0020	-0010	-0.4	-0.4	-0.2	0.0
Douarnenez	48 06N	4 19W	-0010	-0015	-0018	-0008	-0.5	-0.5	-0.3	-0.1

BELGIUM AND HOLLAND

Location	Lat	Long	High Water		Low Water		MHWS	MHWN	MLWN	MLWS
			0200	0700	0200	0800				
HELGOLAND			and	and	and	and	2.7	2.3	0.4	0.0
standard port	54 11N	7 53E	1400	1900	1400	2000				
River Ems										
Nieuwe Staten Zijl	53 14N	7 13E	+0110	+0135	no data	no data	+1.1	+1.1	no data	no data
Delfzijl	53 19N	6 57E	+0020	-0005	-0040	0000	+0.9	+0.9	+0.3	+0.3
Termunterzijl/Termunten	53 18N	7 02E	+0025	0000	-0030	0000	+0.9	+0.9	+0.2	+0.2
Eemshaven	53 26N	6 52E	-0025	-0045	-0115	-0045	+0.5	+0.5	+0.3	+0.3
Schiermonnikoog	53 28N	6 12E	-0120	-0130	-0240	-0220	+0.2	+0.3	+0.3	+0.3
Waddenzee										
Lauwersoog	53 25N	6 12E	-0130	-0145	-0235	-0220	+0.2	+0.3	+0.3	+0.3
Nes	53 26N	5 47E	-0135	-0150	-0245	-0225	+0.1	+0.2	+0.2	+0.2
Holwerd	53 24N	5 53E	-0120	-0135	-0155	-0135	+0.3	+0.4	+0.4	+0.4
West Terschelling	53 21N	5 13E	-0220	-0250	-0335	-0310	-0.4	-0.2	+0.1	+0.2
Vlieland-haven	53 18N	5 06E	-0250	-0320	-0355	-0330	-0.3	-0.2	+0.1	+0.2
Harlingen	53 10N	5 24E	-0155	-0245	-0210	-0130	-0.4	-0.3	-0.1	+0.2
Kornwerderzand	53 04N	5 20E	-0210	-0315	-0300	-0215	-0.5	-0.4	-0.1	+0.2
Den Oever	52 56N	5 00E	-0245	-0410	-0400	-0305	-0.8	-0.6	0.0	+0.2
Oude Schild	53 02N	4 51E	-0310	-0420	-0445	-0400	-0.9	-0.7	0.0	+0.2
Den Helder	52 58N	4 45E	-0410	-0520	-0520	-0430	-0.9	-0.7	0.0	+0.2
			0300	0900	0400	1000				
VLISSINGEN	51 27N	3 36E	and	and	and	and	4.8	3.9	0.9	0.3
standard port			1500	2100	1600	2200				
IJmuiden	52 28N	4 35E	+0145	+0140	+0305	+0325	-2.7	-2.2	-0.6	-0.1
Scheveningen	52 06N	4 16E	+0105	+0100	+0220	+0245	-2.6	-2.1	-0.6	-0.1
Europlatform	52 00N	3 17E	+0005	-0005	-0030	-0055	-2.7	-2.2	-0.6	-0.1
Nieuwe Waterweg − Maassluis	51 55N	4 15E	+0125	+0100	+0110	+0255	-2.8	-2.2	-0.6	0.0
Nieuwe Maas − Vlaardingen	51 54N	4 21E	+0150	+0125	+0135	+0320	-2.8	-2.2	-0.6	0.0
Lek										
Krimpen	51 55N	4 38E	+0230	+0210	+0305	+0430	-3.3	-2.6	-0.7	-0.1
Streefkerk	51 55N	4 45E	+0305	+0310	+0400	+0510	-3.3	-2.5	-0.6	0.0
Schoonhoven	51 57N	4 51E	+0415	+0315	+0435	+0545	-3.1	-2.4	-0.5	+0.1
Oude Maas										
Spijkenisse	51 52N	4 20E	+0155	+0125	+0135	+0315	-3.0	-2.3	-0.7	-0.1
Goidschalxoord	51 50N	4 27E	+0225	+0205	+0235	+0355	-3.4	-2.7	-0.7	-0.1
De Kil										
's-Gravendeel	51 47N	4 38E	+0400	+0310	+0425	+0525	-4.0	-3.2	-0.6	0.0
Merwede										
Dordrecht	51 49N	4 39E	+0205	+0300	+0405	+0505	-3.8	-3.1	-0.7	0.0
Werkendam	51 49N	4 53E	+0425	+0410	+0550	+0650	-4.1	-3.3	-0.6	0.0
Haringvlietsluizen	51 50N	4 02E	+0015	+0015	+0015	-0020	-1.8	-1.6	-0.5	0.0
Ooster Schelde										
Roompot	51 37N	3 40E	-0015	+0005	+0005	-0020	-1.2	-1.0	-0.3	0.0
Colijnsplaat	51 36N	3 51E	+0040	+0035	+0020	+0030	-1.2	−0.9	−0.3	0.0
Kats	51 34N	3 54E	+0055	+0050	+0030	+0050	-1.2	−0.9	−0.3	0.0
Goessche Sas	51 32N	3 56E	+0150	+0120	+0055	+0115	-1.2	−0.9	−0.4	0.0
Wemeldinge	51 31N	4 01E	+0143	+0123	+0100	+0115	-0.9	−0.6	−0.3	0.0
Yerseke	51 30N	4 03E	+0145	+0125	+0105	+0115	-0.6	−0.4	−0.2	0.0
Stavenisse	51 36N	4 01E	+0150	+0120	+0055	+0115	-1.3	−0.9	−0.5	0.0
Zierikzee	51 39N	3 55E	+0040	+0035	+0020	+0030	-1.2	−0.9	−0.3	0.0
Lodijkse Gat	51 30N	4 12E	+0145	+0125	+0105	+0115	-0.7	-0.4	-0.3	0.0
Zijpe										
Philipsdam *West*	51 40N	4 11E	+0215	+0125	+0100	+0110	-1.2	-0.8	-0.5	-0.1
Walcheren − Westkapelle	51 31N	3 27E	-0025	-0015	-0010	-0025	-0.6	-0.5	-0.1	0.0
Wester Schelde										
Breskens	51 24N	3 34E		as Standard Port Vlissengen						
Terneuzen	51 20N	3 49E	+0020	+0020	+0020	+0030	+0.3	+0.3	0.0	0.0
Hansweert	51 27N	4 00E	+0100	+0050	+0040	+0100	+0.6	+0.6	0.0	0.0
Bath	51 24N	4 12E	+0125	+0115	+0115	+0140	+1.0	+0.9	0.0	0.0
Belgium			0000	0500	0000	0600				
ANTWERPEN	51 21N	4 14E	and	and	and	and	5.8	4.8	0.8	0.3
standard port			1200	1700	1200	1800				
Boudewijnsluis	51 17N	4 20E	+0013	+0005	+0025	+0020	0.0	+0.1	0.0	0.0
Royersluis	51 14N	4 24E	+0030	+0015	+0045	+0041	+0.2	+0.3	0.0	0.0
Boom	51 05N	4 22E	+0125	+0110	+0155	+0150	-0.2	0.0	-0.4	-0.2
Gentbrugge	51 03N	3 44E	+0430	+0415	+0630	+0600	-3.9	-3.3	-1.1	-0.4

Location	Lat	Long	High Water		Low Water		MHWS	MHWN	MLWN	MLWS
			0300	0900	0400	1000				
VLISSINGEN	51 27N	3 36E	and	and	and	and	**4.8**	**3.9**	**0.9**	**0.3**
standard port			1500	2100	1600	2200				
Zeebrugge	51 21N	3 12E	-0035	-0015	-0020	-0035	+0.1	0.0	+0.3	+0.1
Blankenberge	51 19N	3 07E	-0040	-0020	-0022	-0037	+0.2	+0.1	+0.3	+0.1
Oostende	51 14N	2 56E	-0055	-0040	-0030	-0045	+0.4	+0.3	+0.3	+0.1
Nieuwpoort	51 09N	2 43E	-0110	-0050	-0035	-0045	+0.6	+0.4	+0.4	+0.1

GERMANY AND DENMARK

Location	Lat	Long	High Water		Low Water		MHWS	MHWN	MLWN	MLWS
			0300	0700	0100	0800				
ESBJERG	55 28N	8 27E	and	and	and	and	**1.6**	**1.4**	**0.2**	**-0.1**
standard port			1500	1900	1300	2000				
Hirtshals	57 36N	9 58E	+0055	+0320	+0340	+0100	-1.3	-1.1	-0.1	+0.1
Hanstholm	57 08N	8 36E	+0100	+0340	+0340	+0130	-1.3	-1.1	-0.1	+0.1
Thyboron	56 42N	8 13E	+0120	+0230	+0410	+0210	-1.2	-1.1	-0.1	+0.1
Torsminde	56 22N	8 07E	+0030	+0050	+0040	+0010	-0.7	-0.7	-0.1	+0.1
Hvide Sande	56 00N	8 70E	-0025	-0010	-0005	-0025	-0.3	-0.3	0.0	+0.1
Blavandshuk	55 33N	8 05E	-0120	-0110	-0050	-0100	+0.2	0.0	+0.1	+0.1
Gradyb Bar	55 26N	8 15E	-0130	-0115	no data	no data	-0.1	-0.2	+0.1	+0.1
Rømø Havn	55 05N	8 34E	-0040	-0005	0000	-0020	+0.3	+0.2	+0.1	+0.1
Højer	54 58N	8 40E	-0020	+0015	no data	no data	+0.8	+0.7	+0.2	+0.1

Location	Lat	Long	High Water		Low Water		MHWS	MHWN	MLWN	MLWS
			0100	0600	0100	0800				
HELGOLAND	54 11N	7 53E	and	and	and	and	**2.7**	**2.3**	**0.4**	**0.0**
standard port			1300	1800	1300	2000				
Lister Tief										
List	55 01N	8 27E	+0252	+0240	+0201	+0210	-0.7	-0.6	-0.2	0.0
Hörnum	54 46N	8 18E	+0223	+0218	+0131	+0137	-0.5	-0.3	-0.2	0.0
Föhr	54 42N	8 35E	+0202	+0157	+0150	+0200	+0.4	+0.4	-0.1	0.0
Amrum-Hafen	54 38N	8 23E	+0138	+0137	+0128	+0134	+0.2	+0.2	-0.1	0.0
Dagebüll	54 44N	8 41E	+0226	+0217	+0211	+0225	+0.6	+0.6	-0.1	0.0
Suderoogsand	54 25N	8 30E	+0116	+0102	+0038	+0122	+0.3	+0.4	+0.1	0.0
Hever										
Husum	54 28N	9 02E	+0205	+0152	+0118	+0200	+1.2	+1.1	+0.1	0.0
Suederhoeft	54 16N	8 42E	+0103	+0056	+0051	+0112	+0.8	+0.7	+0.1	0.0
Linnenplate	54 13N	8 40E	+0047	+0046	+0034	+0046	+0.7	+0.6	+0.1	0.0
Büsum	54 07N	8 52E	+0054	+0049	-0001	+0027	+0.9	+0.9	+0.1	0.0

Location	Lat	Long	High Water		Low Water		MHWS	MHWN	MLWN	MLWS
			0200	0800	0200	0900				
CUXHAVEN	53 52N	8 43E	and	and	and	and	**3.3**	**2.9**	**0.4**	**0.0**
standard port			1400	2000	1400	2100				
River Elbe										
Scharhörn	53 58N	8 28E	-0045	-0047	-0057	-0059	0.0	0.0	0.0	0.0
Brunsbüttel	53 53N	9 08E	+0057	+0105	+0121	+0112	-0.2	-0.2	-0.1	0.0
Otterndorf	53 50N	9 54E	+0022	+0025	+0032	+0028	-0.1	-0.1	0.0	0.0
Freiburg	53 50N	9 18E	+0134	+0145	+0155	+0137	-0.2	-0.2	-0.1	+0.1
Glückstadt	53 47N	9 25E	+0205	+0214	+0220	+0213	-0.2	-0.2	-0.1	+0.1
Stadersand	53 38N	9 32E	+0241	+0245	+0300	+0254	-0.1	0.0	-0.2	+0.1
Schulau	53 34N	9 42E	+0304	+0315	+0337	+0321	+0.1	+0.1	-0.2	+0.1
Seemanshoeft	53 32N	9 53E	+0324	+0332	+0403	+0347	+0.2	+0.3	-0.3	0.0
Hamburg	53 33N	9 58E	+0338	+0346	+0422	+0406	+0.3	+0.3	-0.3	0.0
Harburg	53 28N	10 0E	+0344	+0350	+0430	+0416	+0.4	+0.4	-0.3	0.0
Horumersiel/Wangersiel	53 41N	8 20E	-0041	-0041	-0058	-0103	+0.3	+0.2	+0.1	0.0
Hooksiel	53 38N	8 40E	-0033	-0038	-0100	-0101	+0.5	+0.4	+0.1	0.0
Wilhelmshaven	53 31N	8 08E	-0010	-0016	-0052	-0049	+1.0	+0.8	+0.2	0.0
Harlersiel	53 43N	7 49E	-0111	-0114	-0127	-0134	+0.1	-0.1	0.0	0.0

Location	Lat	Long	High Water		Low Water		MHWS	MHWN	MLWN	MLWS
			0200	0700	0200	0800				
HELGOLAND			and	and	and	and	**2.7**	**2.3**	**0.4**	**0.0**
standard port	54 11N	7 53E	1400	1900	1400	2000				
East Frisian islands and coast										
Spiekeroog	53 45N	7 41E	+0003	-0003	-0031	-0012	+0.4	+0.4	+0.1	+0.1
Neuharlingersiel	53 42N	7 42E	no data	no data	no data	no data	+0.5	+0.5	0.0	0.0
Langeoog	53 43N	7 30E	+0003	-0001	-0034	-0018	+0.3	+0.3	0.0	0.0
Baltrum	53 44N	7 22E	-0010	-0015	-0045	-0030	+0.2	+0.2	0.0	0.0
Norderney *Riffgat*	53 42N	7 10E	-0024	-0030	-0056	-0045	+0.1	+0.1	0.0	0.0
Norddeich Hafen	53 37N	7 10E	-0018	-0017	-0029	-0012	+0.2	+0.2	0.0	0.0
River Ems										
Memmert	53 38N	6 53E	no data	no data	no data	no data	+0.1	+0.1	0.0	0.0

Location	Lat	Long	High Water		Low Water		MHWS	MHWN	MLWN	MLWS
			0200	0700	0200	0800				
HELGOLAND			and	and	and	and	2.7	2.3	0.4	0.0
standard port	54 11N	7 53E	1400	1900	1400	2000				
Borkum *Fischerbalje*	53 33N	6 45E	-0048	-0052	-0124	-0105	0.0	0.0	0.0	0.0
Emshorn	53 30N	6 51E	-0037	-0041	-0108	-0047	+0.1	+0.2	0.0	0.0
Knock	53 20N	7 02E	+0018	+0005	-0028	+0004	+0.6	+0.6	0.0	0.0
Ditzum	53 19N	7 17E	+0100	+0050	+0010	+0040	+1.0	+1.0	0.0	0.0
Emden	53 20N	7 11E	+0041	+0028	-0011	+0022	+0.8	+0.8	0.0	0.0

BISCAY, SPAIN & PORTUGAL

Location	Lat	Long	High Water		Low Water		MHWS	MHWN	MLWN	MLWS
			0000	0600	0000	0600				
BREST	48 23N	4 30W	and	and	and	and	6.9	5.4	2.6	1.0
standard port			1200	1800	1200	1800				
Ile de Sein	48 02N	4 51W	-0005	-0005	-0010	-0005	-0.7	-0.6	-0.2	-0.1
Audierne	48 01N	4 33W	-0035	-0030	-0035	-0030	-1.7	-1.3	-0.6	-0.2
Le Guilvinec	47 48N	4 17W	-0010	-0025	-0025	-0015	-1.8	-1.4	-0.6	-0.1
Lesconil	47 48N	4 13W	-0008	-0028	-0028	-0018	-1.9	-1.4	-0.6	-0.1
Pont l'Abbe River – Loctudy	47 50N	4 10W	-0013	-0033	-0035	-0025	-1.9	-1.5	-0.7	-0.2
Odet River										
Bénodet	47 53N	4 07W	0000	-0020	-0023	-0013	-1.7	-1.3	-0.5	-0.1
Corniguel	47 58N	4 06W	+0015	+0010	-0015	-0010	-2.0	-1.6	-1.0	-0.7
Concarneau	47 52N	3 55W	-0010	-0030	-0030	-0020	-1.9	-1.5	-0.7	-0.2
Iles de Glenan										
Ile de Penfret	47 44N	3 57W	-0005	-0030	-0028	-0018	-1.9	-1.5	-0.7	-0.2
Port Louis	47 42N	3 21W	+0004	-0021	-0022	-0012	-1.8	-1.4	-0.6	-0.1
Lorient	47 45N	3 21W	+0003	-0022	-0020	-0010	-1.8	-1.4	-0.6	-0.2
Ile de Groix										
Port Tudy	47 39N	3 27W	0000	-0025	-0025	-0015	-1.8	-1.4	-0.6	-0.1
Port d'Etel	47 39N	3 12W	+0020	-0010	+0030	+0010	-2.0	-1.3	-0.4	+0.5
Port-Haliguen	47 29N	3 06W	+0015	-0020	-0015	-0010	-1.7	-1.3	-0.6	-0.3
Belle-Ile – Le Palais	47 21N	3 09W	+0007	-0028	-0025	-0020	-1.8	-1.4	-0.7	-0.3
Crac'h River – La Trinité	47 35N	3 01W	+0020	-0020	-0015	-0005	-1.5	-1.1	-0.5	-0.2
Morbihan										
Port-Navalo/Crouesty	47 33N	2 55W	+0030	-0005	-0010	-0005	-2.0	-1.5	-0.8	-0.3
Auray	47 40N	2 59W	+0055	0000	+0020	+0005	-2.0	-1.4	-0.8	-0.2
Arradon	47 37N	2 50W	+0155	+0145	+0145	+0130	-3.7	-2.7	-1.6	-0.5
Vannes	47 39N	2 46W	+0220	+0200	+0200	+0125	-3.6	-2.7	-1.6	-0.5
Le Logeo	47 33N	2 51W	+0155	+0140	+0145	+0125	-3.7	-2.7	-1.6	-0.5
Ile de Houat	47 24N	2 57W	+0010	-0025	-0020	-0015	-1.7	-1.3	-0.6	-0.2
Ile de Hoedic	47 20N	2 52W	+0010	-0035	-0027	-0022	-1.8	-1.4	-0.7	-0.3
Pénerf	47 31N	2 37W	+0020	-0025	-0015	-0015	-1.5	-1.1	-0.6	-0.3
Tréhiguier	47 30N	2 27W	+0035	-0020	-0005	-0010	-1.4	-1.0	-0.5	-0.3
Le Croisic/La Turballe	47 18N	2 31W	+0015	-0040	-0020	-0015	-1.5	-1.1	-0.6	-0.3
Le Pouliguen	47 17N	2 25W	+0020	-0025	-0020	-0025	-1.5	-1.1	-0.6	-0.3
Le Grand-Charpentier	47 13N	2 19W	+0015	-0045	-0025	-0020	-1.5	-1.1	-0.6	-0.3
Pornichet	47 16N	2 21W	+0020	-0045	-0022	-0022	-1.4	-1.0	-0.5	-0.2
La Loire										
St Nazaire	47 16N	2 12W	+0030	-0040	-0010	-0010	-1.1	-0.8	-0.4	-0.2
Donges	47 18N	2 05W	+0040	-0030	0000	0000	-0.9	-0.7	-0.5	-0.4
Cordemais	47 17N	1 54W	+0055	-0005	+0105	+0030	-0.7	-0.5	-0.7	-0.4
Le Pellerin	47 12N	1 46W	+0110	+0010	+0145	+0100	-0.7	-0.5	-0.9	-0.4
Nantes *Chantenay*	47 12N	1 35W	+0135	+0055	+0215	+0125	-0.6	-0.3	-0.8	-0.1
			0500	1100	0500	1100				
BREST	48 23N	4 30W	and	and	and	and	6.9	5.4	2.6	1.0
standard port			1700	2300	1700	2300				
Pornic	47 06N	2 07W	-0050	+0030	-0010	-0010	-1.1	-0.8	-0.4	-0.2
Ile de Noirmoutier										
L'Herbaudière	47 02N	2 18W	-0047	+0023	-0020	-0020	-1.4	-1.0	-0.5	-0.2
Fromentine	46 54N	2 10W	-0045	+0020	-0015	+0005	-1.7	-1.3	-0.8	-0.1
Ile de Yeu										
Port Joinville	46 44N	2 21W	-0025	+0010	-0030	-0030	-1.7	-1.3	-0.6	-0.2
St. Gilles-Croix-de-Vie	46 41N	1 56W	-0032	+0013	-0033	-0033	-1.8	-1.3	-0.6	-0.3
Les Sables d'Olonne/Port										
de Bourgenay	46 30N	1 48W	-0030	+0015	-0035	-0035	-1.7	-1.3	-0.6	-0.3

Location	Lat	Long	High Water		Low Water		MHWS	MHWN	MLWN	MLWS
			0000	0600	0500	1200				
POINTE DE GRAVE	45 34N	1 04W	and	and	and	and	5.4	4.4	2.1	1.0
standard port			1200	1800	1700	2400				
Ile de Ré										
St Martin	46 12N	1 22W	+0007	-0032	-0030	-0025	+0.5	+0.3	+0.2	-0.1
La Pallice	46 10N	1 13W	+0015	-0030	-0025	-0020	+0.6	+0.5	+0.3	-0.1
La Rochelle	46 09N	1 09W	+0015	-0030	-0025	-0020	+0.6	+0.5	+0.3	-0.1
Ile d'Aix	46 01N	1 10W	+0015	-0040	-0030	-0025	+0.7	+0.5	+0.3	-0.1
La Charente – Rochefort	45 57N	0 58W	+0020	-0020	+0040	+0115	+1.0	+0.7	+0.1	+0.4
Le Chapus	45 51N	1 11W	+0015	-0040	-0025	-0015	+0.6	+0.6	+0.4	+0.2
La Cayenne	45 47N	1 08W	+0030	-0015	-0010	-0005	+0.2	+0.2	+0.3	0.0
Pointe de Gatseau	45 48N	1 14W	+0005	-0005	-0015	-0025	-0.1	-0.1	+0.2	+0.2
La Gironde										
Royan	45 37N	1 00W	0000	-0005	-0005	-0005	-0.3	-0.2	0.0	0.0
Richard	45 27N	0 56W	+0018	+0018	+0028	+0033	-0.1	-0.1	-0.4	-0.5
Lamena	45 20N	0 48W	+0035	+0045	+0100	+0125	+0.2	+0.1	-0.5	-0.3
Pauillac	45 12N	0 45W	+0100	+0100	+0135	+0205	+0.1	0.0	-1.0	-0.5
La Reuille	45 03N	0 36W	+0135	+0145	+0230	+0305	-0.2	-0.3	-1.3	-0.7
La Garonne										
Le Marquis	45 00N	0 33W	+0145	+0150	+0247	+0322	-0.3	-0.4	- 1.5	-0.9
Bordeaux	44 52N	0 33W	+0200	+0225	+0330	+0405	-0.1	-0.2	-1. 7	-1 .0
La Dordogne – Libourne	44 55N	0 15W	+0250	+0305	+0525	+0540	-0.7	-0.9	-2.0	-0.4
Bassin d' Arcachon										
Cap Ferret	44 37N	1 15W	-0015	+0005	-0005	+0015	-1.4	-1.2	-0.8	-0.5
Arcachon *Eyrac*	44 40N	1 10W	+0010	+0025	0000	+0020	-1.1	-1.0	-0.8	-0.6
Capbreton	43 39N	1 27W	-0020	-0018	-0002	-0033	-1.0	-1.0	-0.3	-0.3
L'Adour – Boucau	43 31N	1 31W	-0030	-0035	-0025	-0040	-1.2	-1.1	-0.4	-0.3
St Jean de Luz										
Socoa	43 23N	1 40W	-0040	-0045	-0030	-0045	-1.1	-1.1	-0.6	-0.4
Hendaye	43 22N	1 47W	-0045	-0039	-0018	-0044	-1.0	-1.1	-0.5	-0.4
Pasajes	43 20N	1 56W	-0050	-0030	-0015	-0045	-1.2	-1.3	-0.5	-0.5
San Sebastian	43 19N	1 59W	-0110	-0030	-0020	-0040	-1.2	-1.2	-0.5	-0.4
Guetaria	43 18N	2 12W	-0110	-0030	-0020	-0040	-1.0	-1.0	-0.5	-0.4
Motrico	43 18N	2 23W	-0112	-0032	-0022	-0042	-1.0	-1.0	-0.5	-0.4
Lequeitio	43 22N	2 30W	-0115	-0035	-0025	-0045	-1.2	-1.2	-0.5	-0.4
Bermeo	43 25N	2 43W	-0055	-0015	-0005	-0025	-0.8	-0.7	-0.5	-0.4
Abra de Bilbao	43 21N	3 02W	-0125	-0045	-0035	-0055	-1.2	-1.2	-0.5	-0.4
Portugalete *Bilbao*	43 20N	3 02W	-0100	-0020	-0010	-0030	-1.2	-1.2	-0.5	-0.4
Castro Urdiales	43 23N	3 13W	-0040	-0120	-0020	-0110	-1.4	-1.5	-0.6	-0.6
Ria de Santona	43 26N	3 28W	-0005	-0045	+0015	-0035	-1.4	-1.4	-0.6	-0.6
Santander	43 28N	3 47W	-0020	-0100	0000	-0050	-1.3	-1.4	-0.6	-0.6
Ria de Suances	43 27N	4 03W	0000	-0030	+0020	-0020	-1.5	-1.5	-0.6	-0.6
San Vicente de la Barquera	43 23N	4 24W	-0020	-0100	0000	-0050	-1.5	-1.5	-0.6	-0.6
Ria de Tina Mayor	43 24N	4 31W	-0020	-0100	0000	-0050	-1.4	-1.5	-0.6	-0.6
Ribadesella	43 28N	5 04W	+0005	-0020	+0020	-0020	-1.4	-1.3	-0.6	-0.4
Gijon	43 34N	5 42W	-0005	-0030	+0010	-0030	-1.4	-1.3	-0.6	-0.4
Luanco	43 37N	5 47W	-0010	-0035	+0005	-0035	-1.4	-1.3	-0.6	-0.4
Aviles	43 35N	5 56W	-0100	-0040	-0015	-0050	-1.5	-1.4	-0.7	-0.5
San Esteban de Pravia	43 34N	6 05W	-0005	-0030	+0010	-0030	-1.4	-1.3	-0.6	-0.4
Luarca	43 33N	6 32W	+0010	-0015	+0025	-0015	-1.2	-1.1	-0.5	-0.3
Ribadeo	43 33N	7 02W	+0010	-0015	+0025	-0015	-1.4	-1.3	-0.6	-0.4
Ria de Vivero	43 43N	7 36W	+0010	-0015	+0025	-0015	-1.4	-1.3	-0.6	-0.4
Santa Marta de Ortigueira	43 41N	7 51W	-0020	0000	+0020	-0010	-1.3	-1.2	-0.6	-0.4
El Ferrol del Caudillo	43 28N	8 16W	-0045	-0100	-0010	-0105	-1.6	-1.4	-0.7	-0.4
La Coruña	43 22N	8 24W	-0110	-0050	-0030	-0100	-1.6	-1.6	-0.6	-0.5
Ria de Corme	43 16N	8 58W	-0025	-0005	+0015	-0015	-1.7	-1.6	-0.6	-0.5
Ria de Camarinas	43 08N	9 11W	-0120	-0055	-0030	-0100	-1.6	-1.6	-0.6	-0.5
			0500	1000	0300	0800				
LISBOA	38 42N	9 08W	and	and	and	and	3.8	3.0	1.4	0.5
standard port			1700	2200	1500	2000				
Corcubion	42 57N	9 12W	-0005	+0010	+0020	+0035	- 0.5	- 0.4	- 0.2	0.0
Muros	42 46N	9 03W	-0010	+0005	+0015	+0030	- 0.3	- 0.3	- 0.1	0.0
Ria de Arosa										
Villagarcia	42 37N	8 47W	-0020	0000	+0010	+0020	- 0.3	- 0.2	- 0.1	0.0
Ria de Pontevedra										
Marin	42 24N	8 42W	-0010	+0010	+0020	+0030	- 0.5	- 0.4	- 0.2	0.0
Vigo	42 15N	8 43W	-0020	0000	+0005	+0025	- 0.4	- 0.3	- 0.1	0.0
Bayona	42 07N	8 51W	-0025	- 0010	0000	+0015	- 0.3	- 0.3	- 0.1	0.0
La Guardia	41 54N	8 53W	-0020	- 0005	+0005	+0020	- 0.5	- 0.4	- 0.2	- 0.1

Location	Lat	Long	High Water 0500 and 1700	1000 and 2200	Low Water 0500 and 1700	1000 and 2200	MHWS	MHWN	MLWN	MLWS
LISBOA standard port	38 42N	9 08W	0500 and 1700	1000 and 2200	0500 and 1700	1000 and 2200	**3.8**	**3.0**	**1.4**	**0.5**
Viana do Castelo	41 41N	8 50W	-0020	0000	+0010	+0015	-0.3	-0.3	0.0	0.0
Esposende	41 32N	8 47W	-0020	0000	+0010	+0015	-0.6	-0.5	-0.1	0.0
Povoa de Varzim	41 22N	8 46W	-0020	0000	+0010	+0015	-0.3	-0.3	0.0	0.0
Porto de Leixoes	41 11N	8 42W	-0025	-0010	0000	+0010	-0.3	-0.3	-0.1	0.0
Rio Douro										
Entrance	41 09N	8 40W	-0010	+0005	+0015	+0025	-0.6	-0.5	-0.1	0.0
Oporto *Porto*	41 08N	8 37W	+0002	+0002	+0040	+0040	-0.5	-0.4	-0.1	+0.1
Barra de Aveiro	40 39N	8 45W	+0005	+0010	+0010	+0015	-0.6	-0.4	0.0	+0.2
Figueira da Foz	40 09N	8 51W	-0015	0000	+0010	+0020	-0.3	-0.3	-0.1	0.0
Nazare *Pederneira*	39 36N	9 07W	-0030	-0015	-0005	+0005	-0.5	-0.4	0.0	+0.2
Peniche	39 21N	9 22W	-0035	-0015	-0005	0000	-0.3	-0.3	-0.1	+0.1
Ericeira	38 58N	9 25W	-0040	-0025	-0010	-0010	-0.4	-0.3	-0.1	+0.1
River Tagus (Rio Tejo)										
Cascais	38 42N	9 25W	-0040	-0025	-0015	-0010	-0.3	-0.3	+0.1	+0.2
Paco de Arcos	38 41N	9 18W	-0020	-0030	-0005	-0005	-0.4	-0.4	-0.1	0.0
Alcochete	38 45N	8 58W	+0010	+0010	+0010	+0010	+0.5	+0.4	+0.2	+0.1
Vila Franca de Xira	38 57N	8 59W	+0045	+0040	+0100	+0140	+0.3	+0.2	-0.1	+0.4
Sesimbra	38 26N	9 07W	-0045	-0030	-0020	-0010	-0.4	-0.4	0.0	+0.1
Setubal	38 30N	8 54W	-0020	-0015	-0005	+0005	-0.4	-0.3	-0.1	0.0
Porto de Sines	37 57N	8 53W	-0050	-0030	-0020	-0010	-0.4	-0.4	0.0	+0.1
Milfontes	37 43N	8 47W	-0040	-0030	*no data*	*no data*	-0.1	-0.1	+0.1	+0.2
Arrifana	37 17N	8 52W	-0030	-0020	*no data*	*no data*	-0.1	0.0	0.0	+0.2
Enseada de Belixe	37 01N	8 58W	-0050	-0030	-0020	-0015	+0.3	+0.2	+0.3	+0.3
Lagos	37 06N	8 40W	-0100	-0040	-0030	-0025	-0.4	-0.4	0.0	+0.1
Portimao	37 07N	8 32W	-0100	-0040	-0030	-0025	-0.5	-0.4	0.0	+0.2
Ponta do Altar	37 06N	8 31W	-0100	-0040	-0030	-0025	-0.3	-0.3	0.0	+0.1
Enseada de Albufeira	37 05N	8 15W	-0035	+0015	-0005	0000	-0.2	-0.2	+0.1	+0.2
Vilamoura	37 04N	8 07W	-0040	-0020	-0005	0000	-0.2	-0.2	+0.1	+0.2
Cabo de Santa Maria	36 58N	7 52W	-0050	-0030	-0015	+0005	-0.4	-0.4	0.0	+0.1
Rio Guadiana										
Vila Real de Santo António	37 11N	7 25W	-0050	-0015	-0010	0000	-0.4	-0.3	0.0	+0.2
LISBOA standard port	38 42N	9 08W	0500 and 1700	1000 and 2200	0500 and 1700	1100 and 2300	**3.8**	**3.0**	**1.4**	**0.5**
Ayamonte	37 13N	7 25W	-0055	-0045	-0035	-0015	-0.7	-0.6	0.0	-0.1
Ria de Huelva										
Bar	37 08N	6 52W	-0100	-0045	-0025	-0030	-0.6	-0.5	-0.2	-0.1
Huelva, Muelle de Fabrica	37 15N	6 58W	-0050	-0035	-0015	-0020	-0.3	-0.3	-0.2	0.0
Rio Guadalquivir										
Bar	36 45N	6 26W	-0105	-0055	-0040	-0030	-0.6	-0.5	-0.1	-0.1
Bonanza	36 48N	6 20W	-0035	-0020	0000	+0020	-0.8	-0.6	-0.3	0.0
Corta de los Jerónimos	37 08N	6 06W	+0110	+0130	+0155	+0245	-1.2	-0.9	-0.4	0.0
Sevilla	37 23N	6 00W	+0300	+0330	+0410	+0445	-1.7	-1.2	-0.5	0.0
Rota	36 37N	6 21W	-0110	-0050	-0035	-0045	-0.7	-0.6	-0.3	-0.1
Puerto de Santa Maria	36 36N	6 13W	-0054	-0054	-0033	-0033	-0.6	-0.4	-0.3	-0.1
Cadiz										
Puerto Cadiz	36 32N	6 17W	-0100	-0040	-0020	-0035	-0.5	-0.5	-0.2	0.0
La Carraca	36 30N	6 11W	-0040	-0010	0000	-0020	-0.5	-0.4	-0.1	0.0
Sancti-Petri	36 23N	6 13W	-0100	-0050	-0025	-0035	-1.0	-0.8	-0.3	0.0
Cabo Trafalgar	36 11N	6 02W	-0103	-0103	-0034	-0034	-1.4	-1.1	-0.5	-0.1
Rio Barbate	36 11N	5 55W	-0044	-0044	-0015	-0015	-1.9	-1.5	-0.4	+0.1
Punta Camarinal	36 05N	5 48W	-0107	-0107	-0047	-0047	-1.7	-1.4	-0.6	-0.2
GIBRALTAR standard port	36 08N	5 21W	0000 and 1200	0700 and 1900	0100 and 1300	0600 and 1800	**1.0**	**0.7**	**0.3**	**0.1**
Tarifa	36 00N	5 36W	-0038	-0038	-0042	-0042	+0.4	+0.3	+0.3	+0.2
Punta Carnero	36 04N	5 26W	-0010	-0010	0000	0000	0.0	+0.1	+0.1	+0.1
Algeciras	36 07N	5 27W	-0010	-0010	-0010	-0010	+0.1	+0.2	+0.1	+0.1

ENGLISH CHANNEL AND SOUTH BRITTANY

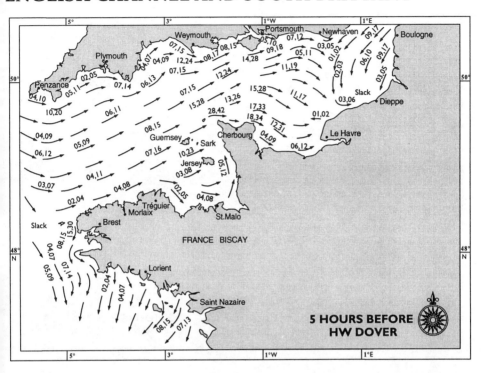

5 HOURS BEFORE HW DOVER

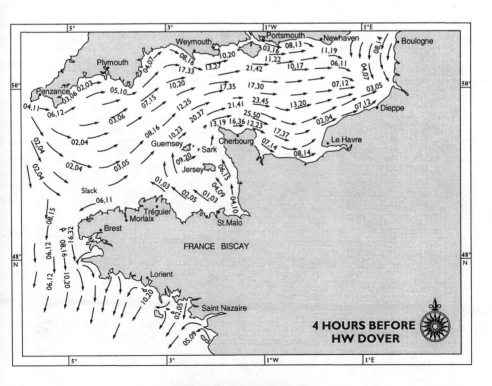

4 HOURS BEFORE HW DOVER

ENGLISH CHANNEL AND SOUTH BRITTANY

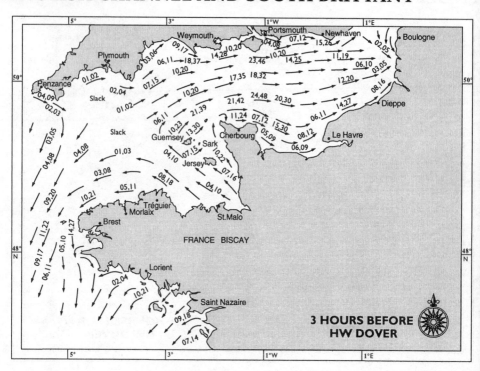

3 HOURS BEFORE HW DOVER

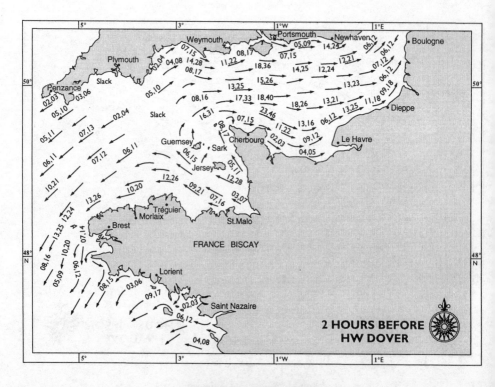

2 HOURS BEFORE HW DOVER

ENGLISH CHANNEL AND SOUTH BRITTANY

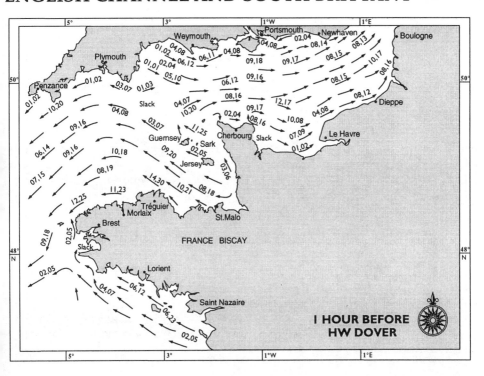

1 HOUR BEFORE HW DOVER

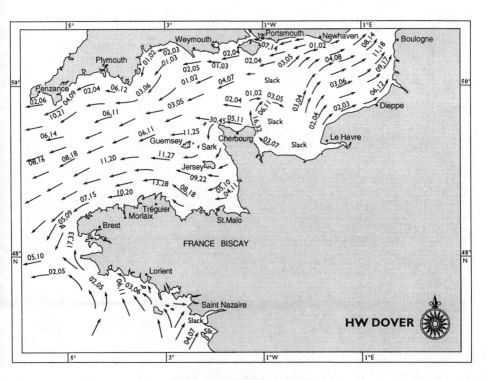

HW DOVER

ENGLISH CHANNEL AND SOUTH BRITTANY

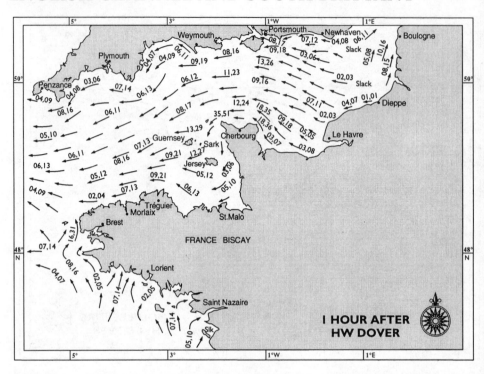

I HOUR AFTER
HW DOVER

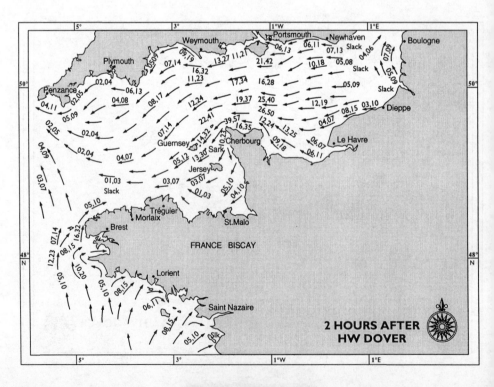

2 HOURS AFTER
HW DOVER

ENGLISH CHANNEL AND SOUTH BRITTANY

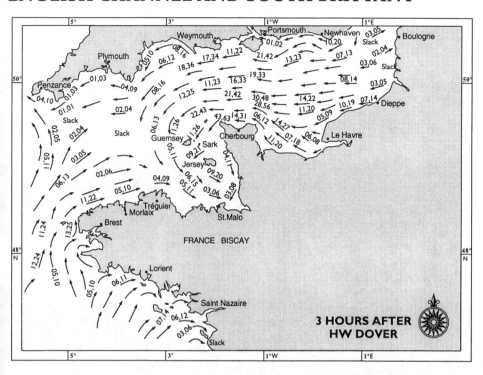

3 HOURS AFTER HW DOVER

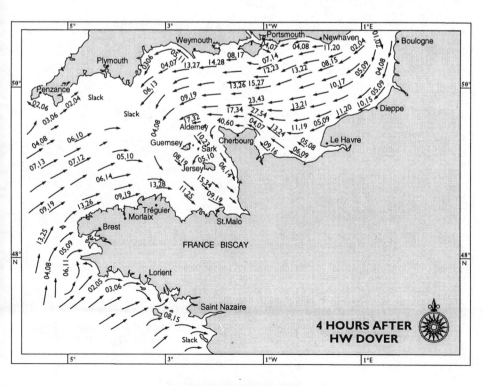

4 HOURS AFTER HW DOVER

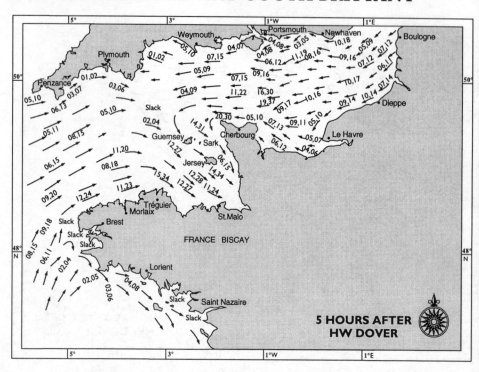

5 HOURS AFTER
HW DOVER

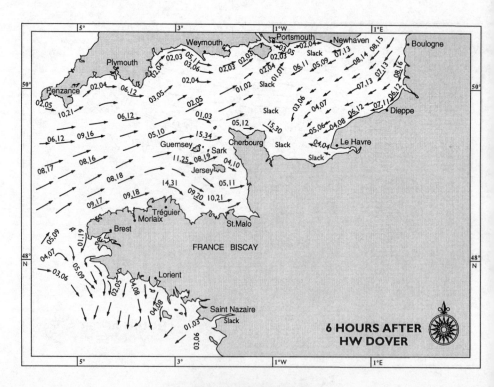

6 HOURS AFTER
HW DOVER

PORTLAND

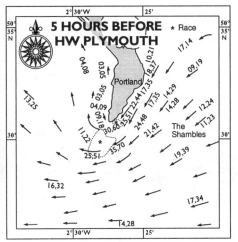

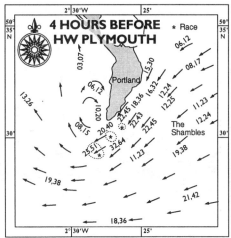

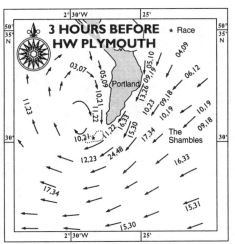

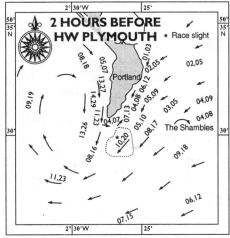

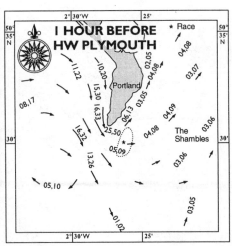

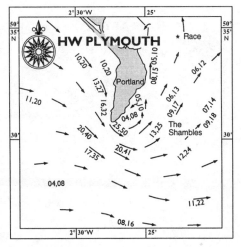

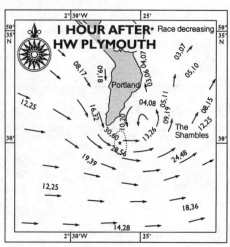

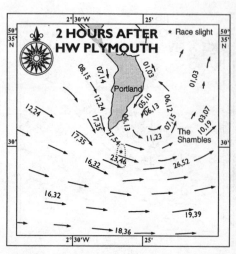

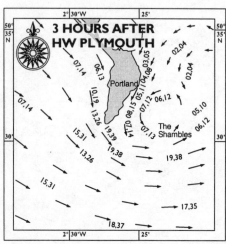

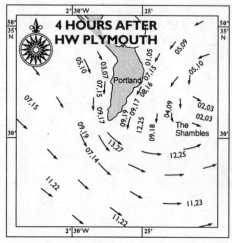

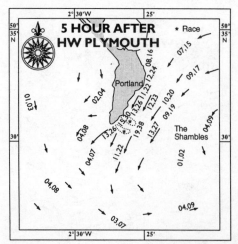

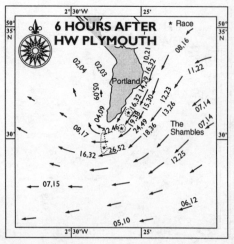

ISLE OF WIGHT

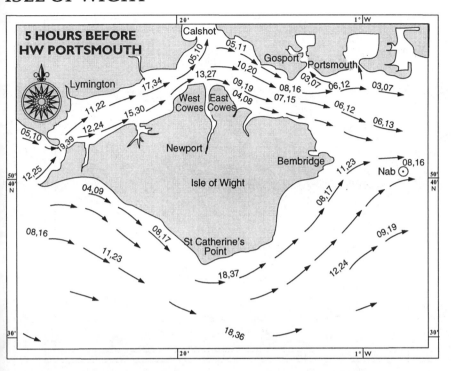

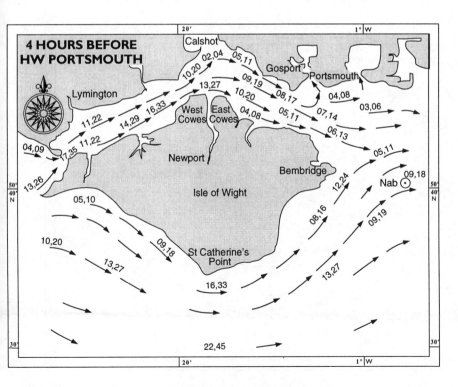

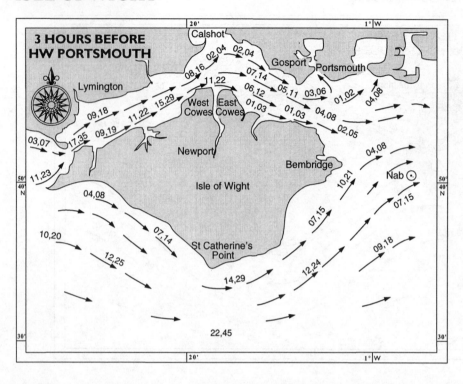

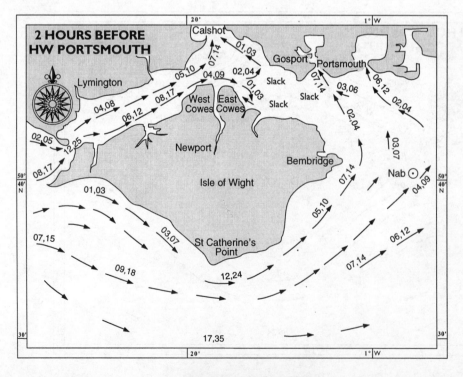

ISLE OF WIGHT

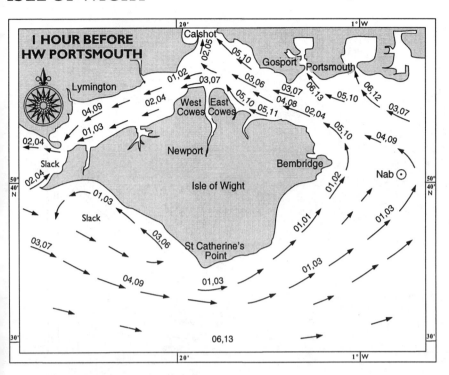

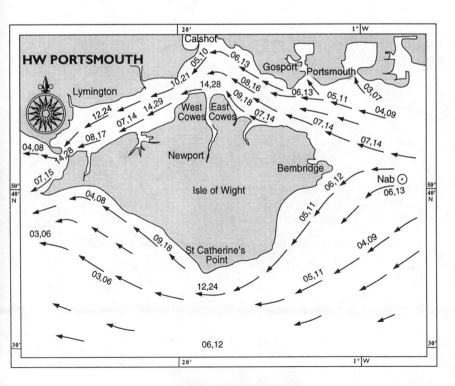

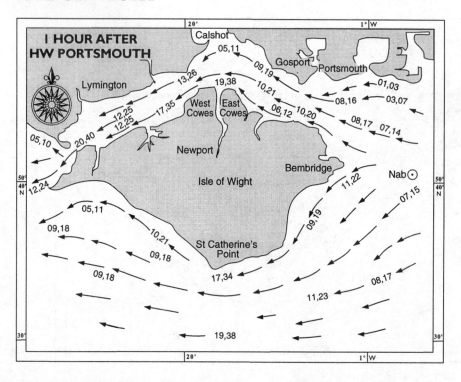

I HOUR AFTER HW PORTSMOUTH

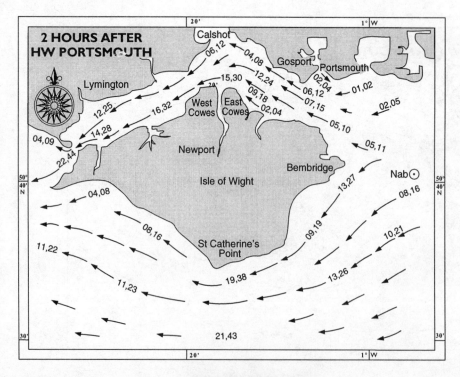

2 HOURS AFTER HW PORTSMOUTH

ISLE OF WIGHT

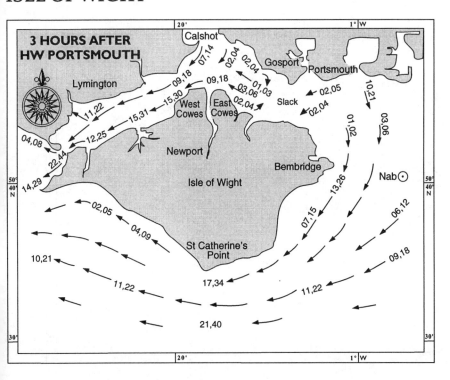

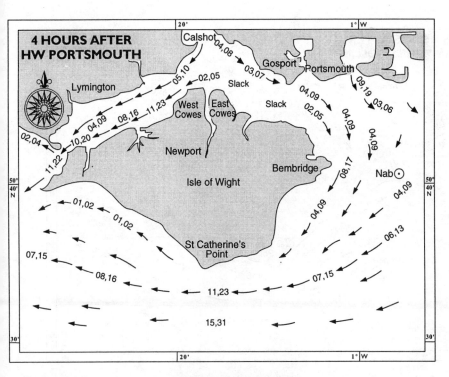

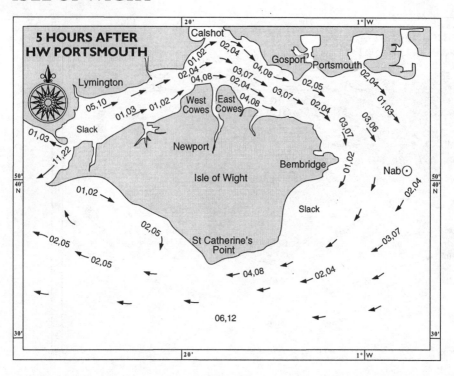

5 HOURS AFTER HW PORTSMOUTH

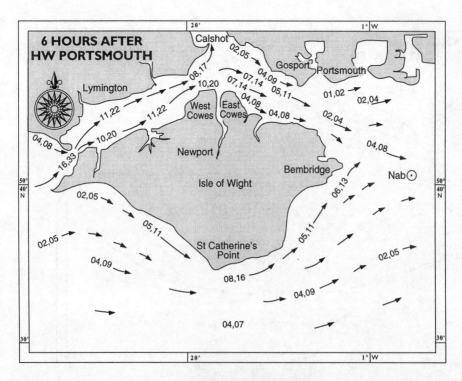

6 HOURS AFTER HW PORTSMOUTH

CHANNEL ISLES

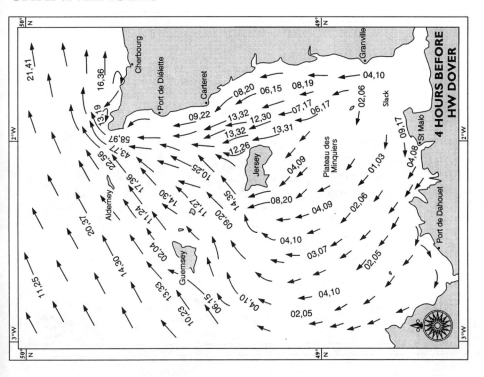

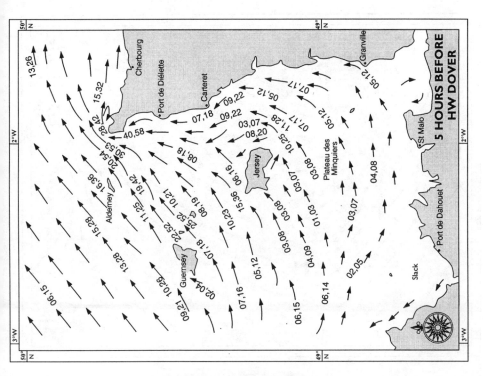

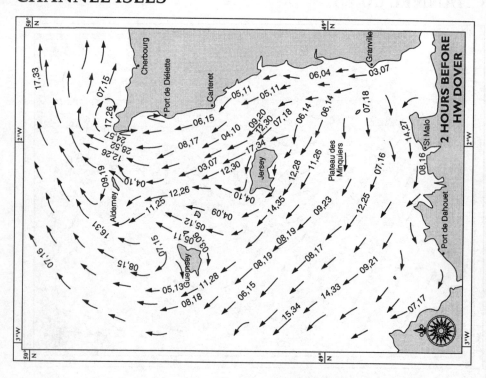

2 HOURS BEFORE HW DOVER

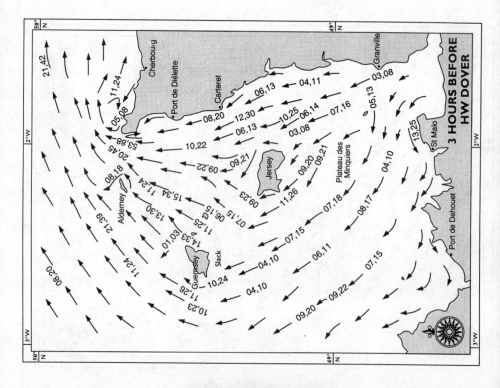

3 HOURS BEFORE HW DOVER

CHANNEL ISLES

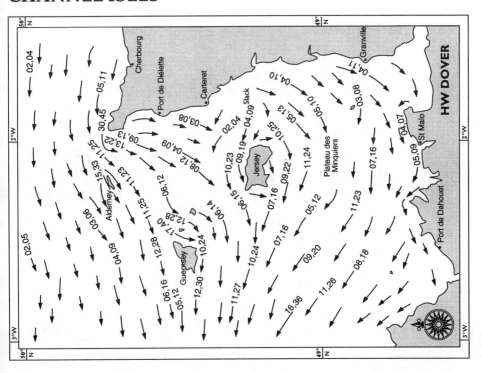

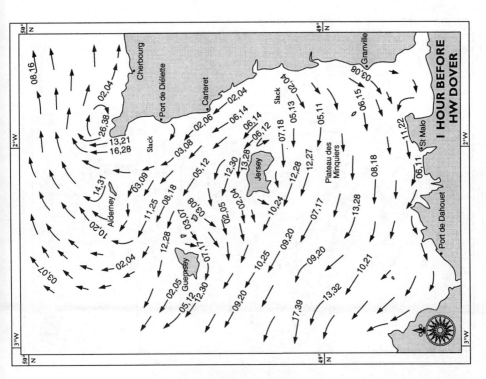

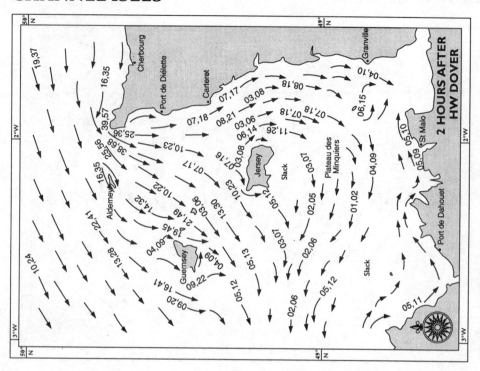

2 HOURS AFTER HW DOVER

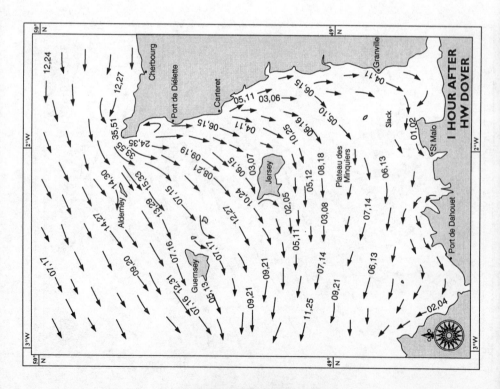

1 HOUR AFTER HW DOVER

CHANNEL ISLES

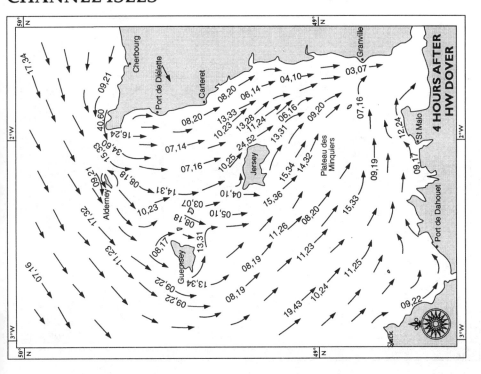

4 HOURS AFTER HW DOVER

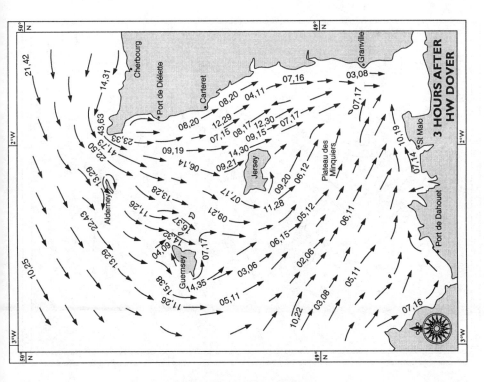

3 HOURS AFTER HW DOVER

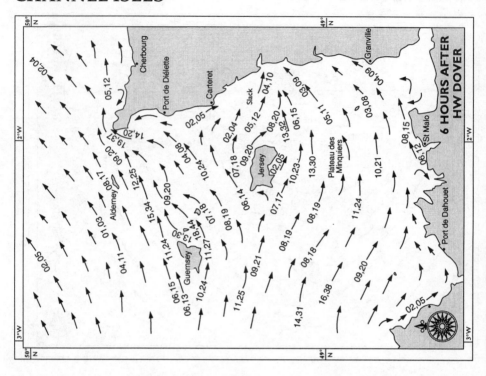

6 HOURS AFTER HW DOVER

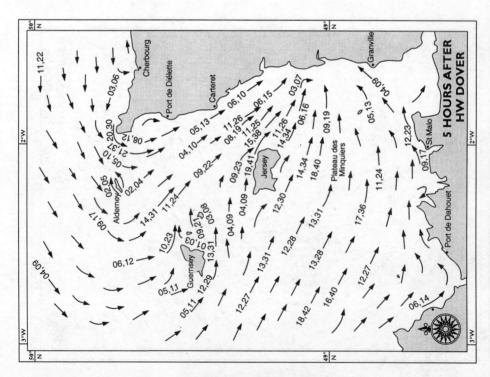

5 HOURS AFTER HW DOVER

NORTH SEA

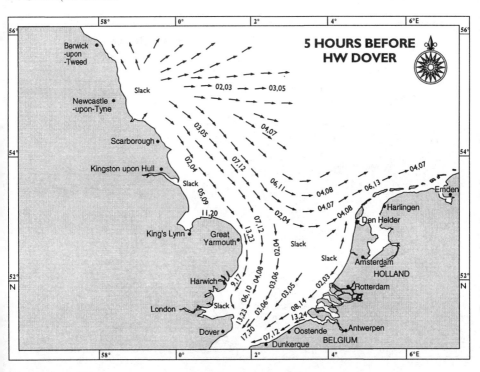

5 HOURS BEFORE HW DOVER

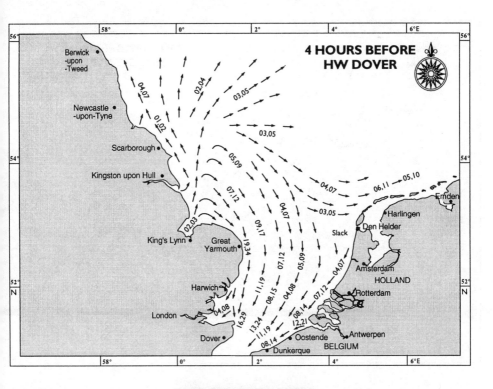

4 HOURS BEFORE HW DOVER

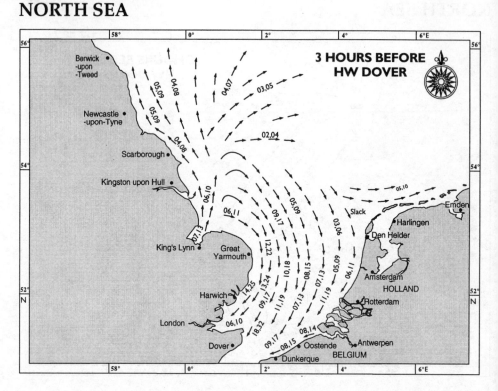

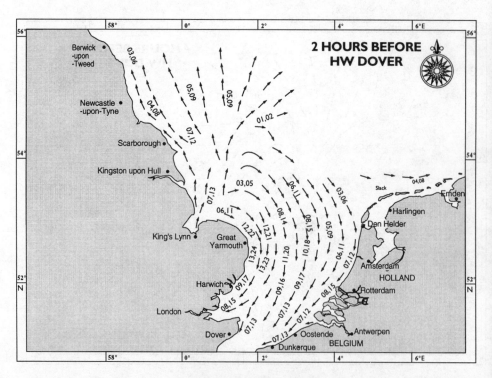

NORTH SEA

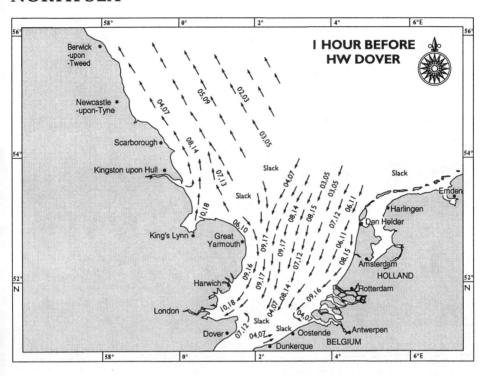

I HOUR BEFORE HW DOVER

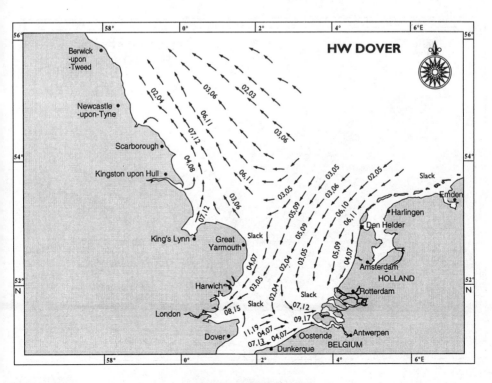

HW DOVER

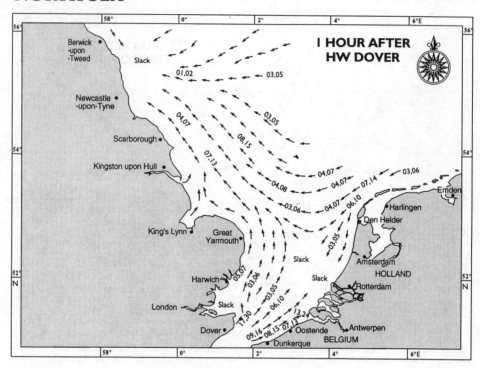

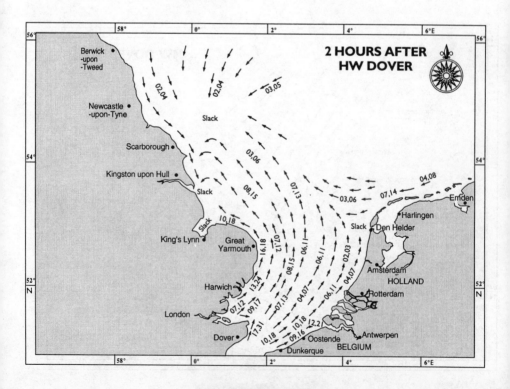

NORTH SEA

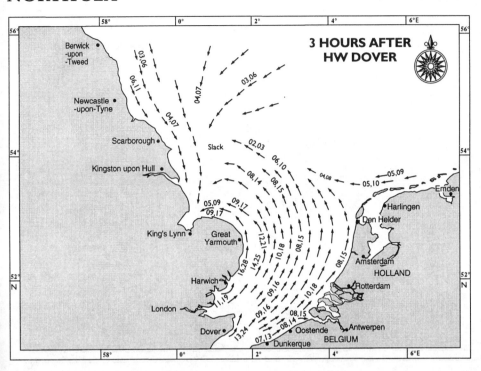

3 HOURS AFTER HW DOVER

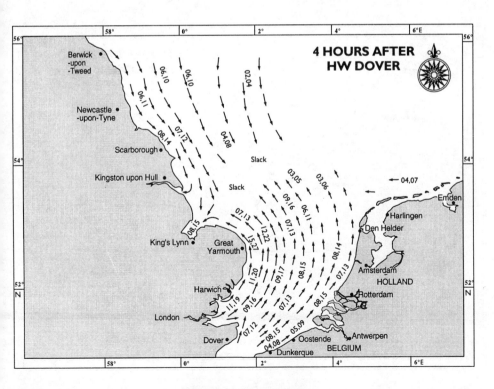

4 HOURS AFTER HW DOVER

NORTH SEA

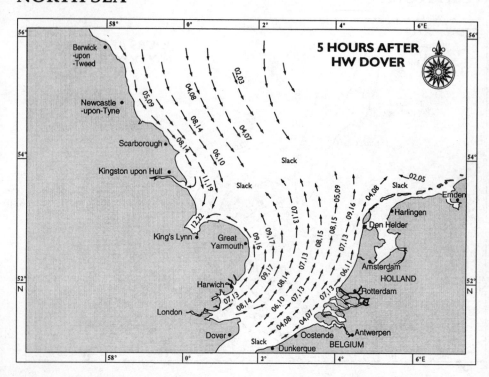

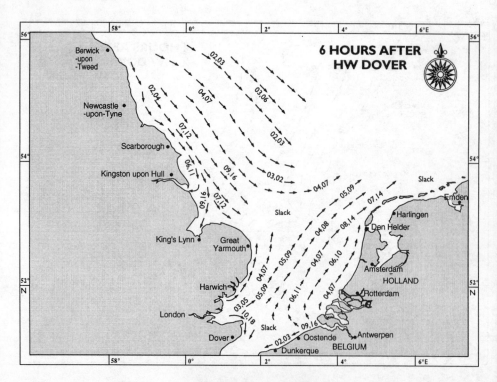

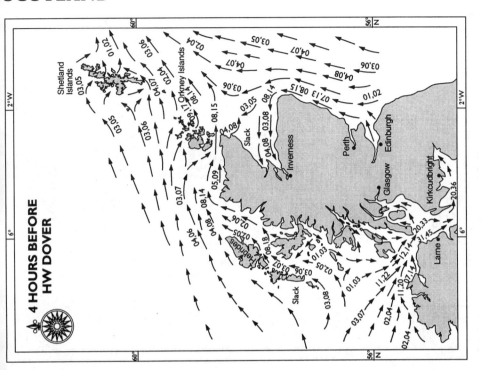

4 HOURS BEFORE HW DOVER

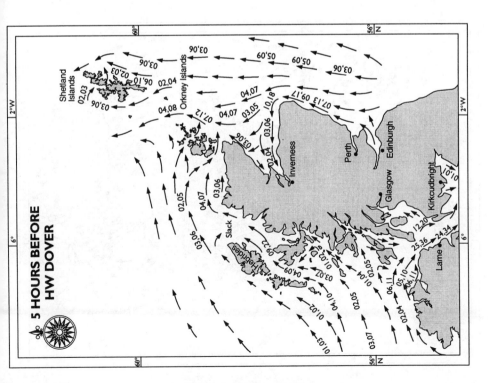

5 HOURS BEFORE HW DOVER

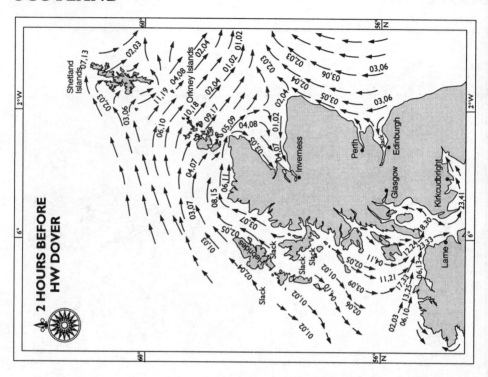

2 HOURS BEFORE
HW DOVER

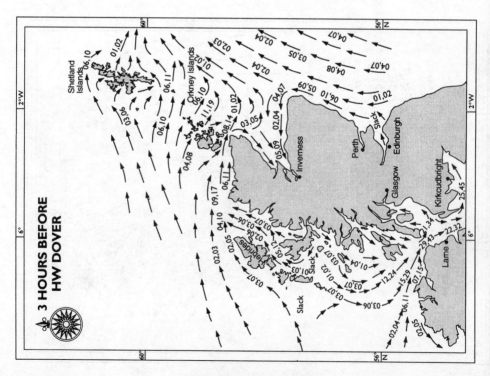

3 HOURS BEFORE
HW DOVER

SCOTLAND

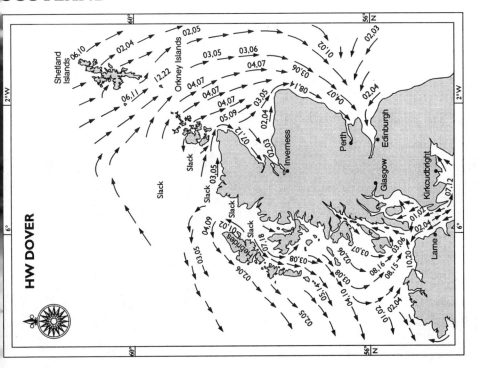

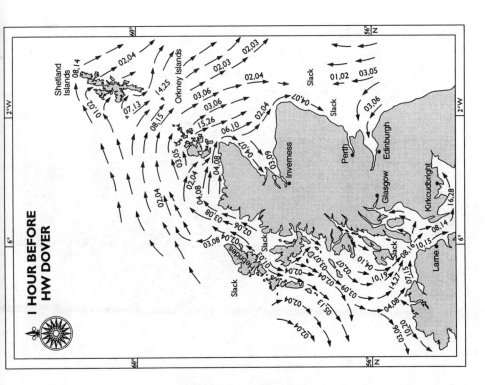

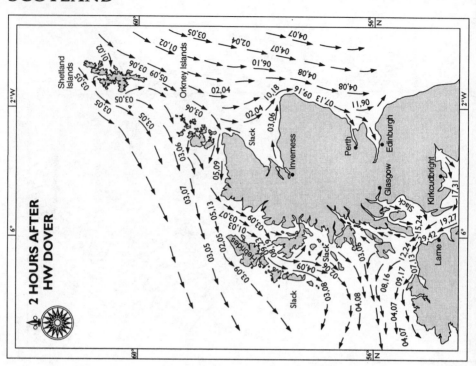

2 HOURS AFTER HW DOVER

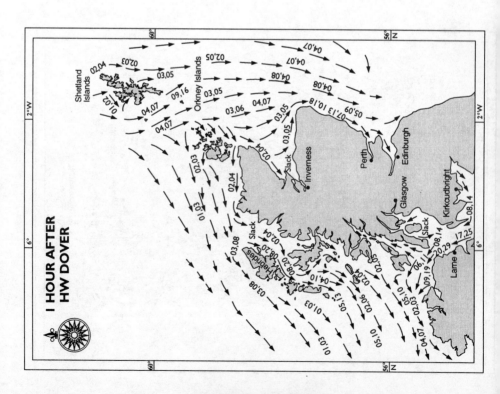

1 HOUR AFTER HW DOVER

SCOTLAND

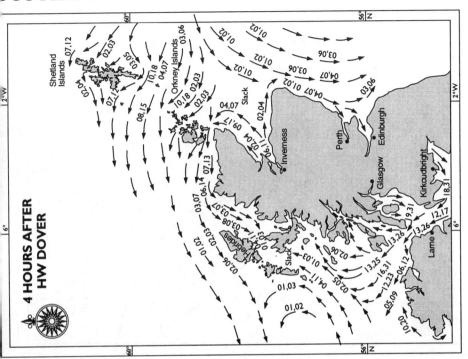

4 HOURS AFTER HW DOVER

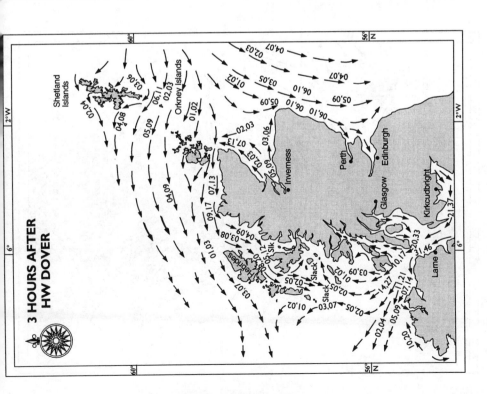

3 HOURS AFTER HW DOVER

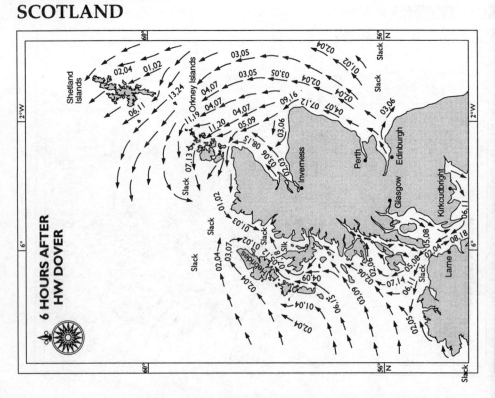

6 HOURS AFTER HW DOVER

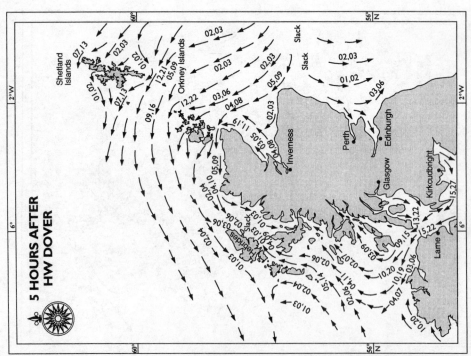

5 HOURS AFTER HW DOVER

CELTIC SEA, IRISH SEA AND WEST IRELAND

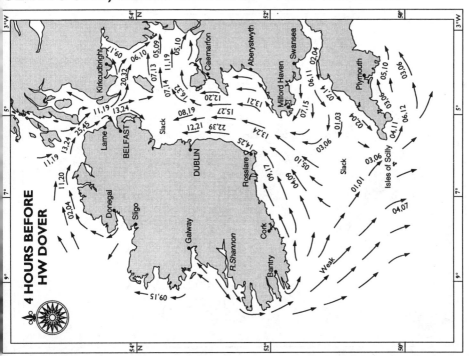

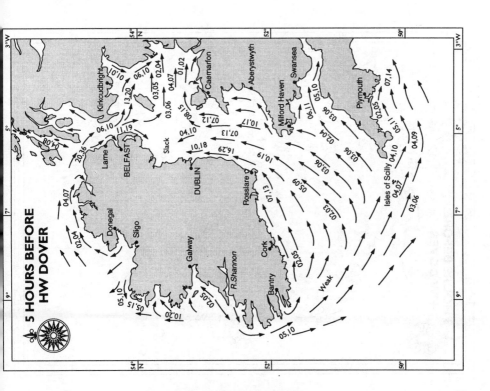

CELTIC SEA, IRISH SEA AND WEST IRELAND

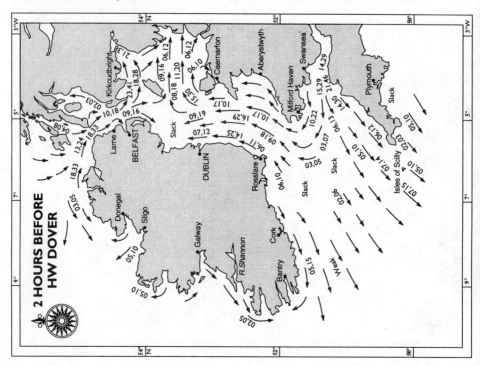

2 HOURS BEFORE HW DOVER

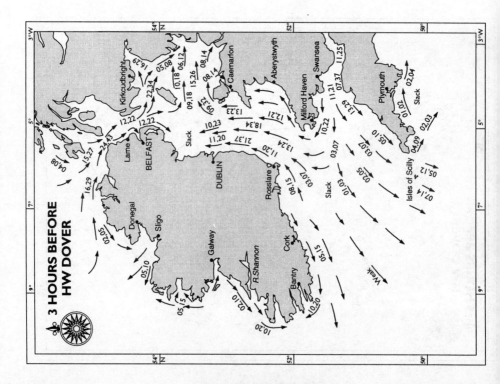

3 HOURS BEFORE HW DOVER

CELTIC SEA, IRISH SEA AND WEST IRELAND

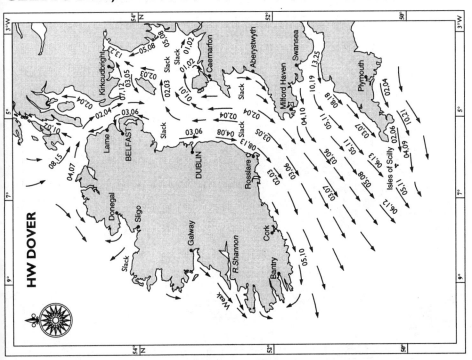

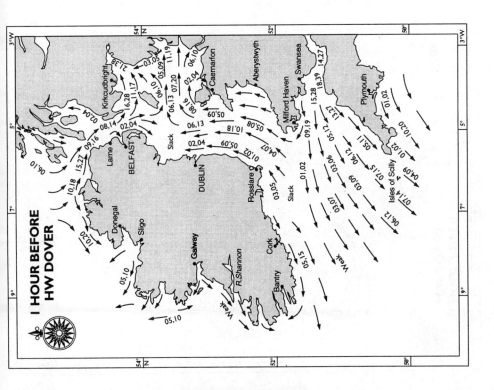

CELTIC SEA, IRISH SEA AND WEST IRELAND

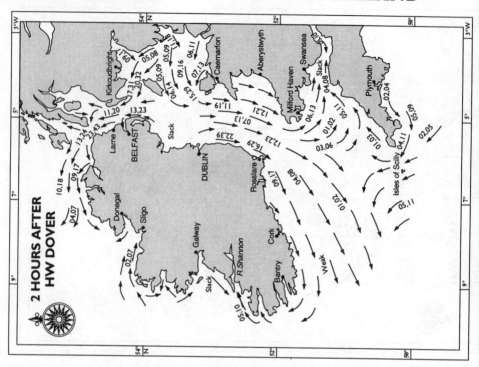

2 HOURS AFTER HW DOVER

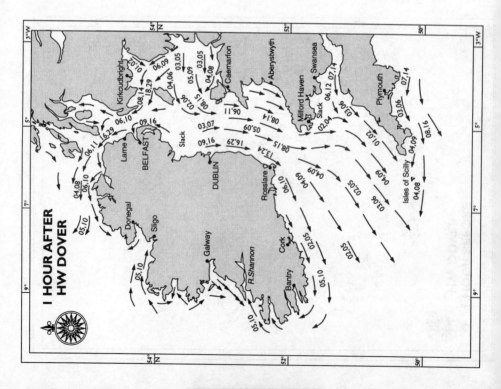

1 HOUR AFTER HW DOVER

CELTIC SEA, IRISH SEA AND WEST IRELAND

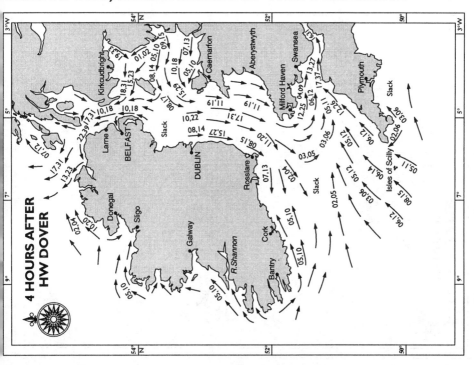

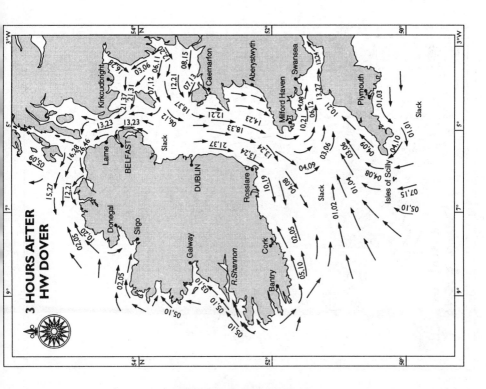

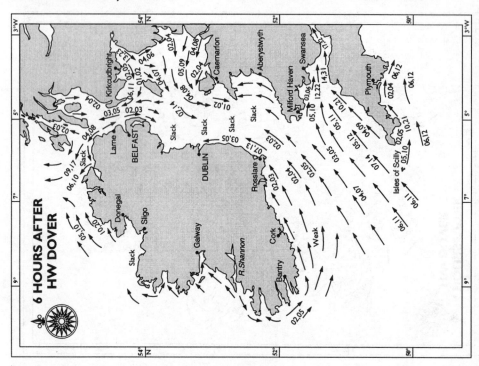

6 HOURS AFTER HW DOVER

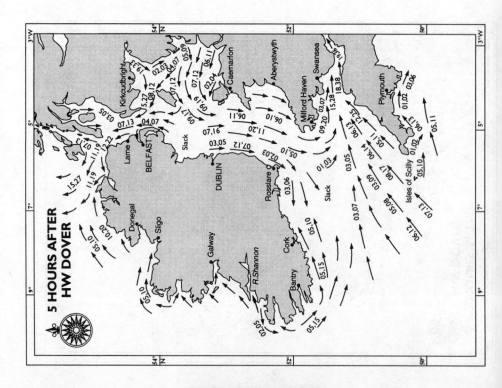

5 HOURS AFTER HW DOVER

SMALL CRAFT CHARTS

UK & Ireland, Wales, France, Belgium, Holland
Germany, Denmark, Spain & Portugal
Seafile ports, waypoints, principal lights pp 302 - 317, radiobeacons pp 318 - 321,
courses and distances

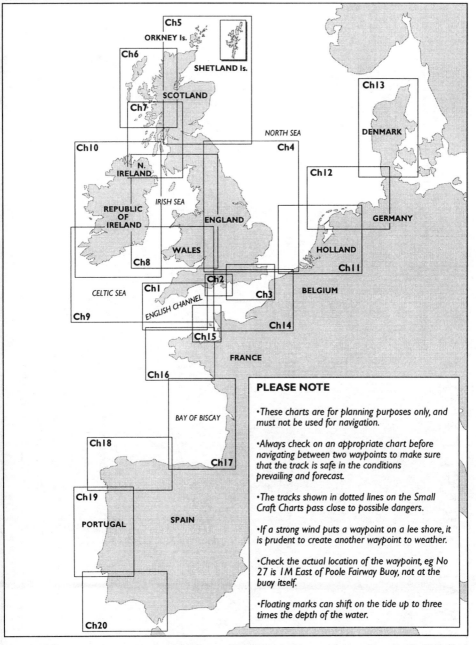

PLEASE NOTE

• These charts are for planning purposes only, and must not be used for navigation.

• Always check on an appropriate chart before navigating between two waypoints to make sure that the track is safe in the conditions prevailing and forecast.

• The tracks shown in dotted lines on the Small Craft Charts pass close to possible dangers.

• If a strong wind puts a waypoint on a lee shore, it is prudent to create another waypoint to weather.

• Check the actual location of the waypoint, eg No 27 is 1M East of Poole Fairway Buoy, not at the buoy itself.

• Floating marks can shift on the tide up to three times the depth of the water.

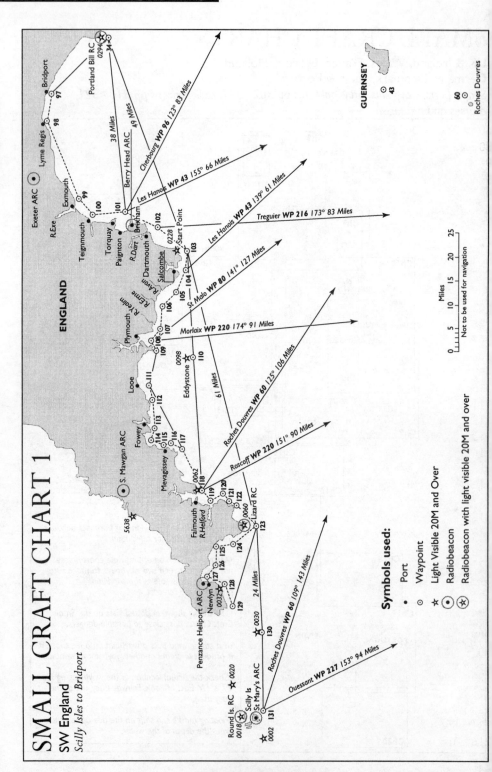

SMALL CRAFT CHART 1

SW England
Scilly Isles to Bridport

ENGLAND

GUERNSEY

Portland Bill RC 0294 341

Bridport 97

Lyme Regis 98

Exeter ARC

R.Exe

Exmouth 99

Teignmouth 100

Torquay 101

Paignton

R.Dart

Brixham 0228

Dartmouth 102

Salcombe 103

Start Point

Berry Head ARC

38 Miles

49 Miles

Cherbourg **WP 96** 125° 83 Miles

Les Hanois **WP 43** 155° 66 Miles

Treguier **WP 216** 173° 83 Miles

Les Hanois **WP 43** 139° 61 Miles

St. Malo **WP 80** 141° 127 Miles

104
105
106
107

R.Yealm
R.Erme

Plymouth 108
109
0098
Eddystone 110

Morlaix **WP 220** 174° 91 Miles

Loe 111
112

Fowey 113
114 116
115 117

61 Miles

Mevagissey

0062
118

Roches Douvres **WP 60** 125° 106 Miles

119 120
121
122
Lizard RC

Roscoff **WP 220** 151° 90 Miles

Falmouth
R.Helford

0060
123

S. Mawgan ARC

5638

124
125
126
127
Newlyn 0032
128
129

24 Miles

Penzance Heliport ARC

Roches Douvres **WP 60** 109° 143 Miles

0030
130

Round Is. RC 0020
0018
Scilly Is
St Mary's ARC
0002
131

Ouessant **WP 227** 153° 94 Miles

43

60
Roches Douvres

Symbols used:

• Port

⊙ Waypoint

✶ Light Visible 20M and Over

⊙ Radiobeacon

⊛ Radiobeacon with light visible 20M and over

Miles

0 5 10 15 20 25

Not to be used for navigation

SMALL CRAFT CHART 1
WAYPOINTS

England South West - *Scilly Isles to Bridport*

34...... Portland Bill - *2M S of*......	50°28.82'N	...... 02°27.32'W
43 ..... Guernsey SW - *1.8M W Les Hanois*	49°26.16'N	.... 02°45.00'W
60 ..... Roches Douvres Lt-*2.5M NE*......	49°08.10'N	.... 02°46.20'W
80 ..... St Malo -*1.3M NW Grande Jardin Lt Bn*	48°41.10'N	.... 02°06.40'W
96 ..... Cherbourg-*0.5M N of W ent*......	49°40.95'N	.... 01°39.35'W
97 ..... Bridport - *1M S of entrance*......	50°41.50'N	.... 02°45.70'W
98 ..... Lyme Regis-*1M SSE on ldg Lts*......	50°42.80'N	.... 02°54.80'W
99 ..... River Exe-*0.3M S of E Exe Lt By*......	50°35.67'N	.... 03°22.30'W
100 ... Teignmouth - *1M E of Bar*......	50°32.30'N	.... 03°27.80'W
101 ... Tor Bay - *1.7M NE of Berry Hd*......	50°25.10'N	.... 03°27.00'W
102 ... Dartmouth - *2M 150° from ent*	50°18.25'N	.... 03°31.60'W
103 ... Start Point - *2M S of*......	50°11.30'N	.... 03°38.47'W
104 ... Salcombe - *1.5M S of bar*	50°11.62'N	.... 03°46.60'W
105 ... Bolt Tail-*1.3M SW of R Avon*......	50°13.60'N	.... 03°53.60'W
106 ... River Erme - *1.5M SSW of Battisborough I.*	50°16.80'N	.... 03°58.50'W
107 ... R Yealm -*1.2M SW of Yealm Hd*	50°17.30'N	.... 04°05.70'W
108 ... Plymouth - *0.9M S of W end of brkwtr*	50°19.13'N	.... 04°09.50'W
109 ... Rame Hd - *0.2M S of*......	50°18.15'N	.... 04°13.30'W
110 ... Eddystone - *1M S of*......	50°09.80'N	.... 04°15.85'W
111 ... Looe - *1.5M SE of entrance*	50°19.80'N	.... 04°25.20'W
112 ... Polperro - *0.7M S of*......	50°19.00'N	.... 04°30.80'W
113 ... Fowey - *1.5M SSW of ent*	50°18.20'N	.... 04°39.50'W
114 ... Charlestown - *1M SE of*......	50°19.00'N	.... 04°44.10'W
115 ... Mevagissey - *0.8M E of*......	50°16.10'N	.... 04°45.50'W
116 ... Gwineas Lt By - *0.2M E of*......	50°14.40'N	.... 04°45.00'W
117 ... Dodman Pt - *1.3M SSE of*......	50°11.90'N	.... 04°47.00'W
118 ... Falmouth - *0.8M S of St Anthony Hd*	50°07.64'N	.... 05°00.90'W
119 ... Helford River -*1M E of ent*	50°05.70'N	.... 05°04.00'W
120 ... Manacles - *0.2M E of*......	50°02.80'N	... 05°01.50'W
121 ... Coverack - *1M E of*......	50°01.30'N	.... 05°04.30'W
122 ... Black Hd - *0.7M SE of*	49°59.70'N	.... 05°05.30'W
123 ... Lizard - *2M S of*......	49°55.50'N	.... 05°12.00'W
124 ... Porth Mellin - *1.7M W of*......	50°00.80'N	.... 05°18.50'W
125 ... Porthleven, *0.4M SW of*......	50°04.50'N	.... 05°19.70'W
126 ... Mountamopus By - *0.2M S*......	50°04.30'N	.... 05°26.20'W
127 ... Penzance - *1.5M SE of and for Mousehole*......	50°06.00'N	.... 05°30.00'W
128 ... Tater Du Lt -*1.5M ESE*......	50°02.50'N	.... 05°32.60'W
129 ... Runnel Stone Lt By - *0.3M S*	50°00.85'N	.... 05°40.30'W
130 ... Wolf Rk - *2M S of*......	49°54.65'N	.... 05°48.50'W
131 ... St Mary's, Scilly - *2M E of St Mary's Sound*	49°54.00'N	.... 06°15.00'W
216 ... Treguier - *4.1M N of Pointe de Chateau*	48°56.20'N	.... 03°14.30'W
220 ... Roscoff - *6M NNE of ent*	48°49.10'N	.... 03°54.30'W
227 ... Ushant Creac'h Lt - *3.5M NW*	48°30.00'N	.... 05°11.30'W

SMALL CRAFT CHART 2

S Central England
Portland to Chichester

Symbols used:

- • Port
- ⊙ Waypoint
- ★ Light Visible 20M and Over
- ⊙ Radiobeacon
- ⊛ Radiobeacon with light visible 20M and over

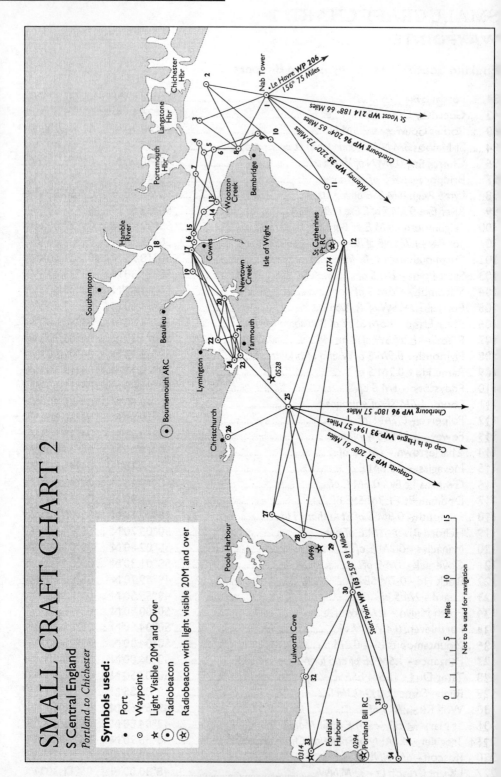

SMALL CRAFT CHART 2
WAYPOINTS

England South Central - *Portland to Chichester*

1	Nab Tower - *0.5M NW of*...	50°40.38'N .... 00°57.55'W
2	Chichester Bar Bn - *0.5M S of*...................................	50°45.38'N .... 00°56.37'W
3	Langstone Fairway Buoy -*0.5M S of*...........................	50°45.78'N .... 01°01.27'W
4	Main Passage - *Dolphin gap off Southsea*	50°45.98'N .... 01°04.02'W
5	Horse Sand Buoy - *Portsmouth ch*.............................	50°45.49'N .... 01°05.18'W
6	Forts- *midway between the two*	50°44.70'N .... 01°05.00'W
7	Gilkicker Point- *0.3M S of*..	50°46.00'N .... 01°08.40'W
8	Bembridge Tide Gauge	50°42.43'N .... 01°04.93'W
9	Bembridge Ledge Buoy	50°41.12'N .... 01°02.72'W
10	West Princessa Buoy - *S of Bembridge*	50°40.12'N .... 01°03.58'W
11	Dunnose Head- *1M off*...	50°35.00'N .... 01°10.00'W
12	St Catherine's Point- *1M S of*...................................	50°33.52'N .... 01°17.80'W
13	Wootton Beacon	50°44.51'N .... 01°12.05'W
14	Peel Bank Buoy- *east Solent*	50°45.46'N .... 01°13.25'W
15	Old Castle Point- *0.3M N of*.....................................	50°46.30'N .... 01°16.50'W
16	Cowes entrance...	50°46.20'N .... 01°17.85'W
17	Egypt Point- *0.4M N of*..	50°46.20'N .... 01°18.70'W
18	Hamble Point Buoy	50°50.12'N .... 01°18.58'W
19	Beaulieu Spit Beacon - *0.3M off*................................	50°46.83'N .... 01°21.50'W
20	Newtown- *0.5M NW of ent*.......................................	50°43.87'N .... 01°25.20'W
21	Yarmouth ent - *0.4M N of*..	50°42.80'N .... 01°30.00'W
22	Lymington, Jack in the basket- *seaward mark*	50°44.24'N .... 01°30.48'W
23	Hurst Narrows- *midway*...	50°42.20'N .... 01°32.40'W
24	Keyhaven-*0.2M E of entrance*....................................	50°42.80'N .... 01°32.80'W
25	Fairway Buoy-*Needles channel*...................................	50°38.20'N .... 01°38.90'W
26	Christchurch - *0.3M E of ent*	50°43.44'N .... 01°43.80'W
27	Poole Fairway Buoy - *1M E of*...................................	50°39.00'N .... 01°53.20'W
28	Swanage - *0.7M NE of pier*	50°37.00'N .... 01°56.00'W
29	Anvil Point - *1.5M SE of*..	50°34.30'N .... 01°56.00'W
30	St Albans Head - *1.5M S of*	50°33.20'N .... 02°03.30'W
31	East Shambles - *1M SE of*	50°30.00'N .... 02°1 8.90'W
32	Lulworth Cove-*0.1M S of ent*	50°36.87'N .... 02°14.80'W
33	Weymouth - *1M E of ent*	50°36.60'N .... 02°25.00'W
34	Portland Bill - *2M S of*...	50°28.82'N .... 02°27.32'W
35	Alderney - Bray Harbour -*1M NNE of*	49°45.00'N .... 02°10.75'W
37	Casquets - *1M W of*...	49°43.38'N .... 02°24.06'W
93	Cap de La Hague - *2M W of*.......................................	49°43.37'N .... 02°00.00'W
96	Cherbourg - *0.5M N of W ent*	49°40.95'N .... 01°39.35'W
103 ..	Start Point - *2M S of*...	50°11.30'N .... 03°38.47'W
206 ..	Le Havre - *0.5M NE of Le Havre LHA*	49°32.00'N .... 00°09.20'W
214 ..	St-Vaast-la-Hougue - *3.0 M ENE of entrance*	49°36.40'N .... 01°11.00'W

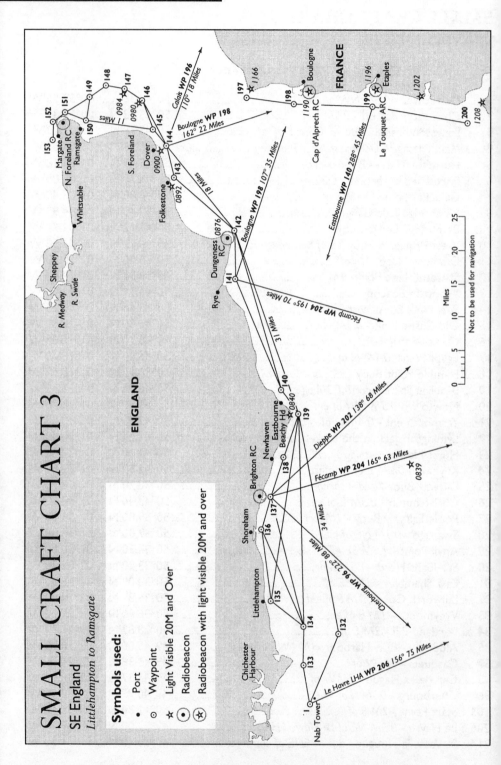

SMALL CRAFT CHART 3

SE England
Littlehampton to Ramsgate

Symbols used:

•	Port
⊙	Waypoint
☆	Light Visible 20M and Over
⊙	Radiobeacon
⊛	Radiobeacon with light visible 20M and over

ENGLAND

FRANCE

Margate
N. Foreland RC
Ramsgate
152
151
153
149
148
147
146
150
145
144
S. Foreland
Dover
0900
143
Folkestone
0892
142
0876
Dungeness RC
141
Rye
140
Eastbourne
Beachy Hd
0840
139
Newhaven
138
Brighton RC
137
136
Shoreham
135
Littlehampton
134
133
132
Chichester Harbour
Nab Tower

Calais **WP 196** 110° 18 Miles
Boulogne **WP 198** 162° 22 Miles
11 Miles
0984 0980
18 Miles
Boulogne **WP 198** 107° 35 Miles
Fécamp **WP 204** 195° 70 Miles
31 Miles
Dieppe **WP 202** 138° 68 Miles
Fécamp **WP 204** 165° 63 Miles
0839
34 Miles
Cherbourg **WP 96** 222° 88 Miles
Le Havre LHA **WP 206** 156° 75 Miles

1166
197
1
198
1190
Cap d'Alprech RC
Boulogne
199
1196
Étaples
Le Touquet ARC
1202
200
1208

Eastbourne **WP 140** 288° 45 Miles

Miles
0   5   10   15   20   25

Not to be used for navigation

SMALL CRAFT CHART   3
WAYPOINTS

England South East - *Littlehampton to Ramsgate*

I .... Nab Tower- *0.5 mile north-west of*	50°40.38'N	00°57.55'W
96 .... Cherbourg - *0.5 mile N of W entrance*	49°40.95'N	01°39.35'W
132 .. Owers Lt by-*0.5 mile S of*	50°36.80'N	00°40.60'W
133 .. Boulder Lt by- *0.1mile N of*	50°41.60'N	00°49.03'W
134 .. East Borough Hd Lt By-*0.1mileN of*	50°41.60'N	00°39.00'W
135 .. Littlehampton entrance-*IM 165°of on leading Lts*	50°47.00'N	00°32.00'W
136 .. Shoreham entrance- *I mile S of on leading Lts*	50°48.50'N	00°14.65'W
137 .. Brighton entrance- *I mile S of*	50°47.50'N	00°06.30'W
138 .. Newhaven entrance- *I mile S of*	50°45.50'N	00°03.60'E
139 .. Beachy Hd- *1.5 miles S of*	50°42.50'N	00°14.60'E
140 .. Eastbourne- *1.2 miles SE of Langney Pt*	50°46.25'N	00°21.10'E
141 .. Rye-*0.1 mile S of Rye Fairway By*	50°53.90'N	00°48.13'E
142 .. Dungeness- *I mile SE of*	50°54.00'N	00°59.65'E
143 .. Folkestone- *0.5 mile SE of breakwater*	51°04.17'N	01°12.35'E
144 .. Dover- *1.2 miles SE of Western entrance*	51°05.80'N	01°21.10'E
145 .. South Foreland-*2 miles E of*	51°08.70'N	01°26.25'E
146 .. South Goodwin Lt By-*0.2 mile SE of*	51°10.45'N	01°32.60'E
147 .. East Goodwin Lt Float-*0.8 mile W of*	51°13.05'N	01°35.10'E
148 .. East Goodwin Lt By-*0.2 mile E of*	51°16.00'N	01°36.00'E
149 .. Goodwin Knoll- *I mile SE of*	51°18.83'N	01°33.40'E
150 .. Ramsgate- *I mile E of; and for Pegwell Bay*	51°19.47'N	01°27.13'E
151 .. North Foreland- *I mile E of*	51°22.50'N	01°28.70'E
152 .. Foreness Pt- *I mile NNE of*	51°24.46'N	01°26.36'E
153 .. Margate-*0.7 miles N of*	51°24.10'N	01°22.50'E
197 .. Cap Gris-Nez -*2.0 miles NW of headland*	50°53.30'N	01°32.50'E
198 .. Boulogne -*2.0 miles WNW of entrance*	50°45.30'N	01°31.50'E
199 .. Étaples -*3.0 miles W of Le Touquet point*	50°32.20'N	01°30.80'E
200 .. St Valéry-sur-Somme - *5M WNW Le Hourdel Pt*	50°15.30'N	01°27.10'E
202 .. Dieppe - *I mile NW of entrance*	49°57.00'N	01°04.00'E
204 .. Fécamp -*IM NW of entrance*	49°46.70'N	00°20.80'E
206 .. Le Havre - *0.5M NE of Le Havre LHA*	49°32.00'N	00°09.20'W

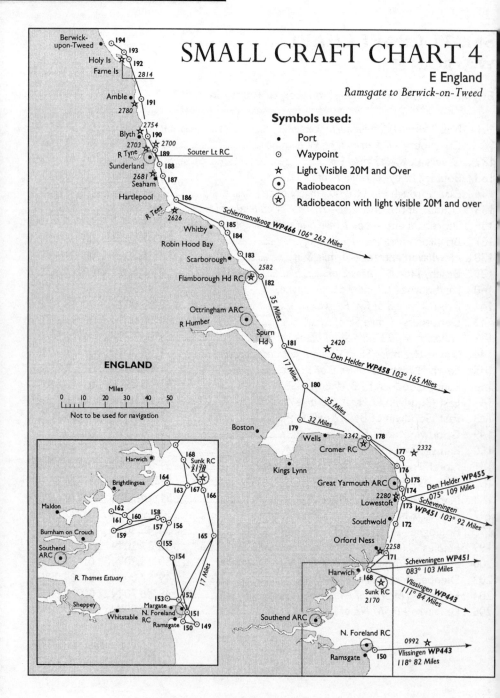

SMALL CRAFT CHART 4
E England
Ramsgate to Berwick-on-Tweed

Symbols used:

- •   Port
- ⊙   Waypoint
- ☆   Light Visible 20M and Over
- ⊙   Radiobeacon
- ⊛   Radiobeacon with light visible 20M and over

Berwick-upon-Tweed • ⊙194
⊙193
Holy Is ☆ ⊙192
Farne Is 2814
Amble • ⊙191
2780
2754
Blyth ☆ ⊙190
2703 ⊙2700
R Tyne ☆ ⊙189   Souter Lt RC
Sunderland ⊙188
2681 ☆ ⊙187
Seaham
Hartlepool ⊙186
R Tees ☆
2626
Schiermonnikoog **WP466** 106° 262 Miles
Whitby • ⊙185
⊙184
Robin Hood Bay
Scarborough • ⊙183
2582
Flamborough Hd RC ⊛ ⊙182
35 Miles
Ottringham ARC ⊙
R Humber
Spurn Hd ⊙181
2420
Den Helder **WP458** 103° 165 Miles
17 Miles
ENGLAND
⊙180
35 Miles
32 Miles
Boston • ⊙179
Wells 2342
Cromer RC ⊛ ⊙178
⊙177 ⊙2332
Kings Lynn
⊙176
Great Yarmouth ARC ⊙ ⊙175
Den Helder **WP455**
⊙174
2280 075° 109 Miles
Lowestoft ☆ ⊙173 Scheveningen
WP451 103° 92 Miles
Southwold • ⊙172
Orford Ness ⊙2258
⊙71   Scheveningen **WP451**
083° 103 Miles
Harwich • ⊙168
Sunk RC ⊛   Vlissingen **WP443**
2170   171° 84 Miles
Southend ARC ⊙
N. Foreland RC ⊙
0992 ☆
Ramsgate • ⊙150   Vlissingen **WP443**
118° 82 Miles

Miles
0   10   20   30   40   50
Not to be used for navigation

Harwich • ⊙168
Sunk RC ⊙2170
⊛2178
Brightlingsea • ⊙164
⊙167
⊙163 ⊙166
Maldon •
⊙162
⊙161 ⊙160 ⊙158
Burnham on Crouch • ⊙159 ⊙157 ⊙156
Southend ARC ⊙ ⊙165
⊙155
⊙154
17 Miles
R. Thames Estuary
⊙152
Sheppey ⊙153
Margate •
N. Foreland RC ⊙151
Whitstable • Ramsgate • ⊙150 ⊙149

SMALL CRAFT CHART 4
WAYPOINTS

England East *Ramsgate to Berwick-on-Tweed*

149 .. Goodwin Knoll-*1M SE of*	51°18.83'N ...	01°33.40'E
150 .. Ramsgate - *1M E Pegwell Bay*	51°19.47'N ...	01°27.13'E
151 .. North Foreland - *1M E*	51°22.50'N	01°28.70'E
152 .. Foreness Pt - *1M NNE of*	51°24.46'N	01°26.36'E
153 .. Margate - *0.7M N of*	51°24.10'N	01°22.50'E
154 .. Fisherman's Gat - *SE turning waypoint*	51°33.30'N	01°25.00'E
155 .. Fisherman's Gat - *NW turning waypoint*	51°36.30'N	01°20.70'E
156 .. Black Deep/Sunk Sand - *turning waypoint*	51°40.94'N	01°25.00'E
157 .. Barrow No2 Lt By - *0.3M NE*	51°42.15'N	01°23.30'E
158 .. Barrow No3 Lt By - *0.3M N*	51°42.30'N	01°20.30'E
159 .. Whitaker channel - *for River Crouch (6M)*	51°40.40'N	01°05.30'E
160 .. Swim Spitway Lt By - *0 .1M SSW*	51°41.83'N	01°08.36'E
161 .. Spitway North-*turning waypt*	51°43.70'N	01°07.10'E
162 .. Colne,Blackwater - *0.3M W Eagle Lt By*	51°44.10'N	01°03.43'E
163 .. NE Gunfleet Lt By - *0.5M NW of*	51°50.25'N	01°27.35'E
164 .. Medusa Lt By - *0.3M SW of*	51°51.00'N	01°20.00'E
165 .. Kentish Knock Lt By - *0.2M E*	51°38.50'N	01°40.80'E
166 .. Trinity Lt By - *0.6M N of*	51°49.65'N	01°36.45'E
167 .. Sunk Lt Float - *0.2M SW of*	51°50.87'N	01°34.80'E
168 .. Cork Lt By-*1M E Harwich Yt ch*	51°55.35'N	01°29.00'E
171 .. Orfordness- *1.5M ESE of*	52°04.20'N	01°37.00'E
172 .. Southwold - *2M ESE of ent*	52°18.00'N	01°43.70'E
173 .. Lowestoft - *2.8M E of ent*	52°28.30'N	01°50.10'E
174 .. Gt Yarmouth - *0.4M WSW of S Corton SCM*	52°32.07'N	01°49.36'E

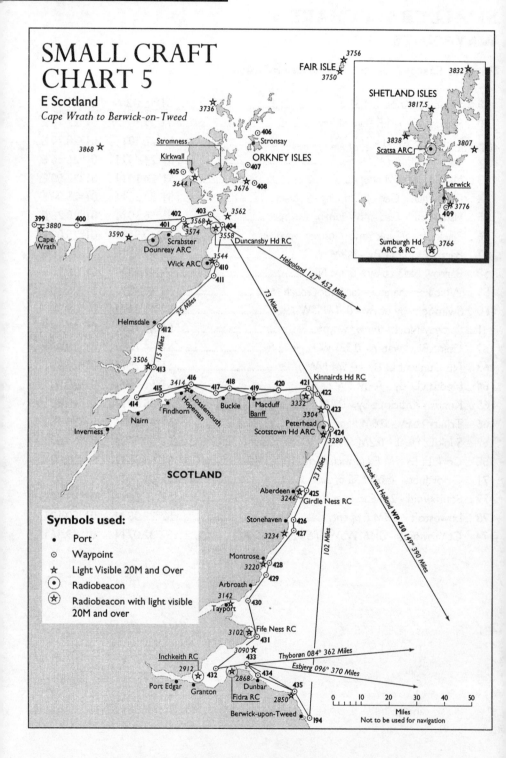

SMALL CRAFT CHART 5

E Scotland
Cape Wrath to Berwick-on-Tweed

Symbols used:

- Port
- ⊙ Waypoint
- ☆ Light Visible 20M and Over
- ⊙ Radiobeacon
- ✪ Radiobeacon with light visible 20M and over

SMALL CRAFT CHART 5
WAYPOINTS

Scotland East - *Cape Wrath to Berwick-upon-Tweed*

194 .. Berwick-upon-Tweed - *1.5M E*	55°45.90'N	01°56.30'W
399 .. Cape Wrath - *2M NW of*	58°38.90'N	05°02.80'W
400 .. Whiten Head - *4.4M N of*	58°39.20'N	04°34.90'W
401 .. Scrabster -*1.4M NE of Holborn Hd*	58°38.60'N	03°30.70'W
402 .. Dunnet Head Lt - *1.7M NW of*	58°41.60'N	03°24.30'W
403 .. Pentl'd Firth -*1.5M NE by N Stroma*	58°43.00'N	03°05.40'W
404 .. Duncansby Head - *2M NE of*	58°39.80'N	02°58.40'W
405 .. Stromness -*2.8M NW Graemsay Lt.*	58°57.10'N	03°23.70'W
406 .. Stronsay - *0.8M NW Ness Lt.*	59°10.00'N	02°35.80'W
407 .. Kirkwall - *1.5M NW of Mull Hd*	58°59.40'N	02°40.40'W
408 .. Copinsay Lt - *2.5M E of*	58°54.10'N	02°35.10'W
409 .. Lerwick - *1.1M SW of Bressay Lt*	60°06.60'N	01°08.60'W
410 .. Wick - *1.6M E of South Hd*	58°25.80'N	03°01.00'W
411 .. Scarlet Hd - *2M E by S*	58°21.90'N	03°02.50'W
412 .. Helmsdale - *1.8M SE of ent*	58°05.50'N	03°36.80'W
413 .. Tarbat Ness Lt - *2M E of*	57°51.80'N	03°42.70'W
414 .. Inverness - *0.5 NE of Frwy By*	57°40.30'N	03°53.30'W
415 .. Findhorn - *2.2M NW of bay*	57°41.45'N	03°40.00'W
416 .. Lossiemouth - *1.7M N*	57°45.20'N	03°16.70'W
417 .. Buckie - *2.0M WNW*	57°41.70'N	03°00.90'W
418 .. Scar Nose - *1.6M N*	57°44.00'N	02°50.90'W
419 .. Banff - *1.3M N of Meavie Pt*	57°41.60'N	02°31.40'W
420 .. Troup Head - *1.8M N*	57°43.50'N	02°17.70'W
421 .. Kinnairds Head - *1.6M N*	57°43.50'N	02°00.20'W
422 .. Cairnbulg Point Lt - *1.9M NE*	57°42.20'N	01°53.70'W
423 .. Rattray Head Lt - *1.8M ENE*	57°37.40'N	01°45.90'W
424 .. Peterhead - *2.1M ESE*	57°29.30'N	01°42.60'W
425 .. Aberdeen - *2M E by N Girdle Ness*	57°08.80'N	01°59.00'W
426 .. Stonehaven - *2M E*	56°57.60'N	02°08.20'W
427 .. Todhead Point Lt - *2.5M E*	56°53.10'N	02°08.30'W
428 .. Montrose - *2.1M E Scurdie Ness Lt*	56°42.10'N	02°22.40'W
429 .. Red Head - *1.8M E of*	56°37.40'N	02°25.30'W
430 .. Tayport - *0.5M E Fairway By*	56°28.60'N	02°36.30'W
431 .. Fife Ness - *2.8M ESE*	56°15.95'N	02°30.30'W
432 .. Granton - *0.5M N Inchkeith By*	56°04.00'N	03°00.00'W
433 .. Bass Rock Lt - *1.5M N*	56°06.10'N	02°38.40'W
434 .. Dunbar - *1.5M NNE*	56°01.76'N	02°30.20'W
435 .. St Abb's Head Lt - *1.5M NE*	55°56.10'N	02°06.40'W
450 .. Hoek van Holland - *1.2M WNW*	51°59.90'N	04°01.00'E

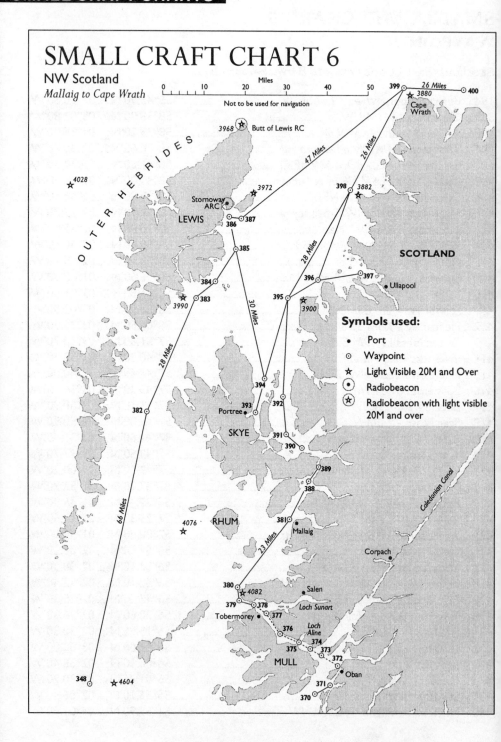

SMALL CRAFT CHART 6

NW Scotland
Mallaig to Cape Wrath

Miles
0 10 20 30 40 50

Not to be used for navigation

26 Miles

399 ⊙ ☆ 3880 ⊙ 400
Cape Wrath

3968 ⊛ Butt of Lewis RC

47 Miles   26 Miles

☆ 4028

3972

398 ⊙ ☆ 3882

Stornoway ARC
LEWIS
⊙ 387
386

385

28 Miles

SCOTLAND

384 ⊙

396 ⊙   ⊙ 397

383
☆ 3990

395 ⊙
☆ 3900

Ullapool

30 Miles

Symbols used:

- • Port
- ⊙ Waypoint
- ☆ Light Visible 20M and Over
- ⊙ Radiobeacon
- ⊛ Radiobeacon with light visible 20M and over

28 Miles

382 ⊙

394 ⊙

393
Portree •   392 ⊙

SKYE

391 ⊙
390 ⊙

389 ⊙

388 ⊙

Caledonian Canal

66 Miles

4076
☆   RHUM

381 ⊙
Mallaig •

23 Miles

Corpach •

380 ⊙ ☆ 4082   Salen •

379 ⊙ 378
Tobermorey •   377

Loch Sunart

376   Loch Aline

375   374
373
MULL   372

371   • Oban

348 ⊙   ☆ 4604   370

SMALL CRAFT CHART 6
WAYPOINTS

Scotland North West - *Mallaig to Cape Wrath*

348 ..	Skerryvore Lt - *6.8M W by N of*	56°20.80'N	07°18.80'W
370 ..	Sound of Insh - *1M SSW of Insh Island*	56°17.60'N	05°41.00'W
371 ..	Kerrera Sound - *0.7M SSW of Rubha Seanach*	56°21.70'N	05°33.90'W
372 ..	Oban - *0.5M WNW of Maiden Isle*	56°26.00'N	05°30.30'W
373 ..	Between Lady's Rock and Eilean Musdile	56°27.20'N	05°36.70'W
374 ..	Sound of Mull - *1.6M SE of Ardtornish Point*	56°30.15'N	05°42.75'W
375 ..	Loch Aline - *0.7M S by W of entrance*	56°31.30'N	05°46.80'W
376 ..	Sound of Mull - *1.8M N of Salen*	56°33.00'N	05°56.30'W
377 ..	Tobermory - *0.9M NE of harbour entrance*	56°38.40'N	06°02.40'W
378 ..	Ardmore Point (Mull) - *0.7M N of*	56°40.00'N	06°07.60'W
379 ..	Point of Ardnamurchan - *2.8M S of*	56°40.90'N	06°13.30'W
380 ..	Point of Ardnamurchan - *1.3M W of*	56°43.60'N	06°15.90'W
381 ..	Mallaig - *1.5 miles WNW of harbour entrance*	57°01.00'N	05°52.10'W
382 ..	Neist Point lt - *4.0M W of*	57°25.45'N	06°54.50'W
383 ..	Sound of Shiant - *2.2M E of Eilean Glas Lt Ho.*	57°51.20'N	06°34.40'W
384 ..	Sound of Shiant- *0.3M NW of Shiants Lt By.*	57°54.80'N	06°26.00'W
385 ..	Kebock Head - *2.3M E of*	58°02.40'N	06°17.00'W
386 ..	Stornoway - *1.2M SE of harbour entrance*	58°10.30'N	06°20.60'W
387 ..	Chicken Head - *M S of*	58°09.80'N	06°15.10'W
388 ..	Sandaig Islands Lt. - *Ms W by N of*	57°10.25'N	05°43.20'W
389 ..	Kyle Rhea (S appr) - *0.6M W of Glenelg*	57°12.75'N	05°38.80'W
390 ..	Loch Alsh (W appr) - *1.0M NW of entrance*	57°17.20'N	05°46.10'W
391 ..	Crowlin Islands - *1.5 M W of*	57°20.70'N	05°53.80'W
392 ..	Inner Sound - *1.7M E Rubha Ard Ghlaisen*	57°29.55'N	05°55.50'W
393 ..	Portree - *1.8M E of town*	57°25.00'N	06°08.00'W
394 ..	Sd of Raasay - *3.1M SE of Rubha nam Brathairean*	57°33.30'N	06°03.80'W
395 ..	Rubha Reidh - *3.0M W of*	57°51.60'N	05°54.40'W
396 ..	Greenstone Point - *1.6M NW of*	57°56.60'N	05°39.20'W
397 ..	Ullapool - *1.7M NE of Cailleach Head Lt.*	57°56.90'N	05°21.80'W
398 ..	Stoerhead Light - *2M NW of*	58°15.80'N	05°26.80'W
399 ..	Cape Wrath - *2M NW of*	58°38.90'N	05°02.80'W
400 ..	Whiten Head - *4.4M N of*	58°39.20'N	04°34.90'W

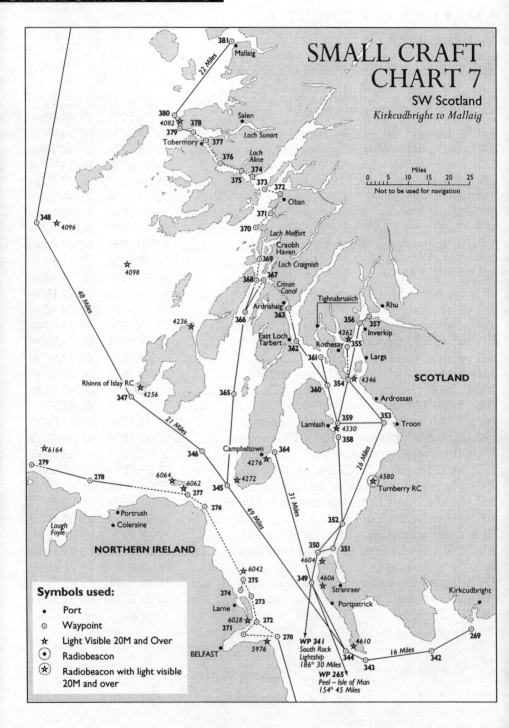

SMALL CRAFT CHART 7

SW Scotland

Kirkcudbright to Mallaig

381
Mallaig

22 Miles

380
4082 378
379
Tobermory 377
376
Salen
Loch Sunart
Loch Aline
374
375 373
372
Oban
371
370
Loch Melfort
Craobh Haven
369
Loch Craignish
367
368
Crinan Canal

Miles
0 5 10 15 20 25
Not to be used for navigation

348
4096

4098

48 Miles

Tighnabruaich
Rhu
356 357
4362 Inverkip
355
Largs

366
363
Ardrishaig
4236
East Loch Tarbert
362
Rothesay
361
SCOTLAND

Rhinns of Islay RC
347 4256
365
360
354 4346
359 Ardrossan
Lamlash 4330
353 Troon
358
Turnberry RC 4580
346
Campbeltown
364
4276
6064
6062
277
345
4272
276
349
350
351
4604
352
31 Miles
49 Miles
26 Miles
16 Miles
343 342

6164
279
278

Portrush
Coleraine
Lough Foyle

NORTHERN IRELAND

6042
275
274
273
Larne
272
6028
271
270
5976
BELFAST

349
4606
Stranraer
Portpatrick
Kirkcudbright
269

WP 341
South Rock Lightship
186° 30 Miles
344
4610
WP 265
Peel – Isle of Man
154° 45 Miles

Symbols used:

- • Port
- ⊙ Waypoint
- ☆ Light Visible 20M and Over
- ⊙ Radiobeacon
- ✪ Radiobeacon with light visible 20M and over

SMALL CRAFT CHART 7

WAYPOINTS
Scotland South West - *Kirkcudbright to Mallaig*

265 .. Peel - *1.0M NW Hbr ent*	54°14.50'N	04°42.50'W
269 .. Kirkcudbright-*1.5M S Little Ross lt*	54°44.50'N	04°05.00'W
270 .. Mew Island light - *1.3M ENE*	54°42.30'N	05°29.90'W
271 .. Belfast -*0.7M ENE No.1 Std Ch By*	54°42.00'N	05°45.20'W
272 .. Black Head light - *1.3M ENE*	54°46.50'N	05°39.20'W
273 .. Isle of Muck - *1.1M NE*	54°51.70'N	05°41.85'W
274 .. Larne Lough-*1M N of Barr's pt*	54°52.50'N	05°46.80'W
275 .. East Maiden Light - *1.7M SW*	54°54.50'N	05°45.50'W
276 .. Torr Head - *0.6M ENE of*	55°12.20'N	06°02.80'W
277 .. Fair Head - *0.9M N of*	55°14.60'N	06°09.00'W
278 .. Lough Foyle -*4.8M NNE Inishowen Hd Lt*	55°17.90'N	06°52.20'W
279 .. Malin Head - *2 miles NNE*	55°25.00'N	07°21.20'W
341 .. South Rock lightship - *1.1M E of*	54°24.30'N	05°20.00'W
342 .. Burrow Head - *2.0 M S of*	54°38.70'N	04°23.00'W
343 .. Mull of Galloway Lt-*1.7M S of*	54°36.40'N	04°51.50'W
344 .. Crammag Head L -*1.8M SW of*	54°38.60'N	05°00.00'W
345 .. Mull of Kintyre Lt - *2.5M SW of*	55°16.90'N	05°51.30'W
346 .. Mull of Kintyre Lt- *10.3M NW of*	55°25.50'N	06°01.50'W
347 .. Rhinns of Islay Lt - *2.2M SW of*	55°38.85'N	06°33.50'W
348 .. Skerryvore Lt - *6.8M W by N of*	56°20.80'N	07°18.80'W
349 .. Killantringan Lt - *4.2M NW of*	54°54.20'N	05°14.70'W
350 .. Corsewall Pt Lt-*1.8M WNW of*	55°01.20'N	05°12.20'W
351 .. Stranraer -*1.0M NNW ent to Loch Ryan*	55°02.40'N	05°05.10'W
352 .. Bennane Head - *1.5M NW of*	55°09.25'N	05°01.80'W
353 .. Troon - *2.1M W of harbour ent*	55°33.10'N	04°44.70'W
354 .. Little Cumbrae Island Lt - *0.8M SW of*	55°42.75'N	04°59.00'W
355 .. Rothesay - *Ent to Rothesay Sound*	55°50.90'N	04°59.60'W
356 .. Firth of Clyde, Cloch Point Lt- *1.3M WSW of*	55°55.95'N	04°54.75'W
357 .. R. Clyde, Kempock Point - *0.9M WNW of*	55°58.10'N	04°50.50'W
358 .. Lamlash - *1.0M SE of S ent*	55°29.80'N	05°03.60'W
359 .. Lamlash - *1.0M E of N ent*	55°32.90'N	05°03.00'W
360 .. Isle of Arran - *2.0M NNE of Sannox Bay*	55°41.60'N	05°08.00'W
361 .. West Kyle - *1.0M E Lamont Shelf IDM*	55°48.35'N	05°11.80'W
362 .. East Loch Tarbert - *1.0 E of Loch*	55°52.20'N	05°22.00'W
363 .. Ardrishaig - *1.3 SSE of hbr ent*	55°59.50'N	05°25.60'W
364 .. Campbeltown-*1.0 NE of Loch ent*	55°26.40'N	05°31.00'W
365 .. Gigha Island - *1.5M W of Cath Sgeir W Cd Mk*	55°39.70'N	05°50.00'W
366 .. Sound of Jura -*2.5M NW of Island of Danna*	55°58.80'N	05°45.50'W
367 .. Loch Crinan - *0.6M NW of Ardnoe Point*	56°06.00'N	05°35.40'W
368 .. Sound of Jura - *2.0M SSW Reisa an t-Sruith I. Lt*	56°06.00'N	05°39.90'W
369 .. Sound of Luing - *0.5M WSW of Ardluing SHM By*	56°11.00'N	05°39.40'W
370 .. Sound of Insh - *1M SSW of Insh Island*	56°17.60'N	05°41.00'W
371 .. Kerrera Sound - *0.7M SSW of Rubha Seanach*	56°21.70'N	05°33.90'W
372 ... Oban-*0.5M WNW of Maiden Isle*	56°26.00'N	05°30.30'W
373 .. Between Lady's Rock and Eilean Musdile	56°27.20'N	05°36.70'W
374 .. Sound of Mull - *1.6M SE of Ardtornish Point*	56°30.15'N	05°42.75'W
375 .. Loch Aline - *0.7M S by W of ent*	56°31.30'N	05°46.80'W
376 .. Sound of Mu -*1.8M N of Salen*	56°33.00'N	05°56.30'W
377 .. Tobermory-*0.9M NE of hbr ent*	56°38.40'N	06°02.40'W
378 .. Ardmore Pt (Mull) - *0.7M N of*	56°40.00'N	06°07.60'W
379 .. Pt of Ardnamurchan - *2.8M S*	56°40.90'N	06°13.30'W
380 .. Pt of Ardnamurchan - *1.3M W*	56°43.60'N	06°15.90'W
381 .. Mallaig-*1.5M WNW of hbr ent*	57°01.00'N	05°52.10'W

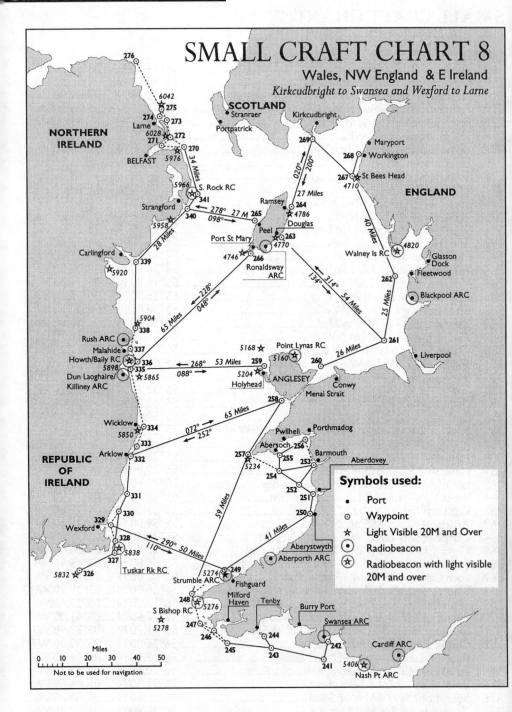

SMALL CRAFT CHART 8
Wales, NW England & E Ireland
Kirkcudbright to Swansea and Wexford to Larne

SMALL CRAFT CHART 8

WAYPOINTS

NW England, Wales & E Ireland - *Kirkcudbright to Swansea*

241 .. Ledge S Cd By - 2M S	51°28.00'N	03°58.60'W
242 .. Swansea - 1M SE Mumbles Hd	51°33.40'N	03°57.00'W
243 .. Caldey Island - 7M SE	51°32.20'N	04°35.20'W
244 .. Tenby - 1M SE Caldey Is	51°37.20'N	04°39.60'W
245 .. Crow Rock -1.3M S of	51°35.40'N	05°03.50'W
246 .. Milford Haven - 1.1M S St Ann's Hd	51°39.70'N	05°10.60'W
247 .. Skokholm Island light - 1.6M W of	51°41.60'N	05°19.70'W
248 .. South Bishop Is Lt - 3.0M NW of	51°53.30'N	05°27.80'W
249 .. Fishguard - 1.5M N Strumble Hd	52°03.40'N	05°04.20'W
250 .. Aberystwyth - 1.5M W	52°24.40'N	04°08.00'W
251 .. Aberdovey - 1.5M W of harbour bar	52°31.70'N	04°07.10'W
252 .. Sarn-y-Bwch W Cd By - 1.1M W	52°34.80'N	04°15.10'W
253 .. Barmouth - 1.2M W of harbour bar	52°42.60'N	04°05.60'W
254 .. Causeway W Cd By - 2M SW	52°39.90'N	04°28.00'W
255 .. Abersoch - 1.2M SE St Tudwal's Is Lt	52°47.20'N	04°26.80'W
256 .. Porthmadog - 1.1M SW Frwy By	52°52.70'N	04°12.50'W
257 .. Bardsey Island light - 4M NNW	52°48.60'N	04°50.30'W
258 .. Menai Strait - 1.4M SW Llanddwyn Is	53°07.30'N	04°26.80'W
259 .. Holyhead - 1M N of W Breakwater	53°21.00'N	04°37.00'W
260 .. Menai Strait- 1.2M N of Puffin Is	53°20.50'N	04°01.50'W
261 .. Liverpool - 0.7M S of Bar Lt Vsl	53°31.30'N	03°20.90'W
262 .. Fleetwood - 2M SW Lune Dp By	53°54.10'N	03°13.00'W
263 .. Douglas - 1.1M W of Douglas Hd Lt	54°08.70'N	04°26.00'W
264 .. Ramsey - 1.3M ENE of S breakwater	54°19.90'N	04°20.20'W
265 .. Peel - 1M NW entrance	54°14.50'N	04°42.50'W
266 .. Pt St Mary - 1.2M S of Kallow Pt	54°02.90'N	04°43.80'W
267 .. St Bees Head Lt - 2M W of	54°30.80'N	03°41.50'W
268 .. Workington - 1M WNW of brkwtr	54°39.40'N	03°36.30'W
269 .. Kirkcudbright - 1.5M S Little Ross Lt	54°44.50'N	04°05.00'W
270 .. Mew Island lighthouse - 1.3M ENE	54°42.30'N	05°29.90'W
271 .. Belfast - 0.7M ENE No.1 Std By	54°42.00'N	05°45.20'W
272 .. Black Head lighthouse - 1.3M ENE	54°46.50'N	05°39.20'W
273 .. Isle of Muck - 1.1M NE	54°51.70'N	05°41.85'W
274 .. Larne Lough - 1M N of Barr's pt	54°52.50'N	05°46.80'W
275 .. East Maiden Lighthouse -1.7M SW	54°54.50'N	05°45.50'W
276 .. Torr Head - 0.6M ENE of	55°12.20'N	06°02.80'W
326 .. Coningbeg Lt - 0.4M N of	52°02.80'N	06°39.30'W
327 .. Carnsore Point - 3.2M ESE of	52°09.40'N	06°16.40'W
328 .. Greenore Point - 1.8M E of	52°14.70'N	06°15.90'W
329 .. Wexford - 1.6M E of entrance	52°20.50'N	06°19.30'W
330 .. W Blackwater Pt Mk - 0.4M W of	52°25.80'N	06°14.00'W
331 .. Cahore Point - 1.7M SE of	52°32.50'N	06°09.90'W
332 .. Arklow - 1.2M E by S	52°47.40'N	06°06.40'W
333 .. Mizen Head (E coast) - 1M ESE	52°51.00'N	06°01.90'W
334 .. Wicklow - 2.6M E of	52°58.90'N	05°57.80'W
335 .. Dun Laoghaire - 2.2M NE of	53°19.60'N	06°04.60'W
336 .. Ben of Howth - 1.4M E of	53°22.40'N	06°00.50'W
337 .. Malahide - 1.5M E of Bar	53°27.00'N	06°04.80'W
338 .. Rockabill light - 1.2M WSW	53°35.30'N	06°02.00'W
339 .. Carlingford Lough	53°58.40'N	06°00.00'W
340 .. Strangford Lough	54°18.40'N	05°27.70'W
341 .. South Rock lightship - 1.1M E of	54°24.30'N	05°20.00'W

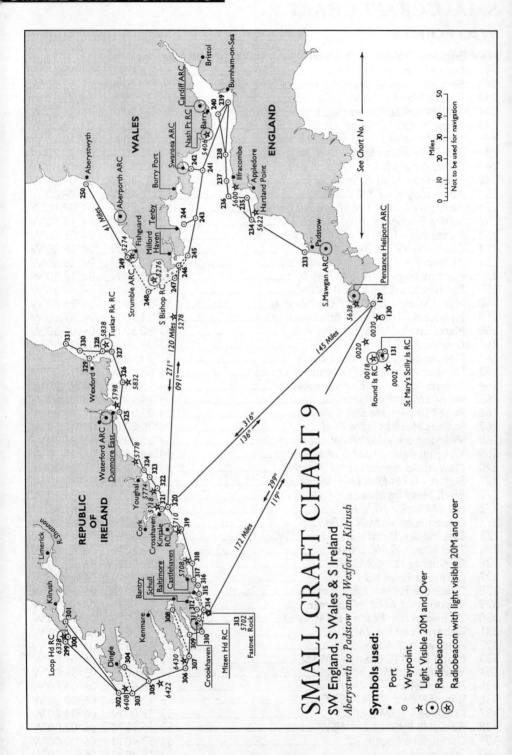

SMALL CRAFT CHART 9

SW England, S Wales & S Ireland
Aberystwth to Padstow and Wexford to Kilrush

Symbols used:

- ⊙ Port
- ∘ Waypoint
- ☆ Light Visible 20M and Over
- ⊙ Radiobeacon
- ⊛ Radiobeacon with light visible 20M and over

SMALL CRAFT CHART 9

WAYPOINTS

SW England, S Wales and S Ireland - *Aberystwyth to Padstow*

129 ..	Runnel Stone Lt By - 0.3M S of	50°00.85'N	05°40.30'W
130 ..	Wolf Rk - 2M S of	49°54.65'N	05°48.50'W
131 ..	St Mary.s, Scilly - 2M E of St Mary.s	49°54.00'N	06°15.00'W
233 ..	Padstow - 2M NW of Stepper Point	50°35.70'N	04°59.10'W
234 ..	Hartland Point - 2.5M NW of	51°02.80'N	04°34.40'W
235 ..	River Taw - 1.6M NW Bideford By	51°06.20'N	04°18.20'W
236 ..	Morte Point - 2.5M NNW of	51°13.60'N	04°15.80'W
237 ..	Ilfracombe - 1.5M N	51°14.20'N	04°06.80'W
238 ..	Foreland Point - 1.5 miles N	51°16.20'N	03°47.20'W
239 ..	Burnham on Sea - 2.6M N	51°15.30'N	03°07.80'W
240 ..	Barry & R.Severn - 2.9M SSW ent	51°21.00'N	03°17.30'W
241 ..	Ledge South Cd By - 2M S of	51°28.00'N	03°58.60'W
242 ..	Swansea - 1M SE Mumbles Hd	51°33.40'N	03°57.00'W
243 ..	Caldey Island - 7 miles SE	51°32.20'N	04°35.20'W
244 ..	Tenby - 1M SE Caldey Island	51°37.20'N	04°39.60'W
245 ..	Crow Rock -1.3M S of	51°35.40'N	05°03.50'W
246 ..	Milford Haven - 1.1M S St Ann's Hd	51°39.70'N	05°10.60'W
247 ..	Skokholm Island light - 1.6M W of	51°41.60'N	05°19.70'W
248 ..	South Bishop Is Lt - 3.0M NW	51°53.30'N	05°27.80'W
249 ..	Fishguard - 1.5M N Strumble Hd	52°03.40'N	05°04.20'W
250 ..	Aberystwyth - 1.5M W of ent	52°24.40'N	04°08.00'W
299 ..	Loop Head light - 1.6M W of	52°33.70'N	09°58.60'W
300 ..	Loop Head light - 1.4 miles S of	52°32.30'N	09°55.80'W
301 ..	Kilrush - 0.9M S of Kilcredaun Lt	52°33.90'N	09°42.50'W
302 ..	Tearaght Island light - 2.5M NW	52°06.20'N	10°42.50'W
303 ..	Great Foze Rock - 1.8M SW	52°00.00'N	10°43.20'W
304 ..	Dingle - 1.2M S of Reenbeg Point	52°05.60'N	10°15.80'W
305 ..	Bray Head - 1.4M W of	51°52.80'N	10°28.00'W
306 ..	The Bull Island light - 1.7M SW	51°34.30'N	10°20.10'W
307 ..	Crow Head - 1.9MS of	51°32.90'N	10°09.40'W
308 ..	Bantry - 0.8M SW Whiddy Island	51°40.00'N	09°32.80'W
309 ..	Sheep's Head light - 1.5M W of	51°32.30'N	09°53.40'W
310 ..	Mizen Head Lt (SW) - 2M SSW	51°25.00'N	09°50.30'W
311 ..	Crookhaven - 1M ESE Streek Hd	51°27.80'N	09°40.30'W
312 ..	Schull - 1M S of Long Island Lt	51°29.20'N	09°32.00'W
313 ..	The Fastnet Rock	51°23.33'N	09°36.16'W
314 ..	Cape Clear - 1.6M SW of	51°24.20'N	09°32.90'W
315 ..	Baltimore - 1.5M Sharbour ent	51°26.90'N	09°23.50'W
316 ..	Toe Head - 1.5M S of	51°27.40'N	09°13.00'W
317 ..	Castle Haven - 1M SE of ent	51°30.30'N	09°09.80'W
318 ..	Galley Head - 1.4M S of	51°30.40'N	08°57.20'W
319 ..	Old Hd of Kinsale Lt - 1.5M SSE	51°34.90'N	08°30.80'W
320 ..	Cork Landfall By - 0.4M E of	51°43.00'N	08°14.80'W
321 ..	Roche's Point Lt - 1.2M S of	51°46.40'N	08°15.40'W
322 ..	Ballycotton Island Lt - 1.2M S	51°48.40'N	07°58.80'W
323 ..	Youghal, S - 1M SE Capel Island	51°52.40'N	07°50.00'W
324 ..	Youghal, SE - 2M SE Blackball PHB	51°54.80'N	07°45.60'W
325 ..	Waterford - 1.4M SSE Dunmore E	52°07.40'N	06°58.80'W
326 ..	Coningbeg lightship - 0.4M N of	52°02.80'N	06°39.30'W
327 ..	Carnsore Point - 3.2M ESE of	52°09.40'N	06°16.40'W
328 ..	Greenore Point - 1.8M E of	52°14.70'N	06°15.90'W
329 ..	Wexford - 1.6M E of entrance	52°20.50'N	06°19.30'W
330 ..	W Blackwater Pt Mk - 0.4M W	52°25.80'N	06°14.00'W
331 ..	Cahore Point - 1.7 miles SE of	52°32.50'N	06°09.90'W

SMALL CRAFT CHART 10
Ireland
All Coast

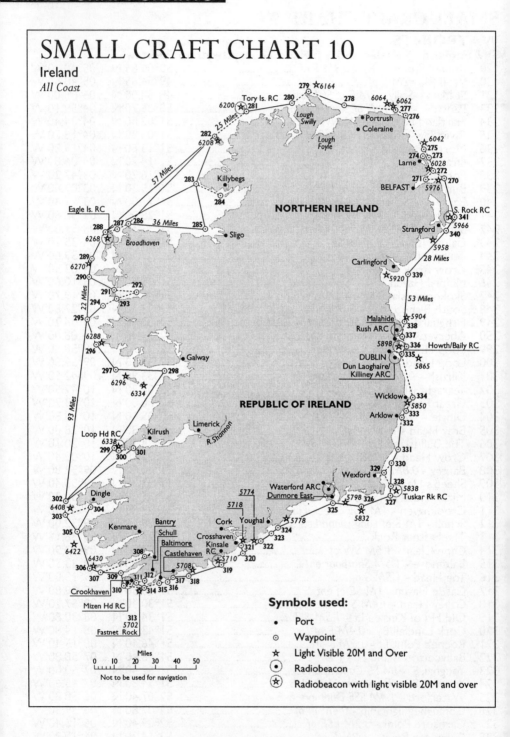

Tory Is. RC 280   279 ☆6164   278   6064   6062
6200◉☆281   ☆277
Lough   ◉276
Swilly   Portrush
282   25 Miles   Coleraine
6208◉☆   Lough   6042
Foyle   ◉☆275
274◉◉273
Larne ●   6028
☆◉272
BELFAST ●   271◉◉☆270
5976

283◉   Killybegs
Eagle Is. RC
284◉   NORTHERN IRELAND   S. Rock RC
288   287◉◉286 36 Miles 285◉   ☆◉341
6268◉☆   Strangford   5966
Broadhaven   ● Sligo   ◉340

289◉   57 Miles   5958
6270◉   Carlingford   28 Miles
290◉   292◉   ●
291◉◉◉294 293◉   ☆5920 ◉339
295◉   53 Miles

6288◉☆   ◉☆5904
296◉   Malahide   ◉338
297◉   ● Galway   Rush ARC(◉)337
6296◉☆ 298◉   5898◉☆◉336 Howth/Baily RC
6334☆   DUBLIN(◉)◉335☆
Dun Laoghaire/   5865
Killiney ARC

REPUBLIC OF IRELAND   Wicklow◉◉334
◉5850
Limerick   Arklow ●◉333
Loop Hd RC   Kilrush   R.Shannon   ◉332
6338◉☆
299◉◉300 301◉   ◉331
◉330
329◉◉ Wexford ●
302◉   Dingle   328
6408◉☆   5774   ◉☆5838
303◉◉304   Waterford ARC 5718   327◉ Tuskar Rk RC
305◉   Kenmare   Dunmore East   5798◉326
☆   Bantry   Cork Youghal ● 325◉ 5832
6422◉   Schull   Crosshaven   ☆5778
6430◉☆ 308◉ Baltimore Kinsale 324◉
306◉☆   Castlehaven RC● 323◉
307◉309◉311◉312 5708◉ 321◉◉322
Crookhaven 310◉ 314◉315 316 317◉318 320◉
Mizen Hd RC   5710◉ 319◉

313
5702
Fastnet Rock

Symbols used:
- ● Port
- ◉ Waypoint
- ☆ Light Visible 20M and Over
- (◉) Radiobeacon
- (☆) Radiobeacon with light visible 20M and over

Miles
0 10 20 30 40 50
Not to be used for navigation

SMALL CRAFT CHART 10

WAYPOINTS
Ireland - *whole*

270 Mew Is Lt-*1.3M ENE* .... 54°42.30'N . 05°29.90'W
271 Belfast -
0.7M ENE No.1 By......... 54°42.00'N . 05°45.20'W
272 Black Hd Lt -*1.3M ENE* 54°46.50'N . 05°39.20'W
273 Isle of Muck-*1.1M NE* .. 54°51.70'N . 05°41.85'W
274 Larne Lough -
1M N of Barr's pt............ 54°52.50'N . 05°46.80'W
275 E Maiden Lt -*1.7M SW* 54°54.50'N . 05°45.50'W
276 Torr Head-
0.6M ENE of.................... 55°12.20'N . 06°02.80'W
277 Fair Head-*0.9M N of*..... 55°14.60'N . 06°09.00'W
278 L. Foyle
4.8M NNE Inishowen Lt 55°17.90'N . 06°52.20'W
279 Malin Head - 2M NNE . 55°25.00'N . 07°21.20'W
280 Lough Swilly-*1M N ent.* 55°18.20'N . 07°34.30'W
281 Tory Island-*1.2M SE of.* 55°14.00'N . 08°11.00'W
282 Rinrawros Pt Lt, Aran-
1.3M NW .... 55°01.75'N . 08°35.40'W
283 Rathlin O'Birne Is Lt
1.9M WSW .... 54°39.20'N . 08°52.90'W
284 Killibegs -
2.4MWNW S.John's Pt Lt 54°34.70'N . 08°31.80'W
285 Sligo-
2.7M N Aughris Hd .... 54°19.50'N . 08°45.30'W
286 The Stags rocks-
1.3M N .... 54°23.40'N . 09°47.40'W
287 Broadhaven-*1M N of bay* .... 54°20.40'N
09°56.00'W
288 Eagle Island-*1.4M NW of* .... 54°17.80'N
10°07.40'W
289 Black Rock -
2.7M NE by N of .... 54°06.20'N . 10°16.60'W
290 Achill Head - 1.4M SW53°57.30'N . 10°17.90'W
291 Clew Bay -
1M SW Achillbeg Is Lt.... 53°50.80'N . 09°57.90'W
292 Westport -
1.5M WSW Inishgort Lt. 53°49.00'N . 09°42.60'W
293 Clew Bay -
1.5M NW Roonah Hd... 53°46.90'N . 09°57.80'W
294 Inishturk Is- 1.2M NW . 53°43.60'N . 10°08.80'W
295 Inishshark Is - 1.8M W 53°36.50'N . 10°21.00'W
296 Slyne Hd It - 1.6M SW . 53°22.90'N . 10°16.00'W
297 Rock Is Lt -
5.3M NW by W of .... 53°11.80'N . 09°58.60'W
298 Galway -
2.3M N Black Hd Lt....... 53°11.50'N . 09°15.80'W
299 Loop Hd It -*1.6M W of* 52°33.70'N . 09°58.60'W
300 Loop Hd It - 1.4M S of. 52°32.30'N . 09°55.80'W
301 Kilrush -
0.9M S Kilcredaun Hd Lt52°33.90'N . 09°42.50'W
302 Tearaght Is Lt-
2.5M NW .... 52°06.20'N . 10°42.50'W
303 Gt Foze Rock-
1.8M SW .... 52°00.00'N . 10°43.20'W
304 Dingle -
1.2M S of Reenbeg Pt .... 52°05.60'N . 10°15.80'W

305 Bray Head - 1.4MW of 51°52.80'N . 10°28.00'W
306 The Bull Is It-*1.7M SW* 51°34.30'N . 10°20.10'W
307 Crow Head -*1.9M S of* 51°32.90'N . 10°09.40'W
308 Bantry -
0.8M SW Whiddy Is .... 51°40.00'N . 09°32.80'W
309 Sheep's Hd Lt-*1.5M W* . 51°32.30'N . 09°53.40'W
310 Mizen Head Lt (SW)-
2M SSW .... 51°25.00'N . 09°50.30'W
311 Crookhaven -
1M ESE Streek Hd .... 51°27.80'N . 09°40.30'W
312 Schull -
1M S of Long Is Lt .... 51°29.20'N . 09°32.00'W
313 The Fastnet Rock .... 51°23.33'N . 09°36.16'W
314 Cape Clear-1.6M SW ... 51°24.20'N 09°32.90'W
315 Baltimore - 1.5M S .... 51°26.90'N . 09°23.50'W
316 Toe Head - 1.5M S of.. 51°27.40'N . 09°13.00'W
317 Castle Haven - 1M SE.. 51°30.30'N . 09°09.80'W
318 Galley Hd-1.4M S of ... 51°30.40'N . 08°57.20'W
319 Old Hd of Kinsale Lt -
1.5M SSE .... 51°34.90'N . 08°30.80'W
320 Cork Landfall By -
0.4M E of .... 51°43.00'N . 08°14.80'W
321 Roche's Point Lt -
1.2M S of .... 51°46.40'N . 08°15.40'W
322 Ballycotton Island Lt -
1.2M S .... 51°48.40'N . 07°58.80'W
323 Youghal,
1M SE Capel Island .... 51°52.40'N . 07°50.00'W
324 Youghal, SE -
2M SE Blackball PHB..... 51°54.80'N . 07°45.60'W
325 Waterford -
1.4M SSE Dunmore E ... 52°07.40'N . 06°58.80'W
326 Coningbeg lightship -
0.4M N .... 52°02.80'N . 06°39.30'W
327 Carnsore Point -
3.2M ESE .... 52°09.40'N . 06°16.40'W
328 Greenore Point -
1.8M E of .... 52°14.70'N . 06°15.90'W
329 Wexford - 1.6M E .... 52°20.50'N . 06°19.30'W
330 W Blackwater Pt Mk -
0.4M W .... 52°25.80'N . 06°14.00'W
331 Cahore Point -
1.7 miles SE of .... 52°32.50'N . 06°09.90'W
332 Arklow - 1.2M E by S ... 52°47.40'N . 06°06.40'W
333 Mizen Head (E coast) -
1M ESE .... 52°51.00'N . 06°01.90'W
334 Wicklow - 2.6M E .... 52°58.90'N . 05°57.80'W
335 Dun Laoghaire -
2.2M NE .... 53°19.60'N . 06°04.60'W
336 Ben of Howth -
1.4M E of .... 53°22.40'N . 06°00.50'W
337 Malahide -
1.5M E of Bar .... 53°27.00'N . 06°04.80'W
338 Rockabill light -
1.2M WSW .... 53°35.30'N . 06°02.00'W
339 Carlingford Lough .... 53°58.40'N . 06°00.00'W
340 Strangford Lough .... 54°18.40'N . 05°27.70'W
341 South Rock lightship -
1.1M E .... 54°24.30'N . 05°20.00'W

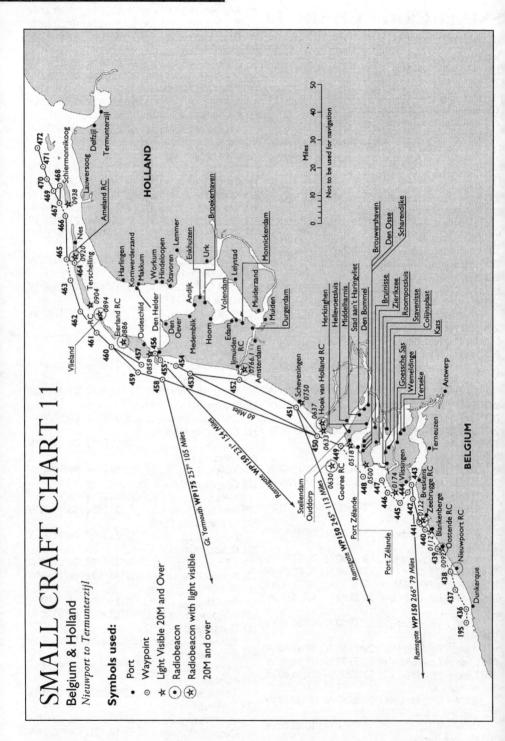

SMALL CRAFT CHART 11

Belgium & Holland
Nieuwport to Termunterzijl

Symbols used:

- Port
- ⊙ Waypoint
- ✶ Light Visible 20M and Over
- ⊙̞ Radiobeacon
- ✪ Radiobeacon with light visible 20M and over

SMALL CRAFT CHART 11
WAYPOINTS

Belgium & Holland - *Nieuwport to Termunterzijl*

150 .. Ramsgate - *1M E of*	51°19.47'N	01°27.13'E
175 .. Gt Yarmouth - *4.7M E*	52°34.33'N	01°52.10'E
195 .. Dunkerque *-2M NW of*	51°05.00'N	02°18.40'E
436 .. Dunkerque - *1.7M NE by E*	51°04.50'N	02°23.50'E
437 .. Trapegeer Stbd By - *0.6M N*	51°09.10'N	02°34.50'E
438 .. Nieuwpoort - *0.9M NW by W*	51°09.80'N	02°41.80'E
439 .. Oostende - *0.5M NW*	51°14.70'N	02°54.50'E
440 .. Blankenberge - *0.8M NW*	51°19.60'N	03°05.60'E
441 .. Zeebrugge - *0.6M NW*	51°22.30'N	03°10.80'E
442 .. Ft Maisonnueve W Cd *-0.3M NE*	51°24.50'N	03°21.60'E
443 .. Vlissingen *-1.4M NE Niewe Sluis Lt*	51°25.50'N	03°32.80'E
444 .. Trawl S cardinal marker - *0.4M N*	51°26.70'N	03°28.30'E
445 .. West Kapelle Lt - *4M W by S*	51°31.30'N	03°20.50'E
446 .. Domburg - *2M NW*	51°35.60'N	03°28.00'E
447 .. Roompotsluis - *S chnl 5M off*	51°36.20'N	03°33.20'E
448 .. Geul Van de Banjaard - *N ent*	51°44.00'N	03°33.00'E
449 .. Haringvlietsluizen - *to S Channel*	51°51.60'N	03°53.20'E
450 .. Hoek van Holland - *1.2M WNW*	52°00.10'N	04°00.30'E
451 .. Scheveningen - *0.7M NW*	52°07.00'N	04°14.80'E
452 .. IJmuiden - *0.7M W by N ent*	52°28.10'N	04°31.10'E
453 .. Petten W Cd Mk - *0.4M W*	52°47.50'N	04°36.20'E
454 .. Grote Kaap Lt - *0.9M W*	52°52.90'N	04°41.40'E
455 .. Den Helder - *1.2M SW Kijkduin Lt*	52°56.90'N	04°41.90'E
456 .. Den Helder - *1.1M N*	52°58.40'N	04°44.10'E
457 .. Molengat Channel - *N entrance*	53°03.00'N	04°41.00'E
458 .. Noorderhaaks I. - *3.2M WSW*	52°57.30'N	04°33.70'E
459 .. Texel - *0.3M W Molengat N Cd*	53°03.70'N	04°39.00'E
460 .. Vlieland - *2.8M W of SW end of Is*	53°13.50'N	04°46.60'E
461 .. Vlieland - *W ent to Stortemelk chnl*	53°19.10'N	04°55.20'E
462 .. Terschelling - *0.4M NW Otto E Cd*	53°25.00'N	05°06.10'E
463 .. Terschelling - *W ent*	53°27.80'N	05°24.00'E
464 .. Borndiep Channel - *1.4M WNW*	53°27.60'N	05°35.60'E
465 .. Ameland Lt - *2.5M N*	53°29.50'N	05°37.40'E
466 .. Ameland - *2.9M NNE of E end*	53°30.40'N	06°00.00'E
467 .. Schiermonnikoog - *N ent*	53°32.60'N	06°06.00'E
468 .. Schiermonnikoog - *W ent*	53°33.20'N	06°17.00'E
469 .. Verkenningston Hubertgat By	53°34.70'N	06°14.40'E
470 .. W'ereems Verkenningston By	53°36.80'N	06°19.80'E
471 .. Riffgat landfall buoy - *0.2M SE*	53°38.80'N	06°27.40'E
472 .. Osterems landfall By - *0.2M S*	53°41.70'N	06°36.20'E

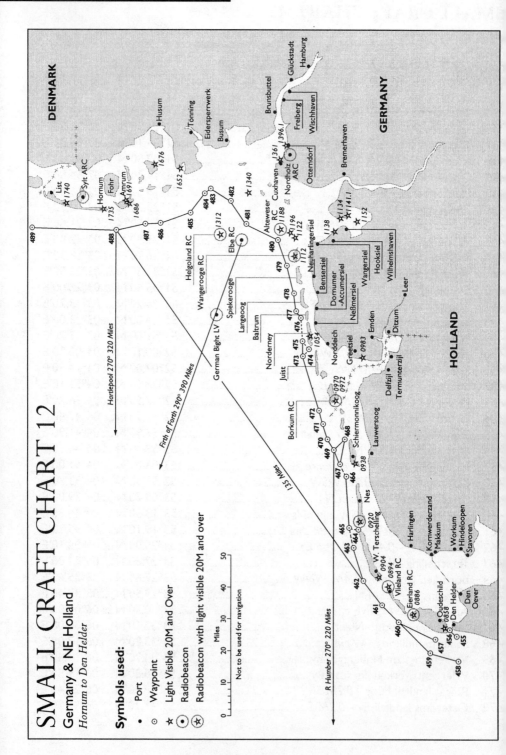

SMALL CRAFT CHART 12

Germany & NE Holland

Hornum to Den Helder

Symbols used:

- • Port
- ⊙ Waypoint
- ☆ Light Visible 20M and Over
- ⊙ Radiobeacon
- ⊛ Radiobeacon with light visible 20M and over

Miles

0 10 20 30 40 50

Not to be used for navigation

SMALL CRAFT CHART 12
WAYPOINTS

Germany & N Holland - *Hornum to Den Helder*

455 .. Den Helder - *1.2M SW Kijkduin Lt*	52°56.90'N	04°41.90'E
456 .. Den Helder - *1.1M N by E Kijkduin Lt*	52°58.40'N	04°44.10'E
457 .. Molengat Channel - *N ent*	53°03.00'N	04°41.00'E
458 .. Noorderhaaks *I.-3.2M WSW*	52°57.30'N	04°33.70'E
459 .. Texel-*0.3M W Molengat NCM*	53°03.70'N	04°39.00'E
460 .. Vlieland-*2.8M W of SW end of I.*	53°13.50'N	04°46.60'E
461 .. Vlieland-*W ent to Stortemelk ch*	53°19.10'N	04°55.20'E
462 .. Terschelling - *0.4M NW Otto ECM*	53°25.00'N	05°06.10'E
463 .. Terschelling - *W ent to Westgat buoyed ch*	53°27.80'N	05°24.00'E
464 .. Borndiep Channel - *1.4M WNW Ameland Lt*	53°27.60'N	05°35.60'E
465 .. Ameland Lt - *2.5M N*	53°29.50'N	05°37.40'E
466 .. Ameland-*2.9M NNE of E end*	53°30.40'N	06°00.00'E
467 .. Schiermonnikoog - *N ent Westgat buoyed ch*	53°32.60'N	06°06.00'E
468 .. Schiermonnikoog - *W ent Lauwers buoyed ch*	53°33.20'N	06°17.00'E
469 .. Verkenningston Hubertgat SWM- *0.2M S*	53°34.70'N	06°14.40'E
470 .. Westereems Verkenningston SWM-*0.2M SE*	53°36.80'N	06°19.80'E
471 .. Riffgat SWM - *0.2M SE*	53°38.80'N	06°27.40'E
472 .. Osterems SWM - *0.2M S*	53°41.70'N	06°36.20'E
473 .. Schluchter SWM - *0.2M S*	53°44.60'N	07°04.20'E

SMALL CRAFT CHART 13
Denmark
Skagen to Hornum

Miles
0 5 10 15 20 25

Not to be used for navigation

Symbols used:

- • Port
- ⊙ Waypoint
- ☆ Light Visible 20M and Over
- ⊙ Radiobeacon
- ⊛ Radiobeacon with light visible 20M and over

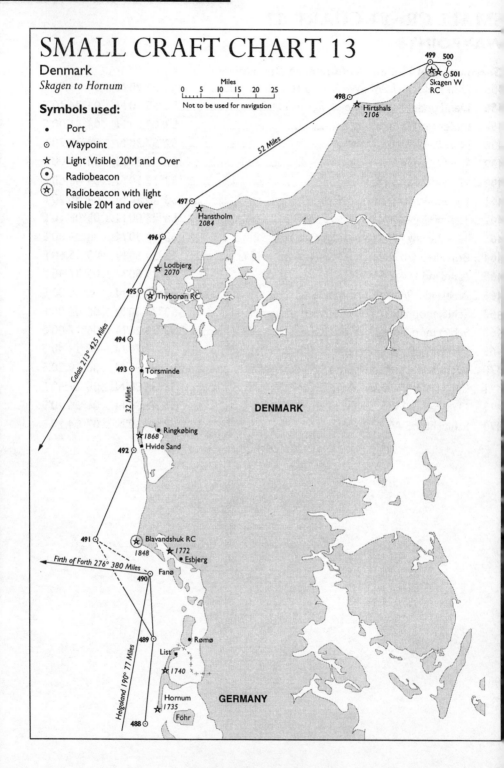

499 500
501
Skagen W
RC

498

Hirtshals
2106

52 Miles

497
Hanstholm
2084

496

Lodbjerg
2070

495 Thyborøn RC

Calais 213° 425 Miles

494

32 Miles

493 • Torsminde

DENMARK

• Ringkøbing
☆1868
492 • Hvide Sand

491 Blavandshuk RC
1848 ☆1772
• Esbjerg
Firth of Forth 276° 380 Miles Fanø
490

489 • Rømø
List
☆1740

Helgoland 190° 77 Miles

Hornum
☆1735
Föhr

GERMANY

488

SMALL CRAFT CHART 13
WAYPOINTS

Denmark & NW Germany - *Skagen to Hornum*

488 .. Hornum - *1.2M W of Holtknobsloch landfall buoy* .... 54°41.10'N .... 08°08.40'E

489 .. Rømø - *0.4M W of Lister Tief landfall buoy* .... 55°05.40'N .... 08°16.40'E

490 .. Esbjerg - *0.5M SW of Grådyb landfall buoy* .... 55°24.30'N .... 08°11.00'E

491 .. Slugen chan N - *9.6M W by N Blavands Huk lt.* .... 55°35.40'N .... 07°48.40'E

492 .. Hvide Sande - *2.7M W of harbour entrance* .... 56°00.00'N .... 08°02.50'E

493 .. Torsminde - *2.7 M W of harbour entrance* .... 56°22.50'N .... 08°02.30'E

494 .. Bovbjerg lt - *2.6M W* .... 56°30.80'N .... 08°03.00'E

495 .. Thyborøn - *0.7M W landfall buoy* .... 56°42.50'N .... 08°07.40'E

496 .. Nørre Vorupør Lt - *3.2M W* .... 56°57.20'N .... 08°16.40'E

497 .. Hanstholm - *1.0M NW landfall buoy* .... 57°08.80'N .... 08°33.70'E

498 .. Hirtshals - *2.3M N by W harbour entrance* .... 57°38.00'N .... 09°56.50'E

499 .. Skagen W Lt - *2.2M N* .... 57°47.10'N .... 10°35.70'E

500 .. Skagen *landfall buoy No.1 - 0.7M S* .... 57°46.40'N .... 10°46.00'E

501 .. Skagen - *3.3M E Skagen Lt* .... 57°44.00'N .... 10°43.50'E

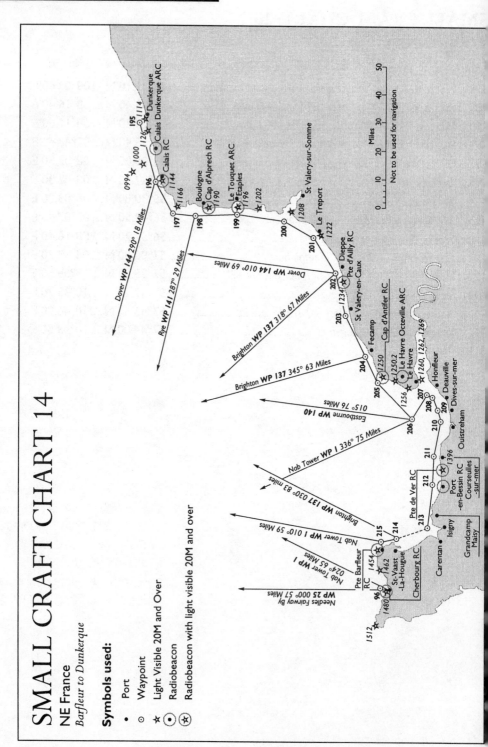

SMALL CRAFT CHART 14

NE France
Barfleur to Dunkerque

Symbols used:

- • Port
- ⊙ Waypoint
- ☆ Light Visible 20M and Over
- ⊙ Radiobeacon
- ⊗ Radiobeacon with light visible 20M and over

Miles

0 10 20 30 40 50

Not to be used for navigation

Calais Dunkerque ARC
Dunkerque 1114
195
1126
1000
0994
Calais RC
196 1144
1166
197
Boulogne
198 Cap d'Alprech RC 190
Le Touquet ARC
199 Etaples 196
1202
200
St Valery-sur-Somme
1208
Le Treport
201 1222
Dieppe
Pte d'Ailly RC
202
1234
St Valery-en-Caux
203
Cap d'Antifer RC
Fecamp
204 1250
1250.2 Le Havre Octeville ARC
205 Le Havre
1256 1260, 1262, 1269
206 207 Honfleur
208 Deauville
209 Dives-sur-mer
210
211 Ouistreham
212 Port 1396
Pte de Ver RC -en-Bessin RC
213 Courseulles
215 214 -sur-mer
Carentan Isigny Grandcamp Maisy
Pte Barfleur 1454
RC 1462
96 St-Vaast
1480 -La-Hougue
1512 Cherbourg RC

Dover WP 144 290° 18 Miles
Rye WP 141 287° 29 Miles
Dover WP 144 010° 69 Miles
Brighton WP 137 318° 67 Miles
Brighton WP 137 345° 63 Miles
Eastbourne WP 140 015° 76 Miles
Nab Tower WP 1 336° 75 Miles
Brighton WP 137 030° 83 miles
Nab Tower WP 1 010° 59 Miles
Nab Tower WP 1 024° 65 Miles
Needles Fairway by WP 25 000° 57 Miles

SMALL CRAFT CHART 14
WAYPOINTS

France North - *Barfleur to Dunkerque*

1	Nab Tower- *0.5M NW*	50°40.38'N	00°57.55'W
25	Fairway Buoy- *Needles channel*	50°38.20'N	01°38.90'W
96	Cherbourg - *0.5M N of W ent*	49°40.95'N	01°39.35'W
137 ..	Brighton entrance- *1M S of*	50°47.50'N	00°06.30'W
140 ..	Eastbourne- *1.2M SE Langney Pt*	50°46.25'N	00°21.10'E
141 ..	Rye-*0.1M S of Fairway By*	50°53.90'N	00°48.13'E
144 ..	Dover- *1.2M SE of W ent*	51°05.80'N	01°21.10'E
195 ..	Dunkerque -*2M NW of ent*	51°05.00'N	02°18.40'E
196 ..	Calais -*2M NW of ent*	50°59.20'N	01°47.70'E
197 ..	Cap Gris-Nez -*2M NW*	50°53.30'N	01°32.50'E
198 ..	Boulogne -*2M WNW of ent*	50°45.30'N	01°31.50'E
199 ..	Étaples -*3M W of Le Touquet pt*	50°32.20'N	01°30.80'E
200 ..	St Valéry-sur-Somme - *5M WNW*	50°15.30'N	01°27.10'E
201 ..	Le Trèport - *2M NW of ent*	50°05.40'N	01°20.40'E
202 ..	Dieppe - *1M NW of ent*	49°57.00'N	01°04.00'E
203 ..	St Valéry-en-Caux -*2M N of ent*	49°54.50'N	00°42.30'E
204 ..	Fécamp -*1M NW of ent*	49°46.70'N	00°20.80'E
205 ..	Cap D'Antifer - *1.8M NW*	49°42.40'N	00°07.80'E
206 ..	Le Havre - *0.5M NE of LHA*	49°32.00'N	00°09.20'W
207 ..	Honfleur - *7.5M W of ent*	49°27.00'N	00°02.50'E
208 ..	Deauville - *3M NNW of ent*	49°24.50'N	00°02.20'E
209 ..	Dives-sur-Mer - *3M NNW*	49°20.70'N	00°07.00'W
210 ..	Ouistreham - *3.6M NNE of ent*	49°21.00'N	00°11.40'W
211 ..	Courseulles-sur-Mer - *3M N*	49°23.40'N	00°27.00'W
212 ..	Port-en-Bessin - *3M NNW*	49°24.00'N	00°43.60'W
213 ..	Grandcamp Maisy - *4M NW*	49°26.70'N	01°06.30'W
214 ..	St-Vaast-la-Hougue - *3M ENE*	49°36.40'N	01°11.00'W
215 ..	Barfleur - *2M NE*	49°42.00'N	01°13.30'W

SMALL CRAFT CHART 15

N Central France & Channel Isles
Cherbourg to Lézardrieux

Symbols used:

- • Port
- ⊙ Waypoint
- ☆ Light Visible 20M and Over
- ⊙ Radiobeacon
- ⊛ Radiobeacon with light visible 20M and over

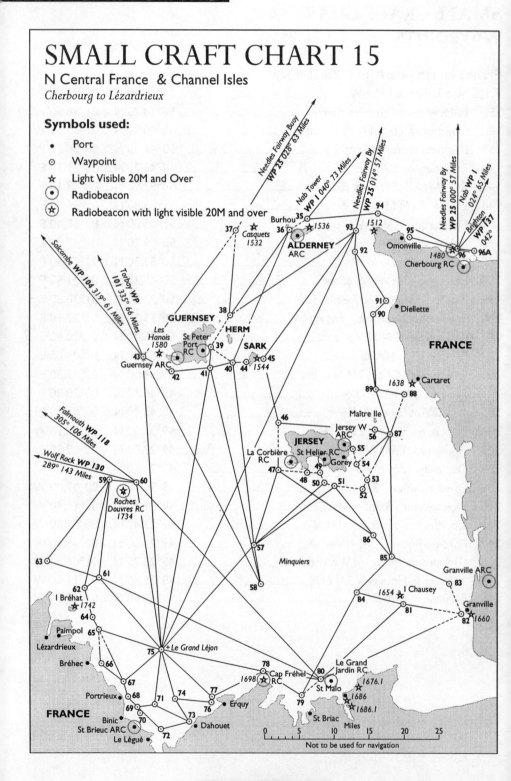

SMALL CRAFT CHART 15
WAYPOINTS

France North Central & Channel Islands - *Cherbourg to Lezardrieux*

1   Nab Tower-*0.5M NW* .... 50°40.38'N . 00°57.55'W
25 Fairway By-
    Needles channel .... 50°38.20'N . 01°38.90'W
35 Alderney, Braye-*1M NNE* 49°45.00'N . 02°10.75'W
36 The Swinge -
    turning way point .... 49°43.50'N . 02°14.40'W
37 Casquets- *1M W of* .... 49°43.38'N . 02°24.06'W
38 Guernsey NE-
    1.2m E of Beaucette .... 49°30.13'N . 02°28.30'W
39 Guernsey St Peter Port -
    0.5M E of ent .... 49°27.40'N . 02°30.70'W
40 Big Russel - *mid way S* .... 49°25.30'N . 02°26.00'W
41 Guernsey SE -
    1M SE of St Martin's Pt ..... 49°24.67'N . 02°30.50'W
42 Guernsey SW -
    1.5M S of Pleinmont Pt ...... 49°24.00'N . 02°40.00'W
43 Guernsey SW -
    1.8M W of Les Hanois .... 49°26.16'N . 02°45.00'W
44 Sark SW-*0.3M S of Brecou* 49°25.47'N . 02°23.30'W
45 Sark E-*1M E of Creux Hbr* 49°25.80'N . 02°19.00'W
46 Jersey NW -
    1.75M NW of Grosnez Pt. 49°16.60'N . 02°16.75'W
47 Jersey SW -
    1M WSW of La Corbiere ... 49°10.46'N . 02°16.32'W
48 Jersey S -
    0.15M S of Normant Pt ..... 49°09.80'N . 02°10.00'W
49 St Helier-*0.3M S of Bkwr* . 49°09.97'N . 02°07.33'W
50 St Helier -
    0.3M S of Demie de Ras ... 49°08.77'N . 02°06.06'W
51 SE Jersey -
    1st turning point going E .... 49°08.05'N . 02°03.35'W
52 SE Jersey -
    2nd turning point to Gorey 49°07.60'N . 01°57.90'W
53 SE Jersey -
    3rd turning point to Gorey. 49°08.70'N . 01°57.20'W
54 Gorey Ent -*298°, 1.6M*.... 49°11.10'N . 01°59.12'W
55 St Catherine - *0.5M SE* ... 49°13.10'N . 02°00.00'W
56 Les Ècrehou -
    1.4M S of Maitre Ile Bn ..... 49°15.70'N . 01°55.50'W
57 NW Minquiers N Cd By -
    0.1M W .... 48°59.70'N . 02°20.65'W
58 SW Minquiers W Cd By -
    0.1M SW .... 48°54.34'N . 02°19.42'W
59 Les Roches Douvres Lt.-
    3M NW of .... 49°08.60'N . 02°52.10'W
60 Les Roches Douvres Lt-
    2.5M NE .... 49°08.10'N . 02°46.20'W
61 Lezardrieux -
    1.5M N La Horaire Bn ...... 48°55.07'N . 02°55.16'W
62 Lezardrieux Approach -
    1.7M NNE .... 48°53.60'N . 02°58.18'W
63 Les Héaux de Brehat -
    3M N of .... 48°57.60'N . 03°05.10'W

64 Ile de Brehat -
    2.5M E by S of .... 48°49.70'N . 02°56.00'W
65 Paimpol-
    1M E Les Charpentiers Bn 48°47.90'N . 02°54.40'W
66 Bréhec -
    0.8M E of Le Taureau Mk .. 48°43.60'N . 02°54.00'W
67 Ile Harbour Lt - *1M NW* 48°40.75'N . 02°49.60'W
68 St Quay Portrieux-*0.2M E*48°38.90'N . 02°48.55'W
69 La Roselière W Cd By-
    0.3M S .... 48°37.25'N . 02°46.40'W
70 Binic-*2M 080° from Bkwtr* 48°36.50'N . 02°45.85'W
71 Caffa E Cd Buoy-*0.3M SE* 48°37.70'N . 02°42.75'W
72 Le Legué Buoy- *0.2M NW*48°34.50'N . 02°41.25'W
73 Dahouet - *1M NW of ent* 48°35.50'N . 02°35.20'W
74 Rohein W Cd Bn-*0.6M SW* 48°38.50'N . 02°38.40'W
75 Grand Léjon Lt Bn-*0.7M NW* 48°44.90'N . 02°40.80'W
76 Erquy-*1M W of* .... 48°38.10'N . 02°30.00'W
77 Cap d'Erquy-*0.M W NW of*48°38.95'N . 02°30.00'W
78 Cap Frehel Lt-*1.1M N of.* 48°42.50'N . 02°19.07'W
79 St Briac-*2M off on approach* 48°38.40'N . 02°10.90'W
80 St Malo -
    1.3M NW Le Grande Jardin Bn 48°41.10'N . 02°06.40'W
81 Iles Chausey -*1M S of ent* 48°51.10'N . 01°49.00'W
82 Granville -
    0.7M SW of Granville Lt Ho. 48°49.62'N . 01°37.55'W
83 Iles Chausey -
    0.5M E of Anvers E Cd By .. 48°54.00'N . 01°40.00'W
84 SE Minquiers E Cd By -
    1M SE .... 48°53.20'N . 01°58.90'W
85 Les Ardentes E Cd By -
    0.2M E .... 48°57.90'N . 01°51.15'W
86 NE Minquiers E Cd By -
    0.1M NE .... 49°00.97'N . 01°55.11'W
87 Les Écrehou SE -
    0.4M SE of Écrevière By .... 49°15.10'N . 01°51.65'W
88 Cartaret - *1.75M SW* ...... 49°20.90'N . 01°49.20'W
89 Cartaret -
    0.3M SW Trs Grunes Cd By . 49°21.65'N . 01°55.30'W
90 Cap de Flamanville-*2M W*.. 49°31.65'N . 01°56.30'W
91 Diellette -
    1M NW of on transit .... 49°33.80'N . 01°53.00'W
92 Cap de La Hague-*4M SSW* 49°40.00'N . 02°00.00'W
93 Cap de La Hague-*2M W*.. 49°43.37'N . 02°00.00'W
94 Cap de La Hague -
    1.5M N of La Plate Lt .... 49°45.50'N . 01°55.70'W
95 Omonville -
    1M E of, in white sector ..... 49°42.55'N . 01°48.25'W
96 Cherbourg -
    0.5M N of W ent .... 49°40.95'N . 01°39.35'W
96a Cherbourg-
    0.5M N of E ent .... 49°40.87'N . 01°35.80'W
101 Tor Bay -
    1.7M NE of Berry Hd ... 50°25.10'N ... 03°27.00'W
104 Salcombe -
    1.5M S of bar .... 50°11.62'N ... 03°46.60'W
118 Falmouth -
    0.8M S of St Anthony Hd 50°07.64'N ... 05°00.90'W
130 Wolf Rk - 2 miles S of. 49°54.65'N ... 05°48.50'W

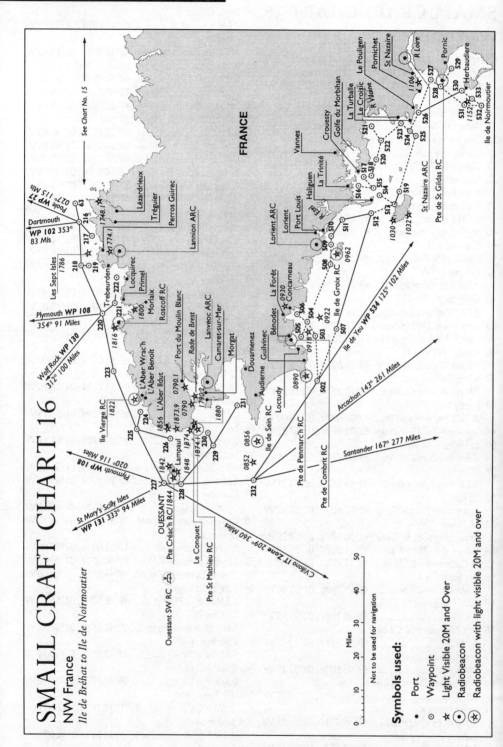

SMALL CRAFT CHART 16

NW France
Ile de Bréhat to Ile de Noirmoutier

FRANCE

See Chart No. 15

Poole WP 37 027° 115 Mls

Dartmouth
WP 102 353°
83 Mls

Plymouth WP 108
354° 91 Miles

Wolf Rock WP 130
312° 100 Miles

Plymouth WP 108
020° 116 Miles

St Mary's Scilly Isles
WP 131 333° 94 Miles

Les Sept Isles
1786

Lézardrieux
Tréguier
Perros Guirec
Lannion ARC

Trébeurden
Locquirec
Primel
Morlaix
Roscoff RC
Port du Moulin Blanc
Rade de Brest
Camaret-sur-Mer
Lanveoc ARC
Morgat

Ile Vierge RC
1822

L'Aber Wrac'h
L'Aber Benoît
L'Aber Ildut

Lampaul

OUESSANT
Pte Créac'h RC 1844

Ouessant SW RC

Le Conquet
Pte St Mathieu RC

Douarnenez
Audierne
Guilvinec
Loctudy
Ile de Sein RC

Bénodet
La Forêt
Concarneau
0930
0922
0918
0911
0890

Pte de Penmarc'h RC

Pte de Combrit RC

Vannes
Crouesty
Golfe du Morbihan
La Turballe
Le Croisic
La Trinité
Haliguen
Port Louis
Lorient
Lorient ARC
R Etel

Ile de Groix RC
0962

Ile de Yeu WP 534 125° 102 Miles

Accachon 143° 261 Miles

Santander 167° 277 Miles

Villaine IT Zone 209° 360 Miles

Le Pouliguen
Pornichet
St Nazaire
R Loire
1106
527
528
529
530
531
532
533
1152
Herbaudiere
Ile de Noirmoutier
526
525
524
523
522
521
520
519
518
517
516
515
514
513
512
511
510
509
508
507
506
505
504
503
502
0856
0852
232
231
230
229
228
227
226
225
224
223
222
221
220
219
218
217
216
63
748.1
1774.1
1816
1855
1873.9
1842
1848
1874
1880
1902
1800
0790.1
0790

R Vilaine
St Nazaire ARC
Pte de St Gildas RC
St Nazaire ARC

1030
1032

FRANCE

Symbols used:

- •   Port
- ◎   Waypoint
- ☆   Light Visible 20M and Over
- ⊙   Radiobeacon
- ⊛   Radiobeacon with light visible 20M and over

Miles

0   10   20   30   40   50

Not to be used for navigation

SMALL CRAFT CHART 16

WAYPOINTS
France North West & Biscay - *Douarnenez to Ile de Noirmoutier*

27	Poole Fairway Buoy - *1M E*	50°39.00'N	01°53.20'W
63	Les Héaux de Brehat - *3M N*	48°57.60'N	03°05.10'W
102	Dartmouth - *2M 150° from ent*	50°18.25'N	03°31.60'W
108	Plymouth - *0.9M S of W end of brkwtr*	50°19.13'N	04°09.50'W
130	Wolf Rk - *2M S of*	49°54.65'N	05°48.50'W
131	St Mary's, Scilly - *2M E of St Mary's Sound*	49°54.00'N	06°15.00'W
216	Treguier - *4.1M N of Pte de Chateau*	48°56.20'N	03°14.30'W
217	Perros Guirec - *2.3M NNW of Port Blanc*	48°52.30'N	03°20.20'W
218	Ile Bono Light - *4M NW*	48°55.50'N	03°33.90'W
219	Ploumanach - *2.7M E of Les Triagoz Light*	48°52.30'N	03°34.60'W
220	Roscoff - *6M NNE of ent*	48°49.10'N	03°54.30'W
221	Morlaix & Primel -*2.2M NW Pte de Primel*	48°45.00'N	03°51.20'W
222	Trebeurden - *1.5M S of Le Crapaud WCM*	48°45.20'N	03°40.50'W
223	Pte de Beg-Pol Lt - *4M N*	48°44.70'N	04°20.80'W
224	L'Aber Wrach, L'Aber Benoit - *1M W of Libenter WCM*	48°37.60'N	04°39.90'W
225	Gr Basse de Portsall WCM - *1.6M N of*	48°38.30'N	04°45.90'W
226	Chenal du Four - *3.9M W of L'Aber Ildut ent*	48°28.30'N	04°51.30'W
227	Ushant Creach Lt - *3.5M NW*	48°30.00'N	05°11.30'W
228	Ushant - *4.9M WSW Lampaul*	48°25.30'N	05°12.30'W
229	Vandrée WCM - *4.8M W*	48°15.30'N	04°55.00'W
230	Chenal du Four, S Ent - *3.5M WSW ent Rade de Brest*	48°17.20'N	04°48.20'W
231	Douarnenez - *1.5M SW Basse Vieille IDM*	48°07.30'N	04°37.20'W
232	Chaussée de Sein WCM - *1.6M SW*	48°02.90'N	05°09.60'W
502	Guilvinec-*5.5M SW hbr ent*	47°44.30'N	04°23.50'W
503	Concarneau appr ch - *2.3M SW I. aux moutons Lt*	47°44.80'N	04°03.90'W
504	Concarneau appr ch -*2.1M ENE I. aux moutons*	47°47.50'N	03°58.80'W
505	Benodet - *3.0M S by E river mouth*	47°48.90'N	04°05.40'W
506	Concarneau - *2.0M SSW hbr ent*	47°50.40'N	03°56.50'W
507	Iles de Glenan -*3M S Jument de Glénan SCM*	47°38.50'N	04°01.30'W
508	Lorient appr - *3.0M NW by W Pen Men Lt (I .Groix)*	47°40.50'N	03°34.20'W
509	Lorient Passe de L'Ouest-*2.5M SW ent*	47°40.50'N	03°25.70'W
510	Lorient S.Chan - *1.5M S by W ent*	47°40.40'N	03°22.50'W
511	R.Etel - *3M SW river mouth*	47°36.60'N	03°15.70'W
512	Quiberon Peninsula Lt - *3.0M W*	47°28.90'N	03°11.80'W
513	Belle Ile - Le Palais - *1.3M NE hbr ent*	47°21.60'N	03°07.50'W
514	Passage de la Teignouse SW ent - *0.7M SW*	47°25.20'N	03°05.20'W
515	Passage de la Teignouse NE ent - *0.7M E*	47°26.90'N	03°00.50'W
516	La Trinite-sur-mer - *1.5M S by E ent*	47°32.70'N	02°59.80'W
517	Golfe du Morbihan -*2.2M S Ent ch*	47°31.00'N	02°55.20'W
518	Chimère SCM - *0.5M SW*	47°28.60'N	02°54.60'W
519	Pointe de Kerdonis Lt -*2M NE*	47°20.20'N	03°01.50'W
520	Pointe de S.Jacques Lt - *1.8M S*	47°27.40'N	02°47.40'W
521	R.Vilaine - *0.7M S Les Mâts SCM*	47°28.50'N	02°34.80'W
522	Ile Dumet Lt. - *1.5M W*	47°24.80'N	02°39.30'W
523	La Turballe/Le Croisic-*2M N Pointe du Croisic*	47°19.80'N	02°32.90'W
524	Plateau du Four - *1.6M ESE Le Four Lt*	47°17.40'N	02°35.80'W
525	Plateau du Four - *0.4M S Goué-Vas SCM*	47°14.60'N	02°38.10'W
526	Le Pouliguen/La Baule/Pornichet- *2M W by S of Pt de Penchâteau*	47°15.00'N	02°27.90'W
527	St. Nazaire - *3.5M Pte Aiguillon Lt*	47°11.40'N	02°17.60'W
528	St. Nazaire - *6.1M Pte Aiguillon Lt*	47°09.00'N	02°19.30'W
529	Pornic - *2.1M WSW Pornic hbr ent*	47°05.70'N	02°10.00'W
530	L'Herbaudière -*1.5M N by E harbour ent*	47°03.10'N	02°17.50'W
531	Ile du Pilier Lt - *1.8M W*	47°02.60'N	02°24.10'W
532	Chaussée des Boeufs - SW ent.	46°56.70'N	02°24.10'W
533	Ile Noirmoutier -*SW ent. Chenal de la Grise*	47°01.10'N	02°20.80'W

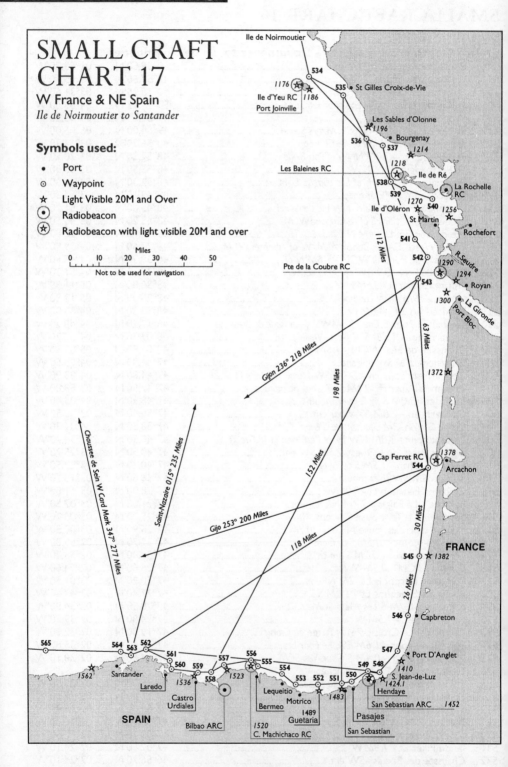

SMALL CRAFT CHART 17

W France & NE Spain

Ile de Noirmoutier to Santander

Symbols used:

- Port
- ⊙ Waypoint
- ☆ Light Visible 20M and Over
- ⊙ Radiobeacon
- ⊛ Radiobeacon with light visible 20M and over

Miles

0   10   20   30   40   50

Not to be used for navigation

Ile de Noirmoutier

534

1176 ⊛ ☆

535 • St Gilles Croix-de-Vie

Ile d'Yeu RC 1186

Port Joinville

Les Sables d'Olonne

☆ 1196

536 ⊙ • Bourgenay

537 ⊙ 1214

1218

Les Baleines RC ⊛ Ile de Ré

538 ⊙ La Rochelle RC ⊛

539 ⊙

1270 540 1256

Ile d'Oléron ☆

St Martin ☆

Rochefort

541 ⊙

R. Seudre

542 ⊙ 1290

1294 • Royan

Pte de la Coubre RC

543 ⊙ 1300 • La Gironde

☆ Port Bloc

112 Miles

63 Miles

1372 ☆

Gijon 236° 218 Miles

198 Miles

Chaussee de Sein W Card Mark 347° 277 Miles

Saint-Nazaire 015° 235 Miles

152 Miles

Cap Ferret RC ⊛ 1378

544 Arcachon

Gijo 253° 200 Miles

118 Miles

30 Miles

FRANCE

545 ⊙ ☆ 1382

26 Miles

546 ⊙ • Capbreton

565 ⊙

564 ⊙ 563 562 ⊙

561 ⊙ 556 ⊙

547 ⊙ • Port D'Anglet

1562 Santander

560 559 ⊙ 557 ⊙ 555 ⊙

549 548 ⊙ ☆

1410

558 ⊙ 1523 554 ⊙

550 ⊙ S. Jean-de-Luz

1424.1

Laredo 1536

553 552 551 ☆

Hendaye

Castro Urdiales

Lequeitio ☆

1483

San Sebastian ARC 1452

Bermeo Motrico

SPAIN

1489

Pasajes

Guetaria

1520

Bilbao ARC C. Machichaco RC

San Sebastian

SMALL CRAFT CHART 17
WAYPOINTS

France- Biscay & NE Spain - *Ile de Nourmontier to Santander*

534 .. Ile d'Yeu,Port Joinville - *2.4M N by E harbour ent*............ 46°46.00'N .... 02°19.60'W

534 .. Ile d'Yeu,Port Joinville - *2.4M N by E harbour ent* .... 46°46.00'N .... 02°19.60'W

535 .. St. Gilles-Croix-da-Vie - *3M SW ent* .... 46°39.70'N .... 01°59.60'W

536 .. Les Sables-d'Olonne - *3.7M SW ent* .... 46°26.30'N .... 01°49.60'W

537 .. Bourgenay - *1.4M SW SWM* .... 46°24.40'N .... 01°43.20'W

538 .. Ile de Ré - *3.0M SW Les Baleines Lt* .... 46°12.70'N .... 01°37.10'W

539 .. La Rochelle appr. chan. - *6.5M NW Pte Chassiron* .... 46°07.40'N .... 01°31.60'W

540 .. La Rochelle Ldg Lts - *6M SW by W harbour ent* .... 46°06.00'N .... 01°17.30'W

541 .. Ile d'Oleron - *3.7M SW Pte Chardonnière* .... 45°54.60'N .... 01°26.70'W

542 .. R.Seudre - *3.0M W Pointe de Gatseau* .... 45°47.80'N .... 01°18.80'W

543 .. R.Gironde-ent. chan. *-7M SW Pte de la Coubre* .... 45°38.20'N .... 01°22.60'W

544 .. Bassin d'Arcachon - *N ent-5M SW Cap Ferret Lt* .... 44°35.00'N .... 01°19.80'W

545 .. Contis Lt - *3.5M W* .... 44°05.70'N .... 01°23.80'W

546 .. Capbreton - *1.9M W by N harbour ent* .... 43°39.80'N .... 01°29.50'W

547 .. Port d'Anglet - *1.7M WNW hbr brkwtr* .... 43°32.80'N .... 01°33.70'W

548 .. St Jean-de-Luz - *1.5M NNW harbour ent* .... 43°25.50'N .... 01°40.80'W

549 .. Hendaye - *1.8M N Cabo Higuer Lt.* .... 43°25.40'N .... 01°47.70'W

550 .. Pasajes - *2.0M N harbour entrance* .... 43°22.30'N .... 01°55.80'W

551 .. San Sebastian - *2.2M N entrance to bay* .... 43°21.80'N .... 01°59.70'W

552 .. Guetaria - *1.8 M N I. de San Antón* .... 43°20.50'N .... 02°11.80'W

553 .. Motrico - *1.8M NE hbr ent* .... 43°20.10'N .... 02°21.00'W

554 .. Lequeitio-*1.8M NNE hbr ent* .... 43°23.60'N .... 02°28.60'W

555 .. Bermeo - *2.2M NNE* .... 43°27.40'N .... 02°41.40'W

556 .. Cabo Machichaco Lt - *1.9M N* .... 43°29.20'N .... 02°45.10'W

557 .. Cabo Villano Lt-*2.3M N* .... 43°28.30'N .... 02°56.60'W

558 .. Abra de Bilbao - *2.0M N of ent* .... 43°24.80'N .... 03°04.80'W

559 .. Castro Urdiales - *1.9M NW of harbour ent* .... 43°24.40'N .... 03°11.00'W

560 .. Laredo - *2M NW Canto de Laredo* .... 43°26.80'N .... 03°22.50'W

561 .. Punta del Pescador - *1.9M NW* .... 43°29.10'N .... 03°24.20'W

562 .. Cabo Ajo Lt - *2.2M N* .... 43°32.90'N .... 03°35.30'W

563 .. Santander - *1.7M N I. de S. Marina* .... 43°30.20'N .... 03°43.70'W

564 .. Cabo Major Lt - *1.7M N* .... 43°31.10'N .... 03°47.40'W

565 .. S Vicente de la Barquera Lt- *9.3M N* .... 43°33.00'N .... 04°23.50'W

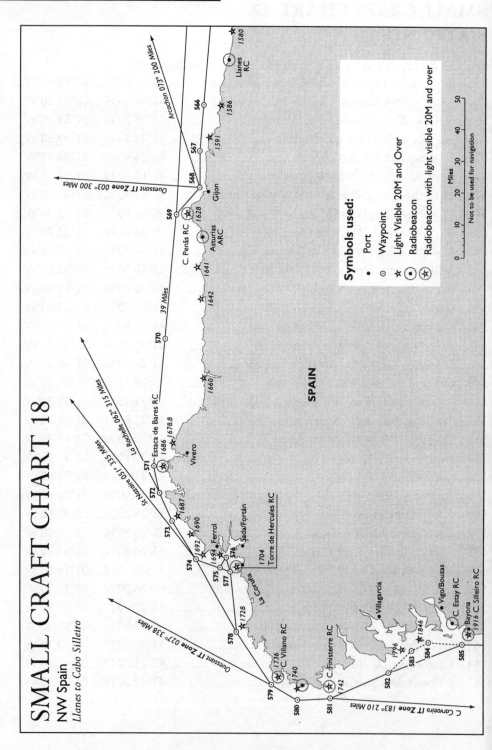

SMALL CRAFT CHART 18

NW Spain
Llanes to Cabo Silleiro

Symbols used:

- Port
- ⊙ Waypoint
- ✪ Light Visible 20M and Over
- ⦿ Radiobeacon
- ⦻ Radiobeacon with light visible 20M and over

Not to be used for navigation

Miles
0 10 20 30 40 50

SPAIN

Llanes RC — *1580*
1586
1591
566
567
568
Gijon
569
1628
C. Peñas RC
Asturias ARC
1641
1642
570
1660
Estaca de Bares RC
571 *1686 678.8*
Vivero
572
1687
573 *1690*
574 *1692* Ferrol
575 *1694* *576*
577 Sada/Fortán
1704
Torre de Hercules RC
La Coruña
578 *1728*
579 *1736*
C. Villano RC
740
580
581 C. Finisterre RC
742
Villagarcia
582
583 *1796*
584 *1846*
Vigo/Bouzas
C. Estay RC
585 Bayona
1916 C. Silleiro RC

Arcachon 073° 200 Miles
Ouessant IT Zone 003° 300 Miles
39 Miles
La Rochelle 062° 315 Miles
St. Nazaire 051° 335 Miles
Ouessant IT Zone 027° 338 Miles
C. Carvoeiro IT Zone 183° 210 Miles

SMALL CRAFT CHART 18
WAYPOINTS

NW Spain - *Llanes to Cabo Silleiro*

566 .. Punta de Somos Lt - *6.3M N* .... 43°34.70'N .. 05°05.00'W

567 .. Tazones Lt - *2.7M N* .... 43°35.60'N .. 05°24.00'W

568 .. Gijon - *1.9M ENE breakwater lt.* .... 43°35.00'N .. 05°38.20'W

569 .. Cabo Peñas Lt - *3.1M N* .... 43°42.50'N .. 05°50.80'W

570 .. Cabo San Augustin Lt - *11.8M N* .... 43°45.80'N .. 06°44.00'W

571 .. Pta de la Estaca de Bares Lt - *2.0M N* .... 43°49.30'N .. 07°41.10'W

572 .. Pta de los Aguillones Lt - *2.5M N* ....43°48.80'N .. 07°52.10'W

573 .. Pta Candelaria Lt - *2.1M NW* .... 43°44.30'N .. 08°04.70'W

574 .. Cabo Prior Lt - *3.4M NW* .... 43°36.70'N .. 08°21.50'W

575 .. Cabo Prioriño Chico Lt - *4.4M WNW* .... 43°29.40'N .. 08°25.80'W

576 .. El Ferrol appro. - *1.4M SW C. Prioriño Chico Lt.* .... 43°26.70'N .. 08°21.80'W

577 .. La Coruña - *3.3M NW Torre de Hercules Lt.* .... 43°25.10'N .. 08°28.00'W

578 .. Sisargas Is. Lt *-2.9M NW* .... 43°23.70'N .. 08°53.50'W

579 .. Cabo Villano Lt - *3.6M NW* .... 43°11.50'N .. 09°16.60'W

580 .. Cabo Toriñano Lt - *2.7M W* .... 43°03.30'N .. 09°21.50'W

581 .. Cabo Finisterre Lt - *4M W* .... 42°52.80'N .. 09°21.60'W

582 .. Cabo Corrubedo Lt - *4.2M WSW* ....42°33.40'N .. 09°10.60'W

583 .. Villagarcia - *2.5M S Isla Salvora Lt* .... 42°25.50'N .. 09°00.70'W

584 .. Vigo - NW appr - *5.0M W Pta Couso Lt.* .... 42°18.60'N .. 08°58.00'W

585 .. Vigo/Bayona - SW appr - *3.8M NW C Silleiro Lt* .... 42°08.70'N .. 08°57.50'W

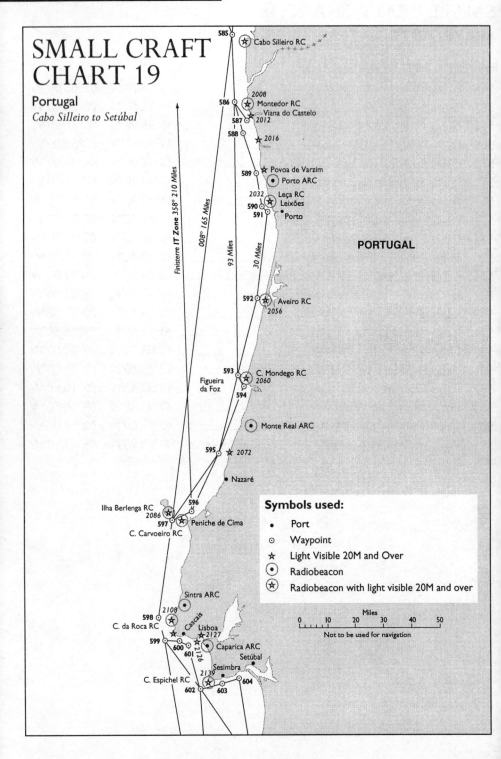

SMALL CRAFT CHART 19

Portugal
Cabo Silleiro to Setúbal

585
Cabo Silleiro RC

2008
586 Montedor RC
587 2012 Viana do Castelo
588

2016

589 Povoa de Varzim
Porto ARC

2032 Leça RC
590 Leixões
591 Porto

Finisterre IT Zone 358° 210 Miles
008° 165 Miles
93 Miles
30 Miles

PORTUGAL

592 Aveiro RC
2056

593 C. Mondego RC
Figueira 2060
da Foz
594

Monte Real ARC

595 2072

Nazaré

596
Ilha Berlenga RC
2086
597 Peniche de Cima
C. Carvoeiro RC

Symbols used:

- • Port
- ⊙ Waypoint
- ☆ Light Visible 20M and Over
- ⊙ Radiobeacon
- ⊛ Radiobeacon with light visible 20M and over

Sintra ARC

2108
598
C. da Roca RC
Cascais
Lisboa
599 2127
600
601 Caparica ARC
Setúbal
Sesimbra
2139
C. Espichel RC
602 603 604

Miles
0 10 20 30 40 50
Not to be used for navigation

SMALL CRAFT CHART 19
WAYPOINTS

Portugal - *Cabo Silleiro to Setubal*

585 .. Vigo/Bayona - SW appro - *3.8 M NW C Silleiro Lt*....... 42°08.70'N .. 08°57.50'W

585 .. Vigo/Bayona - SW appro - *3.8M NW C Silleiro Lt*........ 42°08.70'N .. 08°57.50'W

586 .. Montedor Lt - *3.8M W*.. 41°44.90'N .. 08°57.50'W

587 .. Viano do Castelo (Ldg Lts) - *1.2M from breakwater*... 41°39.20'N .. 08°51.00'W

588 .. Viano do Castelo (Ldg Lts) - *5.5M from breakwater*... 41°35.00'N .. 08°52.00'W

589 .. Póvoa de Varzim - *1.6M WSW harbour entrance*......... 41°21.50'N .. 08°48.10'W

590 .. Porto de Leixões - *2M W breakwater*........................ 41°10.20'N .. 08°45.00'W

591 .. Porto - *1.5M W river mouth*................................. 41°08.50'N .. 08°42.80'W

592 .. Aveiro - *2.0M W breakwater*................................ 40°38.60'N .. 08°48.20'W

593 .. Cabo Mondego Lt - *3.2M W*................................. 40°11.30'N .. 08°58.10'W

594 .. Figueira da Foz - *2.1M W breakwater*..................... 40°08.60'N .. 08°55.00'W

595 .. Nazaré - *2.8M W of harbour entrance*..................... 39°35.40'N .. 09°08.40'W

596 .. Peniche de Cima (Ldg Lts) -
3.2M NE by N of entrance.................... 39°24.50'N .. 09°20.00'W

597 .. Cabo Carvoeiro Lt - *3.0M W by N*........................... 39°22.50'N .. 09°28.30'W

598 .. Cabo da Roca Lt - *3.5M W*................................... 39°47.00'N .. 09°34.20'W

599 .. Cabo Raso Lt - *3.3M SW*..................................... 38°40.40'N .. 09°32.10'W

600 .. Cascais - *1.5M S S. Marta Lt.*............................. 38°40.00'N .. 09°25.20'W

601 .. Lisboa (Ldg Lts) - *5.0M SW Gibalta Lt.*................. 38°38.60'N .. 09°20.50'W

602 .. Cabo Espichel Lt - *3.2M SW*................................. 38°22.50'N .. 09°15.40'W

603 .. Sesimbra (Ldg Lts) - *1.5M S harbour entrance*............. 38°24.80'N .. 09°06.10'W

604 .. Sétubal (Ldg Lts) - *3.5M SW Outão Lt.*................... 38°26.80'N .. 08°58.60'W

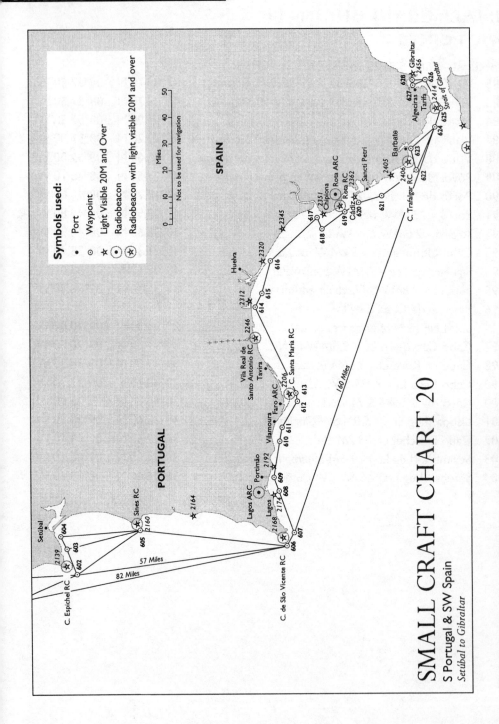

Symbols used:

- Port
- ⊙ Waypoint
- ☆ Light Visible 20M and Over
- ⊙̇ Radiobeacon
- ⊛ Radiobeacon with light visible 20M and over

Miles
0   10   20   30   40   50
Not to be used for navigation

PORTUGAL

SPAIN

Setúbal
2139
604
603
602
C. Espichel RC
2168
2160
605
Sines RC
2164
C. de São Vicente RC
608
607
2168
2172
608
Lagos
Lagos ARC
Portimão
2192
609
610 611
Vilamoura
612 613
2206
Faro ARC
Tavira
Vila Real de
Santo Antonio RC
2246
2312
614
615
2320
616
Huelva
2345
617
618
235/
Chipiona
Rota ARC
Rota RC
619
Cádiz
620
2362
Sancti Petri
621
2405
Barbate
2406
C. Trafalgar RC
622
623
Algeciras
627
628
Tarifa
624 625
626
Gibraltar
2456
241.4
Strait of Gibraltar

57 Miles
82 Miles
160 Miles

SMALL CRAFT CHART 20
S Portugal & SW Spain
Setúbal to Gibraltar

SMALL CRAFT CHART 20
WAYPOINTS

S Portugal & SW Spain - *Setubal to Gibraltar*

602 .. Cabo Espichel - *3.2 M SW* .... 38°22.50'N .... 09°15.40'W

602 .. Cabo Espichel - *3.2M SW* .... 38°22.50'N .... 09°15.40'W

603 .. Sesimbra (Ldg Lts) - *1.5M S harbour entrance* .... 38°24.80'N .... 09°06.10'W

604 .. Sétubal (Ldg Lts) - *3.5M SW Outão Lt.* .... 38°26.80'N .... 08°58.60'W

605 .. Sines - *1M W of breakwater* .... 37°56.30'N .... 08°54.60'W

606 .. Cabo de São Vicente Lt - *3.0M SW* .... 36°59.50'N .... 09°02.50'W

607 .. Pta de Sagres Lt - *2.5M S* .... 36°57.20'N .... 08°56.80'W

608 .. Lagos - *1.4M SE Punta da Piedade Lt* .... 37°04.00'N .... 08°38.80'W

609 .. Portimão - *2.0M S harbour entrance* .... 37°04.40'N .... 08°31.50'W

610 .. Albufeira Lt - *2.6M S* .... 37°02.60'N .... 08°14.80'W

611 .. Vilamoura - *1.6M SSW harbour entrance* .... 37°02.60'N .... 08°08.20'W

612 .. I. da Barreta - *2.0M SW* .... 36°56.50'N .... 07°57.30'W

613 .. Faro/Olhào - *1.0M SSW entrance channel* .... 36°56.70'N .... 07°52.60'W

614 .. Santo António - *2.0M S river mouth* .... 37°08.50'N .... 07°23.60'W

615 .. Fish Haven off Ria Higuerita - *1.2M S* .... 37°05.80'N .... 07°20.00'W

616 .. Huelva - *1M S river mouth* .... 37°05.60'N .... 06°49.60'W

617 .. Chipiona/Sanlúcar (Ldg Lts)- *0.5M WSW By* .... 36°45.70'N .... 06°27.50'W

618 .. Punta del Perro Lt - *3.2M W* .... 36°44.80'N .... 06°30.40'W

619 .. Bahia de Cádiz - *2.2M SSW Punta Candor* .... 36°36.10'N .... 06°24.80'W

620 .. Cadiz - *1.6M W by S Castillo de San Sebastián* .... 36°31.40'N .... 06°20.80'W

621 .. Sancti Petri - *3M SW chan. entrance* .... 36°21.00'N .... 06°15.30'W

622 .. Cabo Trafalgar Lt - *3.6M SW* .... 36°08.50'N .... 06°05.20'W

623 .. Barbate - *1.1M S end of breakwater* .... 36°09.70'N .... 05°55.40'W

624 .. Punta Paloma Lt - *4.7M SSW* .... 35°59.50'N .... 05°45.00'W

625 .. Tarifa - *1.3M S I. de Tarifa Lt.* .... 35°58.80'N .... 05°36.40'W

626 .. Punta Carnero Lt - *1.8M SE* .... 36°03.40'N .... 05°24.00'W

627 .. Algeciras - *1.2M SE end of breakwater* .... 36°08.20'N .... 05°24.40'W

628 .. Gibraltar - *0.8M SW E Head pier* .... 36°08.60'N .... 05°22.80'W

1997 SUNRISE & SUNSET LAT 40°N LONG 00°

The times are GMT. Adjustment for Daylight Saving Time should be made as appropriate. Data is based on Greenwich Meridian. Add 4 min for every degree West and subtract 4 min for every degree East

	JANUARY		FEBRUARY		MARCH		APRIL		MAY		JUNE	
	Rise	Set	Rise	Set	Rise	Set	Rise	Set	Rise	Set	Rise	Set
1	0722	1646	0709	1719	0634	1752	0544	1824	0500	1855	0433	1923
2	0722	1646	0708	1720	0632	1753	0543	1825	0459	1856	0433	1923
3	0722	1647	0707	1722	0631	1754	0541	1826	0458	1857	0432	1924
4	0722	1648	0706	1723	0629	1755	0539	1827	0457	1858	0432	1925
5	0722	1649	0705	1724	0627	1756	0538	1828	0455	1859	0432	1925
6	0722	1650	0704	1725	0626	1757	0536	1829	0454	1900	0432	1926
7	0722	1651	0702	1726	0624	1758	0535	1830	0453	1901	0431	1927
8	0722	1652	0701	1728	0623	1759	0533	1831	0452	1902	0431	1927
9	0722	1653	0700	1729	0621	1800	0532	1832	0451	1903	0431	1928
10	0722	1654	0659	1730	0620	1802	0530	1833	0450	1904	0431	1928
11	0721	1655	0658	1731	0618	1803	0528	1834	0449	1905	0431	1929
12	0721	1656	0657	1732	0617	1804	0527	1835	0448	1906	0431	1929
13	0721	1657	0656	1734	0615	1805	0525	1836	0447	1906	0431	1930
14	0720	1658	0654	1735	0613	1806	0524	1837	0446	1907	0431	1930
15	0720	1659	0653	1736	0612	1807	0522	1838	0445	1908	0431	1931
16	0720	1700	0652	1737	0610	1808	0521	1839	0444	1909	0431	1931
17	0719	1701	0650	1738	0608	1809	0519	1840	0443	1910	0431	1931
18	0719	1703	0649	1739	0607	1810	0518	1841	0442	1911	0431	1932
19	0718	1704	0648	1741	0605	1811	0516	1842	0441	1912	0431	1932
20	0718	1705	0646	1742	0604	1812	0515	1843	0441	1913	0431	1932
21	0717	1706	0645	1743	0602	1813	0514	1844	0440	1914	0431	1932
22	0716	1707	0644	1744	0600	1814	0512	1845	0439	1915	0431	1932
23	0716	1708	0642	1745	0559	1815	0511	1847	0438	1916	0432	1933
24	0715	1710	0641	1746	0557	1816	0509	1848	0438	1916	0432	1933
25	0714	1711	0639	1747	0556	1817	0508	1849	0437	1917	0432	1933
26	0714	1712	0638	1748	0554	1818	0507	1850	0436	1918	0433	1933
27	0713	1713	0636	1750	0552	1819	0505	1851	0436	1919	0433	1933
28	0712	1714	0635	1751	0551	1820	0504	1852	0435	1920	0433	1933
29	0711	1716			0549	1821	0503	1853	0435	1920	0434	1933
30	0710	1717			0547	1822	0501	1854	0434	1921	0434	1933
31	0710	1718			0546	1823			0434	1922		

1997 SUNRISE & SUNSET LAT 40°N LONG 00°

The times are GMT. Adjustment for Daylight Saving Time should be made as appropriate. Data is based on Greenwich Meridian. Add 4 min for every degree West and subtract 4 min for every degree East

	JULY		AUGUST		SEPTEMBER		OCTOBER		NOVEMBER		DECEMBER	
	Rise	Set	Rise	Set	Rise	Set	Rise	Set	Rise	Set	Rise	Set
1	0435	1933	0458	1914	0528	1832	0556	1742	0629	1658	0703	1635
2	0435	1933	0459	1913	0529	1830	0557	1741	0630	1657	0704	1635
3	0436	1932	0500	1912	0529	1828	0558	1739	0631	1655	0705	1635
4	0436	1932	0501	1910	0530	1827	0559	1738	0632	1654	0705	1635
5	0437	1932	0502	1909	0531	1825	0600	1736	0634	1653	0706	1635
6	0437	1932	0503	1908	0532	1824	0601	1734	0635	1652	0707	1635
7	0438	1931	0504	1907	0533	1822	0602	1733	0636	1651	0708	1635
8	0439	1931	0505	1906	0534	1820	0603	1731	0637	1650	0709	1635
9	0439	1931	0506	1905	0535	1819	0604	1730	0638	1649	0710	1635
10	0440	1930	0507	1903	0536	1817	0605	1728	0639	1648	0711	1635
11	0441	1930	0508	1902	0537	1815	0606	1727	0640	1647	0712	1635
12	0441	1929	0509	1901	0538	1814	0607	1725	0642	1646	0712	1635
13	0442	1929	0510	1859	0539	1812	0608	1724	0643	1645	0713	1635
14	0443	1928	0510	1858	0540	1811	0609	1722	0644	1645	0714	1635
15	0444	1928	0511	1857	0541	1809	0610	1721	0645	1644	0715	1636
16	0444	1927	0512	1855	0542	1807	0611	1719	0646	1643	0715	1636
17	0445	1927	0513	1854	0543	1806	0612	1718	0647	1642	0716	1636
18	0446	1926	0514	1853	0544	1804	0614	1716	0648	1642	0717	1637
19	0447	1925	0515	1851	0545	1802	0615	1715	0650	1641	0717	1637
20	0448	1925	0516	1850	0546	1801	0616	1713	0651	1640	0718	1637
21	0448	1924	0517	1848	0546	1759	0617	1712	0652	1640	0718	1638
22	0449	1923	0518	1847	0547	1757	0618	1711	0653	1639	0719	1638
23	0450	1922	0519	1845	0548	1756	0619	1709	0654	1638	0719	1639
24	0451	1921	0520	1844	0549	1754	0620	1708	0655	1638	0720	1640
25	0452	1921	0521	1842	0550	1752	0621	1706	0656	1637	0720	1640
26	0453	1920	0522	1841	0551	1751	0622	1705	0657	1637	0720	1641
27	0454	1919	0523	1839	0552	1749	0623	1704	0658	1637	0721	1642
28	0455	1918	0524	1838	0553	1747	0624	1703	0659	1636	0721	1642
29	0455	1917	0525	1836	0554	1746	0626	1701	0700	1636	0721	1643
30	0456	1916	0526	1835	0555	1744	0627	1700	0702	1636	0722	1644
31	0457	1915	0527	1833			0628	1659			0722	1644

1997 SUNRISE & SUNSET LAT 45°N LONG 00°

The times are GMT. Adjustment for Daylight Saving Time should be made as appropriate. Data is based on Greenwich Meridian. Add 4 min for every degree West and subtract 4 min for every degree East

	JANUARY		FEBRUARY		MARCH		APRIL		MAY		JUNE	
	Rise	Set	Rise	Set	Rise	Set	Rise	Set	Rise	Set	Rise	Set
1	0738	1629	0720	1708	0638	1747	0541	1828	0449	1905	0417	1939
2	0738	1630	0719	1709	0636	1749	0539	1829	0448	1907	0416	1940
3	0738	1631	0718	1711	0635	1750	0537	1830	0447	1908	0416	1941
4	0738	1632	0716	1712	0633	1751	0535	1831	0445	1909	0415	1942
5	0738	1633	0715	1714	0631	1753	0533	1833	0444	1910	0415	1943
6	0738	1634	0714	1715	0629	1754	0532	1834	0442	1912	0414	1943
7	0738	1635	0712	1716	0627	1755	0530	1835	0441	1913	0414	1944
8	0738	1636	0711	1718	0626	1757	0528	1837	0440	1914	0414	1945
9	0737	1637	0710	1719	0624	1758	0526	1838	0438	1915	0413	1945
10	0737	1639	0708	1721	0622	1759	0524	1839	0437	1916	0413	1946
11	0737	1640	0707	1722	0620	1801	0523	1840	0436	1918	0413	1947
12	0736	1641	0705	1724	0618	1802	0521	1842	0435	1919	0413	1947
13	0736	1642	0704	1725	0616	1803	0519	1843	0433	1920	0413	1948
14	0735	1643	0703	1727	0615	1805	0517	1844	0432	1921	0413	1948
15	0735	1645	0701	1728	0613	1806	0516	1845	0431	1922	0413	1948
16	0734	1646	0700	1729	0611	1807	0514	1847	0430	1923	0413	1949
17	0734	1647	0658	1731	0609	1809	0512	1848	0429	1925	0413	1949
18	0733	1648	0656	1732	0607	1810	0510	1849	0428	1926	0413	1950
19	0732	1650	0655	1734	0605	1811	0509	1850	0427	1927	0413	1950
20	0731	1651	0653	1735	0603	1812	0507	1852	0426	1928	0413	1950
21	0731	1652	0652	1736	0601	1814	0505	1853	0425	1929	0413	1950
22	0730	1654	0650	1738	0600	1815	0504	1854	0424	1930	0413	1950
23	0729	1655	0648	1739	0558	1816	0502	1855	0423	1931	0414	1951
24	0728	1657	0647	1741	0556	1818	0500	1857	0422	1932	0414	1951
25	0727	1658	0645	1742	0554	1819	0459	1858	0421	1933	0414	1951
26	0726	1659	0643	1743	0552	1820	0457	1859	0421	1934	0415	1951
27	0725	1701	0642	1745	0550	1821	0456	1900	0420	1935	0415	1951
28	0724	1702	0640	1746	0548	1823	0454	1902	0419	1936	0416	1951
29	0723	1704			0546	1824	0452	1903	0418	1937	0416	1951
30	0722	1705			0545	1825	0451	1904	0418	1938	0417	1951
31	0721	1706			0543	1826			0417	1939		

1997 SUNRISE & SUNSET LAT 45°N LONG 00°

The times are GMT. Adjustment for Daylight Saving Time should be made as appropriate. Data is based on Greenwich Meridian. Add 4 min for every degree West and subtract 4 min for every degree East

	JULY		AUGUST		SEPTEMBER		OCTOBER		NOVEMBER		DECEMBER	
	Rise	Set	Rise	Set	Rise	Set	Rise	Set	Rise	Set	Rise	Set
1	0417	1950	0445	1927	0522	1837	0558	1741	0638	1648	0718	1620
2	0418	1950	0446	1925	0523	1835	0559	1739	0640	1647	0719	1620
3	0418	1950	0447	1924	0524	1834	0600	1737	0641	1645	0720	1619
4	0419	1950	0449	1923	0525	1832	0602	1735	0642	1644	0721	1619
5	0419	1949	0450	1921	0527	1830	0603	1733	0644	1643	0722	1619
6	0420	1949	0451	1920	0528	1828	0604	1731	0645	1642	0723	1619
7	0421	1949	0452	1919	0529	1826	0605	1730	0647	1640	0724	1618
8	0422	1948	0453	1917	0530	1824	0607	1728	0648	1639	0725	1618
9	0422	1948	0454	1916	0531	1822	0608	1726	0649	1638	0726	1618
10	0423	1947	0456	1914	0533	1821	0609	1724	0651	1637	0727	1618
11	0424	1947	0457	1913	0534	1819	0610	1722	0652	1635	0728	1618
12	0425	1946	0458	1911	0535	1817	0612	1721	0653	1634	0729	1618
13	0426	1945	0459	1910	0536	1815	0613	1719	0655	1633	0730	1619
14	0427	1945	0500	1908	0537	1813	0614	1717	0656	1632	0731	1619
15	0427	1944	0502	1907	0538	1811	0616	1715	0658	1631	0731	1619
16	0428	1943	0503	1905	0540	1809	0617	1714	0659	1630	0732	1619
17	0429	1942	0504	1903	0541	1807	0618	1712	0700	1629	0733	1619
18	0430	1942	0505	1902	0542	1805	0619	1710	0702	1628	0733	1620
19	0431	1941	0506	1900	0543	1803	0621	1708	0703	1627	0734	1620
20	0432	1940	0507	1858	0544	1801	0622	1707	0704	1627	0735	1621
21	0433	1939	0509	1857	0546	1800	0623	1705	0706	1626	0735	1621
22	0434	1938	0510	1855	0547	1758	0625	1703	0707	1625	0736	1622
23	0435	1937	0511	1853	0548	1756	0626	1702	0708	1624	0736	1622
24	0436	1936	0512	1852	0549	1754	0627	1700	0709	1624	0736	1623
25	0437	1935	0513	1850	0550	1752	0629	1659	0711	1623	0737	1623
26	0438	1934	0515	1848	0552	1750	0630	1657	0712	1622	0737	1624
27	0440	1933	0516	1846	0553	1748	0631	1656	0713	1622	0737	1625
28	0441	1932	0517	1844	0554	1746	0633	1654	0714	1621	0738	1626
29	0442	1930	0518	1843	0555	1744	0634	1653	0716	1621	0738	1626
30	0443	1929	0519	1841	0557	1743	0636	1651	0717	1620	0738	1627
31	0444	1928	0521	1839			0637	1650			0738	1628

1997 SUNRISE & SUNSET LAT 50°N LONG 00°

The times are GMT. Adjustment for Daylight Saving Time should be made as appropriate. Data is based on Greenwich Meridian. Add 4 min for every degree West and subtract 4 min for every degree East

	JANUARY		FEBRUARY		MARCH		APRIL		MAY		JUNE	
	Rise	Set	Rise	Set	Rise	Set	Rise	Set	Rise	Set	Rise	Set
1	0759	1609	0734	1654	0643	1742	0537	1832	0436	1919	0356	2000
2	0758	1610	0732	1656	0641	1744	0535	1833	0435	1920	0355	2001
3	0758	1611	0731	1658	0639	1745	0533	1835	0433	1922	0354	2002
4	0758	1612	0729	1659	0637	1747	0530	1837	0431	1923	0354	2003
5	0758	1613	0728	1701	0635	1749	0528	1838	0430	1925	0353	2004
6	0758	1615	0726	1703	0633	1750	0526	1840	0428	1926	0353	2005
7	0757	1616	0724	1705	0631	1752	0524	1841	0426	1928	0352	2006
8	0757	1617	0723	1706	0629	1754	0522	1843	0425	1929	0352	2007
9	0756	1618	0721	1708	0627	1755	0520	1844	0423	1931	0351	2007
10	0756	1620	0719	1710	0625	1757	0518	1846	0422	1932	0351	2008
11	0755	1621	0718	1712	0622	1759	0516	1848	0420	1934	0351	2009
12	0755	1622	0716	1713	0620	1800	0513	1849	0418	1935	0351	2009
13	0754	1624	0714	1715	0618	1802	0511	1851	0417	1937	0350	2010
14	0753	1625	0712	1717	0616	1803	0509	1852	0416	1938	0350	2010
15	0753	1627	0711	1718	0614	1805	0507	1854	0414	1939	0350	2011
16	0752	1628	0709	1720	0612	1807	0505	1855	0413	1941	0350	2011
17	0751	1630	0707	1722	0610	1808	0503	1857	0411	1942	0350	2012
18	0750	1631	0705	1724	0607	1810	0501	1858	0410	1944	0350	2012
19	0749	1633	0703	1725	0605	1811	0459	1900	0409	1945	0350	2012
20	0748	1634	0701	1727	0603	1813	0457	1902	0408	1946	0350	2013
21	0747	1636	0659	1729	0601	1815	0455	1903	0406	1947	0351	2013
22	0746	1638	0657	1730	0559	1816	0453	1905	0405	1949	0351	2013
23	0745	1639	0655	1732	0556	1818	0451	1906	0404	1950	0351	2013
24	0744	1641	0654	1734	0554	1819	0449	1908	0403	1951	0351	2013
25	0743	1642	0652	1735	0552	1821	0448	1909	0402	1953	0352	2013
26	0742	1644	0650	1737	0550	1822	0446	1911	0401	1954	0352	2013
27	0740	1646	0647	1739	0548	1824	0444	1912	0400	1955	0353	2013
28	0739	1647	0645	1740	0546	1826	0442	1914	0359	1956	0353	2013
29	0738	1649			0543	1827	0440	1916	0358	1957	0354	2013
30	0736	1651			0541	1829	0438	1917	0357	1958	0354	2013
31	0735	1653			0539	1830			0357	1959		

1997 SUNRISE & SUNSET LAT 50°N LONG 00°

The times are GMT. Adjustment for Daylight Saving Time should be made as appropriate. Data is based on Greenwich Meridian. Add 4 min for every degree West and subtract 4 min for every degree East

	JULY		AUGUST		SEPTEMBER		OCTOBER		NOVEMBER		DECEMBER	
	Rise	Set	Rise	Set	Rise	Set	Rise	Set	Rise	Set	Rise	Set
1	0355	2012	0429	1942	0515	1844	0600	1739	0650	1637	0737	1601
2	0356	2012	0431	1941	0516	1842	0601	1736	0651	1635	0738	1601
3	0356	2012	0432	1939	0518	1840	0603	1734	0653	1634	0739	1600
4	0357	2011	0433	1938	0519	1838	0604	1732	0655	1632	0741	1600
5	0358	2011	0435	1936	0521	1835	0606	1730	0656	1630	0742	1559
6	0359	2010	0436	1934	0522	1833	0608	1728	0658	1629	0743	1559
7	0359	2010	0438	1933	0524	1831	0609	1726	0700	1627	0744	1559
8	0400	2009	0439	1931	0525	1829	0611	1723	0701	1626	0745	1558
9	0401	2009	0441	1929	0527	1827	0612	1721	0703	1624	0746	1558
10	0402	2008	0442	1928	0528	1825	0614	1719	0705	1623	0747	1558
11	0403	2007	0444	1926	0530	1822	0615	1717	0706	1621	0748	1558
12	0404	2006	0445	1924	0531	1820	0617	1715	0708	1620	0749	1558
13	0405	2006	0447	1922	0533	1818	0619	1713	0709	1619	0750	1558
14	0406	2005	0448	1920	0534	1816	0620	1711	0711	1617	0751	1558
15	0407	2004	0449	1918	0536	1814	0622	1709	0713	1616	0752	1558
16	0409	2003	0451	1916	0537	1811	0623	1707	0714	1615	0753	1559
17	0410	2002	0452	1915	0539	1809	0625	1705	0716	1614	0753	1559
18	0411	2001	0454	1913	0540	1807	0627	1703	0718	1612	0754	1559
19	0412	2000	0455	1911	0542	1805	0628	1701	0719	1611	0755	1559
20	0413	1959	0457	1909	0543	1803	0630	1659	0721	1610	0755	1600
21	0414	1957	0458	1907	0545	1800	0631	1657	0722	1609	0756	1600
22	0416	1956	0500	1905	0546	1758	0633	1655	0724	1608	0756	1601
23	0417	1955	0501	1903	0548	1756	0635	1653	0725	1607	0757	1601
24	0418	1954	0503	1901	0549	1754	0636	1651	0727	1606	0757	1602
25	0420	1952	0504	1859	0551	1752	0638	1649	0728	1605	0758	1603
26	0421	1951	0506	1857	0552	1749	0640	1648	0730	1605	0758	1603
27	0422	1950	0507	1855	0554	1747	0641	1646	0731	1604	0758	1604
28	0424	1948	0509	1852	0555	1745	0643	1644	0733	1603	0758	1605
29	0425	1947	0510	1850	0557	1743	0645	1642	0734	1602	0758	1606
30	0426	1946	0512	1848	0558	1741	0646	1640	0735	1602	0759	1607
31	0428	1944	0513	1846			0648	1639			0759	1608

1997 SUNRISE & SUNSET LAT 55°N LONG 00°

The times are GMT. Adjustment for Daylight Saving Time should be made as appropriate. Data is based on Greenwich Meridian. Add 4 min for every degree West and subtract 4 min for every degree East

	JANUARY		FEBRUARY		MARCH		APRIL		MAY		JUNE	
	Rise	Set	Rise	Set	Rise	Set	Rise	Set	Rise	Set	Rise	Set
1	0825	1543	0751	1637	0650	1736	0532	1837	0420	1935	0329	2028
2	0825	1544	0749	1639	0648	1738	0529	1839	0418	1937	0328	2029
3	0824	1545	0747	1641	0645	1740	0527	1841	0416	1939	0327	2030
4	0824	1546	0745	1643	0643	1742	0524	1843	0414	1941	0326	2031
5	0823	1548	0743	1646	0640	1744	0522	1845	0412	1943	0325	2032
6	0823	1549	0741	1648	0638	1746	0519	1847	0410	1945	0324	2034
7	0822	1551	0739	1650	0635	1748	0517	1849	0408	1947	0324	2035
8	0822	1552	0737	1652	0633	1750	0514	1851	0406	1949	0323	2036
9	0821	1554	0735	1654	0630	1752	0512	1853	0404	1951	0322	2036
10	0820	1555	0733	1656	0628	1754	0509	1855	0402	1952	0322	2037
11	0820	1557	0731	1658	0625	1756	0507	1857	0400	1954	0322	2038
12	0819	1559	0729	1700	0623	1758	0504	1858	0358	1956	0321	2039
13	0818	1600	0727	1702	0620	1800	0502	1900	0356	1958	0321	2040
14	0817	1602	0725	1705	0618	1802	0459	1902	0354	2000	0321	2040
15	0816	1604	0723	1707	0615	1804	0457	1904	0352	2001	0320	2041
16	0815	1606	0720	1709	0613	1806	0455	1906	0351	2003	0320	2041
17	0813	1607	0718	1711	0610	1808	0452	1908	0349	2005	0320	2042
18	0812	1609	0716	1713	0608	1810	0450	1910	0347	2007	0320	2042
19	0811	1611	0714	1715	0605	1812	0447	1912	0346	2008	0320	2043
20	0810	1613	0711	1717	0602	1814	0445	1914	0344	2010	0320	2043
21	0808	1615	0709	1719	0600	1816	0443	1916	0343	2012	0320	2043
22	0807	1617	0707	1721	0557	1818	0440	1918	0341	2013	0321	2043
23	0806	1619	0704	1723	0555	1819	0438	1920	0340	2015	0321	2043
24	0804	1621	0702	1725	0552	1821	0436	1922	0338	2016	0321	2043
25	0803	1623	0700	1727	0550	1823	0433	1924	0337	2018	0322	2043
26	0801	1625	0657	1730	0547	1825	0431	1926	0336	2019	0322	2043
27	0759	1627	0655	1732	0545	1827	0429	1928	0334	2021	0323	2043
28	0758	1629	0652	1734	0542	1829	0427	1930	0333	2022	0323	2043
29	0756	1631			0540	1831	0424	1932	0332	2024	0324	2042
30	0754	1633			0537	1833	0422	1933	0331	2025	0325	2042
31	0753	1635			0534	1835			0330	2026		

1997 SUNRISE & SUNSET LAT 55°N LONG 00°

The times are GMT. Adjustment for Daylight Saving Time should be made as appropriate. Data is based on Greenwich Meridian. Add 4 min for every degree West and subtract 4 min for every degree East

	JULY		AUGUST		SEPTEMBER		OCTOBER		NOVEMBER		DECEMBER	
	Rise	Set	Rise	Set	Rise	Set	Rise	Set	Rise	Set	Rise	Set
1	0325	2042	0409	2003	0506	1853	0602	1736	0704	1623	0801	1537
2	0326	2041	0410	2001	0508	1850	0604	1733	0706	1621	0803	1536
3	0327	2041	0412	1959	0510	1848	0606	1731	0708	1619	0804	1535
4	0328	2040	0414	1957	0512	1845	0608	1728	0710	1617	0806	1535
5	0329	2039	0416	1955	0514	1842	0610	1726	0712	1615	0807	1534
6	0330	2039	0418	1953	0515	1840	0612	1723	0714	1613	0808	1533
7	0331	2038	0419	1951	0517	1837	0614	1721	0716	1611	0810	1533
8	0332	2037	0421	1949	0519	1835	0616	1718	0718	1609	0811	1533
9	0333	2036	0423	1946	0521	1832	0618	1716	0720	1607	0812	1532
10	0335	2035	0425	1944	0523	1830	0620	1713	0722	1605	0814	1532
11	0336	2034	0427	1942	0525	1827	0622	1711	0724	1603	0815	1532
12	0337	2033	0429	1940	0527	1825	0623	1708	0726	1602	0816	1532
13	0338	2032	0431	1938	0528	1822	0625	1706	0728	1600	0817	1531
14	0340	2031	0432	1936	0530	1820	0627	1704	0730	1558	0818	1531
15	0341	2030	0434	1933	0532	1817	0629	1701	0732	1557	0819	1531
16	0343	2029	0436	1931	0534	1814	0631	1659	0734	1555	0820	1532
17	0344	2027	0438	1929	0536	1812	0633	1656	0736	1553	0820	1532
18	0345	2026	0440	1926	0538	1809	0635	1654	0738	1552	0821	1532
19	0347	2025	0442	1924	0540	1807	0637	1652	0740	1551	0822	1532
20	0348	2023	0444	1922	0542	1804	0639	1649	0742	1549	0823	1533
21	0350	2022	0446	1919	0543	1802	0641	1647	0744	1548	0823	1533
22	0352	2020	0447	1917	0545	1759	0643	1645	0745	1546	0824	1534
23	0353	2019	0449	1915	0547	1756	0645	1642	0747	1545	0824	1534
24	0355	2017	0451	1912	0549	1754	0647	1640	0749	1544	0824	1535
25	0357	2015	0453	1910	0551	1751	0649	1638	0751	1543	0825	1536
26	0358	2014	0455	1907	0553	1749	0651	1636	0753	1542	0825	1536
27	0400	2012	0457	1905	0555	1746	0653	1633	0754	1540	0825	1537
28	0402	2010	0459	1902	0557	1744	0655	1631	0756	1539	0825	1538
29	0403	2008	0500	1900	0558	1741	0658	1629	0758	1539	0825	1539
30	0405	2006	0502	1858	0600	1738	0700	1627	0759	1538	0825	1540
31	0407	2005	0504	1855			0702	1625			0825	1541

1997 SUNRISE & SUNSET LAT 60°N LONG 00°

The times are GMT. Adjustment for Daylight Saving Time should be made as appropriate. Data is based on Greenwich Meridian. Add 4 min for every degree West and subtract 4 min for every degree East

	JANUARY		FEBRUARY		MARCH		APRIL		MAY		JUNE	
	Rise	Set	Rise	Set	Rise	Set	Rise	Set	Rise	Set	Rise	Set
1	0902	1505	0814	1614	0659	1727	0525	1844	0358	1958	0249	2108
2	0902	1507	0811	1617	0656	1730	0522	1846	0355	2000	0248	2109
3	0901	1508	0809	1620	0653	1732	0519	1849	0353	2003	0246	2111
4	0900	1510	0807	1622	0650	1735	0516	1851	0350	2005	0245	2112
5	0900	1512	0804	1625	0647	1737	0513	1854	0347	2008	0244	2114
6	0859	1513	0802	1627	0644	1740	0510	1856	0345	2010	0243	2115
7	0858	1515	0759	1630	0641	1742	0507	1858	0342	2013	0242	2117
8	0857	1517	0757	1633	0638	1745	0504	1901	0340	2015	0241	2118
9	0856	1519	0754	1635	0635	1747	0501	1903	0337	2018	0240	2119
10	0855	1521	0751	1638	0632	1750	0458	1906	0334	2020	0239	2121
11	0853	1523	0749	1641	0629	1752	0455	1908	0332	2022	0238	2122
12	0852	1525	0746	1643	0626	1755	0452	1911	0330	2025	0238	2123
13	0851	1527	0743	1646	0623	1757	0449	1913	0327	2027	0237	2124
14	0849	1530	0741	1649	0620	1800	0447	1916	0325	2030	0237	2124
15	0848	1532	0738	1651	0617	1802	0444	1918	0322	2032	0236	2125
16	0846	1534	0735	1654	0614	1805	0441	1921	0320	2034	0236	2126
17	0844	1537	0733	1656	0611	1807	0438	1923	0318	2037	0236	2126
18	0843	1539	0730	1659	0608	1810	0435	1926	0316	2039	0236	2127
19	0841	1541	0727	1702	0605	1812	0432	1928	0313	2041	0235	2127
20	0839	1544	0724	1704	0602	1815	0429	1931	0311	2043	0236	2128
21	0837	1546	0721	1707	0559	1817	0426	1933	0309	2046	0236	2128
22	0835	1549	0719	1709	0556	1819	0423	1935	0307	2048	0236	2128
23	0833	1551	0716	1712	0553	1822	0420	1938	0305	2050	0236	2128
24	0831	1554	0713	1715	0550	1824	0417	1940	0303	2052	0237	2128
25	0829	1556	0710	1717	0547	1827	0415	1943	0301	2054	0237	2128
26	0827	1559	0707	1720	0544	1829	0412	1945	0259	2056	0238	2127
27	0825	1601	0704	1722	0541	1832	0409	1948	0257	2058	0238	2127
28	0823	1604	0701	1725	0538	1834	0406	1950	0256	2100	0239	2127
29	0821	1606			0534	1836	0403	1953	0254	2102	0240	2126
30	0818	1609			0531	1839	0401	1955	0252	2104	0241	2126
31	0816	1612			0528	1841			0251	2106		

1997 SUNRISE & SUNSET LAT 60°N LONG 00°

The times are GMT. Adjustment for Daylight Saving Time should be made as appropriate. Data is based on Greenwich Meridian. Add 4 min for every degree West and subtract 4 min for every degree East

	JULY		AUGUST		SEPTEMBER		OCTOBER		NOVEMBER		DECEMBER	
	Rise	Set	Rise	Set	Rise	Set	Rise	Set	Rise	Set	Rise	Set
1	0242	2125	0341	2030	0455	1904	0605	1733	0722	1604	0835	1503
2	0243	2124	0343	2028	0457	1901	0608	1730	0725	1602	0837	1502
3	0244	2123	0345	2025	0459	1858	0610	1727	0727	1559	0839	1500
4	0246	2122	0348	2023	0502	1855	0612	1724	0730	1556	0841	1459
5	0247	2121	0350	2020	0504	1852	0615	1721	0732	1554	0843	1458
6	0248	2120	0352	2018	0507	1849	0617	1718	0735	1551	0844	1457
7	0250	2119	0355	2015	0509	1846	0620	1715	0738	1549	0846	1457
8	0251	2118	0357	2012	0511	1843	0622	1712	0740	1547	0848	1456
9	0253	2116	0400	2010	0514	1839	0625	1709	0743	1544	0849	1455
10	0254	2115	0402	2007	0516	1836	0627	1706	0745	1542	0851	1455
11	0256	2114	0404	2004	0518	1833	0629	1703	0748	1539	0852	1454
12	0258	2112	0407	2001	0521	1830	0632	1700	0750	1537	0854	1454
13	0300	2110	0409	1959	0523	1827	0634	1657	0753	1535	0855	1453
14	0302	2109	0412	1956	0525	1824	0637	1654	0755	1533	0856	1453
15	0303	2107	0414	1953	0528	1821	0639	1651	0758	1531	0857	1453
16	0305	2105	0416	1950	0530	1818	0642	1648	0800	1528	0858	1453
17	0307	2103	0419	1947	0532	1815	0644	1645	0803	1526	0859	1453
18	0309	2102	0421	1945	0535	1812	0647	1643	0805	1524	0900	1453
19	0311	2100	0424	1942	0537	1809	0649	1640	0808	1522	0901	1453
20	0314	2058	0426	1939	0539	1806	0652	1637	0810	1520	0901	1454
21	0316	2056	0428	1936	0542	1803	0654	1634	0813	1518	0902	1454
22	0318	2053	0431	1933	0544	1800	0657	1631	0815	1517	0902	1455
23	0320	2051	0433	1930	0546	1757	0659	1628	0817	1515	0903	1455
24	0322	2049	0436	1927	0549	1754	0702	1626	0820	1513	0903	1456
25	0324	2047	0438	1924	0551	1751	0704	1623	0822	1511	0903	1457
26	0327	2045	0440	1921	0553	1748	0707	1620	0824	1510	0904	1458
27	0329	2042	0443	1918	0556	1745	0709	1617	0826	1508	0904	1459
28	0331	2040	0445	1916	0558	1742	0712	1615	0829	1507	0904	1500
29	0334	2038	0448	1913	0601	1739	0714	1612	0831	1505	0903	1501
30	0336	2035	0450	1910	0603	1736	0717	1609	0833	1504	0903	1502
31	0338	2033	0452	1907			0720	1607			0903	1504

1997 MOONRISE & MOONSET LAT 40°N LONG 00°

The times are GMT. Adjustment for Daylight Saving Time should be made as appropriate. Data is based on Greenwich Meridian. Add 4 min for every degree West and subtract 4 min for every degree East
•• •• *Indicates that this phenomenon does not occur*

	JANUARY Rise	Set	FEBRUARY Rise	Set	MARCH Rise	Set	APRIL Rise	Set	MAY Rise	Set	JUNE Rise	Set
1	•• ••	1126	0053	1141	•• ••	1020	0125	1146	0141	1255	0211	1518
2	0007	1157	0154	1224	0043	1105	0215	1250	0220	1404	0248	1624
3	0106	1229	0255	1313	0142	1156	0301	1359	0258	1513	0327	1730
4	0206	1306	0356	1409	0239	1255	0343	1509	0334	1623	0409	1832
5	0308	1347	0453	1513	0333	1359	0423	1621	0412	1732	0455	1931
6	0412	1434	0547	1622	0423	1508	0501	1733	0451	1839	0545	2024
7	0515	1529	0636	1735	0508	1620	0539	1843	0532	1945	0638	2112
8	0616	1631	0721	1849	0551	1734	0618	1953	0617	2046	0733	2155
9	0712	1739	0801	2002	0631	1847	0659	2100	0705	2143	0829	2233
10	0803	1850	0840	2113	0709	1958	0742	2203	0756	2233	0925	2307
11	0848	2002	0917	2222	0748	2108	0828	2301	0850	2318	1021	2339
12	0929	2113	0954	2328	0827	2215	0917	2354	0945	2358	1116	•• ••
13	1007	2223	1032	•• ••	0908	2318	1008	•• ••	1040	•• ••	1212	0009
14	1043	2330	1113	0031	0951	•• ••	1102	0041	1136	0034	1308	0038
15	1118	•• ••	1156	0130	1037	0017	1156	0123	1232	0107	1406	0108
16	1154	0035	1242	0226	1126	0112	1251	0200	1327	0138	1505	0139
17	1232	0138	1331	0317	1217	0201	1346	0234	1424	0207	1605	0213
18	1313	0239	1422	0404	1310	0245	1442	0306	1521	0237	1706	0251
19	1356	0337	1515	0446	1404	0324	1538	0336	1619	0308	1808	0334
20	1443	0431	1610	0525	1459	0400	1634	0406	1719	0340	1907	0423
21	1534	0520	1705	0600	1554	0434	1732	0436	1820	0416	2004	0519
22	1626	0606	1800	0632	1650	0505	1831	0508	1921	0457	2055	0621
23	1720	0647	1856	0703	1746	0535	1931	0542	2021	0543	2142	0728
24	1815	0724	1952	0732	1843	0605	2031	0619	2118	0634	2224	0836
25	1911	0758	2049	0802	1941	0635	2131	0701	2211	0732	2302	0946
26	2006	0830	2146	0833	2039	0707	2228	0748	2259	0834	2338	1055
27	2102	0900	2245	0905	2138	0742	2323	0841	2342	0940	•• ••	1203
28	2158	0929	2344	0941	2237	0820	•• ••	0939	•• ••	1047	0014	1310
29	2255	0959			2336	0903	0013	1042	0022	1155	0050	1415
30	2353	1030			•• ••	0951	0059	1147	0059	1303	0127	1520
31	•• ••	1103			0032	1046			0135	1410		

1997 MOONRISE & MOONSET LAT 40°N LONG 00°

The times are GMT. Adjustment for Daylight Saving Time should be made as appropriate. Data is based on Greenwich Meridian. Add 4 min for every degree West and subtract 4 min for every degree East
•• •• *Indicates that this phenomenon does not occur*

	JULY		AUGUST		SEPTEMBER		OCTOBER		NOVEMBER		DECEMBER	
	Rise	Set	Rise	Set	Rise	Set	Rise	Set	Rise	Set	Rise	Set
1	0207	1622	0317	1749	0452	1815	0534	1747	0714	1759	0800	1810
2	0251	1722	0411	1830	0548	1845	0629	1817	0812	1839	0855	1905
3	0338	1817	0507	1907	0644	1915	0726	1848	0910	1925	0946	2006
4	0429	1907	0603	1941	0739	1944	0823	1922	1005	2016	1033	2109
5	0523	1951	0658	2013	0835	2014	0920	1959	1058	2112	1115	2215
6	0618	2031	0754	2042	0931	2046	1017	2041	1147	2212	1154	2322
7	0714	2107	0850	2111	1028	2121	1114	2127	1232	2317	1231	•• ••
8	0811	2140	0945	2141	1125	2159	1208	2220	1313	•• ••	1307	0030
9	0906	2210	1041	2212	1223	2243	1300	2318	1352	0024	1343	0138
10	1002	2240	1138	2245	1320	2333	1349	•• ••	1430	0132	1420	0247
11	1058	2309	1236	2321	1415	•• ••	1434	0022	1507	0242	1500	0356
12	1154	2339	1335	•• ••	1507	0029	1516	0129	1545	0353	1544	0503
13	1251	•• ••	1434	0003	1556	0132	1556	0239	1624	0504	1632	0609
14	1350	0011	1532	0051	1642	0240	1634	0351	1707	0615	1724	0710
15	1450	0046	1628	0145	1724	0352	1713	0504	1754	0723	1819	0806
16	1550	0126	1721	0247	1804	0505	1753	0617	1845	0827	1917	0856
17	1651	0212	1809	0354	1843	0619	1835	0729	1939	0926	2015	0939
18	1749	0304	1853	0506	1922	0732	1920	0838	2035	1018	2113	1018
19	1844	0403	1934	0619	2003	0843	2008	0944	2132	1104	2210	1052
20	1934	0509	2013	0732	2045	0953	2059	1044	2229	1144	2306	1123
21	2019	0618	2051	0844	2130	1058	2153	1138	2326	1220	•• ••	1153
22	2101	0730	2129	0954	2218	1159	2248	1226	•• ••	1252	0002	1222
23	2139	0841	2208	1103	2309	1255	2344	1308	0022	1322	0058	1251
24	2216	0952	2250	1208	•• ••	1345	•• ••	1345	0117	1351	0154	1321
25	2252	1101	2335	1310	0002	1429	0040	1419	0213	1420	0251	1354
26	2329	1208	•• ••	1407	0056	1509	0136	1450	0309	1450	0350	1431
27	•• ••	1313	0023	1500	0151	1544	0231	1520	0406	1522	0449	1513
28	0009	1416	0113	1547	0247	1617	0327	1549	0505	1557	0548	1601
29	0051	1516	0207	1630	0342	1648	0423	1619	0603	1636	0645	1654
30	0136	1611	0301	1708	0438	1717	0519	1650	0702	1720	0739	1754
31	0225	1703	0357	1743			0616	1723			0829	1858

1997 MOONRISE & MOONSET LAT 45°N LONG 00°

The times are GMT. Adjustment for Daylight Saving Time should be made as appropriate. Data is based on Greenwich Meridian. Add 4 min for every degree West and subtract 4 min for every degree East
•• •• *Indicates that this phenomenon does not occur*

	JANUARY		FEBRUARY		MARCH		APRIL		MAY		JUNE	
	Rise	Set	Rise	Set	Rise	Set	Rise	Set	Rise	Set	Rise	Set
1	•• ••	1125	0102	1131	•• ••	1009	0138	1133	0148	1249	0208	1523
2	0010	1153	0205	1212	0055	1053	0226	1240	0225	1401	0242	1632
3	0111	1223	0308	1300	0155	1143	0310	1351	0259	1513	0318	1740
4	0214	1257	0409	1356	0252	1241	0349	1504	0333	1626	0358	1844
5	0319	1336	0506	1500	0345	1347	0426	1619	0407	1738	0443	1944
6	0424	1421	0559	1612	0433	1458	0501	1734	0443	1848	0532	2038
7	0528	1515	0645	1727	0516	1613	0536	1848	0522	1956	0625	2125
8	0629	1618	0727	1844	0556	1730	0612	2000	0605	2059	0721	2206
9	0724	1727	0805	2000	0633	1846	0650	2110	0652	2156	0818	2242
10	0813	1841	0840	2114	0708	2001	0731	2215	0743	2246	0916	2314
11	0856	1956	0914	2226	0743	2114	0816	2314	0837	2330	1014	2343
12	0934	2110	0948	2335	0820	2224	0904	•• ••	0934	•• ••	1113	•• ••
13	1009	2223	1024	•• ••	0858	2329	0956	0007	1031	0009	1211	0011
14	1042	2333	1102	0041	0940	•• ••	1050	0053	1129	0042	1310	0038
15	1114	•• ••	1144	0142	1025	0030	1145	0134	1226	0113	1410	0105
16	1147	0041	1229	0239	1113	0125	1242	0210	1325	0141	1511	0134
17	1223	0147	1318	0330	1204	0214	1340	0242	1424	0208	1614	0205
18	1302	0250	1410	0417	1258	0257	1438	0311	1524	0236	1718	0241
19	1344	0349	1504	0458	1354	0335	1536	0339	1625	0304	1821	0322
20	1430	0444	1600	0535	1451	0409	1636	0406	1727	0334	1921	0410
21	1521	0534	1658	0608	1549	0440	1736	0434	1831	0408	2017	0506
22	1614	0618	1756	0638	1647	0509	1838	0503	1934	0446	2107	0609
23	1710	0658	1854	0706	1746	0537	1940	0535	2035	0530	2151	0717
24	1807	0733	1953	0733	1845	0604	2042	0610	2132	0621	2230	0828
25	1905	0805	2052	0800	1945	0632	2143	0650	2224	0718	2306	0940
26	2003	0835	2152	0829	2046	0701	2242	0735	2310	0822	2339	1052
27	2101	0902	2253	0859	2148	0734	2336	0828	2351	0930	•• ••	1203
28	2200	0929	2354	0932	2249	0810	•• ••	0926	•• ••	1039	0012	1313
29	2259	0956			2348	0851	0025	1030	0028	1150	0045	1422
30	•• ••	1025			•• ••	0938	0109	1138	0102	1301	0119	1529
31	0000	1056			0045	1032			0135	1412		

1997 MOONRISE & MOONSET LAT 45°N LONG 00°

The times are GMT. Adjustment for Daylight Saving Time should be made as appropriate. Data is based on Greenwich Meridian. Add 4 min for every degree West and subtract 4 min for every degree East
•• •• *Indicates that this phenomenon does not occur*

	JULY		AUGUST		SEPTEMBER		OCTOBER		NOVEMBER		DECEMBER	
	Rise	Set	Rise	Set	Rise	Set	Rise	Set	Rise	Set	Rise	Set
1	0157	1634	0304	1801	0446	1820	0534	1745	0724	1749	0813	1757
2	0239	1734	0359	1841	0544	1848	0632	1813	0824	1827	0908	1852
3	0325	1830	0456	1916	0642	1915	0731	1842	0923	1912	0959	1953
4	0416	1920	0554	1948	0740	1942	0830	1913	1019	2002	1044	2059
5	0510	2003	0653	2017	0838	2009	0930	1948	1111	2059	1124	2207
6	0607	2042	0751	2044	0937	2039	1029	2028	1159	2201	1200	2318
7	0705	2115	0849	2111	1036	2111	1127	2114	1242	2307	1234	•• ••
8	0803	2146	0947	2138	1136	2148	1222	2207	1321	•• ••	1307	0028
9	0902	2214	1046	2206	1235	2231	1313	2306	1357	0017	1340	0140
10	1000	2241	1145	2237	1333	2320	1400	•• ••	1432	0129	1414	0252
11	1058	2307	1245	2311	1428	•• ••	1443	0011	1506	0242	1451	0403
12	1157	2335	1346	2351	1520	0016	1522	0121	1540	0356	1533	0514
13	1257	•• ••	1447	•• ••	1607	0120	1559	0234	1617	0510	1619	0621
14	1358	0004	1546	0038	1650	0230	1635	0349	1658	0623	1710	0723
15	1500	0037	1641	0132	1729	0345	1710	0506	1742	0734	1806	0819
16	1602	0115	1732	0234	1806	0501	1747	0622	1832	0840	1905	0908
17	1704	0159	1818	0343	1842	0618	1826	0737	1925	0939	2005	0950
18	1803	0251	1900	0457	1918	0735	1909	0849	2022	1031	2105	1027
19	1857	0350	1937	0613	1955	0850	1955	0956	2121	1115	2204	1059
20	1945	0457	2013	0730	2035	1001	2046	1057	2220	1154	2303	1128
21	2027	0609	2048	0845	2118	1109	2140	1151	2319	1227	•• ••	1155
22	2106	0723	2123	0959	2205	1212	2236	1238	•• ••	1257	0001	1221
23	2141	0838	2200	1110	2256	1308	2334	1319	0017	1325	0100	1248
24	2215	0951	2239	1218	2349	1357	•• ••	1354	0115	1352	0159	1316
25	2248	1103	2323	1321	•• ••	1441	0032	1426	0214	1418	0258	1346
26	2323	1214	•• ••	1420	0045	1519	0130	1455	0313	1446	0359	1421
27	2359	1322	0010	1513	0142	1553	0228	1522	0412	1515	0500	1501
28	•• ••	1427	0100	1600	0240	1623	0326	1549	0513	1548	0601	1547
29	0039	1528	0154	1641	0337	1652	0424	1616	0614	1625	0659	1641
30	0123	1625	0250	1718	0435	1719	0523	1644	0715	1708	0752	1741
31	0212	1716	0348	1750			0623	1715			0841	1847

1997 MOONRISE & MOONSET LAT 50°N LONG 00°

The times are GMT. Adjustment for Daylight Saving Time should be made as appropriate. Data is based on Greenwich Meridian. Add 4 min for every degree West and subtract 4 min for every degree East
•• •• *Indicates that this phenomenon does not occur*

	JANUARY Rise	Set	FEBRUARY Rise	Set	MARCH Rise	Set	APRIL Rise	Set	MAY Rise	Set	JUNE Rise	Set
1	•• ••	1124	0113	1119	0006	0956	0153	1118	0157	1241	0204	1529
2	0013	1149	0218	1158	0110	1038	0240	1227	0230	1357	0234	1641
3	0117	1216	0323	1244	0211	1127	0321	1341	0301	1513	0308	1752
4	0223	1246	0425	1340	0308	1226	0357	1458	0331	1629	0345	1859
5	0331	1323	0522	1445	0400	1333	0430	1617	0402	1745	0428	2000
6	0439	1406	0613	1558	0446	1447	0502	1735	0435	1859	0516	2054
7	0545	1459	0656	1717	0526	1605	0533	1853	0511	2009	0609	2140
8	0646	1602	0735	1838	0602	1726	0605	2009	0551	2114	0706	2220
9	0739	1713	0808	1958	0635	1846	0640	2122	0637	2212	0805	2253
10	0826	1829	0840	2116	0707	2005	0718	2229	0727	2302	0906	2323
11	0905	1948	0910	2232	0738	2122	0801	2329	0822	2345	1007	2349
12	0940	2106	0941	2344	0811	2234	0848	•• ••	0920	•• ••	1108	•• ••
13	1011	2223	1014	•• ••	0847	2343	0940	0023	1019	0021	1210	0014
14	1040	2337	1050	0052	0926	•• ••	1035	0108	1120	0052	1312	0038
15	1109	•• ••	1129	0156	1009	0045	1133	0147	1220	0120	1415	0102
16	1139	0048	1213	0254	1057	0140	1232	0221	1322	0146	1520	0127
17	1212	0157	1302	0346	1149	0229	1332	0250	1424	0210	1625	0156
18	1248	0302	1355	0432	1244	0311	1433	0317	1527	0234	1732	0229
19	1329	0404	1451	0512	1342	0348	1535	0342	1631	0259	1836	0308
20	1414	0500	1549	0547	1442	0419	1637	0406	1737	0326	1938	0354
21	1505	0550	1649	0617	1542	0448	1741	0431	1843	0357	2033	0449
22	1559	0634	1750	0644	1643	0514	1845	0457	1948	0433	2121	0553
23	1657	0712	1851	0710	1745	0539	1951	0526	2051	0515	2202	0703
24	1757	0745	1953	0734	1848	0603	2056	0558	2148	0604	2238	0818
25	1857	0814	2056	0758	1951	0628	2159	0636	2239	0702	2310	0934
26	1958	0840	2159	0824	2055	0655	2258	0720	2323	0807	2340	1049
27	2059	0905	2302	0851	2159	0724	2352	0811	•• ••	0917	•• ••	1204
28	2201	0929	•• ••	0921	2303	0757	•• ••	0910	0001	1031	0009	1318
29	2304	0953			•• ••	0836	0039	1016	0035	1145	0039	1430
30	•• ••	1019			0004	0922	0121	1127	0105	1300	0110	1541
31	0008	1047			0101	1016			0135	1414		

1997 MOONRISE & MOONSET LAT 50°N LONG 00°

The times are GMT. Adjustment for Daylight Saving Time should be made as appropriate. Data is based on Greenwich Meridian. Add 4 min for every degree West and subtract 4 min for every degree East
•• •• *Indicates that this phenomenon does not occur*

	JULY		AUGUST		SEPTEMBER		OCTOBER		NOVEMBER		DECEMBER	
	Rise	Set	Rise	Set	Rise	Set	Rise	Set	Rise	Set	Rise	Set
1	0145	1648	0248	1816	0438	1826	0534	1744	0735	1737	0830	1740
2	0225	1750	0345	1854	0539	1851	0635	1808	0837	1813	0925	1836
3	0309	1846	0444	1927	0640	1915	0737	1834	0938	1856	1014	1938
4	0400	1935	0545	1956	0741	1939	0840	1903	1035	1946	1057	2046
5	0455	2018	0646	2022	0843	2004	0942	1936	1127	2043	1134	2158
6	0553	2054	0747	2047	0944	2031	1043	2014	1214	2147	1208	2312
7	0653	2125	0848	2110	1046	2100	1142	2058	1254	2256	1238	•• ••
8	0755	2153	0949	2134	1149	2135	1238	2151	1331	•• ••	1307	0026
9	0856	2218	1051	2200	1250	2215	1329	2251	1403	0009	1336	0142
10	0957	2242	1153	2227	1349	2304	1414	2358	1434	0124	1407	0257
11	1058	2306	1257	2259	1444	•• ••	1454	•• ••	1504	0241	1441	0412
12	1200	2330	1400	2337	1535	0000	1530	0111	1535	0359	1519	0526
13	1303	2357	1502	•• ••	1620	0106	1604	0227	1609	0517	1603	0636
14	1407	•• ••	1602	0022	1700	0218	1635	0347	1646	0634	1654	0740
15	1512	0027	1657	0116	1736	0336	1707	0507	1728	0748	1750	0836
16	1617	0102	1746	0219	1809	0456	1740	0627	1816	0855	1850	0923
17	1720	0144	1830	0330	1841	0618	1816	0746	1909	0955	1952	1004
18	1819	0234	1908	0447	1913	0738	1856	0901	2007	1047	2055	1037
19	1912	0334	1942	0607	1947	0857	1940	1011	2107	1130	2157	1107
20	1958	0442	2013	0728	2024	1012	2030	1113	2209	1206	2259	1133
21	2037	0557	2044	0847	2104	1123	2124	1207	2310	1237	•• ••	1157
22	2112	0715	2116	1004	2150	1227	2222	1253	•• ••	1304	0001	1220
23	2143	0833	2150	1119	2240	1324	2321	1332	0012	1329	0102	1244
24	2213	0951	2227	1230	2334	1413	•• ••	1405	0113	1353	0204	1309
25	2243	1107	2308	1336	•• ••	1455	0022	1434	0214	1416	0307	1337
26	2314	1220	2354	1436	0031	1531	0123	1500	0317	1441	0411	1409
27	2348	1332	•• ••	1529	0130	1603	0224	1525	0419	1507	0514	1446
28	•• ••	1440	0045	1615	0231	1630	0325	1548	0523	1537	0617	1531
29	0026	1543	0139	1655	0331	1656	0426	1612	0627	1611	0715	1624
30	0108	1641	0237	1729	0432	1720	0529	1638	0730	1652	0809	1725
31	0156	1732	0337	1759			0632	1705			0856	1833

1997 MOONRISE & MOONSET LAT 55°N LONG 00°

The times are GMT. Adjustment for Daylight Saving Time should be made as appropriate. Data is based on Greenwich Meridian. Add 4 min for every degree West and subtract 4 min for every degree East
•• •• *Indicates that this phenomenon does not occur*

	JANUARY Rise	Set	FEBRUARY Rise	Set	MARCH Rise	Set	APRIL Rise	Set	MAY Rise	Set	JUNE Rise	Set
1	•• ••	1122	0126	1105	0022	0940	0213	1059	0209	1231	0159	1536
2	0016	1143	0236	1140	0128	1018	0257	1211	0237	1352	0225	1653
3	0125	1206	0343	1224	0231	1107	0334	1328	0304	1513	0255	1808
4	0235	1233	0446	1319	0329	1205	0406	1450	0329	1634	0329	1917
5	0347	1306	0542	1425	0419	1314	0435	1614	0356	1754	0409	2020
6	0458	1347	0630	1542	0501	1432	0502	1737	0424	1912	0455	2114
7	0605	1438	0710	1705	0538	1555	0529	1900	0456	2026	0548	2159
8	0706	1541	0744	1830	0609	1720	0557	2021	0533	2134	0647	2237
9	0758	1654	0813	1955	0638	1846	0628	2137	0617	2232	0749	2307
10	0841	1815	0840	2118	0705	2010	0702	2247	0707	2322	0853	2333
11	0917	1938	0906	2239	0732	2131	0742	2349	0802	•• ••	0958	2356
12	0946	2101	0933	2355	0801	2248	0828	•• ••	0902	0003	1103	•• ••
13	1013	2222	1001	•• ••	0832	2359	0920	0043	1005	0036	1208	0017
14	1038	2341	1034	0107	0908	•• ••	1016	0127	1108	0105	1314	0037
15	1103	•• ••	1110	0214	0950	0104	1116	0204	1213	0129	1421	0058
16	1129	0057	1153	0314	1037	0201	1219	0235	1318	0151	1530	0120
17	1158	0210	1241	0407	1130	0249	1322	0301	1424	0212	1639	0144
18	1231	0319	1335	0452	1227	0329	1427	0324	1531	0232	1749	0214
19	1309	0423	1434	0530	1327	0403	1532	0346	1639	0253	1856	0249
20	1354	0520	1535	0601	1430	0432	1639	0407	1749	0317	1959	0334
21	1444	0610	1639	0629	1534	0457	1747	0428	1859	0344	2053	0428
22	1541	0653	1743	0653	1639	0520	1855	0450	2007	0416	2139	0533
23	1641	0728	1848	0715	1744	0541	2004	0515	2111	0455	2217	0646
24	1744	0759	1954	0735	1851	0602	2112	0543	2209	0544	2248	0805
25	1848	0825	2100	0756	1958	0623	2218	0618	2258	0642	2316	0925
26	1952	0847	2207	0817	2106	0646	2319	0700	2339	0749	2341	1046
27	2057	0909	2315	0841	2214	0712	•• ••	0751	•• ••	0902	•• ••	1205
28	2203	0929	•• ••	0908	2321	0742	0012	0851	0014	1019	0006	1324
29	2310	0949			•• ••	0818	0058	0959	0043	1138	0031	1440
30	•• ••	1011			0024	0902	0136	1113	0109	1258	0059	1555
31	0018	1036			0122	0956			0134	1417		

1997 MOONRISE & MOONSET LAT 55°N LONG 00°

The times are GMT. Adjustment for Daylight Saving Time should be made as appropriate. Data is based on Greenwich Meridian. Add 4 min for every degree West and subtract 4 min for every degree East

•• •• *Indicates that this phenomenon does not occur*

	JULY		AUGUST		SEPTEMBER		OCTOBER		NOVEMBER		DECEMBER	
	Rise	Set	Rise	Set	Rise	Set	Rise	Set	Rise	Set	Rise	Set
1	0130	1705	0228	1835	0428	1834	0534	1742	0749	1722	0851	1719
2	0206	1810	0326	1911	0533	1855	0639	1803	0855	1755	0946	1815
3	0249	1907	0428	1941	0637	1916	0745	1825	0958	1836	1034	1919
4	0339	1955	0532	2006	0742	1936	0851	1850	1056	1925	1114	2030
5	0435	2036	0637	2029	0848	1957	0957	1920	1148	2022	1148	2146
6	0536	2109	0742	2050	0953	2020	1101	1955	1232	2129	1217	2304
7	0639	2137	0847	2110	1059	2047	1202	2038	1310	2241	1243	•• ••
8	0744	2201	0952	2130	1205	2118	1259	2130	1342	2358	1307	0024
9	0849	2223	1057	2152	1309	2156	1348	2231	1411	•• ••	1332	0144
10	0954	2243	1204	2216	1409	2243	1431	2341	1437	0119	1358	0304
11	1059	2303	1311	2244	1505	2340	1508	•• ••	1503	0240	1428	0424
12	1205	2324	1417	2319	1554	•• ••	1540	0058	1529	0403	1503	0542
13	1311	2347	1522	•• ••	1636	0047	1609	0219	1558	0526	1544	0655
14	1419	•• ••	1623	0002	1712	0203	1636	0343	1631	0648	1633	0800
15	1528	0013	1717	0055	1743	0326	1703	0509	1710	0805	1729	0857
16	1636	0045	1804	0159	1812	0451	1732	0634	1755	0915	1831	0943
17	1741	0124	1844	0313	1839	0617	1803	0757	1848	1016	1936	1020
18	1840	0213	1917	0434	1907	0743	1839	0916	1947	1107	2042	1051
19	1931	0313	1947	0559	1936	0906	1921	1029	2050	1148	2149	1117
20	2014	0424	2014	0724	2009	1026	2009	1133	2155	1221	2254	1139
21	2049	0542	2040	0849	2046	1140	2104	1228	2300	1249	•• ••	1159
22	2119	0704	2108	1011	2130	1246	2203	1312	•• ••	1312	0000	1219
23	2146	0827	2137	1130	2219	1344	2305	1349	0005	1333	0105	1239
24	2212	0950	2211	1245	2314	1433	•• ••	1419	0110	1353	0211	1300
25	2237	1111	2249	1354	•• ••	1513	0009	1444	0216	1413	0318	1325
26	2304	1229	2334	1456	0014	1547	0114	1507	0321	1434	0425	1353
27	2334	1344	•• ••	1549	0116	1615	0218	1528	0428	1457	0532	1427
28	•• ••	1456	0024	1634	0220	1639	0324	1548	0536	1523	0637	1510
29	0008	1602	0120	1712	0324	1701	0429	1608	0643	1554	0737	1603
30	0048	1701	0221	1744	0429	1722	0535	1630	0749	1632	0829	1705
31	0135	1752	0324	1811			0642	1654			0914	1816

1997 MOONRISE & MOONSET LAT 60°N LONG 00

The times are GMT. Adjustment for Daylight Saving Time should be made as appropriate. Data is based on Greenwich Meridian. Add 4 min for every degree West and subtract 4 min for every degree East
•• •• *Indicates that this phenomenon does not occur*

	JANUARY		FEBRUARY		MARCH		APRIL		MAY		JUNE	
	Rise	Set	Rise	Set	Rise	Set	Rise	Set	Rise	Set	Rise	Set
1	••••	1120	0145	1045	0043	0918	0240	1033	0223	1219	0153	1545
2	0021	1136	0258	1116	0153	0953	0320	1149	0246	1345	0214	1708
3	0135	1155	0410	1157	0259	1039	0352	1312	0307	1512	0238	1828
4	0251	1216	0515	1250	0356	1138	0419	1440	0327	1640	0307	1943
5	0407	1244	0610	1359	0444	1250	0442	1610	0347	1806	0343	2048
6	0523	1321	0654	1519	0522	1412	0503	1740	0410	1930	0427	2142
7	0634	1409	0728	1648	0553	1541	0524	1909	0437	2049	0521	2225
8	0735	1513	0756	1820	0619	1713	0546	2035	0510	2200	0622	2259
9	0824	1630	0819	1952	0641	1845	0611	2157	0550	2300	0728	2326
10	0902	1756	0840	2121	0702	2015	0641	2312	0639	2349	0836	2347
11	0931	1925	0901	2248	0724	2143	0717	•• ••	0736	•• ••	0946	•• ••
12	0955	2055	0922	•• ••	0747	2305	0801	0017	0839	0027	1056	0005
13	1016	2222	0945	0010	0813	•• ••	0852	0110	0945	0057	1206	0021
14	1035	2347	1013	0127	0845	0022	0951	0153	1054	0121	1317	0037
15	1055	•• ••	1046	0238	0923	0130	1055	0227	1203	0141	1429	0053
16	1116	0109	1126	0341	1009	0228	1201	0253	1313	0158	1543	0110
17	1139	0227	1214	0434	1103	0316	1310	0315	1424	0214	1658	0130
18	1208	0341	1309	0518	1203	0354	1419	0334	1536	0229	1813	0154
19	1243	0448	1411	0553	1307	0424	1530	0351	1650	0246	1924	0225
20	1326	0548	1517	0621	1414	0449	1641	0407	1805	0304	2027	0306
21	1417	0638	1625	0644	1523	0510	1754	0423	1920	0326	2121	0400
22	1515	0718	1734	0704	1633	0528	1908	0440	2033	0354	2203	0506
23	1619	0751	1844	0721	1744	0544	2022	0500	2140	0429	2235	0624
24	1727	0817	1955	0737	1855	0600	2135	0524	2237	0515	2301	0748
25	1835	0838	2106	0753	2008	0617	2245	0554	2324	0613	2323	0914
26	1945	0857	2218	0810	2121	0635	2347	0633	•• ••	0723	2343	1041
27	2055	0913	2331	0828	2233	0656	•• ••	0722	0001	0842	•• ••	1207
28	2206	0929	•• ••	0850	2344	0721	0039	0823	0030	1005	0002	1331
29	2318	0945			•• ••	0753	0122	0935	0054	1130	0022	1454
30	•• ••	1002			0051	0835	0156	1055	0115	1255	0044	1613
31	0031	1021			0150	0928			0134	1421		

1997 MOONRISE & MOONSET LAT 60°N LONG 00°

The times are GMT. Adjustment for Daylight Saving Time should be made as appropriate. Data is based on Greenwich Meridian. Add 4 min for every degree West and subtract 4 min for every degree East
•• •• *Indicates that this phenomenon does not occur*

	JULY		AUGUST		SEPTEMBER		OCTOBER		NOVEMBER		DECEMBER	
	Rise	Set	Rise	Set	Rise	Set	Rise	Set	Rise	Set	Rise	Set
1	0110	1729	0201	1900	0415	1844	0534	1739	0808	1702	0919	1650
2	0142	1837	0302	1932	0525	1901	0645	1755	0918	1731	1015	1746
3	0222	1935	0407	1958	0634	1916	0755	1813	1025	1808	1100	1853
4	0311	2023	0516	2019	0744	1932	0906	1834	1125	1856	1136	2009
5	0408	2100	0626	2037	0854	1948	1017	1858	1216	1955	1205	2131
6	0512	2130	0735	2053	1005	2007	1126	1930	1257	2104	1228	2255
7	0620	2153	0845	2109	1116	2029	1230	2010	1331	2222	1249	•• ••
8	0729	2213	0955	2124	1226	2055	1327	2102	1357	2345	1308	0020
9	0839	2229	1106	2141	1334	2130	1415	2205	1420	•• ••	1327	0147
10	0949	2245	1217	2201	1437	2215	1455	2319	1441	0111	1347	0313
11	1059	2301	1329	2224	1533	2312	1527	•• ••	1501	0240	1411	0439
12	1210	2317	1440	2255	1620	•• ••	1553	0041	1521	0409	1441	0602
13	1322	2335	1549	2334	1657	0023	1616	0208	1544	0538	1518	0720
14	1435	2356	1651	•• ••	1728	0144	1637	0339	1612	0706	1604	0829
15	1549	•• ••	1745	0026	1753	0312	1658	0511	1646	0828	1701	0925
16	1701	0023	1828	0132	1815	0443	1721	0642	1728	0942	1806	1009
17	1809	0058	1902	0251	1837	0616	1746	0812	1820	1045	1915	1043
18	1908	0145	1930	0417	1858	0748	1817	0937	1920	1134	2026	1109
19	1957	0245	1953	0549	1922	0918	1855	1055	2027	1212	2137	1130
20	2035	0359	2015	0721	1950	1044	1942	1201	2136	1241	2248	1147
21	2105	0522	2035	0851	2023	1203	2037	1255	2246	1304	2359	1203
22	2129	0651	2057	1020	2103	1313	2138	1338	2356	1323	•• ••	1218
23	2150	0820	2121	1145	2152	1412	2244	1411	•• ••	1339	0109	1233
24	2210	0949	2149	1305	2248	1500	2353	1436	0106	1355	0220	1250
25	2230	1116	2224	1418	2350	1537	•• ••	1457	0217	1410	0332	1309
26	2251	1240	2306	1523	•• ••	1607	0102	1515	0328	1426	0445	1332
27	2316	1401	2357	1617	0057	1631	0212	1531	0440	1444	0556	1402
28	2346	1518	•• ••	1700	0205	1651	0322	1547	0552	1505	0705	1442
29	•• ••	1628	0055	1735	0314	1708	0432	1602	0705	1531	0806	1533
30	0022	1729	0159	1803	0424	1724	0544	1619	0815	1606	0857	1638
31	0107	1820	0306	1825			0656	1639			0938	1753

MARINAS

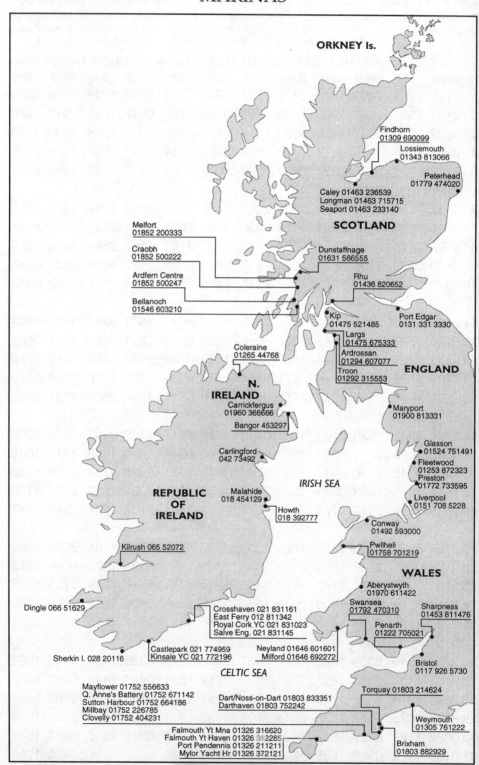

ORKNEY Is.

Findhorn
01309 690099

Lossiemouth
01343 813066

Peterhead
01779 474020

Caley 01463 236539
Longman 01463 715715
Seaport 01463 233140

SCOTLAND

Melfort
01852 200333

Craobh
01852 500222

Ardfern Centre
01852 500247

Bellanoch
01546 603210

Dunstaffnage
01631 566555

Rhu
01436 820652

Kip
01475 521485

Port Edgar
0131 331 3330

Largs
01475 675333

Ardrossan
01294 607077

Troon
01292 315553

ENGLAND

Coleraine
01265 44768

**N.
IRELAND**

Carrickfergus
01960 366666

Bangor 453297

Maryport
01900 813331

Glasson
01524 751491

Fleetwood
01253 872323

Preston
01772 733595

Liverpool
0151 708 5228

Carlingford
042 73492

IRISH SEA

**REPUBLIC
OF
IRELAND**

Malahide
018 454129

Howth
018 392777

Conway
01492 593000

Pwllheli
01758 701219

Kilrush 065 52072

WALES

Aberystwyth
01970 611422

Dingle 066 51629

Swansea
01792 470310

Sharpness
01453 811476

Crosshaven 021 831161
East Ferry 012 811342
Royal Cork YC 021 831023
Salve Eng. 021 831145

Penarth
01222 705021

Castlepark 021 774959
Kinsale YC 021 772196

Neyland 01646 601601
Milford 01646 692272

Sherkin I. 028 20116

Bristol
0117 926 5730

CELTIC SEA

Mayflower 01752 556633
Q. Anne's Battery 01752 671142
Sutton Harbour 01752 664186
Millbay 01752 226785
Clovelly 01752 404231

Dart/Noss-on-Dart 01803 833351
Darthaven 01803 752242

Torquay 01803 214624

Weymouth
01305 761222

Falmouth Yt Mna 01326 316620
Falmouth Yt Haven 01326 312285
Port Pendennis 01326 211121
Mylor Yacht Hr 01326 372121

Brixham
01803 882929

MARINAS

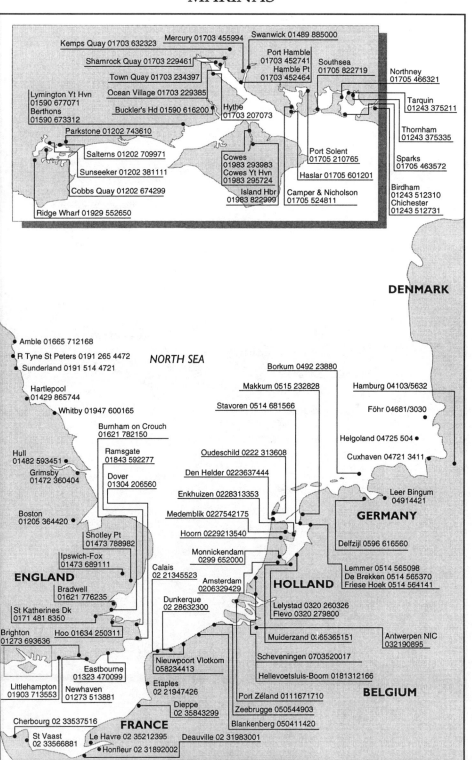

Kemps Quay 01703 632323
Mercury 01703 455994
Swanwick 01489 885000
Shamrock Quay 01703 229461
Port Hamble 01703 452741
Hamble Pt 01703 452464
Southsea 01705 822719
Northney 01705 466321
Town Quay 01703 234397
Ocean Village 01703 229385
Lymington Yt Hvn 01590 677071
Berthons 01590 673312
Buckler's Hd 01590 616200
Hythe 01703 207073
Tarquin 01243 375211
Thornham 01243 375335
Parkstone 01202 743610
Salterns 01202 709971
Cowes 01983 293983
Cowes Yt Hvn 01983 295724
Port Solent 01705 210765
Sparks 01705 463572
Sunseeker 01202 381111
Haslar 01705 601201
Cobbs Quay 01202 674299
Island Hbr 01983 822999
Camper & Nicholson 01705 524811
Birdham 01243 512310
Chichester 01243 512731
Ridge Wharf 01929 552650

DENMARK

Amble 01665 712168
R Tyne St Peters 0191 265 4472
Sunderland 0191 514 4721
NORTH SEA
Hartlepool 01429 865744
Whitby 01947 600165
Borkum 0492 23880
Makkum 0515 232828
Hamburg 04103/5632
Stavoren 0514 681566
Föhr 04681/3030
Burnham on Crouch 01621 782150
Ramsgate 01843 592277
Oudeschild 0222 313608
Helgoland 04725 504
Cuxhaven 04721 3411
Hull 01482 593451
Grimsby 01472 360404
Dover 01304 206560
Den Helder 0223637444
Enkhuizen 0228313353
Leer Bingum 04914421
Boston 01205 364420
Medemblik 0227542175
GERMANY
Shotley Pt 01473 788982
Hoorn 0229213540
Delfzijl 0596 616560
Ipswich-Fox 01473 689111
Monnickendam 0299 652000
Calais 02 21345523
Lemmer 0514 565098
De Brekken 0514 565370
Friese Hoek 0514 564141
ENGLAND
Bradwell 01621 776235
Amsterdam 0206329429
HOLLAND
St Katherines Dk 0171 481 8350
Dunkerque 02 28632300
Lelystad 0320 260326
Flevo 0320 279800
Brighton 01273 693636
Hoo 01634 250311
Muiderzand 0365365151
Antwerpen NIC 032190895
Eastbourne 01323 470099
Nieuwpoort Vlotkom 058234413
Scheveningen 0703520017
Littlehampton 01903 713553
Newhaven 01273 513881
Etaples 02 21947426
Hellevoetsluis-Boom 0181312166
BELGIUM
Cherbourg 02 33537516
Dieppe 02 35843299
Port Zéland 0111671710
St Vaast 02 33566881
Le Havre 02 35212395
Deauville 02 31983001
Zeebrugge 050544903
Honfleur 02 31892002
Blankenberg 050411420
FRANCE

MARINAS

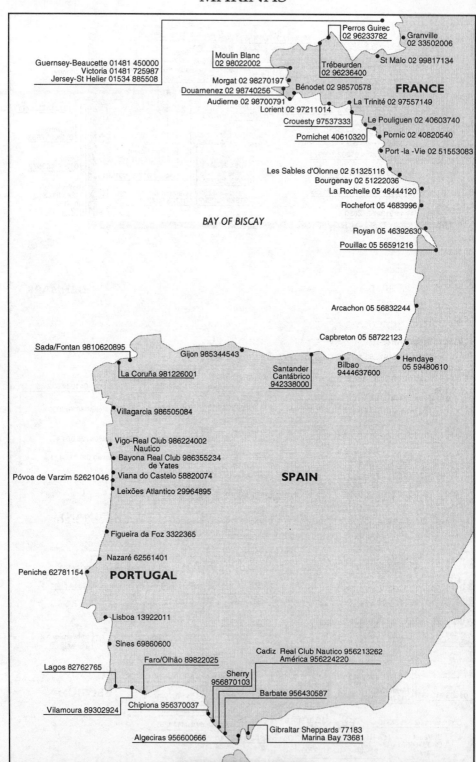

Perros Guirec 02 96233782

Granville 02 33502006

Moulin Blanc 02 98022002

Trébeurden 02 96236400

St Malo 02 99817134

Guernsey-Beaucette 01481 450000
Victoria 01481 725987
Jersey-St Helier 01534 885508

Morgat 02 98270197

Douarnenez 02 98740256

Bénodet 02 98570578

FRANCE

Audierne 02 98700791

Lorient 02 97211014

La Trinité 02 97557149

Crouesty 97537333

Le Pouliguen 02 40603740

Pornichet 40610320

Pornic 02 40820540

Port -la -Vie 02 51553083

Les Sables d'Olonne 02 51325116
Bourgenay 02 51222036
La Rochelle 05 46444120

Rochefort 05 4683996

BAY OF BISCAY

Royan 05 46392630

Pouillac 05 56591216

Arcachon 05 56832244

Capbreton 05 58722123

Sada/Fontan 9810620895

Gijon 985344543

Hendaye 05 59480610

Bilbao 9444637600

La Coruña 981226001

Santander Cantábrico 942338000

Villagarcia 986505084

Vigo-Real Club 986224002 Nautico

Bayona Real Club 986355234 de Yates

Póvoa de Varzim 52621046

Viana do Castelo 58820074

SPAIN

Leixões Atlantico 29964895

Figueira da Foz 3322365

Nazaré 62561401

Peniche 62781154

PORTUGAL

Lisboa 13922011

Sines 69860600

Cadiz Real Club Nautico 956213262
América 956224220

Faro/Olhão 89822025

Lagos 82762765

Sherry 956870103

Barbate 956430587

Vilamoura 89302924

Chipiona 956370037

Gibraltar Sheppards 77183
Marina Bay 73681

Algeciras 956600666

POSITION SECTION

CONTENTS

Principal lights visible 15M and over -

UK South coast 302
UK East coast 303
UK Scotland 303
UK West coast 305
Ireland 306
Belgium 307
Holland 307
Germany 309
Denmark 311
France & Channel Islands 311
Spain 316
Portugal 317
Gibraltar 317
Radiobeacons 318
Emergency D/F service 322
Emergency D/F service chart - UK 324
Emergency D/F service chart - France 325
Distance from dipping light table 326
Speed, time and distance table 327

LIGHTS TO BE CARRIED BY YACHTS

At night or in poor visibilty, yachts must show the following lights:

Sail/power, under 7m ...... All round white
Power under 12m .... All round white plus sidelights
Power over 12m .... White steaming and stern lights plus sidelights
Sail up to 20m .... Masthead tricolour or sternlight plus sidelights
Sail over 12m .... Sternlight and separate sidelights

Arcs

Steaming beam .... White 22·5° abaft the beam through right ahead to 22·5°abaft the other
Stern beam .... White 22·5° abaft the beam through right astern to 22·5°abaft the other
Sidelights .... Red to port and green to starboard 22·5° abaft the beam to right ahead

PRINCIPAL LIGHTS

Range 15M and over

Abbreviations used in List of Lights:

Al Alternating
Bu Blue
Dir Direction light
F Fixed
Fl Flashing
Fl( ) Group flashing
G Green
(hor) Horizontal
intens Intensified sector
Iso Isophase
Lanby Large Automatic Navigational Buoy
Ldg Lts Leading lights
LFl Long flash
Lt F Light-float
Lt V Light-vessel
M Sea miles
m Metres
Mo Morse code light or fog signal
Oc Occulting
Occas Occasional
(P) Provisional, preliminary
Q Quick flashing
R Red
Ra Coast radar station
Racon Radar responder beacon
Radio Coast radio station
RC Circular radiobeacon
RG Radio direction finding station
s Seconds
(T) Temporary
TE Light temporarily extinguished
unintens Unintensified sector
(vert) Vertical
Vi Violet
Vis Visible
VQ Very quick flashing
W White
Y Yellow, amber or orange

SOUTH COAST OF ENGLAND

A0002 Bishop Rock- 49°52'.3N 6°26'.7W Fl(2)W 15s 44m 24M Racon *partially obscured 204°-211°(7°), obscured 211°-233°(22°), 236°-259°(23°)*

A0006 St Mary's- Peninnis Head 49°54'.2N 6°18'.2W FlW 20s 36m 17M *Vis 231°-117°(246°), partially obscured 048°-083°(35°) within 5M*

A0018 Round Island 49°58'.7N 6°19'.3W FlW 10s 55m 24M *Vis 021°-288°(267°) RC*

A0020 Seven Stones Lt F 50°03'.6N 6°04'.3W Fl(3)W 30s 12m 25M *Racon*

A0028 Longships 50°04'.0N 5°44'.8W Iso WR 10s 35m 19/18/15M *R189°-208° (19°), R(unintens)208°-307°(99°), R307°-327° (20°), W327°-189°(222°)*

A0030 Wolf Rock 49°56'.7N 5°48'.5W FlW 15s 34m 23M *Racon*

A0032 Tater-du 50°03'.1N 5°34'.6W Fl(3)W 15s 34m 23M *Vis 241°-074°(193°)*

A0046 Penzance Hbr- S Pier hd 50°07'.0N 5°31'.6W FlWR 5s 11m 17/12 M *R(unintens)159°- 224°(65°), R224°-268°(44°), W268°- 344.5°(76.5°), R344.5°- shore .*

A0060 Lizard 49°57'.6N 5°12'.1W FlW 3s 70m 25M *Vis 250°-120°(230°), ptly vis 235°-250°(15°) RC*

A0062 St Anthony Head 50°08'.4N 5°00'.9W Oc WR 15s 22m 22/20/20M *W295°-004°(69°),R004°- 022°(18°) over Manacle rocks, W(unintens) 022°-100°(78°)W100° -172° (72°)*

A0094 Looe Harbour - Banjo Pier hd 50°21'.0N 4°27'.0W Oc WR 3s 8m 15/12M *W013°-207° (194°), R207°- 267°(60°), W267°-313°(46°), R313°-332°(19°)*

A0098 Eddystone 50°10'.8N 4°15'.9W Fl(2)W 10s 41m 22M *Racon*

A0228 Start Point 50°13'.3 N 3°38'.5W Fl(3)W 10s 62m 25M *Vis 184°-068°(244°)*

A0294 Portland Bill 50°30'.8N 2°27'.3W Fl(4)W 20s 43m 25M *Gradually changes from 1fl to 4fl 221°-244°(23°), 4fl 244°-117°(233°), gradually changes from 4fl to 1fl 117°-141°(24°) RC*

A0314 Portland Harbour NE brkwr SE end, A head 50°35'.1N 2°25'.0W FlW 10s 22m 20M

A0496 Anvil Pt 50°35'.5N 1°57'.5W FlW 10s 45m 24M *Vis 237°-076°(199°)*

A0528 Needles Outer Needle 50°39'.7N 1°35'.4W Oc(2)WRG 20s 24m 17/17/14/14M *R shore-300°, W300°-083°(143°), R(unintens) 083°-212°(129°), W212°-217°(5°), G217°-224°(7°)*

A0774 St Catherine's Pt 50°34'.5N 1°17'.8W FlW 5s 41m 27M *Vis 257°-117°(220°),* F R 35m 17M *Vis 099°-116°(17°) RC*

A0780 Nab 50°40'.0N 0°57'.1W FlW 10s 27m 16M *Racon Vis 300°-120° (180°)*

A0814.1 Shoreham Harbour Ldg Lt 355° Rear 192m from front 50°49'.8N 0°14'.8W FlW 10s 13m 15M *Vis 283°-103°(180°)*

A0839 Greenwich Lt F 50°24'.5N 0°00'.0 FlW 5s 12m 21M *Racon*

A0840 Beachy Head 50°44'.0N 0°14'.6E Fl(2)W 20s 31m 25M *Vis 248°-101°(213°)*

A0876 Dungeness 50°54'.8N 0°58'.7E FlW 10s 40m 27M *RC Partially obscured 078°-shore*

A0892 Folkestone Breakwater head 51°04'.5N 1°11'.8E Fl(2)W 10s 14m 22M

A0900 DOVER HARBOUR - Admiralty pier 51°06'.6N 1°19'.8E FlW 7.5s 21m 20M *Vis 096°-090°(354°), Obscured in The Downs by S Foreland inshore of 226°*

A0924 - S brkwr, W hd 51°06'.8N 1°19'.9E Oc R 30s 21m 18M

A0926 - - Knuckle 51°07'.0N 1°20'.6E Fl(4)WR 10s 15m 15/13M *R059°-239°(180°), W239°-059°(180°)*

A0966 North Foreland 51°22'.5N 1°26'.8E Fl(5)WR 20s 57m 19/16/15M *W shore - 150°, R 150°-181° (31°), R181°-200°(19°), W200°-011°(171°). RC*

A0970 Varne Lt F 51°01'.2N 1°24'.0E Fl R 20s 12m 19M *Racon*

A0980 S Goodwin Lt F 51°07'.9N 1°28'.6E Fl(2)W 30s 12m 21M

A0984 E Goodwin Lt F 51°13'.0N 1°36'.3E FlW 15s 12m 21M *Racon*

A0992 F3 Lt F 51°23'.8N 2°00'.6E FlW 10s 12m 22M *Racon*

EAST COAST OF ENGLAND

A2096 Shornmead 51°27'.0N 0°26'.6E Fl(2)WRG 10s
12m 17/13/13M *G054°- 081.5°(27.5°),
R081.5°-086.2° (4.7°), W086.2°- 088.7°(2.5°),
G088.7°- 141°(52.3°), W141°-205°(64°),
R205°-213°(8°)*

A2118 **TILBURY** Northfleet Lower 51°26'.9N
0°20'.4E **Oc WR 5s** 15m 17/14M *W164°-
271°(107°), R271°-S shore in Gravesend reach*

A2119 **- Northfleet Upper** 51°26'.9N 0°20'.2E
Oc WRG 10s 30m 16/12/12M
*R126°-149°(23°), W149°-159°(10°),
G159°-268°(109°), W268°- 279°(11°)*

A2170 **Sunk Lt F** 51°51'.0N 1°35'.0E Fl(2)W20s
12m 24M RC. *Racon.*

A2258 **Orford Ness** 52°05'.0N 1°34'.6E
Fl W 5s 28m 25M *Racon*
F RG14m 15/14M
R shore-210°, R038°-047°(9°), G047°-shore

A2272 **Southwold** 52°19'.6N 1°41'.0E Fl(4)WR 20s
37m 17/15/14M *R(intens)204°-220°(16°),
W220°- 001°(141°), R001°-032.3°(31.3°)*

A2280 **Lowestoft** 52°29'.2N 1°45'.5E **Fl W 15s** 37m
28M *Partially obsc 347°-shore.*

A2332 **Newarp Lt F** 52°48'.3N 1°55'.8E
Fl W 10s 12m 21M *Racon*

A2342 **Cromer** 52°55'.5N 1°19'.1E
Fl W 5s 84m 23M *Vis 102°-307°(205°). RC.
Racon.*

A2351 **Inner Dowsing Lt F** 53°19'.5N 0°34'.0E
Fl W 10s 12m 15M *Racon*

A2420 **B 1D Dowsing** 53°33'.7N 0°52'.7E
Fl(2)W 10s 28m 22M *Racon*

A2582 **Flamborough Head** 54°07'.0N 0°04'.8W
Fl(4)W 15s 65m 24M *RC*

A2596 **Whitby High** 54°28'.6N 0°34'.0W
Iso WR 10s 73m 18/16M
R128°-143°(15°), W143°-319°(176°)

A2626 **South Gare** 54°38'.8N 1°08'.1W **Fl WR 12s**
16m 20/17M *W020°-274°(254°). R274°-
357°(83°).* **Shown from a structure 84m S,
obscured on a bearing 197.5°(T) 1993**

A2663 **Hartlepool** The Heugh 54°41'.8N 1°10'.5W
Fl(2)W 10s 19m 19M *RG*

A2681 **Sunderland** Roker Pier 54°55'.3N 1°21'.0W
Fl W 5s 25m 23M *Vis 211°-357°(146°)*

A2700 **Tynemouth** Entrance 55°00'.9N 1°24'.1W
Fl(3)W 10s 26m 26M

A2703 **NORTH SHIELDS** Fish Quay. Ldg Lts 258°
Front 55°00'.5N 1°26'.0W **F W** 25m 20M

A2703-1 **- Rear** 220m from front 55°00'.5N 1°26'.2W
F W 39m 20M

A2754 **Blyth** East Pier 55°07'.0N 1°29'.1W
Fl(4)W 10s 19m 21M

A2780 **Coquet** 55°20'.0N 1°32'.2W **Fl(3)WR 30s**
25m 23/19M *R330°-140°(170°), W140°-
163°(23°), R163°-180°(17°), W180°-
330°(150°). Sector boundaries are indeterminate
and may appear as A1WR*

A2810 **Bamburgh** 55°37'.0N 1°43'.3W
Oc(2)WRG 15s 12m 17/13/13M *G122°-
165°(43°), W165°- 175° (10°), R175°-
191°(16°), W191°-238°(47°), R238°-
275°(37°), W275-289°(14°), G289°- 300°(11°)*

A2814 **Farne Is** Longstone. W Side 55°38'.6 N
1°36'.5 W **Fl W 20s** 23m 24M

SCOTLAND

A2850 **St Abb's Head** 55°55'.0N 2°08'.3W
Fl W 10s 68m 26M *Racon*

A2868 **Fidra** 56°04'.4N 2°47'.0W **Fl (4)W 30s**
34m 24M *RC Obscured by Bass Rock. Craig Leith
& Lamb Island*

A2912 **Inchkeith,** Summit 56°02'.0N 3°08'.1W
Fl W 15s 67m 22M *RC*

A2915-4 **BRAEFOOT BAY TERMINAL,** Western
Jetty. Ldg Lts 247°15'. Front 56°02'.2N
3°18'.6W **Fl W 3s** 6m 15M *Vis 237.2°-
257.2°(20°)*

A2915-41 **- Rear**, 88m from front 56°02'.2N 3°18'.7W
Fl W 3s12m 15M *Vis 237.2°-257.2°(20°)
Synchronised with front*

A3060 **Elie Ness** 56°11'.0N 2°48'.6W
Fl W 6s 15m 18M

A3090 **Isle of May** Summit 56°11'.2N 2°33'.3W
Fl(2)W 15s 73m 22M

A3102 **Fife Ness** 56°16'.7N 2°35'.1W **Iso WR 10s**
12m 21/20M *W143°-197°(54°).
R197°-217°(20°). W217°-023°(166°). RC*

A3108 **Bell Rock** 56°26'.1N 2°23'.1W
Fl W 5s 28m 18M *Racon*

A3142 **Tayport** High Lighthouse. Dir Lt 269°
56°27'.2N 2°53'.8W
Dir Iso WRG 3s 24m 22/17/16M *G267°-
268°(1°), W268°-270°(2°), R270°-271°(1°)*

A3220 **Scurdie Ness** 56°42'.1N 2°26'.1W
Fl(3)W 20s 38m 23M *Racon*

A3234 **Todhead** 56°53'.0N 2°12'.8W
Fl(4)W 30s 41m 18M

A3246 **Girdle Ness** 57°08'.3N 2°02'.8W
Fl(2)W 20s 56m 22M *Obscured by Greg Ness
when brg more than about 020°. RC. Racon*

A3280 **Buchan Ness** 57°28'.2N 1°46'.4W
Fl W 5s 40m 28M *Racon*

A3304 **Rattray Head** Ron Rock 57°36'.6N
1°48'.9W
Fl(3)W 30s 28m 24M *Racon*

A3332 **Kinnaird Head** 57°41'.9N 2°00'.1W
Fl W 5s 25m 22M *Vis 092°-297°(205°) RC*

A3394 **BUCKIE HARBOUR** Ldg Lts 125°Front
57°40'.9N 2°57'.5W **Oc R 10s** 15m 15M

A3394.1 **- Rear** 365m from front, 57°40'.7N 2°57'.2W
Iso WG 2s 20m 16/12M *G090°-110°(20°),
W110°-225° (115°)*

A3414 **Covesea Skerries** 57°43'.5N 3°20'.2W
Fl WR 20s 49m 24/20M *W076°-
267°(191°). R267°-282°(15°)*

A3440 **Chanonry** 57°34'.5N 4°05'.4W
Oc W 6s 12m 15M *Vis 148°-073°(285°)*

A3490 **Cromarty** The Ness 57°41'.0N 4°02'.1W
Oc WR 10s 18m 15/11M *R079°-088°(9°),
W088°-0275°(187°)*

A3506 **Tarbat Ness** 57°51'.9N 3°46'.5W
Fl(4)W 30s 53m 24M *Racon*

A3524 **Clythness** 58°18'.7N 3°12'.6W
Fl(2)W 30s 45m 16M

A3544 **Noss Head** 58°28'.8N 3°03'.0W **Fl WR 20s**
53m 25/21M *R shore-191°, W191°-shore*

A3558 **PENTLAND FIRTH** Duncansby Head
58°38'.6N 3°01'.4W **Fl W**12s 67m 24M
Racon. RC

A3562 - **Pentland Skerries** 58°41'.4N 2°55'.4W
Fl(3)W 30s 52m 23M

A3568 - **Swilkie Point** Stroma 58°41'.8N 3°07'.0W
Fl(2)W 20s 32m 26M

A3574 - **Dunnet Head** 58°40'.3N 3°22'.4W
Fl(4)W 30s 105m 23M *RG*

A3578 **Thurso Bay** Little Head. Holborn Head
58°36'.9N 3°32'.4W **Fl WR 10s** 23m 15/11M
W198°-358°(160°), R358°-shore

A3590 **Strathy Point** 58°36'.1'N 4°00'.9 W
Fl W 20s 45m 27M

A3602 **Cantick Head** 58°47'.2N 3°07'.8W
Fl W 20s 35m 18M

A3644 **HOY SOUND** Graemsay Island Ldg Lts
104°'. Front 58°56'.5N 3°18'.4W
Iso W 3s 17m 15M *Vis 070°-255°(185°)*

A3644-1- Rear 1.2M from front 58°56'.2N 3°16'.3W
Oc WR 8s 35m 20/16M *R097°-112°(15°),
W112°- 163° (51°), R163°-178°(15°), W178°-
332°(154°) Obscured on leading line within 0.5M*

A3676 **Copinsay** 58°53'.8N 2°40'.2W
Fl(5)W 30s 79m 21M

A3680 **Auskerry** 59°01'.6N 2°34'.2W
Fl W 20s 34m 18M

A3688 **Kirkwall** Pier. N end 58°59'.3N 2°57'.6W
Iso WRG 5s 13m 15/13/13M *G153°-
183°(30°), W183°-192°(9°), R192°-210°(18°)*

A3700 **Brough of Birsay** 59°08'.2N 3°20'.3W
Fl(3)W 25s 52m 18M

A3718 **Sanday Island** Start Point 59°16'.7N
2°22'.5W Fl(2)W 20s 24m 19M

A3722 **North Ronaldsay** 59°23'.4N 2°22'.8W
Fl W 10s 43m 19M *Racon*

A3736 **Westray** Noup Head 59°19'.9N 3°04'.0W
Fl W 30s 79m 22M *Vis about 335°-
242°(267°). 248-282°(34°) Obscured by cliffs on
easterly bearings within 0.8M, partially obscured
240°-275°(35°)*

A3750 **FAIR ISLE** South. Skadan 59°30'.9N
1°39'.0W
Fl(4)W 30s 32m 24M *Vis 260°- 146°(246°),
but obscured close inshore from 260°- 282°(22°)*

A3756 - **North** Skroo 59°33'.2N 1°36'.5W
Fl(2)W 30s 80m 22M *Vis 086.7°-
358°(271.3°)*

A3766 **Sumburgh Head** 59°51'.3N 1°16'.3W
Fl(3) W 30s 91m 23M *RC*

A3776 **Kirkabister Ness** Bressay 60°07'.2N
1°07'.2W Fl(2)W 20s 32m 23M

A3807 **Out Skerries** Bound Skerry 60°25'.5N
0°43'.5W Fl W 20s 44m 20M

A3812 **YELL SOUND** Firths Voe. N shore
60°27'.2N 1°10'.6W Oc WRG 8s 9m 15/10/
10M *W189°-194°(5°), G194°-257(63°),
W257-263° (6°), R263°-339°(76°),
W339°-066°(87°)*

A3817-5 - **Point of Fethaland** 60°38'.1N 1°18'.6W
Fl(3)WR 15s 65m 24/20M *R080°-103°(23°),
W103°-160°(57°), R160°-206°(46°), W206°-
340°(134°)*

A3822 **SULLOM VOE** Gluss Isle Ldg Lts 194°44'.
Front 60°29'.8N 1°19'.3W F W 39m 19M

A3822-1 - **Rear** 0.75M from front 60°29'.1N 1°19'.5W
FW 69m 19M

A3832 **North Unst** Muckle Flugga 60°51'.3N
0°53'.0W Fl(2) W 20s 66m 22M

A3838 **Esha Ness** 60°29'.3N 1°37'.6W
Fl W 12s 61m 25M

A3845-5 **West Burra Firth** Inner Lt 60°17'.8N
1°32'.0W
F WRG 9m 15/9/9M *G095°-098°(3°),
W098°-102°(4°), R102°- 105°(3°)*

A3860 **Foula** 60°06'.8N 2°03'.7W Fl(3)W 15s 36m
18M *Obscured 123°-221°(98°)*

A3868 **Sule Skerry** 59°05'.0N 4°24'.3W
Fl(2)W 15s 34m 21M *Racon*

A3869 **Rona** (North Rona) 59°07'.3N 5°48'.8W
Fl(3)W 20s 114m 24M

A3880 **Cape Wrath** 58°37'.5N 5°00'.0W
Fl(4)W 30s 122m 24M

A3882 **Stoer Head** Cluas Deas 58°14'.4N 5°24'.0W
Fl W 15s 59m 24M

A3900 **Rubha Reidh** 57°51'.4N 5°48'.6W
Fl(4)W 15s 37m 24M

A3904 **Rona** (South Rona). NE point 57°34'.7N
5°57'.5W Fl W 12s 69m 19M
Vis 050°-358°(308°)

A3944 **Sound of Sleat** SE End. 57°08'.6N 5°46'.4W
Oc W 8s 18m 15M *Vis 157°-030°(233°)*

A3968 **Butt of Lewis** 58°31'.0N 6°15'.7W
Fl W 5s 52m 25M *Vis 056°-320°(264°). RC*

A3972 **Tiumpan Head** 58°15'.6N 6°08'.3W
Fl(2)W 15s 55m 25M

A3976 **Stornoway Harbour** Arnish Point
58°11'.5N 6°22'.2W Fl WR 10s 17m 19/15M
*W088°- 198° (110°), R198°-302°(104°),
W302°-013°(71°)*

A3990 **East Loch Tarbert** Scalpay. Eilean Glas
57°51'.4N 6°38'.5W Fl(3)W 20s 43m 23M
Racon

A4004 **South Uist** Ushenish 57°17'.9N 7°11'.5W
Fl WR 20s 54m 19/15M *W193°-356°(163°).
R356°-013°(17°)*

A4020 **Berneray** W side. Barra Head 56°47'.1N
7°39'.2W Fl W 15s 208m 18M
Obscured by the islands to NE

A4028 **Flannan Isles** Eilean Mór 58°17'.3N
7°35'.4W Fl(2)W 30s 101m 20M *Obscured
in places by islands W of Eilean Mór*

A4064 **Skye Ness Point** Neist Point 57°25'.4N
6°47'.2W Fl W 5s 43m 16M

A4076 **Òigh Sgeir** Near S end. Hyskeir 56°58'.2N
6°40'.9W Fl(3)W 30s 41m 24M

A4082 **Ardnamurchan** 56°43'.6N 6°13'.4W
Fl(2)W 20s 55m 24M *Vis 002°-217°(215°)*

A4092 **Tiree Scarinish** S side of entrance
56°30'.0N 6°48'.2W Fl W 3s 11m 16M
Vis 210°-030°(180°)

A4096 **Skerryvore** 56°19'.4N 7°06'.9W
Fl W 10s 46m 23M *Racon*

A4098 **Dubh Artach** 56°08'.0N 6°37'.9W Fl(2)W
30s 44m 20M **Range 10M(T) 1996**

A4112 **Sound of Mull-** Rubha nan Gall 56°38'.3N
6°03'.9W Fl W 3s 17m 15M

A4170 **Lismore** Eilean Musdile. SW end 56°27'.4N
5°36'.4W Fl W 10s 31m 19M
Vis 237°-208°(331°)

A4236 **Sound of Islay** Rubh'a' Mhàil. Ruvaal
55°56'.2N 6°07'.3W Fl(3)WR 15s 45m 24/
21M *R075°-180°(105°), W180°-075°(255°)*

A4256 **Orsay Island** Rhinns of Islay 55°40'.4N
6°30'.8W **Fl W 5s** 46m 24M
Vis 256°-184°(288°). RC

A4272 **Mull of Kintyre** 55°18'.6N 5°48'.1W
Fl(2)W 20s 91m 24M Vis 347°-178°(191°)
Reduced range (T) 1995

A4274 **Sanda Island** S side 55°16'.5N 5°34'.9W
Fl W 10s 50m 15M Racon

A4276 **Campbeltown Loch** Island Davaar. N Point
55°25'.7N 5°32'.4W **Fl(2)W 10s** 37m 23M
Vis 073°-330°(257°)

A4293 **Skipness** Calibration range 55°46'.7 N
5° 19'.0W **Oc(2)Y 10s** 24M.
Shown when range in use

A4326 **Arran Island** Pladda 55°25'.5N 5°07'.3W
Fl(3)W 30s 40m 17M

A4330 **Holy Island** Pillar Rock Point 55°31'.0N
5°03'.6W **Fl(2)W 20s** 38m 25M

A4346 **Little Cumbrae** Cumbrae Elbow 55°43'.3N
4°57'.9W **Fl W 3s** 31m 23M Vis 334°-
210°(236°)

A4362 **Toward Point** 55°51'.7N 4°58'.7W
Fl W 10s 21m 22M

A4421 **GARELOCK** Beacon No 8N. Dir Lt 080°
55°59'.1N 4°44'.1W **Dir WRG** 4m 16/13/13M
FG075°-077.5°(2.5°),Al WG077.5°-079.5°(2°),
FW079.5°-080.5°(1°),AlWR080.5°-082.5°(2°),
FR082.5°-085°(2.5°)
- **Dir Lt 138° Dir WRG** 4m 16/13/13M
FG132°-134°(2°), AlWG134°-137°(3°),
FW137°-139°(2°), Al WR139°-142°(3°)

A4422 - **Ldg Lts** 356°. Front. Beacon No 7N
56°00'.1N 4°45'.3W **Dir WRG** 5m 16/13/13M
Al WG353°- 355°(2°), FW355°-357°(2°),
Al WR357°-000°(3°),FR000°-002°(2°)
- **Dir Lt 115°**
Dir WRG 5m 16/13/13M
Al WG 111°-114°(3°), FW114°-116°(2°),
Al WR116°-119°(3°), FR119°-121°(2°)

A4422.5 - **Rhu Point** Dir Lt 318° 56°00'.9N 4°47'.1W
Dir WRG 16/13/13M Al WG315°-317°(2°),
FW317°-319°(2°), Al WR319°-321°(2°),
FR321°-325°(4°)

A4423 -**Rhu Narrows** Limekiln Point.
Beacon No 2N Dir Lt 295°
56°00'.7N 4°47'.6W **Dir WRG** 5m 16/13/13M
Al WG291°-294°(3°), FW294°-296°(2°),
Al WR296°-299°(3°), FR299°-301°(2°)

A4423-5 - **Roseneath Bay** Beacon No 3N
Dir Lt 149° 56°00'.1N 4°46'.6W
Dir WRG 9m 16/13/13M
FG144°-145°(1°), Al WG145°-148°(3°),
FW148°-150°(2°),AlWR150°-153°(3°),FR153°-
154°(1°)

A4580 **Turnberry Point** Near castle ruins
55°19'.6N 4°50'.6W **Fl W 15s** 29m 24M

A4582 **Ailsa Craig** 55°15'.1N 5°06'.4W
Fl W 4s 18m 17M Vis 145°-028°(243°)

A4604 **Corsewall Point** 55°00'.5N 5°09'.5W
Fl(5)W 30s 34m 22M Vis 027°-257°(230°)

A4606 **Killantringan** Black Head 54°51'.7N
5°08'.7W **Fl(2)W 15s** 49m 25M

A4608 **Crammag Head** 54°39'.9N 4°57'.8W
Fl W 10s 35m 18M

A4610 **Mull of Galloway** SE end 54°38'.1N
4°51'.4W **Fl W 20s** 99m 28M
Vis 182°-105°(283°)

WEST COAST OF ENGLAND

A4710 **Saint Bees Head** 54°30'.8N 3°38'.1W
Fl(2)W20s 102m 21M Obscured shore-340°

ISLE OF MAN

A4720 **Point of Ayre** 54°24'.9N 4°22'.1W
Fl(4)W 20s 32m 19M Racon

A4746 **Calf of Man** 54°03'.2N 4°49'.6W
Fl W 15s 93m 26M Vis 274°0-190°(276°)

A4770 **Douglas Head** 54°08'.6N 4°27'.9W
Fl W 10s 32m 24M Reduced range shore-220°.
Obscured when bearing more than 037°

A4786 **Maughold Head** 54°17'.7N 4°18'.4W
Fl(3)W 30s 65m 21M

WEST COAST OF ENGLAND

A4820 **Isle of Walney** 54°02'.9N 3°10'.6W
Fl W 15s 21m 23M Obscured 122°-127°(5°)
when within 3M of the shore. RC

WALES

A5160 **Point Lynas** 53°25'.0N 4°17'.3W
Oc W 10s 39m 20M Vis 109°-315°(206°). RC

A5168 **The Skerries** 53°25'.3N 4°36'.4W **Fl(2)W**
10s 36m 22M Racon. **FR** 26m 16M Vis 231°-
254°(23°) **Range reduced (T)** 1996

A5204 **South Stack** 53°18'.4N 4°41'.9W
Fl W 10s 60m 23M Obscured to the northward
by North Stack, and may also be obscured in
Penrhos Bay by the high land of Penrhyn Mawr,
but is visible over the land from the southward
when in line with Rhoscolyn Beacon

A5234 **Bardsey Island** 52°45'.0N 4°47'.9W
Fl(5)W15s 39m 26M Obscured by Bardsey
Island 198°-250°(52°) and inTremadoc Bay when
bearing less than 260°

A5238 **St Tudwal's** 52°47'.9N 5°31'.8W
Fl WR 20s 46m 15/13M W349°-169°(180°),
R169°-221°(52°), W221°-243°(22°),
R243°- 259°(16°), W259°-293°(34°), R293°-
349°(56°),obscured by East Island 211°-231°(20°)

A5274 **Strumble Head** 52°01'. 8N 5°04'.3W
Fl(4)W 15s 45m 26M Vis 038°-257°(219°)

A5276 **South Bishop** 51°51'.1N 5°24'.6W
Fl W 5s 44m 19M RC

A5278 **The Smalls** 51°43'.2N 5°40'.1W
Fl(3)W15s 36m 25M Racon

A5282 **Skokholm Island** 51°41'.6N 5°17'.1W
Fl W 10s 54m 20M Partially obscured
226°- 258°(32°)

A5284 **St Ann's Head** 51°40'.9N 5°10'.4W
Fl WR 5s 48m 18/17/14M W233°-247°(14°),
R247°-285°(38°), R(intens) 285°-314°(29°),
R314°- 332°(18°), W332°-131°(159°), partially
obscured between 124°-129°(5°). Ra

A5286-3 **Watwick Point** Ldg Lt 022°30'. Rear. 0.5M
from front 51°41'.8N 5°09'.2W **FW** 80m 15M
Vis 013.5°-031.5°(18°). Common rear

A5287 **GREAT CASTLE HEAD** Ldg Lts 039°45'.
Front 51°42'.6N 5°07'.0W **Oc W 4s** 27m 15M
Vis 031.2°-048.2°(17°) On request through
Milford Haven Port radio.

A5287-1 - **Little Castle Head** Rear. 890m from front
51°43'.0N 5°06'.6W **Oc W 8s** 53m 15M
Vis 031.2°-048.2°(17°)

A5356 **Burry Port** 51°40'.6N 4°15'.0W **Fl W 5s** 7m
15M

A5358 **Mumbles** 51°34'.0N 3°58'.2W
Fl(4)W 20s 35m 16M

A5406 **Nash** 51°24'.0N 3°33'.1W **Fl(2)WR 10s**
56m 21/20/17M R280°-290°(10°),
W290°097°(167°), R097°- 100°(3°),
R(intens) 100°-104°(4°), R104°- 120°(16°),
W120°-128°(8°). RC

A5426 **Flat Holm** 51°22'.5N 3°07'.0W
Fl(3)WR 10s 50m 16/13M R 106°-
140°(34°),
W140°- 151°(11°) R 151°-203°(52°),
W 203°- 106°(263°)

A5433 **CARDIFF -** Ldg Lts 349° Front 51°27'.7N
3°09'.9W **FW** 4m 17M

A5433.1-**Rear.** 520m from front 51°27'.9N 3°10'.0W
FW 24m 17M

A5454 **River Usk** E Usk 51°32'.4N 2°57'.9W
Fl(2)WRG 10s 11m 15/11/11M W284°-
290°(6°), R290°-017°(87°), W017°-037°(20°),
G037°-115° (78°), W115°-120°(5°)

A5482 **Black Nore Point** 51°29'.1N 2°48'.0W
Fl(2)W 10s 11m 15M Vis 044°-243°(199°),
Obscured by Sand Pt when bearing less than 049°

A5484 **Portishead Point** 51°29'.6N 2°46'.4W
Q(3)W 10s 9m 16M Vis 060°-262°(202°)

A5590 **Lynmouth Foreland** 51°14'.7N 3°47'.1W
Fl(4)W 15s 67m 18M Vis 083°-275°(192°)

A5600 **Bull Point** 51°12'.0N 4°12'.0W **Fl(3)W 10s**
54m 24M Obscured by high ground from
shore -056°

A5610 **BIDEFORD** Instow Ldg Lts 118° Front
51°03'.6N 4°10'.6W **Oc W 6s** 22m 15M Vis
104.5°-131.5°(27°)

A5610.1 - **Rear** 427m from front 51°03'.5N 4°10'.3W
Oc W 10s 38m 15M Vis 103°-133°(30°)

A5616 **LUNDY** Near N point 51°12'.1N 4°40'.6W
Fl W 15s 48m 17M Vis 009°-285°(276°)

A5618 - **SE point** 51°09'.7N 4°39'.3W
Fl W 5s 53m 15M Vis 170°-073°(263°)

A5622 **Hartland Point** 51°01'.3N 4°31'.4W
Fl(6) W 15s 37m 25M

A5638 **Trevose Head** NW end 50°32'.9N
5°02'.1W
Fl W 7.5s 62m 21M

A5670 **Pendeen,** near Watch House 50°09'.8N
5°40'.2W **Fl(4) W 15s** 59m 18M Vis 042°-
240°(198°)

SOUTH COAST OF IRELAND

A5702 **Fastnet** 51°23'.3N 9°36'.1W
Fl W 5s 49m 27M Racon

A5708 **Galley Head** 51°31'.7N 8°57'.1W
Fl(5)W 20s 53m 23M Vis 256°-065°(169°)

A5710 **Old Head of Kinsale** 51°36'.3N 8°31'.9W
Fl(2)W 10s 72m 25M RC

A5718 **Roche's Point** 51°47'.6N 8°15'.3W
Fl WR 3s 30m 20/16M R shore-292°,W292°-
016°(84°), R016°-033°(17°),W(unintens) 033°-
159°(126°). R159°-shore

A5774 **Ballycotton** 51°49'.5N 7°59'.1W
Fl WR 10s 59m 21/17M W238°-048°(170°),
R048°-238°(190°)

A5776 **Youghal** W side of Entrance 51°56'.5N
7°50'.5W **Fl WR 2.5s** 24m 17/13M
W183°-273°(90°), R273°- 295°(22°),
W295°-307°(12°), R307°-351°(44°),
W351°-003°(12°)

A5778 **Mine Head** 51°59'.6N 7°35'.2W
Fl(4)W 20s 87m 28M Vis 228°-052°(184°)

A5798 **Hook Head** 52°07'.3N 6°55'.7W
Fl W 3s 46m 23M Racon

A5800 **Dunmore East** E Pier. Head 52°08'.9N
6°59'.3W **Fl WR 8s** 13m 17/13M
W225°-310°(85°), R310°-004°(54°)

A5832 **Coningbeg Lt F** 52°02'.4N 6°39'.4W
Fl(3)W 30s 12m 24M Racon

EAST COAST OF IRELAND

A5838 **Tuskar** 52°12'.2N 6°12'.4W
Q(2)W 7.5s 33m 24M RC. Racon

A5845 **Arklow Lanby** 52°39'.5N 5°58'.1W
Fl(2)W 12s 12m 15M Racon

A5850 **Wicklow Head** 52°57'.9N 5°59'.8W
Fl(3)W 15s 37m 23M

A5861 **Codling Lanby** 53°03'.0N 5°40'.7W
Fl W 4s 12m 15M Racon

A5865 **Kish Bank** 53°18'.7N 5°55'.3W
Fl(2)W 20s 29m 22M Racon

A5872 **Dun Laoghaire** East Breakwater. Head
53°18'.1N 6°07'.6W **Fl(2)R 10s** 16m 17M

A5882 **PORT OF DUBLIN** Great S Wall. Poolbeg
53°20'.5N 6°09'.0W **Oc(2)R 20s** 20m 15M

A5884 - **North Bull Wall** 53°20'.7N 6°08'.9W
Fl(3)G 10s 15m 15M

A5886 - **N Bank** 53°20'.7N 6°10'.5W
Oc G 8s 10m 16M

A5898 **Ben of Howth** Baily 53°21'.7N 6°03'.1W
Fl W 15s 41m 26M RC

A5904 **Rockabill** 53°35'.8N 6°00'.3W
Fl WR 12s 45m 22/18M W178°-329°(151°),
R329°-178°(209°)

A5910 **DROGHEDA HARBOUR**
Entrance Lts in line about 248°. Front
53°43'.1N 6°14'.9W **Oc W 12s** 8m 15M
Vis 203°-293°(90°)

A5910.1- **Rear** 85m from front 53°43'.1N 6°14'.9W
Oc W 12s 12m 17M Vis 246°-252°(6°)

A5911 - **North Light** 53°43'.4N 6°15'.2W
Fl R 4s 7m 15M Vis 282°-288°(6°)

A5920 **Dundalk Harbour** N training wall
53°58'.5N 6°17'.6W **Fl WR 15s** 10m 21/18M
W124°- 151°(27°), R151°-284°(133°),
W284°-313°(29°), R313°-124°(171°)

A5928 **Haulbowline** 54°01'.2N 6°04'.7W
Fl(3)W 10s 32m 17M

A5958 **St John's Point** 54°13'.6N 5°39'.5W
Q(2)W 7.5s 37m 25M **Fl WR 3s** 14m
15/11M W064°-078°(14°), R078°-shore

A5966 **Strangford Lough** S Rock Lt F 54°24'.5 N
5°21'.9 W **Fl(3)R 30s** 12m 20M RC Racon

A5974 **Donaghadee** 54°38'.7N 5°31'.8W
Iso WR 4s 17m 18/14M W shore-326°. R326°-
shore

A5976 **Mew Island** NE end 54°41'.9N 5°30'.7W
Fl(4)W 30s 37m 24M Racon

A6028 **Black Hd** 54°46'.0N 5°41'.3W
Fl W 3s 45m 27M

A6031 **Chaine Tower** 54°51'.3N 5°47'.8W
Iso WR 5s
23m 16M W230°-240°(10°), R240°-shore

A6042 **Maidens** 54°55'.7N 5°43'.6W
Fl(3)W 20s 29m 24M Racon

A6062 **RATHLIN ISLAND** Altacarry Hd. Rathlin E
55°18'.1N 6°10'.2W **Fl(4)W 20s** 74m 26M
Vis 110°-006°(256°) and 036°-058°(22°). Racon

A6064 - **Rathlin West** 0.5M NE of Bull Point
55°18'.1N 6°16'.7W **Fl R 5s** 62m 22M
Vis 015°-225°(210°)

NORTH COAST OF IRELAND

A6084 **Inishowen** 55°13'.6N 6°55'.7W
Fl(2)WRG 10s 28m 18/14/14M
*G197°-211°(14°), W211°- 249°(38°),
R249°-000°(111°)*

A6164 **Inishtrahull** 55°25'.8N 7°14'.6W
Fl(3)W 15s 59m 25M *Racon*

A6168 **Fanad Head** 55°16'.6N 7°37'.9W
Fl(5)WR 20s 39m 18/14M *R100°-110°(10°),
W110°-313° (203°)R313°-345°(32°),
W345°-100°(115°)*

WEST COAST OF IRELAND

A6200 **Tory Island** 55°16'.4N 8°14'.9W
Fl(4)W 30s 40m 27M *Obscured by land about
277°-302°(25°). RC. Racon*

A6208 **Aranmore** 55°00'.9N 8°33'.6W
Fl(2)W 20s 71m 29M *Obscured by land about
234°-007°(133°) and when bearing about 013°*

A6216 **Rathlin O'Birne** 54°39'.8N 8°49'.9W
Fl WR 15s 35m 18/14M *R195°-307°(112°).
W307°-195°(248°). Racon*

A6224 **Rotten Island** 54°36'.9N 8°26'.3W
Fl WR 4s 20m 15/11M *W255°-008°(113°),
R008°-039°(31°), W039°-208°(169°)*

A6268 **Eagle Island** 54°17'.0N 10°05'.5W
Fl(3)W 10s 67m 23M *RC*

A6270 **Black Rk** 54°04'.0N 10°19'.2W
Fl WR 12s 86m 22/16M *W276°-212°(296°),
R212°-276°(64°)*

A6276 **Achillbeg Is** 53°51'.5N 9°56'.8W **Fl WR 5s**
56m 18/18/15M *R262°-281°(19°), W281°-
342°(61°), R342°-060°(78°),W060°- 092°(32°),
R(intens) 092°-099°(7°), W099°-118°(19°)*

A6288 **Slyne Head** 53°24'.0N 10°14'.0W
Fl(2)W 15s 35m 24M

A6296 **GALWAY BAY** Eeragh 53°08'.9N 9°51'.4W
Fl W 15s 35m 23M *Vis 297°-262°(325°)*

A6298 - **Straw Island** 53°07'.0N 9°37'.9W
Fl(2)W 5s 11m 17M

A6334 - **Inisheer** 53°02'.8N 9°31'.5W **Iso WR 12s**
34m 20/16M *W(partially vis beyond 7M) 225°-
231°(6°), W231°- 245°(14°), R245°-269°(24°),
W269°- 115°(206°). Racon*

A6338 **Loop Head** 52°33'.7N 9°55'.9W
Fl(4)W 20s 84m 23M *Vis 280°-218°(298°).RC*

A6392 **Little Samphire Is** 52°16'.2N 9°52'.9W
Fl WRG 5s 17m 16/13/13M *R262°-275°(13°).
R280°-090°(170°), G090°-140°(50°), W140°-
152°(12°), R152°-172°(20°)*

A6408 **Inishtearaght** 52°04'.5N 10°39'.7W **Fl(2)W
20s** 84m 27M *Vis 318°-221°(263°) Racon*

A6416 **Valentia Harbour** Ft (Cromwell) Pt
51°56'.0N 10°19'.3W **Fl WR 2s** 16m 17/
15M *R304°-351°(47°), W104°-304°(200°)
Obscured from seaward by Doulus Hd when
bearing over 180°*

A6422 **Skelligs Rock** 51°46'.2N 10°32'.5W
Fl(3)W 10s 53m 27M *Vis 262°-115°(213°).*

*Partially obscured by land within 6M 110°-
115°(5°)*

A6430 **Bull Rock** 51°35'.5N 10°18'.1W
Fl W 15s 83m 21M *Vis 220°-186°(326°)*

A6432 **Sheep's Hd** 51°32'.5N 9°50'.8W
Fl(3)WR 15s 83m 18/15M *R007°-
017°(10°), W017°-212°(195°)*

A6434 **Ardnakinna Point** 51°37'.1N 9°55'.0W
Fl(2)WR 10s 62m 17/14M
*R319°-348°(29°), W348°-066°(78°), R066°-
shore*

A6442 **Roancarrigmore** 51°39'.1N 9°44'.8W
Fl WR 3s 18m 18/14M *W312°-050°(98°).
R050°-122°(72°), R(unintens) 122°-242°(120°),
R242°-312°(70°)*

A6448 **Mizen Head** 51°26'.9N 9°49'.2W
Iso W 4s 55m 15M *Vis 313°-133°(180°).Racon*

BELGIUM

B0074 **Nieuwpoort** E Pier. 51°09'.3N 2°43'. 8E
Fl(2)R 14s 26m 16M

B0092 **Oostende** 51°14'.2N 2°55'.9E **Fl(3)W 10s**
63m 27M *Obscured 069.5°-071°(1.5°)*

B0112 **Blankenberge** Cte Jean 51°18'.8N 3°06'.9E
Fl(2)W 8s 30m 20M *Vis 065°-245°(80°)*

B0122 **Zeebrugge** Heist. Mole. Head 51°20'.9N
3°12'.3E **Oc WR 15s** 22m 20/18M *W068°-
145°(77°), R145°-212°(67°), W212°-296°(84°)*

HOLLAND

B0174 **Walcheren** Westkapelle. Common rear.
51°31'.8N 3°26'. 9E **Fl W 3s** 48m 28M
Obscured by the land on certain bearings

B0500 **Zeegat van Brouwershaven**
West Schouwen 51°42'.6N 3°41'.6E
Fl(2+1)W 15s 57m 30M

B0518 **Westhoofd** 51°48'.8N 3°51'.9E
Fl(3)W 15s 55m 30M

B0593-39 **DORDSCHE KIL** De Wacht. Ldg Lts 164°.
Rear. 190m from front 51°44'.6N 4°38'.2E
Iso W 2s 18m 15M

B0593-4 - **Common front** 51°44'.7N 4°38'.1E
Iso W 2s 14m 15M **Iso W 4s** 14m 16M

B0593-41 - **Ldg Lts** 015°. Rear. 500m from front
51°45'.0N 4°38'.2E **Iso W 4s** 20m 16M

B0593-5 - **S-Gravendeel** Ldg Lts 344°. Front
51°46'.1N 4°37'.5E **Iso W 2s** 12m 15M

B0593-51 - **Rear** 125m from front 51°46'.1N 4°37'.5E
Iso W 2s 15m 15M

B0593-7 - **De Wacht** Ldg Lts 183°. Front 51°45'.4N
4°37'.6E **Iso W 8s** 12m 15M

B0593-71 - **Rear** 490m from front 51°45'.1N 4°37'.6E
Iso W 8s 19m 15M

B0593-8 - **N entrance** Ldg Lts 346°30'. Front
51°48'.2N 4°37'.3E **Iso W 4s** 14m 15M

B0593-81 - **Rear** 217m from front 51°48'.3N 4°37'.2E
Iso W 4s 16m 15M

B0593-9 - **Wieldrecht** Ldg Lts 166°30'. Front
51°46'.6N 4°37'.9E **Iso W 4s** 12m 15M

B0593-91 - **Rear** 225m from front 51°46'.5N 4°37'.9E
Iso W 4s 16m 15M

B0630 **Goeree** 51°55'.5N 3°40'.2E
Fl(4)W 20s 31m 28M *RC. Racon*

B0633 **HOOK OF HOLLAND** Maasvlakte
51°58'.2N 4°00'.9E **Fl(5)W 20s** 66m 28M
Vis 340°-267°(287°)

B0637   - **Maasmond Ldg Lts** 112°.Front 51°58'.9N 4°04'.9E **Iso W 4s** 29m 21M Vis 101°-123°(22°), for use of very deep draught vessels

B0637-1 - **Rear** 0.6M from front 51°58'.7N 4°05'.9E **Iso W 4s** 46m 21M Synchronised with front. Vis 101°-123°(22°)

B0638   - **Ldg Lts** 107°. Front 51°58'. 6N 4°07'.6E **Iso R 6s** 29m 18M Vis 099. 5°- 114 .5°(15°). For vessels other than those of very deep draught

B0638-1- **Rear** 450m from front 51° 58'. 5N 4°08''.0E **Iso R 6s** 43m 18M Synchronised with front Vis 099.5°-114. 5°(15°)

B0642   **EUROPOORT** Calandkanaal. Entrance. Ldg Lts 116°.Front 51°57'.6N 4°08'. 8E **Oc G 6s** 29m16M Vis 108.5°-123.5°(15°)

B0642-1-**Rear** 550m from front 51°57'. 5N 4°09'. 2E **Oc G 6s** 43m16M Vis 108.5°-123.5°(15°). Synchronised with front.

B0648-3- **Mississippihaven** E side Ldg Lts 249°30' Rear. 584m from front 51°56'.0N 4°02'.3E **Iso W 3s** 23m15M Vis 242°-257°(15°). Synchronised with front

B0712   **OUDE MAAS** Huis Te Engeland Ldg Lts 157°30' Front 51°52'.9N 4°19'.8E **Iso W 8s** 12m 15M Vis 150°-165°(15°)

B0712-1- **Rear** 115m from front 51°52'.8N 4°19'.8E **Iso W 8s** 14m 15M Vis 150°-165°(15°).

B0713-5- **Botlekbrug** Ldg Lts 161°30'. Front 51°51'.7N 4°20'.3E **Iso W 2s** 13m 15M Vis 154°-169°(15°)

B0713-51- **Rear** 232m from front 51°51'.5N 4°20'.3E **Iso W 2s** 16m 15M Vis 154°-169°(15°). Synchronised with front

B0717-1- **Allemanshaven** Ldg Lts 143°. Front. No 6 51°50'.8N 4°21'.5E **Iso W 4s** 12m 15M Vis 135.5°-150.5°(15°)

B0717-11- **Rear** 186m from front 51°50'.7N 4°21'.6E **Iso W 4s** 15m 15M Vis 135.5°-150.5°(15°).

B0719-2 - **Johannapolder- Oost** Ldg Lts 082°30'. Front 51°50'.7N 4°24'.9E **Iso W 2s** 12m 15M Vis 075°-090°(15°)

B0719-21 - **Rear** 190m from front 51°50'.7N 4°25'.0E **Iso W 2s** 15m 15M Vis 075°-090°(15°). Synchronised with front

B0721-5 - **Johannapolder - West** Ldg Lts 300°30'. Front 51°50'.7N 4°24'.8E **Iso W 8s** 12m 15M Vis 293°-308°(15°)

B0721-51- **Rear** 534m from front 51°50'.9N 4°24'.4E **Iso W 8s** 17m 15M Vis 293°-308°(15°). Synchronised with front

B0721-6 - **Goidschalxpolder-Oost** Ldg Lts 120°30'. Front 51°49'.8N 4°27'.1E **Iso W 4s** 12m 15M Vis 113°-128°(15°)

B0721-61- **Rear** 389m from front 51°49'.7N 4°27'.4E **Iso W 4s** 16m 15M Vis 113°-128°(15°). Synchronised with front

B0722-4 - **Goidschalxpolder-West** Ldg Lts 257°. Front 51°49'.9N 4°26'.9E **Iso W 4s** 12m 15M Vis 249.5°-264.5°(15°)

B0722-41- **Rear** 484m from front 51°49'.8N 4°26'.5E **Iso W 4s** 17m 15M Vis 249.5°-264.5°(15°). Synchronised with front

B0722-8 - **Koedood-Oost** Ldg Lts 077°. Front 51°50'.4N 4°30'.5E **Iso W 4s** 12m 15M Vis 069.5-°084.5°(15°)

B0722-81- **Rear** 510m from front 51°50'.4N 4°30'.9E **Iso W 4s** 17m 15M Vis 069.5°-084.5°(15°). Synchronised with front

B0723   - **Ldg Lts** 291°. Front. No 12 51°50'.3N 4°29'.8E **Iso W 6s** 15M Vis 283.5°-298.5°(15°)

B0723-1 - **Rear** 130m from front 51°50'.3N 4°29'.7E **Iso W 6s** 15M Vis 283.5°-298.5°(15°). Synchronised with front

B0726   - **Ldg Lts** 347°. Front 51°49'.8N 4°33'.5E **Iso W 6s** 15M Vis 339.5°-354.5°(15°)

B0726-1 - **Rear** 50m from front 51°49'.9N 4°33'.5E **F W** 15M Vis 339.5°-354.5°(15°)

B0728-3 - **Puttershoek-West** Ldg Lts 275°30'. Front 51°48'.5N 4°34'.5E **Iso W 4s** 12m 15M Vis 267.5°-282.5°(15°)

B0728-31 - **Rear** 120m from front 51°48'.5N 4°34'.4E **Iso W 4s** 14m 15M Vis 267.5°-282.5°(15°). Synchronised with front

B0730   - **Krabbepolder** Ldg Lts 112°. Front 51°48'.0N 4°37'.7E **Iso W 6s** 15M

B0730-1 - **Rear** 190m from front 51°47'.9N 4°37'.9E **Iso W 6s** 15M Synchronised with front

B0750   **Scheveningen** 52°06'.3N 4°16'.2E **Fl(2)W 10s** 48m 29M Vis 014°-244°(230°)

B0760   **Noordwijk-aan-Zee** 52°14'.9N 4°26'.1E **Oc(3)W 20s** 32m 18M

B0766   **HAVEN VAN IJMUIDEN** Ldg Lts 100°30'. Front 52°27'.8N 4°34'.5E **F WR** 30m 16/13M W050°- 122°(72°), R122°-145°(23°),W145°-160°(15°). RC

B0766-1 - **Ijmuiden** Rear. 570m from front 52°27'.7N 4°35'.0E **Fl W 5s** 52m 29M Vis 019°-199°(180°)

B0842   **Egmond-aan-Zee** 52°37'.2N 4°37'.6E **Iso WR 10s** 36m 18/14M W010°-175°(165°), R175°-188°(13°)

B0852   **ZEEGAT VAN TEXEL** Schulpengat. Ldg Lts 026°30'. Front 53°00'.9N 4°44'.5E **Iso W 4s** 18M Vis 024.5°-028.5°(4°)

B0852-1 - **Den Hoorn** Rear. 0.83M from front 53°01'.6N 4°45'.1E **Oc W 8s** 18M Vis 024°-028.5°(4°)

B0858   - **Kijkduin** Rear 52°57'.4N 4°43'.7E **Fl(4)W 20s** 56m 30M Vis except where obscured by dunes on Texel

B0859   - **Schilbolsnol** 53°00'.6N 4°45'.8E **F WRG** 27m 15/12/11M W338°-002°(24°), G002°-035°(33°), W035°-038°(3°) Ldg sector for Schulpengat, R038°-051°(13°), W051°-68.5°(17.5°)

B0886   **Texel** Eierland 53°11'.0N 4°51'.4E **Fl(2)W 10s** 52m 29M RC

B0894   **ZEGGAT VAN TERSCHELLING** Vlieland. 53°17'.8N 5°03'.6E **Iso W 4s** 53m 20M RC

B0904   - **Terschelling** Brandaris Tower 53°21'.7N 5°12'.9E **Fl W 5s** 55m 29M Visible except when obscured by dunes on Vlieland & Terschelling

B0910   **W Terschelling** Ldg Lts 053°. On dyke. Rear. 1.1M from front 53°22'.0 N 5°14'.7E **Iso W 5s** 14m 19M Vis 045°-061°(16°) Intens 045°-052°(7°) TE1989

B0920   - **Ameland** W end 53°27'.0N 5°37'.6E **Fl(3)W 15s** 57m 30M RC

B0938　**Friesche Zeegat** Schiermonnikoog.
53°29'.2N　6°09'.0E
Fl(4)W 20s 43m 28M **F WR** 29m
15/12M W210°-221°(11°), R221°-230°(9°)

GERMANY

B0970　**BORKUM** Grosser 53°35'.4N 6°39'.8E
Fl(2)W 12s 63m 24M **F WRG** 46m 19/15/
15M G107.4°-109° (1.6°), W109°-111.2°(2.2°),
R111.2°-112.6°(1.4°)

B0972　**- Borkum Kleiner** 53°34'.8N 6°40'.1E
FW 32m 30M Vis 089.9°-090.9°(1°)
Ldg sector for Hubertgat. Ra. RC. ,
Fl W 3s 16M Vis 088°-089.9° (1.9°)
Q(4)W 10s 16M Vis 090.9°-093°(2.1°)

B0976　**- Fischerbalje** 53°33'.2N 6°43'.0E
Oc(2)WRG 16s 15m 16/12/11
R260°-313° (53°),G313°-014° (61°),
W014°-068°(54°) Ldg sector, R068°-123°(55°)

B0983　**Campen** 53°24'.4N 7°01'.0E
FW 62m 30M Vis 127°-127.3°(0.3°)

B1051　**GW/EMS Lt F** 54°10'.0N 6°20'.8E
Iso W 8s 12m 17M Racon

B1052　**German Bight Lt F** 54°10'.8N 7°27'.6E
Iso W 8s 12m 17M RC. Racon

B1054　**Norderney** 53°42'.6 N 7°13'.8 E
Fl(3)W 12s 59m 23M

B1112　**Wangerooge** W end 53°47'.4N
7°51'.5E **Fl R 5s** 60m 23M
FWRG 24m 22/15/17/11/18/10M
R358.5°-008°(9.5°),W008° 018.5° (10.5°),
G018.5°- 055°(36.5°), W055°-060.5° (5.5°),
R060.5°- 065.5°(5°), W065.5°-071°(5.5°),
G(18M)119.4°- 138.8°(19.4°),
W(22M) 138.8°-152.2°(13.4°)
Ldg Sector, R(17M)152.2°- 159.9°(7.7°).RC

B1122　**Wangerooge Fahrwasser** Mellumplate
53°46'.3N 8°05'.6E **FW** 27m 24M Vis 116.1°-
116.4°(0.3°) Ldg sector for outer part of
Wangerooger Fahrwasser **Fl W 4s** 23M
Vis 114°- 115.2°(1.2°)

B1132　**Schillig** 53°41'.8N 8°01'.7E
Oc WR 6s 15m 15/12M W195.8°-221°(25.2°),
R221°-254.5°(33.5°), W254.5°-278.3°(23.8°)

B1134　**Tossens** Ldg Lts 146°. Front 53°34'.5N
8°12'.4E **Oc W 6s** 15m 20M

B1134-1　**- Rear** 2M from front 53°32'.8N 8°14'.4E
Oc W 6s 51m 20M

B1138　**Voslapp** Ldg Lts 164°30'. Front 53°37'.3N
8°06'.8E **Iso W 6s** 15m 24M
Intens on leading line

B1138-1　**- Rear** 2.35M from front 53°34'.9N 8°07'.9E
Iso W 6s 60m 27M Synchronised with front

B1141　**Eckwarden** Ldg Lts 154°. Solthörner Watt.
Front 53°32'.5N 8°13'.1E
Iso WRG 3s 15m 19/12/9/8M
R346°-348°(2°), W348°-028°(40°),
R028°-052°(24°), W(intens)052°-054°(2°)
Ldg sector. G054°- 067.5° (13.5°),
W067.5°- 110°(42.5°), G110°- 152.6°(42.6°),
W(intens) 152.6°-across fairway, with undefined
limit on E side of Ldg line

B1141-1　**- Rear** 1.27M from front 53°31'.3N 8°14'.0E
Iso W 3s 41m 21M Synchronised with front

B1152　**Arngast** 53°28'.9N 8°11'.0E **F WRG** 30m
21/10/16/17/7M W135°-142°(7°), G142°-
150°(8°), W150°-152°(2°), G152°-
174.6°(21.1°), R180.5°- 191°(10.5°), W191°-
213°(22°), R213°-225°(12°), W(10M)286°-
303°(17°),G(7M)303°-314°(11°), **Oc W 6s**
20M Vis 176.4°-177.4°(1°) Ldg sector

B1188　**AlteWeser** 53°51'.9N 8°07'.6E **F WRG** 33m
22/19/17M W288°-352°(64°), R352°-
003°(11°), W003°-017°(14°) Ldg sector for Alte
Weser, G017°-045°(28°), W045°074°(29°),
G074°- 118°(44°), W118°-123°(5°) Ldg sector
of Alter Weser, R123°-140°(17°),G140°-
175°(35°), W175°- 183°(8°),R183°- 196°(13°),
W196°-238°(42°). RC

B1196　**Tegeler Plate** N end 53°47'.9N 8°11'.5E
Oc(3)WRG 12s 21m 21/17/16M W329°-
340°(11°),R340°-014°(34°),W014°-100°(86°),
G100°-116° (16°),W116°-119°(3°) Ldg sector
for Neue Weser, R119°-123°(4°), G123°-
144°(21°), W144°-147°(3°) Ldg sector for Alte
Weser, R147°-264°(117°).

B1198　**Hohe Weg** NE part 53°42'.9N 8°14'.7E
FWRG 29m 19/16/15M W102°-138.5°(36.5°),
G138.5°-142.5°(4°), W142.5°-145.5°(3°),
R145.5°-184°(38.5°), W184°-278.5°(94.5°).

B1214　**ROBBENPLATE** Ldg Lts 122°18'. Front
53°40'.9N 8°23'.0E **Oc W 6s** 15m 17M Intens
on leading line

B1214-1　**- Rear** 0.54M from front 53°40'.6N 8°23'.8E
Oc W 6s 37m 18M Vis 116°-125.5°(9.5°).
Synchronised with front

B1225　**Dwarsgat** Ldg Lts 320°06'. Front 53°43'.2N
8°18'.5E **Iso W 6s** 16m 15M

B1225-1　**- Rear** 0.75M from front 53°43'.7N 8°17'.8E
Iso W 6s 35m 17M. Synchronised with front

B1230-1　**Imsum** Ldg Lts 125°12'**Rear**
1.02M from front 53°35'.8N 8°32'.0E
Oc W 6s 39m 16M Synchronised with front

B1239-1　**Solthorn** Ldg Lts 320°36'. - Rear. 700m from
front 53°38'.6N 8°27'.0E **Iso W 4s** 31m 17M
Synchronised with front

B1240　**Hofe** Ldg Lts 330°48'. Front 53°37'.1N
8°29'.8E **Oc W 6s** 15m 18M

B1240-1　**- Rear** 0.7M from front 53°37'.7N 8°29'.2E
Oc W 6s 35m 18M Synchronised with front

B1256-9　**Bremerhaven Fisheriehafen** Ldg Lts
150°48'. Rear. 0.68M from front 53°31'.3N
8°35'.2E **Oc W 6s** 45m 18M
Synchronised with front

B1257　**- Common front** 53°31'.9N 8°34'.6E
Oc W 6s 17m 18/11M

B1279-9　**Flagbalgersiel Reitsand** Ldg Lts 233°54'.
Front. 480m from rear 53°30'.0N 8°30'.3E
Oc W 6s 18m 15M

B1280　**- Common Rear** 53°29'.9N 8°29'.9E
Oc W 6s 36m 17M

B1280-1　**- Ldg Lt 005°18' Front** 580m from rear
53°29'.6N 8°29'.9E **Oc W 6s** 18m 15M

B1286　**Nordenham** Ldg Lts 355°54'. Front
53°27'.9N 8°29'.4E **Iso W 4s** 15m 16M

B1286-1　**-Rear** 1M from front 53°28'.9N 8°29'.2E
Iso W 4s 41m 19M Synchronised with front

B1288　**GROSSERPATER** Ldg Lts175°54'. Front
53°19'.8N 8°30'.4E **Iso W 4s** 15m 19M
Intens on leading line

B1288-1- **Rear** 0.71M from front 53°19'.1N 8°30'.4E
Iso W 4s 34m 22M *Synchronised with front.*
Intens on leading line

B1294 **REIHERPLATE** Ldg Lts 185°18'. Front
53°25'.6N 8°29'.2E **Oc W 6s** 14m 15M

B1294-1 - **Rear** 850m from front 53°25'.1N 8°29'.2E
Oc W 6s 27m 16M *Synchronised with front*

B1297 **SANDSTEDT** Ldg Lts 021°. Front
53°21'.7N 8°30'.7E **Oc W 6s** 15m 15M
Intens on leading line

B1297-1 - **Rear** 420m from front 53°21'.9N 8°30'.8E
Oc W 6s 23m 15M *Intens on leading line.*
Synchronised with front

B1299-21 **Osterpater** Ldg Lts 173°42'. Rear 250m
from front 53°17'.2N 8°29'.8E
Iso W 4s 21m 15M *Intens on leading line.*
Synchronised with front

B1299-41 **Harriersand** Ldg Lts 007°36'. Rear. 0.5M
from front 53°19'.5N 8°29'.9E
Oc W 6s 22m 15M *Intens on leading line*

B1302-39 **BERNE** Ldg Lts 147°54'. Rear. 220m from
front 53°11'.7N 8°31'.2E **Oc W 6s** 22m 15M
Intens on leading line

B1302-4 - **Common front** 53°11'.8N 8°31'.1E
OcW 6s 15m 15M *Synchronised with rear lights.*
Intens on leading line

B1302-41 **Juliusplate** Ldg Lts 299°36'. Rear 490m from
front 53°11'.9N 8°30'.7E **Iso W 4s** 29m 15M
Intens on leading line

B1303 **LEMWERDER** Ldg Lts 119°36'. Front
53°10'.3N 8°35'.4E **Iso W 4s** 15m 15M

B1303-1 - **Rear** 430m from front 53°10'.2N 8°35'.7E
Iso W 4s 26m 15M *Synchronised with front*

B1312 **Helgoland** 54°11'.0N 7°53'.0E **Fl W 5s**
82m28M

B1332 **Elbe Lt F** 54°00'.0N 8°06'.6E
Iso W 10s 12m 17M *RC. Racon*

B1340 **Grosser Vogelsand** 53°59'.8N 8°28'.7E
Fl(3)W 12s 39m 25M *Vis 085.1°-087.1°(2°).*
Iso W 3s 26M *Vis 091.1°-095.1°(4°).*
Oc W 6s 26M *Vis 095.1°-101.9°(6.8°)*
Fl(4)W 15s19M *Vis 087.1°-091.1°(4°).*
Fl R 3s 15M. *Vis 113°-270°(157°)*

B1344 **Neuwerk** S side 53°55'.0N 8°29'.8E
LFl(3)WRG 20s 38m 16/12/11M
G165.3°-215.3°(50°),W215.3°- 238.8° (23.5°),
R238.8°-321°(82.2°), R343°- 100°(117°)

B1360-9 **CUXHAVEN** Ldg Lts 151°12'. Baumrönne.
Front 1.55M from rear 53°51'.2N 8°44'.2E
Fl W 3s 25m 17M *Vis 143.8°-149.2°(5.4°)*
Iso W 4s 17M *Vis 149.2°-154.2°(5°)*
Fl(2)W 9s 17M *Vis 154.2°-156.7°(2.5°)*

B1361 - **Altenbruch** Common rear 53°49'.9N
8°45'.5E **Iso W 4s** 58m 21M **Iso W 8s** 51m
22M *Intens on leading line. Synchronised with front*

B1361-1 - **Ldg Lts 261°**. Common front 53°50'.1N
8°47'.8E **Iso W 8s** 19m 19M

B1395-9 **BELUM** Ldg Lts 092°48'. Rear 53°50'.1N
8°57'.4E **Iso W 4s** 45m 18M
Vis on leading line only. Synchronised with front

B1396 - **Common front** 53°50'.2N 8°56'.2E
Iso W 4s 23m 18M *Vis on leading line only*

B1396-1 **Otterndorf** Ldg Lts 245°30'. Rear
53°49'.6N 8°54'.1E **Iso W 4s** 52m 21M
Vis on leading line only.Synchronised with front

B1412 **BALJE** Ldg Lts 081°. Front 53°51'.4N
9°02'.7E **Iso W 8s** 24m 17M *Intens on leading
line*

B1412-1 - **Rear** 1.35M from front 53°51'.5N 9°04'.9E
Iso W 8s 54m 21M *Intens on leading line.*
Synchronised with front

B1416 **BRUNSBÜTTEL DER NORD OSTEE
KANAL** Ldg Lts 065°30'.
Schleuseninsel. Front 53°53'.4N 9°08'.5E
Iso W 3s 24m 16M *Vis N 063°*

B1416-1 - **Industriegebiet** Rear. 0.9M from front
53°53'.7N 9°09'.9E **Iso W 3s** 46m 21M
Synchronised with front

B1453-9 **St Margarethen** Ldg Lts 311°48'. Rear.
0.58M from front 53°53'.3N 9°15'.0E **Iso W
8s** 36m 19M *Intens on leading line. Synchronised
with front*

B1454 **SCHEELENKUHLEN** Common front
53°52'.9N 9°15'.7E **Iso W 8s** 20m 18M
Intens on leading line

B1454-1 - **Ldg Lts 089°12'**. Rear. 1M from front
53°52'.9N 9°17'.4E **Iso W 8s** 44m 22M
Synchronised with front

B1456 **GLÜCKSTADT** Ldg Lts 131°48'. Front
53°48'.4N 9°24'.3E **Iso W 8s** 15m 19M
Intens on leading line

B1456-1 - **Rear**. 0.68M from front 53°47'.9N 9°25'.2E
Iso W 8s 30m 21M *Intens on leading line*

B1457-51 **Osterende** Ldg Lts 115°48'. Rear. 0.6M
from front 53°50'.8N 9°21'.3E
Iso W 4s 36m 15M *Synchronised with front*

B1458 **LDG LTS 340°30'** Hollerwettern. Front
53°50'.5N 9°21'.2E **Iso W 4s** 21m 19M
Intens on leading line

B1460 - **Brokdorf**. Rear. 0.9M from front 53°51'.2N
9°20'.9E **Iso W 4s** 44m 22M *Synchronised
with front. Intens on leading line*

B1474 **Ruthensand** Ldg Lts 161°36'. Front
53°43'.3N 9°25'.5E **Oc WRG 6s** 15m 15/12/
11M *G170°- 176.1°(6.1°),W176.1°
177.6°(1.5°), R177.6°- 182°(4.4°)*

B1501 **PAGENSAND** Ldg Lts 345°18'. Front
53°43'.0N 9°29'.4E **Iso W 8s** 20m 15M
Intens on leading line

B1501-1 - **Kollmar**. Rear. 0.7M from front 53°43'.6N
9°29'.1E **Iso W 8s** 40m 16M
Synchronised with front

B1522-1 **Stadersand** Ldg Lts 165°18'. Rear. 785m
from front 53°37'.3N 9°31'.9E **Iso W 8s**
40m 16M

B1540 **LDG LTS 278°18'**. Lühe. Front 53°34'.3N
9°38'.0E **Iso W 4s** 16m 17M

B1540-1 - **Grünendeich**. Rear. 0.82M from front
53°34'.5N 9°36'.6E **Iso W 4s** 36m 21M
Synchronised with front

B1568-1 **Tinsdal** Ldg Lt 286°42'. Rear. 800m from
front 53°34'.0N 9°44'.5E **Iso W 8s** 55m 16M
Synchronised with front. Intens on leading line

B1568-7 **BLANKENESE** Ldg Lts 098°18'.Front
53°33'.5N 9°47'.8E **Iso W 4s** 41m 16M

B1568-71 - **Rear**. 0.8M from front 53°33'.4N 9°49'.0E
Iso W 4s 84m 20M

B1581-7 **HAMBURG** Budendey-Ufer. Ldg Lts 106°42'.
Front 53°32'.4N 9°53'.2E **Iso W 8s** 20m 16M

B1581-71 - **Rear** 0.6M from front 53°32'.3N 9°54'.1E
Iso W 8s 38m 18M

B1606　**Büsum** 54°07'.7N 8°51'.6E Iso **WRG 6s** 22m
17/14/13M W248°-317°(69°), R317°-024°(67°),
W024°-084°(60°), G084°-091.5°(7.5°),
W091.5°-093.5°(2°) Ldg sector for Süder Piep,
R093.5°-097°(3.5°), W097°-148°(51°)

B1624　**St Peter** 54°17'.3N 8°39'.2E **LFl(2)WRG**
15s 23m 15/13/11M R271°-294°(23°),W294°-
325°(31°), R325°344°(19°),W344°-035°(51°),
G035°-056.5°(21.5°), W056.5°-068°(11.5°),
R068°-091°(23°), W091°(23°), W091°-
120°(29°)

B1652　**Westerheversand** 54°22'.5N 8°38'.5E
Oc(3)**WRG 15s** 41m 21/17/16M
W012.2°- 069°(56.8°), G069°-079.5°(10.5°),
W079.5°- 080.5°(1°) Ldg sector for Hever.
R080.5°- 107°(26.5°), W107°-157°(50°),
R157°- 169°(12°), W169°- 206.5°(37.5°),
R206.5°- 218.5° (12°), W218.5°- 233°(14.5°),
R233°-248°(15°)

B1672　**Süderoogsand** Cross light 54°25'.5N
8°28'.7E Iso **WRG 6s** 18m 15/12/11M R240°-
244°(4), W244°-246°(2°), G246°-263°(17°),
W263°- 320°(57°), R320°-338°(18°), W338°-
013°(35°), R013°-048°(35°), W048°-
082.5°(34.5°), R082.5°- 122.5°(40°),W122.5°-
150°(27.5°)

B1676　**PELLWORM** S side. Ldg Lts 041°. Front
54°29'.3N 8°39'.1E Oc **WR 5s** 14m 20/11/8M
W(intens) on leading line.W303.5°-313.5°(10°),
R313.5°-316.5°(3°)

B1676-1- **Rear** 0.8M from front 54°29'.8N 8°40'.0E
Oc **W 5s** 38m 20M Synchronised with front

B1686　**Husumer Au** Amrum 54°37'.9N 8°21'.3E
Fl **W 7.5s** 63m 23M

B1691　**Nebel** 54°38'.8N 8°21'.7E Oc **WRG 5s** 16m
20/15/15M R255.5°-258.5°(3°), W258.5°-
260.5°(2°), G260.5°-263.5°(3°)

B1702　**Nieblum** 54°41'.1N 8°29'.2E Oc(2)**WRG**
10s 11m 19/15/15M G028°-031°(3°),W031°-
032.5°(1.5°), R032.5°-035.5°(3°)

B1718　**Dagebüll** 54°43'.8N 8°41'.4E Iso **WRG 8s**
23m 18/15/15M G042°-043°(1°), W043°-
044.5°(1.5°), R044.5°-047°(2.5°)

B1728　**Amrum** W side. Norddorf 54°40'.3N
8°18'.6E Oc **WRG 6s** 22m 15/12/11M W009°-
032°(23°), G032°-034°(2°), W034°-
036.8°(2.8°)Ldg sector. R036.8°-099°(62.2°),
W099°-146°(47°), R146°-176.5°(30.5°),
W176.5°-178.5°(2°),G178,5°- 188°(9.5°),
G(unintens) 188°- 202°(14°).W (partially obscured) 202°-230°(28°)

B1735　**SYLT Hornum** 54°45'.3N 8°17'.5E
Fl(2)**W 9s** 48m 20M

B1740　**- Kampen** Rote Kliff 54°56'.8N 8°20'.5E **LFl**
WR 10s 62m 20/16M W193°-260°(67°),
W(unintens) 260°-339°(79°),W339°-165°(186°),
R165°-193°(28°)

DENMARK

B1772　**Saedding Strand Ldg Lt** 053°48' Front
55°29'.8N 8°24'.0E Iso **W 2s** 12m 21M

B1772.1 **Middle** 630m from front 55°30'.0N 8°24'.4E
Iso **W 4s** 26m 21M

B1772.2 **Rear** 0.75M from front 55°30'.2N 8°25'.0E
F **W** 36m 18M

B1778　**- South Ldg Lt** 067° Front
55°28'.7N 8°24'.7E F **G** 10m 16M

B1778.1 **- Rear** 55°29'.1N 8°26'.1E
F **G** 21m 16M

B1779　**- North Ldg Lt** 049° Front 55°29'.9N
8°23'.8E F **R** 16m 16M

B1779.1 **Rear** 550m from front 55°30'.1N 8°24'.1E
F **R** 27m 16M

B1848　**Blavandshuk** 55°33'.5N 8°05'.1E
Fl(3) **W 20s** 54m 23M. RC

B1849　**Oksbøl Firing Range South** 55°33'.6N
8°04'.7E A **IFl WR 4s** 35m 16/13M By day
Q W 10M Shown when firing in progress

B1849.4 **-North** 55°37'.3N 8°07'.1E A **IFl WR 4s**
35m 16/13MBy day Q W 10M Shown when
firing in progress

B1868　**Lyngvig** 56°03'.0N 8°06'.3E Fl **W 5s** 53m
22M

B1890　**Thyborøn,** Kanal Approach
56°42'.5N 8°13'.0E Fl (3) **W 10s** 24m 16M
Intens 023.5°-203.5°(180°) RC

B2050.1 **Løgstør Grundge** Ldg Lt 079°. Rear. 1.25M
from front. 56°58'.4N 9°17'.4E Iso **W 4s** 38m
18M Vis 077.25°-080.75°(3.5°) FW(T) 1996

B2070　**Lodbjerg** 56°49'.4N 8°15'.8E
Fl (2) **W 20s** 48m 23M

B2084　**Hanstholm** 57°06'.8N 8°36'.0E
Fl (3) **W 20s** 65m 26M

B2101　**Tranum** 57°10'.8N 9°26'.7E A **I WR 4s** 20m
16/13M Shown when firing in progress

B2106　**Hirtshals** 57°35'.1N 9°56'.6E FFI **W 30s** 57m
F18M Fl 25M **Works in progress (T)** 1996

FRANCE

A0994　**Sandettié Lt F** 51°09'.4N 1°47'.2E
Fl **W 5s** 12m 24M Racon

A1000　**Dunkerque Lanby** 51°03'.1N 1°51'.8E
Fl **W 3s** 10m 25M Racon

A1114　**DUNKERQUE** 51°03'.0N 2°21'.9E
Fl(2)**W 10s** 59m 26M

A1116　**- Jetée Est.** Head 51°03'.6N 2°21'.2E
Fl(2)**R 10s** 12m 16M

A1118　**- Jetée Ouest** Head 51°03'.7N 2°21'.2E
Oc(2+1)**WG 12s** 35m 15/12M
G252°-310°(58°), W310°-252°(302°)

A1126　**- Port Ouest** Ldg Lts 120°. Front 51°01'.7N
2°12'.0E **Dir FG** 16m 21M
Intens 119°-121°(2°).
Irregular characteristics (T) 1993

A1126-1 **—Rear** 600m from front 51°01'.6N 2°12'.5E
Dir F G 30m 21M Intens 119°-121°(2°).
Irregular characteristics (T) 1993

A1144　**CALAIS** Main Light. 50°57'.7N 1°51'.2E
Fl(4)**W 15s** 59m 22M RC.
Vis 073°-260°(187°)

A1146　**- Jetée Est** Head 50°58'.4N 1°50'.5E
Fl(2)**R 6s** 12m 17M

A1166　**Cap Gris-Nez** 50°52'.2N 1°35'.0E
Fl **W 5s** 72m 29M Vis 005°-232°(227°). RG

A1170　**Boulogne** Digue Carnot. 50°44'.5N 1°34'.1E
Fl(2+1)**W 15s** 25m 19M

A1190　**Cap d'Alprech** 50°42'.0N 1°33'.8E
Fl(3)**W 15s** 62m 23M RC

A1196　**LeTouquet** (La Canche) 50°31'.4N 1°35'.6E
Fl(2) **W 10s** 54m 25M

A1202 **Pointe du Haut-Blanc,** Berck-Plage
50°23'.9N 1°33'.7E **Fl W 5s** 44m 23M

A1208 **Baie du Somme,** Cayeux-sur-Mer 50°11'.7N
1°30'.7E **Fl R 5s** 32m 22M

A1220 **Ault** 50°06'.3N 1°27'.2E
Oc(3) WR 12s 95m 18/14M
W040°-175°(135°), R175°-220°(45°)

A1222 **Le Tréport,** Jetée Ouest. Head 50°03'.9N
1°22'.2E **Fl(2)G 10s** 15m 20M

A1234 **Pointe d'Ailly** 49°55'.0N 0°57'.6E
Fl(3)W 20s 95m 31M *RC*

A1244 **Fécamp** Jetée Nord 49°46'.0N 0°21'.9E
Fl(2)W 10s 15m 16M

A1250 **Cap d'Antifer** 49°41'.1N 0°10'.0 E
Fl W 20s 128m 29M *Vis 021°-222°(201°), RC*

A1250.2 **PORT D'ANTIFER** Entrance Ldg Lts
127°30'. Front 49°38'.3N 0°09'.2E
Dir OcW 4s 105m 22M *Vis 127°-128°(1°)*

A1250.21 **-Rear** 430m from front 49°38'.2N 0°09'.4E
Dir OcW 4s 124m 22M *Vis 127°-128°(1°)*

A1250.8 **- 49°39'.5N 0°09'.2E**
Dir Oc WRG 4s 24m 15/13/13M *G068.5°-
078.5°(10°), W078.5°-088.5°(10°), R088.5°-
098.5°(10°)*

A1251.2 **- Bassin de Caux,** Mole Ouest - Elbow Dir Lt
018°30' 49°39'.3N 0°09'.0E
Dir Oc WRG 4s 11m 15/11/11M *G006.5°-
017.5°(11°), W017.5°-019.5°(2°), R019.5°-
036.5°(17°)*

A1251.7 **- Digue M Thieullent** Post 2 49°40'.3N
0°08'.1E
Dir Oc(2)WRG 6s 24m 15/13/13M *G334.5°-
346.5°(12°), W346.5°-358.5°(12°), R358.5°-
004.5°(6.5°)*

A1251.8 **—Post 3,** 49°40'.3N 0°07'.7E
Dir Oc WRG 4s 21m 15/13/13M *R352.5°-
358°.5(6°), W358.5°-010.5°(12°),G010.5°-
022.5°(12°)*

A1256 **Cap de la Hève** 49°30'.8N 0°04'.2E **Fl W 5s**
123m 24M *Vis 225°-196°(331°)*

A1260 **LE HAVRE-** Ldg Lts 106°48', Quai Roger
Meunier, Front 49°29'.0N 0°06'.5E
Dir F W 36m 25M *Intens 106°-108°(2°)*

A1260.1 **—Quai J Couvert** Rear 0.73M from front
49°28'.8N 0°07'.6E **Dir F W** 78m 25M
Intens 106°-108°(2°)

A1261 **- Ldg Lts 090°.** Front 49°29'.6N 0°05'.9E
Dir F R 21m 19M *Intens 089°-091°(2°). Occas*

A1261.1 **—Rear** 680m from front 49°29'.6N 0°06'.4E
Dir F R 43m 19M *Intens 089°-091°(2°) Occas*

A1262 **- Digue Nord** Head 49°29'.2N 0°05'.5E
Fl R 5s 15m 21M

A1269 **- Quai R Meunier** W corner 49°29'.0N
0°06'.4E **Fl(3) W 15s** 4m 23M *Occas*

A1290 **Honfleur** Falaise des Fonds 49°25'.5N
0°12'.9E
Fl(3) WRG 12s 15m 17/13/13M *G040°-
080°(40°), R080°-084°(4°), G084°-100°(16°),
W100°-109°(9°), R109°-162°(53°), G162°-
260°(98°)*

A1377 **OUISTREHAM.** Main Light 49°16'.8N
0°14'.9W **Oc WR 4s** 37m 17/13M *R115°-
151°(36°), W151°-115°(324°)*

A1381 **- Ldg Lts 185°.** Jetée E. Hd. Front 49°17'.2N
0°14'.7W **Dir Oc(3 + 1)R 12s** 10m 17M
Intens 183.5°-186.5°(3°)

A1381.1 **-Rear** 610m from front 49°16'.9N 0°14'.8W
Dir Oc(3 + 1)R 12s 30m 17M
Synchronised with front. Intens 183.5°-186.5°(3°)

A1396 **Ver** 49°20'.3N 0°31'.1W **Fl(3)W 15s** 42m
26M *Obscured by St Aubincliffs when more than
275°. RC*

A1411 **LA MARESQUERIE** Ldg Lts 146°
Front 49°23'.4N 1°02'.8W **Dir Q W** 9m 15M
Vis 144.5°-147.5°(3°)

A1411.1 **- Rear** 102m from front 49°23'.4N 1°02'.8W
Dir QW 12m 15M *Vis 144.5°-147.5°(3°)*

A1412 **ISIGNY-SUR-MER** Ldg Lts 172°30'
Front 49°19'.6N 1°06'.7W
Dir Oc(2+1)W 12s 7m 18M *Intens 170.5°-
174.5°(4°)*

A1412.1 **- Rear** 625m from front 49°19'.3N 1°06'.8W
Dir Oc(2 + 1)W 12s 19m 18M
Synchronised with front. Intens 170.5°-174.5°(4°)

A1418 **Carentan** Ldg Lts 209°30' Front
49°20'.5N 1°11'.1W **Dir Oc(3)R 12s** 6m 18M
Intens 208.2°-210.7°(2.5°)

A1454 **Pointe de Barfleur** 49°41'.8N 1°15'.9W
Fl(2)W 10s 72m 29M
Obscured when bearing less than 088°. RC.

A1462 **Cap Lévi** 49°41'.8N 1°28'.4W **Fl R 5s** 36m
22M

A1480 **CHERBOURG** - Fort de L'Ouest 49°40'.5N
1°38'.8W **Fl(3)WR 15s** 19m 24/20M *W122°-
355°(233°), R355°-122°(127°). RC*

A1484 **-Lts in line** 140°18' & 142°'.12'. Jetée du
Homet, Front 49°39'.6N 1°37'.9W
Dir Q W (2 hor) 5m 17M *63m apart
Intens 137.3°-143.3°(6°) & 139.2°-145.2°(6°).
Marks SW-NE limit of dredged channel.*

A1484.1 **-Gare Maritime** Rear 0.99M from front
49°38'.8N 1°37'.0W **Dir QW** 35m 19M
Intens 140°-142.5°(2.5°)

A1488.1 **-Ldg Lts 192°** Rear 652m from front
49°39'.3N 1°38'.6W **Dir Q G** 26m 15M
Intens 189°-195°(6°)

A1512 **Cap de la Hague**
49°43'.4N 1°57'.3W **Fl W 5s** 48m 23M

ENGLISH CHANNEL

A1518 **Lanby** SW 48°31'.7N 5°49'.1W **Fl W 4s** 10m
20M *RC.* **Replaced by Lt By 10M Racon (T)**
1996

A1520 **Channel Lt F** 49°54'.4N 2°53'.7W
Fl W 15s 12m 25M *Racon*

CHANNEL ISLANDS

A1532 **Casquets** 49°43'.4N 2°22'.7W
Fl(5)W 30s 37m 24M *Racon*

A1536 **ALDERNEY** 49°43'.8N 2°09'.8W
Fl(4)W 15s 37m 28M *Vis 085°-027°(302°)*

A1538 **-Alderney Hbr** Ldg Lts 215° Front 49°43'.4N
2°11'.8W **Q W** 8m 17M *Vis 210°-220°(10°)*

A1538.1 **- Rear** 335m from front 49°43'.2N 2°12'.0W
Q W 17m 18M *Vis 210°-220°(10°)*

A1544 **Sark** Pt Robert 49°26'.2N 2°20'.7W
Fl W 15s 65m 20M *Vis 138°-353°(215°)*

A1548 **GUERNSEY-** Platte Fougère 49°30'.9N
2°29'.0W **Fl WR 10s** 15m 16M
W155°-085°(290°), R085°-155°(70°). Racon

A1560 **- St Peter Port** Ldg Lts 220°, Front
49°27'.4N 2°31'.4W **AI WR 10s** 14m 16M *Vis
187°-007°(180°) RC.*

A1580 **- Les Hanois** 49°26'.2N 2°42'.1W
Fl(2)W 13s 33m 20M *Vis 294°-237°(303°)*

A1584 **JERSEY-** Sorel Point 49°15'.7N 2°09'.4W
LFl WR 7.5s 50m 15M *W095°-112°(17°),
R112°-173° (61°), W173°-230°(57°)
R230°-269°(39°), W269°-273°(4°)*

A1620 **-La Corbière** 49°10'.8N 2°14'.9W
Iso WR 10s 36m 18/16M *W shore-294°,
R294°-328° (34°), W328°-148°(180°),
R148°-shore. RC*

A1622 **- Grosnez Point** 49°15'.5N 2°14'.7W
Fl(2)WR 15s 50m 19/17M
W081°-188°(107°), R188°-241°(53°)

FRANCE

A1638 **Cap de Carteret** 49°22'.4N 1°48'.4W
Fl(2 + 1)W 15s 81m 26M

A1654 **Îles Chausey** 48°52'.2N 1°49'.3W
Fl W 5s 39m 23M

A1660 **Port de Granville** Pte du Roc 48°50'.1N
1°36'.8W **Fl(4)W 15s** 49m 23M

A1670 **La Pierre-de-Herpin** 48°43'.8N 1°48'.9W
Oc(2)W 6s 20m 17M

A1676 **SAINT MALO** - Ldg Lts 089°06' Le Grand
Jardin, Front 48°40'.2N 2°05'.0W
Fl(2)R 10s 24m 15M
*In line 129.7° with A 1686.1 leads through the
channel of Petite Port. Obscured by Cap Fréhel
when bearing less than 097°, by Île de Cézembre
220°-233°(13°), by Grande Conchée 241°-
243°(2°) by Grande Chevreun & Pointe du Meinga
when bearing more than 251°. RC*

A1676.1- **Rochebonne** Rear 4.2M from front
48°40'.3N 1°58'.7W **Dir FR** 40m 24M
Intens 088.2°-089.7°(1.5°)

A1686 **- Ldg Lts** 128°42'. Les Bas-Sablons. Front
48°38'.2N 2°01'.2W **Dir F G** 20m 22M
Intens 127.5°-130.5°(3°)

A1686.1 **- La Balue** Rear 0.9M from front 48°37'.7N
2°00'.2W **Dir FG** 69m 25M
Intens 128.2°-129.7 (1.5°)

A1698 **Cap Fréhel** 48°41'.1N 2°19'.2W
Fl(2)W 10s 85m 29M *RC*

A1713.55 **Portrieux** NE Môle. Elbow 48°39'.0N
2°49'.1W **Dir Iso WRG 4s** 16m 15/11/11M
*W159°-179° (20°), G179°-316°(137°), W316°-
320.5°(4.5°), R320.5°-159°(198.5°)*

A1716 **Le Grand-Léjon** 48°44'.9N 2°39'.9W **Fl(5)WR
20s** 17m 18/14M *R015°-058°(43°), W058°-
283°(225°), R283°-350°(67°), W350°-
015°(25°)*

A1722 **Paimpol** Pointe de Porz-Don 48°47'.5N
3°01'.6W
Oc(2) WR 6s 13m 15/11M *W269°-272°(3°),
R272°-279°(7°)*

A1734 **Roches Douvres** 49°06'.5N 2°48'.8W **Fl W
5s** 60m 28M *RC. RG*

A1738 **Les Héaux de Bréhat**
48°54'.5N 3°05'.2W
Oc(3)WRG 12s 48m 15/11/11M
*R227°-247°(20°), W247°-270°(23°),
G270°-302°(32°), W302°-227°(285°)*

A1742 **Île de Bréhat** Rosédo 48°51'.5N 3°00'.3W
Fl W 5s 29m 20M *RC*

A1748 **LE TRIEUX** Ldg Lts 224°42'. La Croix.
Front 48°50'.3N 3°03'.3W **Dir Oc W 4s**
15m 19M
Intens 215°-235°(20°)

A1748.1- **Bodic**. Rear 2.1M from front 48°48'.8N
3°05'.4W **Dir Q W** 55m 22M
Intens 221°-229°(8°)

A1762.1 **Rivière de Tréguier** Sainte Antoine. Ldg Lt
137°Rear. 0.75M from front 48°51'.1N
3°07'.0W **Dir Oc R 4s** 34m 15M
Intens 134°-140°(6°)

A1770 **PERROS-GUIREC** Passe de l'Ouest. Dir
Lt 143°36' 48°47'.8N 3°23'.4W
Dir Oc(2+1)WRG 12s 78m 15/12/12M
*G133.7°-143.2°(9.5°), W143.2°- 144.8°(1.6°),
R144. 8°-154.3°(9.5°)*

A1774 **- Passe de l'Est.** Ldg Lts 224°30'. Le
Colombier. Front 48°47'.9N 3°26'.7W
Dir Oc(4)W 12s 28m 15M *Intens 214.5°-
234.5°(20°)*

A1774.1 **-Kerprigent**. Rear 1.5M from front
48°46'.9N 3°28'.2W **Dir QW** 79m 21M
Intens 221°-228°(7°)

A1786 **Les Sept-Îles** Île-aux-Moines 48°52'.8N
3°29'.5W **Fl(3)W 15s** 59m 24M *Obscured by
Îliot Rouzic and E end of Île Bono 237°-241°(4°)
and in Baie de Lannion when bearing less than
039°*

A1800 **BAIE DE MORLAIX-** La Lande.
Common rear ldg lt 190°30' & 176° 24'
48°38'.2N 3°53'.1W
Fl W 5s 85m 23M *Obscured by Pointe
Annelouesten when bearing more than 204°*

A1800.1- **Ldg Lts** 176°24'. Île Louet. Front 48°40'.5N
3°53'.4W **Oc(3)WG 12s** 17m 15/10M
*W305°-244°(299°), G244°-305°(61°), Vis
139°-223°(84°) from offshore, except where
obscured by islands*

A1812.1 **Roscoff** Ldg Lts 209° Rear 430m from front
48°43'.4N 3°58'.7W **Oc(2 + 1)W 12s** 24m
15M *Vis 062°-242°(180°)*

A1816 **Île de Batz** 48°44'.8N 4°01'.6W
Fl(4)W 25s 69m 23M

A1822 **Île-Vierge** 48°38'.4N 4°34'.1W
Fl W 5s 77m 27M *Vis 337°-325°(348°). RC*

A1842 **OUESSANT (USHANT)** Le Stiff 48°28'.5N
5°03'.4W **Fl(2)R 20s** 85m 24M

A1844 **- Créac'h** 48°27'.6N 5°07'.8W **Fl(2)W 10s**
70m 32M *Obscured 247°-255°(8°). Racon*

A1848 **- La Jument** 48°25'.4N 5°08'.1W
Fl(3)R 15s 36m 22M *Vis 241°-199°(318°)*

A1850 **- Kéréon (Men-Tensel)** 48°26'.3N 5°01'.6W
Oc(2 + 1) WR 24s 38m 17/7M
W019°-248°(229°), R248°-019°(131°)

A1854 **CHENAL DU FOUR (N PART)** Le Four
48°31'.4N 4°48'.3W **Fl(5)W 15s** 28m 18M

A1856 **- L'Aber-Ildut** 48°28'.3N 4°45'.6W
Dir Oc(2)WR 6s 12m 25/20M
W081°-085°(4°), R085°-087°(2°)

A1873.9 **CHENAL DU FOUR (S PART)** Ldg Lts
007°. Trézien. Rear 48°25'.4N 4°46'.8W
Dir Oc(2)W 6s 84m 20M *Intens 003°-011°(8°)*

A1874 **- Kermorvan** Front 48°21'.7N 4°47'.4W **Fl
W 5s** 20m 22M *Obscured by Pointe de Saint
Mathieu when bearing less than 341°. Front Ldg Lt
137.9° for Chenal de la Helle with 1880*

A1874.1- **Ldg Lts** 158°30'. St Mathieu. Rear 48°19'.8N 4°46'.3W **Fl W 15s** 56m 29M **Dir F W** 54m 28M *Intens F W 157.5°-159.5°(2°) RC*

A1880 **Lochrist** 48°20'.6N 4°45'.7W **Dir Oc(3)W 12s** 49m 22M *Intens 135°-140.°(5°) Rear Ldg Lt 137.9° for Chenal de la Helle with 1874*

A1886 **Les Pierres Noires** 48°18'.7N 4°54'.9W **Fl R 5s** 27m 19M

D0790 **POINTE DU PETIT-MINOU** 48°20'.2N 4°36'.9W **Fl(2)WR 6s** 32 m 19/15M *R Shore-252°, W252°- 260°(8°), R260-307°(47°) W (unintens) 307°-015°(68°), W015-065.5°(50.5°), W070.5° - shore.*

- Ldg Lts 068°. Front **Dir Q W** 30m 23M *Intens 067.3°-068.8°(1.5°)*

D0790.1- **Pointe du Portzic** 48°21'.6N 4°32'.0W **Oc(2)WR 12s** 56m 19/15M *R219°-259°(40°), W259°-338°(79°), R338°-000°(22°), W000°-065.5°(65.5°),W070.5°-219°(148.5°). Vis 041°-069 (28°) when W of Goulet.*

- Rear Dir Q W 54m 22M *Intens 065°-071°(6°)*

D0790.2 - **48°21'.6N 4°32'.0W Dir Q(6) + LFl W 15s** 54m 23M *Intens 045°-050(5°)*

D0818 **Pointe du Toulinguet** 48°16'.8N 4°37'.8W **Oc(3)WR 12s** 49m 15/11M *W shore-028°, R028°- 090°(62°), W090°-shore.*

D0826 **Pointe de Morgat** 48°13'.2N 4°29'.9W **Oc(4)WRG 12s** 77m 15/11/10M *W shore-281°. G281°-301°(20°). W301°-021°(80°), R021°- 043°(22°)*

D0836 **Douarnenez** Pointe du Millier 48°05'.9N 4°27'.9W **Oc(2)WRG 6s** 34m 16/12/11M *G080°- 087°(7°), W087°-113°(26°), R113°-120°(7°), W120°-129°(9°), G129°-148°(19°), W148°-251° (103°), R251°-258°(7°)*

D0852 **CHAUSSÉE DE SEIN** Ar-men 48°03'.0N 4°59'.9W **Fl(3)W 20s** 29m 23M

D0856 **- Main light** Ie de Sein 48°02'.6N 4°52'.1W **Fl(4)W 25s** 49m 29M *RC*

D0870 **Raz de Sein** La Vieille 48°02'.5N 4°45'.4W **Oc(2+1)WRG 12s** 33m17/14/13M *W290°-298°(8°), R298°-325°(27°), W325°-355°(30°), G355°-017°(22°), W017°-035°(18°), G035°-105°(70°), W105°-123°(18°), R123°-158°(35°), W158°-205°(47°).*

D0890 **Pointe de Penmarc'h** Eckmühl 47°47'.9N 4°22'.4W **Fl W 5s** 60m 23M *RC*

D0906 **Loctudy** Pointe de Langoz 47°49'.9N 4°09'.6W **Fl(4)WRG 12s** 12m 15/11/11M *W115°-257°(142°), G257°-284°(27°), W284°-295°(11°), R295°-318°(23°), W318°-328°(10°), R238°-025°(57°)*

D0913.9 **Bénodet.** Rivière Odet Ldg Lts 345°30'. Pointe du Coq. Front. 47°52'.4N 4°06'.6W **Dir Oc(2+1)G 12s** 11m 17M *Intens 345°-347°(2°)*

D0918 **ÎLES DE GLÉNAN** Île-aux-Moutons 47°46'.5N 4°01'.7W **Oc(2)WRG 6s** 18m 15/11/11M *W035°-050°(15°), G050°-063°(13°), W063°-081°(18°), R081°-141°(60°), W141°-292°(151°), R292°-035°(103°)*

- Auxiliary light Dir Oc(2)W 6s 17m 24M *Sychronised with main light. Intens 278.5°-283.5°(5°)*

D0922 **- Penfret** 47°43'.3N 3°57'.2W **Fl R 5s** 36m 21M

D0930 **Concarneau** Beuzec. Rear. 1.34M from front 47°53'.4N 3°54'.0W **Dir Q W** 87m 23M *Intens 026.5°-030.5°(4°)*

D0962 **Île de Groix** Pen-Men 47°38'.9N 3°30'.5W **Fl(4)W 25s** 59m 29M *Vis 309°-275°(326°). RC close NE*

D0970 **Tudy** Pointe des Chats 47°37'.3N 3°25'.3W **Fl R 5s** 16m 19M

D0971-1 **LORIENT** Port Louis. Ldg Lt 057° Rear 740m from front 47°42'.4N 3°21'.3W **Dir QW** 22m 18M

D0976 **- Passe Sud** Ldg Lts 008°30'. Fish Market. Front 47°43'.8N 3°21'.7W **Dir QR** 16m 17M *Intens 006°-011°(5°)*

D0976-1- **Kergroise-La Perrière** Rear. 515m from front 47°44'.1N 3°21'.6W **Dir QR** 34m 16M *Synchronised with front. Intens 006°-011°(5°)*

D0978 **- Île Saint-Michel** Ldg Lts 016°30'. Front 47°43'.5N 3°21'.6W **Dir Oc(3)G 12s** 8m 16M *Intens 014.5°-017.5(3°)*

D0978-1- **Rear** 306m from front 47°43'.7N 3°21'.5W **Dir Oc(3)G 12s** 14m 16M *Synchronised with front. Intens 014.5°-017.5°(3°)*

D0990 **- Keroman** Submarine Base. Ldg Lts 350°. Front. 47°43'.7N 3°21'.9W **Dir Oc(2)R 6s** 25m 15M *Intens 349°-351°(2°)*

D0990-1- **Rear** 91m from front 47°43'.7N 3°21'.9W **Dir Oc(2)R 6s** 31m 15M *Synchronised with front. Intens 349°-351°(2°)*

D0996 **Kernével** Ldg Lts 217° Front 47°43'.1N 3°22'.3W **Dir Q R** 10m 15M *Intens 215°-219°(4°)*

D0996-1 **Rear** 290m from front 47°42'.9N 3°22'.4W **Dir Q R** 18m 15M *Intens 215°-219°(4°)*

D1022 **Passage de la Teignouse** La Teignouse 47°27'.5N 3°02'.8W **Fl WR 4s** 19m 15/11M *W033°-039°(6°), R039°-033°(354°)*

D1030 **BELLE ÎLE** Pointe des Poulains 47°23'.3N 3°15'.1W **Fl W 5s** 34m 23M *Vis 023°-291°(268°)*

D1032 **- Goulphar** 47°18'.7N 3°13'.6W **Fl(2)W 10s** 87m 26M

D1036 **- Pointe de Kerdonis** 47°18'.6N 3°03'.6W **Fl(3)R 15s** 35m 15M *Obscured by Pointes d'Arzic and de Taillefer 025°-129°(104°)*

D1050-1 **Rivière de Crac'h** Ldg Lt 347° Rear. 560m from front 47°34'.4N 3°00'.4W **Dir QW** 21m 15M *Synchronised with front. Intens 337°-357°(20°)*

D1054 **Port-Navalo** 47°32'.9N 2°55'.1W **Oc(3) WRG 12s** 32m 15/11/11M *W155°-220°(65°) G317°-359°(42°) W359°-015°(16°), R015°-105°(90°)*

D1055 **PORT DU CROUESTY** - Ldg Lts 058°. Front 47°32'.6N 2°53'.8W **Dir QW** 10m 19M *Intens 056.5°-059.5°(3°)*

D1055-1 **-Rear** 315m from front 47°32'.7N 2°53'.6W **Dir QW** 27m 19M *Intens 056.5°-059.5°(3°)*

D1064 **La Vilaine Entrance.** Penlan 47°31'.0N 2°30'.2W **Oc(2)WRG 6s** 26m 15/11/11M *R292.5°-025°(92.5°), G025°-052°(27°), W052°-060°(8°), R060°-138°(78°), G138°-180°(42°)*

D1080 **Le Four** 47°17'.9N 2°38'.1W
Fl W 5s 23m 19M

D1090 **LE CROISIC** Ldg Lts 156°. Front 47°18'.0N
2°31'.0W **Dir Oc(2+1)W 12s** 10m 18M
Intens 154°-158°(4°)

D1090-1-**Rear** 116m from front 47°18'.0N 2°30'.9W
Dir Oc(2+1)W 12s 14m 18M *Synchronised
with front. Intens 154°-158°(4°)*

D1096 **ESTUAIRE DE LA LOIRE** La Banche
47°10'.6N 2°28'.1W **Fl(2+1)WR 15s**22m 15/
11M *R266°-280°(14°), W280°-266°(346°)*

D1106 -**Portcé** Ldg Lts 025°30'. Front 47°14'.6N
2°15'.4W **Dir QW** 6m 22M *Intens 024°-7°-
026.2°(1.5°)*

D1106-1-**Rear** 0.75M from front 47°15'.3N 2°14'.9W
Dir QW 36m 27M *Intens 024°-027° (3°)*

D1114 -**Pointe d'Aiguillon** 47°14'.6N 2°15'.8W
Oc(4)WR 12s27m 15/11M W*(unintens) 207°-
233°(26°),* W*233°-293°(60°),* W*297°-300°(3°),
R300°- 327°(27°),* W*327°-023°(86°),* W*027°-
089°(62°)*

D1142 **Paimboeuf** 47°17'.5N 2°01'.9W
Oc(3) WG 12s 9m 16/11M *G shore-123°,
W123°-shore*

D1152 **Baie de Bourgneuf** Île du Pilier 47°02'.6N
2°21'.6W **Fl(3)W 20s** 33m 29M

D1162 **Île de Noirmoutier** Pointe des Dames
47°00'.7N 2°13'.3W **Oc(3)WRG 12s** 34m
19/15/15M *G016.5°-057°(40.5°), R057°-
124°(67°), G124°-165°(41°), W165°-
191°(26°), R191°- 267°(76°), W267°-
357°(90°), R357°-016.5°(19.5°)*

D1174 **Fromentine Bridge** 46°53'.5N 2°09'.0W
Iso W 4s 32m 18M

D1176 **ÎLE D'YEU** Petite Foule 46°43'.1N 2°22'.9W
Fl W 5s 56m 24M. RC

D1186 - **Pointe des Corbeaux** 46°41'.4N 2°17'.1W
Fl(2+1)R 15s 25m 20M *Obscured by the high
land of Île d'Yeu 083°-143°(60°)*

D1189.6 **Saint Gilles-Sur-Vie** Pointe de Grosse Terre
46°41'.6N 1°57'.8W **Fl(4)WR 12s** 25m 17/
13M *W290°-125°(195°), R125°-145°(20°)*

D1196 **LES SABLES D'OLONNE**
L'Armandèche 46°29'.4N 1°48'.3W **Fl(2+1)
W 15s** 42m 24M *Vis 295°-130°(195°)*

D1207 - **Passe du SW** Ldg Lts 033°. Front
46°29'.5N 1°46'.3W **Iso R 4s** 14m 16M
Iso W 4s(T) 1994

D1207-1- **Rear** La Potence 330m from front
46°29'.6N 1°46'.1W **Iso R 4s** 33m 16M
Iso W 4s (T) 1994

D1214 **Pointe du Grouin-du-Cou** 46°20'.7N
1°27'.8W **Fl WRG 5s** 29m 20/16/16M
*R034°-061°(27°), W061°- 117°(56°),
G117°-138°(21°), W138°- 034°(256°)*

D1218 **ÎLE DE RÉ** Les Baleines 46°14'.7N 1°33'.7W
Fl(4)W 15s 53m 27M RC

D1220-1- **Le Fier d'Ars** Ldg Lts 265°. Rear. 370m from
front 46°14'.1N 1°28'.8W **Dir Iso G 4s** 13m
15M *Synchronised with front. Intens 264°-266°(2°)*

D1238 - **Chauveau** 46°08'.1N 1°16'.3W
Oc(2+1)WR 12s 27m 15/11M
*W057°-094°(37°), R094°- 104°(10°),
W104°-342°(238°), R342°-057°(75°)*

D1256 **LA CHARENTE** Île d'Aix 46°00'.6N

1°10'.7W **Fl WR 5s** 24m 24/20M
R103°-118°(15°), W118°-103°(345°)

D1257 - Ldg Lts 115°. Fort de la Pointe. Front
45°58'.0N 1°04'.3W **Dir QR** 8m 19M
Intens 113°-117°(4°)

D1257-1- **Rear** 600m from front 45°57'.9N 1°03'.8W
Dir QR 21m 20M *Intens 113°-117°(4°)*

D1270 **Île D'Oléron** Chassiron 46°02'.9N 1°24'.5W
Fl W 10s 50m 28M *Part obscured 297°-
351°(54°)*

D1290 **LA GIRONDE** La Coubre 45°41'.8N
1°14'.0W **Fl(2)W 10s** 64m 28M RC

D1293-9 - Ldg Lts 081°30'. La Palmyre. Front. 1.1M
from rear 45°39'.6N 1°08'.7W
Dir Iso W 4s 21m 20M
Intens 080.5°-082.5°(2°)

D1294 - **Common rear** 45°39'.8N 1°07'.2W
Dir QW57m 27M*Intens 080.5°082.5°(2°).Ra*
Dir FR 57m 17M *Intens 325.5°-328.5°(3°)*

D1294-1 - Ldg Lts 327° Terre-Nègre. Front. 1.1M from
rear 45°38'.8N 1°06'.3W
Oc(3)WRG 12s 39m 18/14/14M
*R304°-319°(15°), W319°-327°(8°),
G327°-000°(33°), W000°-004°(4°),
G004°- 097°(93°), W097°-104°(7°),
R104°-116°(12°)*

D1300 - **Cordouan** 45°35'.2N 1°10'.4W.
Oc(2+1)WRG12s 60m 22/18/18M
*W014°-126° (112°), G126°-178.5°(52.5°),
W178°.5-250°(71.5°), W(unintens) 250°-
267°(17°), R(unintens)267°- 294.5°(27.5°),
R294.5°-014°(79.5°). Obscured in estuary when
bearing more than 285°*

D1310 - **1st Ldg Lts** 063° St Nicolas. Front
45°33'.8N 1°04'.9W **Dir QG** 22m 16M
Intens 061.5°-064.5°(3°)

D1310-1 - **Pointe de Grave**. Rear. 0.84M from front
45°34'.2N 1°03'.9W
Oc WRG 4s 26m 19/15/15M *W(unintens)
033°-054°(21°), W054°-233.5°(179.5°),
R233.5°-303°(69.5°), W303°-312°(9°),
G312°-330°(18°), W330°-341°(11°).
W(unintens)341°-025°(44°).*

D1312 - Ldg Lts 041°. Le Chay. Front 45°37'.3N
1°02'.4W **Dir QR** 33m 18M
Intens 039.5°-042.5°(3°)

D1312-1 - **Saint-Pierre** Rear. 0.97M from front
45°38'.1N 1°01'.4W **Dir QR** 61m 18M
Intens 039°-043°(4°)

D1372 **Hourtin** 45°08'.5N 1°09'.7W
Fl W 5s 55m 23M

D1378 **Cap Ferret** 44°38'.7N 1°15'.0W
Fl R 5s 53m 27M RC

D1382 **Contis** 44°05'.7N 1°19'.2W
Fl(4)W 25s 50m 23M

D1387-2 **L'ADOUR** Boucau. Ldg Lts 090°.
Front 43°31'.9N 1°31'.2W
Dir QW 9m 19M *Intens 086.5°-093.5°(7°)*

D1387-21 - **Rear** 250m from front 43°31'.9N 1°31'.0W
Dir QW 15m 19M *Intens 086.5°-093.5°(7°)*

D1396 - **La Forme de Radoub** Ldg Lts 205°. Front
43°30'.6N 1°29'.7W **Dir FG** 17m 16M
Intens 203.5°-206.5°(3°)

D1396-1 - **Rear** 147m from front 43°30'.5N 1°29'.8W

Dir FG 24m 16M *Intens 203.5°-206.5°(3°)*

D1410 **Pointe Saint-Martin** 43°29'.6N 1°33'.3W
Fl(2)W 10s 73m 29M

D1414 **BAIE DE SAINT-JEAN-DE-LUZ** Sainte-Barbe. Ldg Lts 101°. Front 43°24'.0N 1°39'.8W
Dir Oc(3+1)R 12s 30m 18M
Intens 095°-107°(12°)

D1416 **- Rear** 340m from front 43°24'.0N 1°39'.5W
Dir Oc(3+1)R 12s 47m 18M *Synchronised with front. Intens 095°-107°(12°)*

D1418 **- Entrance** Ldg Lts 150°42'. Front. Jetée Est 43°23'.3N 1°40'.1W **Dir QG** 18m 16M
Intens 149.5°-152°(2.5°)

D1420 **- Rear** 410m from front 43°23'.1N 1°39'.9W
Dir QG 27m 16M
Intens 149.7°-152.2°(2.5°)

D1424-1 **- Passe D'illarguita** Ldg Lts 138°30'
Bordagain. Rear. 0.77M from front 43°23'.2N 1°40'.4W **Dir QW** 67m 20M
Intens 134.5°-141.5°(7°)

SPAIN

D1452 **Cabo Higuer** 43°23'.6N 1°47'.4W
Fl(2)W 10s 63m 23M
Vis 072°-340°(268°) Aero marine

D1459 **PUERTO DE PASAJES** Ldg Lts 154°49'.
Front 43°20'.0N 1°55'.5W **QW** 67m 18M

D1459-1 **- Rear** 45m from front 43°20'.0N 1°55'.5W
Oc W 3s 86m 18M

D1483 **Igueldo or San Sebastián** 43°19'.3N 2°00'.7W **Fl (2+1)W 15s** 132m 26M

D1489 **Puerto de Guertaria** Isla de San Antón, 43°18'.6N 2°12'.1W **Fl (4)W 15s** 91m 21M

D1502 **Cabo de Santa Catalina** 43°22'.6N 2°30'.6W **Fl (1+3)W 20s** 44m 17M

D1520 **Cabo Machichaco** 43°27'.2N 2°45'.2W
Fl W 7s 120m 24M *RC*

D1523 **Gorliz** 46°26'.0N 2°56'.6W
Fl (1+2)W 16s 163m 22M

D1524 **Puerto de Bilbao** Punta Galea 43°22'.4N 3°02'.0W **Fl (3)W 8s** 82m 19M
Vis 011°-227°(216°)

D1536 **Puerto de Castro - Urdiales,** Castillo de Santa Ana 43°23'.1N 3°12'.9W
Fl (4)W 24s 46m 20M

D1552 **Cabo Ajo** 43°30'.8N 3°35'.3W
Oc (3)W 16s 69m 17M

D1561 **Cabo Mayor** 43°29'.5N 3°47'.4W
Fl (2)W 10s 89m 21M *RC*

D1562 **Ría de Suances** Punta del Torco de Fuera 43°26'.5N 4°02'.6W **Fl (1+2)W 24s** 33m 22M
Obscured close inshore by higher land 091°-113°(22°)

D1580 **Punta San Emeterio** 43°24'.0N 4°32'.1W
Fl W 5s 66m 20M

D1582 **Llanes,** Punta de San Antón 43°25'.2N 4°44'.9W
Oc (4) W 15s 16m 15M *RC*

D1586 **Puerto de Ribadesella** Somos 43°28'.4N 5°05'.0W **Fl(1+2) W 12s** 113m 21M

D1591 **Cabo Lastres** 43°32'.1N 5°18'.0W
Fl W 12s 116m 23M

D1592 **Tazones** 43°32'.9N 5°24'.0W
Oc (3) W 15s 125m 15M

D1596 **Puerto de Gijón** Cabo de Torres

43°34'.4N 5°41'.9W **Fl(2) W 10s** 80m 18M

D1628 **Cabo Peñas** 43°39'.3N 5°50'.9W
Fl(3) W 15s 115m 21M *RC*

D1630 **Ría de Avilés** Punta del Castillo, Avilés 43°35'.8N 5°56'.6W **Oc WR 5s** 38m 15/13M
R091.5°-113°(21.5°) over Bajo El Petón. W113°-091.5°(338.5°)

D1634 **Puerto de San Esteban de Pravia** W Brkwr elbow 43°34'.0N 6°04'.7W
Fl(2)W 12s 19m 15M

D1640 **Puerto de Cudillero** Punta Rebollera 43°33'.9N 6°08'.7W **Oc(4)W 15s** 42m 16M

D1641 **Cabo Vidio** 43°35'.6N 6°14'.7W
Fl W 5s 99m 25M Aeromarine

D1642 **Cabo Busto** 43°34'.1N 6°28'.2W
Fl(4) W 20s 84m 21M Aeromarine

D1657 **Ría de Navia** Cabo de San Augustín 43°33'.8N 6°44'.1W **Oc(2) W 12s** 70m 18M

D1658 **Isla Tapia** 43°34'.4N 6°56'.8W
Fl(1+2) W 19s 22m 18M

D1660 **Ría de Ribadeo** Isla Pancha 43°33'.4N 7°02'.5W **Fl(3+1) W 20s** 26m 21M

D1676 **Puerto de San Ciprián** Punta Atalaya 43°42'.1N 7°26'.1W **Fl(4)W 11s** 39m 15M

D1678.8 **Punta Roncadoira** 43°44'.1N 7°31'.5W
Fl W 7.5s 92m 21M.
Reduced range (T) 1995

D1686 **Punta Estaca de Bares** 43°47'.2N 7°41'.1W
Fl (2)W 7.5s 99m 23M Aeromarine.
Obscured when bearing more than 291°. RC

D1687 **Punta Candelaria** 43°42'.7N 8°02'.8W
Fl(3+1) W 24s 87m 21M

D1690 **Punta de la Frouxeira** 43°37'.1N 8°11'.3W
Fl(5) W 15s 73m 20M

D1692 **Cabo Prior** 43°34'.1N 8°18'.9W
Fl(1+2) W 15s 105m 22M *Vis 055.5°-310° (254.5°)*

D1694 **Cabo Prioriño Chico** 43°27'.5N 8°20'.3W
Fl W 5s 34m 23M

D1704 **Torre de Hércules** 43°23'.2N 8°24'.3W
Fl(4)W 20s 104m 23M *RC*
Obscured in entrance to Ensenada del Orzán

D1728 **Islas Sisargas** 43°21'.6N 8°50'.7W
Fl(3)W 15s 108m 23M

D1736 **Cabo Villano** 43°09'.6N 9°12'.7W
Fl(2)W 15s 102m 28M.
Vis 031.5°-228.5°(197°)RC. Racon

D1740 **Cabo Toriñana** 43°03'.2N 9°17'.9W
Fl(2+1)W 15s 63m 24M
Vis 340.5°-235.5°(255°)

D1742 **Cabo Finisterre** 42°52'.9N 9°16'.3W
Fl W 5s 141m 23M *Obscured when bearing more than 149°. Racon. RC*

D1782 **Punta Insúa** 42°46'.3N 9°07'.6W
F W 26m 15M
Vis 093°-172.5° but obscured 145° 172.5°(27.5°)

D1794 **Cabo Corrubedo** 42°34'.6N 9°05'.4W
Fl(3+2)R 20s *Clear sector Fl(3+2) 089.4°- about 200°(110.6°).***Fl(3)R 20s**
Dangerous sector Fl(3) about 332°- (325° within Ensenada de Corrubedo)- 089.4°(117.4°)

D1796 **Isla Sálvora** 42°27'.9N 9°00'.8W

Fl(3+1)W 20s 38m 21M Fl(3)W 20s
Clear sector Fl(3+1)217°- 126° (269°),
dangerous sector Fl(3) 126°- 160°(34°)
D1846 Isla Ons 42°22'.9N 8°56'.2W
Fl(4)W 24s 126m 25M
D1884 Monte Faro 42°12'.8N 8°54'.9W
Fl(2)W 8s 185m 22M
Obscured 315°-016.5°(61.5°) over Bajos
de Los Castros and Forcados
D1890 CABO ESTAY Ldg Lts 069°20'. Front
42°11'.1N 8°48'.9W Iso W 2s 16m 18M
Vis 066.3°-072.3(6°). Racon
D1890-1- Rear 660m from front 42°11'.3N 8°48'.3W
Oc W 4s 48m 18M *Vis 066.3°-072.3°(6°)*
D1904 Punta Areiño La Guia 42°15'.6N 8°42'.1W
Oc(2+1)W 20s 35m 15M
D1916 Cabo Silleiro 42°06'.2N 8°53'.8W
Fl(2+1)W 15s 83m 24M *Aeromarine. RC*

PORTUGAL
D2008 Promontório de Montedor 41°44'.9N
8°52'.4W Fl(2)W 9.5s 102m 22M *RC*
D2012 VIANA DO CASTELO Rio Lima. Barra Sul
Ldg Lts 012°30'. Castelo de Santiago. SW
battery. Front 41°41'.4N 8°50'.3W
Iso R 4s 14m 23M *Vis 241°-151°(270°)*
D2012-1 - Senhora da Agonia Rear. 500m from front
41°41'.7N 8°50'.2W
Oc R 6s 32m 23M *Vis 005°-020°(15°)*
D2016 Forte da Barra do Rio Cávado
41°32'.5N 8°47'.4W Fl W 5s 20m 21M
D2020 Póvoa de Varzim Regufe
41°22'.4N 8°45'.2W Iso W 6s 29m 15M
D2032 Leça 41°12'.1N 8°42'.6W
Fl(3)W 14s 57m 28M *RC*
D2056 Aveiro 40°38'.6N 8°44'.8W
Fl(4)W 13s 65m 23M *Aeromarine. RC*
D2060 Cabo Mondego 40°11'.4N 8°54'.2W
Fl W 5s 101m 28M. *RC*
D2072 Penedo da Saudade 39°45'.8N 9°01'.8W
Fl(2)W 15s 54m 30M *Aeromarine*
D2086 Ilha Berlenga 39°24'.8N 9°30'.5W
Fl(3)W 20s 120m 27M *RC*
D2088 Cabo Carvoeiro 39°21'.5N 9°24'.4W
Fl(3)R 15s 57m 15M *RC*
D2108 Cabo da Roca 38°46'.8N 9°29'.8W
Fl(4)W 18s 164m 26M. *RC. Aeromarine*
D2110 Forte de São Brás 38°42'.6N 9°29'.1W
Fl(3)W 15s 22m 20M *Vis 324°-189°(225°)*
D2114 CASCAIS Barra do Norte. Ldg Lts 285°.
Nossa Senhora de Guia. Rear 38°41'.6N
9°26'.7W Iso WR 2s 57m 19/16M
W326°-092°(126°), R278°-292°(14°)
D2118 - Forte de Santa Marta
Front 38°41'.3N 9°25'.2W
Oc WR 6s 24m 18/14M
R223°-334°(101°), W334°-098°(124°)
D2126 Forte Bugio 38°39'.5N 9°17'.9W
FIG 5s 27m 21M
D2127 Barra do Sul Ldg Lts 047°. Gibalta. Front
38°41'.8N 9°15'.9W Oc R 3s 30m 21M
Vis 039.5°-054.5°(15°)
D2127-1 - Esteiro Rear. 760m from front 38°42'.1N

9°15'.6W Oc R 6s 81m 21M
Vis 039.5°-054.5°(15°) Racon
D2127-15 Mama Sul 38°43'.7N 9°13'.6W
IsoW 6s 154m 21M
D2139 Cabo Espichel 38°24'.8N 9°12'.9W
Fl W 4s 167m 26M *Aeromarine. RC*
D2151-1 Porto de Setúbal Ldg Lts 040° Azêda. Rear
1.7M from front 38°32'.4N 8°52'.4W
Iso R 6s 71m 17M
D2160 Cabo de Sines 37°57'.5N 8°52'.7W Fl(2)W
15s 50m 26M. *RC. Obscured 001°-003°(2°),*
004°-007°(3°) within 17M.
D2164 Cabo Sardão 37°35'.8N 8°48'.9W
Fl(3)W 15s 66m 23M
D2168 Cabo de São Vicente 37°01'.3N 8°59'.7W
Fl W 5s 84m 32M *Aeromarine RC*
D2174 Ponta da Piedade 37°04'.8N 8°40'.1W
Fl W 7s 49m 20M
D2192 Alfanzina 37°05'.1N 8°26'.5W
Fl(2)W 15s 61m 29M
D2197.2 Vilamoura 37°04'.4N 8°07'.3W
Fl W10s 17m 19M
D2206 Cabo de Santa Maria 36°58'.4N 7°51'.8W
Fl (4)W 17s 49m 25M *Aeromarine. RC.*
Reduced range 17M (T) 1995
D2246 Vila Real de Santo António 37°11'.1N
7°24'.9W Fl W 6.5s 51m 26M *RC*

SPAIN
D2312 Rompido de Cartaya 37°12'.9N 7°07'.6W
Fl(2)W 10s 41m 24M
D2320 Picacho 37°08'.2N 6°49'.5W
Fl(2+4)W 30s 51m 25M
D2345 Higuera 37°00'.6N 6°34'.1W
Fl(3)W 20s 46m 20M
D2351 Chipiona Punta del Perro 36°44'.3N
6°26'.4W FIW 10s 68m 25M. *Racon*
D2355 Rota 36°38'.2N 6°20'.8W
Aero AlFI WG 9s 79m 17M
D2362 Puerto de Cádiz Castilla de San Sebastián
36°31'.8N 6°18'.9W Fl(2) W 10s 38m 25M
Unintens 085°-121°(36°) Obscured over the port
by the houses in the town.
D2405 Cabo Roche 36°17'.8N 6°08'.3W
Fl(4)W 24s 44m 20M
D2406 Cabo Trafalgar 36°11'.0N 6°02'.0W
Fl(2+1)W 15s 50m 22M *Aeromarine. RC*
D2414 Tarifa S. end of peninsula 36°00'.1N
5°36'.5W Fl(3) W R 10s 40m 26/18M
W113°-089°(336°) R089°-113°(24°) RC Racon
D2420 Punta Carnero 36°04'.7N 5°25'.5W
Fl(4)WR 20s 42m 18/9M
W018°-325°(307°), R 325°- 018°(53°)

GIBRALTAR
D2438 Europa Point 36°06'.7N 5°20'.6W
Iso W 10s 49m 19M *Vis 197°-042°(205°),*
intens 067°- 125°(58°) Oc R 10s 15M *Vis 042°-*
067°(25°) FR 44m 15M *Vis 042°-067°(25°)*
D2442 South Mole A head 36°08'.1N 5°21'.8W
Fl W 2s 18m 15M
D2456 Aero light 36°08'.7N 5°20'.5W
Aero Mo (GB)R 10s 405m 30M
Obscured on Westerly bearings within 2M

DIRECTION FINDING RADIOBEACONS

MODE OF EMISSION		
Mode designator	During DF period	During identification
A1A	BFO ON	BFO ON
A2A	BFO ON or OFF - see handbook	BFO OFF
NON A2A	BFO ON	BFO OFF

All beacons are A1A unless othewise shown

ENGLAND SOUTH COAST

Dungeness Lt RC 50°54'.77N 0°58'.67E
DU ··· ··· 300.5 NON A2A 50 M H24
Brighton Marina RC 50°48'.67N 0°05'.95W
BM ···· ·· 294.5 10 M H24
S. Catherine's Point Lt RC
  50°34'.52N 1°17'.80W
CP ···· ···· 293 50 M H24
Bournemouth Aero RC 50°46'.63N 1°50'.47W
BIA ···· ·· ·· 339 NON A2A 15 M H24
Bill of Portland Lt RC 50°30'.82N 2'.27'.30W
PB ···· ···· 309.5 50 M H24
Exeter Aero RC 50°45'.12N 3°17'.62W
EX · ···· 337 NON A2A 15 M HJ
Berry Hd Aero RC 50°23'.88N 3°29'.55W
BHD ···· ···· ··· 318 NON A2A25 M H24
Lizard Lt RC 49°57'.58N 5°12'.07W
LZ ···· ····284.5 70 M H24
Penzance Heliport Aero RC
  50°07'.67N 5°31'.00W
PH ···· ····333 NON A2A 15 M HJ
S. Marys, Scilly Is Aero RC
  49°54'.82N 6°17'.43W
STM ··· - ·· 321 NON A2A 15 M HJ
Round I Lt, Scilly Is RC
  49°58'.70N 6°19'.33W
RR ··· ··· 298.5 150 M H24
S. Mawgan Aero RC 50°26'.51N 4°59'.36W
SM ··· ·· 356.5 NON A2A 20 M H24

ENGLAND EAST COAST

Souter Lt RC 54'.58'.23N 1°21'.80W
SJ ··· ···· 292 50 M H24

Flamborough Hd Lt RC
  54°06'.95N 0°04'.87W
FB ···· ···· 303 70 M H24
Ottringham Aero RC 53°41'.88N 0°06'.14W
OTR ··· - ··· 398.5 30 M H24
Cromer Lt RC 52°55'.45N 1°19'.10E
CM ···· ·· 313.5 50 M H24
GtYarmouth Aero RC 52°38'.10N 1°43'.73E
ND ·· ··· 417 NON A2A 10 M H24
Sunk Lt F RC 51°51'.00N 1°35'.00E
UK ··· ··· 294.5 10 M H24
Southend Aero RC 51°34'.55N 0°42'.12E
SND ··· ·· ··· 362.5 NON A2A 20 M H24
North Foreland RC 51°22'.49N 1°26'.85E
NF ·· ···· 311 50 M H24

SCOTLAND

Turnberry Aero RC 55°18'.80N 4°47'.00W
TRN - ··· ·· 355 NON A2A 25 M H24
Rhinns of Islay Lt RC 55°40'.38N 6°30'.70W
RN ··· ·· 293 70 M H24
Stornoway Aero RC 58°12'.86N 6°19'.49W
SAY ··· ·· ···· 669.5 NON A2A
  60 M H24
Butt of Lewis Lt RC 58°30'.93N 6°15'.72W
BL ···· ···· 289 70 M H24
Dounreay Aero RC 58°34'.90N 3°43'.58W
DO ··· ··· 364.5 NON A2A 15 M H24
Scatsta, Shetland Is AeroRC
  60°27'.68N 1°12'.78W
SS ··· ··· 315.5 NON A2A 25 M HJ
**Sumburgh,
Shetland Is** Aero RC 59°52'.08N 1°16'.35W
SBH ··· ···· ···· 351NON A2A 25 M HJ
**Sumburgh Head Light,
Shetland Is** RC 59°51'.30N 1°16'.37W
SB ··· ···· 304 70 M H24
Duncansby Head Lt RC
  58°38'.67N 3°01'.42W
DY ··· ···· 290.5 50 M H24
Wick Aero RC 58°26'.83N 3°03'.70W
WIK ··· ·· ··· 344 NON A2A 30 M HJ
Kinnairds Hd Lt RC 57°41'.87N 2°00'.13W
KD ··· ··· 301.5 50 M H24
Scotstown Head Aero RC
  57°33'.56N 1°48'.94W
SHD ··· ···· ··· 383 NON A2A 80 M H24
Girdle Ness Lt RC 57°08'.32N 2°02'.83W
GD ··· ··· 311 50 M H24
Fife Ness Lt RC 56°16'.73N 2°35'.10W
FP ···· ···· 305 50 M H24
Inchkeith Lt RC 56°02'.02N 3°08'.08W
NK ·· ···· 286.5 10 M H24
Fidra Lt RC 56°04'.40N 2°47'.02W
FD ···· ··· 290 10 M H24

UK WEST COAST

Cardiff Aero RC   51°23'.57N 3°20'.23W
CDF •••• ••• ••••388.5 NON A2A
                    20 M   H24

Nash Point Lt RC   51°24'.03N 3°33'.06W
NP •• •••• 299.5   50 M H24

Swansea Aero RC   51°36'.10N 4°03'.88W
SWN••• ••• ••320.5 NON A2A 15 M   HJ

South Bishop Lt RC   51°51'.15N 5°24'.65W
SB ••• •••• 290.5   70 M   H24

Strumble Aero RC   52°00'.50N 5°01'.01W
STU ••• - ••• 400   NON A2A 40 M   H24

Aberporth Aero RC   52°06'.92N 4°33'.57W
AP •• •••• 370.5 NON A2A 20 M   H24

Point Lynas Lt RC   53°24'.97N 4°17'.30W
PS •••• ••• 304   50 M   H24

Blackpool Aero RC   53°46'.36N 3°01'.59W
BPL •••• •••• ••••420 NON A2A 15 M   HJ

Walney Island Lt RC   54°02'.92N 3°10'.55W
FN •••• •• 306   50 M   H24

Ronaldsway, Isle of Man Aero RC
                    54°05'.15N 4°36'.45W
RWY ••• ••- •••-359 NON A2A 20 M   HJ

IRELAND

Mizen Head RC   51°27'.05N 9°48'.80W
MZ -- ---•• 300   100 M   H24

Old Head of Kinsale Lt RC
                    51°36'.27N 8°31'.97W
OH ••• •••• 288   50 M   H24

Waterford Aero RC   52°11'.83N 7°05'.33W
WTD ••• - -••• 368   NON A2A 25 M   H24

Tuskar Rock Lt RC   52°12'.15N 6°12'.38W
TR - ••• 286   50 M   H24

Killiney Aero RC   53°16'.17N 6°06'.33W
KLY ••• •••• ••••378 NON A2A 50 M   H24

Baily Lt RC   53°21'.68N 6°03'.09W
BY •••• •••• 289   50 M   H24

Dublin, Rush Aero RC 53°30'.73N 6°06'.60W
RSH ••• ••• •••• 326 NON A2A 30 M   H24

South Rock Lt Float RC
                    54°24'.47N 5°21'.92W
SU ••• ••• 291.5   50 M   H24

Tory Island Lt RC   55°16'.35N 8°14'.92W
TY - •••• 313   100 M   H24

Eagle Island Lt RC   54°16'.98N 10°05'.52W
GL ••• •••• 307   100 M   H24

Loop Head Lt RC   52°33'.65N 9°55'.90W
LP •••• •••• 311.5   50 M   H24

BELGIUM

Nieuwpoort, W Pier Lt RC
                    51°09'.40N 2°43'.08E
NP •• •••• 285   6 M   H24

Oostende RC   51°14'.36N 2°55'.94E
OE --- • 312   40 M   H24

Zeebrugge, N Westdam RC
                    51°21'.66N 3°11'.33E
ZB --- •• •••• 289   6 M   H24

HOLLAND

Goeree Lt RC   51°55'.53N 3°40'.18E
GR --- ••• 296   48 M   H24

Hoek van Holland RC 51°58'.90N 4°06'.83E
HH •••• •••• 288   50 M   H24

IJmuiden Front Lt RC 52°27'.75N 4°34'.55E
YM --•• -- 288.5   20 M   H24

Eierland Lt RC   53°10'.97N 4°51'.40E
ER • •••• 301   20 M   H24

Vlieland Lt RC   53°17'.80N 5°03'.57E
VL •••• •••• 303.5   20 M   H24

Ameland Lt RC   53°27'.02N 5°37'.60E
AD •• -••• 299   50 M   H24

GERMANY

Borkum, Kleiner Lt RC
                    53°34'.78N 6°40'.09E
BE •••• • 302   20 M   H24

Wangerooge Lt RC   53°47'.45N 7°51'.52E
WE ••• • 309.5   20 M   H24

Alte Weser Lt RC   53°51'.85N 8°07'.72E
AR •• •••• 309   20 M   H24

Nordholz Aero RC   53°47'.18N 8°48'.47E
NDO-• -••• ---372 NON A2A 30 M   H24

Elbe Lt F RC   54°00'.00N 8°06'.58E
EL • •••• 298   10 M   H24

German Bight Lt V RC
                    54°10'.80N 7°27'.60E
GB ---• •••• 312   10 M   H24

Westerland/Sylt Aero RC
                    54°51'.45N 8°24'.67E
SLT ••• •••• - 387 NON A2A 25 M   H24

DENMARK

Dan Oil Field Platform DUC-OF-C
Aero RC   55°28'.73N 5°06'.43E
DNF-•• -• ••••349 NON A2A 25 M   H24

Blåvanshuk Lt RC   55°33'.52N 8°05'.07E
BH •••• •••• 296   50 M   H24

Thyborøn Lt RC   56°42'.53N 8°13'.00E
TN - -• 306   100 M   H24

Skagen W Lt RC   57°44'.98N 10°35'.78E
SW ••• ••- 298.5   50 M   H24

CHANNEL ISLANDS

Alderney Aero RC   49°42'.58N 2°11'.90W
ALD •• -•••• •••383 NON A2A 50 M   H24

Castle Brkwr Lt, St. Peter Port,			
Guernsey RC		49°27'.37N 2°31'.37W	
GY --- -•-- 304.5		10 M	H24
Guernsey Aero RC		49°26'.12N 2'.38'.30W	
GRB --- -•- -••••361	NON A2A 30 M		H24
Elizabeth Castle,			
S. Helier, Jersey RC		49°10'.62N 2°07'.50W	
EC •-•-• 306		10 M	H24
La Corbière Lt, Jersey RC			
		49°10'.85N 2°14'.90W	
CB --•- -••• 295.5		20 M	H24
Jersey West Aero RC	49°12'.37N 2°13'.30W		
JW •--- --- 329	NON A2A 25 M		H24

FRANCE

Calais. Dunkerque Aero RC			
		50°59'.88N 2°03'.36E	
MK -- -•- 418		15 M	H24
Calais Main Lt RC		50°57'.73N 1°51'.30E	
CS --•• ••• 312.5		20 M	H24
Cap d'Alprech Lt RC	50°41'.95N 1°33'.83E		
PH •--• -••• 294		20 M	H24
Le Touquet Aero RC	50°32'.13N 1°35'.37E		
LT •--• - 358	A2A	20 M	H24
Pointe d'Ailly Lt RC		49°55'.00N 0°57'.55E	
AL •- -•-• 305.5		50 M	H24
Cap d Antifer Lt RC		49°41'.07N 0°10'.00E	
TI - •• 300		50 M	H24
Le Havre, Octeville Aero RC			
		49°35'.75N 0°11'.00E	
LHO •-•• -••• ---346		15 M	H24
Pointe de Ver Lt RC		49°20'.47N 0°31'.15W	
ER •-•• 310		20 M	H24
Port en Bessin Rear Lt RC			
		49°21'.00N 0°45'.60W	
BS -••• ••• 290		5 M	H24
Pointe de Barfleur Lt RC			
		49°41'.87N 1°15'.87W	
FG •-•- --- 297		70 M	H24
Cherbourg,			
Fort de l'Ouest Lt RC	49°40'.50N 1°38'.87W		
RB •-• -••• 302		20 M	H24
Granville Aero RC		48°55'.10N 1°28'.87W	
GV --- -••- 321		25 M	H24
Le Grand Jardin Lt RC	48°40'.27N 2°04'.90W		
GJ --- -••• 306.5		10 M	H24
Cap Fréhel Lt RC		48°41'.10N 2°19'.07W	
FÉ •-•• ••-•• 286.5		20 M	H24
Saint Brieuc Aero RC	48°34'.10N 2°46'.90W		
SB ••• -••• 353		25 M	H24
Rosédo Lt, Île Bréhat RC			
		48°51'.51N 3°00'.21W	
DO -•- --- 287.5		10 M	H24

Lannion Aero RC		48°43'.25N 3°18'.45W	
LN •--• -• 345		50 M	H 24
Roches Douvres Lt RC			
		49°06'.47N 2°48'.65W	
RD •-• -•• 308		70 M	H24
Roscoff, Bloscon Jty Lt RC			
		48°43'.27N 3°57'.59W	
BC -••• -••• 304.5		10 M	H24
Île Vierge Lt RC		48°38'.38N 4°33'.97W	
VG •••- --- 314		70 M	H24
Pointe de Créac'h Lt,			
Île d'Ouessant RC		48°27'.62N 5°07'.65W	
CA -••• •- 301		100 M	H24
Ouessant SW, Lanby RC			
		48°31'.68N 5°49'.10W	
SW ••• •-- 305.5		10 M	H24
Pointe S Mathieu Lt RC			
		48°19'.85N 4°46'.17W	
SM ••• -- 292.5		50 M	H24
Lanvéoc, Poulmic Aero RC			
		48°17'.07N 4°26'.00W	
BST -••• ••• - 428		80 M	H24
Île de Sein NW Lt RC	48°02'.70N 4°51'.95W		
SN ••• -• 289.5		70 M	H24
Eckmühl Lt,			
Pointe de Penmarc'h RC		47°47'.95N 4°22'.35W	
UH ••• -••• 312		50 M	H24
Pointe de Combrit Lt RC			
		47°51'.92N 4°06'.70W	
CT -••• - 288.5		20 M	H24
Lorient Aero RC		47°45'.75N 3°26'.43W	
LOR •-•• --- ••• 359		80 M	H24
Pen Men, Île de Groix RC			
		47°38'.97N 3°30'.36W	
GX --- -••- 298		50 M	H24
S Nazaire, Montoir Aero RC			
		47°20'.02N 2°02'.57W	
MT --- - 398		50 M	H24
S Nazaire, Pointe de St Gildas Lt RC			
		47°08'.10N 2°14'.67W	
NZ -•• -••• 308.5		40 M	H24
Île d'Yeu Main Lt RC	46°43'.10N 2°22'.90W		
YE -••• • 303		100 M	H24
Les Baleines Lt, Île de Ré RC			
		46°14'.70N 1°33'.60W	
BN -••• -• 299		50 M	H24
La Rochelle, Tour Richelieu Lt RC			
		46°08'.97N 1°10'.27W	
RE •-• • 295.5		40M	H24
Pointe de la Coubre Lt RC			
		45°41'.87N 1°13'.93W	
LK •-•• -•• 292		100 M	H24

Cap Ferret Lt RC   44°38'.77N 1°14'.81W
FT ••••-   286.5   100 M   H24

SPAIN

San Sebastián Aero RC 43°23'.25N 1°47'.65W
HIG ••••-••-•••328   NON A2A 50 M   H24
Cabo Machichaco Lt RC
       43°27'.45N 2°45'.08W
MA --•--   284.5   100M   H24
Bilbao Aero RC   43°19'.43N 2°58'.43W
BLO ••••-••-•••--- 370 NON A2A 70 M   H24
Cabo Mayor Lt RC   43°29'.48N 3°47'.37W
MY --•-•--   304.5   100 M   H24
Llanes Lt RC   43°25'.20N 4°44'.90W
A ••-•-   303.5   50 M   H24
Cabo Peñas Lt RC   43°39'.42N 5°50'.80W
PS •---•-•••   297.5   50 M   H24
Asturias Aero RC   43°33'.57N 6'.01'.50W
AVS •-•••-•••325   NON A2A 60 M   H24
Punta Estaca de Bares Lt RC
       43°47'.17N 7'.41'.07W
BA •---•-•-   309.5   100 M   H24
Torre de Hercules Lt RC
       43°23'.23N 8°24'.30W
L •-••   301.5   50 M   H24
Cabo Villano Lt RC   43°09'.68N 9°12'.60W
VI ••••-••   290.5   100 M   H24
Cabo Finisterre Lt RC 42°53'.00N 9°16'.23W
FI ••••-••   288.5   100 M   H24
Cabo Estay Lt,
Ria de Vigo RC   42°11'.19N 8°48'.73W
VS ••••-•••   312.5   50 M   H24
Cabo Silleiro Lt RC   42°06'.33N 8°53'.70W
RO •••-•---   293.5   100 M   H24

PORTUGAL

Montedor Lt RC   41°44'.95N 8°52'.30W
290   Leça   291.9 A2A

No	Name	Ident	Range	Seq
0945	Montedor	MR --••••	150	1, 4
0949	Leça	LC ••••-••••	100	2, 5
0955	Aveiro	AV •-••••	100	3, 6

Porto Aero RC   41°19'.07N 8°41'.98W
POR ••••-•••-•••327 NON A2A 250 M H24
Leça Lt, Pta Boa Nova RC
       41°12'.50N 8°42'.64W
LC ••••-•••• 291.9   A2A - Grouped with 0945
Aveiro Lt RC   40°38'.47N 8°44'.80W
AV •-•••• 291.9   A2A - Grouped with 0945
Cabo Mondego Lt RC 40°11'.42N 8°54'.20W
287.5

No	Name	Ident	Range	Seq
0957	C Mondego	MD--••••	150	1, 2
0961	C Carvoeiro	CV-•••-••••	150	3, 4
0959	Ilha Berlenga	IB ••-••••	200	5, 6

Monte Real Aero RC   39°54'.54N 8°52'.92W
MTL -- - ••••   336 A2A   150 M   H24
Ilha Berlenga Lt RC   39°24'.83N 9°30'.50W
IB ••-••••   287.3 A2A-Grouped with 0957
Cabo Carvoeiro Lt RC
       39°21'.53N 9°24'.40W
CV -•••-•••-   Grouped with 0957
Sintra Aero RC   38°52'.92N 9°24'.04W
STR •••-•-••• 371   A2A   50 M   H24
Cabo Roca Lt RC   38°46'.70N 9°29'.82W
308

No	Name	Ident	Range	Seq
0963	C Roca RC	•••-••••	100	1, 2
0969	C Espichel	PI •••••-••	50	3, 4
0971	C de Sines	SN •••-••	100	5, 6

Caparica Aero RC   38°38'.62N 9°13'.21W
CP -•••-•••• 389 NON A2A 250 M   H24
Cabo Espichel Lt RC   38°24'.83N 9°12'.90W
PI •••••-••   Grouped with 0963
Cabo de Sines RC   37°57'.48N 8°53'.75W
SN •••-••   Grouped with 0963
Cabo de São Vicente Lt RC
       37°01'.32N 8°59'.70W
305.5   A1A

No	Name	Ident	Range	Seq
0973	São Vicente	VC ••••-••••	200	1, 2
0979	Santa Maria	SM •••-••	50	3, 4
0981	S Antonio	VR ••••-••••	100	5, 6

Lagos Aero RC   37°09'.65N 8°36'.80W
LGS •-•••-•••-••• 364 A2A   100 M   H24
Faro Aero R C   37°00'.43N 7°55'.48W
FAR ••••-••-•••   332A2A   50 M   H24
Cabo de Santa Maria Lt RC
       36°58'.38N 7°51'80W
SM •••-••   Grouped with 0973
Vila Real de Santo Antonio Lt RC
       37°11'.28N 7°24'.90W
VR ••••-•••   Grouped with 0973

SPAIN

Rota Aero RC   36°38'.62N 6°19'.00W
AOG •- ---•-••• 423 NON A2A 100 M   H24
Rota RC   36°37'.69N 6°22'.77W
D -••   303   80 M   H24
Cabo Trafalgar RC   36°11'.06N 6°02'.06W
B -•••   297   50 M   H24
Tarifa Lt RC   36°00'.13N 5°36'.47W
O ---   299   50 M   H24

VHF - EMERGENCY
DIRECTION FINDING SERVICE

This service is for emergency use only. Each direction- finding station is remotely controlled by an HM Coastguard Maritime Rescue Co-ordination Centre or Sub-Centre .Watch is kept on Ch 16. Ship transmits on Ch 16 (distress only) or Ch 67 in order that the station can determine its bearing. Ship's bearing from the station is transmitted on Ch 16 (distress only) or Ch 67.

ENGLAND SOUTH COAST

Berry Head 50°23'.94N 3°28'.97W
Controlled by MRSC Brixham
Boniface 50°36'.20N 1°11'.95W
Controlled by MRSC Solent
Prawle 50°13'.10N 3°42'.48W
Controlled from MRSC Brixham
Fairlight 50°52'.19N 0°38'.83E
Controlled from MRCC Dover
Pendennis 50°08'.68N 5°02'.69W
Controlled by MRCC Falmouth
Grove Point 50°32'.90N 2°25'.13W
Controlled from MRSC Portland
Hartland 51°01'.20N 4°31'.32W
Controlled by MRCC Swansea
Hengistbury Head 50°42'.92N 1°45'.56W
Controlled by MRSC Portland
Lands End 50°08'.13N 5°38'.19W
Controlled by MRCC Falmouth
Langdon Battery 51°07'.91N 1°20'.21E
Controlled by MRCC Dover
Newhaven 50°46'.90N 0°03'.13E
Controlled by MRSC Newhaven
Rame Head 50°18'.99N 4°13'.10W
Controlled by MRSC Brixham
S Mary's, Scilly Isles 49°55'.70N 6°18'.17W
Controlled by MRCC Falmouth
Selsey 50°43'.80N 0°48'.15W
Controlled by MRSC Solent
Trevose Head 50°32'.91N 5°01'.89W
Controlled by MRCC Falmouth

ENGLAND EAST COAST

Bawdsey 51°59'.55N 1°24'.59E
Controlled by MRSC Thames
Caister 52°39'.59N 1°43'.00E
Controlled by MRCC Yarmouth
Crosslaw 55°54'.50N 2°12'.20W
Controlled by MRSC Forth
Easington 53°39'.13N 0°05'.95E
Controlled by MRSC Humber
Flamborough 54°07'.08N 0°05'.12W
Controlled by MRSC Humber
Hartlepool 54°41'.79N 0°10'.47W
Controlled by MRCC Tyne Tees

Hunstanton 52°56'.93N 0°29'.70E
Controlled by MRCC Yarmouth
Langdon Battery 51°07'.91N 1°20'.21E
Controlled by MRCC Dover
Newton 55°31'.01N 1°37'.10W
Controlled by MRSC Tyne/Tees
North Foreland 51°22'.50N 1°26'.82E
Controlled by MRCC Dover
Shoeburyness 51°31'.34N 0°46'.69E
Controlled by MRCC Thames
Trimingham 52°54'.55N 1°20'.73E
Controlled by MRCC Yarmouth
Tynemouth 55°01'.08N 1°24'.90W
Controlled by MRSC Tyne/Tees
Whitby 54°29'.40N 0°36'.25W
Controlled by MRSC Humber

SCOTLAND

Barra 57°00'.81N 7°30'.42W
Controlled by MRSC Stornoway
Compass Head 59°52'.05N 1°16'.30W
Controlled by MRSC Shetland
Dunnet Head 58°40'.31N 3°22'.52W
Controlled by MRSC Pentland
Fife Ness 56°16'.78N 2°35'.25W
Controlled by MRSC Forth
Inverbervie 56°51'.10N 2°15'.65W
Controlled by MRCC Aberdeen
Kilchiaran 55°45'.90N 6°27'.19W
Controlled by MRCC Clyde
Law Hill 55°41'.76N 4°50'.46W
Controlled by MRCC Clyde
Rodel 57°44'.90N 6°57'.41W
Controlled by MRSC Stornoway
Sandwick 58°12'.65N 6°21'.27W
Controlled by MRSC Stornoway
Thrumster 58°23'.55N 3°07'.25W
Controlled by MRSC Pentland
Tiree 56°30'.62N 6°57'.68W
Controlled by MRSC Oban
Wideford Hill 58°59'.29N 3°01'.40W
Controlled by MRSC Pentland
Windyhead 57°38'.90N 2°14'.50W
Controlled by MRCC Aberdeen

UK WEST COAST

Great Ormes Head 53°19'.98N 3°51'.11W
Controlled by MRSC Holyhead
Rhiw 52°49'.98N 4°37'.69W
Controlled by MRSC Holyhead
Orlock Head 54°40'.41N 5°34'.97W
Controlled by MRSC Belfast
S Ann's Head 51°40'.97N 5°10'.52W
Controlled by MRSC Milford Haven
Snaefell 54°15'.82N 4°27'.59W
Controlled by MRSC Liverpool

Walney Island 54°06'.59N 3°15'.88W
Controlled by MRSC Liverpool
West Torr 55°11'.91N 6°05'.60W
Controlled by MRSC Belfast

CHANNEL ISLANDS
Guernsey 49°26'.27N 2°35'.77W
Jersey 49°10'.85N 2°14'.30W

FRANCE
Emergency use only Each station is remotely con-
trolled either by CROSS or a Naval Lookout Sta-
tion. Stations watch on Ch 16,11; 67. Ship trans-
mits on Ch 16 (distress only) or Ch 11 in order
that the station can determine its bearing. Ship's
bearing from the station is transmitted on Ch 16
(distress only) or Ch 11
Gris-Nez H24 50°52'.20N 1°35'.00E
Controlled by CROSS
Jobourg H24 49°41'.10N 1°54'.60W
Controlled by CROSS
Roches-Douvres H24 49°06'.50N 2°48'.80W
Controlled by CROSS-Jobourg
Dunkerque H24 51°03'.40N 2°20'.40E
Controlled by Signal Station
Boulogne HJ 50°44'.00N 1°36'.00E
Controlled by Signal Station
Ault HJ 50°06'.50N 1°27'.50E
Controlled by Signal Station
Dieppe HJ 49°56'.00N 1°05'.20E
Controlled by Signal Station
Fécamp H24 49°46'.10N 0°22'.20E
Controlled by Signal Station
La Hève H24 49°30'.60N 0°04'.20E
Controlled by Signal Station
Villerville HJ 49°23'.20N 0°06'.50E
Controlled by Signal Station
Port-en-Bessin H24 49°21'.10N 0°46'.30W
Controlled by Signal Station
Saint-Vaast HJ 49°34'.50N 1°16'.50W
Controlled by Signal Station
Barfleur H24 49°41'.90N 1°15'.90W
Controlled by Signal Station
Levy HJ 49°41'.70N 1°28'.20W
Controlled by Signal Station
Homet H24 49°39'.50N 1°37'.90W
Controlled by Lookout Stn
La Hague HJ 49°43'.60N 1°56'.30W
Controlled by Signal Station
Carteret HJ 49°22'.40N 1°48'.30W
Controlled by Signal Station
Le Roc HJ 48°50'.10N 1°36'.90W
Controlled by Signal Station
Créach Ouessant H24 48°27'.60N 5 °07'.80W
Controlled by CROSS Corsen
Grouin Cancale HJ 48°42'.60N 1°50'.60W
Controlled by Signal Station

Saint-Cast HJ 48°38'.60N 2°14'.70W
Controlled by Signal Station
S.-Quay-Portrieux H24 48°39'.30N 2°49'.50W
Controlled by Signal Station
Bréhat HJ 48°51'.30N 3°00'.10W
Controlled by Signal Station
Ploumanach H24 48°49'.50N 3°28'.20W
Controlled by Signal Station
Batz HJ 48°44'.80N 4°00'.60W
Controlled by Signal Station
Brignogan H24 48°40'.60N 4°19'.70W
Controlled by Signal Station
Créach Ouessant HJ 48°27'.60N 5°07'.70W
Controlled by Signal Station
Saint-Mathieu H24 48°19'.80N 4°46'.20W
Controlled by Lookout Station
Toulinguet Camaret HJ 48°16'.80N 4°37'.50W
Controlled by Signal Station
Cap de La Chèvre HJ 48°10'.20N 4°33'.00W
Controlled by Signal Station
Pointe du Raz H24 48°02'.30N 4°43'.80W
Controlled by Signal Station
Penmarc'h H24 47°47'.90N 4°22'.40W
Controlled by Signal Station
Beg-Meil HJ 47°51'.30N 3°58'.40W
Controlled by Signal Station
Étel RG H24 47°39'.80N 3°12'.00W
Controlled by CROSS
Beg Melen HJ 47°39'.20N 3°30'.10W
Controlled by Signal Station
Port-Louis H24 47°42'.60N 3°21'.80W
Controlled by Lookout Station
Saint-Julien HJ 47°29'.70N 3°07'.50W
Controlled by Signal Station
Taillefer HJ 47°21'.80N 3°09'.00W
Controlled by Signal Station
Le Talut HJ 47°17'.70N 3°13'.00W
Controlled by Signal Station
Piriac HJ 47°22'.50N 2°33'.40W
Controlled by Signal Station
Chemoulin H24 47°14'.10N 2°17'.80W
Controlled by Signal Station
Saint-Sauveur HJ 46°41'.70N 2°18'.80W
Controlled by Signal Station
Les Baleines HJ 46°14'.60N 1°33'.70W
Controlled by Signal Station
Chassiron HJ 46°02'.80N 1°24'.50W
Controlled by Signal Station
La Coubre H24 45°41'.90N 1°13'.40W
Controlled by Signal Station
Pointe de Grave HJ 45°34'.30N 1°03'.90W
Controlled by Signal Station
Cap Ferret HJ 44°37'.50N 1°15'.00W
Controlled by Signal Station
Messanges HJ 43°48'.80N 1°23'.90W
Controlled by Signal Station
Socoa H24 43°23'.30N 1°41'.10W
Controlled by Signal Station

VHF EMERGENCY DIRECTION FINDING SERVICE

BRITISH ISLES

This Service is for EMERGENCY USE ONLY. Each VHF direction finding station is remotely controlled by a HM Coastguard Marine Co-ordination Centre (MRCC) or Marine Rescue Sub-Centre (MRSC).

Watch is kept on Ch 16
Ship transmits on Ch 16 (distress only) or Ch 67 (Ch 82 Jersey) in order that the Station can determine its bearing
Ship's bearing from the station is transmitted on
Ch 16 (distress only) or Ch 67

Key:
● Signal Stations or
   Naval Lookout Stations

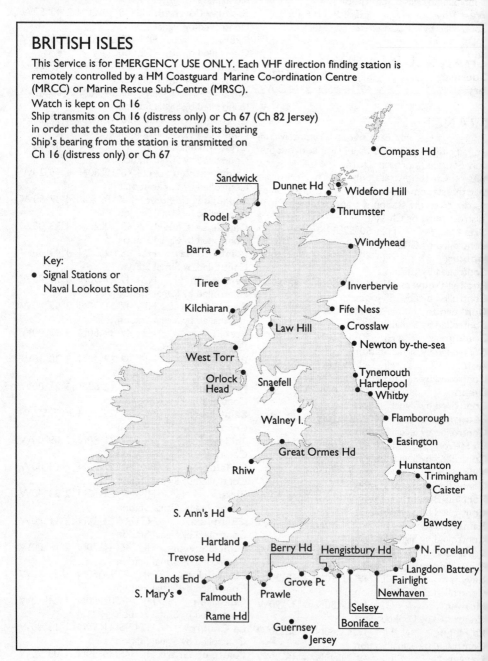

VHF EMERGENCY DIRECTION FINDING SERVICE

FRANCE *Channel and Atlantic Coasts*

This Service is for EMERGENCY USE ONLY. Each VHF direction-finding station is remotely controlled by a Regional Operation Centre for Surveillance and rescue (Cross), Signal Station or Naval Lookout Station.

Cross Stations watch on Ch 16, 11; 67, (when a Maritime rescue operation is already underway on Ch 11)

Signal Stations and Lookout Stations keep a priority watch on Ch 16

Ship transmits on Ch 16 (distress only) or Ch 11 in order that the station can determine its bearing.

Ship's bearing from the station is transmitted on Ch 16 (distress only) or Ch 11

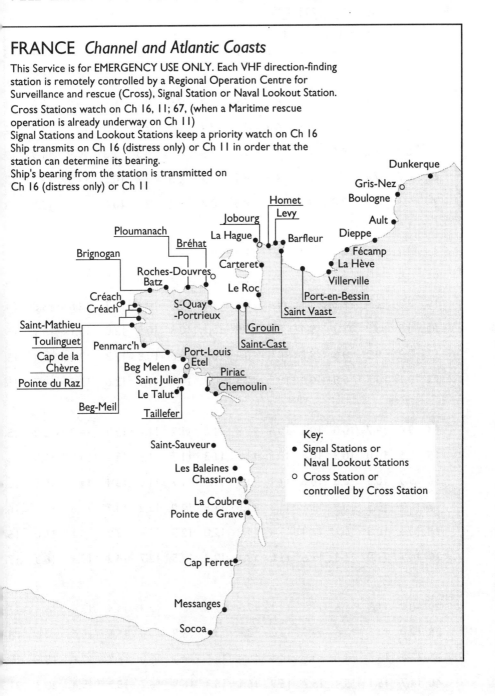

Key:
- ● Signal Stations or Naval Lookout Stations
- ○ Cross Station or controlled by Cross Station

DISTANCE FROM DIPPING LIGHT IN NAUTICAL MILES

Height of eye in feet

Height of light in metres	2	3	4	5	6	7	8	9	10	20	30	40	5
2	4.6	4.9	5.2	5.5	5.7	6.0	6.2	6.4	6.6	8.1	9.2	10.2	11.
3	5.2	5.6	5.9	6.2	6.4	6.6	6.8	7.0	7.2	8.7	9.9	10.8	11
4	5.8	6.1	6.4	6.7	6.9	7.2	7.4	7.6	7.8	9.3	10.4	11.4	12
5	6.3	6.6	6.9	7.2	7.4	7.7	7.9	8.1	8.3	9.8	10.9	11.9	12.
6	6.7	7.1	7.4	7.6	7.9	8.1	8.3	8.5	8.7	10.2	11.3	12.3	13.
7	7.1	7.5	7.8	8.0	8.3	8.5	8.7	8.9	9.1	10.6	11.8	12.7	13.
8	7.5	7.8	8.2	8.4	8.7	8.9	9.1	9.3	9.5	11.0	12.1	13.1	14.
9	7.8	8.2	8.5	8.8	9.0	9.2	9.5	9.7	9.8	11.3	12.5	13.5	14.
10	8.2	8.5	8.8	9.1	9.4	9.6	9.8	10.0	10.2	11.7	12.8	13.8	14.
11	8.5	8.9	9.2	9.4	9.7	9.9	10.1	10.3	10.5	12.0	13.1	14.1	15.
12	8.8	9.2	9.5	9.7	10.0	10.2	10.4	10.6	10.8	12.3	13.4	14.4	15.
13	9.1	9.5	9.8	10.0	10.3	10.5	10.7	10.9	11.1	12.6	13.7	14.7	15.
14	9.4	9.7	10.0	10.3	10.6	10.8	11.0	11.2	11.4	12.9	14.0	15.0	15.
15	9.6	10.0	10.3	10.6	10.8	11.1	11.3	11.5	11.6	13.1	14.3	15.3	16.
16	9.9	10.3	10.6	10.8	11.1	11.3	11.5	11.7	11.9	13.4	14.6	15.5	16.
17	10.2	10.5	10.8	11.1	11.3	11.6	11.8	12.0	12.2	13.7	14.8	15.8	16.
18	10.4	10.8	11.1	11.4	11.6	11.8	12.0	12.2	12.4	13.9	15.1	16.0	16.
19	10.7	11.0	11.3	11.6	11.8	12.1	12.3	12.5	12.7	14.2	15.3	16.3	17.
20	10.9	11.3	11.6	11.8	12.1	12.3	12.5	12.7	12.9	14.4	15.5	16.5	17.
25	12.0	12.3	12.6	12.9	13.2	13.4	13.6	13.8	14.0	15.5	16.6	17.6	18.
30	13.0	13.3	13.6	13.9	14.1	14.4	14.6	14.8	15.0	16.5	17.6	18.6	19.
40	14.7	15.1	15.4	15.7	15.9	16.1	16.3	16.5	16.7	18.2	19.4	20.3	21.
50	16.3	16.6	16.9	17.2	17.4	17.7	17.9	18.1	18.3	19.8	20.9	21.9	22.
60	17.7	18.0	18.3	18.6	18.8	19.1	19.3	19.5	19.7	21.2	22.3	23.3	24.

SPEED, TIME AND DISTANCE IN NAUTICAL MILES

Speed in knots

Time in minutes	1	2	3	4	5	6	7	8	9	10	15	20
1	0.0	0.0	0.1	0.1	0.1	0.1	0.1	0.1	0.2	0.2	0.3	0.3
2	0.0	0.1	0.1	0.1	0.2	0.2	0.2	0.3	0.3	0.3	0.5	0.7
3	0.1	0.1	0.2	0.2	0.3	0.3	0.4	0.4	0.5	0.5	0.8	1.0
4	0.1	0.1	0.2	0.3	0.3	0.4	0.5	0.5	0.6	0.7	1.0	1.3
5	0.1	0.2	0.3	0.3	0.4	0.5	0.6	0.7	0.8	0.8	1.3	1.7
6	0.1	0.2	0.3	0.4	0.5	0.6	0.7	0.8	0.9	1.0	1.5	2.0
7	0.1	0.2	0.4	0.5	0.6	0.7	0.8	0.9	1.1	1.2	1.8	2.3
8	0.1	0.3	0.4	0.5	0.7	0.8	0.9	1.1	1.2	1.3	2.0	2.7
9	0.2	0.3	0.5	0.6	0.8	0.9	1.1	1.2	1.4	1.5	2.3	3.0
10	0.2	0.3	0.5	0.7	0.8	1.0	1.2	1.3	1.5	1.7	2.5	3.3
11	0.2	0.4	0.6	0.7	0.9	1.1	1.3	1.5	1.7	1.8	2.8	3.7
12	0.2	0.4	0.6	0.8	1.0	1.2	1.4	1.6	1.8	2.0	3.0	4.0
13	0.2	0.4	0.7	0.9	1.1	1.3	1.5	1.7	2.0	2.2	3.3	4.3
14	0.2	0.5	0.7	0.9	1.2	1.4	1.6	1.9	2.1	2.3	3.5	4.7
15	0.3	0.5	0.8	1.0	1.3	1.5	1.8	2.0	2.3	2.5	3.8	5.0
16	0.3	0.5	0.8	1.1	1.3	1.6	1.9	2.1	2.4	2.7	4.0	5.3
17	0.3	0.6	0.9	1.1	1.4	1.7	2.0	2.3	2.6	2.8	4.3	5.7
18	0.3	0.6	0.9	1.2	1.5	1.8	2.1	2.4	2.7	3.0	4.5	6.0
19	0.3	0.6	1.0	1.3	1.6	1.9	2.2	2.5	2.9	3.2	4.8	6.3
20	0.3	0.7	1.0	1.3	1.7	2.0	2.3	2.7	3.0	3.3	5.0	6.7
21	0.4	0.7	1.1	1.4	1.8	2.1	2.5	2.8	3.2	3.5	5.3	7.0
22	0.4	0.7	1.1	1.5	1.8	2.2	2.6	2.9	3.3	3.7	5.5	7.3
23	0.4	0.8	1.2	1.5	1.9	2.3	2.7	3.1	3.5	3.8	5.8	7.7
24	0.4	0.8	1.2	1.6	2.0	2.4	2.8	3.2	3.6	4.0	6.0	8.0
25	0.4	0.8	1.3	1.7	2.1	2.5	2.9	3.3	3.8	4.2	6.3	8.3
30	0.5	1.0	1.5	2.0	2.5	3.0	3.5	4.0	4.5	5.0	7.5	10.0
35	0.6	1.2	1.8	2.3	2.9	3.5	4.1	4.7	5.3	5.8	8.8	11.7
40	0.7	1.3	2.0	2.7	3.3	4.0	4.7	5.3	6.0	6.7	10.0	13.3
45	0.8	1.5	2.3	3.0	3.8	4.5	5.3	6.0	6.8	7.5	11.3	15.0
50	0.8	1.7	2.5	3.3	4.2	5.0	5.8	6.7	7.5	8.3	12.5	16.7

COMMUNICATION SECTION

CONTENTS

HM Coastguard chart 329
Radio operation 330
Port and coastal radio stations -
UK South coast 332
UK East coast 334
Scotland... 335
UK West coast.. 337
Ireland... 338
Belgium 339
Holland 339
Germany 340
Denmark 341
France & Channel Islands 342
Spain... 344
Portugal 344
Gibraltar 345
VTS Charts 346

EMERGENCY

MAYDAY distress messages - see inside front cover
MAYDAY RELAY -used as a prefix to pass **MAYDAY** messages
SEE LONCE MAYDAY - used to impose radio silence
PAN PAN - used as a prefix for very urgent messages
concerning safety eg man overboard or medical emergency
SÉCURITÉ - used to prefix an important navigational or weather
warning

THE PHONETIC ALPHABET

A	• –	Alfa	AL-fah	N	– •	November	no-VEM-ber
B	– • • •	Bravo	BRAH-voh	O	– – –	Oscar	OSS-car
C	– • – •	Charlie	CHAR-lee	P	• – – •	Papa	pa-PAH
D	– • •	Delta	DELL-tah	Q	– – • –	Quebec	keh-BECK
E	•	Echo	ECK-oh	R	• – •	Romeo	ROW-me-oh
F	• • – •	Foxtrot	FOKS-trot	S	• • •	Sierra	see-AIR-rah
G	– – •	Golf	GOLF	T	–	Tango	TANG-go
H	• • • •	Hotel	hoh-TELL	U	• • –	Uniform	YOU-nee-form
I	• •	India	IN-dee-ah				or OO-nee-form
J	• – – –	Juliett	JEW-lee-ett	V	• • • –	Victor	VIK-tah
K	– • –	Kilo	KEY-loh	W	• – –	Whiskey	WISS-key
L	• – • •	Lima	LEE-mah	X	– • • –	X-Ray	ECKS-ray
M	– –	Mike	MIKE	Y	– • – –	Yankee	YANG-key
				Z	– – • •	Zulu	ZOO-loo

HM COASTGUARD CHART

SHETLAND MRSC
The Knab, Knab Road,
Lerwick, Shetland ZE1 0AX
Tel: 01595 692976

PENTLAND MRSC
Cromwell Road, Kirkwall, Orkney
KW15 1LN. Tel: 01856 873268

STORNOWAY MRSC
Battery Point, Stornoway
Isle of Lewis HS1 2RT
Tel: 01851 702013

*NORTH & EAST
SCOTLAND REGION*

*WEST OF SCOTLAND
& NORTHERN
IRELAND
REGION*

OBAN MRSC
Boswell House, Argyll Square
Oban PA34 4BD.
Tel: 01631 563720

STIRLING

ABERDEEN MRCC
Marine House, Blaikies Quay
Aberdeen AB1 2PB.
Tel: 01224 592334

FORTH MRSC
Fifeness, Crail, Fife, KY10 3XN
Tel: 01333 450666

**CLYDE
MRCC**
Navy Buildings
Eldon Street
Greenock PA16 7QY.
Tel: 01475 729988

TYNE TEES MRSC
Priory Grounds, Tynemouth, Tyne & Wear
NE30 4DA. Tel: 0191 2572691

BELFAST
MRSC
Bregenz House
Quay Street, Bangor
Co Down BT20 5ED
Tel: 01247 463933

EASTERN REGION

HUMBER MRSC
Lime Kiln Lane,
Bridlington
North Humberside
YO15 2LX
Tel: 01262 672317

HOLYHEAD MRSC
Prince of Wales Road
Holyhead
Anglesey
Gwynedd
LL65 1ET
Tel: 01407
762051

LIVERPOOL
MRSC
Hall Road West
Crosby, Liverpool L23 8SY
Tel: 0151 931 3341

YARMOUTH MRCC
Havenbridge House, 5th Floor
Great Yarmouth NR30 1HA
Tel: 01493 851338

*WESTERN
REGION*

MILFORD HAVEN MRSC
Gorsewood Drive, Hakin
Milford Haven, Dyfed SA73 3ER
Tel: 01646
690909

SWANSEA MRCC
Tutt Head, Mumbles
Swansea SA3 4EX
Tel: 01792 366534

SOUTHAMPTON
COASTGUARD
HEADQUARTERS

THAMES
MRSC
East terrace
Walton-on-Naze
Essex CO14 8PY
Tel: 01255 675518

*SOUTH
WESTERN
REGION*

**DOVER
MRCC**
Langdon Battery
Swingate, Dover
Kent CT15 5NA
Tel: 01304 210008

PORTLAND
MRSC
Custom House Quay
Weymouth
Dorset, DT4 8BE
Tel: 01305 760439

SOLENT
MRSC
44a Marine Parade West
Lee on Solent, Hants PO13 9NR
Tel: 01705 552100

FALMOUTH MRCC
Pendennis Point, Castle Drive
Falmouth, Cornwall TR11 4WZ
Tel: 01326 317575

BRIXHAM
MRSC
Kings Quay,
Brixham
Devon TQ5 9TW
Tel: 01803 882704

SOUTH EASTERN REGION

■ MARITIME RESCUE COORDINATION CENTRE (REGIONAL) MRCC ▲ MARITIME RESCUE SUB CENTRE (DISTRICT) MRSC
—— REGIONAL BOUNDARY ----- DISTRICT BOUNDARY □ MPCU EQUIPMENT STOCKPILE

RADIO OPERATION

Warning

It is illegal, and carries heavy penalties, to transmit radio signals from a yacht unless the YACHT IS LICENSED and has been issued with a call sign. Ask for an application form from any marine electronics company and avoid serious trouble.

Avoiding interference

Before transmitting, first listen on the VHF channel. If occupied, wait for a break before transmitting, or choose another. If you cause interference you must comply immediately with any request from a Coastal Radio Station (CRS) to stop transmitting. The request will indicate how long to desist.

Control of communications

Ship-to-Shore: Except in the case of distress, urgency or safety, communications between ship and CRS are controlled by the latter.

Intership: The ship *called* controls communication. If you call another ship, then it has control. If you are called by a ship, you assume control. If a CRS breaks in, both ships must comply with instructions given. A CRS has better aerials and equipment and thus its transmission and reception areas are greater.

Radio confidentiality

Inevitably that you will overhear people's private conversations on VHF. These must not be reproduced, passed on or used for any purpose.

Voice technique

There are two considerations when operating:
What to say – ie *voice procedure*
How to say it – ie *voice technique*
Clear R/T speech is vital. If a message cannot be understood by the receiving operator it is useless. Anyone can become a good operator by following a few rules: The voice should be pitched at a higher level than for normal conversation. Avoid dropping the voice pitch at the end of a word or phrase. Hold the microphone a few inches in front of the mouth and speak directly into it at a normal level. Speak clearly so that there can be no confusion. Emphasise words with weak syllables; 'Tower', if badly pronounced, could sound like 'tar'. People with strong accents must try to use as understandable a pronunciation as possible. Messages which have to be written down at the receiving station should be sent slowly. This gives time for it to be written down by the receiving operator. Remember, the average reading speed is 250 words a minute, whilst average writing speed is only 20. If the transmitting operator himself writes it down all should be well.

The phonetic alphabet

The syllables to emphasise are underlined.

letter	morse	phonetic	spoken as
A	• —	Alfa	<u>AL</u>-fah
B	— • • •	Bravo	<u>BRAH</u>-voh
C	— • — •	Charlie	<u>CHAR</u>-lee
D	— • •	Delta	<u>DELL</u>-tah
E	•	Echo	<u>ECK</u>-oh
F	• • — •	Foxtrot	<u>FOKS</u>-trot
G	— — •	Golf	<u>GOLF</u>
H	• • • •	Hotel	hoh-<u>TELL</u>
I	• •	India	<u>IN</u>-dee-ah
J	• — — —	Juliett	<u>JEW</u>-lee-ett
K	— • —	Kilo	<u>KEY</u>-loh
L	• — • •	Lima	<u>LEE</u>-mah
M	— —	Mike	<u>MIKE</u>
N	— •	November	no-<u>VEM</u>-ber
O	— — —	Oscar	<u>OSS</u>-car
P	• — — •	Papa	pa-<u>PAH</u>
Q	— — • —	Quebec	keh-<u>BECK</u>
R	• — •	Romeo	<u>ROW</u>-me-oh
S	• • •	Sierra	see-<u>AIR</u>-rah
T	—	Tango	<u>TANG</u>-go
U	• • —	Uniform	<u>YOU</u>-nee-form or <u>OO</u>-nee-form
V	• • • —	Victor	<u>VIK</u>-tah
W	• — —	Whiskey	<u>WISS</u>-key
X	— • • —	X-Ray	<u>ECKS</u>-ray
Y	— • — —	Yankee	<u>YANG</u>-key
Z	— — • •	Zulu	<u>ZOO</u>-loo

Difficult words may be spelled phonetically. Operators precede this with 'I spell'. If the word is pronounceable include it before and after it has been spelt. If an operator sends the message 'I will moor alongside the yacht Coila' he would transmit: 'I will moor alongside the yacht Coila – I spell – Charlie Oscar India Lima Alfa – Coila'. When asked for your international callsign – say it is MGLA4 – transmit: 'My callsign is Mike Golf Lima Alfa Four.'

Phonetic numerals

When numerals are transmitted, the following pronunciations make them easier to understand.

no	morse	spoken as	no	morse	spoken as
1	• — — — —	WUN	2	• • — — —	TOO
3	• • • — —	TREE	4	• • • • —	FOW-ER
5	• • • • •	FIFE	6	— • • • •	SIX
7	— — • • •	SEV-EN	8	— — — • •	AIT
9	— — — — •	NIN-ER	0	— — — — —	ZERO

Numerals are transmitted digit by digit:

numeral	spoken as
44	FOW-ER FOW-ER
90	NIN-ER ZERO
136	WUN TREE SIX
500	FIFE ZERO ZERO
1478	WUN FOW-ER SEV-EN AIT

However, thousands may be spoken as follows:

7000	SEV-EN THOU-SAND

Punctuation

Punctuation marks should be used only where their omission would cause confusion.

mark	word	spoken as
.	Decimal	DAY-SEE-MAL
,	Comma	COMMA
.	Stop	STOP

Procedure words or 'prowords'

These are used to shorten transmissions

All after: Used after proword *'say again'* to request repetition of a portion of a message

All before: Used after proword *say again'* to request repetition of a portion of message

Correct: Reply to repetition of message that was preceded by prowords *'read back for check"*when it has been correctly repeated. Often said twice

Correction: Spoken during the transmission of a message means an error has been made in this transmission. Cancel the last word or group of words. The correct word or group follows.

In figures: Following numeral or group of numerals to be written as figures

In letters: Following numeral or group of numerals to be written as figures as spoken

I say again: I am repeating transmission or portion indicated

I spell: I shall spell the next word or group of letters phonetically

Out: This is the end of working to you

Over: Invitation to reply

Read back: If receiving station is doubtful about accuracy of whole or part of message it may repeat it back to the sending station, preceding the repetition with prowords *'I read back'*.

Say again: Repeat your message or portion referred to ie *'Say again all after'* *'Say again address'* etc

Station calling: Used when a station is uncertain of the calling station's identification

This is: This transmission is from station whose callsign immediately follows

Wait: If a called station is unable to accept traffic immediately, it will reply 'WAIT...........MINUTES'. If probable delay exceeds 10 minutes the reason will be given

Word after or Word before: Used after the proword *'say again'* to request repetition

Wrong: Reply to repetition of message preceded by prowords *'read back'* when it has been incorrectly repeated.

Calls, calling & callsigns

CRSs normally identify themselves by using their geographical name followed by the word Radio, eg Niton Radio, Humber Radio, etc. Vessels normally identify themselves by the name on their licence but the International callsign assigned to the ship may be used in certain cases. If two yachts bear the same name or where some confusion may result, you should give your International callsign when starting communications, and thereafter use your ship's name as callsign.

'All ships' broadcast

Information to be received or used by all who intercept it, eg Gale warnings, navigational warnings, weather forecasts etc, is generally broadcast by CRSs and addressed 'All stations'. No reply is needed.

Establishing communication with CRS

The initial call is always made on a working channel.
• Switch to one of CRS's working channels, pause to ensure no station is transmitting
• Are you are close enough to try low power *(1 watt)* first? Possible at ranges up to 10 miles. Otherwise use high power*(25 watts)* with more battery drain. Then give the callsign of the station called *(up to three times only)* and prowords 'This is'
• The callsign of calling station up to three times only
• Indication of number of R/T calls you have to make
• Proword 'Over.'

If yacht *Vasco* wishes to ring a telephone number in the UK this is the procedure
• 'Niton radio, this is Vasco, Vasco.   One link call please. Over.'

If your call is loud enough to register at Niton, you will hear a regular 'pip' signal which will continue until operator has time to talk. Then he will say
• 'Station calling Niton radio, this is Niton radio. Repeat your call. Over. '

Vasco replies
• 'Niton radio, this is Vasco, Vasco. Callsign MIKE GOLF HOTEL VICTOR FOUR. One link call please. Over.'

Niton radio will reply when ready
• 'Vasco, this is Niton radio. What number do you want? Over.'

Vasco would reply with the number, preceded by arrangements for payment, either by quoting accounting code *'Golf Bravo One Four'*, which together with the callsign allows a British or foreign CRS to send the bill to the owner of the boat's radio licence. Alternatively boat's operator could use phrase *'Yankee Tango Delta'* which stands for *'Yacht Telephone Debit.'* In this case the charge is made to the number called.

• 'Niton, this is Vasco, YANKEE TANGO DELTA ZERO ONE TWO FOUR THREE THREE SEVEN THREE SEVEN EIGHT FIVE THREE NINE. Over.'

Niton radio would reply
• 'Vasco, This is Niton radio. Roger, Stand by.'

Niton radio will then establish connection with the telephone network and call *Vasco* when ready. Beginners repeat callsigns and names unnecessarily. Once communication is established there is no need for repetition.

If you don't hear the pips

Even if before calling, you could hear Niton clearly you might still be out of transmission range, or your VHF might not be transmitting well.

The battery/ies may need charging or the aerial cable has a poor connection. Small faults can drastically reduce your transmitting range. Possibly the aerial for the channel chosen has been optimised for areas east of the CRS and you are to the west. If approaching the CRS wait 15 minutes and call again. If the range is opening, either try again in hope, or try another CRS within range.

Every time you call at high power, you are decreasing battery state and the range your VHF will achieve.

UK SOUTH COAST
COASTAL RADIO

Hours of watch are continuous **H24** unless otherwise shown, **HJ** shows day service only, **HX** no specific hours. Times given for Port Radio Stations are local time except where marked **UT** *ie GMT* but times for Coastal Radio Stations are UT. **ALRS** means Admiralty List of Radio Signals. Calling channels precede a semi colon **;**, preferred channels are marked *****. *Call on a working channel if possible.*

0111 Dover (Coastguard MRCC) Ch 16* 69 (H24) **10 11 67 73 80** (HX)

0113 Hastings Ch 07* 16 66*
Remotely controlled. Traffic lists: **Ch 07:** *0133 0303 0533 0733 0903 0933 1333 1503 1733 1933 2103 2133*

0038 Solent (Coastguard MRSC) Ch 16* 67* (H24) **10 73** (HX)

0040 Niton Ch 04ⁱ* 16 28* 64* 85* 87*
For telephone see Land's End 1)For vessels in the Brighton area. Traffic lists: **Ch 28:** *0233 0303 0633 0733 0903 1033 1433 1503 1833 1933 2103 2233*

0041 Weymouth Bay Ch 05* 16
Remotely controlled. Traffic lists:
Ch 05: *0233 0303 0633 0733 0903 1033 1433 1503 1833 1933 2103 2233*

0042 Brixham (Coastguard MRSC) Ch 16* (H24) **10 67 73** (HX)

0043 Start Point Ch 16 26* 60*
Remotely controlled. Traffic lists:
Ch 26: *0233 0303 0633 0733 0903 1033 1433 1503 1833 1933 2103 2233*

0044 Pendennis Ch 16 62*
Remotely controlled. Traffic lists:
Ch 62: *0233 0303 0633 0733 0903 1033 1433 1503 1833 1933 2103 2233*

0045 Falmouth (Coastguard MRCC) Ch 16* (H24) **110 67 73** (HX)

0046 Land's End Ch 16 27* 64ⁱ*
Telephone: +44(0)1736 871363 *or Freephone:* 0800 378378 *Fax:* +44(0)1736 871684 *1) For vessels in the Scilly Isles area. Traffic lists:* **Ch 27 64:** *0233 0303 0633 0733 0903 1033 1433 1503 1833 1933 2103 2233*

0050 Ilfracombe Ch 05ⁱ* 16
1) For vessels in the Severn area. Remotely controlled. Traffic lists: **Ch 05:** *0233 0303 0633 0733 0903 1033 1433 1503 1833 1933 2103 2233*

0053 Burnham Ch 25*
For commercial traffic in Severn Estuary East of Nash Point. Remotely controlled.

PORT RADIO
RAMSGATE VTS

Call Ramsgate Port Control: **Ch 14 16**
Ramsgate Marina: *Contact Hr Mr. Marina 2h-HW-2h*
DOVER STRAIT Channel Navigation Information Service *CNIS:* **Ch 16 69; 11ⁱ 69˚80** *I Broadcast channel only* **Information:** *Gris Nez Traffic H+10. Additional broadcast at H+25 when visibility is less than 2M*
DOVER VTS *Call Dover Port Control:* **Ch 74; 12 16**
Dover Marina *Call Dover Port Control:* **Ch 74 12 80** *Access: 1.30h-HW-1.30h*
Diesel Fuel *Call Dover Motor Boats:* **Ch 74**
FOLKESTONE *Call Folkestone Port Control:* **Ch 15** *Contact Port Control before entering*
RYE *Call PV 'Rother III':* **Ch 16; 14** *0900-1700 and when vessel expected*

SOVEREIGN YACHT HARBOUR: Ch 15* 16
Lock and Bridges: Ch 17
NEWHAVEN: Ch 16; 12
Newhaven Marina: Ch M 80 *0800-1700*
BRIGHTON MARINA *Call Brighton Control:* **Ch 16 M 80; 11 M 68 80**
SHOREHAM: Ch 14 16; 14
Lady Bee Marina: *Call Shoreham Harbour Radio:* **Ch 14** *Mon-Sat 0800-1830, Sun 0900-1300*
LITTLEHAMPTON: Ch 16; 71 *when vessel expected*
Littlehampton Marina: Ch M 80 *0800-1700*
Arun Yacht Club: *Call Lisboa* **Ch M** *3h-HW-3h*
CHICHESTER *Call patrol craft 'Regnum' or 'Aella':* **Ch 14* 16; 14** *Apr-Sep 0900-1300 1400-1730, Oct-Mar Mon-Fri 0900-1300 1400-1730, Sat 0900-1300. Visiting yachts requiring moorings are advised to make arrangements in advance.*
Chichester Yacht Basin: Ch M *Apr-Sep Mon-Thu 0600-2000, Fri-Sun 0600-2400, Oct-Mar 0800-1700*
Tarquin Yacht Harbour: Ch M 80 *0800-1700. Access 2.30h-HW-2.30h*
Northney Marina: Ch M 80 *0900-1800*
Sparkes Yacht Harbour: Ch M 80 *0900-1800*
LANGSTONE HARBOUR: Ch 12 16; 12 *Apr-Sep 0830-1700, Oct-Mar Mon-Fri 0830-1700 Sat Sun 0830-1300*
Southsea Marina: Ch M* 80 *Access 3h-HW-3h*
PORTSMOUTH Naval Base *Call QHM:* **Ch 11** *Harbour* **Ch 13** *Naval* **Ch 73** *Dockyard Craft*
Portsmouth Commercial Port *Call Portsmouth Hbr Radio:* **Ch 11 14**
Listening Watch: Ch 11 or 13
Camper and Nicholson's Marina: Ch M 80
Haslar Marina: Ch M 80 11
Port Solent Marina: Ch M 80
Fareham Marina: Ch M *0900-1730*
Wicor Marina: Ch 80 *Mon-Sat 0900-1730*
RYDE HARBOUR: Ch 80 *Accessible 2.30h-HW-2h*
BEMBRIDGE *Call Hbr Office BHL:* **Ch 16; 80** *3h-HW-2.30h*
Bembridge Marina: Ch M 80 *3h-HW-2.30h*
SOUTHAMPTON VTS: Ch 12* 14 *Port Operations - Calling and Working* **Ch 16** *Distress, Safety and Calling* **Ch 18 20 22** *Harbour Radar and Selected Operations* **Ch 71 74** *Berthing* **Ch 10** *Pollution*
Information: Ch 14 *every even H+00 0600-2200 Fri-Sun and Bank holidays, Easter - 30 Sep*
Listening Watch: Ch 12
Southampton Patrol: Ch 12 16; 01-28 60-88
Fawley, Esso Marine Terminal: Ch 16; 14 19
Hamble, BP Terminal: Ch 16; 68 *Hr Mr* **Ch 16; 71 74** *Pilots and Tugs* **Ch 46** *BP Hamble* **Ch 10** *Pollution*
Hamble Point Marina: Ch M 80
Hamble Harbour: Ch 68 *HJ*
Hamble water taxi *Blue Star Boats:* **Ch 77**
Hamble Point Marina: Ch M 80
Port Hamble Marina: Ch M 80 33
Mercury Yacht Harbour: Ch M 80
Swanwick Marina: Ch M 80
Hamble Yacht Services: Ch 80 *0900-1700*
Universal Shipyards, Sarisbury Green: Ch M
Foulkes & Son Riverside Boatyard: Ch 08 *Launch*
Hythe Marina: Ch M 80
Ocean Village Marina: Ch M 80; *for fuel call* **Ch 08** *Wyefuel or* **Ch 08** *Mr Diesel*

Shamrock Quay Marina: Ch M 80 *0830-2130*
Town Quay Marina: Ch 80 *Apr-Oct H24*
COWES: Ch 69 *Mon-Fri 0830-1700 and by arrangement*
Chain Ferry: Ch 69
Water Taxi: Ch 08, *also Call 'THUMPER' on* **Ch 77**
Cowes Marina *East Cowes:* **Ch M 80**
Cowes Yacht Haven *West Cowes:* **Ch 80**
Island Harbour *Call Medina Yacht Harbour:* **Ch M 80**
NEWPORT *Port and Yacht Harbour.* **Ch 16; 69*** *0800-1600* **Marina: Ch M 80**
YARMOUTH HARBOUR: Ch 68
LYMINGTON
Lymington Yacht Haven: Ch M 80 *Summer 0800-2100, Winter 0800-1800 UT*
Lymington Marina: Ch M 80 *Summer 0800-2200, Winter 0800-1800*
RIBS Marine: Ch M 80 *0800-1700*
POOLE *Poole Harbour Control:* **Ch 14 16; 14**
Bridge: Ch 14. Water Taxi: Ch 06
Poole Bay Fuels: Ch M *Mon-Fri 0900-1730, weekends in season 0830-1800*
Cobbs Quay Marina: *Call CQ Base:* **Ch M 80** *0800-1700*
Dorset Yacht Co Ltd: Ch M
Salterns Marina: Ch M 80 *0800-2400*
Poole Yacht Club Haven: Ch M 80 *May-Sep 0800-2200*
Sandbanks Yacht Co Ltd: *Call SYC* **Ch M** *0900-1700*
WEYMOUTH: Ch 16; 12 *Summer 0800-2000*
Town Bridge: Ch 12
PORTLAND *Call Portland Harbour Control :* **Ch 13** *Mon-Fri 0800-1600*
BRIDPORT: Ch 16; 11
LYME REGIS: Ch 16; 14 *May-Sep 0900-1200 1600-1800*
EXETER: Ch 16; 06 12 *Mon-Fri 0730-1630 and when vessel expected*
Retreat Boatyard: Ch M *3.30-HW-3.30*
TEIGNMOUTH: Ch 12 16; 12 *Mon-Fri 0800-1700, Sat 0900-1200 and when vessel expected*
TORQUAY: Ch 16; 14 *Oct-Feb Mon-Fri 0900-1300, Mar-Apr Mon-Fri 0900-1300 1400-1700, May-Sep 0900-1300 1400-1700 1800-2200*
Torquay Marina: Ch M 80
BRIXHAM: Ch 16; 14 *May-Sep 0900-1300 1400-1700 1800-2000, Oct-Apr Mon-Fri 0900-1300 1400-1700*
Brixham Marina: Ch M 80
DARTMOUTH: Ch 11 16 *Mon-Fri 0900-1700, Sat 0900-1200*
Britannia Royal Naval College: Ch 71
Dart Haven Marina *Kingswear. Call Dart Haven Marina Mobile 1 or 2 :* **Ch M 80** *0830-1730*
Dart Marina *Sand Quay:* **Ch M 80**
Kingswear Marina *Noss Wks. Call Dart Marina :* **Ch M**
Dartside Quay: Ch M 80 *3-HW-3*
SALCOMBE: Ch 14; 14 *Mon-Thu 0900-1645 Fri 0900-1615, May-Sep Sat Sun 0900-1300 1400-1615* **Hr Mr Launches: Ch 14** *Summer 0600-2200* **Water Taxi** *Call Salcombe Harbour Taxi:* **Ch 12**
Fuel Barge: Ch 06
Winters Marine Ltd: Ch 72 *5h-HW-5h*
HMS CAMBRIDGE *Call Wembury Range:* **Ch 16; 10 11** *when range operating*
PLYMOUTH *Call Longroom Port Control:* **Ch 16; 14** *Commercial* **Ch 16; 08 11 12 13** *Naval*
Devonport Dockyard and Hamoaze: Ch 13 73

Millbay Docks: Ch 16; 12 13 14 *Ferry hrs only*
Sutton Harbour Marina: Ch 16; 12 *Lock* **Ch M 80** *Marina*
Cattewater Harbour: Ch 16; 14 *Mon-Fri 0900-1700*
Mayflower International Marina: Ch M 80
Millbay Marina Village: Ch M 80 *0800-1700*
Queen Anne's Battery Marina: Ch M 80
Clovelly Bay Marina: Ch M 80
Southdown Marina: Ch M 80 *0900-1700*
LOOE HARBOUR: Ch 16 *HX*
FOWEY: Ch 16; 09 11 12* *HX*
Fowey Refueller: Ch 16 10 *Summer 0900-1800, Winter Mon-Fri 0900-1800*
Harbour Launch *Call Port Radio:* **Ch 09** *Apr-Oct*
PAR: Ch 16; 12 *2h-HW-2h*
CHARLESTOWN: Ch 16; 14 *2h-HW-1h only when vessel expected*
MEVAGISSEY: Ch 16; 14 *Summer 0900-2100, Winter 0900-1700*
FALMOUTH: Ch 16 *Calling, Safety and Distress* **Ch 12** *Harbour Working* **Ch 11** *Port Operations Working* **Ch 14** *Alternative Working* **Ch 10** *Pollution* **Ch 12** *Hr Launch 'Killigrew' Mon-Fri 0800-1700*
Port Pendennis Marina: Ch M 80 *Lock gate opens 3h-HW-3h Traffic Lights*
Falmouth Yacht Marina: Ch M 80
Mylor Yacht Harbour: Ch M 80 *0830-1730*
Malpas Marine: Ch M *Mon-Sat 0900-1700. Access 3h-HW-3h*
PENZANCE: Ch 16; 09 12 *Mon-Fri 0830-1630 Sat 0830-1230 2h-HW-1h*
NEWLYN: Ch 16; 09 12 *Mon-Fri 0800-1700, Sat 0800-1200*
OFF LAND'S END TSS *Call Falmouth Coastguard:* **Ch 16; 67**
ST MARY'S, Isles of Scilly: Ch 16; 14 *Summer 0800-1700, Winter Mon-Fri 0800-1700 Sat 0800-1200*
ST IVES: Ch 14 *HX*
HAYLE HARBOUR: CH 16, 14, 18*
NEWQUAY: Ch 16; 14 *Office Hours. Access 3h-HW-3h*
PADSTOW: Ch 16; 12 *Mon-Fri 0830-1630 & 2.30h-HW-1.30h. Access 3h-HW-3h*
BUDE: Ch 16; 12 *When vessel expected*
APPLEDORE-BIDEFORD *Call PV 'Two Rivers':* **Ch 16: 12** *2h-HW*
ILFRACOMBE: Ch 16; 12 *Apr-Oct 0800-2000, when manned, Nov-Mar HX*
Watermouth Harbour: Ch 08 16; 08 12 *3-HW-3*
MINEHEAD: Ch 16; 12 14 *HX*
WATCHET: Ch 16; 09 12 14 *2h-HW*
BRIDGEWATER: Ch 16; 08 *3h-HW when vessel expected*
WESTON SUPER MARE: Uphill Boat Services Ltd: Ch 16 *Mon-Sat 0930-1730, 2 h -HW-2h*
BRISTOL Avonmouth Signal Station *Call Avonmouth Radio:* **Ch 16** *Safety and distress* **Ch 12*** *Calling and working* **Ch 14** *Port operations* **Ch 09** *Alternative Working* **Ch 10** *Pollution*
Royal Portbury Dock: Ch 16; 12 14* *4.15h-HW-3.30h*
Portishead Dock: Ch 16; 12 14* *2.30h-HW-1.30h*
Royal Edward Dock: Ch 16; 12 14*
Bristol City Docks: Ch 14; 11 14* *3h-HW-1h*
Prince Street Bridge: Ch 73
Bristol Floating Harbour: Ch 16; 73 *Mon-Thu 0800-*

1700, Fri 0800-1630, other times 0800-sunset
Netham Lock: Ch 73
Bristol Marina: Ch M 80 *Office Hours, access 3h-HW*
SHARPNESS *Call Sharpness Pierhead:* **Ch 17** *Calling and working* **Ch 16** *Distress & safety* **Ch 09** *Pilots & berthing* **Ch 74** *Canal operations 6h-HW-2h*
LYDNEY: Ch 16; *agreed working channel*
NEWPORT VTIS: Ch 16; 69 71 *4h-HW-4h*
Port: Ch 16; 09 11 *4h-HW-4h*
CARDIFF: Ch 14* 16; 13 *4h-HW-3h*
Penarth Marina: Ch 80 *Access 4h-HW-4h*
BARRY DOCKS: Ch 11* 16; 10 *4h-HW-3h*

UK EAST COAST
COASTAL RADIO

0089 Tyne Tees (Coastguard MRSC) Ch 16* (H24) 10 67 73 (HX)
0093 Whitby Ch 16 25*
Remotely controlled. Traffic lists:
Ch 25: *0233 0303 0633 0703 0903 1033 1433 1503 1833 1903 2103 2233*
0093.1 Humber (Coastguard) Ch 16* (H24) 10 67 73 (HX)
0094 Grimsby Ch 16 27*
Remotely controlled. Traffic lists:
Ch 27: *0133 0303 0533 0703 0903 0933 1333 1503 1733 1933 2103 2133*
0095 Humber Ch 16 26* 85*
1) *For vessels in the Wash. Traffic lists:*
Ch 26: *0133 0303 0533 0733 0903 0933 1333 1503 1733 1933 2103 2133*
0098 Bacton Ch 07* 16
Remotely controlled. Traffic lists:
Ch 07: *0133 0303 0533 0733 0903 0933 1333 1503 1733 1933 2103 2133*
0099 Yarmouth (Coastguard MRSC) 16* (H24) 10 67 73 (HX)
0100 Orfordness Ch 16 62*
Remotely controlled. Traffic lists:
Ch 62: *0133 0303 0533 0733 0903 0933 1333 1503 1733 1933 2103 2133*
0105 Thames Ch 02* 16
Remotely controlled. Traffic lists:
Ch 02: *0133 0303 0533 0733 0903 0933 1333 1503 1733 1933 2103 2133*
0107 Thames (Coastguard MRSC) 16* (H24) 10 67 73 (HX)
0110 North Foreland Ch 16 26*
Remotely controlled. Traffic lists:
Ch 26: *0133 0303 0533 0733 0903 0933 1333 1503 1733 1933 2103 2133*

PORT RADIO

BERWICK: Ch 16; 12 *Mon-Fri 0800-1700*
WARKWORTH HARBOUR: Ch 16; 14
BLYTH: Ch 12 16; 11 12
PORT OF TYNE: Ch 12 16; 11 12* 14
Harbour Launch: Ch 16; 06 08 11 12 14
St Peter's Marina: Ch M 80* *0800-0000, 5h-HW-4h*
SUNDERLAND: Ch 16; 14
SEAHAM: Ch 16; 06 *12* Hr Mr Office 2.30h-HW-1.30h, Operations Office Mon-Fri Office hours*
TEES *Call Tees Port Control:* **Ch 16; 08 11 12 14* 22*** *Port Operations* **Ch 14 16; 08* Ch 14** *Tugs* **Ch 16; 06 11 14** *Port Maintenance Craft*

River Tees Barrage: Ch M
Hartlepool Docks: *Call Tees Port Control*
Hartlepool Yacht Haven: Ch M 80
Hartlepool Yacht Club: Ch M *4.30-HW-4.30*
WHITBY: Ch 11 16; 12 *Mon-Fri 0830-1730, Sat Sun 1000- 1230.* **Bridge: Ch 16; 06 11** *2h-HW-2h*
SCARBOROUGH *Call Scarborough Lthouse:* **Ch 16; 12 16**
BRIDLINGTON: Ch 16; 12* 14 *HX, 3h-HW-3h*
HUMBER VTS: Ch 16 *Calling and Safety* **Ch 12** *Navigation and Safety Information. Intership navigation only:* **Ch 13** *Lower Humber* **Ch 10** *Middle Humber* **Ch 15** *Upper Humber* **Information:** *Weather, tides and navigation,* **Ch 12** *every odd H+03.* **Listening watches: Ch 12** *R Humber & approaches,* **Ch 14** *R Ouse,* **Ch 08** *R Trent (Ouse to Keadby Br),* **Ch 06** *R Trent (Keadby Br to Gainsborough)*
Hull Marina: Ch M* 80 *3h-HW-3h*
South Ferriby Marina: Ch 74 80 *Mon-Fri 0930-1700, Sat Sun & Holidays 1030-1700, 3h-HW-3h*
Tetney Oil Terminal: Ch 73; 21 73 74 *Berthing*
Grimsby Docks: Ch 74; 18 74 79
Grimsby Docks Marina *call Fish Dock Island:* **Ch 74** *2h -HW-2h*
Grimsby Marina: Ch 16; 09 18 *3.30h-HW-2.30h*
Immingham Oil Terminal: Ch 69; 17 19 69 71 73 *Berthing* **Immingham Docks: Ch 19 68; 17 19 68 69 71 73 74** *Docking Instructions*
Saltend Jetties: Ch 22; 09 11 22 *Berthing Instructions*
King George Dock: Ch 11; 09 11 22
Alexandra Dock: Ch 11; 09 11 22 *Docking Instructions*
River Hull Port Operations Service: Ch 22; 11 22 *Mon-Fri 2h-HW-1h, Sat 0900-1100*
Albert Dock: Ch 09; 09 11 22
Blacktoft Jetty: Ch 14; 09 14 19 *2.30h-HW Goole-1.30h*
Goole Docks: Ch 14; 09 14 19
Goole Railway Bridge: Ch 09
Viking Commercial Services Ch 16; 09 19 *4h-HW-1h*
Howdendyke: Ch 09 *Mooring/Unmooring only*
Boothferry Bridge: Ch 09
Selby Railway Bridge: Ch 09 *Inward bound vessels should make contact 10 min in advance*
Selby Toll Bridge: Ch 09 *Outward bound vessels should make contact 10 min in advance.*
Selby Lock: Ch 16 74 *HJ*
Naburn Lock: Ch 16 74
Burton-upon-Stather: Ch 20
Flixborough: Ch 20
Crone: Ch 20
Keadby: Ch 20
Keadby Lock: Ch 16 74
Gunness: Ch 20
West Stockwith, Torksey and Cromwell Locks: Ch 16 74
Gainsborough: Ch 20
BOSTON: Ch 16; 11 12 *Mon-Fri 0700-1700 and 2.30h-HW-1.30h*
Boston Marina: Ch 06 M *2h-HW-2h*
Boston Grand Sluice: Ch 74
Denver Sluice: Ch 73 *when vessel expected*
WISBECH: Ch 16; 09 14* *3h-HW when vessel expected*
PORT SUTTON BRIDGE: Ch 16; 09
KING'S LYNN *Call KLCB:* **Ch 16; 11 12 14*** *Mon-Fri 0800-1730 and 4h-HW-1h*
King's Lynn Docks *Call Docks Radio ABP:* **Ch 14* 16;**

11 *2.30h-HW-1h*
WELLS HARBOUR: Ch 12 16 *when vessel expected,*
2h before HW
GREAT YARMOUTH VTS: 16;12
Port: Ch 12 16; 09 11 12
Haven Bridge: Ch 12
LOWESTOFT: Ch 14* 16; 11. *Yachts may use a bridge*
opening for commercial shipping provided that prior
arrangement has been made with Hr Control on Ch 14
Royal Norfolk & Suffolk Y: Ch14 M*4h-HW-4h*
MUTFORD ROAD BRIDGE: Ch 09 14
SOUTHWOLD: Ch 12* 16; 12 *0800-1800*
FELIXSTOWE FERRY: Ch 08
Felixstowe Ferry Boatyard: Ch 08 16; 08 *4h-HW-4h*
River Deben, Tide Mill Hr: Ch M 80 *0800-1700*
HARWICH, Haven Operations Service: Ch 16
Calling and Safety **Ch 14 71*** *Harbour operations and*
listening watch **Ch 11** *Harbour Services* **Ch 10** *Pollution*
Ch 20 *Harbour radar*
Listening Watch: Ch 71
Parkstone Quay: Ch 16; 18
Shotley Marina: Ch 16 M* 71 80; M 80
Suffolk Yacht Harbour: Ch M* 80 *0815-1715*
Woolverstone Marina: Ch M 80 *Mon-Thu 0800-*
1830, Fri-Sun 0800-2100
IPSWICH Orwell Nav Service: Ch 14* 16; 12 14*
Fox's Marina: Ch M 80 *Mon-Fri 0800-1800, Sat/Sun*
0900-1800
Neptune Marina: *Call Ipswich Pt Radio* **Ch 14** *or* **M**
2h-HW-0.45h
TITCHMARSH MARINA: Ch M 80 *Summer only*
0800-2100, 5h-HW-5h
COLCHESTER: Ch 16 68*; 11 14 68* *Mon-Fri 0900-*
1700 and 2h-HW-1h
West Mersea Marine: Ch M
Brightlingsea: Ch 68 *HJ*
Bradwell Marina: Ch M 80 *Mon-Fri 0830-1700 Sat/*
Sun 0830-2100. Access NOT 1.30h-LW-1.30h
Tollesbury Marina: Ch M 80 *2h-HW-2h*
Tollesbury Saltings Ltd: Ch M 80 *Mon-Sat 0800-1800*
River Bailiff: Ch 16 *0900-1700*
Blackwater Marina: Ch M *0900-2300, 2.30h-HW-*
2.30h
RIVER CROUCH
Burnham Yacht Harbour: Ch M* 80 *0800-1800*
North Fambridge Yacht Centre: Ch M 80 *0900-1730*
West Wick Marina: Ch M 80 *Not 2h-LW-2h*
Rice & Cole, *Burnham on Crouch:* **Ch M** *0900-1700*
Essex Marina: Ch M 80 *Mon-Fri 0800-1745 Sat Sun*
0900-dusk
Halcon Marine Ltd: Ch M *0800-1700, 2h-HW-2h*
Holehaven Marine: Ch 12; 12 M *Mon-Fri 0800-1600*
HAVENGORE BRIDGE: Ch 16; 72 *Office hours*
PORT OF LONDON, Thames Navigation Service
Patrol Launches *Call Thames Patrol:* **Ch 12 13 14 16**
Woolwich Radio *above Crayford Ness:* **Ch 14* 16 22**
Port Control London *below Crayford Ness:* **Ch 09 16**
18 20
Shellhaven: Ch 19
Tilbury Docks: Ch 04
Thames Barrier: Ch 14* 16 22. *All vessels equipped*
with VHF intending to navigate in the Thames Barrier Control
Zone must report to Woolwich Radio on **Ch 14**
King George V Dock Lock *Call KG Control:* **Ch 68**
West India Dock Lock: Ch 68
Gallions Point Marina: Ch 68 *When vessel expected,*

5h-HW-5h
Bow Lock: Ch 16 74
South Dock Marina: Ch M 80 *2h-HW-2h*
Limehouse Marina: Ch 80 *summer 0800-1800, winter*
0900-1630 1h-HW-1h
S Katharine Yacht Haven: Ch M 80. *Access: Summer*
2h-HW-1.30h between 0600 and 2030, Winter 2h-HW-
1.30h between 0800 and 1800.
Chelsea Harbour Ltd: Ch 80 *0900-1700, 1.30h-HW-*
1.30h
Cadogan Pier: Ch 14 *0900-1700*
Brentford Dock Marina: Ch M *1000-1800, 2.3-0h-*
HW-2.30-h
Thames Lock (Brentford): Ch 74 *summer 0800-*
1800 winter 0800-1630
Chiswick Quay Marina: Ch 14 *2h-HW-2h*
MEDWAY Nav Service: Ch 16 74; 11 22 23 74*
BP Kent, Isle of Grain: Ch 16; 73 *While vessels are*
berthing **Kingsferry Bridge: Ch 10**
Gillingham Marina: Ch M 80 *0830-1700*
Medway Pier Marina: Ch M 80 *2h-HW-2h*
Medway Bridge Marina: Ch M 80 *0900-1730, NOT*
2h-LWS-2h
Port Medway Marina: Ch M 80
Hoo Marina: Ch M 80 *3.30h-HW-3.30h*
Elmhaven Marina: Ch M *4h-HW-4h*
Conyer Marina: Ch 16 M 80 *1.30h-HW-1.30h*
WHITSTABLE: Ch 16; 09 12 *Mon-Fri 0800-1700 &*
3h-HW-1h

SCOTLAND
COASTAL RADIO

0065 Portpatrick Ch 16 27*
Traffic lists: **Ch 27:** *0203 0303 0603 0703 0903 1003*
1403 1503 1803 1903 2103 2203
0070 Clyde Ch 16 26*
Remotely controlled. Traffic lists: **Ch 26:** *0203 0303 0603*
0703 0903 1003 1403 1503 1803 1903 2103 2203
0072 Clyde (Coastguard MRSC) 16 (H24) **10 67**
73 (HX)
0073 Islay Ch 16 25*
Remotely controlled. Traffic lists: **Ch 25:** *0203 0303 0603*
0703 0903 1003 1403 1503 1803 1903 2103 2203
0074 Oban Ch 07* 16
Remotely controlled. Traffic lists; **Ch 07:** *as Islay*
0075 Oban (Coastguard MRSC) 16 (H24) **10 67**
73 (HX)
0076 Skye Ch 16 24*
Remotely controlled. Traffic lists: **Ch 24:** *0203 0303 0603*
0703 0903 1003 1403 1503 1803 1903 2103 2203
0079 Stornoway (Coastguard MRSC) 16 (H24) **10**
67 73 (HX)
0080 Wick 16 128*
0081 Pentland (Coastguard MRSC) 16 (H24) **10**
67 73 (HX)
0082 Shetland Ch 16 27*
Remotely controlled. Traffic lists: **Ch 27:** *0233 0303 0633*
0733 0903 1033 1433 1503 1833 1933 2103 2233
0083 Shetland (Coastguard MRSC) 16 (H24) **10**
67 73 (HX)
0085 Buchan 16 25*
Remotely controlled. Traffic lists: **Ch 25:** *0233 0303 0633*
0703 0903 1033 1433 1503 1833 1903 2103 2233
0086 Stonehaven Ch 16 26*
Telephone: 01278 772200 or Freephone: 0800 378378

Fax: 01278 792145. Traffic lists: **Ch 26: 0233 0303 0633
0703 0903 1033 1433 1503 1833 1903 2103 2233**
0086.1 Aberdeen (Coastguard MRCC) 16 (H24)
10 67 73 (HX)
0086.2 Forth (Coastguard MRSC) 10 67 73 (HX)
0087   Forth Ch 16 62*
Remotely controlled. Traffic lists: **Ch 62: 0233 0303 0633
0703 0903 1033 1433 1503 1833 1903 2103 2233**
0088   Cullercoats Ch 16 26*
Traffic lists: **Ch 26: 0233 0303 0633 0703 0903 1033
1433 1503 1833 1903 2103 2233**

PORT RADIO
KIRKUDBRIGHT: Ch 16; 12 *2h-HW-2h*
STRANREAR: Ch 16; 14
GIRVAN: Ch 16; 12 *Mon-Fri 0900-1700*
AYR: Ch 16; 14
TROON: Ch 16; 14 *Mon-Thu 0800-2400, Fri 0800-
2300, other times by request*
Troon Marina: Ch M 80*
IRVINE: Ch 16; 12 *Mon-Fri 0800-1600*
CLYDEPORT: Ch 16; 12 *Clyde Estuary Port Control*
Ch 13 *QHM Faslane* **Ch 73** *Greenock Control* **Ch 16;
11** *Conservancy vessels*
Ardrossan: Ch 16; 12 14
Rothesay, Bute: Ch 16; 12 *May-Sep 0600-2100, Oct-
Apr 0600-1900*
Dunoon: Ch 31; 12 16 31* *Mon-Sat 0700-2035, Sun
0900-2015*
**Finnart Ocean Terminal, Loch Long: Ch 16; 10
12 19**
Largs Yacht Haven: Ch M 80
Rhu Marina: Ch M
Silvers Marine: Ch M *0800-1630*
Kip Marina: Ch M 80
Crinan Boats: Ch 16; 12
Crinan Canal, Ardrishaig: Ch 16 74; 74 *May-Sep
0800-1200 1230-1600 1620-1800, Oct Mon-Sat 0800-
1200 1230-1600, Nov-Apr Mon-Fri 0900-1530*
Ardfern Yacht Centre: Ch M 80 *0830-1730*
Craobh Marina *Loch Shona:* **Ch M 80** *Oct-Apr 0830-
1700, May Jun Sep 0830-1800, Jul Aug 0830-1900*
Kilmelford Yacht Haven *Loch Melfort:* **Ch M* 80** *Mon-
Sat 0830-1700*
Melfort Pier & Harbour: Ch 16; 12
CAMPBELTOWN: Ch 16; 12 14 *Mon-Thu 0845-
1645, Fri 0845-1600*
Tarbert: Ch 16 *0900-1700*
GLENSANDA HARBOUR: Ch 14; 14 *When expected*
OBAN
Port-North Pier: Ch 16; 12 *0900-1700*
Port-Railway Pier: Ch 16; 12 *0700-0100*
Ardoran Marine: Ch 16 *Not 2h-LW-2h*
Tobermory: Ch 16; 12 *Office Hours, listens only*
Clachnaharry Lock: Ch 16 74; 74 *4h-HW-4h*
Dunstaffnage Yacht Haven: Ch M *0900-1700*
Oban Yachts & Marine Services: Ch 16 80; 80
0800-1700
Information *HMCG Oban:* **Ch 67** *Submarine exercise
warning*
CRAIGNURE PIER, Island of Mull: Ch 31 *HX*
GOTT BAY PIER, Tiree: Ch 31
ARINAGOUR PIER, Isle of Coll: Ch 31
CORPACH: Ch 16; 74 *When manned, Mon-Sat 0800-
1700*
ARISAIG: Ch 16; M

MALLAIG: Ch 16; 09 *Office Hours*
KYLE: Ch 11 16
Skye Bridge Crossing: Ch 12
UIG: Ch 16 *HX*
PORTREE HARBOUR, Isle of Skye: Ch 16; 12 *HX*
GAIRLOCH HARBOUR: Ch 16 *HX*
ULLAPOOL: Ch 14 16; 12 *H24 during fishing season,
else office hours*
LOCHINVER: Ch 09 16 *HX*
KINLOCHBERVIE: Ch 06 16 *HX*
LITTLE MINCH and NORTH MINCH *Call
Stornaway Coastguard :* **Ch 16**
STORNAWAY: Ch 16; 12
LOCHMADDY, N Uist: Ch 16; 12
S KILDA: Ch 16; 08 *HJ*
SCRABSTER, Thurso: Ch 16; 12 *0800-2200*
PENTLAND FIRTH Reporting *Call Pentland
Coastguard* **Ch 16**
ORKNEY HARBOURS *Call Orkney Harbour Radio :*
Ch 16; 09 11 20
Flotta Oil Terminal, Scapa Flow: Ch 16; 69
Kirkwall Harbour: Ch 16; 12 *Mon-Fri 0800-1700
and when vessel expected*
Stromness Harbour: Ch 16; 12 *Mon-Fri 0900-1700*
Westray Pier: Ch 16; 14 *When vessel expected*
FAIR ISLE Reporting *Call Shetland Coastguard:* **Ch 16**
LERWICK, Shetland: Ch 16; 11 12*
SCALLOWAY, Shetland: Ch 16; 09 12* *Mon-Fri
0600-1800, Sat 0600-1230*
SULLOM VOE HARBOUR, Shetland: Ch 16
Distress, Safety and Calling **Ch 14 16** *Pilots* **Ch 09**
Tanker Pilot and Tugs **Ch 10** *Port Emergency and Pollution*
Ch 12 14* 20 *Port Control* **Ch 16; 19** *Terminal
Traffic information on request on* **Ch 14** *or* **16**
BALTASOUND HARBOUR: Ch 16 20 *Office hours
or as required*
WICK: Ch 16; 14 *When vessel expected*
INVERGORDON: Ch 11* 16 13
INVERNESS: Ch 16; 06 12 *Mon-Fri 0900-1700 and
when vessel expected*
**Seaport Marina call Clachnaharry Sea Lock: Ch
16 74; 74** *4h-HW-4h*
BURGHEAD: Ch 16; 12 14 *Working Hours and when
vessel expected*
LOSSIEMOUTH: Ch 12 16; 12 *0700-1700 and 1h
before vessel expected*
BUCKIE: Ch 12 16; 12 *H24 on* **Ch 16**
MACDUFF: Ch 16; 12
FRASERBURGH *Call Pilots MCUW4 :* **Ch 16; 12**
PETERHEAD: Ch 14; 14 *Use* **Ch 16** *only in emergency*
Peterhead Asco North Base: Ch 11 *HJ*
Peterhead Asco South Base: Ch 11
ABERDEEN *Call Aberdeen Pt Control:* **Ch 16; 06 11
12* 13**
MONTROSE: Ch 16; 12
DUNDEE: Ch 16; 12*
Royal Tay Yacht Club: Ch M
PERTH: Ch 16; 09
FORTH PORTS *Call Forth Navigation :* **Ch 71; 12 20***
Call on **Ch 71** *and for subsequent reporting unless* **Ch 12**
or **Ch 20** *requested.*
Methil Docks: Ch 16; 14 *3h-HW-1h*
Leith Docks: Ch 16; 12
Braefoot Terminal: Ch 16; 69* *2h before vessel
expected*
Hound Point Terminal: Ch 09

N Queensferry Naval Signal Station: Ch 16 71; 74*

Rosyth Naval Base   Call QHM : Ch 16 74; 13 73 *Mon-Fri 0730-1700*

Grangemouth Docks: Ch 16; 14

BP Grangemouth: Ch 16; 14 19

Port Edgar Marina: Ch M 80* *Apr-Sep 0900-1930, Oct-Mar 0900-1630*

Royal Forth Yacht Club: Call Boswall Ch M 80 *4h-HW-4h*

Eyemouth Harbour: Ch 16; 12 *office hours*

Amble Marina: Ch M* 80 *4h-HW-4h*

UK WEST COAST COASTAL RADIO

0056 Swansea (Coastguard MRCC) 16* (H24) 10 67 73 (HX)

0057 Milford Haven (Coastguard MRSC) 16* (H24) 10 67 73 (HX)

0058 Celtic Ch 16 24*
Remotely controlled. Traffic lists: Ch 24: 0233 0303 0633 0733 0903 1033 1433 1503 1833 1933 2103 2233

0059 Cardigan Bay Ch 03* 16
Remotely controlled. Traffic lists: Ch 03: 0203 0303 0603 0703 0903 1003 1403 1503 1803 1903 2103 2203

0059.1 Holyhead (Coastguard MRSC) 16 (H24) 10 67 73 (HX)

0060 Anglesey Ch 16 26* 28¹*
1) For vessels in the Mersey. Remotely controlled. Traffic lists: Ch 26: 0203 0303 0603 0703 0903 1003 1403 1503 1803 1903 2103 2203

0061 Liverpool (Coastguard MRSC) 16 (H24) 10 67 73 (HX)

PORT RADIO

BROMBOROUGH WHARF: Ch 16 74

NEWPORT VTIS: cH 16; 69 71 *4h-HW-4h*

Port: Ch 16; 09 11 *4h-HW-4h*

CARDIFF: CH 14* 16; 11 14* *4h-HW-3h*

Barrage Control: Ch 72

Penarth Marina: Ch 80 *Access 4h-HW-3h*

BARRY DOCKS: Ch 11* 16; 10 *4h -HW-3h*

PORTHCAWL: Ch 80 *0900-2100*

PORT TALBOT: Ch 12 16; 12

NEATH: Ch 16; 77

SWANSEA: Ch 14; 14 *HJ*

Swansea Marina: Ch 18 80 *Barrage* 80* *Business Hours and locking times 0700-2200*

Saundersfoot: Ch 16; 11 *2.30h-HW-2.30h*

Monkstone Cruising & Sailing Club: Ch M *2.30h-HW-2.30h*

MILFORD HAVEN, Port Information Service: Ch 09 10 11 12* 14 16 67 *Ch 11 12 14 16 -H24*

Patrol Launches *Call Milford Haven Patrol* Ch 06 08 11 12 14 16 67 *Ch 11 12 -H24*

Information: Ch 12 14 *at 0300 0900 1500 2100 approx. Shipping movements during next 24h on* Ch 12 *at 0800- 0830 and 2000-2030 and on request*

Elf Marine Terminal: Ch 14 16 18* *HX*

Milford Docks: Ch 09 12 14 16 *2h-HW*

Milford Marina: Ch 12 M; M *2h-HW*

Texaco Terminal: Ch 14 16 21 *HX*

Gulf Terminal: 14 16 18* *HX*

Pembroke Dock: 13

Port of Pembroke: Ch 12; 68 *Mon-Fri 0700-1900 or when vessel expected*

Neyland Yacht Haven: Ch M 80

Lawrenny Yacht Station: Ch M

FISHGUARD: Ch 16; 14

NEW QUAY: Ch 14 16 *0900-1700, 3h-HW-3h*

ABERAERON: Ch 14 16 *0900-1700, 3h-HW-3h*

ABERYSTWYTH: Ch 16; 14 *3h-HW-3h*

ABERDOVEY: Ch 16; 12 *0900-1700 or as required by tides, 3h-HW-3h*

BARMOUTH HARBOUR: Ch 12* 16; 12 *Apr-Sep 0900-2200, Oct-Mar 0900-1600*

PWLLHELI MARINA: *call Hafen Pwllheli, 5h-HW-5h*

Cyngor Dosbarth Dwytor: *call Pwllheli Harbour Master:* Ch 16; 08 *2h-HW-1.45h*

Abersoch Land & Sea Ltd: Ch M *0800-1700*

PORTHMADOG: Ch16; 12 14 *0900-1715, and when vessel expected, 1.30h-HW-1.30h*

CAERNARVON: Ch 16; 12 14 *3h-HW-3h HJ*

Port Dinorwic Yacht Hr: Ch M *Office Hours*

HOLYHEAD: Ch 16; 14

Holyhead Sailing Club: Ch M

BEAUMARIS & MENAI BRIDGE: Ch 16; 69 *Mon-Fri 0800-1700*

CONWY: Ch 14 16; 06 08 12* 14 71 80 *Apr-Sep 0900-1700, Oct-Mar Mon-Fri 0900-1700 3h-HW-2h.*

Conwy Marina: Ch 80 *3h-HW-4h*

RAYNES JETTY: Ch 16; 14 *4h-HW only when vessel expected*

LLANDDULAS: Ch 16; 14 *4h-HW only when vessel expected*

MOSTYN DOCK AND RIVER DEE PILOTS: 14* 16; 14 *2h-HW or by arrangement*

LIVERPOOL Port Operations and Information
Call Mersey Radio : Ch 16 *Calling and Safety* Ch 12 *Port Ops Calling and Navigation* Ch 09 *Port Ops and Routine Broadcasts* Ch 18* 19 *Port Ops and Radar*

Information: Ch 09 *at 3h before and 2h before HW.*

Listening Watch: Ch 12

Garston Dock: Ch 20

Liverpool Marina: Ch M *2.30h-HW-2.30h*

Blundellsands Sailing Club: Ch M *2h-HW-2h*

Fiddlers Ferry Yacht Haven: Ch M *1h-HW-1h*

Tranmere Oil Stage: Ch 19

Canning Dock: Ch M *2h-HW*

Alfred Dock: Ch 22

Langton Dock: Ch 21

Gladstone Dock: Ch 05

MANCHESTER SHIP CANAL: Ch 14

Listening Watch: Ch 14

Eastham Locks: Ch 07

Stanlow Oil Docks: Ch 14 20

Weaver Nav: Ch 14; 71 73* *H24 except 1800-1900*

Latchford Locks: Ch 14 20

Irlam Locks: Ch 14 20 *Emergency use only*

Barton Locks: Ch 14 20 *Emergency use only*

Mode Wheel Locks: Ch 14 20 *Emergency use only*

PRESTON MARINA: Ch 16; 14 *1.30h-HW Liverpool-1.30h*

Douglas Boatyard: Ch 16 *Mon-Fri 0830-1800 Sat & Sun 1400-1800*

FLEETWOOD Harbour Control: Ch 11 *0400-1100 1600-2300 and when vessel expected*

Fleetwood Docks: Ch 12 *2h-HW-2h*

Fleetwood Harbour Village: Ch 11 12 16; 11 12 *0900-1700*

GLASSON DOCK: Ch 16; 69 *2h-HW-1h*

Glasson Basin Yacht Ltd: Ch 16; 08 *1h-HW*

HEYSHAM: Ch 16; 14 74
BARROW DOCKS: Ch 16; 12
RAMSDEN DOCK: Ch 16 *2.30h-HW*
DOUGLAS, Isle of Man: Ch 16 *Calling-if not possible on* **Ch 12** *and Safety* **Ch 12** *Calling and Port Ops* **Ch 12** *Tugs, PV and Hr Mr* **Information:** *Navigation warnings for all Isle of Man ports are broadcast on* **Ch 12** *at 0133 0533 0733 0933 1333 1733 2133 UT*
CASTLETOWN, Isle of Man: Ch 16; 12 *0830-1700 and when vessel expected*
PORT S MARY, Isle of Man: Ch 16; 12 *HJ and when vessel expected*
PEEL, Isle of Man: Ch 16; 12 *HJ and when vessel expected*
RAMSEY, Isle of Man: Ch 16; 12 *0830-1700 and when vessel expected*
WHITEHAVEN *Call PV 'J T Pears' MZVA :* **Ch 16; 12** *3h-HW-3h*
WORKINGTON: Ch 16; 11 14 *2.30h-HW-2h*
Maryport Marina: Ch 16 M 80 *3.30h-HW-3.30h*
SILLOTH DOCKS: Ch 16; 12 *2.30h-HW-1h*

IRELAND
COASTAL RADIO
0124   Dublin Ch 16 67[1] 83*
1) For safety messages only. Remotely controlled from Malin Hd. Traffic lists: **Ch 83:** *0103 0503 & every odd H+03 (0903-2303)*
0125   Wicklow Head Ch 16 67[1]
1) For safety messages only. Remotely controlled from Dublin. Traffic lists: **Ch 87:** *0103 0503 & every odd H+03 (0903-2303)*
0126   Rosslare Ch 16 23* 67[1]
1) For safety messages only. Remotely controlled from Dublin. Traffic lists: **Ch 23:** *0103 0503 & every odd H+03 (0903-2303)*
0127   Mine Head Ch 16 67[1] 83
1) For safety messages only. Remotely controlled from Dublin. Traffic lists: **Ch 83:** *0103 0503 & every odd H+03 (0903-2303)*
0128   Bantry Ch 16 23* 67[1] 85
1) For safety messages only. Remotely controlled from Valentia. Traffic lists: **Ch 23:** *0333 and every odd H+33 (0733-2303)*
0129   Cork Ch 16 26 67[1]
1) For safety messages only. Remotely controlled from Valentia. Traffic lists: **Ch 26:** *0333 & every odd H+33 (0733-2303)*
0130   Valentia Ch 16 24 28 67[1]
Telephone 353 667 6109 1) Safety information for small craft. Located at Kilvearagh (51°52'N 10°20'W) Traffic lists: **Ch 24:** *0333 & every odd H + 33 (0733-2303)*
0134   Shannon Ch 16 24 28* 67[1]
1) For safety messages only. Remotely controlled from Valentia. Traffic lists: **Ch 28:** *0333 & every odd H + 33 (0733-2303)*
0135   Clifden Ch 16 26* 67[1]
1) For safety messages only. Remotely controlled from Malin Head
0136   Belmullet Ch 16 67[1] 83*
1) For safety messages only. Remotely controlled from Malin Head Traffic lists: **Ch 83:** *0103 0503 & every odd H+03 (0903-2303)*
0137   Glen Head Ch 16 24 67[1]
1) For safety messages only. Remotely controlled from Malin Head. Traffic lists: **Ch 24:** *0103 0503 & every odd H+03 (0903-2303)*
0140   Malin Head Ch 16 23 67[1] 85
Telephone +353(0)77 70103 1) For safety messages only.

Located at Crockalough (55°21'N 7°16'W) Traffic lists: **Ch 23:** *0103 0503 & every odd H+03 (0903-2303)*

PORT RADIO
LONDONDERRY: Ch 12 14*
COLERAINE: Ch 16; 12 *Mon-Fri 0900-1700 and when vessel expected*
Coleraine Marina: Ch M *Office hours*
Seatons Marina: Ch M *HJ*
PORTRUSH: Ch 16; 12 *Mon-Fri 0900-1700, extended Jun-Sep, Sat Sun 0900-1700, Jun-Sep only*
LARNE: Ch 16; 14 *Hr Mr* **Ch 14 16** *Port Information*
CLOGHAN POINT, Terminal: Ch 16; Ch 10 *Pollution* **Ch 14**
KILROOT SALT JETTY: Ch 14* 16 *Mon-Fri 0800-1700*
KILROOT COAL JETTY Call PV 'Sarah McLoughlin': Ch 14* 16
CARRICKFERGUS: Ch 16; 12 14 *3h-HW-1h*
Carrickfergus Marina: Ch M
BELFAST: Ch 12* 16
BP Belfast: Ch 16; 10 19
BANGOR: Ch 16; 11 80 M *When vessel expected*
Bangor Marina: Ch 16; 11 80 M
PORTAVOGIE: Ch 16; 12 14 *Mon-Fri 0900-1700*
STRANGFORD HARBOUR: Ch 16; 12 14 M *Mon-Fri 0900-1700*
Ardglass Harbour: Ch 16; 14 12
Carlingford Marina: Ch 16
Malahide Marina: Ch M
KILLYLEAGH: Ch 16; 12 *HX*
KILKEEL: Ch 16; 12* 14 *Mon-Fri 0900-2000*
WARRENPOINT: Ch 16; 12
GREENORE: Ch 16 *HJ*
DUNDALK: Ch 14 *Mon-Fri 0900-1700*
DROGHEDA: Ch 11 *HX*
HOWTH HARBOUR: Ch 16; 08 *Mon-Fri 0700-2300, Sat Sun HX*
Howth Marina: Ch M 16
DUBLIN: Ch 16 *Distress and Safety* **Ch 12* 13 14** *Port Operations*
Lifting Bridge *Call Eastlink :* **Ch 12 13**
DUN LAOGHAIRE: Ch 14 16; 14
WICKLOW: Ch 16; 02 06 07 08 14 26 27 28
ARKLOW: Ch 16 *HJ*
ROSSLARE: Ch 06; 12* 14 16
WATERFORD: Ch 16; 12 14 *HJ and when expected*
NEW ROSS: Ch 16; 12 14
YOUGHAL: Ch 16; 14 *3h-HW-3h*
CORK: Ch 12 14 16; 12 14
Whitegate Marine Terminal, Cobh: Ch 16; 14
East Ferry Marina: Ch M
Crosshaven Marina: Ch M *Mon-Fri 0830-1700*
Royal Cork Yacht Club Marina: Ch M *0900-2300*
Kinsale YC Marina: Ch M
Castle Park Marina: Ch M
BALTIMORE HARBOUR: Ch 16; 09
BANTRY: Ch 16; 10 11 14
CASTLETOWN BEARHAVEN: Ch 14 16; 14
DINGLE: Ch M 11
FENIT: Ch 16; 14 *HX*
LIMERICK: Ch 16; 12 13 *Office hours & when expected*
Tarbert Oil Jetty: Ch 16; 12 13
Foynes Harbour: Ch 16; 12 13 *Office Hours and when vessel expected*
Aughinish Marine Terminal: Ch 16; 12 13

Dernish Oil Jetty: **Ch 16; 12 13**
Kilrush Creek Marina: **Ch 80**
GALWAY: **Ch 16; 12** 2.30h-HW-1h
ROSSAVEEL: **Ch 16; 12 14** Office Hours
SLIGO: **Ch 16; 12 14** 0900-1700 and when vessel expected
KILLYBEGS: **Ch 16**

BELGIUM
COASTAL RADIO
0155 Oostende Ch 16 27[1,2] **28**[3] **63 78**[3] **85**[2] **87**[1] **88**[1]
Telephone: +32 59 706565 Fax: +32 59 701339
1) For vessels in the vicinity of Zeebrugge
2) For vessels in the vicinity of Oostende
3) For vessels in the vicinity of La Panne
Traffic lists: **Ch 27:** every H+20
0160 Antwerpen
Facilities are located at:

Antwerpen	**Ch 07 16**[1] **24* 27 87**
Konrijk	**Ch 24**[1]
Gent	**Ch 16 24**[1] **81**
Vilvoorde	**Ch 24**[1]
Ronquieres	**Ch 24**[1]
Mol	**Ch 24**[1]
Liege	**Ch 24**[1]

1) For Distress and safety calls only
Traffic lists: **Ch 24:** every H+05

BELGIUM & HOLLAND
PORT RADIO
NIEUWPOORT: **Ch 09 16**
OOSTENDE: **Ch 10**
Lock and Mercator Marina: **Ch 14**
BLANKENBERGE Marina Call Old Chap : **Ch 08**
ZEEBRUGGE Call Zeebrugge Port Control : **Ch 71**
Port Entrance and Port Control **Ch 67** Emergencies
Locks: **Ch 13**
WESTERSCHELDE
Reporting is compulsory within the VTS Schelde and Estuaries area for all Inward-Bound and Outward-Bound vessels. Vessels must maintain a continuous listening watch on the VHF channel for the appropriate Traffic Area including vessels at anchor . Each Traffic Area is marked by buoys and the appropriate Traffic Centre must be called on the relevant channel when a vessel enters the area.
TRAFFIC AREA WANDELAAR: **Ch 65** Traffic Centre **Ch 04** Radar **Ch 67** Emergency . Outward bound vessels report when between buoys A1 bis and Scheur 2.
TRAFFIC AREA ZEEBRUGGE: **Ch 69** Traffic Centre **Ch 04** Radar **Ch 19** Harbour **Ch 67** Emergency . Area see chart. Radar Control Zeebrugge: **Ch 19.** Report when inward/outward bound and within Zeebrugge Hr.
TRAFFIC AREA STEENBANK: **Ch 64** Traffic centre **Ch 67** Emergency
TRAFFIC CENTRE VLISSINGEN/TERNEUZEN: **Ch 14** Traffic Centre Vlissingen, **Ch 03** Traffic Centre Terneuzen, **Ch 21** Radar Vlissingen **Ch 03** Radar Terneuzen **Ch 67** Emergency
Reporting: **Ch 14** Centrale ap Vlissingen **Ch 03** Radar 79 Terneuzen Areas **Ch 21** Vlissingen Harbour
TRAFFIC AREA GENT/TERNEUZEN: **Ch 11** Traffic **Ch 67** Emergency . Call Havendienst Terneuzen or Havendienst Gent as appropriate

TRAFFIC AREA HANSWEERT: **Ch 65** Traffic Centre **Ch 67** Emergency Reporting: In and Out: **Ch 65** Centrale Hansweert, In **Ch 12** Centrale Zandvliet, Out **Ch 14** Centrale Vlissingen
TRAFFIC AREA ANTWERPEN: **Ch 12** Traffic Centre Centrale Zandvliet **Ch 19** Radar Waarde **Ch 21** Radar Saeftinge **Ch 04** Radar Zandvliet **Ch 66** Radar Kruischans **Ch 67** Emergency Reporting: In and Out **Ch 12** Centrale Zandvliet
Information: In Dutch and English every H+50 on **Ch 14** by Vlissingen, every H+05 on **Ch 03** and every H+55 on **Ch 11** by Terneuzen and every H+00 on **Ch 12** by Zandvliet. Traffic lists and navigation warnings between H+05 and H+10 on **Ch 16** by Antwerpen
Vlissingen Call Flushing Port Control: **Ch 09** Port **Ch 22** Locks **Ch 22** Bridge
Braakmanhaven Call DOW Chemical Terneuzen : **Ch 06 13 34; 06 08 11 13 34** Ch 06 13- H24
Terneuzen: **Ch 11** Port **Ch 69** Locks Organisation **Ch 06** Westsluis and Middensuis **Ch 18** Oostsluis
Terneuzen Information: Every H+00 on **Ch 11**
Gent: Ch 05 11
Hansweert Locks: Ch 22
Antwerpen: Ch 74 Calling and Safety **Ch 18** VTS Centre **Ch 13** Bridges **Ch 63** Dock Mr **Ch 02 60** Radar
Antwerpen Locks: Ch 08 11 Boudewijnsluis & Van Cauwelaertsluis **Ch 22** Royerssluis & Kattendijksluis **Ch 03 08** Kallosluis, Zandvlietsluis and Barendrechtsluis **Ch 68** Winthamsluis
Antwerpen Marina Call MIC Marina : **Ch 09** Hr gate normally open 1h-HW-1h

HOLLAND
COASTAL RADIO
0165 Scheveningen
The following stations are remotely controlled by Scheveningen. Call Scheveningen Radio in each case
Coastal Area

Goes	Ch	16	23*
Rotterdam	Ch	16	87*
Scheveningen	Ch	16	83*
Haarlem	Ch	16	25*
Tjerkgaast	Ch	16	
Wieringermeer	Ch	16	27*
Platform L7	Ch	16	84*
Terschelling	Ch	16	78*
Nes	Ch	16	23*
Appingedam	Ch	16	27*
Inland Waters			
Maastricht	Ch	25	
Roermond	Ch	26	
Arcen	Ch	28	
Goes	Ch	25	
Rotterdam	Ch	24*	28
Lopic	Ch	16	86*
Scheveningen	Ch	26	
Markelo	Ch	23	
Haarlem	Ch	23	
Lelystad	Ch	16	83*
Smilde	Ch	24	
Tjerkgaast	Ch	28	
Megen	Ch	07	

Note **Ch 16** is remotely controlled by Netherlands Coast Guard. Call on working channels for routine traffic. Hours of watch **Ch 16 and all working channels:** H24. Traffic

lists: All working channels except **Ch 16:** *every H+05.*
0166 Netherlands Coastguard (IJmuiden) Ch 16

PORT RADIO

OOSTERSCHELDE
Lock *Call Roompotsluis :* **Ch 18.** *Lock operating times: Mon and Thu 0000-2200, Tue and Sun 0600-0000, Wed H24, Fri and Sat 0600-2200.*
Roompot Hr: Ch 31
Wemeldinge Bridges and Locks: Ch 68
Zeelandbrug: Ch 18
Krammer Locks: Ch 22
Kreekraksluizen, Schelde-Rijnkanaal: Ch 20
HARINGVLIET-SLUIZEN Lock & Lift Bridge: Ch 20 *Mon/Thu H24 Fri 0000-2200 Sat/Sun & hols 0800-2000*
HOEK VAN HOLLAND ROADSTEAD *Call Maasmond Entrance :* **Ch 03.** *Yachts should follow a track close W of a line joining buoys MV, MVN and Indusbank N. Before crossing, report vessel's name, position and course. Whilst crossing, maintain continuous listening watch.*
NIEUWE WATERWEG
Keep a continuous listening watch on the following Traffic Centres, as appropriate
Haven Coördinatie Centre *HCC Central Traffic Control:* **Ch 11 14**
Traffic Centre, Hoek van Holland *VCH :* **Ch 13**
Traffic Centre **Ch 01** *Maas Approach* **Ch 03** *Sector Maasmond* **Ch 65** *Sector Waterweg* **Ch 66** *Sector Europort*
Traffic Centre, Botlek *VCB :* **Ch 13** *Traffic Centre* **Ch 80** *Sector Maassluis* **Ch 61** *Sector Botlek*
Traffic Centre, Hartel *VPH :* **Ch 05** *Traffic Centre* **Ch 62** *Sector Oude Maas*
Traffic Centre, Stad: Ch 13 *Traffic Centre* **Ch 60** *Sector Waalhaven* **Ch 63** *Sector Eemhaven*
Traffic Centre Maasboulevard *VPM :* **Ch 81** *Sector Maasbruggen* **Ch 21** *Sector Brienenoord . The area is divided into the following sectors and continuous listening watch should be kept as appropriate:* **Ch 01** *Maasaanloop/ Maas Approach* **Ch 02** *Pilot Maas* **Ch 03** *Maasmond/ Maas Entrance* **Ch 65** *Waterweg* **Ch 66** *Europort* **Ch 80** *Maassluis* **Ch 61** *Botlek* **Ch 62** *Oude Maas* **Ch 05** *Hartel* **Ch 63** *Eemhaven* **Ch 60** *Waalhaven* **Ch 81** *Maasbruggen* **Ch 21** *Brienenoord .*
Other stations within the area
Maassluis Radio-Dirkzwager: Ch 12 *Visibility Reports*
Oude Maas: Ch 13 19
Bridges and Locks: Ch 18 *Botlekbrug and Spijkenisserbrug* **Ch 20** *Brienenoordbrug* **Ch 22** *Altblasserdam Br* **Ch 19** *Dordrecht Br*
Dordrecht: Ch 19 *Traffic Centre* **Ch 04** *Sector Heerjansdam* **Ch 71** *Post Dordrecht* **Ch 74** *Port Authority*
Volkeraksluizen: Ch 18 69 ·
SCHEVENINGEN: Ch 14 *Traffic Centre & Port* **Ch 21** *Radar*
IJMUIDEN
Traffic Centre IJmuiden: Ch 12 *W of IJmuiden Lt buoy*
IJmuiden Port Control: Ch 09 *from IJmuiden Lt buoy to the North Sea Locks*
Seaport Marina, Ijmuiden *Call SPM:* **Ch 74**
NORDZEEKANAAL, Vessel Traffic Services
IJmuiden: Ch 09 *from IJmuiden Lt buoy to the IJmuiden Sluices*
IJmuiden Sluices: Ch 22
Noordzeekanaal: Ch 11 *from IJmuiden Sluices to km 11.2*
Zijkanaal C Sluice: Ch 68
Amsterdam: Ch 14 *Port Control* **Ch 04** *Port Information Amsterdam port basins and the Noordzeekanaal east of km 11.2* **Information: H+00 on all VHF Channels** *when visibility falls below 1000m*
BEVERWIJK: Ch 71 *HX*
ENKHUIZEN or Krabbersgat, Lock: Ch 22. *Lock operates 0300-2300 Weekdays, 0800-2000 Sun and holidays*
DEN HELDER:
VTS: Ch 12. *All vessels equipped with VHF to report when entering/leaving the area, berthing/unberthing, anchoring/ weighing or entering/leaving Koopvaardersschutsluis stating vessel's name, type, position, destination and special details.*
Port Control Den Helder: Ch 14
Moormanbrug Bridge: Ch 18
Koopvaardersschutsluis: Ch 22
DEN OEVER Lock: Ch 20
KORNWERDERZAND Locks: Ch 18
HARLINGEN: Ch 11 *Mon 0000-Sat 2200*
TERSCHELLING:
VTS *Call Brandaris Vessel Traffic Centre:* **Ch 02.** *All vessels must report when entering/leaving the area with the following details: vessel's name and call sign, type, length as certificate of registry, position, where from and bound for, any dangerous cargo and special particulars, and thereafter, keep a continuous listening watch.*
Waddenzee Central Reporting: Ch 04 *Incidents* **Ch 16** *Search and Rescue*
LAUWERSOOG: Ch 09 *Mon 0000-1700, Tue-Wed 0800-1700, Thur-Sat 0700-1500*
Locks: Ch 22 *May-Sep Mon-Fri 0700-2000 Sat 0700- 1900 Sun 0900-1200 1400-1830, Oct-Apr Mon-Fri 0700- 1800 Sat 0700-1700*
Lauwersmeer Firing Range: Ch 71 *Keep listening watch for information on firing times*
EEMSHAVEN: Ch 14 *Port* **Ch 19** *Radar*
DELFZIJL: Ch 14 *Special Regulations apply when visibility falls below 500m,* **information:** *every H+10 on* **Ch 14**
Locks: Ch 11 *Mon-Sat H24*
Bridges: Ch 22 *Mon 0600-Sat 1400*
Farmsumerhaven: Ch 14

GERMANY
COASTAL RADIO

0190 Norddeich Ch 16 28* 61 *Mon-Fri: 0500-1800*
Traffic lists: **Ch 28:** *every H+45*
0200 Bremen Ch 16 25 28*
Remotely controlled from Elbe-Weser
Traffic lists: **Ch 28:** *every H+40*
0205 Helgoland Ch 16 27* 88
Remotely controlled from Elbe-Weser
Traffic lists: **Ch 27:** *every H+20*
0210 Elbe-Weser Ch 01 16 24¹*
Traffic lists: **Ch 24:** *every H+20*
0225 Hamburg Ch 16 27* 83
Remotely controlled from Elbe-Weser.
Traffic lists: **Ch 27:** *every H+40*
0230 Eiderstedt Ch 16 25* 64
Remotely controlled from Elbe-Weser
Traffic lists: **Ch 25:** *every H+40*
0235 Nordfriesland Ch 05 16 26*
Remotely controlled from Elbe-Weser
Traffic lists: **Ch 26:** *every H+50*

PORT RADIO
IMPORTANT: *Before navigating German waterways, all vessels must report to waterway authorities.*
DIE EMS Call Ems Traffic: CH 15 16 18 20 21
Emden Locks: Ch 13 16 *Grosse Seeschleuse - Call*
Emden Lock **Ch 13 16** *Nesserlander Seeschleuse -Call Nesserland Lock*
Leer Bridge: Ch 15
Leer Lock: Ch 13 16
Weener Bridge: Ch 15
Weener Lock: Ch 13 16 *Apr-Oct only Mon-Thu 0700-1600 Fri 0700-sunset Sat and Sun sunrise-sunset UT*
Papenburg Lock: Ch 13 16
BORKUM: Ch 14 16 *All year Mon-Fri 0700-2200, Sep-Apr Sat & Sun 0700-1700, May-Aug Sat 0800-1200 1500-2100 Sun 0700-1100 1400-2000UT . All vessels report arrival/departure.*
NORDDEICH: Ch 14 *Mon 0730-1900,Tue-Fri 0700-1300 1330-1900, Sat & Sun 0800-1200 1230-1730 UT*
NORDENEY: Ch 14 *Mon 0700-1200 1230-1730, Tues 0900-1200 1230-1900, Wed-Sun 0700-1200 1230-1900 UT*
BENSERSIEL: Ch 14 *Oct-Mar Mon-Fri 0700-1230 1330-1700,Apr-Sep Mon-Fri 0700-1900 Sat & Sun 0700-1100 1300-1700 UT*
DEUTSCHE BUCHT: EMS, JADE, WESER and ELBE
Reporting: *Vessels over 50m in length must report on Ch 80 toWSA Wilhemshaven andWSA Cuxhaven and maintain listening watch on specified Channels.* **German Bight Traffic - Ch 16;80*** *Helgoland* **or Ch 16;79*** *Borkum*
Information: *all vessels should monitor* **Ch 79 or Ch 80**
DIE JADE Reporting and Information: Ch 16 20 63 *Traffic - from the sea to Wilhemshaven* **Ch 63** *Radar I - Lt buoy JW5/Jade 1 to Lt buoy 33* **Ch 20** *Radar II - Lt buoy 33 to Lt buoy 60*
Wilhemshaven: Ch 11 16 *Port* **Ch 11 16** *Naval Port* **Ch 13 16** *Lock* **Ch 11** *Bridges*
Varel Lock: Ch 13 *2h-HW-2h*
DIE WESER and DIE HUNTE
Bremerhaven Weser Traffic: Ch 02 04 05 07 16 21 22 82
Bremen Weser Traffic: Ch 16 19 78 81
Hunte Traffic: Ch 16 63
Die Weser and Die Hunte Information *in German : H+20 on* **Ch 02 04 05 07 21 22 82** *by Bremerhaven Weser Traffic, H+30 on* **Ch 19 78 81** *by Bremen Weser Traffic and H+30 on* **Ch 63** *by Hunte Traffic*
Bremerhaven: Ch 12 16
Bremerhaven Locks: Ch 12
Bremerhaven Weser: Ch 14 16
Brake Lock: Ch 10
Elsfleth-Ohrt Railway Bridge: Ch 73
Hunte Lifting Bridge: Ch 73
Oldenburg Railway Bridge: Ch 73 *H24 except Sun and public holidays 0030-0630*
Oldenburg Lock: Ch 20 *Mon-Sat 0500-2100 Sun 0900-1200*
Oslebshausen Lock: Ch 12
Bremen: Ch 03 14 16
Bremen Lock: Ch 20 *Mon-Sat 0500-2100, Sun Oct-Apr 0800-1100 May-Sep 0800-1100 1730-1930*
DIE ELBE
Information, Reporting and Radar for vessels over 50m LOA - consult ALRS.
Cuxhaven Elbe Traffic: Ch 16 71*

Brunsbuttel Elbe Traffic: Ch 16 68*
Cuxhaven Elbe Port: Ch 12* 16
Cuxhaven: Ch 69 *Port* **Ch 69** *Lock - HX*
Brunsbuttel Elbe Port: Ch 12* 16
Oste Bridge *Flood Barrage :* **Ch 16 69.** *Apr-Sep the bridge is opened on request,* **Ch 69**; *Oct-Mar request through* **Ch 03 or 16** *Belum Radar* **or Ch 21** *Cuxhaven Radar.*
Oste Bridge, Geversdorf: Ch 69. *The bridge opens on request for small craft Apr-Sep 0730-1930 UT and every H+00 and H+30.*
Oberndorf Bridge: Ch 68 *Oct-Mar H24, Apr-Sep 1930-0730 UT . The bridge is opened on request by telephone 04752 5 21 .*
Stor Lock: Ch 09 16. *The bridge is opened on request.*
Gluckstadt Lock: Ch 11 *0700-1600 UT and during HW*
Stadersand: Ch 12* 16
Este Lock: Ch 10 16
Este Bridge: Ch 11. *Opened on request.*
HAMBURG
Reporting: *Compulsory for seagoing vessels - see* ALRS *Vol 6 Part 1.*
Hamburg Port: Ch 16; 06 13 14* 73. *Keep listening watch on* **Ch 06.**
Hamburg Elbe Port: Ch 12* 16
Rethe Bridge: Ch 13* 16
Kattwyk Bridge: Ch 13* 16
Harburg Lock: Ch 13 16
Tiefstack Lock: Ch 11
NORD-OSTSEE KANAL, KIEL KANAL: *Keep listening watch as follows:* **Ch 13** *Kiel Kanal I, Brunsbuttel Entr, inward* **Ch 68** *Brunsbuttel Elbe Traffic, Brunsbuttel approaches out* **Ch 13** *Keil Kanal I, Brunsbuttel locks* **Ch 02** *Kiel Kanal II, Brunsbuttel to Breiholz* **Ch 03** *Keil Kanal III, Breiholz to Kiel-Holtenau* **Ch 12** *Kiel Kanal IV, Holtenau Entr, outer hr and locks .*
Information: Ch 02 *by Kiel Kanal II. Also at H+20 and H+50 on* **Ch 03** *by Kiel Kanal III*
Ostermoor: Ch 73
Brieholz: Ch 73
FRIEDRICHSKOOG: Ch 10 *2h-HW-2h*
BÜSUM: Ch 11 16
EIDER Lock: Ch 14 16
HUSUM: Ch 11 16
Information: Ch 11 *every H+00, 4h-HW-2h*
PELLWORM: Ch 11 *0700-1700 UT*
WYK, Fohr: List Ch 11
HELGOLAND: Ch 16 67 *Mon-Fri 0700-1800 Sat 0800-1700 Sun 0800-1000*

DENMARK
COASTAL RADIO
0295 Lyngby: Skagen Ch 04* 16, Hantsholm Ch 01* 16, Hirtshals Ch 16* 66* *Ch 16 H24. Traffic Lists Ch 01 04 66¹: every odd H + 05 (¹ Hirtshals only)*

PORT RADIO
RØMØ HAVN: Ch 16; 10 12 13 HX
ESBJERG: CH 16; 12 13 14
HVIDE SANDE: Ch 16; 12 13 HX
THORSMINDE: Ch 16; 12 13 *0300-1300, 1400-2400 LT*
HANSTOLM HAVN: Ch 16; 12 13 HX
TORUP STRAND: Ch 16 12 13 HX
HIRTSHALS HAVN: Ch 16; 14 HX

FRANCE
COASTAL RADIO
0830 Dunkerque Ch 16 H24 24* 61* 0600-2100(LT)
Remotely controlled from Boulogne
0835 Calais Ch 16 H24 01* 87* 0600-2100 (LT)
Remotely controlled from Boulogne
0840 Boulogne-sur-Mer Ch 16 H24 23* 25* 0600-2100[1] Telephone 21 33 25 26 Fax 21 91 99 71.
0842 Gris-Nez (CROSS) Ch 16 H24 15 76 73 HX
0845 Dieppe Ch 16 H24 02* 24* 0600-2100 (LT)
1) 1 hr earlier during DST. Remotely controlled from Boulogne
0848 Fécamp Ch 16
Remotely controlled from Boulogne
0850 Le Havre Ch 16 H24 23 26* 28* 0600-2100(LT)
Remotely controlled from Boulogne
0855 Rouen Ch 16 H24 25* 27 0600-2100 (LT)
Remotely controlled from Boulogne
0856 Port-en-Bessin Ch 16 H24 03* 0600-2100 (LT)
Remotely controlled from Boulogne
0857 Cherbourg Ch 16 H24 27* 0600-2100 (LT)
Remotely controlled from Boulogne

PORT RADIO
DUNKERQUE: Ch 16; 12* 73*
GRAVELINES Marina: Ch 09 0800-1200 1300-1730
CALAIS *Call Calais Port Traffic :* **Ch 16; 12**
Marina: Ch 12 0800-1200 1400-1800
Hoverport: Ch 20 HX
Ecluse Carnot: Ch 12 16 HX
GRIS NEZ Maritime Traffic Service: Ch 16; 11
Information: Ch 11 H+10. Occasional when visibility less than 2M H+25
CROSS: Ch 16 Distress and Safety, Call CROSS Gris Nez
Ch 15 16 73 SAR Coordination, Call CROSS Gris Nez
11 16 Calling and Information, Call Gris Nez Traffic
BOULOGNE Call Control Tr, Boulogne Port : **Ch 12**
Marina: Ch 09 Summer 0900-1200 1400-1900, Winter 0900-1200 1500-1800
Boulogne Hoverport: Ch 20 HX
LE TREPORT: Ch 16; 12 72 3h-HW-3h
DIEPPE: 12 16; 12* Ch 12 Office Hours, Ch 16 H24
S VALÉRY-EN-CAUX Marina: Ch 09 Lock operates: Day: 2.15h-HW-2.15h, Night: 30m-HW-30m
FÉCAMP: Ch 16; 10 12 3h-HW-1h
Gayant Lock Bassin Freycinet-Call Bureau du Port : **Ch 16**
Berigny Lock Call Ecluse Berigny : **Ch 09**
Marina: Ch 09 Season: 0800-1200 1400-2000, Out of season: 0900-1200 1400-1700
PORT DU HAVRE-ANTIFER: Ch 16 22*; 14 22* 67
LE HAVRE: Ch 16; 12 20 22 Control Tr **Ch 12**
Radar **Ch 67 69** Port Operations
Marina: Ch 09 Season 0800-1200 1400-1800, Out of season Mon-Fri as season, Sat 0800-1200, Sun & holidays closed
LA SEINE Procedure: Call Honfleur when entering and then Rouen while on passage Control Centre: **Ch 73**
HONFLEUR: Ch 16; 11 12 73 2h-HW Le Havre-4h
Locks and Basins: Ch 73 2h-HW Le Havre-4h
TANCARVILLE: Ch 16 Lock: **Ch 18** HX
PORT JÉROME Call PR : **Ch 16; 73**
ROUEN: Ch 16; 68 73*
LOCKS: ROUEN to PARIS
Poses-Amfreville: Ch 18
Notre-Dame-de-la-Gerenne: Ch 22
Mericourt: Ch 18

Andrésy: Ch 22
Bougival: Ch 22
Chatou: Ch 18
Suresnes: Ch 22
Paris-Arsenal: Ch 09
DEAUVILLE-TROUVILLE: Ch 09 0800-1730
Marina Bassin Morny : **Ch 09** 0900-1200 1400-1830
Marina Port-Deauville : **Ch 09** Mon-Fri closed Wed 0900-1200 1400-1800, Sat 0900-1200 1500-1800, Sun & public holidays 1000-1200 1500-1800
PORT GUILLAUME, Dives-Sur-Mer, Marina: Ch 09 24 Neaps 2h-HW-2h, Springs 2.30h-HW-2.30h
CAEN-OUISTREHAM:
Ouistreham Port: Ch 16; 68
Ouistreham Lock: Ch 12 68 2h-HW-3h
Marina: Ch 09 0815-1200 1400-1800
Canal de Caen: Ch 68 and keep listening watch
Caen Marina: Ch 68
COURSELLES-SUR-MER Marina: Ch 09 0900-1200 and 3h-HW-3h
PORT-EN-BESSIN Lock and Bridge : Ch 18 2h-HW-2h
CARENTAN Marina: Ch 09 0800-1800
STVAAST-LA HOUGUE: Ch 09 Season: 2.15h-HW-3h, Out of season: as season 0800-1800 only
CHERBOURG: Port de Commerce Call Le Homet : **Ch 16; 12** Homet Coastguard H24 **Ch 06** Lock 45m-HW-45m **Marina** Call Chantereyne : **Ch 09** 0800-2300

CHANNEL ISLANDS
COASTAL RADIO
0115 St Peter Port Ch 16 20* 62[1]* 67[2]
Telephone: 01481 720672 or 710277 (Shore-Ship Link Call) Fax 01481 714177 (Harbour Master) 1) Available for link calls 2) Available on request for yacht safety messages. Traffic lists: Vessels for which traffic is held are called individually on **Ch 16.** Traffic lists are broadcast on **Ch 20** after the Navigational Warnings at 0133 0533 0933 1333 1733 2133
0120 Jersey Ch 16 25[2]* 67[3] 82[1]
Telephone: +01534 41121 Fax: 01534 499089 1) Direct calling for UK registered vessels. 2) Available for link calls. 3) For small craft distress and safety working. Call on **Ch 16.** **Ch 0** and **Ch 73** may be used for distress, urgency, safety and search and rescue situations. **Ch 10** may be used for oil pollution operations. Traffic lists: Vessels for which traffic is held are called individually on **Ch 16.** Traffic lists are broadcast on **Ch 25** and **82** after the Weather Messages at 0645 LT 0745 LT 1245 1845 2245

PORT RADIO
BRAYE, Alderney: Ch 16; 12 74 Mon-Fri 0800-1200 1400-1700, Sat Sun 0900-1200 1400-1600
S PETER PORT, Guernsey Call Port Control: **Ch 12**
SAINT SAMPSON: Ch 12 Via S Peter Port Port Control
BEAUCETTE Marina, Guernsey: Ch M 80 0830-2030 UT Access 3h-HW-3h
S HELIER, Jersey: Ch 14 Access 3h-HW-3h
GOREY HARBR, Jersey: Ch 74 Summer 3h-HW-3h

FRANCE
COASTAL RADIO
0858 Jobourg Ch 16 H24 21* 0600-2100 (LT)
Remotely controlled from Boulogne
0859 Carteret Ch 16 H24 64* 0600-2100 (LT)
Remotely controlled from Boulogne

0860 **Tobourg (CROSS)** Ch 16 *H24* **67 68** *HX*
0861 **Saint-Malo** Ch 16 *H24* **01* 02*** *0600-2100 (LT)*
Remotely controlled from St Nazaire
0862 **Paimpol** Ch 16 *H24* **84*** *0600-2100¹*
Remotely controlled from Brest-LE Conquet
0863 **Plougasnou** Ch 16 *H24* **81*** *0600-2100 (LT)*
Remotely controlled from Brest-Le Conquet
0864 **Ouessant** Ch 16 *H24* **24* 82*** *0600-2100 (LT)*
Remotely controlled from Brest-Le Conquet
0865 **Brest-Le Conquet** Ch 16 *H24* **26* 28*** *0600-
2100 (LT)*
0866 **Corsen (CROSS)** Ch 16 *H24* **15 67 73** *HX*
0867 **Pont l'Abbe** Ch 16 *H24* **86*** *0600-2100¹*
*1) One hour earlier when DST is in force. Remotely control-
led from Brest-Le Conquet*
0869 **Belle-Île** Ch 16 *H24* **05* 25*** *0600-2100 (LT)*
Remotely controlled from Saint-Nazaire
0870 **Etel (CROSS)** Ch 16 *H24* **11** *HX*
0871 **St-Nazaire** Ch 16 *H24* **23* 24*** *0600-2100 (LT)*
0872 **Saint-Herblain** Ch 16 *H24* **28*** *0600-2100 (LT)*
Remotely controlled from St Nazaire.
0874 **Saint-Hilaire-de-Riez** Ch 16 *H24* **27*** *0600-
2100 (LT)*
Remotely controlled from Saint-Nazaire.
0876 **Île de Ré** Ch 16 *H24* **21* 26*** *0600-2100 (LT)*
Remotely controlled from Bordeaux-Arcachon
0877 **Royan** Ch 16 *H24* **23* 25*** *0600-2100 (LT)*
Remotely controlled from Bordeaux-Arcachon
0878 **Bordeaux** Ch 16 *H24* **27*** *0600-2100 (LT)*
0879 **Soulac (SOUS-CROSS)** Ch 16 *H24* **11** *HX*
0880 **Bordeaux-Arcachon** Ch 16 *H24* **28* 82***
0600-2100 (LT). Remotely controlled from Brest-Le Conquet
0885 **Bayonne** Ch 16 *H24* **24*** *0600-2100 (LT)*
Remotely controlled from Bordeaux-Arcachon

PORT RADIO

JOBOURG *Jobourg Maritime Traffic Service provides a
continuous traffic watch, it also broadcasts information and
provides radar assistance as required. The service works in
liason with Portland Coastguard.*
Jobourg Traffic: Ch 16; 11 80 Information: Ch 80
at H+20 and H+50
**Centre Regional Operationnel de Surveillance et
duSauvetage CROSS : Ch 16** *Distress and Safety* **Ch
15 67 73** *SAR Coordination Call CROSS Jobourg* **Ch 13
16** *Calling* **Ch 16 80** *Info Ch 16-H24, other channels HX*
GRANVILLE: Ch 12 *1.30h-HW-1.30h*
Marina: Ch 09 *Season H24, Out of season & public
holidays 0800-1200 1400-1800*
SAINT MALO: Ch 12 16; 12
Bassin Vauban Marina: Ch 09 *Season 0700-2400
depending on tide, Out of season 0800-1200 1400-1800*
Les Bas Sablons Marina: Ch 09 *Season 0700-2100,
Out of season 0800-1200 1400-1700*
Dinard Marina: Ch 09 *Season 0700-2100, Out of sea-
son 0830-1200 1330-1800*
Rance Lock: Ch 13
Plover-sur-Rance Marina: Ch 13
LE LÉGUÉ, S BRIEUC *Call Légué Port :* **Ch 16; 12**
2h-HW-1.30h and 1h-HW-1h depending on height of tide
SAINT-QUAY PORTRIEUX Marina: Ch 09
PAIMPOL-PONTRIEUX
Paimpol: Ch 09 *2h-HW-2h*
Lézardrieux Marina: Ch 09
Pontrieux Lock: Ch 12 *2h-HW-1h*
Tréguier Marina: Ch 09 *Season Mon-Sat 0800-1200*

*1330-2100, Sun 0800-1000 1600-1800, Out of season
Tue-Sat 0800-1200 1330-1700, Sun and Mon closed*
ROSCOFF-BLOSCON: Ch 16; 12 *0830-1200 1330-
1800*
Marina: Ch 09 *0800-1200 1330-1730*
MORLAIX Marina: Ch 16; 09 *2h-HW-2h*
CORSEN-OUESSANT Maritime Traffic Service:
keep listening watch on **Ch 16**
Ouessant Traffic Control Centre *Call Ouessant Traffic*
Ch 11* 16; 11* 68
Vigie d'Ouessant, *Call Le Stitt:* **Ch 16**
Vigie de Saint-Mathieu: Ch 16
Cap de la Chevre: Ch 16 *HJ*
Vigie du Raz: Ch 16
Information: Ch 79 *every H+10 and H+40*
CORSEN CROSS: Ch 16 *Distress and Safety* **Ch 15
67 73** *SAR* **Ch 16** *Calling* **Ch 16 79** *Information*
BREST: *A compulsory reporting system exists for vessels
over 25m LOA - see ALRS Vol 6 Part 1,*
Port de Commerce: Ch 16; 12
Marina: Ch 09 *Season 0800-2000, Out of season 0830-
1800, Holidays 0900-1200 1400-1900*
DOUARNENEZ: Ch 16; 12 *0800-1200 1330-1730*
Marina: Ch 09 *Season 0700-1200 1330-2100, Out of
season 0800-1200 1300-1700*
SAINT GUENOLE: Ch 12 *HJ*
Le GUILVINEC: Ch 12
LOCTUDY: Ch 12 *Portable VHF Mon-Fri 0630-1200
1400-1900 Sat 0800-1200*
Marina: Ch 09 *Season 0730-2100, Out of season Mon-
Sat 0830-1200 1330-1800, Sun and holidays closed*
PORT-LA-FORÊT Marina: Ch 09 *Season 0800-
2000, Out of season Mon-Sat 0830-1200 1330-1830 Sun
and holidays 0900-1200 1330-1830*
CONCARNEAU: Ch 16; 12
Marina: Ch 09 *Season 0700-2100, Out of season 0900-
1200 1330-1730*
BÉNODET Marina: Ch 09 *Season 0800-2000, Out
of season 0800-1200 1400-1800*
SAINTE-MARINE Marina: Ch 09 *Season 0800-
1200 1500-2000, Out of season 0800-1200 1400-1800*
LORIENT *Call Vigie Port Louis :* **Ch 16; 12**
Marina: Ch 09 *Hrs as Kernevel*
Kernevel Marina *Private :* **Ch 09** *Season 0800-1230
1330-2000, Out of season Mon-Sat 0830-1230 1400-
1800, Sun and holidays 0900-1230*
Kernevel Marina *Public :* **Ch 09** *Season 0830-1900,
Out of season 0830-1230 1400-1800*
ÉTEL CROSS: Ch 16; 11 *Distress and Safety* **Ch 13
16 80** *Information and Calling*
Information: Ch 13 or 80, *following call on* **Ch 16.**
*Urgent navigational messages broadcast on receipt and then
every 2h. Non-urgent navigational messages broadcast 0433
and 2133 after weather forecasts.*
ÉTEL: Ch 16; 13 *Season Mon-Sat 0800-1200 1400-
1800, Sun 1000-1200*
PORT-HALIGUEN Marina: Ch 09 *Season 0800-
1230 1400-2000, Out of season 0900-1200 1400-1800*
LA TRINITÉ-SUR-MER Marina: Ch 09 *Season
0830-1900, Out of season 0830-1230 1400-1800*
LE CROUESTY Marina: Ch 09 *Season 0800-2000,
Out of season 0900-1230 1330-1800*
VANNES Marina: Ch 09 *Season 0830-2100, Out of
season 2.30h-HW-2.30h Morning 0900-1230*
ARZAL-CAMOËL Marina: Ch 09 *Season 0830-
1230 1400-2000, Out of season 0830-1230 1330-1730*

Lock: Ch 18 *HX*
PORNICHET Marina: Ch 09 *Season 0800-2100,
Out of season 0800-2000*
LA LOIRE Signal Station *Call Chemoulin* : **Ch 16**
Reporting system *Compulsory for all commercial vessels* : **Ch 12* 16; 06 12* 14 67 69**
Saint-Nazaire: Ch 12* 16; 06 12* 14 67 69
Information: *Tidal information between Saint-Nazaire and Nantes is automatically broadcast on* **Ch 73** *at H+00, H+15, H+30 and H+45*
Donges: Ch 12 16
Nantes: Ch 12* 16; 06 12* 14 67 69
Pornic Marina: Ch 09
PORT-JOINVILLE, Île D'Yeu, Marina: Ch 09. *Contact the Hr Mr before arrival. Entry to wet basin possible 2h- HW-2h, mooring by arrangement with Hr Mr.*
LES SABLES D'OLONNE: Ch 12 *Hr Mr Mon-Fri 0800-1800, Lock 2h-HW-2h or 1.30h-HW-1.30h depending on tide*
Marina: Ch 09
PORT DE BOURGENAY Marina: Ch 09 16
LA ROCHELLE-PALLICE: Ch 12* 16; 12*
Marina: Ch 09
ROCHEFORT: Ch 16; 12
Marina: Ch 09 *1h-HW-1h*
BORDEAUX *Movement Reporting System. This is compulsory for all vessels in the area extending from BXA Lt buoy to Bordeaux:* **Ch 12** *Hr Mr* **Ch 12; 16** *Radar .*
Information: *The height of water between Le Verdon and Bordeaux is broadcast automatically every 5 min on* **Ch 17.**
Royan: Ch 16; 09 *Ch 09 Season 0800-2000, Out of season 0900-1800 except Sat afternoons and Sun*
Le Verdon: Ch 16; 11 12 14
Pauillac Port: Ch 12
Pauillac Marina: Ch 09
Blaye: Ch 12
Ambes: Ch 12
Bordeaux Port: Ch 16; 12
Bordeaux Marina: Ch 09 *office hours during season*
SOULAC CROSS: Ch 16; 11 *Distress and Safety* **Ch 13 16 79** *Information and Calling* **Ch 16** *H24 Other frequencies HX*
Information: **Ch 13** or **Ch 79** *following announcement on* **Ch 16.** *Urgent navigational information is broadcast on receipt and then every 2h. Non-urgent navigational information is broadcast at 0433 and 2133 after the weather forecast.*
ARCACHON Marina: Ch 09
CAPBRETON: Ch 09
ANGLET Marina: Ch 16; 12 *Season 0700-2000, Out of season* *0730-1830*
BAYONNE: Ch 09 12
HENDAYE Marina: Ch 09

SPAIN
COASTAL RADIO
0901 Pasajes Ch 16 25 26 27*
Remotely controlled from CCR at Bilbao. Traffic lists: **Ch 27:** *0233 0633 0833 1033 1233 1633 1833 2233*
0905 Bilbao Ch 04 16 26*
Remotely controlled from CCR at Bilbao. Traffic lists: **Ch 26:** *0233 0633 0833 1033 1233 1633 1833 2233*
0910 Santander Ch 16 24*
Remotely controlled from CCR at Bilbao. Traffic lists: **Ch 24:** *0233 0633 0833 1033 1233 1633 1833 2233*
0914 Gijón. **Call Gijón Traffic Ch 16 10 15 17.**

Distress and safety only
0916 Cabo Peñas Ch 16 25 26*
Remotely controlled from CCR at Bilbao. Traffic lists: **Ch 26:** *0233 0633 0833 1033 1233 1633 1833 2233*
0918 Navia Ch 16 27*
Remotely controlled from CCR at Bilbao. Traffic lists: **Ch 27:** *0233 0633 0833 1033 1233 1633 1833 2233*
0919 Cabo Ortegal Ch 16 02*
Remotely controlled from CCR at La Coruña. Traffic lists: **Ch 21:** *0303 0703 0903 1103 1303 1703 1903 2303*
0924 Coruña (MRSC) Ch 16
0925 Coruña Ch 16 26*
Remotely controlled from CCR at La Coruña. Traffic lists: **Ch 26:** *0303 0703 0903 1103 1303 1703 1903 2303*
0927 Finisterre Ch 01* 16 22
Remotely controlled from CCR at La Coruña. Traffic lists: **Ch 01:** *0303 0703 0903 1103 1303 1703 1903 2303*
0928 Finisterre. Call FLinisterre Traffic Ch 11 16
Distress and Safety only
0929 Vigo Ch 16 20
Remotely controlled from CCR at La Coruña. Traffic lists: **Ch 20:** *0303 0703 0903 1103 1303 1703 1903 2303*
0930 La Guardia Ch 16 21*
Remotely controlled from CCR at La Coruña.

PORT RADIO
PASAJES Pilots *Call Pasajes Prácticos* : **Ch 16; 11 12 13 14***
BILBAO: Ch 12* 16; 12 13 14
Signal Station: Ch 16; 12 13 *HX*
Petronor Refinery: Ch 16; 11 12 14
SANTANDER Pilots: Ch 16; 06 12 14 *PV* **Ch 16; 09 12* 14** *Office*
GIJÓN Pilots: Ch 16; 11 12 14*
REQUEJADA, SUANCES Pilots: Ch 12 16 *When vessel expected*
AVILÉS Pilots: Ch 12; 06 09 14 16 *PV* **16; 11 12 14*** *Office*
RIBADEO Pilots: Ch 16
PUERTO DE SAN CIPRIÁN: Ch 12 14 16
EL FERROL DEL CAUDILLO Pilots: Ch 14* 16; 10 11 12 13 14 *Ch 14 H24*
LA CORUÑA: Ch 16; 12 *HX*
CORCUBIÓN Pilots: Ch 16; 14 *When vessel expected*
FINISTERRE Maritime Traffic Service: Ch 11 16
Voluntary reporting for non-Spanish vessels
VILLAGARCIA DE AROSA: Ch 16; 12
PUERTO DE MARIN *Call Marin Pilots* : **Ch 16; 06** *When vessel expected*
PUERO DE VIGO *Call Vigo Prácticos* : **Ch 16; 14** *HX*

PORTUGAL
COASTAL RADIO
0935 Arga Ch 16 25 28 83
Remotely controlled from Lisboa
0949 Arestal Ch 16 24 26 85
Remotely controlled from Lisboa
0950 Montejunto Ch 16 23 87
Remotely controlled from Lisboa
0952 Lisboa Ch 16 23 25 26 27 28
0958 Atalaia Ch 16 24 26 85
Remotely controlled from Lisboa
0959 Picos Ch 16 23 27 85
Remotely controlled from Lisboa
0960 Sagres (RadioNavel) Ch 11 16
Remotely controlled from Lisboa
0963 Estoi Ch 16 24 28 86

Remotely controlled from Lisboa

PORT RADIO

CAMINHA *Call Postradcaminha* : **Ch 16; 11** *Mon-Fri 0900-1200 1400-1700*
VIANA DO CASTELO *Call Postradviana* : **Ch 16; 11** *Mon-Fri 0900-1200 1400-1700*
PÓVOA DE VARZIM *Call Postradvarzim* : **Ch 16; 11** *Mon-Fri 0900-1200 1400-1700*
VILA DO CONDE *Call Postradviconde* : **Ch 16; 11** *Mon-Fri 0900-1200 1400-1700*
LEIXÕES *Call Postradleixões* : **Ch 16; 11 13 19 60** Port **Ch 16** *Distress and Safety* **Ch 06 08** *Intership* **Ch 74** *Oil Terminal* **Ch 62** *Marinas*
Radar Station: Ch 12 16; 01 04 09 10 11 14 18 20 61 63 67 68 69 71 79 80 84 *Controls all radar, navigational, tidal and berthing information for Leixoes*
Posto Central: Ch 12; 18 67 68 *0730-1900 UT*
Serviços Maritimos: Ch 12; 18 67 68 *0700-2400*
Bascule Bridge *Call Pónte Movel* : **Ch 12; 18 67 68**
DOURO *Call Postraddouro* : **Ch 16; 11** *Mon-Fri 0900-1200 1400-1700*
AVEIRO *Call Postradaveiro* : **Ch 16; 11** *Mon-Fri 0900-1200 1400-1700*
FIGUEIRA DA FOZ *Call Postradfoz* : **Ch 16; 11** *Mon-Fri 0900-1200 1400-1700*
NAZARÉ *Call Postradnazare* : **Ch 16; 11** *Mon-Fri 0900-1200 1400-1700*
BERLENGA *Call Postradberlenga* : **Ch 16; 11**
PENICHE *Call Postradpeniche* : **Ch 16; 11**
LISBOA *Call Contrololisboa* : **Ch 12 16; 12** *Calling and Safety* **Ch 13** *Intership Safety* **Ch 11 63** *Ship to Shore* **Ch 16; 11** *Control* **Ch 67** *Rescue . When near to Forte de S Juliao, on entering or leaving, vessels should report on* **Ch 12 or 16** *working* **Ch 11** *and when navigating within the hr approach and the hr, maintain continuous listening watch on* **Ch 13.**
Information *In Portuguese* : **Ch 11** *1030 and 1630 UT*
Doca de Pesca *Call Docopesca* : **Ch 03 12** *0100 Mon-0100 Sat*
Doca de Alcântara Lock: Ch 12; 05 *0700 0815 0915 1015 1115 1315 1500 1630 1800 UT*
Rocha Drydocks: Ch 14 74
Lisnave Drydocks, Margueira: Ch 14
Alfeite Sig Station *Call Radiosinaisfaleite* : **Ch 16; 11**
SESIMBRA *Call Postradsesimbra* : **Ch 16; 11** *Mon-Fri 0900-1200 1400-1700*
SETÚBAL *Call Postradsetúbal* : **Ch 16; 11**
SINES *Call Postradsines* : **Ch 16; 11 13**
Serviços Maritimos: Ch 12 16; 01 04 09 10 11 18 20 63 67 68 69 81 84
SAGRES, Posto Radionaval *Call Radnavalsagres:* **Ch 16; 11**
LAGOS *Call Postradlagos* : **Ch 16; 11** *Mon-Fri 0900-1200 1400-1700*
Marina: Ch 16; 62
PORTIMÃO *Call Postradportimão* : **Ch 16; 11** *Mon-Fri 0900-1200 1400-1700*
VILAMOURA Marina *Call Vilamouraradio* : **Ch 62; 20** *Mon-Sat 0900-1230 1400-1800*
FARO *Call Postradfaro* : **Ch 16; 11**
OLHÃO *Call Postradiolhão* : **Ch 16; 11**
Fishery Radio Station: Ch 03; 16 *Mon-Fri 0900-1200 Sat 0700-1200*
VILA REAL DE SANTO ANTÓNIO *Call*

Postradvilareal: **Ch 16; 11** *Mon-Fri 0900-1200 1400-1700*

SPAIN
COASTAL RADIO

1034 Cádiz Ch 16 20* 25 26 27
Remotely controlled from CCR at Málaga. Traffic lists: **Ch 20:** *0233 0633 0833 1033 1233 1633 1833 2233*
1043 Tarifa (MRCC) Ch 16
1044 Tarifa Ch 16 23 24 26 27*
Remotely controlled from CCR at Málaga. Traffic lists: **Ch 27:** *0233 0633 0833 1033 1233 1633 1833 2233*
1045 Algeciras Ch 01* 04 16 20 81
Remotely controlled from CCR at Málaga. Traffic lists: **Ch 01:** *0233 0633 0833 1033 1233 1633 1833 2233*

PORT RADIO

EL ROMPIDO Marina: Ch 09 16 *HX*
PUNTA UMBRÍA Marina: Ch 09 *HX*
Bridge: Call 16; 06 11 12 14* *Huelva Pilots*
PUERTO DE HUELVA *Call Huelva Barra Prácticos for Bar or Huelva Puerto Prácticos for Hr* : **Ch 16; 06 11 12 14***
Marina: Ch 09 16
La Rábida Refinery: Ch 16; 09 *HX*
RIO GUADALQUIVIR *Call Obras Puerto Sevilla* : **Ch 12**
Marina: Ch 09 16
PUERTO SHERRY Marina: Ch 09 16 *HX*
REAL CLUB NAUTICO DE SANTA MARIA Marina: Ch 09 16 *HX*
CÁDIZ
Real Club Nautico de Cadiz: Ch 09 16 *Call Cádiz Prácticos* : **Ch 16; 11 12 14*** *HX*
Cadiz Terminal: Ch 16; 09 *HX*
STRAIT OF GIBRALTAR Vessel Traffic Service *Call Tarifa Traffic* : **Ch 16; 10***
Information: *Urgent messages will be broadcast at any time on* **Ch 10 & Ch 16.** *Routine messages will be broadcast every even H+15 on* **Ch 10.**
ALGECIRAS *Call Algeciras Prácticos* : **Ch 16; 09 12 13** *HX*
Real Club Nautico de Algeciras: Ch 09 16 *HX*
Algeciras Iberia *Call Sea Land Iberia* : **Ch 16; 09** *HX*
Refineria Gibralta *CEPSA* : **Ch 13* 16; 09 11 13**

GIBRALTAR
COASTAL RADIO

1047 Gibraltar Ch 01 02 03 04¹ 16 23 24¹25 27 28¹ 86 87 *1)* **Ch 04** *is exclusively used for Autolink RT.* **Ch 24 & 28** *can be used as 2nd & 3rd choices respectively for Autolink RT services on a shared basis with the operaror during hours of service only.*

PORT RADIO

Port: Ch 16 06* 12* 13 14 *Ch 12* is the Gibraltar Bay Working Channel*
Lloyds Gibraltar Radio: Ch 08 16; 12* 14
Queen's Harbour Master: Ch 08 *Mon-Thu 0800-1630 Fri 0800-1600*
Queensway Quay Marina: Ch 73 *Summer 0830-2030, Winter 0830-2000*
Shepherd Marina: Ch 71 *Mon-Fri 0900-1300, 4130-1800, Sat 0900-1300*
Marina Bay: Ch 73 *Summer 0830-2230, Winter 0830-2030*

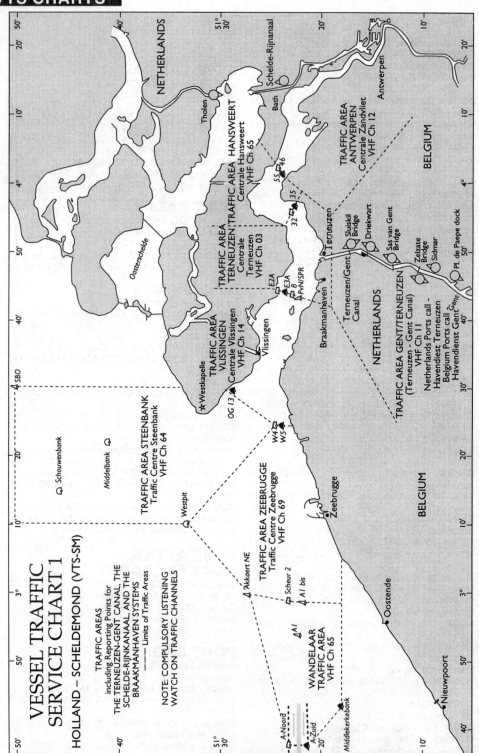

VESSEL TRAFFIC SERVICE CHART 1

HOLLAND – SCHELDEMOND (VTS-SM)

TRAFFIC AREAS
including Reporting Points for
THE TERNEUZEN-GENT CANAL, THE
SCHELDE-RIJNKANAAL, AND THE
BRAAKMANHAVEN SYSTEMS

——— Limits of Traffic Areas

NOTE: COMPULSORY LISTENING
WATCH ON TRAFFIC CHANNELS

NETHERLANDS

BELGIUM

Schelde-Rijnanaal

Tholen

Bath

Antwerpen

TRAFFIC AREA
ANTWERPEN
Centrale Zandvliet
VHF Ch 12

TRAFFIC AREA
HANSWEERT
Centrale Hansweert
VHF Ch 65

Oosterschelde

TRAFFIC AREA
TERNEUZEN
Centrale
Terneuzen
VHF Ch 03

55 / 46

35

32

Terneuzen

Sluiskil
Bridge

Driekwart

Sas van Gent

Zelzate
Bridge

Sidmar

Pt. de Paepe dock

E2A
E3A
8
PvN/SPR

Westkapelle

TRAFFIC AREA
VLISSINGEN
Centrale Vlissingen
VHF Ch 14

Vlissingen

Braakmanhaven

Terneuzen/Gent
Canal

NETHERLANDS

TRAFFIC AREA GENT/TERNEUZEN
(Terneuzen - Gent Canal)
VHF Ch 11
Netherlands Ports call -
Havendiest Terneuzen
Belgium Ports call
Havendienst Gent

OG 13

W4
W5

SBO

Schouwenbank

Middelbank

TRAFFIC AREA STEENBANK
Traffic Centre Steenbank
VHF Ch 64

Westpit

TRAFFIC AREA ZEEBRUGGE
Traffic Centre Zeebrugge
VHF Ch 69

Zeebrugge

BELGIUM

Oostende

Akkaert NE

Scheur 2

A1 bis

A1

WANDELAAR
TRAFFIC AREA
VHF Ch 65

Middelkerkebank

Nieuwpoort

A-Noord

A-Zuid

VESSEL TRAFFIC SERVICES CHART 2

HOLLAND – APPROACHES TO NIEUWE WATERWEG

- - - - - Traffic Separation Scheme

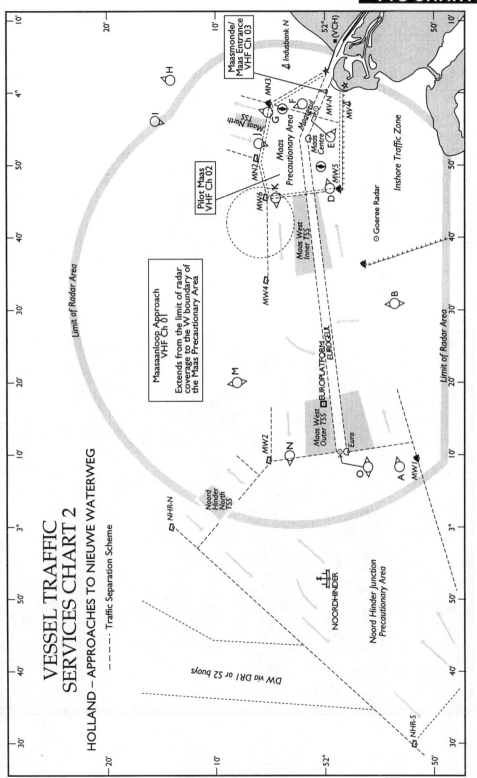

Maasmonde/Maas Entrance VHF Ch 03

Pilot Maas VHF Ch 02

Maasaanloop Approach VHF Ch 01

Extends from the limit of radar coverage to the W boundary of the Maas Precautionary Area

Limit of Radar Area

Maas North TSS

Maas Precautionary Area

Maas West Inner TSS

Maas West Outer TSS

Inshore Traffic Zone

© Goeree Radar

EUROPLATFORM

EUROGEUL

Noord Hinder North TSS

Noord Hinder Junction Precautionary Area

DW via DR1 or S2 buoys

NOORDHINDER

NHR-N

NHR-S

Indusbank N

(VCH)

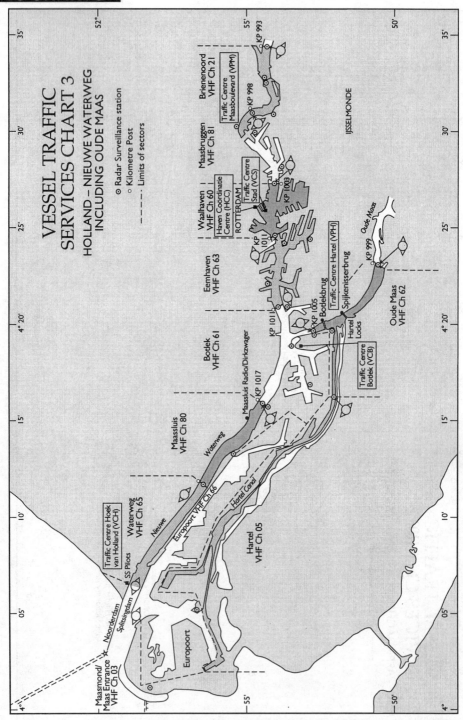

VESSEL TRAFFIC
SERVICES CHART 3

HOLLAND – NIEUWE WATERWEG
INCLUDING OUDE MAAS

⊚ Radar Surveillance station
○ Kilometre Post
– – – Limits of sectors

Brienenoord
VHF Ch 21

Traffic Centre
Maasboulevard (VPM)

IJSSELMONDE

Maasbruggen
VHF Ch 81

Waalhaven
VHF Ch 60

Haven Coordinatie
Centre (HCC)

Traffic Centre
Stad (VCS)

ROTTERDAM

KP 993
KP 998
KP 1003
KP 999

Oude Maas

Eemhaven
VHF Ch 63

Botek
VHF Ch 61

Botlekbrug

Traffic Centre Hartel (VPH)

Spijkenisserbrug

Hartel
Locks

Oude Maas
VHF Ch 62

KP 1011
KP 1005
KP 101

Maassluis Radio/Dirkzwager

Traffic Centre
Botlek (VCB)

KP 1017

Maassluis
VHF Ch 80

Waterweg

Nieuwe

Europoort VHF Ch 66

Hartel Canal

Hartel
VHF Ch 05

Traffic Centre Hoek
van Holland (VCH)

SS Pilots

Waterweg
VHF Ch 65

Noorderdam

Splitsingsdam

Europoort

Maasmond/
Maas Entrance
VHF Ch 03

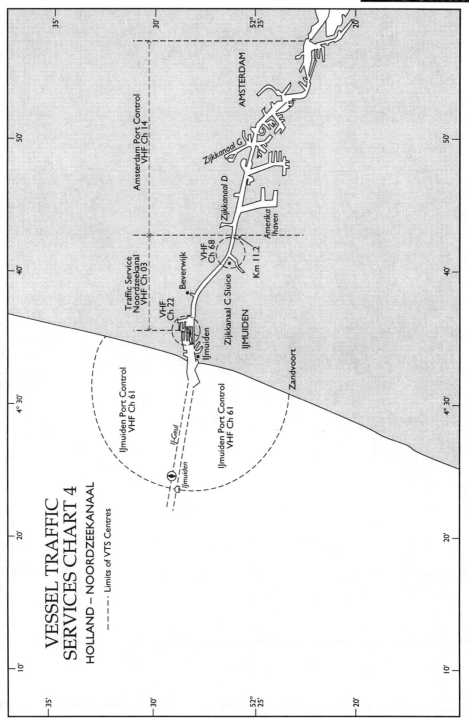

VESSEL TRAFFIC SERVICES CHART 4

HOLLAND – NOORDZEEKANAAL

– – – – Limits of VTS Centres

IJmuiden Port Control
VHF Ch 61

IJ-Geul

IJmuiden

IJmuiden Port Control
VHF Ch 61

Zandvoort

Traffic Service
Noordzeekanaal
VHF Ch 03

VHF
Ch 22

IJmuiden

IJmuiden

Zijkanaal C Sluice

IJMUIDEN

Beverwijk

VHF
Ch 68

Km 11.2

Amerika
haven

Zijkanaal D

Zijkanaal G

Amsterdam Port Control
VHF Ch 14

AMSTERDAM

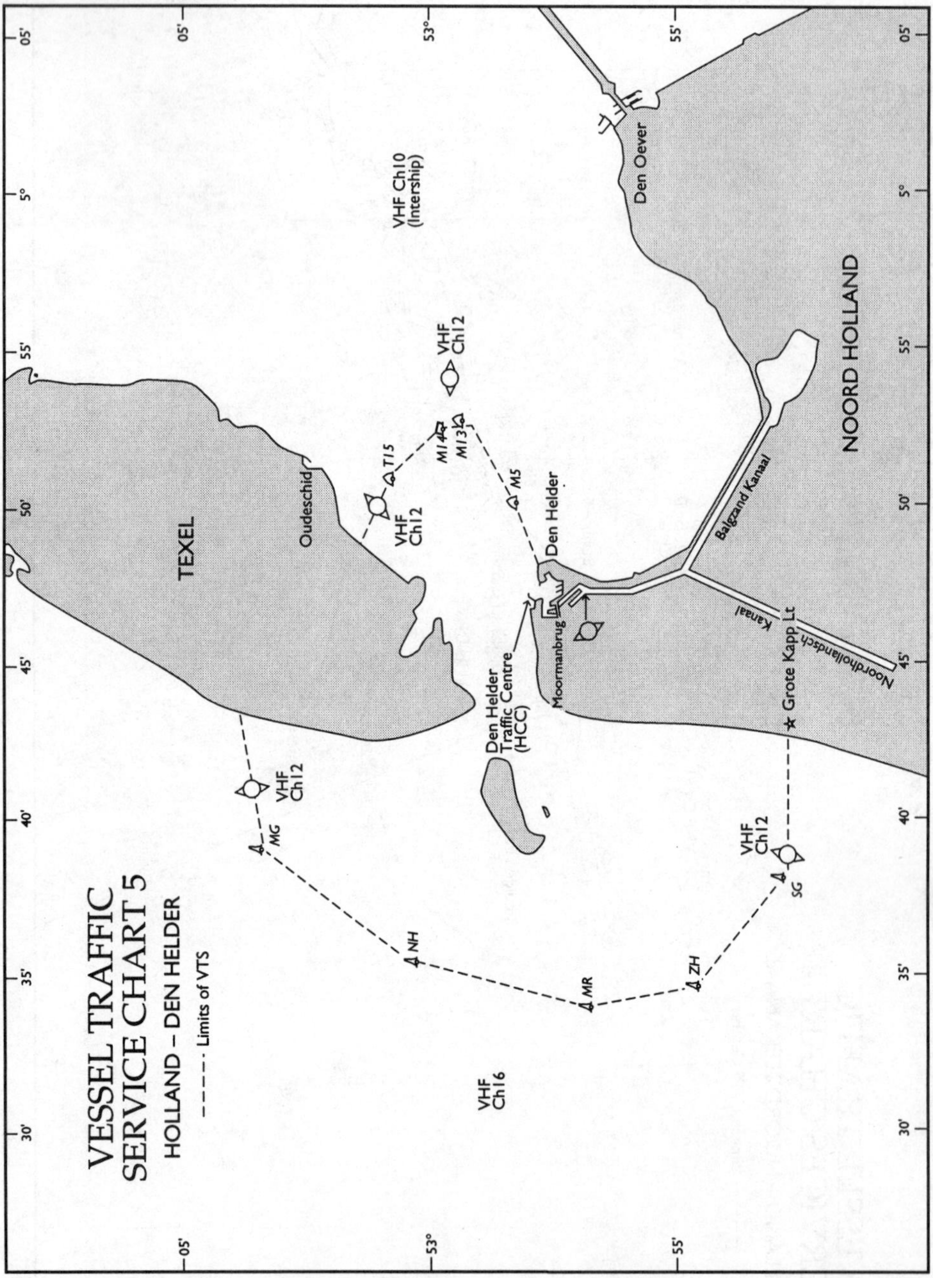

VESSEL TRAFFIC
SERVICE CHART 5
HOLLAND – DEN HELDER

------ Limits of VTS

VHF Ch16

VHF Ch10
(Intership)

NOORD HOLLAND

TEXEL

Oudeschild

Den Helder

Den Helder
Traffic Centre
(HCC)

Moormanbrug

Balgzand Kanaal

Noordhollandsch Kanaal

Grote Kapp Lt

Den Oever

VHF Ch12

VHF Ch12

VHF Ch12

VHF Ch12

VHF Ch12

MG

NH

MR

ZH

SG

MS

M14

M13

T15

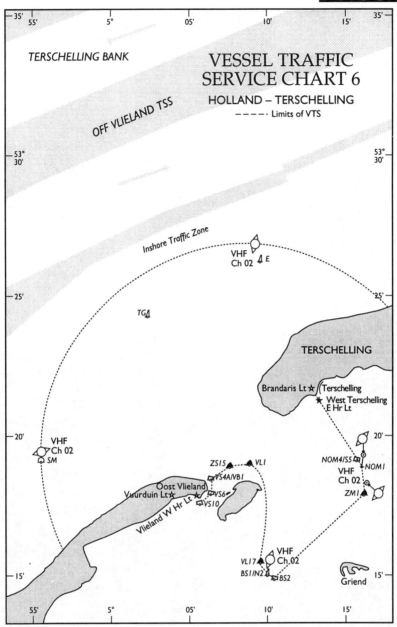

TERSCHELLING BANK

VESSEL TRAFFIC
SERVICE CHART 6
HOLLAND – TERSCHELLING
— — — — · Limits of VTS

OFF VLIELAND TSS

Inshore Traffic Zone

VHF
Ch 02   E

TG

TERSCHELLING

Brandaris Lt ★ Terschelling
★ West Terschelling
E Hr Lt

VHF
Ch 02
SM

ZS15   VLI

VS4A/VB1

Oost Vlieland
Vuurduin Lt★   VS6
VS10

Vlieland W Hr Lt

NOM4/S5   NOM1
VHF
Ch 02
ZM1

VHF
Ch 02
VL17
BS1/N2   BS2

Griend

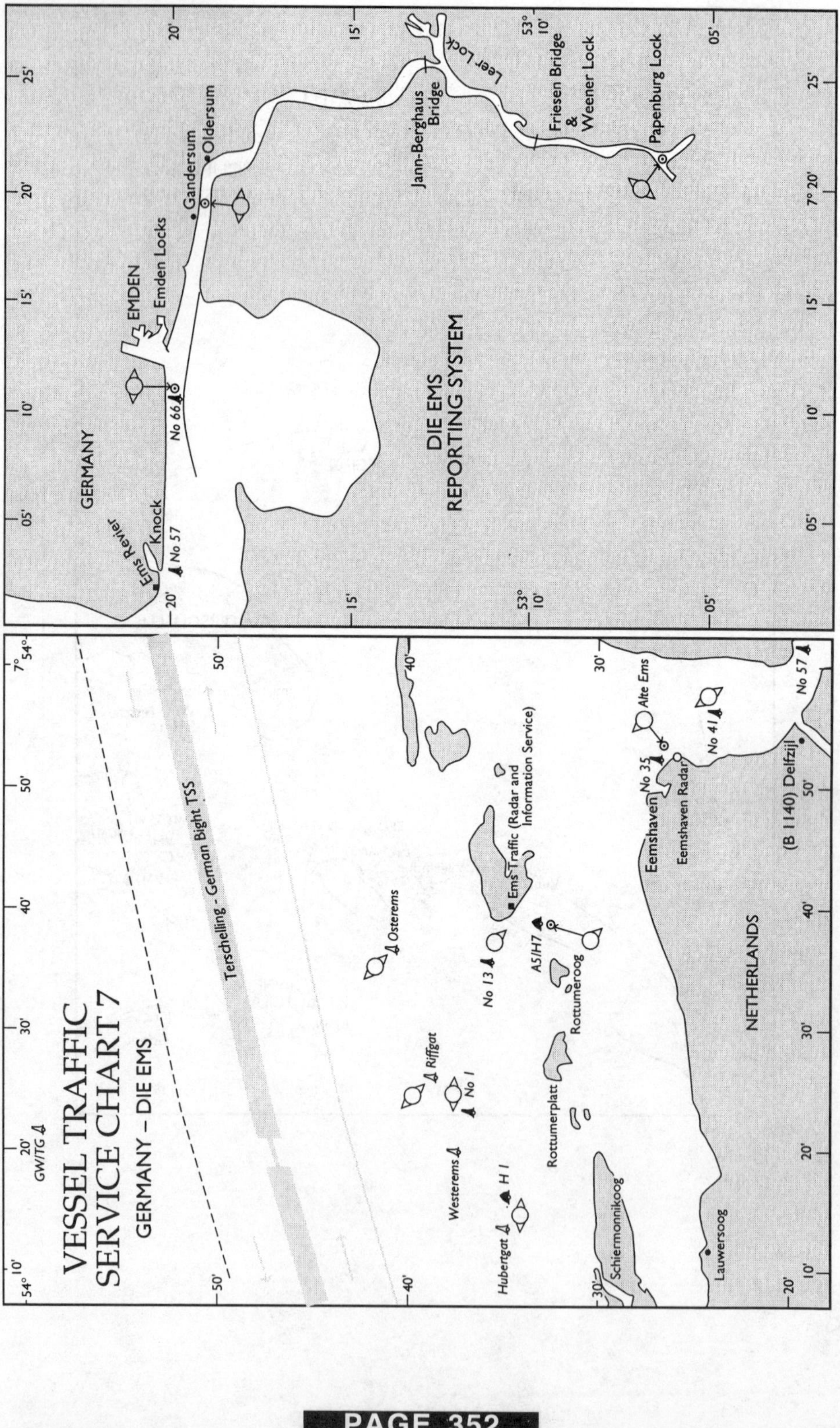

VESSEL TRAFFIC
SERVICE CHART 7
GERMANY – DIE EMS
GW/TG
Hubertgat
H 1
Westerems
Riffgat
No 1
Osterems
Terschelling - German Bight TSS
No 13
A5/H7
Rottumeroog
Rottumerplatt
Schiermonnikoog
Lauwersoog
NETHERLANDS
Ems Traffic (Radar and
Information Service)
Eemshaven
Eemshaven Radar
No 35
Alte Ems
No 41
No 57
(B 1140) Delfzijl
DIE EMS
REPORTING SYSTEM
GERMANY
Ems Revier
Knock
No 57
No 66
EMDEN
Emden Locks
Gandersum
Oldersum
Jann-Berghaus
Bridge
Leer Lock
Friesen Bridge
&
Weener Lock
Papenburg Lock
54°
53°
7°
7° 20'
10'
20'
30'
40'
50'
05'
15'
25'

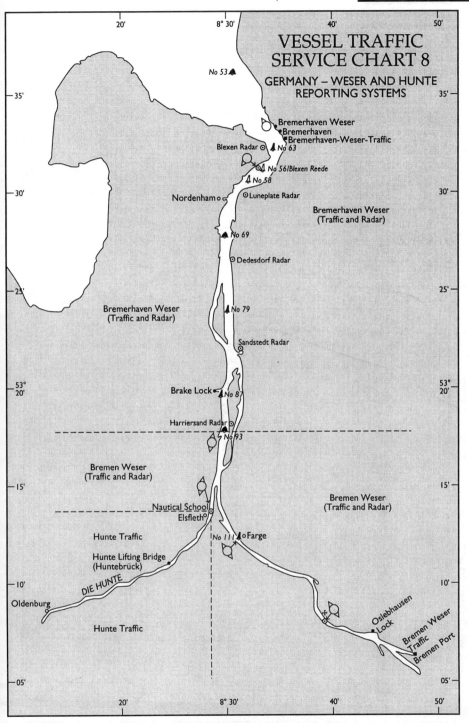

VESSEL TRAFFIC SERVICE CHART 8

GERMANY – WESER AND HUNTE REPORTING SYSTEMS

No 53

Bremerhaven Weser
Bremerhaven
Bremerhaven-Weser-Traffic

Blexen Radar
No 63

No 56/Blexen Reede

No 58

Nordenham
Luneplate Radar

Bremerhaven Weser
(Traffic and Radar)

No 69

Dedesdorf Radar

Bremerhaven Weser
(Traffic and Radar)

No 79

Sandstedt Radar

Brake Lock
No 87

Harriersand Radar
No 93

Bremen Weser
(Traffic and Radar)

Bremen Weser
(Traffic and Radar)

Nautical School
Elsfleth

Hunte Traffic

No 111 Farge

Hunte Lifting Bridge
(Huntebrück)

DIE HUNTE

Oldenburg

Oslebhausen
Lock

Bremen Weser
Traffic

Bremen Port

Hunte Traffic

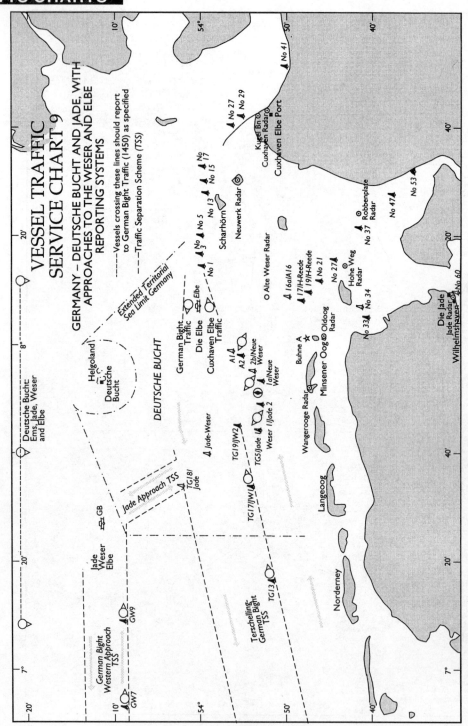

VESSEL TRAFFIC SERVICE CHART 9

GERMANY – DEUTSCHE BUCHT AND JADE, WITH APPROACHES TO THE WESER AND ELBE REPORTING SYSTEMS

– – – – Vessels crossing these lines should report to German Bight Traffic (1450) as specified

– · – · – Traffic Separation Scheme (TSS)

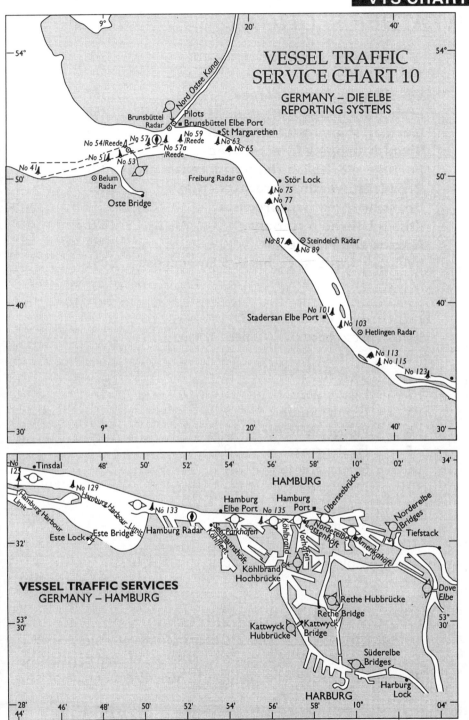

VESSEL TRAFFIC SERVICE CHART 10

GERMANY – DIE ELBE REPORTING SYSTEMS

Nord Ostee Kanal

Pilots
Brunsbüttel Radar
Brunsbüttel Elbe Port
St Margarethen
No 54/Reede
No 57
No 59 /Reede
No 63
No 57a /Reede
No 65
No 51
No 53
No 41

Belum Radar
Freiburg Radar
Stör Lock
No 75
No 77

Oste Bridge

No 87
Steindeich Radar
No 89

Stadersan Elbe Port
No 101
No 103
Hetlingen Radar

No 113
No 115
No 123

VESSEL TRAFFIC SERVICES
GERMANY – HAMBURG

Tinsdal
No 121
No 129
Hamburg Harbour Limit
No 133
Hamburg Elbe Port
Hamburg Port
No 135
HAMBURG
Überseebrücke
Norderelbe Bridges
Hamburg Harbour Limit
Este Lock
Este Bridge
Hamburg Radar
Seemannshöft
Parkhafen
Köhlbrand
Vorhafen
Norderelbe
Lotsenhöft
Amerikahöft
Tiefstack
Köhlfleet
Seemannshöft
Köhlbrand Hochbrücke
Rethe Hubbrücke
Dove Elbe
Rethe Bridge
Kattwyck Hubbrücke
Kattwyck Bridge
Süderelbe Bridges
Harburg Lock
HARBURG

WEATHER SECTION

CONTENTS

UK shipping forecast areas 357
French shipping forecast areas 358
German shipping forecast areas 359
Spanish shipping forecast areas 360
Portugese & Italian shipping forecast areas .. 361
Broadcast weather forecasts - marine 362
Broadcast weather forecasts
- main UK radio stations 381
Navtex and Marinecall 384
Weather forecast terms in 5 languages 385

THE BEAUFORT SCALE

Force	Description	Speed in knots
0	Calm	0
1	Light air	2
2	Light breeze	5
3	Gentle breeze	9
4	Moderate breeze	13
5	Fresh breeze	19
6	Strong breeze	24
7	Near gale	30
8	Gale	37
9	Strong gale	44
10	Storm	52
11	Violent storm	60
12	Hurricane	64

FORECAST TIME DEFINITIONS

Imminent: Expected within 6 hours of time of issue
Soon: Expected within 6 to 12 hours of time of issue
Later: Expected more than 12 hours from of time of issue

TELEPHONE & FAX WEATHER FORECASTS

Please see *page 384* for details of Marinecall telephone and fax weather forecasts

UK SHIPPING FORECAST AREAS

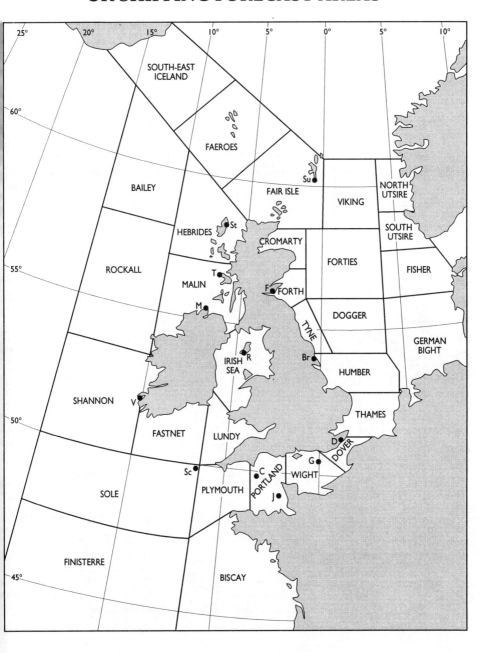

FRENCH SHIPPING FORECAST AREAS

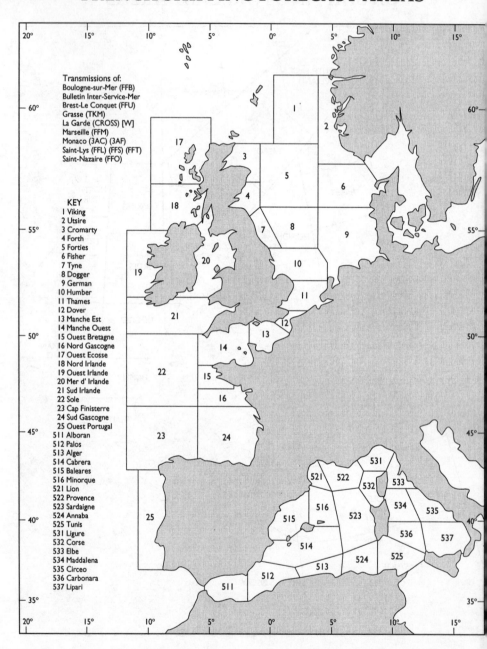

Transmissions of:
Boulogne-sur-Mer (FFB)
Bulletin Inter-Service-Mer
Brest-Le Conquet (FFU)
Grasse (TKM)
La Garde (CROSS) [W]
Marseille (FFM)
Monaco (3AC) (3AF)
Saint-Lys (FFL) (FFS) (FFT)
Saint-Nazaire (FFO)

KEY
1 Viking
2 Utsire
3 Cromarty
4 Forth
5 Forties
6 Fisher
7 Tyne
8 Dogger
9 German
10 Humber
11 Thames
12 Dover
13 Manche Est
14 Manche Ouest
15 Ouest Bretagne
16 Nord Gascogne
17 Ouest Ecosse
18 Nord Irlande
19 Ouest Irlande
20 Mer d' Irlande
21 Sud Irlande
22 Sole
23 Cap Finisterre
24 Sud Gascogne
25 Ouest Portugal
511 Alboran
512 Palos
513 Alger
514 Cabrera
515 Baleares
516 Minorque
521 Lion
522 Provence
523 Sardaigne
524 Annaba
525 Tunis
531 Ligure
532 Corse
533 Elbe
534 Maddalena
535 Circeo
536 Carbonara
537 Lipari

GERMAN SHIPPING FORECAST AREAS

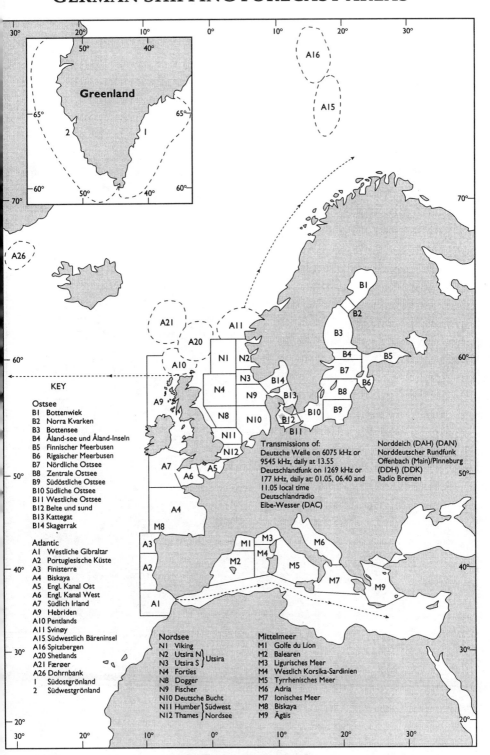

Greenland

2   1

A26

A16

A15

B1

B2

A21   A11   B3

A20   B4   B5

A10   N1   N2   B7

N3   B14   B6

N4   N9   B13   B8

A9   N8   N10   B12   B10   B9

N11   B11

Transmissions of:
Deutsche Welle on 6075 kHz or
9545 kHz, daily at 13.55
Deutschlandfunk on 1269 kHz or
177 kHz, daily at: 01.05, 06.40 and
11.05 local time
Deutschlandradio
Elbe-Wesser (DAC)

Norddeich (DAH) (DAN)
Norddeutscher Rundfunk
Offenbach (Main)/Pinneburg
(DDH) (DDK)
Radio Bremen

N12   A7   A5   A6

KEY

Ostsee
B1   Bottenwiek
B2   Norra Kvarken
B3   Bottensee
B4   Åland-see und Åland-Inseln
B5   Finnischer Meerbusen
B6   Rigaischer Meerbusen
B7   Nördliche Ostsee
B8   Zentrale Ostsee
B9   Südöstliche Ostsee
B10 Südliche Ostsee
B11 Westliche Ostsee
B12 Belte und sund
B13 Kattegat
B14 Skagerrak

Atlantic
A1   Westliche Gibraltar
A2   Portugiesische Küste
A3   Finisterre
A4   Biskaya
A5   Engl. Kanal Ost
A6   Engl. Kanal West
A7   Südlich Irland
A9   Hebriden
A10 Pentlands
A11 Svinøy
A15 Südwestlich Bäreninsel
A16 Spitzbergen
A20 Shetlands
A21 Færøer
A26 Dohrnbank
1   Südostgrönland
2   Südwestgrönland

A8   A3   M3   M1   M6

M4   M2   M5

A2   M7   M9

A1

M8

Nordsee
N1   Viking
N2   Utsira N } Utsira
N3   Utsira S }
N4   Forties
N8   Dogger
N9   Fischer
N10 Deutsche Bucht
N11 Humber } Südwest
N12 Thames } Nordsee

Mittelmeer
M1   Golfe du Lion
M2   Balearen
M3   Ligurisches Meer
M4   Westlich Korsika-Sardinien
M5   Tyrrhenisches Meer
M6   Adria
M7   Ionisches Meer
M8   Biskaya
M9   Ägäis

SPANISH SHIPPING FORECAST AREAS

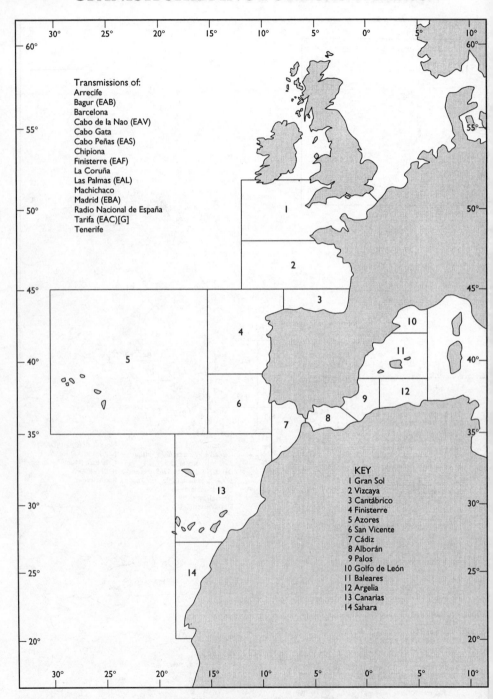

Transmissions of:
Arrecife
Bagur (EAB)
Barcelona
Cabo de la Nao (EAV)
Cabo Gata
Cabo Peñas (EAS)
Chipiona
Finisterre (EAF)
La Coruña
Las Palmas (EAL)
Machichaco
Madrid (EBA)
Radio Nacional de España
Tarifa (EAC)[G]
Tenerife

KEY
1 Gran Sol
2 Vizcaya
3 Cantábrico
4 Finisterre
5 Azores
6 San Vicente
7 Cádiz
8 Alborán
9 Palos
10 Golfo de León
11 Baleares
12 Argelia
13 Canarias
14 Sahara

PORTUGUESE SHIPPING FORECAST AREAS

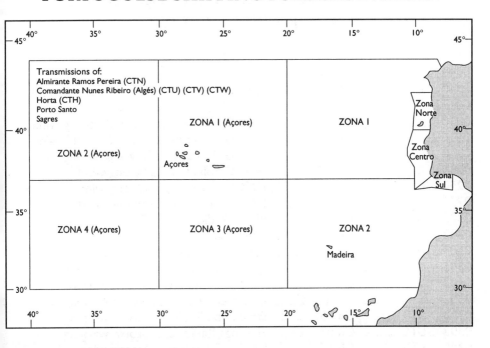

ITALIAN SHIPPING FORECAST AREAS

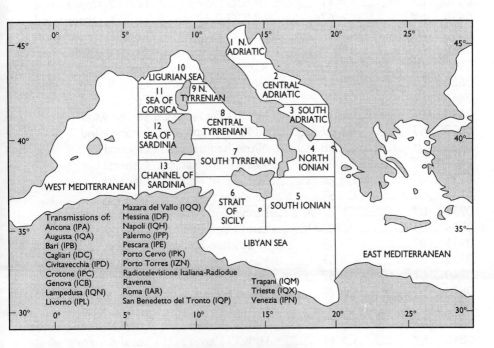

ROUND THE CLOCK WEATHER FORECASTS
UK SOUTH & SOUTH WEST COAST

Time	Ch/Freq	Source	Forecast
0018 .... UT	Ch 28	Niton Radio	Storm warning
0040 .... LT	Ch 67	HMCG Solent	Local & strong wind
0040 .... LT	Ch 11	HMCG Dover	Local & strong wind
0048 .... LT	198 kHz	Radio 4	General
0050 .... LT	Ch 67	HMCG Brixham	Local & strong wind
0140 .... LT	Ch 67	HMCG Falmouth	Local & strong wind
0220 .... LT	Ch 67	HMCG Portland	Local & strong wind
0240 .... LT	Ch 67	HMCG Solent	Strong wind
0240 .... LT	Ch 11	HMCG Dover	Strong wind
0250 .... LT	Ch 67	HMCG Brixham	Strong wind
0303 .... UT	Ch 28	Niton Radio	Storm warning
0303 .... UT	Ch 05	Weymouth Radio	Storm warning
0303 .... UT	Ch 26	Start Point Radio	Storm warning
0303 .... UT	Ch 62	Pendennis Radio	Storm warning
0303 .... UT	Ch 27 64'	Land's End Radio	Storm warning
0303 .... UT	2670 kHz	Land's End Radio	Storm warning
0303 .... UT	Ch 05	Ilfracombe Radio	Storm warning
0303 .... UT	Ch 07	Hastings Radio	Storm warning
0340 .... LT	Ch 67	HMCG Falmouth	Strong wind
0418 .... UT	Ch 28	Niton Radio	Storm warning
0420 .... LT	Ch 67	HMCG Portland	Strong wind
0440 .... LT	Ch 67	HMCG Solent	Local & strong wind
0440 .... LT	Ch 11	HMCG Dover	Local & strong wind
0450 .... LT	Ch 67	HMCG Brixham	Local & strong wind
0540 .... LT	Ch 67	HMCG Falmouth	Local & strong wind
0550 .... LT	198 kHz	Radio 4	Coastal waters
0555 .... LT	198 kHz	Radio 4	General
0620 .... LT	Ch 67	HMCG Portland	Local & strong wind
0640 .... LT	Ch 67	HMCG Solent	Strong wind
0640 .... LT	Ch 11	HMCG Dover	Strong wind
0650 .... LT	Ch 67	HMCG Brixham	Strong wind
0733 .... UT	Ch 28	Niton Radio	General
0733 .... UT	Ch 05	Weymouth Radio	General
0733 .... UT	Ch 26	Start Point Radio	General
0733 .... UT	Ch 62	Pendennis Radio	General
0733 .... UT	Ch 27 64'	Land's End Radio	General
0733 .... UT	2670 kHz	Land's End Radio	General
0733 .... UT	Ch 05	Ilfracombe Radio	General
0733 .... UT	Ch 07	Hastings Radio	General
0740 .... LT	Ch 67	HMCG Falmouth	Strong wind
0818 .... UT	Ch 28	Niton Radio	Storm warning
0820 .... LT	Ch 67	HMCG Portland	Strong wind
0840 .... LT	Ch 67	HMCG Solent	Local & strong wind
0840 .... LT	Ch 11	HMCG Dover	Local & strong wind

UK SOUTH & SOUTH WEST COAST

Time	Ch/Freq	Source	Forecast
0850 .... *LT*	Ch 67	HMCG Brixham	Local & strong wind
0903 .... *UT*	Ch 28	Niton Radio	Storm warning
0903 .... *UT*	Ch 05	Weymouth Radio	Storm warning
0903 .... *UT*	Ch 26	Start Point Radio	Storm warning
0903 .... *UT*	Ch 62	Pendennis Radio	Storm warning
0903 .... *UT*	Ch 27 64'	Land's End Radio	Storm warning
0903 .... *UT*	2670 kHz	Land's End Radio	Storm warning
0903 .... *UT*	Ch 05	Ilfracombe Radio	Storm warning
0903 .... *UT*	Ch 07	Hastings Radio	Storm warning
0940 .... *LT*	Ch 67	HMCG Falmouth	Local & strong wind
1020 .... *LT*	Ch 67	HMCG Portland	Local & strong wind
1040 .... *LT*	Ch 67	HMCG Solent	Strong wind
1040 .... *LT*	Ch 11	HMCG Dover	Strong wind
1050 .... *LT*	Ch 67	HMCG Brixham	Strong wind
1140 .... *LT*	Ch 67	HMCG Falmouth	Strong wind
1218 .... *UT*	Ch 28	Niton Radio	Storm warning
1220 .... *LT*	Ch 67	HMCG Portland	Strong wind
1240 .... *LT*	Ch 67	HMCG Solent	Local & strong wind
1240 .... *LT*	Ch 11	HMCG Dover	Local & strong wind
1250 .... *LT*	Ch 67	HMCG Brixham	Local & strong wind
1340 .... *LT*	Ch 67	HMCG Falmouth	Local & strong wind
1355 .... *LT*	198 kHz	Radio 4	General
1420 .... *LT*	Ch 67	HMCG Portland	Local & strong wind
1440 .... *LT*	Ch 67	HMCG Solent	Strong wind
1440 .... *LT*	Ch 11	HMCG Dover	Strong wind
1450 .... *LT*	Ch 67	HMCG Brixham	Strong wind
1503 .... *UT*	Ch 28	Niton Radio	Storm warning
1503 .... *UT*	Ch 05	Weymouth Radio	Storm warning
1503 .... *UT*	Ch 26	Start Point Radio	Storm warning
1503 .... *UT*	Ch 62	Pendennis Radio	Storm warning
1503 .... *UT*	Ch 27 64'	Land's End Radio	Storm warning
1503 .... *UT*	2670 kHz	Land's End Radio	Storm warning
1503 .... *UT*	Ch 05	Ilfracombe Radio	Storm warning
1503 .... *UT*	Ch 07	Hastings Radio	Storm warning
1540 .... *LT*	Ch 67	HMCG Falmouth	Strong wind
1618 .... *UT*	Ch 28	Niton Radio	Storm warning
1620 .... *LT*	Ch 67	HMCG Portland	Strong wind
1640 .... *LT*	Ch 67	HMCG Solent	Local & strong wind
1640 .... *LT*	Ch 11	HMCG Dover	Local & strong wind
1650 .... *LT*	Ch 67	HMCG Brixham	Local & strong wind
1740 .... *LT*	Ch 67	HMCG Falmouth	Local & strong wind
1750 .... *LT*	198 kHz	Radio 4	General
1820 .... *LT*	Ch 67	HMCG Portland	Local & strong wind
1840 .... *LT*	Ch 67	HMCG Solent	Strong wind
1840 .... *LT*	Ch 11	HMCG Dover	Strong wind

UK SOUTH & SOUTH WEST COAST

Time	Ch/Freq	Source	Forecast
1840 .... *LT*	Ch 11	HMCG Dover	Strong wind
1850 .... *LT*	Ch 67	HMCG Brixham	Strong wind
1933 .... *UT*	Ch 28	Niton Radio	General
1933 .... *UT*	Ch 05	Weymouth Radio	General
1933 .... *UT*	Ch 26	Start Point Radio	General
1933 .... *UT*	Ch 62	Pendennis Radio	General
1933 .... *UT*	Ch 27 64'	Land's End Radio	General
1933 .... *UT*	2670 kHz	Land's End Radio	General
1933 .... *UT*	Ch 05	Ilfracombe Radio	General
1933 .... *UT*	Ch 07	Hastings Radio	General
1940 .... *LT*	Ch 67	HMCG Falmouth	Strong wind
2018 .... *UT*	Ch 28	Niton Radio	Storm warning
2020 .... *LT*	Ch 67	HMCG Portland	Strong wind
2040 .... *LT*	Ch 67	HMCG Solent	Local & strong wind
2040 .... *LT*	Ch 11	HMCG Dover	Local & strong wind
2050 .... *LT*	Ch 67	HMCG Brixham	Local & strong wind
2103 .... *UT*	Ch 28	Niton Radio	Storm warning
2103 .... *UT*	Ch 05	Weymouth Radio	Storm warning
2103 .... *UT*	Ch 26	Start Point Radio	Storm warning
2103 .... *UT*	Ch 62	Pendennis Radio	Storm warning
2103 .... *UT*	Ch 27 64'	Land's End Radio	Storm warning
2103 .... *UT*	2670 kHz	Land's End Radio	Storm warning
2103 .... *UT*	Ch 05	Ilfracombe Radio	Storm warning
2103 .... *UT*	Ch 07	Hastings Radio	Storm warning
2140 .... *LT*	Ch 67	HMCG Falmouth	Local & strong wind
2220 .... *LT*	Ch 67	HMCG Portland	Local & strong wind
2240 .... *LT*	Ch 67	HMCG Solent	Strong wind
2240 .... *LT*	Ch 11	HMCG Dover	Strong wind
2250 .... *LT*	Ch 67	HMCG Brixham	Strong wind
2340 .... *LT*	Ch 67	HMCG Falmouth	Strong wind

Note 1: Land's End transmissions on Ch 64 are for vessels in the Scilly Isles area.

EAST COAST OF ENGLAND

0010 .... *LT*	Ch 67	HMCG Thames	Local & strong wind
0040 .... *LT*	Ch 67	HMCG Yarmouth	Local & strong wind
0048 .... *LT*	198 kHz	Radio 4	General
0150 .... *LT*	Ch 67	HMCG Tyne/Tees	Local & strong wind
0210 .... *LT*	Ch 67	HMCG Thames	Strong wind
0240 .... *LT*	Ch 67	HMCG Yarmouth	Strong wind
0303 .... *UT*	Ch 25	Whitby Radio	Storm warning
0303 .... *UT*	Ch 27	Grimsby Radio	Storm warning
0303 .... *UT*	Ch 26	Humber Radio	Storm warning
0303 .... *UT*	Ch 07	Bacton Radio	Storm warning
0303 .... *UT*	Ch 62	Orfordness Radio	Storm warning
0303 .... *UT*	Ch 02	Thames Radio	Storm warning
0303 .... *UT*	Ch 26	N Foreland Radio	Storm warning

:AST COAST OF ENGLAND

Time	Ch/Freq	Source	Forecast
340 .... *LT*	Ch 67	HMCG Humber	Local & strong wind
350 .... *LT*	Ch 67	HMCG Tyne/Tees	Strong wind
410 .... *LT*	Ch 67	HMCG Thames	Local & strong wind
440 .... *LT*	Ch 67	HMCG Yarmouth	Local & strong wind
540 .... *LT*	Ch 67	HMCG Humber	Strong wind
550 .... *LT*	Ch 67	HMCG Tyne/Tees	Local & strong wind
550 .... *LT*	198 kHz	Radio 4	Coastal waters
555 .... *LT*	198 kHz	Radio 4	General
610 .... *LT*	Ch 67	HMCG Thames	Strong wind
640 .... *LT*	Ch 67	HMCG Yarmouth	Strong wind
703 .... *UT*	Ch 25	Whitby Radio	General
733 .... *UT*	Ch 27	Grimsby Radio	General
733 .... *UT*	Ch 26	Humber Radio	General
733 .... *UT*	Ch 07	Bacton Radio	General
733 .... *UT*	Ch 62	Orfordness Radio	General
733 .... *UT*	Ch 02	Thames Radio	General
733 .... *UT*	Ch 26	N Foreland Radio	General
740 .... *LT*	Ch 67	HMCG Humber	Local & strong wind
750 .... *LT*	Ch 67	HMCG Tyne/Tees	Strong wind
810 .... *LT*	Ch 67	HMCG Thames	Local & strong wind
840 .... *LT*	Ch 67	HMCG Yarmouth	Local & strong wind
903 .... *UT*	Ch 25	Whitby Radio	Storm warning
903 .... *UT*	Ch 27	Grimsby Radio	Storm warning
903 .... *UT*	Ch 26	Humber Radio	Storm warning
903 .... *UT*	Ch 07	Bacton Radio	Storm warning
903 .... *UT*	Ch 62	Orfordness Radio	Storm warning
903 .... *UT*	Ch 02	Thames Radio	Storm warning
903 .... *UT*	Ch 26	N Foreland Radio	Storm warning
940 .... *LT*	Ch 67	HMCG Humber	Strong wind
950 .... *LT*	Ch 67	HMCG Tyne/Tees	Local & strong wind
010 .... *LT*	Ch 67	HMCG Thames	Strong wind
040 .... *LT*	Ch 67	HMCG Yarmouth	Strong wind
140 .... *LT*	Ch 67	HMCG Humber	Local & strong wind
150 .... *LT*	Ch 67	HMCG Tyne/Tees	Strong wind
210 .... *LT*	Ch 67	HMCG Thames	Local & strong wind
240 .... *LT*	Ch 67	HMCG Yarmouth	Local & strong wind
340 .... *LT*	Ch 67	HMCG Humber	Strong wind
350 .... *LT*	Ch 67	HMCG Tyne/Tees	Local & strong wind
355 .... *LT*	198 kHz	Radio 4	General
410 .... *LT*	Ch 67	HMCG Thames	Strong wind
440 .... *LT*	Ch 67	HMCG Yarmouth	Strong wind
503 .... *UT*	Ch 25	Whitby Radio	Storm warning
503 .... *UT*	Ch 27	Grimsby Radio	Storm warning
503 .... *UT*	Ch 26	Humber Radio	Storm warning
503 .... *UT*	Ch 07	Bacton Radio	Storm warning

EAST COAST OF ENGLAND

Time	Ch/Freq	Source	Forecast
1503 .... *UT*	Ch 62	Orfordness Radio....	Storm warnimg
1503 .... *UT*	Ch 02	Thames Radio	Storm warning
1503 .... *UT*	Ch 26	N Foreland Radio....	Storm warning
1540 .... *LT*	Ch 67	HMCG Humber	Local & strong wind
1550 .... *LT*	Ch 67	HMCG Tyne/Tees...	Strong wind
1610 .... *LT*	Ch 67	HMCG Thames	Local & strong wind
1640 .... *LT*	Ch 67	HMCG Yarmouth ...	Local & strong wind
1740 .... *LT*	Ch 67	HMCG Humber	Strong wind
1750 .... *LT*	198 kHz	Radio 4	General
1750 .... *LT*	Ch 67	HMCG Tyne/Tees...	Local & strong wind
1810 .... *LT*	Ch 67	HMCG Thames	Strong wind
1840 .... *LT*	Ch 67	HMCG Yarmouth ...	Strong wind
1903 .... *UT*	Ch 25	Whitby Radio	General
1933 .... *UT*	Ch 27	Grimsby Radio	General
1933 .... *UT*	Ch 26	Humber Radio	General
1933 .... *UT*	Ch 07	Bacton Radio	General
1933 .... *UT*	Ch 62	Orfordness Radio....	General
1933 .... *UT*	Ch 02	Thames Radio	General
1933 .... *UT*	Ch 26	N Foreland Radio....	General
1940 .... *LT*	Ch 67	HMCG Humber	Local & strong wind
1950 .... *LT*	Ch 67	HMCG Tyne/Tees...	Strong wind
2010 .... *LT*	Ch 67	HMCG Thames	Local & strong wind
2040 .... *LT*	Ch 67	HMCG Yarmouth ...	Local & strong wind
2103 .... *UT*	Ch 25	Whitby Radio	Storm warning
2103 .... *UT*	Ch 27	Grimsby Radio	Storm warning
2103 .... *UT*	Ch 26	Humber Radio	Storm warning
2103 .... *UT*	Ch 07	Bacton Radio	Storm warning
2103 .... *UT*	Ch 62	Orfordness Radio....	Storm warning
2103 .... *UT*	Ch 02	Thames Radio	Storm warning
2103 .... *UT*	Ch 26	N Foreland Radio....	Storm warning
2140 .... *LT*	Ch 67	HMCG Humber	Strong wind
2150 .... *LT*	Ch 67	HMCG Tyne/Tees...	Local & strong wind
2210 .... *LT*	Ch 67	HMCG Thames	Strong wind
2240 .... *LT*	Ch 67	HMCG Yarmouth ...	Strong wind
2340 .... *LT*	Ch 67	HMCG Humber	Local & strong wind
2350 .... *LT*	Ch 67	HMCG Tyne/Tees...	Strong wind

WEST COAST OF ENGLAND & IRELAND

Time	Ch/Freq	Source	Forecast
0005 .... *LT*	Ch 67	HMCG Swansea	Local & strong wind
0033 .... *LT*	Ch 83	Dublin Radio	Storm warning
0033 .... *LT*	Ch 87	Wicklow Head	Storm warning
0033 .... *LT*	Ch 23	Rosslare Radio	Storm warning
0033 .... *LT*	Ch 83	Mine Head Radio	Storm warning
0033 .... *LT*	Ch 26	Cork Radio	Storm warning
0033 .... *LT*	Ch 23	Bantry Radio	Storm warning
0033 .... *LT*	Ch 24	Valentia Radio	Storm warning

WEST COAST OF ENGLAND & IRELAND

Time	Ch/Freq	Source	Forecast
0033 .... *LT*	Ch 28	Shannon Radio	Storm warning
0033 .... *LT*	Ch 26	Clifden Radio	Storm warning
0033 .... *LT*	Ch 83	Belmullet Radio	Storm warning
0033 .... *LT*	Ch 24	Glen Head Radio	Storm warning
0033 .... *LT*	Ch 23	Malin Head	Storm warning
0048 .... *LT*	198 kHz	Radio 4	General
0103 .... *LT*	Ch 83	Dublin Radio	General
0103 .... *LT*	Ch 87	Wicklow Head	General
0103 .... *LT*	Ch 23	Rosslare Radio	General
0103 .... *LT*	Ch 83	Mine Head Radio	General
0103 .... *LT*	Ch 26	Cork Radio	General
0103 .... *LT*	Ch 23	Bantry Radio	General
0103 .... *LT*	Ch 24	Valentia Radio	Local
0103 .... *LT*	Ch 28	Shannon Radio	General
0103 .... *LT*	Ch 26	Clifden Radio	General
0103 .... *LT*	Ch 83	Belmullet Radio	General
0103 .... *LT*	Ch 24	Glen Head Radio	General
0103 .... *LT*	Ch 23	Malin Head	General
0205 .... *LT*	Ch 67	HMCG Swansea	Strong wind
0210 .... *LT*	Ch 67	HMCG Liverpool	Local & strong wind
0235 .... *LT*	Ch 67	HMCG Holyhead	Local & strong wind
0303 .... *UT*	Ch 24	Celtic Radio	Storm warning
0303 .... *UT*	Ch 03	Cardigan By Radio	Storm warning
0303 .... *UT*	Ch 26	Anglesey Radio	Storm warning
0303 .... *UT*	Ch 27	Portpatrick Radio	Storm warning
0305 .... *LT*	Ch 67	HMCG Belfast	Local
0335 .... *LT*	Ch 67	HMCG Milfd Hvn	Local & strong wind
0403 .... *LT*	Ch 83	Dublin Radio	General
0403 .... *LT*	Ch 87	Wicklow Head	General
0403 .... *LT*	Ch 23	Rosslare Radio	General
0403 .... *LT*	Ch 83	Mine Head Radio	General
0403 .... *LT*	Ch 26	Cork Radio	General
0403 .... *LT*	Ch 23	Bantry Radio	General
0403 .... *LT*	Ch 24	Valentia Radio	Local
0403 .... *LT*	Ch 28	Shannon Radio	Forecast
0403 .... *LT*	Ch 26	Clifden Radio	General
0403 .... *LT*	Ch 83	Belmullet Radio	General
0403 .... *LT*	Ch 24	Glen Head Radio	General
0403 .... *LT*	Ch 23	Malin Head	General
0405 .... *LT*	Ch 67	HMCG Swansea	Local & strong wind
0410 .... *LT*	Ch 67	HMCG Liverpool	Strong wind
0435 .... *LT*	Ch 67	HMCG Holyhead	Strong wind
0535 .... *LT*	Ch 67	HMCG Milfd Hvn	Strong wind
0550 .... *LT*	198 kHz	Radio 4	Coastal waters
0555 .... *LT*	198 kHz	Radio 4	General

WEST COAST OF ENGLAND & IRELAND

Time	Ch/Freq	Source	Forecast
0605 .... *LT*	Ch 67	HMCG Swansea	Strong wind
0610 .... *LT*	Ch 67	HMCG Liverpool	Local & strong wind
0633 .... *LT*	various	RTE Radio 1& Fm	General
0633 .... *LT*	Ch 83	Dublin Radio	Storm warning
0633 .... *LT*	Ch 87	Wicklow Head	Storm warning
0633 .... *LT*	Ch 23	Rosslare Radio	Storm warning
0633 .... *LT*	Ch 83	Mine Head Radio	Storm warning
0633 .... *LT*	Ch 26	Cork Radio	Storm warning
0633 .... *LT*	Ch 23	Bantry Radio	Storm warning
0633 .... *LT*	Ch 24	Valentia Radio	Storm warning
0633 .... *LT*	Ch 28	Shannon Radio	Storm warning
0633 .... *LT*	Ch 26	Clifden Radio	Storm warning
0633 .... *LT*	Ch 83	Belmullet Radio	Storm warning
0633 .... *LT*	Ch 24	Glen Head Radio	Storm warning
0633 .... *LT*	Ch 23	Malin Head	Storm warning
0635 .... *LT*	Ch 67	HMCG Holyhead	Local & strong wind
0703 .... *UT*	Ch 26	Anglesey Radio	General
0703 .... *UT*	Ch 27	Portpatrick Radio	General
0703 .... *LT*	Ch 83	Dublin Radio	General
0703 .... *LT*	Ch 87	Wicklow Head	General
0703 .... *LT*	Ch 23	Rosslare Radio	General
0703 .... *LT*	Ch 83	Mine Head Radio	General
0703 .... *LT*	Ch 26	Cork Radio	General
0703 .... *LT*	Ch 23	Bantry Radio	General
0703 .... *LT*	Ch 24	Valentia Radio	Local
0703 .... *LT*	Ch 28	Shannon Radio	General
0703 .... *LT*	Ch 26	Clifden Radio	General
0703 .... *LT*	Ch 83	Belmullet Radio	General
0703 .... *LT*	Ch 24	Glen Head Radio	General
0703 .... *LT*	Ch 23	Malin Head	General
0703 .... *UT*	Ch 03	Cardigan Bay Radio	General
0705 .... *LT*	Ch 67	HMCG Belfast	Local
0733 .... *UT*	Ch 24	Celtic Radio	General
0735 .... *LT*	Ch 67	HMCG Milfd Hvn	Local & strong wind
0805 .... *LT*	Ch 67	HMCG Swansea	Local & strong wind
0810 .... *LT*	Ch 67	HMCG Liverpool	Strong wind
0835 .... *LT*	Ch 67	HMCG Holyhead	Strong wind
0903 .... *UT*	Ch 24	Celtic Radio	Storm warning
0903 .... *UT*	Ch 03	Cardigan Bay Radio	Storm warning
0903 .... *UT*	Ch 26	Anglesey Radio	Storm warning
0903 .... *UT*	Ch 27	Portpatrick Radio	Storm warning
0935 .... *LT*	Ch 67	HMCG Milfd Hvn	Strong wind
1003 .... *LT*	Ch 83	Dublin Radio	General
1003 .... *LT*	Ch 87	Wicklow Head	General
1003 .... *LT*	Ch 23	Rosslare Radio	General

WEST COAST OF ENGLAND & IRELAND

Time	Ch/Freq	Source	Forecast
1003 .... LT	Ch 83	Mine Head Radio	General
1003 .... LT	Ch 26	Cork Radio	General
1003 .... LT	Ch 23	Bantry Radio	General
1003 .... LT	Ch 24	Valentia Radio	Local
1003 .... LT	Ch 28	Shannon Radio	General
1003 .... LT	Ch 26	Clifden Radio	General
1003 .... LT	Ch 83	Belmullet Radio	General
1003 .... LT	Ch 24	Glen Head Radio	General
1003 .... LT	Ch 23	Malin Head	General
1005 .... LT	Ch 67	HMCG Swansea	Strong wind
1010 .... LT	Ch 67	HMCG Liverpool	Local & strong wind
1035 .... LT	Ch 67	HMCG Holyhead	Local & strong wind
1105 .... LT	Ch 67	HMCG Belfast	Local
1135 .... LT	Ch 67	HMCG Milfd Hvn	Local & strong wind
1205 .... LT	Ch 67	HMCG Swansea	Local & strong wind
1210 .... LT	Ch 67	HMCG Liverpool	Strong wind
1233 .... LT	Ch 83	Dublin Radio	Storm warning
1233 .... LT	Ch 87	Wicklow Head	Storm warning
1233 .... LT	Ch 23	Rosslare Radio	Storm warning
1233 .... LT	Ch 83	Mine Head Radio	Storm warning
1233 .... LT	Ch 26	Cork Radio	Storm warning
1233 .... LT	Ch 23	Bantry Radio	Storm warning
1233 .... LT	Ch 24	Valentia Radio	Storm warning
1233 .... LT	Ch 28	Shannon Radio	Storm warning
1233 .... LT	Ch 26	Clifden Radio	Storm warning
1233 .... LT	Ch 83	Belmullet Radio	Storm warning
1233 .... LT	Ch 24	Glen Head Radio	Storm warning
1233 .... LT	Ch 23	Malin Head	Storm warning
1235 .... LT	Ch 67	HMCG Holyhead	Strong wind
1303 .... LT	Ch 83	Dublin Radio	General
1303 .... LT	Ch 87	Wicklow Head	General
1303 .... LT	Ch 23	Rosslare Radio	General
1303 .... LT	Ch 83	Mine Head Radio	General
1303 .... LT	Ch 26	Cork Radio	General
1303 .... LT	Ch 23	Bantry Radio	Forecast
1303 .... LT	Ch 24	Valentia Radio	Local
1303 .... LT	Ch 28	Shannon Radio	General
1303 .... LT	Ch 26	Clifden Radio	General
1303 .... LT	Ch 83	Belmullet Radio	General
1303 .... LT	Ch 24	Glen Head Radio	General
1303 .... LT	Ch 23	Malin Head	General
1335 .... LT	Ch 67	HMCG Milfd Hvn	Strong wind
1355 .... LT	198 kHz	Radio 4	General
1405 .... LT	Ch 67	HMCG Swansea	Strong wind
1410 .... LT	Ch 67	HMCG Liverpool	Local & strong wind

WEST COAST OF ENGLAND & IRELAND

Time	Ch/Freq	Source	Forecast
1435 .... *LT*	Ch 67	HMCG Holyhead	Local & strong wind
1503 .... *UT*	Ch 24	Celtic Radio	Storm warning
1503 .... *UT*	Ch 03	Cardigan Bay Radio.	Storm warning
1503 .... *UT*	Ch 26	Anglesey Radio	Storm warning
1503 .... *UT*	Ch 27	Portpatrick Radio	Storm warning
1505 .... *LT*	Ch 67	HMCG Belfast	Local
1535 .... *LT*	Ch 67	HMCG Milfd Hvn	Local & strong wind
1603 .... *LT*	Ch 83	Dublin Radio	General
1603 .... *LT*	Ch 87	Wicklow Head	General
1603 .... *LT*	Ch 23	Rosslare Radio	General
1603 .... *LT*	Ch 83	Mine Head Radio	General
1603 .... *LT*	Ch 26	Cork Radio	General
1603 .... *LT*	Ch 23	Bantry Radio	General
1603 .... *LT*	Ch 24	Valentia Radio	Local
1603 .... *LT*	Ch 28	Shannon Radio	General
1603 .... *LT*	Ch 26	Clifden Radio	General
1603 .... *LT*	Ch 83	Belmullet Radio	General
1603 .... *LT*	Ch 24	Glen Head Radio	General
1603 .... *LT*	Ch 23	Malin Head	General
1605 .... *LT*	Ch 67	HMCG Swansea	Local & strong wind
1610 .... *LT*	Ch 67	HMCG Liverpool	Strong wind
1633 .... *LT*	Ch 26	Clifden Radio	Storm warning
1633 .... *LT*	Ch 83	Belmullet Radio	General
1635 .... *LT*	Ch 67	HMCG Holyhead	Strong wind
1735 .... *LT*	Ch 67	HMCG Milfd Hvn	Strong wind
1750 .... *LT*	198 kHz	Radio 4	General
1805 .... *LT*	Ch 67	HMCG Swansea	Strong wind
1810 .... *LT*	Ch 67	HMCG Liverpool	Local & strong wind
1823 .... *LT*	various	RTE Radio 1 & FM	General
1833 .... *LT*	Ch 83	Dublin Radio	Storm warning
1833 .... *LT*	Ch 87	Wicklow Head	Storm warning
1833 .... *LT*	Ch 23	Rosslare Radio	Storm warning
1833 .... *LT*	Ch 83	Mine Head Radio	Storm warning
1833 .... *LT*	Ch 26	Cork Radio	Storm warning
1833 .... *LT*	Ch 23	Bantry Radio	Storm warning
1833 .... *LT*	Ch 24	Valentia Radio	Storm warning
1833 .... *LT*	Ch 28	Shannon Radio	Storm warning
1833 .... *LT*	Ch 83	Belmullet Radio	Storm warning
1833 .... *LT*	Ch 24	Glen Head Radio	Storm warning
1833 .... *LT*	Ch 23	Malin Head	Storm warning
1835 .... *LT*	Ch 67	HMCG Holyhead	Local & strong wind
1903 .... *UT*	Ch 03	Cardigan Bay Radio.	General
1903 .... *UT*	Ch 26	Anglesey Radio	General
1903 .... *UT*	Ch 27	Portpatrick Radio	General
1903 .... *LT*	Ch 83	Dublin Radio	General

WEST COAST OF ENGLAND & IRELAND

Time	Ch/Freq	Source	Forecast
1903 .... LT	Ch 87	Wicklow Head	General
1903 .... LT	Ch 23	Rosslare Radio	General
1903 .... LT	Ch 83	Mine Head Radio	General
1903 .... LT	Ch 26	Cork Radio	General
1903 .... LT	Ch 23	Bantry Radio	General
1903 .... LT	Ch 24	Valentia Radio	Local
1903 .... LT	Ch 28	Shannon Radio	General
1903 .... LT	Ch 26	Clifden Radio	General
1903 .... LT	Ch 83	Belmullet Radio	General
1903 .... LT	Ch 24	Glen Head Radio	General
1905 .... LT	Ch 67	HMCG Belfast	Local
1933 .... UT	Ch 24	Celtic Radio	General
1935 .... LT	Ch 67	HMCG Milfd Hvn	Local & strong wind
2005 .... LT	Ch 67	HMCG Swansea	Local & strong wind
2010 .... LT	Ch 67	HMCG Liverpool	Strong wind
2033 .... LT	Ch 83	Belmullet Radio	General
2035 .... LT	CH 67	HMCG Holyhead	Strong wind
2103 .... UT	Ch 24	Celtic Radio	Storm warning
2103 .... UT	Ch 03	Cardigan Bay Radio	Storm warning
2103 .... UT	Ch 26	Anglesey Radio	Storm warning
2103 .... UT	Ch 27	Portpatrick Radio	Storm warning
2135 .... LT	Ch 67	HMCG Milfd Hvn	Strong wind
2203 .... LT	Ch 83	Dublin Radio	General
2203 .... LT	Ch 87	Wicklow Head	General
2203 .... LT	Ch 23	Rosslare Radio	General
2203 .... LT	Ch 83	Mine Head Radio	General
2203 .... LT	Ch 26	Cork Radio	General
2203 .... LT	Ch 23	Bantry Radio	General
2203 .... LT	Ch 24	Valentia Radio	Local
2203 .... LT	Ch 28	Shannon Radio	General
2203 .... LT	Ch 26	Clifden Radio	General
2203 .... LT	Ch 83	Belmullet Radio	General
2203 .... LT	Ch 24	Glen Head Radio	General
2203 .... LT	Ch 23	Malin Head	General
2205 .... LT	Ch 67	HMCG Swansea	Strong wind
2210 .... LT	Ch 67	HMCG Liverpool	Local & strong wind
2235 .... LT	Ch 67	HMCG Holyhead	Local & strong wind
2305 .... LT	Ch 67	HMCG Belfast	Local
2335 .... LT	Ch 67	HMCG Milfd Hvn	Local & strong wind

SCOTLAND

Time	Ch/Freq	Source	Forecast
0020 .... LT	Ch 67	HMCG Clyde	Local
0048 .... LT	198 kHz	Radio 4	General
0105 .... LT	Ch 67	HMCG Shetland	Local & strong wind
0110 .... LT	Ch 67	HMCG Stornoway	Local
0135 .... LT	Ch 67	HMCG Pentland	Local & strong wind

SCOTLAND

Time	Ch/Freq	Source	Forecast
0205 .... LT	Ch 67	HMCG Forth	Local & strong wind
0240 .... LT	Ch 67	HMCG Oban	Local & strong wind
0303 .... UT	Ch 27	Portpatrick Radio	Storm warning
0303 .... UT	Ch 26	Clyde Radio	Storm warning
0303 .... UT	Ch 25	Islay Radio	Storm warning
0303 .... UT	Ch 07	Oban Radio	Storm warning
0303 .... UT	Ch 24	Skye Radio	Storm warning
0303 .... UT	Ch 05	Lewis Radio	Storm warning
0303 .... UT	Ch 27	Shetland Radio	Storm warning
0303 .... UT	Ch 25	Buchan Radio	Storm warning
0303 .... UT	Ch 26	Stonehaven Radio	Storm warning
0303 .... UT	Ch 28	Wick Radio	Storm warning
0303 .... UT	Ch 24	Forth Radio	Storm warning
0303 .... UT	Ch 26	Cullercoats Radio	Storm warning
0305 .... LT	Ch 67	HMCG Shetland	Strong wind
0320 .... LT	Ch 67	HMCG Aberdeen	Local & strong wind
0335 .... LT	Ch 67	HMCG Pentland	Strong wind
0405 .... LT	Ch 67	HMCG Forth	Strong wind
0420 .... LT	Ch 67	HMCG Clyde	Local
0440 .... LT	Ch 67	HMCG Oban	Strong wind
0505 .... LT	Ch 67	HMCG Shetland	Local & strong wind
0510 .... LT	Ch 67	HMCG Stornoway	Local
0520 .... LT	Ch 67	HMCG Aberdeen	Strong wind
0535 .... LT	Ch 67	HMCG Pentland	Local & strong wind
0550 .... LT	198 kHz	Radio 4	Coastal waters
0555 .... LT	198 kHz	Radio 4	General
0605 .... LT	Ch 67	HMCG Forth	Local & strong wind
0640 .... LT	Ch 67	HMCG Oban	Local & strong wind
0703 .... UT	Ch 27	Portpatrick Radio	General
0703 .... UT	Ch 26	Clyde Radio	General
0703 .... UT	Ch 25	Islay Radio	General
0703 .... UT	Ch 07	Oban Radio	General
0703 .... UT	Ch 24	Skye Radio	General
0703 .... UT	Ch 05	Lewis Radio	General
0703 .... UT	Ch 27	Shetland Radio	General
0703 .... UT	Ch 25	Buchan Radio	General
0703 .... UT	Ch 26	Stonehaven Radio	General
0703 .... UT	Ch 28	Wick Radio	General
0703 .... UT	Ch 24	Forth Radio	General
0703 .... UT	Ch 26	Cullercoats Radio	General
0705 .... LT	Ch 67	HMCG Shetland	Strong wind
0720 .... LT	Ch 67	HMCG Aberdeen	Local & strong wind
0735 .... LT	Ch 67	HMCG Pentland	Strong wind
0805 .... LT	Ch 67	HMCG Forth	Strong wind
0820 .... LT	Ch 67	HMCG Clyde	Local

SCOTLAND

Time	Ch/Freq	Source	Forecast
0840 .... *LT*	Ch 67	HMCG Oban	Strong wind
0903 .... *UT*	Ch 27	Portpatrick Radio	Storm warning
0903 .... *UT*	Ch 26	Clyde Radio	Storm warning
0903 .... *UT*	Ch 25	Islay Radio	Storm warning
0903 .... *UT*	Ch 07	Oban Radio	Storm warning
0903 .... *UT*	Ch 24	Skye Radio	Storm warning
0903 .... *UT*	Ch 05	Lewis Radio	Storm warning
0903 .... *UT*	Ch 27	Shetland Radio	Storm warning
0903 .... *UT*	Ch 25	Buchan Radio	Storm warning
0903 .... *UT*	Ch 26	Stonehaven Radio	Storm warning
0903 .... *UT*	Ch 28	Wick Radio	Storm warning
0903 .... *UT*	Ch 24	Forth Radio	Storm warning
0903 .... *UT*	Ch 26	Cullercoats Radio	Storm warning
0905 .... *LT*	Ch 67	HMCG Shetland	Local & strong wind
0910 .... *LT*	Ch 67	HMCG Stornoway	Local
0920 .... *LT*	Ch 67	HMCG Aberdeen	Strong wind
0935 .... *LT*	Ch 67	HMCG Pentland	Local & strong wind
1005 .... *LT*	Ch 67	HMCG Forth	Local & strong wind
1040 .... *LT*	Ch 67	HMCG Oban	Local & strong wind
1105 .... *LT*	Ch 67	HMCG Shetland	Strong wind
1120 .... *LT*	Ch 67	HMCG Aberdeen	Local & strong wind
1135 .... *LT*	Ch 67	HMCG Pentland	Strong wind
1205 .... *LT*	Ch 67	HMCG Forth	Strong wind
1220 .... *LT*	Ch 67	HMCG Clyde	Local
1240 .... *LT*	Ch 67	HMCG Oban	Strong wind
1305 .... *LT*	Ch 67	HMCG Shetland	Local & strong wind
1310 .... *LT*	Ch 67	HMCG Stornoway	Local
1320 .... *LT*	Ch 67	HMCG Aberdeen	Strong wind
1335 .... *LT*	Ch 67	HMCG Pentland	Local & strong wind
1355 .... *LT*	198 kHz	Radio 4	General
1405 .... *LT*	Ch 67	HMCG Forth	Local & strong wind
1440 .... *LT*	Ch 67	HMCG Oban	Local & strong wind
1503 .... *UT*	Ch 27	Portpatrick Radio	Storm warning
1503 .... *UT*	Ch 26	Clyde Radio	Storm warning
1503 .... *UT*	Ch 25	Islay Radio	Storm warning
1503 .... *UT*	Ch 07	Oban Radio	Storm warning
1503 .... *UT*	Ch 24	Skye Radio	Storm warning
1503 .... *UT*	Ch 05	Lewis Radio	Storm warning
1503 .... *UT*	Ch 27	Shetland Radio	Storm warning
1503 .... *UT*	Ch 25	Buchan Radio	Storm warning
1503 .... *UT*	Ch 26	Stonehaven Radio	Storm warning
1503 .... *UT*	Ch 28	Wick Radio	Storm warning
1503 .... *UT*	Ch 24	Forth Radio	Storm warning
1503 .... *UT*	Ch 26	Cullercoats Radio	Storm warning
1505 .... *LT*	Ch 67	HMCG Shetland	Strong wind

SCOTLAND

Time	Ch/Freq	Source	Forecast
1520 .... *LT*	Ch 67	HMCG Aberdeen	Local & strong wind
1535 .... *LT*	Ch 67	HMCG Pentland	Strong wind
1605 .... *LT*	Ch 67	HMCG Forth	Strong wind
1620 .... *LT*	Ch 67	HMCG Clyde	Local
1640 .... *LT*	Ch 67	HMCG Oban	Strong wind
1705 .... *LT*	Ch 67	HMCG Shetland	Local & strong wind
1710 .... *LT*	Ch 67	HMCG Stornoway ..	Local
1720 .... *LT*	Ch 67	HMCG Aberdeen	Strong wind
1735 .... *LT*	Ch 67	HMCG Pentland	Local & strong wind
1750 .... *LT*	198 kHz	Radio 4	General
1805 .... *LT*	Ch 67	HMCG Forth	Local & strong wind
1840 .... *LT*	Ch 67	HMCG Oban	Local & strong wind
1903 .... *UT*	Ch 27	Portpatrick Radio	General
1903 .... *UT*	Ch 26	Clyde Radio	General
1903 .... *UT*	Ch 25	Islay Radio	General
1903 .... *UT*	Ch 07	Oban Radio	General
1903 .... *UT*	Ch 24	Skye Radio	General
1903 .... *UT*	Ch 05	Lewis Radio.............	General
1903 .... *UT*	Ch 27	Shetland Radio	General
1903 .... *UT*	Ch 25	Buchan Radio	General
1903 .... *UT*	Ch 26	Stonehaven Radio....	General
1903 .... *UT*	Ch 28	Wick Radio	General
1903 .... *UT*	Ch 24	Forth Radio	General
1903 .... *UT*	Ch 26	Cullercoats Radio....	General
1905 .... *LT*	Ch 67	HMCG Shetland	Strong wind
1920 .... *LT*	Ch 67	HMCG Aberdeen	Local & strong wind
1935 .... *LT*	Ch 67	HMCG Pentland	Strong wind
2005 .... *LT*	Ch 67	HMCG Forth	Strong wind
2020 .... *LT*	Ch 67	HMCG Clyde	Local
2040 .... *LT*	Ch 67	HMCG Oban	Strong wind
2103 .... *UT*	Ch 27	Portpatrick Radio	Storm warning
2103 .... *UT*	Ch 26	Clyde Radio	Storm warning
2103 .... *UT*	Ch 25	Islay Radio	Storm warning
2103 .... *UT*	Ch 07	Oban Radio	Storm warning
2103 .... *UT*	Ch 24	Skye Radio	Storm warning
2103 .... *UT*	Ch 05	Lewis Radio.............	Storm warning
2103 .... *UT*	Ch 27	Shetland Radio	Storm warning
2103 .... *UT*	Ch 25	Buchan Radio	Storm warning
2103 .... *UT*	Ch 26	Stonehaven Radio....	Storm warning
2103 .... *UT*	Ch 28	Wick Radio	Storm warning
2103 .... *UT*	Ch 24	Forth Radio	Storm warning
2103 .... *UT*	Ch 26	Cullercoats Radio....	Storm warning
2105 .... *LT*	Ch 67	HMCG Shetland	Local & strong wind
2110 .... *LT*	Ch 67	HMCG Stornoway ..	Local
2120 .... *LT*	Ch 67	HMCG Aberdeen	Strong wind

SCOTLAND

Time	Ch/Freq	Source	Forecast
2135....*LT*	Ch 67	HMCG Pentland	Local & strong wind
2205....*LT*	Ch 67	HMCG Forth	Local & strong wind
2240....*LT*	Ch 67	HMCG Oban	Local & strong wind
2305....*LT*	Ch 67	HMCG Shetland	Strong wind
2320....*LT*	Ch 67	HMCG Aberdeen	Local & strong wind
2335....*LT*	Ch 67	HMCG Pentland	Strong wind

BELGIUM, HOLLAND, GERMANY & DENMARK

Time	Ch/Freq	Source	Forecast	
0048....*LT*	198 kHz	BBC Radio 4	General	
0340....*LT*	1713/1890/2824 kHz	Scheveningen Radio	Local	Eng
0348....*UT*	518 kHz	IJmuiden Cstguard	Storm warnings	Eng
0550....*LT*	198 kHz	Radio 4	Coastal waters	
0555....*LT*	198 kHz	Radio 4	General	Eng
0600....*LT*	91.7/94.2/95.7/98.5MHz, & 927 kHz	Belgische Radio	Local	
0633....*LT*	Ch 61	Dunkerque Radio	Local	
0633....*LT*	Ch 23	Boulogne Radio	Local	
0648....*UT*	518 kHz	Oostende Radio	Strong breeze	Eng
0700....*LT*	91.7/94.2/95.7/98.5MHz, & 927 kHz	Belgische Radio	Local	
0700....*LT*	Ch 26	Elbe-Weser Radio	Elbe-Weser Local	
0700....*LT*	Ch 25	Elbe-Weser Radio	Eiderstedt Local	
0700....*LT*	Ch 26	Elbe-Weser Radio	Nordfriesland Local	
0700....*LT*	Ch 27	Elbe-Weser Radio	Helgoland Local	
0700....*LT*	Ch 28	Norddeich	Local	
0703....*LT*	1692 kHz	Boulogne Radio	General	
0705....*LT*	See table	Scheveningen Ra	Local	
0748....*UT*	518 kHz	IJmuiden Cstguard	Storm warnings	Eng
0800....*LT*	91.7/94.2/95.7/98.5MHz, & 927 kHz	Belgische Radio	Local	
0820....*UT*	Ch 27	Oostende Radio	Local	Eng
0900....*LT*	91.7/94.2/95.7/98.5MHz, & 927 kHz	Belgische Radio	Local	
0920....*UT*	438/449/516.5 kHz	Lyngby Radio	Danish areas 2/9	Eng
0940....*LT*	1713/1890 kHz	Scheveningen Ra	Local	Eng
1148....*UT*	518 kHz	IJmuiden Cstguard	Storm warnings	Eng
1200....*UT*	Ch 26	Elbe-Weser Radio	Elbe-Weser Local	
1200....*UT*	Ch 25	Elbe-Weser Radio	Eiderstedt Local	
1200....*UT*	Ch 26	Elbe-Weser Radio	Nordfriesland Local	
1200....*UT*	Ch 27	Elbe-Weser Radio	Helgoland Local	
1200....*UT*	Ch 28	Norddeich	Local	
1205....*LT*	See table	Scheveningen Ra	Local	

BELGIUM, HOLLAND, GERMANY & DENMARK

Time	Ch/Freq	Source	Forecast	
1220 .... UT	438/449/516.5 kHz			
		Lyngby Radio	Danish Areas 2/9	Eng
1355 .... LT	198 kHz	BBC Radio 4	General	
1433 .... LT	Ch 61	Dunkerque Radio	Local	
1433 .... LT	Ch 23	Boulogne Radio	Local	
1540 .... LT	1713/1890 kHz			
		Scheveningen Ra	Local	Eng
1548 .... UT	518 kHz	IJmuiden Cstguard ...	Storm warnings	Eng
1700 .... LT	91.7/94.2/95.7/98.5MHz, & 927 kHz			
		Belgische Radio	Local	
1720 .... UT	Ch 27	Oostende Radio	Strong breeze	Eng
1750 .... LT	198 kHz	BBC Radio 4	General	Eng
1800 .... LT	Ch 26	Elbe-Weser Radio ...	Elbe-Weser Local	
1800 .... LT	Ch 25	Elbe-Weser Radio ...	Eiderstedt Local	
1800 .... LT	Ch 26	Elbe-Weser Radio ...	Nordfriesland Local	
1800 .... LT	Ch 27	Elbe-Weser Radio ...	Helgoland Local	
1800 .... LT	Ch 28	Norddeich	Local	
1805 .... LT	See table	Scheveningen Ra	Local	
1820 .... UT	438/449/516.5 kHz			
		Lyngby Radio	Danish Areas 2-9 Eng	
1848 .... UT	518 kHz	Oostende Radio	Strong breeze	Eng
1948 .... UT	518 kHz	IJmuiden Cstguard ...	Storm warnings	Eng
2140 .... LT	1713/1890 kHz			
		Scheveningen Ra	Local	Eng
2200 .... LT	91.7/94.2/95.7/98.5MHz, & 927 kHz			
		Belgische Radio	Local	
2305 .... LT	See table	Scheveningen Ra	Local	
2320 .... UT	438/449/516.5 kHz			
		Lyngby Radio	Danish Areas 2-9	Eng
2348 .... UT	518 kHz	IJmuiden Cstguard ...	Storm warnings	Eng
2400 .... LT	198 kHz	Radio 4	General	Eng

Boulogne Radio broadcasts Storm warnings on 442.5 kHz every H+18 and H+48 in French when storm is imminent.

Gris-Nez CROSS broadcasts Storm warnings on Ch 11 every H+10 and H+25 and, on request, Local Weather Forecasts on Ch 68 and 79 in English

Antwerpen Radio broadcasts strong breeze warnings for the Schelde every H+03 and H+48 in English on Ch 24.

Scheveningen Radio broadcasts storm warnings in English and Dutch every H+05 and local forecasts as schedule above on the following Channels:

Rotterdam	Ch 87	Goes	Ch23
Scheveningen	Ch 83	Haarlem	Ch 25
Lelystad	Ch 83	Wieringermeer	Ch 27
Platform L7	Ch 84	Terschelling	Ch 78
Nes	Ch 23	Appingedam	Ch 27

BELGIUM, HOLLAND, GERMANY & DENMARK

German Traffic Centres weather messages

German Bight traffic	Ch 79 80	Every H+00
Ems traffic	Ch 15 18 20 21	Every H+50
Jade traffic	Ch 20 63	Every H+10
Bremerhaven traffic	Ch 02 04 05 07 21 22 82	Every H+20
Bremen Weser traffic	Ch 19 78 81	Every H+30
Hunte traffic	Ch 63	Every H+30
Cuxhaven Elbe traffic	Ch 03 05 18 19 21	Every H+55
Brunsbtl Elbe traffic	Ch 04 05 18 21 22 60 66 67	Every H+05
Kiel Kanal II E.bound	Ch 02	Every H+15, H+45
Kiel Kanal III W.bound	Ch 03	Every H+20,H+50
Wismar Traffic	Ch 14	0230 0630 0930 1230 1530 1830 2130
Warnmunde Traffic	Ch 14	0115 then every odd H+15 from 0500 to 2100
Stralsund Traffic	Ch 14	0235 then every even H+35 from0600 to 2200 *LT*
Sassnitz Traffic	Ch 14	0230 then every even H+30 from 0600 to 2200 *LT*
Wolgast Traffic	Ch14	Every odd H+15 from 0700-2100 *LT*

FRANCE AND CHANNEL ISLANDS

0048 .... *LT*	198 kHz	BBC Radio 4	General	*Eng*
0307 .... *UT*	Ch 25 82	Jersey Radio	Storm warning	*Eng*
0433 .... *LT*	Ch 80	Penmarc'h Radio	Local	
0433 .... *LT*	Ch 79	Chassiron Radio	Local	
0438 .... *LT*	Ch 80	Étel Radio	Local	
0438 .... *LT*	Ch 79	Soulac Radio	Local	
0443 .... *LT*	Ch 80	Kerrouault Radio	Local	
0443 .... *LT*	Ch 79	Cap Ferret Radio	Local	
0448 .... *LT*	Ch 80	L'Armandèche Ra	Local	
0448 .... *LT*	Ch 79	Contis Radio	Local	
0453 .... *LT*	Ch 79	Biarritz Radio	Local	
0550 .... *LT*	198 kHz	Radio 4	Coastal waters	
0555 .... *LT*	198 kHz	Radio 4	General	*Eng*
0633 .... *LT*	Ch 87	Calais Radio	Local	
0633 .... *LT*	Ch 02	Dieppe Radio	Local	
0633 .... *LT*	Ch 26	Le Havre Radio	Local	
0633 .... *LT*	Ch 03	Port-en-Bessin Ra	Local	
0633 .... *LT*	Ch 27	Cherbourg Radio	Local	
0645 .... *LT*	Ch 25 82	Jersey Radio	Local	*Eng*
0703 .... *LT*	1692 kHz	Boulogne Radio	General	
0733 .... *LT*	Ch 02	Sainte-Malo Radio	Local	

FRANCE AND CHANNEL ISLANDS

Time	Ch/Freq	Source	Forecast	
0733 .... LT .... Ch 21 .... Île de Ré Radio .... General				
0733 .... LT .... Ch 23 .... Royan Radio .... General				
0733 .... LT .... Ch 24 .... Bayonne Radio .... General				
0733 .... LT .... Ch 81 .... Plougasnou Radio .... General				
0733 .... LT .... Ch 82 .... Ouessant Radio .... General				
0733 .... LT .... Ch 82 : .... Arcachon Radio .... General				
0733 .... LT .... Ch 84 .... Paimpol Radio .... General				
0733 .... LT .... Ch 86 .... Pont L'Abbé Radio .. General				
0733 .... LT .... Ch 02 .... Saint-Malo Radio ..... General				
0733 .... LT .... Ch 25 .... Belle-Île Radio .... General				
0733 .... LT .... Ch 23 .... Saint Nazaire Ra ...... General				
0733 .... LT .... Ch 28 .... Saint-Herblain Ra ..... General				
0733 .... LT .... Ch 27 .... SHilaire de Riez R ... General				
0745 .... LT .... Ch 80 .... Jobourg (CROSS) ... General				
0745 .... LT .... Ch 25 82 .... Jersey Radio .... Local				Eng
0829 .... LT .... 101.3MHz .... R. France Amorique General				
0845 .... LT .... Ch 25 82 .... Jersey Radio .... (May-Aug only)				Eng
0907 .... UT .... Ch 25 82 .... Jersey Radio .... Storm warning				Eng
1229 .... LT .... 101.3MHz .... R. France Amorique General				
1245 .... UT .... Ch 25 82 .... Jersey Radio .... Local				Eng
1355 .... LT .... 198 kHz .... BBC Radio 4 .... General				Eng
1433 .... LT .... Ch 87 .... Calais Radio .... Local				
1433 .... LT .... Ch 02 .... Dieppe Radio .... Local				
1433 .... LT .... Ch 26 .... Le Havre Radio .... Local				
1433 .... LT .... Ch 03 .... Port-en-Bessin Ra .... Local				
1433 .... LT .... Ch 27 .... Cherbourg Radio ..... Local				
1507 .... UT .... Ch 25 82 .... Jersey Radio .... Storm warning				Eng
1533 .... LT .... Ch 26 .... Le Conquet Radio ... General				
1533 .... LT .... Ch 21 .... Île de Ré Radio .... General				
1533 .... LT .... Ch 23 .... Royan Radio .... General				
1533 .... LT .... Ch 24 .... Bayonne Radio .... General				
1533 .... LT .... Ch 81 .... Plougasnou Radio .... General				
1533 .... LT .... Ch 82 .... Ouessant Radio .... General				
1533 .... LT .... Ch 82 .... Arcachon Radio .... General				
1533 .... LT .... Ch 84 .... Paimpol Radio .... Forecast				
1533 .... LT .... Ch 86 .... Pont L'Abbé Radio .. General				
1533 .... LT .... Ch 02 .... Sainte-Malo Radio ... General				
1533 .... LT .... Ch 25 .... Belle-Île Radio .... General				
1533 .... LT .... Ch 23 .... Saint Nazaire Ra ...... General				
1533 .... LT .... Ch 28 .... Saint-Herblain Ra ..... General				
1533 .... LT .... Ch 27 .... S Hilaire de Riez R .. General				
1750 .... LT .... 198 kHz .... BBC Radio 4 .... General				
1829 .... LT .... 101.3MHz .... R. France Amorique General				
1833 .... LT .... 1692 kHz .... Boulogne Radio .... General				
1845 .... UT .... Ch 25 82 .... Jersey Radio .... Local				Eng

FRANCE AND CHANNEL ISLANDS

Time	Ch/Freq	Source	Forecast	
2107 .... UT	Ch 25 82	Jersey Radio	Storm warning	Eng
2133 .... LT	Ch 79	Chassiron Radio	Local	
2133 .... LT	Ch 80	Jobourg (CROSS) ...	General	
2133 .... LT	Ch 80	Penmarc'h Radio	Local	
2138 .... LT	Ch 80	Étel Radio	Local	
2138 .... LT	Ch 79	Soulac Radio	Local	
2143 .... LT	Ch 80	Kerrouault Radio	Local	
2143 .... LT	Ch 79	Cap Ferret Radio	Local	
2148 .... LT	Ch 80	L'Armandèche Ra	Local	
2148 .... LT	Ch 79	Contis Radio	Local	
2153 .... LT	Ch 79	Biarritz Radio	Local	
2245 .... UT	Ch 25 82	Jersey Radio	Local	
2400 .... LT	198 kHz	Radio 4	General	Eng

Jobourg (CROSS) broadcasts on Ch 80 storm warnings every H+10 and H+50 in French and English and bulletins for Cap de la Hague to Penmarc'h on 0703 and 1903 LT (Granville) and 0715 and 1915 LT (Jobourg)

SPAIN & PORTUGAL

0005 .... UT	Ch 12,13,14	Coruña	Areas 1-5
0130 .... UT	Ch 11	Leixões Radio	Leixões
0250 .... UT	518 kHz	Algés Radio	Norte/Centro/Sul Eng
0405 .... UT	Ch 12,13,14	Coruña	Areas 1-5
0650 .... UT	518 kHz	Algés Radio	Norte/Centro/Sul Eng
0735 .... UT	2657 kHz	Ramos Pereira	Norte/Centro
0748 .... UT	449 kHz	Cabo Peñas Radio ...	General
0803 .... UT	1677 kHz	Cabo Peñas Radio ...	Areas 1-4
0803 .... UT	1764 kHz	Finisterre Radio	Areas 1-4
0805 .... UT	Ch 12,13,14	Coruña	Areas 1-5
0818 .... UT	511.5 kHz	Finisterre Radio	Areas 4, 6
0830 .... UT	Ch 26	Coruña	Areas 1-4
0833 .... UT	1698 kHz	Coruña Radio	Areas 1-4
0835 .... UT	Ch 11	Sagres Radio	Centro/Sul
0900 .... UT	518 kHz	Tarifa VTS	Areas 6-9, 12 Eng
0903 .... UT	1707 kHz	Machichaco	Areas 1-4
1000 .... LT	See table	Radio España	Areas 4, 6-9, 11
1030 .... UT	Ch 11	Lisboa	Lisboa
1030 .... UT	Ch 11	Sagres Radio	Sagres
1030 .... UT	Ch 11	Setúbal	Setúbal
1050 .... UT	518 kHz	Algés Radio	Norte/Centro/Sul Eng
1103 .... UT	1656 kHz	Chipiona Radio	Areas 6-8
1103 .... UT	1704 kHz	Tarifa Radio	Areas 6-8
1118 .... UT	445 kHz	Tarifa Radio	General
1205 .... UT	Ch 12,13,14	Coruña	Areas 1-5
1300 .... LT	see table	Radio España	Areas 4, 6-9, 11
1450 .... UT	518 kHz	Algés Radio	Norte/Centro/Sul Eng
1535 .... UT	2657 kHz	Ramos Pereira	Norte/Centro

SPAIN & PORTUGAL

Time	Ch/Freq	Source	Forecast
1605 .... *UT*	Ch 12,13,14	Coruña	Areas 1-5
1630 .... *UT*	Ch 11	Leixões Radio	Leixões
1630 .... *UT*	Ch 11	Lisboa	Lisboa
1630 .... *UT*	Ch 11	Sagres Radio	Sagres
1630 .... *UT*	Ch 11	Setúbal	Setúbal
1700 .... *LT*	see table	Radio España	Areas 4, 6-9, 11
1703 .... *UT*	1677 kHz	Cabo Peñas Radio	Areas 1-4
1703 .... *UT*	1764 kHz	Finisterre Radio	Areas 1-4
1718 .... *UT*	472 kHz	Finisterre Radio	Areas 4, 6
1733 .... *UT*	1707 kHz	Machichaco	Areas 1-4
1733 .... *UT*	1698 kHz	Coruña Radio	Areas 1-4
1733 .... *UT*	1656 kHz	Chipiona Radio	Areas 6-8
1733 .... *UT*	1704 kHz	Tarifa Radio	Areas 6-8
1748 .... *UT*	449 kHz	Cabo Peñas Radio	General
1818 .... *UT*	445 kHz	Tarifa Radio	General
1850 .... *UT*	518 kHz	Algés Radio	Norte/Centro/Sul *Eng*
2005 .... *UT*	Ch 12,13,14	Coruña	Areas 1-5
2030 .... *UT*	Ch 26	Coruña	Areas 1-4
2035 .... *UT*	Ch 11	Sagres Radio	Centro/Sul
2100 .... *LT*	See table	Radio España	Areas 4, 6-9, 11
2100 .... *UT*	518 kHz	Tarifa VTS	Areas 6-9, 12 *Eng*
2250 .... *UT*	518 kHz	Algés Radio	Norte/Centro/Sul
2335 .... *UT*	2657 kHz	Ramos Pereira	Norte/Centro

Gijón (MRCC) transmits weather messages every even H+15 (0015-2215) UT. Finisterre (MRCC) transmits weather messages H+33 every 4h commencing 0233 UT. After announcement on Ch 16, Tarifa VTS broadcasts on Ch 10 every even H+15 actual wind and visibility at Tarifa followed by forecast for Straits of Gibraltar, Cadiz Bay and Alboran in English and Spanish.

Radio España	kHz	Range	Radio España	kHz	Range
Madrid	585	100-200	La Coruña	639	100
Tenerife	621	100	Zaragoza	639	20
Bilbao	639	20	Sevilla	684	125-250

GIBRALTAR

Gibraltar Broadcasting Corporation

A	1458kHz	**B**	91.3 MHz
C	92.6 MHz	**D**	100.5 MHz

Weather messages in English -1300 broadcast in Spanish

A-D: 0730 0830 0930 1130 1530 1740-1755 *Mon-Fri*
0630 0730 0830 1130 *Sat*   1030 1230 *Sun*
A-D: 0630 0730 0830 1130 1740-1755 *Mon-Fri*
0630 0730 0830 1130 Sat 0730 0830 1130 *Sun*
BFBS Gibraltar broadcasts on 93.5 MHz and 97.8 MHz as follows:
General Shipping Forcast 0745 0845 1130 1715 2345 *LT Mon-Fri* and 0845 0945 1230 *LT Sat, Sun*. Also a forecast for Gibraltar every H+06 (0700-2400) *LT Mon-Fri* and every H+06 (0700-1000 1200-1400) *LT Sat, Sun*

BBC & COMMERCIAL RADIO STATIONS

All times are LOCAL

National
BBC Radio 4 **198 kHz**
Daily Shipping Bulletins 0048 approx, 0555 1355 1750. Inshore Waters 0053 approx.

Hants/Sussex/Isle of Wight
I.O.Wight Radio **1242 kHz**
Weather reports on hour every H+00. Coastal reports 0630 0730 0830 1630 1730 1830

Worthing/Portsmouth
Spirit FM **96.6 MHz 102.3 MHz**
Weather messages every H+00 (0600-0200 following day). Weather forecasts 0630 0730 0830 1630 1730 1830.

Littlehampton/Weymouth
Radio Solent **1359 kHz 999 KHz**
96.1 MHz 103.8 MHz
Mon-Fri 0735 0835 1130 1230 1325 1425 1525 1625 1735 1835 2305 LT Sat: 0635 0735 0835 0935 1035 1135 1235 1310 1757 LT Sun: 0735 0905 1505 2305 LT
Best direct from the local Meteorological Office.
Shipping Fcst, reports from southern coastal stations, Portland and Solent Coastguard reports, shipping movements (additional bcst Mon-Fri at 0850), tide times. For the coastal area from Littlehampton to Weymouth, including the Isle of Wight and the Solent. Additional Sailing (Small Craft) Information is also bcst Mon-Fri: 0535 0635 0745, Sat & Sun: 0633 0745 LT
Wx Fcst summaries bcst after each news bulletin: Mon-Fri: Every 30 mins from 0500-0830, then every hour from 0900-1600, then every 30 mins from 1630-1830, then every hour from 1900-2300 LT Sat: Every 30 mins from 0600-0900, then every hour from 1000-1500, then 1800 LT. Sun: Every 30 mins from 0600-0800, then every hour from 0900-1800, then 2305 LT.

Solent/Weymouth
2CR FM & Classic Gold
828 kHz 102.3 MHz
0730 and 0830 and every H+03 (0600-2000).

Dorset Coast
BBC Dorset FM **103.8MHz**
Mon-Fri 0733 and 0833. Sat 1310.

Wessex FM **97.2 MHz 96.0 MHz**
General every H+00 (0600-2400) after news bulletin. Coastal Mon-Fri 0630 0730 0830 1320 1630 1730. Sat, Sun 0730 0830 1320.

North and South Devon Coasts
BBC Radio Devon **801 kHz 855 kHz**
990 kHz 1458 kHz 94.8 MHz
95.8MHz 96.0 MHz 103.4 MHz
kHz frequencies Mon-Fri 0635 0758 0858 1312 1735 1835 2215 2315. MHz frequencies Mon-Fri 0655 0732 0755 0832 0855 1312 1735 1835 2215 2315. All frequencies Sat 0633 0758 0858 1312 2302. All frequencies Sun 0634 0835 0930 1205 1305 2300

Lyme Regis/Start Point
Gemini Radio **666 kHz 954 kHz**
96.4 MHz 97MHz 103 MHz
Every H +00 and H+30 (0600-2400) and 0725 and 0825, also small craft information Sat, Sun 0920.

Cornwall/Scilly
Pirate FM **102.2MHz 102.8MHz**
Every H+00 (0600-2400) after news bulletin.

North Devon Coast
Lantern Radio **96.2 MHz**
Every H+00 (0600-0100).

Avon and Somerset
Orchard FM 102.6 MHz
Every H+00 (0600-0100 following day) after news bulletin.

Bristol Channel
GWR and Brunel Classic Gold
96.3MHz and 1260 kHz
Every H+00 and H+30 (H24)

Ilfracombe/Gower Peninsula
Galaxy 101 **97.2 MHz 101 MHz**
Weather messages every H+50 (0550-1750).

Llanelli/Barry
Sound Wave & Swansea Sound
1170 kHz & 96.4 MHz
Weather messages every H+30 and Mon-Fri: (1170 kHz only) 0725 0825 0925. Sat & Sun: (1170 kHz only) 0825 1005.

South Wales
Cardiff Broadcasting Co **1305 kHz**
1359 kHz 97.4 MHz 103.2 MHz
Every H+00 (H24).

BBC Radio Cymru/Wales
Radio Wales - English **657 kHz**
882 kHz 1125 kHz
Radio Cymru -Welsh **92.4-94.6 MHz**

96.8 MHz 103.5-105 MHz
BBC Radio Wales: Mon-Fri 0658 0758 0903 1000 1100 1200 1259 1400 1500 1600 1700 1734 1800 1900 2000 2100 2200. Sat 0600 0700 0800 0900 1003 1100 1200 1259 1700 1759. Sun 0700 0800 0859 1000 1259 1400 1500 1600 1700 1759 1900 2000.

BBC Radio Cymru: Mon-Fri 0728 0758 0824 0900 1000 1100 1200 1300-1315 1500 1600 1759 2200. Sat 0700 0800 0900 1200 1300 1700 1800. Sun 0700 0800 0900 1100 1300 1600 1700 1800 2200

Holyhead/Blackpool
Radio City (Liverpool) (including City FM) 96.7 MHz 1548 kHz
Every H+00 (H24) and every H+30 (kHz only).

BBC Radio Merseyside 1485 kHz 95.8 MHz
Mon-Fri 0705 0805 1208 1310 1605 1705 1743. Sat 0742

Southport/Morecombe Bay
BBC Radio Lancashire 855 kHz 1557 kHz 95.5 MHz 103.9 MHz 104.5 MHz
Mon-Fri 0615 0645 0715 0815 0845 1245 1645 1745. Sat 0615 0645 0715 0745 0815 0845. Sun 0630 0805 1255.

Lancashire Coast
Radio Wave 96.5 MHz
Weather messages every H+00 (H24) after news bulletin.

Tory Island/Ballycastle
Q102.9FM 102.9MHz
Every H+00 (0600-2400).

NE Coast of Northern Ireland
Downtown Radio (including Cool FM) 1026 kHz 96.4 MHz 96.6 MHz 97.4 MHz 102.4 MHz
Every H+00 after news bulletin.

Fleetwood/Ravenglass
The Bay 96.9 FM 96.9 MHz 102.3 MHz 103.2 MHz
Every H+00 (0500-2400).

Cumbria
BBC Radio Cumbria 756kHz 837kHz 1458kHz 95.6MHz 96.1MHz 95.2MHz 104.2 MHz
Mon-Fri 0633 0733 0833 1310 1710 1810. Sat-Sun 0705 0732 0832 1315.

Clyde/Solway
West Sound 1035 kHz 96.5MHz

96.7 MHz 97.0 MHz 97.5 MHz 103 MHz Every H+00 (0600-1805).

Firth of Clyde
Radio Clyde 1152 kHz 97.0 MHz 102.5 MHz 103.3 MHz
Mon-Fri every H+00 except 0300 0800 0900 1100. Sat every H+00 (0000-0200 0400-0900 1200-1400 1800 2200 2300). Sun every H+00 (0000-0200 0400-1000 1200-1400 1600 1900 2200 2300).

Scotland General
BBC Radio Scotland 810 kHz 94.3 MHz 93.1 MHz 92.8 MHz 92.7 MHz 93.6 MHz 92.9 MHz 93.7 MHz 93.0 MHz 93.5 MHz 93.9 MHz 93.3 MHz 93.6 MHz 94.0 MHz
Detailed forecast Sat: 0700. Summary forecast Mon-Fri 0628 0658 0758 then every H+00 (0900-1200 1400-1600) then 1758 2157 2357. Sat, Sun 0658 then every H+00 (0900-1300) then 1758 2158.

NW Scottish Coast
Nevis Radio 96.6 MHz
0710 0730 0810 0830 0910 0930 then every H+06 (1000-2400) after news bulletin.

Caithness/Fraserburgh
Moray Firth Radio 1107 kHz 96.6 MHz 97.4 MHz
Every H+00 (0600-1800) after news bulletin.

150M radius from Bressay
Shetland Islands Broadcasting Co 96.2 MHz
Full Forecast: 0730. General forecast every H+00

North East Scotland
NECR 102.1 FM
0605 1150 1750 2350 and every H+50 (0700-2400) before news bulletin.

Firth of Forth
Forth FM Radio 1548 kHz 97.3 MHz
Mon-Fri every H+00 (0600-1900) after news bulletin. Sat, Sun every H+00 (0600-1400) after news bulletin.

Skelton/Berwick-upon-Tweed
BBC Radio Newcastle 1450 kHz 95.4 MHz 96.0 MHz 104.4 MHz
Mon-Fri 0655 0755 0855 1155 1255 1655 1755. Sat, Sun 0755 0855 0955

Holy Island/St Abb's Head
Radio Borders 95.7 MHz 103.4 MHz
Every H+00 (H24).

Whitby/Berwick-upon-Tweed
Century FM   96.2 MHz 96.4 MHz
100.7 MHz 101.8 MHz
Weather messages every H+00 and H+30.

Hartlepool/Whitley Bay
Sun City   103.4 MHz
0630 Coastal forecast and general forecasts every H+05 and H+40 (0600-2200).

N Yorks/Cleveland/Co Durham
TFM 96.6
96.6 MHz
Mon-Fri every H+00 and H+30 (0600-1000) then H+00 (1000-1800 2200-0100) after news bulletin. Sat, Sun every H+00 (0700-1300) after news bulletin.

Hartlepool/Flamborough Head
BBC Radio Cleveland   95.0 MHz
95.8 MHz
Coastal forecasts: Mon-Fri 0645 0745 0845 1345 1645 1715 1815. Sat 0645 0745 0945 1245 1345. Sun 0745 0845 0945.

Tyne/Humber
BBC Radio York   666 kHz 1260 kHz
95.5 MHz 103.7 MHz 109.3 MHz
Mon-Fri 0600 0700 0800 1230 1330 1730 1830. Sat 0710 1810. Sun 0710 0810 1145.

Humber/Wash
BBC Radio Lincolnshire   1368 kHz
94.9 MHz 104.7 MHz
Mon-Fri 0615 0745 1145 1650 1803. Sat 0720 0845 1145 1445. Sun 0650 0850 1145. Also after news bulletin Mon-Fri every H+00 (0600-1900) 2100 2200 2300 and 0630 0730 0830 1230 1730. After news bulletin Sat 0700 0800 0900 1000 1100 1200 1300 1400 and 0730 0830. After news bulletin Sun 0700 0800 0900 1000 1200.

River Humber and Central Yorkshire Coast
Viking FM   96.9 FM
Up to the hour before news every H+00 Mon-Fri (0600-2300). Sat, Sun (0700-2300).

The Wash
KL FM 96.7 Radio   96.7 MHz
Every H+00 and Mon-Fri every H+30 (0600-0900).

Yarmouth/Clacton-on-Sea
BBC Radio Suffolk   95.5 MHz
103.9 MHz
Sailing forecast Mon-Fri: 0617 0717 0817 1330 1717 1810. Sat, Sun: 0707 0807 1305. General forecast Mon-Fri every H+00 (0600-

2300) plus 0530 0630 0650 0730 0750 0830 1230 1250 1630 1730 1750. Sat: every H+00 (0700-1400) then 1600 1800 2100 2200 2300 plus 0750 1250. Sun: every H+00 (0700-1500) then 1800 2200 2300 plus 0750 1250.

Wells/Southwold
Amber Radio (including Broadlands
102.4 Radio and SGR FM Radio)
1152 kHz 1170 kHz 1251 kHz
at 0704 0805 1305 1704 1805.
102.4 MHz 96.1 MHz 96.4 MHz
97.1 MHz
at 0603 0703 0804 0903 1002 1102 1203 1304 1402 1502 1603 1703 1804. Then every H+02 (1900-0500) and Shipping forecast Humber, Thames at 0905 on kHz transmissions and 0903 and 0645 (Sat) on MHz transmissions.

Lowestoft/Dungeness
Invicta Supergold   603 kHz 1242 kHz
Weather messages every H+00 (0600-2300) with summary every H+30 (0630-0930, 1630-1930).

Essex Coast
Essex FM (including Breze Radio)
1359 kHz 1431 kHz 96.3 MHz
102.6 MHz
Every H+00.

Thames/Felixstowe
BBC Radio Essex   729 kHz 765 kHz
1530 kHz 95.3 MHz 103.5 MHz
0640 0740 1740 1840.

Gravesend/Dungeness
BBC Radio Kent
Wrotham   96.7 MHz
Folkestone   97.6 MHz
Swingate   104.2 MHz
Weather messages Mon-Fri 0740 0840 1315 1740. Sat, Sun 0740 0840 1310. General forecast every H+00 (0600-0000) after news bulletin.

Channel Islands
BBC Radio Guernsey
1116 kHz 93.2 MHz
Mon-Fri 0812 1235. Sat 0810. Sun 0905.

BBC Radio Jersey   1026 kHz 88.8 MHz
Mon-Fri 0635 0810 1835.Sat, Sun 0735
Island FM   93.7 MHz 104.7 MHz
Every H+30.

NAVTEX

Navtex is an international system for receiving, in printed form, weather and navigational information at sea. The information is transmitted from shore-based stations on a single narrow-band frequency. It is received by any vessel carrying a Navtex receiver and is printed onto a paper roll to tear off and read so providing data that can be studied and evaluated easily. Information is transmitted routinely at set times - see *table* - but vital information is transmitted straightaway and is repeated with scheduled transmissions. Information can be pre-selected for non-printing, thereby keeping print output to a minimum. Transmissions have a four digit prefix - the first denotes transmitting station, the second, subject matter. The two subsequent are message serial numbers.

Message Categories:

A	Navigational warnings
B	Meteorological warnings
C	Ice reports
D	Search and rescue
E	Meteorological forecasts
F	Pilot service messages
G	DECCA messages
H	LORAN messages
I	OMEGA messages
J	SATNAV messages
K	Other electronic Navaid messages
L	Navigational warnings for drilling rig movements
V	Amplified Navigational Warnings given under A
WXY	Special Service - trial only
Z	No message on hand

Navtex stations in areas covered by Small Craft Almamac

Navarea 1

Station	Routine Transmission Times
L Rogaland	0148 0548 0948 1348 1748 2148
P IJmuiden	0348 0748 1148 1548 1948 2348
T Oostende	0248 0648 1048 1448 1848 2248
G Cullercoats	0048 0448 0848 1248 1648 2048
S Niton	0018 0418 0818 1218 1618 2018
O Portpatrick	0130 0530 0930 1330 1730 2130

Navarea 2

Station	Routine Transmission Times
A Le Stiff	0000 0400 0800 1200 1600 2000
D La Coruña	0430 0830 1630 2030
R Algés	0250 0650 1050 1450 1850 2250
G Tarifa	0100 0500 0900 1300 1700 2100

MARINECALL

Marinecall provides telephone and fax weather forecasts. Calls cost 39p per minute cheap rate, 49p at all other times. For a *spoken* 2 day local forecast phone **0891-500 +** the area number shown on the accompanying map. For a *printed fax* 2 day local forecast fax **0336-400 +** the area number shown on the accompanying map. For *current* weather conditions updated hourly phone **0891-226 +** the area number shown on the map. For *printed fax* 2-5 day area planning forecasts use the following numbers:

North West Scotland *0336-400468*
North Sea *0336-400469* Biscay *0336-400470*
Channel *0336-400471*
Southern North Sea *0336-400472*
Irish Sea *0336-400473*
Channel Islands *0336-400466* National *0336-400450*

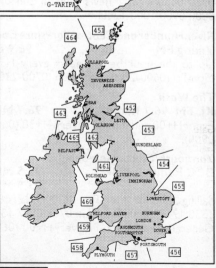

FOREIGN WEATHER TERMS

English	German	French	Spanish	Dutch
Air mass	Luftmasse	Masse d'air	Massa de aire	Luchtmassa
Anticyclone	Antizyklonisch	Anticyclone	Anticiclón	Hogedrukgebied
Area	Gebiet	Zone	Zona	Gebied
Backing wind	Rückdrehender Wind	Vent reculant	Rolar el viento	Krimpende wind
Barometer	Barometer	Baromètre	Barómetro	Barometer
Breeze	Brise	Brise	Brisa	Bries
Calm	Flaute	Calme	Calma	Kalmte
Centre	Zentrum	Centre	Centro	Centum
Clouds	Wolken	Nuages	Nube	Wolken
Cold	Kalt	Froid	Frio	Koud
Cold front	Kaltfront	Front froid	Frente frio	Kou front
Cyclonic	Zyklonisch	Cyclonique	Ciclonica	Cycloonachtig
Decrease	Abnahme	Affaiblissement	Disminución	Afnemen
Deep	Tief	Profond	Profundo	Diep
Deepening	Vertiefend	Approfondissant	Ahondamiento	Verdiepend
Depression	Sturmtief	Dépression	Depresión	Depressie
Direction	Richtung	Direction	Direción	Richting
Dispersing	Auflösend	Se dispersant	Disipación	Oplossend
Disturbance	Störung	Perturbation	Perturbación	Verstoving
Drizzle	Niesel	Bruine	Lioviena	Motregen
East	Ost	Est	Este	Oosten
Extending	Ausdehnung	S'étendant	Extension	Uitstrekkend
Extensive	Ausgedehnt	Etendu	General	Uitgebreid
Falling	Fallend	Descendant	Bajando	Dalen
Filling	Auffüllend	Secomblant	Relleno	Vullend
Fog	Nebel	Brouillard	Niebla	Nevel
Fog bank	Nebelbank	Ligne de brouillard	Banco de niebla	Mist bank
Forecast	Vorhersage	Prévision	Previsión	Vooruitzicht
Frequent	Häufig	Fréquent	Frecuenta	Veelvuldig
Fresh	Frisch	Frais	Fresco	Fris
Front	Front	Front	Frente	Front
Gale	Sturm	Coup de vent	Temporal	Storm
Gale warning	Sturmwarnung	Avis de coup de vent	Aviso de temporal	Stormwaarschuwing
Good	Gut	Bon	Bueno	Goed
Gradient	Druckunterschied	Gradient	Gradiente	Gradiatie
Gust, squall	Bö	Rafalle	Ráfaga	Windvlaag
Hail	Hagel	Grêle	Granizo	Hagel
Haze	Diesig	Brume	Calina	Nevel
Heavy	Schwer	Abondant	Abunante	Zwaar

English	German	French	Spanish	Dutch
High	Hoch	Anticyclone	Alta presión	Hoog
Increasing	Zunehmend	Augmentant	Aumentar	Toenemend
Isobar	Isobar	Isobare	Isobara	Isobar
Isolated	Vereinzelt	Isolé	Aislado	Verspreid
Lightning	Blitze	Eclair de foudre	Relampago	Bliksem
Local	Örtlich	Locale	Local	Plaatselijk
Low	Tief	Dépression	Baja presión	Laag
Mist	Dunst	Brume légere	Nablina	Mist
Moderate	Mäßig	Modéré	Moderado	Matig
Moderating	Abnehmend	Se modérant	Medianente	Matigend
Moving	Bewegend	Se déplacant	Movimiento	Bewegend
North	Nord	Nord	Septentrional	Noorden
Occluded	Okklusion	Couvert	Okklusie	Bewolkt
Poor	Schlecht	Mauvais	Mal	Slecht
Precipitation	Niederschlag	Précipitation	Precipitación	Neerslag
Pressure	Druck	Pression	Presión	Druk
Rain	Regen	Pluie	lluvia	Regen
Ridge	Hochdruckbrücke	Crête	Cresta	Rug
Rising	Ansteigend	Montant	Subiendo	Stijgen
Rough	Rauh	Agitée	Bravo o alborotado	Ruw
Sea	See	Mer	Mar	Zee
Seaway	Seegang	Haute mer	Alta mar	Zee
Scattered	Vereinzelt	Sporadiques	Difuso	Verspreid
Shower	Schauer	Averse	Aguacero	Bui
Slight	Leicht	Un peu	Leicht	Licht
Slow	Langsam	Lent	Lent	Langzaam
Snow	Schnee	Neige	Nieve	Sneeuw
South	Süd	Sud	Sur	Zuiden
Storm	Sturm	Tempête	Temporal	Storm
Sun	Sonne	Soleil	Sol	Zon
Swell	Schwell	Houle	Mar de fondo	Deining
Thunder	Donner	Tonnerre	Tormenta	Donder
Thunderstorm	Gewitter	Orage	Tronada	Onweer
Trough	Trog, Tiefausläufer	Creux	Seno	Trog
Variable	Umlaufend	Variable	Variable	Veranderlijk
Veering	Rechtdrehend	Virement de vent	Dextrogiro	Ruimende wind
Warm front	Warmfront	Front chaud	Frente calido	Warm front
Weather	Wetter	Temps	Tiempo	Weer
Wind	Wind	Vent	Viento	Wind
Weather report	Wetterbericht	Météo	Previsión meteorologica	Weer bericht

REFERENCE SECTION

CONTENTS

Foreign glossary of general terms 388
Common conversion tables 396
Marine VHF transmitting frequencies 397
Index 398
Sounds and shapes signals 400

Nautical miles to Kilometres
multiply by 1.8520

Nt Miles	km
0.25	0.46
0.5	0.93
0.75	1.39
1	1.85
2	3.70
3	5.56
4	7.41
5	9.26
10	18.52
15	27.78
20	37.04
30	55.56
40	74.08
50	92.60
100	185.20

Kilometres to Nautical miles
multiply by 0.5400

km	Nt Miles
0.25	0.14
0.5	0.27
0.75	0.41
1	0.54
2	1.08
3	1.62
4	2.16
5	2.70
10	5.40
15	8.10
20	10.80
30	16.20
40	21.60
50	27.00
100	54.00

Feet to Metres
multiply by 0.3048

feet	metres
0.25	0.08
0.5	0.15
0.75	0.23
1	0.30
2	0.61
3	0.91
4	1.22
5	1.52
10	3.05
15	4.57
20	6.10
30	9.14
40	12.19
50	15.24
100	30.48

Metres to Feet
multiply by 3.2810

metres	feet
0.25	0.82
0.5	1.64
0.75	2.46
1	3.28
2	6.56
3	9.84
4	13.12
5	16.41
10	32.81
15	49.22
20	65.62
30	98.43
40	131.24
50	164.05
100	328.10

GLOSSARY OF FOREIGN TERMS

English	German	French	Spanish	Dutch
Ashore				
Ashore	An Land	A terre	A tierra	Aan land
Airport	Flughafen	Aéroport	Aeropuerto	Vliegveld
Bank	Bank	Banque	Banco	Bank
Boathoist	Bootskran	Travelift	Travelift	Botenlift
Boatyard	Bootswerft	Chantier naval	Astilleros	Jachtwerf
Bureau de change	Wechselstelle	Bureau de change	Cambio	Geldwisselkantoor
Bus	Bus	Autobus	Autobús	Bus
Chandlery	Yachtausrüster	Shipchandler	Efectos navales	Scheepswinkel
Chemist	Apotheke	Pharmacie	Farmacia	Apotheek
Dentist	Zahnarzt	Dentiste	Dentista	Tandarts
Doctor	Arzt	Médecin	Médico	Dokter
Engineer	Motorenservice	Ingénieur/mécanique	Mecánico	Ingenieur
Ferry	Fähre	Ferry/transbordeur	Ferry	Veer/Pont
Garage	Autowerkstatt	Station service	Garage	Garage
Harbour	Hafen	Port	Puerto	Haven
Hospital	Krankenhaus	Hôpital	Hospital	Ziekenhuis
Mast crane	Mastenkran	Grue	Grúa	Masten kraan
Post office	Postamt	Bureau de poste/PTT	Correos	Postkantoor
Railway station	Bahnhof	Gare de chemin de fer	Estación de ferrocaril	Station
Sailmaker	Segelmacher	Voilier	Velero	Zeilmaker
Shops	Geschäfte	Boutiques	Tiendas	Winkels
Slip	Slip	Cale	Varadero	Helling
Supermarket	Supermarkt	Supermarché	Supermercado	Supermarkt
Taxi	Taxi	Taxi	Taxis	Taxi
Village	Ort	Village	Pueblo	Dorp
Yacht club	Yachtclub	Club nautique	Club náutico	Jacht club

Engine and machinery

English	German	French	Spanish	Dutch
Air filter	Luftfilter	Filtre à air	Filtro a aire	Lucht filter
Battery	Batterie	Batterie/accumulateur	Baterías	Accu
Bilge pump	Bilgepumpe	Pompe de cale	Bomba de achique	Bilge pomp
Carburettor	Vergaser	Carburateur	Carburador	Carburateur
Charging	Laden	Charger	Cargador	Opladen
Compression	Kompression	Compression	Compresión	Compressie
Cooling water	Kühlwasser	Eau de refroidissement	Agua refrigerado	Koelwater
Diesel	Diesel	Diésel/gas-oil	Gas-oil	Diesel olie
Diesel engine	Dieselmotor	Moteur diésel	Motor a gas-oil	Diesel motor
Dynamo	Lichtmaschine	Alternateur	Alternador	Dynamo
Electrical wiring	Elektrik	Réseau électrique	Circuito eléctrico	Elektrische bedrading

English	German	French	Spanish	Dutch
Engine mount	Motorenfundament	Support moteur	Bancada del motor	Motorsteun
Engine oil	Maschinenöl	Huile de moteur	Aceite motor	Motor Olie
Exhaust pipe	Auspuff	Tuyau d'échappement	Tubos de escape	Uitlaat
Fuel filter	Kraftstoffilter	Filtre de fuel	Filtro de combustible	Brandstoffilter
Fuel tank	Tank, Kraftstofftank	Réservoir à fuel	Tanque de Combustible	Brandstof tank
Fuse	Sicherung	Fusible	Fusible	Zekering
Gearbox	Getriebe	Transmission	Transmisión	Versnelling
Generator	Generator	Groupe électrogène	Generador	Generator
Grease	Fett	Graisse	Grasa	Vet
Head gasket	Zylinderkopfdichtung	Joint de culasse	Junta de culata	Koppakking
Holding tank	Schmutzwassertank	Réservoir à eaux usées	Tanque aguas negras	Vuil-watertank
Inboard engine	Einbaumotor	Moteur in-bord	Motor intraborda	Binnen boord motor
Injectors	Einspritzdüsen	Injecteurs	Inyectores	Injectoren
Main engine	Hauptmaschine	Moteur principal	Motor	Hoofdmotor
Outboard engine	Außenborder	Moteur hors-bord	Motor fuera borda	Buitenboord motor
Petrol	Benzin	Essence	Gasolina	Benzine
Petrol engine	Benzinmotor	Moteur à essence	Motor a gasolina	Benzine motor
Propeller	Propeller	Hélice	Hélice	Schroef
Propeller bracket	Propeller-Halterung	Chaise	Arbotante	Schroefsteun
Regulator	Regler	Régulateur de charge	Regulador	Regulateur
Shaft	Welle	Arbre d'hélice	Eje	As
Spark plug	Zündkerze	Bougie	Bujia	Bougie
Starter	Starter	Démarreur	Arranque	Start motor
Stern gland	Stopfbuchse	Presse étoupe	Bocina	Schroefasdoorvoer
Throttle	Gas	Accélérateur	Acelerador	Gashendel
Water tank	Wassertank	Réservoir à eau	Tanque de agua	Water tank
Water pump	Wasserpumpe	Pompe à eau	Bomba de agua	Water pomp

General yachting terms

English	German	French	Spanish	Dutch
One	Eins	Un	Uno	Een
Two	Zwei	Deux	Duo	Twee
Three	Drei	Trois	Tres	Drie
Four	Vier	Quatre	Cuatro	Vier
Five	Fünf	Cinq	Cinco	Vijf
Six	Sechs	Six	Seis	Zes
Seven	Sieben	Sept	Siete	Zeven
Eight	Acht	Huit	Ocho	Acht
Nine	Neun	Neuf	Nueve	Negen
Ten	Zehn	Dix	Diez	Tien
Aft	Achtern, achteraus	En arriere	Atrás	Achter
Ahead	Voraus	En avant	Avante	Vooruit
Anchor	Anker	Ancre	Ancia	Anker

English	German	French	Spanish	Dutch
Anchor chain	Ankerkette	Chaîne d'ancre	Cadena	Ankerketting
Anchor warp	Ankerleine	Orin	Cabo	Ankerlijn
Anchor winch	Ankerwinsch	Guindeau	Molinete	Anker lier
Babystay	Babystag	Babystay	Babystay	Baby stag
Backstay	Achterstag	Pataras	Estay de popa	Achterstag
Beating	Kreuzen	Au près	Ciñendo a rabier	Kruisen
Bilge	Bilge	Galbord	Sentina	Bilge
Bilge keel	Kimmkiel	Bi-quilles	Quillas de balance	Door lopende kiel
Block	Block	Poulie	Motón	Blok
Boat	Boot	Bateau	Barco	Boot
Boom	Baum	Bôme	Botavara	Giek
Bow	Bug	Etrave	Proa	Boeg
Bridgedeck	Brückendeck	Bridgedeck	Bridgedeck	Brug dek
Cabin	Kajüte	Cabine	Cabina	Kajuit
Cap shrouds	Oberwanten	Gal haubans	Obenques altos	Zalingkap
Centreboard	Schwert	Dérive	Orza	Midzwaard
Cockpit	Cockpit	Cockpit	Bañera	Cockpit
Companionway	Niedergang	Descente	Entrada cámera	Gangboord
Cruising chute	Cruising chute	Spi asymétrique	MPS	Cruising chute
Cutter stay	Kutterstag	Etai intermédiaire	Estay de tringqueta	Kotter stag
Deck	Deck	Pont	Cubierta	Dek
Dinghy	Jolle	You-you	Chinchorro	Bijboot
Fender	Fender	Défense	Defensa	Stootwil
Ferry	Fähre	Ferry	Ferry	Veer boot
Fin keel	Kurzkiel	Quille courte	Quilla de aleta	Fin kiel
Foresail	Vorsegel	Voile avant/foc	Foque	Fok
Forestay	Vorstag	Etai	Estay	Voorstag
Genoa	Genua	Génois	Génova	Genua
Halyard	Fall	Drisse	Driza	Val
Hull	Rumpf	Carène	Carena	Romp
Inflatable	Schlauchboot	Gonflable	Bote Hinchable	Opblaasbare boot
Jumper	Jumpstag	Guignol	Violín	Trui
Keel	Kiel	Quille	Quilla	Kiel
Long keel	Langkiel	Quille longue	Quilla corrida	Doorlopende kiel
Lower shrouds	Unterwanten	Bas haubans	Obenques bajos	Beneden zaling
Mainsail	Großsegel	Grand' voile	Mayor	Grootzeil
Mast	Mast	Mât	Mast	Mast
Mizzen	Besan	Artimon	Mesana	Bezaan
Motoring	Motoren	Naviguer au moteur	Navegar a motor	Met motor aan
Navigate	Navigieren	Naviguer	Navegar	Navigeren
Port	Backbord	Bâbord	Babor	Bakboord
Pulpit	Bugkorb	Balcon arrière	Púlpito	Preekstoel

English	German	French	Spanish	Dutch
Pushpit	Heckkorb	Balcon avant	Balcón de popa	Hekrailing
Railing	Reling	Rambarde	Guardamencebos	Railing
Reaching	Raumschodts	Au portant	Viento a través	Ruime wind
Rigging	Rigg	Gréement	Jarcia	Verstaging
Rope	Tauwerk	Cordage	Cabo	Touw
Rudder	Ruder	Safran/gouvernail	Pala de Timón	Roer
Running	Vorm Wind	Vent arrière	Viento a favor	Voor de wind
Running backstay	Backstag	Bastaque	Burde volanto	Bakstag
Sail batten	Segellatte	Latte	Sables	Zeillat
Sailing	Segeln	Naviguer à la voile	Navegar a velas	Zeilen
Shackle	Schäkel	Manille	Grillete	Harp
Sheet	Schoot	Ecoute	Escota	Schoot
Ship	Schiff	Navire	Buque	Schip
Shrouds	Wanten	Haubans	Obenques	Zaling
Spinnaker	Spinnaker	Spi	Spi	Spinnaker
Spinnaker boom	Spinnakerbaum	Tangon de spi	Tangon	Spinnaker boom
Stanchion	Seerelingsstütze	Chandelier	Candelero	Scepter
Starboard	Steuerbord	Tribord	Estribor	Stuurboord
Staysail	Stagsegel	Trinquette	Trinquete	Stagzeil
Steamer	Dampfer	Vapeur	Buque de vapor	Vrachtschip
Stern	Heck	Arrière	Popa	Spiegel
Storm jib	Sturmfock	Tourmentin	Tormentin	Storm fok
Storm trysail	Trysegel	Voile de cap	Vela de capa	Trysail
Superstructure	Aufbau	Superstructure	Superestructura	Bovenbouw
Tender	Beiboot	Annexe	Anexo (bote)	Bijboot
Tiller	Pinne	Barre franche	Caña	Helmstok
Toe rail	Fußleiste	Rail de fargue	Regala	Voetrail
Topsides	Rumpfseiten	Oeuvres mortes	Obra muerta	Romp
Underwater hull	Unterwasserschiff	Oeuvres vives	Obra viva	Onderwaterschip
Upwind	Am Wind	Au vent	Vienta en contra	Aan de wind
Wheel	Rad	Barre à roue	Rueda	Stuurwiel
Winch	Winsch	Winch	Winche	Lier
Working jib	Arbeitsfock	Foc de route	Foque	Werk fok
Yacht	Yacht	Yacht	Yate	Jacht

Navigation

English	German	French	Spanish	Dutch
Abeam	Querab	A côté	Por el través	Naast
Ahead	Voraus	Avant	Avante	Voor
Astern	Achteraus	Arrière	Atrás	Achter
Bearing	Peilung	Cap	Maración	Peiling
Buoy	Tonne	Bouée	Boya	Boei
Binoculars	Fernglas	Jumelles	Prismáticos	Verrekijker
Channel	Kanal	Chenal	Canal	Kanaal

FOREIGN GLOSSARY

English	German	French	Spanish	Dutch
Chart	Seekarte	Carte	Carta náutica	Zeekaart
Compass	Kompass	Compas	Compás	Kompas
Compass course	Kompass Kurs	Cap du compas	Rumbo de aguja	Kompas koers
Current	Strömung	Courant	Coriente	Stroom
Dead reckoning	Koppelnavigation	Estime	Estimación	Gegist bestek
Degree	Grad	Degré	Grado	Graden
Deviation	Deviation	Déviation	Desvio	Deviatie
Distance	Entfernung	Distance	Distancia	Afstand
Downstream	Flußabwärts	En aval	Río abajo	Stroom afwaards
East	Ost	Est	Este	Oost
Ebb	Ebbe	Jusant	Marea menguante	Eb
Echosounder	Echolot	Sondeur	Sonda	Dieptemeter
Estimated position	Gegißte Position	Point estimé	Posición estimado	Gegiste positie
Fathom	Faden	Une brasse	Braza	Vadem
Feet	Fuß	Pieds	Pie	Voet
Flood	Flut	Flot	Flujo de marea	Vloed
GPS	GPS	GPS	GPS	GPS
Handbearing compass	Handpeilkompass	Compas de relèvement	Compás de marcaciones	Handpeil kompas
Harbour guide	Hafenhandbuch	Guide du port	Guia del Puerto	Havengids
High water	Hochwasser	Peine mer	Altamer	Hoog water
Latitude	Geographische Breite	Latitude	Latitud	Breedte
Leading lights	Feuer in Linie	Alignement	Luz de enfilación	Geleide lichten
Leeway	Abdrift	Dérive	Hacia sotavento	Drift
Lighthouse	Leuchtturm	Phare	Faro	Vuurtoren
List of lights	Leuchtfeuer Verzeichnis	Liste des feux	Listude de Luces	Lichtenlijst
Log	Logge	Loch	Corredera	Log
Longitude	Geographische Länge	Longitude	Longitud	Lengte
Low water	Niedrigwasser	Basse mer	Bajamar	Laag water
Metre	Meter	Mètre	Metro	Meter
Minute	Minute	Minute	Minuto	Minuut
Nautical almanac	Nautischer Almanach	Almanach nautique	Almanaque náutico	Almanak
Nautical mile	Seemeile	Mille nautique	Milla marina	Zeemijl
Neap tide	Nipptide	Morte-eau	Marea muerta	Dood tij
North	Nord	Nord	Norte	Noord
Pilot	Lotse	Pilote	Práctico	Loods/Gids
Pilotage book	Handbuch	Instructions nautiques	Derrotero	Vaarwijzer
RDF	Funkpeiler	Radio gonio	Radio-gonió	Radio richtingzoeker
Radar	Radar	Radar	Radar	Radar
Radio receiver	Radio, Empfänger	Récepter radio	Receptor de radio	Radio ontvanger
Radio transmitter	Sender	Emetteur radio	Radio-transmisor	Radio zender
River outlet	Flußmündung	Embouchure	Embocadura	Riviermond
South	Süd	Sud	Sud, Sur	Zuid

English	German	French	Spanish	Dutch
Spring tide	Springtide	Vive-eau	Marea viva	Springtij/springvloed
Tide	Tide, Gezeit	Marée	Marea	Getijde
Tide tables	Tidenkalender	Annuaire des marées	Anuario de mareas	Getijdetafel
True course	Wahrer Kurs	Vrai cap	Rumbo	Ware Koers
Upstream	Flußaufwärts	En amont	Río arriba	Stroom opwaards
VHF	UKW	VHF	VHF	Marifoon
Variation	Mißweisung	Variation	Variación	Variatie
Waypoint	Wegpunkt	Point de rapport	Waypoint	Waypoint/Route punt
West	West	Ouest	Oeste	West

Officialdom

English	German	French	Spanish	Dutch
Certificate of registry	Schiffszertifikat	Acte de franchisation	Documentos de matrícuia	Zeebrief
Check in	Einklarieren	Enregistrement	Registrar	Check-in
Customs	Zoll	Douanes	Aduana	Douane
Declare	Verzollen	Déclarer	Declarar	Aangeven
Harbour master	Hafenmeister	Capitaine du port	Capitán del puerto	Havenkantoor
Insurance	Versicherung	Assurance	Seguro	Verzekering
Insurance certificate	Versicherungspolice	Certificat d'assurance	Certificado deseguro	Verzekeringsbewijs
Passport	Paß	Passeport	Pasaporte	Paspoort
Police	Polizei	Police	Policía	Politie
Pratique	Verkehrserlaubnis	Pratique	Prático	Verlof tot ontscheping
Register	Register	Liste de passagers	Lista de tripulantes/rol	Register
Ship's log	Logbuch	Livre de bord	Cuaderno de bitácora	Logboek
Ship's papers	Schiffspapiere	Papiers de bateau	Documentos del barco	Scheepspapieren
Surveyor	Gutachter	Expert maritime	Inspector	Opzichter

Safety/Distress

English	German	French	Spanish	Dutch
Assistance	Hilfeleistung	Assistance	Asistencia	Assistentie
Bandage	Verband	Pansement	Vendas	Verband
Burns	Verbrennung	Brûlures	Quemadura	Brand wond
Capsize	Kentern	Chavirage	Volcó	Omslaan
Coastguard	Küstenwache	Garde de côte	Guarda costas	Kust wacht
Dismasted	Mastbruch	Démâtè	Desarbolar	Mastbreuk
Distress	Seenot	Détresse	Pena	Nood
Distress flares	Signalraketen	Fusées de détresse	Bengalas	Nood signaal
Doctor	Doktor	Médecin	Médico	Doktor/Arts
EPIRB	EPIRB	Balise	Baliza	EPIRB
Emergency	Notfall	Urgence	Emergencias	Noodgeval
Exhaustion	Erschöpfung	Epuisement	Agotamiento	Uitputting
Fever	Fieber	Fièvre	Fiebre	Koorts
Fire extinguisher	Feuerlöscher	Extincteur	Extintor	Brand blusser
First aid	Erste Hilfe	Premier secours	Primeros auxillos	Eerste kulp
Fracture	Fraktur	Cassure	Fractura	Breuk
Grounded	Aufgelaufen	Echoué	Encallado	Vastgelopen

English	German	French	Spanish	Dutch
Harness	Lifebelt	Harnais	Arnés de seguridad	Harnas/Tuig
Headache	Kopfschmerz	Mal à la tête	Dolor de cabeza	Hoofdpÿn
Heart attack	Herzanfall	Crise cardiaque	Ataque corazón	Hart aanval
Helicopter	Hubschrauber	Hélicoptère	Helicóptero	Helikopter
Hospital	Krankenhaus	Hôpital	Hospital	Ziekenhuis
Illness	Krankheit, Übelkeit	Maladie	Enfermo	Ziekte
Injury	Verletzung	Blessure	Lesión	Verwonding
Jackstay	Strecktau	Contre-étai	Violín	Veiligheidstag
Lifeboat	Rettungsboot	Canot de sauvetage	Lancha de salvamento	Reddingsboot
Liferaft	Rettungsinsel	Radeau de sauvetage	Balsa salvavidas	Reddingsvlot
Lifejacket	Schwimmweste	Gilet de sauvetage	Chaleco salvavidas	Reddingsvest
Man overboard	Mann über Bord	Homme à la mer	Hombre al agua	Man over boord
Pulse	Puls	Poux	Pulso	Hartslag
Rest	Ruhen	Repos	Reposo	Rust
Seacock	Seeventil	Vanne	Grifos de fondo	Afsluiter
Seasickness	Seekrankheit	Mal de mer	Mareo	Zeeziekte
Seaworthy	Seetüchtig	Marin	Marinero	Zeewaardig
Shock	Schock	Choc	Choque	Shock
Sinking	Sinken	En train de couler	Hundiendo	Zinken
Sleep	Schlaf	Sommeil	Sueño	Slaap
Tow line	Schleppleine	Filin de remorque	Cabo	Sleeplÿn
Unconscious	Bewußtlos	Inconscient	Inconsciente	Buiten bewustzijn
Wound	Wunde	Blessure	Herida	Wond

Signs and warnings

English	German	French	Spanish	Dutch
Anchoring	Ankern	Mouiller l'ancre	Fondear	Ankeren
Breakwater	Außenmole	Brise-lame	Escolera	Pier
Cable	Kabel	Encablure	Cadena	Kabel
Catwalk	Schlengel	Passerelle	Pasarela	Looplank
Commercial port	Handelshafen	Port de commerce	Puerto comercial	Commerciele haven
Customs office	Zollamt	Bureau de douane	Aduanas	Douane kantoor
Depth	Wassertiefe	Profondeur	Profundidad	Diepte
Dries	Trockenfallend	Découvrant	Descubierto	Droogvallen
Drying port	Trockenfallender Hafen	Port d'échouage	Puerto secarse	Droogvallende haven
Ferry terminal	Fährterminal	Gare maritime	Terminal marítmo	Veerboot steiger
Firing range	Schießgebiet	Zone de tir	Zona de tiro	Schietbaan
Fishing harbour	Fischereihafen	Port de pêche	Puerto de pesca	Vissershaven
Foul ground	unreiner Grund	Fond maisain	Fondo sucio	Slechte grond
Guest berths	Gastliegeplätze	Place visiteurs	Amarradero visitantes	Gasten plaatsen
Harbour entrance	Hafeneinfahrt	Entrée du port	Entradas	Haveningang
Harbour office	Hafenmeisterei	Capitainerie	Capitania	Havenmeester
Hazard	Hindernis	Danger	Peligro	Gevaar
Height	Höhe	Hauteur	Alturas	Hoogte

English	German	French	Spanish	Dutch
Jetty	Steg	Jetée	Malecón	Steiger
Landing place	Anlegeplatz	Point d'accostage	Embarcadero	Plaats om aan land te gaan
Lock	Schleuse	Ecluse	Esclusa	Sluis
Marina	Marina	Marina	Marina	Marina
Mooring	Anlegen	Mouillage	Fondeadero	Meerplaats
Permitted	Erlaubt	Permis	Permitido	Toegestaan
Pier	Pier, Mole	Appontement/quai	Muelle	Pier
Prohibited	Verboten	Interdit	Prohibido	Verboden
Prohibited area	Sperrgebiet	Zone interdite	Zona de phrohibida	Verboden gebied
Swell	Schwell	Houle	Mar de fondo	Golfslag
Swing bridge	Klappbrücke	Pont tournant	Puente giratorio	Klapbrug
Underwater	Unterwasser	Sous-marin	Debajo del agua	Onder water
Wreck	Wrack	Epave	Naufrago	Wrak
Yacht club	Yachtclub	Club nautique	Club náutico	Jachtclub
Yacht harbour	Yachthafen	Port de plaisance	Puerto deportive	Jachthaven

English
Useful phrases

English	German	French
Can I moor here please	Kann ich hier festmachen?	Puis-je accoster ici s'il vous plait?
How far is it to....?	Wie weit ist es nach ..... ?	Est -ce loin jusqu'à...?
How much does that cost?	Was kostet es?	Combien est-il?
Is there enough water?	Ist dort genug Wassertiefe?	Y a-t-il du fond?
Let go aft	Achtern loswerfen.	Larguer à l'arrière
Let go foreward	Vorne loswerfen.	Larguer à l'avant
Make fast aft	Können Sie bitte achtern festmachen?	Amarrer à l'arrière
Make fast foreward	Können Sie bitte vorne festmachen?	Amarrer à l'avant
Please direct me to......?	Bitte zeigen Sie mir den Weg nach	S'il vous plait, vevillez m'indiquer le chemin à...?
Please take my line	Können Sie bitte die Leine annehmen?	Prenez mon amarre, s'il vous plait
Where can I get...?	Wo kann ich ..... bekommen?	Où puis-je obtenir...?
Where can I moor?	Wo kann ich festmachen?	Où puis-je accoster?

English	Spanish	Dutch
Can I moor here please	Puedo atracar aqui por favor?	Mag ik hier aanleggen?
How far is it to....?	A que distancia esta ...?	Hoe ver is het naar...?
How much does that cost?	Cudnto cuesta ...?	Hoeveel kost het?
Is there enough water?	Hay bastante agua?	Is er genoeg water?
Let go aft	Suelta los cabos del amarre de popa	Achter losgooien
Let go foreward	Suelta los cabos del amarre de proa	Voor losgooien
Make fast aft	Asegurar los amarres de popa	Achter vastleggen
Make fast foreward	Asegurar los amarres de proa	Voor vastleggen
Please direct me to......?	Por favor, digame a ...?	Kunt u my de weg naar .. wÿzen
Please take my line	Por favor cojan mi cabo	Kunt u mijn landvast aanpakken?
Where can I get...?	Donde puedo conseguir ...?	Waar kan ik...verkrijgen?
Where can I moor?	Dondo puedo atracar?	Waar kan ik vastmaken?

CONVERSION TABLES

Sq inches to sq millimetres multiply by **645.20**	645.2	0.002	**Sq millimetres to sq inches** multiply by **0.0016**
Inches to millimetres multiply by **25.40**	25.40	0.04	**Millimetres to inches** multiply by **0.0394**
Sq feet to square metres multiply by **0.093**	0.09	10.76	**Sq metres to sq feet** multiply by **10.7640**
Inches to centimetres multiply by **2.54**	2.54	0.39	**Centimetres to inches** multiply by **0.3937**
Feet to metres multiply by **0.305**	0.31	3.28	**Metres to feet** multiply by **3.2810**
Nautical miles to kilometres multiply by **1.852**	1.85	0.54	**Kilometres to nautical miles** multiply by **0.5400**
Miles to kilometres multiply by **1.609**	1.61	0.62	**Kilometres to miles** multiply by **0.6214**
Miles to nautical miles multiply by **0.8684**	0.87	1.15	**Nautical miles to miles** multiply by **1.1515**
HP to metric HP multiply by **1.014**	1.01	0.99	**Metric HP to HP** multiply by **0.9862**
Pounds per sq inch to kg per sq centimetre multiply by **0.0703**	0.07	4.22	**Kg per sq centimetre to pounds per sq inch** multiply by **14.2200**
HP to kilowatts multiply by **0.746**	0.75	1.34	**Kilowatts to HP** multiply by **1.341**
Cu inches to cu centimetres multiply by **16.39**	16.39	0.06	**Cu centimetres to cu inches** multiply by **0.0610**
Gallons to litres multiply by **4.540**	4.54	0.22	**Litres to gallons** multiply by **0.2200**
Pints to litres multiply by **0.5680**	0.57	1.76	**Litres to pints** multiply by **1.7600**
Pounds to kilogrammes multiply by **0.4536**	0.45	2.21	**Kilogrammes to pounds** multiply by **2.2050**

MARINE VHF TRANSMITTING FREQUENCIES

Distress, safety & calling

Ch	MHz	MHz	Note
75	156.7625	156.7875	Guard-band - do not use
16	156.800	156.800	Distress, safety & calling
76	156.8125	156.8375	Guard-band - do not use
67	156.375	156.375	Small ships safety channel
70	156.525	156.525	Digital selective calling

Intership
Channels listed in order of preference of use
Channels: 06, 08, 10, 13, 09, 72, 73, 69, 67, 77, 15, 17

Port operations - single frequency
Channels listed in order of preference of use
Channels: 12, 14, 11, 13, 09, 68, 71, 74, 10, 67, 69, 73, 17, 15

Port operations - two frequency
Channels listed in order of preference of use
Channels: 20, 22, 18, 19, 21, 05, 07, 02, 03, 01, 04, 78, 82, 79, 81, 80, 60, 63, 66, 62, 65, 64, 61, 84

Ship movements - single frequency
Channels listed in order of preference of use
Channels: 11, 68, 12, 69, 13, 71, 14, 74, 67, 10, 73, 09, 17, 15

Ship movements - two frequency
Channels listed in order of preference of use
Channels: 79, 80, 61, 64, 65, 62, 66, 63, 60, 81, 82, 84, 78, 04, 01, 03, 02, 07, 05, 21, 19, 18, 20, 22

Public correspondence
Channels listed in order of preference of use
Channels: 26, 27, 25, 24, 23, 28, 04, 01, 03, 02, 07, 05, 84, 87, 86, 83, 85, 88, 61, 64, 65, 62, 66, 63, 60, 82, 78, 81

Transmitting frequencies

Ch	Ship stations	Coast stations
01	156.050 MHz	160.650 MHz
02	156.100 MHz	160.700 MHz
03	156.150 MHz	160.750 MHz
04	156.200 MHz	160.800 MHz
05	156.250 MHz	160.850 MHz
06	156.300 MHz	
07	156.350 MHz	160.950 MHz
08	156.400 MHz	
09	156.450 MHz	156.450 MHz
10	156.500 MHz	156.500 MHz
11	156.550 MHz	156.550 MHz
12	156.600 MHz	156.600 MHz
13	156.650 MHz	156.650 MHz
14	156.700 MHz	156.700 MHz
15	156.750 MHz	156.750 MHz
16	**156.800 MHz**	**156.800 MHz**
17	156.850 MHz	156.850 MHz
18	156.900 MHz	161.500 MHz
19	156.950 MHz	161.550 MHz
20	157.000 MHz	161.600 MHz
21	157.050 MHz	161.650 MHz
22	157.100 MHz	161.700 MHz
23	157.150 MHz	161.750 MHz
24	157.200 MHz	161.800 MHz
25	157.250 MHz	161.850 MHz
26	157.300 MHz	161.900 MHz
27	157.350 MHz	161.950 MHz
28	157.400 MHz	162.000 MHz
60	156.025 MHz	160.625 MHz
61	156.075 MHz	160.675 MHz
62	156.125 MHz	160.725 MHz
63	156.175 MHz	160.775 MHz
64	156.225 MHz	160.825 MHz
65	156.275 MHz	160.875 MHz
66	156.325 MHz	160.925 MHz
67	156.375 MHz	156.375 MHz
68	156.425 MHz	156.425 MHz
69	156.475 MHz	156.475 MHz
70	156.525 MHz	156.525 MHz
71	156.575 MHz	156.575 MHz
72	156.625 MHz	
73	156.675 MHz	156.675 MHz
74	156.725 MHz	156.725 MHz
77	156.875 MHz	
78	156.925 MHz	161.525 MHz
79	156.975 MHz	161.575 MHz
80	157.025 MHz	161.625 MHz
81	157.075 MHz	161.675 MHz
82	157.125 MHz	161.725 MHz
83	157.175 MHz	161.775 MHz
84	157.225 MHz	161.825 MHz
85	157.275 MHz	161.875 MHz
86	157.325 MHz	161.925 MHz
87	157.375 MHz	161.975 MHz
88	157.425 MHz	162.025 MHz

SMALL CRAFT ALMANAC INDEX

Admiralty Chart Symbols ...... back cover
Communication Section 328
Contents 3
Conversion Tables 396
Distance to Horizon Table 6
Distance from Dipping Light Table ... 326
Distress .... front cover
Ephemera
　Sunrise & sunset 278
　Moonrise & moonset 288
Flags .... front cover
Forecast Definitions 356
Foreign Glossary 388
HM Coastguard Chart 329
IALA Buoyage .... back cover
Light Recognition .... back cover
Lights
　England South coast 302
　England East coast 303
　Scotland 303
　England West coast 305
　Isle of Man 305
　Wales 305
　Ireland 306
　Belgium 307
　Holland 307
　Germany 309
　Denmark 311
　France 311
　Channel Islands 312
　Spain 316
　Portugal 317
　Gibraltar 317
Lights to be carried on yachts 301
Marinas 298
Marinecall 384
Navtex 384
Phonetic Alphabet 328
Planning Section 5
Position Section 301
Radio
　Radiobeacons 318
　Emergency D/F Service 322
　Emergency D/F Service chart - UK 324
　Emergency D/F Service chart - France 325
　Radio operation 330
　Port & coastal radio -
　England South coast 332
　England East coast 334
　Scotland 335
　UK West coast 337
　Ireland 338
　Belgium 339
　Holland 339

Germany 340
Denmark 341
France 342
Channel Islands 342
Spain 344
Portugal 344
Gibraltar 345
VHF Transmitting Frequencies 397
Reference Section 387
Secondary Port Tidal Data 178
Sounds and Shapes Signals 400
Small Craft Charts
　Key chart 237
　1 S W England 238
　2 S Central England 240
　3 SE England 242
　4 E England 244
　5 E Scotland 246
　6 NW Scotland 248
　7 SW Scotland 250
　8 Wales, NW England & E Ireland 252
　9 SW England, S Wales & S Ireland 254
　10 Ireland 256
　11 Belgium & Holland 258
　12 Germany & NE Holland 260
　13 Denmark 262
　14 NE France 264
　15 N Central France & Channel Islands 266
　16 NW France 268
　17 W France & NE Spain 270
　18 NW Spain 272
　19 Portugal 274
　20 S Portugal & SW Spain 276
Standard Port Positions 6
Tidal Streams
　English Channel & S. Brittany 199
　Portland 205
　Isle of Wight 207
　Channel Isles 213
　North Sea 219
　Scotland 225
　Celtic Sea, Irish Sea & W. Ireland 231
Tide Tables - Standard Ports
　Aberdeen predictions 55
　Aberdeen curves 162
　Antwerpen predictions 103
　Antwerpen curves 172
　Avonmouth predictions 79
　Avonmouth curves 167
　Belfast predictions 79
　Belfast curves 168
　Bremerhaven predictions 103
　Brest predictions 127
　Brest curves 176

Calais predictions 127	Plymouth predictions 7
Calais curves 173	Plymouth curves 153
Cherbourg predictions 127	Pointe de Grave predictions 127
Cherbourg curves 175	Pointe de Grave curves 176
Cobh predictions 79	Poole Entrance predictions 7
Cobh curves 169	Poole Entrance curves 154
Cuxhaven predictions 103	Portland predictions 7
Cuxhaven curves 171	Portland curves 153
Dieppe predictions 127	Portsmouth predictions 7
Dieppe curves 174	Portsmouth curves 155
Dover predictions 7	River Tees predictions 31
Dover curves 156	River Tees curves 160
Dublin predictions 79	River Tyne predictions 31
Dublin curves 167	River Tyne curves 160
Dunkerque predictions 103	Rosyth predictions 55
Dunkerque curves 173	Rosyth curves 161
Esbjerg predictions 103	Rotterdam predictions 103
Esbjerg curves 170	Rotterdam curves 171
Galway predictions 79	St Helier predictions 7
Galway curves 169	St Helier curves 152
Gibraltar predictions 127	St Malo predictions 127
Gibraltar curves 177	St Malo curves 175
Greenock predictions 55	St Mary's,Scilly Isles predictions 7
Greenock curves 164	St Mary's,Scilly Isles curves 152
Harwich predictions 31	Sheerness predictions 31
Harwich curves 158	Sheerness curves 157
Helgoland predictions 103	Shoreham predictions 7
Helgoland curves 170	Shoreham curves 155
Holyhead predictions 79	Southampton predictions 7
Holyhead curves 165	Southampton curves 154
Hoek van Holland predictions 103	Swansea predictions 79
Hoek van Holland curves 171	Swansea curves 166
Immingham predictions 31	Ullapool predictions 55
Immingham curves 159	Ullapool curves 163
Le Havre predictions 127	Vlissingen predictions 103
Le Havre curves 174	Vlissingen curves 172
Leith predictions 55	Walton-the-Naze predictions 31
Leith curves 161	Walton-the-Naze curves 158
Lerwick predictions 55	Wick predictions 55
Lerwick curves 163	Wick curves 162
Lisboa predictions 127	**Tidal Calculations** 151
Lisboa curves 177	**Tidal Time Differences on Dover** 4
Liverpool predictions 55	**Vessel Traffic Service Charts** 346
Liverpool curves 165	**Waypoints** 239
London Bridge predictions 31	**Weather Section** 356
London Bridge curves 157	**Weather**
Londonderry predictions 79	Beaufort scale 356
Londonderry curves 168	UK shipping forecast areas 357
Lowestoft predictions 31	French shipping forecast areas 358
Lowestoft curves 159	German shipping forecast areas 359
Margate predictions 31	Spanish shipping forecast areas 360
Margate curves 156	Portuguese shipping forecast areas 361
Milford Haven predictions 79	Broadcast weather forecasts -*marine* ... 362
Milford Haven curves 166	Broadcast weather forecasts
Oban predictions 55	*- main UK radio stations* 381
Oban curves 164	Weather terms in 5 languages 385

SOUNDS

VESSELS IN SIGHT OF ONE ANOTHER

Short blast ◄ - about 1 second, Long blast ●◄ - about 5 seconds

◄   I am turning to **Starboard**

◄ ◄   I am turning to **Port**

◄ ◄ ◄   My engines are going **Astern**

◄ ◄ ◄ ◄ ◄ - *at least* **Look Out**

In a narrow channel

●◄ ●◄ ◄   I intend to overtake you on your **Starboard** side

●◄ ●◄ ◄ ◄   I intend to overtake you on your **Port** side

●◄ ◄ ●◄ ◄   In response to the above two signals - **Agreed** (Morse C - affirmative)

Approaching a bend in the channel
or a harbour wall which restricts visibility

●◄   Look out - I am coming

●◄   Reply to above - so am I

VESSELS IN FOG

●◄   Power vessel under way (every 2 mins)

●◄ ●◄   Power vessel stopped (every 2 mins)

●◄ ◄ ◄   All the lame ducks - not under command, restricted, sailing, fishing or towing - (every 2 mins)(Morse D - I am manoeuvring with difficulty)

●◄ ◄ ◄ ◄   Last vessel in tow (immediately after tug signal)

🔔 5 seconds   At anchor (bell, every minute)

🔔 5 seconds +

🔔 5 seconds   At anchor over 100m (bell forward, gong aft, every minute)

◄ ●◄ ◄   At anchor, in addition to above, to warn approaching vessel

Yachts under 12m are not obliged to sound the fog signals listed above, but if they do not, they *must* make some efficient noise every two minutes

SHAPES

◆	Towing vessel - length of tow over 200m	▼	Sailing vessel under sail *and* power
●◆●	Restricted vessel	●	Vessel at anchor
●●	Vessel not under command	⧓	Fishing vessel
▮	Vessel constrained by her draught	⧖	Fishing vessel below 20m